American Casebook Series

Hornbook Series and Basic Legal Texts

Nutshell Series

of

WEST PUBLISHING COMPANY
P. O. Box 3526
St. Paul, Minnesota 55165
March, 1978

CIVIL PROCEDURE—Continued

Cound, Friedenthal and Miller's Cases and Materials on Civil Procedure, 2nd Ed., 1186 pages, 1974 with 1978 Supplement (Casebook)

Cound, Friedenthal and Miller's Cases on Pleading, Discovery and Joinder, 643 pages, 1968 (Casebook)

Ehrenzweig and Louisell's Jurisdiction in a Nutshell, 3rd Ed., 291 pages, 1973 (Text)

Federal Rules of Civil-Appellate-Criminal Procedure—West Law School Edition, 334 pages, 1977

Hodges, Jones and Elliott's Texas Cases and Materials on Texas Trial and Appellate Procedure, 2nd Ed., 745 pages, 1974 (Casebook)

Hodges, Jones, and Elliott's Texas Cases and Materials on the Judicial Process Prior to Trial in Texas, 2nd Ed., 871 pages, 1977 (Casebook)

Karlen's Procedure Before Trial in a Nutshell, 258 pages, 1972 (Text)

Karlen and Joiner's Cases and Materials on Trials and Appeals, 536 pages, 1971 (Casebook)

Karlen, Meisenholder, Stevens and Vestal's Cases on Civil Procedure, 923 pages, 1975 (Casebook)

Koffler and Reppy's Hornbook on Common Law Pleading, 663 pages, 1969 (Text)

McBaine's Cases on Introduction to Civil Procedure, 399 pages, 1950 (Casebook)

McCoid's Cases on Civil Procedure, 823 pages, 1974 (Casebook)

Park's Computer-Aided Exercises on Civil Procedure, 118 pages, 1976 (Coursebook)

Shipman's Hornbook on Common-Law Pleading, 3rd Ed., 644 pages, 1923 (Text)

Siegel's Hornbook on New York Practice, 1011 pages, 1978 (Text)

See also Federal Jurisdiction and Procedure

COMMERCIAL LAW

Bailey's Secured Transactions in a Nutshell, 377 pages, 1976 (Text)

Epstein and Martin's Basic Uniform Commercial Code Teaching Materials, 599 pages, 1977 (Casebook)

Henson's Hornbook on Secured Transactions under the U.C.C., 364 pages, 1973 (Text)

Murray's Commercial Law, Problems and Materials, 366 pages, 1975 (Coursebook)

COMMERCIAL LAW—Continued

Nordstrom and Clovis' Problems and Materials on Commercial Paper, 458 pages, 1972 (Casebook)

Nordstrom and Lattin's Problems and Materials on Sales and Secured Transactions, 809 pages, 1968 (Casebook)

Nordstrom's Hornbook on Sales, 600 pages, 1970 (Text)

Selected Commercial Statutes, 1144 pages, 1976

Speidel, Summers and White's Teaching Materials on Commercial and Consumer Law, 2nd Ed., 1475 pages, 1974 (Casebook)

Stone's Uniform Commercial Code in a Nutshell, 507 pages, 1975 (Text)

Uniform Commercial Code, Official Text with Comments, 816 pages, 1972

UCC Article Nine Reprint, 128 pages, 1976

Weber's Commercial Paper in a Nutshell, 2nd Ed., 361 pages, 1975 (Text)

White and Summers' Hornbook on the Uniform Commercial Code, 1086 pages, 1972 (Text)

COMMUNITY PROPERTY

Burby's Cases on Community Property, 4th Ed., 342 pages, 1955 (Casebook)

Huie's Texas Cases and Materials on Marital Property Rights, 681 pages, 1966 (Casebook)

Verrall's Cases and Materials on California Community Property, 3rd Ed., 547 pages, 1977 (Casebook)

COMPARATIVE LAW

Langbein's Comparative Criminal Procedure: Germany, 172 pages, 1977 (Casebook)

CONFLICT OF LAWS

Cramton, Currie and Kay's Cases-Comments-Questions on Conflict of Laws, 2nd Ed., 1021 pages, 1975 (Casebook)

Ehrenzweig's Treatise on Conflict of Laws, 824 pages, 1962 (Text)

Ehrenzweig's Conflicts in a Nutshell, 3rd Ed., 432 pages, 1974 (Text)

Goodrich and Scoles' Hornbook on Conflict of Laws, 4th Ed., 483 pages, 1964 (Text)

Scoles and Weintraub's Cases and Materials on Conflict of Laws, 2nd Ed., 966 pages, 1972 (Casebook)

CONSTITUTIONAL LAW

Engdahl's Constitutional Power in a Nutshell: Federal and State, 411 pages, 1974 (Text)

CONSTITUTIONAL LAW—Continued

Ginsburg's Constitutional Aspects of Sex-Based Discrimination, 129 pages, 1974 (Casebook)—reprint from Davidson, Ginsburg and Kay's Cases on Sex-Based Discrimination, 1974

Lockhart, Kamisar and Choper's Cases-Comments-Questions on Constitutional Law, 4th Ed., 1664 pages plus Appendix, 1975, with 1977 Supplement (Casebook)

Lockhart, Kamisar and Choper's Cases-Comments-Questions on the American Constitution, 4th Ed., 1249 pages plus Appendix, 1975, with 1977 Supplement (Casebook)—reprint from Lockhart, et al. Cases on Constitutional Law, 4th Ed., 1975

Lockhart, Kamisar and Choper's Cases and Materials on Constitutional Rights and Liberties, 4th Ed., 1244 pages plus Appendix, 1975, with 1977 Supplement (Casebook)—reprint from Lockhart, et al. Cases on Constitutional Law, 4th Ed., 1975

Miller's Presidential Power in a Nutshell, 328 pages, 1977 (Text)

Nowak, Rotunda and Young's Hornbook on Constitutional Law, 974 pages, 1978 (Text)

Vieira's Civil Rights in a Nutshell, 279 pages, 1978 (Text)

CONSUMER LAW

Epstein's Consumer Protection in a Nutshell, 322 pages, 1976 (Text)

Kripke's Text-Cases-Materials on Consumer Credit, 454 pages, 1970 (Casebook)

McCall's Consumer Protection, Cases, Notes and Materials, 594 pages, 1977, with 1977 Statutory Supplement (Casebook)

Schrag's Cases and Materials on Consumer Protection, 2nd Ed., 197 pages, 1973 (Casebook)—reprint from Cooper, et al. Cases on Law and Poverty, 2nd Ed., 1973

Selected Commercial Statutes, 1144 pages, 1976

Uniform Consumer Credit Code, Official Text with Comments, 218 pages, 1974

CONTRACTS

Calamari & Perillo's Cases and Problems on Contracts, approximately 1100 pages, August 1978 (Casebook)

Calamari and Perillo's Hornbook on Contracts, 2nd Ed., 878 pages, 1977 (Text)

Corbin's Text on Contracts, One Volume Student Edition, 1224 pages, 1952 (Text)

CONTRACTS—Continued

Freedman's Cases and Materials on Contracts, 658 pages, 1973 (Casebook)

Fuller and Eisenberg's Cases on Basic Contract Law, 3rd Ed., 1043 pages, 1972 (Casebook)

Jackson's Cases on Contract Law in Modern Society, 1404 pages, 1973 (Casebook)

Reitz's Cases on Contracts as Basic Commercial Law, 763 pages, 1975 (Casebook)

Schaber and Rohwer's Contracts in a Nutshell, 307 pages, 1975 (Text)

Simpson's Hornbook on Contracts, 2nd Ed., 510 pages, 1965 (Text)

COPYRIGHT

Nimmer's Cases and Materials on Copyright and Other Aspects of Law Pertaining to Literary, Musical and Artistic Works, 828 pages, 1971, with 1977 Supplement (Casebook)

See also Patent Law

CORPORATIONS

Hamilton's Cases on Corporations—Including Partnerships and Limited Partnerships, 998 pages, 1976, with 1976 Statutory Supplement and 1977 Case Supplement (Casebook)

Henn's Cases on Corporations, 1279 pages, 1974, with 1974 Statutes, Forms and Case Study Supplement (Casebook)

Henn's Hornbook on Corporations, 2nd Ed., 956 pages, 1970 (Text)

CORRECTIONS

Krantz's Cases and Materials on the Law of Corrections and Prisoners' Rights, 1130 pages, 1973, with 1977 Supplement (Casebook)

Krantz's Law of Corrections and Prisoners' Rights in a Nutshell, 353 pages, 1976 (Text)

Model Rules and Regulations on Prisoners' Rights and Responsibilities, 212 pages, 1973

Popper's Post-Conviction Remedies in a Nutshell, approximately 360 pages, April 1978 (Text)

CREDITOR'S RIGHTS

Epstein's Debtor-Creditor Relations in a Nutshell, 309 pages, 1973 (Text)

Epstein and Landers' Debtors and Creditors: Cases and Materials, 722 pages, 1978 (Casebook)

MacLachlan's Hornbook on Bankruptcy, 500 pages, 1956 (Text)

Riesenfeld's Cases and Materials on Creditors' Remedies and Debtors'

CREDITOR'S RIGHTS—Continued

Protection, 2nd Ed., 808 pages, 1975, with 1975 Statutory Supplement and 1977 Supplement Update (Casebook)

Selected Bankruptcy Statutes, 486 pages, 1974

CRIMINAL LAW AND CRIMINAL PROCEDURE

Cohen and Gobert's Problems in Criminal Law, 297 pages, 1976 (Problem book)

Davis' Police Discretion, 176 pages, 1975 (Text)

Dix and Sharlot's Cases and Materials on Criminal Law, 1360 pages, 1973 (Casebook)

Federal Rules of Civil-Appellate-Criminal Procedure—West Law School Edition, 334 pages, 1977

Grano's Problems in Criminal Procedure, 171 pages, 1974 (Problem book)

Heymann and Kenety's The Murder Trial of Wilbur Jackson: A Homicide in the Family, 340 pages, 1975 (Case Study)

Israel and LaFave's Criminal Procedure in a Nutshell, 2nd Ed., 404 pages, 1975 (Text)

Johnson's Criminal Law: Cases, Materials and Text on Substantive Criminal Law in its Procedural Context, 878 pages, 1975, with 1977 Supplement (Casebook)

Kamisar, LaFave and Israel's Cases, Comments and Questions on Modern Criminal Procedure, 4th Ed., 1572 pages, plus Appendix, 1974, with 1978 Supplement (Casebook)

Kamisar, LaFave and Israel's Cases, Comments and Questions on Basic Criminal Procedure, 4th Ed., 790 pages, 1974, with 1978 Supplement (Casebook)—reprint from Kamisar, et al. Modern Criminal Procedure, 4th Ed., 1974

LaFave's Modern Criminal Law: Cases, Comments and Questions, 789 pages, 1978 (Casebook)

LaFave and Scott's Hornbook on Criminal Law, 763 pages, 1972 (Text)

Loewy's Criminal Law in a Nutshell, 302 pages, 1975 (Text)

Uniform Rules of Criminal Procedure—Approved Draft, 407 pages, 1974

Uviller's The Processes of Criminal Justice: Adjudication, 991 pages, 1975, with 1977 Supplement (Casebook)

Uviller's The Processes of Criminal Justice: Investigation, 744 pages, 1974, with 1977 Supplement (Casebook)

CRIMINAL LAW AND CRIMINAL PROCEDURE—Continued

Vorenberg's Cases on Criminal Law and Procedure, 1044 pages, 1975, with 1977 Supplement (Casebook)

See also Corrections, Juvenile Justice

DECEDENTS ESTATES

See Wills, Trusts and Estates

DOMESTIC RELATIONS

Clark's Cases and Problems on Domestic Relations, 2nd Ed., 918 pages, 1974, with 1977 Supplement (Casebook)

Clark's Hornbook on Domestic Relations, 754 pages, 1968 (Text)

Kay's Sex-Based Discrimination in Family Law, 305 pages, 1974 (Casebook)—reprint from Davidson, Ginsburg and Kay's Cases on Sex-Based Discrimination, 1974

Krause's Cases and Materials on Family Law, 1132 pages, 1976 (Casebook)

Krause's Family Law in a Nutshell, 400 pages, 1977 (Text)

Paulsen's Cases and Selected Problems on Family Law and Poverty, 2nd Ed., 200 pages, 1973 (Casebook)—reprint from Cooper, et al. Cases on Law and Poverty, 2nd Ed., 1973

DRUG ABUSE

Uelmen and Haddox's Cases on Drug Abuse and the Law, 564 pages, 1974, with 1977 Supplement (Casebook)

EDUCATION LAW

Morris' The Constitution and American Education, 833 pages, 1974 (Casebook)

EMPLOYMENT DISCRIMINATION

Cooper, Rabb and Rubin's Fair Employment Litigation: Text and Materials for Student and Practitioner, 590 pages, 1975 (Coursebook)

Player's Federal Law of Employment Discrimination in a Nutshell, 336 pages, 1976 (Text)

Sovern's Cases and Materials on Racial Discrimination in Employment, 2nd Ed., 167 pages, 1973 (Casebook)—reprint from Cooper et al. Cases on Law and Poverty, 2nd Ed., 1973

See also Women and the Law

ENVIRONMENTAL LAW

Currie's Cases and Materials on Pollution, 715 pages, 1975 (Casebook)

Federal Environmental Law, 1600 pages, 1974 (Text)

ENVIRONMENTAL LAW—Continued

Hanks, Tarlock and Hanks' Cases on Environmental Law and Policy, 1242 pages, 1974, with 1976 Supplement (Casebook)

Rodgers' Hornbook on Environmental Law, 956 pages, 1977 (Text)

See also Natural Resources

EQUITY

See Remedies

ESTATE PLANNING

Casner and Stein's Estate Planning under the Tax Reform Act of 1976, 456 pages, 1978 (Coursebook)

Lynn's An Introduction to Estate Planning, 274 pages, 1975 (Text)

EVIDENCE

Broun and Meisenholder's Problems in Evidence, 130 pages, 1973 (Problem book)

Cleary and Strong's Cases, Materials and Problems on Evidence, 2nd Ed., 1124 pages, 1975 (Casebook)

Federal Rules of Evidence for United States Courts and Magistrates, 323 pages, 1975

Lempert and Saltzburg's A Modern Approach to Evidence: Text, Problems, Transcripts and Cases, 1231 pages, 1977 (Casebook)

McCormick, Elliott and Sutton's Cases and Materials on Evidence, 4th Ed., 1088 pages, 1971 (Casebook)

McCormick's Hornbook on Evidence, 2nd Ed., 938 pages, 1972 (Text)

Rothstein's Evidence in a Nutshell, 406 pages, 1970 (Text)

FEDERAL JURISDICTION AND PROCEDURE

Currie's Cases and Materials on Federal Courts, 2nd Ed., 1040 pages, 1975, with 1977 Supplement (Casebook)

Currie's Federal Jurisdiction in a Nutshell, 228 pages, 1976 (Text)

Federal Rules of Civil-Appellate-Criminal Procedure—West Law School Edition, 334 pages, 1977

Forrester and Moye's Cases and Materials on Federal Jurisdiction and Procedure, 3rd Ed., 917 pages, 1977 (Casebook)

Merrill and Vetri's Problems on Federal Courts and Civil Procedure, 460 pages, 1974 (Problem book)

Wright's Hornbook on Federal Courts, 3rd Ed., 818 pages, 1976 (Text)

FUTURE INTERESTS

See Wills, Trusts, and Estates

HOUSING AND URBAN DEVELOPMENT

Berger's Cases and Materials on Housing, 2nd Ed., 254 pages, 1973 (Casebook)—reprint from Cooper et al. Cases on Law and Poverty, 2nd Ed., 1973

Krasnowiecki's Cases and Materials on Housing and Urban Development, 697 pages, 1969, with 1969 Statutory Supplement (Casebook)

See also Land Use

INSURANCE

Keeton's Cases on Basic Insurance Law, 2nd Ed., 1086 pages, 1977

Keeton's Basic Text on Insurance Law, 712 pages, 1971 (Text)

Keeton's Case Supplement to Keeton's Basic Text on Insurance Law, approximately 350 pages, May 1978 (Casebook)

Keeton's Programmed Problems in Insurance Law, 243 pages, 1972 (Text Supplement)

INTERNATIONAL LAW

Friedmann, Lissityzyn and Pugh's Cases and Materials on International Law, 1205 pages, 1969, with 1972 Supplement (Casebook)

Jackson's Legal Problems of International Economic Relations, 1097 pages, 1977, with Statutory Supplement (Casebook)

Kirgis' International Organizations in Their Legal Setting, 1016 pages, 1977 (Casebook)

INTRODUCTION TO LAW

Dobbyn's So You Want to go to Law School, Revised First Edition, 206 pages, 1976 (Text)

Kinyon's Introduction to Law Study and Law Examinations in a Nutshell, 389 pages, 1971 (Text)

See also Legal Method and Legal System

JUDICIAL ADMINISTRATION

Carrington, Meador and Rosenberg's Justice on Appeal, 263 pages, 1976 (Casebook)

Nelson's Cases and Materials on Judicial Administration and the Administration of Justice, 1032 pages, 1974 (Casebook)

JURISPRUDENCE

Christie's Text and Readings on Jurisprudence—The Philosophy of Law, 1056 pages, 1973 (Casebook)

JUVENILE JUSTICE

Fox's Cases and Materials on Modern Juvenile Justice, 1012 pages, 1972 (Casebook)

Fox's Juvenile Courts in a Nutshell, 2nd Ed., 275 pages, 1977 (Text)

LABOR LAW

Gorman's Labor Law-Unionization and Collective Bargaining, 914 pages, 1976 (Text)

Oberer and Hanslowe's Cases and Materials on Labor Law—Collective Bargaining in a Free Society, 1091 pages, 1972, with 1972 Statutory Supplement, and 1975 Case Supplement (Casebook)

See also Employment Discrimination, Social Legislation

LAND FINANCE—PROPERTY SECURITY

Maxwell, Riesenfeld, Hetland and Warren's Cases on California Security Transactions in Land, 2nd Ed., 584 pages, 1975 (Casebook)

Nelson and Whitman's Cases on Real Estate Finance and Development, 1064 pages, 1976 (Casebook)

Osborne's Cases and Materials on Secured Transactions, 559 pages, 1967 (Casebook)

Osborne's Hornbook on Mortgages, 2nd Ed., 805 pages, 1970 (Text)

LAND USE

Beuscher, Wright and Gitelman's Cases and Materials on Land Use, 2nd Ed., 1133 pages, 1976 (Casebook)

Hagman's Cases on Public Planning and Control of Urban and Land Development, 1208 pages, 1973, with 1976 Supplement (Casebook)

Hagman's Hornbook on Urban Planning and Land Development Control Law, 706 pages, 1971 (Text)

See also Housing and Urban Development

LAW AND ECONOMICS

Manne's The Economics of Legal Relationships—Readings in the Theory of Property Rights, 660 pages, 1975 (Text)

See also Regulated Industries

LAW AND MEDICINE—PSYCHIATRY

King's The Law of Medical Malpractice in a Nutshell, 340 pages, 1977 (Text)

LEGAL RESEARCH AND WRITING

Cohen's Legal Research in a Nutshell, 3rd Ed., 415 pages, 1978 (Text)

LEGAL RESEARCH AND WRITING—C't'd

How to Find the Law With Special Chapters on Legal Writing, 7th Ed., 542 pages, 1976. Problem book available (Coursebook)

Rombauer's Legal Problem Solving—Analysis, Research and Writing, 3rd Ed., approximately 350 pages, May 1978. Problem Supplement available (Casebook)

Statsky's Legal Research, Writing and Analysis: Some Starting Points, 180 pages, 1974 (Text)—reprint from Statsky's Introduction to Paralegalism, 1974

Statsky and Wernet's Case Analysis and Fundamentals of Legal Writing, 576 pages, 1977 (Text)

Weihofen's Legal Writing Style, 323 pages, 1961 (Text)

LEGAL CLINICS

Cooper, Rabb and Rubin's Fair Employment Litigation: Text and Materials for Student and Practitioner, 590 pages, 1975 (Coursebook)

Freeman and Weihofen's Cases and Text on Clinical Law Training—Interviewing and Counseling, 506 pages, 1972 (Casebook)

LEGAL PROFESSION

Aronson's Problems in Professional Responsibility, 280 pages, 1978 (Problem book)

Mellinkoff's The Conscience of a Lawyer, 304 pages, 1973 (Text)

Mellinkoff's Lawyers and the System of Justice, 983 pages, 1976 (Casebook)

Pirsig and Kirwin's Cases and Materials on Professional Responsibility, 3rd Ed., 667 pages, 1976, with 1977 Supplement (Casebook)

LEGAL HISTORY

See Legal Method and Legal System

LEGAL METHOD AND LEGAL SYSTEM

Aldisert's Readings, Materials and Cases in the Judicial Process, 948 pages, 1976 (Casebook)

Fryer and Orentlicher's Cases and Materials on Legal Method and Legal System, 1043 pages, 1967 (Casebook)

Greenberg's Judicial Process and Social Change, 666 pages, 1977 (Coursebook)

Kempin's Historical Introduction to Anglo-American Law in a Nutshell, 2nd Ed., 280 pages, 1973 (Text)

Kimball's Historical Introduction to the Legal System, 610 pages, 1966 (Casebook)

LEGAL METHOD AND LEGAL SYSTEM
—Continued

Leflar's Appellate Judicial Opinions, 343 pages, 1974 (Text)

Mashaw and Merrill's Introduction to the American Public Law System, 1095 pages, 1975 (Casebook)

Murphy's Cases and Materials on Introduction to Law—Legal Process and Procedure, 772 pages, 1977 (Casebook)

Smith's Cases and Materials on the Development of Legal Institutions, 757 pages, 1965 (Casebook)

Statsky's Legislative Analysis: How to Use Statutes and Regulations, 216 pages, 1975 (Text)

LEGISLATION

Davies' Legislative Law and Process in a Nutshell, 279 pages, 1975 (Text)

Nutting and Dickerson's Cases and Materials on Legislation, 5th Ed., 744 pages, 1978 (Casebook)

Statsky's Legislative Analysis: How to Use Statutes and Regulations, 216 pages, 1975 (Text)

LOCAL GOVERNMENT

McCarthy's Local Government Law in a Nutshell, 386 pages, 1975 (Text)

Michelman and Sandalow's Cases-Comments-Questions on Government in Urban Areas, 1216 pages, 1970, with 1972 Supplement (Casebook)

Stason and Kauper's Cases and Materials on Municipal Corporations, 3rd Ed., 692 pages, 1959 (Casebook)

Valente's Cases and Materials on Local Government Law, 928 pages, 1975 (Casebook)

MASS COMMUNICATION LAW

Gillmor and Barron's Cases and Comment on Mass Communication Law, 2nd Ed., 1007 pages, 1974 (Casebook)

Zuckman and Gayne's Mass Communications Law in a Nutshell, 431 pages, 1977 (Text)

MORTGAGES

See Land Finance—Property Security

NATURAL RESOURCES LAW

Trelease, Bloomenthal and Geraud's Cases and Materials on Natural Resources Law, 1131 pages, 1965 (Casebook)

See also Environmental Law

OFFICE PRACTICE

Binder and Price's Legal Interviewing and Counseling: A Client-Centered Approach, 232 pages 1977 (Text)

OFFICE PRACTICE—Continued

Edwards and White's Problems, Readings and Materials on the Lawyer as a Negotiator, 484 pages, 1977 (Casebook)

Freeman and Weihofen's Cases and Text on Clinical Law Training—Interviewing and Counseling, 506 pages, 1972 (Casebook)

Shaffer's Legal Interviewing and Counseling in a Nutshell, 353 pages, 1976 (Text)

Strong and Clark's Law Office Management, 424 pages, 1974 (Casebook)

OIL AND GAS

Hemingway's Hornbook on Oil and Gas, 486 pages, 1971 (Text)

Huie, Woodward and Smith's Cases and Materials on Oil and Gas, 2nd Ed., 955 pages, 1972 (Casebook)

See also Natural Resources

PARTNERSHIP

See Agency—Partnership

PATENT LAW

Choate's Cases and Materials on Patent Law, 1060 pages, 1973 (Casebook)

See also Copyright

POVERTY LAW

Brudno's Poverty, Inequality, and the Law: Cases-Commentary-Analysis, 934 pages, 1976 (Casebook)

Cooper, Dodyk, Berger, Paulsen, Schrag and Sovern's Cases and Materials on Law and Poverty, 2nd Ed., 1208 pages, 1973 (Casebook)

Cooper and Dodyk's Cases and Materials on Income Maintenance, 2nd Ed., 449 pages, 1973 (Casebook)—reprint from Cooper et al. Cases on Law and Poverty, 2nd Ed., 1973

LaFrance, Schroeder, Bennett and Boyd's Hornbook on Law of the Poor, 558 pages, 1973 (Text)

See also Social Legislation

PRODUCTS LIABILITY

Noel and Phillips' Cases on Products Liability, 836 pages, 1976 (Casebook)

Noel and Phillips' Products Liability in a Nutshell, 365 pages, 1974 (Text)

PROPERTY

Aigler, Smith and Tefft's Cases on Property, 2 volumes, 1339 pages, 1960 (Casebook)

Bernhardt's Real Property in a Nutshell, 425 pages, 1975 (Text)

Browder, Cunningham and Julin's Cases on Basic Property Law, 2nd Ed., 1397 pages, 1973 (Casebook)

LAW SCHOOL PUBLICATIONS — Continued

PROPERTY—Continued

Burby's Hornbook on Real Property, 3rd Ed., 490 pages, 1965 (Text)

Chused's A Modern Approach to Property: Cases—Notes—Materials, approximately 1150 pages, May 1978 (Casebook)

Cohen's Materials for a Basic Course in Property, approximately 600 pages, July 1978 (Casebook)

Donahue, Kauper and Martin's Cases on Property, 1501 pages, 1974 (Casebook)

Moynihan's Introduction to Real Property, 254 pages, 1962 (Text)

Phipps' Titles in a Nutshell, 277 pages, 1968 (Text)

Smith and Boyer's Survey of the Law of Property, 2nd Ed., 510 pages, 1971 (Text)

Uniform Eminent Domain Code, Official Text with Comments, 160 pages, 1975

Uniform Land Transactions Act, 1975 Official Text with Comments, 170 pages, 1976

See also Housing and Urban Development, Land Finance, Land Use

REAL ESTATE

See Land Finance

REGULATED INDUSTRIES

Morgan's Cases and Materials on Economic Regulation of Business, 830 pages, 1976 (Casebook)

Pozen's Financial Institutions: Cases, Materials and Problems on Investment Management, 844 pages, 1978 (Casebook)

White's Teaching Materials on Banking Law, 1058 pages, 1976, with 1976 Statutory Supplement (Casebook)

See also Mass Communication Law

REMEDIES

Cribbet's Cases and Materials on Judicial Remedies, 762 pages, 1954 (Casebook)

Dobbs' Hornbook on Remedies, 1067 pages, 1973 (Text)

Dobbs' Problems in Remedies, 137 pages, 1974 (Problem book)

Dobbyn's Injunctions in a Nutshell, 264 pages, 1974 (Text)

McClintock's Hornbook on Equity, 2nd Ed., 643 pages, 1948 (Text)

McCormick's Hornbook on Damages, 811 pages, 1935 (Text)

O'Connell's Remedies in a Nutshell, 364 pages, 1977 (Text)

Van Hecke, Leavell and Nelson's Cases and Materials on Equitable Remedies

REMEDIES—Continued

and Restitution, 2nd Ed., 717 pages, 1973 (Casebook)

Wright's Cases on Remedies, 498 pages, 1955 (Casebook)

York and Bauman's Cases and Materials on Remedies, 2nd Ed., 1381 pages, 1973 (Casebook)

REVIEW MATERIALS

Ballantine's Problems

Burby's Law Refreshers

Smith's Review

SECURITIES REGULATION

Ratner's Materials on Securities Regulation, 893 pages, 1975, with 1977 Supplement (Casebook)

Ratner's Securities Regulation in a Nutshell, 300 pages, 1978 (Text)

SOCIAL LEGISLATION

Brudno's Income Redistribution Theories and Programs: Cases-Commentary-Analysis, 480 pages, 1977 (Casebook) —reprint from Brudno's Poverty, Inequality and the Law, 1976

Cooper and Dodyk's Cases and Materials on Income Maintenance, 2nd Ed., 449 pages, 1973 (Casebook)—reprint from Cooper et al. Cases on Law and Poverty, 2nd Ed., 1973

Malone, Plant and Little's Cases on the Employment Relation, 1055 pages, 1974, with 1977 Supplement (Casebook)

See also Poverty Law

SURETYSHIP

Osborne's Cases on Suretyship, 221 pages, 1966 (Casebook)

Simpson's Hornbook on Suretyship, 569 pages, 1950 (Text)

TAXATION

Chommie's Hornbook on Federal Income Taxation, 2nd Ed., 1051 pages, 1973 (Text)

Chommie's Review of Federal Income Taxation, 90 pages, 1973 (Text)

Hellerstein and Hellerstein's Cases on State and Local Taxation, 4th Ed., approximately 1120 pages, April 1978 (Casebook)

Kragen and McNulty's Cases and Materials on Federal Income Taxation, 2nd Ed., 1107 pages, 1974, with 1977 Supplement (Casebook)

Kramer and McCord's Problems for Federal Estate and Gift Taxes, 206 pages, 1976 (Problem book)

Lowndes, Kramer and McCord's Hornbook on Federal Estate and Gift Taxes, 3rd Ed., 1099 pages, 1974 (Text)

LAW SCHOOL PUBLICATIONS — Continued

TAXATION—Continued

McCord's 1976 Estate and Gift Tax Reform–Analysis, Explanation and Commentary, 377 pages, 1977 (Text)

McNulty's Federal Estate and Gift Taxation in a Nutshell, 343 pages, 1973 (Text)

McNulty's Federal Income Taxation of Individuals in a Nutshell, 2nd Ed., approximately 320 pages, May 1978 (Text)

Rice's Problems and Materials in Federal Estate and Gift Taxation, 3rd Ed., 474 pages, 1978 (Casebook)

Rice's Problems and Materials in Federal Income Taxation, 2nd Ed., 589 pages, 1971 (Casebook)

Rose and Raskind's Advanced Federal Income Taxation: Corporate Transactions–Cases, Materials and Problems, 955 pages, 1978 (Casebook)

Selected Federal Taxation Statutes and Regulations, 1321 pages, 1977

Soboloff's Federal Income Taxation of Corporations and Stockholders in a Nutshell, 374 pages, 1978 (Text)

TORTS

Green, Pedrick, Rahl, Thode, Hawkins, Smith, and Treece's Cases and Materials on Torts, 2nd Ed., 1360 pages, 1977 (Casebook)

Green, Pedrick, Rahl, Thode, Hawkins, Smith and Treece's Advanced Torts: Injuries to Business, Political and Family Interests, 544 pages, 1977 (Casebook)—reprint from Green, et al Cases and Materials on Torts, 2nd Ed., 1977

Keeton's Computer-Aided and Workbook Exercises on Tort Law, 164 pages, 1976 (Coursebook)

Keeton and Keeton's Cases and Materials on Torts, 2nd Ed., 1200 pages, 1977 (Casebook)

Kionka's Torts: Injuries to Persons and Property in a Nutshell, 434 pages, 1977 (Text)

Prosser's Hornbook on Torts, 4th Ed., 1208 pages, 1971 (Text)

Shapo's Cases on Tort and Compensation Law, 1244 pages, 1976 (Casebook)

See also Products Liability

TRADE REGULATION

Oppenheim and Weston's Cases and Materials on Unfair Trade Practices and Consumer Protection, 3rd Ed., 1065 pages, 1974, with 1977 Supplement (Casebook)

See also Antitrust, Regulated Industries

TRIAL ADVOCACY

Hegland's Trial and Practice Skills in a Nutshell, approximately 380 pages, May 1978 (Text)

Jean's Trial Advocacy (Student Edition), 473 pages, 1975 (Text)

McElhaney's Effective Litigation, 457 pages, 1974 (Casebook)

TRUSTS

See Wills, Trusts and Estates

WATER LAW

Trelease's Cases and Materials on Water Law, 2nd Ed., 863 pages, 1974 (Casebook)

See also Natural Resources

WILLS, TRUSTS AND ESTATES

Atkinson's Hornbook on Wills, 2nd Ed., 975 pages, 1953 (Text)

Averill's Uniform Probate Code in a Nutshell, 425 pages, 1978 (Text)

Bogert's Hornbook on Trusts, 5th Ed., 726 pages, 1973 (Text)

Clark, Lusky and Murphy's Cases and Materials on Gratuitous Transfers, 2nd Ed., 1102 pages, 1977 (Casebook)

Gulliver's Cases and Materials on Future Interests, 624 pages, 1959 (Casebook)

Gulliver's Introduction to the Law of Future Interests, 87 pages, 1959 (Casebook)

Halbach (Editor)—Death, Taxes, and Family Property: Essays and American Assembly Report, 189 pages, 1977 (Text)

Mennell's Cases and Materials on California Decedent's Estates, 566 pages, 1973 (Casebook)

Powell's Cases on Trusts and Wills, 639 pages, 1960 (Casebook)

Simes' Hornbook on Future Interests, 2nd Ed., 355 pages, 1966 (Text)

Turrentine's Cases and Text on Wills and Administration, 2nd Ed., 483 pages, 1962 (Casebook)

Uniform Probate Code, 5th Ed., Official Text With Comments, 384 pages, 1977

WOMEN AND THE LAW

Davidson, Ginsburg and Kay's Text, Cases and Materials on Sex-Based Discrimination, 1031 pages, 1974, with 1975 Supplement (Casebook)

See also Employment Discrimination

WORKMEN'S COMPENSATION

See Social Legislation

CIVIL PROCEDURE
CASES AND MATERIALS

SECOND EDITION

By

JOHN J. COUND
Professor of Law, University of Minnesota

JACK H. FRIEDENTHAL
Professor of Law, Stanford University

ARTHUR R. MILLER
Professor of Law, Harvard University

AMERICAN CASEBOOK SERIES

ST. PAUL, MINN.
WEST PUBLISHING CO.
1974

C.F. & M.Cs.Civ.Proc.2d Ed. ACB
5th Reprint—1978

To our teachers,

Richard H. Field and Benjamin Kaplan of the Harvard Law School, who first unlocked the door for us and who will not be surprised if we seem, on occasion, to have mislaid the key.

*

PREFACE

In preparing a Second Edition of this book, we have been fortunate in having the benefit of many comments of colleagues from the large number of schools in which the First Edition has been used since its publication in 1968. These responses have been gratifying in confirming our own conclusion that the First Edition was a highly successful teaching tool, regardless of the precise form of the Civil Procedure course being taught or of the specific material covered in it. As a result, this Second Edition preserves the same basic format and much of the material found in the First Edition.

Why then is a Second Edition necessary? Certainly a revision cannot be justified simply to achieve relatively trivial improvements or merely to replace the original text with more recent matter of similar substantive content. The reason for this volume is that since publication of the First Edition there have been important developments in several areas of procedure, notably pretrial discovery and class actions, which give rise to intellectually stimulating questions and policy considerations that require inclusion in a contemporary casebook. Thus, the chapter on discovery has been updated in light of the 1970 amendments to the Federal Rules of Civil Procedure and the new cases interpreting them. The chapter on class actions has been substantially reworked and expanded, as is befitting that area of growing concern. In addition the chapter has been moved from the end of the book, where it appeared in the First Edition, so that it now follows Chapter Six, which deals with the general problems of joinder of parties and claims. We believe it is now preferable, although by no means necessary, to treat class actions (and perhaps interpleader and intervention) after joinder of claims and parties and before the chapters on discovery, pretrial, and trial in order that the special problems raised in class suits may be considered in the context of these chapters.

In addition to these significant alterations, the new edition contains other notable changes that should prove helpful to the student's understanding of the material. First, we have reorganized and augmented much of the personal jurisdiction material. Second, we have streamlined portions of the chapter on modern pleading and have encompassed within it the material on methods of challenging pleadings, which previously had been included, along with summary judgment and default, in the chapter on adjudication without trial. Third, we have rearranged the discussion of the final judgment rule in the chapter on appeals. Fourth, we have added new material on a variety of subjects, including "sewer" service, jury trial in state courts, and burdens of persuasion. Finally, as one might expect, we have updated the authorities throughout the book and, where appropriate, have substituted newer, more interesting cases and materials.

PREFACE

This Second Edition, like the First, has been planned and executed in the belief that a course in Civil Procedure should be one of the most exciting and entertaining intellectual experiences in a student's law-school career. Our primary purpose has been to produce a device for teaching rather than a tool for research, and several consequences have flowed from this choice.

We have looked for modern cases in which the facts are interesting, in which the conflicting policies seem to be in equipoise, or in which the context has extrinsic fascination, rather than for cases whose opinions offer tight little monographs on various aspects of procedure. After all, a student's preparation and participation in class discussion frequently are in direct proportion to the extent to which the materials are interesting and involving.

The notes and questions that follow nearly every principal case have been designed for the most part to encourage deeper analysis of the problems raised in the principal cases rather than to fill the student with additional detail. At the same time, we have tried to provide sufficient and selective references to secondary sources for the student who wishes to look further.

We have not aimed at a "hard" book. Civil procedure is sufficiently mysterious to law students that its ability to challenge survives best when presented in a clear and simple environment. The danger is not of patronizing students, but of losing them. In the textual survey in Chapter One, in the long note on "the nature of the trial process" in Chapter Eleven and in brief-er introductions to other sections of the book, we have tried to tell students where they are going, and through extensive cross-referencing and questions we have tried to force them to review where they have been.

We have not concentrated on the law of any one jurisdiction, although there is substantial emphasis on the operation of the Federal Rules of Civil Procedure, which have served as a model and focal point for serious discussion and implementation of procedural reform in a large majority of the states. In general the book operates on a comparative basis, except in contexts in which this approach has more limited utility than an in-depth exploration of a single system.

A careful attempt has been made to strike a balance between exploration of underlying philosophical problems and analysis of day-to-day matters that arise frequently in office practice or in the courts. Our theory is that a mixture of both is necessary to give students a comprehensive understanding of procedure. How else can they learn why, even today, after so many years of study, revision, and reform, major proposals for alteration of adjective law are still being made, and, undoubtedly, will continue to be made in the years to come? In addition, considerable use has been made of historical material, not only when it is directly relevant to today's system, as in the study of the right to jury trial, but also in contexts in which it is necessary for a true grasp of the basic problems.

PREFACE

Because courses in civil procedure vary greatly not only as to the hours allotted but also as to whether they are mandatory or optional and as to the year during which students are expected to take them, the materials in this edition are designed to provide maximum pedagogical flexibility. The cases and subjects covered have been selected primarily for a comprehensive, year-long course beginning in the first term of the law student's first year; yet they may easily be divided into two or more quite different subjects to be given either as preliminary or advanced courses. The modest expansion of the Second Edition was intended in part to enhance this quality.

The first chapter of this casebook sets forth a basic, textual statement of a procedural system's framework, without which an understanding of any particular part of the system is difficult, if not impossible. This initial discussion defines those procedural terms necessary for comprehending legal opinions, whether they be of a procedural or substantive character. This, we believe, is an important function of a course in procedure, especially when it forms part of the first year curriculum. The textual analysis, which can be assigned for study with little or no class discussion, is followed by a series of illustrative cases designed to raise the basic problems of a procedural system, to illustrate the interplay among its various aspects, and to highlight many of the points in the earlier text. An effort has been made to select cases that can be handled with relative dispatch so that the introduction does not become a de facto study of the entire course. In general, Chapter One is intended to let students form some idea as to the nature of the litigation "forest" before attempting to make them master of any of its "trees."

After the first chapter, the structure of the book proceeds in a chronological fashion. The authors believe that this is the most logical way to teach civil procedure because it permits students to see the evolution and maturation of the litigation process. Furthermore, by putting personal and subject-matter jurisdiction and the materials dealing with the history of civil procedure before such subjects as pleading, joinder, and discovery, first year students are given some "breathing time" in which to absorb enough substantive law from torts, contracts, and property courses to enable them to grasp the significance of such matters as "pleading a cause of action," "contributory negligence," and "joint and several interests." Finally, the authors have concluded that despite its conceptual difficulty, personal jurisdiction is a much more teachable and exhilarating introduction to civil procedure than is pleading.

The chapter on jurisdiction includes an extensive treatment of the federal courts. An investigation of a single system in detail seems the best way to impress students with the significance attached by courts to the concept of jurisdiction over the subject matter. The length of this material is greater than is customary in a civil procedure book, but part of it may readily be treated at the end of the course or be eliminated. We believe that without a working knowledge of such concepts as diversity of citizenship and ancillary jurisdiction, the procedural ramifications of the Erie doctrine and such indisputably procedural problems as joinder cannot be properly understood.

We have concluded that to omit a plenary section on common-law pleading, the forms of action, equity, and the nineteenth century reforms (as many procedure casebooks do) would only lead to the introduction of this material in driblets by lecture during the study of modern pleading and other subjects with no substantial saving in time and probably at a cost in comprehension. At the same time we have eschewed the temptation to overcompensate for the disappearance of courses in equity; we have not attempted to cover the substantive doctrines of that discipline in a historical note. Although we believe history is invaluable to the study of modern procedure, the modern pleading chapter has been planned as a choate whole, and does not require the coverage of the earlier background chapter.

The materials in this volume refer to and are augmented by a Supplement, which contains not only the federal statutes and rules governing procedure, as is traditional, but also comparative state provisions. In some cases other materials, such as notes of Advisory Committees, also are included. Thus at a glance students are able to see the different solutions put forth for particular procedural problems and are induced to explore the reasons why one rule has not been universally acclaimed as "superior" and adopted by all jurisdictions. Use of the Supplement has the added advantage of permitting teachers and students to keep abreast of interesting alterations in the often-changing statutes and rules governing Civil Procedure, without constant revision of the casebook itself. Our practice has been to revise and reissue the Supplement every two years, adding recent significant cases, thereby achieving considerable flexibility at a minimal cost to students.

All teachers of civil procedure are well aware of how difficult it is for students to grapple with problems in the abstract; for example in the field of pleading they may have only a vague notion of what a pleading looks like. The Supplement therefore also contains an illustrative problem, showing how a case develops in practice and samples of the documents that might actually have formed a portion of the record. It is important to note that these samples are not designed as models to be emulated. To the contrary, they often contain defects intended to induce students to criticize them in light of knowledge they have obtained from the cases and classroom discussion.

The cases and excerpts from other materials obviously have been extensively edited in order to shorten them and clarify issues for discussion. Except in a few situations, the materials from the First Edition have not been

PREFACE

significantly shortened in preparing the Second Edition. With regard to footnotes: the same numbering appears in the casebook as appears in the original sources; editors' footnotes are indicated by letters.

The authors are deeply grateful to a host of people who have helped us in the preparation of this volume, the original edition, and the Supplement. Among those deserving special mention for their aid are Prudence Beatty Abram, Sam L. Abram, (Professor) Barry B. Boyer, William M. Burns, Bertram Carp, Raymond Fisher, Jo Anne Friedenthal, (Professor) Joseph J. Kalo, (Professor) Mary Kay Kane, (Professor) Linda Silberman, and Donna Silverberg. We also are grateful to the following people for their great assistance in handling the manuscript, proofs, and a variety of other operations. Robert H. Goldman, Frederick W. Lambert, John J. McGonagle, Franklin N. Meyer, Norman A. Platt, and Martin C. Recchuite. Nor should we overlook the enormous secretarial assistance provided us by Virginia Hunt, Vivian Kurkjian, Beverly O'Leary, and Evelyn Roodhouse, the numerous helpful suggestions offered to us by our colleagues Professors Barbara Babcock, Edward H. Cooper, and Charles W. Wolfram, or the patience of our wives.

J. J. C.
J. H. F.
A. R. M.

April, 1974

*

SUMMARY OF CONTENTS

SUMMARY OF CONTENTS

SUMMARY OF CONTENTS

*

TABLE OF CONTENTS

TABLE OF CONTENTS

TABLE OF CONTENTS

TABLE OF CONTENTS

TABLE OF CONTENTS

TABLE OF CONTENTS

TABLE OF CONTENTS

TABLE OF CONTENTS

TABLE OF CONTENTS

TABLE OF CONTENTS

TABLE OF CONTENTS

TABLE OF CASES

The more significant cases, including the principal cases, are in Italic type. A selection of other cases cited in this book are in Roman. References are to Pages in this volume.

TABLE OF CASES

TABLE OF CASES

TABLE OF CASES

TABLE OF CASES

TABLE OF CASES

TABLE OF CASES

TABLE OF CASES

TABLE OF CASES

TABLE OF CASES

TABLE OF AUTHORITIES

References are to Pages

TABLE OF AUTHORITIES

TABLE OF AUTHORITIES

TABLE OF AUTHORITIES

TABLE OF AUTHORITIES

TABLE OF AUTHORITIES

TABLE OF AUTHORITIES

TABLE OF AUTHORITIES

TABLE OF AUTHORITIES

TABLE OF AUTHORITIES

TABLE OF AUTHORITIES

†

CIVIL PROCEDURE

CHAPTER 1

A SURVEY OF THE CIVIL ACTION

SECTION A. THE CONCERN AND CHARACTER OF PROCEDURE

The law of procedure is the body of rules that governs or provides the framework of the judicial process. The judicial process, in turn, guides the operation of courts in the determination of legal controversies, or as Wigmore defined the process, the decision "by an agent of state power, [of] a controversy existing between two individuals (or the State and an individual), by rational (not merely personal) considerations, purporting to rest on justice and law (i. e. the community's general sense of order)." [a] These definitions are terribly inadequate, and they contain question-begging elements that need definition themselves. But further explication would lead into endless philosophical debate. As stated these definitions will serve our purpose at this time if you understand from them the following points: (1) The judicial process deals not with abstract questions or hypothetical situations but with actual controversies between real parties. (2) These controversies are such that the community will direct its collective force to their resolution. (3) This resolution proceeds not arbitrarily but according to some standards of general application. (4) These standards are applied in a proceeding that follows some fixed lines set out by a system of rules known as procedure.

A distinctive element of the procedure for resolving legal controversies is the *adversary system.* This element is indeed central to the whole subject, and unless it is understood it becomes well nigh impossible to explain, much less to justify, most of our procedural law. It means that the responsibility for beginning suit, for shaping the issues, and for producing evidence rests almost entirely upon the parties to the controversy; the court takes almost no active part, it does not do its own investigating, it rarely even asks a question. Contrasted with the methods of scientific or historical research, this system of finding answers seems sometimes to reduce the whole operation to a game. Yet although the adversary system certainly is not the only possible approach to dispute resolution, it remains a significant element of most judicial systems.[b]

[a] Wigmore, *The Judicial Function,* in *Science of Legal Method* xxvi, xxviii (1917).

[b] For a general discussion of the adversary system in continental procedure, see Millar, *The Formative Principles of Civil Procedure,* and Engelmann, *A History of Continental Civil Procedure* 6–27 (1927).

There are, of course, many degrees between the antipodes of complete control by the parties and complete control by the court, and most systems of procédure fall somewhere between these extremes. In recent times there has been a trend toward increasing the affirmative or active functions of the court that reflects the larger trend away from the "sporting" or "game" theory of litigation. Nonetheless, it cannot be questioned that in the United States the primary responsibility and control over almost all phases of the judicial process continue to reside in the parties.

The reasons for the prevalence of the adversary system are manifold, but four postulates are certainly among the most important: (1) A truer decision will be reached as the result of a contest directed by interested parties. (2) The parties, who after all are the persons principally interested in the resolution of the controversy, should bear the major burden of the time and energy required. (3) Although impartial investigation may be better when no final decision need be reached, setting up sides makes easier the type of yes-or-no decision that is thought to be necessary in a law suit. (4) Since resort to law has replaced the resort to force that characterized primitive ages, the atavistic instinct to do battle is better satisfied by a means of settling disputes that is very much in the hands of the parties.

It is by no means clear that these arguments, or others that may be advanced, justify the extent to which the responsibility for directing legal contests is conferred upon the parties under our rules. The fact that every civilized state has seen fit to furnish an official method for the settlement of private disputes indicates that there is more than a merely personal interest in their resolution. When one reflects on the fact that the adversary system often means that victory will turn on considerations other than the justice or true merits of the cause, there is reason to believe that we have permitted it to take an exaggerated place in our judicial scheme. But the system remains and its presence will color every facet of this course. Full understanding of the materials in this book will require your constant attention to its existence as well as critical analysis of its shortcomings.

There is but one test of a good system of procedure: *Does it tend to the just and efficient determination of legal controversies?* [c] In this connection you must understand one thing: despite the fact that this course is only an introduction to procedure, you are not to assume that your function simply is to digest uncritically the law you read. It is a part of your process of learning to examine, "to wash in cynical acid," each rule, each form, each principle you learn. But while doing so keep in mind that many, diverse, and complex are the aspects of both justice and efficiency.

---

[c] Compare this statement with the principle of construction laid down for the federal courts in Federal Rule of Civil Procedure 1. The Federal Rules will be found in the Supplement.

SECTION B. AN OUTLINE OF THE PROCEDURE IN A CIVIL ACTION

———

The first step in a lawsuit strictly speaking is not a matter of law, certainly not a matter of the law of civil procedure. As already suggested, lawsuits do not begin themselves. Someone must first decide to sue someone else. If this decision is made intelligently, the person choosing to sue must have weighed several matters, among which at least three are basic.

A potential litigant obviously feels aggrieved or would not be thinking of a lawsuit. But he or she must further consider whether the grievance is one for which the law furnishes relief. There are a great many hurts a person may feel that the law will not redress. He loses his girl friend to another and wealthier suitor; she is offended by the paint on her neighbor's house; he has worked for weeks to persuade a grocer to buy his brand of peas, and sees the sale go to a competitor; she has been holding a plot of ground for speculation expecting industry to move in and the area is zoned for residential use; he slips on a spot of grease in the county courthouse but the county is immune from suit. If the injury is among those not redressable by a court of law, litigation would be a fruitless and wasteful exercise.

Even if he concludes that his grievance is one for which the courts will grant relief, a potential litigant must consider the probability of winning a lawsuit. He must ask whether he can find and bring into court the person who has injured him; whether he can produce the witnesses and documents that will prove his case; whether this proof will be believed; whether his adversary can justify his conduct or establish any defenses to the action; and whether his (or rather his attorney's) estimate of the law will turn out to be correct.

Then, and perhaps most important of all, he must consider whether what is won will be worth the time, the effort, and the expense it will cost, and he must weigh against this the alternatives to suit, among them settlement, arbitration, self-help, and letting matters rest. What form will the relief take? Most frequently it will be restricted to a judgment for damages. If this is true he must decide whether his injury is one for which a monetary payment will be satisfactory. Assuming it is, will defendant be rich enough to pay? How difficult will a judgment be to collect? How expensive? Will he end up with enough to pay his lawyer and the other litigation expenses that undoubtedly will be incurred? Even in a context in which the court may grant specific relief—for example, an order directing the opposing party to do something or to stop doing something—will compliance by defendant be possible? Worthwhile? Sufficient? In the same vein, he also must consider whether there are risks not directly tied to the suit: Will he win the reputation of a crank? Will he antagonize people whose goodwill he needs? Will the action publicize an error of judgment on his part or open his private affairs to public gaze?

Only after he has thoughtfully resolved these and similar questions will the prospective plaintiff be ready for the steps that follow. Let us now consider those steps in the light of a relatively uncluttered hypothetical case:

> Aikins, while crossing the street in front of her private home, was struck and seriously injured by an automobile driven by Beasley. On inquiry, Aikins found that the automobile was owned by Cecil and that Beasley apparently had been in Cecil's employ. Beasley was predictably without substantial assets and a judgment against him for Aikins' injuries promised little material compensation. But Cecil was wealthy, and Aikins was advised that if she could establish that Beasley had indeed been working for Cecil and had been negligent, she then could recover from Cecil. Aikins decided to sue Cecil for $50,000.

1. SELECTING A PROPER COURT

Aikins initially must determine in which court to bring the action. She probably will have some choice, but it will be a limited one. This is true because the court selected must have *jurisdiction over the subject matter* (that is, the constitution and statutes under which the court operates must have conferred upon it power to decide this type of case) and must also have *jurisdiction over the person* of Cecil (that is, Cecil must be subject or amenable to suit in the state in which the court is located).

Aikins probably will bring suit in a state court, for as we shall shortly see the subject-matter jurisdiction of the federal courts is severely limited. If the court organization of Aikins' state is typical, there will be courts of *original jurisdiction* in which cases are brought and tried, and one court of *appellate jurisdiction* that sits, with rare exceptions, only to review the decisions of lower courts. (In many states there will be a group of intermediate courts of appellate jurisdiction.) The courts of original jurisdiction probably consist of one set of courts of *general jurisdiction* and several sets of courts of *inferior jurisdiction*. The courts of general jurisdiction are organized into districts comprising for the most part several counties, although the largest or most populous counties each may constitute single districts. These district courts hear cases of many kinds and are competent to grant every kind of relief, but in order to bring a case in one of them plaintiff must have a claim for more than a specific amount, perhaps two or three thousand dollars. The courts of inferior jurisdiction will include municipal courts, whose jurisdiction resembles that of the district courts except that the claims they hear are of less importance; justice-of-the-peace courts, which hear very minor matters; and specialized tribunals such as the probate courts. Since Aikins' injuries are quite serious and her claim correspondingly large, she will, if she sues in a state court, bring the action in one of the district courts.

The Federal Government of course also operates a system of courts. The principal federal courts are the United States District Courts, courts of original jurisdiction of which there is at least one in every state; the eleven United States Courts of Appeals, each of which reviews the decisions of federal district courts in the several states within its circuit (with the exception of the Court of Appeals for the District of Columbia Circuit); and the Supreme Court of the United States, which not only reviews the decisions of federal courts but also reviews decisions of state courts that turn on an issue of federal law.

The jurisdiction over the subject-matter of the United States District Courts extends to many, but by no means all, cases involving federal law, and also to many cases, similar to Aikins', that do not involve federal law; the latter are cases in which there is *diversity of citizenship* (the parties are citizens of different states or one of them is a citizen of a foreign country) and the required *amount in controversy* (more than $10,000) is at stake. Diversity jurisdiction, in common with most of the federal courts' jurisdiction, is not *exclusive*; the state courts also are competent to hear these cases. But if Cecil is not a citizen of Aikins' state, Aikins may bring an action for $50,000 in a federal court. Indeed, in these circumstances, if Aikins sued Cecil in a state court in Aikins' home state Cecil could *remove* the action from the state court in which it was commenced to the federal district court in that state.[d]

It is not enough that the court selected by Aikins has jurisdiction over the subject-matter, however. That court, whether state or federal, must be one in which Cecil can be required to appear. This generally means that Cecil must reside or be found in the state in which the court sits. But the restrictions on a court's jurisdiction over the person have been expanding in recent decades, and if Cecil is not present in Aikins' state but he directed Beasley to drive there, Aikins probably will be able to bring the action in that state. (Even in the event that these facts cannot be established, and Cecil cannot be found in Aikins' state, he can be sued there, if he owns property in that state, but the judgment will be limited to the value of that property.)

Not every court that has jurisdiction over the subject-matter and jurisdiction over the person of defendant will hear a case. It also is necessary that an action be brought in a court having proper *venue*. Thus, although every court in Aikins' state could assert personal jurisdiction over Cecil if he was within its

d If Cecil is not a citizen of Aikins' state and Beasley is, then one of the considerations Aikins will have in deciding to join Beasley as a defendant is the effect on the availability of subject-matter jurisdiction in the federal courts. If Aikins wants to be in the federal court, she should not join Beasley; if Aikins wants to begin and stay in a state court, she should join him. In the latter case, there will not be complete diversity between the plaintiff on the one side and the defendants on the other.

boundaries, that state's statutes typically will provide that the case should be brought in a court whose district includes the county in which either Aikins or Cecil lives. Similarly, although Cecil might be found in a number of states, he can be sued in a federal court only in a district in which he or Aikins resides or where the claim arose.

Jurisdiction over the subject-matter is jealously guarded, and cannot be waived. If Aikins and Cecil are both citizens of the same state, a federal court will refuse to hear the action even though both are anxious that it do so. Jurisdiction over the person and venue, on the other hand, essentially are protections for defendant, who may waive them if he wishes.

2.   COMMENCING THE ACTION

After the court has been selected, Aikins must give notice to Cecil by *service of process*. The process typically consists of a *summons,* which directs defendant to appear and defend under penalty of *default*; that is, unless defendant answers the summons, a judgment will be entered against him. Service of process generally is achieved by *personal service*; the summons is physically delivered to the defendant or is left at his home, sometimes by the plaintiff or her attorney, sometimes by a public official such as a sheriff or a United States marshal. If Cecil lives in another state, but the circumstances are such that a court in Aikins' state may assert jurisdiction over Cecil, the summons may be personally delivered to him, or some form of *substituted service*, such as sending the papers by registered mail or delivering the summons to his agent within Aikins' state, may be employed. Even if Cecil cannot be located, service in yet another form, usually by *publication* in a newspaper for a certain length of time, may be allowed, although the validity of this kind of service in the type of case Aikins is bringing against Cecil is in serious question today. The United States Supreme Court repeatedly has emphasized that service must be of a kind reasonably calculated to bring the action to defendant's notice and from this perspective service by publication is marginal at best.

3.   PLEADING AND PARTIES

With the summons, Aikins usually will serve on Cecil the first of the *pleadings,* commonly called the *complaint*. This is a written statement that will contain Aikins' claim against Cecil. What should be required of such a statement? Obviously it may vary from a simple assertion that Cecil owes her $50,000, to a second-by-second narration of the accident, closely describing the scene and the conduct of each party, followed by a gruesome recital of Aikins' medical treatment and her prognosis for recovery. No procedural system insists upon either of these extremes, but systems do vary greatly in the detail required in the peadings. The degree of detail required largely reflects the purposes that the pleadings are expected to serve. These purposes are many, but three objectives are particularly relevant and to the extent that a procedural system regards one rather than another as crucial, we may expect to find differing amounts of detail required.

First, the system may desire the pleadings to furnish a basis for identifying and separating the legal and factual contentions involved so that the legal issues—and hopefully through them the entire case—may be disposed of at an early stage. Thus, suppose that Cecil's liability for Beasley's driving depends upon the degree of independence with which Beasley was working at the time of the accident. A dispute on this issue might exist on either or both of two elements. The parties might disagree as to what Beasley's duties were, and they might disagree as to whether those duties put Beasley so much under the control of Cecil that the law will impose liability on Cecil for Beasley's actions. The first disagreement would be a question of fact, and there would be no alternative to trying the suit and letting the finder of fact (usually the jury) decide the truth. But if there was agreement on that first element, a question of law would be presented by the second issue, which could be determined by the judge without a trial. The objective of which we are speaking would be fully served in such a case only if the pleadings set forth exactly what Beasley's job required him to do. It would be very inadequately served if the complaint only stated that "Beasley was driving the car on Cecil's business."

Second, the pleadings may be intended to establish in advance what a party proposes to prove at trial so that his opponent will know what contentions he must prepare to meet. If this objective is regarded as very important it will not be enough for the complaint to state that Beasley was negligent, or that Aikins suffered serious bodily injuries. It must say that Beasley was speeding, or was not keeping a proper look-out, or had inadequate brakes, or describe some other act of negligence and say that Aikins suffered a concussion, or a broken neck, or fractures of three ribs, or other injuries.

Third, the pleadings may be intended to give each party only a general notice of his opponent's contentions, in which event the system would rely upon subsequent stages of the lawsuit to identify the legal and factual contentions of the parties and to enable each to prepare to meet the opponent's case. In such a case a complaint similar to that in Form 9 of the Federal Rules would be sufficient.

Obviously each of the first two objectives is desirable. It is a waste of everybody's time to try lawsuits when the underlying legal claim is inadequate to support a judgment, and it is only fair that a person called upon to defend a judicial proceeding should know what he is alleged to have done. But to achieve the first objective fully may require pleading after pleading in order to expose and sharpen the issues; if detail is insisted upon, a long time may be consumed in producing it. Moreover, a single pleading oversight may eliminate a contention necessary to one party's case that easily could have been proven, but which will be held to have been waived. To achieve the second objective through the pleadings will mean that the parties must take rigid positions as to their factual contentions at the very beginning when they do not know what they will learn about their cases by the time trial begins. Either the first or second objective, if fully pursued, requires that the parties adhere to the positions taken in the pleadings. They could not be permitted to introduce evidence in conflict with the pleadings or to change them. For to the extent that *variances* between pleading and proof or *amendments* to the pleadings are permitted, the objectives will be lost. The court frequently will find itself forced either to depart from these objectives or to tolerate cases turning on the skill of the lawyers rather than on the merits of the controversy.

Following the service of Aikins' complaint, Cecil must respond. He may challenge the complaint by a *motion to dismiss*. This motion may challenge the court's jurisdiction over the subject-matter or Cecil's person, the service of process, or venue. It also may be a *motion to dismiss for failure to state a claim or cause of action* (or a *demurrer*). For the purpose of this motion, the facts alleged in the complaint are accepted as true, and the court considers whether, on this assumption, plaintiff has shown that the pleader is entitled to legal relief.

There are three general situations in which such a motion might be granted. First, the complaint may clearly show that the injury is one for which the law furnishes no redress; for example, when plaintiff simply alleges that "defendant has made faces at me." Second, plaintiff may have failed to include an allegation on a necessary part of the case; for example, Aikins might have alleged the accident, her injuries, and Beasley's negligence, and have forgotten to allege that Beasley was Cecil's servant. Third, the complaint may be so general or so confused that the court finds that it does not give adequate notice of what plaintiff's claim is; this would be true, for example, of a complaint in which Aikins merely said, "Cecil injured me and owes me $50,000," although complaints far more specific have fallen on this ground. Obviously, the extent to which motions to dismiss will be granted on the second and third grounds will vary with the degree of detail that the particular system requires of its pleadings.

If the motion to dismiss is denied, or if none is made, Cecil must file an *answer*. In this pleading, he must admit or deny the allegations made by Aikins in the complaint. Moreover if Cecil wishes to rely on certain contentions called *affirmative defenses*, he must plead them in the answer. Thus, if he wishes to contend that Aikins was negligent in the manner in which she tried to cross the street and that this negligence was also a cause of the accident, he must in many states plead this in the answer; if the answer only denied the allegations in Aikins' complaint, Cecil may not advance at trial the contention that Aikins' negligence caused the accident.

There may be further pleadings, particularly a *reply* by Aikins. But the tendency today is to close the pleadings after the answer, and if Cecil has raised new matters in his answer, they automatically are taken as denied by Aikins. There is one major exception: if Cecil has a claim against Aikins, particularly one that arises out of the same occurrence being sued upon by Aikins, Cecil may plead this claim as a *counterclaim* as part of the answer. This is in essence a complaint by Cecil, and Aikins will have to respond to it just as Cecil had to respond to the original complaint.

The original action between Aikins and Cecil may expand in terms of the number of parties, and this frequently will occur at the pleading stage. For example, although Aikins decided not to sue Beasley, Cecil might *implead* Beasley, asking that Beasley be held liable to him for whatever amount he may be found liable to Aikins, since his liability depends upon Beasley having been at fault. Cecil will decide whether to do this in light of a number of practical concerns, including the effect Beasley's presence will have on the *Aikins v. Cecil* suit.

---

4.   OBTAINING INFORMATION PRIOR TO TRIAL

In our discussion of the objectives of pleading, it was noted that some procedural systems do not regard the pleadings as the appropriate vehicle for enabling the parties to prepare for trial. The procedure viewed as primarily charged with this function is pretrial *discovery*. This is a generic term for several methods of obtaining information from an opposing party or from witnesses.

The chief method is to take *depositions* of parties and witnesses. In this procedure, the person whose deposition is to be taken is questioned by lawyers for each side through direct and cross-examination; the *deponent's* statements are taken down and transcribed. The device is useful in finding information that is relevant to the case, including unearthing leads as to other witnesses or documents; it also is useful in laying a basis for impeaching a witness who attempts to change his story at trial. The two parties almost certainly will want depositions taken of each other, as well as of Beasley; the depositions of Aikins and Cecil will be particularly important because they are treated as admissions, and can be used by their adversaries as evidence at trial. The deposition of even a nonparty witness who is unavailable at trial in some circumstances may be used in place of live testimony.

Another device especially adapted to probing the content of an opponent's case is *written interrogatories*, which usually may be addressed only to a party to the suit. (The availability of interrogatories may be one reason why Aikins might join Beasley as a defendant with Cecil or why Cecil might implead Beasley.) These interrogatories are answered by the party with counsel's aid, and the answers will not be as spontaneous as they would be on a deposition; on the other hand interrogatories will require him to supply some information that he does not carry in his head but can get, and may be even more valuable than the deposition in finding out what he will try to prove. Thus, information regarding Beasley's employment that Cecil cannot be expected to have in his mind may best be exposed in this way.

Other discovery devices include *orders for the production of documents,* such as the service record of Cecil's automobile, and *requests for admissions*, which will remove uncontested issues from the case. A particularly useful device for Cecil will be a court order directing Aikins to submit to a *physical examination* by a physician of Cecil's choice so that he may determine the real extent of Aikins' alleged injuries.

The availability of discovery, now increasing in scope and use throughout the country, has had its effect on the philosophy of pleadings. This is not simply because it enables parties to prepare for trial better than pleadings ever did. Of more significance perhaps is the fact that if broad discovery is allowed, it is senseless to make parties take rigid positions with respect to the issues at the very beginning of the lawsuit before they have had the chance to utilize these very useful devices for obtaining information. In addition, the availability of discovery does much to make summary judgment, which is discussed below, a viable and fair procedure, since it enables a party to ascertain those issues on which the opposing party has no evidence, and it also gives the opponent a real chance to develop such evidence.

---

5. SUMMARY JUDGMENT

One of the basic difficulties with attempting to resolve cases at the pleading stage is that the allegations of the parties must be accepted as true for the purpose of ruling on a motion to dismiss. Thus, if plaintiff tells a highly unlikely but possible story in the complaint, the court cannot dismiss the complaint even though it does not believe the allegations or think that the plaintiff will be able to prove the tale. The judge is not the person and the pleading stage is not the time to resolve questions of fact.

But in some cases it will be possible to supplement the pleadings with additional documents to show that an apparent issue that is decisive of the case is spurious. This is done by a motion for *summary judgment*. This motion can be supported by demonstrating that the crucial issue will have to be resolved in the mover's favor at trial, because the opposing party will be unable to produce any admissible evidence in support of his position on the issue.   For example, suppose that it is Cecil's position that prior to the accident he had fired Beasley, but that Beasley had secreted keys to Cecil's automobile and had taken Cecil's car without permission shortly before the accident. On the face of the pleadings, we have only an allegation that Beasley was Cecil's employee and a denial of that allegation; thus, the pleadings seem to present a question of credibility that cannot be resolved at this stage.   Cecil now moves for summary judgment, alleging that this issue is not a genuine one; he accompanies his motion with affidavits of his own and two other witnesses that he had fired Beasley; a deposition of the garage attendant indicating that he had been instructed not to allow Beasley to have the car, and that it was taken without Cecil's knowledge; and a deposition of Beasley to the effect that he had been fired, but wanted to use the car once more for his own purposes.   It is now incumbent upon Aikins to show that the issue is genuine; Aikins cannot rely simply upon her own assertion that all this is not so; after all she has no personal knowledge of the facts.   Aikins must convince the court that she has admissible evidence that Beasley still was acting as Cecil's employee in driving the car at the time of the accident.   If Aikins fails to do so, judgment will be entered against her.

It should be noted that in ruling on a motion for summary judgment the judge does not decide which side is telling the truth.   If Aikins presents an affidavit of a witness who says that he was present when Cecil claims he fired Beasley, and says further that Cecil told Beasley that this was only a subterfuge and that he wanted him to continue to work for him but to pretend to steal the car, summary judgment will not be appropriate even though the judge is firmly convinced that Aikins' affiant is lying.

6. SETTING THE CASE FOR TRIAL

After discovery is completed, and if the case has not been terminated by dismissal, summary judgment, or settlement, it must be set for *trial*.   Typically either party may file a *note of issue*, at which time the case will be given a number and placed on a *trial calendar*.   These calendars have become extremely long in many courts, and the case may have to wait a year, three years, or more before it is called for trial, especially if a jury trial has been requested.

7. THE JURY AND ITS SELECTION

In most actions for damages, the parties have a right to have the facts tried by a *jury*. This right is assured in the federal courts by the Seventh Amendment to the Constitution, and is protected in the courts of most states by similar constitutional provisions. If there is a right to a trial by jury, either party may assert it, but if neither wishes to do so, a judge will try the facts as well as the law. Largely for historical reasons growing out of a division of authority in the English court structure, there are many civil actions in which neither party has a right to a jury trial; these include most cases in which plaintiff wants an order directing or prohibiting specified action by defendant rather than a judgment for damages—a so-called *equitable* remedy.

If a jury has been demanded, the first order of business at trial will be to impanel the jurors. A large number of persons, selected in an impartial manner from voting lists, tax rolls, or street directories, will have been ordered to report to the courthouse for jury duty at a given term of court. The prospective jurors will be questioned—usually by the judge but sometimes by the lawyers—as to their possible biases. If one of the persons called has prior knowledge of the case or is a personal friend of one of the parties, he or she probably will be successfully *challenged for cause* and excused. But suppose Aikins is an architect and her lawyer finds that one of the jury panel has recently constructed a house and believes that he was greatly overcharged for its design and construction; this will likely not be enough to persuade the judge to excuse him, but fearing the juror may be prejudiced against his client, Aikins' lawyer will probably exercise one of the small number of *peremptory challenges* allowed for which no reason need be given. Ultimately, a panel of twelve, or, with increasing frequency, a panel of less than twelve, hopefully unbiased jurors will be selected.

8. THE TRIAL

After the jurors have been sworn, plaintiff's lawyer will make an *opening statement*, in which he will describe for the jury what the case is about, what contentions he will make, and how he will prove them. Defendant's lawyer also may make an opening statement at this time, but he may reserve the right to do so until he is ready to present his own case. Following the opening statement, plaintiff's lawyer calls his witnesses one by one. Each witness is first questioned by the lawyer who has called that witness—this is the *direct examination;* then the lawyer for the other side has the opportunity to *cross-examine* him; this may be followed by *re-direct* and *re-cross* examination, and even further stages. The judge maintains some control over the length and tenor of the examination, and in particular will see to it that the stages beyond cross-examination are not prolonged.

Just as the primary responsibility for introducing evidence is on the lawyers, so too is the responsibility for objecting to evidence that is thought to be inadmissible under the rules of evidence. Suppose that Aikins' lawyer asks: "What happened while you were lying on the ground after the accident?" To which Aikins replies: "The driver of the car came over and said that he had been going too fast and he was sorry." Aikins' answer is objectionable because it contains *hearsay evidence*; that is, it repeats what someone else has said for the purpose of proving the truth of what was said. The judge will not raise this issue himself, however; it is up to Cecil's counsel to object, and then the judge must rule on the objection. This particular issue is not an easy one, for Aikins' answer may well come within one of the exceptions to the rule excluding hearsay evidence. This kind of issue will recur continually throughout the trial and the judge must be prepared to make instantaneous rulings if the trial is to proceed with dispatch. Small wonder that evidentiary rulings form a major source of the errors raised on appeal, but at the same time appellate courts are very reluctant to disturb the trial judge's determination. What happens if the judge rules that Aikins' answer is inadmissible? He will instruct the jury to disregard it. Can a juror who has heard such an important confession totally drive it from his or her mind?

Documents, pictures, and other tangible items may be put into evidence, but unless their admissibility has been stipulated in advance, they will be introduced through witnesses. For example, if Aikins' lawyer has had pictures taken of the accident scene and wishes to get them to the jury, he will call the photographer as a witness, have her testify that she took pictures of the scene, and then show them to the photographer who will identify them as the pictures she took. At this point they may be formally introduced into evidence.

When plaintiff's lawyer has called all of his witnesses, and their examinations are over, plaintiff will *rest*. At this point, defendant's lawyer may ask for a *directed verdict* for defendant on the ground that plaintiff has not established a prima facie case; the thrust of the motion is that plaintiff has not introduced enough evidence to permit the jury to find in her favor. If the motion is denied, defendant may rest and choose to rely on the jury's agreeing with him, but in almost all cases he will proceed to present witnesses of his own and these witnesses will be exposed to the same process of direct and cross-examination. When defendant has rested, plaintiff may present additional evidence to meet any new matter raised by defendant's witnesses. In turn, defendant, after plaintiff rests, may meet any new matter presented by plaintiff. This procedure will continue until both parties rest. Again, the trial judge will maintain considerable control to prevent the protraction of these latter stages.

When both parties have rested, either or both may move for a directed verdict. Again this motion asks the trial judge to rule that under the evidence presented, viewed most favorably to the nonmoving party, the jury cannot find in his or her favor. If these motions are denied, the case must be submitted to the jury.

9. SUBMITTING THE CASE TO THE JURY

At this stage the judge and the lawyers will confer out of the jury's hearing with regard to the content of the judge's *instructions* or *charge* to the jury. Each lawyer may submit proposed instructions, which the trial judge will grant or deny, but the judge is under a duty to charge the jury on the basic aspects of the case in any event. If a party's lawyer has neither requested a particular instruction nor objected to the judge's charge, however, he will generally not be permitted to claim on appeal that the charge was erroneous.

Ordinarily the lawyers will make their final arguments to the jury before the judge delivers the charge. The lawyers will review the evidence from their own points of view, and may suggest how the jury should weigh certain items and resolve specific issues, but it is improper for the lawyers to discuss a matter that has been excluded or has never been introduced. In other words, they are arguing, not testifying.

In the instructions the judge will summarize the facts and issues, tell the jury about the substantive law to be applied on each issue, give general information on determining the credibility of witnesses, and state who has the *burden of persuasion* on each issue of fact. The burden of persuasion in a civil case ordinarily requires that one party prove his contention on a given issue by a preponderance of the evidence. On most issues Aikins will carry this burden but on an affirmative defense such as contributory negligence the burden probably will be on Cecil. What the burden means is that if a juror is unable to resolve an issue in her mind, she should find on that issue against the party who has the burden. In the federal courts and in some states, the judge may comment on the evidence, as long as he emphasizes that his comments represent his own opinion and that the jurors should not feel bound by it; judicial comment is very rare, however, and in many states it is not permitted at all.

Following the charge, the jury retires to reach its *verdict*. The verdict, the jury's decision, will be of a type chosen by the judge. There are three types, of which by far the most common is the *general verdict*. This verdict permits the jurors to determine the facts and apply the law on which they have been charged to those facts; it is simple in form in that only the conclusion as to who prevails, and the amount of the damages, if that party is a claimant, is stated. A second type is the *general verdict with interrogatories*, which combines the form of the general verdict with several key questions that are designed to test the jury's understanding of the issues. Suppose that the accident occurred five miles away from Beasley's appointed route. Aikins' evidence is that Beasley detoured to have the vehicle's brakes fixed; Cecil's is that Beasley was going to visit his sweetheart. The judge might charge the jury that in the former event, but not in the latter, Beasley was acting within the scope of his employment and Cecil would be liable for his negligence, and he might direct the jury, in addition to rendering a verdict for Aikins or for Cecil, to answer the question, "Why did Beasley depart from his route?"

If the general verdict were for Aikins, but the jury's answer was that Beasley was driving to his sweetheart's home, the judge would order judgment for Cecil, for if the answer is inconsistent with the verdict, the answer controls. The third type of verdict is the *special verdict*, in which all of the factual issues in the case are submitted to the jury as questions without instructions as to their legal effect; the judge applies the law to the jury's answers and determines which party prevails.

Traditionally, only a unanimous jury verdict has been effective. In many states, and by consent of the parties in the federal courts, a nonunanimous verdict by the jurors may stand in a civil action. If the minimum number of jurors required for a verdict are unable to reach agreement, the jury is said to be *hung*, and a new trial before a different jury is necessary.

10. POST-TRIAL MOTIONS

After the jury has returned its verdict, judgment will be entered thereon, but the losing party will have an opportunity to make certain post-trial motions. There may be a motion for a *judgment notwithstanding the verdict* (commonly called a *judgment n. o. v.,* from the Latin non obstante veredicto); this motion raises the same question as a motion for a directed verdict. The losing party also may move for a *new trial*; the grounds for this motion are many, and may include assertions that the judge erred in admitting certain evidence, that the charge was defective, that attorneys, parties, or jurors have been guilty of misconduct, that the damages found are excessive or inadequate, or that the verdict is against the clear weight of the evidence. Should these motions fail, it is sometimes possible to reopen a judgment, even several months after the trial, on the grounds of clerical mistake, newly discovered evidence, or fraud, but the occasions on which relief is granted are very rare.

11. THE JUDGMENT AND ITS ENFORCEMENT

The *judgment* is the final determination of the lawsuit, absent an appeal. Judgment may be rendered on default when the defendant does not appear; or following the granting of a demurrer, a motion to dismiss, or a motion for summary judgment; or upon the jury's verdict, or the findings of fact and conclusions of law of the trial judge in a nonjury case. The judgment may be in the form of an award of money to plaintiff, a declaration of rights between the parties, specific recovery of property, or an order requiring or prohibiting some future activity. When defendant has prevailed, the judgment generally will not be "for" anything nor will it order anything; it simply will provide that plaintiff takes nothing by her complaint.

In most cases a judgment for plaintiff will not order defendant to do anything; typically it will simply state that plaintiff shall recover a sum of money from defendant. This does not necessarily mean that defendant will pay. It is up to plaintiff to collect the money. *Execution* is the common method of forcing the losing party to satisfy a money judgment, if the loser does not do so voluntarily. A *writ of execution* is issued by the court commanding an officer—usually the sheriff—to seize property of the losing party and, if necessary, to sell it at public sale and use the proceeds to satisfy plaintiff's judgment.

When plaintiff's recovery takes the form of an *injunction* requiring defendant to do something or to stop doing something, the judgment (in this context typically called the *decree*) is said to operate against defendant's person (in personam). Its sanction is direct, and if defendant fails to obey, he may be held in *contempt of court* and punished by fine or imprisonment.

Costs provided by statute and certain out-of-pocket disbursements are awarded the prevailing party and included in the judgment. Usually these costs are nominal in relation to the total expense of litigation and include only such items as the clerk's fee and witnesses' mileage. In the United States, in contrast to England, attorney's fees are not recoverable as costs in ordinary litigation.

----

12.   APPEAL

Every judicial system provides for review by an appellate court of the decisions of the trial court. Generally a party has the right to appeal any judgment to at least one higher court. When the system contains two levels of appellate courts, appeal usually lies initially to one of the intermediate courts; review at the highest level is only at the discretion of that court except in certain classes of cases. Thus, in the federal courts, district-court decisions are reviewed by the courts of appeals, but review in the United States Supreme Court must be sought in most cases by a *petition for a writ of certiorari*, which that Court may deny as a matter of discretion without reaching any conclusion as to the merits of the case.[e] The discretion of a higher-level appellate court generally is exercised so that only cases whose legal issues are of broad importance are taken.

The *record* on appeal will contain the pleadings, at least a portion of the *transcript of the trial* (the court reporter's verbatim record of the trial), and

----

[e] In a few cases, a direct appeal lies from the district court to the Supreme Court.

the orders and rulings relevant to the appeal.   The parties present their contentions to the appellate court by written *briefs* and in addition, in most cases, by *oral argument*.   The appellate court may review any ruling of law by the trial judge, although frequently it will limit the scope of its review by holding that particular matters were within the trial judge's discretion or that the error if any was not prejudicial, that is, it did not substantially affect the outcome of the case.   There are constitutional limits to the review of a jury's verdict, but even when these limits do not apply—for example, when the judge has sat without a jury—an appellate court rarely will re-examine a question of fact, for a cold record does not convey the nuances of what the trier observed, notably the demeanor of the witnesses.

The appellate court has the power to *affirm, reverse,* or *modify* the judgment of the trial court.   If it reverses, it may order that judgment be entered or it may *remand* the case to the trial court for a new trial or other proceedings not inconsistent with its decision.   The decision of an appellate court usually is accompanied by a written *opinion,* signed by one of the judges hearing the appeal, there always being more than one judge deciding an appeal.   Concurring and dissenting opinions also may be filed.   The opinions of a court are designed to set forth the reasons for a decision and to furnish guidance to lower courts, lawyers, and the public.   You will spend much of your time in law school—and afterwards—reading the opinions of appellate courts.   Unfortunately, although trial courts frequently deliver opinions when ruling on motions or sitting without a jury, these are seldom published.

There is an important distinction between the *reviewability* of a particular ruling of a trial judge and its *appealability*.   For example, a trial judge's ruling excluding certain evidence at trial as hearsay is reviewable; that is, when the judgment is appealed, that ruling may be assigned as error and the appellate court will consider whether it was correct.   But trial would be impossible if an appeal could be taken from every ruling.   Thus, appeals lie only from judgments and from certain orders made in the course of litigation when immediate review is deemed so important that a delay in the action during appeal can be tolerated.   Judicial systems differ in the extent to which *interlocutory orders* can be appealed.   In the federal system, very little other than a final judgment can be taken to the courts of appeals; in some states, on the other hand, many kinds of orders can be appealed.

A good example of the contrast between the two approaches can be seen by looking at the consequences of an order denying a motion to dismiss.   Suppose that Cecil moves to dismiss Aikins' complaint on the grounds that even on Aikins' view of the facts Cecil is not responsible for the conduct of Beasley, and this motion is denied.   In the federal courts such an order would not be appealable; it does not terminate the lawsuit; indeed the disposition of the motion means that the action will continue.   In many states, however, this question could be taken immediately to a higher court for a ruling, while the other stages of the litigation waited.

The question as to which system is better is not easy to answer.   One may argue in favor of the federal practice that everything should be done at one level before going to the next, that too much time is taken in waiting for appellate courts to decide these questions serially, and that no appeal may ever be necessary, since Cecil may prevail anyway. But on the other hand, if the appellate court holds at this early stage that Aikins has no claim against Cecil we will save the time necessary for discovery and trial.

One point worth noting is that the resolution of the question of the appealability of interlocutory orders has an important bearing on the procedural developments within a given system. In the case of motions to dismiss, for example, if denials are not appealable, the law on this subject will be made largely in the trial courts. The trial judge who is in doubt may tend to deny such motions rather than to grant them, and his decision generally will not be disturbed; even though the ruling theoretically is reviewable after final judgment, by that time the significance of the ruling on the pleadings may have been displaced by more substantive questions. If the denial is appealable, a tactical consideration is added and such motions will be resorted to more frequently, inasmuch as they will afford defendant an additional opportunity to delay trial and thus to wear down his opponent. With respect to other procedural rulings—as in the discovery area—the absence of an interlocutory appeal will strengthen the hand of the trial judge; he will in fact, if not in theory, be given a wider discretion because fewer of his rulings will come before the appellate courts and when they do they will be enmeshed in a final judgment, which will make it easy to conclude that any error was not prejudicial.

---

13. THE CONCLUSIVENESS OF JUDGMENTS

After the appeal and whatever further proceedings may take place, or, if no appeal is taken, when the time for appeal expires, the judgment is final. It cannot be challenged in another proceeding. It is *res judicata*, a thing decided, and now at rest. Defining the scope and effect of this finality is one of the most complex tasks in the entire law of procedure.

SECTION C. A NOTE ON REMEDIES

The remedies that may be obtained in a modern civil action should principally be viewed as a part of the substantive law: contract law, tort law, commercial law, labor law, and so forth. Yet because the goal of a lawsuit is the remedy and the means of securing it is procedural, there necessarily is a close relationship between them. For example, the range of available remedies in a case may be limited by the manner in which plaintiff has pleaded and on the other hand certain procedural aspects of the case, such as whether it is tried to a judge or a jury may be determined by the remedy that is being sought; again, whether a person may be joined as a party may depend on the relief that is being sought, and conversely certain remedies may be available only if all interested persons can be joined.

Without question, the most important relationship between procedure and remedies grows out of the existence in English law of two great branches of jurisprudence administered in different courts: common law and equity; the latter was envisioned as complementary to the former. There are two special facts about equity that are important for our purpose. First, already alluded to, it had no jury. Second, the injunction was a creature of equity and remained in its sole custody so long as the two branches remained distinct. From this heritage two consequences of immense significance for the law of procedure result. One, the right of a trial by jury in the United States today, especially in the federal courts, is determined by inquiring whether the matter in question was a subject of legal or equitable cognizance in 1791—the date of the Seventh Amendment—and to some extent this question depends on the remedy sought since the availability of injunctive relief was one font of equity's jurisdiction. Two, just as equity was regarded as a special kind of law to be resorted to only when the common law was inadequate, so too the injunction— and most forms of specific relief, even in those limited circumstances in which it is available at law—has been and still is regarded as a form of exceptional relief, to be allowed only when the ordinary remedy of damages is inadequate.

The most important types of relief that a court may award in a civil action fall into three categories: *declarative, specific,* and *compensatory.* Declarative relief consists simply in a court's defining the rights and duties of the parties in a particular legal context. Suppose a person believes that an agreement he has entered into is not a valid contract and that he is under no obligation to perform it; however, he is afraid to act on this belief in the face of another's insistence that he perform, because if the contract is enforceable the damages for the nonperformance will be great. In these circumstances he may seek a declaratory judgment asking the court to determine whether he is under a duty to perform. This type of relief is not as common as those discussed below and its availability often is limited by statute. In numerous situations, however, it is invaluable.

Specific relief consists generally of an order directing conduct. Defendant may be commanded to return a jewel he has taken from plaintiff, to stop operating a pig farm in a residential neighborhood, to deliver a car he has contracted to sell, or to refrain from opening a barbershop next door to a person to whom he has just sold his former barbershop. Obviously, specific relief is not possible in all cases. For example, no kind of specific relief will compensate or cure Aikins in our hypothetical case; Beasley cannot retroactively be ordered not to run into her. On the other hand, in some kinds of cases specific relief is available almost as a matter of course. A person who has contracted to sell a house or a piece of land ordinarily will be ordered to perform the agreement, for the law regards each bit of real property as unique. But beyond the real-property context, specific relief will be given only if damages would be completely inadequate. Thus, if you order a tuxedo from a tailor who fails to perform his promise to deliver it, it is unlikely that any remedy except damages will be forthcoming. The reasons for this are not purely historical. There is a burden on the court in ordering and supervising performance of a decree of specific performance that is avoided if a simple judgment for money damages is entered; moreover, specific performance might impose a hardship or at least an indignity on the tailor not commensurate with the advantage to be gained by your receiving this tailor's garment rather than one from another tailor. But it may well be asked whether our courts today are not being too reluctant to grant that form of relief that will most adequately redress plaintiff's grievance. See Wright, *The Law of Remedies as a Social Institution,* 18 U.Det.L.J. 376 (1955).

Compensatory relief calls for a judgment that defendant pay plaintiff a certain sum of money. But you should recognize that when we speak of compensation—of the remedy of damages—although we are speaking of one form of relief, it can be computed in accordance with many measures. In your action against the tailor, for example, if you had struck a good bargain, you might claim the difference between the price you agreed to pay and the value the tuxedo would have had if the tailor had performed the promise; or you might claim only the money you had advanced as a down payment; or you might claim the amount you paid for opera tickets you were unable to use without the tuxedo. In many contexts the difference in amount that could be collected under these theories might be substantial.

Again there is a considerable difference in the process of measuring the damages sustained in losing 100 shares of General Motors stock, your leg, your reputation, or your peace of mind. Although it frequently is said that damages are recoverable only if they can be measured with a reasonable degree of certainty, this rule has come to require little more than a demonstration of as much certainty as the subject being measured permits. The fertile minds of lawyers and judges never cease in their quest for new immeasurables. (What is reasonable compensation for being born a bastard? *Cf.* Zepeda v. Zepeda, 41 Ill.App.2d 240, 190 N.E.2d 849 (1963), certiorari denied 379 U.S. 945, 85 S.Ct. 444, 13 L.Ed.2d 545 (1964).)

There is a final point to be considered in evaluating the adequacy of any judicial remedy: how much of it will be consumed by the cost of litigation? As we have noted, the costs awarded to a successful plaintiff will not, in most cases, reimburse him for the fees of his lawyer or for many other substantial costs of a suit, such as the expense of investigation or the fees of expert witnesses. Although it is not possible to give any meaningful figure for the cost of an average trial, some notion may be drawn from such typically suggested *minimum* fees as $50 for the drawing of a complaint (exclusive of interview and investigation), $75 for appearance on any contested motion, and $150 a day for trial. Since these are suggested minimum charges, it can be assumed that as the stakes rise the fees will be correspondingly higher.

In most personal-injury actions plaintiff's cost of recovery must be computed differently because the attorney will be retained on a contingent-fee agreement; that is, the attorney will receive a percentage—typically one-third —of plaintiff's judgment. See Gair v. Peck, 6 N.Y.2d 97, 188 N.Y.S.2d 491, 160 N.E.2d 43 (1959). Thus, in a real sense, an adequate legal remedy is not one that simply compensates plaintiff for a loss but is one that covers both the loss and the cost of recovering it. This distinction has not been ignored by many triers of fact. Indeed, it has been suggested that damages for pain and suffering are "a make-weight to help personal-injury-plaintiffs pay attorney fees and other expenses of litigation." Morris, *The Insurance Principle: Compulsory Insurance*, in *University of Chicago Law School Conference on Insurance* 173, 179 (1954). See generally Finman, *Civil Litigation and Professional Responsibility* 87–101 (1966).

SECTION D. ILLUSTRATIVE CASES

The cases that follow have been selected to illustrate many of the basic concepts, doctrines, and devices about which you have just read. This group of cases is designed to furnish examples of a broad spectrum of procedural problems, and it has been arranged for the most part to present these problems in the order in which they were discussed in the preceding text. Three factors have dominated the choice of the cases: First, each focuses on a specific issue that is typical of a range of problems involving a particular principle and at the same time throws some light on the policies that underlie the principle itself. Second, none of the cases is a "sitting duck"; in each instance strong reasons can be advanced for and against the court's result. Third, each case arises in a context that you can understand and presents an issue about which you should be able to form an opinion, however hesitant it may be. Another purpose of these cases is to help you develop a familiarity with procedural language and a feeling for procedural problems. You must, of course, consider the cases from the perspective of the courts that decided them, seeking to understand not only their rulings but why they were made, asking what alternatives were before them, and thinking through the consequences of those alternatives. But if the full pedagogical objectives of these cases are to be achieved, you also must regard each of them as a practical lawyer's problem—or rather a problem presenting difficulties and opportunities to the lawyers on the opposite sides. You must inquire why they acted as they did and what else they might have done; finally, you must ask in what position the decision has left them and what if anything they should do next.

1. THE AUTHORITY OF THE COURT TO PROCEED WITH THE ACTION

The plaintiff, having decided to sue, must determine in what court to bring the action. A court must be chosen that has jurisdiction over the subject matter of the suit and in which jurisdiction over the person of the defendant may be obtained. In the following case, the word "jurisdiction" is used without either of these modifiers. But from the context and from the information you have been given above you should be able to identify the kind of jurisdiction involved.

CAPRON v. VAN NOORDEN

Supreme Court of the United States, 1804.
6 U.S. (2 Cranch) 126, 2 L.Ed. 229.

Error to the [United States] circuit court of North Carolina. The proceedings stated Van Noorden to be late of Pitt county, but did not allege Capron, the plaintiff, to be an alien, nor a citizen of any state, nor the place of his residence.

Upon the general issue, in an action of trespass on the case, a verdict was found for the defendant, Van Noorden, upon which judgment was rendered.

The writ of error was sued out by Capron, the plaintiff below, who assigned for error, among other things, first, "that the circuit court aforesaid is a court of limited jurisdiction, and that by the record aforesaid it doth not appear, as it ought to have done, that either the said George Capron, or the said Hadrianus Van Noorden, was an alien at the time of the commencement of said suit, or at any other time, or that one of the said parties was at that or any other time, a citizen of the state of North Carolina where the suit was brought, and the other a citizen of another state; or that they the said George and Hadrianus were, for any cause whatever, persons within the jurisdiction of the said court, and capable of suing and being sued there." And, secondly, "that by the record aforesaid it manifestly appeareth that the said circuit court had not any jurisdiction of the cause aforesaid, nor ought to have held plea thereof or given judgment therein, but ought to have dismissed the same, whereas the said court hath proceeded to final judgment therein."

Harper, for the plaintiff in error, stated the only question to be whether the plaintiff had a right to assign for error the want of jurisdiction in that court to which he had chosen to resort. * * *

The defendant in error did not appear, but the citation having been duly served, the judgment was reversed.

NOTES AND QUESTIONS

1.   The Supreme Court obviously regarded the defect in this case as extremely serious.   Does the fact that it was the plaintiff who brought the case to the Supreme Court make this particularly clear?   Why?   Why is such significance attached to an error of this kind?

2.   Read Article III, Section 2, of the United States Constitution, which is set out in the Supplement.   What specific language in that Section is pertinent to the Supreme Court's opinion in *Capron*?

3.   The Supreme Court reversed the judgment of the lower court.   What was the effect of this reversal?   Does it mean that Capron wins the lawsuit?   If not, why had he sought review in the appellate court?

4.   Those of you who have studied American government or political science may recall that one year before *Capron* was decided by the Supreme Court, the broad issue of the case had been involved in MARBURY v. MADISON, 5 U.S. (1 Cranch) 137, 2 L.Ed. 60 (1803), the case that is the cornerstone of judicial review in the United States.   In what way was it there involved?

Unlike the federal courts, which only exercise the limited subject matter jurisdiction bestowed by the Constitution, as further restricted by acts of Congress, state courts of general jurisdiction have jurisdiction over the subject matter of a very broad spectrum of lawsuits.   Indeed questions of the competence of those courts to decide a particular kind of case rarely arise. But before any court may proceed, it also must have the power to require the appearance of the defendant.   In the next case, the court must decide whether it has that power, and whether it will exercise it.

TICKLE v. BARTON

Supreme Court of Appeals of West Virginia, 1956.
142 W.Va. 188, 95 S.E.2d 427.

HAYMOND, Judge.   The plaintiff, Richard Tickle, an infant, who sues by his next friend, instituted this action of trespass on the case in the Circuit Court of McDowell County in March, 1955, to recover damages from the defendants, Raymond Barton, a resident of Austinville, Virginia, and Lawrence Coleman, for personal injuries inflicted upon him by a motor vehicle, owned by the defendant Raymond Barton and operated by his agent the defendant Lawrence Coleman,   *   *   *   in that county which the plaintiff alleges were caused by the negligence of the defendants.

*   *   *   [A first attempt to serve Barton had been made and the validity of this service was still undecided at the time the instant decision was rendered.]

On December 5, 1955, one of the attorneys for the plaintiff caused an alias process to be issued against the defendants   *   *   *   and delivered it to a deputy sheriff for service upon the defendant Barton in McDowell County; and in the evening of December 6, 1955, that process was served by the deputy upon the defendant Barton in person at the War Junior High School in the town of War in that county where he appeared to attend a banquet which was held there at that time.

Issue/procedure → By his amended plea in abatement No. 2, the defendant Barton challenged the validity of the service of the alias process upon him on the ground that he had been induced to come to that place in McDowell County by trickery, artifice and deceit practiced upon him by the attorney for the plaintiff.

The circuit court overruled the demurrer of the plaintiff to the amended plea in abatement and   *   *   *   certified its ruling upon the demurrer to this Court on the joint application of the plaintiff and the defendant Barton.

After reciting the prior proceedings in this case, the amended plea in abatement alleges in substance that after procuring alias process for the purpose of causing it to be served upon the defendant Barton in McDowell County, and inducing him to come to the Junior High School in the town of War in that county, an attorney representing the plaintiff in this action, in the evening of December 5, 1955, called by telephone the defendant Barton at his home in Austinville, Virginia, and wrongfully and deceitfully represented that, in behalf of the sponsors of a banquet honoring a championship high school football team to be held at the Junior High School in the town of War,   *   *   *   he extended an invitation to the defendant Barton, whose son had been a member of an earlier football team of that school, to attend the banquet; that during that telephone conversation between them the attorney, though requested to do so by the defendant Barton, did not disclose his identity except to say that he called him in behalf of the sponsors to extend the defendant Barton a special invitation to attend the banquet; that the defendant Barton before being so invited did not know that the banquet would be held and did not intend to attend it; that he did not know or suspect the identity of the attorney, or realize that the telephone call was a trick or device to entice, induce and inveigle him to come into McDowell County to be served with process in this action; that the attorney was not connected with any of the sponsors of the banquet and was not authorized by them to invite the defendant Barton to attend it; that the attorney called the defendant Barton and invited him to the banquet solely for the purpose of tricking, deceiving and inveigling him to come to the town of War in order to obtain personal service   *   *   *   upon him   *   *   *; that the defendant Barton, believing that the invitation was extended in good faith, by a person authorized to extend it, and not suspecting the real purpose of the telephone call, accepted the invitation and informed the attorney that he would be present at the banquet and on December 6, 1955, left Austinville, Virginia, and went to the town of War with the intention of attending it; that, when he entered the high school where the banquet was held   *   *   *   he was served by the deputy sheriff with the alias process   *   *   *; that the service of the alias process upon the defendant Barton, having been procured by trickery, deceit and subterfuge which was not realized or suspected by him, is, for that reason, null and void and of no force or effect and does not confer upon the Circuit Court of McDowell County jurisdiction of the person of the defendant Barton in this action.

The amended plea in abatement also alleges, on information and belief, that after the defendant Barton had left his home   *   *   *   the attorney for the plaintiff   *   *   *   made a telephone call to the residence of the defendant Barton, or caused some other person to make such call, and inquired of the wife of the defendant Barton if he intended to attend the banquet and was informed by her that he had left his home to attend it   *   *   *.

The amended plea in abatement further avers that   *   *   *   the attorney for the plaintiff denied that he had made, or procured any person to make, either of the foregoing telephone calls, and denied that he had any knowledge whatsoever of either of them.

The question certified to this Court for decision is whether the allegations of the amended plea in abatement, which insofar as they are material and are well pleaded must be considered as true upon demurrer, are sufficient to render invalid the personal service of process upon the defendant Barton   *   *   *.

Procedural Question

  *   *   *   In 42 Am.Jur., Process, Section 35, the general principle is stated thus:

  *   *   *   "[I]f a person resident outside the jurisdiction of the court and the reach of its process is inveigled, enticed, or induced, by any false representation, deceitful contrivance, or wrongful device for which the plaintiff is responsible, to come within the jurisdiction of the court for the purpose of obtaining service of process on him in an action brought against him in such court, process served upon him through such improper means is invalid, and upon proof of such fact the court will, on motion, set it aside."   *   *   *

Statutory Rationale

The foregoing principle applies to the party when such service is procured by his agent or by someone acting for and in his behalf.   *   *   *

In Economy Electric Company v. Automatic Electric Power and Light Plant, 185 N.C. 534, 118 S.E. 3, the court, discussing service of process by fraudulent means, used this language: "Where service of process is procured by fraud, that fact may be shown, and, if shown seasonably, the court will refuse to exercise its jurisdiction and turn the plaintiff out of court. The law will not lend its sanction or support to an act, otherwise lawful, which is accomplished by unlawful means.   *   *   *   Such a fraud is one affecting the court itself and the integrity of its process.   *   *   *   The objection, strictly, is not that the court is without jurisdiction, but that it ought not, by reason of the alleged fraud, to take or to hold jurisdiction of the action.   *   *   *"

Precedant

Under the material allegations of the amended plea in abatement which, as already indicated, must be considered as true upon demurrer, the defendant Barton was induced or enticed to come into McDowell County by the unauthorized invitation extended to him by the attorney for the plaintiff whose purpose at the time was to obtain personal service upon the defendant Barton   *   *   *; the defendant Barton knew that the present action against him was pending in the circuit court by reason of the service of the original process upon him   *   *   *   but he did not suspect or realize that he would be served with process while present in McDowell County to attend the banquet; he was induced to come into that county by the invitation to the banquet; and he would not have come into that jurisdiction if the attorney for the plaintiff had disclosed his identity and his real purpose in extending the invitation, all of which he concealed from the defendant Barton.

*   *   *

The amended plea in abatement is sufficient on demurrer and the action of the circuit court in overruling the demurrer was correct.

It should perhaps be emphasized that, as the factual allegations of the amended plea in abatement have not been denied at this stage of this action by any pleading filed by the plaintiff, the question of the truth or the falsity of those allegations is not before this Court   *   *   *.

Ruling affirmed.

GIVEN, Judge (dissenting).

My disagreement with the majority is not as to the rule of law laid down. I think the rule a salutary one, and masterfully stated. I do not believe, however, that the facts properly pleaded, and the inferences which may be rationally drawn therefrom, bring the facts of this case within the influence of the rule.

Stripped of all explanatory language, and of many allegations of conclusions of fact,   *   *   *   the plea in abatement charges no more than that the attorney, by telephone, inquired at defendant's home whether defendant intended to attend a certain social function to be held in McDowell County, to which defendant was then invited by the attorney; that the attorney, though requested to give his name, did not do so; that the attorney later, or someone for him, again by telephone, inquired whether defendant had decided to attend the social function, and was advised that defendant had made arrangements to attend; and that the attorney caused process to be served on defendant while attending the social function.   *   *   *   The principal, if not only, fact of wrongdoing, if wrongdoing, alleged against the attorney was his failure to inform defendant of the identity of the telephone caller.   *   *   *   It seems to me that the facts properly alleged can not be held to establish fraud or wrongdoing. At most, they would simply show that the attorney took advantage of an opportunity, the holding of the social function in McDowell County and the interest of defendant's son in the holding of the function, to try to obtain proper service of process, which was no more than a duty owed his client. In considering the questions arising, it should be kept in mind that defendant had full knowledge of the institution of the action against him in McDowell County, of the fact that he had questioned the validity of the service of other process issued in that action, and of the fact that the alleged cause of action arose in McDowell County, where ordinarily it would have been triable.

*   *   *

NOTES AND QUESTIONS

1. Did the court in this case decide that West Virginia courts do not have jurisdiction over the person of the defendant (assuming his story is true), or that those courts should not exercise jurisdiction in these circumstances even though they have it?

2. When should a court be able to demand that a person appear before it and defend an action? In what circumstances should this demand be permitted against a nonresident? Why should a nonresident be subject to suit if he is served with process within the state? Insofar as these reasons are concerned, should it make any difference why he is present in the state?

3. In thinking about the cases you read, you should consider how the court might approach the problem presented by a particular case with certain facts changed. For example, should service in West Virginia in the following situations be treated in the same way as it was under the facts alleged in the principal case? (a) Tickle had asked Barton to appear as a witness in a suit against a third party involved in the accident; (b) Tickle had asked Barton to come to West Virginia to discuss settling the case; (c) Tickle had telephoned Barton and falsely told him that his son lay critically injured in a West Virginia hospital; (d) Tickle (like the Sheriff of Nottingham) had scheduled a football banquet in West Virginia that he knew Barton (like Robin Hood) would be unable to resist attending, although he did not personally invite him.

4. When the case is reconsidered by the West Virginia Circuit Court on remand, Barton's lawyer must prove his allegations if Barton is to avoid trial in West Virginia. What problems do you foresee in his being able to prove them, and how should he proceed to do so?

5. You will later become familiar with state statutes that confer upon their courts power to summon out-of-state motorists to defend actions arising out of their operating automobiles within the state. Tickle had first sought to serve Barton under a statute of this type, but because the accident had occurred on private property rather than a West Virginia public highway, a serious question as to the statute's application existed; this uncertainty prompted the second attempt at service discussed in the case.

---

2. DEFINING AND DETERMINING THE CASE BEFORE TRIAL

At this point, you should re-read the part of the Outline of a Civil Action that deals with pleading, especially the portion that discusses the "three general situations" in which a motion to dismiss for failure to state a claim might be granted. Is the court in the following case saying that the plaintiff has not properly pleaded its case or that it has no case at all?

FOLEY-CARTER INS. CO. v. COMMONWEALTH LIFE INS. CO.

United States Circuit Court of Appeals, Fifth Circuit, 1942.
128 F.2d 718.

HUTCHESON, Circuit Judge.   The suit, on an implied contract for commissions, based upon the reasonable value of plaintiff's services in the sale of a parcel of real estate, The Taylor Arcade, was in two counts, each count in 13 paragraphs.   The second count adopted the first 11 paragraphs of the first count and added to the 12th and the 13th paragraphs, the allegation, that defendant in bad faith and for the purpose of attempting to deprive plaintiff of a commission while taking advantage of its services,   *   *   *   sold the property direct at a reduced price to plaintiff's customer.   *   *   *   The 8th, 11th, 12th, and 13th paragraphs, set out the grounds of the claim.   These, as plaintiff sets them out, are;   "plaintiff informed the defendant company that it intended to endeavor to induce Haige, the tenant, to purchase the entire property and inquired the asking price, and the defendant authorized and directed plaintiff to offer the property for sale to Haige at the asking price of $350,-000, well knowing and understanding by reason of the previous activities and services conducted and performed that plaintiff as successor to Foley-Carter Insurance Company, would endeavor to induce Haige to purchase the property and that plaintiff would and should receive from the defendant the usual and customary real estate commissions of 5% of the sales price in the event that plaintiff should succeed in inducing him to purchase the property at said asking price or at such modified price as the defendant might subsequently accept before the agency was revoked,   *   *   *   if plaintiff was the effective or procuring cause of Haige's becoming the purchaser of the property."   It was further alleged that plaintiff went to work endeavoring to get Haige to purchase the property at the asking price and continued to work uninterruptedly for the defendant endeavoring to effect the sale;   that while plaintiff was continuing his negotiations, defendant, without inquiry of or notice to plaintiff, contacted Haige directly, reduced the asking price of $350,000 to the sum of $215,000 and on September 1, 1938, did sell the property to him for that sum.

It was further alleged: that plaintiff was the procuring cause of the sale; that it acted throughout in the utmost good faith, made diligent efforts to persuade Haige to purchase the property and by its efforts succeeded in interesting him as a prospective purchaser;   that defendant had availed itself of the benefit of the services of plaintiff and thereby had become liable to pay plaintiff 5% on $215,000.

*   *   *   Defendant moved under Rule 12(b)   *   *   *   to dismiss the petition for "failure to state a claim upon which relief can be granted." The motion was sustained and this appeal to test the correctness of that ruling followed.   *   *   *

Appellee   *   *   *   insists that no recoverable claim is set out.   We agree with appellee.   The law governing suits for commissions is simple and well understood.   They may be either on express or on implied contracts.   If on an express contract the petition should show the express agreement for commissions and that the agreement was complied with. If on an implied contract, the petition should state facts from which a contract for commissions will be implied and facts showing performance by plaintiff of that contract. Plaintiff's suit is upon an implied contract. Its petition must therefore be searched first for facts from which a contract for commissions will be implied, and second, for facts from which it might be found that the contract thus implied has been performed.

Rationale ——→ Subjected to that test plaintiff's petition fails in both respects. As to the existence of the implied contract, instead of alleging facts from which an agreement to pay a commission if Haige should buy the property by direct purchase from defendant could be implied, the petition negatives such an implication. For, it alleges merely that advised by plaintiff on February 15, 1938, that it intended to endeavor to induce Haige to buy the property, defendant in response to plaintiff's inquiry for the asking price, on March 10, 1938, authorized and directed plaintiff to offer the property for sale to Haige at the asking price of $350,000; and that while plaintiff was conducting the negotiations, for sale at that price, defendant, without inquiry of or notice to the plaintiff, contacted Haige directly, reduced the asking price of $350,000 to $215,000 and on September 1, 1938, sold the property to him for that sum. There is no allegation that plaintiff ever asked for or obtained authority to sell or to offer the property at any different price than the $350,000 given it as the asking price; none from which it could be inferred that defendant gave it an exclusive agency, or in any manner agreed that it would not offer the property itself direct to Haige; none from which it could be implied that plaintiff would be entitled to a commission on a sale made direct by the owner to Haige. Plaintiff's allegations that defendant, "well knowing and understanding by reason of the previous activities of its predecessor," that plaintiff would endeavor to induce Haige to purchase the property and that should plaintiff succeed in inducing him to purchase the property at the asking price or at such modified price as the defendant might subsequently accept before the agency was revoked, are not allegations of facts from which the agreement sought to be, can in law be, implied. They are merely conclusions of the pleader which are not only not supported by the facts alleged but contrary to them. Upon the issue of the performance of the contract sought to be implied, plaintiff's petition leaves it in even worse case. For it alleges no single fact from which any reasonable mind could conclude that plaintiff * * * was the procuring cause of the sale by defendant made to its tenant, six months later, for the price of $215,000, $135,000, less than the price at which plaintiff, according to his own pleading, had been offering it.

The petition in Paragraph 11 does allege; that plaintiff went to work endeavoring to get Haige to purchase the property at the price of $350,000; that it pointed out the advantages to Haige, as tenant, of purchasing the property; that it continued to work uninterruptedly in endeavoring to effect the sale; and that Haige had never definitely refused to be interested in the purchase of the property. Too, Paragraph 13 does contain the conclusions that plaintiff was the procuring cause of the sale; that it succeeded in interesting Haige as a prospective purchaser; and that defendant took advantage of plaintiff's valuable services in urging the purchase upon Haige. But it does not contain a single allegation of fact from which reasonable minds could infer that its efforts in offering the property at $350,000 were the procuring cause of the sale by the owner direct for $215,000. A case for the recovery of commissions is not made out by merely alleging, as here, that an agent * * * is entitled to recover commissions on a sale made direct by the owner at a price so far below, here $135,000, the asking price at which plaintiff was offering the property, as to negative as matter of law, that the plaintiff was or could have been the procuring cause of the sale. Plaintiff, in the circumstances he alleges, must do something more than plead by way of conclusion that he was the procuring cause of the sale. Nor is plaintiff's case at all bettered by the conclusion added in the second count, that defendant did what he did in bad faith to deprive plaintiff of a commission, for reasonable minds could not reach the conclusion that in order to deprive an agent of a commission of five per cent on a sale at $350,000, the only price plaintiff was authorized to offer the property for, the owner cut the price $135,000.

The judgment was right. It is affirmed.

McCORD, Circuit Judge (dissenting). I think the majority opinion draws too fine a distinction as to what is an allegation of fact and what is a conclusion of the pleader. I am of opinion that under the liberal rules now obtaining in Federal Courts the allegations of the complaint presented questions to be determined on the merits. The parties should have been allowed to fully develop the facts, and the court erred in dismissing the cause on the pleadings. * * *

NOTES AND QUESTIONS

1. Which of the three objectives of pleading discussed in the Outline of a Civil Action, in connection with the content of a complaint, pp. 7–8, supra, was most significantly involved in this case? Could plaintiff have established a good cause of action without producing evidence that was inconsistent with the complaint?

2. In ROSEN v. TEXAS CO., 161 F.Supp. 55 (S.D.N.Y.1958), on a motion to dismiss under Federal Rule of Civil Procedure 12(b) (6), Judge Dimock said:

> Under a system of procedure where the function of pleading was to reach and define the issues or to develop the facts a glance would suffice to demonstrate the insufficiency of the complaint. * * *

> Even after a score of years of experience it is still doubtful just how much a complaint must state to avoid dismissal. * * * The principle is now expressed by many courts by the statement that a complaint will not be dismissed for failure to state a claim on which relief can be granted "unless it appears to a certainty that plaintiff is entitled to no relief under any state of facts which could be proved in support of the claim." * * *

This would seem to mean that all a plaintiff need state is what he wants from the court, but the Advisory Committee on the Rules seems to cling to the words of Rule 8(a) that the pleader must show that he is entitled to relief. In the Advisory Committee's Report of Proposed Amendments, October 1955, pp. 18–19, and Preliminary Draft, May 1954, pp. 8, 9, * * * the Committee stated its opinion that Rule 8(a) "requires the pleader to disclose adequate information as to the basis of his claim for relief as distinguished from a bare averment that he wants relief and is entitled to it".

* * *

These motions have, all to no purpose, consumed a large amount of time of counsel for defendant in making them, of counsel for plaintiff in opposing them and of the court in considering and determining them and the progress of the litigation has been correspondingly delayed. It is my personal belief that the profession would do well to accept the fact that little can be accomplished by motions on the pleadings. The very uncertainty as to what constitutes a statement of a "claim upon which relief can be granted" demonstrates the unimportance of the question. We all should realize that the place of pleadings and motions thereon has been taken by interrogatories, depositions and discovery.

3. In deciding the motion to dismiss in *Foley-Carter,* should any significance have been given to the availability of discovery procedures to the parties? Of what relevance is the availability or nonavailability of other pretrial motions, such as summary judgment, that also might terminate the litigation before trial?

4. What was the effect of the dismissal in *Foley-Carter?* Should the plaintiff have been permitted to amend the complaint and start again? Could the plaintiff interpose a new and slightly altered complaint that would survive another motion to dismiss?

The purposes of discovery are many. The most important are the obtaining of evidence for one's own case and the ferreting out of weaknesses in the opponent's. Usually the party seeking discovery is asking about something of which he is ignorant or uncertain, but sometimes he seeks information about a matter within his own knowledge. In reading the next case, you should ask why the plaintiff is so determined to obtain the answers and why the defendant is equally determined that she shall not have them.

BOLDT v. SANDERS

Supreme Court of Minnesota, 1961.
261 Minn. 160, 111 N.W.2d 225.

OTIS, Justice. This matter comes before the court on the petition of defendant * * * for a writ of prohibition to enjoin the trial court from enforcing its order requiring defendant to answer certain of plaintiffs' interrogatories. The action here involved is one for damages arising out of personal injuries which plaintiffs allege Ella Boldt experienced as a passenger in a car which collided with one driven by defendant   *   *   *. In their complaint plaintiffs allege that the injuries Mrs. Boldt received are permanent and disabling. Defendant admits the accident but denies plaintiffs have been injured or damaged as alleged in their complaint.

On April 1, 1960, the deposition of Mrs. Boldt was taken by defendant. She then testified that she had never had any previous automobile accident, accidental fall, or any other kind of accident, and that she had suffered no previous injuries. On November 25, 1960, plaintiffs submitted to defendant under Rules 26.02 and 33   *   *   * f   the following interrogatories, among others:

"4. Do you have information indicating that the plaintiff Ella Boldt was injured at any time prior to the accident described in Plaintiffs' Complaint?

"5. If your answer to No. 4 is 'Yes,' then give the following information relative to each accident:

"a. Give the date upon which the injury occurred;

"b. Identify the place where the injury occurred;

"c. Give the name and address of each person known to you having information relative to the accident or circumstances causing the injury;

"d. Give the name and address of each physician or other person who rendered treatment to the plaintiff Ella Boldt in connection with the injury."

In response defendant stated:

"4. We decline to answer this question on the ground that it is not pertinent to the issues in the above litigation, is known to the plaintiff, if any other accidents occurred and would serve in the event of a trial of this action only for impeachment.

"5. See answer to No. 4."

Thereupon, the motion of plaintiffs to compel defendant to answer these interrogatories   *   *   * was granted   *   *   * following which our alternative writ of prohibition was issued.

Defendant earnestly contends that the information plaintiffs seek to elicit is exempt from discovery because it is known to plaintiffs and its use is contemplated only for impeachment purposes. Defendant cites in support of his position Bogatay v. Montour R. Co., D.C.W.D.Pa., 177 F.Supp. 269, where the trial court held that the defendant railroad was not required to disclose any evidence it had marshalled concerning the physical activities of plaintiff subsequent to the date of the accident. The court stated that the observations of witnesses and the existence of movies or pictures constituted potential impeaching evidence, the disclosure of which would subvert the spirit of a local rule

---

f So far as pertinent, these rules were the same as Federal Rules of Civil Procedure 26(b) and 33 before 1970. Their substance now appears in Federal Rules 26(b)(1) and 33(a) and (b).

protecting such evidence from discovery. The court further observed that the evidence could be revealed to the court at pretrial so that the judge might determine whether it was of a substantive nature or merely impeachment.

* * *

In * * * [*Discovery and Pre-trial Procedure in Federal Courts,* 12 Okla.L.Rev. 321, 324 (1959)], Judge Stephen S. Chandler * * * had this to say about divulging impeachment material:

> * * * "In his court, the writer requires that all signed statements taken from witnesses, moving pictures to show malingering, in fact all evidence, including that intended for purposes of possible impeachment or rebuttal, be furnished to opposing counsel. This is a cardinal requirement for the reason that if any instrument or fact remains undisclosed, the lawyer concealing it feels he has an advantage. While such a situation exists, the whole picture presented by the lawsuit is distorted and obscured because the true situation is not apparent to all."

* * * Defendant's entire argument proceeds on the premise that defendant's evidence which plaintiffs seek to elicit constitutes the unblemished truth which, if prematurely disclosed, will prevent defendant from revealing to the jury the sham and perjury inherent in plaintiffs' claims. While defendant disclaims such assumption, it is implicit in his position that witnesses whose testimony is designed to impeach invariably have a monopoly on virtue and that evidence to which the attempted impeachment is directed is, without exception, fraudulent.

Let us assume hypothetically that a claimant has sustained injuries for which he seeks to recover damages and that he has been in no previous accident and has suffered no prior disability or illness and has been incapacitated solely as a result of the accident in question. The hypothetical defendant, on the other hand, has resorted to fraud and perjury in fabricating pictures of what purport to be plaintiff's physical activities subsequent to the accident, and has manufactured evidence to prove that plaintiff sustained his injuries in prior accidents. It is the defendant's position that under the assumed circumstances plaintiff is foreclosed from discovering the perjured testimony which is about to be foisted upon him because it is essentially impeachment. In other words, the defendant would have us adopt a rule that no opportunity may be afforded either party to impeach evidence which is itself impeachment, but both must await the uncertain fate which befalls litigants when confronted for the first time in the courtroom with surprise testimony for which they are wholly unprepared.

For us to revert to this philosophy would be judicial retrogression undermining the whole purpose of the rules of civil procedure. It would inevitably lead us back to the "poker hand" concept of litigation, rewarding artifice and camouflage. We do not believe the rights of the parties should be determined in such a murky atmosphere. It is essential to the achievement of justice that all of the admissible evidence be brought to light in time for both parties to evaluate it and adequately prepare for trial or settlement with full knowledge of the facts.

Not only may impeaching testimony be the subject of impeachment itself, but in this case the information which plaintiff seeks bears on the fundamental issue of the nature and extent of the injuries which Mrs. Boldt sustained in this accident. She is entitled to know what evidence defendant will produce on this issue in view of his denial that her condition is serious or is attributable to this accident.

*   *   *

Holding

We therefore hold that no evidence which will be admissible at the trial is exempt from discovery under Rules 26.02 and 33 unless the affected party invokes a valid privilege. We do not decide, however, whether such party may thereafter waive his privilege at the trial and introduce such testimony, nor do we suggest that pretrial discovery is limited to what is admissible in evidence.

*   *   *

The writ of prohibition is therefore discharged.

NOTES AND QUESTIONS

1. The issue raised by the principal case is discussed in Note, *Pre-Trial Discovery of Impeachment Evidence: A Need to Reexamine Arizona's New Rule*, 7 Ariz.L.Rev. 283 (1966), in which it is suggested that in the case of evidence as to matters within the knowledge of the inquiring party, the party interrogated be allowed to determine whether he will use the evidence for impeachment purposes only, in which event it will not be subject to discovery. Would this be a good rule?

2. * * * [T]he common law * * * *recognized no rule requiring prior notice* of intended evidence to be given to the opponent or furnishing legal process for obtaining such information * * *.

It might be supposed that, in the court of Chancery, a bill for discovery served as a means of evading the strict common-law rule, and that thereby a notice could be compulsorily obtained of the evidence intended to be produced by the opponent. But there was here no radical departure from the established doctrine of the common law; it was a policy, not of one Court rather than another Court, but of the whole legal system * * * [of England].

* * * It is true that, to a limited extent * * * the result of a bill of discovery would usually be the revelation of some portion of information not before known to the applicant. But the general theory remained, and the rule was strictly enforced, that the adversary's own evidence was not to be revealed on a bill for discovery.

In short, equitable discovery involved no more than the negation of the party's privilege at common-law trials not to testify *against* his own cause, and was not intended to give relief against the common-law principle which refused to exact before trial a disclosure of the tenor of the evidence intended to be given *for* his cause.

6 Wigmore, *Evidence* §§ 1845, 1846, at 378, 380 (3d ed. 1940).

Interrogatories: includes attorney

3. Why did plaintiff in *Boldt* use Rule 33 interrogatories rather than Rule 30 depositions? ← D may not know   A: Better Device

4. What is a writ of prohibition? Why was it used in the circumstances of this case? Reread pp. 17–18, *supra*.

In ruling on a motion to dismiss for failure to state a claim as in *Foley-Carter*, the judge must accept as true the allegations in the complaint. If the defendant files an answer denying those allegations, the denials are only assertions of the defendant and do not demonstrate whose story is correct. The motion for summary judgment enables a party to show that there is admissible evidence to support his allegations and to call for a similar showing by the opposing party. The judge will not try to decide a factual dispute when each party has shown that he has evidence on an issue. But if it becomes clear that one party cannot begin to prove his allegations, there is no "genuine issue" and a futile trial may be avoided by granting the motion.

ALDERMAN v. BALTIMORE & OHIO R. CO.

United States District Court, Southern District of West Virginia, 1953.
113 F.Supp. 881.

MOORE, Chief Judge. Plaintiff * * * brings this action against defendant, * * * to recover for personal injuries sustained by her as a result of the derailment of one of defendant's trains near Adrian, West Virginia, on February 14, 1952.

Plaintiff was not a fare-paying passenger. She was traveling on a trip pass, which afforded her free transportation * * *. The following conditions were printed on the pass: "In consideration of the issuance of this free pass, I hereby assume all risk of personal injury and loss of or of damage to property from whatever causes arising, and release the company from liability therefor, and I hereby declare that I am not prohibited by law from receiving free transportation and that this pass will be lawfully used."

Plaintiff in her original complaint charged defendant with negligence in the maintenance of its tracks and the operation of its train. After a pre-trial conference, at which the legal effect of the release from liability contained in the pass was discussed, plaintiff filed an amended complaint charging defendant with wilful or wanton conduct.

On the basis of the amended pleadings and supporting affidavits filed by defendant, defendant moved for summary judgment under Rule 56 * * *.

It is undisputed that the derailment was caused by a break in one of the rails as the train was passing over the track. It is also shown by defendant's affidavits, and not denied, that the break in the rail was due to a transverse fissure inside the cap of the rail, which broke vertically under the weight of the train; that such a fissure is not visible upon inspection; that such defects occur in both new and old rails; and that a visual inspection was in fact made of this particular rail the day preceding the accident and the defect was not discovered.

Since plaintiff was an intrastate passenger, and since the accident occurred in West Virginia, the law of West Virginia governs both the effect to be given to the release and the degree of care which defendant owed plaintiff. * * *

However, counsel have been unable to direct the Court's attention to, and the Court has not found, any West Virginia decision which has determined the effect which a release from liability contained in a pass has upon the carrier's duty to the holder of such a pass. * * *

Since the Federal statute and the West Virginia statute authorizing the issuance of free passes are similar, 49 U.S.C.A. § 1(7), and W.Va.Code, Ch. 24, Art. 3, § 4, it is pertinent to examine the United States Supreme Court decisions construing the Federal statute. The Supreme Court has held that a carrier may contract against liability for negligent injury to one who accepts a free pass * * *; but that for reasons of public policy it cannot relieve itself of liability for wilful or wanton acts. * * *

I am therefore of opinion that the sole duty imposed upon defendant under the facts of this case was to refrain from wilfully or wantonly injuring plaintiff.

In Kelly v. Checker White Cab, Inc., 131 W.Va. 816 at page 822; 50 S. E.2d 888 at page 892, the West Virginia court, quoting from 29 Cyc. 510 said: " ' "In order that one may be held guilty of wilful or wanton conduct, it must be shown that he was conscious of his conduct, and conscious, from his knowledge of existing conditions, that injury would likely or probably result from his conduct, and that with reckless indifference to consequences he consciously and intentionally did some wrongful act or omitted some known duty which produced the injurious result." ' " * * *

The substance of plaintiff's contention that defendant wilfully injured her is that defendant used old and obsolescent rails in its tracks, knowing that the use of these rails made derailments reasonably probable. It is charged that defendant used old rails because the cost of derailments was less than the cost of replacing the old rails, and that for this reason defendant was willing to take the risk of derailments.

I am of opinion that the complaint fails to state sufficient facts to substantiate a charge of wilfulness, as that term is defined by the West Virginia court. It is clear that plaintiff has stated a charge of negligence; but that is not the test in this case. To establish wilfulness it would be necessary to charge that defendant knew of this particular defect in the rail; that the defect would probably result in a break in the rail if the train were run over it, causing a derailment of the train; and that defendant, with this knowledge of existing conditions, and the likelihood or probability of an injury resulting from its conduct, intentionally drove its train over the defective rail with an indifference to the consequences. The undenied affidavits of defendant show clearly that plaintiff cannot establish these facts.

At the hearing of this motion, counsel for plaintiff moved for a continuance of the hearing to enable him to substantiate a newspaper report to the effect that defendant was using old and obsolescent rails in its tracks because the cost of derailments was cheaper than the cost of replacing the rails. The motion was denied since this contention, even if it were true, merely has a bearing ⟵ Wrong! on an issue of negligence, and not upon the question of wilful conduct. Plaintiff does not contend that she can establish that defendant knew of the particular defect in the rail that caused the derailment.

For the reasons stated above, defendant's motion for summary judgment will be sustained. * * *

NOTES AND QUESTIONS

1. If very specific allegations of all of the facts giving rise to the plaintiff's cause of action were required to be set forth in the complaint, would it have been possible to handle the *Alderman* case by a motion to dismiss or a demurrer? To the extent that this would have been possible, does the case present a strong argument for more specific pleading of facts? In this connection, consider whether the court should have ruled as it did if the motion for summary judgment had been made immediately upon the service of the complaint and before plaintiff had an opportunity to utilize the discovery process. What provision does Federal Rule of Civil Procedure 56 make for this contingency? Analytically, the motion for summary judgment can be thought of as a demurrer-plus. You should not forget, however, that if summary judgment is to be a fair and effective device, it must frequently be preceded by discovery, so that each party will have an opportunity to disclose the gaps in her opponent's case and to cure any defects in her own.

2. Should a court always grant a motion for summary judgment if the requirements of Rule 56 are met? In KENNEDY v. SILAS MASON CO., 334 U.S. 249, 256–57, 68 S.Ct. 1031, 1034, 92 L.Ed. 1347, 1350–51 (1948), Mr. Justice Jackson, speaking for the Court, said:

> * * * [S]ummary procedures, however salutary where issues are clear-cut and simple, present a treacherous record for deciding issues of far-flung import, on which this Court should draw inferences with caution from complicated courses of legislation, contracting and practice.
>
> We consider it the part of good judicial administration to withhold decision of the ultimate questions involved in this case until this or another record shall present a more solid basis of findings based on litigation or on a comprehensive statement of agreed facts. While we might be able, on the present record, to reach a conclusion that would decide the case, it might well be found later to be lacking in the thoroughness that should precede judgment of this importance and which it is the purpose of the judicial process to provide.

3. A motion for summary judgment may be useful even though the moving party believes it will be unsuccessful. For what reasons, other than a hope of obtaining judgment, might a defendant in a case like *Alderman* make such a motion?

---

3. JUDGE AND JURY

You will probably be surprised (and perhaps dismayed) by the comparatively small part of this course devoted to the actual process of trial. It is true that the trial, if one occurs, is the most important and most interesting stage of a lawsuit. But most of the "law" about trials is the subject-matter of the course in Evidence. The most important aspect of trial with which this course is concerned is the division of functions between judge and jury and the various ways in which the judge acts to insure that the jury performs its proper function. In this section, we look at four of those ways: the instruction of the jury as to the law it shall apply, the form that the verdict takes, judicial control over the matters the jury may consider, and the taking from the jury of its power to decide a case when the evidence is inadequate.

A. INSTRUCTING THE JURY

Broadly stated, it is a function of the judge to decide questions of law and a function of the jury to decide questions of fact. But in most cases the jury's final decision will be that one or the other party is entitled to judgment and the jury must apply the law to the facts to reach this decision. Therefore the jury must be told what the law is. The vehicle for this is the judge's charge to the jury, which comes at the end of the trial, immediately before the jury retires to consider its verdict.

An important issue concerning these instructions is how far the adversary system should extend to this stage of the lawsuit. Counsel for both parties may request that particular instructions be given to the jury, and when there is a dispute between them as to the law, they ordinarily will submit conflicting requests. The judge must resolve such conflicts, and it is the court's duty in any event to instruct the jury whether or not the parties make specific requests. The judge, even though an expert on the law, may err. To what extent is it the responsibility of counsel to attempt to correct the trial judge? The next case involves not only this question, but it also introduces you to the question of allocating the burden of proof (or burden of persuasion). Why is there any rule that says one party or the other has this burden?

ALEXANDER v. KRAMER BROS. FREIGHT LINES, INC.

United States Court of Appeals, Second Circuit, 1959.
273 F.2d 373.

SWAN, Circuit Judge. The present action is a sequel to a collision between two tractor-trailer trucks on the Pennsylvania Turnpike in or near Somerset, Pennsylvania. It occurred * * * about six o'clock in the morning, when there was spotty fog on the Turnpike. The corporate plaintiff owned one of the trucks. It was badly damaged and its operator, the plaintiff Alexander, sustained serious injuries. The other truck was owned by the defendant corporation. Its answer to the complaint denied any negligence on its part and set up the defense of contributory negligence on the part of the plaintiffs. The jury found a verdict for the plaintiffs. * * *

Because of the character of the questions raised, a very brief statement concerning the testimony will suffice. The only eye witnesses to the accident were drivers of the two trucks. The drivers' stories were contradictory and raised issues as to the exact location of the accident and the manner in which it occurred. Both trucks were proceeding westerly. Alexander testified that the collision occurred where there was an entrance to the Turnpike from the right, that defendant's truck cut in ahead of him, and that the fog was such that he could not see the entering truck in time to avoid hitting it. Holman, defendant's driver, denied that he entered from the right and claimed that plaintiff's truck had been following for some time before it ran into the rear end of his truck. Thus the issues of negligence and contributory negligence raised questions of credibility for the jury.

The first question for consideration is whether the judgment should be reversed because of the court's erroneous charge as to the burden of proof of contributory negligence, despite defendant's failure to request a charge on that subject or to object or take exception to the charge given, as required by Rule 51 * * *. Appellant contends that he is excused from complying with the Rule by what occurred in colloquy with the court near the close of the plaintiffs' case. In the colloquy, the court stated that "the burden of proof of contributory negligence is on the defendant." Counsel for plaintiffs expressed agreement with the statement, and counsel for defendant said, "I take an exception," to which the court replied, "Yes, I give you that exception." The plaintiff then rested, and defendant proceeded to put in its case.

* * * Under the [applicable law] the plaintiffs in an action where death has not resulted * * * carry the burden of proving freedom from contributory negligence. The cases now relied upon by appellant to prove the charge wrong were never brought to the trial court's attention either in the col-

loquy or at the time when counsel submitted numerous requests to charge on other matters. Had they been, it seems probable that Judge Inch would have changed the view he expressed in colloquy. The obvious purpose of the requirement in Rule 51 that objection must be made to matters in the charge in order to assign them as error, is to permit the trial judge to evaluate the objection and correct his charge if further thought persuades him of its error. This purpose is not fulfilled by taking an exception to a statement made by the judge several days prior to the time for charging the jury when nothing was before the judge requiring a ruling in respect to the statement made in colloquy. Certainly an exception under such circumstances does not meet the literal requirement of Rule 51 and, in our opinion, it is an insufficient excuse for failure to object or except to the charge.

The cases relied upon by the appellant deal either with situations where an exception was taken at the time of the charge and the question is whether the exception was sufficiently explicit, or to cases involving evidentiary rulings where exception was taken at the time of the ruling but no further exception was taken at the time of the charge. * * * Nor do we think the instant case of the exceptional character in which an appellate court will sometimes correct an error in the charge in the absence of objection or exception. See Troupe v. Chicago, D. & G. Bay Transit Co., 2 Cir., 234 F.2d 253, 260.

* * *

Judgment affirmed.

NOTES AND QUESTIONS

1. The opinion in this case speaks of the "burden of proof of contributory negligence." In this book, we use the term "burden of persuasion" when we are referring to the kind of burden involved in *Alexander*. There is another kind of burden—the burden of initially putting in evidence on an issue, without which the issue is not in the case at all. This kind of burden we call the "burden of production." The two kinds of burden are distinct, but the term "burden of proof" often is used to mean either of them. For this reason we avoid it. Ordinarily the burden of production and the burden of persuasion on an issue are placed on the same party. But not always. For example, when a defense is one that is seldom raised, it might be a waste of time to require the plaintiff in every case to introduce evidence refuting it; the burden of production would be placed on the defendant. But once there is enough evidence on the issue to go to the jury, the court might rule that the plaintiff should have the burden of persuasion— that is, establishing that the defense is not valid—as the plaintiff does on most issues. See generally McCormick, *Evidence* § 336 (2d ed. 1973).

2. What factors should be considered in determining whether the burden of persuasion on the issue of contributory negligence should be placed on plaintiff or defendant? Are these the same factors that should be involved in deciding who shall be required to plead on the issue of contributory negligence? Why might the two burdens be placed differently?

3. In the *Troupe* case, cited at the end of the principal case, Judge Frank, in a concurring opinion, said, at 234 F.2d 260–61:

> On the negligence issue, the judge, at defendant's request, charged, "It is enough if the steps and paint are commonly used and accepted in the industry at the time." This was as obvious an error, on a material matter, as one can imagine. For the Supreme Court, this court and others have often held that usual practices, by others in the same industry or trade, similar to a defendant's practices, do not constitute a defense in a negligence action.

> My colleagues indicate that, were it not for our reversal on the unseaworthiness issue, they would probably have disregarded this error. I cannot agree. My colleagues refer to Rule 51 and the fact that, before the jury retired, plaintiffs' counsel did not state distinctly that he objected and the grounds of the objection. My colleagues concede that, in an exceptional case, we may review errors not "saved" by a proper objection. They suggest this is not an exceptional case, relying on a statement in United States v. Atkinson, 297 U.S. 157, 160, 56 S.Ct. 391, 392, 80 L.Ed. 555. There the Supreme Court, set forth, in the disjunctive, two grounds for reviewing such errors:

> (1) "the errors are obvious
>
> *or*
>
> (2) they otherwise seriously affect the fairness, integrity, or public reputation of judicial proceedings."

> My colleagues stress the second ground. But the first ground alone suffices, as the cases make clear. And here, as observed above, the error was magnificently obvious. A litigant surely has the right to assume that a federal trial judge knows the elementary substantive legal rules, long established by the precedents, and that therefore the judge will act accordingly, without prompting by the litigant's lawyer.

Was the trial judge's error in *Alexander* "obvious"? What factors are relevant to this question?

B. THE FORM OF THE VERDICT

In most cases, the jury is asked to return a "general verdict." In substance, the jury simply says, "We find for the plaintiff and fix damages at *x* dollars" or "We find for the defendant." But as previously discussed in the Outline, pp. 14–15, supra, there are two variations on the general verdict. One is the special verdict, in which the jury is asked to answer questions as to the facts; the judge then applies the law to the facts as found by the jury. The other is the general verdict with interrogatories; the jury is told to return a verdict in the same form as a general verdict, but in addition it is told to answer certain questions about the facts of the case. If those answers are not consistent with the general verdict, the answers control. There are a number of reasons for using the special verdict or the general verdict with interrogatories. For example, in a complicated case, the special verdict obviates the necessity of instructing the jury about the law and permits it to concentrate on determining the facts. But you should bear in mind that both of these forms of verdict also are devices for controlling the jury—for preventing the jury from ignoring the law and simply deciding the case for the party the jurors want to win.

DINIERO v. UNITED STATES LINES CO.

United States Court of Appeals, Second Circuit, 1961.
288 F.2d 595, 91 A.L.R.2d 770.
Certiorari denied 368 U.S. 831, 82 S.Ct. 54, 7 L.Ed.2d 34.

MEDINA, Circuit Judge. * * * Julio Diniero, a Junior Third Assistant Engineer aboard the S. S. Pioneer Land, owned by United States Lines Company, claimed to have suffered such repeated strains in his back in the performance of his duties as to cause a ruptured disc with resultant pain and suffering, culminating some years later in a fusion operation and the removal of the disc. According to Diniero's testimony, there was a blow-down valve located below a floor plate * * *. There was a slot in the floor plate and normally the valve could be opened or closed as circumstances required by using a reach rod. For a variety of reasons * * * which include the absence of a reach rod and defects in the valve, Diniero said the only way he could operate the valve was by removing the deck plate, crouching down and moving the wheel of the valve by the use of a wrench. He claimed the injuries to his back were the effect of repeatedly operating the valve under these difficult conditions. The shipowner * * * claimed there was nothing wrong with the valve, nor any necessity to remove the floor plate or to use a wrench. The eight day trial was devoted to * * * the controverted issue of liability, and there was also considerable medical proof on the general subject of whether Diniero's trouble was due to a long continued condition caused by a degenerative disc disease and having no relation whatever to the operation of the blow-down valve * * *.

At the close of the evidence the trial judge submitted the case to the jury in a wholly unexceptionable charge. In an endeavor to assist the jury in its deliberations, however, * * * he submitted eight questions to be signed and returned as the verdict of the jury. The last two were in the form of a general verdict for plaintiff or defendant, questions 2 to 6 [related] * * * to unseaworthiness, negligence, contributory negligence and proximate cause. The trouble was caused by question number 1, as follows:

> "Did the plaintiff injure himself aboard the Pioneer Land because in operating the blow-down valve he had to remove the floor plates, then crouch and exert physical effort with a wrench and not his hand to stop it from leaking?
> "Answer yes or no."

After some hours of deliberation and the receipt of a number of communications from the jury, the trial judge withdrew all the questions, told the jury to disregard them and bring in a general verdict in the usual form; and, after further deliberations the jury brought in a verdict in favor of the seaman for $46,150.   *   *   *

The position of the shipowner is that   *   *   *   Rule 49(b) authorizes the submission of written interrogatories but does not authorize the withdrawal of such interrogatories, after they have once been submitted and the jury has commenced its deliberations thereon.   The shipowner further argues that question number 1 related to "one or more issues of fact the decision of which is necessary to a verdict," and that   *   *   *   it was a clear abuse of discretion to withdraw a proper and material interrogatory, relating to an issue that must necessarily be decided in plaintiff's favor, if plaintiff was to recover any damages whatever.   To permit such withdrawal, the shipowner claims, would defeat the very purpose of   *   *   *   Rule 49(b), and smooth the way for a reluctant jury, unable to agree on the facts basic to recovery, to do "popular justice" through the medium of "an old-fashioned verdict."

*   *   *

The jury commenced their deliberations at 2:45 p. m.   At 5:40 p. m. the trial judge received a note from the jury reading: "Your Honor, could we ask for your interpretation of the word 'had' in the second line, first question? Did the plaintiff injure himself?"

Appellant's counsel assures us that the question and the explanation given by the trial judge is just as simple as   *   *   *   whether he was injured in the manner described by him in his testimony.   What the trial judge said, however, is as follows:

> "What I was trying to find out by the first question was whether or not plaintiff injured himself on board this ship, assuming that he had to remove the plates, assuming that he had to crouch down, and assuming he exerted this pressure with the wrench instead of his hand?
>
> "So in answer to your specific question as to the interpretation of the word 'had' it means that I assumed that he had to remove the plates, and he had to do this, and he had to do that.   I didn't mean to take away from you the question as to whether he did in fact have to do that.   In other words, the purpose of the question is to find out whether the plaintiff injured himself on board the ship in the manner that he described.   The defendant claims that he did not.   So the first question that I wanted answered was did he injure himself aboard the ship by doing what he said he did?
>
> "If you find that he didn't remove the plates or he didn't bend down, or he didn't crouch, or he didn't have to, or he didn't do it, those questions will be answered as you go on further down by your answers to the other questions.

"But in my first question I assumed as a fact, accepted the plaintiff's testimony, that he had to bend down, that he had to crouch, that he had to remove the plates.

"What I wanted to find out was, assuming all of that, did he injure himself on board the Pioneer Land.

"Now I hope that is clear. If it isn't you can write me another note."

The jury retired again at 5:50 p. m. and returned with another note at 6:40 p. m. * * * as follows: "Your Honor, we cannot agree on question one. It appears there is no chance for agreement." Thereupon the trial judge withdrew all the questions from the consideration of the jury and asked them to see if they could not agree on a general verdict.

* * * [T]he jury still could not soon reach agreement. At 9:22 p. m. the jury informed the trial judge that "it finds it impossible to arrive at a unanimous agreement in this case." The trial judge thereupon read a quotation from Allen v. United States, 1896, 164 U.S. 492, 501, 17 S.Ct. 154, 41 L.Ed. 528, and returned the jury for further deliberations at 9:30 p. m. * * * At 10:30 p. m. the verdict was announced and the jury polled.

There was an inherent ambiguity in question one, and it is plain enough that the explanation failed to remove the ambiguity. Under these circumstances we think it was not an abuse of discretion to withdraw the questions and give the jury an opportunity to agree upon a general verdict. * * * It was a matter of judgment whether to attempt some further elucidation of the question, or to declare a mistrial, or to withdraw all the questions and authorize a general verdict. We cannot say the decision made here under the circumstances of this case was wrong, particularly as the jury continued its deliberations from about 6:45 p. m. until 10:30 p. m., after the withdrawal of the questions.

* * *

Other cases present the problem in its simplest form. After the submission of material and proper interrogatories, there is a delay of a few hours and the trial judge of his own motion, or on the application of plaintiff's counsel, calls in the jury, withdraws the questions, tells the jury to bring in a general verdict over the objection of defendant's counsel, and shortly thereafter the jury returns a verdict for the plaintiff. This has been held to be an abuse of discretion and ground for reversal. * * * The reason is that the action of the trial judge would probably be prejudicial to defendant. * * * This is a good general rule, and we agree with it. But it has no application to the case before us now, as the interrogatory causing all the difficulty here was unclear and ambiguous. The withdrawal of all the questions was for the purpose of eliminating the confusion caused by the formulation of an improper question. And it is to be noted that a confusing and improperly worded interrogatory cannot fairly be considered a "material" question, or one the answer to which "is necessary to a verdict." Under the circumstances it was, we think, good judgment to withdraw all the questions. Certainly we cannot say to do so was an abuse of discretion.

Affirmed.

NOTES AND QUESTIONS

1. Do you believe the interrogatory as first given to the jury was ambiguous? What are the possible meanings of the question? Could the jury answer the question "No" under any of these meanings and still find for plaintiff? If the jury had answered the interrogatory "No," and a reviewing court found that there was no evidence at all to support a finding that Diniero was *not* required to remove the plate, crouch down, and turn the valve with a wrench, but that a genuine issue existed on the question whether his condition was caused by this work, would the reviewing court be required to reverse a verdict for defendant that was based on the answer to the first interrogatory?

2. Could the jury have properly reached a decision for plaintiff without resolving the issue that the judge said in his explanation he intended the interrogatory to present? If it could not, was it proper to withdraw the interrogatory altogether and say to the jury: "What I am going to do, in an effort to see whether you can agree, I am going to ask you to forget all of the questions I gave you and see whether you can't agree on a general verdict. * * * I think that might relieve the situation some. I hope you can come to some agreement." (Judge's Instruction, quoted from the Petition for a Writ of Certiorari, p. 11.)

3. Do you think the judge's explanation of the interrogatory was clear? Read it again very carefully before you decide. Then reflect upon the fact that it was delivered orally to the jurors. Do you think they could properly understand it? When the jury is asked to return a general verdict, the charge, frequently including very complex instructions on the law, is given orally, and although the jurors may ask to have parts of it repeated, they usually are not given a copy. From the experience in this case do you think written instructions would be a better idea? What advantages and disadvantages do you see in written instructions?

4. The use of special verdicts and general verdicts with interrogatories is sometimes criticized as atomizing the jury's deliberations and making a unanimous result more difficult to reach. Assume that in an ordinary automobile accident case, six members of the jury believe that the defendant was going too fast but the other six believe that he was not; moreover, the latter group of jurors believes that the defendant was not looking where he was going, but the first group believes that the defendant was. Could the jury return a unanimous verdict for the plaintiff? For defendant? Would the problem be aggravated by the use of a special verdict or a general verdict with interrogatories? For a perceptive discussion of the general problem, see Ginsburg, *Special Findings and Jury Unanimity in the Federal Courts*, 65 Colum.L.Rev. 256 (1965).

5. ALLEN v. UNITED STATES, 164 U.S. 492, 17 S.Ct. 154, 41 L.Ed. 528 (1896), which the trial court in *Diniero* quoted to the jury, involved a variation on what has come to be called the "dynamite charge," an instruction sometimes given in the principal charge but more frequently given only to a jury that has been unable to reach a unanimous verdict for either party after a substantial period

of time. In *Allen* this charge was given sometime after the main charge. Its content was,

> in substance, that in a large proportion of cases absolute certainty could not be expected; that, although the verdict must be the verdict of each individual juror, and not a mere acquiescence in the conclusion of his fellows, yet they should examine the question submitted with candor, and with a proper regard and deference to the opinions of each other; that it was their duty to decide the case if they could conscientiously do so; that they should listen, with a disposition to be convinced, to each other's arguments; that, if much the larger number were for conviction, a dissenting juror should consider whether his doubt was a reasonable one which made no impression upon the minds of so many men, equally honest, equally intelligent with himself. If, upon the other hand, the majority were for acquittal, the minority ought to ask themselves whether they might not reasonably doubt the correctness of a judgment which was not concurred in by the majority.

Id. at 501, 17 S.Ct. at 157, 41 L.Ed. at 530–31. The United States Supreme Court said:

> While, undoubtedly, the verdict of the jury should represent the opinion of each individual juror, it by no means follows that opinions may not be changed by conference in the jury room. The very object of the jury system is to secure unanimity by a comparison of views, and by arguments among the jurors themselves. It certainly cannot be the law that each juror should not listen with deference to the arguments, and with a distrust of his own judgment, if he finds a large majority of the jury taking a different view of the case from what he does himself. It cannot be that each juror should go to the jury room with a blind determination that the verdict shall represent his opinion of the case at that moment, or that he should close his ears to the arguments of men who are equally honest and intelligent as himself.

Id. at 501, 17 S.Ct. at 157, 41 L.Ed. at 530. Does this opinion adequately answer the objections that may be made to such a charge?

The *Allen* charge has recently come under increasingly strong criticism. See United States v. Thomas, 449 F.2d 1177 (D.C.Cir.1971); American Bar Ass'n Project on Minimum Standards for Criminal Justice, *Trial by Jury* 145–58 (Approved Draft, 1968).

C. THE JURY'S DELIBERATION

After the judge completes the charge, the jury retires to deliberate in private. Extensive precautions are taken to insure that the jury is undisturbed and unheard during this period. The jury will have been instructed to decide the case in accordance with the law as explained by the judge and on only the evidence that has been brought forward in the trial. It clearly is improper for the jury to ignore what the judge has said about the law or to speculate about what evidence that was not introduced might have proved. It also is improper for the jurors to decide the case on the basis of their own personal knowledge of the facts of the case. Indeed, if a juror has specific knowledge of the facts, it should be disclosed at the beginning of the trial, and that juror probably will be excused from serving. But a more difficult question is presented by a juror's more general knowledge and experience as it relates to the case. A strength of the jury system is thought to be that it brings together a cross-section of community standards and experienced judgments. At the same time, the parties are not able to meet the special knowledge of jurors of which they are unaware. How should the line between general experience and special knowledge be drawn?

TEXAS EMPLOYERS' INS. ASS'N v. PRICE

Court of Civil Appeals of Texas, Eastland, 1960.
336 S.W.2d 304.

COLLINGS, Justice. Loyal Grant Price brought suit * * * to set aside an award of the Industrial Accident Board * * *. The defendant Texas Employers' Insurance Association answered by general denial and specifically pleaded that plaintiff's alleged injury did not result in total or permanent incapacity, but that any injury plaintiff may have received resulted only in partial and temporary incapacity, or resulted from other injuries and diseases or a combination thereof. * * *

The case was tried before a jury which found that plaintiff received an accidental injury while working for the Port Houston Iron Works, Inc.; * * * that such injury was the producing cause of total disability; that total disability began November 27, 1957; that such disability was permanent and was not partial * * *. Judgment was entered for the plaintiff for $13,415.96 in a lump sum with interest thereon at the legal rate. * * *

[margin note: Jury found total disability]

[margin note: Proc. Posture]
[margin note: D appeals]

In appellant's first four points it is contended that there was no evidence, and in the alternative that the evidence was insufficient to support the findings that any total incapacity sustained by appellee was permanent and the finding that appellee sustained total and permanent incapacity was so against the great weight and preponderance of the evidence as to be clearly wrong and unjust. * * *

In support of its contention in this respect, appellant further urges that appellee's own doctor testified that his back had been improved by the operation and stated that he "would estimate his (appellee's) partial permanent disability as approximately twenty percent as applied to general deficiency." This testimony is not consistent with the finding of the jury and the testimony of appellee to the effect that he has sustained total and permanent incapacity. It is the province of the jury, however, to determine the weight to be given evidence and to reconcile conflicts or inconsistencies therein. * * * The matter under consideration was not one for experts and skilled witnesses alone. Appellee testified that he could not work without pain, that his back was getting worse, that he was having to wear a brace with which he had previously been fitted by Dr. Brelsford. Dr. Brelsford testified that appellee had sustained permanent incapacity although not total, but that he would not pass him to follow his trade. The fact that appellee's testimony was in conflict with expert opinion testimony concerning the extent of his disability did not, under the circumstances, render it insufficient to support the verdict. * * *

Appellant further urges that the court erred in refusing to grant a new trial on the ground of jury misconduct. The evidence concerning some of the alleged jury misconduct was conflicting and would support a finding that such misconduct did not occur. The implied findings of the court in support of the order overruling appellant's motion for a new trial, which findings have support in the evidence, are binding on us. * * *

Holding

The existence of one of the alleged acts of jury misconduct is shown conclusively and in our opinion constitutes reversible error. The question whether the incapacity of appellee was total and permanent or only permanent partial was close, as already indicated. It is our opinion that the evidence supports the finding of total permanent incapacity and that such finding is not against the great weight and preponderance of the evidence. But it is further noted that appellee's own doctor testified, in effect, that his disability was approximately twenty percent partial. It is undisputed that one of the jurors related his personal experiences to persuade the jury that appellee was totally and permanently incapacitated. The witness stated to the jury as follows:

> "I said it has been my experience that in employment that if a man has an injury and it is obvious, such as, a scar on his back if he is being examined by a doctor for employment that he would want a statement from that man concerning that injury, and if he mentioned a back injury I doubted very much if he would get employment. The reason that came out was we were discussing whether or not the injury was partial or total."

The juror testified that he got this experience in union work; that he had read a letter from his company concerning back injuries showing that the company wanted to be more careful in hiring people with such injuries and that he told the jury about this experience. He testified that, in making the above statements to the jury, he was attempting to persuade a juror to come over to his side of the case; that he felt it was proper to give the jury the benefit of his personal knowledge and experience; and that was what he did. He further stated that he knew from experience that appellee could not get a job with Rohm and Haas, Shell Oil Company, Sinclair, or any other company that has a union contract or employee benefits and so advised the jury. He stated his opinion to the jury that appellee should receive total and permanent disability because he could not pass the physical examination he would be required to take; that it had been his experience that companies were very strict about whom they hire and that prospective employees were required to pass a most rigid physical examination. In this connection the juror testified that he also stated to the jury that there might be some jobs that appellee could handle but that he had a doubt whether appellee "could compete favorably on the labor market." The above evidence is undisputed. It shows that a juror related his personal experiences to the jury concerning the practice of company employers in hiring and employing workmen, and that the purpose and effect of such statements was to show that appellee was totally incapacitated. It was misconduct for the juror to relate to the other jurors his own personal experience as original evidence of material facts to be considered in their deliberation. * * * Considered in connection with the entire record, we are of the opinion that the misconduct shown was material and that it reasonably appears that injury probably resulted to appellant. * * *

For the reasons stated the judgment of the trial court is reversed and the cause is remanded.

NOTES AND QUESTIONS

1. Why is it misconduct for a juror "to relate to the other jurors his own personal experience as original evidence of material facts to be considered in their deliberation" ? In HEAD v. HARGRAVE, 105 U.S. 45, 49–50, 26 L.Ed. 1028, 1030 (1881), a case involving the value of legal services, Mr. Justice Field said:

> It was the province of the jury to weigh the testimony of the attorneys as to the value of the services, by reference to their nature, the time occupied in their performance, and other attending circumstances, and by applying to it their own experience and knowledge of the character of such services. To direct them to find the value of the services from the testimony of the experts alone, was to say to them that the issue should be determined by the opinions of the attorneys, and not by the exercise of their own judgment of the facts on which those opinions were given. * * * So far from laying aside their own general knowledge and ideas, the jury should have applied that knowledge and those ideas to the matters of fact in evidence in determining the weight to be given to the opinions expressed; and it was only in that way that they could arrive at a just conclusion. While they cannot act in any case upon particular facts material to its disposition resting in their private knowledge, but should be governed by the evidence adduced, they may, and to act intelligently they must, judge of the weight and force of that evidence by their own general knowledge of the subject of inquiry. If, for example, the question were as to the damages sustained by a plaintiff from a fracture of his leg by the carelessness of a defendant, the jury would ill perform their duty and probably come to a wrong conclusion, if, controlled by the testimony of the surgeons, not merely as to the injury inflicted, but as to the damages sustained, they should ignore their own knowledge and experience of the value of a sound limb. Other persons besides professional men have knowledge of the value of professional services; and, while great weight should always be given to the opinions of those familiar with the subject, they are not to be blindly received, but are to be intelligently examined by the jury in the light of their own general knowledge; they should control only as they are found to be reasonable.

Can the principal case be reconciled with this language?

2. The issue of jury misconduct is complicated by the doctrine, recognized in most jurisdictions but enforced with varying strictness, that a jury verdict may not be impeached by evidence that comes from the jurors themselves. Texas, in which the *Price* case arose, goes much further than most states, in allowing inquiry into the jury's deliberations. See Pope, *The Mental Operations of Jurors,* 40 Texas L.Rev. 849 (1962). In KILGORE v. GREYHOUND CORP., 30 F.R.D. 385, 388 (E.D.Tenn.1962), in which the issue concerned an unsupervised and unauthorized study of the scene of the accident by a juror and his report thereon to his fellows, it was said:

won't question jury in way it arrived at verdict [handwritten margin note]

> Any time a new trial is sought on the basis of the misconduct of a juror, or the receipt and consideration by a jury of improper evidence which may have had prejudicial effect on the jurors, the Court is forced to choose between the possibility that a party litigant may have been done an injustice, and, on the other hand, the possibility that the Court will inflict a public injury which will result if jurors are permitted to testify regarding what happened in the jury room.

> In the case at bar the Court had no way of ascertaining the truth of the matter without allowing a limited departure from the general rule. The Court felt that the least public injury would result in determining from the allegedly offending juror the facts as to the nature and extent of his purported misconduct, because in this way the Court could appraise the character of the extraneous influence on the jury and decide whether it was of such nature as might reasonably have been prejudicial to the plaintiff Kilgore.

What is the possible "public injury" of which this court speaks? Why are jurors generally prohibited from impeaching their verdict? Is one reason a fear that if the jury's processes are too closely examined the theoretical underpinnings of the system may be impaired?

3. The question of the extent to which jurors may rely on their own experience and knowledge may arise in contexts other than jury misconduct. In *Head v. Hargrave*, Note 1, supra, the issue was the denial of a requested instruction that the jury was not bound by the expert testimony. Again the issue may be raised in terms of a question whether there is sufficient evidence to sustain a particular verdict. *Compare* Holt v. Pariser, 161 Pa.Super. 315, 54 A.2d 89 (1947) (holding that a jury could properly find reasonable a very long delay in the repair of a truck in light of a wartime shortage of parts, although no evidence of the reason for the delay had been introduced), *with* Harris v. Pounds, 185 Miss. 688, 187 So. 891 (1939) (holding that a jury in a timber-growing county could not properly find that a hardwood log 15 feet in length and 12 inches in diameter was too heavy to be safely carried by six men over rough, uneven ground in the absence of evidence as to its weight).

D. TAKING THE CASE FROM THE JURY

The most direct and drastic example of jury control occurs in those cases in which it is held that there is no evidence on which a reasonable jury could find for a particular party (usually the plaintiff, but sometimes the defendant). If the judge makes this determination at the close of the evidence, she will direct the jury to return a verdict for the other party. Even after the jury has returned a verdict for one party, the judge in most systems may order that judgment be entered for the other party "notwithstanding the verdict," if she decides that the case should not have been submitted to the jury. The judge also has the power to set aside the verdict and order a new trial on the ground that the verdict is against the great weight of the evidence or because of mistakes or erroneous rulings during trial. Clearly when these devices are used, the jury is more than "controlled"; it is eliminated from the process. If such devices were not available, the jury could decide a case any way it wanted without respect to the evidence or the law. But if the devices are not very severely restricted, the right to jury trial can be negated.

LAVENDER v. KURN

Supreme Court of the United States, 1946.
327 U.S. 645, 66 S.Ct. 740, 90 L.Ed. 916.

On Writ of Certiorari to the Supreme Court of the State of Missouri.

Mr. Justice MURPHY delivered the opinion of the Court.

* * *

Petitioner, the administrator of the estate of L. E. Haney, brought this suit under the [Federal Employers' Liability] Act against the respondent trustees of the St. Louis-San Francisco Railway Company (Frisco) and the respondent Illinois Central Railroad Company. It was charged that Haney, while employed as a switch-tender by the respondents in the switchyard of the Grand Central Station in Memphis, Tennessee, was killed as a result of respondents' negligence. Following a trial * * *, the jury returned a verdict in favor of petitioner and awarded damages in the amount of $30,000. * * * On appeal, however, the Supreme Court of Missouri reversed the judgment, holding that there was no substantial evidence of negligence to support the submission of the case to the jury. * * *

[Haney was employed by the Illinois Central which owned the yards; Frisco's trains used the yards, and part of Haney's wages were paid by Frisco.]

The Illinois Central tracks run north and south directly past and into the Grand Central Station. About 2700 feet south of the station the Frisco tracks cross at right angles to the Illinois Central tracks. A westbound Frisco train wishing to use the station must stop some 250 feet or more west of this crossing and back into the station over a switchline curving east and north. The events in issue center about the switch several feet north of the main Frisco tracks at the point where the switch line branches off. This switch controls the tracks at this point.

It was very dark on the evening of December 21, 1939. At about 7:30 p.m. a westbound interstate Frisco passenger train stopped on the Frisco main line, its rear some 20 or 30 feet west of the switch. Haney, in the performance of his duties, threw or opened the switch to permit the train to back into the station. The respondents claimed that Haney was then required to cross to the south side of the track before the train passed the switch; and the conductor of the train testified that he saw Haney so cross. But there was also evidence that Haney's duties required him to wait at the switch north of the track until the train had cleared, close the switch, return to his shanty near the crossing and change the signals from red to green to permit trains on the Illinois Central tracks to use the crossing. The Frisco train cleared the switch, backing at the rate of 8 or 10 miles per hour. But the switch remained open and the signals still were red. Upon investigation Haney was found north of the track near the switch lying face down on the ground, unconscious. An ambulance was called, but he was dead upon arrival at the hospital.

Haney had been struck in the back of the head, causing a fractured skull from which he died. There were no known eye-witnesses to the fatal blow. Although it is not clear there is evidence that his body was extended north and south, the head to the south. Apparently he had fallen forward to the south; his face was bruised on the left side from hitting the ground and there were marks indicating that his toes had dragged a few inches southward as he fell. His head was about 5½ feet north of the Frisco tracks. Estimates ranged from 2 feet to 14 feet as to how far west of the switch he lay.

The injury to Haney's head was evidenced by a gash about two inches long from which blood flowed. The back of Haney's white cap had a corresponding black mark about an inch and a half long and an inch wide, running at an angle downward to the right of the center of the back of the head. A spot of blood was later found at a point 3 or 4 feet north of the tracks. The conclusion following an autopsy was that Haney's skull was fractured by "some fast moving small round object." One of the examining doctors testified that such an object might have been attached to a train backing at the rate of 8 or 10 miles per hour. But he also admitted that the fracture might have resulted from a blow from a pipe or club or some similar round object in the hands of an individual.

Petitioner's theory is that Haney was struck by the curled end or tip of a mail hook hanging down loosely on the outside of the mail car of the backing train. This curled end was 73 inches above the top of the rail, which was 7 inches high. The overhang of the mail car in relation to the rails was about 2 to 2½ feet. The evidence indicated that when the mail car swayed or moved around a curve the mail hook might pivot, its curled end swinging out as much as 12 to 14 inches. The curled end could thus be swung out to a point 3 to 3½ feet from the rail and about 73 inches above the top of the rail. Both east and west of the switch, however, was an uneven mound of cinders and dirt rising at its highest points 18 to 24 inches above the top of the rails. Witnesses differed as to how close the mound approached the rails, the estimates varying from 3 to 15 feet. But taking the figures most favorable to the petitioner, the mound extended to a point 6 to 12 inches north of the overhanging side of the mail car. If the mail hook end swung out 12 to 14 inches it would be 49 to 55 inches above the highest parts of the mound. Haney was $67\frac{1}{2}$ inches tall. If he had been standing on the mound about a foot from the side of the mail car he could have been hit by the end of the mail hook, the exact point of contact depending upon the height of the mound at the particular point. His wound was about 4 inches below the top of his head, or $63\frac{1}{2}$ inches above the point where he stood on the mound—well within the possible range of the mail hook end.

Respondents' theory is that Haney was murdered. They point to the estimates that the mound was 10 to 15 feet north of the rail, making it impossible for the mail hook end to reach a point of contact with Haney's head. Photographs were placed in the record to support the claim that the ground was level north of the rail for at least 10 feet. * * * It also appears that many hoboes and tramps frequented the area at night in order to get rides on freight trains. Haney carried a pistol to protect himself. This pistol was found loose under his body by those who came to his rescue. It was testified, however that the pistol had apparently slipped out of his pocket or scabbard as he fell. Haney's clothes were not disarranged and there was no evidence of a struggle or fight. No rods, pipes or weapons of any kind, except Haney's own pistol, were found near the scene. Moreover, his gold watch and diamond ring were still on him after he was struck. Six days later his unsoiled billfold was found on a high board fence about a block from the place where Haney was struck and near the point where he had been placed in an ambulance. It contained his social security card and other effects, but no money. His wife testified that he "never carried much money, not very much more than $10." Such were the facts in relation to respondents' theory of murder.

Finally, one of the Frisco foremen testified that he arrived at the scene shortly after Haney was found injured. He later examined the fireman's side of the train very carefully and found nothing sticking out or in disorder. In explaining why he examined this side of the train so carefully he stated that while he was at the scene of the accident "someone said they thought that train No. 106 backing in to Grand Central Station is what struck this man" and that Haney "was supposed to have been struck by something protruding on the side of the train." The foreman testified that these statements were made by an unknown Illinois Central switchman standing near the fallen body of Haney. The foreman admitted that the switchman "didn't see the accident." This testimony was admitted by the trial court over the strenuous objections of respondents' counsel that it was mere hearsay falling outside the *res gestae* rule.

The jury was instructed that Frisco's trustees were liable if it was found that they negligently permitted a rod or other object to extend out from the side of the train as it backed past Haney and that Haney was killed as the direct result of such negligence, if any. The jury was further told that Illinois Central was liable if it was found that the company negligently maintained an unsafe and dangerous place for Haney to work, in that the ground was high and uneven and the light insufficient and inadequate, and that Haney was injured and killed as a direct result of the said place being unsafe and dangerous. This latter instruction as to Illinois Central did not require the jury to find that Haney was killed by something protruding from the train.

The Supreme Court, in upsetting the jury's verdict against both the Frisco trustees and the Illinois Central, admitted that "It could be inferred from the facts that Haney could have been struck by the mail hook knob *if* he were standing on the south side of the mound and the mail hook extended out as far as 12 or 14 inches." * * * But it held that "all reasonable minds would agree that it would be mere speculation and conjecture to say that Haney was struck by the mail hook" and that "plaintiff failed to make a submissible case on that question." It also ruled that there "was no substantial evidence that the uneven ground and insufficient light were cause or contributing causes of the death of Haney." Finally, the Supreme Court held that the testimony of the foreman as to the statement made to him by the unknown switchman was inadmissible under the *res gestae* rule since the switchman spoke from what he had heard rather than from his own knowledge.

* * *

The evidence we have already detailed demonstrates that there was evidence from which it might be inferred that the end of the mail hook struck Haney in the back of the head, an inference that the Supreme Court admitted could be drawn. That inference is not rendered unreasonable by the fact that Haney apparently fell forward toward the main Frisco track so that his head was 5½ feet north of the rail. He may well have been struck and then wandered in a daze to the point where he fell forward. The testimony as to blood marks some distance away from his head lends credence to that possibility, indicating that he did not fall immediately upon being hit. When that is added to the evidence most favorable to the petitioner as to the height and swing-out of the hook, the height and location of the mound and the nature of Haney's duties, the inference that Haney was killed by the hook cannot be said to be unsupported by probative facts or to be so unreasonable as to warrant taking the case from the jury.

It is true that there is evidence tending to show that it was physically and mathematically impossible for the hook to strike Haney. And there are facts from which it might reasonably be inferred that Haney was murdered. But such evidence has become irrelevant upon appeal, there being a reasonable basis in the record for inferring that the hook struck Haney. The jury having made that inference, the respondents were not free to relitigate the factual dispute in a reviewing court. Under these circumstances it would be an undue invasion of the jury's historic function for an appellate court to weigh the conflicting evidence, judge the credibility of witnesses and arrive at a conclusion opposite from the one reached by the jury. * * *

It is no answer to say that the jury's verdict involved speculation and conjecture. Whenever facts are in dispute or the evidence is such that fair-minded men may draw different inferences, a measure of speculation and conjecture is required on the part of those whose duty it is to settle the dispute by choosing what seems to them to be the most reasonable inference. Only when there is a complete absence of probative facts to support the conclusion reached does a reversible error appear. But where, as here, there is an evidentiary basis for the jury's verdict, the jury is free to discard or disbelieve whatever facts are inconsistent with its conclusion. And the appellate court's function is exhausted when that evidentiary basis becomes apparent.   *   *   *

We are unable, therefore, to sanction a reversal of the jury's verdict against Frisco's trustees. Nor can we approve any disturbance in the verdict as to Illinois Central. The evidence was uncontradicted that it was very dark at the place where Haney was working and the surrounding ground was high and uneven. The evidence also showed that this area was entirely within the domination and control of Illinois Central   *   *   *. It was not unreasonable to conclude that these conditions constituted an unsafe and dangerous working place   *   *   *.

In view of the foregoing disposition of the case, it is unnecessary to decide whether the allegedly hearsay testimony was admissible under the *res gestae* rule. Rulings on the admissibility of evidence must normally be left to the sound discretion of the trial judge in actions under the Federal Employers' Liability Act. But inasmuch as there is adequate support in the record for the jury's verdict apart from the hearsay testimony, we need not determine whether that discretion was abused in this instance.

The judgment of the Supreme Court of Missouri is reversed and the case is remanded for whatever further proceedings may be necessary not inconsistent with this opinion.

The CHIEF JUSTICE and Mr. Justice FRANKFURTER concur in the result.

Mr. Justice REED dissents.

NOTES AND QUESTIONS

1. -Why does a trial judge or an appellate court have the power to take a case away from the jury or to set aside its verdict? Could a court effectively exercise this control if the rule regarding a jury's inability to use its own knowledge were different than as stated in *Texas Employers' Ins. Ass'n v. Price*, p. 47, supra?

2. In PENNSYLVANIA R. CO. v. CHAMBERLAIN, 288 U.S. 333, 339, 53 S.Ct. 391, 393, 77 L.Ed. 819, 822–23 (1933), the Supreme Court, in approving a directed verdict for defendant, said:

   *   *   * At most there was an inference to that effect drawn from observed facts which gave equal support to the opposite inference *   *   *.

   We, therefore, have a case belonging to that class of cases where proven facts give equal support to each of two inconsistent inferences;

in which event, neither of them being established, judgment, as a matter of law, must go against the party upon whom rests the necessity of sustaining one of these inferences as against the other, before he is entitled to recover.

Is this language consistent with the opinion of the Court in the principal case? Is there a difference between cases in which the evidence simply fails to point one way or the other, and cases in which the evidence on one side is overwhelming in terms of taking a case away from the jury? Would *Lavender* have been decided in the same way if the evidence that Haney was murdered was much stronger than it was?

2. When the *Lavender* case is remanded to the Missouri Supreme Court, what should that court do? In this connection, do you agree with the United States Supreme Court that it was unnecessary to determine whether evidence of the statement of the unknown switchman was improperly admitted?

---

4. REVIEW ON APPEAL

The grounds for appeal are chiefly mistakes of law—an erroneous ruling that the court had jurisdiction, an improper admission of evidence, or an incorrect instruction to the jury. Even if an error of law has been committed, the appellate court must be convinced that the error was prejudicial, and that the case probably would not have come out the same if the error had not occurred. In the event of an erroneous ruling on jurisdiction the prejudice is obvious. But appellate courts are reluctant to reverse merely because an error has been committed during the trial.

An appellate court rarely will reverse a decision on the ground that a question of fact was decided improperly. If there has been a jury, the constitutional right to jury trial itself is involved in such a ruling by an appellate court. See Amendment VII to the United States Constitution, which is set out in the Supplement. When there has been no jury, no constitutional problem is involved, but it may be asked whether a broad scope of review of the trial judge's findings of fact will not encourage needless appeals and denigrate the function of the trial judge.

HICKS v. UNITED STATES

United States Court of Appeals, Fourth Circuit, 1966.
368 F.2d 626.

SOBELOFF, Circuit Judge: This action was brought under the Federal Tort Claims Act, 28 U.S.C. § 1346, to recover damages for the death of Carol Greitens. The plaintiff, administrator of her estate, alleges that death was due to the negligence of the doctor on duty at the dispensary of the United States Naval Amphibious Base, Little Creek, Virginia, in diagnosing and treating her illness. The District Court, concluding that the evidence was insufficient to establish that the doctor was negligent, or that his concededly erroneous diagnosis and treatment was the proximate cause of her death, dismissed the complaint. *   *   *

The decedent, 25 years of age, had been a diabetic since the age of 13, although the condition was under control. *   *   * Mrs. Greitens' husband brought her to the dispensary at about 4 a.m. on August 25, 1963, suffering from intense abdominal pain and continual vomiting which had begun suddenly an hour before. The corpsman on duty in the examining room procured her medical records, obtained a brief history, took her blood pressure, pulse, temperature, and respiration and summoned the doctor on duty, then asleep in his room at the dispensary. The doctor arrived 15 or 20 minutes later and after questioning the patient concerning her symptoms, felt her abdomen and listened to her bowel sounds with the aid of a stethoscope. Recording his diagnosis on the chart as gastroenteritis, he told Mrs. Greitens that she had a "bug" in her stomach, prescribed some drugs for the relief of pain, and released her with instructions to return in eight hours. The examination took approximately ten minutes.

The patient returned to her home, and after another episode of vomiting, took the prescribed medicine and lay down. At about noon, she arose and drank a glass of water, vomited immediately thereafter and fell to the floor unconscious. She was rushed to the dispensary, but efforts to revive her were unsuccessful. She was pronounced dead at 12:48 p. m. and an autopsy revealed that she had a high obstruction, diagnosed formally as an abnormal congenital peritoneal hiatus with internal herniation into this malformation of some of the loops of the small intestine. Death was due to a massive hemorrhagic infarction of the intestine resulting from its strangulation.

I

The plaintiff contends that the doctor at the dispensary did not meet the requisite standard of care and skill demanded of him by the law of Virginia. Compliance with this standard, the plaintiff maintains, would have required a more extended examination and immediate hospitalization. More specifically, plaintiff's expert witnesses, two general practitioners in the Norfolk-Virginia Beach area, testified that, according to prevailing practice in the community, the doctor should have inquired whether the patient had had diarrhea and should have made a rectal examination to determine whether the patient was suffering from an obstruction rather than from gastroenteritis. While the latter condition does not ordinarily require immediate radical treatment, a high obstruction is almost invariably lethal unless promptly operated upon. Plaintiff's experts further testified that on observing the symptoms manifested by Mrs. Greitens, the procedure of general practitioners in the community would have been to order immediate hospitalization. *   *   *

The standard of care which Virginia law exacts from a physician, in this case a general practitioner, is * * * [such that] if he uses ordinary care in reaching his diagnosis, and thereafter acts upon it, he incurs no liability, even if the diagnosis proves to be a mistake in judgment.

It is undisputed that the symptoms of high obstruction and of gastroenteritis are quite similar. The District Court placed great emphasis on this fact as an indication that the doctor's erroneous diagnosis was not negligent, but was merely an error of judgment. It would seem, however, that where the symptoms are consistent with either of two possible conditions, one lethal if not attended to promptly, due care demands that a doctor do more than make a cursory examination and then release the patient. * * * The fact that an intestinal obstruction is a rare occurrence, and that some form of gastroenteritis is the more likely of the two conditions, does not excuse the failure to make inquiries and perform recognized additional tests that might have served to distinguish the one condition from the other. The dispensary doctor himself, as well as the experts for both sides, agreed that an inquiry as to diarrhea and a rectal examination were the "proper procedure" and "the accepted standard" in order to be able to rule out gastroenteritis and to make a definite diagnosis of high intestinal obstruction. If he had made the inquiry which he admits was the accepted standard, he would at least have been alerted to the fact that the case was one calling for close observation with a view to immediate surgical intervention if the graver diagnosis were confirmed. In these circumstances, failure to make this investigation constitutes a lack of due care on the part of the physician. * * * Only if a patient is adequately examined, is there no liability for an erroneous diagnosis.

Our conclusion that the physician was negligent in his diagnosis and treatment of the patient is not inconsistent with * * * [Rule] 52(a), which declares that the trial judge's findings of fact are not to be disturbed unless clearly erroneous. This Rule comes into play primarily where the trial judge as fact finder has had to reconcile conflicting testimony. Where the veracity of witnesses is in issue, the decision is for the judge who has had the opportunity to see and evaluate the witnesses' demeanor. * * * But we are dealing here with the testimony of expert witnesses who are not in controversy as to the basic facts; thus, the opportunity of the trial court to observe the witnesses is of limited significance. It has often been held that where the trial court's conclusions are based on undisputed facts, they are not entitled to the finality customarily accorded basic factual findings under Rule 52(a). * * *

The question before us is not one of fact in the usual sense, but rather whether the undisputed facts manifest negligence. Although the absence of a factual dispute does not *always* mean that the conclusion is a question of law, it becomes so *here* since the ultimate conclusion to be drawn from the basic facts, i. e., the existence or absence of negligence, is actually a question of law. For this reason, the general rule has been that when a judge sitting without a jury makes a determination of negligence his conclusion, as distinguished from the evidentiary findings leading to it, is freely reviewable on appeal. * * *

The determination of negligence involves not only the formulation of the legal standard, but more particularly in this case, its application to the evidentiary facts as established; and since these are uncontested, there is no basis for applying the "clearly erroneous" rule.   *   *   *

The government's expert opined that the dispensary physician exercised "average judgment," but analysis of his entire testimony points unavoidably to the opposite conclusion.   Revealing are his statements that it was wrong not to inquire about diarrhea, conceding that "that is one question that one usually asks," and that given a patient with abdominal pain of one hour's duration, it is too soon "to expect anybody to come up with a proper diagnosis."   Furthermore, his opinion was predicated upon a factual assumption not permissible in this case.   His assumption was that the dispensary physician had made only a "working" or "tentative" diagnosis   *   *   *.   However, the uncontradicted evidence indicates that this was not a "tentative" diagnosis.

The examining doctor himself testified that he had already considered and ruled out at the beginning of his examination the possibility of an obstruction without making the additional differentiating diagnostic tests.   He said that his only reason for asking the patient to return eight hours later was because her diabetic condition could become complicated by a case of gastroenteritis.   *   *   *   By releasing the patient, the dispensary physician made his diagnosis final, allowing no further opportunity for revision   *   *   *.

On careful scrutiny, therefore, the government's expert is seen to have demonstrated that the examiner did *not* conform to the required standard of care.   Coupled with the explicit testimony of the plaintiff's experts, the government's testimony leads us inevitably to the conclusion that the doctor was negligent as a matter of law.   We think that the District Court gave undue weight to the purely conclusory opinion of the government witness.   The District Court is not bound by his statement that "average judgment" had been exercised, nor are we bound by it.   Only the standard of care is to be established by the testimony of experts.   If under the undisputed facts the defendant failed to meet that standard it is not for the expert but for the court to decide whether there was negligence.

*   *   *

Judgment reversed and cause remanded for the determination of damages.

NOTES AND QUESTIONS

1.   Would the court of appeals have reached the same result if the judgment appealed from had been based on the verdict of a jury rather than the findings of a judge?   Why is there any difference between the standard enunciated in *Lavender v. Kurn* and that in Federal Rule of Civil Procedure 52(a)?

2.   Is the question whether certain conduct is negligent one of law or of fact?   Legal scholars have long debated the issue.   See pp. 837–38, infra.   In any event, the issue ordinarily is left to the jury.   Why?   Are the reasons for giving the issue to the jury any less persuasive when the finder of fact is a judge sitting without a jury?   Is there a difference if the standard of care to be applied by

the judge sitting without a jury must be derived from the testimony of experts? Why?

3. What considerations should govern an appellate court's decision to overturn a trial judge's findings? Is the only basis for the "clear error" rule, the opportunity of the trial judge to observe the witnesses' demeanor? For a vigorous argument that it is not, see Reay v. Butler, 95 Cal. 206, 213–14, 30 P. 208, 209 (1892).

5. CONCLUSIVENESS OF JUDGMENTS

Lawsuits are designed to settle disputes. An idealist might argue that nothing should be considered settled until it is settled *right*. A pragmatist could counter that nothing is settled at all unless it is settled *finally*. Cosmic questions may be debated endlessly, but controversies between individuals that are expected to result in enforceable judgments for damages or orders that must be obeyed under penalty of contempt must come to an end if the judicial process is to work at all. Res judicata requires that occasionally we let a judgment stand even when we become convinced that it was wrongly decided. A doctrine that only correct decisions have res judicata effect would furnish no finality at all.

Couna = This concept is absolutely essential – can't apply res judicata to action

The following case decided almost 300 years ago raises the same doubts that res judicata cases raise today: Is the decision fair to the plaintiff? Would an opposite decision be fair to the defendant?

P not permitted to split cause of actions
1) must bring suit for all remedies growing out of a cause of action

FETTER v. BEALE, 1 Ld.Raym. 339, 91 Eng.Rep. 1122 (King's Bench 1697). Plaintiff had brought an action for battery against defendant and recovered £11. Subsequently "part of his skull by reason of the said battery came out of his head," and plaintiff brought another action. Plaintiff's counsel argued that "this action differed from the nature of the former * * * because the recovery in the former action was only for the bruise and battery, but here there is a maihem by the loss of the skull."

Judgement replaces cause of action in case for P,
Judgment bars the cause when P looses.

And per totam Curiam, the jury in the former action considered the nature of the wound, and gave damages for all the damages that it had done to the plaintiff; and therefore a recovery in the said action is good here. And it is the plaintiff's fault, for if he had not been so hasty, he might have been satisfied for this loss of the skull also. Judgment for the defendant * * *.

A particularly difficult question of res judicata is presented when it is alleged that the first decision—now advanced as conclusive—was rendered by a court that lacked jurisdiction over the subject matter. This group of Illustrative Cases began with a decision that demonstrated the grave concern of the United States Supreme Court to keep the federal courts from deciding cases outside their constitutional and statutory jurisdiction. Res judicata was not involved in *Capron v. Van Noorden*; the trial court's decision was reversed in the ordinary course of appellate review. What if the plaintiff in that case had not sought a writ of error but had permitted the decision to become final and then instituted another action?

DES MOINES NAVIGATION & R. CO. v. IOWA HOMESTEAD CO.

Supreme Court of the United States, 1887.
123 U.S. 552, 8 S.Ct. 217, 31 L.Ed. 202.

Error to the Supreme Court of the State of Iowa.

Mr. Chief Justice WAITE delivered the opinion of the court.

This suit was brought by the Iowa Homestead Company against the Des Moines Navigation and Railroad Company to recover the same taxes for the years 1864 to 1871, both inclusive, which formed part of the subject matter of the litigation between the same parties in Homestead Co. v. Valley Railroad, 17 Wall. 153 * * *. The Railroad Company set up the decree in its favor in that suit as a bar to the present action, and to this the Homestead Company replied "that the decree or judgment referred to is null and void, for the reason that the courts of the United States had no jurisdiction of said suit, and no legal power or authority to render said decree or judgment."

[margin note: Q. shall null judg. have force?]

* * * It must be conceded that the Homestead Company and the Navigation and Railroad Company were both Iowa corporations, and, therefore, in law, citizens of the same State; but the defendants * * * who caused the removal to be made [from the Iowa state court to the United States Circuit Court], were citizens of the State of New York. After the removal was effected, all the above named defendants, as well as * * * the Navigation and Railroad Company, appeared, filed answers, and defended the action. The Homestead Company took issue on all the answers, and actually contested the matters in dispute with the Navigation and Railroad Company, as well as the other defendants, in the Circuit Court, and in this court on appeal, without taking any objection to the jurisdiction.

The precise question we have now to determine is whether the adjudication by this court, under such circumstances, of the matters then and now at issue between the Homestead Company and the Navigation and Railroad Company was absolutely void for want of jurisdiction. The point is not whether it was error in the Circuit Court to take jurisdiction of the suit, or of so much of it as related to the Navigation and Railroad Company, originally, but as to the binding effect of the decree of this court so long as it remains in force, and is not judicially annulled, vacated, or set aside.

* * *

It was settled by this court at a very early day, that, although the judgments and decrees of the Circuit Courts might be erroneous, if the records failed to show the facts on which the jurisdiction of the court rested, such as that the plaintiffs were citizens of different States from the defendants, yet that they were not nullities, and would bind the parties until reversed or otherwise set aside. * * * In 1825, McCormick v. Sullivant, 10 Wheat. 192, was decided by this court. There a decree in a former suit was pleaded in bar of the action. To this a replication was filed, alleging that the proceedings in the former suit were *coram non judice,* the record not showing that the complainants and defendants in that suit were citizens of different States; but this court held on appeal that "the courts of the United States are courts of *limited,* but not of *inferior,* jurisdiction. If the jurisdiction be not alleged in the proceedings, their judgments and decrees may be reversed for that cause on a writ of error or appeal; but until reversed they are conclusive between the parties and their privies." "But they are not nullities." There has never been any departure from this rule.

It is said, however, that these decisions apply only to cases where the record simply fails to show jurisdiction. Here it is claimed that the record shows there could be no jurisdiction, because it appears affirmatively that the Navigation and Railroad Company, one of the defendants, was a citizen of the same State with the plaintiff. But the record shows, with equal distinctness, that all the parties were actually before the court, and made no objection to its jurisdiction. The act of 1867, under which the removal was had, provided that when a suit was pending in a state court "in which there is a controversy between a citizen of the State in which the suit is brought and a citizen of another State, * * * such citizen of another State, * * * if he will make and file an affidavit stating that he has reason to and does believe that, from prejudice or local influence, he will not be able to obtain justice in such state court, may * * * file a petition in such state court for the removal of the suit" into the Circuit Court of the United States, and, when all things have been done that the act requires, "it shall be * * * the duty of the state court to * * * proceed no further with the suit," and, after the record is entered in the Circuit Court, "the suit shall then proceed in the same manner as if it had been brought there by original process." [g]

In the suit now under consideration there was a separate and distinct controversy between the plaintiff, a citizen of Iowa, and each of the citizens of

---

[g] The Judiciary Act of 1789 had been interpreted by the Supreme Court to require complete diversity of citizenship (all the plaintiffs being of a citizenship different from that of any defendant) for removal. It was widely argued that the 1867 statute referred to in the *Des Moines* case, because of a difference in language, did not have the same requirement. The Supreme Court held that the 1867 statute did require complete diversity, Case of the Sewing Machine Companies, 85 U.S. (18 Wall.) 553, 21 L.Ed. 914 (1874), but this decision came a year *after* the Court's decision in the Homestead Company's first suit in which the issue had not been raised.

New York, who were defendants. Each controversy related to the several tracts of land claimed by each defendant individually, and not as joint owner with the other defendants. Three of the citizens of New York caused to be made and filed the necessary affidavit and petition for removal, and thereupon, by common consent apparently, the suit as an entirety was transferred to the Circuit Court for final adjudication as to all the parties. * * * Whether in such a case the suit could be removed was a question for the Circuit Court to decide when it was called on to take jurisdiction. If it kept the case when it ought to have been remanded, or if it proceeded to adjudicate upon matters in dispute between two citizens of Iowa, when it ought to have confined itself to those between the citizens of Iowa and the citizens of New York, its final decree in the suit could have been reversed, on appeal, as erroneous, but the decree would not have been a nullity. To determine whether the suit was removable in whole or in part or not, was certainly within the power of the Circuit Court. The decision of that question was the exercise and the rightful exercise of jurisdiction, no matter whether in favor of or against taking the cause. Whether its decision was right, in this or any other respect, was to be finally determined by this court on appeal. As the Circuit Court entertained the suit, and this court, on appeal, impliedly recognized its right to do so, and proceeded to dispose of the case finally on its merits, certainly our decree cannot, in the light of prior adjudications on the same general question, be deemed a nullity. It was, at the time of the trial in the present case in the court below, a valid and subsisting prior adjudication of the matters in controversy, binding on these parties, and a bar to this action. In refusing so to decide, the court failed to give full faith and credit to the decree of this court * * * and this was error.

* * *

NOTES AND QUESTIONS

1. Where a court has jurisdiction over the parties and determines that it has jurisdiction over the subject matter, the parties cannot collaterally attack the judgment on the ground that the court did not have jurisdiction over the subject matter, unless the policy underlying the doctrine of res judicata is outweighed by the policy against permitting the court to act beyond its jurisdiction.

Restatement, Judgments § 10(1) (1942). How can the two policies of which the Restatement speaks be weighed against one another? What factors should be regarded as important in making such a decision?

2. Was it critical to the Supreme Court's opinion in this case that the first case had been heard and determined by the Supreme Court itself? Would the case have been decided differently if no review had been sought in the first case at all?

3. Was the fact that the question of jurisdiction was a doubtful one at the time the first *Homestead Company* case arose relevant to the Supreme Court's decision in the second case?

4. Suppose that the issue of jurisdiction is raised in a case and erroneously decided. Is this a factor arguing for or against the application of res judicata in a second action?

5. Since it is clear in the principal case that in the suit before the Court there is no diversity of citizenship and the writ of error is to the Supreme Court of Iowa, what is the basis for appellate jurisdiction in the United States Supreme Court?

CHAPTER 2

SELECTING THE PROPER COURT

SECTION A. JURISDICTION OVER THE PARTIES TO THE ACTION

---

1. THE TRADITIONAL BASES OF JURISDICTION

A. NATURAL PERSONS

PENNOYER v. NEFF

Supreme Court of the United States, 1877.
95 U.S. 714, 24 L.Ed. 565.

Error to the Circuit Court of the United States for the District of Oregon.

Mr. Justice FIELD delivered the opinion of the court:

This is an action to recover the possession of a tract of land, of the alleged value of $15,000, situated in the State of Oregon. The plaintiff asserts title to the premises by a patent of the United States issued to him in [March] 1866, under the Act of Congress of September 27th, 1850, 9 Stat. at L., 496, usually known as the Donation Law of Oregon. The defendant claims to have acquired the premises under a sheriff's deed, made upon a sale of the property on execution issued upon a judgment recovered against the plaintiff in one of the circuit courts of the State. The case turns upon the validity of this judgment.

It appears from the record that the judgment was rendered in February, 1866, in favor of J. H. Mitchell, for less than $300, including costs, in an action brought by him upon a demand for services as an attorney; that, at the time the action was commenced and the judgment rendered, the defendant therein, the plaintiff here, was a non-resident of the State; that he was not personally served with process, and did not appear therein; and that the judgment was entered upon his default in not answering the complaint, upon a constructive service of summons by publication.

The Code of Oregon provides for such service when an action is brought against a non-resident and absent defendant, who has property within the State. It also provides, where the action is for the recovery of money or damages, for the attachment of the property of the non-resident. And it also declares that no natural person is subject to the jurisdiction of a court of the State, "unless he appear in the court, or be found within the State, or be a resident thereof, or have property therein; and in the last case, only to the extent of such property at the time the jurisdiction attached." Construing this latter provision to mean that, in an action for money or damages where a defendant does not appear in the court, and is not found within the State, and is not a resident thereof, but has property therein, the jurisdiction of the court extends only over such property, the declaration expresses a principle of general, if not universal, law. The authority of every tribunal is necessarily restricted by the territorial limits of the State in which it is established. Any attempt to exercise authority beyond those limits would be deemed in every other forum, as has been said by this court, an illegitimate assumption of power, and be resisted as mere abuse. * * * In the case against the plaintiff, the property here in controversy sold under the judgment rendered was not attached, nor in any way brought under the jurisdiction of the court. Its first connection with the case was caused by a levy of the execution. It was not, therefore, disposed of pursuant to any adjudication, but only in enforcement of a personal judgment, having no relation to the property, rendered against a non-resident without service of process upon him in the action, or his appearance therein. The court below did not consider that an attachment of the property was essential to its jurisdiction or to the validity of the sale, but held that the judgment was invalid from defects in the affidavit upon which the order of publication was obtained, and in the affidavit by which the publication was proved.

There is some difference of opinion among the members of this court as to the rulings upon these alleged defects. The majority are of opinion that, inasmuch as the statute requires, for an order of publication, that certain facts shall appear by affidavit *to the satisfaction of the court or judge*, defects in such affidavit can only be taken advantage of on appeal, or by some other direct proceeding, and cannot be urged to impeach the judgment collaterally. The majority of the court are also of opinion that the provision of the statute requiring proof of the publication in a newspaper to be made by the "affidavit of the printer, or his foreman, or his principal clerk," is satisfied when the affidavit is made by the editor of the paper. The term "printer," in their judgment, is there used not to indicate the person who sets up the type—he does not usually have a foreman or clerks—it is rather used as synonymous with publisher. * * *

If, therefore, we were confined to the rulings of the court below upon the defects in the affidavits mentioned, we should be unable to uphold its decision. But it was also contended in that court, and is insisted upon here, that the judgment in the State Court against the plaintiff was void for want of personal service of process on him, or of his appearance in the action in which it was rendered, and that the premises in controversy could not be subjected to the payment of the demand of a resident creditor except by a proceeding *in rem*; that is, by a direct proceeding against the property for that purpose. If these positions are sound, the ruling of the Circuit Court as to the invalidity of that judgment must be sustained, notwithstanding our dissent from the reasons upon which it was made. And that they are sound would seem to follow from two well established principles of public law respecting the jurisdiction of an independent State over persons and property. The several States of the Union are not, it is true, in every respect independent, many of the rights and powers which originally belonged to them being now vested in the government created by the Constitution. But, except as restrained and limited by that instrument, they possess and exercise the authority of independent States, and the principles of public law to which we have referred are applicable to them. One of these principles is, that every State possesses exclusive jurisdiction and sovereignty over persons and property within its territory. As a consequence, every State has the power to determine for itself the civil *status* and capacities of its inhabitants; to prescribe the subjects upon which they may contract, the forms and solemnities with which their contracts shall be executed, the rights and obligations arising from them, and the mode in which their validity shall be determined and their obligations enforced; and also to regulate the manner and conditions upon which property situated within such territory, both personal and real, may be acquired, enjoyed and transferred. The other principle of public law referred to follows from the one mentioned; that is, that no State can exercise direct jurisdiction and authority over persons or property without its territory.   *   *   *   The several States are of equal dignity and authority, and the independence of one implies the exclusion of power from all others. And so it is laid down by jurists, as an elementary principle, that the laws of one State have no operation outside of its territory, except so far as is allowed by comity; and that no tribunal established by it can extend its process beyond that territory so as to subject either persons or property to its decisions. *   *   *

But as contracts made in one State may be enforceable only in another State, and property may be held by non-residents, the exercise of the jurisdiction which every State is admitted to possess over persons and property within its own territory will often affect persons and property without it. To any influence exerted in this way by a State affecting persons resident or property situated elsewhere, no objection can be justly taken; whilst any direct exertion of authority upon them, in an attempt to give exterritorial operation to its laws, or to enforce an exterritorial jurisdiction by its tribunals, would be deemed an encroachment upon the independence of the State in which the persons are domiciled or the property is situated, and be resisted as usurpation.

Thus the State, through its tribunals, may compel persons domiciled within its limits to execute, in pursuance of their contracts respecting property elsewhere situated, instruments in such form and with such solemnities as to transfer the title, so far as such formalities can be complied with; and the exercise of this jurisdiction in no manner interferes with the supreme control over the property by the State within which it is situated. Penn v. Ld. Baltimore, 1 Ves., 444; Massie v. Watts, 6 Cranch, 148; Watkins v. Holman, 16 Pet., 25; Corbett v. Nutt, 10 Wall., 464, 19 L.Ed. 976.

So the State, through its tribunals, may subject property situated within its limits owned by non-residents to the payment of the demand of its own citizens against them; and the exercise of this jurisdiction in no respect infringes upon the sovereignty of the State where the owners are domiciled. Every State owes protection to its own citizens; and, when non-residents deal with them, it is a legitimate and just exercise of authority to hold and appropriate any property owned by such non-residents to satisfy the claims of its citizens. It is in virtue of the State's jurisdiction over the property of the non-resident situated within its limits that its tribunals can inquire into that non-resident's obligations to its own citizens, and the inquiry can then be carried only to the extent necessary to control the disposition of the property. If the non-resident have no property in the State, there is nothing upon which the tribunals can adjudicate.

In personam judg's w/o personal service are subject to Fraud

     * * * If, without personal service, judgments *in personam*, obtained *ex parte* against non-residents and absent parties, upon mere publication of process, which, in the great majority of cases, would never be seen by the parties interested, could be upheld and enforced, they would be the constant instruments of fraud and oppression. Judgments for all sorts of claims upon contracts and for torts, real or pretended, would be thus obtained, under which property would be seized, when the evidence of the transactions upon which they were founded, if they ever had any existence, had perished.

Sub. service valid only when state has acted to take prop. into possession.

     Substituted services by publication, or in any other authorized form, may be sufficient to inform parties of the object of proceedings taken where property is once brought under the control of the court by seizure or some equivalent act. The law assumes that property is always in the possession of its owner, in person or by agent; and it proceeds upon the theory that its seizure will inform him, not only that it is taken into the custody of the court, but that he must look to any proceedings authorized by law upon such seizure for its condemnation and sale. * * * In other words, such service may answer in all actions which are substantially proceedings *in rem*. But where the entire object of the action is to determine the personal rights and obligations of the defendants, that is, where the suit is merely *in personam*, constructive service in this form upon a non-resident is ineffectual for any purpose. Process from the tribunals of one State cannot run into another State, and summon parties there domiciled to leave its territory and respond to proceedings against them. Publication of process or notice within the State where the tribunal sits cannot create any greater obligation upon the non-resident to appear. Process sent to him out of the State, and process published within it, are equally unavailing in proceedings to establish his personal liability.

     The want of authority of the tribunals of a State to adjudicate upon the obligations of non-residents, where they have no property within its limits, is not denied by the court below; but the position is assumed that, where they have property within the State, it is immaterial whether the property is in the first instance brought under the control of the court by attachment or some other equivalent act, and afterwards applied by its judgment to the satisfaction of demands against its owner; or such demands be first established in a personal action, and the property of the non-resident be afterwards seized and sold on execution. But the answer to this position has already been given in the statement, that the jurisdiction of the court to inquire into and determine his obligations at all is only incidental to its jurisdiction over the property. Its jurisdiction in that respect cannot be made to depend upon facts to be ascertained after it has tried the cause and rendered the judgment. If the judgment be previously void, it will not become valid by the subsequent discovery of property of the defendant, or by his subsequent acquisition of it. The judgment, if void when rendered, will always remain void; it cannot occupy the doubtful position of being valid if property be found, and void if there be none. Even if the position assumed were confined to cases where the non-resident defendant possessed property in the State at the commencement of the action, it would still make the validity of the proceedings and judgment depend upon the question whether, before the levy of the execution, the defendant had or had not disposed of the property. If, before the levy, the property should be sold, then, according to this position, the judgment would not be binding. This doctrine would introduce a new element of uncertainty in judicial proceedings. The contrary is the law; the validity of every judgment depends upon the jurisdiction of the court before it is rendered, not upon what may occur subsequently. * * *

The force and effect of judgments rendered against non-residents without personal service of process upon them, or their voluntary appearance, have been the subject of frequent consideration in the courts of the United States and of the several States, as attempts have been made to enforce such judgments in States other than those in which they were rendered, under the provision of the Constitution requiring that "Full faith and credit shall be given in each State to the public Acts, records and judicial proceedings of every other State;" and the Act of Congress providing for the mode of authenticating such Acts, records and proceedings, and declaring that, when thus authenticated, "They shall have such faith and credit given to them in every court within the United States as they have by law or usage in the courts of the State from which they are or shall be taken." In the earlier cases, it was supposed that the Act gave to all judgments the same effect in other States which they had by law in the State where rendered. But this view was afterwards qualified so as to make the Act applicable only when the court rendering the judgment had jurisdiction of the parties and of the subject-matter, and not to preclude an inquiry into the jurisdiction of the court in which the judgment was rendered, or the right of the State itself to exercise authority over the person or the subject-matter. * * *

Since the adoption of the 14th Amendment to the Federal Constitution, the validity of such judgments may be directly questioned, and their enforcement in the State resisted, on the ground that proceedings in a court of justice to determine the personal rights and obligations of parties over whom that court has no jurisdiction do not constitute due process of law. Whatever difficulty may be experienced in giving to those terms a definition which will embrace every permissible exertion of power affecting private rights, and exclude such as is forbidden, there can be no doubt of their meaning when applied to judicial proceedings. They then mean a course of legal proceedings according to those rules and principles which have been established in our systems of jurisprudence for the protection and enforcement of private rights. To give such proceedings any validity, there must be a tribunal competent by its constitution —that is, by the law of its creation—to pass upon the subject-matter of the suit; and, if that involves merely a determination of the personal liability of the defendant, he must be brought within its jurisdiction by service of process within the State, or his voluntary appearance.

Sub. service effective only when:

1) property in suit brought under control by state

2) judgment sought directed against property

Except in cases affecting the personal *status* of the plaintiff, and cases in which that mode of service may be considered to have been assented to in advance as hereinafter mentioned, the substituted service of process by publication allowed by the law of Oregon and by similar laws in other States, where actions are brought against non-residents, is effectual only where, in connection with process against the person for commencing the action, property in the State is brought under the control of the court, and subjected to its disposition by process adapted to that purpose, or where the judgment is sought as a means of reaching such property or affecting some interest therein; in other words, where the action is in the nature of a proceeding *in rem.*   *   *   *

Holding Rationale

Proceeding against person where direct object is disposal of property is, If, a proceeding in rem

It is true that, in a strict sense, a proceeding *in rem* is one taken directly against property, and has for its object the disposition of the property, without reference to the title of individual claimants; but, in a larger and more general sense, the terms are applied to actions between parties, where the direct object is to reach and dispose of property owned by them, or of some interest therein. Such are cases commenced by attachment against the property of debtors, or instituted to partition real estate, foreclose a mortgage, or enforce a lien. So far as they affect property in the State, they are substantially proceedings *in rem* in the broader sense which we have mentioned.

    *   *   *

Holding →

It follows from the views expressed that the personal judgment recovered in the State Court of Oregon against the plaintiff herein, then a non-resident of the State, was without any validity, and did not authorize a sale of the property in controversy.

To prevent any misapplication of the views expressed in this opinion, it is proper to observe that we do not mean to assert, by anything we have said, that a State may not authorize proceedings to determine the *status* of one of its citizens towards a non-resident, which would be binding within the State, though made without service of process or personal notice to the non-resident. The jurisdiction which every State possesses, to determine the civil *status* and capacities of all its inhabitants involves authority to prescribe the conditions on which proceedings affecting them may be commenced and carried on within its territory. The State, for example, has absolute right to prescribe the conditions upon which the marriage relation between its own citizens shall be created, and the causes for which it may be dissolved. One of the parties guilty of acts for which, by the law of the State, a dissolution may be granted, may have removed to a State where no dissolution is permitted. The complaining party would, therefore, fail if a divorce were sought in the State of the defendant; and if application could not be made to the tribunals of the complainant's domicil in such case, and proceedings be there instituted without personal service of process or personal notice to the offending party, the injured citizen would be without redress.   *   *   *

Neither do we mean to assert that a State may not require a non-resident entering into a partnership or association within its limits, or making contracts enforceable there, to appoint an agent or representative in the State to receive service of process and notice in legal proceedings instituted with respect to such partnership, association or contracts, or to designate a place where such service may be made and notice given, and provide upon their failure, to make such appointment or to designate such place that service may be made upon a public officer designated for that purpose, or in some other prescribed way, and that judgments rendered upon such service may not be binding upon the non-residents both within and without the State.   *   *   *   Nor do we doubt that a State, on creating corporations or other institutions for pecuniary or charitable purposes, may provide a mode in which their conduct may be investigated, their obligations enforced, or their charters revoked, which shall require other than personal service upon their officers or members.   *   *   *

[margin note: ref. to Corp. - Power over corp. domiciled or created in the State]

In the present case, there is no feature of this kind and, consequently, no consideration of what would be the effect of such legislation, in enforcing the contract of a non-resident, can arise.   The question here respects only the validity of a money judgment rendered in one State, in an action upon a simple contract against the resident of another, without service of process upon him, or his appearance therein.

Judgment affirmed.

[The dissenting opinion of Mr. Justice HUNT is omitted.]

NOTES AND QUESTIONS

1.   SMITH v. GIBSON, 83 Ala. 284, 285, 3 So. 321 (1887):

> The general rule is, that every country has jurisdiction over all persons found within its territorial limits, for the purposes of actions in their nature transitory.   It is not a debatable question, that such actions may be maintained in any jurisdiction in which the defendant may be found, and is legally served with process.   However transiently the defendant may have been in the State, the summons having been in the State, the summons having been legally served upon him, the jurisdiction of his person was complete, in the absence of a fraudulent inducement to come.

Should this territorial concept of jurisdiction permit valid service to be made in an airplane while it is flying over the state in which the action is brought? Does the altitude of the plane at the time of service have any bearing on the effectiveness of the service? If not, can we predict that service in a space vehicle will be valid as long as it takes place above a spot on earth that is within the court's territorial competence? See Grace v. MacArthur, 170 F.Supp. 442 (E.D.Ark.1959).

2.   In BLACKMER v. UNITED STATES, 284 U.S. 421, 438–39, 52 S.Ct. 252, 255, 76 L.Ed. 375, 383 (1932), petitioner, an American citizen, sought reversal of a contempt conviction resulting from his refusal to comply with a subpoena issued by an American court and served upon him in France in connection with a proceeding that grew out of the Teapot Dome Scandal.   Service was authorized by federal statute.   The Supreme Court concluded that no violation of due process had taken place because

> the jurisdiction of the United States over its absent citizen, so far as the binding effect of its legislation is concerned, is a jurisdiction in personam, as he is personally bound to take notice of the laws that are applicable to him and to obey them.   *   *   *   The question of the validity of the provision for actual service of the subpoena in a foreign country is one that arises solely between the   *   *   *   United States and the citizen.

The mere giving of such a notice to the citizen in the foreign country of the requirement of his government that he shall return is in no sense an invasion of any right of the foreign government and the citizen has no standing to invoke any such supposed right.

The *Blackmer* principle was applied to state-court litigation in MILLIKEN v. MEYER, 311 U.S. 457, 462–63, 61 S.Ct. 339, 342–43, 85 L.Ed. 278, 283, 132 A.L.R. 1357, 1360–61 (1940). Milliken sued Meyer, a Wyoming resident, in a Wyoming state court. Personal service was effected in Colorado under a Wyoming statute that permitted such service, in lieu of service by publication, on absent residents. Meyer did not appear and an in personam judgment was entered against him. Four years later Meyer asked a Colorado court to restrain Milliken's enforcement of the Wyoming judgment. The United States Supreme Court held the Wyoming judgment valid and entitled to full faith and credit. According to the Court:

> * * * Domicile in the state is alone sufficient to bring an absent defendant within the reach of the state's jurisdiction for purposes of a personal judgment by means of appropriate substituted service. * * * [T]he authority of a state over one of its citizens is not terminated by the mere fact of his absence from the state. The state which accords him privileges and affords protection to him and his property by virtue of his domicile may also exact reciprocal duties.

The Court's opinion made no attempt to distinguish among "resident," "domicile," and "citizen." What factors are relevant in deciding whether defendant's relationship with the forum state is sufficient to invoke the *Milliken* doctrine?

Do *Blackmer* and *Milliken* fall within the scope of the statement in *Pennoyer* that "every State has the power to determine for itself the civil *status* and capacities of its inhabitants," or do they involve a different basis of jurisdiction? Jurisdiction based on status is discussed in *Developments in the Law—State-Court Jurisdiction*, 73 Harv.L.Rev. 909, 966–80 (1960); Comment, *Jurisdiction to Annul*, 6 Stan.L.Rev. 153 (1953).

3. ADAM v. SAENGER, 303 U.S. 59, 67–68, 58 S.Ct. 454, 458, 82 L.Ed. 649, 654–55 (1938). The Beaumont Export & Import Co., a Texas corporation, brought suit against Montes in a California state court. In accordance with California procedure, Montes filed a cross-action against the corporation. The corporation then defaulted, its suit was dismissed, and Montes obtained a default judgment on his cross-action. Montes later assigned his judgment to Adam, who sought to enforce it in a Texas court. The Texas court refused to recognize the California judgment, holding that California law did not permit service of the complaint in the cross-action on the corporation's attorney, and that the corporation had not been otherwise "present" in California for purposes of jurisdiction. The United States Supreme Court reversed, holding that the method of service in the cross-action was authorized by California law and the judgment was entitled to full faith and credit:

> There is nothing in the Fourteenth Amendment to prevent a state from adopting a procedure by which a judgment *in personam* may be rendered in a cross-action against a plaintiff in its courts, upon service of process or of appropriate pleading upon his attorney of record. The plaintiff having, by his voluntary act in demanding justice from the defendant, submitted himself to the jurisdiction of the court, there is noth-

ing arbitrary or unreasonable in treating him as being there for all purposes for which justice to the defendant requires his presence. It is the
price which the state may exact as the condition of opening its courts to
the plaintiff.

Compare KANE v. NEW JERSEY, 242 U.S. 160, 37 S.Ct. 30, 61 L.Ed. 222
(1916), in which the Supreme Court upheld a New Jersey statute requiring a
nonresident motorist to file a formal instrument appointing the Secretary of State
his attorney for service of process in any legal action arising out of the operation
of an automobile before he could operate the vehicle on New Jersey's highways.
How does the type of consent involved in *Adam* differ from that in *Kane*? Can
the concept of jurisdiction by consent be reconciled with *Pennoyer's* emphasis on
the territorial power of the states as the basis for the exercise of jurisdiction? See
generally Ehrenzweig, *The Transient Rule of Personal Jurisdiction: The "Power"
Myth and Forum Conveniens,* 65 Yale L.J. 289 (1956).

4.   The civil-law tradition with regard to personal jurisdiction is somewhat
different from our own. Whereas the cornerstone of the common-law's concept of
jurisdiction historically has been defendant's presence, domicile has been the key
in The Netherlands and Switzerland, plaintiff's nationality has been of great importance in France, and domicile and the situs of property have been of major significance in Germany. "In this area of law, differences among civil-law countries
are as great as differences between given civil-law and common-law countries."
de Vries & Lowenfeld, *Jurisdiction in Personal Actions—A Comparison of Civil
Law Views,* 44 Iowa L.Rev. 306, 344 (1959).

5.   Should Mr. Justice Field's opinion in *Pennoyer* be read as requiring attachment before service in a quasi in rem action? Consider the following:

> Following *Pennoyer v. Neff,* there was some question as to when
> the property must be seized. On the one hand it was said that it may be
> any time before the final judgment while on the other, *Pennoyer* was in-
> terpreted to mean that service by publication, or otherwise, upon non-resi-
> dents, gave the required notice only when it was coupled with a prior
> seizure of the defendant's property within the state. The [New York]
> Court of Appeals interpreted the Civil Practice Act as providing that
> "no order of publication in an action to recover a sum of money only
> against a non-resident may be made except upon proof that his property
> has been seized." Hence plaintiff was required to show the issuance and
> levy of a warrant of attachment before an order of service by publication
> could be granted or other service outside the state effected.

1 Weinstein, Korn & Miller, *New York Civil Practice* ¶ 314.18. For a contrary
view, see Closson v. Chase, 158 Wis. 346, 149 N.W. 26 (1914). See generally
Note, *The Requirement of Seizure in the Exercise of Quasi in Rem Jurisdiction:
Pennoyer v. Neff Re-Examined,* 63 Harv.L.Rev. 657 (1950).

HESS v. PAWLOSKI

Supreme Court of the United States, 1927.
274 U.S. 352, 47 S.Ct. 632, 71 L.Ed. 1091.

In Error to the Superior Court of Worcester County, Massachusetts.

Mr. Justice BUTLER delivered the opinion of the Court.

This action was brought by defendant in error to recover damages for personal injuries. The declaration alleged that plaintiff in error negligently and wantonly drove a motor vehicle on a public highway in Massachusetts, and that by reason thereof the vehicle struck and injured defendant in error. Plaintiff in error is a resident of Pennsylvania. No personal service was made on him, and no property belonging to him was attached. The service of process was made in compliance with chapter 90, General Laws of Massachusetts, as amended by Stat.1923, c. 431, § 2, the material parts of which follow:

"The acceptance by a nonresident of the rights and privileges conferred by section three or four, as evidenced by his operating a motor vehicle thereunder, or the operation by a nonresident of a motor vehicle on a public way in the commonwealth other than under said sections, shall be deemed equivalent to an appointment by such nonresident of the registrar or his successor in office, to be his true and lawful attorney upon whom may be served all lawful processes in any action or proceeding against him, growing out of any accident or collision in which said nonresident may be involved while operating a motor vehicle on such a way, and said acceptance or operation shall be a signification of his agreement that any such process against him which is so served shall be of the same legal force and validity as if served on him personally. Service of such process shall be made by leaving a copy of the process with a fee of two dollars in the hands of the registrar, or in his office, and such service shall be sufficient service upon the said nonresident: Provided, that notice of such service and a copy of the process are forthwith sent by registered mail by the plaintiff to the defendant, and the defendant's return receipt and the plaintiff's affidavit of compliance herewith are appended to the writ and entered with the declaration. * * * "

Plaintiff in error appeared specially for the purpose of contesting jurisdiction, and filed an answer in abatement and moved to dismiss on the ground that the service of process, if sustained, would deprive him of his property without due process of law, in violation of the Fourteenth Amendment. The court overruled the answer in abatement and denied the motion. The Supreme Judicial Court held the statute to be a valid exercise of the police power, and affirmed the order. * * * At the trial the contention was renewed and again denied. Plaintiff in error excepted. The jury returned a verdict for defendant in error. The exceptions were overruled by the Supreme Judicial Court. * * * Thereupon the superior court entered judgment. The writ of error was allowed by the Chief Justice of that court.

The question is whether the Massachusetts enactment contravenes the due process clause of the Fourteenth Amendment.

The process of a court of one state cannot run into another and summon a party there domiciled to respond to proceedings against him. Notice sent outside the state to a nonresident is unavailing to give jurisdiction in an action against him personally for money recovery. Pennoyer v. Neff * * *. There must be actual service within the state of notice upon him or upon some one authorized to accept service for him. Goldey v. Morning News, 156 U.S. 518, 15 S.Ct. 559, 39 L.Ed. 517. A personal judgment rendered against a nonresident, who has neither been served with process nor appeared in the suit, is without validity. McDonald v. Mabee, 243 U.S. 90, 37 S.Ct. 343, 61 L.Ed. 608, L.R.A.1917F, 458. The mere transaction of business in a state by nonresident natural persons does not imply consent to be bound by the process of its courts. Flexner v. Farson, 248 U.S. 289, 39 S.Ct. 97, 63 L.Ed. 250. The power of a state to exclude foreign corporations, although not absolute, but qualified, is the ground on which such an implication is supported as to them. Pennsylvania Fire Insurance Co. v. Gold Issue Mining Co., 243 U.S. 93, 96, 37 S.Ct. 344, 61 L.Ed. 610. But a state may not withhold from nonresident individuals the right of doing business therein. The privileges and immunities clause of the Constitution (section 2, art. 4), safeguards to the citizens of one state the right "to pass through, or to reside in any other state for purposes of trade, agriculture, professional pursuits, or otherwise." And it prohibits state legislation discriminating against citizens of other states. * * *

Motor vehicles are dangerous machines, and, even when skillfully and carefully operated, their use is attended by serious dangers to persons and property. In the public interest the state may make and enforce regulations reasonably calculated to promote care on the part of all, residents and nonresidents alike, who use its highways. The measure in question operates to require a nonresident to answer for his conduct in the state where arise causes of action alleged against him, as well as to provide for a claimant a convenient method by which he may sue to enforce his rights. Under the statute the implied consent is limited to proceedings growing out of accidents or collisions on a highway in which the nonresident may be involved. It is required that he shall actually receive and receipt for notice of the service and a copy of the process. And it contemplates such continuances as may be found necessary to give reasonable time and opportunity for defense. It makes no hostile discrimination against nonresidents, but tends to put them on the same footing as residents. Literal and precise equality in respect of this matter is not attainable; it is not required. * * * The state's power to regulate the use of its highways extends to their use by nonresidents as well as by residents. * * * And, in advance of the operation of a motor vehicle on its highway by a nonresident, the state may require him to appoint one of its officials as his agent on whom process may be served in proceedings growing out of such use. Kane v. New Jersey * * *. That case recognizes power of the state to exclude a nonresident until the formal appointment is made. And, having the power so to exclude, the state may declare that the use of the highway by the nonresident is the equivalent of the appointment of the registrar as agent on whom process may be served. * * * The difference between the formal and implied appointment is not substantial, so far as concerns the application of the due process clause of the Fourteenth Amendment.

Judgment affirmed.

NOTES AND QUESTIONS

1. Is there any difference between the notion of "consent" as used in *Hess* and as used in *Adam v. Saenger*, p. 72, supra? What are the "pros" and "cons" of using "consent," given either before or after the commencement of an action, as a determinant of jurisdiction? Can you think of situations in which the parties should not be able to "consent" to jurisdiction? Could a nonresident motorist negate the implication of a consent to service under the Massachusetts statute by writing to the registrar in advance of an automobile trip to that state? To what extent can a state actually condition access to its highways upon consent to suit without being accused of placing an improper burden on interstate commerce, *cf.* Castle v. Hayes Freight Lines, Inc., 348 U.S. 61, 75 S.Ct. 191, 99 L.Ed. 68 (1954), or of denying the privileges and immunities guaranteed under Article IV, Section 2 of the United States Constitution? If the basis for the *Hess* decision is the state's power to condition use of its highways, does this mean that the type of service used in *Hess* is unavailable when the state cannot exclude the defendant, such as is the case with transportation on navigable waters? See Tardiff v. Bank Line, Ltd., 127 F.Supp. 945 (E.D.La.1954).

2. In FLEXNER v. FARSON, 248 U.S. 289, 39 S.Ct. 97, 63 L.Ed. 250 (1919), which is cited in *Hess*, the question before the Court was the validity of a Kentucky judgment against a partnership doing business in Kentucky through an agent. Mr. Justice Holmes, writing for the Court, rejected the argument that the partnership had consented to suit by doing business in Kentucky.

> * * * [T]he consent that is said to be implied in such cases is a mere fiction, founded upon the accepted doctrine that the States could exclude foreign corporations altogether, and therefore could establish this obligation as a condition to letting them in. * * * The State had no power to exclude [these] * * * defendants * * *.

Note that in *Hess* the Court made no attempt to distinguish *Flexner*. Can it be distinguished or was *Flexner* overruled by *Hess* by implication?

Compare HENRY L. DOHERTY & CO. v. GOODMAN, 294 U.S. 623, 55 S.Ct. 553, 79 L.Ed. 1097 (1935), in which the principle of *Hess* was applied to permit Iowa to assert jurisdiction over a nonresident individual who had established an office in Iowa to sell corporate securities, a business that had been heavily regulated by the Iowa legislature. The cause of action sued upon involved a securities transaction in Des Moines, Iowa. By what sequence of reasoning might one conclude that *Goodman* follows from *Hess?*

In *Goodman,* the *Flexner* case was distinguished on two grounds: First, service in *Flexner* "was made upon one not then agent for the defendants." Service in *Goodman* was made on an individual who was a resident manager when the sale contract was made and when process was served. Second, under the Iowa law involved in *Goodman,* "neither her citizens nor nonresidents could freely engage in the business of selling securities." No comparable law applied in *Flexner.* Are these factors persuasive?

3. Would a nonresident-motorist statute that purported to assert jurisdiction over any cause of action that arises out of the presence of defendant's vehicle within the state, or over people other than the driver of the vehicle be constitutional? Would such a statute be wise? See generally Langley v. Bunn, 225 Ark. 651, 284 S.W.2d 319 (1955); Leighton v. Roper, 300 N.Y. 434, 91 N.E.2d 876, 18 A.L.R.2d 537 (1950); Dambach, *Personal Jurisdiction: Some Current Problems and Modern Trends*, 5 U.C.L.A.L.Rev. 198, 199–211 (1958); Stumberg, *Extension of Nonresident Motorist Statutes to Those Not Operators*, 44 Iowa L. Rev. 268 (1959); Note, *Nonresident Motorist Statutes—Their Current Scope*, 44 Iowa L.Rev. 384 (1959).

B. CORPORATIONS

KURLAND, THE SUPREME COURT, THE DUE PROCESS CLAUSE AND THE IN PERSONAM JURISDICTION OF STATE COURTS—FROM PENNOYER TO DENCKLA: A REVIEW, 25 U.Chi. L.Rev. 569, 577–86 (1958):

A domestic corporation is subject to suit in the courts of the state of its incorporation, whether because it is a creature of that state and therefore necessarily subject to its control, or because it is "domiciled" there, or because it is "present" there.

Foreign corporations have proved more difficult to fit into the concepts which underlie the principles of personal jurisdiction relating to individuals, for it has been thought necessary to speak in "fictive" terms whether the term used is the corporation's "citizenship," its "domicile," its "consent," or its "presence." "Until toward the middle of the [nineteenth] century, the idea seems to have been widely prevalent that foreign attachment was the only process available against them." In some measure the difficulties flowed from a notion phrased by Mr. Chief Justice Taney in Bank of Augusta v. Earle [38 U.S. (13 Pet.) 519, 588, 10 L.Ed. 274, 308 (1839)]:

> * * * a corporation can have no legal existence out of the bundaries [sic] of the sovereignty by which it is created. It exists only in contemplation of law, and by force of the law; and where that law ceases to operate, and is no longer obligatory, the corporation can have no existence. It must dwell in the place of its creation; and cannot migrate to another sovereignty.

This apparently did not mean that a corporation was precluded from engaging in activities beyond the borders of the state of its incorporation, but only that any activity which it conducted outside the state of its incorporation was dependent upon the permission of the government within whose jurisdiction it desired to operate. * * *

As the corporate form of business became more and more the common method of carrying on economic activity, it became incumbent on the courts to make provision for suits by and against such entities in foreign states. Two major theories evolved and merged into a third, none of which proved satisfactory. The first was the "consent" theory, which quickly prevailed in the Supreme Court. The second was a theory of "presence," which became necessary in order to fill the gaps which the "consent" theory did not cover, but which required the rejection of the Taney dictum in Bank of Augusta v. Earle. The third was the "doing business" notion.

1. *"Consent."* The consent thesis rested on the proposition that, since a foreign corporation could not carry on business within a state without the permission of that state, the state could impose as a condition of engaging in business within its borders a requirement that the corporation appoint an agent to receive service of process within the state. Thus, in Lafayette Insurance Co. v. French [59 U.S. (18 How.) 404, 407, 15 L.Ed. 451, 452 (1855)], Mr. Justice Curtis, speaking for all but one member of the Court, said:

> A corporation created by Indiana can transact business in Ohio only with the consent, express or implied, of the latter state. [Bank of Augusta v. Earle, 38 U.S. 519, 10 L.Ed. 274] 13 Pet. 519. This consent may be accompanied by such conditions as Ohio may think fit to impose; and these conditions must be deemed valid and effectual by other States, and by this court, provided they are not repugnant to the constitution or laws of the United States, or inconsistent with those rules of public law which secure the jurisdiction and authority of each State from encroachment by all others, or that principle of natural justice which forbids condemnation without opportunity for defence.

The limitations of "public law" and "natural justice" were necessarily vague, and were ultimately to be merged into the Due Process Clause when the Fourteenth Amendment became effective. * * * The important limitations on the conditions which could be imposed by the state were set forth later by Mr. Justice Field in St. Clair v. Cox [106 U.S. 350, 356, 1 S.Ct. 354, 360, 27 L.Ed. 222, 225 (1882)]:

> The State may, therefore, impose as a condition upon which a foreign corporation shall be permitted to do business within her limits, that it shall stipulate that in any litigation *arising out of its transactions in the State*, it will accept as sufficient the service of process on its agents or persons specially designated; and the condition would be eminently fit and just. And such condition and stipulation may be implied as well as expressed.

Field reiterated the primary limitation that "the corporation be engaged in business in the State, and the agent be appointed to act there." The Court later made it clear, too, that the agent must be one who would be likely to inform the corporation of the receipt and content of the process and if service were made on an official or person designated by the state that such person be re-

quired to forward notice of the suit to the defendant. The "consent" which a *Probs w/ "Consent"*
state could demand was held to be a valid base for jurisdiction of the federal
courts within that state as well as of state courts.

Q: One of the questions resulting from the adoption of this thesis was
whether, if implied consent was confined to cases arising out of transactions
within the state as stated in St. Clair v. Cox, the consent secured by the actual
appointment of an agent by the corporation was similarly limited. Three of
America's greatest jurists [Cardozo, Hand, and Holmes] answered the question in the negative. * * * One may wonder how, in rejecting the fiction
of consent for the corporations which have not appointed agents, these three
could have found "a true consent" in the appointment of an agent in conformity with statutes, especially when the statutes have not suggested different treatment for extorted actual consent and the equally unwilling implied consent.
* * * One may wonder, too, why, if it is the Due Process Clause—or a
"principle of natural justice"—which denied the power of the state to imply
consent to suit on claims arising out of transactions occurring elsewhere than
within the state, it did not also deny to the state the power to extort such a consent in writing. Certainly the St. Clair case on which these cases are predicated
drew no such distinction.

There was still another major difficulty with the consent thesis. The
Privileges and Immunities Clause did not prohibit a state from excluding a foreign corporation. This point was made pellucidly in Paul v. Virginia [75
U.S. (8 Wall.) 168, 19 L.Ed. 357 (1868)] in language quite reminiscent of
Taney's in Bank of Augusta v. Earle * * *. But insurance, which was
the subject of the business involved in that case, was not then considered "interstate commerce." And it soon became established law that a foreign corporation could not be prevented by a state from carrying on interstate commerce
within its borders. It would seem to follow that if the state's power to exact
consent to be sued depended on its power to exclude, and it could not exclude,
it could not exact such consent. Nonetheless, the Court continued to hold that
foreign corporations were subject to the jurisdiction of state courts, even if the
business they carried on within the state was interstate commerce.

                    *   *   *

2. *"Presence."* The presence doctrine afforded an equally defective pattern, for it necessarily rejected the theme of Bank of Augusta and Paul v. Virginia, that a corporation cannot exist beyond the limits of the state which created it. From time to time, however, the Supreme Court spoke as though the issue were one of presence rather than consent. Thus, Mr. Justice Brandeis said
in Philadelphia and Reading R.R. v. McKibbin [243 U.S. 264, 265, 37 S.Ct.
280, 61 L.Ed. 710, 711–12 (1917)], "A foreign corporation is amenable to
process to enforce a personal liability, in the absence of consent, only if it is
doing business within the State in such manner and to such extent as to warrant
the inference that it is present there." And very distinguished authorities in
other courts adopted this approach to the problem. The presence theory, unlike the consent doctrine, would sustain jurisdiction against corporations on

claims which did not arise out of the business done within the state, a position which the Supreme Court never openly espoused. On the other hand, under that doctrine, the departure from the state by the corporation by ceasing to do business therein would preclude later assertion of jurisdiction even as to claims which grew out of the business it had once done there. The implied consent theory would sustain jurisdiction under such circumstances.

In the same fashion in which he had removed the mask of the consent theory, Judge Hand exposed the false face of the presence thesis. In Hutchinson v. Chase and Gilbert [45 F.2d 139, 141 (2d Cir.1930)], he wrote for a court made up of three of the most capable judges ever to sit on any American bench:

> It scarcely advances the argument to say that a corporation must be 'present' in the foreign state, if we define that word as demanding such dealings as will subject it to jurisdiction, for then it does no more than put the question to be answered. * * * It is difficult, to us it seems impossible, to impute the idea of locality to a corporation, except by virtue of those acts which realize its purposes. The shareholders, officers and agents are not individually the corporation, and do not carry it with them in all their legal transactions. It is only when engaged upon its affairs that they can be said to represent it, and we can see no qualitative distinction between one part of its doings and another, so they carry out the common plan. If we are to attribute locality to it at all, it must be equally present wherever any part of its work goes on, as much in the little as in the great.

> When we say therefore, that a corporation may be sued only where it is 'present,' we understand that the word is used, not literally, but as shorthand for something else. It might indeed be argued that it must stand suit upon any controversy arising out of legal transactions entered into where the suit was brought, but that would impose upon it too severe a burden. On the other hand, it is not plain that it ought not, upon proper notice, to defend suits arising out of foreign transactions, if it conducts a continuous business in the state of the forum. * * * But a single transaction is certainly not enough, whether a substantial business subjects that corporation to jurisdiction generally, or only as to local transactions. There must be some continuous dealings in the state of the forum; enough to demand trial away from its home.

> This last appears to us to be really the controlling consideration, expressed shortly by the word 'presence,' but involving an estimate of the inconveniences which would result from requiring it to defend, where it has been sued. We are to inquire whether the extent and continuity of what it has done in the state in question makes it reasonable to bring it before one of its courts. Nor is it anomalous to make the question of jurisdiction depend upon a practical test. * * * This does not indeed avoid the uncertainties, for it is as

hard to judge what dealings make it just to subject a foreign corporation to local suit, as to say when it is 'present,' but at least it puts
the real question, and that is something.   *   *   *

In his conclusion, Judge Hand once again foreshadowed the doctrine which the
Supreme Court would later adopt:

> In the end there is nothing more to be said than that all the de-
> fendant's local activities, taken together, do not make it reasonable
> to impose such a burden upon it.   It is fairer that the plaintiffs
> should go to Boston than that the defendant should come here.
> Certainly such a standard is no less vague than any that the courts
> have hitherto set up; one may look from one end of the decisions
> to the other and find no vade mecum.

[45 F.2d at 142]

3. *"Doing Business."* The courts thus came round to using either the consent thesis or the presence thesis, depending largely upon which would support
jurisdiction over the nonresident corporation.   No notice was taken of the underlying inconsistency between the two doctrines.   The application of either
created difficulties, for whichever was chosen it became necessary to determine
whether the foreign corporation was "doing business" within the state, either
to decide whether its "consent" could properly be "implied," or to discover
whether the corporation was "present."   The law reports became cluttered
with decisions as to what constituted "doing business."   The cases drew fine
lines which made little sense in terms of either theory.   *   *   *

The real difficulty underlying these attempts to work out a rationale for
personal jurisdiction lay in the fact that the doctrines were borrowed from laws
relating to wholly independent sovereignties which were not relevant to jurisdictions joined in a federation.   The basic premise for such decisions was "that
a judgment   *   *   *   is necessarily something to be enforced and that a
state which is physically impotent to enforce its judgments should be treated as
legally incompetent to adjudicate.   *   *   *"   But with the Full Faith and
Credit Clause as an overriding principle, such a premise only puts the question;
it does not answer it.   The real question becomes not whether a state could itself enforce a judgment, but rather under what circumstances the national
power should be used to assist the extraterritorial enforcement of a state's
judicial decrees.   The great importance of Pennoyer v. Neff is that it identified the test under the Full Faith and Credit Clause with the test under the
Due Process Clause, making a judgment which would not be enforceable beyond the borders of the state unenforceable within its boundaries.   If there
are reasons, concerned with the state's relationship with the litigation, why a
judgment is not entitled to extrastate enforcement, those reasons should be
sufficient to sustain attack within the state.   Although Pennoyer suggested
this principle, there remained the necessity for fixing criteria for determining
when the absence of the state's physical power would be supplemented by the
command of the national sovereign, criteria which must necessarily change
with the basic changes in our methods of carrying on economic activity and

with the changes in means of transportation and communication. The attempts to adapt old language to new problems proved unhappy in their result.

With doctrine in so bad a state of disrepair, the time had long since passed for the Supreme Court to acknowledge the truth of Holmes' dictum that "[t]he Constitution is not to be satisfied with a fiction." International Shoe Co. v. Washington afforded the Court an opportunity to begin to set its house in order in this field.

INTERNATIONAL SHOE CO. v. WASHINGTON

Supreme Court of the United States, 1945.
326 U.S. 310, 66 S.Ct. 154, 90 L.Ed. 95, 161 A.L.R. 1057.

Appeal from the Supreme Court of the State of Washington.

Mr. Chief Justice STONE delivered the opinion of the Court.

Issues:

The questions for decision are (1) whether, within the limitations of the due process clause of the Fourteenth Amendment, appellant, a Delaware corporation, has by its activities in the State of Washington rendered itself amenable to proceedings in the courts of that state to recover unpaid contributions to the state unemployment compensation fund exacted by state statutes, * * * and (2) whether the state can exact those contributions consistently with the due process clause of the Fourteenth Amendment.

The statutes in question set up a comprehensive scheme of unemployment compensation, the costs of which are defrayed by contributions required to be made by employers to a state unemployment compensation fund. The contributions are a specified percentage of the wages payable annually by each employer for his employees' services in the state. The assessment and collection of the contributions and the fund are administered by respondents. Section 14(c) of the Act, Wash.Rev.Stat.1941 Supp., § 9998—114c, authorizes respondent Commissioner to issue an order and notice of assessment of delinquent contributions upon prescribed personal service of the notice upon the employer if found within the state, or, if not so found, by mailing the notice to the employer by registered mail at his last known address. That section also authorizes the Commissioner to collect the assessment by distraint if it is not paid within ten days after service of the notice. * * *

Int'l. Shoe argues it is not an employer:

In this case notice of assessment for the years in question was personally served upon a sales solicitor employed by appellant in the State of Washington, and a copy of the notice was mailed by registered mail to appellant at its address in St. Louis, Missouri. Appellant appeared specially before the office of unemployment and moved to set aside the order and notice of assessment on the ground that the service upon appellant's salesman was not proper service upon appellant; that appellant was not a corporation of the State of Washington and was not doing business within the state; that it had no agent within the state upon whom service could be made; and that appellant is not an employer and does not furnish employment within the meaning of the statute.

The motion was heard on evidence and a stipulation of facts by the appeal tribunal which denied the motion and ruled that respondent Commissioner was entitled to recover the unpaid contributions. That action was affirmed by the Commissioner; both the Superior Court and the Supreme Court affirmed. * * * Appellant in each of these courts assailed the statute as applied, as a violation of the due process clause of the Fourteenth Amendment, and as imposing a constitutionally prohibited burden on interstate commerce.

* * * Appellant is a Delaware corporation, having its principal place of business in St. Louis, Missouri, and is engaged in the manufacture and sale of shoes and other footwear. It maintains places of business in several states, other than Washington, at which its manufacturing is carried on and from which its merchandise is distributed interstate through several sales units or branches located outside the State of Washington.

[margin note: Desc. of Int'l. Shoe's business activity.]

Appellant has no office in Washington and makes no contracts either for sale or purchase of merchandise there. It maintains no stock of merchandise in that state and makes there no deliveries of goods in intrastate commerce. During the years from 1937 to 1940, now in question, appellant employed eleven to thirteen salesmen under direct supervision and control of sales managers located in St. Louis. These salesmen resided in Washington; their principal activities were confined to that state; and they were compensated by commissions based upon the amount of their sales. The commissions for each year totaled more than $31,000. Appellant supplies its salesmen with a line of samples, each consisting of one shoe of a pair, which they display to prospective purchasers. On occasion they rent permanent sample rooms, for exhibiting samples, in business buildings, or rent rooms in hotels or business buildings temporarily for that purpose. The cost of such rentals is reimbursed by appellant.

The authority of the salesmen is limited to exhibiting their samples and soliciting orders from prospective buyers, at prices and on terms fixed by appellant. The salesmen transmit the orders to appellant's office in St. Louis for acceptance or rejection, and when accepted the merchandise for filling the orders is shipped f.o.b. from points outside Washington to the purchasers within the state. All the merchandise shipped into Washington is invoiced at the place of shipment from which collections are made. No salesman has authority to enter into contracts or to make collections.

The Supreme Court of Washington was of opinion that the regular and systematic solicitation of orders in the state by appellant's salesmen, resulting in a continuous flow of appellant's product into the state, was sufficient to constitute doing business in the state so as to make appellant amenable to suit in its courts. But it was also of opinion that there were sufficient additional activities shown to bring the case within the rule frequently stated, that solicitation within a state by the agents of a foreign corporation plus some additional activities there are sufficient to render the corporation amenable to suit brought in the courts of the state to enforce an obligation arising out of its activities there. * * * The court found such additional activities in the salesmen's display

[margin note: Washington's Argument:]

of samples sometimes in permanent display rooms, and the salesmen's residence within the state, continued over a period of years, all resulting in a substantial volume of merchandise regularly shipped by appellant to purchasers within the state. The court also held that the statute as applied did not invade the constitutional power of Congress to regulate interstate commerce and did not impose a prohibited burden on such commerce.

Appellant's argument, renewed here, that the statute imposes an unconstitutional burden on interstate commerce need not detain us. * * *

Appellant also insists that its activities within the state were not sufficient to manifest its "presence" there and that in its absence the state courts were without jurisdiction, that consequently it was a denial of due process for the state to subject appellant to suit. It refers to those cases in which it was said that the mere solicitation of orders for the purchase of goods within a state, to be accepted without the state and filled by shipment of the purchased goods interstate, does not render the corporation seller amenable to suit within the state. * * * And appellant further argues that since it was not present within the state, it is a denial of due process to subject it to taxation or other money exaction. It thus denies the power of the state to lay the tax or to subject appellant to a suit for its collection.

Historically the jurisdiction of courts to render judgment in personam is grounded on their de facto power over the defendant's person. Hence his presence within the territorial jurisdiction of a court was prerequisite to its rendition of a judgment personally binding him. Pennoyer v. Neff * * *. But now that the capias ad respondendum has given way to personal service of summons or other form of notice, due process requires only that in order to subject a defendant to a judgment in personam, if he be not present within the territory of the forum, he have certain minimum contacts with it such that the maintenance of the suit does not offend "traditional notions of fair play and substantial justice." Milliken v. Meyer * * *. See Holmes, J., in McDonald v. Mabee, 243 U.S. 90, 91, 37 S.Ct. 343, 61 L.Ed. 608, L.R.A. 1917F, 458. * * *

Since the corporate personality is a fiction, although a fiction intended to be acted upon as though it were a fact * * * it is clear that unlike an individual its "presence" without, as well as within, the state of its origin can be manifested only by activities carried on in its behalf by those who are authorized to act for it. To say that the corporation is so far "present" there as to satisfy due process requirements, for purposes of taxation or the maintenance of suits against it in the courts of the state, is to beg the question to be decided. For the terms "present" or "presence" are used merely to symbolize those activities of the corporation's agent within the state which courts will deem to be sufficient to satisfy the demands of due process. L. Hand, J., in Hutchinson v. Chase & Gilbert * * *. Those demands may be met by such contacts of the corporation with the state of the forum as make it reasonable, in the context of our federal system of government, to require the corporation to defend the particular suit which is brought there. An "estimate of the inconveniences" which would result to the corporation from a trial away from its "home" or principal place of business is relevant in this connection. * * *

"Presence" in the state in this sense has never been doubted when the activities of the corporation there have not only been continuous and systematic, but also give rise to the liabilities sued on, even though no consent to be sued or authorization to an agent to accept service of process has been given. * * * Conversely it has been generally recognized that the casual presence of the corporate agent or even his conduct of single or isolated items of activities in a state in the corporation's behalf are not enough to subject it to suit on causes of action unconnected with the activities there. * * * To require the corporation in such circumstances to defend the suit away from its home or other jurisdiction where it carries on more substantial activities has been thought to lay too great and unreasonable a burden on the corporation to comport with due process.

While it has been held in cases on which appellant relies that continuous activity of some sorts within a state is not enough to support the demand that the corporation be amenable to suits unrelated to that activity * * *, there have been instances in which the continuous corporate operations within a state were thought so substantial and of such a nature as to justify suit against it on causes of action arising from dealings entirely distinct from those activities. * * *

Finally, although the commission of some single or occasional acts of the corporate agent in a state sufficient to impose an obligation or liability on the corporation has not been thought to confer upon the state authority to enforce it, Rosenberg Bros. & Co. v. Curtis Brown Co., 260 U.S. 516, 43 S.Ct. 170, 67 L.Ed. 372, other such acts, because of their nature and quality and the circumstances of their commission, may be deemed sufficient to render the corporation liable to suit. Cf. Kane v. New Jersey * * *; Hess v. Pawloski * * *. True, some of the decisions holding the corporation amenable to suit have been supported by resort to the legal fiction that it has given its consent to service and suit, consent being implied from its presence in the state through the acts of its authorized agents. * * * But more realistically it may be said that those authorized acts were of such a nature as to justify the fiction. * * *

It is evident that the criteria by which we mark the boundary line between those activities which justify the subjection of a corporation to suit, and those which do not, cannot be simply mechanical or quantitative. The test is not merely, as has sometimes been suggested, whether the activity, which the corporation has seen fit to procure through its agents in another state, is a little more or a little less. * * * Whether due process is satisfied must depend rather upon the quality and nature of the activity in relation to the fair and orderly administration of the laws which it was the purpose of the due process clause to insure. That clause does not contemplate that a state may make binding a judgment in personam against an individual or corporate defendant with which the state has no contacts, ties, or relations. * * *

excercise of priv.
in doing business in
State gives rise to
obligations.

But to the extent that a corporation exercises the privilege of conducting activities within a state, it enjoys the benefits and protection of the laws of that state. The exercise of that privilege may give rise to obligations; and, so far as those obligations arise out of or are connected with the activities within the state, a procedure which requires the corporation to respond to a suit brought to enforce them can, in most instances, hardly be said to be undue.   *   *   *

Rationale

1) Shoe had regular
systematic conduct
establishing ties
w/ state

— oblig. arose out
of those activities

Applying these standards, the activities carried on in behalf of appellant in the State of Washington were neither irregular nor casual. They were systematic and continuous throughout the years in question. They resulted in a large volume of interstate business, in the course of which appellant received the benefits and protection of the laws of the state, including the right to resort to the courts for the enforcement of its rights. The obligation which is here sued upon arose out of those very activities. It is evident that these operations establish sufficient contacts or ties with the state of the forum to make it reasonable and just according to our traditional conception of fair play and substantial justice to permit the state to enforce the obligations which appellant has incurred there. Hence we cannot say that the maintenance of the present suit in the State of Washington involves an unreasonable or undue procedure.

2) Service on agent
was sufficient

— agent establishes
presence
"minimal contacts"

— Mailed, too.

We are likewise unable to conclude that the service of the process within the state upon an agent whose activities establish appellant's "presence" there was not sufficient notice of the suit, or that the suit was so unrelated to those activities as to make the agent an inappropriate vehicle for communicating the notice. It is enough that appellant has established such contacts with the state that the particular form of substituted service adopted there gives reasonable assurance that the notice will be actual.   *   *   *   Nor can we say that the mailing of the notice of suit to appellant by registered mail at its home office was not reasonably calculated to apprise appellant of the suit.   *   *   *

Holding:

Appellant having rendered itself amenable to suit upon obligations arising out of the activities of its salesmen in Washington, the state may maintain the present suit in personam to collect the tax laid upon the exercise of the privilege of employing appellant's salesmen within the state. For Washington has made one of those activities, which taken together establish appellant's "presence" there for purposes of suit, the taxable event by which the state brings appellant within the reach of its taxing power. The state thus has constitutional power to lay the tax and to subject appellant to a suit to recover it. The activities which establish its "presence" subject it alike to taxation by the state and to suit to recover the tax.   *   *   *

Affirmed.

Mr. Justice JACKSON took no part in the consideration or decision of this case.

Mr. Justice BLACK delivered the following opinion.
  *   *   *

I believe that the Federal Constitution leaves to each State, without any "ifs" or "buts," a power to tax and to open the doors of its courts for its citizens to sue corporations whose agents do business in those States. Believing that the Constitution gave the States that power, I think it a judicial deprivation to condition its exercise upon this Court's notion of "fair play," however appealing that term may be. Nor can I stretch the meaning of due process so far as to authorize this Court to deprive a State of the right to afford judicial protection to its citizens on the ground that it would be more "convenient" for the corporation to be sued somewhere else.

There is a strong emotional appeal in the words "fair play," "justice," and "reasonableness." But they were not chosen by those who wrote the original Constitution or the Fourteenth Amendment as a measuring rod for this Court to use in invalidating State or Federal laws passed by elected legislative representatives. No one, not even those who most feared a democratic government, ever formally proposed that courts should be given power to invalidate legislation under any such elastic standards. Express prohibitions against certain types of legislation are found in the Constitution, and under the long settled practice, courts invalidate laws found to conflict with them. This requires interpretation, and interpretation, it is true, may result in extension of the Constitution's purpose. But that is no reason for reading the due process clause so as to restrict a State's power to tax and sue those whose activities affect persons and businesses within the State, provided proper service can be had. Superimposing the natural justice concept on the Constitution's specific prohibitions could operate as a drastic abridgment of democratic safeguards they embody * * *.

NOTES AND QUESTIONS

1. According to the Vermont Supreme Court in SMYTH v. TWIN STATE IMPROVEMENT CORP., 116 Vt. 569, 80 A.2d 664, 25 A.L.R.2d 1193 (1951), *International Shoe* "left undecided whether isolated tortious activity could result in a proper subjection of a foreign corporation to suit in the forum when the cause of action arose out of that activity." Is it really true that the *International Shoe* opinion leaves this matter "undecided"? The court went on to assume jurisdiction over a Massachusetts corporation that had contracted to re-roof plaintiff's house and allegedly had done so negligently. *International Shoe* was then described as part of a "dual trend in jurisdictional decisions: in defining the court with jurisdiction, a trend from the court with immediate power over the defendant to the court where the parties may most conveniently settle their dispute; and in defining due process of law, a trend from the emphasis on territorial limitations of courts to emphasis on providing notice and an opportunity to be heard."

2. PERKINS v. BENGUET CONSOLIDATED MINING CO., 342 U.S. 437, 446, 72 S.Ct. 413, 418, 96 L.Ed. 485, 493 (1952). Defendant, a Philippine corporation doing systematic and continuous business in Ohio during the Japanese occupation of the Philippines, was sued by a nonresident of Ohio in an Ohio state court on a cause of action that had arisen outside the state. The Ohio courts quashed service, and the United States Supreme Court, relying on *International Shoe*, held:

> The instant case takes us one step further to a proceeding *in personam* to enforce a cause of action not arising out of the corporation's activities in the state of the forum. * * * [W]e find no require-

ment of federal due process that either *prohibits* Ohio from opening its courts to the cause of action here presented or *compels* Ohio to do so. (Emphasis in original.)

On remand the Ohio courts refused to quash summons. 158 Ohio St. 145, 107 N.E.2d 203 (1952).

In FISHER GOVERNOR CO. v. SUPERIOR COURT, 53 Cal.2d 222, 225–26, 1 Cal.Rptr. 1, 3–4, 347 P.2d 1, 3–4 (1959), a wrongful death action growing out of an explosion in Idaho, plaintiffs served defendant, an Iowa corporation by delivering the papers to a California manufacturers' agent who sold defendant's products. The California Supreme Court ordered the process quashed. In his opinion for the Court, Justice Traynor said:

> Although a foreign corporation may have sufficient contacts with a state to justify an assumption of jurisdiction over it to enforce causes of action having no relation to its activities in that state * * * more contacts are required for the assumption of such extensive jurisdiction than sales and sales promotion within the state by independent nonexclusive sales representatives. * * * To hold otherwise would subject any corporation that promotes the sales of its goods on a nationwide basis to suit anywhere in the United States without regard to other considerations bearing on "the fair and orderly administration of the laws which it was the purpose of the due process clause to insure." * * * Accordingly, we must look beyond defendant's sales activities in this state to determine whether jurisdiction may constitutionally be assumed.

> The interest of the state in providing a forum for its residents * * *; or in regulating the business involved * * *; the relative availability of evidence and the burden of defense and prosecution in one place rather than another * * *; the ease of access to an alternative forum * * *; the avoidance of multiplicity of suits and conflicting adjudications * * *; and the extent to which the cause of action arose out of defendant's local activities * * * are all relevant to this inquiry. * * *

> None of these considerations supports an assumption of jurisdiction in plaintiffs' actions.

Compare BRYANT v. FINNISH NATIONAL AIRLINE, 15 N.Y.2d 426, 260 N.Y.S.2d 625, 208 N.E.2d 439 (1965), in which jurisdiction was upheld in an action that was unrelated to the forum. The airline did not fly to or from New York and its sole contact with the state was a small office to receive reservations for travel on Finnair's European flights. Plaintiff was a New York resident. Is this result consistent with *International Shoe?* Is it distinguishable from *Perkins?*

3. For a discussion of the various factors considered by state courts in determining whether a corporation's activities have had sufficient impact on the forum state to warrant an assertion of jurisdiction, see generally Morgan v. Heckle, 171 F.Supp. 482 (E.D.Ill.1959); *Developments in the Law—State Court Jurisdiction,* 73 Harv.L.Rev. 909, 919–35 (1960); Note, *Recent Interpretations of "Doing Business" Statutes,* 44 Iowa L.Rev. 345 (1959); Note, *Jurisdiction over Foreign Corporations—An Analysis of Due Process,* 104 U.Pa.L.Rev. 381 (1955). See 4 Wright & Miller, *Federal Practice and Procedure: Civil* §§ 1067–69, 1073 (1969), for a discussion of the cases applying the "doing business" test since *International Shoe.*

2. CONTEMPORARY NOTIONS ABOUT THE BASES OF JURISDICTION

Read the selected state jurisdictional statutes in the Supplement.

GRAY v. AMERICAN RADIATOR & STANDARD SANITARY CORP.

Supreme Court of Illinois, 1961.
22 Ill.2d 432, 176 N.E.2d 761.

KLINGBIEL, Justice. Phyllis Gray appeals from a judgment of the circuit court of Cook County dismissing her action for damages. The issues are concerned with the construction and validity of our statute providing for substituted service of process on nonresidents. Since a constitutional question is involved, the appeal is direct to this court.

The suit was brought against the Titan Valve Manufacturing Company and others, on the ground that a certain water heater had exploded and injured the plaintiff. The complaint charges, *inter alia*, that the Titan company, a foreign corporation, had negligently constructed the safety valve; and that the injuries were suffered as a proximate result thereof. Summons issued and was duly served on Titan's registered agent in Cleveland, Ohio. The corporation appeared specially, filing a motion to quash on the ground that it had not committed a tortious act in Illinois. Its affidavit stated that it does no business here; that it has no agent physically present in Illinois; and that it sells the completed valves to defendant, American Radiator & Standard Sanitary Corporation, outside Illinois. The American Radiator & Standard Sanitary Corporation (also made a defendant) filed an answer in which it set up a cross claim against Titan, alleging that Titan made certain warranties to American Radiator, and that if the latter is held liable to the plaintiff it should be indemnified and held harmless by Titan. The court granted Titan's motion, dismissing both the complaint and the cross claim.

Section 16 of the Civil Practice Act provides that summons may be personally served upon any party outside the State; and that as to nonresidents who have submitted to the jurisdiction of our courts, such service has the force and effect of personal service within Illinois. (Ill.Rev.Stat.1959, chap. 110, par. 16.) Under section 17(1) (b) a nonresident who, either in person or through an agent, commits a tortious act within this State submits to jurisdiction. * * * The questions in this case are (1) whether a tortious act was committed here, within the meaning of the statute, despite the fact that the Titan corporation had no agent in Illinois; and (2) whether the statute, if so construed, violates due process of law.

The first aspect to which we must direct our attention is one of statutory construction. Under section 17(1) (b) jurisdiction is predicated on the committing of a tortious act in this State. It is not disputed, for the purpose of this appeal, that a tortious act was committed. The issue depends on whether it was committed in Illinois, so as to warrant the assertion of personal jurisdiction by service of summons in Ohio.

The wrong in the case at bar did not originate in the conduct of a servant physically present here, but arose instead from acts performed at the place of manufacture. Only the consequences occurred in Illinois. It is well established, however, that in law the place of a wrong is where the last event takes place which is necessary to render the actor liable. Restatement, Conflict of Laws, sec. 377. A second indication that the place of injury is the determining factor is found in rules governing the time within which an action must be brought. In applying statutes of limitation our court has computed the period from the time when the injury is done. * * * We think it is clear that the alleged negligence in manufacturing the valve cannot be separated from the resulting injury; and that for present purposes, like those of liability and limitations, the tort was committed in Illinois.

Titan seeks to avoid this result by arguing that instead of using the word "tort," the legislature employed the term "tortious act"; and that the latter refers only to the act or conduct, separate and apart from any consequences thereof. We cannot accept the argument. To be tortious an act must cause injury. The concept of injury is an inseparable part of the phrase. In determining legislative intention courts will read words in their ordinary and popularly understood sense. * * * We think the intent should be determined less from technicalities of definition than from considerations of general purpose and effect. To adopt the criteria urged by defendant would tend to promote litigation over extraneous issues concerning the elements of a tort and the territorial incidence of each, whereas the test should be concerned more with those substantial elements of convenience and justice presumably contemplated by the legislature. As we observed in Nelson v. Miller, 11 Ill.2d 378, 143 N.E. 2d 673, the statute contemplates the exertion of jurisdiction over nonresident defendants to the extent permitted by the due-process clause.

[left margin handwritten note: Contemplation of exertion of Ill. Statute: "to extent permitted by due"]

The Titan company contends that if the statute is applied so as to confer jurisdiction in this case it violates the requirement of due process of law. The precise constitutional question thus presented has not heretofore been considered by this court. In the Nelson case the validity of the statute was upheld in an action against a nonresident whose employee, while physically present in Illinois, allegedly caused the injury. The *ratio decidendi* was that Illinois has an interest in providing relief for injuries caused by persons having "substantial contacts within the State." A standard of fairness or reasonableness was announced, within the limitation that defendant be given a realistic opportunity to appear and be heard. * * *

Under modern doctrine the power of a State court to enter a binding judgment against one not served with process within the State depends upon

For party not in state, Jurisd. depends on:

1) minimum contacts

2) reasonable method of notification

two questions: first, whether he has certain minimum contacts with the State * * * and second, whether there has been a reasonable method of notification. See International Shoe Co. v. State of Washington * * *; Nelson v. Miller * * *. In the case at bar there is no contention that section 16 provides for inadequate notice or that its provisions were not followed. Defendant's argument on constitutionality is confined to the proposition that applying section 17(1) (b), where the injury is defendant's only contact with the State, would exceed the limits of due process.

A proper determination of the question presented requires analysis of those cases which have dealt with the quantum of contact sufficient to warrant jurisdiction. Since the decision in Pennoyer v. Neff * * * the power of a State to exert jurisdiction over nonresidents has been greatly expanded, particularly with respect to foreign corporations. * * * [In International Shoe Co. v. Washington,] the court pointed out that the activities of the corporation in Washington were not only continuous and systematic but also gave rise to the liability sued on. It was observed that such operations, which resulted in a large volume of business, established "sufficient contacts or ties with the state of the forum to make it reasonable and just according to our traditional conception of fair play and substantial justice to permit the state to enforce the obligations which appellant has incurred there." * * *

Where the business done by a foreign corporation in the State of the forum is of a sufficiently substantial nature, it has been held permissible for the State to entertain a suit against it even though the cause of action arose from activities entirely distinct from its conduct within the State. Perkins v. Benguet Consolidated Mining Co. * * *. But where such business or other activity is not substantial, the particular act or transaction having no connection with the State of the forum, the requirement of "contact" is not satisfied. Hanson v. Denckla * * * [p. 134, infra].

In the case at bar the defendant's only contact with this State is found in the fact that a product manufactured in Ohio was incorporated in Pennsylvania, into a hot water heater which in the course of commerce was sold to an Illinois consumer. The record fails to disclose whether defendant has done any other business in Illinois, either directly or indirectly; and it is argued, in reliance on the International Shoe test, that since a course of business here has not been shown there are no "minimum contacts" sufficient to support jurisdiction. We do not think, however, that doing a given volume of business is the only way in which a nonresident can form the required connection with this State. Since the International Shoe case was decided the requirements for jurisdiction have been further relaxed, so that at the present time it is sufficient if the act or transaction itself has a substantial connection with the State of the forum.

In McGee v. International Life Insurance Co., 355 U.S. 220, 78 S.Ct. 199, 201, 2 L.Ed.2d 223, suit was brought in California against a foreign insurance company on a policy issued to a resident of California. The defendant was not served with process in that State but was notified by registered mail at its place of business in Texas, pursuant to a statute permitting such service in suits on insurance contracts. The contract in question was delivered in California, the premiums were mailed from there and the insured was a resident of that State when he died, but defendant had no office or agent in California nor did it solicit any business there apart from the policy sued on. After referring briefly to the International Shoe case the court held that "it is sufficient for purposes of due process that the suit was based on *a contract* which had substantial connection" with California. (Emphasis supplied.)

McGee holding

In Smyth v. Twin State Improvement Corp. * * * the court discussed the principal authorities on the question and concluded, *inter alia*, that "continuous activity within the state is not necessary as a prerequisite to jurisdiction."

In Nelson v. Miller * * * the commission of a single tort within this State was held sufficient to sustain jurisdiction under the present statute. The defendant in that case, a resident of Wisconsin, was engaged in the business of selling appliances. It was alleged that in the process of delivering a stove in Illinois, an employee of the defendant negligently caused injury to the plaintiff. In holding that the defendant was not denied due process by being required to defend in Illinois, this court observed at page 390 of 11 Ill.2d, at page 680 of 143 N.E.2d: "The defendant sent his employee into Illinois in the advancement of his own interests. While he was here, the employee and the defendant enjoyed the benefit and protection of the laws of Illinois, including the right to resort to our courts. In the course of his stay here the employee performed acts that gave rise to an injury. The law of Illinois will govern the substantive rights and duties stemming from the incident. Witnesses, other than the defendant's employee, are likely to be found here, and not in Wisconsin. In such circumstances, it is not unreasonable to require the defendant to make his defense here."

Whether the type of activity conducted within the State is adequate to satisfy the requirement depends upon the facts in the particular case. * * * The question cannot be answered by applying a mechanical formula or rule of thumb but by ascertaining what is fair and reasonable in the circumstances. In the application of this flexible test the relevant inquiry is whether defendant engaged in some act or conduct by which he may be said to have invoked the benefits and protections of the law of the forum. * * * The relevant decisions since Pennoyer v. Neff show a development of the concept of personal jurisdiction from one which requires service of process within the State to one which is satisfied either if the act or transaction sued on occurs there or if defendant has engaged in a sufficiently substantial course of activity in the State, provided always that reasonable notice and opportunity to be heard are afforded. * * * [T]he trend in defining due process of law is away from the emphasis on territorial limitations and toward emphasis on providing adequate notice and opportunity to be heard: from the court with immediate power over the defendant, toward the court in which both parties can most conveniently settle their dispute.

In the McGee case the court commented on the trend toward expanding State jurisdiction over nonresidents, observing that: "In part this is attributable to the fundamental transformation of our national economy over the years. Today many commercial transactions touch two or more States and may involve parties separated by the full continent. With this increasing nationalization of commerce has come a great increase in the amount of business conducted by mail across state lines. At the same time modern transportation and communication have made it much less burdensome for a party sued to defend himself in a State where he engages in economic activity."

It is true that courts cannot "assume that this trend heralds the eventual demise of all restrictions on the personal jurisdiction of state courts." Hanson v. Denckla * * *. An orderly and fair administration of the law throughout the nation requires protection against being compelled to answer claims brought in distant States with which the defendant has little or no association and in which he would be faced with an undue burden or disadvantage in making his defense. It must be remembered that lawsuits can be brought on frivolous demands or groundless claims as well as on legitimate ones, and that procedural rules must be designed and appraised in the light of what is fair and just to both sides in the dispute. * * *

In the case at bar defendant does not claim that the present use of its product in Illinois is an isolated instance. While the record does not disclose the volume of Titan's business or the territory in which appliances incorporating its valves are marketed, it is a reasonable inference that its commercial transactions, like those of other manufacturers, result in substantial use and consumption in this State. To the extent that its business may be directly affected by transactions occurring here it enjoys benefits from the laws of this State, and it has undoubtedly benefited, to a degree, from the protection which our law has given to the marketing of hot water heaters containing its valves. Where the alleged liability arises, as in this case, from the manufacture of products presumably sold in contemplation of use here, it should not matter that the purchase was made from an independent middleman or that someone other than the defendant shipped the product into this State.

With the increasing specialization of commercial activity and the growing interdependence of business enterprises it is seldom that a manufacturer deals directly with consumers in other States. The fact that the benefit he derives from its laws is an indirect one, however, does not make it any the less essential to the conduct of his business; and it is not unreasonable, where a cause of action arises from alleged defects in his product, to say that the use of such products in the ordinary course of commerce is sufficient contact with this State to justify a requirement that he defend here.

As a general proposition, if a corporation elects to sell its products for ultimate use in another State, it is not unjust to hold it answerable there for any damage caused by defects in those products. Advanced means of distribution and other commercial activity have made possible these modern methods of doing business, and have largely effaced the economic significance of State lines. By the same token, today's facilities for transportation and communication have removed much of the difficulty and inconvenience formerly encountered in defending lawsuits brought in other States.

Unless they are applied in recognition of the changes brought about by technological and economic progress, jurisdictional concepts which may have been reasonable enough in a simpler economy lose their relation to reality, and injustice rather than justice is promoted. Our unchanging principles of justice * * * should be scrupulously observed by the courts. But the rules of law which grow and develop within those principles must do so in the light of the facts of economic life as it is lived today. Otherwise the need for adaptation may become so great that basic rights are sacrificed in the name of reform, and the principles themselves become impaired.

The principles of due process relevant to the issue in this case support jurisdiction in the court where both parties can most conveniently settle their dispute. The facts show that the plaintiff, an Illinois resident, was injured in Illinois. The law of Illinois will govern the substantive questions, and witnesses on the issues of injury, damages and other elements relating to the occurrence are most likely to be found here. Under such circumstances the courts of the place of injury usually provide the most convenient forum for trial. * * * In Travelers Health Association v. Commonwealth of Virginia, 339 U.S. 643, 70 S.Ct. 927, 94 L.Ed. 1154, a Nebraska insurance corporation was held subject to the jurisdiction of a Virginia regulatory commission although it had no paid agents within the State and its only contact there was a mail-order business operated from its Omaha office. The court observed, by way of *dictum*, that "suits on alleged losses can be more conveniently tried in Virginia where witnesses would most likely live and where claims for losses would presumably be investigated. Such factors have been given great weight in applying the doctrine of *forum non conveniens.* * * * And prior decisions of this Court have referred to the unwisdom, unfairness and injustice of permitting policyholders to seek redress only in some distant state where the insurer is incorporated. The Due Process Clause does not forbid a state to protect its citizens from such injustice." 339 U.S. at page 649, 70 S.Ct. at page 930, 94 L.Ed. 1161–1162. We think a similar conclusion must follow in the case at bar.

We are aware of decisions, cited by defendant, wherein the opposite result was reached on somewhat similar factual situations. See Erlanger Mills, Inc. v. Cohoes Fibre Mills, Inc., 4 Cir., 239 F.2d 502; Hellriegel v. Sears Roebuck & Co., D.C.N.D.Ill.E.D., 157 F.Supp. 718; Johns v. Bay State Abrasive Products Co., D.C.D.Md., 89 F.Supp. 654. Little purpose can be served, however, by discussing such cases in detail, since the existence of sufficient "contact" depends upon the particular facts in each case. In any event we think the better rule supports jurisdiction in cases of the present kind. We conclude accordingly that defendant's association with this State is sufficient to support the exercise of jurisdiction.

* * *

Reversed and remanded, with directions.

NOTES AND QUESTIONS

1. A case similar to *Gray* is HOAGLAND v. SPRINGER, 75 N.J.Super. 560, 569, 183 A.2d 678, 683 (App.Div.1962), in which a tractor engine owned by Springer exploded in New Jersey, injuring plaintiff driver. Also joined as defendants were the manufacturer of the engine (Cummins Engine Co., an Indiana corporation); the distributor that had sold and installed the engine (Cummins Diesel Michigan, a Michigan corporation); and the company that had serviced the engine prior to the explosion (Cummins Diesel Metropolitan, a Delaware corporation doing business in New Jersey). Cummins Diesel Michigan, one of over fifty distributors and dealers throughout the country connected by Cummins' teletype network, objected to New Jersey's assertion of jurisdiction, but without success:

> We cannot disregard the economic realities of the situation exposed by the record in this case. Indiana [Cummins Engine] and its distributors form one, cohesive, economic unit. In the pursuit of business profits and their general economic well-being they are all concerned with the successful selling and servicing of Indiana's products, but for whose existence neither the mother company nor its distributors would have any reason for being. That Cummins was organized on the basis of a parent-manufacturer selling its products through independent distributors was a decision reached by its officers and directors, perhaps in an effort to avoid future difficulties with federal and state tax laws and other legislation.

> On the basis of the record, it cannot reasonably be believed that the Cummins management intended, by having independent distributors, to divorce them completely or effectively from Indiana. * * * All distributors had a form of rapid communication, one with the other and with the mother company, in order to effect quick delivery of needed parts from one distributor or another should Indiana not be able to fulfill that need. Furthermore, in an obvious effort to attract customers, keep them satisfied, and permit the Cummins family to meet competition, arrangements were made so that a product sold by one distributor would be serviced by another * * *. There is also the fact that sales had over the past few years been consummated between Michigan [Cummins Diesel] and Metropolitan, the one buying from the other. Indeed, it would not be unreasonable to say that Metropolitan was Michigan's special agent * * * for the servicing of products bought from Michigan.

See also Gelfand v. Tanner Motor Tours, Ltd., 385 F.2d 116 (2d Cir.1967) ("independent" agents); Comment, *Jurisdiction over Parent Corporations*, 51 Calif.L.Rev. 574 (1963).

2. FEATHERS v. McLUCAS, 15 N.Y.2d 443, 463–64, 261 N.Y.S.2d 8, 23–24, 209 N.E.2d 68, 79–80, certiorari denied 382 U.S. 905, 86 S.Ct. 241, 15 L.Ed.2d 158 (1965). Plaintiffs were injured by the explosion of a tractor-drawn tank of liquid propane gas on a highway near their home in New York. The tank had been manufactured in Kansas and sold to a Missouri corporation, "presumably with knowledge that the latter would mount the tank on a wheelbase and then sell it to * * * a Pennsylvania corporation, which operated as a licensed interstate carrier." The applicable New York statute, N.Y.C.P.L.R. 302(2), which was based upon the Illinois statute involved in *Gray*, permitted jurisdiction over a non-

domiciliary "if, in person or through an agent, he * * * commits a tortious act within the state." In refusing to assert jurisdiction over the Kansas manufacturer, the New York court criticized the conclusion in *Gray* that a tort had been committed in Illinois for purposes of that state's jurisdiction statute:

> * * * It certainly does not follow that, if the "place of wrong" for purposes of conflict of laws is a particular state, the "place of the commission of a tortious act" is also that same state for purposes of interpreting a statute conferring jurisdiction, on that basis, over nonresidents. * * * Moreover, the place of the "tort" is not necessarily the same as the place of defendant's commission of the "tortious act." * * *
>
> In sum, then, it is our conclusion, based not only on the plain language of the statute but on its legislative history, that * * * [N.Y.C. P.L.R. 302(2)] covers only a tortious act committed (by a nondomiciliary) in this state. * * *

SINGER v. WALKER, decided jointly with *Feathers*, involved a geologist's hammer manufactured in Illinois and shipped to a retail dealer in New York City; the hammer broke and injured plaintiff while he was using it in Connecticut. The New York court again held that no tortious act had been committed within the state, but asserted jurisdiction under N.Y.C.P.L.R. 302(1) on the ground that the company's shipment of "substantial quantities" of its products into the state and solicitation of business there through representatives and printed advertising amounted to the "transaction of business" in New York. Chief Judge Desmond concurred in the result, but disagreed with the holding that no tortious act had been committed in the state:

> * * * [T]he totality of an actionable tort such as is charged here (involving manufacturer's products liability) consists of three elements: defective manufacture, distribution to purchaser, and a resulting injury. Each of these is a "tortious act" or, in other words, "part of a tort." * * * Singer's is a much stronger case than Gray for the application of such a long-arm statute since the defendant manufacturer in Gray did not directly send its product into Illinois at all. * * *

See generally Homburger, *The Reach of New York's Long-Arm Statute: Today and Tomorrow,* 15 Buffalo L.Rev. 61 (1965).

In 1966, the New York legislature amended Section 302 to reach defendants in cases like *Feathers* and *Singer*. Is the text of the current New York provision, which is set out in the Supplement, broader or narrower than the Illinois act? In what ways? Examine the text of Article 1 of the Uniform Interstate and International Procedure Act, which also appears in the Supplement. In what ways is it broader or narrower than the Illinois and New York acts? For a discussion of *Feathers* and related New York tort cases, see 1 Weinstein, Korn & Miller, *New York Civil Practice* ¶¶ 302.10–.10a.

3. In O'BRIEN v. COMSTOCK FOODS, INC., 123 Vt. 461, 464–65, 194 A.2d 568, 570–71 (1963), the Vermont Supreme Court refused to apply the statute construed in *Smyth v. Twin State Improvement Co.,* p. 87, supra, to an action by a Vermont plaintiff who had been injured in Vermont by glass in a can of beans packaged in New York by a New York corporation.

> The vital factor in the statute is the intentional and affirmative action on the part of the non-resident defendant in pursuit of its corporate purposes within this jurisdiction. * * *

The bare allegation that the defendant at Newark, New York put its product "into the stream of commerce," without more, is insufficient to show a voluntary contact or an intentional participation in Vermont. The fact that the can of beans was ultimately purchased and consumed here does not cure the defect.

* * *

Unlike the Supreme Court of Illinois in *Gray* * * *, we cannot infer that the defendant's products have substantial use and consumption in Vermont.

What policy considerations might have led the Vermont Supreme Court to take a more conservative approach than the Illinois Supreme Court toward the assertion of jurisdiction over foreign corporations? What type of proof would satisfy the Vermont court's desire for "intentional and affirmative action" by defendant? See also Mann v. Equitable Gas Co., 209 F.Supp. 571 (N.D.W.Va.1962).

4. Perhaps the best known decision reaching a result opposed to that in *Gray*, is ERLANGER MILLS, INC. v. COHOES FIBRE MILLS, INC., 239 F.2d 502, 509 (4th Cir.1956). In that case a New York corporation was held not amenable to suit in North Carolina on the basis of a single shipment of allegedly defective goods into that state pursuant to an order placed in New York by a North Carolina corporation. The applicable North Carolina statute provided for jurisdiction over foreign corporations when the cause of action arose "out of the production, manufacture, or distribution of goods by such corporation with the reasonable expectation that those goods are to be used or consumed in this state." In holding that the statute was invalid as applied to the facts of the case, the court stated:

> The Constitution * * * contemplates that the boundaries between the states shall have continued significance for some purposes though not for all. If one State may, without violation of the due process clause, extend the authority of its courts beyond its boundaries over persons and situations not sufficiently related to that State, the separate identity of the States will be reduced to a mere fiction. Individual states could undertake at the expense of other States to enlarge the sphere of their authority to nationwide dimensions. It requires no flight of fancy to foresee the resulting maze of lawsuits adjudicating the interests of persons having only the faintest and most remote links with the State exercising authority. If the due process clause is not effective to restrain such extensions of local power, then the federal system is likely to be transformed into something very different from anything we have known.

The *Erlanger* approach has not been widely followed.

5. One section of the Illinois long-arm statute construed in *Gray* permits jurisdiction to be asserted over nonresidents on a cause of action arising from the transaction of any business in the state. This section was invoked in CONN v. WHITMORE, 9 Utah 2d 250, 255, 342 P.2d 871, 874–75 (1959), in which plaintiff, an Illinois resident, mailed a list of horses being offered for sale to defendant in Utah. Defendant asked a friend in Illinois to inspect the horses and subsequently sent a letter accepting the offer and enclosing partial payment for the horses. An employee was then dispatched to bring them to Utah. A dispute developed, and plaintiff successfully sued in Illinois to recover the balance of the pur-

chase price. When plaintiff attempted to enforce the judgment in Utah, the courts of that state refused to accord it full faith and credit:

> * * * It is important to bear in mind that it was not the defendant Utah resident who took the initiative by going into Illinois to transact business, nor did he engage in any activity resulting in injury or damage there. Quite the contrary, it was the plaintiff resident of Illinois who proselyted for business in Utah, and whose proffer the defendant accepted here. He agreed to the terms offered and completed his contract of purchase in Utah * * *.

> Brief reflection will bring to mind difficulties to be encountered if the ordering of merchandise in a foreign state by mail and taking delivery through a designated carrier, whether private or common, is to be deemed "doing business" in a foreign state, which will draw one into the orbit of the jurisdiction of its courts. * * * A person contemplating business in another state would have only two alternatives: either subject himself to the jurisdiction of the foreign court if any dispute arises, or refrain from doing such business. * * * Mail order houses, for example, accept and fill orders from all over the country. If they could sue on their own accounts in their own state where it would be highly inconvenient for out-of-state customers to defend, then forward the judgments to the jurisdictions where the customers live, demanding full faith and credit for them, this would effectively prevent the customers from presenting a meritorious defense where one existed. The ultimate result would be to dissuade customers from doing business across state lines by mail.

Should the minimum contacts test suggested by *International Shoe* and *Gray* be applied any differently to individual, as opposed to corporate, defendants?

The *Conn* rationale was applied and extended in FOURTH NORTHWESTERN NAT. BANK v. HILSON INDUSTRIES, INC., 264 Minn. 110, 115–18, 117 N.W.2d 732, 735–36 (1962), in which a Minnesota corporation brought suit in a court of that state on promissory notes executed by defendant in Ohio. The notes had been executed in an attempt to resolve a dispute that had grown out of an order for machinery sent by Hilson in Ohio. Defendant was not doing business nor engaging in a sales campaign in Minnesota and had no agents or employees there. The applicable Minnesota statute permitted the assertion of jurisdiction when a foreign corporation made a contract with a resident "to be performed in whole or in part by either party in Minnesota." After reviewing the precedents, the Minnesota Supreme Court dismissed the action:

> We believe it is significant that * * * [certain earlier Minnesota cases] all resulted in the protection of *individuals* damaged in one way or another by nonresident defendants who sold their products in this state or whose products found their way here and caused injury to a Minnesota resident. In each instance the nonresident defendant had been the aggressor, so to speak, and had had substantial contact with the forum, invoking its protection for the privilege of doing business here. It had subjected itself to the reciprocal obligation of amenability to suit in return for the right to compete for sales in our market places. However, there is a sharp distinction between suing a nonresident seller and invoking * * * [the long-arm statute] against a nonresident buyer.

* * * We are not confronted with a relatively defenseless holder of a small claim who is in effect denied justice by being required to
travel to a foreign jurisdiction. We have, instead, a corporate resident
plaintiff who has taken the initiative in response to a nonresident corporation's inquiries. The nonresident corporation enjoys no particular privilege or protection in purchasing products from the resident seller, none
akin to the rights exercised by a party seeking to distribute its products
within the forum state. * * * The only connection with Minnesota
in this case, however remote, is the fact that the notes are payable here.
* * * Fixing the place of payment at plaintiff's business residence is
hardly the kind of commercial benefit to defendand [sic] that must be
balanced by a countervailing capitulation to jurisdiction. * * * For
these reasons we believe that less than the minimum contacts required by
"traditional notions of fair play and substantial justice" have been proved.

Would it have been possible to make the distinction that the *Hilson* court made
between buyers and sellers if the case had arisen under the Illinois or New York
long-arm statute? Is such a distinction desirable, or should the *Hilson* rationale
be verbalized in different terms?

6. As a result of *International Shoe* many state legislatures have enacted
broad long-arm statutes to conform to the Supreme Court's view as to when per-
sonal jurisdiction can be asserted consistent with due process considerations.
This, in turn, has resulted in a growing volume of literature on the various statutes.
A few of the more general articles are the following: Currie, *The Growth of
the Long Arm: Eight Years of Extended Jurisdiction in Illinois,* 1963 U.Ill.
L.F. 533; Foster, *Judicial Economy, Fairness and Convenience of Place of Trial:
Long-Arm Jurisdiction in District Courts,* 47 F.R.D. 73 (1969); Homburger,
The Reach of New York's Long-Arm Statute: Today and Tomorrow, 15 Buffalo
L.Rev. 61 (1965); Comment, *Long-Arm and Quasi in Rem Jurisdiction and the
Fundamental Test of Fairness,* 69 Mich.L.Rev. 300 (1970); Comment, *In Per-
sonam Jurisdiction Over Nonresident Manufacturers in Product Liability Actions,*
63 Mich.L.Rev. 1028 (1965); and *Developments in the Law—State Court Juris-
diction,* 73 Harv.L.Rev. 909 (1960).

BUCKEYE BOILER CO. v. SUPERIOR COURT OF
LOS ANGELES COUNTY

Supreme Court of California, 1969.
71 Cal.2d 893, 80 Cal.Rptr. 113, 458 P.2d 57.

PETERS, Justice. Petitioner, The Buckeye Boiler Company, seeks a
writ of mandate to compel the respondent superior court to quash the service of summons upon it in an action for personal injuries brought by real
party in interest Wayman P. Flynt. * * *

The record shows that on or about March 15, 1967, while acting in
the course of his employment at the General Electric Company's plant in
Ontario, California, plaintiff was injured by the explosion of a pressure
tank containing an unidentified liquid and being used in connection with
a system for the spraying of liquid under air pressure. The tank, it is al-

leged, bore a metal name plate with the legend: "The Buckeye Boiler Company, Dayton, Ohio. Built 1960—150 lbs, maximum;" and was, according to the record, being put to a use for which it was intended when manufactured. While receiving treatment in a California hospital for his injuries resulting from the explosion, plaintiff it is claimed suffered a fall, after which he was stricken with left hemiplegia, that is, total paralysis of his entire left side.

Plaintiff sued Buckeye, alleging inter alia negligent manufacture of the pressure vessel, manufacturer's strict liability, and breach of warranty. By amended complaint, plaintiff joined as defendants the doctor by which and the hospital in which he was treated for his injuries [hereinafter "medical defendants"], alleging that the fall he suffered resulted from their negligence, and further alleging that he is in doubt whether his hemiplegic condition resulted from the explosion, the negligence of the doctor and hospital, or both.

* * *

The medical defendants consist of a California corporation and an individual who is a California resident, both of whom allegedly cannot be sued in any other state on plaintiff's asserted causes of action. All witnesses of the accident reside in California.

Buckeye is a foreign corporation, organized and existing under the laws of the State of Ohio, with its principal place of business and principal offices in Dayton, Ohio. It manufactures pressure vessels which have numerous and varied uses. Sales are solicited outside Ohio in interstate commerce both directly and through independent manufacturers' representatives who sell Buckeye's products on a commission basis in Ohio, Kentucky, Michigan, Indiana, Pennsylvania, New Jersey, New York, Connecticut, Maryland, Delaware, North Carolina, South Carolina, West Virginia, Virginia, Georgia, Florida, and Alabama. Buckeye does not advertise its products.

Buckeye has no agent, office, sales representative, exclusive agency or exclusive sales outlet, warehouse, stock of merchandise, property, or bank account in California. It does not sell on consignment to, and has no commission agreement with, any person or entity in California. However, for a period of five years prior to plaintiff's injury, and continuing to the present, Buckeye has sold pressure tanks to Cochin Manufacturing Company, an Ohio corporation, which maintains a manufacturing plant in South San Francisco, California. Cochin orders some tanks directly from that plant; the purchases of other tanks are negotiated through its Ohio office. Buckeye ships the tanks (priced at $55 to $60 each) directly to the Cochin plant in South San Francisco. Annual gross sales to Cochin during the last two or three years have ranged from $25,000 to $35,000. Cochin manufactures hydraulic automobile lifts for service stations; it incorporates the tanks purchased from Buckeye into these lifts and then sells the lifts to purchasers throughout California and in other states.   Cochin apparently does not re-sell Buckeye's tanks for other uses.

Buckeye claims that other than sales to Cochin it has had "no contact with anyone in the State of California" and that it has not sold any of its products to the General Electric Company between January 1960 and the present.   However, Buckeye admits that it has no records of its sales prior to 1962.

Buckeye ships to the Cochin plant in South San Francisco tanks iden-tified in its invoices as "Hydraulic Oil Tanks" which are generally 14 inches in diameter and 75 inches in height.   Apparently the exploding tank which allegedly injured plaintiff was approximately 10 inches in diameter and 16 inches in height.   There is no evidence in the record before us, other than the evidence of size and general type of use, to indicate what significant dif-ferences there may be between the tanks purchased by Cochin and the tank which allegedly injured plaintiff.[2]

Plaintiff is unable to establish where his employer purchased the ex-ploding tank.   The chief of the purchasing department at General Electric's Ontario, California, plant testified that the company has no record of pur-chasing the tank in question, or any other item, from Buckeye.   He also testified that the department destroys records more than five years old. However, he stated that it was the department's policy to purchase equip-ment, whenever possible, from suppliers located within the State of Cali-fornia.

Section 411, subdivision 2, of the Code of Civil Procedure authorizes service of process on foreign corporations "doing business in this state." This section exerts the full power of the state, consistent with the due proc-ess clause, to subject foreign corporations to the jurisdiction of California courts.   *   *   *

A defendant not literally "present" in the forum state may not be re-quired to defend itself in that state's tribunals unless the "quality and na-ture of the defendant's activity" in relation to the particular cause of ac-tion makes it fair to do so.   *   *   *   Such a defendant's activity must consist of "an act done or transaction consummated in the forum State" or "some [other] act by which the defendant purposefully avails itself of the privilege of conducting activities within the forum State, thus invoking the benefits and protections of its laws."   (Hanson v. Denckla,   *   *   * [p. 134, infra] 357 U.S. at pp. 251, 253, 78 S.Ct. at pp. 1238, 1240.) Furthermore, unless the defendant's forum-related activity reaches such extensive or wide-ranging proportions as to make the defendant sufficiently "present" in the forum state to support jurisdiction over it concerning causes of action which are unrelated to that activity   *   *   *   the particu-lar cause of action must arise out of or be connected with the defendant's forum-related activity.   *   *   *

2 In a brief filed with this court Buckeye for the first time claims that the tanks purchased by Cochin bear "no relation" to the tank that injured plaintiff.

Once it is established that the defendant has engaged in activity of the requisite quality and nature in the forum state and that the cause of action is sufficiently connected with this activity, the propriety of an assumption of jurisdiction depends upon a balancing of the inconvenience to the defendant in having to defend itself in the forum state against both the interest of the plaintiff in suing locally and the interrelated interest of the state in assuming jurisdiction.   *   *   *   In other words, once the threshold of sufficient activity by the defendant has been passed, the question of the propriety of subjecting the defendant to the jurisdiction of the forum involves both a consideration of fairness to the plaintiff   *   *   *   and a determination of whether, from a standpoint of the logical and orderly distribution of interstate litigation, the forum state is what Professor Ehrenzweig has termed a "forum conveniens."   (See Ehrenzweig, The Transient Rule of Personal Jurisdiction: The "Power" Myth and Forum Conveniens (1956) 65 Yale L.J. 289, 312   *   *   *.)

The forum state, of course, has an interest in opening its courts to residents seeking redress   *   *   *   particularly when its courts are the only ones accessible to them as a practical matter.   It also has an interest, from the standpoint of the orderly administration of the laws, in assuming jurisdiction in cases where most of the evidence, testimonial and otherwise, is within its borders and where prevailing choice of law principles dictate the application of local law to the major issues involved.   *   *   *

The plaintiff, of course, has an interest in presenting his claim in court and in obtaining relief if it is warranted.   As already indicated, suit in a local court may be his only practical opportunity to accomplish this objective. Both the plaintiff and the state may have an interest in avoiding multiple and possibly conflicting adjudications.   *   *   *   On the other hand, a nonresident defendant which derives economic benefit from activity in the forum state and thus does more than a purely local business ordinarily has very little basis for complaining of inconvenience when required to defend itself in that state.   *   *   *

A manufacturer engages in economic activity within a state as a matter of "commercial actuality" whenever the purchase or use of its product within the state generates gross income for the manufacturer and is not so fortuitous or unforeseeable as to negative the existence of an intent on the manufacturer's part to bring about this result.   *   *   *

A manufacturer's economic relationship with a state does not necessarily differ in substance, nor should its amenability to jurisdiction necessarily differ, depending upon whether it deals directly or indirectly with residents of the state.   *   *   *

A manufacturer whose products pass through the hands of one or more middlemen before reaching their ultimate users cannot disclaim responsibility for the total distribution pattern of the products.   If the manufacturer sells its products in circumstances such that it knows or should reasonably anticipate that they will ultimately be resold in a particular state, it should be held to have purposefully availed itself of the market for its products in that state.   *   *   *   In Regie Nationale Des Usines Renault v. Superior Court, 208 Cal.App.2d 702, 703, 25 Cal.Rptr. 530, 531, the court refused to exempt the defendant, a French corporation, from jurisdiction in a suit apparently for personal injuries although the defendant did not sell its cars directly in California but rather "inaugurate[d] a flow of its products to   *   *   *   California" through a "Chain of sales" involving a wholly-owned American subsidiary and independently-owned distributorships and dealerships.   The court held that the indirect manner in which the defendant dealt with California consumers "effect[s] little, if any, alteration in the jurisdictional situation."   *   *   *

The same focus on actual economic benefit should be made in cases where the middlemen between the defendant manufacturer and the consumer include intermediate manufacturers who incorporate the original manufacturer's products into their own as components thereof.   *   *   *

When a plaintiff is allegedly injured in the forum state by a defect in a nonresident manufacturer's product, the question whether that product's use or purchase was an isolated instance or part of a continuous course of business in the state is relevant but not necessarily decisive in determining the existence or nonexistence of the requisite jurisdictional activity. *   *   *   Only if isolated use or purchase conclusively establishes lack of foreseeability that the product will enter the state is the isolation necessarily fatal to jurisdiction over the manufacturer; in that event there is a manifest lack of purposeful activity on the part of the manufacturer.

"Manifest lack of purposeful activity"

In the present case, it is clear that defendant derives substantial economic benefit from the sale and use of its products in California; it currently derives about $30,000 annually in gross sales revenues from its direct sales of certain pressure tanks to the Cochin Manufacturing Company plant in South San Francisco.   On the basis of these sales alone, defendant is purposefully engaging in economic activity within California as a matter of "commercial actuality."

The trial court was warranted in concluding that defendant's total economic activity in California consists of its direct sales to Cochin and some indeterminate amount of additional sales activity, direct or indirect; and that at some time during or subsequent to 1960 (the date of manufacture of the tank that allegedly injured the plaintiff) and prior to 1962 (the year prior to which defendant has no sales records) defendant sold the pressure tank that allegedly injured plaintiff either directly to the General Electric plant in Ontario, California,[6] or through one or more intermediate parties.   This tank may be the only Buckeye pressure tank ever sold in, or

6 Defendant claims that it has not sold any of its products to General Electric between January 1960 and the present.   However, defendant admits that it has no records of its pre-1962 sales.

for use in, California other than the tanks sold to Cochin. Or it may be only one of a substantial number of pressure tanks purchased in, or for use in, California through the channels of interstate commerce in which defendant distributes many of its products. It is very possible that a number of the firms to which defendant sells its pressure tanks in the eastern half of the United States resell some of these tanks, either alone or as components of their own products, to customers in California. This distinct possibility is not negated by Buckeye's somewhat evasive statement in its response to plaintiff's interrogatories that other than its sales to Cochin it has had "no contact with anyone in the State of California."

But whether the pressure tank that injured plaintiff is one of a number of tanks sent into California by Buckeye through a "chain of sales" * * * or is the subject of an isolated California transaction apart from Buckeye's sales to Cochin, plaintiff's cause of action appears to arise from Buckeye's economic activity in California, the totality of its sales of pressure tanks to California customers or to other customers for foreseeable resale or use in California.

Buckeye did not allege before the trial court that the tank which allegedly injured plaintiff arrived in California in a manner so fortuitous and unforeseeable as to demonstrate that its placement here was not purposeful.[7] Nor did Buckeye there allege that the burden of defending the present action in California would be substantially different in its nature and extent than the burden of defending actions which might arise from sales of pressure tanks to Cochin. If Buckeye can demonstrate both of these propositions,[9] an assumption of jurisdiction might well be inappropriate since it might then be said that plaintiff's cause of action neither arose from nor was connected with any purposeful activity by Buckeye within the State of California. Since Buckeye's position in the trial court was based in significant measure upon Court of Appeal decisions that have been disapproved for applying the purposeful activity test in too mechanical a fashion it should be afforded the opportunity of making the sort of evidentiary showing suggested above before the trial court, a showing which appeared unnecessary under those decisions.

[7] The record shows only that this tank may be the only Buckeye tank in California other than tanks sold to Cochin and that it may not have been sold directly to General Electric Company (see fn. 6, *supra*).

[9] The plaintiff has the burden of showing that a defendant is doing business in California for purposes of section 411 of the Code of Civil Procedure. * * * Consistent with this rule, it would seem that where, as in the present case, the plaintiff establishes that the defendant is a manufacturer which frequently does not deal directly with the ultimate purchasers or users of its products; that its products are put to "numerous and varied uses" which are not readily apparent to the average person; that a substantial amount of its business is conducted through the channels of interstate commerce; and that the defendant does engage in some substantial economic activity within the state, it is reasonable to require the defendant to carry the burden of making the sort of showing outlined above in order to avoid jurisdiction over a cause of action such as that involved in the present case. * * *

The interests of both the plaintiff and the State of California appear to substantially outweigh any inconvenience of which defendant may complain in being required to defend the present action in California. The state has a substantial interest in affording the plaintiff, a California resident, a forum in which he may seek whatever redress is warranted, especially where, as here, it is quite likely that the plaintiff cannot, for financial as well as possible physical reasons, pursue his claim in the distant state where the defendant has its principal place of business. The plaintiff, in the present case, also has a peculiar interest in litigating locally. The distinct preponderance of relevant evidence is located within California. Not only are all witnesses and records concerning explosion of the tank and the extent of plaintiff's injuries here, but a major piece of evidence concerning the question of defective manufacture—the tank itself—is also here. Choice of law principles followed in California and Ohio both appear to dictate the application of California law to the major substantive issues likely to be involved. * * * Finally, there may be a multiplicity of suits with possibly conflicting results if plaintiff is forced to sue defendant Buckeye in Ohio and the medical defendants in California. It will be recalled that plaintiff alleged in his amended complaint that he is in doubt whether his present incapacitating hemiplegic condition was caused by the explosion or by the negligence of the medical defendants or both. He fears that if he is required to sue defendant Buckeye in Ohio and the medical defendants in California, the defendant(s) in each case may be able to avoid liability for this condition by pointing the finger at the absent defendant(s).

The plaintiff has made a sufficient prima facie showing that his injury arose from or is connected with purposeful activity in California— direct and indirect sales of pressure tanks—which produces economic benefit for Buckeye as a matter of "commercial actuality." A balancing of inconvenience to the defendant against the interests of the state and the plaintiff in having the present litigation in California strongly favors the local jurisdiction.

The alternative writ of mandamus is discharged and the application for a peremptory writ is denied.

TRAYNOR, C. J., and McCOMB, TOBRINER, MOSK, BURKE and SULLIVAN, JJ., concur.

NOTES AND QUESTIONS

1. Reread the description of the California Supreme Court's decision in *Fisher Governor Co. v. Superior Court*, p. 88, supra. Are *Fisher* and *Buckeye* distinguishable? Does *Buckeye* overrule *Fisher*?

2. Note the California Supreme Court's statement that the "cause of action appears to arise from * * * sales of pressure tanks to California customers or to other customers for foreseeable resale or use in California." What facts are provided in the court's opinion to support this conclusion? Does *Buckeye* extend California's jurisdiction beyond constitutional limits? See generally

Gorfinkel & Lavine, *Long-Arm Jurisdiction in California Under New Section 410.10 of the Code of Civil Procedure,* 21 Hast.L.J. 1163, 1192 (1970); Note, *The Development of In Personam Jurisdiction over Individuals and Corporations in California: 1849–1970,* 21 Hast.L.J. 1105, 1155 (1970).

3. Of what significance is the court's placing the burden on defendant to show that the presence of the exploding tank in California was fortuitous and that the burden of defending in California would be "substantially different" from defending in its own state. What would defendant have to show to meet this burden? Is there any likelihood that the defendant could have met its burden in *Buckeye* given the absence of records relating to sales prior to 1962? Is it fair to conclude that one of the reasons why the court places the ultimate burden of proof on defendants is to encourage them to forego jurisdictional challenges because of the difficulties and costs involved?

4. Note that the court in *Buckeye* seems to be saying that even if a defendant is found to have had sufficient contacts with the forum to satisfy the requirements of due process, the power of the court to proceed with the action still would depend "upon a balancing of the inconvenience to the defendant in having to defend itself in the forum state against both the interest of the plaintiff in suing locally and the interrelated interest of the state in assuming jurisdiction." Is it possible that there are cases that meet the "minimum contacts" requirement but would fail this balancing test? If so, is it clear that the action should be dismissed? Has the California court raised the question of *forum non conveniens* to constitutional dimensions? See pp. 249–55, *infra,* particularly Note 2 on p. 255, indicating that a California court will not dismiss if the plaintiff is from that state.

SECTION B. JURISDICTION BASED UPON POWER OVER PROPERTY

PENNINGTON v. FOURTH NATIONAL BANK, 243 U.S. 269, 271–72, 37 S.Ct. 282, 282–83, 61 L.Ed. 713 (1917):

The 14th Amendment did not, in guarantying due process of law, abridge the jurisdiction which a state possessed over property within its borders, regardless of the residence or presence of the owner. That jurisdiction extends alike to tangible and to intangible property. Indebtedness due from a resident to a nonresident—of which bank deposits are an example—is property within the state. * * * It is, indeed, the species of property which courts of the several states have most frequently applied in satisfaction of the obligations of absent debtors. * * * Substituted service on a nonresident by publication furnishes no legal basis for a judgment in personam. * * * But garnishment or foreign attachment is a proceeding quasi in rem. * * * The thing belonging to the absent defendant is seized and applied to the satisfaction of his obligation. The Federal Constitution presents no obstacle to the full exercise of this power.

* * * The power of the state to proceed against the property of an absent defendant is the same whether the obligation sought to be enforced is an admitted indebtedness or a contested claim. * * * It is likewise immaterial that the claim is, at the commencement of the suit, inchoate, to be perfected only by time or the action of the court. The only essentials to the exercise of the state's power are presence of the res within its borders, its seizure at the commencement of proceedings, and the opportunity of the owner to be heard.

NOTES AND QUESTIONS

1. What is the situs of corporate stock for purposes of attachment—the corporation's place of incorporation, the domicile of the shareholder, or the state in which the stock certificates actually are located? See generally Note, *Attachment of Corporate Stock: The Conflicting Approaches of Delaware and the Uniform Stock Transfer Act*, 73 Harv.L.Rev. 1579 (1960).

2. Prior to 1963, the federal courts had no general original quasi in rem jurisdiction. This was a curious limitation since the federal courts permitted the removal of actions initially commenced in a state court by attachment. See Rorick v. Devon Syndicate, Ltd., 307 U.S. 299, 59 S.Ct. 877, 83 L.Ed. 1303 (1939). In 1963 this inconsistency was eliminated by the amendment of Federal Rule 4(e). Full discussions of this topic are found in Carrington, *The Modern Utility of Quasi in Rem Jurisdiction*, 76 Harv.L.Rev. 303 (1962); B. Currie, *Attachment and Garnishment in the Federal Courts*, 59 Mich.L.Rev. 337 (1961). See also 4 Wright & Miller, *Federal Practice and Procedure: Civil* §§ 1119–23 (1969).

Quasi in rem jurisdiction in the federal courts also specifically is provided for in 28 U.S.C. § 1655 in connection with certain types of claims to land when defendant cannot be served personally within the state. See Blume, *Actions Quasi in Rem Under Section 1655, Title 28, U.S.C.*, 50 Mich.L.Rev. 1 (1951).

HARRIS v. BALK

Supreme Court of the United States, 1905.
198 U.S. 215, 25 S.Ct. 625, 49 L.Ed. 1023.

Error to the Supreme Court of the State of North Carolina.

* * *

The facts are as follows: The plaintiff in error, Harris, was a resident of North Carolina at the time of the commencement of this action, in 1896, and prior to that time was indebted to the defendant in error, Balk, also a resident of North Carolina, in the sum of $180, for money borrowed from Balk by Harris * * *. During the year above mentioned one Jacob Epstein, a resident of Baltimore, in the state of Maryland, asserted that Balk was indebted to him in the sum of over $300. In August, 1896, Harris visited Baltimore * * * and while he was in that city temporarily on August 6, 1896, Epstein caused to be issued out of a proper court in Baltimore a foreign or nonresident writ of attachment against Balk, attaching the debt due Balk from Harris, which writ the sheriff at Baltimore laid in the hands of Harris, with a summons to appear in the court at a day named. With that attachment, a writ of summons and a short declaration against Balk (as provided by the Maryland statute) were also delivered to the sheriff, and by him set up at the courthouse door, as required by the law of Maryland. Before the return day of the attachment writ Harris left Baltimore, and returned to his home in North Carolina. He did not contest the garnishee process, which was issued to garnish the debt which Harris owed Balk. After his return Harris made an affidavit on August 11, 1896, that he owed Balk $180, and stated that the amount had been attached by Epstein, of Baltimore, and by his counsel in the Maryland proceeding Harris consented therein to an order of condemnation against him as such garnishee for $180, the amount of his debt to Balk. Judgment was thereafter entered against the garnishee, and in favor of the plaintiff, Epstein, for $180. After the entry of the garnishee judgment, condemning the $180 in the hands of the garnishee, Harris paid the amount of the judgment to one Warren, an attorney of Epstein, residing in North Carolina. On August 11, 1896, Balk commenced an action against Harris before a justice of the peace in North Carolina, to recover the $180 which he averred Harris owed him. The plaintiff in error, by way of answer to the suit, pleaded in bar the recovery of the Maryland judgment and his payment thereof, and contended that it was conclusive against the defendant in error in this action, because that judgment was a valid judgment in Maryland, and was therefore entitled to full faith and credit in the courts of North Carolina. This contention was not allowed by the trial court, and judgment was accordingly entered against Harris for the amount of his indebtedness to Balk, and that judgment was affirmed by the supreme court of North Carolina. The ground of such judgment was that the Maryland court obtained no jurisdiction to attach or garnish the debt due from Harris to Balk, because Harris was but temporarily in the state, and the situs of the debt was in North Carolina.

Mr. Justice PECKHAM, after making the foregoing statement, delivered the opinion of the court:

* * *

The defendant in error contends that the Maryland court obtained no jurisdiction to award the judgment of condemnation, because the garnishee, although at the time in the state of Maryland, and personally served with process therein, was a nonresident of that state, only casually or temporarily within its boundaries; that the situs of the debt due from Harris, the garnishee, to the defendant in error herein, was in North Carolina, and did not accompany Harris to Maryland; that, consequently, Harris, though within the state of Maryland, had not possession of any property of Balk, and the Maryland state court therefore obtained no jurisdiction over any property of Balk in the attachment proceedings, and the consent of Harris to the entry of the judgment was immaterial. The plaintiff in error, on the contrary, insists that, though the garnishee were but temporarily in Maryland, yet the laws of that state provide for an attachment of this nature if the debtor, the garnishee, is found in the state, and the court obtains jurisdiction over him by the service of process therein; that the judgment, condemning the debt from Harris to Balk, was a valid judgment, provided Balk could himself have sued Harris for the debt in Maryland. This, it is asserted, he could have done, and the judgment was therefore entitled to full faith and credit in the courts of North Carolina.

The cases holding that the state court obtains no jurisdiction over the garnishee if he be but temporarily within the state proceed upon the theory that the situs of the debt is at the domicil either of the creditor or of the debtor, and that it does not follow the debtor in his casual or temporary journey into another state, and the garnishee has no possession of any property or credit of the principal debtor in the foreign state.

            *   *   *

Attachment is the creature of the local law; that is, unless there is a law of the state providing for and permitting the attachment, it cannot be levied there. If there be a law of the state providing for the attachment of the debt, then, if the garnishee be found in that state, and process be personally served upon him therein, we think the court thereby acquires jurisdiction over him, and can garnish the debt due from him to the debtor of the plaintiff, and condemn it, provided the garnishee could himself be sued by his creditor in that state. We do not see how the question of jurisdiction *vel non* can properly be made to depend upon the so-called original situs of the debt, or upon the character of the stay of the garnishee, whether temporary or permanent, in the state where the attachment is issued. Power over the person of the garnishee confers jurisdiction on the courts of the state where the writ issues. * * * If, while temporarily there, his creditor might sue him there and recover the debt, then he is liable to process of garnishment, no matter where the situs of the debt was originally. We do not see the materiality of the expression "situs of the debt," when used in connection with attachment proceedings. If by situs is meant the place of the creation of the debt, that fact is immaterial. If it be meant that the obligation to pay the debt can only be enforced at the situs thus fixed, we think it plainly untrue. The obligation of the debtor to pay his debt clings to and accompanies him wherever he goes. He is as much bound to pay his debt in a foreign state when therein sued upon his obligation by his creditor, as he was in the state where the debt was contracted. * * * It would be no defense to such suit for the debtor to plead that he was only in the foreign state casually or temporarily. * * * It is nothing but the obligation to pay which is garnished or attached. This obligation can be enforced by the courts of the foreign state after personal service of process therein, just as well as by the courts of the domicil of the debtor. If the debtor leave the foreign state without appearing, a judgment by default may be entered, upon which execution may issue, or the judgment may be sued upon in any other state where the debtor might be found. In such case the situs is unimportant. It is not a question of possession in the foreign state, for possession cannot be taken of a debt or of the obligation to pay it, as tangible property might be taken possession of. Notice to the debtor (garnishee) of the commencement of the suit, and notice not to pay to his creditor, is all that can be given, whether the garnishee be a mere casual and temporary comer, or a resident of the state where the attachment is laid. His obligation to pay to his creditor is thereby arrested, and a lien created upon the debt itself.   *   *   *

There can be no doubt that Balk, as a citizen of the state of North Carolina, had the right to sue Harris in Maryland to recover the debt which Harris owed him. Being a citizen of North Carolina, he was entitled to all the privileges and immunities of citizens of the several states, one of which is the right to institute actions in the courts of another state. The law of Maryland provides for the attachment of credits in a case like this.   *   *   *

It thus appears that Balk could have sued Harris in Maryland to recover his debt, notwithstanding the temporary character of Harris' stay there; it also appears that the municipal law of Maryland permits the debtor of the principal debtor to be garnished, and therefore if the court of the state where the garnishee is found obtains jurisdiction over him, through the service of process upon him within the state, then the judgment entered is a valid judgment. *   *   *

It seems to us, therefore, that the judgment against Harris in Maryland, condemning the $180 which he owed to Balk, was a valid judgment, because the court had jurisdiction over the garnishee by personal service of process within the state of Maryland.

It ought to be and it is the object of courts to prevent the payment of any debt twice over. Thus, if Harris, owing a debt to Balk, paid it under a valid judgment against him, to Epstein, he certainly ought not to be compelled to pay it a second time, but should have the right to plead his payment under the Maryland judgment. It is objected, however, that the payment by Harris to Epstein was not under legal compulsion. Harris in truth owed the debt to Balk, which was attached by Epstein. He had, therefore, as we have seen, no defense to set up against the attachment of the debt.   *   *   *   As he was absolutely without defense, there was no reason why he should not consent to a judgment impounding the debt, which judgment the plaintiff was legally entitled to, and which he could not prevent.   *   *   *

But most rights may be lost by negligence, and if the garnishee were guilty of negligence in the attachment proceeding, to the damage of Balk, he ought not to be permitted to set up the judgment as a defense. Thus it is recognized as the duty of the garnishee to give notice to his own creditor, if he would protect himself, so that the creditor may have the opportunity to defend himself against the claim of the person suing out the attachment. *   *   *   While the want of notification by the garnishee to his own creditor may have no effect upon the validity of the judgment against the garnishee (the proper publication being made by the plaintiff), we think it has and ought to have an effect upon the right of the garnishee to avail himself of the prior judgment and his payment thereunder. This notification by the garnishee is for the purpose of making sure that his creditor shall have an opportunity to defend the claim made against him in the attachment suit. Fair dealing requires this at the hands of the garnishee. In this case, while neither the defendant nor the garnishee appeared, the court, while condemning the credits attached, could not, by the terms of the Maryland statute, issue the writ of execution unless the plaintiff gave bond or sufficient security before the court awarding the execution, to make restitution of the money paid if the defendant should, at any time within a year and a day, appear in the action and show that the plaintiff's claim, or some part thereof, was not due to the plaintiff. The defendant in error, Balk, had notice of this attachment, certainly within a few days after the issuing thereof and the entry of judgment thereon, because he sued the plaintiff in error to recover his debt within a few days after his (Harris') return to North Carolina, in which suit the judgment in Maryland was set up by Harris as a plea in bar to Balk's claim. Balk, therefore, had an opportunity for a year and a day after the entry of the judgment to litigate the question of his liability in the Maryland court * * *. He, however, took no proceedings to that end, so far as the record shows, and the reason may be supposed to be that he could not successfully defend the claim, because he admitted in this case that he did, at the time of the attachment proceeding, owe Epstein some $344.

* * *

The judgment of the Supreme Court of North Carolina must be reversed, and the cause remanded for further proceedings not inconsistent with the opinion of this court.

Reversed.

Mr. Justice HARLAN and Mr. Justice DAY dissented.

NOTES AND QUESTIONS

1. SEIDER v. ROTH, 17 N.Y.2d 111, 269 N.Y.S.2d 99, 216 N.E.2d 312 (1966). Plaintiffs, residents of New York, were injured in an automobile accident in Vermont, allegedly as a result of the negligence of defendant Lemiux, who resided in Quebec. Plaintiffs sought to attach the contractual obligation of Hartford Accident and Indemnity Company to defend and indemnify Lemiux under an automobile liability insurance policy that had been issued in Canada. Hartford does business in New York and the attachment papers were served on it in New York; Lemiux was personally served in Quebec. In a four to three decision, the New York Court of Appeals upheld the attachment on the ground that the contractual obligation constituted a debt that was subject to attachment. The dissenters argued that "the so-called 'debt' * * * is a mere promise * * * to *defend and indemnify* the Canadian resident *if a suit is commenced* and *if damages are awarded* against the insured. * * * In other words, the promise to defend the insured is assumed to furnish the jurisdiction for a civil suit which must be validly commenced before the obligation to defend can possibly accrue." (Emphasis in original.) Is *Seider* distinguishable from *Harris*? The *Seider* case is noted in 51 Minn.L.Rev. 158; 33 Brooklyn L.Rev. 368; 18 Syracuse L.Rev. 631; 35 U.Cin.L.Rev. 691.

The New York Court of Appeals reaffirmed *Seider* in SIMPSON v. LOEHMANN, 21 N.Y.2d 305, 287 N.Y.S.2d 633, 234 N.E.2d 669 (1967). However, four separate opinions were written, none of which commanded a majority of the court and four of the seven judges labelled *Seider* unhealthy. The result in *Simpson* seems to have been reached strictly on the basis of stare decisis. Reading the opinions together, the New York court appears to have viewed the insurer as the real party of interest. In practical effect, therefore, the *Seider-Simpson* procedure establishes a right of action directly against the insurer despite the absence of any legislation to that effect in New York.

Among the many writings criticizing the two New York cases are Stein, *Jurisdiction by Attachment of Liability Insurance,* 43 N.Y.U.L.Rev. 1075 (1968); Comment, *Garnishment of Intangibles; Contingent Obligations and the Interstate Corporation,* 67 Colum.L.Rev. 550 (1967); Comment, *Jurisdiction in Rem and the Attachment of Intangibles: Erosion of the Power Theory,* 1968 Duke L.J. 725. Not surprisingly, one federal district court held the New York approach unconstitutional. Podolsky v. Devinney, 281 F.Supp. 488 (S.D.N.Y.1968).

In a per curiam opinion denying reargument in *Simpson,* 21 N.Y.2d 990, 238 N.E.2d 319, 290 N.Y.S.2d 914 (1968), the Court of Appeals attempted to protect the *Seider-Simpson* practice from constitutional challenge by stating that the value of the attached property would be limited by the face amount of the insurance policy and making it clear that the judgment could not exceed that amount even though the defendant appeared and defended on the merits. The latter point is particularly interesting since New York has a statute that seems to reject such a limitation on the effect of a defendant's appearance in quasi in rem actions. N.Y.C.P.L.R. § 320(c). See pages 179–86, infra on challenging the court's jurisdiction.

In light of these modifications, the Second Circuit, in an opinion by Judge Friendly, upheld the constitutionality of the *Seider-Simpson* practice. MINICHI-ELLO v. ROSENBERG, 410 F.2d 106 (2d Cir.1968). On rehearing in banc 410 F.2d 117 (2d Cir. 1969), certiorari denied 396 U.S. 844, 90 S.Ct. 69, 24 L.Ed. 2d 94 (1969), a majority of the court concluded that New York had the constitutional power to provide its residents a forum for an action against a nonresident involving an out-of-state accident by attaching the nonresident's interest in a liability insurance policy issued by an insurance company doing business in New York. In response to the contention that the *Seider-Simpson* procedure does not protect the out-of-state defendant when the claim exceeds the policy limits because the action will be taken to have adjudicated defendant's liability and then can be used against him in an action for the deficiency, Judge Friendly stated:

> * * * Whatever the right rule may be as to *quasi in rem* judgments generally, we think it clear that neither New York nor any other state could constitutionally give collateral estoppel effect to a *Seider* judgment when the whole theory behind this procedure is that it is in effect a direct action against the insurer and that the latter rather than the insured will conduct the defense. To be sure it may be cold comfort to a nonresident defendant to have our assurance that if some state should be so misguided as to consider a New York *Seider* judgment as concluding him, he will be able to have this ruling overturned by the Supreme Court of the United States. But we cannot fairly hold that New York has denied due process merely because of the possibility that some other state may do so.

Id. at 112.

Judge Anderson dissented strongly. The essence of his objection to the majority's conclusions is as follows:

> A balancing of considerations of fairness to the parties, of litigational convenience, and of the interests of the state (which is to say the interest of its citizens) (1) in compensating the injured party, both for his own sake and to prevent him from becoming a public charge, (2) in compensating its medical and other creditors, and (3) in deterring tortious conduct, leads, on the one hand to a finding that a direct action statute in the state where an accident occurs is fair and reasonable in the due process sense. On the other hand, a similar weighing of interests leads to the conclusion that a direct action statute purporting to provide a New York forum for a New York plaintiff, regardless of other local contacts or considerations, is unreasonable and parochial in the due process sense. It is one thing to require a resident of Alaska to make trips to New York to respond to an action arising out of an accident with a resident of New York in New York state to which the Alaskan had gone, and quite another to make him do so for an accident which occurred in Alaska when the New Yorker elected to go to Alaska and use its highways.

Id. at 116–17. Other cases holding the *Seider-Simpson* procedure constitutional include Rintala v. Shoemaker, 362 F.Supp. 1044 (D.Minn.1973); Turner v. Evers, 31 Cal.App.3d Supp. 11, 107 Cal.Rptr. 390 (Super.Ct.1973).

Would the *Seider-Simpson* procedure be constitutional if invoked by a nonresident of the forum state? See Farrell v. Piedmont Aviation, Inc., 295 F.Supp. 228 (S.D.N.Y.1968), affirmed 411 F.2d 812 (2d Cir.1969), certiorari denied 396 U.S. 840, 90 S.Ct. 103, 24 L.Ed.2d 91 (1969). See generally Rosenberg, *One Procedural Genie Too Many or Putting Seider Back Into Its Bottle,* 71 Colum. L.Rev. 660 (1971). Can the procedure be utilized to obtain jurisdiction when the claim that is asserted is unrelated to the insurer's liability on the policy or its duty to defend the insured?

2. Are there any limitations that should be placed on a court when it exercises jurisdiction under a *Seider* type attachment? Consider ROSENTHAL v. WARREN, 342 F.Supp. 246 (S.D.N.Y.1972), a wrongful death action by a New York domiciliary for the alleged negligence and malpractice of a doctor and a hospital. Quasi in rem jurisdiction in New York was obtained over the doctor, a citizen of Massachusetts, by attaching the obligation of the debtor's liability insurer. The operation that allegedly caused the death had been performed in Massachusetts. Defendants interposed an affirmative defense based on the Massachusetts Death Statute, which limited the damages that might be recovered. The court granted plaintiff's motion for a partial summary judgment striking that defense and held that New York law, which placed no dollar limit on recovery, governed. Is this decision sound?

SECTION C. THE REQUIREMENT OF REASONABLE NOTICE AND AN OPPORTUNITY TO BE HEARD

McDONALD v. MABEE, 243 U.S. 90, 91–92, 37 S.Ct. 343, 343–44, 61 L.Ed. 608, 609–10 (1917). In a suit upon a promissory note, defendant Mabee contended that a prior Texas judgment against him on the same note was a bar to the action. At the time the first action was commenced Mabee was a domiciliary of Texas and his family was residing in that state, but he had left the state with intent to establish a domicile elsewhere. Service in the earlier action was attempted through publication in a newspaper once a week for four successive weeks after Mabee's departure from the state; Mabee never appeared in the action. The United States Supreme Court, reversing the Texas Supreme Court, held that the prior Texas judgment was void under the Fourteenth Amendment:

> The foundation of jurisdiction is physical power, although in civilized times it is not necessary to maintain that power throughout proceedings properly begun, and although submission to the jurisdiction by appearance may take the place of service upon the person. * * * No doubt there may be some extension of the means of acquiring jurisdiction beyond service or appearance, but the foundation should be borne in mind. * * *

> There is no dispute that service by publication does not warrant a personal judgment against a nonresident. * * * When the former suit was begun, Mabee, although technically domiciled in Texas, had left the state intending to establish his home elsewhere. Perhaps in view of his technical position and the actual presence of his family in the state a summons left at his last and usual place of abode would have been enough. But it appears to us that an advertisement in a local newspaper is not sufficient notice to bind a person who has left a state intending not to return. To dispense with personal service the substitute that is most likely to reach the defendant is the least that ought to be required if substantial justice is to be done. We repeat also that the ground for giving subsequent effect to a judgment is that the court rendering it had acquired power to carry it out; and that it is going to the extreme to hold such power gained even by service at the last and usual place of abode.

In WUCHTER v. PIZZUTTI, 276 U.S. 13, 48 S.Ct. 259, 72 L.Ed. 446, 57 A.L.R. 1230 (1928), the Supreme Court invalidated a New Jersey nonresident-motorist statute similar to the one involved in *Hess v. Pawloski*, p. 74, supra, because it did not expressly require the Secretary of State to communicate notice of the commencement of the action to the nonresident. In fact, notice actually was given by the Secretary of State. According to the Supreme Court: "Every statute of this kind * * * should require the plaintiff bringing the suit to show in the summons to be served the post office address or residence of the defendant being sued, and should impose either on the plaintiff himself or upon the official receiving service or some other, the duty of communication by mail or otherwise with the defendant." Justices Brandeis, Holmes, and Stone dissented. Compare Washington ex rel. Bond & Goodwin & Tucker, Inc. v. Superior Court, 289 U.S. 361, 53 S.Ct. 624, 77 L. Ed. 1256, 89 A.L.R. 653 (1933) (*Wuchter* held inapplicable to statute providing for service on foreign corporation).

MULLANE v. CENTRAL HANOVER BANK & TRUST CO.

Supreme Court of the United States, 1950.
339 U.S. 306, 70 S.Ct. 652, 94 L.Ed. 865.

Appeal from the Court of Appeals of New York.

Mr. Justice JACKSON delivered the opinion of the Court.

This controversy questions the constitutional sufficiency of notice to beneficiaries on judicial settlement of accounts by the trustee of a common trust fund established under the New York Banking Law * * *. The New York Court of Appeals considered and overruled objections that the statutory notice contravenes requirements of the Fourteenth Amendment and that by allowance of the account beneficiaries were deprived of property without due process of law. * * * The case is here on appeal * * *.

Common trust fund legislation is addressed to a problem appropriate for state action. Mounting overheads have made administration of small trusts undesirable to corporate trustees. In order that donors and testators of moderately sized trusts may not be denied the service of corporate fiduciaries, the District of Columbia and some thirty states other than New York have permitted pooling small trust estates into one fund for investment administration. The income, capital gains, losses and expenses of the collective trust are shared by the constituent trusts in proportion to their contribution. By this plan, diversification of risk and economy of management can be extended to those whose capital standing alone would not obtain such advantage.

Statutory authorization for the establishment of such common trust funds is provided in the New York Banking Law, § 100–c * * *. Under this Act a trust company may, with approval of the State Banking Board, establish a common fund and, within prescribed limits, invest therein the assets of an unlimited number of estates, trusts or other funds of which it is trustee. Each participating trust shares ratably in the common fund, but exclusive management and control is in the trust company as trustee, and neither a fiduciary nor any beneficiary of a participating trust is deemed to have ownership in any particular asset or investment of this common fund. The trust company must keep fund assets separate from its own, and in its fiduciary capacity may not deal with itself or any affiliate. Provisions are made for accountings twelve to fifteen months after the establishment of a fund and triennially thereafter. The decree in each such judicial settlement of accounts is made binding and conclusive as to any matter set forth in the account upon everyone having any interest in the common fund or in any participating estate, trust or fund.

Trust affected by Judicial Settlement

In January, 1946, Central Hanover Bank and Trust Company established a common trust fund in accordance with these provisions, and in March, 1947, it petitioned the Surrogate's Court for settlement of its first account as common trustee. During the accounting period a total of 113 trusts, approximately half *inter vivos* and half testamentary, participated in the common trust fund, the gross capital of which was nearly three million dollars. The record does not show the number or residence of the beneficiaries, but they were many and it is clear that some of them were not residents of the State of New York.

Notice of settlement by Publication.

1 a week for 4 weeks

The only notice given beneficiaries of this specific application was by publication in a local newspaper in strict compliance with the minimum requirements of N. Y. Banking Law § 100–c(12): "After filing such petition [for judicial settlement of its account] the petitioner shall cause to be issued by the court in which the petition is filed and shall publish not less than once in each week for four successive weeks in a newspaper to be designated by the court a notice or citation addressed generally without naming them to all parties interested in such common trust fund and in such estates, trusts or funds mentioned in the petition, all of which may be described in the notice or citation only in the manner set forth in said petition and without setting forth the residence of any such decedent or donor of any such estate, trust or fund."

Summary of notice

Thus the only notice required, and the only one given, was by newspaper publication setting forth merely the name and address of the trust company, the name and the date of establishment of the common trust fund, and a list of all participating estates, trusts or funds.

At the time the first investment in the common fund was made on behalf of each participating estate, however, the trust company, pursuant to the requirements of § 100–c(9), had notified by mail each person of full age and sound mind whose name and address was then known to it and who was "entitled to share in the income therefrom * * * [or] * * * who would be entitled to share in the principal if the event upon which such estate, trust or fund will become distributable should have occurred at the time of sending such notice." Included in the notice was a copy of those provisions of the Act relating to the sending of the notice itself and to the judicial settlement of common trust fund accounts.

Upon the filing of the petition for the settlement of accounts, appellant was, by order of the court pursuant to § 100–c(12), appointed special guardian and attorney for all persons known or unknown not otherwise appearing who had or might thereafter have any interest in the income of the common trust fund; and appellee Vaughan was appointed to represent those similarly interested in the principal.   There were no other appearances on behalf of any one interested in either interest or principal.

Appellant appeared specially, objecting that notice and the statutory provisions for notice to beneficiaries were inadequate to afford due process under the Fourteenth Amendment, and therefore that the court was without jurisdiction to render a final and binding decree.   Appellant's objections were entertained and overruled, the Surrogate holding that the notice required and given was sufficient.   *   *   *   A final decree accepting the accounts has been entered, affirmed by the Appellate Division of the Supreme Court   *   *   * and by the Court of Appeals of the State of New York   *   *   *.

The effect of this decree, as held below, is to settle "all questions respecting the management of the common fund."   We understand that every right which beneficiaries would otherwise have against the trust company, either as trustee of the common fund or as trustee of any individual trust, for improper management of the common trust fund during the period covered by the accounting is sealed and wholly terminated by the decree.   *   *   *

We are met at the outset with a challenge to the power of the State—the right of its courts to adjudicate at all as against those beneficiaries who reside without the State of New York.   It is contended that the proceeding is one *in personam* in that the decree affects neither title to nor possession of any *res*, but adjudges only personal rights of the beneficiaries to surcharge their trustee for negligence or breach of trust.   Accordingly, it is said, under the strict doctrine of Pennoyer v. Neff   *   *   *   the Surrogate is without jurisdiction as to nonresidents upon whom personal service of process was not made.

Distinctions between actions *in rem* and those *in personam* are ancient and originally expressed in procedural terms what seems really to have been a distinction in the substantive law of property under a system quite unlike our own.   *   *   *   The legal recognition and rise in economic importance of incorporeal or intangible forms of property have upset the ancient simplicity of property law and the clarity of its distinctions, while new forms of proceedings have confused the old procedural classification.   American courts have sometimes classed certain actions as *in rem* because personal service of process was not required, and at other times have held personal service of process not required because the action was *in rem*.   *   *   *

Judicial proceedings to settle fiduciary accounts have been sometimes termed *in rem*, or more indefinitely *quasi in rem*, or more vaguely still, "in the nature of a proceeding *in rem*."   It is not readily apparent how the courts of New York did or would classify the present proceeding, which has some characteristics and is wanting in some features of proceedings both *in rem* and *in personam*.   But in any event we think that the requirements of the Fourteenth Amendment to the Federal Constitution do not depend upon a classification for which the standards are so elusive and confused generally and which, being primarily for state courts to define, may and do vary from state to state.   Without disparaging the usefulness of distinctions between actions *in rem* and those

Fiduciary accts:
in rem
quasi in rem   } ?
in nature of in rem

in personam in many branches of law, or on other issues, or the reasoning which underlies them, we do not rest the power of the State to resort to constructive service in this proceeding upon how its courts or this Court may regard this historic antithesis. It is sufficient to observe that, whatever the technical definition of its chosen procedure, the interest of each state in providing means to close trusts that exist by the grace of its laws and are administered under the supervision of its courts is so insistent and rooted in custom as to establish beyond doubt the right of its courts to determine the interests of all claimants, resident or nonresident, provided its procedure accords full opportunity to appear and be heard.

Quite different from the question of a state's power to discharge trustees is that of the opportunity it must give beneficiaries to contest. Many controversies have raged about the cryptic and abstract words of the Due Process Clause but there can be no doubt that at a minimum they require that deprivation of life, liberty or property by adjudication be preceded by notice and opportunity for hearing appropriate to the nature of the case.

In two ways this proceeding does or may deprive beneficiaries of property. It may cut off their rights to have the trustee answer for negligent or illegal impairments of their interests. Also, their interests are presumably subject to diminution in the proceeding by allowance of fees and expenses to one who, in their names but without their knowledge, may conduct a fruitless or uncompensatory contest. Certainly the proceeding is one in which they may be deprived of property rights and hence notice and hearing must measure up to the standards of due process.

Personal service of written notice within the jurisdiction is the classic form of notice always adequate in any type of proceeding. But the vital interest of the State in bringing any issues as to its fiduciaries to a final settlement can be served only if interests or claims of individuals who are outside of the State can somehow be determined. A construction of the Due Process Clause which would place impossible or impractical obstacles in the way could not be justified.

Against this interest of the State we must balance the individual interest sought to be protected by the Fourteenth Amendment. This is defined by our holding that "The fundamental requisite of due process of law is the opportunity to be heard." Grannis v. Ordean, 234 U.S. 385, 394, 34 S.Ct. 779, 783, 58 L.Ed. 1363. This right to be heard has little reality or worth unless one is informed that the matter is pending and can choose for himself whether to appear or default, acquiesce or contest.

The Court has not committed itself to any formula achieving a balance between these interests in a particular proceeding or determining when constructive notice may be utilized or what test it must meet. Personal service has not in all circumstances been regarded as indispensable to the process due to residents, and it has more often been held unnecessary as to nonresidents.
* * *

An elementary and fundamental requirement of due process in any proceeding which is to be accorded finality is notice reasonably calculated, under all the circumstances, to apprise interested parties of the pendency of the action and afford them an opportunity to present their objections. * * * The notice must be of such nature as reasonably to convey the required information * * * and it must afford a reasonable time for those interested to make their appearance * * *. But if with due regard for the practicalities and peculiarities of the case these conditions are reasonably met the constitutional requirements are satisfied. * * *

But when notice is a person's due, process which is a mere gesture is not due process. The means employed must be such as one desirous of actually informing the absentee might reasonably adopt to accomplish it. The reasonableness and hence the constitutional validity of any chosen method may be defended on the ground that it is in itself reasonably certain to inform those affected, compare Hess v. Pawloski * * * with Wuchter v. Pizzutti * * *, or, where conditions do not reasonably permit such notice, that the form chosen is not substantially less likely to bring home notice than other of the feasible and customary substitutes.

It would be idle to pretend that publication alone as prescribed here, is a reliable means of acquainting interested parties of the fact that their rights are before the courts. It is not an accident that the greater number of cases reaching this Court on the question of adequacy of notice have been concerned with actions founded on process constructively served through local newspapers. Chance alone brings to the attention of even a local resident an advertisement in small type inserted in the back pages of a newspaper, and if he makes his home outside the area of the newspaper's normal circulation the odds that the information will never reach him are large indeed. The chance of actual notice is further reduced when as here the notice required does not even name those whose attention it is supposed to attract, and does not inform acquaintances who might call it to attention. In weighing its sufficiency on the basis of equivalence with actual notice we are unable to regard this as more than a feint.

Nor is publication here reinforced by steps likely to attract the parties' attention to the proceeding. It is true that publication traditionally has been acceptable as notification supplemental to other action which in itself may reasonably be expected to convey a warning. The ways of an owner with tangible property are such that he usually arranges means to learn of any direct attack upon his possessory or proprietary rights. Hence, libel of a ship, attachment of a chattel or entry upon real estate in the name of law may reasonably be expected to come promptly to the owner's attention. When the state within which the owner has located such property seizes it for some reason, publication or posting affords an additional measure of notification. A state may indulge the assumption that one who has left tangible property in the state either has abandoned it, in which case proceedings against it deprive him of nothing * * * or that he has left some caretaker under a duty to let him know that it is being jeopardized. * * *

In the case before us there is, of course, no abandonment. On the other hand these beneficiaries do have a resident fiduciary as caretaker of their interest in this property. But it is their caretaker who in the accounting becomes their adversary. Their trustee is released from giving notice of jeopardy, and no one else is expected to do so. Not even the special guardian is required or apparently expected to communicate with his ward and client, and, of course, if such a duty were merely transferred from the trustee to the guardian, economy would not be served and more likely the cost would be increased.

This Court has not hesitated to approve of resort to publication as a customary substitute in another class of cases where it is not reasonably possible or practicable to give more adequate warning. Thus it has been recognized that, in the case of persons missing or unknown, employment of an indirect and even a probably futile means of notification is all that the situation permits and creates no constitutional bar to a final decree foreclosing their rights. * * *

Those beneficiaries represented by appellant whose interests or whereabouts could not with due diligence be ascertained come clearly within this category. As to them the statutory notice is sufficient. However great the odds that publication will never reach the eyes of such unknown parties, it is not in the typical case much more likely to fail than any of the choices open to legislators endeavoring to prescribe the best notice practicable.

Nor do we consider it unreasonable for the State to dispense with more certain notice to those beneficiaries whose interests are either conjectural or future or, although they could be discovered upon investigation, do not in due course of business come to knowledge of the common trustee. Whatever searches might be required in another situation under ordinary standards of diligence, in view of the character of the proceedings and the nature of the interests here involved we think them unnecessary. We recognize the practical difficulties and costs that would be attendant on frequent investigations into the status of great numbers of beneficiaries, many of whose interests in the common fund are so remote as to be ephemeral; and we have no doubt that such impracticable and extended searches are not required in the name of due process. The expense of keeping informed from day to day of substitutions among even current income beneficiaries and presumptive remaindermen, to say nothing of the far greater number of contingent beneficiaries, would impose a severe burden on the plan, and would likely dissipate its advantages. These are practical matters in which we should be reluctant to disturb the judgment of the state authorities.

Accordingly we overrule appellant's constitutional objections to published notice insofar as they are urged on behalf of any beneficiaries whose interests or addresses are unknown to the trustee.

As to known present beneficiaries of known place of residence, however, notice by publication stands on a different footing. Exceptions in the name of necessity do not sweep away the rule that within the limits of practicability notice must be such as is reasonably calculated to reach interested parties. Where the names and post office addresses of those affected by a proceeding are at hand, the reasons disappear for resort to means less likely than the mails to apprise them of its pendency.

The trustee has on its books the names and addresses of the income beneficiaries represented by appellant, and we find no tenable ground for dispensing with a serious effort to inform them personally of the accounting, at least by ordinary mail to the record addresses. * * * Certainly sending them a copy of the statute months and perhaps years in advance does not answer this purpose. The trustee periodically remits their income to them, and we think that they might reasonably expect that with or apart from their remittances word might come to them personally that steps were being taken affecting their interests.

We need not weigh contentions that a requirement of personal service of citation on even the large number of known resident or nonresident beneficiaries would, by reasons of delay if not of expense, seriously interfere with the proper administration of the fund. Of course personal service even without the jurisdiction of the issuing authority serves the end of actual and personal notice, whatever power of compulsion it might lack. However, no such service is required under the circumstances. This type of trust presupposes a large number of small interests. The individual interest does not stand alone but is identical with that of a class. The rights of each in the integrity of the fund and the fidelity of the trustee are shared by many other beneficiaries. Therefore notice reasonably certain to reach most of those interested in objecting is likely to safeguard the interests of all, since any objections sustained would inure to the benefit of all. We think that under such circumstances reasonable risks that notice might not actually reach every beneficiary are justifiable.
* * *

The statutory notice to known beneficiaries is inadequate, not because in fact it fails to reach everyone, but because under the circumstances it is not reasonably calculated to reach those who could easily be informed by other means at hand. However it may have been in former times, the mails today are recognized as an efficient and inexpensive means of communication. Moreover, the fact that the trust company has been able to give mailed notice to known beneficiaries at the time the common trust fund was established is persuasive that postal notification at the time of accounting would not seriously burden the plan.

We hold the notice of judicial settlement of accounts required by the New York Banking Law § 100–c(12) is incompatible with the requirements of the Fourteenth Amendment as a basis for adjudication depriving known persons whose whereabouts are also known of substantial property rights. Accordingly the judgment is reversed and the cause remanded for further proceedings not inconsistent with this opinion.

Reversed.

Mr. Justice DOUGLAS took no part in the consideration or decision of this case.

[The dissenting opinion of Mr. Justice BURTON is omitted.]

NOTES AND QUESTIONS

1. In WALKER v. CITY OF HUTCHINSON, 352 U.S. 112, 116, 77 S.Ct. 200, 202, 1 L.Ed.2d 178, 182 (1956), appellant's land was taken by condemnation by the City of Hutchinson, Kansas. Notice of the proceeding was given by publication in the official city paper of Hutchinson. After the time for appealing the condemnation report had run, Walker commenced an equitable proceeding in a Kansas state court alleging that he never had been notified of the condemnation proceeding and that the newspaper publication, which was authorized by Kansas statute, was not sufficient notice to satisfy the Fourteenth Amendment. The Kansas courts denied Walker's request to enjoin the City of Hutchinson from entering or trespassing on the property. The United States Supreme Court reversed, stating in part:

> Measured by the principles stated in the Mullane case, we think that the notice by publication here falls short of the requirements of due process. * * * In Mullane we pointed out many of the infirmities of such notice and emphasized the advantage of some kind of personal notice to interested parties. In the present case there seem to be no compelling or even persuasive reasons why such direct notice cannot be given. Appellant's name was known to the city and was on the official records. Even a letter would have apprised him that his property was about to be taken and that he must appear if he wanted to be heard as to its value.

The implications of *Walker* are discussed in Comment, *In Rem Actions—Adequacy of Notice*, 25 Tenn.L.Rev. 495 (1958).

2. A similar case is SCHROEDER v. CITY OF NEW YORK, 371 U.S. 208, 83 S.Ct. 279, 9 L.Ed.2d 255, 89 A.L.R.2d 1398 (1962), which involved an attempt by New York City to acquire the right to divert water from a river that flowed through Mrs. Schroeder's land. Despite the fact that her name and address were readily ascertainable from public records, no attempt at personal notice was made. Instead, notice of the city's acquisition was published in several newspapers with limited circulations and notices were posted on trees along the river. Neither the newspapers nor the notices carried Mrs. Schroeder's name and no notices were posted on her land. The Supreme Court held the New York scheme unconstitutional.

3. Can *Mullane*, *Walker*, and *Schroeder* be reconciled with the statement in *Pennoyer*, p. 65, supra, that "substituted service by publication, or in any other authorized form, may be sufficient to inform parties of the object of proceedings taken where property is once brought under the control of the court by seizure or some equivalent act"? In light of these decisions are there any instances in which it is safe to say that attachment plus publication is a sufficient procedure to establish jurisdiction? Should the fact that a state has a significant interest in the speedy and final termination of particular disputes relating to realty or personalty within its borders, as in probate proceedings, have an effect on the constitutionality of the kind of notice given to potential claimants? See Stevens v. Torregano, 192 Cal.App.2d 105, 13 Cal.Rptr. 604 (1st Dist.1961). Should the intelligence or the actual reading habits of a particular defendant be relevant?

FUENTES v. SHEVIN

Supreme Court of the United States, 1972.
407 U.S. 67, 92 S.Ct. 1983, 32 L.Ed.2d 556.

Appeal from the United States District Court for the Southern District of Florida.

Mr. Justice STEWART delivered the opinion of the Court.

*   *   *

I

The appellant in No. 5039, Margarita Fuentes, is a resident of Florida. She purchased a gas stove and service policy from the Firestone Tire and Rubber Company (Firestone) under a conditional sales contract calling for monthly payments over a period of time. A few months later, she purchased a stereophonic phonograph from the same company under the same sort of contract. The total cost of the stove and stereo was about $500, plus an additional financing charge of over $100. Under the contracts, Firestone retained title to the merchandise, but Mrs. Fuentes was entitled to possession unless and until she should default on her installment payments.

For more than a year, Mrs. Fuentes made her installment payments. But then, with only about $200 remaining to be paid, a dispute developed between her and Firestone over the servicing of the stove. Firestone instituted an action in a small claims court for repossession of both the stove and the stereo, claiming that Mrs. Fuentes had refused to make her remaining payments. Simultaneously with the filing of that action and before Mrs. Fuentes had even received a summons to answer its complaint, Firestone obtained a writ of replevin ordering a sheriff to seize the disputed goods at once.

*   *   *

Shortly thereafter, Mrs. Fuentes instituted the present action in a federal district court, challenging the constitutionality of the Florida prejudgment replevin procedures under the Due Process Clause of the Fourteenth Amendment. She sought declaratory and injunctive relief against continued enforcement of the procedural provisions of the state statutes that authorize prejudgment replevin.

The appellants in No. 5138 filed a very similar action in a federal district court in Pennsylvania, challenging the constitutionality of that State's prejudgment replevin process. Like Mrs. Fuentes, they had had possessions seized under writs of replevin. Three of the appellants had purchased personal property—a bed, a table, and other household goods—under installment sales contracts like the one signed by Mrs. Fuentes; and the sellers of the property had obtained and executed summary writs of replevin, claiming that the appellants had fallen behind in their installment payments. The experience of the fourth appellant, Rosa Washington, had been more bizarre. She had been divorced from a local deputy sheriff and was engaged in a dispute with him over the custody of their son. Her former husband, being familiar with the routine forms used in the replevin process, had obtained a writ that ordered the seizure of the boy's clothes, furniture, and toys.

In both No. 5039 and No. 5138, three-judge district courts were convened to consider the appellants' challenges to the constitutional validity of the Florida and Pennsylvania statutes. The courts in both cases upheld the constitutionality of the statutes. * * * [5]

II

Under the Florida statute challenged here, "[a]ny person whose goods or chattels are wrongfully detained by any other person * * * may have a writ of replevin to recover them * * *." Fla.Stats. § 78.01, F.S.A. There is no requirement that the applicant make a convincing showing before the seizure that the goods are, in fact, "wrongfully detained." Rather, Florida law * * * requires only that the applicant file a complaint, initiating a court action for repossession and reciting in conclusory fashion that he is "lawfully entitled to the possession" of the property, and that he file a security bond * * *. On the sole basis of the complaint and bond, a writ is issued "command[ing] the officer to whom it may be directed to replevy the goods and chattels in possession of defendant * * * and to summon the defendant to answer the complaint." Fla.Stats. § 78.08. If the goods are "in any dwelling house or other building or enclosure," the officer is required to demand their delivery; but if they are not delivered, "he shall cause such house, building or enclosure to be broken open and shall make replevin according to the writ * * *." Fla.Stats. § 78.10, F.S.A.

Thus, at the same moment that the defendant receives the complaint seeking repossession of property through court action, the property is seized from him. He is provided no prior notice and allowed no opportunity whatever to challenge the issuance of the writ. *After* the property has been seized, he will eventually have an opportunity for a hearing, as the defendant in the trial of the court action for repossession, which the plaintiff is required to pursue. And he is also not wholly without recourse in the meantime. For under the Florida statute, the officer who seizes the property must keep it for three days, and during that period the defendant may reclaim possession of the property by posting his own security bond in double

---

[5] Since the announcement of this Court's decision in Sniadach v. Family Finance Corp., 395 U.S. 337, 89 S.Ct. 1820, 23 L.Ed.2d 349 summary prejudgment remedies have come under constitutional challenge throughout the country. The summary deprivation of property under statutes very similar to the Florida and Pennsylvania statutes at issue here has been held unconstitutional by at least two courts. * * * Applying *Sniadach* to other closely related forms of summary prejudgment remedies, some courts have construed that decision as setting forth general principles of procedural due process and have struck down such remedies. * * * Other courts, however, have construed *Sniadach* as closely confined to its own facts and have upheld such summary prejudgment remedies. * * *

its value. But if he does not post such a bond, the property is transferred to
the party who sought the writ, pending a final judgment in the underlying
action for repossession.   *   *   *

The Pennsylvania law differs, though not in its essential nature, from
that of Florida. As in Florida, a private party may obtain a prejudgment
writ of replevin through a summary process of *ex parte* application, although
a prothonotary rather than a court clerk issues the writ. As in Florida, the
party seeking the writ may simply post with his application a bond in double
the value of the property to be seized.   *   *   *   There is no opportunity for a prior hearing and no prior notice to the other party. On this basis,
a sheriff is required to execute the writ by seizing the specified property.
Unlike the Florida statute, however, the Pennsylvania law does not require
that there *ever* be opportunity for a hearing on the merits of the conflicting
claims to possession of the replevied property. The party seeking the writ
is not obliged to initiate a court action for repossession. Indeed, he need
not even formally allege that he is lawfully entitled to the property.   *   *   *
If the party who loses property through replevin seizure is to get even a post-
seizure hearing, he must initiate a lawsuit himself. He may also, as under
Florida law, post his own counterbond within three days after the seizure to
regain possession.   *   *   *

III

*   *   *

Prejudgment replevin statutes like those of Florida and Pennsylvania
are derived from this ancient possessory action [common law replevin] in
that they authorize the seizure of property before a final judgment. But
the similarity ends there. As in the present cases, such statutes are most commonly used by creditors to seize goods allegedly wrongfully detained—not
wrongfully taken—by debtors. At common law, if a creditor wished to invoke state power to recover goods wrongfully detained, he had to proceed
through the action of debt or detinue. These actions, however, did not provide for a return of property before final judgment. And, more importantly,
on the occasions when the common law did allow prejudgment seizure by
state power, it provided some kind of notice and opportunity to be heard
to the party then in possession of the property, and a state official made
at least a summary determination of the relative rights of the disputing
parties before stepping into the dispute and taking goods from one of them.

IV

For more than a century the central meaning of procedural due process has been clear: "Parties whose rights are to be affected are entitled to
be heard; and in order that they may enjoy that right they must be notified." Baldwin v. Hale, 68 U.S. 223, 1 Wall. 223, 17 L.Ed. 531.   *   *   *
It is equally fundamental that the right to notice and an opportunity to be

heard "must be granted at a meaningful time and in a meaningful manner." Armstrong v. Manzo, 380 U.S. 545, 552, 85 S.Ct. 1187, 1191, 14 L.Ed.2d 62.

The primary question in the present cases is whether these state statutes are constitutionally defective in failing to provide for hearings "at a meaningful time." The Florida replevin process guarantees an opportunity for a hearing after the seizure of goods, and the Pennsylvania process allows a post-seizure hearing if the aggrieved party shoulders the burden of initiating one. But neither the Florida nor Pennsylvania statute provides for notice or an opportunity to be heard *before* the seizure. * * *

The constitutional right to be heard is a basic aspect of the duty of government to follow a fair process of decisionmaking when it acts to deprive a person of his possessions. The purpose of this requirement is not only to ensure abstract fair play to the individual. Its purpose, more particularly, is to protect his use and possession of property from arbitrary encroachment— to minimize substantively unfair or mistaken deprivations of property, a danger that is especially great when the State seizes goods simply upon the application of and for the benefit of a private party. So viewed, the prohibition against the deprivation of property without due process of law reflects the high value, embedded in our constitutional and political history, that we place on a person's right to enjoy what is his, free of governmental interference. * * *

The requirement of notice and an opportunity to be heard raises no impenetrable barrier to the taking of a person's possessions. But the fair process of decision-making that it guarantees works, by itself, to protect against arbitrary deprivation of property. For when a person has an opportunity to speak up in his own defense, and when the State must listen to what he has to say, substantively unfair and simply mistaken deprivations of property interests can be prevented. It has long been recognized that "fairness can rarely be obtained by secret, one-sided determination of facts decisive of rights. * * * [And n]o better instrument has been devised for arriving at truth than to give a person in jeopardy of serious loss notice of the case against him and opportunity to meet it." Joint Anti-Fascist Refugee Committee v. McGrath, 341 U.S. 123, 170–172, 71 S.Ct. 624, 647, 95 L.Ed. 817 (Frankfurter, J., concurring).

If the right to notice and a hearing is to serve its full purpose, then, it is clear that it must be granted at a time when the deprivation can still be prevented. At a later hearing, an individual's possessions can be returned to him if they were unfairly or mistakenly taken in the first place. Damages may even be awarded to him for the wrongful deprivation. But no later hearing and no damage award can undo the fact that the arbitrary taking that was subject to the right of procedural due process has already occurred. "This Court has not * * * embraced the general proposition that a wrong may be done if it can be undone." Stanley v. Illinois, 405 U.S. 645, 647, 92 S.Ct. 1208, 1210, 31 L.Ed.2d 551.

This is no new principle of constitutional law. The right to a prior hearing has long been recognized by this Court under the Fourteenth and Fifth Amendments. Although the Court has held that due process tolerates variances in the *form* of a hearing "appropriate to the nature of the case," Mullane v. Central Hanover Tr. Co.,   *   *   *   and "depending upon the importance of the interests involved and the nature of the subsequent proceedings [if any]," Boddie v. Connecticut, 401 U.S. 371, 378, 91 S.Ct. 780, 786, 28 L.Ed.2d 113, the Court has traditionally insisted that, whatever its form, opportunity for that hearing must be provided before the deprivation at issue takes effect.   *   *   *   "That the hearing required by due process is subject to waiver, and is not fixed in form does not affect its root requirement that an individual be given an opportunity for a hearing *before* he is deprived of any significant property interest, except for extraordinary situations where some valid governmental interest is at stake that justifies postponing the hearing until after the event." Boddie v. Connecticut, *supra*, 401 U.S., at 378–379, 91 S.Ct., at 786 (emphasis in original).

The Florida and Pennsylvania prejudgment replevin statutes fly in the face of this principle. To be sure, the requirements that a party seeking a writ must first post a bond, allege conclusorily that he is entitled to specific goods, and open himself to possible liability in damages if he is wrong, serve to deter wholly unfounded applications for a writ. But those requirements are hardly a substitute for a prior hearing, for they test no more than the strength of the applicant's own belief in his rights.[13] Since his private gain is at stake, the danger is all too great that his confidence in his cause will be misplaced. Lawyers and judges are familiar with the phenomenon of a party mistakenly but firmly convinced that his view of the facts and law will prevail, and therefore quite willing to risk the costs of litigation. Because of the understandable, self-interested fallibility of litigants, a court does not decide a dispute until it has had an opportunity to hear both sides—and does not generally take even tentative action until it has itself examined the support for the plaintiff's position. The Florida and Pennsylvania statutes do not even require the official issuing a writ of replevin to do that much.

The minimal deterrent effect of a bond requirement is, in a practical sense, no substitute for an informed evaluation by a neutral official. More specifically, as a matter of constitutional principle, it is no replacement for the right to a prior hearing that is the only truly effective safeguard against arbitrary deprivation of property. While the existence of these other, less effective, safeguards may be among the considerations that affect the form of hearing demanded by due process, they are far from enough by themselves to obviate the right to a prior hearing of some kind.

13 They may not even test that much. For if an applicant for the writ knows that he is dealing with an uneducated, uninformed consumer with little access to legal help and little familiarity with legal procedures, there may be a substantial possibility that a summary seizure of property—however unwarranted—may go unchallenged, and the applicant may feel that he can act with impunity.

V

The right to a prior hearing, of course, attaches only to the deprivation of an interest encompassed within the Fourteenth Amendment's protection. In the present cases, the Florida and Pennsylvania statutes were applied to replevy chattels in the appellants' possession. The replevin was not cast as a final judgment; most, if not all, of the appellants lacked full title to the chattels; and their claim even to continued possession was a matter in dispute. Moreover, the chattels at stake were nothing more than an assortment of household goods. Nonetheless, it is clear that the appellants were deprived of possessory interests in those chattels that were within the protection of the Fourteenth Amendment.

A

A deprivation of a person's possessions under a prejudgment writ of replevin, at least in theory, may be only temporary. The Florida and Pennsylvania statutes do not require a person to wait until a post-seizure hearing and final judgment to recover what has been replevied. Within three days after the seizure, the statutes allow him to recover the goods if he, in return, surrenders other property—a payment necessary to secure a bond in double the value of the goods seized from him.[14] But it is now well settled that a temporary, nonfinal deprivation of property is nonetheless a "deprivation" in the terms of the Fourteenth Amendment. * * *

* * * When officials of Florida or Pennsylvania seize one piece of property from a person's possession and then agree to return it if he surrenders another, they deprive him of property whether or not he has the funds, the knowledge and the time needed to take advantage of the recovery provision. The Fourteenth Amendment draws no bright lines around three-day, 10-day or 50-day deprivations of property. Any significant taking of property by the State is within the purview of the Due Process Clause. While the length and consequent severity of a deprivation may be another factor to weigh in determining the appropriate form of hearing, it is not decisive of the basic right to a prior hearing of some kind.

B

The appellants who signed conditional sales contracts lacked full legal title to the replevied goods. The Fourteenth Amendment's protection of "property," however, has never been interpreted to safeguard only the rights

---

14 The appellants argue that this opportunity for quick recovery exists only in theory. They allege that very few people in their position are able to obtain a recovery bond, even if they know of the possibility. Appellant Fuentes says that in her case she was never told that she could recover the stove and stereo and that the deputy sheriff seizing them gave them at once to the Firestone agent, rather than holding them for three days. She further asserts that of 442 cases of prejudgment replevin in small claims courts in Dade County, Florida, in 1969, there was not one case in which the defendant took advantage of the recovery provision.

of undisputed ownership. Rather, it has been read broadly to extend protection to "any significant property interest" * * *.

The appellants were deprived of such an interest in the replevied goods —the interest in continued possession and use of the goods. * * * They had acquired this interest under the conditional sales contracts that entitled them to possession and use of the chattels before transfer of title. In exchange for immediate possession, the appellants had agreed to pay a major financing charge beyond the basic price of the merchandise. Moreover, by the time the goods were summarily repossessed, they had made substantial installment payments. Clearly, their possessory interest in the goods, dearly bought and protected by contract, was sufficient to invoke the protection of the Due Process Clause.

Their ultimate right to continued possession was, of course, in dispute. If it were shown at a hearing that the appellants had defaulted on their contractual obligations, it might well be that the sellers of the goods would be entitled to repossession. But even assuming that the appellants had fallen behind in their installment payments, and that they had no other valid defenses, that is immaterial here. The right to be heard does not depend upon an advance showing that one will surely prevail at the hearing. * * *

C

Nevertheless, the district courts rejected the appellants' constitutional claim on the ground that the goods seized from them—a stove, a stereo, a table, a bed, and so forth—were not deserving of due process protection, since they were not absolute necessities of life. The courts based this holding on a very narrow reading of Sniadach v. Family Finance Corp., supra, and Goldberg v. Kelly, * * * [397 U.S. 254, 90 S.Ct. 1011, 25 L.Ed. 2d 287 (1970)], in which this Court held that the Constitution requires a hearing before prejudgment wage garnishment and before the termination of certain welfare benefits. They reasoned that *Sniadach* and *Goldberg*, as a matter of constitutional principle, established no more than that a prior hearing is required with respect to the deprivation of such basically "necessary" items as wages and welfare benefits.

This reading of *Sniadach* and *Goldberg* reflects the premise that those cases marked a radical departure from established principles of procedural due process. They did not. Both decisions were in the mainstream of past cases, having little or nothing to do with the absolute "necessities" of life but establishing that due process requires an opportunity for a hearing before a deprivation of property takes effect. * * * While *Sniadach* and *Goldberg* emphasized the special importance of wages and welfare benefits, they did not convert that emphasis into a new and more limited constitutional doctrine.

* * *

VI

There are "extraordinary situations" that justify postponing notice and opportunity for a hearing. Boddie v. Connecticut, supra, 401 U.S., at 379, 91 S.Ct., at 786. These situations, however, must be truly unusual. Only in a few limited situations has this Court allowed outright seizure without opportunity for a prior hearing. First, in each case, the seizure has been directly necessary to secure an important governmental or general public interest. Second, there has been a special need for very prompt action. Third, the State has kept strict control over its monopoly of legitimate force; the person initiating the seizure has been a government official responsible for determining, under the standards of a narrowly drawn statute, that it was necessary and justified in the particular instance. Thus, the Court has allowed summary seizure of property to collect the internal revenue of the United States, to meet the needs of a national war effort, to protect against the economic disaster of a bank failure, and to protect the public from misbranded drugs and contaminated food.

The Florida and Pennsylvania prejudgment replevin statutes serve no such important governmental or general public interest. They allow summary seizure of a person's possessions when no more than private gain is directly at stake.[29] * * *

Nor do the broadly drawn Florida and Pennsylvania statutes limit the summary seizure of goods to special situations demanding prompt action. There may be cases in which a creditor could make a showing of immediate danger that a debtor will destroy or conceal disputed goods. But the statutes before us are not "narrowly drawn to meet any such unusual condition." Sniadach v. Family Finance Corp., supra, 395 U.S. at 339, 89 S.Ct. at 1821. And no such unusual situation is presented by the facts of these cases.

The statutes, moreover, abdicate effective state control over state power. Private parties, serving their own private advantage, may unilaterally invoke state power to replevy goods from another. No state official participates in the decision to seek a writ; no state official reviews the basis for the claim to repossession; and no state official evaluates the need for immediate seiz-

---

[29] By allowing repossession without an opportunity for a prior hearing, the Florida and Pennsylvania statutes may be intended specifically to reduce the costs for the private party seeking to seize goods in another party's possession. Even if the private gain at stake in repossession actions were equal to the great public interests recognized in this Court's past decisions, * * * the Court has made clear that the avoidance of the ordinary costs imposed by the opportunity for a hearing is not sufficient to override the constitutional right. * * *

[The] * * * cost of an opportunity to be heard before repossession should not be exaggerated. For we deal here only with the right to an *opportunity* to be heard. Since the issues and facts decisive of rights in repossession suits may very often be quite simple, there is a likelihood that many defendants would forgo their opportunity, sensing the futility of the exercise in the particular case. And, of course, no hearing need be held unless the defendant, having received notice of his opportunity takes advantage of it.

ure. There is not even a requirement that the plaintiff provide any information to the court on these matters. The State acts largely in the dark.

VII

Finally, we must consider the contention that the appellants who signed conditional sales contracts thereby waived their basic procedural due process rights. The contract signed by Mrs. Fuentes provided that "in the event of default of any payment or payments, Seller at its option may take back the merchandise * * *." The contracts signed by the Pennsylvania appellants similarly provided that the seller "may retake" or "repossess" the merchandise in the event of a "default in any payment." These terms were parts of printed form contracts, appearing in relatively small type and unaccompanied by any explanations clarifying their meaning.

* * * For a waiver of constitutional rights in any context must, at the very least, be clear. The contractual language relied upon must, on its face, amount to a waiver.

The conditional sales contracts here simply provided that upon a default the seller "may take back," "may retake" or "may repossess" merchandise. The contracts included nothing about the waiver of a prior hearing. They did not indicate *how* or *through what process*—a final judgment, self-help, prejudgment replevin with a prior hearing, or prejudgment replevin without a prior hearing—the seller could take back the goods. Rather, the purported waiver provisions here are no more than a statement of the seller's right to repossession upon occurrence of certain events. * * *

VIII

We hold that the Florida and Pennsylvania prejudgment replevin provisions work a deprivation of property without due process of law insofar as they deny the right to a prior opportunity to be heard before chattels are taken from their possessor. Our holding, however, is a narrow one. We do not question the power of a State to seize goods before a final judgment in order to protect the security interests of creditors so long as those creditors have tested their claim to the goods through the process of a fair prior hearing. The nature and form of such prior hearings, moreover, are legitimately open to many potential variations and are a subject, at this point, for legislation—not adjudication. * * *

For the foregoing reasons, the judgments of the district courts are vacated and these cases are remanded for further proceedings consistent with this opinion.

It is so ordered.

Vacated and remanded.

Mr. Justice POWELL and Mr. Justice REHNQUIST did not participate in the consideration or decision of these cases.

Mr. Justice WHITE, with whom THE CHIEF JUSTICE and Mr. Justice BLACKMUN join, dissenting.

* * * [The dissenters first noted that state proceedings were in progress when these actions were commenced so that jurisdiction should have been refused because there was an adequate remedy at law.]

Second: * * *.

The narrow issue, as the Court notes, is whether it comports with due process to permit the seller, pending final judgment, to take possession of the property through a writ of replevin served by the sheriff without affording the buyer opportunity to insist that the seller establish at a hearing that there is reasonable basis for his claim of default. The interests of the buyer and seller are obviously antagonistic during this interim period: the buyer wants the use of the property pending final judgment; the seller's interest is to prevent further use and deterioration in his security. By the Florida and Pennsylvania law the property is for all intents and purposes placed in custody and immobilized during this time. The buyer loses use of the property temporarily but is protected against loss; the seller is protected against deterioration of the property but must undertake by bond to make the buyer whole in the event the latter prevails.

In considering whether this resolution of conflicting interests is unconstitutional, much depends on one's perceptions of the practical considerations involved. The Court holds it constitutionally essential to afford opportunity for a probable cause hearing prior to repossession. Its stated purpose is "to prevent unfair and mistaken deprivations of the property." But in these typical situations, the buyer-debtor has either defaulted or he has not. If there is a default, it would seem not only "fair," but essential, that the creditor be allowed to repossess; and I cannot say that the likelihood of a mistaken claim of default is sufficiently real or recurring to justify a broad constitutional requirement that a creditor do more than the typical state law requires and permits him to do. Sellers are normally in the business of selling and collecting the price for their merchandise. I could be quite wrong, but it would not seem in the creditor's interest for a default occasioning repossession to occur; as a practical matter it would much better serve his interests if the transaction goes forward and is completed as planned. Dollar and cents considerations weigh heavily against false claims of default as well as against precipitate action that would allow no opportunity for mistakes to surface and be corrected. Nor does it seem to me that creditors would lightly undertake the expense of instituting replevin actions and putting up bonds.

* * * Viewing the issue before us in this light, I would not construe the Due Process Clause to require the creditors to do more than they have done in these cases to secure possession pending final hearing. Certainly, I would not ignore, as the Court does, the creditor's interest in preventing further use and deterioration of the property in which he has substantial interest. Surely under the Court's own definition, the creditor has a "property" interest as deserving of protection as that of the debtor. At least the debtor, who is very likely uninterested in a speedy resolution that could terminate his use of the property, should be required to make those payments, into court or otherwise, upon which his right to possession is conditioned. * * *

Third: The Court's rhetoric is seductive, but in end analysis, the result it reaches will have little impact and represents no more than ideological tinkering with state law. It would appear that creditors could withstand attack under today's opinion simply by making clear in the controlling credit instruments that they may retake possession without a hearing, or, for that matter, without resort to judicial process at all. Alternatively, they need only give a few days' notice of a hearing, take possession if hearing is waived or if there is default; and if hearing is necessary merely establish probable cause for asserting that default has occurred. It is very doubtful in my mind that such a hearing would in fact result in protections for the debtor substantially different from those the present laws provide. On the contrary, the availability of credit may well be diminished or, in any event, the expense of securing it increased.

None of this seems worth the candle to me. The procedure which the Court strikes down is not some barbaric hangover from bygone days. The respective rights of the parties in secured transactions have undergone the most intensive analysis in recent years. * * *

NOTES AND QUESTIONS

1. The *Fuentes* case is analyzed in 22 Buffalo L.Rev. 17; 86 Harv.L. Rev. 85; 10 Houston L.Rev. 201; 33 La.L.Rev. 62; 51 N.C.L.Rev. 111; 40 Tenn.L.Rev. 125; 4 Tex.Tech.L.Rev. 23; and 25 Vand.L.Rev. 1251.

2. Can you draft a replevin statute that would provide for prejudgment seizure and be consistent with the constitutional requirements set out in *Fuentes*? A number of states have attempted to do so. See, e. g., Cal.Code Civ.Proc. §§ 537–61 (1972) (interim statute).

3. How sound is the dissent's argument that creditors can avoid the restrictions of *Fuentes* by providing in their financing contracts that they may retake possession of property without a hearing? Consider D. H. OVERMYER CO. v. FRICK CO., 405 U.S. 174, 92 S.Ct. 775, 31 L.Ed.2d 124 (1972), in which the Court held that a clause authorizing a creditor upon default to use a confession of judgment procedure and secure the entry of judgment against a debtor without service of process or notice was not per se violative of the Fourteenth Amendment requirements of prejudgment notice and a hearing. The Court noted that the parties to the agreement had equal bargaining power and that the debtor had knowingly waived its rights to notice and a hearing. It then concluded that the applicable state procedure provided adequate safeguards because it authorized the vacation of a confessed judgment if a valid defense was shown. Compare KOSCHES v. NICHOLS, 68 Misc.2d 795, 327 N.Y.S.2d 968 (N.Y.City Civ.Ct.1971), in which the court stated:

> * * * The court also recognizes that, in these adhesion agreements where the buyer has no alternative but to purchase on credit, the

parties are not in equal bargaining position. The era of the company store where the purchaser had no place else to go may not be dead. * * * Needless to say, the clauses giving the seller the right to enter a debtor's residence and seize the goods without a court order are unconscionable.

Id. at 797. See also Hopson, *Cognovit Judgments: An Ignored Problem of Due Process and Full Faith and Credit,* 29 U.Chi.L.Rev. 111 (1961).

4. As the Court in *Fuentes* noted, its holding as to replevin statutes was an application of its earlier decision in SNIADACH v. FAMILY FINANCE CORP., 395 U.S. 337, 89 S.Ct. 1820, 23 L.Ed.2d 349 (1969), which struck down a Wisconsin prejudgment wage garnishment procedure as violative of Due Process guarantees. To what other types of situations might *Sniadach* apply? Should it apply to temporary restraining orders, which under Federal Rule 65(b) may be obtained without notice or a hearing? In light of *Fuentes,* what is the status of pre-action attachment for purposes of establishing quasi in rem jurisdiction? See, e. g., Schneider v. Margossian, 349 F.Supp. 741 (D.Mass.1972). For an excellent discussion of the implications of *Sniadach, Fuentes,* and other cases in the same vein, see Countryman, *The Bill of Rights and the Bill Collector,* 15 Ariz.L.Rev. 521 (1973).

SECTION D. JURISDICTION OVER PARTIES AND PROPERTY: LIMITATIONS

HANSON v. DENCKLA

Supreme Court of the United States, 1958.
357 U.S. 235, 78 S.Ct. 1228, 2 L.Ed.2d 1283.

[Dora Browning Donner, while a domiciliary of Pennsylvania, executed a trust instrument in Wilmington, Delaware in 1935. The trust reserved the income to Mrs. Donner during her life; the principal and any undistributed income were to pass on her death as appointed in the last instrument she might execute and deliver to the trustee or pursuant to her last will and testament in the absence of any such instrument. In 1949, Mrs. Donner, then a domiciliary of Florida, executed the last of a series of appointments relevant to this dispute. On the same day she executed her last will and testament, which contained a residuary clause covering any property over which she might have a power of appointment that had not been effectively exercised prior to her death. She died domiciled in Florida in 1952. Claiming that the power of appointment had been ineffectively exercised, the residuary legatees brought an action in Florida seeking a determination that the Delaware trust passed under the residuary clause of the will. The beneficiaries who would be entitled to the property if the power had been effectively exercised and the Delaware trustee were named as defendants and given notice and an opportunity to appear, although only the executrix and some of the beneficiaries were personally served. Those defendants that did appear challenged the court's jurisdiction on the ground that the Delaware trustee was an indispensable party and Florida could not constitutionally assert jurisdiction over it.   The Florida court found that it had jurisdiction over the trustee for the purpose of the action, concluded that the trust was invalid and that the exercise of the power of appointment was ineffective to pass title, and held that the trust property therefore passed under the will.   Before the Florida judgment was rendered, an action was commenced in Delaware to determine who was entitled to share the trust assets, which were situated in Delaware.   With minor exceptions, the parties were the same as in the Florida action.   Nonresident defendants were served by registered mail.   When the Florida judgment was rendered, the legatees under the will unsuccessfully urged it as res judicata of the Delaware action.   The Delaware court ultimately held the trust and the exercise of the power of appointment valid under Delaware law.]

Certiorari to the Supreme Court of Florida and certiorari to the Supreme Court of Delaware.

Mr. Chief Justice WARREN delivered the opinion of the Court. * * *

The issues for our decision are, *first*, whether Florida erred in holding that it had jurisdiction over the nonresident defendants, and *second*, whether Delaware erred in refusing full faith and credit to the Florida decree. * * *

No. 107, The Florida Appeal. * * * [The Court initially decided it had no jurisdiction by way of appeal but treated the papers as a petition for certiorari.]

Appellants charge that this judgment is offensive to the Due Process Clause of the Fourteenth Amendment because the Florida court was without jurisdiction. * * * The alleged defect is the absence of those "affiliating circumstances" without which the courts of a State may not enter a judgment imposing obligations on persons (jurisdiction *in personam*) or affecting interests in property (jurisdiction *in rem* or *quasi in rem*).[12]   While the *in rem* and *in personam* classifications do not exhaust all the situations that give rise to jurisdiction, they are adequate to describe the affiliating circumstances suggested here, and accordingly serve as a useful means of approach to this case.

In rem jurisdiction.   Founded on physical power, McDonald v. Mabee, * * * the *in rem* jurisdiction of a state court is limited by the extent of its power and by the coordinate authority of sister States.   The basis of the jurisdiction is the presence of the subject property within the territorial jurisdiction of the forum State. * * * Tangible property poses no problem for the application of this rule, but the situs of intangibles is often a matter of controversy.   In considering restrictions on the power to tax, this Court has concluded that "jurisdiction" over intangible property is not limited to a single State. * * * Whether the type of "jurisdiction" with which this opinion deals may be exercised by more than one State we need not decide.   The parties seem to assume that the trust assets that form the subject matter of this action were located in Delaware and not in Florida.   We can see noth-

---

12 * * * For convenience of terminology this opinion will use "*in rem*" in lieu of "*in rem* and *quasi in rem*."

ing in the record contrary to that assumption, or sufficient to establish a situs in Florida.

The Florida court held that the presence of the subject property was not essential to its jurisdiction. Authority over the probate and construction of its domiciliary's will, under which the assets might pass, was thought sufficient to confer the requisite jurisdiction. But jurisdiction cannot be predicated upon the contingent role of this Florida will. Whatever the efficacy of a so-called "*in rem*" jurisdiction over assets admittedly passing under a local will, a state acquires no *in rem* jurisdiction to adjudicate the validity of *inter vivos* dispositions simply because its decision might augment an estate passing under a will probated in its courts. If such a basis of jurisdiction were sustained, probate courts would enjoy nationwide service of process to adjudicate interests in property with which neither the State nor the decedent could claim any affiliation. The settlor-decedent's Florida domicile is equally unavailing as a basis for jurisdiction over the trust assets. For the purpose of jurisdiction *in rem* the maxim that personalty has its situs at the domicile of its owner is a fiction of limited utility. * * * The maxim is no less suspect when the domicile is that of a decedent. In analogous cases, this Court has rejected the suggestion that the probate decree of the State where decedent was domiciled has an *in rem* effect on personalty outside the forum State that could render it conclusive on the interests of nonresidents over whom there was no personal jurisdiction. * * * The fact that the owner is or was domiciled within the forum State is not a sufficient affiliation with the property upon which to base jurisdiction *in rem*. Having concluded that Florida had no *in rem* jurisdiction, we proceed to consider whether a judgment purporting to rest on that basis is invalid in Florida and must therefore be reversed.

Prior to the Fourteenth Amendment an exercise of jurisdiction over persons or property outside the forum State was thought to be an absolute nullity, but the matter remained a question of state law over which this Court exercised no authority. With the adoption of that Amendment, any judgment purporting to bind the person of a defendant over whom the court had not acquired *in personam* jurisdiction was void within the State as well as without. Pennoyer v. Neff * * *. Nearly a century has passed without this Court being called upon to apply that principle to an *in rem* judgment dealing with property outside the forum State. The invalidity of such a judgment within the forum State seems to have been assumed—and with good reason. Since a State is forbidden to enter a judgment attempting to bind a person over whom it has no jurisdiction, it has even less right to enter a judgment purporting to extinguish the interest of such a person in property over which the court has no jurisdiction. Therefore, so far as it purports to rest upon jurisdiction over the trust assets, the judgment of the Florida court cannot be sustained.
* * *

In personam jurisdiction. Appellees' stronger argument is for *in personam* jurisdiction over the Delaware trustee. They urge that the circumstances of this case amount to sufficient affiliation with the State of Florida to empower its courts to exercise personal jurisdiction over this nonresident defendant. Principal reliance is placed upon McGee v. International Life Ins. Co., 355 U.

S. 220, 78 S.Ct. 199, 2 L.Ed.2d 223.   In McGee the Court noted the trend of expanding personal jurisdiction over nonresidents.   As technological progress has increased the flow of commerce between States, the need for jurisdiction over nonresidents has undergone a similar increase.   At the same time, progress in communications and transportation has made the defense of a suit in a foreign tribunal less burdensome.   In response to these changes, the requirements for personal jurisdiction over nonresidents have evolved from the rigid rule of Pennoyer v. Neff   *   *   *   to the flexible standard of International Shoe Co. v. State of Washington   *   *   *.   But it is a mistake to assume that this trend heralds the eventual demise of all restrictions on the personal jurisdiction of state courts.   See Vanderbilt v. Vanderbilt, 354 U.S. 416, 418, 77 S.Ct. 1360, 1362, 1 L.Ed.2d 1456.   Those restrictions are more than a guarantee of immunity from inconvenient or distant litigation.   They are a consequence of territorial limitations on the power of the respective States.   However minimal the burden of defending in a foreign tribunal, a defendant   *   may not be called upon to do so unless he has had the "minimal contacts" with that State that are a prerequisite to its exercise of power over him.   *   *   *

We fail to find such contacts in the circumstances of this case.   The defendant trust company has no office in Florida, and transacts no business there. None of the trust assets has ever been held or administered in Florida, and the record discloses no solicitation of business in that State either in person or by mail.   *   *   *

The cause of action in this case is not one that arises out of an act done or transaction consummated in the forum State.   In that respect, it differs from McGee   *   *   *   and the cases there cited.   In McGee, the nonresident defendant solicited a reinsurance agreement with a resident of California.   The offer was accepted in that State, and the insurance premiums were mailed from there until the insured's death.   Noting the interest California has in providing effective redress for its residents when nonresident insurers refuse to pay claims on insurance they have solicited in that State, the Court upheld jurisdiction because the suit "was based on a contract which had substantial connection with that State."   In contrast, this action involves the validity of an agreement that was entered without any connection with the forum State.   The agreement was executed in Delaware by a trust company incorporated in that State and a settlor domiciled in Pennsylvania.   The first relationship Florida had to the agreement was years later when the settlor became domiciled there, and the trustee remitted the trust income to her in that State.   From Florida Mrs. Donner carried on several bits of trust administration that may be compared to the mailing of premiums in McGee.   But the record discloses no instance in which the *trustee* performed any acts in Florida that bear the same relationship to the agreement as the solicitation in McGee.   Consequently, this suit cannot be said to be one to enforce an obligation that arose from a privilege the defendant exercised in Florida.   *   *   *   This case is also different from McGee in that there the State had enacted special legislation   *   *   *   to exercise what McGee called its "manifest interest" in providing effective redress for citizens who had been injured by nonresidents engaged in an activity that the State treats as exceptional and subjects to special regulation.   * * *

The execution in Florida of the powers of appointment under which the beneficiaries and appointees claim does not give Florida a substantial connection with the contract on which this suit is based. It is the validity of the trust agreement, not the appointment, that is at issue here. For the purpose of applying its rule that the validity of a trust is determined by the law of the State of its creation, Florida ruled that the appointment amounted to a "republication" of the original trust instrument in Florida. For choice-of-law purposes such a ruling may be justified, but we think it an insubstantial connection with the trust agreement for purposes of determining the question of personal jurisdiction over a nonresident defendant. The unilateral activity of those who claim some relationship with a nonresident defendant cannot satisfy the requirement of contact with the forum State. The application of that rule will vary with the quality and nature of the defendant's activity, but it is essential in each case that there be some act by which the defendant purposefully avails itself of the privilege of conducting activities within the forum State, thus invoking the benefits and protections of its laws.   * * *

It is urged that because the settlor and most of the appointees and beneficiaries were domiciled in Florida the courts of that State should be able to exercise personal jurisdiction over the nonresident trustees. This is a non-sequitur. With personal jurisdiction over the executor, legatees, and appointees, there is nothing in federal law to prevent Florida from adjudicating concerning the respective rights and liabilities of those parties. But Florida has not chosen to do so. As we understand its law, the trustee is an indispensable party over whom the court must acquire jurisdiction before it is empowered to enter judgment in a proceeding affecting the validity of a trust. It does not acquire that jurisdiction by being the "center of gravity" of the controversy, or the most convenient location for litigation. The issue is personal jurisdiction, not choice of law. It is resolved in this case by considering the acts of the trustee. As we have indicated, they are insufficient to sustain the jurisdiction.

Because it sustained jurisdiction over the nonresident trustees, the Florida Supreme Court found it unnecessary to determine whether Florida law made those defendants indispensable parties in the circumstances of this case. Our conclusion that Florida was without jurisdiction over the Delaware trustee, or over the trust corpus held in that State, requires that we make that determination in the first instance. As we have noted earlier, the Florida Supreme Court has repeatedly held that a trustee is an indispensable party without whom a Florida court has no power to adjudicate controversies affecting the validity of a trust. For that reason the Florida judgment must be reversed not only as to the nonresident trustees but also as to appellants, over whom the Florida court admittedly had jurisdiction.

No. 117, The Delaware Certiorari. The same reasons that compel reversal of the Florida judgment require affirmance of the Delaware one. Delaware is under no obligation to give full faith and credit to a Florida judgment invalid in Florida because offensive to the Due Process Clause of the Fourteenth Amendment. * * * Even before passage of the Fourteenth Amendment this Court sustained state courts in refusing full faith and credit to judgments entered by courts that were without jurisdiction over nonresident defendants. D'Arcy v. Ketchum, 11 How. 165, 13 L.Ed. 648; Hall v. Lanning, 91 U.S. 160, 23 L.Ed. 271. * * * Since Delaware was entitled to conclude that Florida law made the trust company an indispensable party, it was under no obligation to give the Florida judgment any faith and credit— even against parties over whom Florida's jurisdiction was unquestioned.

* * *

The judgment of the Delaware Supreme Court is affirmed, and the judgment of the Florida Supreme Court is reversed and the cause is remanded for proceedings not inconsistent with this opinion.

* * *

Mr. Justice BLACK, whom Mr. Justice BURTON and Mr. Justice BRENNAN join, dissenting.

* * *

In light of the * * * circumstances it seems quite clear to me that there is nothing in the Due Process Clause which denies Florida the right to determine whether Mrs. Donner's appointment was valid as against its statute of wills. This disposition, which was designed to take effect after her death, had very close and substantial connections with that State. Not only was the appointment made in Florida by a domiciliary of Florida, but the primary beneficiaries also lived in that State. In my view it could hardly be denied that Florida had sufficient interest so that a court with jurisdiction might properly apply Florida law, if it chose, to determine whether the appointment was effectual. * * * True, the question whether the law of a State can be applied to a transaction is different from the question whether the courts of that State have jurisdiction to enter a judgment, but the two are often closely related and to a substantial degree depend upon similar considerations. It seems to me that where a transaction has as much relationship to a State as Mrs. Donner's appointment had to Florida its courts ought to have power to adjudicate controversies arising out of that transaction, unless litigation there would impose such a heavy and disproportionate burden on a nonresident defendant that it would offend what this Court has referred to as "traditional notions of fair play and substantial justice." Milliken v. Meyer * * *; International Shoe Co. v. State of Washington * * *. So far as the nonresident defendants here are concerned I can see nothing which approaches that degree of unfairness. Florida, the home of the principal contenders for Mrs. Donner's largess, was a reasonably convenient forum for all. Certainly there is nothing fundamentally unfair in subjecting the corporate trustee to the jurisdiction of the Florida courts. It chose to maintain business relations with Mrs. Donner in that State for eight years, regularly communicating with her with respect to the business of the trust including the very appointment in question.

Florida's interest in the validity of Mrs. Donner's appointment is made more emphatic by the fact that her will is being administered in that State. It has traditionally been the rule that the State where a person is domiciled at the time of his death is the proper place to determine the validity of his will, to construe its provisions and to marshal and distribute his personal property. Here Florida was seriously concerned with winding up Mrs. Donner's estate and with finally determining what property was to be distributed under her will. In fact this suit was brought for that very purpose.

The Court's decision that Florida did not have jurisdiction over the trustee (and inferentially the nonresident beneficiaries) stems from principles stated the better part of a century ago in Pennoyer v. Neff * * *. But as the years have passed the constantly increasing ease and rapidity of communication and the tremendous growth of interstate business activity have led to a steady and inevitable relaxation of the strict limits on state jurisdiction announced in that case. In the course of this evolution the old jurisdictional landmarks have been left far behind so that in many instances States may now properly exercise jurisdiction over nonresidents not amenable to service within their borders. Yet further relaxation seems certain. Of course we have not reached the point where state boundaries are without significance, and I do not mean to suggest such a view here. There is no need to do so. For we are dealing with litigation arising from a transaction that had an abundance of close and substantial connections with the State of Florida.

Perhaps the decision most nearly in point is Mullane v. Central Hanover Bank & Trust Co. * * *. In upholding the State's jurisdiction the Court emphasized its great interest in trusts administered within its boundaries and governed by its laws. * * * Also implicit in the result was a desire to avoid the necessity for multiple litigation with its accompanying waste and possibility of inconsistent results. It seems to me that the same kind of considerations are present here supporting Florida's jurisdiction over the nonresident defendants.

Even if it be assumed that the Court is right in its jurisdictional holding, I think its disposition of the two cases is unjustified. It reverses the judgment of the Florida Supreme Court on the ground that the trustee may be, but need not be, an indispensable party to the Florida litigation under Florida law. At the same time it affirms the subsequent Delaware judgment. Although in form the Florida case is remanded for further proceedings not inconsistent with the Court's opinion, the effect is that the Florida courts will be obliged to give full faith and credit to the Delaware judgment. This means the Florida courts will never have an opportunity to determine whether the trustee is an indispensable party. * * * In my judgment the proper thing to do would be to hold the Delaware case until the Florida courts had an opportunity to decide whether the trustee is an indispensable party. * * *

Mr. Justice DOUGLAS, dissenting.

* * * Florida has such a plain and compelling relation to these out-of-state intangibles * * * and the nexus between the settlor and trustee is so close, as to give Florida the right to make the controlling determination

even without personal service over the trustee and those who claim under it. We must remember this is not a suit to impose liability on the Delaware trustee or on any other absent person. It is merely a suit to determine interests in those intangibles. * * * Under closely analogous facts the California Supreme Court held in Atkinson v. Superior Court, 49 Cal.2d 338, 316 P.2d 960, that California had jurisdiction over an absent trustee. I would hold the same here. The decedent was domiciled in Florida; most of the legatees are there; and the absent trustee through whom the others claim was an agency so close to the decedent as to be held to be privy with her—in other words so identified in interest with her as to represent the same legal right.

NOTES AND QUESTIONS

1. The principal case has provoked a considerable amount of writing including Kurland, *The Supreme Court, the Due Process Clause and the In Personam Jurisdiction of State Courts—From Pennoyer to Denckla: A Review*, 25 U. Chi.L.Rev. 569 (1958); Scott, *Hanson v. Denckla*, 72 Harv.L.Rev. 695 (1959); *Developments in the Law—State-Court Jurisdiction*, 73 Harv.L.Rev. 909, 960–65 (1960).

2. Note that the opinions by the Chief Justice and Mr. Justice Black agree that the question whether a court may apply its own law to a controversy is to be decided by a standard that differs from the standard used to decide the question whether the court can adjudicate the controversy at all. That is, the constitutional power to apply local law is of a different dimension from the constitutional power to assert jurisdiction. Can you articulate the way the majority and dissenting opinions in *Hanson* characterize this difference? Can this difference be justified? Might it be appropriate to allow a court to adjudicate any controversy to which it might apply local law under the applicable choice-of-law rule? What defects do you see in such a standard?

3. The primary beneficiaries under the appointment executed in 1949 by Mrs. Donner were the children of Mrs. Donner's daughter Elizabeth, who were to receive approximately $400,000. The residuary legatees under Mrs. Donner's will were her other two daughters, who were going to receive over $1,000,000 from other sources in any event. The effect of the Florida decision invalidating the appointment was to augment the amount received by the other two daughters at the expense of Elizabeth's family. To what extent, therefore, might *Hanson* simply reflect the Supreme Court's distaste for an "unfair" result under Florida law?

4. Note that the Florida court had jurisdiction over the executrix and she was the person who had the duty to turn the securities over to the beneficiaries. How is this situation distinguishable from that in *Harris v. Balk,* p. 107, supra?

ATKINSON v. SUPERIOR COURT, 49 Cal.2d 338, 342–43, 345–48, 316 P.2d 960, 963–69 (1957), certiorari denied 357 U.S. 569, 78 S.Ct. 1381, 2 L.Ed.2d 1546 (1958). Plaintiff musicians attacked the validity of certain collective bargaining and related trust agreements between their employers and the American Federation of Musicians. Plaintiffs' theory was that the union had violated its duty as collective bargaining agent in agreeing that certain royalty payments, allegedly wages, be diverted to a trust created to further the public's knowledge and appreciation of music. The union and the employers were personally served in California; the trustee was served in New York pursuant to a court order, but did not appear. The lower court held that it had no jurisdiction over the trustee, who was an indispensable party to the action. The California Supreme Court, however, upheld quasi in rem jurisdiction:

> * * * Plaintiffs claim that the employers' obligation to make the payments involved is one owing to them instead of to a trustee. That obligation is a chose in action and is therefore personal property within the meaning of the statutory provisions. Being an intangible, it has no situs in fact. * * * The question presented, therefore, is whether the chose in action in question may be treated as being within this state * * * for purposes of exercising in rem or quasi in rem jurisdiction over it in these actions.

> Plaintiffs rely on cases holding that having jurisdiction over the obligor, the state has power to enforce the obligation and cut off the right, if any, of a nonresident claimant * * *. Defendants contend, however, that in the case of ordinary choses in action such power is limited to situations in which the local claimant admits the validity of the local debtor's obligation to the nonresident and seeks to reach the interest he admits is the property of the nonresident. * * *

> It is significant that with respect to jurisdiction to tax intangibles * * *, jurisdiction over foreign corporations * * *, and jurisdiction to adjudicate trust obligations * * *, emphasis is no longer placed on actual or physical presence but on the bearing that local contacts have to the question of overall fair play and substantial justice. A similar change in emphasis has been taking place with respect to personal jurisdiction over individuals. * * *

> In the present case, since the trustee is not and has not been a resident of California, section 417 of the Code of Civil Procedure precludes the entry of a personal judgment against him, and it is therefore unnecessary to determine whether his activities as trustee have sufficient connection with this state constitutionally to justify an assumption of personal jurisdiction without service of process here. The relevant contacts with this state are significant, however, in deciding whether due process permits exercising a more limited or quasi in rem jurisdiction to determine his and plaintiffs' interests in the intangibles in question.

> We find no relevance in the distinction defendants seek to make between jurisdiction to take over a nonresident's claim to a chose in action admittedly his and jurisdiction to establish that

it was never his. In both situations the nonresident can protect his interest in the property only by submitting to the jurisdiction of the court. It is true that in the former situation he must litigate a controversy solely between himself and his creditor unrelated to pre-existing rights in the obligation garnished, whereas in the latter situation pre-existing conflicting rights to the obligation itself are involved; but this distinction alone has no bearing on the fairness of making him appear.   *   *   *

The obligation plaintiffs seek to enforce grows out of their employment by defendants here. The payments involved are alleged to be consideration for work performed in this state. The Federation defendant is before the court. Under these circumstances, fairness to plaintiffs demands that they be able to reach the fruits of their labors before they are removed from the state. Moreover, fairness to the defendants who are personally before the court also demands that the conflicting claims of the trustee be subject to final adjudication. Even if we were to hold that his absence prevents the granting of the provisional remedies here sought, plaintiffs would not be foreclosed thereby from asserting that payment to him did not discharge the employers' obligation to them and that the Federation was independently liable for damages for breach of its fiduciary duty. The evil of exposing the obligor to actions to enforce the same obligation in two jurisdictions with the attendant risk of double liability would not be obviated.   *   *   *

NOTES AND QUESTIONS

1. The Supreme Court's denial of certiorari in *Atkinson* came one week after it decided *Hanson*. Are the two cases inconsistent? In view of the fact that *Mullane v. Central Hanover Bank & Trust Co.*, p. 115, supra and *Atkinson* amply demonstrate the weaknesses in the historic distinctions among in personam, in rem, and quasi in rem jurisdiction, isn't Chief Justice Warren's opinion in *Hanson* retrogressive? See generally Traynor, *Is This Conflict Really Necessary?*, 37 Texas L.Rev. 657 (1959).

2. Note that unlike most of the earlier cases in this Chapter, *Hanson* and *Atkinson* are cases involving multiple parties and claims. In both cases the court undoubtedly was concerned about the possible unavailability of any other, or any other reasonably effective, forum in which to litigate. For example, consider the effect in terms of alternative locations for bringing suit of a holding in *Atkinson* that California was an impermissible forum? From this perspective can it be said that California had jurisdiction by "necessity" in *Atkinson?*

JUDICIAL CONSTRAINTS ON THE APPLICATION
OF STATE LONG-ARM STATUTES

Despite the broad wording of many state long-arm statutes, a number of courts have imposed various limitations on their application. A few illustrative cases will serve to indicate the character of these restrictions.

In HAYNES v. JAMES H. CARR, INC., 427 F.2d 700 (4th Cir.), certiorari denied 400 U.S. 942, 91 S.Ct. 238, 27 L.Ed.2d 245 (1970), an action by an injured general contractor's employee against the subcontractor and the Pacific Lumber Inspection Bureau, the court considered the applicability of Virginia's long-arm statute, Va.Code Ann. § 8–812, which provides for the assertion of personal jurisdiction over nonresidents who cause tortious injury in the state. The Fourth Circuit affirmed the district court's holding that since the Lumber Inspection Bureau did not solicit business in Virginia or engage in any other persistent course of conduct there, it was not subject to Virginia's jurisdiction statute even though the Bureau stamped some of the lumber shipped into the state and later sent an employee to inspect the broken truss that had caused plaintiff's injury. Is this case distinguishable from *Gray?*

In SINGER, PPA v. PIAGGIO & C. (s. p. a.), 420 F.2d 679 (1st Cir. 1970), the court considered the Massachusetts long-arm statute, M.G.L.A. c. 223A, § 3, which permits the assertion of personal jurisdiction over nonresidents on causes of action arising from defendant's contracting to supply services or things in the Commonwealth. Plaintiff, a citizen of Pennsylvania, purchased a motor scooter in that state made by defendant in Italy. When plaintiff subsequently was injured in Florida allegedly as a result of a manufacturing defect, he attempted to sue defendant in Massachusetts, asserting that defendant was doing business there because it sold its products under a franchise agreement to a Massachusetts corporation. The district court denied jurisdiction and the First Circuit affirmed, holding that since the action did not specifically arise from and was not connected with any shipment or services within the Commonwealth the statute was inapplicable. Is there any way to harmonize this case with *Buckeye Boiler?* See also Ratliff v. Cooper Labs., Inc., 444 F.2d 745 (4th Cir.1971).

In SAFARI OUTFITTERS, INC. v. SUPERIOR COURT IN & FOR THE CITY & COUNTY OF DENVER, 167 Colo. 456, 448 P.2d 783 (1968), defendant, an out-of-state corporation obtained a writ of prohibition to prevent the Superior Court from exercising in personam jurisdiction over it pursuant to the state long-arm statute, 1965 Perm.Supp., C.R.S. §§ 37–1–26, 37–1–27. The Colorado Supreme Court held that (1) the corporation's advertisement of its services in national magazines that were distributed within the state, (2) its interstate telephone conversations and correspondence with plaintiff, and (3) its receipt of out-of-state checks drawn on a Colorado bank were not sufficient to establish minimum contacts with the state so as to meet the due process limitations for exercising jurisdiction.

WESTERN UNION TEL. CO. v. COMMONWEALTH OF PENN-SYLVANIA, 368 U.S. 71, 82 S.Ct. 199, 7 L.Ed.2d 139 (1961). Pennsylvania sought to escheat funds that were held by Western Union as unclaimed money orders that had been purchased in Pennsylvania for forwarding funds to persons both within and without the state. Western Union challenged Pennsylvania's claim on the ground that an escheat judgment would not protect the company from multiple liability either in Pennsylvania or other states because the judgment would not be binding on subsequent claimants since service by publication, which had been utilized, did not give the Pennsylvania court jurisdiction. Moreover, the company argued that other states also might try to escheat the funds and would not be bound by a Pennsylvania judgment because they could not be made parties to the proceeding. In connection with this allegation, the trial court found that New York already had seized and escheated some of the same monies that were being claimed in the Pennsylvania action. Nonetheless, the Pennsylvania court went on to declare the unclaimed obligations escheated and this conclusion was upheld by the state supreme court. The United States Supreme Court reversed and held that Pennsylvania had no power to escheat the money. It stated:

> Pennsylvania does not claim and could not claim that the same debts or demands could be escheated by two states. * * * And our prior opinions have recognized that when a state court's jurisdiction purports to be based, as here, on the presence of property within the State, the holder of such property is deprived of due process of law if he is compelled to relinquish it without assurance that he will not be held liable in another jurisdiction or in a suit brought by a claimant who is not bound by the first judgment. * * * Applying that principle, there can be no doubt that Western Union has been denied due process by the Pennsylvania judgment here unless the Pennsylvania courts had power to protect Western Union from any other claim, including the claim of the State of New York that these obligations are property "within" New York and are therefore subject to escheat under its laws. But New York was not a party to this proceeding and could not have been made a party, and, of course, New York's claims could not be cut off where New York was not heard as a party. Moreover, the potential multi-state claims to the "property" which is the subject of this escheat make it not unlikely that various States will claim *in rem* jurisdiction over it. Therefore, Western Union was not protected by the Pennsylvania judgment, for a state court judgment need not be given full faith and credit by other States as to parties or property not subject to the jurisdiction of the court that rendered it. * * *

> The claims of New York * * * were presented to us in both the brief and oral argument of that State as *amicus curiae*. In

presenting its claims New York also called our attention to the potential claims of other States for escheat based on their contacts with the separate phases of the multistate transactions out of which these unclaimed funds arose, including: the State of residence of the payee, the State of the sender, the State where the money order was delivered, and the State where the fiscal agent on which the money order was drawn is located. Arguments more than merely plausible can doubtless be made to support claims of all these and other States to escheat all or parts of all unclaimed funds held by Western Union. And the large area of the company's business makes it entirely possible that *every State* may now or later claim a right to participate in these funds. * * * [T]o require it to pay this money to Pennsylvania before New York has had its full day in court might force Western Union to pay a single debt more than once and thus take its property without due process of law.

Our Constitution has wisely provided a way in which controversies between States can be settled without subjecting individuals and companies affected by those controversies to a deprivation of their right to due process of law. Article III, § 2 of the Constitution gives this Court original jurisdiction of cases in which a State is a party. * * *

The rapidly multiplying state escheat laws, originally applying only to land and other tangible things but recently moving into the elusive and wide-ranging field of intangible transactions have presented problems of great importance to the States and persons whose rights will be adversely affected by escheats. This makes it imperative that controversies between different States over their right to escheat intangibles be settled in a forum where all the States that want to do so can present their claims for consideration and final authoritative determination. Our Court has jurisdiction to do that. * * *

Id. at 75–77, 79–80, 82 S.Ct. at 201–02, 203–04.

NOTES AND QUESTIONS

1. Is *Western Union* a jurisdiction by "necessity" case? Does it establish a general principle that a holder of property is deprived of due process if she is forced to relinquish the property without assurance that she will be secure from liability to another claimant not bound by the judgment? If so, doesn't such a rule present difficulties when the dispute is not between two states and the original jurisdiction of the Supreme Court cannot be invoked? For example, what alternative is open to a state court when one of the claimants is a nonresident over whom the court cannot obtain jurisdiction and there is no other forum that can secure jurisdiction over all parties? Does *Atkinson* provide a partial answer to this dilemma? What about interpleader? See pp. 605–29, infra. Can *Western Union* be harmonized with *Mullane, Hanson,* and *Atkinson?*

2. Some of the ambiguities of *Western Union* were resolved in TEXAS v. NEW JERSEY, 379 U.S. 674, 85 S.Ct. 626, 13 L.Ed.2d 596 (1965), in which the Supreme Court took original jurisdiction over a dispute among New Jersey,

Pennsylvania, and Texas over the power to escheat certain intangible personal property held by the Sun Oil Company. Florida intervened after the commencement of the action. Texas claimed the power to escheat the property on the ground that it was the state with the most significant "contacts" with the debts; New Jersey's claim was premised on the fact that Sun Oil Company was incorporated in that state; Pennsylvania argued that it had a paramount claim because Sun's principal place of business was in that state; and Florida theorized that since the debts were the property of the creditors and not the Sun Oil Company, the right to escheat "should be accorded to the State of the creditor's last known address as shown by the debtor's books and records." The court adopted the Florida approach.

> * * * Adoption of such a rule involves a factual issue simple and easy to resolve, and leaves no legal issue to be decided. * * * [T]he rule recognizes that the debt was an asset of the creditor. The rule * * * will tend to distribute escheats among the States in the proportion of the commercial activities of their residents.

Is *Texas v. New Jersey* inconsistent with *Harris v. Balk*? In what ways?

3. In UNITED STATES ex rel. MAYO v. SATAN AND HIS STAFF, 54 F.R.D. 282 (W.D.Pa.1971), plaintiff applied to proceed under the civil rights act in forma pauperis. He alleged that on numerous occasions Satan caused plaintiff "misery and unwarranted threats" and "has placed deliberate obstacles in his path and has caused plaintiff's downfall." The court denied the application for a number of reasons, including the following:

> * * * We question whether plaintiff may obtain personal jurisdiction over the defendant in this judicial district. The complaint contains no allegation of residence in this district. While the official reports disclose no case where this defendant has appeared as defendant there is an unofficial account of a trial in New Hampshire where this defendant filed an action of mortgage foreclosure as plaintiff. The defendant in that action was represented by the preeminent advocate of that day, and raised the defense that the plaintiff was a foreign prince with no standing to sue in an American Court. This defense was overcome by overwhelming evidence to the contrary. Whether or not this would raise an estoppel in the present case we are unable to determine at this time.

BUCKLEY v. NEW YORK POST CORP.

United States Court of Appeals, Second Circuit, 1967.
373 F.2d 175.

FRIENDLY, Circuit Judge. Buckley, a resident of Connecticut, brought this action in the Superior Court of Fairfield County in that state, against New York Post Corporation, a Delaware corporation having its principal place of business in New York City, to recover damages for libel. He claimed that two editorials appearing in April 1965 had been published maliciously and with reckless disregard of the truth. The Post, having removed the action to the United States District Court, sought dismissal on the ground that it was not subject to service of process in Connecticut.

Buckley asserted that two sections of Connecticut's "long-arm" statute * * *, G.S. § 33–411(c) (3) and (4), gave the court jurisdiction.

The sections subject a foreign corporation to suit in the state "on any cause of action arising as follows:

> (3) out of the production, manufacture or distribution of goods by such corporation with the reasonable expectation that such goods are to be used or consumed in this state and are so used or consumed   *   *   *; or (4) out of tortious conduct in this state, whether arising out of repeated activity or single acts   *   *   *."

Answers to interrogatories disclosed that for a two year period ending May 1, 1965, an average of 1707 copies of the daily and 2100 copies of the weekend edition of the Post were distributed to persons in Connecticut   *   *   *; that the Post received news dispatches relating to Connecticut from the Associated Press in New York City and from five Connecticut contributors; that it carried advertisements for not more than 15 Connecticut resorts once or twice weekly during the spring and summer, for four Connecticut restaurants once a week, and for three New York stores which indicated a Connecticut branch in some of their advertising. The figures as to papers distributed to persons and corporations in Connecticut did not include copies sold in New York City with the expectation they would be taken into Connecticut by residents returning home from work; the number of these was stated to be "indeterminable." The district judge held that the case was within subdivision (3) but not within subdivision (4); he dismissed the complaint on the ground that application of the long-arm statute to the Post under the circumstances would violate the due process clause of the Fourteenth Amendment.

I.

[The court initially held that subdivision (3) of the Connecticut statute was inapplicable.]

*   *   *

II.

On the other hand, it would seem hard to deny that distributing two thousand copies of a libel about a resident in Connecticut is "tortious conduct in this state," under any ordinary meaning of those words in subdivision (4). *   *   * Indeed, the original Restatement of Conflict of Laws, applying Professor Beale's "last event" approach, stated that "Where harm is done to the reputation of a person, the place of wrong is where the defamatory statement is communicated" and gave as an example that when A, broadcasting in state X, slanders B who is well and favorably known in state Y and the broadcast is heard there, "The place of wrong is Y." § 377 at 457 (1934). While the "last event" approach has been discredited as a basis for choice of law, *   *   * it does not follow that the influence of the concept on the thinking of legislators has been eradicated to such a point that they would not consider the distribution of a libel of a resident to constitute tortious conduct in the state. *   *   *

The defendant contends that, however all this might stand as a matter of the normal interpretation of language, the "single publication" rule with respect to newspapers and other aggregate communications, Restatement (Second), Torts § 577A (Tent.Draft No. 11, 1965), requires a different conclusion * * *.

To hold that the single-publication rule exempts a publisher of a newspaper or magazine or a broadcaster from a long-arm statute that would otherwise have been applicable would be quite as artificial as the "last event" approach of the first Conflicts Restatement * * *. Elliptical statements that a libel by newspaper is "complete" upon publication, though often accurate enough in their particular context, should not obscure that the purpose of the single publication rule is not to deprive a plaintiff defamed in another state of a privilege to sue there which the legislature had granted generally to persons injured by wrongful conduct within its borders, but rather to protect the defendant—and the courts—from a multiplicity of suits, an almost endless tolling of the statute of limitations, and diversity in applicable substantive law. * * * These goals can be sufficiently accomplished by holding that the plaintiff must collect all his damages in one action, that the statute of limitations begins to run on the initial publication, and that substantive issues will be governed by a single law * * *. [D]efamed persons have rights too; the interests of the defendant are not so dominant as to require a mechanical application of the single publication rule in such a manner that circulating a libel outside that state should be treated as if it never occurred. * * *

The impropriety of reading a tortious conduct statute like subdivision (4) so as not to permit suit in the state of the plaintiff's residence when a libel had been distributed there would be plainer if, unlike the case before us, that state was far removed from the state of initial publication and plaintiff was unknown in the latter. That would not only compel the plaintiff to travel to a distant place to enforce his rights but would enshrine as the only forum a state far removed from the evidence and unfamiliar with the plaintiff's reputation and thus with the damage done by the libel. But if Connecticut meant to permit a local suit by one of its residents unknown in Illinois who was libelled by a Chicago magazine circulating within Connecticut, it also meant to give a more widely known resident similar rights with respect to a libel in a New York City newspaper. * * * In the absence of any relevant decisions by Connecticut courts pointing in the direction of Insull, we decline to apply that decision to the construction of the Connecticut long-arm statute. Whether the circulation in that state of a libel of a person not residing or generally known there would also constitute "tortious conduct in the state," we need not here determine.

III.

This brings us to the question whether subjecting the New York Post to this suit in Connecticut would violate rights accorded it by the Federal Constitution.

* * * There has been a "movement away from the bias favoring the defendant," in matters of personal jurisdiction "toward permitting the plaintiff

to insist that the defendant come to him" when there is a sufficient basis for doing so. Von Mehren & Trautman, Jurisdiction to Adjudicate: A Suggested Analysis, 79 Harv.L.Rev. 1121, 1128 (1966). * * *

Despite some language emphasizing considerations peculiar to insurance, it would not be difficult to extrapolate from the *McGee* decision and opinion a general principle that the due process clause imposes no bar to a state's asserting personal jurisdiction, of course on proper notice, in favor of a person within its border who suffers damage from the breach of a contract the defendant was to perform there or a tort the defendant committed there. Once we free our minds from traditional thinking that the plaintiff must inevitably seek out the defendant, such a doctrine would not seem to violate basic notions of fair play; any view that it does must rest on an inarticulate premise, which a legislature is free to question, that plaintiffs are much more given to making unjust claims than defendants are to not paying just ones. Indeed, when the operative facts have occurred where the plaintiff sues, the convenience of both parties would often be served by a trial there, and the chief benefit to the defendant of a rule requiring the plaintiff to seek him out is the impediment this creates to the bringing of any suit at all. * * * Unfairness inconsistent with notions of fair play occurs only when a defendant is "compelled to defend himself in a court of a State with which he has no relevant connection." D. Currie, [*The Growth of the Long Arm: Eight Years of Extended Jurisdiction in Illinois*, 1963 U.Ill.L.F. 533,] at 534. And inflicting harm within a state would appear to meet whatever further constitutional requirement may arise from "territorial limitations on the power of the respective States." See Hanson v. Denckla * * *. We would thus perceive no constitutional problem in Connecticut's summoning the New York Post to answer in its courts for a tort—other than defamation—alleged to have been committed in Connecticut upon a Connecticut resident even if that had been a wholly isolated event. * * *

IV.

The Fifth Circuit has recently held, however, that "First Amendment considerations surrounding the law of libel require a greater showing of contact to satisfy the due process clause than is necessary in asserting jurisdiction over other types of tortious activity," New York Times Co. v. Connor, 365 F.2d 567, 572 (1966). The court did not say just what would be constitutionally sufficient, except that a daily circulation of 395 and a Sunday circulation of 2455, some advertising revenue not calculable from the opinion but apparently small, rare trips to solicit advertising, occasional staff visits, and a few purchases of stories from free-lance writers in the state, were not enough. In so ruling the court followed its earlier decision in Buckley v. New York Times Co., 338 F.2d 470 (5 Cir. 1964), where it had held that the sale in Louisiana of 391 copies of the daily and 1784 of the Sunday Times, together with other activities generally similar to those described above, did not provide sufficient contacts to satisfy due process. The only normative principle we can extract from the opinions is that jurisdiction over an action against an out-of-state newspaper for circulating a libel within the state, even when brought by a resident, cannot be asserted consistently with due process "where the size of his circulation does not balance the danger of this liability." 365 F.2d at 572.[8]

We are not sure whether the law made by these hard cases was good or bad. Newspapers, magazines, and broadcasting companies are businesses conducted for profit and often make very large ones. Like other enterprises that inflict damage in the course of performing a service highly useful to the public, such as providers of food or shelter or manufacturers of drugs designed to ease or prolong life, they must pay the freight; and injured persons should not be relegated to forums so distant as to make collection of their claims difficult or impossible unless strong policy considerations demand. We cannot but wonder whether the Connor court would have felt the same way if the *dramatis personae*, instead of being "Bull" Connor and a newspaper internationally known for its high standards, had been an esteemed local educator or clergyman and an out-of-state journal with a taste for scandal which had circulated 395 copies of a libel stating he had corrupted the morals of the young. Hazards to publishers from libel actions have recently been much mitigated by the development of substantive principles under the First Amendment, notably in New York Times Co. v. Sullivan, 376 U.S. 254, 84 S.Ct. 710, 11 L.Ed.2d 686 (1964), whose teaching * * * seems likely to be extended at least to candidates for public office and persons like this plaintiff who have projected themselves into public controversy. * * * It is a legitimate question whether this will not sufficiently protect communications media without superimposing a necessarily vague First Amendment standard upon the application of long-arm statutes and thereby possibly creating undue hardship for a plaintiff like our traduced educator or clergyman.

If * * * mass media should be protected not merely by appropriate substantive defenses to defamation actions but also by procedural rules that will enable them to have burdensome suits dismissed without the necessity of a trial and an appeal, such considerations go not to "jurisdiction" over the defendant, which must exist quite as much when he circulates a libel within a state as when he sends a leaking can of poison there, but to the consistency with the First Amendment's objectives of the state's exercising such jurisdiction in a particular case. The basis for dismissal, in other words, would not be the minimum contacts requirement of the Fourteenth Amendment due process clause as such * * *; the office served by the Fourteenth Amendment would be simply the making of the First applicable to the states. * * * Such a distinction has the merit of focusing attention on the facts allegedly creating hardship in each case without mandating a uniform rule that would apply whether the place to which a newspaper is summoned to defend a libel suit is twenty-five or twenty-five hundred miles from the point of publication, as a jurisdictional due process approach that necessarily focuses at

---

[8] The context makes clear that what the court meant was not liability as such but the added danger of being sued in the state of circulation before "local juries incensed by the out-of-state newspaper's coverage of local events" rather than in the state of publication.

least in part on state boundaries might well do. Putting the matter in a slightly different way, the First Amendment could be regarded as giving *forum non conveniens* special dimensions and constitutional stature in actions for defamation against publishers and broadcasters.

Once this point is correctly analyzed, the lack of basis for constitutional objection to Connecticut's holding The New York Post to answer Buckley's complaint becomes clear. * * * The record affords no ground for a prediction that the added danger of a plaintiff's verdict from having a libel suit by a resident tried in Connecticut rather than in New York—presumably rather slight—would cause the Post to forgo the substantial revenues from these sales and thus deprive Connecticut readers of its news and editorials, as might have been the case if the Times were subjected to repeated libel suits in southern states for articles on racial problems. Beyond this, the Post's argument neglects the many respects in which the southwestern corner of Connecticut and New York City, although divided by a state boundary, are economically and intellectually one. While the Post was unable to determine how many copies are tucked each day under the arms of commuters bound for Greenwich, Stamford, New Canaan and other places in Connecticut, we do not have to shut our eyes to what a trip to Grant [sic] Central Station late any afternoon would reveal. The population center of Fairfield County, to which Connecticut was proposing to summon the Post, is only 40 miles from the Empire State Building, and a goodly number of its adult males make the trip to New York City every working day. For us to say that although the First Amendment would not protect the Post against having to answer a defamed Buffalonian in Buffalo or a Plattsburgher in Plattsburgh, the existence of a state border permits it to invoke the First Amendment as a bar to having to defend a libel suit by a Fairfielder in Fairfield County, Connecticut, would substitute formalism for the reality that should be requisite before a court applies the Amendment so as to forbid a state's exercising a jurisdiction over a non-resident that it could do in the case of any other tort.

The order dismissing the complaint for want of jurisdiction over the defendant is reversed.

[A concurring opinion by Judge Medina is omitted.]

NOTES AND QUESTIONS

1. CURTIS PUBLISHING CO. v. BIRDSONG, 360 F.2d 344 (5th Cir. 1966), was a libel action that arose out of an article in the Saturday Evening Post concerning the riots that occurred when James Meredith became the first Black to register at the University of Mississippi. Plaintiff Birdsong, the Commander of the Mississippi Highway Patrol and a resident of that state, brought the action in Alabama, presumably to gain the benefit of that state's more expansive long-arm statute. Curtis, a Pennsylvania corporation, had mailed nearly 70,000 copies of the allegedly offending article into Alabama. The Fifth Circuit Court of Appeals quashed service without considering whether the jurisdiction statute encompassed the case or whether the requisite minimum contacts existed. The court felt that it was unnecessary to discuss these requirements because the forum state must have "a sufficient interest in the litigation to justify, under the due process clause, the

exercise of extra-territorial jurisdiction." Since there was "no rational nexus between Alabama and the parties or the injury," that state was "not a constitutionally permissible forum," largely because of dangers to interstate commerce.

Is *Birdsong* inconsistent with *Buckley*? Which case is better reasoned? Why? Can you think of any considerations other than the First Amendment concerns that may act as a restraint on the assertion of personal jurisdiction in situations in which there is no due-process objection?

2. In CURTIS PUBLISHING CO. v. GOLINO, 383 F.2d 586 (5th Cir. 1967), the Fifth Circuit distinguished its earlier decision in *New York Times Co. v. Connor*, which is discussed in the principal case, and held Curtis amenable to process in Louisiana in an action concerning an alleged libel in the Saturday Evening Post. The *Connor* case was distinguished on the ground that a newspaper, being inherently a localized venture, was entitled to a greater degree of immunity from jurisdictional pressures than a national magazine. According to the court: "To argue that periodic law suits resulting from circulation of the Post will chill the desire of Curtis to actively encourage the widest possible circulation is clearly out of line with economic realities." The circulation of the Saturday Evening Post in Louisiana at the time of the *Golino* decision was about fifty thousand copies a week, which comprised approximately one percent of the Post's total circulation.

Many of the problems raised by the *Connor, Golino,* and *Buckley* decisions are discussed in Carrington & Martin, *Substantive Interests and the Jurisdiction of State Courts,* 66 Mich.L.Rev. 227 (1967); Comment, *Constitutional Limitations to Long Arm Jurisdiction in Newspaper Libel Cases,* 34 U.Chi.L.Rev. 436 (1967); Comment, *Long-Arm Jurisdiction Over Publishers: To Chill a Mocking Word,* 67 Colum.L.Rev. 342 (1967).

3. Evaluate the following passage from ST. CLAIR v. RIGHTER, 250 F. Supp. 148 (W.D.Va.1966), in light of the evolution in thinking about personal jurisdiction from *Pennoyer* to *Buckley*:

> It is possible that the law is moving more and more toward the idea that choice of law is jurisdictional, and that the fact that the law of the place is applicable provides the minimum contact necessary to permit the state to exercise *in personam* jurisdiction under the Due Process clause of the Fourteenth Amendment.

SECTION E.   JURISDICTION OVER PARTIES AND PROPERTY: A POSTSCRIPT

To what extent has the territorial theory of jurisdiction survived? In considering this query, think about the broad conceptual framework of *Pennoyer* as well as its strict holding. The following passage, taken from Hazard, *A General Theory of State-Court Jurisdiction,* 1965 Sup.Ct.Rev. 241, 281–88, provides a valuable framework for analysis.

> Ever since *International Shoe, Pennoyer v. Neff* has been eligible for oblivion. Chief Justice Traynor plainly suggested [in *Atkinson v. Superior Court,* p. 141, supra] that the step be taken,

and that all jurisdictional problems be approached as ones of the existence of minimum contacts between the forum and the transaction in litigation. Surely this is not difficult to conceive in the present posture of the law.

1.   The "long-arm" statutes are settling into familiar application in multistate tort and contract cases. If drafted to embrace multiparty litigation—disastrous accidents, claims for impleader in manufacturer's liability cases, and the like—they would close a gap that has long existed in the remedial system of the United States. * * * This would supply the jurisdictional basis for the damage actions that are the general run of litigation.

2.   The presence of a res—a tract of land, a fund—is of no peculiar jurisdictional significance but is rather the transactional event that provides a legitimate basis for plenary jurisdiction pursuant to the minimum-contacts rule. The process is issued to nonresidents in such cases in order to comply with *Mullane's* notice requirement. That process, because it issues from a state having minimum contacts with the litigated transaction, has potency in virtue of *International Shoe* to permit entry of whatever judgment is necessary to determine the controversy, without regard to limitations formerly associated with in rem proceedings.

3.   The attachment cases are appropriately limited by the minimum-contacts rule to situations where either the obligation secured by the attachment arose from a transaction with local elements, in which case there is plenary jurisdiction because of minimum contacts anyway, or where the plaintiff can show that attachment is probably necessary if he is to realize on his claim, in which case attachment is employed for its proper use as a security device. Since these two categories include practically all the cases where attachment is presently employed, only minor practical change will result from this revised conceptualization. Serious inconvenience regarding the place of trial occasioned by attachment as a security device can be avoided or mitigated by dismissal conditioned upon a bond being posted by defendant to meet judgment liability should it ultimately be established.

In this scheme of things, there are two defects that inhibit acceptance of a general minimum-contacts theory of jurisdiction. The first is that the vagueness of the minimum-contacts general principle can make jurisdictional litigation uncertain at the trial level and frequent at the appellate level. The second is that it provides no solution to the problem of the claimant who cannot be located or identified—he being among those constituting "all the world" that were concluded by in rem proceedings.

The first defect can be resolved by the technique of particularization—arbitrary particularization if you will—within the general minimum-contacts framework. This technique is manifested legislatively in the "long-arm" statutes, though they could be greatly improved upon. * * *

There are differences between the problem of the person who can be identified but not located and that of the person who cannot even be identified. * * * First, the problem of notifying him turns on the degree of effort that must be expended in seeking him. Second, he is a person against whom it may be practical to obtain a compensatory judgment. On the other hand, the unidentified person—"unknown heirs" are the prototype—may be nonexistent, so that efforts to find him will necessarily prove futile. Moreover, the unidentified person is never in practical terms the target of a compensatory claim because it is impossible to identify "his" property and thus to realize redress. As to him, the only litigating objective can be to foreclose claims he may have against others.

With these differences in mind, it is not difficult to put the identified but unlocated person into place in the minimum-contacts framework. The limiting case here would be where, in an action for damages or other compensatory relief, reasonable effort is made to deliver notice but notice is in fact not delivered to the defendant. Can a valid judgment for compensatory relief be granted in such a case? This depends on whether the condition of rendering a valid judgment under the Due Process Clause is defined as the giving of notice or the making a reasonable effort to give notice. If the former, then the plaintiff is helpless to obtain compensation—for example, from the defendant's insurance company —unless he can actually deliver notice to the defendant. The Supreme Court has never gone beyond holding that due process requires a reasonable opportunity to be heard and that reasonable effort to give notice of the hearing sufficiently affords that opportunity. But the Supreme Court has never passed on the precise question raised, although many lower courts have. The problem has arisen recurrently under the automobile "long-arm" statutes. Most courts have ducked the issue by reading—sometimes by straining to read—the local state statute to require actual notice. Those courts that have faced the issue all appear to have held that failure of actual delivery of notice does not preclude valid judgment, so long as a reasonable and technically punctilious effort has been made, i. e., there has been compliance with a statutory procedure that is itself reasonable. And this seems a correct analysis of the due process requirement as established by the Supreme Court.

This brings us to the last stage of the analysis, the problem of the person who cannot be identified. By hypothesis such a person cannot be given notice of the proceedings despite reasonable efforts to identify and locate him within the state and without. Yet there are necessities that require proceedings that can close the door conclusively on all future disputation. * * * The trust accounting in *Mullane* was such a case, decedents' estates are such cases, and so are bankruptcy, quiet-title, and many other proceedings conventionally denominated in rem proceedings.

The traditional device of foreclosing the absentee is notice by publication. Indeed, achievement of the objective of finality is the only real justification for service by publication, and the tradition and the need no doubt will keep the ceremony of service by publication a part of the law of jurisdiction. * * *

The more appropriate approach, it seems to me, is the notion of bar by statute of limitation. This notion has pervaded the law of jurisdiction to an extent perhaps not fully appreciated. The fact is that the prototype foreign attachment proceeding, that of the Lord Mayor's Court of London, was not conclusive on the absentee debtor until the expiration of a year and a day after judgment. The same was true also of the Maryland statute in *Harris v. Balk*. Most probate statutes fix a period for claims, and so do the bankruptcy laws. Escheat and abandoned property forfeitures are predicated on the bar of time, as are many statutory quiet-title procedures. Many procedures that are not explicitly founded on the principle of limitation are nevertheless consonant with it— "absconding debtors" and "unknown heirs," the typical personages, do not become such overnight.

On this analysis, the problem of serving notice on [an] unknown absentee disappears. The claims of those who cannot be found are concluded instead by an official signal—such as the commencement of proceedings—that time is running, and the imposition of bar when it has done so. The limiting case would be that of an absentee who ultimately proved to have been an incompetent: Could the bar of time validly be raised to his claims? The Supreme Court has indicated it can, and there is no reason to suppose a retreat from this view. That being so, the minimum-contacts principle, particularized in needful special areas, attended by a notice requirement, and supplemented by systems of time bar, provides an adequate general theory of state-court jurisdiction.

Another gaze into the future appears in von Mehren & Trautman, *Jurisdiction to Adjudicate: A Suggested Analysis*, 79 Harv.L.Rev. 1121, 1164, 1166–68, 1172–75, 1177–79 (1966). After expressing dissatisfaction with the current breakdown of jurisdiction in terms of in personam, in rem, or quasi in rem, the authors recategorize as follows: 1) unlimited general jurisdiction permits the judgment to speak "without restriction to any of the judgment debtor's assets" regardless of the nature of the controversy; 2) limited general jurisdiction again permits the adjudication of any controversy but the resulting judgment can affect only a specified fund or assets; and 3) specific jurisdiction limits the court's power to adjudicate "to matters arising out of—or intimately related to—the affiliating circumstances on which the jurisdictional claim is based." The authors' prognosis is as follows:

> * * * We suggest that significant changes are probable in two directions. First, a more functional and less mechanical methodology will emerge, just as it has in the field of choice of law. Second, the landscape that we have surveyed will gradually change; in particular, specific jurisdiction will come into sharper relief and form a considerably more significant part of the scene. At the same time, the contours of present forms of specific jurisdiction will be modified substantially and entirely new forms may emerge. And if such a development does occur, there should be repercussions elsewhere; some of the principal bases of jurisdiction of the past may become exceptional and occasional devices.
> * * *
> What policies should inform these developments and give content to "reason" and "fairness"? We submit that specific jurisdiction—with its characteristic feature of permitting the plaintiff to require the defendant to come, as it were, to him—is appropriate in two distinct classes of cases: (1) when the traditional jurisdictional bias in favor of the defendant is not justified; (2) when very strong considerations of convenience, relating not only to the plaintiff but also to the taking of evidence and other litigational considerations, point to a particular community. * * *
> Why should the jurisdictional rule in *Hess v. Pawloski* favor the plaintiff? We suggest that the explanation lies in the multistate character of the defendant's activity giving rise to the underlying controversy, as compared with the localized nature of the plaintiff's. In addition, the defendant's activity foreseeably involved the risk of serious harm to individuals in communities other than his own. These two elements, taken together, and quite apart from considerations of litigational convenience, justify requiring the defendant to come to the plaintiff. The result is rendered still easier by the fact that the nonresident motorist—after the development of automobile insurance—usually does not handle his own case as a private person but is defended by representatives of his insurance company, whose activities are multistate and whose rates ultimately reflect the economic cost to defendants of requiring them to come to plaintiffs.

These observations suggest a point about specific jurisdiction that we consider basic to its future development: in any class of cases in which the controversy arises out of conduct that is essentially multistate on the part of the defendant, and essentially local on the part of the plaintiff, an argument exists for reversing the jurisdictional preference traditionally accorded defendants. This argument becomes very strong when the defendants as a class are regularly engaged in extensive multistate activity that will produce litigation from time to time, while the plaintiffs as a class are localized in their activities. The insurance cases illustrate this proposition splendidly: insurance companies are engaged in extensive multistate activity, and their economic and legal existence is not localized; on the other hand, plaintiffs who bring actions against an insurance company typically lead a localized economic and legal existence.

* * * [W]e now consider briefly a second form of specific jurisdiction, in which strong considerations of convenience, relating not only to the plaintiff but also to the taking of evidence and other litigational considerations, point to a particular community. * * * [J]urisdiction based on these considerations has been exercised sporadically in litigation involving multiple or indeterminate parties. The traditional bases for such exercises of jurisdiction have been the location of land or other assets in the community; and more recently, the establishment in the forum state of a legal entity, such as the trust in the *Mullane* case, has been recognized as an appropriate basis for the exercise of what might be called jurisdiction by necessity. Another form of jurisdiction by necessity may also eventually emerge: the assertion of jurisdiction in the interest of justice in those rare cases in which no forum that is appropriate under conventional standards is prepared to act. Hints of such an approach can be found, but the proposition should be generalized even though as long as the world remains reasonably ordered, the occasions for asserting jurisdiction on this basis will be exceedingly rare.

It seems too early to explore in any detail the appropriate contours of specific jurisdiction for dispersed parties associated in a common venture, but some guidelines may be suggested. Otherwise intractable situations involving such matters as assessment of the shareholders of an insolvent bank, determinations affecting members of a fraternal benefit association, and settlement of the accounts of a trustee can be handled by recognizing specific jurisdiction in the most obvious forum. Often only one obvious jurisdiction will exist—the place of incorporation of the bank or fraternal benefit association or the place of administration of the common trust fund, if those places are in fact the true headquarters of the common venture and there are no other states with substantially equivalent jurisdictional claims. * * *

Considerably more difficult are cases in which two jurisdictions have relatively equal claims. In such situations, if a particular community with strong jurisdictional claims also offers intrinsic guarantees against an aberrational or unfair choice-of-law process, this community should for that reason be preferred over another community with roughly equivalent jurisdictional claims but lacking comparable guarantees. For example, in the situation presented by *Hanson v. Denckla*, Florida was perhaps from the sheerly litigational point of view at least as convenient a forum as Delaware. However, on the issue presented—the validity of a trust—intrinsic guarantees of neutrality and objectivity in the choice-of-law process operate in Delaware—the seat of the trust—and are absent in Florida. * * *

If specific jurisdiction enjoys the growth and undergoes the refinement just described, other changes should occur in the coming decades in the accepted bases for assuming jurisdiction to adjudicate. For reasons that have already been suggested, ultimately only general jurisdiction and specific jurisdiction should be recognized, and the only relationship basing *general* jurisdiction should come to be habitual residence except in those rare situations in which the defendant has no substantial connection with any community. *Limited* general jurisdiction should disappear entirely as various forms of specific jurisdiction emerge to permit a community to adjudicate in those situations that, in the past, have furnished the only legitimate justification for the spectrum of limited genral jurisdiction cases that today runs from *Pennoyer v. Neff* through *Harris v. Balk* and perhaps even beyond.

Historically, the phenomenon of limited general jurisdiction is understandable. Specific jurisdiction was largely or completely unknown and enforcement of a foreign judgment was often difficult if not impossible. As a result the litigational convenience of proceeding where assets could be found was great, and the methodology through which jurisdictional problems were approached gave an apparent justification for such practices, concealing the true difficulties. Often, too, the presence of defendant's assets was symptomatic of other activities, or of relationships of the defendant to the forum, that functionally justified requiring the defendant to come to the plaintiff. But today all this is changing. Ultimately, all that should remain of *Pennoyer v. Neff, Harris v. Balk,* and their progeny is specific jurisdiction to secure assets against dissipation and concealment while a controversy is being litigated in an appropriate forum. The functions heretofore performed, often unfairly, by limited general jurisdiction can more rationally be performed by specific jurisdiction, which offers protection against the unfairness of requiring a defendant to litigate any and every question wherever his assets can be found * * *.

For much the same reasons, general jurisdiction based on presence, which often produces unfair results quite comparable to those reached under limited general jurisdiction, should disappear. It is, of course, appropriate to preserve some place where the defendant can be sued on any cause of action. But we submit that only the common arena of the defendant's activities should be such a place. For an individual, the sole community where it is fair to require him to litigate any cause of action is his habitual residence; for a corporation, it is the corporate headquarters— presumably both the place of incorporation and the principal place of business, where these differ. If specific jurisdiction matures to its full potential and is subjected to the tests based on fairness elaborated above, jurisdiction should be abandoned for many situations in which it is now asserted.

SECTION F. SERVICE OF PROCESS

---

1. SUFFICIENCY OF SERVICE OF PROCESS

A. THE ETIQUETTE OF SERVICE

WYMAN v. NEWHOUSE

United States Circuit Court of Appeals, Second Circuit, 1937.
93 F.2d 313.

MANTON, Circuit Judge. This appeal is from a judgment entered dismissing the complaint on motion before trial. The action is on a judgment entered by default in a Florida state court, a jury having assessed the damages. The recovery there was for money loaned, money advanced for appellee, and for seduction under promise of marriage.

* * *

Appellant and appellee were both married, but before this suit appellant's husband died. They had known each other for some years and had engaged in meretricious relations.

The affidavits submitted by the appellee * * * established that he was a resident of New York and never lived in Florida. On October 25, 1935, while appellee was in Salt Lake City, Utah, he received a telegram from the appellant, which read: "Account illness home planning leaving. Please come on way back. Must see you." Upon appellee's return to New York he received a letter from appellant stating that her mother was dying in Ireland; that she was leaving the United States for good to go to her mother; that she could not go without seeing the appellee once more; and that she wanted to discuss her affairs with him before she left. Shortly after the receipt of this letter, they spoke to each other on the telephone, whereupon the appellant repeated, in a hysterical and distressed voice, the substance of her letter. Appellee promised to go to Florida in a week or ten days and agreed to notify her when he would arrive. This he did, but before leaving New York by plane he received a letter couched in endearing terms and expressing love and affection for him, as well as her delight at his coming. Before leaving New York, appellee telegraphed appellant, suggesting arrangements for their accommodations together while in Miami, Fla. She telegraphed him at a hotel in Washington, D. C., where he was to stop en route, advising him that the arrangements requested had been made. Appellee arrived at 6 o'clock in the morning at the Miami Airport and saw the appellant standing with her sister some 75 feet distant. He was met by a deputy sheriff who, upon identifying appellee, served him with process in a suit for $500,000. A photographer was present who attempted to take his picture. Thereupon a stranger introduced himself and offered to take appellee to his home, stating that he knew a lawyer who was acquainted with the appellant's attorney. The attorney whom appellee was advised to consult came to the stranger's home and seemed to know about the case. The attorney invited appellee to his office, and upon his arrival he found one of the lawyers for the appellant there. Appellee did not retain the Florida attorney to represent him. He returned to New York by plane that evening and consulted his New York counsel, who advised him to ignore the summons served in Florida. He did so, and judgment was entered by default. * * *

These facts and reasonable deductions therefrom convincingly establish that the appellee was induced to enter the jurisdiction of the state of Florida by a fraud perpetrated upon him by the appellant in falsely representing her mother's illness, her intention to leave the United States, and her love and affection for him, when her sole purpose and apparent thought was to induce him to come within the Florida jurisdiction so as to serve him in an action for damages. * * *

This judgment is attacked for fraud perpetrated upon the appellee which goes to the jurisdiction of the Florida court over his person. A judgment procured fraudulently, as here, lacks jurisdiction and is null and void. * * * A fraud affecting the jurisdiction is equivalent to a lack of jurisdiction. * * * The appellee was not required to proceed against the judgment in Florida. His equitable defense in answer to a suit on the judgment is sufficient. A judgment recovered in a sister state, through the fraud of the party procuring the appearance of another, is not binding on the latter when an attempt is made to enforce such judgment in another state. * * *

The appellee was not required to make out a defense on the merits to the suit in Florida. * * * An error made in entering judgment against a party over whom the court had no jurisdiction permits a consideration of the jurisdictional question collaterally. The complaint was properly dismissed.

Judgment affirmed.

NOTES AND QUESTIONS

1. Reread *Tickle v. Barton*, p. 23, supra. Which case presents a stronger case for quashing service—*Wyman* or *Tickle*? Why? Would the result have been the same in *Wyman* if Mr. Newhouse had been in Florida and the trickery had been used to "flush him out of hiding"? See Gumperz v. Hofmann, 245 App.Div. 622, 283 N.Y.S. 823 (1st Dep't 1935), affirmed 271 N.Y. 544, 2 N.E. 2d 687 (1936).

2. WESTERN STATES REFINING CO. v. BERRY, 6 Utah 2d 336, 313 P.2d 480 (1957). Defendant, an Idaho citizen, was invited to Utah by plaintiff to negotiate a dispute. When discussions proved fruitless, plaintiff had process served on defendant before the latter could leave the state. The Utah Supreme Court quashed the service.

> * * * It is our opinion that when plaintiff extends an invitation to defendant to enter the jurisdiction for settlement negotiations, equity and good conscience will not permit plaintiff to take sharp advantage of defendant's presence in the jurisdiction so long as defendant is in the jurisdiction for the purpose for which plaintiff invited him. One who is invited into a jurisdiction to discuss compromise and settlement of a disputed matter will not be subject to service of process in that matter, if he comes into the jurisdiction for the sole purpose of discussing compromise and settlement, by the one extending the invitation, for a reasonable period involved in coming to the negotiations and returning therefrom, as well as during the period of actual presence at the negotiations, unless the party extending the invitation advises him at the time the invitation is extended that he will be served with process immediately if settlement negotiations fail.

Id. at 337–38, 313 P.2d 481–82. According to the dissenting justice:

> This decision opens the door to the unscrupulous nonresident present in the state, who, on being served by a resident, need only conveniently to state that he is present in the state at the invitation of the plaintiff for the purpose of settling a claim, thus inoculating himself against the indignities of the process server. Before such immunity should be granted, there should be a finding of an allurement, enticement, trickery, fraud, legal or otherwise, or some other kind of bad faith on the part of him, who did the inviting to negotiate, as the great weight of authority requires. The trial court in this case found that there was *not* any such trickery, bad faith or fraud * * *. In my opinion, the majority attacks the integrity of two members of the bar, neither of whom, in the opinion of this writer, has ever had the reputation of taking "sharp advantage" of others.

Id. at 339, 313 P.2d at 482–83. Would the *Berry* case make sense if Utah had a "long-arm" statute that permitted the assumption of jurisdiction over the Idaho defendant by service in Idaho?

3.   SIRO v. AMERICAN EXPRESS CO., 99 Conn. 95, 121 A. 280 (1923). Although the Express Company was not a "resident" of Connecticut, it was selling its travelers' checks in that state through the United States Bank in Hartford. To secure jurisdiction over the Express Company, plaintiff's attorney had a friend purchase $620 worth of checks at the Bank with money supplied by the attorney and endorse and deposit the checks to the attorney's credit in another bank. Pursuant to a prearranged plan, the debt of $620 running from the United States Bank to defendant created by the purchase of the travelers' checks was then "attached." The Supreme Court of Connecticut, after acknowledging the rule that a "court will not exercise a jurisdiction which rests upon a service of process on a defendant who has been decoyed, enticed or induced to come within its reach by any false representation, deceitful contrivance or wrongful device for which the plaintiff is responsible," concluded that there was "nothing in the conduct of the plaintiff which should be regarded in law as a breach of faith with the defendant, or as a false representation or deceitful contrivance, and nothing by which the defendant was enticed or induced to bring its property within the jurisdiction." Can *Siro* be harmonized with *Wyman*? See generally Annot., 98 A.L. R.2d 551 (1964).

4.   Consider NOWELL v. NOWELL, 24 Conn.Sup. 314, 190 A.2d 233 (1963), in which defendant was advised that process could not be served in Connecticut on Sunday and thus entered the jurisdiction on a Sunday to retrieve some personal effects held by his former wife. The wife, noting that the law permitted service after sundown on Sunday asked him to come to the house after tea and when he did so he was served by the sheriff. The court upheld service on the ground that defendant had not been fraudulently induced to enter the forum. Is this case distinguishable from *Wyman?*

———

McKELWAY, PROFILES—PLACE AND LEAVE WITH, New Yorker, August 24, 1935, 23–26:

* * *   In a little frame house near the intersection of Rogers and Flatbush Avenues in Brooklyn there lived until a few years ago an old lady named Mrs. Katherina Schnible. She was seventy-two and a little lame. She owned the house and rented out the first two floors as apartments, but there were mortgages and she had not met the payments. She knew the bank that held the mortgages was about to foreclose * * *. Her son, who lived with her, went out to work at eight in the morning and did not return until six, so from eight till six every day, except Sunday, Mrs. Schnible stayed in her room on the third floor and refused to open the door, no matter who knocked. Came a day when she heard a heavy footfall on the first landing, heard somebody running frantically up the first flight of stairs, heard a man's voice shouting something. Then the footsteps came closer, up the second flight of stairs, and right outside her door she heard yelled the word "Fire!" Mrs. Schnible opened her door and hobbled hurriedly into the hall. "Hello, Mrs. Schnible," said a man standing there. "Here's a summons for you." He handed her the papers, and the proceedings were begun which eventually put Mrs. Schnible out of her house.

Harry Grossman, who was the man in the hall, is regarded by those who employ him as the champion process-server of the day. He is an instrument of justice and his profession is a corner-stone of civil law, but not many of the people he serves appreciate that.   *   *   *   Grossman has been cursed by hundreds of defendants, many of them distinguished citizens. Defendants have thrown him down flights of stairs and shoved him off porches. He has been pinched, slapped, punched, and kicked by scores of individuals, and he was beaten up one time by a family of seven.

      *   *   *

"Place and leave with" is the legal phrase for what a process-server must do with a summons when he goes out to serve papers on a defendant, but the courts never have explained precisely what that means. Where the process-server must place the papers is still a nice legal question. A process-server once threw a summons-and-complaint at James Gordon Bennett and hit him in the chest with it, but the courts held that this was not a proper service. Another famous case in the lawbooks tells of a defendant named Martin, who in 1893 hid himself under his wife's petticoats and refused to receive the papers. The process-server saw him crouching there, so he put the papers on what seemed to be the defendant's shoulder, and went away. The Supreme Court rendered a decision which held that "where a person, to avoid service of summons, shelters himself in his wife's petticoats, the laying of the papers on his shoulder will be a sufficient service."   *   *   *

Grossman has never bothered to look up legal precedents for his actions; he simply places the papers in the hands of the defendant and leaves them there. On innumerable occasions he has had to use ingenuity in order to get close enough to the defendant to do this, and only once has he been forced to depart from a literal interpretation of the legal phrase. That was in the case of an elderly lady, who, like Mrs. Schnible, was trying to hide from him. This lady, whose name was Mrs. Mahoney, refused to leave her apartment in the East Side tenement she owned, and Grossman's routine tricks   *   *   * failed to budge her. He knew she was there, because he had wheedled his way into a flat across the court from her and had seen her sitting at her kitchen table in front of an open window, peeling potatoes. Grossman went home to his own apartment in Brooklyn and thought for a while, and then began to practice throwing the summons. He put rubber bands around the paper to make it compact, placed a salad bowl on the dining-room table, and practiced all that afternoon, throwing the subpoena into the bowl from the middle of the living-room. He went back next morning to the flat across the court from Mrs. Mahoney's kitchen. She came into the kitchen a little before noon, puttered around for a while, and then sat down at the table with a bowl of potatoes in front of her and began placidly to peel them. Grossman leaned out of his window and tossed the subpoena. The papers landed in the bowl just as the old lady reached into it. "There you are, Mrs. Mahoney!" Grossman shouted. "There's a foreclosure paper for you!" The courts never questioned his method of placing these papers, and Mrs. Mahoney lost her property.

Tens of thousands of papers have to be served in the course of a year in this city, and the majority of them are handled for the law firms by process-serving agencies, which rely for their profits on quantity and a quick turnover. * * * Cases involving expert dodgers or stubborn hug-the-hearths usually are turned over to private detective agencies, and the detective agencies usually hire Grossman to serve the papers. When the Electrical Research Product Institute sued the Fox Film Corporation for $15,000,000 in 1930, the lawyers for the plaintiff, naturally, surmised that it would be difficult to "place and leave with" William Fox, Winfield Sheehan, and other defendants, the papers summoning them to come to court. Grossman received the assignment through a detective agency. He got in to see Fox by having a telegram sent from Boston saying that Mr. Grossman had "closed the theatre deal" and would call on Fox at eleven o'clock the next morning. When Grossman reached Fox's office, the film executive's secretary told him Mr. Fox had received the wire but was not sure what deal it was that had been closed. "My God," said Grossman, "the theatre deal—that's what deal! If this is the way I am to be received, never mind—to hell with it!" He started out, and the secretary called him back. "Just wait one moment," she said. "I'll tell Mr. Fox." She opened a door marked "Private" and went into an inner office. Grossman followed her and handed Fox the subpoena. Fox started up from his desk indignantly, but Grossman's indignation expressed itself first. "You, a multi-millionaire!" Grossman shouted. "Is it decent, is it nice, for a multi-millionaire who can be sued for fifteen million dollars to hide from me? Why don't you take the papers like a man?" This so flabbergasted Fox that he sank back in his chair, and Grossman went through the corporation's offices unimpeded and served papers on Sheehan, two vice-presidents, the secretary, and the treasurer.

* * * Harry established a reputation as an adroit private detective before he was old enough to serve subpoenas. * * * But after he had passed his eighteenth birthday and had begun to serve summonses and subpoenas, it was evident to his employer, and to everybody else who knew him, that he had found a vocation in which he might expect to excel. During his first year he served Maude Adams by posing as a youthful adorer. When she came out of the stage entrance at the Empire Theatre after a performance one evening, Grossman stepped in front of her holding in his left hand a bouquet of jonquils. "Are you Maude Adams?" he asked. "Oh, are those really for me?" she exclaimed, reaching for the flowers, "No, but this is," said Grossman, jerking back the bouquet. With his right hand he served her with a summons. He still remembers that he had paid fifty cents for the jonquils and that he was able to sell them back to the florist for twenty.

His ability to become more indignant at the attitude of defendants than defendants are at his actions has saved Grossman from bodily injury on many occasions. One of his early triumphs involved Gutzon Borglum. The sculptor was at that time modelling life-size figures in a studio in the Gramercy Park section. Grossman entered by means of what he calls the rush act. A maid opened the door and Grossman rushed past her, saying perfunctorily "Is Mr. Borglum in?" Borglum was chipping stone on a nearly completed nude. "Here's a summons for you, Mr. Borglum," said Grossman. "Of all the effrontery," began the sculptor. "You * * * you * * * you ought to be * * *." Then Grossman began to shout. "How about you?" he asked. "Shouldn't you maybe be ashamed of yourself? You and your naked women!" He went out spluttering with indignation, leaving Borglum speechless, clutching the summons in his hand.

"SEWER" SERVICE

In UNITED STATES v. BRAND JEWELERS, INC., 318 F.Supp. 1293 (S.D.N.Y.1970), noted in 37 Brooklyn L.Rev. 426, 84 Harv.L. Rev. 1930, 46 N.Y.U.L.Rev. 367, 20 J.Pub.L. 337, 24 Vand.L.Rev. 829, 17 Wayne L.Rev. 1287, 1971 Wis.L.Rev. 665, it was held that the United States had standing to seek an injunction preventing defendant from systematically obtaining default judgments against economically disadvantaged defendants by utilizing so-called "sewer" service techniques, by which the process server simply disposes of the papers and makes a false affidavit of service. The actions were for the purchase price of consumer goods sold on "easy credit terms" by door-to-door salesmen. The court reasoned that continuously failing to make proper service of process or preparing false affidavits of service imposed "a burden on interstate commerce." Moreover, defendants' alleged conduct was held to be "state action" so that the United States had standing to sue to end a widespread unconstitutional deprivation of property without due process of law.

B. THE TECHNIQUE OF SERVICE

ROVINSKI v. ROWE, 131 F.2d 687, 689 (6th Cir.1942). Rowe brought suit against Rovinski in a Michigan state court, service of process being effected under the state's nonresident motorist statute. Rovinski moved to dismiss on the ground that he was a resident of Michigan, and hence not amenable to service under the statute. After the action was dismissed, Rowe commenced a diversity action against Rovinski in a federal court. Service of process was made under Federal Rule of Civil Procedure 4(d)(1), by leaving a copy of the summons and complaint with Rovinski's mother, at the address that he had given as his residence in an affidavit supporting his motion to dismiss in the prior state action. Rovinski again attacked service, contending that his "dwelling place and usual place of abode" had been in Minnesota for the past two years, and that he had returned to his mother's house only to visit, even though he considered it his legal residence. The district court held the service of process valid, and the Sixth Circuit affirmed:

In construing * * * Rule 4(d)(1) liberally, the district court effectuated the declared purpose of the Supreme Court Advisory Committee in submitting a service of process rule, which would provide "a good deal of freedom and flexibility in service." * * * That the rule should be liberally construed seems logical, when consideration is given to the fact that uncertainty of its applicability to varying situations would be increased by strict construction. This is apparent from the irreconcilable conflict among state courts upon the meaning and interpretation of the expression "usual place of abode." * * *

The wide diversity of opinion may be illustrated by two examples. On the one hand, delivery of process to defendant's wife at an apartment in Miami Beach, Florida, where his family had been living for about two months and where he had previously visited them, but from which he had departed to his permanent home in another state, was held *sufficient* under a Florida statute * * *. On the other hand, delivery of service of process to the father of a minor defendant at the family home where the defendant had lived up to the time of his enlistment in the United States Army less than one month previously was held *insufficient* under a New Jersey statute * * *.

The only pertinent reported Federal decision is Skidmore v. Green, D.C.N.Y., 33 F.Supp. 529, 530, wherein service was upheld under Rule 4(d)(1) against a peregrinating policeman, who, after retiring from the New York force, spent most of his time traveling about the country in an automobile and trailer. Process had been delivered at the home of defendant's brother which, in the application for his New York automobile license, defendant had given as his address. In his application for his South Carolina automobile license, he had stated that he was a resident of New York. The district judge commented that "so far as the migratory nature of his life" permitted of any place of abode or dwelling house, that place was his brother's home.

NOTE

Identifying a person's usual place of abode often is difficult. For example, in FIRST NAT. BANK & TRUST CO. OF TULSA v. INGERTON, 207 F.2d 793 (10th Cir.1953), defendants, who were horse owners, appeared to change their residence whenever their horses moved to a new race track. Their furniture was stored in a warehouse in Raton, New Mexico, and some of their possessions were left at a hotel there, at which they continued to receive mail. Process was served on defendants' daughter at a furnished home that they had rented for one month in Denver, Colorado. The trial court later quashed the service on the ground that defendants' usual place of abode was Raton. The appellate court affirmed but Judge Murrah dissented noting that

> * * * for the purpose of notice and service, consideration ought undeniably be given to the living habits of the defendant. If the defendant is an itinerant without any fixed dwelling or residence, * * * the migratory nature of the defendant becomes important to the question * * *. [T]he record clearly shows that as race horse owners, the Ingertons' usual place of abode was wherever their horses happened to be running.

Id. at 795, 796.

NATIONAL EQUIPMENT RENTAL, LTD. v. SZUKHENT

Supreme Court of the United States, 1964.
375 U.S. 311, 84 S.Ct. 411, 11 L.Ed.2d 354.

Certiorari to the United States Court of Appeals for the Second Circuit.

Mr. Justice STEWART delivered the opinion of the Court.

* * * The petitioner is a corporation with its principal place of business in New York. It sued the respondents, residents of Michigan, in a New York federal court, claiming that the respondents had defaulted under a farm equipment lease. The only question now before us is whether the person upon whom the summons and complaint were served was "an agent authorized by appointment" to receive the same, so as to subject the respondents to the jurisdiction of the federal court in New York.

The respondents obtained certain farm equipment from the petitioner under a lease executed in 1961. The lease was on a printed form less than a page and a half in length, and consisted of 18 numbered paragraphs. The last numbered paragraph, appearing just above the respondents' signatures and printed in the same type used in the remainder of the instrument, provided that "the Lessee hereby designates Florence Weinberg, 47–21 Forty-first Street, Long Island City, N. Y., as agent for the purpose of accepting service of any process within the State of New York." The respondents were not acquainted with Florence Weinberg.

In 1962 the petitioner commenced the present action by filing in the federal court in New York a complaint which alleged that the respondents had failed to make any of the periodic payments specified by the lease. The Marshal delivered two copies of the summons and complaint to Florence Weinberg. That same day she mailed the summons and complaint to the respondents, together with a letter stating that the documents had been served upon her as the respondents' agent for the purpose of accepting service of process in

New York, in accordance with the agreement contained in the lease. The petitioner itself also notified the respondents by certified mail of the service of process upon Florence Weinberg.

Upon motion of the respondents, the District Court quashed service of the summons and complaint, holding that, although Florence Weinberg had promptly notified the respondents of the service of process and mailed copies of the summons and complaint to them, the lease agreement itself had not explicitly required her to do so, and there was therefore a "failure of the agency arrangement to achieve intrinsic and continuing reality." * * * The Court of Appeals affirmed * * * and we granted certiorari * * *.

We need not and do not in this case reach the situation where no personal notice has been given to the defendant. Since the respondents did in fact receive complete and timely notice of the lawsuit pending against them, no due process claim has been made. The case before us is therefore quite different from cases where there was no actual notice * * *. Similarly, as the Court of Appeals recognized, this Court's decision in Wuchter v. Pizzutti * * * is inapposite here. * * * Wuchter dealt with the limitations imposed by the Fourteenth Amendment upon a statutory scheme by which a State attempts to subject nonresident individuals to the jurisdiction of its courts. The question presented here, on the other hand, is whether a party to a private contract may appoint an agent to receive service of process within the meaning of Federal Rule of Civil Procedure 4(d) (1), where the agent is not personally known to the party, and where the agent has not expressly undertaken to transmit notice to the party.

The purpose underlying the contractual provision here at issue seems clear. The clause was inserted by the petitioner and agreed to by the respondents in order to assure that any litigation under the lease should be conducted in the State of New York. The contract specifically provided that "This agreement shall be deemed to have been made in Nassau County, New York, regardless of the order in which the signatures of the parties shall be affixed hereto, and shall be interpreted, and the rights and liabilities of the parties here determined, in accordance with the laws of the State of New York." And it is settled, as the courts below recognized, that parties to a contract may agree in advance to submit to the jurisdiction of a given court, to permit notice to be served by the opposing party, or even to waive notice altogether. * * *

Under well-settled general principles of the law of agency Florence Weinberg's prompt acceptance and transmittal to the respondents of the summons and complaint pursuant to the authorization was itself sufficient to validate the agency, even though there was no explicit previous promise on her part to do so. * * *

We deal here with a Federal Rule, applicable to federal courts in all 50 States. But even if we were to assume that this uniform federal standard should give way to contrary local policies, there is no relevant concept of state law which would invalidate the agency here at issue. In Michigan, where the respondents reside, the statute which validates service of process under the circumstances present in this case contains no provision requiring that the appointed agent expressly undertake to notify the principal of the service of process. Similarly, New York law, which it was agreed should be applicable to the lease provisions, does not require any such express promise by the agent in order to create a valid agency for receipt of process.   *   *   *

It is argued, finally, that the agency sought to be created in this case was invalid because Florence Weinberg may have had a conflict of interest. This argument is based upon the fact that she was not personally known to the respondents at the time of her appointment and upon a suggestion in the record that she may be related to an officer of the petitioner corporation. But such a contention ignores the narrowly limited nature of the agency here involved. Florence Weinberg was appointed the respondents' agent for the single purpose of receiving service of process. An agent with authority so limited can in no meaningful sense be deemed to have had an interest antagonistic to the respondents, since both the petitioner and the respondents had an equal interest in assuring that, in the event of litigation, the latter be given that adequate and timely notice which is a prerequisite to a valid judgment.

A different case would be presented if Florence Weinberg had not given prompt notice to the respondents, for then the claim might well be made that her failure to do so had operated to invalidate the agency. We hold only that, prompt notice to the respondents having been given, Florence Weinberg was their "agent authorized by appointment" to receive process within the meaning of Federal Rule of Civil Procedure 4(d) (1).

Judgment of Court of Appeals reversed and case remanded.

Mr. Justice BLACK, dissenting.

*   *   *   I disagree with   *   *   *   [the Court's] holding, believing that (1) whether Mrs. Weinberg was a valid agent upon whom service could validly be effected under Rule 4(d) (1) should be determined under New York law and that we should accept the holdings of the federal district judge and the Court of Appeals sitting in New York that under that State's law the purported appointment of Mrs. Weinberg was invalid and ineffective; (2) if however, Rule 4(d) (1) is to be read as calling upon us to formulate a new federal definition of agency for purposes of service of process, I think our formulation should exclude Mrs. Weinberg from the category of an "agent authorized by appointment   *   *   *   to receive service of process"; and (3) upholding service of process in this case raises serious questions as to whether these Michigan farmers have been denied due process of law in violation of the Fifth and Fourteenth Amendments.

*   *   *

The end result of today's holding is not difficult to foresee. Clauses like the one used against the Szukhents—clauses which companies have not inserted, I suspect, because they never dreamed a court would uphold them—will soon find their way into the "boilerplate" of everything from an equipment lease to a conditional sales contract. Today's holding gives a green light to every large company in this country to contrive contracts which declare with force of law that when such a company wants to sue someone with whom it does business, that individual must go and try to defend himself in some place, no matter how distant, where big business enterprises are concentrated, like, for example, New York, Connecticut, or Illinois, or else suffer a default judgment.   In this very case the Court holds that by this company's carefully prepared contractual clause the Szukhents must, to avoid a judgment rendered without a fair and full hearing, travel hundreds of miles across the continent, probably crippling their defense and certainly depleting what savings they may have, to try to defend themselves in a court sitting in New York City.   I simply cannot believe that Congress, when by its silence it let Rule 4(d) (1) go into effect, meant for that rule to be used as a means to achieve such a far-reaching, burdensome, and unjust result.   Heretofore judicial good common sense has, on one ground or another, disregarded contractual provisions like this one, not encouraged them.   It is a long trip from San Francisco—or from Honolulu or Anchorage—to New York, Boston, or Wilmington.   And the trip can be very expensive, often costing more than it would simply to pay what is demanded.   The very threat of such a suit can be used to force payment of alleged claims, even though they be wholly without merit.   This fact will not be news to companies exerting their economic power to wangle such contracts.   *   *   *

Mr. Justice BRENNAN, with whom THE CHIEF JUSTICE and Mr. Justice GOLDBERG join, dissenting.

I would affirm.   In my view, federal standards and not state law must define who is "an agent authorized by appointment" within the meaning of Rule 4(d) (1).   *   *   *   In formulating these standards I would, *first*, construe Rule 4(d) (1) to deny validity to the appointment of a purported agent whose interests conflict with those of his supposed principal   *   *   *.   *Second,* I would require that the appointment include an explicit condition that the agent after service transmit the process forthwith to the principal.   Although our decision in Wuchter v. Pizzutti   *   *   *   dealt with the constitutionality of a state statute, the reasoning of that case is persuasive that, in fashioning a federal agency rule, we should engraft the same requirement upon Rule 4(d) (1).   *Third,* since the corporate plaintiff prepared the printed form contract, I would not hold the individual purchaser bound by the appointment without proof, in addition to his mere signature on the form, that the individual understandingly consented to be sued in a State not that of his residence.   *   *   *   It offends common sense to treat a printed form which closes an installment sale as embodying terms to all of which the individual knowingly assented.   The sales pitch aims solely at getting the signature on the form and wastes no time explaining or even mentioning the print.   *   *   *

NOTES AND QUESTIONS

1.   In appraising cases such as *Rovinski* and *Szukhent,* remember that neither jurisdiction, in the "power" sense, nor actual notice is in issue.   The basic

inquiry is whether the court should refrain from taking the case in view of the technique used to serve process. Under what circumstances should the manner of service be a limiting factor? Do the policies underlying *Fuentes v. Shevin*, p. 123, supra, cast doubt on the procedure used in *Szukhent*?

2. How defective must a summons be before it will be stricken by the Court? In THARP v. THARP, 228 Minn. 23, 36 N.W.2d 1 (1949), the summons stated:

> You are hereby summoned to appear within twenty days after service of this summons * * * and defend the above entitled action in the court aforesaid; and in case of your failure to do so, judgment will be rendered against you in the sum of * * *.

> G. F. Mantz,
> Attorney for Plaintiff,
> Oak Grove and Hennepin,
> Minneapolis, Minnesota.

Defendant moved to quash service and plaintiff cross-moved to amend the summons to conform it to the statute. By the time the motions were heard, the statute of limitations on plaintiff's claim had run. The Minnesota court held the summons "fatally defective." Evaluate the following reasons for the result.

> The statute requires the summons to designate a place within the state at which the defendant is required to serve his answer upon the subscriber to the summons. The summons here is entirely lacking in this requirement. It directs defendant * * * to appear in the district court at any time within 20 days to defend the lawsuit. That is materially different from directing defendant to serve an answer within 20 days on the subscriber at his office. Nothing is said about the effect of a failure to answer. * * *

> In passing, it may be noted that the subscriber designates his address as "Oak Grove and Hennepin," a metropolitan street intersection. "Oak Grove and Hennepin" may be a "specified place within the state," in the words of the statute, but it is rather indefinite as a place where an answer may be served.

> * * *

> Here, defendant would obviously be prejudiced where, if an amendment were granted, a defense which would bar the cause of action would be destroyed. Since the summons was so fatally defective as in effect to be no summons at all, the amendment proposed by plaintiff would breathe life into a cause of action which had expired.

Id. at 26–27, 36 N.W.2d at 3–4. See also Pinkham v. Jennings, 123 Me. 343, 122 A. 873 (1923) (summons that did not have seal or signature vacated just before trial despite fact that defendant had answered complaint); Rockefeller v. Hein, 176 Misc. 659, 28 N.Y.S.2d 266 (Sup.Ct.1941) (failure to include defendant's name invalidated summons).

3. How can a plaintiff prepare a valid summons when he can describe but cannot identify defendant? Is there any way by which plaintiff can toll the statute of limitations when he doesn't have time to locate and identify defendant? Does the solution to this problem depend on whether the jurisdiction deems an action commenced when the complaint is filed or when service actually is effected

upon defendant? See generally Note, *Designation of Defendants by Fictitious Names—Use of John Doe Complaints*, 46 Iowa L.Rev. 773 (1961).

4. When service is made pursuant to a statute permitting service by registered mail, return receipt requested, what are the consequences of a failure to present a signed receipt? If a signed receipt is mandatory, can defendant avoid service merely by refusing delivery of the letter or by refusing to sign the receipt? See generally Olsen v. Dairyland Mut. Ins. Co., 248 F.Supp. 639 (D.Mont.1966); Annot., 95 A.L.R.2d 1033 (1964).

5. Note the elaborate provision for service of process in a foreign country in Federal Rule of Civil Procedure 4(i). A comparable provision is found in Section 2.01 of the Uniform Interstate and International Procedure Act. 9B Uniform Laws Ann. 305, 315–18 (1966). The intention of these provisions is to provide American attorneys with an extremely flexible framework to permit accommodation to the widely divergent procedures for service of process employed by the various nations of the world. This accommodation is necessary in order to avoid violating the sovereignty of other countries by committing acts within their borders that they may consider to be "official" and to maximize the likelihood that the judgment rendered in the action in this country will be recognized and enforced abroad. Service of process in a foreign country and other procedural aspects of civil litigation having multi-national incidents are discussed in Miller, *International Cooperation in Litigation Between the United States and Switzerland: Unilateral Procedural Accommodation in a Test Tube*, 49 Minn.L.Rev. 1069, 1075–86 (1965); Comment, *Revitalization of the International Judicial Assistance Procedures of the United States: Service of Documents and Taking of Testimony*, 62 Mich.L.Rev. 1375, 1377–86 (1964). See also 4 Wright & Miller, *Federal Practice and Procedure: Civil* §§ 1133–36 (1969).

RETURN OF SERVICE

After the process server has delivered the papers to the defendant, he must file a return, which should contain the basic facts relating to the service to demonstrate that defendant actually has been served and given notice that he is required to appear in court. Thus, although the actual service of process and not the proof of that act is a prerequisite to the court assuming jurisdiction, it has been held that a proper return ordinarily is necessary in order for the trial court to conclude it has jurisdiction.

Should the process server's return of service be considered conclusive or merely presumptive evidence that service has been effected? Consider the rationale advanced by the Supreme Court in MIEDREICH v. LAUEN-STEIN, 232 U.S. 236, 34 S.Ct. 309, 58 L.Ed. 584 (1914), in which plaintiff sought to vacate a mortgage foreclosure judgment rendered in a prior suit. She was not a resident of the county in which the action was brought, was not served with process, and had no knowledge of the prior proceeding; the sheriff had made a false return of summons. The Supreme Court upheld the prior judgment:

> In the present case the * * * original party in the foreclosure proceeding did all that the law required in the issue of and

attempt to serve process; and, without fraud or collusion, the sheriff made a return to the court that service had been duly made. * * * [A]lthough contrary to the fact, in the absence of any attack upon it, the court was justified in acting upon such return as upon a true return. If the return is false the law of the State * * * permitted a recovery against the sheriff upon his bond. We are of the opinion that this system of jurisprudence, with its provisions for safeguarding the rights of litigants, is due process of law. It may result, unfortunately, * * * that the recovery upon the sheriff's bond will not be an adequate remedy, but statutes must be framed and laws administered so as to protect * * * all litigants and other persons who derive rights from the judgments of courts. * * * [T]he purchaser at the sheriff's sale had a right to rely upon the record * * *.

Id. at 246, 34 S.Ct. at 312, 58 L.Ed. at 591. Is it significant that *Miedreich* involves a collateral attack on the sheriff's return? Would the result have been the same if a direct attack in the original proceeding had been involved? Compare Gamlen Chem. Co. v. Dacar Chem. Prods. Co., 57 F.Supp. 574 (W.D.Pa.1964).

In some situations the return will not resolve issues of fact and it will not be treated as conclusive with regard to them. For example, when a corporate defendant is served, the return of service is not conclusive on the question whether the person served actually was an agent of defendant.

---

2. IMMUNITY FROM PROCESS

STATE EX REL. SIVNKSTY v. DUFFIELD

Supreme Court of Appeals of West Virginia, 1952.
137 W.Va. 112, 71 S.E.2d 113.

[On June 30, 1951, while vacationing in Gilmer County, West Virginia, petitioner Sivnksty's automobile struck and injured two children who were walking along the highway. He was arrested on charges of reckless driving, and, being unable to post bond, was incarcerated in the county jail until his trial on July 2. While he was in jail awaiting trial, Sivnksty was served with process in a tort action brought by one of the children in the Circuit Court of Gilmer County. Sivnksty was found guilty of the criminal charge and his appeals from that conviction failed.

Sivnksty made a special appearance in the civil action and filed a plea in abatement, alleging that the court was without jurisdiction because at the time of service he was a nonresident of the county and a prisoner in the county jail.

The court sustained a demurrer to the plea in abatement, whereupon Sivnksty petitioned the Supreme Court of Appeals of West Virginia for a writ of prohibition against the judge of the trial court. A stipulation was filed with the appellate court stating that Sivnksty had entered Gilmer County on June 30, 1951, with the intention of remaining there through the Fourth of July holiday and that he left the county immediately upon his release on appeal bond following his conviction on July 2, 1951.]

RILEY, President. * * *

The sole question presented by this record is: In the circumstances of this case was the petitioner immune from civil process at the time he was served with process in the civil action? Petitioner asserts here that the mere fact that he intended, when he came into Gilmer County, to remain for a period of a few days could not render his continuing presence in Gilmer County, after he was arrested, one of a voluntary status, when he was, in fact, incarcerated in the county jail there against his will.

The original and prime purpose for which the privilege of immunity from civil process on nonresidents of a county or state charged with crime therein was the protection of the court itself from interference with its judicial processes. Thus, originally the rule was asserted as the privilege of the court to secure the administration of justice free from outside interference or influence. Later the rule was enlarged for the protection of suitors, witnesses, jurors, and court officials from process, both in civil and criminal cases. Whited v. Phillips, 98 W.Va. 204, 205, 206, 126 S.E. 916, 917, 40 A.L.R. 83. In the Whited case the Court said: "It is well said that, if there is ever a time when a man should be relieved of all other concerns, and when he should be permitted to use unhampered his every faculty, it is when he is on trial under charge of a crime. Judicial reasoning also recognizes the right of a man, ordinarily, to be tried by a jury in the vicinity in which he resides, so that he may have such advantage and safeguard there as his conduct and character shall merit."

In addition the privilege of immunity from civil process of a nonresident of a county or state, charged with crime therein, has underlying it the public policy that a person charged with crime in a county of which he is a nonresident will not be deterred from appearing before the courts of that county or state by the threat of civil or other process; and thus a person so charged with crime because of the immunity extended will be encouraged to return to the county or state in which he is charged with crime to respond to the criminal process.

* * *

In the syllabus to Whited v. Phillips, supra, perhaps the leading case in this jurisdiction, bearing on the instant subject matter, this Court held: "A non-resident of West Virginia, who voluntarily and without compulsion of law, submits himself to the jurisdiction of a state court, in answer to an indictment therein against him, and who is not at the time a fugitive from justice, is privileged while attending court from service of process in a civil suit." In this jurisdiction the immunity rule has been applied to a case in which a defendant in a civil action was served with process while he was in a county, of which he was not a resident, in obedience to a citation from a member of the Department of Public Safety to answer a criminal charge. Morris v. Calhoun, 119 W.Va. 603, pt. 3 syl., 195 S.E. 341. It has also been applied to a case in which a person charged with a criminal offense in a county of which he was a nonresident, was arrested therefor in that county and later released on bond on his own recognizance, and who, in pursuance of such recognizance, returned to the county to answer the charge on the day set for trial. Lang v. Shaw, 113 W.Va. 628, syl., 169 S.E. 444. But in the case of State ex rel. Godby v. Chambers, 130 W.Va. 115, pt. 2 syl., 42 S.E.2d 255, 256, * * * the Court refused the writ of prohibition on the ground that after petitioner's conviction, sentence, and incarceration on a misdemeanor charge, the reason for the application of the immunity rule was not present, and that in that case there was no criminal process within the meaning of the immunity rule. * * *

In the instant case the petitioner went to Gilmer County of his own volition: he did not enter the county in response to a criminal process, because at the time of his entry therein he had committed no crime, and there was pending against him no criminal case. * * * In Crusco v. Strunk Steel Co., 365 Pa. 326, 74 A.2d 142, 20 A.L.R.2d 160, the Pennsylvania Supreme Court held that a defendant residing outside of a county in which a civil action had been commenced, and who was arrested on a warrant issued on an information of the plaintiff in the civil action and brought within the county, was not immune from civil process merely because of his status as a criminal defendant. For an excellent collation of authorities, see annotation in 20 A.L.R.2d 160, pages 163 to 189 * * *. In 72 C.J.S., Process, § 82, the rule is well stated as follows: "A person confined in jail on a criminal charge or imprisoned on conviction for such charge is subject to service of civil process, irrespective of the question of residence, at least if he was voluntarily in the jurisdiction at the time of the arrest and confinement." * * *

As the petitioner did not come and was not brought into Gilmer County under criminal process, the reason for the application of the immunity rule is not present, and he is not entitled to the writ of prohibition prayed for.

Writ denied.

LOVINS, Judge (dissenting). Being of the opinion that the refusal of a writ of prohibition in this case virtually emasculates the principle relative to immunity of a litigant from the service of judicial process in the circumstances here shown, I respectfully dissent.

The rule of immunity of a litigant in attendance upon a court from the service of judicial process is of ancient origin. * * *

Originally the rule of immunity applied only to the judges and attaches of a court, but gradually it has been extended to cover witnesses and litigants as well. It seems to have been founded on reasons of public policy in that service of process on a judge or official of a court would interfere with the orderly administration of justice and would detract from the dignity of the court. An additional reason in modern decisions has been assigned: that a witness should be free of fear, embarrassment, vexation and harassment while attending a court as a witness in one cause and therefore should be immune from service in a different cause. The same reason has been assigned for the protection of a litigant, that he should not be vexed by the service of process in another action or criminal prosecution.

In this jurisdiction there is no statute dealing with the subject of immunity from service of judicial process to a person to whom the rule applies. The law on the subject will be found in the opinion of this court in Whited v. Phillips, supra, and cases subsequently decided by this court hereinafter cited. This court in the Whited case used the following language: "Judicial reasoning also recognizes the right of a man, ordinarily, to be tried by a jury in the vicinity in which he resides, so that he may have such advantage and safeguard there as his conduct and character shall merit. An additional argument for the extension of the rule is that a person should not ordinarily be drawn into a foreign jurisdiction 'and there be exposed to entanglements in litigation far from home, which means he shall be attended with augmented expense.' "   *   *   *

The specific question here considered is: May a defendant in a criminal charge, confined in jail on such charge and unable to furnish bail bond, be served with process commencing a civil action based on the same facts as those involved in the criminal prosecution?

An examination of the various authorities will disclose that the courts of last resort which have considered this question are not in accord and that the authorities are in confusion with respect to the same.   *   *   *

In the instant case, Sivnksty came into Gilmer County voluntarily for the purpose of fishing. While there, he had an accident and thereafter was incarcerated in the jail. His presence in Gilmer County, originally voluntary, became involuntary.   *   *   *   I think whether Sivnksty came into Gilmer County voluntarily or otherwise has no pertinency to the question here presented.

Sivnksty will be forced to trial in a county far from his residence, among strangers. Even though he may have led an exemplary life and may have had a good reputation in the county of his residence, he would derive little or no benefit from those factors. In addition, he was harassed in his defense of the criminal charge by the institution of the civil suit against him while the criminal charge was still pending. This case is dissimilar from State ex rel. Godby v. Chambers, supra. In that case, the defendant had already been convicted.

Another element enters into this case. It is a matter of common knowledge that in this day and age there is much travel by motor vehicles. Under the rule laid down in the majority opinion, the luckless motorist, who has the misfortune to have an accident injuring persons or property in a county or state far from his residence, may be arrested and incarcerated in jail on a criminal charge, based on a real or fancied violation of an ordinance or statute having no connection with the accident, and while so incarcerated, the person suffering the injury would immediately commence an action in his own home county for the recovery of alleged damages. This could and may lead to widespread abuse of judicial process.

* * *

NOTES AND QUESTIONS

1. Although immunity from process serves the legitimate goals of furthering the presence of witnesses at judicial and quasi-judicial proceedings and permitting government officials to discharge their duties, when carried to extremes it ignores the resident plaintiff's desire to litigate in a local forum. What limitations could be imposed on a witness' immunity from process in order to reach some form of balance between the competing interests? Should immunity be denied when the witness furthers some personal goal by entering the state to testify or would such a test be too evanescent to enforce? See St. John v. Superior Court, 178 Cal.App.2d 794, 3 Cal.Rptr. 535 (2d Dist.1960); Franklin v. Superior Court, 98 Cal.App.2d 292, 220 P.2d 8 (1st Dist.1950). See also Recent Development, 48 Calif.L.Rev. 867 (1960). Should a nonresident attorney be exempt from process while in a state representing a client on a matter unrelated to the suit in which he is served? What if it is related? See State ex rel. Johnson v. Tautges, 146 Neb. 439, 20 N.W.2d 232 (1945). Should immunity depend upon whether the forum is a "convenient" one for defendant? What would be the ingredients of such a standard? See Note, *Immunity of Non-Resident Participants in a Judicial Proceeding from Service of Process—A Proposal for Renovation*, 26 Ind.L.J. 459 (1951).

2. Does it make any sense to grant a defendant who can be reached outside the state under a long-arm statute immunity from process when she is within the state for a purpose that otherwise would qualify for immunity? See generally Keeffe & Roscia, *Immunity and Sentimentality*, 32 Cornell L.Q. 471 (1947).

3. EBERLIN v. PENNSYLVANIA R. R., 402 Pa. 520, 522, 167 A.2d 155, 156–57 (1961).

> The privilege of exemption from service of civil process enjoyed by a nonresident suitor or witness in a civil action is not a privilege of the individual but of the court itself and exists that the business of the court might be expedited and justice duly administered. * * * The privilege is only extended as judicial necessities require and should be denied if the court feels that under the circumstances the judicial necessity is not great enough to require it.

Under what circumstances should a court deny immunity to a witness or governmental official as a matter of discretion? See Lamb v. Schmitt, 285 U.S. 222, 52 S.Ct. 317, 76 L.Ed. 720 (1932); 61 Colum.L.Rev. 278 (1961). See generally 4 Wright & Miller, *Federal Practice and Procedure: Civil* §§ 1076–81 (1969).

4. In many instances immunity from process is governed by statute. For example, 22 U.S.C. §§ 252–54, and 288d(b) grant immunity to certain representatives of foreign governments, their families, and members of their households. What justification is there for giving these people immunity?

SECTION G. CHALLENGING THE JURISDICTION OF THE COURT

HARKNESS v. HYDE

Supreme Court of the United States, 1878.
98 U.S. 476, 25 L.Ed. 237.

Error to the Supreme Court of the Territory of Idaho.

Mr. Justice FIELD delivered the opinion of the court.

This was an action to recover damages for maliciously and without probable cause procuring the seizure and detention of property of the plaintiff under a writ of attachment. It was brought in September, 1873, in a district court of the Territory of Idaho for the county of Oneida. The summons, with a copy of the complaint, was soon afterwards served by the sheriff of the county on the defendant, at his place of residence, which was on the Indian reservation, known as the Shoshonee reservation.

The defendant thereupon appeared specially by counsel appointed for the purpose, and moved the court to dismiss the action, on the ground that the service thus made upon him on the Indian reservation was outside of the bailiwick of the sheriff, and without the jurisdiction of the court. Upon stipulation of the parties, the motion was adjourned to the Supreme Court of the Territory, and was there overruled. * * * The case was then remanded to the District Court, and the defendant filed an answer to the complaint. Upon the trial which followed, the plaintiff obtained a verdict for $3,500. Upon a motion for a new trial, the amount was reduced to $2,500; for which judgment was entered. On appeal to the Supreme Court of the Territory, the judgment was affirmed. The defendant thereupon brought the case here, and now seeks a reversal of the judgment, for the alleged error of the court in refusing to dismiss the action for want of jurisdiction over him.

* * *

On the 3d of July, 1868, a treaty with the Shoshonee Indians was ratified, by which, among other things, that portion of the country within which service of process on the defendant was made in this case was set apart for their "absolute and undisturbed use and occupation;" * * *. The territory reserved, therefore, was as much beyond the jurisdiction, legislative or judicial, of the government of Idaho, as if it had been set apart within the limits of another country, or of a foreign State. * * * The process of one of its courts, consequently, served beyond those lines, could not impose upon the defendant any obligation of obedience, and its disregard could not entail upon him any penalties. The service was an unlawful act of the sheriff. The court below should, therefore, have set it aside on its attention being called to the fact that it was made upon the defendant on the reservation. * * *

The right of the defendant to insist upon the objection to the illegality of the service was not waived by the special appearance of counsel for him to move the dismissal of the action on that ground, or what we consider as intended, that the service be set aside; nor, when that motion was overruled, by their answering for him to the merits of the action. Illegality in a proceeding by which jurisdiction is to be obtained is in no case waived by the appearance of the defendant for the purpose of calling the attention of the court to such irregularity; nor is the objection waived when being urged it is overruled, and the defendant is thereby compelled to answer. He is not considered as abandoning his objection because he does not submit to further proceedings without contestation. It is only where he pleads to the merits in the first instance, without insisting upon the illegality, that the objection is deemed to be waived.

The judgment of the Supreme Court of the Territory, therefore, must be reversed, and the case remanded with directions to reverse the judgment of the District Court for Oneida County, and to direct that court to set aside the service made upon the defendant; and it is

So ordered.

––––––––

CORBETT v. PHYSICIANS' CAS. ASS'N OF AMERICA, 135 Wis. 505, 511–12, 115 N.W. 365, 367–68 (1908):

* * * The following language by Dixon, C. J., in Alderson v. White [32 Wis. 308] * * * is often quoted as an unmistakable indication of the doctrine prevailing in this state:

"The party seeking to take advantage of want of jurisdiction in every such case, must object on that ground alone, and keep out of court for every other purpose. If he goes in for any purpose incompatible with the supposition that the court has no power or jurisdiction on account of defective service of process upon him, he goes in and submits for all the purposes of personal jurisdiction with respect to himself, and cannot afterwards be heard to make the objection. It is a general appearance on his part, equivalent in its effect to proof of due personal service of process."

It will be thus seen that the right to proceed to a trial on the merits after a decision against the defendant on the jurisdictional question, efficiently saving an objection to the ruling in that regard, is not recognized as having any place in our practice. The quoted language was only a reiteration, in effect, of what was said in Lowe v. Stringham [14 Wis. 222] * * *.

"We think it is also a waiver of such a defect for the party, after making his objection, to plead and go to trial on the merits. To allow him to do this, would be to give him this advantage. After objecting that he was not properly in court, he could go in, take his chance of a trial on the merits, and if it resulted in his favor, insist upon the judgment as good for his benefit, but if it resulted against him, he could set it all aside upon the ground that he had never been properly got into court at all. * * * * a

––––––––

a Wisconsin abandoned the rule described in *Corbett* in 1960 by enacting a statute providing that personal jurisdiction objections are not waived by joining them with other defenses. Wis.Stat.Ann. § 262.16(2).

Read Federal Rules of Civil Procedure 12(b), (g), and (h) and the accompanying material in the Supplement.

———

ORANGE THEATRE CORP. v. RAYHERSTZ AMUSEMENT CORP., 139 F.2d 871, 874 (3d Cir.1944):

* * * Rule 12 has abolished for the federal courts the age-old distinction between general and special appearances. A defendant need no longer appear specially to attack the court's jurisdiction over him. He is no longer required at the door of the federal courthouse to intone that ancient abracadabra of the law, de bene esse, in order by its magic power to enable himself to remain outside even while he steps within. He may now enter openly in full confidence that he will not thereby be giving up any keys to the courthouse door which he possessed before he came in. This, of course, is not to say that such keys must not be used promptly. If the defense of lack of jurisdiction of the person is not raised by motion before answer or in the answer itself it is by the express terms of paragraph (h) of Civil Procedure Rule 12 to be treated as waived, not because of the defendant's voluntary appearance but because of his failure to assert the defense within the time prescribed by the rules.

NOTES AND QUESTIONS

1. Note that a party always can consent to the court's exercise of personal jurisdiction or waive any objection there may be to it. Probably the most common situations in which this occurs are when defendant does not interpose a timely challenge to jurisdiction or when defendant fails to consolidate a personal jurisdiction objection with other pretrial motions as is required by Rule 12(g). In some situations the consent is given prior to the institution of litigation. As has been seen earlier in this Chapter, the consent may be express or implied, see pp. 72–73, supra, and often is embodied in a cognovit note or confession of judgment, see pp. 133–34, supra.

2. For many years, Texas procedure did not provide for a special appearance. As a result, a foreign defendant could not contest the jurisdiction of a Texas court and was forced either to make a general appearance and contest the merits or to default and rely on a collateral attack in a subsequent suit on the Texas judgment. The nonresident defendant's dilemma was compounded when he owned property in Texas that could be seized to satisfy any judgment that might be entered against him in the action. In YORK v. TEXAS, 137 U.S. 15, 11 S. Ct. 9, 34 L.Ed. 604 (1890), the Supreme Court upheld the Texas practice against a challenge to its constitutionality under the Fourteenth Amendment. The Court concluded that the availability of collateral attack was all that due process required. In order to circumvent the rigors of the Texas practice, a defendant would employ the ruse of having an amicus curiae "suggest" the absence of jurisdiction to the Texas court. See Fishbein v. Thorton, 247 S.W.2d 404 (Tex.Civ.App. 1952). Finally, in 1962, Texas Rule of Civil Procedure 120a was promulgated to permit a special appearance to challenge jurisdiction. See generally Thode, *In Personam Jurisdiction; Article 2031B, the Texas "Long Arm" Jurisdiction Stat-*

ute; and the Appearance to Challenge Jurisdiction in Texas and Elsewhere, 42 Texas L.Rev. 279 (1964). See also Gorfinkel, *Special Appearance in California— The Need for Reform,* 5 U.S.F.L.Rev. 25 (1970).

COLLATERAL ATTACK ON PERSONAL JURISDICTION

If defendant makes a special appearance to contest jurisdiction, loses on the issue, and then leaves the jurisdiction without defending on the merits, may he challenge jurisdiction again in a subsequent action on the judgment? Consider BALDWIN v. IOWA STATE TRAVELING MEN'S ASS'N, 283 U.S. 522, 51 S.Ct. 517, 75 L.Ed. 1244 (1931). In that case respondent attempted to attack a judgment rendered against it in a Missouri federal district court. The company had appeared in the prior suit and had moved to set aside service and dismiss the case for a lack of personal jurisdiction, alleging that (1) it was an Iowa corporation, (2) it had never been present in Missouri, and (3) the person who had been served was not a proper agent for receiving process. The motion was overruled after a full hearing on affidavits and briefs; judgment subsequently was entered against the respondent. Suit then was brought in Iowa to enforce the judgment. In rejecting the respondent's attempt to attack the first judgment collaterally, the Supreme Court stated:

> * * * It is of no moment that the appearance was a special one expressly saving any submission to such jurisdiction. That fact would be important upon appeal from the judgment, and would save the question of the propriety of the court's decision on the matter, even though, after the motion had been overruled, the respondent had proceeded, subject to a reserved objection and exception, to a trial on the merits. * * * The special appearance gives point to the fact that the respondent entered the Missouri court for the very purpose of litigating the question of jurisdiction over its person. It had the election not to appear at all. * * * It had also the right to appeal from the decision of the Missouri District Court. * * *

> Public policy dictates that there be an end of litigation; that those who have contested an issue shall be bound by the result of the contest; and that matters once tried shall be considered forever settled as between parties. We see no reason why this doctrine should not apply in every case where one voluntarily appears, presents his case and is fully heard, and why he should not, in the absence of fraud, be thereafter concluded by the judgment of the tribunal to which he has submitted his cause.

Id. at 524–26, 51 S.Ct. at 517–18. See also pp. 203–05, infra. The special appearance is discussed in *Developments in the Law—State-Court*

Jurisdiction, 73 Harv.L.Rev. 909, 991–97 (1960); Note, *Special Appearance in California,* 10 Stan.L.Rev. 711 (1958).

CHESHIRE NAT. BANK v. JAYNES

Supreme Judicial Court of Massachusetts, 1916.
224 Mass. 14, 112 N.E. 500.

RUGG, C. J.   This is an action of contract brought by a national banking corporation domiciled in the state of New Hampshire against a resident of the state of Connecticut, upon whom no personal service has been made, but whose property has been attached by trustee process under the statute making provision for reaching the property of a non-resident.   * * *   The defendant filed a special appearance, whereby he has undertaken by apt words not to submit himself generally to the jurisdiction of the court, but only so far as is necessary in order to protect his interest in the goods, effects and credits in the hands of the alleged trustees.   * * *   [T]he superior court has ruled that a non-resident defendant could not "appear, answer to the merits and defend the case for the purpose of protecting his rights in property trusteed or attached and at the same time by 'special appearance' repudiate the jurisdiction of the court.   If he is in court claiming its protection upon the merits of the case, he must submit to the obligations which the court places upon every litigant before it."   The correctness of this ruling is challenged.

This precise question does not appear to have been decided.   It has been determined that a valid personal judgment cannot be rendered against a non-resident defendant who is not served with process within the state and who does not appear.   When property of a non-resident defendant is attached within the state, valid judgment may be entered, enforceable against such property but possessing no further validity unless such non-resident defendant is served personally with process within the state, or appears.   * * *   A non-resident defendant may ignore the proceedings in the courts of another jurisdiction when not served with process in that other jurisdiction and when no valid attachment of his property is made.   When attempt is made to affect his rights by judgment obtained in the absence of service of process or attachment of property, he may show its invalidity in the courts of any forum, either under the "full faith and credit" clause of the federal Constitution or under general principles of international comity.   * * *   Perhaps it would be competent for the Legislature to enact, without violating any provision of the federal Constitution, that no one may voluntarily appear in our courts to contest any question there pending, even when some of the property is held under attachment, without at the same time submitting himself wholly to the jurisdiction of our courts for all purposes of the proceeding.   York v. Texas * * *.

But that question is not now presented and expressly is left open.   R. L. c. 170, § 1, which governs this matter, makes no such provision.   * * *   [I]t does not disclose a purpose to impose upon a non-resident defendant the burden of entering a general appearance in order to protect his property rights so far as they are put in peril by effectual attachment of his property upon the original writ. It does not by apt words cover a situation like that now presented. So far as there is implication from the words used, it seems to be that the action shall not be maintained without service with process within this commonwealth (unless there is voluntary general appearance) except so far as it may affect property held under effectual attachment. The provisions for notice to a non-resident defendant in sections 6 and 9 of the same chapter, do not manifest a purpose to compel him to appear generally if he appears at all. Indeed, reading sections 1, 6 and 9 together, and giving them all appropriate force, they are quite satisfied by interpreting them to mean that when effectual attachment of property of a non-resident is made, the best kind of notice which can be given under the circumstances shall issue in order to afford him opportunity to come into court and be heard on the question whether the property so attached ought to be held to satisfy a judgment in accordance with the terms of section 1.

*   *   *

Treating the question as one of general law, quite uncontrolled by statute, the same result is reached. It was said by Chief Justice Parsons in Bissell v. Briggs, 9 Mass. 462, at 468, 6 Am.Dec. 88:

" *   *   *   [A] debtor living in Massachusetts may have goods, effects, or credits in New Hampshire, where the creditor lives. The creditor there may lawfully attach these, pursuant to the laws of that state, in the hands of the bailiff, factor, trustee, or garnishee, of his debtor; and on recovering judgment, those goods, effects, and credits, may lawfully be applied to satisfy the judgment; and the bailiff, factor, trustee, or garnishee, if sued in this state for those goods, effects, or credits, shall in our courts be protected by that judgment, the court in New Hampshire having jurisdiction of the cause for the purpose of rendering that judgment, and the bailiff, factor, trustee, or garnishee, producing it, not to obtain execution of it here, but for his own justification. If, however, those goods, effects, and credits, are insufficient to satisfy the judgment, and the creditor should sue an action on that judgment in this state to obtain satisfaction, he must fail, because the defendant was not personally amenable to the jurisdiction of the court rendering the judgment. And if the defendant after the service of the process of foreign attachment, should either in person have gone into the state of New Hampshire, or constituted an attorney to defend the suit, so as to protect his goods, effects, or credits, from the effect of the attachment, he would not thereby have given the court jurisdiction of his person   *   *   *. It would be unreasonable to oblige any man living in one state, and having effects in another state, to make himself amenable to the courts of the last state, that he might defend his property there attached."

*   *   *   While the allusion to the injustice of requiring a non-resident to surrender himself wholly to the jurisdiction of the courts of a foreign state, in order to defend his property there attached, was by way of illustration rather than exact adjudication, it was employed to illuminate an essential step in the

reasoning by which the decision was reached, and therefore was something more than a mere obiter dictum. It states a sound principle. It is decisive of the question at bar.

It may be urged that to reach this conclusion is to impair the doctrine of res judicata, in that it compels a plaintiff to try the merits of his case and be barred by his failure, while no such decisive result inheres in defeat to the defendant. But this consequence does not follow. It is elementary law that the doctrine of res judicata does not operate as an estoppel unless it is mutual and affects both parties alike. * * * In a situation like that at bar, the plaintiff puts his cause in issue no further than does the defendant. The bar of whatever judgment may be rendered, where a non-resident defendant appears specially merely for the purpose of protecting his interest in attached property, extends no further against the plaintiff than it does against the defendant. It relates only to the property of the defendant held under effectual attachment. The record of the judgment and the form of the execution when rendered against the defendant, explicitly show this. It runs only against the property so attached, and not otherwise. The record of the judgment when against the plaintiff should be equally categorical in showing that the plaintiff has failed to establish his case only against the property attached, and not that he has failed generally to establish a cause of action against the defendant. In such case the question of the general liability of the defendant to the plaintiff has not been put in issue, because the defendant has chosen to rely on his strict right by confining his appearance to the protection of the property alone and not to submit himself to the general jurisdiction of the court. When a defendant pursues this course he cannot at the same time claim the boon of general judgment if he wins, and the shelter of his special appearance if he loses. He cannot gamble with jurisdiction and invoke its benefit if favorable and repudiate its force if adverse. He must select his ground in advance and abide by the issue. If he stands only upon the special ground, he is entitled upon success only to a judgment which protects that property but which goes no further and will afford no shield against further prosecution of the plaintiff's claim against other property or against him personally, provided effectual attachment or personal service may be made.

The plaintiff, by instituting his action and making the effectual attachment of property, offers to the defendant the alternative, first, of coming into court generally and settling all issues by submitting to the jurisdiction of the court with the attendant advantage of ending that cause of action by a final judgment, or second, of appearing specially and protecting only the property attached and settling only that question and nothing else. The adjudication will be exactly commensurate with the alternative accepted by the defendant. This result is one of fairness and justice to both parties.

* * *

Exceptions sustained.

NOTES AND QUESTIONS

1. The courts that have considered the problem of the limited appearance since the *Cheshire* case have reached inconsistent results. Several states have taken a position contrary to *Cheshire* in recent years. See Minn.Rule Civ.Proc. 4.04(2), 27A M.S.A.; N.Y.C.P.L.R. 320(c), both of which are set out in the Supplement. See also pp. 111–13, supra. State cases denying the right of limited appearance include Sands v. Lefcourt Realty Corp., 35 Del.Ch. 340, 117 A.2d 365 (Sup.Ct. 1955), and State ex rel. Methodist Old People's Home v. Crawford, 159 Or. 377, 80 P.2d 873 (1938). See also Frumer, *Jurisdiction and Limited Appearance in New York: Dilemma of the Nonresident Defendant,* 18 Fordham L.Rev. 73 (1949).

In SALMON FALLS MFG. CO. v. MIDLAND TIRE & RUBBER CO., 285 F. 214, 217 (6th Cir.1922), a case originally commenced in an Ohio state court and then removed to a federal court, the court followed *Cheshire* with the following caveat: "[H]ad defendant, while protesting against the court's jurisdiction to render personal judgment without reference to the value of the attached property, yet asked relief on the merits beyond that value, whether before or in connection with the making of its protest, [he] would be deemed to have appeared generally, and so to have waived lack of personal jurisdiction." *But see* Norris, Inc. v. M. H. Reed & Co., 278 F. 19 (5th Cir.1922); Grant v. Kellogg Co., 3 F.R.D. 229 (S.D.N.Y.1943), affirmed on other grounds 154 F.2d 59 (2d Cir.1946). Should a federal court exercising original quasi in rem jurisdiction under Rule 4 (e) permit a limited appearance or should it follow the practice of the state in which it is sitting? See generally *Restatement, Judgments* § 40 (1942); 4 Wright & Miller, *Federal Practice and Procedure: Civil* § 1123 (1969); *Developments in the Law—State-Court Jurisdiction,* 73 Harv.L.Rev. 909, 953–54 (1960); Note, *"Special" Appearances to Contest the Merits in Attachment Suits,* 97 U.Pa.L.Rev. 403 (1949).

2. UNITED STATES v. BALANOVSKI, 236 F.2d 298, 302 (2d Cir.1956), certiorari denied 352 U.S. 968, 77 S.Ct. 357, 1 L.Ed.2d 322 (1957). Action to recover income taxes on sales of personalty shipped to Argentina and to foreclose a federal tax lien on funds held by defendants in two United States banks. Jurisdiction was based upon 28 U.S.C. § 1655, which permits the enforcement of a lien against an absent defendant. Defendants appeared to challenge the federal court's quasi in rem and in personam jurisdiction and then defended on the merits.

> Since the defendants appeared and defended on the merits, the court acquired power to render a judgment *in personam* conditional only upon the validity of the original *quasi-in-rem* jurisdiction. The parties cannot complain of inconvenience, since they have come into the jurisdiction. They have had their day in court on the issues which would settle both the right to the funds and personal liability; there is no constitutional problem. * * * If the parties or if other assets are found in the United States, a rule against personal jurisdiction will only bring on further litigation, which the taxpayers will lose on the merits by collateral estoppel or *stare decisis.* Thus a rule against personal jurisdiction would be merely a mandate for further fruitless litigation.

Is it clear that there is no "constitutional problem"?

SECTION H. JURISDICTION OVER THE SUBJECT MATTER OF THE ACTION—THE COURT'S COMPETENCY

1. BASIC PRINCIPLES

As was described briefly in Chapter One, pp. 4–6, supra, most Anglo-American jurisdictions have distributed judicial power to hear disputes among a variety of courts. In many instances this is accomplished by segregating certain types of controversies from the mainstream of litigation and giving special courts subject-matter jurisdiction over them, as usually is done with domestic relations and probate matters, and formerly was true of "actions at law" and "suits in equity." As described by one commentator:

> * * *   In practically all states * * * there are separate courts for large and small cases with an arbitrary line of division between them. There are usually separate courts of first instance and of review. Separate courts of probate, criminal courts, courts of equity, and courts for causes arising in certain localities are common. Jurisdiction of the same kind is often apportioned among several different courts, each exercising only a designated and restricted part of it, as where certain appeals must be taken to one reviewing court and other appeals to another. Sometimes different courts with concurrent jurisdiction in certain classes of cases and exclusive jurisdiction in others are established. It is not uncommon to find a large number of municipal courts in the various cities of the same state, no two of which exercise the same jurisdiction. And as a final complication, the legislature is constantly shifting and changing the jurisdiction of the various courts, practically every change involving litigation to construe the meaning and ascertain the effect of the legislative act.

Sunderland, *Problems Connected with the Operation of a State Court System,* 1950 Wis.L.Rev. 585, 585–86. As you gain familiarity with the materials in this Section give some thought to the extent to which historical allocations of subject-matter jurisdiction over matters such as probate, divorce, disputes involving land, and patents continue to make sense.

Probably the most common method of limiting judicial power is by providing that the court only can adjudicate controversies involving more than a certain minimum or less than a stated maximum amount of money, or its equivalent. These rules often are designed to direct the quantitative and qualitative flow of litigation into the various courts within a jurisdiction. Thus, for example, it is provided by statute, 28 U.S.C. § 1332, that cases in the federal courts based solely on diversity of citizenship must involve more than $10,000. If a dispute does not, it cannot be instituted in a federal court and must be brought in a state court. Amount-in-controversy restrictions also are common in state systems. These often provide that a plaintiff cannot bring his action in a particular court—typically called a court of inferior, limited, or special jurisdiction—if the amount involved exceeds a statutorily established jurisdictional maximum. What factors are relevant in choosing appropriate jurisdictional amount figures? Are the same factors relevant for both the state and federal courts?

Because of the limitations imposed upon the federal judicial system by Article III of the United States Constitution and by the Congress, the federal subject-matter jurisdiction scheme provides an excellent model for study. For this reason, and because it is desirable to examine some of the basic characteristics of the federal courts and the ways in which they interact, and occasionally conflict, with state courts, the materials in this Section are largely federal. In studying them, remember that many of the problems that will be considered have counterparts under state subject-matter jurisdiction allocations. Visualize the way in which they should be solved on the state level and try to identify subject-matter jurisdiction problems that are peculiarly nonfederal.

2. THE SUBJECT-MATTER JURISDICTION OF THE FEDERAL COURTS—FEDERAL QUESTIONS

MISHKIN, THE FEDERAL "QUESTION" IN THE DISTRICT COURTS, 53 Colum.L.Rev. 157, 157–60 (1953):

Although the framers of our Constitution could not agree upon whether there should be any federal trial courts at all, it was generally conceded at the Convention that the national judicial power should, in some form, extend to cases arising under the laws of the new government. However, though the first Congress did exercise its option to establish a system of "inferior" national tribunals, it did not assign to them general jurisdiction over cases of that type. With the exception of an extremely shortlived statute enacted just after the end of the eighteenth century, it was not until 1875 that the federal courts were given initial cognizance of all types of federal question cases. *　*　*

Whatever may have been the circumstances and needs during the first century of our country's history, there seems to be little doubt that today, with the expanding scope of federal legislation, the exercise of power over cases of this sort constitutes one of the major purposes of a full independent system of national trial courts. The alternative would be to rely entirely upon United States Supreme Court review of state court decisions. But, at least in our present judicial system, Supreme Court pronouncements as to any particular segment of national law are comparatively few. Consequently, sympathetic handling of the available Supreme Court rulings assumes a role of substantial importance in achieving widespread, uniform effectuation of federal law. Presumably judges selected and paid by the central government, with tenure during good behavior—and that determined by the Congress—and probably even somewhat insulated by a separate building, are more likely to give full scope to any given Supreme Court decision, and particularly ones unpopular locally, than are their state counterparts. By the same token, should a district judge fail, or err, a more sympathetic treatment of Supreme Court precedents can be expected from federal circuit judges than from state appellate courts.

Thus, the exercise of federal question jurisdiction by lower federal tribunals presumably permits the Supreme Court to confine itself (insofar as any such distinction can be drawn) to the solving of new problems rather than the policing of old solutions, without the loss that might otherwise be entailed in the effectuation of national rights. Further, the fact that the lower federal bench is chosen by officials of the national government under the same procedure as the members of the high Court suggests a greater similarity in the interpretation of national law, even on first impression, among the several parts of the national system than between the Supreme Court and any state system, or among the various state tribunals themselves. Insofar as this is true, it also promotes a more uniform, correct application of federal law in that significant group of cases where, either because of the novelty of the question, disproportionate expense or for other reasons, recourse to the Supreme Court has previously either not been attempted or been precluded. Finally, it might even be argued that the very existence of an alternative forum stimulates state courts to give a more attentive treatment to claims of federal right.

These factors suggest that it is desirable that Congress be competent to bring to an initial national forum all cases in which the vindication of federal policy may be at stake. However, it does not follow from this that at any given time all such cases should in fact be brought before the federal courts. There are other considerations which must enter into any decision as to the actual use of the national judiciary. For example, there are limits on the volume of litigation which they can handle without an expansion which might not be warranted by the advantages to be gained; the hardships which the geographic location of these courts may impose on the litigants and a willingness to trust that a party's self-interest will lead him to bring or remove an appropriate case to the federal courts might well justify the current rule that federal question jurisdiction is, for the most part, shared by the local courts; in some circumstances, such as where the validity of state action may be at issue, it may avoid friction and wasted effort, without sacrificing national authority, to allow the initial adjudication to be made by the state's tribunals subject to ultimate review by the United States Supreme Court. Other factors could easily be added. In any event, it should be clear that while the power of Congress must of necessity extend to an extremely wide range of cases, the actual assignment of all such suits to the national courts might well prove unwise and self-defeating.

————

Read 28 U.S.C. §§ 1331, 1334, 1337, 1338, 1343, 1345, and 1346, which are in the Supplement.

————

GULLY v. FIRST NAT. BANK IN MERIDIAN, 299 U.S. 109, 112–13, 117–18, 57 S.Ct. 96, 97–98, 100, 81 L.Ed. 70, 72, 74–75 (1936):

How and when a case arises "under the Constitution or laws of the United States" has been much considered in the books. Some tests are well established. To bring a case within the statute, a right or immunity created by the Constitution or laws of the United States must be an element, and an essential one, of the plaintiff's cause of action. * * * The right or immunity must be such that it will be supported if the Constitution or laws of the United States are given one construction or effect, and defeated if they receive another. * * * A genuine and present controversy, not merely a possible or conjectural one, must exist with reference thereto * * * and the controversy must be disclosed upon the face of the complaint, unaided by the answer or by the petition for removal. * * *

This Court has had occasion to point out how futile is the attempt to define a "cause of action" without reference to the context. * * * To define broadly and in the abstract "a case arising under the Constitution or laws of the United States" has hazards of a kindred order. What is needed is something of that common-sense accommodation of judgment to kaleidoscopic situations which characterizes the law in its treatment of problems of causation. One could carry the search for causes backward, almost without end. * * * Instead, there has been a selective process which picks the substantial causes out of the web and lays the other ones aside. As in problems of causation, so here is the search for the underlying law. If we follow the ascent far enough, countless claims of right can be discovered to have their source or their operative limits in the provisions of a federal statute or in the Constitution itself with its circumambient restrictions upon legislative power. To set bounds to the pursuit, the courts have formulated the distinction between controversies that are basic and those that are collateral, between disputes that are necessary and those that are merely possible. We shall be lost in a maze if we put that compass by.

LOUISVILLE & NASHVILLE R.R. v. MOTTLEY

Supreme Court of the United States, 1908.
211 U.S. 149, 29 S.Ct. 42, 53 L.Ed. 126.

Appeal from the Circuit Court of the United States for the Western District of Kentucky * * *.

The appellees (husband and wife), being residents and citizens of Kentucky, brought this suit in equity in the circuit court of the United States for the western district of Kentucky against the appellant, a railroad company and a citizen of the same state. * * *

The bill alleged that in September, 1871, plaintiffs, while passengers upon the defendant railroad, were injured by the defendant's negligence, and released their respective claims for damages in consideration of the agreement for transportation during their lives, expressed in the contract. It is alleged that the contract was performed by the defendant up to January 1, 1907, when the defendant declined to renew the passes. The bill then alleges that the refusal to comply with the contract was based solely upon that part of the act of Congress of June 29, 1906 (34 Stat. at L. 584, chap. 3591, U.S.Comp.Stat. Supp. 1907, p. 892), which forbids the giving of free passes or free transportation. The bill further alleges: First, that the act of Congress referred to does not prohibit the giving of passes under the circumstances of this case; and, second, that, if the law is to be construed as prohibiting such passes, it is in conflict with the 5th Amendment of the Constitution, because it deprives the plaintiffs of their property without due process of law. The defendant demurred to the bill. The judge of the circuit court overruled the demurrer, entered a decree for the relief prayed for, and the defendant appealed directly to this court.

Mr. Justice MOODY, after making the foregoing statement, delivered the opinion of the court:

Two questions of law were raised by the demurrer to the bill, were brought here by appeal, and have been argued before us. They are, first, whether * * * the act of Congress of June 29, 1906 * * * makes it unlawful to perform a contract for transportation of persons who, in good faith, before the passage of the act, had accepted such contract in satisfaction of a valid cause of action against the railroad; and, second, whether the statute, if it should be construed to render such a contract unlawful, is in violation of the 5th Amendment of the Constitution of the United States. We do not deem it necessary, however, to consider either of these questions, because, in our opinion, the court below was without jurisdiction of the cause. Neither party has questioned that jurisdiction, but it is the duty of this court to see to it that the jurisdiction of the circuit court, which is defined and limited by statute, is not exceeded. * * *

There was no diversity of citizenship, and it is not and cannot be suggested that there was any ground of jurisdiction, except that the case was a "suit * * * arising under the Constitution or laws of the United States." 25 Stat.

Original cause of action was breach of contract. The Unconstitutionality went to defense against gov. answer

at L. 434, chap. 866, U.S.Comp.Stat.1901, p. 509. It is the settled interpretation of these words, as used in this statute, conferring jurisdiction, that a suit arises "under the Constitution and laws of the United States" only when the plaintiff's statement of his own cause of action shows that it is based upon those laws or that Constitution. It is not enough that the plaintiff alleges some anticipated defense to his cause of action, and asserts that the defense is invalidated by some provision of the Constitution of the United States. Although such allegations show that very likely, in the course of the litigation, a question under the Constitution would arise, they do not show that the suit, that is, the plaintiff's original cause of action, arises under the Constitution. In Tennessee v. Union & Planters' Bank, 152 U.S. 454, 38 L.Ed. 511, 14 S.Ct.Rep. 654, the plaintiff, the state of Tennessee, brought suit in the circuit court of the United States to recover from the defendant certain taxes alleged to be due under the laws of the state. The plaintiff alleged that the defendant claimed an immunity from the taxation by virtue of its charter, and that therefore the tax was void, because in violation of the provision of the Constitution of the United States, which forbids any state from passing a law impairing the obligation of contracts. The cause was held to be beyond the jurisdiction of the circuit court, the court saying, by Mr. Justice Gray (p. 464): "A suggestion of one party, that the other will or may set up a claim under the Constitution or laws of the United States, does not make the suit one arising under that Constitution or those laws." Again, in Boston & M. Consol. Copper & S. Min. Co. v. Montana Ore Purchasing Co., 188 U.S. 632, 47 L.Ed. 626, 23 S.Ct.Rep. 434, the plaintiff brought suit in the circuit court of the United States for the conversion of copper ore and for an injunction against its continuance. The plaintiff then alleged, for the purpose of showing jurisdiction, in substance, that the defendant would set up in defense certain laws of the United States. The cause was held to be beyond the jurisdiction of the circuit court, the court saying, by Mr. Justice Peckham (pp. 638, 639):

"It would be wholly unnecessary and improper, in order to prove complainant's cause of action, to go into any matters of defense which the defendants might possibly set up, and then attempt to reply to such defense, and thus, if possible, to show that a Federal question might or probably would arise in the course of the trial of the case. To allege such defense and then make an answer to it before the defendant has the opportunity to itself plead or prove its own defense is inconsistent with any known rule of pleading, so far as we are aware, and is improper.

"The rule is a reasonable and just one that the complainant in the first instance shall be confined to a statement of its cause of action, leaving to the defendant to set up in his answer what his defense is, and, if anything more than a denial of complainant's cause of action, imposing upon the defendant the burden of proving such defense.

"Conforming itself to that rule, the complainant would not, in the assertion or proof of its cause of action, bring up a single Federal question. The presentation of its cause of action would not show that it was one arising under the Constitution or laws of the United States.

"   *   *   *   "

*   *   *   The application of this rule to the case at bar is decisive against the jurisdiction of the circuit court.

It is ordered that the judgment be reversed and the case remitted to the circuit court with instructions to dismiss the suit for want of jurisdiction.

NOTES AND QUESTIONS

1. What justifications are there for the Supreme Court's disposition of *Mottley*? Why should subject-matter jurisdiction depend on technical pleading rules and the content of the complaint? Following the Court's decision, the Mottleys commenced an action in a Kentucky state court. The case ultimately was brought to the United States Supreme Court by appeal from the highest court in Kentucky on the question of the validity and construction of the 1906 Act; three years after the Supreme Court dismissed the federal action it examined the merits of the Mottleys' contentions and decided in favor of the railroad. In light of this history, what was gained by the original dismissal? Consider the proposal of the American Law Institute, *Study of the Division of Jurisdiction Between State and Federal Courts,* Official Draft, § 1312(d) (1969), which provides that a federal court may retain jurisdiction even when the complaint does not present a claim within its original jurisdiction if defendant introduces a federal defense or counterclaim.

2. Would there have been jurisdiction in the principal case if the railroad had sought, as it can today, a judicial declaration, see pp. 18–21, supra, under the Declaratory Judgment Act, 28 U.S.C. §§ 2201–2202, to the effect that the 1906 Act had rendered the passes invalid? See SKELLY OIL CO. v. PHILLIPS PETROLEUM CO., 339 U.S. 667, 673–74, 70 S.Ct. 876, 880, 94 L.Ed. 1194, 1200–01 (1950), in which suit was brought for a declaration that certain contracts had not been terminated. The effectiveness of an attempted termination by defendant depended on whether the Federal Power Commission had issued a certificate of public convenience and necessity under the Federal Natural Gas Act. In denying jurisdiction, the Court said: "To sanction suits for declaratory relief as within the jurisdiction of the District Courts merely because, as in this case, artful pleading anticipates a defense based on federal law would contravene the whole trend of jurisdictional legislation by Congress, disregard the effective functioning of the federal judicial system and distort the limited procedural purposes of the Declaratory Judgment Act." How would the assertion of jurisdiction in *Skelly* have done all of those things? See also Note, *Federal Question Jurisdiction of the Federal Courts and the Declaratory Judgment Act,* 4 Vand.L.Rev. 827 (1951).

BIVENS v. SIX UNKNOWN NAMED AGENTS OF FEDERAL BUREAU OF NARCOTICS

United States Supreme Court, 1971.
403 U.S. 388, 91 S.Ct. 1999, 29 L.Ed.2d 619.

Certiorari to the United States Court of Appeals for the Second Circuit.

Mr. Justice BRENNAN delivered the opinion of the Court.

* * *

This case has its origin in an arrest and search carried out on the morning of November 26, 1965. Petitioner's complaint alleged that on that day respondents, agents of the Federal Bureau of Narcotics acting under claim of federal authority, entered his apartment and arrested him for alleged narcotics violations. The agents manacled petitioner in front of his wife and children, and threatened to arrest the entire family. They searched the apartment from stem to stern. Thereafter, petitioner was taken to the federal courthouse in Brooklyn, where he was interrogated, booked, and subjected to a visual strip search.

On July 7, 1967, petitioner brought suit in Federal District Court. In addition to the allegations above, his complaint asserted that the arrest and search were effected without a warrant, and that unreasonable force was employed in making the arrest; fairly read, it alleges as well that the arrest was made without probable cause. Petitioner claimed to have suffered great humiliation, embarrassment, and mental suffering as a result of the agents' unlawful conduct, and sought $15,000 damages from each of them. The District Court, on respondents' motion, dismissed the complaint on the ground, *inter alia*, that it failed to state a cause of action. * * * The Court of Appeals, one judge concurring specially, affirmed on that basis. * * * We granted certiorari. * * * We reverse.

I

Respondents do not argue that petitioner should be entirely without remedy for an unconstitutional invasion of his rights by federal agents. In respondents' view, however, the rights that petitioner asserts—primarily rights of privacy—are creations of state and not of federal law. Accordingly, they argue, petitioner may obtain money damages to redress invasion of these rights only by an action in tort, under state law, in the state courts. In this scheme the Fourth Amendment would serve merely to limit the extent to which the agents could defend the state law tort suit by asserting that their actions were a valid exercise of federal power: if the agents were shown to have violated the Fourth Amendment, such a defense would be lost to them and they would stand before the state law merely as private individuals. Candidly admitting that it is the policy of the Department of

Justice to remove all such suits from the state to the federal courts for decision,[b] respondents nevertheless urge that we uphold dismissal of petitioner's complaint in federal court, and remit him to filing an action in the state courts in order that the case may properly be removed to the federal court for decision on the basis of state law.

We think that respondents' thesis rests upon an unduly restrictive view of the Fourth Amendment's protection against unreasonable searches and seizures by federal agents, a view that has consistently been rejected by this Court. Respondents seek to treat the relationship between a citizen and a federal agent unconstitutionally exercising his authority as no different from the relationship between two private citizens. In so doing, they ignore the fact that power, once granted, does not disappear like a magic gift when it is wrongfully used. An agent acting—albeit unconstitutionally—in the name of the United States possesses a far greater capacity for harm than an individual trespasser exercising no authority other than his own. * * * Accordingly, as our cases make clear, the Fourth Amendment operates as a limitation upon the exercise of federal power regardless of whether the State in whose jurisdiction that power is exercised would prohibit or penalize the identical act if engaged in by a private citizen. It guarantees to citizens of the United States the absolute right to be free from unreasonable searches and seizures carried out by virtue of federal authority. And "where federally protected rights have been invaded, it has been the rule from the beginning that courts will be alert to adjust their remedies so as to grant the necessary relief." Bell v. Hood, 327 U.S., at 684, 66 S.Ct., at 777 (footnote omitted) * * *.

First. Our cases have long since rejected the notion that the Fourth Amendment proscribes only such conduct as would, if engaged in by private persons, be condemned by state law. * * * And our recent decisions regarding electronic surveillance have made it clear beyond peradventure that the Fourth Amendment is not tied to the niceties of local trespass laws. * * * In light of these cases, respondents' argument that the Fourth Amendment serves only as a limitation on federal defenses to a state law claim, and not as an independent limitation upon the exercise of federal power, must be rejected.

Second. The interests protected by state laws regulating trespass and the invasion of privacy, and those protected by the Fourth Amendment's guarantee against unreasonable searches and seizures, may be inconsistent or even hostile. Thus, we may bar the door against an unwelcome private intruder, or call the police if he persists in seeking entrance. The availability of such alternative means for the protection of privacy may lead the State to restrict imposition of liability for any consequent trespass. A private citizen, asserting no authority other than his own, will not normally be liable in trespass if he demands, and is granted, admission to another's house.

---

[b] Removal is authorized by 28 U.S.C. § 1442(a), which is in the Supplement. The subject is discussed at pp. 230–37, infra.

* * * But one who demands admission under a claim of federal authority stands in a far different position. * * * The mere invocation of federal power by a federal law enforcement official will normally render futile any attempt to resist an unlawful entry or arrest by resort to the local police; and a claim of authority to enter is likely to unlock the door as well. * * * "In such cases there is no safety for the citizen, except in the protection of the judicial tribunals, for rights which have been invaded by the officers of the government, professing to act in its name. There remains to him but the alternative of resistance, which may amount to crime." United States v. Lee, 106 U.S. 196, 219, 1 S.Ct. 240, 259, 27 L.Ed. 171 (1882). Nor is it adequate to answer that state law may take into account the different status of one clothed with the authority of the Federal Government. For just as state law may not authorize federal agents to violate the Fourth Amendment, * * * neither may state law undertake to limit the extent to which federal authority can be exercised. * * * The inevitable consequence of this dual limitation on state power is that the federal question becomes not merely a possible defense to the state law action, but an independent claim both necessary and sufficient to make out the plaintiff's cause of action. * * *

Third. That damages may be obtained for injuries consequent upon a violation of the Fourth Amendment by federal officials should hardly seem a surprising proposition. Historically, damages have been regarded as the ordinary remedy for an invasion of personal interests in liberty. * * * Of course, the Fourth Amendment does not in so many words provide for its enforcement by an award of money damages for the consequences of its violation. But "it is * * * well settled that where legal rights have been invaded, and a federal statute provides for a general right to sue for such invasion, federal courts may use any available remedy to make good the wrong done." Bell v. Hood, 327 U.S., at 684, 66 S.Ct., at 777 (footnote omitted). The present case involves no special factors counselling hesitation in the absence of affirmative action by Congress. * * * Nor are we asked in this case to impose liability upon a congressional employee for actions contrary to no constitutional prohibition, but merely said to be in excess of the authority delegated to him by the Congress. Wheeldin v. Wheeler, 373 U.S. 647, 83 S.Ct. 1441, 10 L.Ed.2d 605 (1963). Finally, we cannot accept respondents' formulation of the question as whether the availability of money damages is necessary to enforce the Fourth Amendment. For we have here no explicit congressional declaration that persons injured by a federal officer's violation of the Fourth Amendment may not recover money damages from the agents, but must instead be remitted to another remedy, equally effective in the view of Congress. The question is merely whether petitioner, if he can demonstrate an injury consequent upon the violation by federal agents of his Fourth Amendment rights, is entitled to redress his injury through a particular remedial mechanism normally available in the federal courts. * * * "The very essence

[handwritten margin note:] This is a direct cause of action arising out of vio. of Constitution + thus is not a mere possibility of defense.

of civil liberty certainly consists in the right of every individual to claim the protection of the laws, whenever he receives an injury." Marbury v. Madison, 1 Cranch 137, 163, 2 L.Ed. 60 (1803). Having concluded that petitioner's complaint states a cause of action under the Fourth Amendment, * * * we hold that petitioner is entitled to recover money damages for any injuries he has suffered as a result of the agents' violation of the Amendment.

* * * The judgment of the Court of Appeals is reversed and the case is remanded for further proceedings consistent with this opinion.

* * *

Mr. Justice HARLAN, concurring in the judgment.

* * *

For the reasons set forth below, I am of the opinion that federal courts do have the power to award damages for violation of "constitutionally protected interests" and I agree with the Court that a traditional judicial remedy such as damages is appropriate to the vindication of the personal interests protected by the Fourth Amendment.

I

I turn first to the contention that the constitutional power of federal courts to accord Bivens damages for his claim depends on the passage of a statute creating a "federal cause of action." Although the point is not entirely free of ambiguity, I do not understand either the Government or my dissenting Brothers to maintain that Bivens' contention that he is entitled to be free from the type of official conduct prohibited by the Fourth Amendment depends on a decision by the State in which he resides to accord him a remedy. Such a position would be incompatible with the presumed availability of federal equitable relief, if a proper showing can be made in terms of the ordinary principles governing equitable remedies. * * * However broad a federal court's discretion concerning equitable remedies, it is absolutely clear—at least after Erie R. Co. v. Tompkins, * * * [p. 265, infra]—that in a nondiversity suit a federal court's power to grant even equitable relief depends on the presence of a substantive right derived from federal law. * * * Thus the interest which Bivens claims—to be free from official conduct in contravention of the Fourth Amendment—is a federally protected interest. * * * Therefore, the question of judicial *power* to grant Bivens damages is not a problem of the "source" of the "right"; instead, the question is whether the power to authorize damages as a judicial remedy for the vindication of a federal constitutional right is placed by the Constitution itself exclusively in Congress' hands.

II

The contention that the federal courts are powerless to accord a litigant damages for a claimed invasion of his federal constitutional rights until

Congress explicitly authorizes the remedy cannot rest on the notion that the decision to grant compensatory relief involves a resolution of policy considerations not susceptible of judicial discernment. Thus, in suits for damages based on violations of federal statutes lacking any express authorization of a damage remedy, this Court has authorized such relief where, in its view, damages are necessary to effectuate the congressional policy underpinning the substantive provisions of the statute.   *   *   *

If it is not the nature of the remedy which is thought to render a judgment as to the appropriateness of damages inherently "legislative," then it must be the nature of the legal interest offered as an occasion for invoking otherwise appropriate judicial relief. But I do not think that the fact that the interest is protected by the Constitution rather than statute or common law justifies the assertion that federal courts are powerless to grant damages in the absence of explicit congressional action authorizing the remedy. Initially, I note that it would be at least anomalous to conclude that the federal judiciary—while competent to choose among the range of traditional judicial remedies to implement statutory and common-law policies, and even to generate substantive rules governing primary behavior in furtherance of broadly formulated policies articulated by statute or Constitution   *   *   * —is powerless to accord a damages remedy to vindicate social policies which, by virtue of their inclusion in the Constitution, are aimed predominantly at restraining the Government as an instrument of the popular will.

More importantly, the presumed availability of federal equitable relief against threatened invasions of constitutional interests appears entirely to negate the contention that the status of an interest as constitutionally protected divests federal courts of the power to grant damages absent express congressional authorization. Congress provided specially for the exercise of equitable remedial powers by federal courts, see Act of May 8, 1792, § 2, 1 Stat. 276; C. Wright, Law of Federal Courts 257 (2d ed., 1970), in part because of the limited availability of equitable remedies in state courts in the early days of the Republic.   *   *   *   And this Court's decisions make clear that, at least absent congressional restrictions, the scope of equitable remedial discretion is to be determined according to the distinctive historical traditions of equity as an institution,   *   *   *.   The reach of a federal district court's "inherent equitable powers," Textile Workers Union v. Lincoln Mills, 353 U.S. 448, 460, 77 S.Ct. 912, 919–920, 1 L.Ed.2d 972 (Burton, J., concurring in result), is broad indeed   *   *   *.

If explicit congressional authorization is an absolute prerequisite to the power of a federal court to accord compensatory relief regardless of the necessity or appropriateness of damages as a remedy simply because of the status of a legal interest as constitutionally protected, then it seems to me that explicit congressional authorization is similarly prerequisite to the exercise of equitable remedial discretion in favor of constitutionally protected interests. Conversely, if a general grant of jurisdiction to the federal courts by Congress is thought adequate to empower a federal court to grant equitable relief for all areas of subject-matter jurisdiction enumerated therein, see 28 U.S.C. § 1331(a), then it seems to me that the same statute is sufficient to empower a federal court to grant a traditional remedy at law.   *   *   *

Mr. Justice BLACK, dissenting.

*   *   *   There can be no doubt that Congress could create a federal cause of action for damages for an unreasonable search in violation of the Fourth Amendment.   Although Congress has created such a federal cause of action against *state* officials acting under color of state law, it has never created such a cause of action against federal officials.   If it wanted to do so, Congress could, of course, create a remedy against federal officials who violate the Fourth Amendment in the performance of their duties.   But the point of this case and the fatal weakness in the Court's judgment is that neither Congress nor the State of New York has enacted legislation creating such a right of action.   For us to do so is, in my judgment, an exercise of power that the Constitution does not give us.

Even if we had the legislative power to create a remedy, there are many reasons why we should decline to create a cause of action where none has existed since the formation of our Government.   The courts of the United States as well as those of the States are choked with lawsuits.   The number of cases on the docket of this Court have reached an unprecedented volume in recent years.   A majority of these cases are brought by citizens with substantial complaints—persons who are physically or economically injured by torts or frauds or governmental infringement of their rights; persons who have been unjustly deprived of their liberty or their property; and persons who have not yet received the equal opportunity in education, employment, and pursuit of happiness that was the dream of our forefathers.   Unfortunately, there have also been a growing number of frivolous lawsuits, particularly actions for damages against law enforcement officers whose conduct has been judicially sanctioned by state trial and appellate courts and in many instances even by this Court.   My fellow Justices on this Court and our brethren throughout the federal judiciary know only too well the time-consuming task of conscientiously poring over hundreds of thousands of pages of factual allegations of misconduct by police, judicial, and corrections officials.   *   *   *

We sit at the top of a judicial system accused by some of nearing the point of collapse.   Many criminal defendants do not receive speedy trials and neither society nor the accused are assured of justice when inordinate delays occur.   Citizens must wait years to litigate their private civil suits. Substantial changes in correctional and parole systems demand the attention of the lawmakers and the judiciary.   If I were a legislator I might well find these and other needs so pressing as to make me believe that the resources of lawyers and judges should be devoted to them rather than to civil damage actions against officers who generally strive to perform within constitutional bounds. There is also a real danger that such suits might deter officials from the *proper* and honest performance of their duties.

All of these considerations make imperative careful study and weighing of the arguments both for and against the creation of such a remedy under the Fourth Amendment. I would have great difficulty for myself in resolving the competing policies, goals, and priorities in the use of resources, if I thought it were my job to resolve those questions. But that is not my task. The task of evaluating the pros and cons of creating judicial remedies for particular wrongs is a matter for Congress and the legislatures of the States. Congress has not provided that any federal court can entertain a suit against a federal officer for violations of Fourth Amendment rights occurring in the performance of his duties. A strong inference can be drawn from creation of such actions against state officials that Congress does not desire to permit such suits against federal officials. * * *

I dissent.

[The dissenting opinions of Mr. Chief Justice BURGER and Mr. Justice BLACKMUN are omitted.]

NOTES AND QUESTIONS

1. In WHEELDIN v. WHEELER, 373 U.S. 647, 83 S.Ct. 1441, 10 L.Ed.2d 605 (1963), the Court held that there was no federal cause of action on behalf of a citizen to recover a damage remedy for abuse of process by a congressional employee. *Bivens* distinguishes this case on the ground that defendant's actions in *Wheeldin* were not contrary to a constitutional prohibition but merely were in excess of the authority granted him by the Congress. Why couldn't the Court have created a federal common law damage right in the *Wheeldin* situation, as it did in *Bivens?* Consider the arguments advanced by the dissent in *Wheeldin*, written by Mr. Justice Brennan, who was joined by Mr. Chief Justice Warren and Mr. Justice Black, concerning the possible sources of federal common law for establishing a private remedy.[c]

>   * * * As the Court of Appeals correctly apprehended, the gravamen of the complaint is the notion of a tort of malicious abuse of federal process by a federal officer. This to me raises a number of questions. Does the complaint state a claim actionable under common-law principles? If so, and if the claim is a creature of state law, may it nevertheless be entertained in the federal courts? Under what theory, if any, can the claim be deemed federal and within the original jurisdiction of the Federal District Courts? * * *

[c] The discussion in the dissenting opinion of the possible application of pendent jurisdiction has been omitted. This source of federal subject-matter jurisdiction is discussed at pp. 220–25, infra.

* * * [Assuming the claim is actionable under state law, one theory for sustaining federal court jurisdiction over it] builds from Smith v. Kansas City Title & Trust Co., 255 U.S. 180, 41 S.Ct. 243, 65 L.Ed. 577. A shareholder sued to enjoin the Trust Company, a Missouri corporation, from investing in certain federal bonds, on the ground that the Act of Congress authorizing their issuance was unconstitutional. It was claimed that under Missouri law an investment in securities the issuance of which had not been authorized by a valid law was *ultra vires* and enjoinable. The cause of action, thus, was state-created. Nevertheless this Court held that the action was one arising under federal law within the meaning of the predecessor section to 28 U.S.C. § 1331(a). * * * Smith remains firm authority for the principle that "where federal law has inserted itself into the texture of state law, a claim founded on the national legislation could be brought into a federal forum" even if the right of action was state-created. * * * Stated differently, "in the Smith case the claim under federal law was an essential ingredient of the plaintiff's case, without which he could assert no right to relief." Hart and Wechsler, [The Federal Courts and the Federal System] * * * at 766. In short, there is federal-question jurisdiction if a proposition of federal law is inherent in the plaintiff's claim. * * *

How does the instant complaint fare under this standard? The matter is not free from doubt, but it is arguable, at least, that inherent in a claim to abuse of federal process by a federal officer are certain propositions drawn from the network of federal statutory and constitutional provisions governing congressional investigations. * * * Concretely, the instant complaint asserts that respondent's use of congressional process was unauthorized and was for an "unjustifiable end" * * *; surely the contours of this authority and the classification of justifiable and unjustifiable ends of congressional process are matters of federal law. Thus, just as Smith is a case "where state law incorporates federal standards by reference," * * * so here a basic element of the common-law tort is the body of federal law authorizing and defining the issuance of federal legislative process. I do not wish, however, to be understood as suggesting that the analogy is perfect.

I come now to the question whether petitioner Dawson's cause of action may be deemed created by federal law apart from the Fourth Amendment. It is not claimed that any federal statute in terms confers a remedy in damages for malicious abuse of federal process by a federal officer. But it is argued that such a remedy (1) may be implied from the Act of Congress respecting the issuance of subpoenas by the House Un-American Activities Committee and its subcommittees, and (2) is given by the federal common law.

The Legislative Reorganization Act of 1946, c. 753, § 121(b), House Rule XI(1) (q) (2), 60 Stat. 828, provides in part: "Subpenas [sic] may be issued under the signature of the chairman of the committee [on Un-American Activities] or any subcommittee, or by any member designated by any such chairman * * *." If this provision be interpreted to prohibit respondent from issuing the Committee's subpoenas on his own, may a right of action in damages be implied in favor of one injured as a direct consequence of respondent's unlawful use of such a subpoena? I see no reason why it may not. * * * Increasingly, the tendency in the federal courts has been to infer private rights of action from federal statutes unless to do so would defeat manifest congressional purpose. * * * We must presume that Congress, in specifying the conditions for the lawful delegation of the Committee on Un-American Activities' subpoena power, was mindful of the grave injustices which might be done to individuals as a result of the flouting of those conditions. * * *

A final approach to the problem of founding federal jurisdiction is by way of the federal common law. * * * [I]n a wide variety of cases the federal courts have assumed to fashion federal common-law rights. Ordinarily, to be sure, such fashioning is done under the aegis of a more specific jurisdictional grant than 28 U.S.C. § 1331(a). But I * * * would recognize the existence of federal common-law rights of action "wherever necessary or appropriate" for dealing with "essentially federal matters." Plainly, this test supports recognition of a federal cause of action on the facts of the instant complaint. * * * [W]here, as here, it is alleged that a federal officer acting under color of federal law has so abused his federal powers as to cause unjustifiable injury to a private person, I see no warrant for concluding that state law must be looked to as the sole basis for liability. Under such circumstances, no state interest is infringed by a generous construction of federal jurisdiction, and every consideration of practicality and justice argues for such a construction. * * *

Id. at 654–66, 83 S.Ct. at 1447–53, 10 L.Ed.2d at 613–20. See also Katz, *The Jurisprudence of Remedies: Constitutional Legality and the Law of Torts in Bell v. Hood*, 117 U.Pa.L.Rev. 1 (1968).

2. The question whether a case is one "arising under" the Constitution or laws of the United States often is difficult to resolve and a variety of standards have been advanced. See, e. g., Cohen, *The Broken Compass: The Requirement that a Case Arise "Directly" Under Federal Law*, 115 U.Pa.L.Rev. 890 (1967). In spite of the confusion, the American Law Institute has chosen not to propose a new statutory definition of the test in its proposals. American Law Institute, *Study of the Division of Jurisdiction Between State and Federal Courts*, Official Draft, 178–79 (1969). For a discussion of the statutory development of federal question jurisdiction, see Hart & Wechsler, *The Federal Courts and the Federal System* 844–50 (2d ed., Bator, Mishkin, Shapiro & Wechsler, 1973).

3. Neither the federal-question nor the diversity-of-citizenship jurisdiction statutes confer exclusive jurisdiction on the federal courts, although Congress undoubtedly has the power to do so. Areas in which Congress has given the federal courts exclusive jurisdiction include, *inter alia*, bankruptcy, 28 U.S.C. § 1334, patents and copyrights, 28 U.S.C. § 1338(a), actions against foreign consuls and vice-consuls, 28 U.S.C. § 1351, actions to recover a fine, penalty, or forfeiture under federal law, 28 U.S.C. § 1355, and actions involving certain seizures, 28 U.S.C. § 1356. What factors should motivate Congress in choosing between a grant of concurrent or exclusive jurisdiction? See Note, *Ex-*

Certain areas of exclusive, as opposed to concurrent, federal jurisdiction.

clusive Jurisdiction of the Federal Courts in Private Civil Actions, 70 Harv.L. Rev. 509 (1957). Should the result in *Mottley* have been different if the anticipated defense involved a matter that was within the exclusive, rather than the concurrent, jurisdiction of the federal courts?

4.   What would be the effect on a state-court action to collect moneys due under a patent licensing agreement if defendant asserted a defense that the patent was invalid under the Patent Act's test of invention? Examine the text of 28 U.S.C. § 1338(a), which is in the Supplement, to see if it helps you in answering this question. Under what circumstances should Congress, if it decides upon exclusive federal jurisdiction over a particular area of substantive law, create a special tribunal rather than vest jurisdiction in the district courts? Among the existing specialized federal courts are the Court of Claims, the Tax Court, and the Court of Customs and Patent Appeals.

DIRECT AND COLLATERAL ATTACK ON A JUDGMENT FOR LACK OF SUBJECT-MATTER JURISDICTION

If neither the parties nor the court notice the absence of subject-matter jurisdiction at any time during the original proceeding, can defendant successfully raise the lack of jurisdiction as a defense to a subsequent proceeding by plaintiff to enforce the decree? Would it make any difference for purposes of collateral attack if the issue of jurisdiction had been raised and litigated in the original action and it had been decided that the court did have power to proceed? In grappling with this problem reconsider *Capron v. Van Noorden,* p. 22, supra, and *Des Moines Navigation & R. R. v. Iowa Homestead Co.,* p. 61, supra, and recall that one of the oldest pieces of jurisdiction dogma is the maxim that a judgment rendered by a court that lacked jurisdiction over the subject matter (or the "cause," to use the older terminology) is void and a nullity. See, e. g., The Case of the Marshalsea, 10 Co.Rep. 68b, 77 Eng.Rep. 1027 (K.B. 1613); Elliott v. Piersol, 26 U.S. (1 Pet.) 328, 7 L.Ed. 164 (1828). Of course, the subject is considerably more complex than the dogma would indicate and *Des Moines* demonstrates that collateral attack is not always an available technique for challenging a judgment on the ground that the rendering court lacked subject-matter jurisdiction.

Section 10 of the Restatement of Judgments analyzes the question of the availability of collateral attack in terms of balancing the policies underlying res judicata and finality of judgments, which are treated in detail in Chapter Fourteen, against the policy of prohibiting a court from exceeding the powers conferred upon it by the legislature or the jurisdiction's organic law. It lists the following factors to be weighed in determining whether or not collateral attack should be permitted:

(a) the lack of jurisdiction over the subject matter was clear;

(b) the determination as to jurisdiction depended upon a question of law rather than of fact;

(c) the court was one of limited and not of general jurisdiction;

(d) the question of jurisdiction was not actually litigated;

(e) the policy against the court's acting beyond its jurisdiction is strong.

The Supreme Court has had to deal with problems of collateral attack on numerous occasions. In CHICOT COUNTY DRAINAGE DIST. v. BAXTER STATE BANK, 308 U.S. 371, 60 S.Ct. 317, 84 L.Ed. 329 (1940), the judgment under attack had been rendered by a district court sitting as a court of bankruptcy under a statute that was later declared unconstitutional. The Supreme Court refused to allow attack:

> * * * If the general principles governing the defense of res judicata are applicable * * * [respondents], having the opportunity to raise the question of invalidity, were not the less bound by the decree because they failed to raise it.

> * * * The lower federal courts are all courts of limited jurisdiction, that is, with only the jurisdiction which Congress has prescribed. But none the less they are courts with authority * * * to determine whether or not they have jurisdiction to entertain the cause and for this purpose to construe and apply the statute under which they are asked to act. Their determinations of such questions, while open to direct review, may not be assailed collaterally.

Id. at 375–76, 60 S.Ct. at 319, 84 L.Ed. at 333.

Exception →

But collateral attack was allowed by the Court in KALB v. FEUERSTEIN, 308 U.S. 433, 60 S.Ct. 343, 84 L.Ed. 370 (1940), decided the same day as *Chicot*. The questions for decision in *Kalb* were whether a state court had jurisdiction to render a judgment confirming a foreclosure sale while the mortgagor's petition under the Bankruptcy Act was pending in a bankruptcy court, and, if not, whether the mortgagor was prohibited from attacking the state-court judgment collaterally. The Court answered both questions in the negative:

> It is generally true that a judgment by a court of competent jurisdiction bears a presumption of regularity and is not thereafter subject to collateral attack. But Congress, because its power over the subject of bankruptcy is plenary, may by specific bankruptcy legislation create an exception to that principle and render judicial acts taken with respect to the person or property of a debtor whom the bankruptcy law protects nullities and vulnerable collaterally. * * *

> We think the language and broad policy of the * * * Act conclusively demonstrate that Congress intended to, and did deprive the Wisconsin County Court of the power and jurisdiction to continue or maintain in any manner the foreclosure proceedings

against appellants without the consent   *   *   *   of the bankruptcy court   *   *   *.

Id. at 438–40, 60 S.Ct. at 346, 84 L.Ed. at 374–75.

Which of the Restatement categories seems determinative of the *Kalb* case? Are *Chicot* and *Kalb* reconcilable? A fuller discussion of *Chicot* and *Kalb* can be found in Boskey & Braucher, *Jurisdiction and Collateral Attack: October Term, 1939,* 40 Colum.L.Rev. 1006 (1940).

A more recent example of the Supreme Court's attitude toward collateral attack can be found in DURFEE v. DUKE, 375 U.S. 106, 84 S.Ct. 242, 11 L.Ed.2d 186 (1963), which involved a dispute over title to a tract of bottom land on the Missouri River, which forms the boundary between Nebraska and Missouri. A Missouri federal district court allowed collateral attack on a Nebraska judgment quieting title, on the ground that considerations of territorial sovereignty outweighed the policies of res judicata. The Nebraska court's subject-matter jurisdiction depended on whether the land was within Nebraska, which "depended entirely upon a factual question— whether a shift in the river's course had been caused by avulsion or accretion." The question had been fully litigated in the Nebraska action. The Supreme Court reversed:

>   *   *   *   [W]hile it is established that a court in one State, when asked to give effect to the judgment of a court in another State, may constitutionally inquire into the foreign court's jurisdiction to render that judgment, the modern decisions of this Court have carefully delineated the permissible scope of such an inquiry. From these decisions there emerges the general rule that a judgment is entitled to full faith and credit—even as to questions of jurisdiction—when the second court's inquiry discloses that those questions have been fully and fairly litigated and finally decided in the court which rendered the original judgment.   *   *   *
>
> To be sure, the general rule of finality of jurisdictional determinations is not without exceptions. Doctrines of federal preemption or sovereign immunity may in some contexts be controlling. Kalb v. Feuerstein   *   *   *. But no such overriding considerations are present here.

Id. at 111–14, 84 S.Ct. at 245–47, 11 L.Ed.2d at 191–93.

Are there situations in which defects in subject-matter jurisdiction should be immune from direct attack? See Dobbs, *Beyond Bootstrap: Foreclosing the Issue of Subject-Matter Jurisdiction Before Final Judgment,* 51 Minn.L.Rev. 491 (1967).

3. THE SUBJECT-MATTER JURISDICTION OF THE FEDERAL COURTS—DIVERSITY OF CITIZENSHIP

Article III, Section 2 of the United States Constitution, extends the judicial power of the United States to controversies "between Citizens of different States * * * and between a State, or the Citizens thereof, and Foreign States, Citizens or Subjects."[d]   The current scope of the diversity jurisdiction granted to the federal courts by Congress is set out in 28 U.S.C. § 1332. One of the most important limitations on federal diversity jurisdiction is the rule of "complete diversity" announced by Chief Justice Marshall in STRAW-BRIDGE v. CURTISS, 7 U.S. (3 Cranch) 267, 2 L.Ed. 435 (1806). The rule provides in effect that there is no diversity jurisdiction if any plaintiff is a citizen of the same state as any defendant, no matter how many parties are involved in the litigation. The precise status of the complete diversity doctrine is a subject of considerable debate because it is not clear whether the *Strawbridge* decision was simply a construction of the diversity statute then in force or was intended by Chief Justice Marshall as a constitutional limitation on federal-court jurisdiction. See also p. 624, infra.

The origin and purposes of diversity of citizenship jurisdiction have long been the subject of vigorous debate. The most widely accepted rationale was offered by Chief Justice Marshall in BANK OF THE UNITED STATES v. DEVAUX, 9 U.S. (5 Cranch) 61, 87, 3 L.Ed. 38, 45 (1809):

> However true the fact may be, that the tribunals of the states will administer justice as impartially as those of the nation, * * * it is not less true that the constitution itself either entertains apprehensions on this subject, or views with such indulgence the possible fears and apprehensions of suitors, that it has established national tribunals for the decision of controversies * * * between citizens of different states.

Another argument that has been advanced to justify diversity jurisdiction is that the availability of a federal tribunal during our nation's formative period afforded some measure of security to investors developing the southern and western portions of the country. Analyses of the historical origins of the diversity jurisdiction can be found in Frank, *Historical Bases of the Federal Judicial System*, 13 Law & Contemp.Prob. 1 (1948); Friendly, *The Historic Basis of the Diversity Jurisdiction*, 41 Harv.L.Rev. 483 (1928); and Phillips & Christenson, *The Historical and Legal Background of the Diversity Jurisdiction*, 46 A.B.A.J. 959 (1960).

Assuming that diversity jurisdiction was created to protect out-of-state litigants against local prejudice and that it has helped speed the economic growth of the country, are these realistic or meaningful bases for continuing

---

d Controversies between a citizen of a state and an alien technically are denominated "alienage cases," but may be considered as diversity cases for purposes of this Section.

diversity jurisdiction today?   If not, are there other reasons that are more persuasive for retaining or even enlarging the scope of diversity jurisdiction? In what ways should the existing diversity scheme be modified to make it more rational and responsive to current conditions?   In this regard, examine American Law Institute, *Study of the Division of Jurisdiction Between State and Federal Courts,* Official Draft, §§ 1301–02, 111–34 (1969).   A bill containing the Institute's proposals has been introduced in the Congress, S. 1876, 92d Cong., 1st Sess. (1971), and hearings have been held but the legislation has not emerged from the subcommittee.   For a detailed analysis of the proposal, see Currie, *The Federal Courts and the American Law Institute,* 36 U.Chi.L.Rev. 1, 268 (1968, 1969).   See also Burdick, *Diversity Jurisdiction under the American Law Institute Proposals: Its Purpose and Effect on State and Federal Courts,* 48 No.Dak.L.Rev. 1 (1971).

Diversity cases currently represent approximately thirty per cent of the case load of the federal courts.   Nearly half of these actions arise out of automobile accidents.   See generally *Diversity Jurisdiction: A Symposium—Appendix: Statistical Analyses of Diversity Jurisdiction,* 40 Ind.L.J. 511, 586–98 (1965).   In view of the amount of federal judicial time and energy devoted to diversity cases, it is not surprising that the utility of diversity jurisdiction has been the subject of sharp debate.   Several of the numerous conflicting views can be found in Frankfurter, *Distribution of Judicial Power Between United States and State Courts,* 13 Cornell L.Q. 499 (1928);   Marbury, *Why Should We Limit Federal Diversity Jurisdiction?,* 36 A.B.A.J. 379 (1960);   Moore & Weckstein, *Diversity Jurisdiction: Past, Present, and Future,* 43 Texas L.Rev. 1 (1964).   Statistical data on the actual existence of local prejudice against out-of-state parties, or whether an attorney's belief in the existence of such prejudice is a factor influencing forum choice, is sparse and inconclusive.   *Compare* Summers, *Analysis of Factors that Influence Choice of Forum in Diversity Cases,* 47 Iowa L.Rev. 933 (1962), *with* Note, *The Choice Between State and Federal Court in Diversity Cases in Virginia,* 51 Va.L.Rev. 178 (1965).

JANZEN v. GOOS

United States Court of Appeals, Eighth Circuit, 1962.
302 F.2d 421.

BLACKMUN, Circuit Judge.   This action was dismissed for lack of diversity jurisdiction.   The plaintiff has appealed.

The suit   *   *   *   on behalf of a decedent's widow and six minor children, as next of kin, is for the alleged wrongful death of the decedent on November 20, 1960, resulting from injuries sustained in a Nebraska automobile accident.   The complaint, by the widow as special administratrix of her husband's estate, alleges that she is a citizen of Kansas, that the two defendants are citizens of Nebraska, and that the amount in controversy exceeds the minimum specified by 28 U.S.C.A. § 1332 * * *. Each of the defendants, prior to filing an answer, moved that the action be dismissed for lack of the requisite diversity of citizenship. Their motions were sustained.

* * * The parties stipulated, * * * (a) that the decedent was a resident of Richardson County, Nebraska; (b) that he died in that state on November 20, 1960, as a result of injuries received in an accident; (c) that on February 9, 1961, the plaintiff was the widow of the decedent and was a citizen and resident of Stella, Nebraska; (d) that on that date she filed in the County Court of Richardson County, Nebraska, a petition for her appointment as administratrix of her husband's estate; (e) that on March 6, 1961, the plaintiff was appointed as such administratrix; (f) that letters of administration were issued to her by that court on March 15, 1961; (g) that on May 17, 1961, the plaintiff

> "moved with her entire family to 809 East 6th Street, Newton, Kansas. She was living there with her family on July 14, 1961, and if permitted to testify would testify that she was living there with the intention of residing there permanently";

(h) that the complaint in the present action was filed in the United States District Court for the District of Nebraska on July 14, 1961; (i) that at that time the plaintiff was still serving in the capacity of Nebraska administratrix * * *.

Construction of 28 U.S.C.A. § 1332. Statutes conferring diversity jurisdiction upon the federal courts are to be strictly construed. * * * Consequently, "if a plaintiff's allegations of jurisdictional facts are challenged by the defendant, the plaintiff bears the burden of supporting the allegations by competent proof". Thomson v. Gaskill, * * * p. 446 of 315 U.S., p. 675 of 62 S.Ct.; McNutt v. General Motors Acceptance Corp., 1936, 298 U.S. 178, 189, 56 S.Ct. 780, 80 L.Ed. 1135; KVOS, Inc. v. Associated Press, 1936, 299 U.S. 269, 278, 57 S.Ct. 197, 81 L.Ed. 183. Therefore, although the complaint before us properly alleges facts sufficient for diversity jurisdiction, the situation is not one, as the plaintiff suggests, for the application of the rule that, for purposes of a motion to dismiss, the allegations of the complaint are to be taken as true. * * * Instead, the challenge to the diversity jurisdiction, raised by the motions here, places the allegation of the plaintiff's complaint that she is a citizen of Kansas flatly in issue and she is required to establish this feature of her case. * * * This she must do by a preponderance of the evidence * * * or * * * by proof which is "clear and convincing."

Citizenship and its acquisition. Citizenship and domicile are synonymous for purposes of § 1332. * * * The existence of diversity of citizenship is to be determined not as of the time the cause of action arises but as of the time suit is instituted. * * *

Any person, sui juris, may make a bona fide change of domicile or citizenship at any time. * * * However, one may have only one domicile at a time and a domicile once established persists until a new one is acquired. * * * Once acquired, it is presumed to continue until it is shown to have been changed. * * *

This court has expressed itself as to the requirements of the acquisition of a domicile for diversity purposes:

> "To acquire a domicil of choice, the law requires the physical presence of a person at the place of the domicil claimed, coupled with the intention of making it his present home. When these two facts concur, the change in domicil is instantaneous. Intention to live permanently at the claimed domicil is not required. If a person capable of making his choice honestly regards a place as his present home, the motive prompting him is immaterial."

Spurgeon v. Mission State Bank, 1945, 151 F.2d 702, 705–706, certiorari denied 327 U.S. 782, 66 S.Ct. 682, 90 L.Ed. 1009. * * *

The effect of representative capacity. When an action is brought by an administrator or other fiduciary and the governing state law authorizes that fiduciary to bring suit in his own name as the real party in interest, it is the fiduciary's personal citizenship, not the identity of the state from which he receives his appointment or the citizenship of the persons for whose benefit the action is brought, which is pertinent in the ascertainment of the existence of diversity. Mecom v. Fitzsimmons Drilling Co., 1931, 284 U.S. 183, 186, 52 S.Ct. 84, 76 L.Ed. 233 * * *.

Even the appointment of a non-resident as a wrongful death representative for the avowed purpose of providing diversity, so long as it is bona fide and lawful, has been held not to run afoul of 28 U.S.C.A. § 1359 relating to improper or collusive acts in the invocation of jurisdiction. Motive, thus, is immaterial. * * *

From all the foregoing we conclude that until May 17, 1961, the plaintiff was a citizen of Nebraska; that the fact the present action is one instituted by the plaintiff in a representative capacity does not negate the governing character of her personal citizenship in the determination of diversity; that the vital date for the ascertainment of diversity is July 14, 1961, when the action was instituted; that the plaintiff has the burden of proof on the diversity issue; that her continuing to serve as a Nebraska representative does not prevent or deny her acquisition of citizenship in another state; and that her motive, whatever it may have been, in effecting her removal to Kansas is immaterial. This brings us, then, to the ultimate analysis of the district court's conclusion that diversity of citizenship did not exist.

The court's determination of absence of diversity here (which, as noted above, we treat as a specific finding of fact to that effect) is not to be set aside unless clearly erroneous. * * * Having in mind the legal principles outlined above and the initial conclusions we have expressed, we feel compelled to conclude that the trial court's determination that diversity of citizenship was not established was clearly erroneous within Rule 52(a) as so defined.

We repeat: there is no question that until May 17, 1961, the plaintiff was and had been a citizen of Nebraska. But there also is no question, in view of the stipulation, that on that date the plaintiff moved with her entire family of six minor children to Newton, Kansas, and that the plaintiff "was living there with her family" on the date the present action was instituted. As the defendant points out, residence does not equate with citizenship and this portion of the stipulation, which cannot be disregarded by the trial court, may not in and of itself establish citizenship. The stipulation, however, goes on to state that the plaintiff would testify that she was living in Kansas with the intention of residing there permanently. This, if believed, brings the intent factor, essential in domicile and citizenship, to coincide with the other essential factor of physical presence and, again if believed, establishes plaintiff's case and fulfills her burden of proof on the diversity issue.

* * *

Reversed and remanded for further proceedings.

NOTES AND QUESTIONS

1. What advantages are there to the rule that diversity is to be ascertained as of the time suit is instituted rather than as of the date the cause of action arises or any other date? The American Law Institute has recommended that the principal case and others like it be legislatively overruled by means of a provision stating that executors and administrators be deemed citizens of the same state as the decedent. American Law Institute, *Study of the Division of Jurisdiction Between State and Federal Courts,* Official Draft, § 1301(b)(4), and comments at 117–19 (1969). Is this sound?

2. Is it relevant that the choice of a particular person to bring an action affecting a number of people is motivated by a desire to create or destroy diversity of citizenship? *Cf.* Mecom v. Fitzsimmons Drilling Co., 284 U.S. 183, 52 S.Ct. 84, 76 L.Ed. 233 (1931). See Note, *Federal Jurisdiction—Appointment of an Out-of-State Administratrix to Gain Diversity Jurisdiction,* 96 U.Pa.L.Rev. 897 (1948); Note, *Appointment of Non-resident Administrators to Create Federal Diversity Jurisdiction,* 73 Yale L.J. 873 (1964). Note that in *Janzen* the court held that if the appointment was valid under state law, there was no need to inquire into the motives behind the appointment of an administrator. Several recent cases indicate that this permissive attitude is undergoing serious re-evaluation and that the validity of an appointment under state law is only one of the factors that the court should consider when determining whether the parties have tried to "manufacture" jurisdiction in violation of 28 U.S.C. § 1359. See McSparran v. Weist, 402 F.2d 867 (3d Cir.1968), certiorari denied 395 U.S. 903, 89 S.Ct. 1739, 23 L.Ed.2d 217 (1969). See also 6 Wright & Miller, *Federal Practice and Procedure: Civil* § 1557 (1971). What are the disadvantages of a "particularistic" or "ad hoc" approach to this problem?

3. SMITH v. SPERLING, 354 U.S. 91, 77 S.Ct. 1112, 1 L.Ed.2d 1205 (1957), was a derivative action on behalf of Warner Brothers (a Delaware corporation), against United States Pictures, Inc. (another Delaware corporation), certain directors of Warner, and others challenging the fairness of various agreements between Warner and United. The district court ordered Warner realigned as a plaintiff and the action was dismissed for lack of diversity of citizen-

ship; the Ninth Circuit affirmed. The Supreme Court reversed in a five-to-four decision holding that it was improper to engage in a trial of the issues as part of the jurisdiction determination and that the issue whether the management is antagonistic to the stockholder so as to be aligned as a defendant should be determined on the face of the pleadings and by considering the nature of the controversy.

The *Smith* case was relied on by the plaintiff in REED v. ROBILIO, 248 F. Supp. 602 (W.D.Tenn.1965), a suit by the daughter of a deceased partner on behalf of her father's executor to impose a constructive trust upon the purchase of her father's interest in the partnership and to have the interest reconveyed to the partnership with an accounting for profits. The suit was brought against the purchasers of the partnership interest, as well as the surviving partner, his sister, and two brothers. A second cause of action on behalf of the executor of plaintiff's mother sought rescission of a subsequent partnership agreement between the mother and the purchasers of the deceased partner's interest. The executors of the estates of plaintiff's father and mother were named as defendants because of their unwillingness to bring suit against the purchasers. Plaintiff was a citizen of New York; the purchasers of the partnership interest and the executors were citizens of Tennessee. After a trial on the merits the action was dismissed on the ground that the executors had to be realigned as plaintiffs, thereby destroying diversity of citizenship. "It * * * appears from the nature of the claim asserted in the complaint and the relief sought, and from the plaintiff's own admissions, that the executors' real interests in this suit are identifiable with the side of the plaintiff rather than with the side of the individual defendants." The court, in a lengthy opinion discussing many of the realignment cases, rejected the notion that the executors' hostility toward plaintiff was sufficient for denying realignment. Cf. 376 F.2d 392 (6th Cir. 1967).

4. 28 U.S.C. § 1332(a)(2) authorizes the assertion of jurisdiction over actions involving more than $10,000 that are between "citizens of a State, and foreign states or citizens or subjects thereof." Is an alien, who also is a stateless person a citizen or subject of a foreign state for purposes of that statute? See Blair Holdings Corp. v. Rubinstein, 133 F.Supp. 496 (S.D.N.Y.1955).

5. What is the status for diversity purposes of a corporation that is incorporated in two or more states? Are there situations in which one or more of the states of incorporation should be ignored in determining diversity of citizenship? These problems are explored in the trial and appellate court opinions in Gavin v. Hudson & Manhattan R. R., 90 F.Supp. 172 (D.N.J.), reversed 185 F.2d 104 (3d Cir.1950). See also Friedenthal, *New Limitations on Federal Jurisdiction,* 11 Stan.L.Rev. 213, 236–41 (1959); Note, *Citizenship of Multi-State Corporations for Diversity Jurisdiction Purposes,* 48 Iowa L.Rev. 410 (1963). What is the citizenship of an unincorporated association for diversity purposes? See Comment, *Diversity Jurisdiction for Unincorporated Associations,* 75 Yale L.J. 138 (1965).

6. It generally is accepted that a corporation can have only one principal place of business for purposes of applying 28 U.S.C. § 1332. How does a court determine what that is? Is it where the stockholders or board of directors meet, where operational policy is fixed, where the greatest amount of corporate property or employees are located, or where the largest amount of revenue is earned? What

other factors might be relevant? *Compare* Kelly v. United States Steel Corp., 284 F.2d 850 (3d Cir.1960), *with* Scot Typewriter Co. v. Underwood Corp., 170 F.Supp. 862 (S.D.N.Y.1959). See generally Friedenthal, Note 5, supra at 222–25; Moore & Weckstein, *Corporations and Diversity of Citizenship Jurisdiction: A Supreme Court Fiction Revisited*, 77 Harv.L.Rev. 1426 (1964); Comment, *A Corporation's Principal Place of Business for Federal Diversity Jurisdiction*, 38 N.Y.U.L.Rev. 148 (1963).

7. In NATIONAL MUT. INS. CO. v. TIDEWATER TRANSFER CO., 337 U.S. 582, 69 S.Ct. 1173, 93 L.Ed. 1556 (1949), five Justices upheld the constitutionality of the provision in Section 1332(d) treating the District of Columbia as a state for diversity purposes. The decision is unique because a majority of the Court rejected the argument that citizens of the District were citizens of a state within the meaning of Article III of the Constitution and a differently constituted majority rejected the argument that the statute was a valid exercise of Congress' power under Article I of the Constitution to enact legislation for the inhabitants of the District. Yet these were the only two arguments advanced to sustain the statute's constitutionality.

---

4. THE SUBJECT-MATTER JURISDICTION OF THE FEDERAL COURTS—AMOUNT IN CONTROVERSY

HORTON v. LIBERTY MUTUAL INS. CO.

Supreme Court of the United States, 1961.
367 U.S. 348, 81 S.Ct. 1570, 6 L.Ed.2d 890.

Certiorari to the United States Court of Appeals for the Fifth Circuit.

Mr. Justice BLACK delivered the opinion of the Court.

* * *

Petitioner, Horton, was injured while working for an employer in Texas insured by the respondent, Liberty Mutual Insurance Company. Pursuant to the Texas Workmen's Compensation Law, petitioner filed a claim with the Texas Industrial Accident Board against his employer and the respondent insurance company alleging that he had been totally and permanently incapacitated and claiming the maximum recovery under the law of $35 per week for 401 weeks, or a total of $14,035. After administrative hearings the Board decided that petitioner would be disabled for only 30 weeks and accordingly made an award of only $1,050. * * * [T]he respondent * * *, the very day of the award, filed this diversity case in the United States District Court to set aside the award, alleging that petitioner had claimed, was claiming and would claim $14,035, but denying that petitioner was entitled to recover anything at all under Texas law. One week later the petitioner, who also was dissatisfied with the award, filed an action in the state court to set aside the Board's award and to recover in that court the full $14,035. After that, petitioner moved to dismiss the respondent's federal court suit on the ground that the value of the "matter in controversy" was only the amount of the award, $1,050, and not the amount of his claim of $14,035, although he also contemporaneously filed, subject to his motion to dismiss, what he designated as a compulsory counterclaim for the full amount he had claimed before the Texas Board and in his Texas State Court suit. The District Court held that the "matter in controversy" in the federal action was only the amount of the $1,050 award that the respondent company had asked the court to set aside. In so holding the District Court relied on National Surety Corp. v. Chamberlain,[4] in which another District Court in Texas had reached the same conclusion as to jurisdiction largely on the basis of what it deemed to have been the purpose of Congress in enacting the 1958 amendment to 28 U.S.C. § 1332 * * *, which amendment rather severely cut down the jurisdiction of Federal District Courts, particularly in state workmen's compensation cases. The Court of Appeals reversed * * *.

First. It is true, as the Chamberlain opinion pointed out, that the purpose and effect of the 1958 amendment were to reduce congestion in the Federal District Courts partially caused by the large number of civil cases that were being brought under the long-standing $3,000 jurisdictional rule. This effort to reduce District Court congestion followed years of study by the United States Judicial Conference and the Administrative Office of the United States Courts, as well as by the Congress. To accomplish this purpose the 1958 amendment took several different but related steps. It raised the requisite jurisdictional amount from $3,000 to $10,000 in diversity and federal question cases; it provided that a corporation is to be deemed a citizen not only of the State by which it was incorporated but also of the State where it has its principal place of business; and, most importantly here, it also for the first time forbade the *removal* of state workmen's compensation cases from state courts to United States District Courts. By granting district judges a discretionary power to impose costs on a federal court plaintiff if he should "recover less than the sum or value of $10,000," the amendment further manifested a congressional purpose to discourage the trying of suits involving less than $10,000 in federal courts. In discussing the question of state workmen's compensation cases, the Senate Report on the amendment evidenced a concern not only about the problem of congestion in the federal courts, but also about trial burdens that claimants might suffer by having to go to trial in federal rather than state courts due to the fact that the state courts are likely to be closer to an injured worker's home and may also provide him with special procedural advantages in workmen's compensation cases.

The foregoing are some of the appealing considerations that led the District Court to conclude that it would frustrate the congressional purpose to permit insurers to file workmen's compensation suits in federal courts when Congress had deliberately provided that such suits could not be removed to federal courts if filed by claimants in state courts. But after the most deliberate study of the whole problem by lawyers and judges and after its consideration by law-

4 171 F.Supp. 591.

yers on the Senate Judiciary Committee in the light of statistics on both removals and original filings, Congress used language specifically barring removal of such cases from state to federal courts and at the same time left unchanged the old language which just as specifically permits civil suits to be filed in federal courts in cases where there are both diversity of citizenship and the prescribed jurisdictional amount.   In this situation we must take the intent of Congress with regard to the filing of diversity cases in Federal District Courts to be that which its language clearly sets forth.   Congress could very easily have used language to bar filing of workmen's compensation suits by the insurer as well as removal of such suits, and it could easily do so still.   We therefore hold that under the present law the District Court has jurisdiction to try this civil case between citizens of different States if the matter in controversy is in excess of $10,000.

Second.   We agree with petitioner that determination of the value of the matter in controversy for purposes of federal jurisdiction is a federal question to be decided under federal standards,[10] although the federal courts must, of course, look to state law to determine the nature and extent of the right to be enforced in a diversity case.   *   *   *

The general federal rule has long been to decide what the amount in controversy is from the complaint itself, unless it appears or is in some way shown that the amount stated in the complaint is not claimed "in good faith." [12]   In deciding this question of good faith we have said that it "must appear to a legal certainty that the claim is really for less than the jurisdictional amount to justify dismissal." [13]   The complaint of the respondent company filed in the District Court, while denying any liability at all and asking that the award of $1,050 against it be set aside, also alleges that petitioner Horton has claimed, now claims and will claim that he has suffered total and permanent disability and is entitled to a maximum recovery of $14,035, which, of course, is in excess of the $10,000 requisite to give a federal court jurisdiction of this controversy. No denial of these allegations in the complaint has been made, no attempted disclaimer or surrender of any part of the original claim has been made by petitioner, and there has been no other showing, let alone a showing "to a legal certainty," of any lack of good faith on the part of the respondent in alleging that a $14,035 claim is in controversy.   It would contradict the whole record as well as the allegations of the complaint to say that this dispute involves only $1,050.   The claim before the Board was $14,035; the state court suit of petitioner asked that much; the conditional counterclaim in the federal court claims the same amount.   Texas law under which this claim was created and has its being leaves the entire $14,035 claim open for adjudication in a *de novo* court trial, regardless of the award.   Thus the record before us shows beyond a doubt that the award is challenged by both parties and is binding on neither;

[handwritten margin note: Determination of amount = amount stated in complaint in good faith. ✓]

[10] See, e. g., Shamrock Oil & Gas Corp. v. Sheets, 313 U.S. 100, 104, 61 S.Ct. 868, 870, 85 L.Ed. 1214.

[12] St. Paul Mercury Indemnity Co. v. Red Cab Co., 303 U.S. 283, 288, 58 S.Ct. 586, 590, 82 L.Ed. 845, and cases there cited.

[13] Id., 303 U.S. at page 289, 58 S.Ct. at page 590.   *   *   *

that petitioner claims more than $10,000 from the respondent and the respondent denies it should have to pay petitioner anything at all.   No matter which party brings it into court, the controversy remains the same; it involves the same amount of money and is to be adjudicated and determined under the same rules.   Unquestionably, therefore, the amount in controversy is in excess of $10,000.

* * *

The Court of Appeals was right in holding that the District Court had jurisdiction of this case and its judgment is affirmed.

Affirmed.

Mr. Justice CLARK, with whom THE CHIEF JUSTICE, Mr. Justice BRENNAN and Mr. Justice STEWART join, dissenting.

The Court turns a new furrow in the field of diversity jurisdiction today and, in so doing, plows under a rule of almost a quarter of a century's standing —the rule that in determining jurisdiction, "the sum claimed by the plaintiff controls if the claim is apparently made in good faith."   St. Paul Mercury Indemnity Co. v. Red Cab Co. * * *.   This is the first time the Court has let a plaintiff affix jurisdiction by prophesying what the defendant would or might claim, rather than by stating what the plaintiff itself did claim.   In so generously construing the statute, the Court confounds the test heretofore applied in diversity cases.   It also nullifies the result of "years of study by the United States Judicial Conference and the Administrative Office of the United States Courts, as well as by the Congress" * * * in the adoption of the Act of July 25, 1958 * * * increasing the jurisdictional amount in diversity cases to $10,000.   Once again the United States District Courts in Texas will be flooded by compensation cases,[1] and the Congress once again will be obliged to amend the diversity statute.   Moreover, today's decision practically wipes out the long-existing distinction between declaratory judgment actions and conventional suits. * * *   For these reasons I must dissent.

* * *

The jurisdictional limits of Federal District Courts are bounded on one side by the Constitution and on the other by the enactments of Congress.   Only that judicial power expressly granted by statute may be exercised by the *nisi prius* courts. * * *   In the light of such history, this Court has repeatedly held that such jurisdiction is to be narrowly interpreted.

* * *   In most cases, the determination of the amount in controversy is exceedingly simple, e. g., liquidated damages.   However, where the relief sought is difficult to define in terms of money, or is of differing value to the parties, the statute does not admit of ready application.   To clarify these situations, this Court, in St. Paul Mercury Indemnity Co. v. Red Cab Co., supra, 303 U.S. at page 288, 58 S.Ct. at page 590, stated: "[U]nless the law gives a

---

[1] In 1957, 2,147 workmen's compensation cases were commenced in the United States District Courts of Texas.   S.Rep. No. 1830, 85th Cong., 2d Sess. 8, U.S. Code Cong. & Adm.News 1958, p. 3105.

different rule, *the sum claimed by the plaintiff controls* if the claim is apparently made in good faith." (Emphasis added.)

The application of the foregoing rules to the problem here results in a simple solution. At the time respondent filed its complaint, there was enforceable against it a liability in the amount of $1,050. If petitioner defaulted, the District Court would set aside the Board award. If respondent lost and petitioner filed no counterclaim, the judgment could only be for $1,050. It was only if petitioner counterclaimed for an amount in excess of the jurisdictional amount of $10,000, that respondent could have controverted a claim cognizable in federal court. It seems impossible to avoid the conclusion that the Court is allowing diversity jurisdiction to be predicated upon a counterclaim which might possibly be filed by petitioner. Even a "disclaimer or surrender of [a] * * * part of the original claim" would not change the Court's insistence upon looking to the alleged counterclaim if that were more than the respondent's claim, for the jurisdictional minimum. Apparently the Court would require a "denial of these allegations" that petitioner will claim an amount in excess of the jurisdictional limit before considering the respondent's prayer to set aside the Board's award as the source of the jurisdictional amount. * * * Not only is this in patent conflict with St. Paul Mercury Indemnity Co. v. Red Cab Co., supra, but it distorts the meaning of Rule 3, Federal Rules of Civil Procedure, which states, "[a] civil action is commenced by filing a complaint with the court." Here the Court evidently holds that if the complaint, insufficient to meet the jurisdictional standards, alleges that a possible compulsory counterclaim, sufficient to meet such standards, may be filed by the defendant, federal jurisdiction attaches. Certainly we have never permitted a District Court to acquire jurisdiction under 28 U.S. C. § 1331(a) * * * where the plaintiff does not allege a federal question but claims that the defendant will raise such an issue. * * *

In essence, the Court has permitted respondent to turn its suit into an action for a declaratory judgment without meeting the requirements of the Declaratory Judgments Act. 28 U.S.C. § 2201 * * *. That Act provides that "[i]n a case of actual controversy within its jurisdiction * * * any court of the United States, *upon the filing of an appropriate pleading, may declare* the rights and other legal relations of any interested party seeking such declaration * * *." (Emphasis added.)

* * *

Finally today's decision effectively emasculates the recent congressional attempt to limit diversity jurisdiction, especially in workmen's compensation cases. * * * Workmen's compensation cases were singled out and specifically dealt with because they "arise and exist only by virtue of State laws. No Federal question is involved and no law of the United States is involved in these cases." * * * [S. Rep. No. 1830, 85th Cong., 2d Sess. 8], U.S. Code Cong. & Adm.News 1958, p. 3106. * * *

To further limit the number of diversity cases, the Congress enacted 28 U.S.C. § 1332(b) * * *. This provision makes little sense when applied to the result now approved by the Court. If respondent were to obtain the relief it sought, namely, to have the Board's award of less than $10,000 "vacated, set aside, voided and declared to be of no further force and effect," it is clear that costs could be assessed against it under § 1332(b). This produces an anomalous situation which the Court must implicitly approve. Respondent has no hope of avoiding possible liability under the cost sanction of § 1332(b). This is so because the relief it obtains must be measured against the jurisdictional minimum "without regard" for Horton's possible counterclaim. We are therefore left with the strange result that while respondent has met the requirements of § 1332(a), yet under § 1332(b) it will be liable for costs for failing to meet the same requirements.

Moreover, the Senate Report expressed concern for the problems of the injured employee in federal court   *   *   *.   While 28 U.S.C. § 1332 does not specifically prohibit the filing of original workmen's compensation cases, a clearer expression of congressional dislike for saddling federal courts with such cases could hardly be imagined. We should, therefor, give effect to this policy wherever possible. Not only does the decision today fail to do this, but the Court goes out of its way to defeat the congressional intent.   *   *   *   It is now an unequal race to the courthouse door—a race which the insurers will invariably win, since they have resident counsel in Austin (the location of the Texas Industrial Accident Board) who quickly secure news of Board awards and are thus enabled to "beat" the workman in the choice of forums. Thus, the Court—contrary to the specifically expressed intention of the Congress—grants the insurance companies the option of going into federal court, with all its attendant difficulties to the already overburdened federal judiciary and the impecunious workman.   *   *   *   Congress closed the back door and locked it tight in 1958, only to have the Court break down the front door today and hang out the welcome sign.

NOTES AND QUESTIONS

1. Note that in *Horton* the defendant only had asserted his claim conditionally so that as a technical matter no counterclaim was before the court when it determined jurisdiction. Does this mean that the Supreme Court held that the amount-in-controversy requirement may be satisfied if plaintiff simply alleges that defendant will interpose a counterclaim at some future date? Of what importance is the fact that *Horton* involved a claim under the Texas Workmen's Compensation Law, which provided for an action de novo to set aside the Board's award so that the issues before the court were identical to those that previously were before the Board? Some courts have limited *Horton* to Texas compensation cases because of this fact. See, e. g., Insurance Co. of No. America v. Keeling, 360 F.2d 88 (5th Cir.), certiorari denied 385 U.S. 840, 87 S.Ct. 91, 17 L.Ed.2d 73 (1966).

2. Given the *St. Paul* and *Horton* approach, will a court ever dismiss an inflated claim in an action for unliquidated damages? Consider the following passage from TURNER v. WILSON LINE OF MASSACHUSETTS, 242 F.2d 414, 419 (1st Cir.1957), a wrongful death and survival action in which plaintiff

sought to recover for decedent's pain and suffering in the hours preceding his death from carbon monoxide poisoning:

> The amount of money appropriate as compensation for pain and suffering [in a survival action] cannot be determined by any precise measure or rule. * * * Severe or excruciating pain, even for only a period of time measured by minutes, might warrant an award of over $3,000 whether or not coupled with fear of impending death. So also would mild pain if suffered for months or years. But here we have a case of mild pain, perhaps no more than severe discomfort, * * * not severe enough to cause the sufferer to quit work or fear impending death, and lasting for not more than some 7 or 8 hours. The court's judgment as to what a reasonable jury would award as maximum damages for such pain and suffering is subjective. So is ours. In this situation about all that we can or need to say is that we agree with the District Court [in dismissing the complaint].

Does this amount to a holding that plaintiff's claim was not made in "good faith"? Is it a "legal certainty" that no reasonable jury would award more than the jurisdictional amount under the circumstances of the *Turner* case?

3. If a question of jurisdictional amount is raised as in *Turner,* what types of evidence and information should the court be allowed to consider in ruling on a motion to dismiss? To what extent may the court examine the merits to determine the jurisdiction question? May the court hear argument on the question whether the elements of plaintiff's purported injuries are compensable under the governing law? See McDonald v. Patton, 240 F.2d 424 (4th Cir.1957).

4. In ARNOLD v. TROCCOLI, 344 F.2d 842 (2d Cir.1965), plaintiff's personal injury action for $15,000, which originally had been brought for $6,000 in a state court, was dismissed as a colorable claim asserted for the sole purpose of conferring federal jurisdiction. There appeared to be no justification for the increase in claimed damages, and plaintiff's counsel admitted that the switch from state to federal court was made because of the congested condition of the state courts. In the course of its opinion, the Second Circuit examined statistics prepared by New York's Judicial Conference showing that 97% of all accident claims in New York result in settlements or judgments of less than $10,000. Of what relevance is this statistic in determining whether plaintiff's claim is "in excess of $10,000"? What if plaintiff discovers new facts during pretrial proceedings that show that any possible recovery cannot reach the jurisdictional amount, and his attorney files a written stipulation to that effect? Must the action be dismissed or is it saved by the fact that the original claim was made in "good faith"? See National Sur. Corp. v. City of Excelsior Springs, 123 F.2d 573 (8th Cir.1941).

5. In an action on a life or disability insurance policy involving installment payments that eventually may aggregate more than the jurisdictional amount, does it make any difference that there are conditions on the payment of installments, such as the continued disability of the beneficiary, that may prevent the beneficiary from ever collecting such an amount? See Aetna Cas. & Sur. Co. v. Flowers, 330 U.S. 464, 67 S.Ct. 798, 91 L.Ed. 1024 (1947). Can a group of creditors assign their claims to one person and thereby satisfy the $10,000 requisite? Does it make any difference if there is some legitimate reason for the assignment? See Kramer v. Caribbean Mills, Inc., 394 U.S. 823, 89 S.Ct. 1487, 23 L.Ed.2d 9 (1969).

The liberal joinder provisions of the Federal Rules raise a number of questions as to whether "aggregation" can be used to meet the jurisdictional amount.

See Wright, *Federal Courts* § 33 (2d ed. 1970). See also *Snyder v. Harris*, p. 587, infra. Consider whether a federal court can assert jurisdiction in the following situations:

(a) One plaintiff suing one defendant claiming $3000 property damage and $9000 personal injury resulting from an automobile accident. *Yes – P can combine claim (probably dont have to even be related)*

(b) Two plaintiffs, each with a claim for $7,000 arising out of one accident, suing one defendant. *No – cant merge claims of separate P's*

depends on the nature of the obligation (c) One plaintiff suing two defendants seeking $7,000 from each defendant. *No – dont join claims of 2 or more parties*

(d) One plaintiff suing one defendant for $8,000, defendant asserting a compulsory counterclaim for $6,000. *No (split)*

(e) Insurance company seeking a declaratory judgment that it is not liable on an insurance policy to two beneficiaries in the amount of $6,000 to each beneficiary. *Yes (split) 1 policy w/ $12000 liability*

(f) Two plaintiffs suing a single defendant; one plaintiff has a claim for $15,000 and the other has a separate and distinct claim for $5,000 that will involve many of the same items of proof.

6. How does a court determine whether the jurisdictional-amount requirement has been satisfied when the object of plaintiff's action is something other than the recovery of damages, such as the abatement of a nuisance or an injunction against the enforcement of a tax statute or a municipal ordinance on the ground that it is unconstitutional? For example, if a riparian property owner seeks to enjoin an upstream proprietor from polluting the river, should the court measure the jurisdictional amount in terms of whether the decline in value of plaintiff's property due to the pollution is more than $10,000 or whether it will cost defendant more than $10,000 to abate the nuisance? May the court uphold jurisdiction if either of these figures exceeds the jurisdictional amount? If the aggregate of these two figures is over $10,000? See Comment, *Federal Jurisdiction: Amount in Controversy in Suits for Nonmonetary Remedies*, 46 Calif.L. Rev. 601 (1958).

7. In American Law Institute, *Study of the Division of Jurisdiction Between State and Federal Courts*, Official Draft, § 1311 (1969), it is proposed that there be no amount in controversy requirement in original federal-question cases in order to assure that disputes involving serious matters arising under the Constitution, laws, or treaties of the United States always can be heard in a federal court. In the commentary to that proposal the Institute states:

> Figures showing actual experience as to amount involved suggest that a substantial portion of federal question jurisdiction does involve "petty controversies" in terms of the amount in controversy. But these cases must be tried in some forum. To impose a jurisdictional amount requirement that would keep such cases out of federal court would require them to be heard in state court. In cases within the diversity jurisdiction, where parties are relying entirely on state law, it is not inappropriate to require the states to provide a forum for cases involving a small amount. Where the right relied on is federal, the national government should bear the burden of providing a forum to parties who wish to be heard in federal court.

Id. at 174.

5. THE SUBJECT-MATTER JURISDICTION OF THE FEDERAL COURTS—PENDENT AND ANCILLARY CLAIMS

UNITED MINE WORKERS OF AMERICA v. GIBBS

Supreme Court of the United States, 1966.
383 U.S. 715, 86 S.Ct. 1130, 16 L.Ed.2d 218.

Certiorari to the United States Court of Appeals for the Sixth Circuit.

Mr. Justice BRENNAN delivered the opinion of the Court.

Respondent Paul Gibbs was awarded compensatory and punitive damages in this action against petitioner United Mine Workers of America (UMW) for alleged violations of § 303 of the Labor Management Relations Act, 1947, and of the common law of Tennessee. The case grew out of the rivalry between the United Mine Workers and the Southern Labor Union over representation of workers in the southern Appalachian coal fields. Tennessee Consolidated Coal Company, not a party here, laid off 100 miners of the UMW's Local 5881 when it closed one of its mines in southern Tennessee during the spring of 1960. Late that summer, Grundy Company, a wholly owned subsidiary of Consolidated, hired respondent as mine superintendent to attempt to open a new mine on Consolidated's property at nearby Gray's Creek through use of members of the Southern Labor Union. As part of the arrangement, Grundy also gave respondent a contract to haul the mine's coal to the nearest railroad loading point.

On August 15 and 16, 1960, armed members of Local 5881 forcibly prevented the opening of the mine, threatening respondent and beating an organizer for the rival union. The members of the local believed Consolidated had promised them the jobs at the new mine; they insisted that if anyone would do the work, they would. * * * George Gilbert, the UMW's field representative for the area including Local 5881 * * * [had] explicit instructions from his international union superiors to establish a limited picket line, to prevent any further violence, and to see to it that the strike did not spread to neighboring mines. There was no further violence at the mine site * * *.

Respondent lost his job as superintendent, and never entered into performance of his haulage contract. He testified that he soon began to lose other trucking contracts and mine leases he held in nearby areas. Claiming these effects to be the result of a concerted union plan against him, he sought recovery not against Local 5881 or its members, but only against petitioner, the International. The suit was brought in the United States District Court for the Eastern District of Tennessee, and jurisdiction was premised on allegations of secondary boycotts under § 303. The state law claim, for which jurisdiction was based upon the doctrine of pendent jurisdiction, asserted "an unlawful conspiracy and an unlawful boycott aimed at him and [Grundy] to maliciously, wantonly and willfully interfere with his contract of employment and with his contract of haulage."

* * * The jury's verdict was that the UMW had violated both § 303 and state law. Gibbs was awarded $60,000 as damages under the employment contract and $14,500 under the haulage contract; he was also awarded $100,-000 punitive damages. On motion, the trial court set aside the award of damages with respect to the haulage contract on the ground that damage was unproved. It also held that union pressure on Grundy to discharge respondent as supervisor would constitute only a primary dispute with Grundy, as respondent's employer, and hence was not cognizable under § 303. Interference with employment was cognizable as a state claim, however, and a remitted award was sustained on the state law claim. * * * The Court of Appeals for the Sixth Circuit affirmed. * * * We granted certiorari. * * *

I.

A threshold question is whether the District Court properly entertained jurisdiction of the claim based on Tennessee law.

* * * The Court held in Hurn v. Oursler, 289 U.S. 238, 53 S.Ct. 586, 77 L.Ed. 1148, that state law claims are appropriate for federal court determination if they form a separate but parallel ground for relief also sought in a substantial claim based on federal law. The Court distinguished permissible from non-permissible exercises of federal judicial power over state law claims by contrasting "a case where two distinct grounds in support of a single cause of action are alleged, one only of which presents a federal question, and a case where two separate and distinct causes of action are alleged, one only of which is federal in character. In the former, where the federal question averred is not plainly wanting in substance, the federal court, even though the federal ground be not established, may nevertheless retain and dispose of the case upon the nonfederal *ground*; in the latter it may not do so upon the nonfederal *cause of action*." 289 U.S., at 246, 53 S.Ct., at 589. The question is into which category the present action fell.

Hurn was decided in 1933, before the unification of law and equity by the Federal Rules of Civil Procedure. At the time, the meaning of "cause of action" was a subject of serious dispute * * *. The Court in *Hurn* identified what it meant by the term by citation of Baltimore S. S. Co. v. Phillips, 274 U.S. 316, 47 S.Ct. 600, 71 L.Ed. 1069, a case in which "cause of action" had been used to identify the operative scope of the doctrine of *res judicata*. In that case the Court had noted that " 'the whole tendency of our decisions is to require a plaintiff to try his whole cause of action and his whole case at one time,' " 274 U.S., at 320, 47 S.Ct., at 602, and stated its holding in the following language, quoted in part in the *Hurn* opinion:

> "Upon principle, it is perfectly plain that the respondent [a seaman suing for an injury sustained while working aboard ship] suffered but one actionable wrong, and was entitled to but one recovery, whether his injury was due to one or the other of several dis-

tinct acts of alleged negligence, or to a combination of some or all of them. In either view, there would be but a single wrongful invasion of a single primary right of the plaintiff, namely, the right of bodily safety, whether the acts constituting such invasion were one or many, simple or complex.

"A cause of action does not consist of facts, but of the unlawful violation of a right which the facts show. The number and variety of the facts alleged do not establish more than one cause of action so long as their result, whether they be considered severally or in combination, is the violation of but one right by a single legal wrong. The mere multiplication of grounds of negligence alleged as causing the same injury does not result in multiplying the causes of action. The facts are merely the means, and not the end. They do not constitute the cause of action, but they show its existence by making the wrong appear.' " Id., at 321, 47 S.Ct. at 602.

Had the Court found a jurisdictional bar to reaching the state claim in *Hurn*, we assume that the doctrine of *res judicata* would not have been applicable in any subsequent state suit. But the citation of *Baltimore S. S.* shows that the Court found that the weighty policies of judicial economy and fairness to parties reflected in *res judicata* doctrine were in themselves strong counsel for the adoption of a rule which would permit federal courts to dispose of the state as well as the federal claims.

With the adoption of the Federal Rules of Civil Procedure and the unified form of action   *   *   *   much of the controversy over "cause of action" abated. The phrase remained as the keystone of the *Hurn* test, however, and   *   *   *   has been the source of considerable confusion. Under the Rules, the impulse is toward entertaining the broadest possible scope of action consistent with fairness to the parties; joinder of claims, parties and remedies are strongly encouraged. Yet because the *Hurn* question involves issues of jurisdiction as well as convenience, there has been some tendency to limit its application to cases in which the state and federal claims are, as in *Hurn*, "little more than the equivalent of different epithets to characterize the same group of circumstances." 289 U.S., at 246, 53 S.Ct. at 590.

This limited approach is unnecessarily grudging. Pendent jurisdiction, in the sense of judicial *power*, exists whenever there is a claim "arising under [the] Constitution, the Laws of the United States, and Treaties made, or which shall be made, under their Authority   *   *   *." U.S.Const., Art. III, § 2, and the relationship between that claim and the state claims made in the complaint permits the conclusion that the entire action before the court comprises but one constitutional "case." The federal claim must have substance sufficient to confer subject matter jurisdiction on the court. Levering & Garrigues Co. v. Morrin, 289 U.S. 103, 53 S.Ct. 549, 77 L.Ed. 1062. The state and federal claims must derive from a common nucleus of operative fact. But if, considered without regard for their federal or state character, a plaintiff's claims are such that he would ordinarily be expected to try them all in one judicial proceeding, then, assuming substantiality of the federal issues, there is *power* in federal courts to hear the whole.

That power need not be exercised in every case in which it is found to exist. It has consistently been recognized that pendent jurisdiction is a doctrine of discretion, not of plaintiff's right. Its justification lies in considerations of judicial economy, convenience and fairness to litigants; if these are not present a federal court should hesitate to exercise jurisdiction over state claims, even though bound to apply state law to them, Erie R. Co. v. Thompkins * * * [p. 229, infra]. Needless decisions of state law should be avoided both as a matter of comity and to promote justice between the parties, by procuring for them a surer footed reading of applicable law. Certainly, if the federal claims are dismissed before trial, even though not insubstantial in a jurisdictional sense, the state claims should be dismissed as well. Similarly, if it appears that the state issues substantially predominate, whether in terms of proof, of the scope of the issues raised, or of the comprehensiveness of the remedy sought, the state claims may be dismissed without prejudice and left for resolution to state tribunals. There may, on the other hand, be situations in which the state claim is so closely tied to questions of federal policy that the argument for exercise of pendent jurisdiction is particularly strong. In the present case, for example, the allowable scope of the state claim implicates the federal doctrine of pre-emption; while this interrelationship does not create statutory federal question jurisdiction, Louisville & N. R. Co. v. Mottley, * * * its existence is relevant to the exercise of discretion. Finally, there may be reasons independent of jurisdictional considerations, such as the likelihood of jury confusion in treating divergent legal theories of relief, that would justify separating state and federal claims for trial, Fed.Rules Civ.Proc. 42(b); if so, jurisdiction here, too, should ordinarily be refused.

The question of power will ordinarily be resolved on the pleadings. But the issue whether pendent jurisdiction has been properly assumed is one which remains open throughout the litigation. Pretrial procedures or even the trial may reveal a substantial hegemony of state law claims, or likelihood of jury confusion, which could not have been anticipated at the pleading stage. Although it will of course be appropriate to take account in this circumstance of the already completed course of the litigation, dismissal of the state claim might even then be merited. For example, it may appear that the plaintiff was well aware of the nature of his proofs and the relative importance of his claims; recognition of a federal court's wide latitude to decide ancillary questions of state law does not imply that it must tolerate a litigant's effort to impose upon it what is in effect only a state law case. Once it appears that a state claim constitutes the real body of a case, to which the federal claim is only an appendage, the state claim may fairly be dismissed.

We are not prepared to say that in the present case the District Court exceeded its discretion in proceeding to judgment on the state claim. * * *

It is true that the § 303 claims ultimately failed and that the only recovery allowed respondent was on the state claim. We cannot confidently say, however, that the federal issues were so remote or played such a minor role at the trial that in effect the state claim only was tried. Although the District Court dismissed as unproved the claims that petitioner's secondary activities included attempts to induce coal operators other than Grundy to cease doing business with respondent, the court submitted the § 303 claims relating to Grundy to the jury. The jury returned verdicts against petitioner on those claims, and it was only on petitioner's motion for a directed verdict and a judgment *n. o. v.* that they were set aside. * * * Although there was some risk of confusing the jury in joining the state and federal claims—especially since, as will be developed, differing standards of proof of UMW involvement applied—the possibility of confusion could be lessened by employing a special verdict form, as the District Court did. Moreover, the question whether the permissible scope of the state claim was limited by the doctrine of pre-emption afforded a special reason for the exercise of pendent jurisdiction; the federal courts are particularly appropriate bodies for the application of pre-emption principles. We thus conclude that although it may be that the District Court might, in its sound discretion, have dismissed the state claim, the circumstances show no error in refusing to do so.

* * *

[The Court went on to hold that the plaintiff could not recover damages for conspiracy under Tennessee common law on the basis of the record.]

Reversed.

THE CHIEF JUSTICE took no part in the decision of this case.

[A concurring opinion by Mr. Justice HARLAN, joined by Mr. Justice CLARK, is omitted.]

NOTES AND QUESTIONS

1. To what extent are *Hurn v. Oursler* and *United Mine Workers of America v. Gibbs* inconsistent with the notion that the subject-matter jurisdiction of the federal courts is limited by Article III of the Constitution and whatever enabling legislation Congress chooses to enact? Surely convenience and judicial administration, although admirable goals, cannot always be used to override basic tenets regarding the distribution of judicial business in a federal system. In this connection, consider the following passage:

> * * * [T]he exercise of pendent jurisdiction must be judged by whether it furthers some federal policy. Measured by that test pendent jurisdiction serves two purposes. First, it ensures that litigants will not be dissuaded from maintaining their federal rights in a federal court solely because they can dispose of all claims by one litigation in the state but not the federal forum. When jurisdiction over the federal claim is exclusive in the federal judiciary, only pendent jurisdiction makes possible a complete remedy for vindication of the plaintiff's rights. Second, assuming that the litigants are in a federal forum, pendent jurisdiction serves the interest of avoiding piecemeal litigation, thus promoting judicial economy and greater expedition for the litigants. In respect to judicial economy, one must reject the idea * * * of a dichotomy between the state and federal judicial systems; rather they are copartners in the judicial endeavor to effectuate justice throughout the nation with the least burden on national and individual resources.

Note, *The Evolution and Scope of the Doctrine of Pendent Jurisdiction in the Federal Courts*, 62 Colum.L.Rev. 1018, 1044 (1962). See also Note, *Problems of Parallel State and Federal Remedies*, 71 Harv.L.Rev. 513 (1958); Note, *Pendent Jurisdiction: An Expanding Concept in Federal Court Jurisdiction*, 51 Iowa L. Rev. 151 (1965). The principal case is discussed in Note, *UMW v. Gibbs and Pendent Jurisdiction*, 81 Harv.L.Rev. 657 (1968), and is criticized in Shakman, *The New Pendent Jurisdiction of the Federal Courts*, 20 Stan.L.Rev. 262 (1968).

2. When is the federal question that forms the basis for a claim of pendent jurisdiction "plainly wanting in substance"? In LEVERING & GARRIGUES CO. v. MORRIN, 289 U.S. 103, 53 S.Ct. 549, 77 L.Ed. 1062 (1933), decided shortly before *Hurn* and cited in *Gibbs*, the Supreme Court said:

> * * * [T]he federal question averred may be plainly unsubstantial either because obviously without merit, or "because its unsoundness so clearly results from the previous decisions of this court as to foreclose the subject and leave no room for the inference that the questions sought to be raised can be the subject of controversy."

Is this an adequate test? A number of federal courts apply a somewhat different test and deny pendent jurisdiction when the federal claim is dismissed on the pleadings. See, e. g., Strachman v. Palmer, 177 F.2d 427 (1st Cir.1949); Walters v. Shari Music Publishing Corp., 193 F.Supp. 307 (S.D.N.Y.1961). What are the advantages, if any, of this test? Is it more or less permissive than the one suggested in *Levering*?

3. The aspect of *Hurn* that caused the most interpretive difficulties was the requirement that the state and federal claims merely be two distinct grounds of a "single cause of action" rather than "two separate and distinct causes of action." What considerations are relevant to the question whether two claims are but aspects of a "single cause of action"? See generally Armstrong Paint & Varnish Works v. Nu-Enamel Corp., 305 U.S. 315, 59 S.Ct. 191, 83 L.Ed. 195 (1938); Kleinman v. Betty Dain Creations, Inc., 189 F.2d 546 (2d Cir.1951). See generally Comment, *Discretionary Federal Jurisdiction Over the Pendent Cause*, 46 Ill.L.Rev. 646 (1951). What is the test for pendency that emerges from *Gibbs*? Is it any easier to apply than the *Hurn* test?

4. Section 1338(b) of Title 28 was enacted in 1948, at least in part, to overcome a number of restrictive applications of the *Hurn* doctrine in the area of patents, copyrights, and trademarks. See generally Note, *The Doctrine of Hurn v. Oursler and the New Judicial Code*, 37 Iowa L.Rev. 406 (1952). Note that the statute speaks of "a substantial and related claim" under the federal statutes. Section 1338(b) was not intended to limit the scope of pendent jurisdiction to those cases enumerated in the statute and a host of cases since its enactment have applied the *Hurn* doctrine in a variety of other contexts. Many of the cases are classified in Note, *The Evolution and Scope of the Doctrine of Pendent Jurisdiction in the Federal Courts*, 62 Colum.L.Rev. 1018, 1034–42 (1962).

5. Should the considerations of judicial economy and party convenience underlying pendent subject-matter jurisdiction also allow the court to assert pendent personal jurisdiction for purposes of adjudicating the nonfederal claim? For example, if jurisdiction over defendant has been effected pursuant to a federal statute providing for nationwide service of process, but defendant would not be subject to process in the forum state for purposes of the joined state claim, must the court dismiss the latter? See Robinson v. Penn Central Co., 484 F.2d 553 (3d Cir.1973); Price v. United Mine Workers of America, 336 F.2d 771 (6th Cir.1964), certiorari denied 380 U.S. 913, 85 S.Ct. 899, 13 L.Ed.2d 799 (1965).

DERY v. WYER

United States Court of Appeals, Second Circuit, 1959.
265 F.2d 804.

HINCKS, Circuit Judge. In November, 1953, plaintiff's intestate, a brakeman employed by the Long Island Railroad Company, was killed when he was knocked from the side of a moving freight car by a gate post located on the land of McKeon Lumber Company. Under the Federal Employers' Liability Act, 45 U.S.C.A. § 51 et seq., the plaintiff-administratrix, a citizen of New York, brought an action against the defendant as trustee of the Railroad. The defendant filed a third-party complaint against the Lumber Company, claiming full indemnity for any loss for which it might be held liable to the plaintiff. Both the Railroad and the Lumber Company were citizens of New York. With the litigation in this posture, the plaintiff's action was settled for $30,-000; thereafter the third-party action was tried to the court, upon an agreed stipulation of the facts. Judge Abruzzo decided that both the Railroad and the Lumber Company were at fault. The situation, he held, was governed by the terms of a written agreement between the parties * * *. His judgment therefore provided that each should contribute $15,000 to this settlement. From this judgment the Railroad appeals claiming to be entitled to complete indemnity.

The district court's jurisdiction over the third-party complaint was not questioned below but at our request the point was briefed by the parties and is before us now. The questions for decision are whether the district court had jurisdiction to entertain the third-party complaint, independent grounds of federal jurisdiction being absent; and whether federal jurisdiction over the third-party claim, if it once attached, survived the settlement of the main action upon which federal jurisdiction depended. We think that both questions must be answered in the affirmative.

The contemporary sanction for third-party procedure in the federal courts is Rule 14 of the Federal Rules of Civil Procedure * * *.

To understand the basic theory of Rule 14 it is necessary to remember that in the Federal Rules of Civil Procedure the word "claim" has a somewhat broader connotation than that which prior to the Rules pertained to a "cause of action." "It is used to denote the aggregate of operative facts which give rise to a right enforceable in the courts." Original Ballet Russe v. Ballet Theatre, 2 Cir., 133 F.2d 187, 189. * * * The same aggregate or core of facts may give rise not only to rights in the plaintiff against the defendant but also to rights in the defendant against third parties. Under Rule 14, as amended, in the discretion of the court a defendant in the very action which determines the plaintiff's right against him may have a determination of any right of his against another which arises out of the same transaction or set of facts which gave rise to the plaintiff's claim. It is the theory of the Rule that the defendant's right against the third party is merely the outgrowth of the same aggregate or core of facts which is determinative of the plaintiff's claim. In this view, the court which has jurisdiction over the aggregate of facts which constitutes the plaintiff's claim needs no additional ground of jurisdiction to determine the third-party claim which comprises the same core of facts. It is, we think, in this sense that the court is said to have ancillary jurisdiction over the third-party claim.

The great weight of authority amongst the federal district courts is to the effect that when federal jurisdiction over the subject-matter of the main action once attaches the court has ancillary jurisdiction to decide a third-party dispute growing out of the same core of facts and hence within the scope of the Rule even though the dispute, separately considered, is lacking in the attributes of federal jurisdiction. * * * In a number of appellate court opinions there is discussion which clearly supports that conclusion. * * *

Our conclusion as to the ancillary character of a third-party claim under Rule 14 is fortified by cases in the cognate field of compulsory counterclaims under Rule 13. This court is committed to the majority rule that such a counterclaim—even one which impleads a new party—may rest on ancillary jurisdiction without need for an independent ground of federal jurisdiction. * * *

A rule of procedure, of course, however convenient and salutary it may be, is without efficacy to extend the jurisdiction of a court. See Hurn v. Oursler * * *; Fed.Rules Civ.Proc., Rule 82. But Rule 14 does not extend jurisdiction. It merely sanctions an impleader procedure which rests upon the broad conception of a claim as comprising a set of facts giving rise to rights flowing both to and from a defendant. For solution of the incidental jurisdictional problems which often attend utilization of the procedure, the concept of ancillary jurisdiction, which long antedated the Federal Rules, may often be drawn upon. * * * In this case, we hold, the jurisdiction which the court below had acquired over the plaintiff's claim was broad enough to comprehend jurisdiction of the ancillary third-party claim and that the ancillary jurisdiction attached when the impleader was accomplished.

We also hold that the ancillary jurisdiction over the third-party complaint was not lost when the main cause of action was settled. Generally, in a diversity action, if jurisdictional prerequisites are satisfied when the suit is begun, subsequent events will not work an ouster of jurisdiction. * * * This result is not attributable to any specific statute or to any language in the statutes which confer jurisdiction. It stems rather from the general notion that the sufficiency of jurisdiction should be determined once and for all at the threshold and if found to be present then should continue until final disposition of the action. * * *   *Rationale*

Considerations of policy, as well as the foregoing analogies, accord with our conclusion. If the main claim and the third-party claim are tried together and a decision or a settlement in favor of the plaintiff is announced on the main claim in advance of decision of the third-party claim, to hold that the determination of the main claim ousted the court of jurisdiction over the ancillary claim would in many cases entail a serious waste of effort by both the judge and the litigants. The natural tendency would be to discourage settlements.

And the same considerations, though perhaps to a lesser degree, would tend to discourage adjudications on motions and settlements in advance of trial. Confusion would result from such doctrine not only as to the timing but also as to the nature of the event causing loss of the ancillary jurisdiction. If the jurisdictional loss were held not to flow from a settlement of the main claim after trial, can it consistently be held that a settlement thereof at some pre-trial stage will operate to terminate jurisdiction over the third-party claim? Is an out-of-court agreement of settlement an operative jurisdictional factor, or must the agreement be translated into a judicial order to dismiss the claim as moot or to enforce the settlement? Not infrequently, if ancillary jurisdiction were thus subject to defeasance, the third-party claim might be time-barred although, to be sure, that seems not to be an immediate hazard in this case. In short, a rule that ancillary jurisdiction of a third-party claim terminates on a determination of the main claim will seriously impair the utility of the Rule, breed confusion and generate many sterile jurisdictional disputes.

*   *   *

Affirmed

LUMBARD, Circuit Judge (dissenting).

*   *   *

The exercise of federal jurisdiction over a state claim, without statutory authorization, requires the use of the court's ancillary power to extend federal jurisdiction to its constitutional limits. *   *   * The invocation of such extrastatutory power cannot turn on the mere exercise of discretion, as would be the case if the litigants' convenience were the test, but must be justified by a compelling and definable federal interest. *   *   *

Here Judge HINCKS, in my view misconstruing the rationale of Hurn v. Oursler, maintains that merely because the third-party dispute grows out of the "same core of facts" as the federal claim, a federal court may exercise ancillary jurisdiction over both disputes. But the application of the principle of Hurn v. Oursler depends not on the mere identity of facts that may happen to underlie both a federal and state claim, but on the necessity to prevent a federal litigant from being subjected to the risk of inconsistent verdicts or other prejudice which may stem from his being compelled to prove the same facts twice. As a consequence, Judge HINCKS fails to inquire into whether the railroad would be prejudiced by being required to re-establish the facts on which its federal liability is based in an action on the indemnity contract in a state court.

By its motion to implead the third-party defendant, the Railroad seeks to protect itself from the hazards of relitigation. The question the district court should have asked in passing on the motion was whether the Railroad, the defendant in the main action, would be subject to the risk of substantial injury if its motion were denied. Had this question been asked in this case it would have appeared, on the inspection of New York law which governs the state indemnity claim, that none of the facts relevant to the establishment of the federal claim could be relitigated in a state court. Under the law of New York, although the indemnitor does not expressly stipulate in the indemnity contract to be bound by a recovery against the indemnitee in an action to which he is not a party, the indemnitee may make such a recovery conclusive against the indemnitor by giving him notice of the pending action and an opportunity to defend against it.   *   *   *   Once such notice was given to the Lumber Company, any subsequent federal judgment that the Railroad breached its non-delegable duty under the Federal Employers Liability Act to provide a safe place for plaintiff's intestate to work would be conclusive against the Lumber Company.

*   *   *

NOTES AND QUESTIONS

1. Notice that in the principal case the issue is whether the court has ancillary jurisdiction over a claim by the original defendant against the third-party defendant. Should the ancillary-jurisdiction concept apply to a claim by the third-party defendant against the original defendant; to a claim by the third-party defendant against the original plaintiff, *compare* Heintz & Co. v. Provident Tradesmens Bank & Trust Co., 30 F.R.D. 171 (E.D.Pa.1962), *with* James King & Son, Inc. v. Indemnity Ins. Co., 178 F.Supp. 146 (S.D.N.Y.1959); or to a claim by plaintiff against the third-party defendant, *compare* Pasternack v. Dalo, 17 F.R.D. 420 (W.D.Pa.1955), *with* Myer v. Lyford, 2 F.R.D. 507 (M.D. Pa.1942)? What are the relevant considerations in each of these cases? In what other contexts might ancillary jurisdiction be appropriate? See generally Moore v. New York Cotton Exchange, 270 U.S. 593, 46 S.Ct. 367, 70 L.Ed. 750 (1926); Fraser, *Ancillary Jurisdiction and the Joinder of Claims in the Federal Courts*, 33 F.R.D. 27 (1964); Note, *Ancillary Process and Venue in the Federal Courts*, 73 Harv.L.Rev. 1164 (1960); Note, *The Ancillary Concept and the Federal Rules*, 64 Harv.L.Rev. 968 (1951); Note, *Ancillary Jurisdiction of the Federal Courts*, 48 Iowa L.Rev. 383 (1963). Should the availability of ancillary jurisdiction depend on whether the federal claim is one within the exclusive jurisdiction of the federal courts? Reconsider the related question in Note 3 on p. 202, supra.

2. One of the first important cases on ancillary jurisdiction was FREEMAN v. HOWE, 65 U.S. (24 How.) 450, 16 L.Ed. 749 (1860). Initially, a diversity action was commenced by Freeman, a United States marshal, involving the attachment of a number of railroad cars. Several mortgagees then successfully brought a state replevin action against Freeman. The United States Supreme Court, reviewing the replevin action, held that a state court could not interfere with property previously placed under the control of a federal court. The Court rejected the argument that a state forum was necessary because the mortgagees could not have asserted their claim in a federal court inasmuch as diversity of citizenship was lacking, on the ground that a claim to property in the control of a federal court may be asserted without regard to the citizenship of the parties and it will be viewed as ancillary to the suit out of which the taking of the property arose.

3. The concept of ancillary jurisdiction has been applied in diversity litigation when diversity of citizenship between the original defendant and the third-party defendant was absent. See, e. g., Brandt v. Olson, 179 F.Supp. 363 (N.D. Iowa 1959). Does the notion of ancillary jurisdiction have any application in the realm of personal, as opposed to subject-matter, jurisdiction?

4. In addition to ancillary jurisdiction, the student should be familiar with the evanescent concept of protective jurisdiction, which is premised on the notion that in substantive areas in which Congress has power to legislate it may enact a jurisdiction statute that becomes a "law of the United States" under Article III. A federal court then is able to hear cases within the ambit of the jurisdiction

statute, although the substantive aspects of the action might be governed by state law. In some instances the jurisdiction provision has served as a mandate to the federal courts to develop federal common law. See Textile Workers Union of America v. Lincoln Mills, 353 U.S. 448, 77 S.Ct. 912, 1 L.Ed.2d 972 (1957); Bickel & Wellington, *Legislative Purpose and the Judicial Process: The Lincoln Mills Case,* 71 Harv.L.Rev. 1 (1957). See also Note, *Protective Jurisdiction and Adoption as Alternative Techniques for Conferring Jurisdiction on Federal Courts in Consumer Class Actions,* 69 Mich.L.Rev. 710 (1971).

---

6. THE SUBJECT-MATTER JURISDICTION OF THE FEDERAL COURTS—REMOVAL

Read 28 U.S.C. § 1441 in the Supplement.

SHAMROCK OIL & GAS CORP. v. SHEETS, 313 U.S. 100, 105–09, 61 S.Ct. 868, 871–72, 85 L.Ed. 1214, 1217–19 (1941), presented the question whether a plaintiff could remove a state-court action to the federal courts because defendant had interposed a counterclaim. Mr. Justice Stone, writing for a unanimous court, held no.

     Section 12 of the Judiciary Act of 1789 * * * declared that "if a suit be commenced in any state court against an alien * * * or * * * against a citizen of another state, and the matter in dispute exceeds" the jurisdictional amount "and the defendant shall, at the time of entering his appearance in such state court, file a petition for the removal of the cause," it shall be removable to the circuit court. In West v. Aurora City, 6 Wall. 139, 18 L.Ed. 819, this Court held that removal of a cause from a state to a federal court could be effected under § 12 only by a defendant against whom the suit is brought by process served upon him. Consequently a non-citizen plaintiff in the state court, against whom the citizen-defendant had asserted in the suit a claim by way of counterclaim which, under state law, had the character of an original suit, was not entitled to remove the cause. The Court ruled that the plaintiff, having submitted himself to the jurisdiction of the state court, was not entitled to avail himself of a right of removal conferred only on a defendant who has not submitted himself to the jurisdiction.

     By § 3 of the Act of 1875 * * * the practice on removal was greatly liberalized. It authorized "either party, or any one or more of the plaintiffs or defendants entitled to remove any suit" from the state court to do so upon petition in such suit to the state court "before or at the term at which said cause could be first tried and before the trial thereof." These provisions were continued. until the adoption of the provisions of the present statute so far as now material by the Act of 1887 * * *.

We cannot assume that Congress, in thus revising the statute, was unaware of the history which we have just detailed, or certainly that it regarded as without significance the omission from the earlier act of the phrase "either party," and the substitution for it of the phrase authorizing removal by the "defendant or defendants" in the suit, or the like omission of the provision for removal at any time before the trial, and the substitution for it of the requirement that the removal petition be filed by the "defendant" at or before the time he is required to plead in the state court.

* * *

Not only does the language of the Act of 1887 evidence the Congressional purpose to restrict the jurisdiction of the federal courts on removal, but the policy of the successive acts of Congress regulating the jurisdiction of federal courts is one calling for the strict construction of such legislation. * * *

NOTES AND QUESTIONS

1. Why should Section 1441(b) permit a defendant to remove a federal-question action when plaintiff has commenced it in a state court of competent jurisdiction and presumably is content to have it adjudicated in a local forum? Is defendant's right of removal consistent with the denial of original or removal jurisdiction when plaintiff anticipates or defendant raises a federal defense, as in the *Mottley* case? See Wechsler, *Federal Jurisdiction and the Revision of the Judicial Code,* 13 Law & Contemp. Prob. 216, 233–34 (1948).

2. It frequently is said that a federal court's power to hear a case under its removal jurisdiction is derivative, which means that the state court from which the action is removed must have had jurisdiction over it. This has led to the anomalous result that if the action falls within the exclusive jurisdiction of the federal courts—e. g., antitrust and copyright actions—a federal court cannot accept it by way of removal because the state court never had subject-matter jurisdiction over the dispute. See General Investment Co. v. Lake Shore & M. S. Ry., 260 U.S. 261, 43 S.Ct. 106, 67 L.Ed. 244 (1922); Martinez v. Seaton, 285 F.2d 587 (10th Cir.1961), certiorari denied 366 U.S. 946, 81 S.Ct. 1677, 6 L.Ed.2d 856 (1961).

3. Is it permissible for plaintiff to seek recovery for "no more than $10,000" in order to defeat defendant's right of removal? See Capps v. New Jellico Coal Co., 87 F.Supp. 369 (E.D.Tenn. 1950). May plaintiff prevent an out-of-state defendant from removing by joining an in-state defendant? Section 1304(b) of the American Law Institute, *Study of the Division of Jurisdiction Between State and Federal Courts,* Official Draft, 141–47 (1969), provides that an out-of-state defendant may remove the entire action if she could have done so had she been sued alone.

4. The removal procedure is set out in 28 U.S.C. § 1446, which is in the Supplement. Prior to 1948, an application for removal was made in the state court, which frequently led to a federal-state conflict over the case. Once the case has been removed it is governed by federal procedure. See Freeman v. Bee Machine Co., 319 U.S. 448, 63 S.Ct. 1146, 87 L.Ed. 1509 (1943). A federal court may correct an erroneous removal by remanding the case to the state court. See 28 U.S.C. § 1447.

TWENTIETH CENTURY-FOX FILM CORP. v. TAYLOR

United States District Court, Southern District of New York, 1965.
239 F.Supp. 913.

WEINFELD, District Judge.   The plaintiff, Twentieth Century-Fox Film Corporation, moves to remand this action to the New York State Supreme Court whence it was removed to this Court on the petition of the defendant Richard Burton.   The action is one of a series of litigations arising out of the production of the motion picture "Cleopatra," in which Burton and Elizabeth Taylor, now husband and wife, play principal roles.   Twentieth Century-Fox seeks to recover substantial damages based upon five separate causes of action, the first and fifth of which are against Taylor individually, the second against Burton individually, and the third and fourth against them severally and jointly.

Plaintiff, a Delaware corporation, alleges its principal place of business is New York.   Taylor is a citizen of the United States, but is not a citizen of any state.   Burton is a British subject, not resident in any state of the United States.

I.   REMOVAL OF THE SECOND CAUSE OF ACTION.

Had Burton, an alien, been named as the sole defendant, removability could not be questioned, since the case would be within the original diversity jurisdiction of this Court.   And so, too, it is beyond challenge that had Taylor been named as the sole defendant, the action would have been non-removable. However, the joinder of the claims against them enabled Burton to remove the entire case to this Court upon his allegation that the second cause of action, pleaded solely against him, came within the purview of 28 U.S.C. § 1441 (c)   *   *   *.

The section, with its "separate and independent claim or cause of action" removability standard, was enacted in 1948, according to the revisers of the Judicial Code, to avoid the confusion which had beset the earlier "separable controversy" test and also in the hope that it would "somewhat decrease the volume of Federal litigation."   The new provision had its first, and thus far only, consideration by the Supreme Court in American Fire & Cas. Co. v. Finn.[7] There the plaintiff, a Texas citizen, joined two foreign insurance companies and their local agent, also a Texas citizen, claiming that either of the companies was alternatively liable for a fire loss under a policy issued by each separately, or that the agent was liable for failure to keep the property insured. The Court, in upholding an attack upon removal jurisdiction by the very defendant which had successfully invoked it in the courts below but had failed in the action itself, held:

> "   *   *   *   where there is a single wrong to plaintiff, for which relief is sought, arising from an interlocked series of transactions, there is no separate and independent claim or cause of action under
> § 1441(c)."

[7] 341 U.S. 6, 71 S.Ct. 534, 95 L.Ed. 702 (1951).

In applying the test to the case before it, the Court attached significant weight to the circumstances that "[t]he single wrong for which relief is sought is the failure to pay compensation for the loss on the property"; that the "facts in each portion of the complaint" involved the local agent, plaintiff's co-citizen; that the damages arose from a single incident; and that each of the three claims asserted involved "substantially the same facts and transactions," and consequently concluded that removal was improper.

Twentieth Century-Fox, relying heavily upon Finn, contends that the acts and conduct of the two defendants set forth in the first four causes of action are so interlaced that in substantial measure they give rise to and establish the two individual causes of action for breach of each respective employment agreement, as well as the two causes of action, one for the inducement of the breach, and the other for tortious interference—that, as in Finn, in plaintiff's words, "one 'fire' both induced and resulted in the simultaneous breach of two employment contracts so as to render this action [the second cause of action] not removable as a 'separate and independent cause of action' for breach of one of the agreements."

The statutory test is more easily stated than applied. When multiple defendants are alleged to have contributed concurrently or jointly to a single tortious impact and claims are stated against alternative defendants, removal is uniformly denied. But the courts are split as to removability where one defendant is accused of breach of contract and another is charged with inducing or exploiting the breach, and where co-insurers are sued on separate contracts covering a single loss. The present case, however, fits none of these categories. Having examined the judicial gloss which Finn and other decisions have put on section 1441(c), the Court concludes that the "second cause of action," the basis of Burton's removal petition, constitutes "a separate and independent claim or cause of action" within the statute.   *   *   *

[handwritten margin note: as w/ 2 insurance co.'s + 1 defendant.]

The first cause of action is against Taylor individually for breach of her contract, and specifies a series of acts and conduct which gives rise to the claim. These include allegations that she failed to perform her services with diligence, care and attention; that she reported for work in an unfit condition; that she allowed herself to become unphotographable and unfit to perform her services; that she failed to report for work; that she failed to report on time; that she suffered herself to be held up to scorn, ridicule and unfavorable publicity by her public conduct; and that she conspired with and induced others to breach their agreements with plaintiff.

The second cause of action against Burton for breach of his employment contract contains allegations of conduct identical to those charged against Taylor. There are, however, allegations that he breached the contract in other respects.

The third cause of action against Taylor and Burton, individually and jointly, charges that each induced the other, and others, to breach the respective employment agreements as set forth in the first and second causes of action; this cause of action specifies that each induced the other:

> "30.(a) * * * to engage in conduct with each other although each was to public knowledge at these times, married to another, so as to hold the other up to public scorn and ridicule;

> "30.(b) * * * not to abide by and observe reasonable and customary rules, directives, regulations and orders for conduct and deportment during the course of production * * *."

The fourth cause of action against Taylor and Burton, individually and jointly, charges interference with and injury to plaintiff's business and property rights by the acts and conduct complained of in the prior causes of action.

The fifth cause of action is solely against Taylor and alleges that she is the alter ego of MCL Films, S.A., and seeks a declaratory judgment that any money due from Twentieth Century-Fox to MCL may be set off against any judgment against Taylor.

The hard core of the rationale of the Finn holding is that the plaintiff suffered a single wrong arising out of the fire, which entitled him to but one recovery, sought alternatively against one of the three defendants. The situation here is quite unlike that. Basically there are two separate and distinct employment contracts, one with each defendant, for services of a highly specialized and individual nature. This circumstance at once negates rather than supports plaintiff's position that individual breaches of the two separate contracts give rise to a single wrong and a single claim for damages.

The contracts were entered into on different dates. Taylor performed services almost a year before Burton entered into his agreement. Each alleged breach, predicated upon individual acts, gives rise to a separate wrong and a separate claim for damages unrelated to the breach of the employment contract with the other defendant. The fact that the services were to be rendered by each performer in the production of one film does not coalesce violations of the two separate contracts into a single wrong. While it is true that the same kind or type of conduct is asserted to constitute the breach of each separate contract, it does not follow that the acts resulted, as plaintiff charges, in the "simultaneous breach of two employment agreements." For example, it is alleged that each defendant rendered himself or herself unfit to perform required services; failed to report for work; to report on time; and refused to follow directions. But it is not alleged, and it does not appear from the complaint, that one defendant's violation of contractual duty is necessarily related to the other; that their alleged absences from work or tardiness in appearing, or refusal to follow directions occurred simultaneously, at the same place or under similar circumstances. Moreover, as already noted, there are some allegations of breaches different in the one cause of action from the other. Thus, Taylor is charged with having permitted herself to become unphotographable. No such claim is made against Burton. On the other hand, charges are made against him that are not made against her—to wit, that he disabled himself from performing in the manner directed and at times and places required; that he failed or refused to perform to the best of his ability with due regard to the efficient production of the picture; that he circulated and disseminated news stories and issued other publicity without prior approval contrary to his agreement.

It is true that the individual acts alleged in support of the respective claims against each defendant for breach of his or her contract serve, upon additional allegations of joint conduct, as the basis for the third and fourth causes of action—the tort claims. However, these allegations of joint conduct which underlie the tort claims do not destroy the independent character of the cause of action against Burton for breach of his individual agreement—the single wrong attributed to Burton still remains one of the plaintiff's separate claims.

The claim against him individually is not governed by the operative facts required to establish, nor does it turn upon, any other cause of action. The amount of damages claimed from Burton for his alleged breach is $5,000,000; that sought from Taylor for her alleged breach is $20,000,000. A recovery by Twentieth Century-Fox in its suit against her for breach of her contract will not foreclose recovery against Burton for breach of his, and vice versa. * * * Similarly with respect to the tort actions, a disposition of them will not necessarily be dispositive of the second cause of action against Burton. First, one cannot be charged with inducing a breach of his own contract. Then, should it be found there was no breach of the agreement, it would end any claim of inducement, and even should it be found that there has been a breach, it would not necessarily follow that it was the result of tortious conduct or inducement on the part of any third person. In sum, plaintiff here charges more than a single wrong; it seeks more than a single recovery.

* * * And finally, in no respect has the second cause of action any relationship whatsoever to the fifth cause of action involving the status of Taylor and a Swiss corporation. The motion to remand on the ground that the suit was not removable under Section 1441(c) is denied.

II.   THE REMAINING CAUSES OF ACTION.

The plaintiff further moves, in the event the second cause of action is deemed separate and independent, that the Court remand the other four claims, nonremovable in and of themselves, to the State Court. It urges that such a course is constitutionally compelled and, if not, is justified as a matter of discretion. Neither ground is persuasive.

Plaintiff's constitutional contention may be summarized as follows: Article III, Section 2, of the Constitution authorizes the Federal courts to adjudicate only those controversies arising between parties of diverse citizenship or cases involving Federal questions; Twentieth Century-Fox and defendant Taylor are not of diverse citizenship within the meaning of the Article; the claims or causes of action asserted against Taylor clearly raise no Federal question; therefore they cannot be carried into the Federal courts on the coattails of the separate and independent cause of action which plaintiff brought against defendant Burton; to the extent Section 1441(c) authorizes the transfer of the separate nondiversity, nonfederal question claims against Taylor, it confers jurisdiction upon the Federal courts in excess of the judicial power authorized in

Article III, Section 2. The unconstitutionality of this grant of jurisdiction, argues plaintiff, is underscored by the fact that the 1948 requirement of a separate and independent cause of action as a predicate for removal necessarily means that such a claim or cause of action is so "unrelated," "disassociated," or "isolated" from the joined and otherwise nonremovable claims as to foreclose the application of pendant and ancillary jurisdiction doctrines to justify Federal retention of such claims. * * *

First, the presumption of constitutionality which cloaks all legislation is, in this instance, strengthened by nearly a century of usage and judicial decision upholding the jurisdiction of Federal courts to remove not only a controversy between diverse citizens, but the entire case, including nonfederal, nondiversity claims of other citizens. * * *

The plaintiff's basic position is that the rule of Strawbridge v. Curtiss, requiring diversity of citizenship between all plaintiffs and all defendants, expresses a limitation inherent in Article III, Section 2, rather than a construction of the Judiciary Act of 1789. Chief Justice Marshall's decision in Strawbridge clearly purported only to construe "The words of the act of congress." There is nothing in the opinion to justify attributing to Marshall, who was after all profoundly aware of the difference between construing a statute and expounding the Constitution, any purpose to impose an inflexible, narrow view upon the grant of jurisdiction contained in Article III. The Supreme Court has never so read his opinion. * * * In Finn, the Supreme Court itself noted that the revisers carefully provided "an opportunity" for state courts to adjudicate nonfederal causes of action, implying that such claims may be federally retained. * * * In numerous other contexts the Federal courts have declined to apply the rule of complete diversity. Thus, the jurisdictional requirements of the Federal Interpleader Act have been held satisfied by "minimal diversity," by diverse citizenship of any two adverse claimants. Similarly, less than complete diversity has been found sufficient in class actions and in intervention suits by co-citizens. * * *

Finally, and wholly apart from the foregoing analysis, Section 1441(c) finds support in Congressional power under the "necessary and proper" clause of Article I, Section 8. Since 1875 Congress has manifested concern lest the removal jurisdiction result in the fragmentation of litigation. * * * Although Congress in 1948 narrowed the category of removable claims, requiring of them a greater degree of disassociation than was true of the "separable controversies" * * *, it still retained power to effectuate a policy against fragmentation of litigation. * * * Where considerations of convenience and economy of litigation dictated, the expansive "necessary and proper" clause frequently has been relied upon to sustain judicial power beyond the strict limits of Article III, assuming arguendo that the Article commands complete diversity. * * * And the whole notion of removal, nowhere provided for in the Constitution, is itself a creature of Congressional power "[t]o make all Laws which shall be necessary and proper for carrying into Execution * * * all Powers vested by this Constitution." * * * To the extent that "separate and independent" claims relate to the same transaction or series of transactions and thus involve overlapping items of proof, as in the instant case, retention of them by this Court places no greater strain on Article III than do many accepted applications of the ancillary jurisdiction doctrine. Since the power of Congress to make a Federal forum available to a diversity litigant in Burton's position is unquestioned, this Court is of the view that Congress has the concomitant power to provide that, once the litigant exercises his right to remove, he may be relieved of the burden of multiple trials in different jurisdictions, at least where some degree of duplication is involved.

* * *

As to plaintiff's alternative motion addressed to the Court's discretion, it is abundantly clear that, despite the "separate and independent" quality of the second cause of action, at least the first four claims have some common problems. Items of proof may overlap and the same witnesses may be called to testify with relation to all four claims. To splinter the case and to require a separate trial in this Court, and another in the State Court as to those claims, would needlessly waste the time and effort of all concerned—litigants, witnesses, counsel and courts. The parties are already embroiled in enough litigation here and in California; it would be unreasonable further to proliferate the litigation. Accordingly, the alternative motion to remand the first, third and fourth causes of action is denied. As to the fifth cause of action for a declaratory judgment against Taylor alone, this has no relationship of any kind to the individual claims against Burton, or for that matter to the claims asserted against him and Taylor jointly and severally. The motion for remand of the fifth claim is granted.

* * *

NOTES AND QUESTIONS

1. What policies underlie the removability of (a) "a separate and independent claim or cause of action" and (b) "the entire case," including "otherwise non-removable claims or causes of action," when a removable separate and independent claim is present?

2. In *Hurn v. Oursler,* quoted at length in *United Mine Workers v. Gibbs,* pp. 221–22, supra, the Supreme Court limited pendent jurisdiction by saying that "the rule does not go so far as to permit a federal court to assume jurisdiction of a separate and distinct non-federal cause of action because it is joined in the same complaint with a federal cause of action." How is this consistent with the requirement in Section 1441(c) that a federal claim must be "separate and independent" before the otherwise nonremovable claims can be heard in a federal court? See generally Cohen, *Problems in the Removal of a "Separate and Independent Claim or Cause of Action,"* 46 Minn.L.Rev. 1 (1961); Lewin, *The Federal Courts' Hospitable Back Door—Removal of "Separate and Independent" Non-Federal Causes of Action,* 66 Harv.L.Rev. 423 (1953); Moore & Van Dercreek, *Multi-party, Multi-claim Removal Problems: The Separate and Independent Claim Under Section 1441(c),* 46 Iowa L.Rev. 489 (1961); Comment, *Diversity Removal Where the Federal Court Would Not Have Original Jurisdiction: A Suggested Reform,* 114 U.Pa.L.Rev. 709 (1966).

SECTION I. VENUE

1. GENERAL PRINCIPLES

STEVENS, VENUE STATUTES: DIAGNOSIS AND PROPOSED
CURE, 49 Mich.L.Rev. 307, 307–15 (1951):

Venue　*　*　*　means the place of trial in an action within a state.
Given a cause of action, and having decided what court has jurisdiction over
the subject matter, the lawyer must lay the venue, that is, select the place of
trial. In making this decision, the lawyer in every state of the United States
turns in the first instance, not to common law, but to statute, constitutional
provision or rule of court. And he finds that the "proper" venue of his action
depends upon the theory of his claim, the subject matter of his claim, the parties involved, or a combination of these factors.

Most codes make provision for the place of trial in local actions, and all
codes provide in one way or another for venue in transitory actions arising both
within and without the state. Many states make special provision for divorce
actions, actions against executors, and actions for the specific recovery of personal property. Most states also provide for venue in actions against residents,
against nonresidents, against corporations, domestic and foreign, against partnerships, associations and individuals doing business in the state, and against
the state, or a county, or a city or public officers generally or specifically. The
nature of the plaintiff, as a resident or nonresident, corporation, domestic or
foreign, or political entity, is another factor frequently considered and provided for. *　*　*

A comparative study of contemporary venue provisions reveals some thirteen different fact situations upon which venue statutes are predicated.

A. *Where the subject of action or part thereof is situated.* The common
law concept of actions which were local because the facts could have occurred
only in a particular place still persists. As might well be expected, the proper
venue for such actions is the county where the subject of the action is situated.
There is, however, considerable variation from state to state as to what types of
cases are local and fall into this category. *　*　*

This type of venue　*　*　*　is based upon the idea that the court of
the county in which the res, which is the subject matter of the suit, is located is
best able to deal with the problem. The local sheriff can attach, deliver or execute upon the property. The local clerk can make the necessary entries with a
minimum of red tape where title to land is affected. Trial convenience is
served where "a view" is necessary or of value in reaching a determination.
Third parties can readily ascertain, at a logical point of inquiry, the status of a
res in which they may be interested.

It is submitted that these factors are of sufficient importance in this type of case to outweigh other considerations such as convenience of parties or witnesses in the selection of place of trial.   *   *   *

B. *Where the cause of action, or part thereof, arose or accrued.* Convenience of witnesses is the most logical reason for venue provisions allowing the action to be brought in the county where the cause of action, or part thereof, arose or accrued. And since convenience of witnesses is a very practical problem in the trial of a law suit, one would expect to find venue based upon the place where the cause of action arose or accrued a rather common, and general, provision.   *   *   *

The idea behind this type of venue provision   *   *   *   is sound and popular.   *   *   *   However, its usefulness has been somewhat impaired by difficulties arising out of problems of statutory interpretation. First, what do the words "arose" and "accrued" mean? Second, what is the difference, if any, between "arose" and "accrued"? And, third, what is the meaning of the phrase "or part thereof"?   *   *   *

C. *Where some fact is present or happened.* There is a sizeable group of statutes which provide for trial of the action in the county where some particular fact or fact situation related to, but no part of, the cause of action is present or happened.   *   *   *

If the purpose of venue is trial convenience, either of parties, or witnesses, or the court or court officials, then it is hard to find any real justification for this group of venue provisions. Most if not all of them are examples of singling out certain specific types of actions for special treatment where a need for special treatment is not or at least no longer [is] apparent.   *   *   *

D. *Where the defendant resides.* Convenience of the defendant is the reason usually given for venue statutes which provide for the place of trial in the county where the defendant resides—the theory probably being, as suggested by Professor E. R. Sunderland, "that since the plaintiff controls the institution of the suit he might behave oppressively toward the defendant unless restrained."   *   *   *

E. *Where the defendant is doing business.*   *   *   *   Convenience of the defendant, and of witnesses, appears to be the reason behind such provisions where they are tied to causes of action arising out of the doing of business in the state. Convenience of the defendant, and even more clearly, convenience of the plaintiff, by providing a county in which to lay the venue against a non-resident individual, partnership, company or corporation without undue inconvenience to defendant, is served by the broader type of provision—against certain classes of defendants generally.   *   *   *

F. *Where defendant has an office or place of business, or an agent, or representative, or where an agent or officer of defendant resides.* [These venue statutes]   *   *   *   are quite common where a corporation, company or some other type of business organization is the defendant. Convenience of the plaintiff, rather than the defendant, is the moving consideration behind such statutes in most instances.   *   *   *

G. *Where the plaintiff resides.*   *   *   *

Convenience of the plaintiff is the obvious reason behind venue statutes of this nature. Convenience of plaintiff's witnesses may or may not be served, depending upon the nature of the action. * * * In certain types of cases against certain classes of defendants—such as an action on a foreign cause of action against a nonresident—this type of provision is both logical and practical. * * *

H.   *Where the plaintiff is doing business.* * * * Obviously the convenience of the plaintiff is the sole consideration behind such a provision. It is submitted that other factors of trial convenience such as convenience of witnesses and of the defendant are more important, and that in view of the number of adherents to this ground of venue, it would be wise to advocate its abandonment. * * *

I. *Where the defendant may be found.* Venue based upon the county where the defendant may be found is in accord with the common law doctrine that the right of action follows the person. * * *

It is difficult to find any sound reason for venue based upon where the defendant may be found. It serves no useful purpose—no trial convenience of either witnesses or parties. It is a good example of a historical hang-over—a type of provision which has long since outlived its usefulness. The problem which this type of provision was designed to solve was and is not one of venue but of service of process. * * *

J. *Where the defendant may be summoned or served.* Another group of statutes, also based upon the common law doctrine that the right of action follows the person, provides that venue may be laid in the county where the defendant may be summoned, or served with process. * * *

The comments which were made with respect to venue based upon where the defendant may be found apply with equal force to this type of provision. * * *

K. *In the county designated in the plaintiff's complaint.* * * *

Venue provisions of this type give the plaintiff an unnecessary economic advantage not warranted by convenience of parties or witnesses. In the interests of justice and trial convenience they should be eliminated.

L. *In any county.* The broadest venue provision on the books is that which provides that the plaintiff may lay the venue in any county. * * *

M. *Where the seat of government is located.* * * *

Statutes of this sort have a sound and practical reason behind them. With one exception, this type of provision is reserved for actions by or against governmental units or agencies. Convenience of the government appears to be the controlling factor.

NOTES AND QUESTIONS

1. See also Blume, *American Civil Procedure* 309–10 (1955); Report of the Temporary Commission on the Courts of the State of New York, *First*

Preliminary Report of the Advisory Committee on Practice and Procedure 495–552 (1957).

2. What should be the underlying goals of a venue system? Is it really necessary to superimpose notions of venue on a soundly conceived jurisdictional system, especially one with a long-arm statute? What statistics and empirical data do you think are relevant to deciding where contract, tort, and property actions should be brought? Indeed, should venue depend on the nature of the plaintiff's action at all? In what ways should the venue system for the federal courts differ from the ways in which the states allocate judicial business among their courts?

2. LOCAL AND TRANSITORY ACTIONS

REASOR-HILL CORP. v. HARRISON

Supreme Court of Arkansas, 1952.
220 Ark. 521, 249 S.W.2d 994.

GEORGE ROSE SMITH, Justice. Petitioner asks us to prohibit the circuit court of Mississippi County from taking jurisdiction of a cross-complaint filed by D. M. Barton. In the court below the petitioner moved to dismiss the cross-complaint for the reason that it stated a cause of action for injury to real property in the state of Missouri. When the motion to dismiss was overruled the present application for prohibition was filed in this court.

The suit below was brought by the Planters Flying Service to collect an account for having sprayed insecticide upon Barton's cotton crop in Missouri. In his answer Barton charged that the flying service had damaged his growing crop by using an adulterated insecticide, and by cross-complaint he sought damages from the petitioner for its negligence in putting on the market a chemical unsuited to spraying cotton. The petitioner is an Arkansas corporation engaged in manufacturing insecticides and is not authorized to do business in Missouri.

The question presented is one of first impression: May the Arkansas courts entertain a suit for injuries to real property situated in another State? For the respondent it is rightly pointed out that if the suit is not maintainable Barton has no remedy whatever. The petitioner cannot be served with summons in Missouri; so unless it is subject to suit in Arkansas it can escape liability entirely by staying out of Missouri until the statute of limitations has run. * * * The petitioner answers this argument by showing that with the exception of the Supreme Court of Minnesota every American court that has passed upon the question (and there have been about twenty) has held that jurisdiction does not exist.

We agree that the weight of authority is almost unanimously against the respondent, although in some States the rule has been changed by statute and in others it has been criticized by the courts and restricted as narrowly as possible. But before mechanically following the majority view we think it worthwhile to examine the origin of the rule and the reasons for its existence.

The distinction between local and transitory actions was recognized at the beginning of the fourteenth century in the common law of England. Before then all actions had to be brought where the cause of action arose, because the members of the jury were required to be neighbors who would know something of the litigants and of the dispute as well. But when cases were presented that involved separate incidents occurring in different communities the reason for localizing the action disappeared, for it was then impossible to obtain a jury who knew all the facts. Consequently the courts developed the distinction between a case that might have arisen anywhere, which was held to be transitory, and one that involved a particular piece of land, which was held to be local. * * *

As between judicial districts under the same sovereign the rule has many advantages and has been followed in America. As between counties our statutes in Arkansas require that actions for injury to real estate be brought where the land lies. * * * But we permit the defendant to be served anywhere in the State * * * ; so that plaintiff is not denied a remedy even though the defendant is a resident of another county.

The English courts, in developing the law of local and transitory actions, applied it also to suits for injuries to real property lying outside England. If, for example, there had been a trespass upon land in France, the courts would not permit the plaintiff to bring suit in England, even though the defendant lived in England and could not be subjected to liability in France. The American courts, treating the separate States as independent sovereigns, have followed the English decisions.

In the United States the leading case is unquestionably Livingston v. Jefferson, Fed.Cas.No.8411, 1 Brock 203. That suit was a part of the famous litigation between Edward Livingston and Thomas Jefferson; see Beveridge's Life of John Marshall, vol. 4, pp. 100–116. The case was heard by Marshall as circuit justice and Tyler as district judge. Both agreed that the suit, which was for a wrongful entry upon land in Louisiana, could not be maintained in Virginia. In Marshall's concurring opinion he examined the English precedents and concluded that the law was so firmly established that the court was bound to follow it, though Marshall expressed his dissatisfaction with a rule which produced "the inconvenience of a clear right without a remedy."

Since then the American courts have relied almost uniformly upon the Livingston case in applying the rule to interstate litigation in this country. At least three reasons have been offered to justify the rule, but it is easy to show that each reason is more applicable to international controversies than to interstate disputes.

First, the ground most frequently relied upon is that the courts are not in a position to pass upon the title to land outside the jurisdiction. As between nations this reasoning may be sound. The members of this court have neither the training nor the facilities to investigate questions involving the ownership of land in France, in Russia, or in China. But the same difficulties do not exist with respect to land in another State. In our library we have the statutes and decisions of every other State, and it seldom takes more than a few hours to find the answer to a particular question. Furthermore, the American courts do not hesitate to pass upon an out-of-state title when the issue arises in a transitory action. If, for example, Barton had charged that this petitioner converted a mature crop in Missouri and carried it to Arkansas, our courts would decide the case even though it became necessary to pass upon conflicting claims of title to the land in Missouri. Again, a suit for damages for nonperformance of a contract to purchase land is transitory and may be maintained in another State, even though the sole issue is the validity of the seller's title. To put an extreme example, suppose that two companion suits, one local and one transitory, were presented to the same court together. In those States where the courts disclaim the ability to pass upon questions of title in local actions it might be necessary for the court to dismiss the local action for that reason and yet to decide the identical question in the allied transitory case.

Second, it has been argued that since the tort must take place where the land is situated the plaintiff should pursue his remedy before the defendant leaves the jurisdiction. This argument, too, has merit when nations are concerned. A sovereign, by its control of passports and ports of entry, may detain those who wish to cross its borders. But the citizens of the various States have a constitutional right to pass freely from one jurisdiction to another. * * * In the case at bar * * * Barton could hardly be expected to discover the damage and file an attachment suit before the pilot returned to his landing field in Arkansas.

Third, there is an understandable reluctance to subject one's own citizens to suits by aliens, especially if the other jurisdiction would provide no redress if the situation were reversed. * * * One may have some sympathy for this position in international disputes, but it has no persuasive effect when the States are involved. We do not feel compelled to provide a sanctuary in Arkansas for those who have willfully and wrongfully destroyed property, torn down houses, uprooted crops, polluted streams, and inflicted other injuries upon innocent landowners in our sister States. Yet every jurisdiction which follows the rule of the Livingston case affords that refuge to any person— whether one of its citizens or not—who is successful in fleeing from the scene of such misdeeds.

The truth is that the majority rule has no basis in logic or equity and rests solely upon English cases that were decided before America was discovered and in circumstances that are not even comparable to those existing in our Union. Basic principles of justice demand that wrongs should not go unredressed. * * * Under the majority rule we should have to tell Barton that he would have been much better off had the petitioner stolen his cotton outright instead of merely damaging it. And the only reason we could give for this unfortunate situation would be that English juries in the thirteenth century were expected to have personal knowledge of the disputes presented to them.   We prefer to afford this litigant his day in court.

Writ denied.

GRIFFIN SMITH, C. J., concurs.

McFADDIN and WARD, JJ., dissent.

McFADDIN, Justice (dissenting).

* * *

The majority in the present case candidly admits that every American Jurisdiction—save only the State of Minnesota—has followed the holding in the original case of Livingston v. Jefferson   * * *   yet the majority, in seeing fit to depart from such time honored holding, advances three reasons, which do not seem to me to be sufficient for such a radical departure.

In the first place, the majority says that we have ample facilities to determine the land laws of other States in the United States.   * * *   This statement about the size of the law library seems rather weak, because land actions are tried in lower courts and not in the Supreme Court library.   Just because we have a fine law library does not mean that we are prepared to determine the title to lands in Texas,[4] Missouri, Vermont, or any other State.   But if we have the jurisdiction which the majority claims, then we could determine ejectment actions involving ownership of lands in other States.   We might undertake to do this, but the Full Faith and Credit clause of the U.S. Constitution would not require the Sister State to recognize our judgment.   * * *

Secondly, the majority says that the rule, requiring that an action be brought in the jurisdiction in which the land is situated, is a good rule between Nations, but is not good as between States in the American Union.   For answer to this, I say: I have always understood that each of the American States is Sovereign; that the Federal Government is a government of delegated powers; and that all powers not delegated to the Federal Government are retained by the States and the People.   Surely the majority is not attempting to reduce our American States to the level of mere local administrative units.   Yet such, unfortunately, is the natural conclusion to which the majority opinion would carry us, when it concedes one rule for Nations and another for States.

Thirdly, the majority says that it does not desire to afford Arkansas Citizens a sanctuary from damage actions by citizens of other States.   This is an argument that should be made—if at all—in the Legislative branch of Government, rather than in a judicial opinion.   It is for the Legislative Department to determine when and where actions may be prosecuted.

   * * *   I desire now to call attention to the Annotation in 42 A.L.R. 196 * * *.   That Annotation lists the many, many cases that have considered the question here involved;   and each Court—with the sole excep-

---

[4] The writer knows by experience that only one skilled in Texas Land Law can successfully handle an action of Trespass to Try Title in the State of Texas.

tion of Minnesota—has seen fit to follow the great weight of authority which has come down to us from the common law. In matters affecting real property particularly, we should leave undisturbed the ancient land-marks.[7]   *   *   *

Because of the views herein stated, I respectfully dissent from the majority in the case at bar; and I am authorized to state that Mr. Justice WARD concurs in this dissent.

QUESTIONS

In those jurisdictions following the "majority" or "local action" rule, can the parties consent to a waiver of the venue objection to actions involving foreign land? See, e. g., Taylor v. Sommers Bros. Match Co., 35 Idaho 30, 204 P. 472 (1922). If not, doesn't the local-transitory action distinction really raise a more serious problem than simply a defect in venue? Why does the dissenting opinion in *Reasor-Hill* say that a judgment in ejectment rendered by the Arkansas courts involving lands in other states would not be entitled to full faith and credit? See Fall v. Eastin, 215 U.S. 1, 30 S.Ct. 3, 54 L.Ed. 65 (1909).

---

3. VENUE IN THE FEDERAL COURTS

Read 28 U.S.C. § 1391 in the Supplement.

BLUME, PLACE OF TRIAL OF CIVIL CASES, 48 Mich.L.Rev. 1, 34–37 (1949):

*   *   *   [The] rules governing venue in the federal courts [in the Judiciary Act of 1789] can be summarized as follows: (1) All local actions must be commenced and tried in the district in which the cause of action arose—ordinarily, where the property involved is situated. (2) Actions by the United States may be commenced and tried in the district in which the defendant resides or in any district in which he is found. (3) Actions by aliens may be commenced and tried in the district in which the defendant resides or in any district in which he is found. (4) Actions against aliens may be commenced and tried in any district in which the defendant is found. (5) Actions between citizens of different states may be commenced and tried in the district in which the defendant resides or in any district in which he is found, provided the plaintiff or defendant is a citizen of the state *"where the suit is brought."*

1. *Local actions*

The familiar case of *Livingston v. Jefferson* (1811) was an action by a citizen of New York against a citizen of Virginia in the circuit court for Virginia where the defendant resided. The action was for trespass to land situated

---

[7] Proverbs 22:28, "Remove not the ancient landmark, which thy fathers have set."

in New Orleans. The court had jurisdiction over the defendant sufficient for a judgment in personam, but declined to take jurisdiction of the case because the land was situated outside the district. Under the English common law the action was local, not transitory. The court was aware that its decision meant that most likely the plaintiff could not maintain his action at all. * * * Being in personam, the action had to be commenced in the district in which the defendant resided or in a district in which he could be found. Being local it had to be commenced where the land was situated. Unless process could run from the land to the defendant, or the defendant should go to the land, no action could be maintained.

* * *

2. *Transitory actions*

Under the English common law a transitory action was one which could be "laid" in any county, subject to the right of the defendant to have the venue changed to the county in which the cause of action wholly arose. Under the federal practice there is no transitory action of the English type, but two kinds of local actions: (1) actions which must be commenced and tried where the cause of action arose; ordinarily, where the property involved is situated, and (2) actions which must be commenced and tried where the defendant resides or where he may be found. Local actions of the first kind are the same as the local actions of the English common law. Local actions of the second kind were unknown to the common law, and, insofar as the federal courts are concerned, were introduced by the Judiciary Act of 1789.

One of the chief problems involved in the establishment of a federal judicial system was place of trial. Distances were great and means of transportation poor. * * * One of the reasons for the separation of the colonies from England had been threats to drag the colonists from their homes to stand trial at distant places. To the people of 1789, place of trial was a matter of great importance, and without safeguards for defendants a federal system of trial courts would not be acceptable.

The early English rule that a civil action must be "laid" in the county in which the cause of action arose was grounded at first on necessity because of the jury. After this necessity disappeared the rule was continued for local actions because the place thus provided was ordinarily as convenient as any other which might be selected. The rule had the virtue of not favoring either the plaintiff or the defendant. If events involved in an action had occurred in a county it was fair to try the action in that county. Witnesses, ordinarily, would be found in the county and could attend court without great inconvenience. A view by the jury could be had. While it is never possible to say in advance what place will be convenient for the trial of a particular case, if a general rule of convenience is to be made for all cases, the rule requiring trial where the cause of action arose has very great merit. By comparison, the rule adopted by the Judiciary Act of 1789 was wholly irrational. That a person might reside in a certain district or might be travelling through a certain district was not reason for saying it would be convenient to try an action against him in that district.

The "statutory" local action created by the Judiciary Act of 1789 is concerned with the locality of the defendant in two respects, place of his residence and place of his presence. Since the place of residence of a natural person is his usual place of abode, there is, ordinarily, only one such place. When place of trial is the place of the defendant's residence, the plaintiff has no choice. When, however, the place of trial may be any place where the defendant is served with process, possibilities of choice multiply as the defendant travels outside his district. There is, however, at any given time only one place in which he may be sued.   *   *   *

NOTES AND QUESTIONS

1. Changes in the statute governing venue in the federal courts, 28 U.S.C. § 1391, reflect the need to conform venue to the expanding notions of jurisdiction. In 1939, when the Supreme Court decided NEIRBO CO. v. BETHLEHEM SHIPBUILDING CORP., 308 U.S. 165, 60 S.Ct. 153, 84 L.Ed. 167 (1939), the general venue statute required that diversity actions be brought "in the district of the residence of either the plaintiff or the defendant." In *Neirbo,* defendant Bethlehem objected to venue in New York on the ground that it was not incorporated under the laws of that state. Prior cases had held that "residence" meant "state of incorporation" in the case of corporations. The Supreme Court held that Bethlehem's appointment of an agent to receive service of process in New York, an act required by the laws of that state as a condition of doing business there, was a "voluntary act" that gave "actual consent by Bethlehem to be sued in the courts of New York, federal as well as state." e

A similar argument was advanced by plaintiff in OLBERDING v. ILLINOIS CENT R. CO., 346 U.S. 338, 74 S.Ct. 83, 98 L.Ed. 39 (1953). The railroad, an Illinois corporation, brought suit in a Kentucky district court against Olberding, a citizen of Indiana and owner of a truck that had caused the derailment of an Illinois Central train by striking a railroad overpass in Kentucky. Jurisdiction over Olberding was asserted under a nonresident-motorist statute similar to the one upheld in *Hess v. Pawloski*, p. 74, supra. The venue statute enacted in 1948 required that a diversity action be brought "only in the judicial district where all plaintiffs or all defendants reside." Plaintiff argued, on the basis of *Hess* and *Neirbo,* that Olberding had impliedly consented to a waiver of his federal venue objection by driving into Kentucky. This contention was rejected by Mr. Justice Frankfurter:

> It is true that   *   *   *   there has been some fictive talk to the
> effect that the reason why a non-resident can be subjected to a state's
> jurisdiction is that the non-resident has "impliedly" consented to be sued
> there. In point of fact, however, jurisdiction in these cases does not rest
> on consent at all.   *   *   *   The potentialities of damage by a motorist,
> in a population as mobile as ours, are such that those whom he injures
> must have opportunities of redress against him provided only that he
> is afforded an opportunity to defend himself. We have held that this is
> a fair rule of law   *   *   *   and that the requirements of due process
> are therefore met. Hess v. Pawloski   *   *   *.   But to conclude from this

e The adoption of Section 1391(c) in 1948 solved most of the corporate venue questions left open by *Neirbo.* Does the text of Section 1391(c) create any interpretive difficulties? See Wright, *Federal Courts* § 42 (2d ed. 1970).

holding that the motorist, who never consented to anything and whose consent is altogether immaterial, has actually agreed to be sued and has thus waived his federal venue rights is surely to move in the world of Alice in Wonderland.

Id. at 340–41, 74 S.Ct. at 85–86, 98 L.Ed. at 43. *Neirbo* was distinguished as involving "actual consent." Mr. Justice Reed dissented, saying: "I see no difference of substance between the signing of a paper under the New York statute upon which Neirbo is based and the acceptance, by action in driving a motor car, of the privilege of using state highways under the Kentucky statute."

Olberding was legislatively overruled in 1963 by the addition of a new Section 1391(f), providing for venue in tort claims "arising out of the manufacture, assembly, repair, ownership, maintenance, use or operation of an automobile * * * in the judicial district wherein the act or omission complained of occurred." This section was repealed in 1966, and the phrase "where the claim for relief arose" was added to subsections (a) and (b).

2. Is venue proper if A, a resident of X, brings a diversity action against B, a resident of Y, and C, a resident of Z, in a federal court sitting in Z on a cause of action that did not arise in Z? Would the court's venue be proper if the action were based on federal-question jurisdiction? Suppose A, a resident of X, sues B, a resident of Y, in a state court in Z. If B attempts to remove the action to the federal court in Z on the ground that diversity jurisdiction exists, can A defeat removal by asserting a lack of venue? See 28 U.S.C. § 1441(a).

3. Various questions arise in applying the venue requirements when an action involves multiple claims or multiple parties. For example, can a properly impleaded third-party defendant secure a dismissal of the third-party claim for lack of venue if the venue in the principal action is proper? Would it make any difference if the subject-matter jurisdiction over the third-party claim is merely ancillary to the jurisdiction over the principal action? See Brandt v. Olson, 179 F.Supp. 363 (N.D.Iowa 1959). See also Van Alstyne, *Venue of Mixed Actions in California*, 44 Calif.L.Rev. 685 (1956).

4. For venue purposes, should an unincorporated association be held to "reside" in any state in which one of its members resides, only in the state in which all of its members reside, in any state in which the association is doing business, or only in the state in which the association has its principal place of business? This question was resolved by the Supreme Court in DENVER & R. G. W. R. CO. v. BROTHERHOOD OF RAILROAD TRAINMEN, 387 U.S. 556, 559–62, 87 S.Ct. 1746, 1748–50, 18 L.Ed.2d 954, 958–59 (1967):

> * * * [W]e think that the question of the proper venue for such a defendant * * * should be determined by looking to the residence of the association itself rather than that of its individual members. Otherwise, § 1391(b) would seem to require either holding the association not suable at all where its members are residents of different States, or holding that the association "resides" in any State in which any of its members resides. The first alternative * * * removes federal-question litigation from the federal courts unnecessarily; the second is patently unfair to the association when it is remembered that venue is primarily a matter of convenience of litigants and witnesses.

* * *

We think it most nearly approximates the intent of Congress to recognize the reality of the multi-state, unincorporated association such as a labor union and to permit suit against that entity, like the analogous corporate entity, wherever it is "doing business."

5.   Compare Section 1391 with the American Law Institute's federal venue proposals, which are set out in the Supplement following that statute.   What differences are there between the two?   What are the objectives of the American Law Institute's proposals?   Various aspects of federal venue are discussed and proposals for its revision are set forth in Bunn, *Jurisdiction and Practice of the Courts of the United States* 118 (5th ed. 1949); Barrett, *Venue and Service of Process in the Federal Courts—Suggestions for Reform*, 7 Vand.L.Rev. 608 (1954).

6.   Can the parties contractually agree on a forum for litigating any action arising out of that contract?   Can they designate a place other than those provided in the general venue statutes?   See *National Equipment Rental, Ltd. v. Szukhent*, p. 168, supra.   What are some of the factors the court should consider in deciding whether to uphold the stipulation?   See Recent Decision, 62 Mich. L.Rev. 1242 (1964).

---

4.   FORUM NON CONVENIENS AND TRANSFER OF VENUE

GULF OIL CORP. v. GILBERT

Supreme Court of the United States, 1947.
330 U.S. 501, 67 S.Ct. 839, 91 L.Ed. 1055.

[Plaintiff Gilbert brought a $365,000 tort action based on diversity of citizenship in the Southern District of New York, alleging that Gulf Oil had carelessly delivered gasoline to plaintiff's warehouse in Virginia, causing a fire and explosion.   Gulf Oil was organized under the laws of Pennsylvania, was qualified to do business in both Virginia and New York, and had appointed agents to receive service of process in both states.   On motion of the defendant, the New York district court dismissed the action in accordance with New York's principles of *forum non conveniens*; the Court of Appeals disagreed as to the applicability of New York law and reversed on the basis of a restrictive view of the application of the doctrine in the federal courts.   The Supreme Court granted certiorari.]

Mr. Justice JACKSON delivered the opinion of the Court.
* * *

I.

It is conceded that the venue statutes of the United States permitted the plaintiff to commence his action in the Southern District of New York and empower that court to entertain it.   But that does not settle the question whether it must do so.   Indeed the doctrine of *forum non conveniens* can never apply if there is absence of jurisdiction or mistake of venue.

This Court, in one form of words or another, has repeatedly recognized the existence of the power to decline jurisdiction in exceptional circumstances. As formulated by Mr. Justice Brandeis the rule is: "Obviously, the proposition that a court having jurisdiction must exercise it, is not universally true; else the admiralty court could never decline jurisdiction on the ground that the litigation is between foreigners. Nor is it true of courts administering other systems of our law. Courts of equity and of law also occasionally decline, in the interest of justice, to exercise jurisdiction, where the suit is between aliens or nonresidents, or where for kindred reasons the litigation can more appropriately be conducted in a foreign tribunal." Canada Malting Co., Ltd. v. Paterson Steamships, Ltd., 285 U.S. 413, 422, 423, 52 S.Ct. 413, 415, 76 L.Ed. 837.

We later expressly said that a state court "may in appropriate cases apply the doctrine of *forum non conveniens*." * * * Even where federal rights binding on state courts under the Constitution are sought to be adjudged, this Court has sustained state courts in a refusal to entertain a litigation between a nonresident and a foreign corporation or between two foreign corporations. * * * It has held the use of an inappropriate forum in one case an unconstitutional burden on interstate commerce. * * * On substantially *forum non conveniens* grounds we have required federal courts to relinquish decision of cases within their jurisdiction where the court would have to participate in the administrative policy of a state. * * *

It is true that in cases under the Federal Employers' Liability Act, 45 U. S.C.A. § 51 et seq., we have held that plaintiff's choice of a forum cannot be defeated on the basis of *forum non conveniens*. But this was because the special venue act under which those cases are brought was believed to require it. Baltimore & Ohio R. Co. v. Kepner, 314 U.S. 44, 62 S.Ct. 6, 86 L.Ed. 28, 136 A.L.R. 1222. * * * Those decisions do not purport to modify the doctrine as to other cases governed by the general venue statutes.

But the court below says that "The Kepner case * * * warned against refusal of jurisdiction in a particular case controlled by congressional act; here the only difference is that congressional act, plus judicial interpretation (under the Neirbo case), spells out the result." 153 F.2d at page 885. The Federal Employers' Liability Act, however, which controlled decision in the Kepner case, specifically provides where venue may be had in any suit on a cause of action arising under that statute. What the court below refers to as "congressional act, plus judicial interpretation," is the general statute of venue in diversity suits, plus our decision that it gives the defendant "a personal privilege respecting the venue, or place of suit, which he may asert, or may waive, at his election," Neirbo Co. v. Bethlehem Shipbuilding Corp., Ltd. * * *. The Federal Employers' Liability Act, as interpreted by Kepner, increases the number of places where the defendant may be sued and makes him accept the plaintiff's choice. * * * But the general venue statute plus the Neirbo interpretation do not add up to a declaration that the court must respect the choice of the plaintiff, no matter what the type of suit or issues involved. The two taken together mean only that the defendant may consent to be sued, and it is proper for the federal court to take jurisdiction, not that the plaintiff's choice cannot be questioned. The defendant's consent to be sued extends only to give the court jurisdiction of the person; it assumes that the court, having the parties before it, will apply all the applicable law, including, in those cases were it is appropriate, its discretionary judgment as to whether the suit should be entertained. In all cases in which the doctrine of *forum non conveniens* comes into play, it presupposes at least two forums in which the defendant is amenable to process; the doctrine furnishes criteria for choice between them.

II.

The principle of *forum non conveniens* is simply that a court may resist imposition upon its jurisdiction even when jurisdiction is authorized by the letter of a general venue statute. These statutes are drawn with a necessary generality and usually give a plaintiff a choice of courts, so that he may be quite sure of some place in which to pursue his remedy. But the open door may admit those who seek not simply justice but perhaps justice blended with some harassment. A plaintiff sometimes is under temptation to resort to a strategy of forcing the trial at a most inconvenient place for an adversary, even at some inconvenience to himself.

Many of the states have met misuse of venue by investing courts with a discretion to change the place of trial on various grounds, such as the convenience of witnesses and the ends of justice. The federal law contains no such express criteria to guide the district court in exercising its power. But the problem is a very old one affecting the administration of the courts as well as the rights of litigants, and both in England and in this country the common law worked out techniques and criteria for dealing with it.

Wisely, it has not been attempted to catalogue the circumstances which will justify or require either grant or denial of remedy. The doctrine leaves much to the discretion of the court to which plaintiff resorts, and experience has not shown a judicial tendency to renounce one's own jurisdiction so strong as to result in many abuses.

If the combination and weight of factors requisite to given results are difficult to forecast or state, those to be considered are not difficult to name. An interest to be considered, and the one likely to be most pressed, is the private interest of the litigant. Important considerations are the relative ease of access to sources of proof; availability of compulsory process for attendance of unwilling, and the cost of obtaining attendance of willing, witnesses; possibility of view of premises, if view would be appropriate to the action; and all other practical problems that make trial of a case easy, expeditious and inexpensive. There may also be questions as to the enforcibility of a judgment if one is obtained. The court will weigh relative advantages and obstacles to fair trial. It is often said that the plaintiff may not, by choice of an inconvenient forum, "vex," "harass," or "oppress" the defendant by inflicting upon him expense or trouble not necessary to his own right to pursue his remedy. But unless the balance is strongly in favor of the defendant, the plaintiff's choice of forum should rarely be disturbed.

Factors of public interest also have place in applying the doctrine. Administrative difficulties follow for courts when litigation is piled up in congested centers instead of being handled at its origin. Jury duty is a burden that ought not to be imposed upon the people of a community which has no relation to the litigation. In cases which touch the affairs of many persons, there is reason for holding the trial in their view and reach rather than in remote parts of the country where they can learn of it by report only. There is a local interest in having localized controversies decided at home. There is an appropriateness, too, in having the trial of a diversity case in a forum that is at home with the state law that must govern the case, rather than having a court in some other forum untangle problems in conflict of laws, and in law foreign to itself.

*   *   *

III.

Turning to the question whether this is one of those rather rare cases where the doctrine should be applied, we look first to the interests of the litigants.

The plaintiff himself is not a resident of New York, nor did any event connected with the case take place there, nor does any witness with the possible exception of experts live there. No one connected with that side of the case save counsel for the plaintiff resides there, and he has candidly told us that he was retained by insurance companies interested presumably because of subrogation. *   *   *   The only justification for trial in New York advanced here is one rejected by the district court and is set forth in the brief as follows: "This Court can readily realize that an action of this type, involving as it does a claim for damages in an amount close to $400,000, is one which may stagger the imagination of a local jury which is surely unaccustomed to dealing with amounts of such a nature. Furthermore, removed from Lynchburg, the respondent will have an opportunity to try this case free from local influences and preconceived notions which make it difficult to procure a jury which has no previous knowledge of any of the facts herein."

This unproven premise that jurors of New York live on terms of intimacy with $400,000 transactions is not an assumption we easily make. Nor can we assume that a jury from Lynchburg and vicinity would be "staggered" by contemplating the value of a warehouse building that stood in their region, or of merchandise and fixtures such as were used there, nor are they likely to be staggered by the value of chattels which the people of that neighborhood put in storage. It is a strange argument on behalf of a Virginia plaintiff that the community which gave him patronage to make his business valuable is not capable of furnishing jurors who know the value of the goods they store, the building they are stored in, or the business their patronage creates. And there is no specification of any local influence, other than accurate knowledge of local conditions, that would make a fair trial improbable. The net of this is that we cannot say the District Court was bound to entertain a provincial fear of the provincialism of a Virginia jury. That leaves the Virginia plaintiff without even a suggested reason for transporting this suit to New York.

Defendant points out that not only the plaintiff, but every person who participated in the acts charged to be negligent, resides in or near Lynchburg. It also claims a need to interplead an alleged independent contractor which made the delivery of the gasoline and which is a Virginia corporation domiciled in Lynchburg, that it cannot interplead in New York. There also are approximately 350 persons residing in and around Lynchburg who stored with plaintiff the goods for the damage to which he seeks to recover. The extent to which they have left the community since the fire and the number of them who will actually be needed is in dispute. The complaint alleges that defendant's conduct violated Lynchburg ordinances. Conditions are said to require proof by firemen and by many others. The learned and experienced trial judge was not unaware that litigants generally manage to try their cases with fewer witnesses than they predict in such motions as this. But he was justified in concluding that this trial is likely to be long and to involve calling many witnesses, and that Lynchburg, some 400 miles from New York, is the source of all proofs for either side with possible exception of experts. Certainly to fix the place of trial at a point where litigants cannot compel personal attendance and may be forced to try their cases on deposition, is to create a condition not satisfactory to court, jury or most litigants. Nor is it necessarily cured by the statement of plaintiff's counsel that he will see to getting many of the witnesses to the trial and that some of them "would be delighted to come to New York to testify." * * *

The court likewise could well have concluded that the task of the trial court would be simplified by trial in Virginia. If trial was in a state court, it could apply its own law to events occurring there. If in federal court by reason of diversity of citizenship, the court would apply the law of its own state in which it is likely to be experienced. The course of adjudication in New York federal court might be beset with conflict of laws problems all avoided if the case is litigated in Virginia where it arose.

We are convinced that the District Court did not exceed its powers or the bounds of its discretion in dismissing plaintiff's complaint and remitting him to the courts of his own community. * * *

Reversed.

[Mr. Justice REED and Mr. Justice BURTON dissented without formal opinion; a dissenting opinion by Mr. Justice BLACK, joined by Mr. Justice RUTLEDGE has been omitted.]

NOTES AND QUESTIONS

1. A *forum non conveniens* motion is not the only remedy available to a defendant who objects to plaintiff's choice of forum. If another court within the same state is a more appropriate tribunal, defendant may move for a transfer of the action. But this technique is unavailable when more than one state is

involved. Defendant also may institute a suit in another court to enjoin plaintiff from proceeding in the objectionable forum. See generally Comment, *Injunctions Against Suits In Foreign Jurisdictions,* 10 La.L.Rev. 302, 302–12 (1950). However, defendant usually must demonstrate that plaintiff chose the forum to gain some form of advantage or to harass defendant.

> * * * This requirement, which is not part of the doctrine of forum non conveniens, may have arisen from judicial concern about the disruptive effect of injunctions against suit on interstate relations. * * *

> Occasionally, injunctions are issued without regard either for the criteria of trial convenience or the propriety of plaintiff's motive, but rather to promote interests local to the enjoining forum. Some courts, for example, have sought to prevent the "exportation" of particular classes of claims arising within the state; others have issued injunctions in order to guarantee the application of local law to controversies based on domestic incidents.

> Similarly, in applying the doctrine of forum non conveniens, the forum's interest in relieving court congestion often affects its determination of the desirability of transferring an action to another jurisdiction. * * *

> But a choice between the two remedies is not always available. * * * Many states reject the doctrine [of *forum non conveniens*] entirely; † and of those in which it is applied, relief is unlikely if either party is a resident of the forum state.

Comment, *Forum Non Conveniens, Injunctions Against Suit and Full Faith and Credit,* 29 U.Chi.L.Rev. 740, 747–50 (1962).

The principal defect of an injunction to restrain parties from proceeding in another court is the fact that frequently they are unenforceable; if the enjoining court cannot subject plaintiff or his property to its control, the threat of contempt proceedings may be ineffective. Moreover the original forum occasionally will issue a counterinjunction to restrain defendant from enforcing the injunction purporting to direct the parties to refrain from proceeding in the original action. See, e. g., James v. Grand Trunk W.R. Co., 14 Ill.2d 356, 152 N.E.2d 858 (1958). This procedure obviously may have a detrimental effect on the relations among state courts or between federal and state courts. See generally Note, *State Injunction of Proceedings in Federal Courts,* 75 Yale L.J. 150 (1965).

Another approach to the problem of the inconvenient forum is for the court to grant a motion by defendant to stay the proceedings on the assumption that plaintiff will then institute another action in a more convenient locale. Often the stay is conditioned on defendant's making himself available in the alternative forum. See, e. g., Wis.Stat.Ann. § 262.19 in the Supplement under 28 U.S.C. § 1404(a). How does this procedure differ from the *forum non conveniens* practice described in *Gulf Oil Corp. v. Gilbert?* What are the respective merits of dealing with the inconvenient-forum problem by dismissal, transfer, injunction, or stay? To what extent must the court investigate the availability of jurisdiction in the alternative forum when it employs each of these techniques?

---

† E. g., Missouri, State ex rel. Southern Ry. v. Mayfield, 362 Mo. 101, 240 S.W.2d 106, certiorari denied 342 U.S. 871, 72 S.Ct. 107, 96 L.Ed. 655 (1951).

For a discussion of the English approach to the problem of the inconvenient forum, see Comment, *Forum Conveniens—Basis of Jurisdiction in the Commonwealth*, 13 Am.J.Comp.L. 583 (1964).

2. Congress enacted 28 U.S.C. § 1404(a), which is in the Supplement, the year after the decision in *Gulf Oil*. What differences are there between the doctrine of *forum non conveniens* and the procedure under Section 1404(a)? Does it make any difference whether Section 1404(a) has superseded or merely supplemented the doctrine of *forum non conveniens* as a basis for preventing a case from being heard in an inconvenient federal forum? See Norwood v. Kirkpatrick, 349 U.S. 29, 75 S.Ct. 544, 99 L.Ed. 789 (1955). For an excellent discussion of the factors that might influence a judge to grant a transfer, see Kitch, *Section 1404(a) of the Judicial Code: In the Interest of Justice or Injustice?*, 40 Ind.L.J. 99 (1965).

In THOMSON v. CONTINENTAL INS. CO., 66 Cal.2d 738, 59 Cal. Rptr. 101, 427 P.2d 765 (1967), the court refused to apply *forum non conveniens* against a plaintiff who was a resident of the forum state. Could a federal court in California grant a transfer motion in a diversity case against a resident plaintiff if it otherwise was in the interests of justice?

3. Can plaintiffs as well as defendants transfer an action under Section 1404 (a)? What circumstances might motivate a plaintiff to request a transfer of venue? See generally Torres v. Walsh, 221 F.2d 319 (2d Cir.), certiorari denied 350 U.S. 836, 76 S.Ct. 72, 100 L.Ed. 746 (1955); Philip Carey Mfg. Co. v. Taylor, 286 F.2d 782 (6th Cir.1961); Korbel, *The Law of Federal Venue and Choice of the Most Convenient Forum*, 15 Rutgers L.Rev. 607 (1961).

4. To what degree does the availability of transfer under 28 U.S.C. § 1404 (a) mitigate the inconvenience to defendants that might be caused by the assertion of quasi in rem jurisdiction in cases like *Seider v. Roth* and *Simpson v. Loehmann*, pp. 111–13, supra.

HOFFMAN v. BLASKI

Supreme Court of the United States, 1960.
363 U.S. 335, 80 S.Ct. 1084, 4 L.Ed.2d 1254.

Certiorari to the United States Court of Appeals for the Seventh Circuit.

Mr. Justice WHITTAKER delivered the opinion of the Court.

* * *

The instant cases present the question whether a District Court, in which a civil action has been properly brought, is empowered by § 1404(a) to transfer the action, on the motion of the defendant, to a district in which the plaintiff did not have a *right* to bring it.

Respondents, Blaski and others, residents of Illinois, brought this patent infringement action in the United States District Court for the Northern District of Texas against one Howell and a Texas corporation controlled by him, alleging that the defendants are residents of, and maintain their only place of business in, the City of Dallas, in the Northern District of Texas, where they are infringing respondents' patents. After being served with process and filing their answer, the defendants moved, under § 1404(a), to transfer the action to the United States District Court for the Northern District of Illinois. Respondents objected to the transfer on the ground that, inasmuch as the defendants did not reside, maintain a place of business, or infringe the patents in, and could not have been served with process in, the Illinois district, the courts of that district lacked venue over the action and ability to command jurisdiction over the defendants; that therefore that district was not a forum in which the respondents had a right to bring the action, and, hence, the court was without power to transfer it to that district. Without mentioning that objection or the question it raised, the District Court found that "the motion should be granted for the convenience of the parties and witnesses in the interest of justice," and ordered the case transferred to the Illinois district. Thereupon, respondents moved in the Fifth Circuit for leave to file a petition for a writ of mandamus directing the vacation of that order. That court, holding that "[t]he purposes for which § 1404(a) was enacted would be unduly circumscribed if a transfer could not be made 'in the interest of justice' to a district where the defendants not only waive venue but to which they seek the transfer," denied the motion.   *   *   *

Upon receipt of a certified copy of the pleadings and record, the Illinois District Court assigned the action to Judge Hoffman's calendar. Respondents promptly moved for an order remanding the action on the ground that the Texas District Court did not have power to make the transfer order and, hence, the Illinois District Court was not thereby vested with jurisdiction of the action. After expressing his view that the "weight of reason and logic" favored "retransfer of this case to Texas," Judge Hoffman, with misgivings, denied the motion. Respondents then filed in the Seventh Circuit a petition for a writ of mandamus directing Judge Hoffman to reverse his order. After hearing and rehearing, the Seventh Circuit, holding that "[w]hen Congress provided [in § 1404(a)] for transfer [of a civil action] to a district 'where it might have been brought,' it is hardly open to doubt but that it referred to a district where the plaintiff   *   *   *   had a right to bring the case," and that respondents did not have a *right* to bring this action in the Illinois district, granted the writ, one judge dissenting.   *   *   *

Petitioners' "thesis" and sole claim is that § 1404(a), being remedial,   *   *   *   should be broadly construed, and, when so construed, the phrase "where it might have been brought" should be held to relate not only to the time of the bringing of the action but also to the time of the transfer; and that "if at such time the transferee forum has the power to adjudicate the issues of the action, it is a forum in which the action might *then* have been brought." (Emphasis added.) They argue that in the interim between the bringing of the action and the filing of a motion to transfer it, the defendants may move their residence to, or, if corporations, may begin the transaction of business in, some other district, and, if such is done, the phrase "where it might have been brought" should be construed to empower the District Court to transfer the action, on motion of the defendants, to such other district; and that, similarly, if, as here, the defendants move to transfer the action to some other district and consent to submit to the jurisdiction of such other district, the latter district should be held one "in which the action might *then* have been brought." (Emphasis added.) ·

We do not agree. We do not think the § 1404(a) phrase "where it might have been brought" can be interpreted to mean, as petitioners' theory would require, "where it may now be rebrought, with defendants' consent."
* * *

It is not to be doubted that the transferee courts, like every District Court, had jurisdiction to entertain actions of the character involved, but it is obvious that they did not acquire jurisdiction over these particular actions when they were brought in the transferor courts. The transferee courts could have acquired jurisdiction over these actions only if properly brought in those courts, or if validly transferred thereto under § 1404(a). Of course, venue, like jurisdiction over the person, may be waived. A defendant, properly served with process by a court having subject matter jurisdiction, waives venue by failing seasonably to assert it, or even simply by making default. * * * But the power of a District Court under § 1404(a) to transfer an action to another district is made to depend not upon the wish or waiver of the defendant but, rather, upon whether the transferee district was one in which the action "might have been brought" by the plaintiff.

The thesis urged by petitioners would not only do violence to the plain words of § 1404(a), but would also inject gross discrimination. That thesis, if adopted, would empower a District Court, upon a finding of convenience, to transfer an action to any district desired by the *defendants* and in which they were willing to waive their statutory defenses as to venue and jurisdiction over their persons, regardless of the fact that such transferee district was not one in which the action "might have been brought" by the plaintiff. Conversely, that thesis would not permit the court, upon motion of the *plaintiffs* and a like showing of convenience, to transfer the action to the same district, without the consent and waiver of venue and personal jurisdiction defenses by the defendants. Nothing in § 1404(a), or in its legislative history, suggests such a unilateral objective and we should not, under the guise of interpretation, ascribe to Congress any such discriminatory purpose.

* * *

Inasmuch as the respondents (plaintiffs) did not have a right to bring these actions in the respective transferee districts, it follows that the judgments of the Court of Appeals were correct and must be affirmed.

Affirmed.

[A concurring opinion by Mr. Justice STEWART and a dissenting opinion by Justices FRANKFURTER, HARLAN, and BRENNAN have been omitted. Both of these opinions pertained only to Hoffman v. Blaski.]

Mr. Justice FRANKFURTER, whom Mr. Justice HARLAN and Mr. Justice BRENNAN join, dissenting.*

The problem in this case is of important concern to the effective administration of justice in the federal courts. * * * Section 1404(a) was devised to avoid needless hardship and even miscarriage of justice by empowering district judges to recognize special circumstances calling for special relief. It provides that an action, although begun in a place falling within the normally applicable venue rubric may be sent by the District Court to go forward in another district much more appropriate when judged by the criteria of judicial justice.

* * *

The part of § 1404(a) the meaning of which is at issue here is its last phrase * * *. The significance of this phrase is this: even though a place be found to be an overwhelmingly more appropriate forum from the standpoint of "convenience" and "justice," the litigation may not be sent to go forward there unless it is a place where the action "might have been brought." Upon the scope to be given this phrase thus depends almost entirely the effectiveness of § 1404(a) to insure an appropriate place of trial, when the action is begun in an oppressive forum.

One would have to be singularly unmindful of the treachery and versatility of our language to deny that as a mere matter of English the words "where it might have been brought" may carry more than one meaning. * * *

On the face of its words alone, the phrase may refer to * * * venue, amenability to service, or period of limitations, to all of them or to none of them, or to others as well. * * *

I submit that it is not clear from the words themselves, and the experience in the lower courts gives compelling proof of it. At least 28 District Courts, located in all parts of the Nation, have had to give concrete meaning to the set of words in controversy. These are the judges who are, to use a familiar but appropriate phrase, on the firing line, who are in much more intimate, continuous touch with the needs for the effective functioning of the federal judicial system at the trial level than is this Court. They have not found the last phrase of § 1404(a) unambiguous. * * *

The experience in the Courts of Appeals is also revealing. Of the six cases where defendants have moved for transfer, in only two has it been held that the defendant's consent to the transfer is not relevant in determining whether the place to which transfer is proposed is a place where the action "might have been brought," and these are the two decisions of the Seventh Circuit now before us. * * *

Surely, the Court creates its own verbal prison in holding that "the plain words" of § 1404(a) dictate that transfer may not be made in this case al-

---

* This opinion applies only to the companion case of Sullivan v. Behimer, which raised the same question as Hoffman v. Blaski. [Footnote by the Court.]

though transfer concededly was in the interest of "convenience" and "justice." Moreover, the Court, while finding the statutory words "plain," decides the case by applying, not the statutory language, but a formula of words found nowhere in the statute, namely, whether plaintiffs had "a right to bring these actions in the respective transferee districts." This is the Court's language, not that of Congress. * * * There can be expected to be very few, if any, alternative forums in a given case where the plaintiff has a "right" to sue, considering that that means places of unobjectionable venue where the defendant is amenable to service of process and where there are no other impediments such as a statute of limitations which the defendant can rely on to defeat the action.

* * * At the crux of the business, as I see it, is the realization that we are concerned here not with a question of a limitation upon the power of a federal court but with the place in which that court may exercise its power. We are dealing, that is, not with the jurisdiction of the federal courts, which is beyond the power of litigants to confer, but with the locality of a lawsuit, the rules regulating which are designed mainly for the convenience of the litigants. * * *

In light of the nature of rules governing the place of trial in the federal system * * *, what are the competing considerations here? The transferee court in this case plainly had and has jurisdiction to adjudicate this action with the defendant's acquiescence. As the defendant, whose privilege it is to object to the place of trial, has moved for transfer, and has acquiesced to going forward with the litigation in the transferee court, it would appear presumptively, unless there are strong considerations otherwise, that there is no impediment to effecting the transfer so long as "convenience" and "justice" dictate that it be made. It does not counsel otherwise that here the plaintiff is to be sent to a venue to which he objects, whereas ordinarily, when the defendant waives his privilege to object to the place of trial, it is to acquiesce in the plaintiff's choice of forum. This would be a powerful argument if, under § 1404(a), a transfer were to be made whenever requested by the defendant. Such is not the case, and this bears emphasis. A transfer can be made under § 1404(a) to a place where the action "might have been brought" only when "convenience" and "justice" so dictate, not whenever the defendant so moves. A legitimate objection by the plaintiff to proceeding in the transferee forum will presumably be reflected in a decision that the interest of justice does not require the transfer, and so it becomes irrelevant that the proposed place of transfer is deemed one where the action "might have been brought." * * *

On the other hand, the Court's view restricts transfer, when concededly warranted in the interest of justice, to protect no legitimate interest on the part of the plaintiff. And by making transfer turn on whether the defendant could have been served with process in the transferee district on the day the action was brought, the Court's view may create difficult problems in ascertaining that fact, especially in the case of non-corporate defendants. These are problems which have no conceivable relation to the proper administration of a provision meant to assure the most convenient and just place for trial.

    *   *   *

The relevant legislative history of § 1404(a) is found in the statement in the Reviser's Notes, accompanying the 1948 Judicial Code, that § 1404(a) "was drafted in accordance with the doctrine of forum non conveniens." Under that doctrine, the remedy for an inconvenient forum was not to transfer the action, but to dismiss it. In Gulf Oil Corp. v. Gilbert   *   *   *   we held that "[i]n all cases in which the doctrine of *forum non conveniens* comes into play, it presupposes at least two forums in which the defendant is amenable to process; the doctrine furnishes criteria for choice between them." It is entirely "in accordance" with this view of the doctrine of *forum non conveniens* to hold that transfer may be made at the instance of the defendant regardless of the plaintiff's right as an original matter to sue him in the transferee court, so long as the defendant stipulates to going forward with the litigation there. Indeed, to hold otherwise as the Court does is to limit § 1404(a) to a much narrower operation than the nonstatutory doctrine of *forum non conveniens*. Investigation has disclosed several *forum non conveniens* cases, one of them in this Court, where dismissal of the action on the defendant's motion was made upon the condition of the defendant's voluntary submission to the jurisdiction of another more convenient forum when that forum was not available to the plaintiff as of right over the defendant's objection.   *   *   *

The only consideration of the Court not resting on the "plain meaning" of § 1404(a) is that it would constitute "gross discrimination" to permit transfer to be made with the defendant's consent and over the plaintiff's objection to a district to which the plaintiff could not similarly obtain transfer over the defendant's objection.   *   *   *   Transfer cannot be made under this statute unless it is found to be in the interest of "convenience" and in the interest of "justice." Whether a party is in any sense being "discriminated" against through a transfer is certainly relevant to whether the interest of justice is being served. If the interest of justice is being served, as it must be for a transfer to be made, how can it be said that there is "discrimination" in any meaningful sense? Moreover, the transfer provision cannot be viewed in isolation in finding "discrimination." It, after all, operates to temper only to a slight degree the enormous "discrimination" inherent in our system of litigation, whereby the sole choice of forum, from among those where service is possible and venue unobjectionable, is placed with the plaintiff.   *   *   *

If anything is plain, from its history and from its words, it is that § 1404(a) means to afford a balance, a compromise, between these two extremes. It is in this spirit that its provisions must be read. In the ordinary course the regular venue rules are to prevail, with no preliminary litigation to determine the actual convenience. But the statute means to allow for cases where the ordinary rules are found to work a great hardship; there, actual convenience is to prevail.

NOTES AND QUESTIONS

1. To what extent does the decision in the principal case favor plaintiffs at the expense of defendants? How does the transferor court determine whether defendant is amenable to service in the transferee district? Does *Blaski* require the movant to demonstrate conclusively that defendant was amenable to process in the transferee district court at the time the action was commenced, or should a lesser showing be sufficient? See Dill v. Scuka, 198 F.Supp. 808 (E.D.Pa.1961); Comment, *The Requirement of Personal Jurisdiction When Transferring an Action Under Section 1404(a)*, 57 Nw.U.L.Rev. 456 (1962).

In Sections 1302, 1305–1306 of the American Law Institute's *Study of the Division of Jurisdiction Between State and Federal Courts*, Official Draft (1969), which are set out in the Supplement following 28 U.S.C. § 1391, it is proposed that in diversity cases transfer may be allowed to any district except one where one or more plaintiffs and all the moving defendants would be barred from invoking jurisdiction in an original action. Plaintiff may obtain a transfer to any district where venue would be proper and defendant would be amenable to process. In Section 1315 the Institute proposes that a federal question case may be transfered to any district and if venue is improper in the transferor court, transfer may be to any district in which there would be proper venue. These proposals are criticized in Kitch, *Section 1404(a) of the Judicial Code: In the Interest of Justice or Injustice?*, 40 Ind.L.J. 99 (1965).

2. Is the fact that the action would be barred by the statute of limitations in the transferee district relevant to the decision of a motion under Section 1404 (a)? To what extent should the transferee court attempt to reach the same result on the merits that would have been rendered by the transferor court? Must the transferee court apply the law of the transferor court? See generally Van Dusen v. Barrack, 376 U.S. 612, 84 S.Ct. 805, 11 L.Ed.2d 945 (1964); Headrick v. Atchison, Topeka & Santa Fe R. R., 182 F.2d 305 (10th Cir.1950). These questions will be renewed in the next Chapter.

3. Section 1406(a) permits the district court to dismiss "or if it be in the interest of justice" to transfer a case to any district in which it could have been brought when it was brought initially in a court in which venue was improper. This provision should be distinguished from Section 1404(a), which presupposes that venue in the district of commencement is proper.

One of the more interesting cases involving Section 1406(a) is GOLDLAWR, INC. v. HEIMAN, 369 U.S. 463, 82 S.Ct. 913, 8 L.Ed.2d 39 (1962), a treble-damage action under the antitrust laws commenced in the Eastern District of Pennsylvania against a number of defendants. On motion, the district court found both a lack of personal jurisdiction and improper venue and transferred the case to the Southern District of New York, where venue was proper and defendants could be reached by process. The New York federal court, however, dismissed the case on the ground that the Pennsylvania court could not transfer the action because it lacked personal jurisdiction. The Supreme Court reversed.

    * * * The problem which gave rise to the enactment of the section was that of avoiding the injustice which had often resulted to plaintiffs from dismissal of their actions merely because they had made an erroneous guess with regard to the existence of some elusive fact of the kind upon which venue provisions often turn. Indeed, this case is itself a typical example of the problem sought to be avoided, for dismissal here would have resulted in plaintiff's losing a substantial part of its cause of action under the statute of limitations merely because it made a mistake in thinking that the respondent corporations could be "found" or that they "transact * * * business" in the Eastern District of Pennsylvania. The language and history of § 1406(a) * * * show a congressional purpose to provide as effective a remedy as possible to avoid precisely this sort of injustice.

The language of § 1406(a) is amply broad enough to authorize the transfer of cases, however wrong the plaintiff may have been in filing his case as to venue, whether the court in which it was filed had personal jurisdiction over the defendants or not. The section is thus in accord with the general purpose which has prompted many of the procedural changes of the past few years—that of removing whatever obstacles may impede an expeditious and orderly adjudication of cases and controversies on their merits. When a lawsuit is filed, that filing shows a desire on the part of the plaintiff to begin his case and thereby toll whatever statutes of limitation would otherwise apply. The filing itself shows the proper diligence on the part of the plaintiff which such statutes of limitation were intended to insure. If by reason of the uncertainties of proper venue a mistake is made, Congress, by the enactment of § 1406(a), recognized that "the interest of justice" may require that the complaint not be dismissed but rather that it be transferred in order that the plaintiff not be penalized * * *.

Id. at 466–67, 82 S.Ct. at 915–16, 8 L.Ed.2d at 42. Mr. Justice Harlan and Mr. Justice Stewart dissented for the following reasons.

The notion that a District Court may deal with an *in personam* action in such a way as possibly to affect a defendant's substantive rights without first acquiring jurisdiction over him is not a familiar one in federal jurisprudence. No one suggests that Congress was aware that * * * § 1406(a) might be so used when it enacted that statute. The "interest of justice" of which the statute speaks * * * is assuredly not a one-way street. And it is incongruous to consider, as the Court's holding would seem to imply, that in the "interest of justice" Congress sought in § 1406(a) to deal with the transfer of cases where *both* venue and jurisdiction are lacking in the district where the action is commenced, while neglecting to provide any comparable alleviative measures for the plaintiff who selects a district where venue is proper but where personal jurisdiction cannot be obtained.

Id. at 467–68, 82 S.Ct. at 916, 8 L.Ed.2d at 43.

The *Goldlawr* decision leaves open a number of questions that raise doubts as to its soundness. Suppose that plaintiff commences an action in a district court that patently lacks personal jurisdiction one day before the expiration of the applicable statute of limitations and ten days later moves to transfer the action to a district in which venue and jurisdiction are proper. If plaintiff is permitted to transfer, hasn't defendant lost the benefit of the statute of limitations? Put another way, shouldn't plaintiff be required to institute an action in a district having personal jurisdiction over defendant prior to the end of the limitations period? *Cf.* Skilling v. Funk Aircraft Co., 173 F.Supp. 939 (W.D.Mo.1959). Furthermore, shouldn't defendant be guaranteed an opportunity to contest the transfer motion? If the court lacks personal jurisdiction over her, how will defendant know that the action has been instituted and a transfer motion made? An even broader question is to what extent *Goldlawr* results in plaintiff abdicating the obligation to choose an appropriate forum in which defendant is amenable to suit and foisting that task upon the federal courts. In HYDROTHERM, INC. v. BASTIAN-MORLEY CO., 207 F.Supp. 744, 745 (E.D.N.Y.1962), the court suggested:

> It must now be unimportant to decide whether a corporation is amenable to suit in one or another district; if it is incorporated in a state of the United States, it is suable in some district court and federal [subject matter] jurisdiction having been invoked, all that remains is to ascertain the appropriate district * * * [citing *Goldlawr*].

The ramifications of the *Goldlawr* case are discussed in Note, *Change of Venue in Absence of Personal Jurisdiction Under 28 U.S.C. §§ 1404(a) and 1406(a)*, 30 U.Chi.L.Rev. 735 (1963); Comment, *Personal Jurisdiction Requirements Under Federal Change of Venue Statutes*, 1962 Wis.L.Rev. 342.

4. Should the defendant be able to obtain a transfer under Section 1404(a) of a quasi in rem action when the jurisdiction of the transferor court is based entirely on the seizure of defendant's property? If transfer is permitted what should happen to the property that was attached? See Note, *Transfer of Quasi In Rem Action under 28 U.S.C. § 1404(a): A Study in the Interpretation of "Civil Actions,"* 31 U.Chi.L.Rev. 373 (1964).

CHAPTER 3

ASCERTAINING THE APPLICABLE LAW

Civil actions involving citizens of a single state and a transaction that occurred entirely within the boundaries of that state do not present any problems of choosing the proper body of substantive law to be applied in determining the rights and liabilities of the parties. However, as soon as the litigation touches two or more states, one is likely to be confronted with a serious question of choosing between two or more sources of law. For example, suppose plaintiff and defendant, both citizens of State X, are involved in an automobile accident or agree to perform a contract or engage in a transfer of property in State Y. Should questions pertaining to defendant's alleged negligence or failure to perform the contract or the ownership of the property be decided under the law of State X or the law of State Y? Should the choice be made in the same way in tort, contract, and property actions? The complexity of these questions increases if plaintiff and defendant are citizens of different states and the event, relationship, or property that forms the predicate of the controversy can be traced to a third, and perhaps a fourth or fifth, state. The student will be exposed to problems of this type on numerous occasions during the civil procedure course and must learn to recognize them. However, formal education in the philosophy of choosing among the laws of two or more states must be postponed until the course in conflict of laws.

This Chapter is devoted to choice-of-law problems of a somewhat different dimension. Let us suppose that plaintiff is a citizen of State X and defendant is a citizen of State Y and that plaintiff has decided to litigate a tort or contract claim against defendant in a federal district court in State Y. What law should the federal court apply to adjudicate this action? The law of State X? Of State Y? Federal law? Would the answer be different if, assuming personal jurisdiction could be acquired, the action was commenced in a federal district court in State X? The problem of choosing between federal and state law also is present when a state court is called upon to decide cases arising under federal statutes or cases in which federal rights and liabilities are in issue. As one might surmise, the process of choosing between the law of two states and that of choosing between federal and state law are analogous. In some situations, particularly diversity cases, they are intertwined. This Chapter will explore some of the problems created by the application of state law in the federal courts and the role of federal law in the state courts.

A final observation before beginning: If the law applied by one court differs materially from that applied by another, an attorney interested in achieving a particular result for a client obviously may wish to steer the lawsuit, if the jurisdiction and venue rules permit, to a particular tribunal. To what extent should a court take account of this type of forum manipulation in choosing the law to be applied?

SECTION A. STATE LAW IN THE FEDERAL COURTS—DIVERSITY JURISDICTION

ERIE RAILROAD CO. v. TOMPKINS

Supreme Court of the United States, 1938.
304 U.S. 64, 58 S.Ct. 817, 82 L.Ed. 1188, 114 A.L.R. 1487.

Certiorari to the Circuit Court of Appeals for the Second Circuit.

Mr. Justice BRANDEIS delivered the opinion of the Court.

The question for decision is whether the oft-challenged doctrine of Swift v. Tyson [41 U.S. (16 Pet.) 1, 10 L.Ed. 865 (1842)] shall now be disapproved.

Tompkins, a citizen of Pennsylvania, was injured on a dark night by a passing freight train of the Erie Railroad Company while walking along its right of way at Hughestown in that state. He claimed that the accident occurred through negligence in the operation, or maintenance, of the train; that he was rightfully on the premises as licensee because on a commonly used beaten footpath which ran for a short distance alongside the tracks; and that he was struck by something which looked like a door projecting from one of the moving cars. To enforce that claim he brought an action in the federal court for Southern New York, which had jurisdiction because the company is a corporation of that state. It denied liability; and the case was tried by a jury.

The Erie insisted that its duty to Tompkins was no greater than that owed to a trespasser. It contended * * * that its duty to Tompkins, and hence its liability, should be determined in accordance with the Pennsylvania law; that under the law of Pennsylvania, as declared by its highest court, persons who use pathways along the railroad right of way—that is, a longitudinal pathway as distinguished from a crossing—are to be deemed trespassers; and that the railroad is not liable for injuries to undiscovered trespassers resulting from its negligence, unless it be wanton or wilful. Tompkins denied that any such rule had been established by the decisions of the Pennsylvania courts; and contended that, since there was no statute of the state on the subject, the railroad's duty and liability is to be determined in federal courts as a matter of general law.

The trial judge refused to rule that the applicable law precluded recovery. The jury brought in a verdict of $30,000; and the judgment entered thereon was affirmed by the Circuit Court of Appeals, which held * * * that it was unnecessary to consider whether the law of Pennsylvania was as contended, because the question was one not of local, but of general, law, and that "upon questions of general law the federal courts are free, in absence of a local statute, to exercise their independent judgment as to what the law is; and it is well settled that the question of the responsibility of a railroad for injuries caused by its servants is one of general law. * * * Where the public has made open and notorious use of a railroad right of way for a long period of time and without objection, the company owes to persons on such permissive pathway a duty of care in the operation of its trains.   *   *   * It is likewise generally recognized law that a jury may find that negligence exists toward a pedestrian using a permissive path on the railroad right of way if he is hit by some object projecting from the side of the train."

The Erie had contended that application of the Pennsylvania rule was required, among other things, by section 34 of the Federal Judiciary Act of September 24, 1789, c. 20, 28 U.S.C. § 725, which provides: "The laws of the several States, except where the Constitution, treaties, or statutes of the United States otherwise require or provide, shall be regarded as rules of decision in trials at common law, in the courts of the United States, in cases where they apply." [a]

*   *   *

First.   Swift v. Tyson   *   *   *   held that federal courts exercising jurisdiction on the ground of diversity of citizenship need not, in matters of general jurisprudence, apply the unwritten law of the state as declared by its highest court; that they are free to exercise an independent judgment as to what the common law of the state is—or should be; and that, as there stated by Mr. Justice Story, "the true interpretation of the 34th section limited its application to state laws, strictly local, that is to say, to the positive statutes of the state, and the construction thereof adopted by the local tribunals, and to rights and titles to things having a permanent locality, such as the rights and titles to real estate, and other matters immovable and intra-territorial in their nature and character. It never has been supposed by us, that the section did apply, or was designed to apply, to questions of a more general nature, not at all dependent upon local statutes or local usages of a fixed and permanent operation, as, for example, to the construction of ordinary contracts or other written instruments, and especially to questions of general commercial law, where the state tribunals are called upon to perform the like functions as ourselves, that is, to ascertain, upon general reasoning and legal analogies, what is the true exposition of the contract or instrument, or what is the just rule furnished by the principles of commercial law to govern the case."

*   *   *   The federal courts assumed, in the broad field of "general law," the power to declare rules of decision which Congress was confessedly without power to enact as statutes. Doubt was repeatedly expressed as to the correctness of the construction given section 34, and as to the soundness of the rule which it introduced. But it was the more recent research of a competent scholar, who examined the original document, which established that the construction given to it by the Court was erroneous; and that the purpose of the section was merely to make certain that, in all matters except those in which some federal law is controlling, the federal courts exercising jurisdiction in diversity of citizenship cases would apply as their rules of decision the law of the state, unwritten as well as written.[5]

[a] The current version of this provision, 28 U.S.C. § 1652, applies to "civil actions" instead of to "trials at common law." The statute is set out in the Supplement.

[5] Charles Warren, New Light on the History of the Federal Judiciary Act of 1789 (1923) 37 Harv.L.Rev. 49, 51–52, 81–88, 108.

Criticism of the doctrine became widespread after the decision of Black & White Taxicab & Transfer Co. v. Brown & Yellow Taxicab & Transfer Co., 276 U.S. 518, 48 S.Ct. 404, 72 L.Ed. 681, 57 A.L.R. 426. There, Brown & Yellow, a Kentucky corporation owned by Kentuckians, and the Louisville & Nashville Railroad, also a Kentucky corporation, wished that the former should have the exclusive privilege of soliciting passenger and baggage transportation at the Bowling Green, Ky., railroad station; and that the Black & White, a competing Kentucky corporation, should be prevented from interfering with that privilege. Knowing that such a contract would be void under the common law of Kentucky, it was arranged that the Brown & Yellow reincorporate under the law of Tennessee, and that the contract with the railroad should be executed there. The suit was then brought by the Tennessee corporation in the federal court for Western Kentucky to enjoin competition by the Black & White; an injunction issued by the District Court was sustained by the Court of Appeals; and this Court, citing many decisions in which the doctrine of Swift v. Tyson had been applied, affirmed the decree.

Second. Experience in applying the doctrine of Swift v. Tyson, had revealed its defects, political and social; and the benefits expected to flow from the rule did not accrue. Persistence of state courts in their own opinions on questions of common law prevented uniformity; and the impossibility of discovering a satisfactory line of demarcation between the province of general law and that of local law developed a new well of uncertainties.

On the other hand, the mischievous results of the doctrine had become apparent. Diversity of citizenship jurisdiction was conferred in order to prevent apprehended discrimination in state courts against those not citizens of the state. Swift v. Tyson introduced grave discrimination by noncitizens against citizens. It made rights enjoyed under the unwritten "general law" vary according to whether enforcement was sought in the state or in the federal court; and the privilege of selecting the court in which the right should be determined was conferred upon the noncitizen. Thus, the doctrine rendered impossible equal protection of the law. In attempting to promote uniformity of law throughout the United States, the doctrine had prevented uniformity in the administration of the law of the state.

The discrimination resulting became in practice far-reaching. This resulted in part from the broad province accorded to the so-called "general law" as to which federal courts exercised an independent judgment. In addition to questions of purely commercial law, "general law" was held to include the obligations under contracts entered into and to be performed within the state, the extent to which a carrier operating within a state may stipulate for exemption from liability for his own negligence or that of his employee; the liability for torts committed within the state upon persons resident or property located there, even where the question of liability depended upon the scope of a property right conferred by the state; and the right to exemplary or punitive damages. Furthermore, state decisions construing local deeds, mineral conveyances, and even devises of real estate, were disregarded.

In part the discrimination resulted from the wide range of persons held entitled to avail themselves of the federal rule by resort to the diversity of citizenship jurisdiction. Through this jurisdiction individual citizens willing to remove from their own state and become citizens of another might avail themselves of the federal rule. And, without even change of residence, a corporate citizen of the state could avail itself of the federal rule by reincorporating under the laws of another state, as was done in the Taxicab Case.

The injustice and confusion incident to the doctrine of Swift v. Tyson have been repeatedly urged as reasons for abolishing or limiting diversity of citizenship jurisdiction. Other legislative relief has been proposed. If only a question of statutory construction were involved, we should not be prepared to abandon a doctrine so widely applied throughout nearly a century. But the unconstitutionality of the course pursued has now been made clear, and compels us to do so.

Third. Except in matters governed by the Federal Constitution or by acts of Congress, the law to be applied in any case is the law of the state. And whether the law of the state shall be declared by its Legislature in a statute or by its highest court in a decision is not a matter of federal concern. There is no federal general common law. Congress has no power to declare substantive rules of common law applicable in a state whether they be local in their nature or "general," be they commercial law or a part of the law of torts. And no clause in the Constitution purports to confer such a power upon the federal courts. As stated by Mr. Justice Field when protesting in Baltimore & Ohio R. R. Co. v. Baugh, 149 U.S. 368, 401, 13 S.Ct. 914, 927, 37 L.Ed. 772, against ignoring the Ohio common law of fellow-servant liability: "I am aware that what has been termed the general law of the country—which is often little less than what the judge advancing the doctrine thinks at the time should be the general law on a particular subject—has been often advanced in judicial opinions of this court to control a conflicting law of a state. I admit that learned judges have fallen into the habit of repeating this doctrine as a convenient mode of brushing aside the law of a state in conflict with their views. And I confess that, moved and governed by the authority of the great names of those judges, I have, myself, in many instances, unhesitatingly and confidently, but I think now erroneously, repeated the same doctrine. But, notwithstanding the great names which may be cited in favor of the doctrine, and notwithstanding the frequency with which the doctrine has been reiterated, there stands, as a perpetual protest against its repetition, the constitution of the United States, which recognizes and preserves the autonomy and independence of the states, —independence in their legislative and independence in their judicial departments. Supervision over either the legislative or the judicial action of the states is in no case permissible except as to matters by the constitution specifically authorized or delegated to the United States. Any interference with either, except as thus permitted, is an invasion of the authority of the state, and, to that extent, a denial of its independence."

The fallacy underlying the rule declared in Swift v. Tyson is made clear by Mr. Justice Holmes.[23] The doctrine rests upon the assumption that there is

---

[23] Kuhn v. Fairmont Coal Co., 215 U.S. 349, 370–372, 30 S.Ct. 140, 54 L.Ed. 228; Black & White Taxicab, etc., Co. v. Brown & Yellow Taxicab, etc., Co., 276 U.S. 518, 532–536, 48 S.Ct. 404, 408, 409, 72 L.Ed. 681, 57 A.L.R. 426.

"a transcendental body of law outside of any particular State but obligatory within it unless and until changed by statute," that federal courts have the power to use their judgment as to what the rules of common law are; and that in the federal courts "the parties are entitled to an independent judgment on matters of general law":

"But law in the sense in which courts speak of it today does not exist without some definite authority behind it. The common law so far as it is enforced in a State, whether called common law or not, is not the common law generally but the law of that State existing by the authority of that State without regard to what it may have been in England or anywhere else. * * *

"The authority and only authority is the State, and if that be so, the voice adopted by the State as its own [whether it be of its Legislature or of its Supreme Court] should utter the last word."

Thus the doctrine of Swift v. Tyson is, as Mr. Justice Holmes said, "an unconstitutional assumption of powers by the Courts of the United States which no lapse of time or respectable array of opinion should make us hesitate to correct." In disapproving that doctrine we do not hold unconstitutional section 34 of the Federal Judiciary Act of 1789 or any other act of Congress. We merely declare that in applying the doctrine this Court and the lower courts have invaded rights which in our opinion are reserved by the Constitution to the several states.

Fourth. The defendant contended that by the common law of Pennsylvania * * * the only duty owed to the plaintiff was to refrain from willful or wanton injury. The plaintiff denied that such is the Pennsylvania law. In support of their respective contentions the parties discussed and cited many decisions of the Supreme Court of the state. The Circuit Court of Appeals ruled that the question of liability is one of general law; and on that ground declined to decide the issue of state law. As we hold this was error, the judgment is reversed and the case remanded to it for further proceedings in conformity with our opinion.

Reversed.

Mr. Justice CARDOZO took no part in the consideration or decision of this case.

Mr. Justice BUTLER (dissenting).
* * *

Defendant's petition for writ of certiorari presented two questions: Whether its duty toward plaintiff should have been determined in accordance with the law as found by the highest court of Pennsylvania, and whether the evidence conclusively showed plaintiff guilty of contributory negligence. Plaintiff contends that, as always heretofore held by this Court, the issues of negligence and contributory negligence are to be determined by general law against which local decisions may not be held conclusive * * *.

No constitutional question was suggested or argued below or here. And as a general rule, this Court will not consider any question not raised below and presented by the petition. * * * Here it does not decide either of the questions presented, but, changing the rule of decision in force since the foundation of the government, remands the case to be adjudged according to a standard never before deemed permissible.

* * *

The doctrine of * * * [Swift v. Tyson] has been followed by this Court in an unbroken line of decisions. So far as appears, it was not questioned until more than 50 years later, and then by a single judge.[1] Baltimore & O. Railroad Co. v. Baugh, 149 U.S. 368, 390, 13 S.Ct. 914, 37 L.Ed. 772. * * *

And since that decision, the division of opinion in this Court has been of the same character as it was before. In 1910, Mr. Justice Holmes, speaking for himself and two other Justices, dissented from the holding that a court of the United States was bound to exercise its own independent judgment in the construction of a conveyance made before the state courts had rendered an authoritative decision as to its meaning and effect. Kuhn v. Fairmont Coal Co., 215 U.S. 349, 30 S.Ct. 140, 54 L.Ed. 228. But that dissent accepted (215 U. S. 349, at page 371, 30 S.Ct. 140, 54 L.Ed. 228) as "settled" the doctrine of Swift v. Tyson, and insisted (215 U.S. 349, at page 372, 30 S.Ct. 140, 54 L. Ed. 228) merely that the case under consideration was by nature and necessity peculiarly local.

* * *

So far as appears, no litigant has ever challenged the power of Congress to establish the rule as construed. It has so long endured that its destruction now without appropriate deliberation cannot be justified. There is nothing in the opinion to suggest that consideration of any constitutional question is necessary to a decision of the case. By way of reasoning, it contains nothing that requires the conclusion reached. Admittedly, there is no authority to support that conclusion. Against the protest of those joining in this opinion, the Court declines to assign the case for reargument. It may not justly be assumed that the labor and argument of counsel for the parties would not disclose the right conclusion and aid the Court in the statement of reasons to support it. Indeed, it would have been appropriate to give Congress opportunity to be heard before divesting it of power to prescribe rules of decision to be followed in the courts of the United States. * * *

The course pursued by the Court in this case is repugnant to the Act of Congress of August 24, 1937, 50 Stat. 751, 28 U.S.C.A. §§ 17 and note, 349a, 380a and note, 401. It declares that: "Whenever the constitutionality of any Act of Congress affecting the public interest is drawn in question in any court of the United States in any suit or proceeding to which the United States, or any agency thereof, or any officer or employee thereof, as such officer or employee, is not a party, the court having jurisdiction of the suit or proceeding shall certify such fact to the Attorney General. In any such case the court shall

---

[1] Mr. Justice Field filed a dissenting opinion.

permit the United States to intervene and become a party for presentation of evidence * * * and argument upon the question of the constitutionality of such Act. * * * " If defendant had applied for and obtained the writ of certiorari upon the claim that, as now held, Congress has no power to prescribe the rule of decision, section 34 as construed, it would have been the duty of this Court to issue the prescribed certificate to the Attorney General in order that the United States might intervene and be heard on the constitutional question. * * * Congress intended to give the United States the right to be heard in every case involving constitutionality of an act affecting the public interest. In view of the rule that, in the absence of challenge of constitutionality, statutes will not here be invalidated on that ground, the Act of August 24, 1937 extends to cases where constitutionality is first "drawn in question" by the Court. * * *

I am of opinion that the constitutional validity of the rule need not be considered, because under the law, as found by the courts of Pennsylvania and generally throughout the country, it is plain that the evidence required a finding that plaintiff was guilty of negligence that contributed to cause his injuries, and that the judgment below should be reversed upon that ground.

Mr. Justice McREYNOLDS concurs in this opinion.

Mr. Justice REED (concurring in part).

I concur in the conclusion reached in this case, in the disapproval of the doctrine of Swift v. Tyson, and in the reasoning of the majority opinion, except in so far as it relies upon the unconstitutionality of the "course pursued" by the federal courts.

The "doctrine of Swift v. Tyson," as I understand it, is that the words "the laws," as used in section 34 of the Federal Judiciary Act of September 24, 1789, do not include in their meaning "the decisions of the local tribunals." * * *

To decide the case now before us and to "disapprove" the doctrine of Swift v. Tyson requires only that we say that the words "the laws" include in their meaning the decisions of the local tribunals. As the majority opinion shows, by its reference to Mr. Warren's researches and the first quotation from Mr. Justice Holmes, that this Court is now of the view that "laws" includes "decisions," it is unnecessary to go further and declare that the "course pursued" was "unconstitutional," instead of merely erroneous.

The "unconstitutional" course referred to in the majority opinion is apparently the ruling in Swift v. Tyson that the supposed omission of Congress to legislate as to the effect of decisions leaves federal courts free to interpret general law for themselves. I am not at all sure whether, in the absence of federal statutory direction, federal courts would be compelled to follow state decisions. There was sufficient doubt about the matter in 1789 to induce the first Congress to legislate. No former opinions of this Court have passed upon it. * * * If the opinion commits this Court to the position that the Congress is without power to declare what rules of substantive law shall govern the federal courts, that conclusion also seems questionable. The line between procedural and substantive law is hazy, but no one doubts federal power over procedure. * * * The Judiciary Article, 3, and the "necessary and proper" clause of article 1, § 8, may fully authorize legislation, such as this section of the Judiciary Act.

* * *

NOTES

1. Reactions to the *Erie* decision voiced shortly after it was handed down include Shulman, *The Demise of Swift v. Tyson*, 47 Yale L.J. 1336 (1938); Tunks, *Categorization and Federalism: "Substance" and "Procedure" after Erie Railroad v. Tompkins*, 34 Ill.L.Rev. 271 (1939). More recent treatments of the subject are found in Clark, *State Law in the Federal Courts: the Brooding Omnipresence of Erie v. Tompkins*, 55 Yale L.J. 267 (1946); Friendly, *In Praise of Erie—And of the New Federal Common Law*, 39 N.Y.U.L.Rev. 383 (1964); Hill, *The Erie Doctrine and the Constitution*, 53 Nw.U.L.Rev. 427, 541 (1958); Kurland, *Mr. Justice Frankfurter, the Supreme Court and the Erie Doctrine in Diversity Cases*, 67 Yale L.J. 187 (1957). Perhaps the strongest attack on the *Erie* doctrine in the literature is found in Keeffe, Gilhooley, Bailey & Day, *Weary Erie*, 34 Cornell L.Q. 494 (1949).

2. To what extent, if any, does the result in *Erie* rest upon a constitutional ground? What provision or provisions in the Constitution must be considered in deciding this question? If the conclusion reached in *Erie* is mandated by the Constitution, does this mean that neither the Congress nor the Supreme Court could alter the result? Of what relevance is the *Erie* decision to the Federal Rules of Civil Procedure? Does the case apply to all diversity actions? What about federal question cases? See, e.g., Commissioner of Internal Revenue v. Bosch, 387 U.S. 456, 87 S.Ct. 1776, 18 L.Ed.2d 886 (1967).

GUARANTY TRUST CO. OF NEW YORK v. YORK

Supreme Court of the United States, 1945.
326 U.S. 99, 65 S.Ct. 1464, 89 L.Ed. 2079.

Certiorari to the Circuit Court of Appeals for the Second Circuit.

Mr. Justice FRANKFURTER delivered the opinion of the Court.

* * *

In May, 1930, Van Sweringen Corporation issued notes to the amount of $30,000,000. Under an indenture of the same date, petitioner, Guaranty Trust Co., was named trustee with power and obligations to enforce the rights of the noteholders in the assets of the Corporation and of the Van Sweringen brothers. In October, 1930, petitioner, with other banks, made large advances to companies affiliated with the Corporation and wholly controlled by the Van

Sweringens. In October, 1931, when it was apparent that the Corporation could not meet its obligations, Guaranty cooperated in a plan for the purchase of the outstanding notes on the basis of cash for 50% of the face value of the notes and twenty shares of Van Sweringen Corporation's stock for each $1,000 note. * * *

Respondent York received $6,000 of the notes as a gift in 1934, her donor not having accepted the offer of exchange. In April, 1940, three accepting noteholders began suit against petitioner, charging fraud and misrepresentation. Respondent's application to intervene in that suit was denied * * * and summary judgment in favor of Guaranty was affirmed. * * * After her dismissal * * * respondent, on January 22, 1942, began the present proceedings.

The suit, instituted as a class action on behalf of non-accepting noteholders and brought in a federal court solely because of diversity of citizenship, is based on an alleged breach of trust by Guaranty in that it failed to protect the interests of the noteholders in assenting to the exchange offer and failed to disclose its self-interest when sponsoring the offer. Petitioner moved for summary judgment, which was granted, upon the authority of the * * * [earlier] case. On appeal, the Circuit Court of Appeals, one Judge dissenting, found that the * * * [prior] decision did not foreclose this suit, and held that in a suit brought on the equity side of a federal district court that court is not required to apply the State statute of limitations that would govern like suits in the courts of a State where the federal court is sitting even though the exclusive basis of federal jurisdiction is diversity of citizenship. * * *

TC
Fed Crt not bound to state law in Equity Suit

In view of the basis of the decision below, it is not for us to consider whether the New York statute would actually bar this suit were it brought in a State court. Our only concern is with the holding that the federal courts in a suit like this are not bound by local law.

Issue

* * *

Our starting point must be the policy of federal jurisdiction which Erie R. Co. v. Tompkins * * * embodies. In overruling Swift v. Tyson * * * Erie R. Co. v. Tompkins did not merely overrule a venerable case. It overruled a particular way of looking at law which dominated the judicial process long after its inadequacies had been laid bare. * * * Law was conceived as a "brooding omnipresence" of Reason, of which decisions were merely evidence and not themselves the controlling formulations. Accordingly, federal courts deemed themselves free to ascertain what Reason, and therefore Law, required wholly independent of authoritatively declared State law, even in cases where a legal right as the basis for relief was created by State authority and could not be created by federal authority and the case got into a federal court merely because it was "between Citizens of different States" under Art. III, § 2 of the Constitution * * *.

In exercising their jurisdiction on the ground of diversity of citizenship, the federal courts, in the long course of their history, have not differentiated in their regard for State law between actions at law and suits in equity. Although § 34 of the Judiciary Act of 1789 * * * directed that the "laws of the several States * * * shall be regarded as rules of decision in trials of common law * * *," this was deemed, consistently for over a hundred years, to be merely declaratory of what would in any event have governed the federal courts and therefore was equally applicable to equity suits. * * * Indeed, it may fairly be said that the federal courts gave greater respect to State-created "substantive rights," Pusey & Jones Co. v. Hanssen, 261 U.S. 491, 498, 43 S.Ct. 454, 456, 67 L.Ed. 763, in equity than they gave them on the law side, because rights at law were usually declared by State courts and as such increasingly flouted by extension of the doctrine of Swift v. Tyson, while rights in equity were frequently defined by legislative enactment and as such known and respected by the federal courts. * * *

Partly because the States in the early days varied greatly in the manner in which equitable relief was afforded and in the extent to which it was available, * * * Congress provided that "the forms and modes of proceeding in suits * * * of equity" would conform to the settled uses of courts of equity. * * * But this enactment gave the federal courts no power that they would not have had in any event when courts were given "cognizance," by the first Judiciary Act, of suits "in equity." From the beginning there has been a good deal of talk in the cases that federal equity is a separate legal system. And so it is, properly understood. The suits in equity of which the federal courts have had "cognizance" ever since 1789 constituted the body of law which had been transplanted to this country from the English Court of Chancery. But this system of equity "derived its doctrines, as well as its powers, from its mode of giving relief." Langdell, Summary of Equity Pleading (1877) xxvii. In giving federal courts "cognizance" of equity suits in cases of diversity jurisdiction, Congress never gave, nor did the federal courts ever claim, the power to deny substantive rights created by State law or to create substantive rights denied by State law.

This does not mean that whatever equitable remedy is available in a State court must be available in a diversity suit in a federal court, or conversely, that a federal court may not afford an equitable remedy not available in a State court. * * * State law cannot define the remedies which a federal court must give simply because a federal court in diversity jurisdiction is available as an alternative tribunal to the State's courts. Contrariwise, a federal court may afford an equitable remedy for a substantive right recognized by a State even though a State court cannot give it. Whatever contradiction or confusion may be produced by a medley of judicial phrases severed from their environment, the body of adjudications concerning equitable relief in diversity cases leaves no doubt that the federal courts enforced State-created substantive rights if the mode of proceeding and remedy were consonant with the traditional body of equitable remedies, practice and procedure, and in so doing they were enforcing rights created by the States and not arising under any inherent or statutory federal law.

* * *

And so this case reduces itself to the narrow question whether, when no recovery could be had in a State court because the action is barred by the statute of limitations, a federal court in equity can take cognizance of the suit because there is diversity of citizenship between the parties. Is the outlawry, according to State law, of a claim created by the States a matter of "substantive rights" to be respected by a federal court of equity when that court's jurisdiction is dependent on the fact that there is a State-created right, or is such statute of "a mere remedial character," * * * which a federal court may disregard?

Matters of "substance" and matters of "procedure" are much talked about in the books as though they defined a great divide cutting across the whole domain of law. But, of course, "substance" and "procedure" are the same keywords to very different problems. Neither "substance" nor "procedure" represents the same invariants. Each implies different variables depending upon the particular problem for which it is used. * * * And the different problems are only distantly related at best, for the terms are in common use in connection with situations turning on such different considerations as those that are relevant to questions pertaining to ex post facto legislation, the impairment of the obligations of contract, the enforcement of federal rights in the State courts and the multitudinous phases of the conflict of laws. * * *

Here we are dealing with a right to recover derived not from the United States but from one of the States. When, because the plaintiff happens to be a non-resident, such a right is enforceable in a federal as well as in a State court, the forms and mode of enforcing the right may at times, naturally enough, vary because the two judicial systems are not identic. But since a federal court adjudicating a state-created right solely because of the diversity of citizenship of the parties is for that purpose, in effect, only another court of the State, it cannot afford recovery if the right to recover is made unavailable by the State nor can it substantially affect the enforcement of the right as given by the State.

And so the question is not whether a statute of limitations is deemed a matter of "procedure" in some sense. The question is whether such a statute concerns merely the manner and the means by which a right to recover, as recognized by the State, is enforced, or whether such statutory limitation is a matter of substance in the aspect that alone is relevant to our problem, namely, does it significantly affect the result of a litigation for a federal court to disregard a law of a State that would be controlling in an action upon the same claim by the same parties in a State court?

It is therefore immaterial whether statutes of limitation are characterized either as "substantive" or "procedural" in State court opinions in any use of those terms unrelated to the specific issue before us. Erie R. Co. v. Tompkins was not an endeavor to formulate scientific legal terminology. It expressed a policy that touches vitally the proper distribution of judicial power between State and federal courts. In essence, the intent of that decision was to insure that, in all cases where a federal court is exercising jurisdiction solely because of the diversity of citizenship of the parties, the outcome of the litigation in the

Fed must = state

shouldn't be different results

federal court should be substantially the same, so far as legal rules determine the outcome of a litigation, as it would be if tried in a State court. The nub of the policy that underlies Erie R. Co. v. Tompkins is that for the same transaction the accident of a suit by a non-resident litigant in a federal court instead of in a State court a block away, should not lead to a substantially different result. * * * A policy so important to our federalism must be kept free from entanglements with analytical or terminological niceties.

Plainly enough, a statute that would completely bar recovery in a suit if brought in a State court bears on a State-created right vitally and not merely formally or negligibly. As to consequences that so intimately affect recovery or non-recovery a federal court in a diversity case should follow State law. * * *

Diversity jurisdiction is founded on assurance to non-resident litigants of courts free from susceptibility to potential local bias. The Framers of the Constitution, according to Marshall, entertained "apprehensions" lest distant suitors be subjected to local bias in State courts, or, at least, viewed with "indulgence the possible fears and apprehensions" of such suitors. Bank of the United States v. Deveaux, 5 Cranch 61, 87, 3 L.Ed. 38. And so Congress afforded out-of-State litigants another tribunal, not another body of law. The operation of a double system of conflicting laws in the same State is plainly hostile to the reign of law. Certainly, the fortuitous circumstance of residence out of a State of one of the parties to a litigation ought not to give rise to a discrimination against others equally concerned but locally resident. The source of substantive rights enforced by a federal court under diversity jurisdiction, it cannot be said too often, is the law of the States. * * *

The judgment is reversed and the case is remanded for proceedings not inconsistent with this opinion.

So ordered.

Reversed.

Mr. Justice ROBERTS and Mr. Justice DOUGLAS took no part in the consideration or decision of this case.

[Mr. Justice RUTLEDGE dissented in an opinion in which Mr. Justice MURPHY joined.]

NOTES AND QUESTIONS

1. Examine the text of Federal Rules of Civil Procedure 4(f), 15(c), and 35(a). Which of them are capable of being outcome-determinative? Are any of the other Rules vulnerable to attack under the *York* philosophy? Are the arguments for the application of the outcome test advanced by Mr. Justice Frankfurter in *York* controlling when the effect will be to prevent the application of a Federal Rule or are there countervailing considerations? If *York* requires the displacement of a Federal Rule in favor of a contrary state practice, is the uniform application of that Rule so seriously compromised that there is no purpose in the federal courts retaining it?

Going beyond the Federal Rules, isn't it true that virtually any aspect of the procedural process, including such things as the condition of court calendars, the quality of the judges, and the selection of juries, has the capacity to be outcome-determinative? If *York* embraces matters such as these, is there any justification for the continuation of federal diversity jurisdiction?

2.   Evaluate the following passage:

The *York* case, of necessity, spelled death to the hope for a complete-ly uniform federal procedure.   When its doctrine is logically applied, each important step in a diversity action must be examined in the light of two systems of law—first, under the Federal Rules, and then under the law of the state in which the federal court sits.   In one state, a particular Rule might not clash with a local law or decision which significantly bears upon the outcome of a litigation.   Under such circumstances, the Rule should prevail, although the determination as to its applicability is actually made under state law.   In another state, the same Rule might conflict in some substantial way with that state's policy or law.   In such instances, state law, and not the Rule, will govern a federal court's deci-sion.

Merrigan, *Erie to York to Ragan—A Triple Play on the Federal Rules,* 3 Vand.L. Rev. 711, 717 (1950).   See also Symposium, *Federal Trials and the Erie Doctrine,* 51 Nw.U.L.Rev. 338 (1956); Note, *Erie R. R. v. Tompkins and the Federal Rules,* 62 Harv.L.Rev. 1030 (1949).

3.   The early application of *York* to the Federal Rules is best exemplified by the holdings in a trio of cases all decided by the Supreme Court on the same day.   In RAGAN v. MERCHANTS' TRANSFER & WAREHOUSE CO., 337 U.S. 530, 69 S.Ct. 1233, 93 L.Ed. 1520 (1949), the Court held that an action in which the complaint had been filed within the applicable state limitations period, thereby commencing the action for purposes of Federal Rule 3, was barred because process had not been served until after the expiration of the limitations period and under Kansas law service of process was necessary to commence an action and thus toll the statute of limitations.   In COHEN v. BENEFICIAL INDUSTRIAL LOAN CORP., 337 U.S. 541, 69 S.Ct. 1221, 93 L.Ed. 1528 (1949), the Court held applicable a New Jersey statute requiring plaintiff in a shareholder deriva-tive suit to post a security-for-expenses bond, although Federal Rule 23.1, which ostensibly governs such cases, does not require a bond.   Both of these cases are discussed in *Hanna v. Plumer,* p. 284, infra.   The third case, WOODS v. INTER-STATE REALTY CO., 337 U.S. 535, 69 S.Ct. 1235, 93 L.Ed. 1524 (1949), held that a Tennessee corporation that had not qualified to do business in Mississippi could not maintain a diversity action in a federal court in that state when the Mis-sissippi state courts were closed to it.   Strong dissents were filed in *Ragan, Cohen,* and *Woods.*

BYRD v. BLUE RIDGE RURAL ELECTRIC
COOPERATIVE, INC.

Supreme Court of the United States, 1958.
356 U.S. 525, 78 S.Ct. 893, 2 L.Ed.2d 953.

Certiorari to the United States Court of Appeals for the Fourth Circuit.

Mr. Justice BRENNAN delivered the opinion of the Court.

This case was brought in the District Court for the Western District of South Carolina. Jurisdiction was based on diversity of citizenship. * * * The petitioner, a resident of North Carolina, sued respondent, a South Carolina corporation, for damages for injuries allegedly caused by the respondent's negligence. He had judgment on a jury verdict. The Court of Appeals for the Fourth Circuit reversed and directed the entry of judgment for the respondent. * * *

The respondent is in the business of selling electric power to subscribers in rural sections of South Carolina. The petitioner was employed as a lineman in the construction crew of a construction contractor. The contractor, R. H. Bouligny, Inc., held a contract with the respondent * * * for the building of some * * * power lines, the reconversion to higher capacities of * * * existing lines, and the construction of 2 new substations and a breaker station. The petitioner was injured while connecting power lines to one of the new substations.

One of respondent's affirmative defenses was that under the South Carolina Workmen's Compensation Act, the petitioner—because the work contracted to be done by his employer was work of the kind also done by the respondent's own construction and maintenance crews—had the status of a statutory employee of the respondent and was therefore barred from suing the respondent at law because obliged to accept statutory compensation benefits as the exclusive remedy for his injuries. Two questions concerning this defense are before us: (1) whether the Court of Appeals erred in directing judgment for respondent without a remand to give petitioner an opportunity to introduce further evidence; and (2) whether petitioner, state practice notwithstanding, is entitled to a jury determination of the factual issues raised by this defense.

* * *

[The Supreme Court initially decided to remand the case to the trial court to provide the petitioner an opportunity to introduce evidence on the question of whether the respondent was a statutory employer.]

A question is also presented as to whether on remand the factual issue is to be decided by the judge or by the jury. The respondent argues on the basis of the decision of the Supreme Court of South Carolina in Adams v. Davison-Paxon Co., 230 S.C. 532, 96 S.E.2d 566, that the issue of immunity should be decided by the judge and not by the jury. That was a negligence action brought in the state trial court against a store owner by an employee of an independent contractor who operated the store's millinery department. The trial judge denied the store owner's motion for a directed verdict made upon the ground that [South Carolina Code, 1952] § 72–111 barred the plaintiff's action. The jury returned a verdict for the plaintiff. The South Carolina Supreme Court reversed, holding that it was for the judge and not the jury to decide on the evidence whether the owner was a statutory employer, and that the store owner had sustained his defense.   *   *   *

The respondent argues that this state-court decision governs the present diversity case and "divests the jury of its normal function" to decide the disputed fact question of the respondent's immunity under § 72–111. This is to contend that the federal court is bound under Erie R. Co. v. Tompkins   *   *   *   to follow the state court's holding to secure uniform enforcement of the immunity created by the State.

First. It was decided in Erie R. Co. v. Tompkins that the federal courts in diversity cases must respect the definition of state-created rights and obligations by the state courts. We must, therefore, first examine the rule in Adams v. Davison-Paxon Co. to determine whether it is bound up with these rights and obligations in such a way that its application in the federal court is required.   *   *   *

The Workmen's Compensation Act is administered in South Carolina by its Industrial Commission. The South Carolina courts hold that, on judicial review of actions of the Commission under § 72–111, the question whether the claim of an injured workman is within the Commission's jurisdiction is a matter of law for decision by the court, which makes its own findings of fact relating to that jurisdiction. The South Carolina Supreme Court states no reasons in Adams v. Davison-Paxon Co. why, although the jury decides all other factual issues raised by the cause of action and defenses, the jury is displaced as to the factual issue raised by the affirmative defense under § 72–111.   *   *   *   A State may, of course, distribute the functions of its judicial machinery as it sees fit. The decisions relied upon, however, furnish no reason for selecting the judge rather than the jury to decide this single affirmative defense in the negligence action. They simply reflect a policy   *   *   *   that administrative determination of "jurisdictional facts" should not be final but subject to judicial review. The conclusion is inescapable that the Adams holding is grounded in the practical consideration that the question had theretofore come before the South Carolina courts from the Industrial Commission and the courts had become accustomed to deciding the factual issue of immunity without the aid of juries. We find nothing to suggest that this rule was announced as an integral part of the special relationship created by the statute. Thus the requirement appears to be merely a form and mode of enforcing the immunity   *   *   *   and not a rule intended to be bound up with the definition of the rights and obligations of the parties.   *   *   *

Second. But cases following Erie have evinced a broader policy to the effect that the federal courts should conform as near as may be—in the absence of other considerations—to state rules even of form and mode where the state rules may bear substantially on the question whether the litigation would come out one way in the federal court and another way in the state court if the federal court failed to apply a particular local rule. E. g., Guaranty Trust Co. of New York v. York, supra; Bernhardt v. Polygraphic Co., 350 U.S. 198, 76 S.Ct. 273, 100 L.Ed. 199. Concededly the nature of the tribunal which tries issues may be important in the enforcement of the parcel of rights making up a cause of action or defense, and bear significantly upon achievement of uniform enforcement of the right. It may well be that in the instant personal-injury case the outcome would be substantially affected by whether the issue of immunity is decided by a judge or a jury. Therefore, were "outcome" the only consideration, a strong case might appear for saying that the federal court should follow the state practice.

But there are affirmative countervailing considerations at work here. The federal system is an independent system for administering justice to litigants who properly invoke its jurisdiction. An essential characteristic of that system is the manner in which, in civil common-law actions, it distributes trial functions between judge and jury and, under the influence—if not the command—of the Seventh Amendment, assigns the decisions of disputed questions of fact to the jury. * * * The policy of uniform enforcement of state-created rights and obligations * * * cannot in every case exact compliance with a state rule—not bound up with rights and obligations—which disrupts the federal system of allocating functions between judge and jury. * * * Thus the inquiry here is whether the federal policy favoring jury decisions of disputed fact questions should yield to the state rule in the interest of furthering the objective that the litigation should not come out one way in the federal court and another way in the state court.

We think that in the circumstances of this case the federal court should not follow the state rule. It cannot be gainsaid that there is a strong federal policy against allowing state rules to disrupt the judge-jury relationship in the federal courts. In Herron v. Southern Pacific Co., [283 U.S. 91, 51 S.Ct. 383, 75 L.Ed. 857 (1931)] * * * the trial judge in a personal-injury negligence action brought in the District Court for Arizona on diversity grounds directed a verdict for the defendant when it appeared as a matter of law that the plaintiff was guilty of contributory negligence. The federal judge refused to be bound by a provision of the Arizona Constitution which made the jury the sole arbiter of the question of contributory negligence. This Court sustained the action of the trial judge, holding that "state laws cannot alter the essential character or function of a federal court" because that function is not in any sense a local matter, and state statutes which would interfere with the appropriate performance of that function are not binding upon the federal court under either the Conformity Act or the 'Rules of Decision' Act." Id., 283 U.S. at page 94, 51 S.Ct. at page 384. Perhaps even more clearly in light of the influence of the Seventh Amendment, the function assigned to the jury "is an essential factor in the process for which the Federal Constitution provides." Id., 283 U.S. at page 95, 51 S.Ct. at page 384. Concededly the Herron case was decided before Erie R. Co. v. Tompkins, but even when Swift v. Tyson * * * was governing law and allowed federal courts sitting in diversity cases to disregard state decisional law, it was never thought that state statutes or constitutions were similarly to be disregarded.   *   *   *   Yet Herron held that state statutes and constitutional provisions could not disrupt or alter the essential character or function of a federal court.[14]

Third. We have discussed the problem upon the assumption that the outcome of the litigation may be substantially affected by whether the issue of immunity is decided by a judge or a jury. But clearly there is not present here the certainty that a different result would follow   *   *   *   or even the strong possibility that this would be the case   *   *   *. There are factors present here which might reduce that possibility. The trial judge in the federal system has powers denied the judges of many States to comment on the weight of evidence and credibility of witnesses, and discretion to grant a new trial if the verdict appears to him to be against the weight of the evidence. We do not think the likelihood of a different result is so strong as to require the federal practice of jury determination of disputed factual issues to yield to the state rule in the interest of uniformity of outcome.[15]

The Court of Appeals did not consider other grounds of appeal raised by the respondent because the ground taken disposed of the case. We accordingly remand the case to the Court of Appeals for the decision of the other questions, with instructions that, if not made unnecessary by the decision of such questions, the Court of Appeals shall remand the case to the District Court for a new trial of such issues as the Court of Appeals may direct.

Reversed and remanded.

*   *   *

[Mr. Justice WHITTAKER concurred in Part I of the Court's opinion but dissented from Part II on the ground that the South Carolina rule requiring "its courts—not juries—to determine whether jurisdiction over the subject matter of cases like this is vested in its Industrial Commission" should be honored by a federal court. Mr. Justice FRANKFURTER and Mr. Justice HARLAN dissented on the ground that the evidence required the District Court to direct a verdict for the respondent.]

NOTES AND QUESTIONS

1. Does the *Byrd* decision have any application to matters other than the distribution of functions between judge and jury in the federal courts? Are there any other aspects of "an independent system for administering justice" that re-

[14] Diederich v. American News Co., 10 Cir., 128 F.2d 144, decided after Erie R. Co. v. Tompkins, held that an almost identical provision of the Oklahoma Constitution, art. 23, § 6, O.S.1951 was not binding on a federal judge in a diversity case.

[15] Stoner v. New York Life Ins. Co., 311 U.S. 464, 61 S.Ct. 336, 85 L.Ed. 284, is not contrary. It was there held that the federal court should follow the state rule defining the evidence sufficient to raise a jury question whether the state-created right was established. But the state rule did not have the effect of nullifying the function of the federal judge to control a jury submission as did the Arizona constitutional provision which was denied effect in Herron. The South Carolina rule here involved affects the jury function as the Arizona provision affected the function of the judge: The rule entirely displaces the jury without regard to the sufficiency of the evidence to support a jury finding of immunity.

quire the application of federal standards in a diversity action despite the possibility of the type of difference in outcome deplored in the *York* case? See generally Hill, *The Erie Doctrine and the Constitution*, 53 Nw.U.L.Rev. 427, 541 (1958); Meador, *State Law and the Federal Judicial Power*, 49 Va.L.Rev. 1082 (1963); Smith, *Blue Ridge and Beyond: A Byrd's-Eye View of Federalism in Diversity Litigation*, 36 Tul.L.Rev. 443 (1962); Vestal, *Erie R. R. v. Tompkins: A Projection*, 48 Iowa L.Rev. 248 (1963); Comment, *The Constitutional Power of Congress to Control Procedure in the Federal Courts*, 56 Nw.U.L.Rev. 560 (1961); Note, *Of Lawyers and Laymen: A Study of Federalism, the Judicial Process, and Erie*, 71 Yale L.J. 344 (1961).

A number of circuit courts have attempted to balance state and federal interests in the fashion suggested by *Byrd* in areas outside the judge-jury relationship. E. g., Monarch Ins. Co. v. Spach, 281 F.2d 401 (5th Cir.1960) (a prior inconsistent statement held admissible despite a Florida statute requiring its exclusion on the theory that Federal Rule 43(a) reflected a federal policy); Iovino v. Waterson, 274 F.2d 41 (2d Cir.1959), certiorari denied 362 U.S. 949, 80 S.Ct. 860, 4 L.Ed.2d 867 (1960) (substitution of a nonresident administrator permitted under Federal Rule of Civil Procedure 25(a), although New York would not have permitted it). See also Hope v. Hearst Consol. Publications, Inc., 294 F.2d 681 (2d Cir.1961), certiorari denied 368 U.S. 956, 82 S.Ct. 399, 7 L.Ed.2d 388 (1962). Compare Allstate Ins. Co. v. Charneski, 286 F.2d 238 (7th Cir.1960) (action for judgment declaring insurance company's nonliability dismissed because of state's public policy against such actions and in favor of joining the insurance company in the action by the injured party).

How does a federal court identify and then weigh the competing state and federal policies? What sources are available to it in pursuing this inquiry? In ALLSTATE INS. CO. v. CHARNESKI, referred to in the preceding paragraph, the Seventh Circuit, after reviewing the major *Erie*-doctrine cases and concluding that a Wisconsin court would dismiss the declaratory judgment action before it, employed the following reasoning:

> First, as to the State of Wisconsin. This is not a case where a federal declaratory judgment action is filed in a state which has no statute providing for such relief. Wisconsin has passed a general statute providing declaratory relief. However, this statute was held not applicable * * * [by the Wisconsin Supreme Court] because it conflicted with the Wisconsin state policy of providing direct actions against insurance companies. This is a declaration of the *substantive* law of Wisconsin. The Wisconsin Supreme Court held that to allow declaratory relief in such circumstances would undercut its policy of direct actions against an insurance company and thereby concluding the action—defining the rights of the insurer, the insured, and the injured party—in a single suit. This holding represents a legitimate and proper implementation of Wisconsin policy. * * *

> The federal interest to be served here is slight. There is the general interest of a court controlling its own procedure. There is the general policy evidenced by the federal Declaratory Judgments Act. However, no right to jury trial, guaranteed by the Seventh Amendment, is involved here, as in Byrd. The cause of action arising from the accident, the issue

of coverage of the policy, and the rights of the insured, the insurer and the injured parties are intimately connected with Wisconsin law and have no connection with the federal government except that the latter provides a fair and orderly forum in which to try the diversity case. Finally, relief under the Federal act is expressly discretionary. Such relief is permissive and not absolute. Declaratory relief "may" be granted, and need not be when it would create an unnecessary federal-state conflict.

286 F.2d at 244. Is the court's analysis of the Wisconsin and federal policies adequate? Is it persuasive?

2.   In BERNHARDT v. POLYGRAPHIC CO. OF AMERICA, INC., 350 U.S. 198, 203, 76 S.Ct. 273, 276, 100 L.Ed. 199, 205 (1956), plaintiff brought an action in a Vermont state court for damages resulting from his discharge by defendant. Defendant removed the action to a federal district court and moved for a stay pending arbitration in New York pursuant to the contract. The district court denied the stay, ruling that under *Erie* the arbitration provision was governed by Vermont law, which permitted revocation of an agreement to arbitrate any time before an award was made. The Second Circuit reversed on the ground that arbitration merely relates to the form of the trial. The Supreme Court disagreed and reversed and remanded stating:

> * * * If the federal court allows arbitration where the state court would disallow it, the outcome of litigation might depend on the courthouse where suit is brought. For the remedy by arbitration, whatever its merits or shortcomings, substantially affects the cause of action created by the State. The nature of the tribunal where suits are tried is an important part of the parcel of rights behind a cause of action. The change from a court of law to an arbitration panel may make a radical difference in ultimate result. Arbitration carries no right to trial by jury that is guaranteed both by the Seventh Amendment and by Ch. 1, Art. 12th, of the Vermont Constitution. Arbitrators do not have the benefit of judicial instruction on the law; they need not give their reasons for their results; the record of their proceedings is not as complete as it is in a court trial; and judicial review of an award is more limited than judicial review of a trial * * *.

Are *Bernhardt* and *Byrd* consistent or has the latter impliedly overruled the former?

3.   Between 1960 and 1965, one of the most debated subjects in procedural circles was whether a federal court in a diversity action should employ a federal or state standard to determine the existence or nonexistence of in personam jurisdiction over a foreign corporation. By and large the post-*Byrd* cases appear to have opted for the state standard. E. g., Arrowsmith v. United Press Int'l, 320 F.2d 219 (2d Cir.1963) (en banc), apparently overruling a contrary two-to-one decision in Jaftex Corp. v. Randolph Mills, Inc., 282 F.2d 508 (2d Cir.1960). See also Jennings v. McCall Corp., 320 F.2d 64 (8th Cir.1963); Smartt v. Coca Cola Bottling Corp., 318 F.2d 447 (6th Cir.1963).

If *Erie* is constitutionally based, does Congress or do the federal courts have the power to establish jurisdictional standards for diversity actions? Putting the question another way, are jurisdictional rules substantive or procedural within the meaning of *Erie* and *York* or don't they fall entirely within either category? Would a federal test for personal jurisdiction promote or discourage forum-shopping?

Assuming federal power, have either Congress or the federal courts established a clear test for amenability to suit in a federal court? Is the standard in *International Shoe Co. v. Washington,* p. 82, supra, relevant? What about Federal Rule of Civil Procedure 4 or 28 U.S.C. §§ 1391, 1693? A lengthy dialogue on these questions is offered by the late Judge Clark and Judge Friendly in the *Jaftex* and *Arrowsmith* cases. See also 4 Wright & Miller, *Federal Practice and Procedure: Civil* § 1075 (1969).

4. If, as suggested by the Court in *Byrd,* the Seventh Amendment requires a federal court to honor the jury-trial guarantee in diversity cases, why is the *Guaranty Trust* case even relevant to the problem in *Byrd?* Would you articulate the "outcome-determinative" test any differently after *Byrd?*

Read 28 U.S.C. § 2072 (Rules Enabling Act) in the Supplement.

HANNA v. PLUMER

Supreme Court of the United States, 1965.
380 U.S. 460, 85 S.Ct. 1136, 14 L.Ed.2d 8.

Certiorari to the United States Court of Appeals for the First Circuit.

Mr. Chief Justice WARREN delivered the opinion of the Court.

The question to be decided is whether, in a civil action where the jurisdiction of the United States District Court is based upon diversity of citizenship between the parties, service of process shall be made in the manner prescribed by state law or that set forth in Rule 4(d)(1) of the Federal Rules of Civil Procedure.

On February 6, 1963, petitioner, a citizen of Ohio, filed her complaint in the District Court for the District of Massachusetts, claiming damages in excess of $10,000 for personal injuries resulting from an automobile accident in South Carolina, allegedly caused by the negligence of one Louise Plumer Osgood, a Massachusetts citizen deceased at the time of the filing of the complaint. Respondent, Mrs. Osgood's executor and also a Massachusetts citizen, was named as defendant. On February 8, service was made by leaving copies of the summons and the complaint with respondent's wife at his residence, concededly in compliance with Rule 4(d) (1) * * *. Respondent filed his answer on February 26, alleging, *inter alia,* that the action could not be maintained because it had been brought "contrary to and in violation of the provisions of Massachusetts General Laws (Ter.Ed.) Chapter 197, Section 9." That section provides:

> "Except as provided in this chapter, an executor or administrator shall not be held to answer to an action by a creditor of the deceased which is not commenced within one year from the time of his giving bond for the performance of his trust, or to such an ac-

tion which is commenced within said year unless before the expiration thereof the writ in such action has been served by delivery in hand upon such executor or administrator or service thereof accepted by him or a notice stating the name of the estate, the name and address of the creditor, the amount of the claim and the court in which the action has been brought has been filed in the proper registry of probate. * * * "

On October 17, 1963, the District Court granted respondent's motion for summary judgment, citing Ragan v. Merchants Transfer & Warehouse Co. * * * and Guaranty Trust Co. of New York v. York * * * in support of its conclusion that the adequacy of the service was to be measured by § 9, with which, the court held, petitioner had not complied. On appeal, petitioner * * * argued that Rule 4(d) (1) defines the method by which service of process is to be effected in diversity actions. The Court of Appeals for the First Circuit, finding that "[r]elatively recent amendments [to § 9] evince a clear legislative purpose to require personal notification within the year," [1] concluded that the conflict of state and federal rules was over "a substantive rather than a procedural matter," and unanimously affirmed. * * *

We conclude that the adoption of Rule 4(d) (1), designed to control service of process in diversity actions, neither exceeded the congressional mandate embodied in the Rules Enabling Act nor transgressed constitutional bounds, and that the Rule is therefore the standard against which the District Court should have measured the adequacy of the service. Accordingly, we reverse the decision of the Court of Appeals.

Fed rule is standard

* * * Under the cases construing the scope of the Enabling Act, Rule 4(d) (1) clearly passes muster. Prescribing the manner in which a defendant is to be notified that a suit has been instituted against him, it relates to the "practice and procedure of the district courts." * * *

"The test must be whether a rule really regulates procedure,—the judicial process for enforcing rights and duties recognized by substantive law and for justly administering remedy and redress for

---

[1] Section 9 is in part a statute of limitations, providing that an executor need not "answer to an action * * * which is not commenced within one year from the time of his giving bond * * *." This part of the statute, the purpose of which is to speed the settlement of estates, * * * is not involved in this case, since the action clearly was timely commenced. (Respondent filed bond on March 1, 1962; the complaint was filed February 6, 1963; and the service—the propriety of which is in dispute—was made on February 8, 1963.) * * *.

Section 9 also provides for the manner of service. Generally, service of process must be made by "delivery in hand." * * * The purpose of this part of the statute, which *is* involved here, is, as the court below noted, to insure that executors will receive actual notice of claims. * * * Actual notice is of course also the goal of Rule 4(d) (1); however, the Federal Rule reflects a determination that this goal can be achieved by a method less cumbersome than that prescribed in § 9. In this case the goal seems to have been achieved; although the affidavit filed by respondent in the District Court asserts that he had neither been served in hand nor accepted service, it does not allege lack of actual notice.

disregard or infraction of them." Sibbach v. Wilson & Co., 312 U.S. 1, 14, 61 S.Ct. 422, 426, 85 L.Ed. 479.

In Mississippi Pub. Corp. v. Murphree, 326 U.S. 438, 66 S.Ct. 242, 90 L.Ed. 185, this Court upheld Rule 4(f), which permits service of a summons anywhere within the State (and not merely the district) in which a district court sits:

> "We think that Rule 4(f) is in harmony with the Enabling Act * * *. Undoubtedly most alterations of the rules of practice and procedure may and often do affect the rights of litigants. Congress' prohibition of any alteration of substantive rights of litigants was obviously not addressed to such incidental effects as necessarily attend the adoption of the prescribed new rules of procedure upon the rights of litigants who, agreeably to rules of practice and procedure, have been brought before a court authorized to determine their rights. * * * The fact that the application of Rule 4(f) will operate to subject petitioner's rights to adjudication by the district court for northern Mississippi will undoubtedly affect those rights. But it does not operate to abridge, enlarge or modify the rules of decision by which that court will adjudicate its rights." Id., at 445–446, 66 S.Ct. at 246.

Thus were there no conflicting state procedure, Rule 4(d) (1) would clearly control. National Equipment Rental, Limited v. Szukhent * * * [p. 133, supra]. However, respondent, focusing on the contrary Massachusetts rule, calls to the Court's attention another line of cases, a line which—like the Enabling Act—had its birth in 1938. Erie R. Co. v. Tompkins, * * * overruling Swift v. Tyson, * * * held that federal courts sitting in diversity cases, when deciding questions of "substantive" law, are bound by state court decisions as well as state statutes. The broad command of Erie was therefore identical to that of the Enabling Act: federal courts are to apply state substantive law and federal procedural law. However, as subsequent cases sharpened the distinction between substance and procedure, the line of cases following Erie diverged markedly from the line construing the Enabling Act. * * *

Respondent, by placing primary reliance on York and Ragan, suggests that the Erie doctrine acts as a check on the Federal Rules of Civil Procedure, that despite the clear command of Rule 4(d) (1), Erie and its progeny demand the application of the Massachusetts rule. Reduced to essentials, the argument is: (1) Erie, as refined in York, demands that federal courts apply state law whenever application of federal law in its stead will alter the outcome of the case. (2) In this case, a determination that the Massachusetts service requirements obtain will result in immediate victory for respondent. If, on the other hand, it should be held that Rule 4(d) (1) is applicable, the litigation will continue, with possible victory for petitioner. (3) Therefore, Erie demands application of the Massachusetts rule. The syllogism possesses an appealing simplicity, but is for several reasons invalid.

In the first place, it is doubtful that, even if there were no Federal Rule making it clear that in hand service is not required in diversity actions, the Erie rule would have obligated the District Court to follow the Massachusetts procedure. "Outcome determination" analysis was never intended to serve as a talisman. Byrd v. Blue Ridge Rural Elec. Cooperative * * *. Indeed, the message of York itself is that choices between state and federal law are to be made not by application of any automatic, "litmus paper" criterion, but rather by reference to the policies underlying the Erie rule. Guaranty Trust Co. of New York v. York * * *.

The Erie rule is rooted in part in a realization that it would be unfair for the character or result of a litigation materially to differ because the suit had been brought in a federal court. * * * The decision was also in part a reaction to the practice of "forum-shopping" which had grown up in response to the rule of Swift v. Tyson. * * * That the York test was an attempt to effectuate these policies is demonstrated by the fact that the opinion framed the inquiry in terms of "substantial" variations between state and federal litigation. * * * Not only are nonsubstantial, or trivial, variations not likely to raise the sort of equal protection problems which troubled the Court in Erie; they are also unlikely to influence the choice of a forum. The "outcome-determination" test therefore cannot be read without reference to the twin aims of the Erie rule: discouragement of forum-shopping and avoidance of inequitable administration of the laws.[9]

The difference between the conclusion that the Massachusetts rule is applicable, and the conclusion that it is not, is of course at this point "outcome-determinative" in the sense that if we hold the state rule to apply, respondent prevails, whereas if we hold that Rule 4(d) (1) governs, the litigation will continue. But in this sense *every* procedural variation is "outcome-determinative." For example, having brought suit in a federal court, a plaintiff cannot then insist on the right to file subsequent pleadings in accord with the time limits applicable in state courts, even though enforcement of the federal timetable will, if he continues to insist that he must meet only the state time limit, result in determination of the controversy against him. So it is here. Though choice of the federal or state rule will at this point have a marked ef-

[marginal handwritten note: 2 fears from Erie 1) forum-shopping 2) inequitable adm. of the laws]

[9] The Court of Appeals seemed to frame the inquiry in terms of how "important" Section 9 is to the State. In support of its suggestion that Section 9 serves some interest the State regards as vital to its citizens, the court noted that something like Section 9 has been on the books in Massachusetts a long time, that Section 9 has been amended a number of times, and that Section 9 is designed to make sure that executors receive actual notice. * * * The apparent lack of relation among these three observations is not surprising, because it is not clear to what sort of question the Court of Appeals was addressing itself. One cannot meaningfully ask how important something is without first asking "important for what purpose?" Erie and its progeny make clear that when a federal court sitting in a diversity case is faced with a question of whether or not to apply state law, the importance of a state rule is indeed relevant, but only in the context of asking whether application of the rule would make so important a difference to the character or result of the litigation that failure to enforce it would unfairly discriminate against citizens of the forum State, or whether application of the rule would have so important an effect upon the fortunes of one or both of the litigants that failure to enforce it would be likely to cause a plaintiff to choose the federal court.

fect upon the outcome of the litigation, the difference between the two rules would be of scant, if any, relevance to the choice of a forum. Petitioner, in choosing her forum, was not presented with a situation where application of the state rule would wholly bar recovery; [10] rather, adherence to the state rule would have resulted only in altering the way in which process was served.[11] Moreover, it is difficult to argue that permitting service of defendant's wife to take the place of in hand service of defendant himself alters the mode of enforcement of state-created rights in a fashion sufficiently "substantial" to raise the sort of equal protection problems to which the Erie opinion alluded.

There is, however, a more fundamental flaw in respondent's syllogism: the incorrect assumption that the rule of Erie R. Co. v. Tompkins constitutes the appropriate test of the validity and therefore the applicability of a Federal Rule of Civil Procedure. The Erie rule has never been invoked to void a Federal Rule. It is true that there have been cases where this Court has held applicable a state rule in the face of an argument that the situation was governed by one of the Federal Rules. But the holding of each such case was not that Erie commanded displacement of a Federal Rule by an inconsistent state rule, but rather that the scope of the Federal Rule was not as broad as the losing party urged, and therefore, there being no Federal Rule which covered the point in dispute, Erie commanded the enforcement of state law. * * * (Here, of course, the clash is unavoidable; Rule 4(d) (1) says—implicitly, but with unmistakable clarity—that in hand service is not required in federal courts.) At the same time, in cases adjudicating the validity of Federal Rules, we have not applied the York rule or other refinements of Erie, but have to this day continued to decide questions concerning the scope of the Enabling Act and the constitutionality of specific Federal Rules in light of the distinction set forth in Sibbach. * * *

Nor has the development of two separate lines of cases been inadvertent. The line between "substance" and "procedure" shifts as the legal context changes. * * * It is true that both the Enabling Act and the Erie rule say, roughly, that federal courts are to apply state "substantive" law and federal "procedural" law, but from that it need not follow that the tests are identical. For they were designed to control very different sorts of decisions. When a situation is covered by one of the Federal Rules, the question facing the court is a far cry from the typical, relatively unguided Erie choice: the court has been instructed to apply the Federal Rule, and can refuse to do so only if the Advisory Committee, this Court, and Congress erred in their prima facie judgment that the Rule in question transgresses neither the terms of the Enabling Act nor constitutional restrictions.

10 * * *
Similarly, a federal court's refusal to enforce the New Jersey rule involved in Cohen v. Beneficial Indus. Loan Corp. * * * might well impel a stockholder to choose to bring suit in the federal, rather than the state, court.

11 * * * We cannot seriously entertain the thought that one suing an estate would be led to choose the federal court because of a belief that adherence to Rule 4(d) (1) is less likely to give the executor actual notice than Section 9, and therefore more likely to produce a default judgment. Rule 4(d) (1) is well designed to give actual notice, as it did in this case. * * *

We are reminded by the Erie opinion that neither Congress nor the federal courts can, under the guise of formulating rules of decision for federal courts, fashion rules which are not supported by a grant of federal authority contained in Article I or some other section of the Constitution; in such areas state law must govern because there can be no other law. But the opinion in Erie, which involved no Federal Rule and dealt with a question which was "substantive" in every traditional sense   *   *   *, surely neither said nor implied that measures like Rule 4(d) (1) are unconstitutional. For the constitutional provision for a federal court system (augmented by the Necessary and Proper Clause) carries with it congressional power to make rules governing the practice and pleading in those courts, which in turn includes a power to regulate matters which, though falling within the uncertain area between substance and procedure, are rationally capable of classification as either. *   *   *   Neither York nor the cases following it ever suggested that the rule there laid down for coping with situations where no Federal Rule applies is coextensive with the limitation on Congress to which Erie had adverted. Although this Court has never before been confronted with a case where the applicable Federal Rule is in direct collision with the law of the relevant State, courts of appeals faced with such clashes have rightly discerned the implications of our decisions.

> "One of the shaping purposes of the Federal Rules is to bring about uniformity in the federal courts by getting away from local rules. This is especially true of matters which relate to the administration of legal proceedings, an area in which federal courts have traditionally exerted strong inherent power, completely aside from the powers Congress expressly conferred in the Rules. The purpose of the Erie doctrine, even as extended in York and Ragan, was never to bottle up federal courts with 'outcome-determinative' and 'integral-relations' stoppers—when there are 'affirmative countervailing [federal] considerations' and when there is a Congressional mandate (the Rules) supported by constitutional authority." Lumbermen's Mutual Casualty Co. v. Wright, 322 F.2d 759, 764 (C.A. 5th Cir. 1963).[16]

Erie and its offspring cast no doubt on the long-recognized power of Congress to prescribe housekeeping rules for federal courts even though some of those rules will inevitably differ from comparable state rules. *   *   *   Thus, though a court, in measuring a Federal Rule against the standards contained in the Enabling Act and the Constitution, need not wholly blind itself to the degree to which the Rule makes the character and result of the federal litigation stray from the course it would follow in state courts,   *   *   *   it cannot be forgotten that the Erie rule, and the guidelines suggested in York, were created to serve another purpose altogether. To hold that a Federal Rule of Civil Procedure must cease to function whenever it alters the mode of enforcing state-created rights would be to disembowel either the

---

[16] To the same effect, see D'Onofrio Construction Co. v. Recon Co., 255 F.2d 904, 909–910 (C.A.1st Cir. 1958).

Constitution's grant of power over federal procedure or Congress' attempt to exercise that power in the Enabling Act. Rule 4(d) (1) is valid and controls the instant case.

Reversed.

Mr. Justice BLACK concurs in the result.

Mr. Justice HARLAN, concurring.

It is unquestionably true that up to now Erie and the cases following it have not succeeded in articulating a workable doctrine governing choice of law in diversity actions. I respect the Court's effort to clarify the situation in to-day's opinion. However, in doing so I think it has misconceived the constitutional premises of Erie and has failed to deal adequately with those past decisions upon which the courts below relied.

Erie was something more than an opinion which worried about "forum-shopping and avoidance of inequitable administration of the laws," * * * although to be sure these were important elements of the decision. I have always regarded that decision as one of the modern cornerstones of our federalism, expressing policies that profoundly touch the allocation of judicial power between the state and federal systems. Erie recognized that there should not be two conflicting systems of law controlling the primary activity of citizens, for such alternative governing authority must necessarily give rise to a debilitating uncertainty in the planning of everyday affairs. And it recognized that the scheme of our Constitution envisions an allocation of law-making functions between state and federal legislative processes which is undercut if the federal judiciary can make substantive law affecting state affairs beyond the bounds of congressional legislative powers in this regard. * * *

The short-hand formulations which have appeared in some past decisions are prone to carry untoward results that frequently arise from oversimplification. The Court is quite right in stating that the "outcome determinative" test of Guaranty Trust Co. of New York v. York * * * if taken literally, proves too much, for any rule, no matter how clearly "procedural," can affect the outcome of litigation if it is not obeyed. In turning from the "outcome" test of Guaranty back to the unadorned forum-shopping rationale of Erie, however, the Court falls prey to like oversimplification, for a simple forum-shopping rule also proves too much; litigants often choose a federal forum merely to obtain what they consider the advantages of the Federal Rules of Civil Procedure or to try their cases before a supposedly more favorable judge. To my mind the proper line of approach in determining whether to apply a state or a federal rule, whether "substantive" or "procedural," is to stay close to basic principles by inquiring if the choice of rule would substantially affect those primary decisions respecting human conduct which our constitutional system leaves to state regulation. If so, Erie and the Constitution require that the state rule prevail, even in the face of a conflicting federal rule.

The Court weakens, if indeed it does not submerge, this basic principle by finding, in effect, a grant of substantive legislative power in the constitutional provision for a federal court system * * *, and through it, setting up the Federal Rules as a body of law inviolate. * * * So long as a reasonable man could characterize any duly adopted federal rule as "procedural," the Court, unless I misapprehend what is said, would have it apply no matter how seriously it frustrated a State's substantive regulation of the primary conduct and affairs of its citizens.   Since the members of the Advisory Committee, the Judicial Conference, and this Court who formulated the Federal Rules are presumably reasonable men, it follows that the integrity of the Federal Rules is absolute.   Whereas the unadulterated outcome and forum-shopping tests may err too far towards honoring state rules, I submit that the Court's "arguably procedural, *ergo* constitutional" test moves too fast and far in the other direction.

The courts below relied upon this Court's decisions in Ragan v. Merchants Transfer & Warehouse Co. * * * and Cohen v. Beneficial Indus. Loan Corp. * * *. Those cases deserve more attention than this Court has given them, particularly Ragan which, if still good law, would in my opinion call for affirmance of the result reached by the Court of Appeals. * * *

In Ragan * * * the Court held that for purposes of the Kansas statute of limitations a diversity tort action commenced only when service was made upon the defendant. * * * I think that the decision was wrong. At most, application of the Federal Rule would have meant that potential Kansas tort defendants would have to defer for a few days the satisfaction of knowing that they had not been sued within the limitations period.   The choice of the Federal Rule would have had no effect on the primary stages of private activity from which torts arise, and only the most minimal effect on behavior following the commission of the tort.   In such circumstances the interest of the federal system in proceeding under its own rules should have prevailed.

Cohen * * * held that a federal diversity court must apply a state statute requiring a small stockholder in a stockholder derivative suit to post a bond securing payment of defense costs as a condition to prosecuting an action. Such a statute is not "outcome determinative"; the plaintiff can win with or without it.   The Court now rationalizes the case on the ground that the statute might affect the plaintiff's choice of forum * * * but as has been pointed out, a simple forum-shopping test proves too much.   The proper view of Cohen is in my opinion, that the statute was meant to inhibit small stockholders from instituting "strike suits," and thus it was designed and could be expected to have a substantial impact on private primary activity.   Anyone who was at the trial bar during the period when Cohen arose can appreciate the strong state policy reflected in the statute.   I think it wholly legitimate to view Federal Rule 23 as not purporting to deal with the problem.   But even had the Federal Rules purported to do so, and in so doing provided a substantially less effective deterrent to strike suits, I think the state rule should still have prevailed. * * *

It remains to apply what has been said to the present case. * * * The evident intent of * * * [the Massachusetts] statute is to permit an executor to distribute the estate which he is administering without fear that further liabilities may be outstanding for which he could be held personally liable. If the Federal District Court in Massachusetts applies Rule 4(d) (1) of the Federal Rules of Civil Procedure instead of the Massachusetts service rule, what effect would that have on the speed and assurance with which estates are distributed? As I see it, the effect would not be substantial. It would mean simply that an executor would have to check at his own house or the federal courthouse as well as the registry of probate before he could distribute the estate with impunity. As this does not seem enough to give rise to any real impingement on the vitality of the state policy which the Massachusetts rule is intended to serve, I concur in the judgment of the Court.

NOTES AND QUESTIONS

1. Does the *Hanna* decision require the conclusion that district courts should apply a uniform federal test for determining personal jurisdiction in all diversity cases? See Note 3 on p. 283, supra. Reread *National Equipment Rental, Ltd. v. Szukhent,* p. 168, supra. Reconsider the question on p. 186, supra, whether a federal court exercising quasi in rem jurisdiction under Rule 4(e) should permit a limited appearance or follow state practice. What should the answer be in a diversity case? See U. S. Industries, Inc. v. Gregg, 58 F.R.D. 469 (D.Del.1973).

2. Does the majority opinion in *Hanna* actually hold, as Mr. Justice Harlan's concurrence suggests, that a state's "substantive regulation of the primary conduct and affairs of its citizens" may be "frustrated" by "any duly adopted federal rule"? Does the Enabling Act provide any restraining influence in this context? To what extent does *Hanna* revive *Swift v. Tyson?* See Stason, *Choice of Law Within the Federal System: Erie Versus Hanna,* 52 Cornell L.Q. 377 (1967). *Hanna* is subjected to a careful analysis in McCoid, *Hanna v. Plumer: The Erie Doctrine Changes Shape,* 51 Va.L.Rev. 884 (1965). Do you think that *Hanna* creates too extensive an exception to the "outcome-determinative" test? In thinking about that question consider whether any of the cases cited in Note 3 on p. 277, supra, would be decided differently after *Hanna?* See generally Ely, *The Irrepressible Myth of Erie,* 87 Harv.L.Rev. 693 (1974).

3. What is the effect of *Hanna* on state statutes that close the doors of the state courts to suits by foreign corporations that have not registered to do business in the state? Can the diversity clause in Article III of the Constitution be said to exude a federal policy that there be a forum in every state for the protection of foreign corporations? Does anything turn on the nature of the policies underlying the state statute? See Szantay v. Beech Aircraft Corp., 349 F.2d 60 (4th Cir. 1965). Compare the earlier decisions in Angel v. Bullington, 330 U.S. 183, 67 S.Ct. 657, 91 L.Ed. 832 (1947), and *Woods v. Interstate Realty Co.,* p. 277, supra.

4. Given *Hanna,* in what situations might a federal court employ a *Byrd*-analysis? Does anything remain of the "outcome-determinative test"? Consider the following case. Plaintiff, a resident of Virginia, was injured in Virginia by a machine manufactured by a Kentucky corporation. Because Virginia had no long-arm statute at the time, the plaintiff brought suit in a federal court in Kentucky within Virginia's two-year statute of limitations but after Kentucky's one-year period had expired, relying on some precedent indicating that the Vir-

ginia limitations period applied because that was the state where the cause of action arose. This reliance proved misplaced when the Court of Appeals of Kentucky, in another case, suddenly announced that the Kentucky statute of limitations applied in cases of this type. The Kentucky federal court, feeling bound by this new rule, thereupon dismissed the action and an appeal to the Sixth Circuit was unsuccessful. In the meantime Virginia had enacted a long-arm statute. Plaintiff then commenced an action in a federal court in that state. However, the Virginia statute of limitations had run while the Kentucky federal suit was pending. Defendant moved to dismiss on the ground that the action would be time barred in a Virginia state court and therefore should be time barred in a Virginia federal court, relying on *Guaranty Trust*. Plaintiff argued that because the federal court system is a unitary one, the Virginia statute of limitations had been tolled by the pendency of the Kentucky federal court suit. What result? ATKINS v. SCHMUTZ MFG. CO., 435 F.2d 527 (4th Cir.1970), certiorari denied 402 U.S. 932, 91 S.Ct. 1526, 28 L.Ed.2d 867 (1971).

SECTION B.   THE PROBLEM OF ASCERTAINING STATE LAW

MASON v. AMERICAN EMERY WHEEL WORKS

United States Court of Appeals, First Circuit, 1957.
241 F.2d 906.

MAGRUDER, Chief Judge. Whit Mason, a citizen of Mississippi, filed his complaint in the United States District Court for the District of Rhode Island against The American Emery Wheel Works, a Rhode Island corporation. The case was one in tort for personal injuries alleged to have been suffered by the plaintiff in Mississippi as a result of negligent misfeasance by the defendant in putting out in commerce without adequate care and inspection, a dangerously defective emery wheel. According to the allegations of the complaint, at some time prior to the date of the accident defendant negligently manufactured, inspected and tested a certain emery wheel designed for attachment to a bench grinder; that due to such negligence the emery wheel was not reasonably fit for the use for which it was intended, but on the contrary subjected to a risk of personal injury all persons lawfully using a bench grinder with the emery wheel attached * * *.

On the face of the complaint it did not specifically appear that plaintiff was not in privity of contract with defendant. The answer of defendant, in addition to denying negligence, and denying that it had manufactured the particular emery wheel which had caused plaintiff's injuries, also set forth as a "First Defense" that the complaint failed to state a claim upon which relief might be granted, and as a "Fourth Defense" that defendant "owed no duty to the said plaintiff as there is no privity of contract between the plaintiff and the defendant."

* * * Plaintiff's evidence tended to show that a certain emery wheel * * * was purchased by the Hoover Company, a New Jersey corporation, from the defendant for attachment to a bench grinding machine made by the Hoover Company; that the Hoover Company affixed to the said bench grinding machine, with emery wheel attached, a label indicating that the bench grinder had been manufactured by Miller Falls Company, a Massachusetts corporation; that said bench grinder * * * was successively sold by the Hoover Company to Miller Falls Company, by the latter to Komp Equipment Company, and finally by Komp Equipment Company to T. H. Pearce Company, the plaintiff's employer; * * * that while plaintiff was using it in the ordinary and proper manner the emery wheel disintegrated and exploded in plaintiff's face, causing the injuries complained of.

At the conclusion of the plaintiff's case defendant made an oral motion to dismiss the complaint under Rule 41(b) * * *. This motion to dismiss was granted by the district court, and an order was entered dismissing the complaint, from which the present appeal was taken.

Since the injury was inflicted in Mississippi, the district court, no doubt correctly under now familiar authorities, deemed itself to be obliged to apply the Mississippi local law to determine the tort liability, if any, of a manufacturer to one not in privity of contract with him. * * * The district court came to the conclusion "reluctantly" that it was bound by the Mississippi law as declared in Ford Motor Co. v. Myers, 1928, 151 Miss. 73, 117 So. 362; that the "harsh rule" of Mississippi as so declared, "contrary to the great weight of authority" elsewhere, was that a manufacturer was not liable for negligence in the manufacture of appliances which could and would become highly dangerous when put to the uses for which they are intended, where there is no privity of contract between the user and the manufacturer.

Ford Motor Co. v. Myers, supra, was the only Mississippi case relied upon, or even referred to, by the district court. In that case the Supreme Court of Mississippi, in a half-page opinion, did in fact apply what was at one time the prevailing rule, in holding that Ford Motor Company as the manufacturer of a truck owed no duty of care to a remote subvendee of the truck who was injured when the truck collapsed and plunged into a ditch because of a defect which could have been detected by reasonable inspection by the manufacturer before the vehicle left the factory.

* * *

MacPherson v. Buick Motor Co., [217 N.Y. 382, 111 N.E. 1050 (1916)] * * * started a new trend in this particular field of the law, and its substantive result has found favor in § 395 of the * * * Restatement of Torts. If the Supreme Court of Mississippi had recently reconsidered the rule it applied in Ford Motor Co. v. Myers, supra, and had decided to adhere to it on the ground of stare decisis, no doubt the federal courts would have had to accept the local law as so declared. But it would be gratuitous and unwarranted to assume that the Supreme Court of Mississippi would now so hold, when we bear in mind the readiness of other courts, in conservative jurisdictions at that, to overrule their earlier holdings and to bring their jurisprudence into accord with what is now the overwhelming weight of authority. * * * In Anderson v. Linton, 7 Cir., 1949, 178 F.2d 304, the court of appeals declined to accept as the local law of Iowa what it narrowly construed to be a dictum of the Supreme Court of Iowa enunciating the old ruling of nonliability in Larrabee v. Des Moines Tent & Awning Co., 1920, 189 Iowa 319, 178 N.W. 373. * * *

Of course it is not necessary that a case be explicitly overruled in order to lose its persuasive force as an indication of what the law is. A decision may become so overloaded with illogical exceptions that by erosion of time it may lose its persuasive or binding force even in the inferior courts of the same jurisdiction. And where, as in Ford Motor Co. v. Myers, the Supreme Court of Mississippi, twenty or thirty years ago, applied an old rule which has since been generally discredited elsewhere, it is relevant to consider what the Supreme Court of Mississippi has subsequently said on the point. * * * We think that appellant herein rightly stresses the importance of E. I. Du Pont De Nemours & Co. v. Ladner, 1954, 221 Miss. 378, 73 So.2d 249. In that very recent case, the Supreme Court of Mississippi was able to dispose of the particular issue on another ground without the necessity of expressly overruling its earlier decision in Ford Motor Co. v. Myers. But the court did take occasion, in a long and careful opinion, to indicate its awareness of the modern trend in the area * * *. And it quoted, with apparent approval, many more recent authorities in support of the "modern doctrine." (Ibid.) We think it is fair to infer from this latest expression by the Supreme Court of Mississippi that it is prepared to reconsider and revise the rule it applied in Ford Motor Co. v. Myers whenever it may have before it a case that squarely presents the issue. We have no doubt that when this occasion does come to pass, the Supreme Court of Mississippi will declare itself in agreement with the more enlightened and generally accepted modern doctrine.

A judgment will be entered vacating the order of the District Court, dismissing the complaint and remanding the case to the District Court for further proceedings not inconsistent with this opinion.

HARTIGAN, Circuit Judge (concurring).

I concur in the opinion of the court but I am constrained to comment briefly. We were informed in oral argument by counsel for the appellee that the district court in deciding this case had before it both the Ford and the Du Pont decisions. Moreover, the district court knew from the official Mississippi report that the MacPherson case, then approximately twelve years old, had been considered and rejected by the Mississippi Supreme Court sitting in the Ford case. Therefore, "reluctantly" Judge Day adopted the Ford holding since it, as the only binding and conclusive statement of Mississippi law on the issue, had not been expressly modified or overruled. * * *

We, however, have inferred from pure dicta in the Du Pont case and from the status of the law elsewhere on this issue that Mississippi is prepared to discard the Ford rule and adopt the modern rule. I believe this is a sound inference since the dicta in the Du Pont case though not expressly mentioning

Ford, is sufficiently clear and the Ford rule is sufficiently outdated. Yet, in doing so I realize that we present a difficult problem for district judges when they must apply the Erie doctrine to situations wherein the considerations as between conflicting holdings and dicta are not as clearly defined as they are here. The question of how clear dicta must be to prevail over a prior controlling decision does not lend itself to easy solution.

NOTES AND QUESTIONS

1. The history of the privity rule in Mississippi following *Mason* is interesting. Relying heavily on Judge Magruder's opinion, the Fifth Circuit held in GREY v. HAYES–SAMMONS CHEM. CO., 310 F.2d 291 (5th Cir.1962), that under Mississippi law a lack of privity was not a bar to a claim by a Mississippi consumer against a manufacturer of a cotton spray. The Fifth Circuit reached similar conclusions in Necaise v. Chrysler Corp., 335 F.2d 562 (5th Cir.1964), and Putman v. Erie City Mfg. Co., 338 F.2d 911 (5th Cir.1964). Finally, the Mississippi Supreme Court, in STATE STOVE MFG. CO. v. HODGES, 189 So.2d 113 (Miss.1966), certiorari denied sub nom. Yates v. Hodges, 386 U.S. 912, 87 S.Ct. 860, 17 L.Ed.2d 784 (1967), reconsidered the privity question and overruled its decision in *Ford Motor Co. v. Myers*. In doing so, however, the court did not cite either the First Circuit's decision in *Mason* or the series of decisions in the Fifth Circuit.

2. What is the basis for Judge Magruder's statement in *Mason*: "Since the injury was inflicted in Mississippi, the district court, no doubt correctly under now familiar authorities, deemed itself to be obliged to apply the Mississippi local law"? Isn't the lesson of *Erie* and *Guaranty* that a federal court sitting in diversity litigation is obliged to apply the law of the state in which it is sitting, which in the *Mason* case is Rhode Island and not Mississippi? Yet, in *Erie* itself—a case that originated in the New York federal courts—Mr. Justice Brandeis seemed to apply Pennsylvania law—the place of the accident. Can you articulate one or more theories to justify the application of Pennsylvania law in *Erie* and Mississippi law in *Mason*?

In KLAXON CO. v. STENTOR MFG. CO., 313 U.S. 487, 61 S.Ct. 1020, 85 L.Ed. 1477 (1941), the Supreme Court held that in order to promote the desired uniform application of substantive law within a state, a federal court must use the conflict-of-laws rules of the state in which it is sitting in diversity actions. Accord, Sampson v. Channell, 110 F.2d 754 (1st Cir.), certiorari denied 310 U.S. 650, 60 S.Ct. 1099, 84 L.Ed. 1415 (1940). Is there any persuasive argument for the conclusion that the question of which state's law should be applied by a federal court in a diversity action, when the transaction or event that is the subject of the lawsuit had contacts with one or more states other than the forum state, is to be resolved according to a federal rule? See generally Wright, *Federal Courts* § 57 (2d ed. 1970); Baxter, *Choice of Law and the Federal System*, 16 Stan.L.Rev. 1 (1963); Cook, *The Federal Courts and the Conflict of Laws*, 36 Ill. L.Rev. 493 (1942); Hart, *The Relations Between State and Federal Law*, 54 Colum.L.Rev. 489, 513–15 (1954); Horowitz, *Toward a Federal Common Law of Choice of Law*, 14 U.C.L.A.L.Rev. 191 (1967); Weintraub, *The Erie Doctrine and State Conflict of Laws Rules*, 39 Ind.L.J. 228 (1964). Would a federal conflict-of-laws rule applicable to all cases brought in the federal courts be valid?

3. Mr. Justice Stone in WEST v. AMERICAN TEL. & TEL. CO., 311 U.S. 223, 236–37, 61 S.Ct. 179, 183, 85 L.Ed. 139, 144 (1940):

A state is not without law save as its highest court has declared it. There are many rules of decision commonly accepted and acted upon by the bar and inferior courts which are nevertheless laws of the state although the highest court of the state has never passed upon them. In those circumstances a federal court is not free to reject the state rule merely because it has not received the sanction of the highest state court, even though it thinks the rule is unsound in principle or that another is preferable. State law is to be applied in the federal as well as the state courts and it is the duty of the former in every case to ascertain from all the available data what the state law is and apply it rather than to prescribe a different rule, however superior it may appear from the viewpoint of "general law" and however much the state rule may have departed from prior decisions of the federal courts.   * * *

Where an intermediate appellate state court rests its considered judgment upon the rule of law which it announces, that is a datum for ascertaining state law which is not to be disregarded by a federal court unless it is convinced by other persuasive data that the highest court of the state would decide otherwise.

To what extent must a federal court adhere to state trial and intermediate court decisions? *Compare* Fidelity Union Trust Co. v. Field, 311 U.S. 169, 61 S. Ct. 176, 85 L.Ed. 109 (1940) (decisions of intermediate state court followed), *with* King v. Order of United Commercial Travelers, 333 U.S. 153, 68 S.Ct. 488, 92 L.Ed. 608 (1948) (unreported decision of South Carolina county court of common pleas not followed because of its lack of precedential effect in state courts). Can you perceive any negative effects the strict adherence to state trial-court decisions by federal courts may have on the development of state law? Would such a practice augment or deter forum shopping? The problems encountered by a federal court in ascertaining state law are discussed in Clark, *State Law in the Federal Courts: The Brooding Omnipresence of Erie v. Tompkins*, 55 Yale L.J. 267, 290–95 (1946); Kurland, *Mr. Justice Frankfurter, The Supreme Court and the Erie Doctrine in Diversity Cases*, 67 Yale L.J. 187, 204–18 (1957).

4. Should a federal court sitting in diversity jurisdiction accord an *unreported* state decision any weight? Would a federal court be bound by a state statute that provided: "Only such cases as are hereafter reported in accordance with the provisions of this section shall be recognized by and receive the official sanction of any court within the state"? See Gustin v. Sun Life Assur. Co., 154 F.2d 961 (6th Cir.), certiorari denied 328 U.S. 866, 66 S.Ct. 1374, 90 L. Ed. 1636 (1946). What should a federal court do when the courts of the state in which it is sitting have not considered the particular problem before the federal court? May it refuse to accept jurisdiction over the case? See Meredith v. City of Winter Haven, 320 U.S. 228, 64 S.Ct. 7, 88 L.Ed. 9 (1943); Daily v. Parker, 152 F.2d 174 (7th Cir.1945). Should it stay its own proceeding and allow the litigants to seek a declaratory judgment from a state court? See also United Services Life Ins. Co. v. Delaney, 328 F.2d 483 (5th Cir.1964). What problems are created by such a procedure? See Agata, *Delaney, Diversity and Delay: Abstention or Abdication?*, 4 Houston L.Rev. 422 (1966).

5.   In POMERANTZ v. CLARK, 101 F.Supp. 341, 345–46 (D.Mass.1951), a diversity action by policyholders against directors of an insurance company to retrieve for the company certain sums allegedly improvidently and illegally loaned, Judge Wyzanski held that no action was maintainable under Massachusetts law and stated:

> In considering whether   *   *   *   [to create] an exception to the Massachusetts rule that before bringing a derivative suit a member must first lay his case before the body of members, the never-to-be-forgotten caution is that this Court is not free to render such decision as seems to it equitable, just and in accordance with public policy and responsive to all those jurisprudential criteria which so often enter into what Justice Cardozo called "The Nature of the Judicial Process." A federal judge sitting in a diversity jurisdiction case has not a roving commission to do justice or to develop the law according to his, or what he believes to be the sounder, views. His problem is less philosophical and more psychological. His task is to divine the views of the state court judges.   *   *   *

> The eminence of the Massachusetts Supreme Judicial Court, an eminence not surpassed by any American tribunal, is in large measure due to its steadiness, learning and understanding of the durable values long prized in this community. Subtle variations and blurred lines are not characteristic of that court. Principles are announced and adhered to in broad magisterial terms. The emphasis is on precedent and adherence to the older ways, not on creating new causes of action or encouraging the use of novel judicial remedies that have sprung up in less conservative communities. Here abides the ancient faith in the right of men to choose their own associates, make their own arrangements, govern themselves and thus grow in responsibility without much in the way of either hindrance or help from the state. This basic philosophy permeates the Massachusetts rules governing derivative suits   *   *   *.

Compare Judge Friendly's observation in Nolan v. Transocean Air Lines, 276 F. 2d 280, 281 (2d Cir.1960): "Our principal task, in this diversity of citizenship case, is to determine what the New York courts would think the California courts would think on an issue about which neither has thought."

6.   When a diversity case is transferred under either Section 1404(a) or Section 1406(a), what law will the transferee court apply? Should it make any difference whether the transfer was sought by plaintiff or by defendant or whether a state court in the transferor district would have dismissed the action on the basis of *forum non conveniens?* See generally Van Dusen v. Barrack, 376 U.S. 612, 84 S.Ct. 805, 11 L.Ed.2d 945 (1964); Headrick v. Atchison, Topeka & Santa Fe Ry. Co., 182 F.2d 305 (10th Cir.1950).

SECTION C.   FEDERAL "COMMON LAW"

MISHKIN, THE VARIOUSNESS OF "FEDERAL LAW": COMPE-
TENCE AND DISCRETION IN THE CHOICE OF NATIONAL AND
STATE RULES FOR DECISION, 105 U.Pa.L.Rev. 797, 798–800 (1957):

* * *   Although *Erie's* holding that a federal court was bound to
apply state law came specifically in a case brought within the jurisdiction of a
national tribunal only by reason of diversity of citizenship, its impact was
immediately felt more widely, extending to litigation directly involving the
United States.   Insofar as *Erie* represented a reversal of attitude and expressed a strong policy favoring a single substantive rule on a given issue regardless of the court in which the case is presented, that extension is undoubtedly warranted; issues related to operations of the national government may
conceivably arise in either federal or state courts and in such cases, as elsewhere, the source of the governing rule should not turn upon litigants' choice
of forum.   In this aspect, *Erie* serves to focus the general policy of identifying the appropriate source of authority as to any issue regardless of the court
—state or federal—in which the question is presented.

However, insofar as *Erie* represents authority for the required application of state law by federal courts, it is not controlling on problems implicated
in the operation of a congressional program.   From this aspect, *Erie's* basic
holding was a determination that the particular subject matter involved was beyond the law-making competence of the federal courts; that the area was one
where state law governed of its own authority, and the mere grant of jurisdiction to adjudicate a case did not carry with it the power to declare an independent "general" rule displacing that authority.   These propositions are inapposite to problems which bear substantial relation to an established federal operation.   As to such questions, state law cannot govern of its own force; there
must be competence in the federal judiciary to declare the governing law.

Such competence is essential to the effective implementation of the legislative powers committed to the national government by the Constitution.
* * *   [E]xclusive reliance upon statutory provision for the solution of
all problems is futile.   Beyond the political realities which will at times compel
congressional by-passing of any issue—thus leaving it open until pending litigation forces court resolution—lie such simpler pressures as shortness of time
and, perhaps most important, the severe limits of human foresight.   Together,
these factors combine to make the concept of statutory enactment as a totally
self-sufficient and exclusive legislative process entirely unreal.   At the very
least, effective Constitutionalism requires recognition of power in the federal
courts to declare, as a matter of common law or "judicial legislation," rules
which may be necessary to fill in interstitially or otherwise effectuate the statutory patterns enacted in the large by Congress.   In other words, it must mean
recognition of federal judicial competence to declare the governing law in an
area comprising issues substantially related to an established program of government operation.

D'OENCH, DUHME & CO. v. FEDERAL DEPOSIT INS. CORP., 315 U.S. 447, 471–72, 62 S.Ct. 676, 686, 86 L.Ed. 956, 969 (1942) (Jackson, J., concurring):

> A federal court sitting in a non-diversity case such as this does not sit as a local tribunal. In some cases it may see fit for special reasons to give the law of a particular state highly persuasive or even controlling effect, but in the last analysis its decision turns upon the law of the United States, not that of any state. Federal law is no juridical chameleon, changing complexion to match that of each state wherein lawsuits happen to be commenced because of the accidents of service of process and of the application of the venue statutes. It is found in the federal Constitution, statutes, or common law. Federal common law implements the federal Constitution and statutes, and is conditioned by them. Within these limits, federal courts are free to apply the traditional common-law technique of decision and to draw upon all the sources of the common law in cases such as the present.   *   *   *

CLEARFIELD TRUST CO. v. UNITED STATES, 318 U.S. 363, 63 S. Ct. 573, 87 L.Ed. 838 (1943). The United States brought suit to recover the proceeds of a stolen government payroll check. The check had been cashed with a forged signature and ultimately had been tendered for payment by the Clearfield Trust Company. The United States could not recover if the law of Pennsylvania, the state in which the transaction took place, was applied because the government had "unreasonably delayed" in giving notice of the forgery to the Trust Company. The Supreme Court held that the effectiveness of the Trust Company's express guarantee of prior endorsements on a government check was controlled by federal law, stating:

*** Desirability of a uniform law is plain.

> In our choice of the applicable federal rule we have occasionally selected state law.   *   *   *   But reasons which may make state law at times the appropriate federal rule are singularly inappropriate here. The issuance of commercial paper by the United States is on a vast scale and transactions in that paper from issuance to payment will commonly occur in several states. The application of state law, even without the conflict of laws rules of the forum, would subject the rights and duties of the United States to exceptional uncertainty. It would lead to great diversity in results by making identical transactions subject to the vagaries of the laws of the several states.

Id. at 367, 63 S.Ct. at 575, 87 L.Ed. at 842.

The Court went on to hold that the "federal" rule on the subject was that the Trust Company was required to show that it had been damaged by the government's delay in giving notice. Does the difference between the Pennsylvania and the "federal" rule of law have any practical significance? Would the federal government's administrative practices with regard to payroll checks be altered if state law applied?

BANK OF AMERICA NAT. TRUST & SAV. ASS'N v. PARNELL

Supreme Court of the United States, 1956.
352 U.S. 29, 77 S.Ct. 119, 1 L.Ed.2d 93.

Certiorari to the United States Court of Appeals for the Third Circuit.

Mr. Justice FRANKFURTER delivered the opinion of the Court.

Petitioner, alleging diversity of citizenship, brought suit in the District Court for the Western District of Pennsylvania alleging that in September and October 1948 two individual defendants, Parnell and Rocco, and two corporate defendants, the First National Bank in Indiana and the Federal Reserve Bank of Cleveland, had converted 73 Home Owners' Loan Corporation bonds which belonged to petitioner.   *   *   *

At the trial it appeared that these bonds were bearer bonds with payment guaranteed by the United States. They carried interest coupons calling for semi-annual payment. They were due to mature May 1, 1952, but pursuant to their terms, had been called on or about May 1, 1944. On May 2, 1944, the bonds disappeared while petitioner was getting them ready for presentation to the Federal Reserve Bank for payment. In 1948 they were presented to the First National Bank for payment by Parnell on behalf of Rocco. The First National Bank forwarded them to the Federal Reserve Bank of Cleveland. It cashed them and paid the First National Bank, which issued cashier's checks to Parnell. Parnell then turned the proceeds over to Rocco less a fee—there was conflicting testimony as to whether the fee was nominal or substantial.

The principal issue at the trial was whether the respondents took the bonds in good faith, without knowledge or notice of the defect in title. On this issue the trial judge charged:

"As I have indicated, however, in the case—and if you find in this case that the plaintiff owned these bonds, that they were stolen from it—then the burden of proof so far as this plaintiff is concerned is to show that fact, that these bonds were owned by it, that they were lost by it in the manner as shown by its evidence. Then the two defendants, Parnell and the bank, not claiming to be owners for value, but as conduits for redemption, must come forward and they then have the burden of showing that they acted innocently, honestly, and in good faith. *   *   *"

The jury brought in verdicts for petitioner against both respondents. On appeal, the Court of Appeals for the Third Circuit, the seven circuit judges sitting *en banc*, reversed, with three judges dissenting. It held that the District Court had erred in treating the case as an ordinary diversity case and in regarding state law as governing the rights of the parties and the burden of proof. * * * It considered our decision in Clearfield Trust Co. v. United States * * * controlling and held that federal law placed the burden of proof on petitioner to show notice and lack of good faith on the part of respondents. The court further found that there was no evidence of bad faith by the First National Bank since the bonds were not "overdue" as a matter of federal law when presented to it and therefore directed entry of judgment for it. The court found that there was evidence of bad faith on the part of Parnell but ordered a new trial because of the erroneous instructions.

The dissenters agreed in applying the doctrine of the Clearfield Trust case to determine the nature of the contract and the rights and duties of the United States as a party but not the rights of private transferees among themselves. They, like the majority, looked to federal law to determine whether the bonds were "overdue paper" when presented to the First National Bank. They concluded that since the respondent bank knew of the call as to it, the bonds became demand paper and that the bank took the paper an unreasonable length of time after maturity, as advanced by the call.

In the view of the dissenters, state law was controlling with respect to proof of good faith and the burden thereon. They found that state law placed the burden of proof on respondents to demonstrate their good faith, and that there was sufficient evidence to support the jury's verdict that the burden of proving good faith had not been sustained even if, with respect to the respondent bank, the bonds were not to be regarded as demand paper taken an unreasonable time after maturity, as advanced by the call.

* * *

The District Court in this suit, based on diversity jurisdiction, for the conversion in Pennsylvania of pieces of paper of defined value, deemed itself a court of Pennsylvania in which, in view of the nature of the claim, Pennsylvania law would govern. * * * But respondents claim, and the Court of Appeals sustained them, that the decision in Clearfield Trust Co. v. United States * * * compels the application of federal law to the entire case. The Court of Appeals misconceived the nature of this litigation in holding that the Clearfield Trust case controlled. * * *

Securities issued by the Government generate immediate interests of the Government. * * * But they also radiate interests in transactions between private parties. The present litigation is purely between private parties and does not touch the rights and duties of the United States. The only possible interest of the United States in a situation like the one here, exclusively involving the transfer of Government paper between private persons, is that the floating of securities of the United States might somehow or other be adversely affected by the local rule of a particular State regarding the liability of a converter. This is far too speculative, far too remote a possibility to justify the application of federal law to transactions essentially of local concern.

We do not mean to imply that litigation with respect to Government paper necessarily precludes the presence of a federal interest, to be governed by federal law, in all situations merely because it is a suit between private parties, or that it is beyond the range of federal legislation to deal comprehensively with Government paper. We do not of course foreclose such judicial or legislative action in appropriate situations by concluding that this controversy over burden of proof and good faith represents too essentially a private transaction not to be dealt with by the local law of Pennsylvania where the transactions took place. Federal law of course governs the interpretation of the nature of the rights and obligations created by the Government bonds themselves. A decision with respect to the "overdueness" of the bonds is therefore a matter of federal law, which, in view of our holding, we need not elucidate.

This conclusion requires reversal of the judgments of the Court of Appeals but not reinstatement of the judgments of the District Court. The Court of Appeals did not originally consider all the points raised by respondents. Moreover, since the Court of Appeals misconceived the applicable law, it is for that court to review the judgments of the District Court in the light of the controlling state law. The Court of Appeals has not decided what the governing state law on burden of proof is, and it is the court which should so decide. Likewise, if state law casts the burden on respondents to demonstrate their good faith, it is for the Court of Appeals to assess the evidence in light of that standard.

* * *

Reversed and remanded.

Mr. Justice BLACK and Mr. Justice DOUGLAS, dissenting.

We believe that the "federal law merchant" which Clearfield Trust Co. v. United States * * * held applicable to transactions in the commercial paper of the United States should be applicable to all transactions in that paper. * * * Not until today has a distinction been drawn between suits by the United States on that paper and suits by other parties to it. But the Court does not stop there. Because this is "essentially a private transaction," it is to be governed by local law. Yet the nature of the rights and obligations created by commercial paper of the United States Government is said to be controlled by federal law. Thus, federal law is to govern some portion of a dispute between private parties, while that portion of the dispute which is "essentially of local concern" is to be governed by local law. The uncertainties which inhere in such a dichotomy are obvious. * * *

The virtue of a uniform law governing bonds, notes, and other paper issued by the United States is that it provides a certain and definite guide to the rights of all parties rather than subjecting them to the vagaries of the law of many States. The business of the United States will go on without that uniformity. But the policy surrounding our choice of laws is concerned with the convenience, certainty, and definiteness in having one set of rules governing the rights of all parties to government paper, as contrasted to multiple rules. If the rule of the Clearfield Trust case is to be abandoned as to some parties, it should be abandoned as to all and we should start afresh on this problem.

UNITED STATES v. YAZELL, 382 U.S. 341, 86 S.Ct. 500, 15 L.Ed.2d 404 (1966). The Small Business Administration made a disaster loan to Yazell and his wife, respondent, following flood damage to the children's clothing store they operated in Texas. The loan was individually negotiated. After default by the Yazells on the note, and foreclosure of the mortgage, the Government brought suit against the Yazells for the deficiency. Mrs. Yazell moved for summary judgment on the ground that under the Texas law of coverture she had no capacity to bind herself personally by contract unless she had first obtained a court decree removing her disability to contract. She had not done so. The district court granted the motion and the court of appeals affirmed, rejecting the Government's contention that even in the absence of any express federal statute or regulation on the matter or any indication in the loan contract itself, questions of capacity to contract with the Small Business Administration and to subject property to liability on such a contract are governed by federal and not local law. The Supreme Court affirmed on the ground that there was no federal interest that required local law to be overridden. The Court stated:

> * * * [I]t seems clear (1) that the SBA was aware and is chargeable with knowledge that the contract would be subject to the Texas law of coverture; (2) that both the SBA and the Yazells entered into the contract without any thought that the defense of coverture would be unavailable to Mrs. Yazell with respect to her separate property as provided by Texas law; and (3) that, in the circumstances, the United States is seeking the unconscionable advantage of recourse to assets for which it did not bargain.

> * * * Undeniably there is always a federal interest to collect moneys which the Government lends. In this case, the federal interest is to put the Federal Government in position to levy execution against Mrs. Yazell's separate property * * *. Every creditor has the same interest in this respect; every creditor wants to collect. The United States, as sovereign, has certain preferences and priorities, but neither Congress nor this Court has ever asserted that they are absolute. For example, no contention will or can be made that the United States may by judicial fiat collect its loan with total disregard of state laws such as homestead exemptions. * * *

The Government asserts that this overriding federal interest can be found in the unlimited right of the Federal Government to choose the persons with whom it will contract * * *. Realistically, in terms of Yazell's case, this has nothing to do with our problem: The loan was made to enable Yazell to reopen the store after the disaster of the flood. The SBA chose its contractors with knowledge of the limited office of Mrs. Yazell's signature under Texas law. * * * If they had "chosen" Mrs. Yazell as their contractor in the sense that her separate property would be liable for the loan, presumably they would have said so, and they would have proceeded with the formalities necessary under Texas law to have her disability removed. * * *

We do not here consider the question of the constitutional power of the Congress to override state law in these circumstances by direct legislation or by appropriate authorization to an administrative agency coupled with suitable implementing action by the agency. We decide only that this Court, in the absence of specific congressional action, should not decree in this situation that implementation of federal interests requires overriding the particular state rule involved here. Both theory and the precedents of this Court teach us solicitude for state interests, particularly in the field of family and family-property arrangements. They should be overridden by the federal courts only where clear and substantial interests of the National Government, which cannot be served consistently with respect for such state interests, will suffer major damage if the state law is applied.

Id. at 346, 348–50, 352, 86 S.Ct. at 503–07, 15 L.Ed.2d at 407–10.

NOTES AND QUESTIONS

1. Is *Yazell* consistent with *Clearfield*? Does it follow from *Parnell*? Of what relevance is the fact that the loan was "individually negotiated" with knowledge of the Texas law of coverture? Is there really a more important federal interest in *Yazell* than the Court's opinion would lead the reader to believe existed? If so, what is it? See also Wallis v. Pan American Pet. Corp., 384 U.S. 63, 86 S. Ct. 1301, 16 L.Ed.2d 369 (1966) (suggestion that Congress enacts legislation against a background of the total *corpus juris* of the states).

2. BANCO NACIONAL de CUBA v. SABBATINO, 376 U.S. 398, 84 S. Ct. 923, 11 L.Ed.2d 804 (1964), involved the proceeds of a sugar shipment claimed by petitioner, Banco Nacional de Cuba (Banco), a financial agent of the Cuban government, by reason of Cuba's expropriation of the property of Compania Azucarera Vertientes-Camaguey (C.A.V.), a Cuban corporation predominantly owned by Americans. Petitioner tendered the bills of lading for the sugar to Farr, Whitlock & Co. (Farr) who in turn negotiated the bills for the purchase price but did not pay the proceeds to petitioner because Sabbatino, a temporary receiver for the assets of C.A.V. appointed by a New York state court, also claimed them and had procured a state court order directing Farr to turn the proceeds over to him.

Banco then brought suit in the Southern District of New York alleging that Farr had illegally converted the bills of lading and seeking recovery of the proceeds and an injunction to prevent Sabbatino from exercising any dominion over the proceeds. The court granted summary judgment against petitioner on the ground that the Cuban expropriation decree was unenforceable, despite the act-of-state doctrine,[b] because it violated international law.

[b] The act-of-state doctrine has been defined as follows: "Every sovereign state is bound to respect the independence of every other sovereign state, and the courts of one country will not sit in judgment on the acts of the government of another, done within its own territory. Redress of grievances by reason of such acts must be obtained through the means open to be availed of by sovereign powers as between themselves." Underhill v. Hernandez, 168 U.S. 250, 252, 18 S.Ct. 83, 84, 42 L.Ed. 456 (1897).

The Second Circuit affirmed but the Supreme Court reversed, holding that the act-of-state doctrine proscribed any challenge of the Cuban expropriation decree. In discussing the nature of the act-of-state doctrine and whether state or federal law controlled its application in a federal diversity case, the Supreme Court said:

> The act of state doctrine does * * * have "constitutional" underpinnings. It arises out of the basic relationships between branches of government in a system of separation of powers. It concerns the competency of dissimilar institutions to make and implement particular kinds of decisions in the area of international relations. The doctrine as formulated in past decisions expresses the strong sense of the Judicial Branch that its engagement in the task of passing on the validity of foreign acts of state may hinder rather than further this country's pursuit of goals both for itself and for the community of nations as a whole in the international sphere. * * * Whatever considerations are thought to predominate, it is plain that the problems involved are uniquely federal in nature. If federal authority, in this instance this Court, orders the field of judicial competence in this area for the federal courts, and the state courts are left free to formulate their own rules, the purposes behind the doctrine could be as effectively undermined as if there had been no federal pronouncement on the subject.
>
> * * * [A]n issue concerned with a basic choice regarding the competence and function of the Judiciary and the National Executive in ordering our relationships with other members of the international community must be treated exclusively as an aspect of federal law. It seems fair to assume that the Court did not have rules like the act of state doctrine in mind when it decided Erie * * *.
>
> The Court in the pre-Erie act of state cases, although not burdened by the problem of the source of applicable law, used language sufficiently strong and broad-sweeping to suggest that state courts were not left free to develop their own doctrines * * *. We are not without other precedent for a determination that federal law governs; there are enclaves of federal judge-made law which bind the States. A national body of federal-court-built law has been held to have been contemplated by § 301 of the Labor Management Relations Act * * *. Principles formulated by federal judicial law have been thought by this Court to be necessary to protect uniquely federal interests * * *. Of course the federal interest guarded in all these cases is one the ultimate statement of which is derived from a federal statute. Perhaps more directly in point are the bodies of law applied between States over boundaries and in regard to the apportionment of interstate waters.
>
> In Hinderlider v. La Plata River Co., 304 U.S. 92, 110, 58 S.Ct. 803, 811, 82 L.Ed. 1202, in an opinion handed down the same day as Erie and by the same author, Mr. Justice Brandeis, the Court declared, "For whether the water of an interstate stream must be apportioned between the two States is a question of 'federal common law' upon which neither the statutes nor the decisions of either State can be conclusive." Although the suit was between two private litigants and the relevant States could not be made parties, the Court considered itself free to determine the effect of an interstate compact regulating water apportion-

ment.   The decision implies that no State can undermine the federal interest in equitably apportioned interstate waters even if it deals with private parties.   This would not mean that, absent a compact, the apportionment scheme could not be changed judicially or by Congress, but only that apportionment is a matter of federal law.   * * *   The problems surrounding the act of state doctrine are, albeit for different reasons, as intrinsically federal as are those involved in water apportionment or boundary disputes.[c]

Id. at 423–27, 84 S.Ct. at 938–40, 11 L.Ed.2d 821–23.   See generally Note, *The Federal Common Law,* 82 Harv.L.Rev. 1512 (1969).

Is *Sabbatino* consistent with *Parnell* and *Yazell?*   Note that in *Sabbatino* the federal policy emanates directly from the Constitution's grant of power over foreign affairs—a power that is basically "political" and one that is primarily exercised by the Executive, not the Legislature or the Judiciary.   Should this make any difference?   Why are the federal courts more competent to declare rules of decision bearing on foreign policy than the state courts?   Federal common law in the labor relations field is the subject of Textile Workers Union v. Lincoln Mills, 353 U.S. 448, 77 S.Ct. 912, 1 L.Ed.2d 972 (1957).

3.   Does federal common law extend to an application to abate a public nuisance created by the pollution of ambient air or an interstate waterway?   Of what relevance is the fact that the particular remedy sought is not one of those prescribed by the Congress?   Is there federal question jurisdiction on the basis of federal common law or must the requirements for diversity jurisdiction be met?   These and several other interesting questions are discussed in Illinois v. City of Milwaukee, Wisconsin, 406 U.S. 91, 92 S.Ct. 1385, 31 L.Ed.2d 712 (1972).

4.   In FREE v. BLAND, 369 U.S. 663, 82 S.Ct. 1089, 8 L.Ed.2d 180 (1962), the issue was whether Texas community-property law could be applied to determine the ownership of United States Savings Bonds; the application of Treasury Department Regulations would have led to a different result.   Is the rationale of the *Parnell* case controlling?   What law should a federal court apply to an unfair competition claim appended to an action under the Copyright, Patent, or Trademark Act pursuant to 28 U.S.C. § 1338(b)?   See Bulova Watch Co. v. Stolzberg, 69 F.Supp. 543 (D.Mass.1947);   Comment, *Pendent Jurisdiction—Applicability of the Erie Doctrine,* 24 U.Chi.L.Rev. 543 (1957).   A uniform federal standard was chosen in O'BRIEN v. WESTERN UNION TEL. CO., 113 F.2d 539 (1st Cir.1940), which involved the question of the liability of telegraph companies for the negligent misdelivery of telegrams and the handling of telegrams containing defamatory matter.   The court apparently felt that the application of different state tests for tort liability might upset the federal government's regulation of rates.

5.   Statements in *Parnell* should not mislead the student into believing that the *Erie* philosophy is not relevant to federal-question cases.   See Hill, *State Procedural Law in Federal Nondiversity Litigation,* 69 Harv.L.Rev. 66 (1955);   Hill,

---

c Insofar as the *Sabbatino* decision prevented a court from examining the merits of cases involving expropriation, it has been legislatively qualified by 22 U.S.C. § 2370(e) (2).   See also the several opinions in First Nat. City Bank v. Banco Nacional de Cuba, 406 U.S. 759, 92 S.Ct. 1808, 32 L.Ed.2d 466 (1972).   See generally Edwards, *The Erie Doctrine in Foreign Affairs Cases,* 42 N.Y.U.L.Rev. 674 (1967).

The Erie Doctrine in Bankruptcy, 66 Harv.L.Rev. 1013 (1953). This point is made very succinctly in MATERNALLY YOURS, INC. v. YOUR MATERNITY SHOP, INC., 234 F.2d 538, 540–41 n. 1 (2d Cir.1956), in which the court remarked that "it is the *source* of the right sued upon, and not the ground on which federal jurisdiction over the case is founded, which determines the governing law." Various aspects of federal "common law" are discussed in Friendly, *In Praise of Erie—And the New Federal Common Law,* 39 N.Y.U.L.Rev. 383 (1964); Hart, *The Relations Between State and Federal Law,* 54 Colum.L.Rev. 489, 530–35 (1954); Hill, *The Law-Making Power of the Federal Courts: Constitutional Preemption,* 67 Colum.L.Rev. 1024 (1967); Comment, *Erie Limited: The Confines of State Law in the Federal Courts,* 40 Cornell L.Q. 561 (1955); Note, *The Competence of Federal Courts to Formulate Rules of Decision,* 77 Harv.L. Rev. 1084 (1964); Comment, *Rules of Decision in Nondiversity Suits,* 69 Yale L.J. 1428 (1960).

    6. In most instances in which the federal courts incorporate or adopt state law, the reason is that the Congress has failed to deal with one or more facets of a federally regulated area and it would be burdensome for the federal courts to forge their own rules or it would be confusing if they applied an independent federal standard. E. g., De Sylva v. Ballentine, 351 U.S. 570, 76 S.Ct. 974, 100 L.Ed. 1415 (1956) (the word "children" in the Copyright Act construed in accordance with the California Probate Code); Cope v. Anderson, 331 U.S. 461, 67 S.Ct. 1340, 91 L.Ed. 1602 (1947) (state statute of limitations applied in action to enforce statutory liability of shareholders of national banks). The task confronting a federal court when it is instructed by the Congress or decides on its own to incorporate state law bears a certain similarity, but is not identical, to the process by which a federal court ascertains and applies state law under the compulsion of the *Erie* doctrine. See pp. 293–98, supra. What are the differences between the two processes? To what extent should a federal court be bound by the local construction and details of the state law it incorporates?

    The federal courts have borrowed heavily from the states in the realm of procedure. Indeed, until the advent of the Federal Rules, the federal courts were instructed by the Congress to conform their procedure "as nearly as may be" to that employed by the courts of the state in which they were sitting. 17 Stat. 196 (1872). Incorporation of state practice did not end with the advent of the Federal Rules. For example, Federal Rules of Civil Procedure 4(d) (2), (6), (7), and (e) permit service in the manner prescribed by state law, Rule 17(b) refers a number of questions regarding capacity to sue or be sued to state law, Rule 43(a) employs state rules pertaining to the admissibility of evidence,[d] Rule 62(f) authorizes the grant of certain stays of execution when they would be available under state law, and Rule 64 permits the use of state provisional remedies for the purpose of securing satisfaction of the ultimate judgment.

    [d] This rule would be modified if the Proposed Rules of Evidence for United States Courts and Magistrates are adopted. See p. 866, infra.

SECTION D. FEDERAL LAW IN THE STATE COURTS

———

State courts often are called upon to construe and apply federal law. Indeed, the Congress has created several statutory causes of action, such as actions under the Federal Employers' Liability Act, that can be asserted by plaintiff in either a state or federal court but which defendant cannot remove from a state court. When a state attempts to adjudicate such a right, *(federal right)* the Supremacy Clause, United States Const. Art. VI, requires the application of federal law. Ward v. Love County, 253 U.S. 17, 40 S.Ct. 419, 64 L.Ed. 751 (1920).[e] A federally created right also may become germane to a state-court action when it is interposed as a defense to a claim based on state law. For example, in an action for royalties due under a contract licensing the use of a copyright or patent, defendant commonly will assert that the copyright or patent is invalid under the substantive tests established by the Copyright or Patent Act or that the copyright or patent has been used in violation of the federal antitrust laws. See, e. g., Sola Elec. Co. v. Jefferson Elec. Co., 317 U.S. 173, 63 S.Ct. 172, 87 L.Ed. 165 (1942). By way of further example, federal law may become relevant to a state lawsuit because of the presence of some federal interest or policy, which often springs out of its proprietary or governmental activities, or because one of the parties asserts a right protected by the United States Constitution. Finally, federal decisional law may come into play because it provides precedents bearing on issues being litigated before the state court in a nonfederal action.

———

DICE v. AKRON, CANTON & YOUNGSTOWN RAILROAD CO.

Supreme Court of the United States, 1952.
342 U.S. 359, 72 S.Ct. 312, 96 L.Ed. 398.

Certiorari to the Supreme Court of Ohio.

Opinion of the Court by Mr. Justice BLACK, announced by Mr. Justice DOUGLAS.

Petitioner, a railroad fireman, was seriously injured when an engine in which he was riding jumped the track. Alleging that his injuries were due to respondent's negligence, he brought this action for damages under the Federal Employers' Liability Act, 35 Stat. 65, 45 U.S.C. § 51 et seq., in an Ohio court of common pleas. Respondent's defenses were (1) a denial of negligence and

———

e The extent to which a state court may be *compelled* to adjudicate a federal cause of action in a situation in which it has a nondiscriminatory basis for declining jurisdiction is less certain. See generally Testa v. Katt, 330 U.S. 386, 67 S.Ct. 810, 91 L.Ed. 967 (1947); McKnett v. St. Louis & San Francisco Ry., 292 U.S. 230, 54 S.Ct. 690, 78 L.Ed. 1227 (1934).

(2) a written document signed by petitioner purporting to release respondent in full for $924.63. Petitioner admitted that he had signed several receipts for payments made him in connection with his injuries but denied that he had made a full and complete settlement of all his claims. He alleged that the purported release was void because he had signed it relying on respondent's deliberately false statement that the document was nothing more than a mere receipt for back wages.

After both parties had introduced considerable evidence the jury found in favor of petitioner and awarded him a $25,000 verdict. The trial judge later entered judgment notwithstanding the verdict. In doing so he reappraised the evidence as to fraud, found that petitioner had been "guilty of supine negligence" in failing to read the release, and accordingly held that the facts did not "sustain either in law or equity the allegations of fraud by clear, unequivocal and convincing evidence." This judgment notwithstanding the verdict was reversed by the Court of Appeals of Summit County, Ohio, on the ground that under federal law, which controlled, the jury's verdict must stand because there was ample evidence to support its finding of fraud. The Ohio Supreme Court, one judge dissenting, reversed the Court of Appeals' judgment and sustained the trial court's action, holding that: (1) Ohio, not federal, law governed; (2) under that law petitioner, a man of ordinary intelligence who could read, was bound by the release even though he had been induced to sign it by the deliberately false statement that it was only a receipt for back wages; and (3) under controlling Ohio law factual issues as to fraud in the execution of this release were properly decided by the judge rather than by the jury. * * *

First. We agree with the Court of Appeals of Summit County, Ohio, and the dissenting judge in the Ohio Supreme Court and hold that validity of releases under the Federal Employers' Liability Act raises a federal question to be determined by federal rather than state law. Congress in § 1 of the Act granted petitioner a right to recover against his employer for damages negligently inflicted. State laws are not controlling in determining what the incidents of this federal right shall be. * * * Manifestly the federal rights affording relief to injured railroad employees under a federally declared standard could be defeated if states were permitted to have the final say as to what defenses could and could not be properly interposed to suits under the Act. Moreover, only if federal law controls can the federal Act be given that uniform application throughout the country essential to effectuate its purposes. * * * Releases and other devices designed to liquidate or defeat injured employees' claims play an important part in the federal Act's administration. * * * Their validity is but one of the many interrelated questions that must constantly be determined in these cases according to a uniform federal law.

Second. In effect the Supreme Court of Ohio held that * * * the negligence of an innocent worker is sufficient to enable his employer to benefit by its deliberate fraud. Application of so harsh a rule to defeat a railroad employee's claim is wholly incongruous with the general policy of the Act to give railroad employees a right to recover just compensation for injuries negligently inflicted by their employers. And this Ohio rule is out of harmony with modern judicial and legislative practice to relieve injured persons from the effect of releases fraudulently obtained. * * * We hold that the correct federal rule is that * * * a release of rights under the Act is void when the employee is induced to sign it by the deliberately false and material statements of the railroad's authorized representatives made to deceive the employee as to the contents of the release. The trial court's charge to the jury correctly stated this rule of law.

Third. Ohio provides and has here accorded petitioner the usual jury trial of factual issues relating to negligence. But Ohio treats factual questions of fraudulent releases differently. It permits the judge trying a negligence case to resolve all factual questions of fraud "other than fraud in the factum." The factual issue of fraud is thus split into fragments, some to be determined by the judge, others by the jury.

It is contended that since a state may consistently with the Federal Constitution provide for trial of cases under the Act by a nonunanimous verdict, Minneapolis & St. Louis R. Co. v. Bombolis, 241 U.S. 211, 36 S.Ct. 595, 60 L.Ed. 961, Ohio may lawfully eliminate trial by jury as to one phase of fraud while allowing jury trial as to all other issues raised. The Bombolis case might be more in point had Ohio abolished trial by jury in all negligence cases including those arising under the federal Act. But Ohio has not done this. It has provided jury trials for cases arising under the federal Act but seeks to single out one phase of the question of fraudulent releases for determination by a judge rather than by a jury. * * *

We have previously held that "The right to trial by jury is 'a basic and fundamental feature of our system of federal jurisprudence'" and that it is "part and parcel of the remedy afforded railroad workers under the Employers' Liability Act." Bailey v. Central Vermont R. Co., 319 U.S. 350, 354, 63 S.Ct. 1062, 1064, 87 L.Ed. 1444. We also recognized in that case that to deprive railroad workers of the benefit of a jury trial where there is evidence to support negligence "is to take away a goodly portion of the relief which Congress has afforded them." It follows that the right to trial by jury is too substantial a part of the rights accorded by the Act to permit it to be classified as a mere "local rule of procedure" for denial in the manner that Ohio has here used. * * *

Reversed and remanded with directions.

Mr. Justice FRANKFURTER, whom Mr. Justice REED, Mr. Justice JACKSON and Mr. Justice BURTON join, concurring for reversal but dissenting from the Court's opinion.

Ohio, as do many other States, maintains the old division between law and equity as to the mode of trying issues, even though the same judge administers both. * * * [I]n all cases in Ohio, the judge is the trier of fact on this issue of fraud, rather than the jury. It is contended that the Federal Employers' Liability Act requires that Ohio courts send the fraud issue to a jury in

Dissent:
requiring fed
rule forces
upset of state's
settled distribution
of authority

the cases founded on that Act. To require Ohio to try a particular issue before a different fact-finder in negligence actions brought under the Employers' Liability Act from the fact-finder on the identical issue in every other negligence case disregards the settled distribution of judicial power between Federal and State courts where Congress authorizes concurrent enforcement of federally-created rights.

* * *

In 1916 the Court decided without dissent that States in entertaining actions under the Federal Employers' Liability Act need not provide a jury system other than that established for local negligence actions. States are not compelled to provide the jury required of Federal courts by the Seventh Amendment. Minneapolis & St. L. R. Co. v. Bombolis * * *. In the thirty-six years since this early decision after the enactment of the Federal Employers' Liability Act, 35 Stat. 65 (1908), the Bombolis case has often been cited by this Court but never questioned. Until today its significance has been to leave to States the choice of the fact-finding tribunal in all negligence actions, including those arising under the Federal Act. * * *

Although a State must entertain negligence suits brought under the Federal Employers' Liability Act if it entertains ordinary actions for negligence, it need conduct them only in the way in which it conducts the run of negligence litigation. The Bombolis case directly establishes that the Employers' Liability Act does not impose the jury requirements of the Seventh Amendment on the States *pro tanto* for Employers' Liability litigation. If its reasoning means anything, the Bombolis decision means that, if a State chooses not to have a jury at all, but to leave questions of fact in all negligence actions to a court, certainly the Employers' Liability Act does not require a State to have juries for negligence actions brought under the Federal Act in its courts. Or, if a State chooses to retain the old double system of courts, common law and equity * * * surely there is nothing in the Employers' Liability Act that requires traditional distribution of authority for disposing of legal issues as between common law and chancery courts to go by the board. * * * So long as all negligence suits in a State are treated in the same way, by the same mode of disposing equitable, non-jury, and common law, jury issues, the State does not discriminate against Employers' Liability suits nor does it make any inroad upon substance.

Ohio and her sister States with a similar division of functions between law and equity are not trying to evade their duty under the Federal Employers' Liability Act * * *. The States merely exercise a preference in adhering to historic ways of dealing with a claim of fraud; they prefer the traditional way of making unavailable through equity an otherwise valid defense. The State judges and local lawyers who must administer the Federal Employers' Liability Act in State courts are trained in the ways of local practice; it multiplies the difficulties and confuses the administration of justice to require, on purely theoretical grounds, a hybrid of State and Federal practice in the State courts as to a single class of cases. Nothing in the Employers' Liability Act or in the judicial enforcement of the Act for over forty years forces such judicial

hybridization upon the States. The fact that Congress authorized actions un-
der the Federal Employers' Liability Act to be brought in State as well as in
Federal courts seems a strange basis for the inference that Congress overrode
State procedural arrangements controlling all other negligence suits in a State
* * *. Such an inference is admissible, so it seems to me, only on the theory
that Congress included as part of the right created by the Employers' Liability
Act an assumed likelihood that trying all issues to juries is more favorable to
plaintiffs. * * *

Even though the method of trying the equitable issue of fraud which the
State applies in all other negligence cases governs Employers' Liability cases,
two questions remain for decision: Should the validity of the release be tested
by a Federal or a State standard? And if by a Federal one, did the Ohio
courts in the present case correctly administer the standard? If the States afford courts for enforcing the Federal Act, they must enforce the substance of
the right given by Congress. They cannot depreciate the legislative currency
issued by Congress—either expressly or by local methods of enforcement that
accomplish the same result. * * * In order to prevent diminution of railroad workers' nationally-uniform right to recover, the standard for the validity
of a release of contested liability must be Federal. * * *

NOTES AND QUESTIONS

1. In what ways is the question of what law governs the right to jury trial
in *Dice* the same or distinguishable from the question of the governing law in
Byrd? Is the process of applying federal law in a state court identical to the process
of applying state law in a federal court under the *Erie* doctrine? Note, *State Enforcement of Federally Created Rights*, 73 Harv.L.Rev. 1551 (1961). Under
what circumstances might a state court ignore federal law when it deems it to be
inconsistent with its own law or policy? By what method is uniform construction
and application of federal law by state courts assured? How does a state court determine which aspects of federal law it must apply? For example, must it apply
federal common law? What should the state court do if the decisions of the
lower federal courts are in conflict on a particular point? See United States ex
rel. Lawrence v. Woods, 432 F.2d 1072 (7th Cir.1970); People ex rel. Ray
v. Martin, 294 N.Y. 61, 73, 60 N.E.2d 541, 547 (1945), affirmed 326 U.S. 496,
66 S.Ct. 307, 90 L.Ed. 261 (1946); Breckline v. Metropolitan Life Ins. Co.,
406 Pa. 573, 578, 178 A.2d 748, 751 (1962). See generally Cullison, *State
Courts, State Law, and Concurrent Jurisdiction of Federal Questions*, 48 Iowa
L.Rev. 230 (1963).

2. Under what circumstances might a state court or legislature voluntarily
incorporate or apply federal law to a state-created right? Would such an incorporation or application present a federal question for purposes of original jurisdiction in the federal district courts or appellate jurisdiction in the United States
Supreme Court? See generally Hart, *The Relations Between State and Federal Law*,
54 Colum.L.Rev. 489, 536–38 (1954); Note, *Supreme Court Review of State
Interpretations of Federal Law Incorporated by Reference*, 66 Harv.L.Rev. 1498
(1953). Are the federal courts bound by the state construction of the incorporated
federal law?

3. In BROWN v. WESTERN RY. OF ALABAMA, 338 U.S. 294, 70 S.Ct. 105, 94 L.Ed. 100 (1949), respondent demurred to petitioner's complaint in an action brought in a Georgia state court under the Federal Employers' Liability Act. The theory of the demurrer was that the complaint failed to "set forth a cause of action and is otherwise insufficient in law." The Georgia courts sustained the demurrer on the basis of a state practice rule requiring pleading allegations to be construed "most strongly against the pleader." The Supreme Court reversed, stating in part:

> It is contended that this construction of the complaint is binding on us. The argument is that while state courts are without power to detract from "substantive rights" granted by Congress in FELA cases, they are free to follow their own rules of "practice" and "procedure." To what extent rules of practice and procedure may themselves dig into "substantive rights" is a troublesome question at best * * *. [C]ases in this Court point up the impossibility of laying down a precise rule to distinguish "substance" from "procedure." Fortunately, we need not attempt to do so. A long series of cases previously decided, from which we see no reason to depart, makes it our duty to construe the allegations of this complaint ourselves in order to determine whether petitioner has been denied a right of trial granted him by Congress. This federal right cannot be defeated by the forms of local practice. * * *

> Strict local rules of pleading cannot be used to impose unnecessary burdens upon rights of recovery authorized by federal laws. * * * Should this Court fail to protect federally created rights from dismissal because of over-exacting local requirements for meticulous pleadings, desirable uniformity in adjudication of federally created rights could not be achieved.

Id. at 296, 298–99, 70 S.Ct. at 106, 108, 94 L.Ed. at 102–04. Of what relevance is the presence or absence under Georgia practice of a right to replead following a demurrer?

CHAPTER 4

THE DEVELOPMENT OF MODERN PROCEDURE

SECTION A. COMMON-LAW PLEADING

STEPHEN, THE PRINCIPLES OF PLEADING IN CIVIL ACTIONS 37, 147–50 (Tyler ed. 1882): [a]

In the course of administering justice between litigating parties there are two successive objects: to ascertain the subject for decision, and to decide. It is evident that, towards the attainment of the first of these results, there is, in a *general* point of view, only one satisfactory mode of proceeding; and that this consists in making each of the parties state his own case, and collecting, from the opposition of their statements, the points of the legal controversy. Thus far, therefore, the course of every system of judicature is the same. It is common to them all to require, on behalf of each contending party, before the decision of the cause, a statement of his case. But from this point the coincidence naturally ceases. In the style of the contending statements, (called in forensic language *the pleadings*,) the principles on which they are framed, the manner in which they govern or affect the subsequent course of the cause, and the degree of attention paid to their construction, each different code of law exhibits some material difference of practice.   *   *   *

The manner of allegation in our courts may be said to have been first methodically formed and cultivated as a science in the reign of Edward I [1272–1307]. From this time the judges began systematically to prescribe and enforce certain *rules of statement*   *   *   *. None of them seem to have been originally of legislative enactment, or to have had any authority except usage or judicial regulation; but, from the general perception of their wisdom and utility, they acquired the character of fixed and positive institutions, and grew up into an entire and connected *system of pleading*.   *   *   *

As the object of all pleading or judicial allegation is to ascertain the subject for decision, so the main object of that system of pleading established in the common law of England is to ascertain it by the production of an *issue*; and this appears to be peculiar to that system.   *   *   *

The author is of opinion that this peculiarity of coming to issue took its rise in the practice of *oral* pleading. It seems a natural incident of that practice, to compel the pleaders to short and terse allegations, applying to each oth-

---

[a] This edition is based upon Stephen's own second edition of 1827, which is the last of his editions before the reform of common-law pleading in England in 1834.

315

er by way of answer, in somewhat of a logical form, and at length reducing the controversy to a precise point. For while the pleading was *merely* oral, * * * the court and the pleaders would have to rely exclusively on their memory for retaining the tenor of the discussion; and the development of some precise question or issue would then be a very convenient practice, because it would prevent the necessity of reviewing the different statements, and leave no burden on the memory but that of retaining the question itself so developed. And even after the practice of recording was introduced, the same brief and logical forms of allegation would naturally continue to be acceptable, while the pleadings were still *viva voce* * * *.

A co-operative reason for coming to issue was the variety of the modes of decision which the law assigned to different kinds of question. * * * As questions of law were decided by the *court,* and matters of fact referred to other kinds of investigation, it was, in the first place, necessary to settle whether the question in the cause or issue was a matter of *law* or *fact.* Again, if it happened to be a matter of fact, it required to be developed in a form sufficiently specific to show what was the method of trial appropriate to the case. And, unless the state of the question were thus adjusted between the parties, it is evident that they would not have known whether they were to put themselves on the judgment of the court or to go to trial; nor, in the latter case, whether they were to prepare themselves for trial by jury or for one of the other various modes of deciding [the] matter of fact.

NOTES

1. The change from oral to written pleadings cannot be dated precisely. The shift began in the late fourteenth century and extended into the second half of the sixteenth. Predictably the change increased the rigor and technicality of the pleading rules.

> * * * [T]his system of oral pleading had one great advantage over the later system of written pleadings. It made for far greater freedom in the statement of the case. * * * [W]hen all objections to the writ and process had been disposed of * * * the debate between the opposing counsel, carried on subject to the advice or the rulings of the judge, allowed the parties considerable latitude in pleading to the issue. Suggested pleas will, after a little discussion, be seen to be untenable; a proposition to demur will, after a few remarks by the judge, be obviously the wrong move. The counsel feel their way towards an issue which each can accept and allow to be enrolled. In fact, * * * it was not the strictness of the rules of pleading which hindered justice, it was rather the strictness and elaboration of the rules of process.

3 Holdsworth, *A History of English Law* 635 (4th ed. 1935). See also Maitland, *Introduction,* in *3 Yearbooks of Edward II,* 20 Selden Soc'y lxvi, lxviii (1905). Milsom, *Historical Foundations of the Common Law* 28–37, 39–40 (1969), contains a good description of oral pleadings as well as an excellent explanation of the Yearbooks, from which most of our knowledge of early pleading is derived; this book is a particularly valuable reference for most of the matters covered in this Chapter.

2. In this discussion we are concerned with pleading in the royal courts. It should be noted that at the time of the Norman Conquest (1066) and for a century or more afterward the ordinary recourse of suitors was not to the royal courts but to local, or communal, courts and to feudal courts in which a lord heard cases involving his tenants. The royal courts existed primarily to try offenses against the king's laws and to hear cases involving his tenants-in-chief, which came before the king in his capacity as a feudal lord. Gradually, however, these royal courts began to absorb business from the communal and feudal courts.

A person with a grievance against another sought justice from the king, and the king issued a *writ*, ordering the sheriff to bring the other person before the king's judges to answer the complaint. In the course of the twelfth century this pattern became standardized. When it became established that the king's courts would hear a particular kind of case—for example, an action for assault, an action for debt, an action for the possession of land—the complainant in such a case could obtain a writ from the king's chief minister, the chancellor, as a matter of course. See Milsom, *Historical Foundations of the Common Law* 22–25 (1969).

The writ, strictly speaking, was simply the document that commenced the action, similar in function to the modern summons; but each writ came to embody a *form of action,* a concept that governed the method of commencing the suit, the substantive requirements of the case, the manner of trial, and the type of sanction that would attend the eventual judgment. We will study the forms of action in detail in Section B of this Chapter. See pp. 329–49, infra. For the present it is enough to say that there was a writ for each type of case—or form of action —that the royal courts would hear; thus, for example, there was a writ of trespass, a writ of debt, and a writ of nuisance. If plaintiff selected a writ that did not fit the case, the action would fail. If there was no writ that fit the case, and the chancellor would not draw up a new one, plaintiff could obtain no relief in the royal courts. Among the elements of the case controlled by the writ, or form of action chosen, was the mode of decision of which Stephen speaks.

3. The "modes of decision" for issues of fact, referred to in the extract from Stephen, were, at an early date, "trial" by ordeal, by combat, and by oath. These were not trials in the sense in which we now understand and use that term; rather they were proofs undertaken by one of the parties (or both in the case of combat) at the direction of the court. "Since the trial was a matter of form, and the judgment was a determination what form it should take, the judgment naturally came before the trial. It determined, not only what the trial should be, but how it should be conducted and when, and what the consequence should be of this or that result." Thayer, *A Preliminary Treatise on Evidence at the Common Law* 9 (1898).

Ordeal—proof by carrying a red-hot iron unscathed or by sinking when thrown into a pool of water [b]—disappeared in England after it was proscribed by the Lateran Council in 1215. Combat—waged by champions of the parties—was resisted as a Norman importation, and during the reign of Henry II (1154–1189) an early form of jury began to supplant it, although it was not formally abolished until 1819. Thayer, op. cit. supra at 34–45.

---

[b] See Lea, *Superstition and Force* 252, 279 (3d ed. 1878). In ordeal by water, it was thought that the water would reject the evildoer; a rope was tied to the person making the proof in the hope that if proved innocent he could be kept from drowning.

For our purpose the most important of these early methods of proof was that by oath, or as more generally known, *wager of law* or *compurgation*. It required one of the parties to swear to his case with strict and elaborate formalities, accompanied by a number of "oath-helpers," usually twelve, who swore to the truthfulness of the party's oath, or in later periods to their belief in its truth. If all went as prescribed, he prevailed; but if the party or any of the "helpers" made an error by using a wrong word, that party lost.

It is hard for us to say how this ancient procedure worked in practice, hard to tell how easy it was to get oath-helpers who would swear falsely, hard to tell how much risk there was in an ordeal. The rational element of law must, it would seem, have asserted itself in the judgment which decided how and by whom the proof should be given; the jurisprudence of the old courts must have been largely composed of the answers to this question; * * * for example, we can see that even before the Norman Conquest the man who has been often accused has to go to the ordeal instead of being allowed to purge himself with oath-helpers.

Maitland, *Equity, Also the Forms of Action at Common Law* 310 (1909).

The importance of this procedure in legal history lies in the fact that a right to wage one's law was firmly established in certain classes of cases by the last half of the twelfth century, long before the jury began to emerge as an instrument for fact-determination. In its original form the jury, developed as a body for valuing property for taxes, decided cases on its own knowledge rather than after hearing witnesses. See Thayer, op. cit. supra at 47–136. Even in this form suitors saw in the jury a more rational mode of trial, and sought to use forms of action such as trespass, which having developed at a relatively late period did not provide a right to wager of law.[c] Thus, as we shall see in Section B of this Chapter, judicial development of the law for four-and-a-half centuries was channeled and motivated to a substantial degree by increasingly successful attempts to avoid the older modes of trial.[d]

---

1. A BRIEF OVERVIEW OF COMMON-LAW PLEADING

The basic structure of common-law pleading was simple and well-calculated to bring the parties to an issue of law or of fact. It was based on the following analysis. A substantive response to a claim—other than an expression of total agreement—will fall into one of three categories: (1) A party can deny that the alleged facts, even if true, give the claimant any legal right; (2)

---

[c] A similar desire to avoid trial by combat was among the causes for the desuetude of the writ of right, once the most important action. Preference for jury trial also encouraged the expanding jurisdiction of royal courts at the expense of the feudal courts since the jury was found only in the former.

[d] For a time in the fourteenth century it seemed that wager of law might be denied when the facts were well known to witnesses, but this development aborted. Fifoot, *History and Sources of the Common Law—Tort and Contract* 28–29 (1949). By the last quarter of the sixteenth century, however, "a defendant proposing to wage his law was somehow examined and admonished." Milsom, *Historical Foundations of the Common Law* 292–93 (1969).

a party can deny that the alleged facts are true; or (3) a party can say that even if the alleged facts are true and taken alone would establish a right, additional facts not mentioned by the claimant negate that right. Responses (1) and (2) raise issues of law and of fact respectively. Response (3) does not itself raise a contested issue; there is as yet no necessary disagreement between the parties. To raise the necessary issue the claimant must respond to the response, and this response also may fall into any of the three categories. If this response is again of type (3) no issue will have been raised and the process must continue. (How do the Federal Rules avoid the necessity for further pleading after a type (3) response? See Federal Rules 7(a) and 8(d).)

Of course the real process was more complex than this. Plaintiff's claim was set forth in the *declaration*. This document had to meet many formal requirements that might differ from one type of case to another. But stripped of much verbiage, and stated in modern English, it might have said: "Defendant promised to deliver a horse to plaintiff and plaintiff promised to pay 100 dollars for it, but defendant has refused to deliver the horse."

[margin note: 1) Declaration by TP]

At this point, defendant had to *demur* or *plead*. A demurrer would challenge the legal sufficiency of the declaration. Thus prior to STRANGBOROUGH & WARNERS CASE, 4 Leon. 3, 74 Eng.Rep. 686 (K.B. 1589), the modern language declaration set out above would have failed on demurrer, because a promise was not regarded as good consideration for a promise until that decision. A demurrer also would succeed if plaintiff had chosen the wrong writ (or form of action). There were also a great many technical sins that the declaration might commit, but by statute, 27 Eliz. 1, c. 5, § 1 (1585) and 4 Anne c. 16, § 1 (1705), unless these defects were raised by a *special demurrer,* which precisely spelled out the faults, they were waived. If a demurrer was sustained, plaintiff was out of court, although he generally was free to begin again if he could correct the mistake, as by suing in another form of action if the original form was incorrect. If the demurrer was quashed, judgment was entered for plaintiff.[e]

[margin note: 2) Δ demurs or pleads]

If defendant did not demur, he responded to the declaration in a *plea*. Pleas were of two types, *dilatory* and *peremptory*. Dilatory pleas did not deny the merits of plaintiff's claim, but challenged plaintiff's right to have the court hear the case; they included pleas to the jurisdiction of the court, pleas of a variance between the declaration and the writ, and pleas that the case must be suspended (when, for example, one of the parties was under age at the time of suit). A peremptory plea, or *plea in bar*, was on the merits. If defendant denied that he had promised to sell the horse, the plea was a *traverse;* a traverse terminated the pleadings and the case would go to trial to dispose of the issue raised by plaintiff's allegation and defendant's denial. But suppose defendant wanted to allege that at the time of the purported contract he was a minor;

[margin note: 2 types of Pleas 1) dilatory 2) premptory]

---

[e] Defendant could apply for leave to withdraw a demurrer and plead over after the demurrer was quashed, but the courts did not give leave freely. See Brahmah v. Roberts, 1 Bing. (N.C.) 481, 131 Eng.Rep. 1202 (C.P. 1835).

defendant would then plead by *confession and avoidance,* that is, admit the allegations of the declaration and seek to avoid them by pleading minority. If defendant followed this course, no issue would have been reached, and plaintiff would have to respond.

Plaintiff's response might be a demurrer to defendant's plea, which would raise the question whether minority was a defense to the agreement he had pleaded and defendant had confessed.[f] Or plaintiff might plead in a *replication*, either traversing defendant's allegation of his age, or confessing it, and alleging that defendant had lied about his age when making the contract. If plaintiff pleaded in confession and avoidance, defendant would again have to respond, by demurrer or by *rejoinder*. The pleas in confession and avoidance theoretically might go on indefinitely, and in some of the cases we read of a *surrejoinder*, a *rebutter*, and a *surrebutter*. Lack of formal names beyond that point suggests that even the ingenuity of the common-law pleader may have had its limits.

The common-law pleading system may seem ornate to you, even after only the brief description on the preceding pages. Yet bear in mind that this is only a skeletal outline. When the outline is filled in with special instances, inexplicable exceptions, arbitrary rules, and untraversable fictions, the result is one of the most complex and snare-ridden creations ever devised by man. Let us look at a common-law record and decision. (The reporter of the case, it should be noted, is the victorious lawyer, Saunders.)

VEALE v. WARNER

Court of King's Bench, 1670.
1 Wms. Saund. 323, 326, 85 Eng.Rep. 463, 468.

Be it remembered that * * * before our lord the King at Westminster came Thomas Veale Esquire * * * and brought here * * * his certain bill against William Warner, * * * in the custody of the marshal, &c. of a plea of debt: and there are pledges of prosecution, to wit, John Doe and Richard Roe; which said bill follows in these words, * * * [Veale] complains of [Warner] * * * that he render to him 2000l., of lawful money of England, which he owes to, and unjustly detains from him; for that whereas the said William, * * * at London aforesaid, to wit, in the parish of St. Mary-le Bow in the ward of Cheap, by his certain writing obligatory, sealed * * * and to the Court of our said lord the King now here shewn, * * * acknowledged himself to be held and firmly bound to * * * [Veale] in the said 2000l. to be paid to the said Thomas when he should be thereunto requested. Nevertheless, the said William (although often requested) hath not yet paid the said 2000l. to the said Thomas, but to pay the same to him hath hitherto alto-

---

f After a successful demurrer to a dilatory plea, judgment was not entered for plaintiff, but by an order *respondeat ouster*, defendant was directed to plead over.

gether refused, and yet refuses, to the damage of him the said Thomas of 100l.: and therefore he brings suit, &c.

And [Warner] * * * comes and defends the wrong and injury when, &c. and prays oyer of the said writing obligatory, and it is read to him, &c. He also prays oyer of the condition of the said writing, &c. and it is read to him in these words, to wit: "The condition of this obligation is such, that if * * * [Warner] shall and do in all things well and truly stand to, obey, abide, perform, fulfil, and keep the award * * * of John Coggs, gent. and John Foxwell, arbitrators * * * to arbitrate * * * and determine of and concerning all and all manner of action and actions, cause and causes of actions, suits, bills, bonds, specialties, judgments, executions, extents, quarrels, controversies, trespasses, damages, and demands whatsoever, at any time heretofore had, made, moved, brought, commenced, sued, prosecuted, done, suffered, committed, or depending by or between the said parties, * * * then this obligation to be void and of none effect, or else to remain in full force and virtue." Which being read and heard, the said William saith, that * * * [Veale] ought not to have his aforesaid action against him, because he saith that * * * the arbitrators in the said condition named, * * * made their award * * * that [Warner] * * * should satisfy, content, and pay to [Veale] * * * the full sum of 3169l. 16s. and 3d. of lawful money of England. And they further awarded that [Warner] * * * should seal, and as his deed deliver to [Veale] * * * a full and general release and discharge of all and all manner of actions, and causes of actions, suits, bills, bonds, specialties, judgments, executions, extents, quarrels, controversies, trespasses, damages, and demands whatsoever, at any time before the date of the bond brought here into Court had, made, moved, commenced, sued, prosecuted, committed, or depending by or between the said parties. And * * * [Warner] further saith, that he the said William * * * paid to * * * [Veale] the said sum * * * and also, then and there did seal, and as his deed deliver to * * * [Veale] the said full release * * * and this he is ready to verify: wherefore he prays judgment if the said Thomas ought to have or maintain his said action thereof against him &c.

And * * * [Veale] saith, that he by any thing by * * * [Warner] above in pleading alleged, ought not to be barred from having his said action thereof against the said William, because he saith that * * * [Warner] did not pay the said sum * * * as the said William hath above thereof in pleading alleged; and this he prays may be inquired of by the country, &c.

And * * * [Warner] saith that * * * [Veale] ought not to be admitted to say that he the said William hath not paid the said sum * * * because he saith that he the said Thomas, * * * by his certain writing acknowledged that he the said William had paid the said sum to the said Thomas * * * and this he is ready to verify: wherefore he prays judgment if the said Thomas ought to be admitted, against his own acknowledgment, to say, that he the said William hath not paid the said sum of money, &c.

Demurrer and joinder in demurrer.

* * *

And now in this term the plaintiff moved to have judgment. And Saunders for the defendant objected that the plaintiff could not have judgment, because it appeared by the record that the award was void, being all to be performed by the defendant and nothing by the plaintiff: and, therefore, if the award is void, it is not material whether the defendant has performed it or not, although he has pleaded a performance of it. And now he has acknowledged the contrary by his waiver of the issue offered by the plaintiff and pleading a bad rejoinder. And the plaintiff and defendant have both agreed, that the award pleaded by the defendant was the true award made by the arbitrators, which is altogether vicious. But if the plaintiff would have helped himself, he ought to have shewn the other part of the award before he assigned the breach, which he has not done here; and therefore he cannot have judgment.

And of such opinion was the whole Court clearly. But they would not give judgment for the defendant, because they conceived it was a trick in pleading; but they gave the plaintiff leave to discontinue on payment of costs. And Kelynge Chief Justice, reprehended Saunders for pleading so subtlely on purpose to trick the plaintiff by the omission of the other part of the award. But it was a case of the greatest hardship on the defendant; for the bond of submission was only in the penalty of 2000l., and the arbitrators had awarded him to pay 3100l., being 1100l. more than the real penalty of the bond; when in truth there was nothing at all due to the plaintiff, but he was indebted to the defendant. And afterwards the defendant exhibited an English bill in the Exchequer, disclosing bad practice of the plaintiff with the arbitrators, and had relief against the bond: and so this matter was at rest. * * *

NOTES AND QUESTIONS

1. "[B]efore our lord the King at Westminster." *Veale v. Warner* was brought in the Court of King's Bench, one of the three royal common-law courts, maintaining separate existence until merged in the High Court of Justice in 1873. The others were the Court of Common Pleas and the Court of Exchequer. All three developed out of the *Curia Regis* (the King's Court), which at the time of the Norman Conquest and for a period thereafter performed administrative and judicial functions in conjunction with the king. The first offshoot was Exchequer, which originally was charged with the collection and administration of the king's finances, but by 1250 had acquired full judicial jurisdiction. Next to develop separate status was Common Pleas, established by Henry II as the primary tribunal to hear cases not involving the crown. The remaining part of the King's Court supervised Common Pleas through the writ of error, and heard matters particularly touching the king's interests, such as criminal actions and cases involving his tenants in chief; it developed into King's Bench, but the fiction was maintained that hearings before that tribunal were before the king

himself. See Plucknett, *A Concise History of the Common Law* 143–51 (5th ed. 1956).

2. "[H]is * * * bill against William Warner, in the custody of the marshal, &c." Common Pleas was supposed to have exclusive jurisdiction over actions of debt, such as *Veale v. Warner.* But the judges and lawyers of each common-law court zealously sought to expand the jurisdiction of their tribunal, and *Veale v. Warner* illustrates one method by which King's Bench accomplished this. Not all common-law proceedings were commenced by writ; to an undefined extent each court could proceed on a *bill,* which was a complaint addressed directly to the court. See 2 Holdsworth, *A History of English Law* 339 (3d ed. 1923). One instance in which a court clearly could proceed on a bill was an action against one of the court's officers or a person within its custody, and such a bill might be brought on a cause of action that ordinarily was not within the jurisdiction of the court. Thus, a plaintiff who desired to bring an action of debt in King's Bench would first charge defendant with trespass, and by a "bill of Middlesex" that court would order the sheriff of Middlesex to arrest defendant and deliver him to the custody of the marshal of the Marshalsea—the court's prison; once defendant was within the custody of King's Bench, plaintiff could proceed against him by bill in the action of debt. Predictably, the arrest and commitment eventually became wholly fictitious, but defendant was not permitted to challenge the allegation that they had occurred. A similar device used to expand the jurisdiction of Exchequer was the writ of *quo minus,* by which a debtor to the crown could bring suit in that court on the theory that anyone withholding money from the debtor was rendering him unable to pay what was owed the king; in time, the allegation of plaintiff's debt to the king also became untraversable. See Plucknett, op. cit. supra at 161, 387; Milsom, *Historical Foundations of the Common Law* 53–59 (1969).

3. "[P]ledges of prosecution." The original writ in a lawsuit directed the sheriff, to whom it was addressed, to take some action, conditioned on plaintiff's "mak[ing] you secure of prosecuting his claim." Thus plaintiff had to furnish sureties, who would be liable to pay a fine that was imposed upon unsuccessful claimants. As the names of the pledges in the case suggest, the requirement became a sham. Nevertheless, the declaration could fail because satisfaction of the requirement was not alleged.

4. "[I]n the parish of St. Mary-le Bow in the ward of Cheap." As the jury originally decided cases on its own knowledge, it was necessary that jurors be drawn from the vicinity in which a transaction had occurred; the action therefore had to be brought near the place at which it arose, and the declaration had to show this. Since an English court could not summon jurors from abroad, technically it would have been impossible to bring an action on a contract made outside England. In such cases, however, plaintiff made an untraversable allegation that the contract had been made in the aforesaid parish and ward of the city of London. See Sack, *Conflict of Laws in the History of English Law,* in 3 *Law: A Century of Progress* 342, 370 (1937). Some cases actually must have arisen there, but you cannot tell from the records which they are.

5. "[T]o the Court * * * now here shown"; "prays oyer." A plaintiff suing upon a deed or a bond made profert of the document—that is, the plaintiff formally tendered it to the court, although it was strictly speaking not a part of the pleading. If defendant wanted to get the document in the pleadings in order to raise a question of law about it, she had to demand oyer of it, which

meant that defendant was entitled to read it and copy as much of it as she chose into the plea. At this point you might conclude that if defendant demurred, she would be demurring to her own pleading, but even though the document was set out in the plea, it was treated as if it were a part of the declaration. See Sutton, *Personal Actions at Common Law* 103 (1929), which is a particularly valuable introduction to common-law pleading. In what way does this process resemble the modern motion for summary judgment? See pp. 10–11, supra.

6. "[W]herefore he prays judgment if the said Thomas ought to have or maintain his said action." This is the standard conclusion of a pleading in confession and avoidance. Compare the conclusion of plaintiff's replication in the next paragraph of the report of the case. Why was defendant's allegation that he had performed the bond treated as a matter of confession and avoidance?

7. "[W]herefore he prays judgment if the said Thomas ought to be admitted, against his own acknowledgement, to say." Plaintiff in his replication had traversed defendant's claim of payment. Thus the replication already had created an issue, and defendant's rejoinder could not be one of the three responses described in the Overview of Common Law Pleading, pp. 318–19, supra; it is a plea of estoppel, and as stated in Saunders' argument waives the issue created by the traverse in plaintiff's replication. Why was this rejoinder "bad"? Did it allege that the award had been paid?

8. Why did Saunders, a thoroughly capable lawyer, file what he knew was an inadequate rejoinder? The answer lies in a peculiar facet of the demurrer:

> * * * [O]*n demurrer the court will consider the whole record, and give judgment for the party, who on the whole, appears to be entitled to it.* Thus, on demurrer to the replication, if the court think the replication bad, but perceive a substantial fault in the *plea,* they will give judgment, not for the defendant, but the plaintiff, provided the *declaration* be good; but if the declaration also be bad in substance, then, upon the same principle, judgment would be given for the defendant.

Stephen, *The Principles of Pleading in Civil Actions* 160 (Tyler ed. 1882). Thus, by making a rejoinder that he knew plaintiff would demur to, Saunders baited the trap he had set in his plea.

9. "[A]n English bill in the Exchequer." That part of the report of *Veale v. Warner* beginning, "But it was a case of the greatest hardship * * *" is not a part of the record, but is simply the reporter's justification of his own tactics. An English bill was a bill in equity, so-called because it was written in English rather than in the Latin of the common-law courts. As we will see, many instances of fraud and overreaching did not constitute defenses at law, but when such factors were established equity would enjoin a victorious plaintiff from enforcing the judgment at law. See pp. 358–59, infra. But how could such relief be obtained in Exchequer, which was a common-law court? The answer is that Exchequer had an equity side; "duplicating to some extent the Chancery during the seventeenth and eighteenth centuries," "its history * * * [was] by far the most obscure of all the English jurisdictions." Plucknett, op. cit. supra Note 2, at 185–86.

2. THE QUEST FOR A SINGLE ISSUE: PATHS AND PITFALLS

As indicated in the extract from Stephen with which this discussion began, the principal aim of common-law pleading was the production of a single issue; in many ways, the most serious problems in common-law pleading grew out of this persistent drive. To achieve the goal of singleness of issue, it was necessary to prohibit *duplicity* in pleading. That term did not connote fraud, but simply meant raising more than one issue in a pleading. Thus, in our example concerning the sale of the horse, defendant might wish to deny that he had made any promise *and* to assert that he was a minor at the time *and* to contend that a promise was not good consideration for another promise. There would be nothing devious or inconsistent in claiming all three defenses, but he was not permitted to do so. The traverse, the plea in confession and avoidance, and the demurrer were mutually exclusive.

A procedure was available that, in effect, permitted a party to delay the "demurrer." After trial and verdict for plaintiff, defendant could *move to arrest the judgment*, thereby raising the question whether the pleadings could support the judgment. In the case of a verdict for defendant, plaintiff's equivalent motion was for *judgment notwithstanding the verdict*—a term that has now come to identify a motion on a quite different theory. See p. 15, supra. By following this procedure, however, a party could not escape the expense of trial (costs not being awarded to the prevailing party on such a motion), and that party assumed the risk that the defect in a pleading might be cured by a later pleading or aided by the verdict; in any event, a fault that required the use of a special demurrer would not support such a delayed motion. Nonetheless, the practice became very popular, and Sir Edward Coke advised:

> * * * When the matter in fact will clearly serve for your client, although your opinion is that the plaintiff has no cause of action, yet take heed you do not hazard the matter upon a demurrer; in which, upon the pleading, * * * more perhaps will arise than you thought of; but first take advantage of the matters of fact, * * * and never at first demur in law, when after the trial of the matters in fact, the matters in law * * * will be saved to you.

THE LORD CROMWELL'S CASE, 4 Co.Rep. 12b, 14a, 76 Eng.Rep. 877, 884 (K.B. 1578–1581). See Chitty, *A Treatise on Pleading* *662.

No such procedure was available to the party who wanted to deny his adversary's allegations and at the same time advance affirmative allegations of his own. For the plea in confession and avoidance had to give *color*. "As a term of pleading, * * * ["color"] signifies an apparent or prima facie right; and the meaning of the rule, that every pleading in confession and avoidance must give color, is, that it must admit an apparent right in the opposite party, and rely, therefore, on some new matter by which that apparent right is defeat-ed." Stephen, *The Principles of Pleading in Civil Actions* 206–07 (Tyler ed. 1882). A plea in confession and avoidance that failed to give color was doomed, even though it revealed a defense that could have been raised by traverse. In GIBBONS v. PEPPER, 1 Ld.Raym. 38, 91 Eng.Rep. 922 (K.B. 1695), an action for running down plaintiff, defendant admitted the trespass but pleaded that his horse had become so frightened he could not control it; on demurrer the court ordered judgment for plaintiff, holding that if defendant's facts were true there had been no battery at all and the plea should have been a traverse.

Out of this rule that a party could not plead new matter without confessing the opposing party's prima-facie right grew one of the weirder formulae of common-law pleading—the giving of *express color*. See Stephen, op. cit. supra at 210–15; Sutton, *Personal Actions at Common Law* 186–99 (1929). Today, we mercifully are spared the necessity of learning the hoary details that surrounded this device, but a brief look at it will illustrate the complexities of the system that lay beneath the surface of our original simple outline.

Suppose that plaintiff had brought an action of trespass against defendant for entering on plaintiff's land, and that the only genuine issue in the case was the title to the land, defendant contending that although plaintiff had been in possession of the land, defendant was the true owner. If defendant denied the trespass by a traverse, she would be permitted to establish her own title as a defense. However, even if the only issue concerning her title was a question of law, there would have to be a full trial and the case would be decided by a jury under the guidance of the judge. Trial could not be avoided unless defendant somehow could introduce the new matter—her claim of title—into the pleadings and thereby permit it to be made the subject of a demurrer. Yet under the rule that required a plea in confession and avoidance to give color to plaintiff's claim, defendant could not assert new matter without confessing plaintiff's apparent right. The solution of express color was for defendant to confess the existence of a plausible, but imperfect, title in plaintiff, and then to assert her own title by way of avoidance. Having done this, plaintiff could not traverse the confession—even though it was the sheerest fiction—for that would leave two issues in the case; he had to respond to the matter pleaded in avoidance, and when the validity of defendant's claim turned on a question of law, the appropriate response would be a demurrer. You should note, however, that although giving express color enabled defendant to introduce her claim of title into the case, defendant was not able at the same time to deny that she had entered the land at all.[g]

[g] Another device by which defendant could introduce her title into the pleadings in order to make it possible to dispose of the case on a demurrer was the *special traverse*. Defendant would assert her own title in the first part of her plea (this portion being called the "inducement"), and follow this with a denial of the declaration prefaced with the words *absque hoc* (without this). The conclusion of the plea was in the form found in a plea of confession and avoidance, rather than "to the country" as in the common traverse. See Note 6 on p. 324, supra. Plaintiff could

The insistence on arriving at a single issue also prohibited raising more than one issue of fact in a pleading. The fault could be challenged only by a special demurrer, and over a long period the strictness of the prohibition against multiple issues relaxed, but it never ceased to pose a problem for the pleader. Originally a declaration could not state more than one cause of action; at an early date, however, plaintiffs were permitted to join causes of action arising under the same writ, and, as long as they were stated in separate counts, different versions of the same cause of action could be pleaded.[h] Defendant was permitted to plead separately to each count, and indeed might demur to one, traverse a second, and confess and avoid a third. But defendant could not plead two or more defenses to a single count and the ability to deny more than one of its allegations was severely restricted. By a statute, 4 Anne c. 16, § 4 (1705), this was changed to allow more than one plea to a count with the court's permission, but as long as common-law pleading survived there could be no more than one replication to a plea.

As a consequence of these rules, a defendant who did not demur was safest if he could make a defense under a plea of the *general issue,* which challenged plaintiff's whole case.[i] This plea spared defendant the necessity of spelling out his defense, which meant that he did not have to divulge it to plaintiff or run the risk of misstating it. More importantly, the general issue in effect permitted defendant to traverse a number of plaintiff's allegations and, in addition, to raise defenses that ordinarily would be matters of confession and avoidance. Of course not all defenses could be raised under the general issue, and knowing which defenses had to be specially pleaded in particular forms of action was a matter of subtle learning. Although the whole theoretical structure of common-law pleading and its quest for a single issue was threatened by the general issue, inexorable pressures—particularly in the eighteenth century—gradually expanded its scope and availability. In conjunction with the common counts—a particularly cryptic form of declaration in contract, which will be discussed in Section B, p. 349, infra—the plea of the general issue permitted some cases to come to trial with the issues not only unnarrowed, but indeed undisclosed. A good example of the prob-

---

then tender issue on defendant's denial, or challenge the legal sufficiency of the inducement by a demurrer. See Stephen, op. cit. supra at 181–99; Sutton, op. cit. supra at 170–77.

h This privilege was widely used because of the strictness of the rule against *variances* between pleading and proof. A good example of the prohibition on variances is Latham v. Rutley, 2 B. & C. 20, 107 Eng.Rep. 290 (K.B. 1823). Plaintiff who had pleaded breach of a contract to carry and deliver goods safely was nonsuited because he proved a contract to carry and deliver goods safely, fire and robbery excepted, even though the verdict established that the loss was not caused by either fire or robbery.

i Plaintiff's equivalent to the plea of the general issue, the replication *de injuria,* was less frequently available, and in most cases plaintiff was permitted to seize on only one facet of the plea. The most famous illustration is Crogate's Case, 8 Coke 66b, 77 Eng.Rep. 574 (K.B. 1608), which forms the basis for a brilliant satire on the common-law system. Hayes, *Crogate's Case: A Dialogue in Ye Shades on Special Pleading,* in 9 Holdsworth, *A History of English Law* 417 (2d ed. 1938).

lem was stated by Henry Brougham in a seminal speech to Parliament on law reform:

> * * * The plaintiff declares, that the defendant, being indebted to him for so much money had and received to the use of the said plaintiff * * * undertook and faithfully promised to pay it, but broke his engagement; and the count is thus framed, the self-same terms being invariably used, whatever be the cause of action which can be brought into Court under this head. * * * In the first place, such is the declaration for money paid by one individual to another, for the use and benefit of the plaintiff; this is what alone the words of the count imply, but to express this they are rarely, indeed, made use of. 2dly, The self-same terms are used on suing for money received on a consideration that fails, and used in the same way to describe all the endless variety of cases which can occur of such failure * * *. 3dly, The same words are used * * * to recover money paid under mistake of fact. 4thly, To recover money paid by one person to a stakeholder, in consideration of an illegal contract made with another person. 5thly, Money paid to revenue officers for releasing the goods illegally detained, of the person paying. 6thly, To try the right to any office, instead of bringing an assize. 7thly, To try the liability of the landlord for rates levied on his tenant. What information, then, does such a declaration give?

> * * *

> In the [form of action of] *indebitatus assumpsit*, from which I took my first example, * * * under [a plea of the general issue] no less than eight different defences may be set up; as, for instance, a denial of the contract, payment, usury, gaming, infancy, coverture, accord and satisfaction, release.

Brougham, *Present State of the Law* 70–71, 73 (1828).

Thus the pleadings in the English common-law courts immediately preceding the period of reform that began in 1825 presented a strange potpourri of ornate and sinuous paths toward an elusive single issue side by side with a series of pleading rules that fostered abstract and unilluminating statements of dispute. Indeed, as we shall see in Section D of this Chapter, it was the broad scope of the general issue that furnished the chief impetus to the earliest reform. But first we must look into that other peculiar contribution of common-law procedure—the forms of action.

SECTION B. THE FORMS OF ACTION

1. THE DEVELOPMENT OF THE FORMS— CHIEFLY OF TRESPASS

MAITLAND, EQUITY, ALSO THE FORMS OF ACTION AT COMMON LAW 296, 298–99, 304–05, 314–15, 332, 335, 342–47, 359–61 (1909):

Let it be granted that one man has been wronged by another; the first thing that he or his advisers have to consider is what form of action he shall bring. It is not enough that in some way or another he should compel his adversary to appear in court and should then state in the words that naturally occur to him the facts on which he relies and the remedy to which he thinks himself entitled. No, English law knows a certain number of forms of action, each with its own uncouth name * * *. This choice is not merely a choice between a number of queer technical terms, it is a choice between methods of procedure adapted to cases of different kinds.

* * * '[A] form of action' has implied a particular original process, a particular mesne process, a particular final process, a particular mode of pleading, of trial, of judgment. But further to a very considerable degree the substantive law administered in a given form of action has grown up independently of the law administered in other forms. Each procedural pigeon-hole contains its own rules of substantive law, and it is with great caution that we may argue from what is found in one to what will probably be found in another; each has its own precedents. It is quite possible that a litigant will find that his case will fit some two or three of these pigeon-holes. If that be so he will have a choice, which will often be a choice between the old, cumbrous, costly, on the one hand, the modern, rapid, cheap, on the other. Or again he may make a bad choice, fail in his action, and take such comfort as he can from the hints of the judges that another form of action might have been more successful. * * * Lastly he may find that, plausible as his case may seem, it just will not fit any one of the receptacles provided by the courts and he may take to himself the lesson that where there is no remedy there is no wrong.

* * * So long as the forms of action were still in use, it was difficult to tell the truth about their history. There they were, and it was the duty of judges and text writers to make the best of them, to treat them as though they formed a rational scheme provided all of a piece by some all-wise legislator. * * * It was difficult to discover, difficult to tell, the truth, difficult to say that these forms of action belonged to very different ages, expressed very different and sometimes discordant theories of law, had been twisted and tortured to inappropriate uses, were the monuments of long forgotten political

struggles; above all it was difficult to say of them that they had their origin and their explanation in a time when the king's court was but one among many courts. But now,   *   *   *   the truth might be discovered and be told, and one part of the truth is assuredly this that throughout the early history of the forms of action there is an element of struggle, of struggle for jurisdiction. In order to understand them we must not presuppose a centralized system of justice   *   *   *; rather we must think that the forms of action, the original writs, are the means whereby justice is becoming centralized, whereby the king's court is drawing away business from other courts.

*   *   *   I shall attempt a sketch in brief outline of the order in which the different forms of action are developed.   *   *   *

I.   1066—1154.   The first [period]   *   *   *   would end with the great reforms of Henry II.   Litigation of an ordinary kind still takes place chiefly in the communal and feudal courts; even the king's court may be considered as a feudal court, a court of and for the king's tenants in chief. *   *   *   His court is concerned chiefly with (1) the pleas of the crown, *i.e.* cases in which royal rights are concerned, (2) litigation between the king's tenants in chief—for such tenants it is the proper feudal court, (3) complaints of default of justice in lower courts.   *   *   *

II.   1154—1189.   The legislative activity of Henry II's reign marks a second period.   Under Henry II the exceptional becomes normal.   He places royal justice at the disposal of anyone who can bring his case within a certain formula.   From the end of his reign we have Glanvill's book, and we see already a considerable apparatus of writs   *   *   *; they have assumed distinct forms, forms which they will preserve until the nineteenth century   *   *   *; each writ is the beginning of a particular form of action.   *   *   *

As regards those claims which in after days give rise to the personal actions, those actions which, as we say, are founded on contract or founded on tort, Glanvill has but little to tell us; they are seldom prosecuted in the king's court.   But the action of Debt is known there.   *   *   *

III.   1189–1272.   This, our third period, extending from the death of Henry II to the accession of Edward I, is a period of rapid growth *   *   *.   New writs are freely invented, though towards the end of Henry III's reign this gives rise to murmurs   *   *   *.   There is now a large store of original writs which are writs of course (*brevia de cursu*), that is to say, they may be obtained from the subordinate officers of the royal chancery   *   *   *.

Meanwhile the actions which came to be known as personal make their appearance.   The oldest seems to be 'Debt-Detinue'   *   *   *.   Gradually this action divides itself into two, Detinue for a specific chattel, Debt for a sum of money—this differentiation takes place early in the thirteenth century.   As in Detinue the judgment given for the plaintiff awards him either the chattel itself, or its value; and, as the defendant thus has the option of giving back the chattel or paying its value, Bracton is led to make the important remark that there is no real action for chattels—an important remark, for it is the foundation of all our talk about real and personal property.   To Debt and Detinue we

must now add Replevin, the action for goods unlawfully taken in distress.
* * * Covenant also has appeared * * *. Gradually the judges
came to the opinion that the only acceptable evidence of a covenant is a sealed
writing, and one of the foundations of our law of contract is thus laid.
* * *

   But the most important phenomenon is the appearance of Trespass—that
fertile mother of actions. Instances of what we can not but call actions of trespass are found even in John's reign, but I think it clear that the writ of trespass
did not become a writ of course until very late in Henry III's reign. Now trespass * * * has its roots in criminal law * * *. The old criminal
action (yes, action) was the Appeal of Felony * * *. It was but slowly
supplanted by indictment—the procedure of the common accuser set going by
Henry II, the appeal on the other hand being an action brought by a person aggrieved by the crime.

        * * * The new phenomenon appears about the year 1250, it is an ac-
tion which might be called an attenuated appeal based on an act of violence.
* * * The action of trespass is founded on a breach of the king's peace:
—with force and arms the defendant has assaulted and beaten the plaintiff,
broken the plaintiff's close, or carried off the plaintiff's goods; he is sued for
damages. The plaintiff seeks not violence but compensation, but the unsuccessful defendant will also be punished and pretty severely. In other actions
the unsuccessful party has to pay an amercement for making an unjust, or resisting a just claim; the defendant found guilty of trespass is fined and imprisoned. What is more, the action for trespass shows its semi-criminal nature in
the process that can be used against a defendant who will not appear—if he
will not appear, his body can be seized and imprisoned; if he can not be
found, he may be outlawed. We thus can see that the action of trespass is one
that will become very popular with plaintiffs because of the stringent process
against defendants. I very much doubt whether in Henry III's day the action
could as yet be used save where there really had been what we might fairly call
violence and breach of the peace; but gradually the convenience of this new
action showed itself. In order to constitute a case for 'Trespass *vi et armis*,' it
was to the last necessary that there should be some wrongful application of
physical force to the defendant's lands or goods or person—but a wrongful
step on his land, a wrongful touch to his person or chattels was held to be force
enough and an adequate breach of the king's peace. This action then has the
future before it.

        * * *

   IV. 1272–1307. The reign of 'the English Justinian' may be treated as
a period by itself—a period of statutory activity. Statutes made by king and
parliament now interfere with many details both of substantive law and of procedure. * * * The whole system stiffens. Men have learnt that a power to
invent new remedies is a power to create new rights and duties, and it is no
longer to be suffered that the chancellor or the judges should wield this power.
How far the process of crystallisation had gone, how rigid the system was becoming, we learn from a section of the Statute of Westminster II, 13 Edw. I c.

24 (1285). Men have been obliged to depart from the Chancery without getting writs, because there are none which will exactly fit their cases, although
these cases fall within admitted principles. It is not to be so for the future
* * *. 'And whensoever from henceforth it shall fortune in the Chancery,
that in one case a writ is found, and in a like case falling under like law, and
requiring like remedy, is found none, the clerks of the Chancery shall agree in
making the writ; or * * * let the cases be written in which they can not
agree, and let them refer them until the next Parliament, and by consent of
men learned in the law, a writ shall be made, lest it might happen after that the
court should long time fail to minister justice unto complainants.' * * *
[W]hen we say that but little use was made of this Statute there is one great
exception. It is regarded as the statutory warrant for the variation of the writs
of trespass so as to suit special cases, until at length—about the end of the Middle Ages—lawyers perceive that they have a new form 'Trespass upon the special case' or 'Case.' * * * It is worth noting that a writ issued by the Chancery is not necessarily a good writ. The justices may quash it as contrary to
law, and in the later Middle Ages the judges are conservative * * *. At any
rate the tale of common law (*i.e.* non-statutory) actions was now regarded as
complete. The king's courts had come to be regarded as omnicompetent
courts, they had to do all the important civil justice of the realm and to do it
with the limited supply of forms of action which had been gradually accumulated in the days when feudal justice and ecclesiastical justice were serious competitors with royal justice.

V.   1307–1833. * * *

From Edward I's day onwards trespass *vi et armis* is a common action.
We may notice three main varieties—unlawful force has been used against the
body, the goods, the land of the plaintiff; so we have trespass in assault and
battery, trespass *de bonis asportatis, trespass quare clausum fregit.* * * *

I have already said that the writ-making power wielded by the king and
his Chancellor was gradually curbed by our parliamentary constitution, and in
Edward I's day it has become necessary to tell the Chancery that it is not to be
too pedantic, but may make variations in the old formulas when a new case
falls under an old rule. * * * [T]he most important use made of this
liberty consisted in some extensions of the action of trespass. Gradually during Edward III's reign we find a few writs occurring which in form are extremely like writs of trespass—and they are actually called writs of trespass—
but the wrong complained of does not always consist of a direct application of
unlawful physical force * * *; sometimes the words *vi et armis* do not
appear. Sometimes there is no mention of the king's peace. Still they are spoken of as writs of trespass * * *. The plaintiff is said to bring an action
upon his case, or upon the special case, and gradually it becomes apparent that
really a new and a very elastic form of action has thus been created. I think
that lawyers were becoming conscious of this about the end of the fourteenth
century. Certain procedural differences have made their appearance—when
there is *vi et armis* in the writ, then the defendant if he will not appear may be
taken by *capias ad respondendum* or may be outlawed—this can not be if there

is no talk of force and arms or the king's peace.   Thus Case falls apart from Trespass—during the fifteenth century the line between them becomes always better marked.   *   *   *

Case becomes a sort of general residuary action; much, particularly, of the modern law of negligence developed within it.   Sometimes it is difficult to mark off case from trespass.

NOTES AND QUESTIONS

1.   Case developed into a remedy not only for wrongs that were similar to those governed by trespass, but for wrongs that were much more similar to those for which the action of debt was appropriate.   Yet case never lost its roots in trespass.   Why didn't actions of debt on the case develop?   See Kiralfy, *The Action on the Case* 3, 44 (1951).

2.   Maitland's conclusions that trespass grew out of the appeal of felony and that case drew its authority from the Statute of Westminster II are debatable. Others have found the root of trespass in the assize of novel disseisin, in the proceedings of local courts, and in *queralae* ("innominate" actions without writ frequently found in the records of royal courts throughout the thirteenth century). The diversity of opinion is comprehensively reported in Fifoot, *History and Sources of the Common Law—Tort and Contract* 44–56, 66–74 (1949), a book of very great value in the study of the forms.   See also Milsom, *Historical Foundations of the Common Law* 244–70 (1969).

3.   "This action of *trespass*   *   *   *   *on the case* is   *   *   *   so called because the plaintiff's whole case or cause of complaint is set forth at length in the original writ."   3 Blackstone, *Commentaries* *122.   The writ in trespass was shorter and more stylized than that in case, the particular facts being set forth only in the declaration.   For the contrast, compare the writs in Stephen, *The Principles of Pleading in Civil Actions* 48, 50–52 (Tyler ed. 1882).

In England's American colonies, the distinctions between the forms of action, although recognized, were not enforced with the rigor that characterized the procedure of the mother country.   For example, there are instances of the use of both trespass and case for the specific recovery of chattels and real property, and trover and assumpsit frequently were not distinguished from case. Ejectment, when it was still regarded as a modern improvement in England, was unused in New England because of its technicalities.   See Morris, *Studies in the History of American Law* 46–59 (2d ed. 1959).   Since law books were scarce in the colonies, and many of the judges were laymen, these developments were to be expected.   The most technical applications of the forms of action in this country came during the first half of the nineteenth century after the bar had grown in influence, and texts such as Blackstone had become available.   See, e. g., Adams v. Hemmenway, 1 Mass. 145 (1804); Wilson v. Smith, 10 Wend. 324 (N.Y. 1833).

2. THE LINES BLUR

A. TRESPASS OR CASE?

SCOTT, an Infant, by his next Friend v. SHEPHERD, an Infant, by Guardian

Court of Common Pleas, 1773.
2 Wm.Bl. 892, 96 Eng.Rep. 525.

Trespass and assault * * *. On not guilty pleaded, the cause came on to be tried before Nares, J., * * * when the jury found a verdict for the plaintiff with 100£. damages, subject to the opinion of the Court on this case: * * * [D]efendant threw a lighted squib, made of gunpowder, &c. from the street into the market-house, * * * where a large concourse of people were assembled; which lighted squib, * * * fell upon the standing of one Yates, who sold gingerbread, &c. That one Willis instantly, and to prevent injury to himself and the said wares of the said Yates, took up the said lighted squib from off the said standing, and then threw it across the said market-house, when it fell upon another standing there of one Ryal, * * * who instantly, and to save his own goods from being injured, took up the said lighted squib from off the said standing, and then threw it to another part of the said market-house, and, in so throwing it, struck the plaintiff * * * in the face therewith, and the combustible matter then bursting, put out one of the plaintiff's eyes. Qu. If this action be maintainable?

* * *

NARES, J., was of opinion, that trespass would well lie in the present case. That the natural and probable consequence of the act done by the defendant was injury to somebody, and therefore the act was illegal at common law. * * * Being therefore unlawful, the defendant was liable to answer for the consequences, be the injury mediate or immediate. * * * The principle I go upon is what is laid down in *Reynolds and Clark,* Stra. 634, that if the act in the first instance be unlawful, trespass will lie. Wherever therefore an act is unlawful at first, trespass will lie for the consequences of it. * * * [Defendant] * * * is the person, who, in the present case, gave the mischievous faculty to the squib. That mischievous faculty remained in it till the explosion. No new power of doing mischief was communicated to it by Willis or Ryal. It is like the case of a mad ox turned loose in a crowd. The person who turns him loose is answerable in trespass for whatever mischief he may do. The intermediate acts of Willis and Ryal will not purge the original tort in the defendant. But he who does the first wrong is answerable for all the consequential damages. * * *

BLACKSTONE, J., was of opinion, that an action of trespass did not lie for Scott against Shepherd upon this case. He took the settled distinction to be, that where the injury is immediate, an action of trespass will lie; where it is only consequential, it must be an action on the case: *Reynolds and Clarke,* Lord Raym. 1401. * * * The lawfulness or unlawfulness of the original act is not the criterion; though something of that sort is put into Lord Raymond's mouth in Stra. 635 * * *. But this cannot be the general rule; for it is held by the Court in the same case, that if I throw a log of timber into the highway, (which is an unlawful act), and another man tumbles over it, and is hurt, an action on the case only lies, it being a consequential damage; but if in throwing it I hit another man, he may bring trespass, because it is an immediate wrong. Trespass may sometimes lie for the consequences of a lawful act. If in lopping my own trees a bough accidentally falls on my neighbour's ground, and I go thereon to fetch it, trespass lies. * * * But then the entry is of itself an immediate wrong. And case will sometimes lie for the consequence of an unlawful act. If by false imprisonment I have a special damage, as if I forfeit my recognizance thereby, I shall have an action on the case. * * * Yet here the original act was unlawful, and in the nature of trespass. So that lawful or unlawful is quite out of the case; the solid distinction is between direct or immediate injuries on the one hand, and mediate or consequential on the other. And trespass never lay for the latter. If this be so, the only question will be, whether the injury which the plaintiff suffered was immediate, or consequential only; and I hold it to be the latter. The original act was, as against Yates, a trespass; not as against Ryal, or Scott. The tortious act was complete when the squib lay at rest upon Yates's stall. He, or any bystander, had, I allow, a right to protect themselves by removing the squib, but should have taken care to do it in such a manner as not to endamage others. But Shepherd, I think, is not answerable in an action of trespass and assault for the mischief done by the squib in the new motion impressed upon it, and the new direction given it, by either Willis or Ryal; who both were free agents, and acted upon their own judgment. This differs it from the cases put of turning loose a wild beast or a madman. They are only instruments in the hand of the first agent. Nor is it like diverting the course of an enraged ox, or of a stone thrown, or an arrow glancing against a tree; because there the original motion, the vis impressa, is continued, though diverted. Here the instrument of mischief was at rest, till a new impetus and a new direction are given it, not once only, but by two successive rational agents. But it is said that the act is not complete, nor the squib at rest, till after it is spent or exploded. It certainly has a power of doing fresh mischief, and so has a stone that has been thrown against my windows, and now lies still. Yet if any person gives that stone a new motion, and does farther mischief with it, trespass will not lie for that against the original thrower. No doubt but Yates may maintain trespass against Shepherd. And, according to the doctrine contended for, so may Ryal and Scott. Three actions for one single act! nay, it may be extended in infinitum. If a man tosses a football into the street, and after being kicked about by one hundred people, it at last breaks a tradesman's windows; shall he have trespass against the man who first produced it? Surely only against the man who gave it that mischievous direction. But it is said, if Scott has no action against Shepherd, against whom must he seek his remedy? I give no opinion whether case would lie against Shepherd for the consequential damage; though, as at present advised, I think, upon the circumstances, it would. But I think, in strictness of law, trespass would lie against Ryal, the immediate actor in this unhappy business. * * * The throwing it across the market-house, instead of brushing it down, or throwing [it] out of the open sides into the street, (if it was not meant to continue the sport, as it is called), was at least an unnecessary and incautious act. Not even menaces from others are sufficient to justify a trespass against a third person; much less a fear of danger to either his goods or his person;—nothing but inevitable necessity. * * * And I admit that the defendant is answerable in trespass for all the direct and inevitable effects caused by his own immediate act.—But what is his own immediate act? The throwing the squib to Yates's stall. * * * But he is not responsible for the acts of other men. * * * In our case the verdict is suspended till the determination of the Court. And though after verdict the Court will not look with eagle's eyes to spy out a variance, yet, when a question is put by the jury upon such a variance, and it is made the very point of the cause, the Court will not wink against the light, and say that evidence, which at most is only applicable to an action on the case, will maintain an action of trespass. * * * The same evidence that will maintain trespass, may also frequently maintain case, but not e converso. Every action of trespass with a "per quod" includes an action on the case. I may bring trespass for the immediate injury, and subjoin a "per quod" for the consequential damages;—or may bring case for the consequential damages, and pass over the immediate injury * * *. But if I bring trespass for an immediate injury, and prove at most only a consequential damage, judgment must be for the defendant; *Gates and Bailey*, Tr. 6 Geo. 3, 2 Wils. 313. * * *

GOULD, J., was of the same opinion with Nares, J., that this action was well maintainable.—The whole difficulty lies in the form of the action, and not in the substance of the remedy. The line is very nice between case and trespass upon these occasions: I am persuaded there are many instances wherein both or either will lie. I agree with brother Nares, that wherever a man does an unlawful act, he is answerable for all the consequences; and trespass will lie against him, if the consequence be in nature of trespass. But, exclusive of this, I think the defendant may be considered in the same view as if he himself had personally thrown the squib in the plaintiff's face. The terror impressed upon Willis and Ryal excited self-defence, and deprived them of the power of recollection. * * *

DE GREY, C.J. This case is one of those wherein the line drawn by the law between actions on the case and actions of trespass is very nice and delicate. Trespass is an injury accompanied with force, for which an action of trespass vi et armis lies against the person from whom it is received. The question here is, whether the injury received by the plaintiff arises from the force of the original act of the defendant, or from a new force by a third person. I agree with my brother Blackstone as to the principles he has laid down, but not in his application of those principles to the present case. The real question certainly does not turn upon the lawfulness or unlawfulness of the original act; for actions of trespass will lie for legal acts when they become trespasses by accident * * *. They may also not lie for the consequences even of illegal acts, as that of casting a log in the highway, &c.—But the true question is, whether the injury is the direct and immediate act of the defendant; and I am of opinion, that in this case it is. The throwing the squib was an act unlawful and tending to affright the bystanders. So far, mischief was originally intended; not any particular mischief, but mischief indiscriminate and wanton. Whatever mischief therefore follows, he is the author of it * * *. Every one who does an unlawful act is considered as the doer of all that follows. * * * I look upon all that was done subsequent to the original throwing as a continuation of the first force and first act, which will continue till the squib was spent by bursting. And I think that any innocent person removing the danger from himself to another is justifiable; the blame lights upon the first thrower. * * * It has been urged, that the intervention of a free agent will make a difference: but I do not consider Willis and Ryal as free agents in the present case, but acting under a compulsive necessity for their own safety and self-preservation. * * *

Postea to the plaintiff.

NOTES AND QUESTIONS

1. This case, which appears here as reported by Justice Blackstone, also is reported at length in 3 Wils.K.B. 403, 95 Eng.Rep. 1124. That report sets out the pleadings and arguments, as well as somewhat different versions of the opinions.

2. In what ways does Justice Blackstone differ from Chief Justice De Grey? From Justice Nares? On what facts might Chief Justice De Grey and Justice Nares reach a different result? Chief Justice De Grey and Justice Gould? Since Justice Blackstone believes an action in case would lie against Shepherd, is there really any substantive difference between him and his brethren? Would they have agreed with him that Scott could have maintained an action against Ryal? What would have been the nature of that action? In light of *Gibbons v. Pepper,* p. 326, supra, would actions of trespass lie against both Shepherd and Ryal? In the report of *Scott v. Shepherd* referred to in Note 1, Justice Gould is quoted as expressly stating that no action would lie against Ryal or Willis.

3. As noted by Justice Blackstone, plaintiff in an action of trespass might recover damages for consequential injuries if he established the trespass; the allegation of these injuries in the declaration was prefaced by the words *"per quod."* For examples, see Anthon, *American Precedents of Declarations* 413, 422 (1810). In GATES v. BAYLEY, 2 Wils.K.B. 313, 95 Eng.Rep. 830 (C.P.1766), cited by Justice Blackstone, plaintiff brought an action of trespass "for taking and impounding [his] cattle, and keeping them in the pound so closely confined together, that by reason thereof one of the beasts died." Defendant pleaded as a justification that he had taken the cattle because they were doing damage to his property, and the jury found for him on this issue, although it also found that defendant had confined the cattle improperly and had thus caused the death of one. Since defendant had not taken the cattle wrongfully, the trespass was not made out,

and the court held therefore that there could be no recovery for the *per quod* (or aggravation) even though it might have constituted a wrong actionable in case.

4. Trials ordinarily were held at common law before a single judge and a jury. After verdict, if the losing party wanted the judgment of the entire court on a question of law that was involved in the case, that party asked for a rule *nisi*. A hearing before the court *en banc* was then held, and if that court sustained the rulings of the trial judge it denied the rule; otherwise, it made the rule *absolute*. When a verdict was taken subject to the opinion of the court *en banc*, as in *Scott v. Shepherd*, the ordinary procedure of applying for a rule *nisi* was unnecessary. Therefore, instead of denying a rule or making it absolute, the order of the court *en banc* was in the form of a *postea* to the prevailing party, which authorized the entry of judgment.

B. CASE CAPTURES NEGLIGENCE

The close of the eighteenth century brought before the judges a great number of cases of a kind theretofore little known but which ever since have glutted our courts: running-down accidents and vehicular collisions. Echoes of Lord Raymond's distinction in *Reynolds v. Clarke* were less frequently heard, but the categories of direct and indirect injuries became mixed with those of wilful and negligent conduct, often in a context complicated by the involvement of servants. Matters would not stay within the simple confines that Justice Blackstone envisioned.

DAY v. EDWARDS, 5 T.R. 648, 101 Eng.Rep. 361 (K.B.1794), was an action in case against a defendant who had driven his cart "so furiously, negligently and improperly" that it "struck with great force and violence * * * against plaintiff's carriage." Plaintiff's lawyer touched on all the elements that had been or would become significant—legality, indirectness, negligence; the "act of driving * * * in consequence of which the injury arose, was a legal one in itself, although negligently exercised," he said. But Lord Kenyon merely repeated the immediate injury-consequential injury distinction, found that plaintiff "complains of the immediate act," and gave judgment for defendant.

One year later in MORLEY v. GAISFORD, 2 H.Bl. 441, 126 Eng.Rep. 639 (C.P.1795), Common Pleas held case was proper when defendant's servant was alleged to have "badly, ignorantly, and negligently" driven a cart against plaintiff's chaise, saying "it was difficult to put a case where the master could be considered as a trespasser for an act of his servant, which was not done at his command."

The *Morley* holding clearly turned on the issue of a master's liability in trespass, but when plaintiffs brought an action of case against defendants for having "so incautiously, carelessly, negligently, and inexpertly managed, steered and directed" their ship that it collided with plaintiffs' vessel, their counsel relied upon *Morley* solely for the proposition that trespass lay for wilful conduct and case for negligence, and two of the three judges accepted it.[j] OGLE v. BARNES, 8 T.R. 188, 101 Eng.Rep. 1338 (K.B.1799). Lord Kenyon continued to insist upon the distinction between an immediate and a consequential injury, but he agreed that case was proper, since the charge was that by reason of defendants' negligence, their ship sailed against plaintiffs' vessel.

By 1803, we find defendant in LEAME v. BRAY, 3 East 593, 102 Eng. Rep. 724 (K.B.), challenging an action of trespass for a highway collision on the ground that the evidence showed his conduct to be negligent only, and that the action should therefore have been case. The court, however, reaffirmed its position in *Day v. Edwards*, that trespass lay for an immediate injury. Justice Lawrence, who had sat in *Ogle*, explained now that "what I principally relied on there was, that it did not appear that the mischief happened from the personal acts of the defendants: it might have happened from the operation of the wind and tide counteracting their personal efforts at the time: or indeed they might not even have been on board." He did retain this much of the wilfulness-negligence distinction, however: "It is more convenient that the action should be trespass than case; because if it be laid in trespass, no nice points can arise upon the evidence by which the plaintiff may be turned round upon the form of action * * *; for [in case] if any of the witnesses should say that in his belief the defendant did the injury wilfully, the plaintiff will run the risk of being nonsuited."

Common Pleas, which now clearly favored case for these actions, twice suggested that *Leame* be reconsidered, but King's Bench under Lord Ellenborough stood fast. In HALL v. PICKARD, 3 Camp. 187, 170 Eng.Rep. 1350 (K.B.1812), however, he raised the question whether it "may * * * be worthy of consideration, whether, in those instances where trespass may be maintained, the party may not waive the trespass, and proceed for the tort?" Later cases built on this suggestion until at last WILLIAMS v. HOLLAND, 10 Bing. 112, 131 Eng.Rep. 848 (C.P.1833), was accepted as settling the matter:

> The declaration * * * states the ground of action to be an injury occasioned by the carelessness and negligence of the Defendant in driving his own gig; * * * and the jury have found in the very terms of the declaration, that the jury [sic] was so occasioned. Under such a form of action, therefore, and with such a finding by the jury, the present objection ought not to prevail, unless some positive and inflexible rule of law, or some authority too strong to be overcome, is brought forward in its support. * * *

---

j Although the issue of a master's liability for a servant's trespasses, having introduced negligence into the controversy, did not play an active role in the remaining struggle, it later became the focus of the question whether a corporation can be guilty of trespass, since being incorporeal a corporation can act only through its agents. See Sharrod v. London & N.W.R. Co., 4 Ex. 580, 154 Eng.Rep. 1345 (Exch.1849).

But upon examining the cases cited in argument, both in support of, and in answer to, the objection, we cannot find one in which it is distinctly held, that the present form of action is not maintainable under the circumstances of this case.

For as to *Leame v. Bray*, * * * the only rule established is, that an action of trespass might be maintained, not that an action on the case could not. The case of *Savignac v. Roome*, in which the Court held that case would not lie where the defendant's servant wilfully drove against the plaintiff's carriage, was founded on the principle, that no action would lie against the master for the wilful act of his servant; and in that of *Day v. Edwards*, * * * the question * * * arising upon a special demurrer, where the Court could look to nothing but the legal construction of the declaration, is very differently circumstanced from this, where the jury have found that negligence was the ground of the injury.

* * * [T]he late case of *Moreton v. Hardern* [4 B. & C. 223, 107 Eng.Rep. 1042 (K.B.1825)], appears to us to go the full length of deciding, that where the injury is occasioned by the carelessness and negligence of the Defendant, although it be occasioned by his immediate act, the Plaintiff may, if he thinks proper, make the negligence of the Defendant the ground of his action, and declare in case. * * *

We think the case last above referred to has laid down a plain and intelligible rule, that where the injury is occasioned by the carelessness and negligence of the Defendant, the Plaintiff is at liberty to bring an action on the case, notwithstanding the act is immediate, so long as it is not a wilful act * * *.

---

3. THE LOSS AND DETENTION OF PERSONAL PROPERTY

The writ of detinue lay when defendant had possession of plaintiff's personal property and refused to relinquish it. The writ would lie, for example, against a bailee who refused to redeliver bailed goods or an executor who withheld the title-deed to an heir's real property. Although the gist of the action was wrongful detention, rather than wrongful taking, detinue would lie against a thief. But in this type of case trespass *de bonis asportatis* was preferred because detinue had several drawbacks: Defendant had a right to wage his law, and could deliver up the property in lieu of paying damages, even though it was damaged, for detinue did not lie for mere harm to goods.

Not surprisingly, plaintiffs began to try to substitute an action on the case in circumstances that seemed to call for detinue. They succeeded, first in the situation in which detinue was clearly inadequate—when the goods had spoiled—and then in situations in which its remedy might be appropriate but its mode of trial was unsatisfactory. See Fifoot, *History and Sources of the Common Law—Tort and Contract* 102–04 (1949). By 1500, case was essentially an alternative to detinue, and in the course of the sixteenth century a distinct species of case developed—the action of trover.[k] The form of this new action was predicated upon a fiction—plaintiff alleged that he had lost goods, that they had been found by defendant and were now in that party's possession, and that defendant refused to deliver them upon request. Loss and finding soon became recognized as formal allegations only, but the allegations concerning the request for return of the goods and defendant's refusal to deliver retained some significance; after all, your bailee cannot be considered to have committed a tort if you have not asked for your goods back. What might constitute a legitimate, conditional refusal to deliver—as in the case of a finder who wished to check the credentials of a claimant—became an important issue. Apart from the fact that defendant was not entitled to wage his law, trover differed from detinue in this respect: Plaintiff was under no obligation to take back the goods, and in an action against a thief was under no obligation to demand them. The essence of trover was the conversion of the goods.

What is a conversion? The term has troubled the courts for several hundred years, but the most famous definition is that of Chief Justice Holt, in BALDWIN v. COLE, 6 Mod. 212, 87 Eng.Rep. 964 (K.B.1705): "[W]hat is a conversion, but an assuming upon one's self the property and right of disposing another's goods; and he that takes upon himself to detain another man's goods from him without cause, takes upon himself the right of disposing of them * * *." Is this really helpful? Consider the following case.

BUSHEL v. MILLER

Court of King's Bench, 1718.
1 Strange 128, 93 Eng.Rep. 428.

Upon the Custom-House quay there is a hut, where particular porters put in small parcels of goods, if the ship is not ready to receive them when they are brought upon the quay. The porters, who have a right in this hut, have each particular boxes or cupboards, and as such the defendant had one. The plaintiff being one of the porters puts in goods belonging to A and lays them so that the defendant could not get to his chest without removing them. He accordingly does remove them about a yard from the place where they lay, towards the door, and without returning them into their place goes away, and the goods are lost. The plaintiff satisfies A of the value of the goods, and brings trover against the defendant. And upon the trial two points were ruled by the C. J.

---

[k] So distinct that case became the ameliorative for certain deficiencies in trover.

1. That the plaintiff having made satisfaction to A for the goods, had thereby acquired a sufficient property in them to maintain trover.

2. That there was no conversion in the defendant. The plaintiff by laying his goods where they obstructed the defendant from going to his chest, was in that respect a wrong-doer. The defendant had a right to remove the goods, so that thus far he was in no fault. Then as to the not returning the goods to the place where he found them; if this were an action of trespass, perhaps it might be a doubt; but he was clear it could not amount to a conversion.

NOTES AND QUESTIONS

1. Plaintiff's goods were delivered by a ship's captain to defendant wharfingers to be held for plaintiff. The goods were then lost or stolen from defendants. Could defendants be said to have converted them? In ROSS v. JOHNSON, 5 Burrow 2825, 98 Eng.Rep. 483 (K.B. 1772), Lord Mansfield said case, not trover, was the only remedy: "[I]n order to maintain trover, there must be an injurious conversion. This is not to be deemed a refusal to deliver the goods. They can't deliver them: it is not in their power to do it. It is a bare omission."

2. If defendant so negligently kept twenty barrels of plaintiff's butter that "they were become of little value," would trover lie? See Walgrave v. Ogden, 1 Leon. 224, 74 Eng.Rep. 205 (K.B. 1590).

3. Defendant picked up a china doll in a shop to examine it and then dropped it with predictable results? Would trover lie?

———

HARTOP v. HOARE, 2 Strange 1187, 93 Eng.Rep. 1117 (K.B. 1743). Plaintiff left a sealed bag of jewels for safekeeping with a goldsmith, who broke the seals and took the jewels to defendants' shop, and pawned them there. Plaintiff then brought an action of trover against defendants. The court held:

1. [The goldsmith] * * * is a mere bailee for safe custody only, without any authority to open the bag the jewels were in; and he was a trespasser in so doing. * * *

2. As to the defendants, though they came honestly by them, yet they are within the general rule of caveat emptor, unless something appears particularly to exempt them. What they rely upon is, that they are purchasers of them in a market overt, it being found that they bought them in an open shop, where they dealt in jewels, which according to the custom of London is a market overt for that purpose.

To this it was properly answered by the plaintiff, that this custom not being found, the Court cannot judicially take notice of it * * *.

We are all of opinion, the plaintiff must have judgment.

QUESTIONS

1. What is a market overt? What is its significance?

2. Would trespass lie against defendants in this case? Would it lie against them if the goldsmith originally had stolen the jewels out of plaintiff's possession?

GORDON v. HARPER

Court of King's Bench, 1796.
7 T.R. 9, 101 Eng.Rep. 828.

In trover for certain goods, being household furniture * * *. [Plaintiff leased a house with the goods in question to A for a term still extant at the time of trial. While A was in possession under the lease, defendant sheriff seized the goods in execution of a judgment against B, who had sold the furniture to plaintiff sometime before the lease. Defendant after the seizure sold the goods.]

LORD KENYON, Ch. J. The only point for the consideration of the Court in the case of *Ward* v. *Macauley* [4 T.R. 489, 100 Eng.Rep. 1135 (K.B. 1791)] was, whether in a case like the present, the landlord could maintain an action of trespass against the sheriff for seizing goods, let with a house, under an execution against the tenant; and it was properly decided that no such action could be maintained. What was said further by me in that case, that trover was the proper remedy, was an extrajudicial opinion, to which upon further consideration I cannot subscribe. The true question is, whether when a person has leased goods in a house to another for a certain time, whereby he parts with the right of possession during the term to the tenant, and has only a reversionary interest, he can notwithstanding recover the value of the whole property pending the existence of the term in an action of trover. The very statement of the proposition affords an answer to it. If, instead of household goods, the goods here taken had been machines used in manufacture, which had been leased to a tenant, no doubt could have been made but that the sheriff might have seized them under an execution against the tenant, and the creditor would have been entitled to the beneficial use of the property during the term: the difference of the goods then cannot vary the law. * * * I forbear to deliver any opinion as to what remedy the landlord has in this case, not being at present called upon so to do: but it is clear that he cannot maintain trover.

ASHHURST, J. I have always understood the rule of law to be, that in order to maintain trover the plaintiff must have a right of property in the thing, and a right of possession, and that unless both these rights concur, the action will not lie. * * *

GROSE, J. The only question is whether trover will lie where the plaintiff had neither the actual possession of the goods taken at the time, nor the right of possession. * * * Where goods are delivered to a carrier, the owner has still a right of possession as against a tort-feasor, and the carrier is no more than his servant. But here it is clear that the plaintiff had no right of possession; and he would be a trespasser if he took the goods from the tenant: then by what authority can he recover them from any other person during the term? * * *

LAWRENCE, J. * * *. Now here if the taking of the goods by the sheriff determined the interest of the tenant in them, and revested it in the landlord, I admit that the latter might maintain trover for them * * *: but it is clearly otherwise; for here the tenant's property and interest did not determine by the sheriff's trespass, and the tenant might maintain trespass against the wrong-doer, and recover damages. * * *

Postea to the defendant.

NOTES AND QUESTIONS

1. Plaintiff pawned a jeweled hatband to X for 25 pounds with no certain time fixed for redemption. X delivered it to defendant, and then died. Plaintiff tendered 25 pounds to the executrix, who refused it, and then demanded the hatband of defendant. Would trover lie? See Ratcliff v. Davies, Croke Jac. 244, 79 Eng.Rep. 210 (K.B. 1611).

2. Plaintiff leased a farm with cattle to Y for one year. After a few months, Y sold the cattle to defendant and absconded. What theory might be used to allow plaintiff to bring trover against defendant? See Swift v. Moseley, 10 Vt. 208 (1838).

4. THE CREATION OF CONTRACT LAW

A. SPECIAL ASSUMPSIT

Glanvill said, shortly before 1200: "[I]t is not the custom of the court of the lord king to protect private agreements, nor does it concern itself with such contracts as can be considered to be like private agreements." *The treatise on the laws and customs of the realm of England commonly called Glanvill*, Bk. X [18] (Hall ed. 1965). By the middle of the fourteenth century, there remained a good deal of truth in this. Two forms of action, each with significant shortcomings, lay for breach of contract—the writs of covenant and debt. Covenant required a sealed instrument and did not lie when debt was available. Debt lay only when an agreement had been fully performed by one party and he was entitled to a sum certain, and as in the case of detinue, defendant was entitled to wage his law, unless the agreement was sealed. Again plaintiffs resorted to case as a safety valve for the deficiencies of covenant and debt, but progress was slower than it had been in the evasion of detinue, perhaps because the effort was not so much to avoid a particular writ as to create a new area of substantive law.

By 1400, plaintiff could maintain case against a defendant who had carried out his promise so badly that plaintiff was in a worse position than before defendant made his promise. Thus in 1370 case was held to lie against a defendant who having undertaken to cure plaintiff's horse, treated it so negligently that it died. WALDON v. MARSHALL, Y.B. Mich. 43 Ed. 3, f. 33, pl. 38. Chief Justice Cavendish, in an action against a surgeon for maiming plaintiff while trying to cure him, said "this action of covenant of necessity is maintained without specialty, since for every little thing a man cannot always have a Clerk to make a specialty for him." THE SURGEON'S CASE, Y.B. Hil. 48 Ed. 3, f. 6, pl. 11 (K.B.1375). But case did not lie for nonfeasance. Through the fifteenth century there were occasional departures, but the courts seemed always to return to this rule. Then suddenly it was abandoned for good and a new form of action developed from case and received judicial acceptance—special assumpsit.

No single case seems to have established assumpsit as a remedy for nonperformance of a promise, but shortly after 1500 it had become the accepted view. In a note in the Yearbooks, it appears that Chief Justice Fineux of King's Bench in 1506 said that for nonfeasance as well as misfeasance, "I shall have an *accion sur mon cas,* and I will not need to sue out a *Subpoena.*" Nota, Y.B. Mich. 21 Hen. 7, f. 41, pl. 66. What is the significance of a subpoena? See p. 351, infra. Does this suggest a possible reason for the common-law courts' abandonment of the distinction? See Fifoot, *History and Sources of the Common Law—Tort and Contract* 337 (1949).

B.   GENERAL ASSUMPSIT

Special assumpsit filled a major gap left by the action of debt, but it did not take the place of debt, as trover substantially had taken the place of detinue. For another century, argument flared on the question whether assumpsit would lie for a debt. Gradually it was established that if a person, who already was indebted to another, made a fresh promise to pay the debt, assumpsit would lie for a breach of that promise, even though it would not have lain for the debt itself. The question then arose whether the fresh promise actually had to be made, or assumpsit would lie even when the promise was a fiction. In part, the answer lay in the desires of two courts to draw business to themselves; debt was the exclusive province of Common Pleas, while assumpsit with its background in trespass could be brought there or in King's Bench.[1] For thirty years they squabbled over the matter.

---

[1] For other factors in the background of general assumpsit, see Milsom, *Historical Foundations of the Common Law* 292–97 (1969).

SLADE'S CASE

Court of Exchequer Chamber, 1602.
4 Co.Rep. 92b, 76 Eng.Rep. 1074.

John Slade brought an action on the case in the King's Bench against Humphrey Morley * * * and declared, that whereas the plaintiff * * * was possessed of a close of land * * * and being so possessed, the plaintiff * * * the said close had sowed with wheat and rye, which wheat and rye * * * were grown into blades, the defendant, in consideration that the plaintiff, at the special instance and request of the said Humphrey, had bargained and sold to him the said blades of wheat and rye growing upon the said close, * * * assumed and promised the plaintiff to pay him 16l. * * *: and for non-payment thereof * * * the plaintiff brought the said action: the defendant pleaded *non assumpsit modo et forma*; and on the trial of this issue the jurors gave a special verdict, *sc.* that the defendant bought of the plaintiff the wheat and rye in blades growing upon the said close * * * and further found, that between the plaintiff and the defendant there was no other promise or assumption but only the said bargain * * *. And for the honour of the law, and for the quiet of the subject in the appeasing of such diversity of opinions * * * the case was openly argued before all the Justices of England, and Barons of the Exchequer, * * * and after many conferences between the justices and Barons, it was resolved, that the action was maintainable, and that the plaintiff should have judgment. And in this case these points were resolved:—1. That although an action of debt lies upon the contract, yet the bargainor may have an action on the case, or an action of debt at his election * * *. 3. It was resolved, that every contract executory imports in itself an *assumpsit*, for when one agrees to pay money, or to deliver anything, thereby he assumes or promises to pay, or deliver it, and therefore when one sells any goods to another, and agrees to deliver them at a day to come, and the other in consideration thereof agrees to pay so much money as such a day, in that case both parties may have an action of debt, or an action on the case on *assumpsit*, for the mutual executory agreement of both parties imports in itself reciprocal actions upon the case, as well as actions of debt, and therewith agrees the judgment in *Read and Norwood's case*, Pl. Com. 128. 4. It was resolved, that the plaintiff in this action on the case on assumpsit should not recover only damages for the special loss (if any be) which he had, but also for the whole debt, so that a recovery or bar in this action would be a good bar in an action of debt brought upon the same contract * * *. And as to the objection which has been made, that it would be mischievous to the defendant that he should not wage his law, forasmuch as he might pay it in secret: to that it was answered, that it should be accounted his folly that he did not take sufficient witnesses with him to prove the payment he made: but the mischief would be rather on the other party, for now experience proves that men's consciences grow so large that the respect of their private advantage rather induces men (and chiefly those who have declining estates) to perjury * * *.

NOTE

In *Norwood v. Read*, cited in the third resolution in *Slade's Case*, Queen's Bench, in 1558, had allowed assumpsit on a decedent's debt against executors who argued that the action was unfair, because the decedent could have waged his law but they could not wage it on his behalf. The case had been seriously questioned, but its citation in *Slade's Case* presaged the end of the executor's immunity. The blow fell in PINCHON'S CASE, 9 Co.Rep. 86b, 77 Eng.Rep. 859 (K.B.1612).

You should remember in considering the demise of wager of law that at this time, and for two centuries more, parties were incompetent to testify at a trial. The enactment of the Statute of Frauds, 29 Charles 2, c. 3 (1677), which required several kinds of contracts to be in writing is attributed by many to the problem of proof posed by the result in *Slade's Case*. See, e. g., Plucknett, *A Concise History of the Common Law* 648 (5th ed. 1956).

The recognition of *indebitatus assumpsit* (literally, "being indebted, he promised"), or *general assumpsit*, did more than deliver the quietus to debt. The contract-like sanction it imposed upon an obligation that did not really arise out of an actual promise provided the structure for wholly new developments. When A has delivered goods to B or has performed services for the latter, it may be presumed that A expects payment and B expects to pay; but the common law had furnished no remedy in the absence of an actual agreement. Now a new action of quantum meruit developed based upon an implied promise to pay the reasonable value of the goods or services, not unlike the imputed promise to pay the debt that furnished the basis for *Slade's Case*. Even more significant was the extension of this same formula into circumstances in which a promise to pay was the last thing in defendant's mind.

LAMINE v. DORRELL

Court of Queen's Bench, 1705.
2 Ld.Raym. 1216, 92 Eng.Rep. 303.

In an indebitatus assumpsit for money received by the defendant to the use of the plaintiff as administrator of J. S. on non assumpsit pleaded, upon evidence the case appeared to be, that J. S. died intestate possessed of certain Irish debentures; and the defendant pretending to a right to be administrator, got administration granted to him, and by that means got these debentures into his hands, and disposed of them: then the defendant's administration was repealed, and administration granted to the plaintiff, and he brought this action against the defendant for the money he sold the debentures for. And it being objected upon the evidence, that this action would not lie, because the defendant sold the debentures as one that claimed a title and interest in them, and therefore could not be said to receive the money for the use of the plaintiff, which indeed he received to his own use; but the plaintiff ought to have brought trover or detinue for the debentures: the point was saved to the defendant, and now the Court was moved, and the same objection made.

Powell Justice. It is clear the plaintiff might have maintained detinue or trover for the debentures * * *. But the plaintiff may dispense with the wrong, and suppose the sale made by his consent, and bring an action for the money they were sold for, as money received to his use. * * *

Holt Chief Justice. These actions have crept in by degrees. * * * So the defendant in this case pretending to receive the money the debentures were sold for in the right of the intestate, why should he not be answerable for it to the intestate's administrator? If an action of trover should be brought by the plaintiff for these debentures after judgment in this indebitatus assumpsit, he may plead this recovery in bar of the action of trover, in the same manner as it would have been a good plea in bar for the defendant to have pleaded to the action of trover, that he sold the debentures, and paid to the plaintiff in satisfaction. * * * This recovery may be given in evidence upon not guilty in the action of trover, because by this action the plaintiff makes and affirms the act of the defendant in the sale of the debentures to be lawful, and consequently the sale of them is no conversion.

* * *

———

MOSES v. MACFERLAN, 2 Burrow 1005, 97 Eng.Rep. 676 (K.B. 1760). Plaintiff had endorsed four promissory notes to defendant under a written agreement that he should not be liable thereon; in defendant's suit in a Court of Conscience (a small claims court), however, the agreement was not recognized, and plaintiff was found liable for six pounds, which he paid. (On these facts, would *Lamine v. Dorrell* support an action for money had and received?) Lord Mansfield said:

2d objection.—"That no assumpsit lies, except upon an express or implied contract: but here it is impossible to presume any contract to refund money, which the defendant recovered by an adverse suit."

Answer. If the defendant be under an obligation, from the ties of natural justice, to refund; the law implies a debt, and gives this action, founded in the equity of the plaintiff's case, as it were upon a contract ("quasi ex contractu," as the Roman law expresses it).

* * *

Money may be recovered by a right and legal judgment; and yet the iniquity of keeping that money may be manifest, upon grounds which could not be used by way of defence against the judgment.

* * *

Suppose a man recovers upon a policy for a ship presumed to be lost, which afterwards comes home;—or upon the life of a man presumed to be dead, who afterwards appears;—or upon a representation of a risque deemed to be fair, which comes out afterwards to be grossly fraudulent.

* * *

One great benefit, which arises to suitors from the nature of this action, is, that the plaintiff needs not state the special circumstances from which he concludes "that, ex aequo & bono, the money received by the defendant, ought to be deemed as belonging to him:" he may declare generally, "that the money was received to his use;" and make out his case, at the trial.

* * *

This kind of equitable action to recover back money, which ought not in justice to be kept, is very beneficial, and therefore much encouraged. It lies only for money which, ex aequo et bono, the defendant ought to refund: it does not lie for money paid by the plaintiff, which is claimed of him as payable in point of honor and honesty, although it could not have been recovered from him by any course of law; as in payment of a debt barred by the Statute of Limitations, or contracted during his infancy, or to the extent of principal and legal interest upon an usurious contract, or, for money fairly lost at play: because in all these cases, the defendant may retain it with a safe conscience, though by positive law he was barred from recovering.

An important procedural result of the development of indebitatus assumpsit was a new manner of pleading contract actions. The declaration in money had and received, as Lord Mansfield noted in *Moses v. MacFerlan*, was broad in the extreme. See also p. 328, supra. The declarations in other actions derived from indebitatus assumpsit were equally broad. In HIBBERT v. COURTHOPE, Carthew 276, 90 Eng.Rep. 764 (K.B.1694), the court said it was necessary only that the declaration show the debt was not a debt on record or under seal, for debt was still the appropriate writ in such cases—" and any general words, by which that may be made to appear, are sufficient." Pleaders seized upon this liberality to develop what became known as the "common counts," standardized allegations concealing virtually all of the particulars of an action. The principal common counts were for money had and received, for goods sold and delivered, for work done, for money lent, for money paid by plaintiff to the use of defendant, and for money due on an account stated. See Fifoot, *History and Sources of the Common Law— Tort and Contract* 369–70, 393–94 (1949).

SECTION C. THE OTHER SYSTEM: EQUITY

1. THE RISE OF CHANCERY

MAITLAND, EQUITY, ALSO THE FORMS OF ACTION AT COMMON LAW 2–10 (1909):

In Edward I's day, at the end of the thirteenth century, three great courts have come into existence * * *.

One of the three courts, namely, the Exchequer, is more than a court of law. From our modern point of view it is not only a court of law but a 'government office'. * * * What we should call the 'civil service' of the country is transacted by two great offices or 'departments'; there is the Exchequer which is the fiscal department, there is the Chancery which is the secretarial department, while above these there rises the king's permanent Council. At the head of the Chancery stands the Chancellor, usually a bishop; he is we may say the king's secretary of state for all departments, he keeps the king's great seal and all the already great mass of writing that has to be done in the king's name has to be done under his supervision.

He is not as yet a judge, but already he by himself or his subordinates has a great deal of work to do which brings him into a close connexion with the administration of justice. One of the duties of that great staff of clerks over which he presides is to draw up and issue those writs whereby actions are begun in the courts of law—such writs are sealed with the king's seal. * * *

But by another route the Chancellor is brought into still closer contact with the administration of justice. Though these great courts of law have been established there is still a reserve of justice in the king. Those who can not get relief elsewhere present their petitions to the king and his council praying for some remedy. * * * In practice a great share of this labour falls on the Chancellor. He is the king's prime minister, he is a member of the council, and the specially learned member of the council. It is in dealing with these petitions that the Chancellor begins to develop his judicial powers.

* * * Very often the petitioner requires some relief at the expense of some other person. He complains that for some reason or another he can not get a remedy in the ordinary course of justice and yet he is entitled to a remedy. He is poor, he is old, he is sick, his adversary is rich and powerful, will bribe or will intimidate jurors, or has by some trick or some accident acquired an advantage of which the ordinary courts with their formal procedure will not deprive him. The petition is often couched in piteous terms, the king is asked to find a remedy for the love of God and in the way of charity. Such petitions are referred by the king to the Chancellor. Gradually in the course of the

fourteenth century petitioners, instead of going to the king, will go straight to the Chancellor * * *. Now one thing that the Chancellor may do in such a case is to invent a new writ and so provide the complainant with a means of bringing an action in a court of law. But in the fourteenth century the courts of law have become very conservative and are given to quashing writs which differ in material points from those already in use. But another thing that the Chancellor can do is to send for the complainant's adversary and examine him concerning the charge that has been made against him. Gradually a procedure is established. The Chancellor having considered the petition, or 'bill' as it is called, orders the adversary to come before him and answer the complaint. The writ whereby he does this is called a <u>subpoena</u>—because it <u>orders the man to appear upon pain of forfeiting a sum of money</u> * * *. It is very different from the old writs whereby actions are begun in the courts of law. They tell the defendant what is the cause of action against him * * *. The subpoena, on the other hand, will tell him merely that he has got to come before the Chancellor and answer complaints made against him by A. B. Then when he comes before the Chancellor he will have to answer on oath, and sentence by sentence, the bill of the plaintiff. * * * The defendant will be examined upon oath and the Chancellor will decide questions of fact as well as questions of law.

I do not think that in the fourteenth century the Chancellors considered that they had to administer any body of substantive rules that differed from the ordinary law of the land. * * * The complaints that come before them are in general complaints of indubitable legal wrongs * * * of which the ordinary courts take cognizance, wrongs which they ought to redress. * * * However this sort of thing can not well be permitted. * * * And so the Chancellor is warned off the field of common law—he is not to hear cases which might go to the ordinary courts, he is not to make himself a judge of torts and contracts, of property in lands and goods.

But then just at this time it is becoming plain that the Chancellor is doing some convenient and useful works that could not be done, or could not easily be done by the courts of common law. He has taken to enforcing uses or trusts. * * * No doubt they were troublesome things, things that might be used for fraudulent purposes, and statutes were passed against those who employed them for the purpose of cheating their creditors or evading the law of mortmain. But I have not a doubt that they were very popular, and I think we may say that had there been no Chancery, the old courts would have discovered some method of enforcing these fiduciary obligations. That method however must have been a clumsy one. A system of law which will never compel, which will never even allow, the defendant to give evidence, a system which sends every question of fact to a jury, is not competent to deal adequately with fiduciary relationships. On the other hand the Chancellor had a procedure which was very well adapted to this end.

* * * And then there were some other matters that were considered to be fairly within his jurisdiction. An old rhyme allows him 'fraud, accident,

and breach of confidence'—there were many frauds which the stiff old procedure of the courts of law could not adequately meet, and 'accident,' in particular the accidental loss of a document, was a proper occasion for the Chancellor's interference.

 * * *   In James I's day occurred the great quarrel between Lord Chancellor Ellesmere and Chief Justice Coke which finally decided that the Court of Chancery was to have the upper hand over the courts of law. If the Chancery was to carry out its maxims about trust and fraud it was essential that it should have a power to prevent men from going into the courts of law and to prevent men from putting in execution the judgments that they had obtained in courts of law. In fraud or in breach of trust you obtain a judgment against me in a court of law; I complain to the Chancellor, and he after hearing what you have to say enjoins you not to put in force your judgment, says in effect that if you do put your judgment in force you will be sent to prison. Understand well that the Court of Chancery never asserted that it was superior to the courts of law; it never presumed to send to them such mandates as the Court of King's Bench habitually sent to the inferior courts, telling them that they must do this or must not do that or quashing their proceedings * * *. It was addressed not to the judges, but to the party. * * * For all this, however, it was natural that the judges should take umbrage at this treatment of their judgments. Coke declared that the man who obtained such an injunction was guilty of the offence denounced by the Statutes of Praemunire, that of calling in question the judgments of the king's courts in other courts (these statutes had been aimed at the Papal curia). King James had now a wished-for opportunity of appearing as supreme over all his judges, and all his courts
 * * *.

ARGUMENTS Proving from ANTIQUITY the Dignity, Power, and Jurisdiction of the COURT OF CHANCERY

1 Chan.Rep. (App.) 1, 20, 23–24, 49–50, 21 Eng.Rep. 576, 581–82, 588 (1616).

 * * *

His said Majesty being informed of this Difference between his two Courts of Chancery and King's Bench, * * * directed, That his Attorney General, calling to him the Rest of his Learned Counsel, should peruse the * * * Precedents, and certify his Majesty the Truth thereof with their Opinions.

 * * *

And afterwards a Case was presented to his Majesty as followeth.

THE CASE.

A. hath a Judgment and Execution in the King's Bench or Common Pleas against B. in an Action of Debt of £1000, and in an *Ejectione Firmae* of the Manor of D. B. complains in the Chancery to be relieved against these Judgments according to Equity and Conscience, allowing the Judgment to be lawful and good by the Rigour and strict Rules of the Law, and the Matter in Equity to be such, as the Judges of the Common Law being no Judges of Equity, but bound by their Oaths to do the Law, cannot give any Remedy or Relief for the same, either by Error or Attaint, or by any other Means.

QUESTION.

Whether the Chancery may relieve B. in this or such like Cases, or else leave him utterly remediless and undone? And if the Chancery be restrained herein by any Statute of Praemunire, then by what Statute, and by what Words in any Statute is the Chancery so restrained, and Conscience and Equity excluded, banished and damned?

Which Case his Majesty referred again to his said Attorney and Learned Counsel * * *.

* * *

Upon which Certificate the King gave his Judgment as followeth.

Forasmuch as Mercy and Justice be the true Supporters of our Royal Throne, and that it properly belongeth unto us in our Princely Office to take Care and provide, that our Subjects have equal and indifferent Justice ministred unto them: And that where their Case deserveth to be relieved in Course of Equity by Suit in our Court of Chancery, they should not be abandoned and exposed to perish under the Rigor and Extremity of our Laws, We in our Princely Judgment * * * do approve, ratify and confirm, * * * the Practice of our Court of Chancery * * *. And do will and command that our Chancellor, or Keeper of the Great Seal for the Time being, shall not hereafter desist to give unto our Subjects, * * * such Relief in Equity (notwithstanding any Proceedings at the Common Law against them) as shall stand with the Merit and Justice of their Cause, and with the former, ancient and continued Practice and Presidency of our Chancery have done. * * *

NOTE

Sir Edward Coke, Lord Chief Justice of the Court of King's Bench, who had led the fight to keep the common-law courts free of the domination of Chancery, was deposed four months after the King's ruling. The words of his successor, Henry Montagu, on taking the oath of office suggest how effectively the matter was closed: "I will not be a heady judge. * * * I will be glad of good counsel, and I will not be busy in stirring questions, especially of jurisdictions." See 1 Campbell, *The Lives of the Chief Justices of England* 355–56 (1849).

Details of the controversy between Chancery and the common-law courts may be found in 1 Holdsworth, *A History of English Law* 459–65 (6th ed. 1938); Dawson, *Coke and Ellesmere Disinterred: The Attack on the Chancery in 1616*, 36 Ill.L.Rev. 127 (1941). On the history of equity, see also Walsh, *Equity* 1–40 (1930); Adams, *The Origin of English Equity*, 16 Colum.L.Rev. 87 (1916).

BEALE, EQUITY IN AMERICA, 1 Cambridge L.J. 21, 22–23 (1921):

At about the time of the English Revolution colonies came to be more rigorously governed. Most of the old charters were forfeited, and a new provincial form of government was established; and from that time the Judges were appointed, through the royal governors, by the Crown, and they came to be regarded, naturally, as the enemies of popular rights and as creatures of the Crown. The situation at about the time of the American Revolution was that Judges in the North were still regarded as tools of the King and as enemies of the popular will.   *   *   *

In the South conditions were very different. The ruling class was well satisfied with the condition of affairs in England, and, although there were popular uprisings in some parts of the South, notably in Virginia and Maryland, the power of the aristocracy on the whole was never shaken. They determined the laws, they had no distrust of Judges, and in those States there was no desire to hamper a Judge or to exalt the jury at his expense.   *   *   *

We should not be surprised, therefore, to find that in the North at least the people were very jealous of giving any jurisdiction to the Court of Equity, there being no jury in that Court. Equity seemed to the people of America, a hundred years ago even, as a non-popular method of applying law, which it was the duty of the people alone to deal with. The Courts administering equity were, so to speak, royalist persons administering the law of an effete monarchy which had never taken foothold in the democratic part of America. The consequence was that in New England there was no equity jurisdiction and very little admixture of equity in the law. The law administered was the strictly legal portion of the law; and the books cited, when they came to cite books, were the reports of the common law Courts. In New York there was a Chancellor from the time of the original constitution; but that Chancellor was not supposed to be a Judge who administered the English system of equity.   *   *   *

Pennsylvania never had any Court of equity. The law, however, had more of what they regarded as equitable doctrines in it than the law of Massachusetts * * *. In New Jersey and Delaware, however, and throughout the South, there was set up at the time of our Revolution a separate Court of Chancery, sitting beside the Common Law Court and administering the principles of English equity.

NOTE

See also von Moschzisker, *Equity Jurisdiction in the Federal Courts,* 75 U.Pa. L.Rev. 287 (1927); Walsh, *The Growing Function of Equity in the Development of the Law,* in 3 *Law: A Century of Progress* 139, 145–55 (1937); Wilson, *Courts of Chancery in the American Colonies,* 28 American L.Rev. 226 (1884), reprinted in 2 *Select Essays in Anglo-American Legal History* 779 (1908).

2. PROCEDURE IN EQUITY

BOWEN, PROGRESS IN THE ADMINISTRATION OF JUSTICE DURING THE VICTORIAN PERIOD, 1 Select Essays in Anglo-American Legal History 516, 524–27 (1907):

* * *   A bill in a Chancery suit was a marvellous document, which stated the plaintiff's case at full length and three times over.   There was first the part in which the story was circumstantially set forth.   Then came the part which "charged" its truth against the defendant—or, in other words, which set it forth all over again in an aggrieved tone.   Lastly came the interrogating part, which converted the original allegations into a chain of subtly framed inquiries addressed to the defendant, minutely dovetailed and circuitously arranged so as to surround a slippery conscience and to stop up every earth.   No layman, however intelligent, could compose the 'answer' without professional aid.   It was inevitably so elaborate and so long, that the responsibility for the accuracy of the story shifted, during its telling, from the conscience of the defendant to that of his solicitor and counsel, and truth found no difficulty in disappearing during the operation.   * * *   [The form of the answer] often rendered necessary a re-statement of the plaintiff's whole position, in which case an amended bill was drawn requiring another answer, until at last the voluminous pleadings were completed and the cause was at issue.   By a system which to lawyers in 1887 appears to savour of the Middle Ages, the evidence for the hearing was thereupon taken by interrogatories written down beforehand upon paper and administered to the witnesses in private before an examiner or commissioner.   At this meeting none of the parties were allowed to be present, either by themselves or their agents, and the examiner himself was sworn to secrecy.   If cross-examined at all (for cross-examination under such conditions was of necessity somewhat of a farce), the witnesses could only be cross-examined upon written inquiries prepared equally in advance by a counsel who had never had the opportunity of knowing what had been said during the examination-in-chief.   * * *   On the day of the publication of the depositions copies were furnished to the parties at their own expense; but, from that moment, no further evidence was admissible, nor could any slip in the proofs be repaired, except by special permission of the court, when, if such leave was granted, a fresh commission was executed with the same formalities and in the same secret manner as before.   The expense of the pleadings, of the preparation for the hearing, and of the other stages of the litigation may be imagined, when we recollect that it was a necessary maxim of the Court of Chancery that all parties interested in the result must be parties to the suit.   If, for example, relief was sought against a breach of trust, all who were interested in the trust estate had to be joined, as well as all who had been privy to the breach of trust itself.   During the winding journey of the cause towards its termination, whenever any death occurred, bills of review or supplemental suits became necessary to reconstitute the charmed circle of litigants which had been broken. On every such catastrophe the plaintiff had again to begin wearily to weave his web, liable on any new death to find it unravelled and undone. It was satirically observed that a suit to which fifty defendants were necessary parties (a perfectly possible contingency) could never hope to end at all, since the yearly average of deaths in England was one in fifty, and a death, as a rule, threw over the plaintiff's bill for at least a year. The hearing in many cases could not terminate the cause. Often inquiries or accounts were necessary, and had still to be taken under the supervision of a master. Possibly some issue upon the disputed facts required to be sent for trial at the assizes, or a point of law submitted to a common law court. In such cases, the verdict of the jury, or the opinions of the court so taken, in no way concluded the conscience of the Court of Chancery. It resumed charge of the cause again, when the intermediate expedition to the common law was over, and had the power, if it saw fit, to send the same issue to a new trial, or to disregard altogether what had been the result. * * * When a cause had reached its final stage—when all inquiries had been made, all parties represented, all accounts taken, all issues tried—justice was done with vigour and exactitude. Few frauds ever in the end successfully ran the gauntlet of the Court of Chancery. But the honest suitor emerged from the ordeal victorious rather than triumphant, for too often he had been ruined by the way.

NOTES AND QUESTIONS

1. What differences do you find between procedure at common law and procedure in equity as it is described by Bowen? What are the differences in pleading, the manner of receiving evidence, the attitude toward singleness of issue, and the determination of questions of fact? Are these differences interrelated? Is the attitude toward singleness of issue related to the way in which factual issues are decided? To the method of pleading? To the manner of taking and receiving evidence? Is the manner of taking and receiving evidence related to the method of pleading? Would either of these facets of equity procedure have been practical if issues of fact were decided in equity as they were at common law? The rules of evidence, which are chiefly concerned with the exclusion of testimony of doubtful value, were developed in the common-law courts and were never strictly applied in equity. How is this fact related to the differences in equity and common-law procedure?

2. Section 30 of the Judiciary Act of 1789, 1 Stat. 88, provided that "the mode of proof by oral testimony and examination of witnesses in open court" should obtain in equity actions. This provision was weakened in 1802 by permitting written evidence when that was the practice in the state in which the federal court was sitting. In 1842 plenary power was conferred on the Supreme Court to control the matter. Thereafter, and until the Equity Rules of 1912 were issued, written depositions were the ordinary course in federal equity. See Millar, *Civil Procedure of the Trial Court in Historical Perspective* 270–72 (1952) (also discussing the state practices); 2 Street, *Federal Equity Practice* 994–1000 (1909).

The elements of procedure in equity discussed in the foregoing materials are significant because of their impact on the substantive and remedial doctrines of equity. Together with the method of enforcing equity decrees, which is discussed below, these elements largely determined the type of case that equity would hear and the disposition it would order. As you read the materials that follow ask yourself how these differences between law and equity may explain the particular equitable approach in question.

3. THE UNIQUE CHARACTER OF EQUITABLE RELIEF

A. SPECIFIC RELIEF

The ordinary judgment of a common-law court consisted of a declaration of a legal relationship. When plaintiff prevailed in the action, this declaration in all but rare instances was that plaintiff was entitled to a sum of money from defendant. Even this declaration was not an order that defendant pay the sum; if defendant did not pay, plaintiff had to take further steps to execute the judgment. The decree in equity, on the other hand, was an order directed at defendant; imprisonment and fines were used not only to coerce compliance, but to punish disobedience. This difference between the remedies in the two systems of courts was summed up in the maxim that equity acts in personam and not in rem. The primary means by which equity acted in personam was the injunction—an order directing defendant to perform or to stop performing an act.

The injunction and other forms of specific relief shaped the substantive doctrines of equity. See Ames, *Law and Morals*, in *Lectures on Legal History* 435, 444 (1913). But it affected the common law as well in at least three important ways. First, the availability of specific relief through the injunction or specific performance when compensatory relief through a judgment for damages would be inadequate was the chief basis for drawing common-law causes into equity. As a result equity now dominates many areas of controversy originally governed by the common law, because damages are an impotent remedy in such cases; a good example is nuisance. Similarly the enforcement of contracts for the sale of real property has become principally a concern of equity, because specific performance is ordered as a matter of course. Second, the availability of specific relief in equity has effectively dampened pressures to develop common-law remedies in that direction. Third, the injunction was the means by which equity imposed its substantive doctrines on the common-law courts. As noted in the extract from Maitland, if the chancellor found that a common-law judgment had been obtained by fraud, the equity court did not purport to negate it; the chancellor simply took the equally effective step of threatening the judgment creditor with jail if the latter sought to enforce it. In similar fashion equity enjoined the bringing of suits in inconvenient fora and compelled interpleader and class actions in multiparty suits.

A plaintiff who sought specific relief also might have sustained an injury that an injunction could not cure. But there was no necessity for choosing between equitable relief and compensatory damages. A "clean-up" doctrine gave Chancery authority to accord full relief in any case of which it had cognizance even though giving such relief might mean redressing injuries for which there was an adequate remedy at law. See pp. 806–07, infra.

B.   AVAILABILITY OF RELIEF

You must not think that the doctrine of the adequate remedy at law was the only restriction on the use of equitable remedies. Equity carefully husbanded its power. It was reluctant to issue orders that it might not be able to enforce or that might involve it in detailed supervision of a transaction. Traditionally, equity would not direct a party to take action outside its territorial jurisdiction or order specific performance of a building or personal services contract. For other reasons, activity that might be criminal ordinarily would not be enjoined. While the Court of Star Chamber flourished there was no call for criminal jurisdiction in equity, and after that court was abolished in 1642, Chancery, perhaps for fear of meeting a similar fate, refrained from encroaching on this particular domain of the common-law courts. What aspects of Chancery procedure might have seemed particularly odious in criminal cases to people who celebrated the common law as the palladium of their liberty?

The availability of equitable relief also was hedged by doctrines of fairness and justice. Thus the opinions of the chancellor continually repeat that he who seeks equity must do equity, that he must come into equity with "clean hands," that equity abhors a forfeiture, and that equity will not protect one who sleeps on his rights. Is there any reason why these ideas should have been applied only in equity?

C.   FRAUD

Fraud often is spoken of as a fount of equitable jurisdiction. Yet the common law also permitted actions for fraud, and defenses as well. Why was protection against fraud thought to be a peculiarly equitable concern? For at least two reasons. For one thing, it was a function of equity's getting there first and going further. The common law would not recognize fraud as a defense to an action on a sealed instrument.   Thus, before the rise of assumpsit, at a time when most of the agreements that were enforced by the courts were under seal, equity furnished the only remedy for fraud in the great bulk of cases.   When simple contracts—to which fraud was a common-law defense— became enforceable, Chancery sustained its lead by developing the doctrine of constructive fraud, a doctrine in which the rigid technicalities of the common- law fraud concept played little part.   The second reason lay in equity's proce- dure.   In a famous passage, in which Blackstone was at pains to deny that eq- uity was inherently any more concerned with fairness or justice than the com- mon law, he explained:

> When facts, or their leading circumstances, rest only in the knowledge of the party, a court of equity applies itself to his con- science, and purges him upon oath with regard to the truth of the transaction;   and, that being once discovered, the judgment is the same in equity as it would have been at law.   *   *   *
>
> From   *   *   *   [this] fruitful source, the compulsive dis- covery upon oath, the courts of equity have acquired a jurisdiction over almost all matters of fraud;   all matters in the private knowl- edge of the party, which, though concealed, are binding in con- science   *   *   *.

3 Blackstone, *Commentaries* *437.

Equity implemented its concern with fraud in two ways.   First, by deny- ing its own relief to fraudulent complainants, and second, by enjoining legal suitors from pressing their claims or enforcing their judgments.   The fraud concept in the latter case has come to be known as an "equitable defense," to- gether with such doctrines as accident, undue influence, and estoppel.   Of course, the term "equitable defense" does not indicate a defense in an equity suit, but connotes an effective—if not technical—defense to an action at law.

D.   DISCOVERY

Equity and the common law should not be thought of as conflicting sys- tems.   In many respects the relationship was one of cooperation, especially af- ter the confrontation of 1616.   The most important aspect of this mutual assist- ance, for our purposes, was discovery, by which a party at law might obtain through equity much of the information necessary for his case.   The procedure and the limitations are set forth by Lord Chief Baron Abinger:

> *   *   *   A party has a right to compel the production of a document in which he has an equal interest, though not equal in degree, yet to a certain extent equal, with the party who detains it from him.   In that case he may file a bill of discovery, in order to

have the possession of it, and the inspection of it. A party has also a right to file a bill of discovery for the purpose of obtaining such facts as may tend to prove his case; and if those facts are either in possession of the other party, or, if they consist of documents in possession of the other party, in which he either has an interest, or which tend to prove his case, and have no relation to the case of the other party, he has a right to have them produced, and he may file a bill of discovery, in order to aid him in law or in equity, to exhibit those documents in evidence, or compel a statement of those facts. * * * Has he a right, as against the defendant, to discover the defendant's case? * * * The ground on which he files his bill, is to make the defendant discover what is material to his (the plaintiff's) case; but he has no right to say to the defendant, "Tell me what your title is—tell me what your case is—tell me how you mean to prove it—tell me the evidence you have to support it—disclose the documents you mean to make use of in support of it—tell me all these things, that I may find a flaw in your title." Surely that is not the principle of a bill of discovery.

COMBE v. CITY OF LONDON, 4 Y. & C. Ex. 139, 154, 160 Eng.Rep. 953, 959 (Exch.1840). What aspects of equitable procedure explain the availability of discovery in equity? In this connection, reread those portions of Maitland and Bowen in this Section dealing with the pleadings and the taking of evidence in equity.

SECTION D. REFORM: NEW PLEADING, ABOLITION OF THE FORMS, AND THE MERGER OF LAW AND EQUITY

---

1. THE NEW PROCEDURE EMERGES

The first significant reform in procedure occurred in England in the period between 1825 and 1834. Chancery practice was substantially reformed during these years. One form of writ was adopted for all three common-law courts. All but three real actions were abolished. Debt and detinue were reshaped. Wager of law was ended.

The capstone of the reform was a body of new rules of pleading, drafted by a committee that included Henry Stephen, author of the treatise frequently cited earlier in this Chapter, and Sir James Parke, who, as a judge of the Court of Exchequer, was to become the foremost expositor of the new rules. Many of their recommendations were distinct improvements on existing practice;

one—not accepted—would have permitted the joinder of counts in trespass and case, and amendments from the one form of action to the other. The principal defect the commissioners found in the existing system of pleading, however, was the ubiquitous availability of the general issue.

> * * * Consisting, as that plea does, of a mere summary denial of the case stated by the plaintiff, and giving no notice of any defensive allegation on which the defendant means to rely, it sends the whole case on either side to trial, without distinguishing the fact from the law, and without defining the exact question or questions of fact to be tried. It not unfrequently, therefore, happens, that the parties are taken by surprise, and find themselves opposed by some unexpected matter of defence or reply, which, from the want of timely notice, they are not in due condition to resist.

Second Report, Commissioners on Courts of Common Law 45 (1830). In addition, the commissioners attributed to pleas of the general issue "the unnecessary accumulation of proof," the failure to raise questions of law by demurrer, the imposition of the duty to separate law and fact upon the busy *nisi prius* judge, and the proliferation of new trials. This position was reflected by the new rules announced under the authority of an Act of Parliament by the judges of all three common-law courts at Hilary Term, 1834, and known as the Hilary Rules; the defenses that could be proved under a plea of the general issue were greatly reduced, and special pleading was substantially restored. 2 C. & M. 1–30, 149 Eng. Rep. 651–63 (1834).

The result was a disaster. "Under the common-law system the matter was bad enough with a pleading question decided in every sixth case. But under the Hilary Rules it was worse. Every fourth case decided a question on the pleadings. Pleading ran riot." Whittier, *Notice Pleading*, 31 Harv.L.Rev. 501, 507 (1918).[m] Fortunately, corrective action was not long in coming. The Common Law Procedure Acts of 1852, 1854, and 1860 weakened the forms of action, expanded joinder, and liberalized pleading. Finally, the Judicature Acts of 1873 and 1875 combined Chancery and the common-law courts into one Supreme Court of Judicature, fused law and equity, and abolished the forms of action. See 15 Holdsworth, *A History of English Law* 104-38 (Goodhart & Hanbury ed. 1965).

[m] The Hilary Rules, it has been argued, also affected substantive law:

> * * * The vagueness of the general issue permitted a certain flexibility in the law which Lord Mansfield, for one, had taken advantage of. Now that special pleading was required in such cases, this vagueness had to yield before statements so precise that subtle changes which had taken place in substantive law were forced into light, and found to be inconsistent with older authorities which now became of great importance. Hence the doctrine of consideration hardened along seventeenth-century lines, and the distinction between different forms of action was emphasized anew, although in the preceding century it had become of less vital importance.

Plucknett, *A Concise History of the Common Law* 416 (5th ed. 1956). See also Holdsworth, *The New Rules of Pleading of the Hilary Term, 1834,* 1 Cambridge L.J. 261 (1923).

Meanwhile in the United States,[n] a new constitution in New York in 1846 abolished the Court of Chancery and directed the legislature to provide for the appointment of commissioners to "revise, reform, simplify, and abridge" the civil procedure of the state. N.Y. Const. 1846 Art. VI, § 24. The legislature implemented this directive in 1847 and expressly charged the newly-appointed commissioners to "provide for the abolition of the present forms of actions and pleadings in cases at common law; for a uniform course of proceeding in all cases whether of legal or equitable cognizance, and for the abandonment * * * of any form and proceeding not necessary to ascertain or preserve the rights of the parties." N.Y. Laws 1847, c. 59, § 8.

FIRST REPORT OF THE COMMISSIONERS ON PRACTICE AND PLEADINGS (New York) 73–74, 87, 123–24, 137–38, 140–41, 144 (1848):

The history of jurisprudence, both in this state and in England, * * * affords a most convincing proof of the wisdom of the measure adopted by the people of this state, in abolishing the distinction between law and equity tribunals. Notwithstanding their separate existence, they had, under the institutions of this state, but one common object, the administration of justice—depending not upon the mere discretion of the court, but ascertained by fixed and certain rules of law. And yet, while they were kept distinct, though their jurisdictions continually encroached upon each other, there were certain rules, not well defined, but yet existing, by which their powers were distinguished. It is, therefore, no matter of surprise, that the books are filled with cases, in which the injustice has been imposed upon parties, of suffering the loss of a substantial right, because of a mistake in the choice of a forum, before which its enforcement was sought. * * *

From the period [in which the forms of action developed] * * * —a period comparatively benighted and ignorant, in all that is valuable in science—to the present, these forms have been adhered to with a sort of bigoted devotion. While the principles of legal science have expanded and adapted themselves to the exigencies of each successive age, through which they have passed, we find ourselves met with the standing argument against improvement, that the time-honored institutions of ages must be held sacred, and that these forms, which may have been well suited to the age in which they originated, must be left untouched.

* * * It seems to us, clear, that neither the forms of remedies, nor the mode in which they are stated, require the complexity, in which both are now enveloped. The embarrassments, to which they have given rise, have resulted from no difficulty in determining the real rights of parties, but simply

---

[n] The textual discussion is limited to states with a common-law heritage. Louisiana had adopted a system based on Spanish law with only one form of action by 1812, the year it was admitted to the Union. Texas experimented briefly with separate systems but by 1845 had a unitary system based on Spanish-Mexican jurisprudence.

in the means of enforcing them; and in this respect, we feel no hesitation in recommending, that the retention of forms, which serve no valuable purpose, should no longer constitute a portion of the remedial law of this state.
*   *   *

The rules respecting parties in the courts of law, differ from those in the courts of equity. The blending of the jurisdictions makes it necessary to revise these rules, to some extent. In doing so, we have had a three-fold purpose in view: first, to do away with the artificial distinctions existing in the courts of law, and to require the real party in interest to appear in court as such: second, to require the presence of such parties as are necessary to make an end of the controversy: and third, to allow otherwise great latitude in respect to the number of parties who may be brought in.
*   *   *

The courts of law generally administer justice betweee [sic] those parties only who stand in the same relation to *   *   * [each] other; while courts of equity bring before them various parties, standing in different relations, that the whole controversy may be settled, if possible, in one suit, and others avoided. This reasonable and just rule, we would adopt for all actions. *   *   *

As has been already remarked, the change in the mode of pleading is the key of the reform which we propose. Without this, we should despair of any substantial and permanent improvement in our modes of legal controversy.
*   *   *

The pleadings, we have said, are the written allegations of the parties of the cause of action on one side, and the defence on the other. Their object is three-fold: to present the facts on which the court is to pronounce the law; to present them in such a manner, as that the precise points in dispute shall be perceived, to which the proofs may be directed; and to preserve the record of the rights determined. Not one of these objects is gained by the law of pleading as it now exists in this state.
*   *   *

There are many treatises and books of forms, indispensable to the lawyer, on the mode of pleading and the forms of the allegations. The rules and the commentaries upon them, form one of the most technical and abstruse branches of the law *   *   *. We are *   *   * disposed to pronounce it a system of dialectics, very fit for the schoolmen with whom it originated, but unfit for the practical business of life.

So unfit has it been found, that in instances almost numberless, the legislature and the courts have departed from it and gone to the other extreme.
*   *   * A form of plea was devised which in many cases would virtually deny every material allegation of the declaration without disclosing any particular defence. The courts from time to time have admitted new defences under these general issues, and still further to encourage them, a statute has been passed allowing the defendant to plead the general issue, and with it give notice of any defence, which he could not otherwise introduce under such issue.
*   *   *

Besides the general issues, we have general declarations, or in technical language, common counts. These have been so contrived as to give no information of the particular demand. They also have been encouraged by the courts and numberless demands allowed to be proven under them. * * *

In truth the arguments of those who defend the present system destroy each other. One is the advantage of having the question of fact drawn out so precisely, that the court and jury may see what they have to try, and the parties be prepared with their proofs; the other is the advantage of having the facts stated in so general a form, that the allegations shall cover any state of facts that may appear on the trial, or in other words, the advantage of having no question of fact drawn out by the pleadings at all.

* * *

Disentangling the questions and separating those of fact and of law, is rarely effected by the present system of pleading at common law. * * * This is necessarily so, so long as the pleadings state the conclusions of fact, instead of the facts themselves. * * *

Following the report of the commissioners, the New York legislature enacted a Code of Civil Procedure, commonly called the Field Code after David Dudley Field, the most influential of the commissioners. N.Y. Laws 1848, c. 379. This Code proved to be the prototype for numerous state codes—at one time more than one-half the states had codes patterned to some degree after the Field Code—and the precursor of the Federal Rules. Among its most important provisions were the following:

§ 69. [§ 62]° The distinction between actions at law and suits in equity, and the forms of all such actions and suits, heretofore existing, are abolished; and, there shall be in this state, hereafter, but one form of action, for the enforcement or protection of private rights and the redress of private wrongs, which shall be denominated a civil action.

§ 140. [§ 118] All the forms of pleading heretofore existing, inconsistent with the provisions of this act, are abolished * * *.

§ 142. [§ 120] The complaint shall contain:

1. * * *

2. A statement of the facts constituting the cause of action, in ordinary and concise language, without repetition, and in such a manner as to enable a person of common understanding to know what is intended;

° The New York legislature added several sections to the Code in 1849, and renumbered the provisions first enacted in 1848 with some very slight changes in language. N.Y. Laws 1849, c. 438. Because the 1849 version became the best known, it is used here. Section numbers in brackets refer to the sections of the 1848 Code.

3. A demand of the relief, to which the plaintiff supposes himself entitled. If the recovery of money be demanded, the amount thereof shall be stated.

§ 156. [§ 132] No other pleading shall be allowed than the complaint, answer, reply and demurrers.

§ 159. [§ 136] In the construction of a pleading, for the purpose of determining its effect, its allegations shall be liberally construed, with a view to substantial justice between the parties.

§ 176. [§ 151] The court shall, in every stage of an action, disregard any error, or defect in the pleadings or proceedings, which shall not affect the substantial rights of the adverse party; and no judgment shall be reversed or affected by reason of such error or defect.

NOTES AND QUESTIONS

1. In 1851 the New York legislature amended Section 142(2) to read: "A plain and concise statement of the facts constituting a cause of action without unnecessary repetition." N.Y. Laws 1851, c. 479, § 1.

2. Compare Federal Rule of Civil Procedure 8(a)(2) and Section 142(2) of the Field Code in its original and amended forms. What differences do you find? What significance attaches to these differences?

———

ABADIE v. CARRILLO, 32 Cal. 172 (1867). Plaintiffs brought suit on a complaint in which they alleged only that "the defendant was indebted to the plaintiffs in the sum of   *   *   *   [$1004.20] on an account for goods sold and delivered by the plaintiffs to the defendant, at his request   *   *   *   and that no part thereof has been paid." A demurrer on the ground that "the complaint does not state the value of the goods, or a promise to pay the sum claimed" was overruled, and the Supreme Court of California affirmed. In a concurring opinion, Justice Sanderson said:

*   *   *   The fundamental rule in our system of pleading requires a statement of the facts constituting the cause of action or defence in ordinary and concise language, so that the precise matters intended may appear upon the face of the pleading, and the opposite party need not be put upon his outside knowledge for the purpose of ascertaining what is meant. I do not think the common counts satisfy this rule, and must regard their retention as impairing the symmetry of our system; but a contrary view was adopted at the outset, and has been uniformly adhered to since. The matter is not of sufficient importance to justify us in disturbing a rule so long settled.   *   *   *

QUESTIONS

Is the decision in *Abadie* consistent with Sections 140 and 142(2) of the Field Code? Does the pleading in that case satisfy the objectives set by the Commissioners in their report? Turn to the Supplement and compare Form 5 in the Appendix of Official Forms to the Federal Rules. What effect should the acceptance of the common counts under the Field Code have had on the interpretation given to Section 142(2) when complaints that did not use the common counts were challenged?

———

Although the division between law and equity in the federal courts never took the form of separate courts or judges of law and equity, the two were separately administered in the federal system until 1938. From the beginning, procedure at law was conformed to that of the state in which the court was held, but—due in part to the fact that some states had no system of equity in 1789—equity procedure in the federal courts was governed by acts of the Congress and rules promulgated by the Supreme Court. See p. 356, supra. In 1915, Congress provided that when "a suit at law should have been brought in equity or a suit in equity should have been brought at law, the court shall order any amendments to the pleadings which may be necessary to conform them to the proper practice," and that in "all actions at law equitable defenses may be interposed by answer, plea, or replication without the necessity of filing a bill on the equity side of the court." 38 Stat. 956. See generally Holtzoff, *Equitable and Legal Rights and Remedies Under the New Federal Procedure*, 31 Calif.L.Rev. 127 (1943). After an extended period of agitation for reform, Congress, in 1934, passed the Rules Enabling Act, 28 U.S.C. § 2072, authorizing the United States Supreme Court to promulgate rules of procedure for the district courts. The Federal Rules of Civil Procedure were the result. These Rules established a uniform procedure in all federal district courts, abolished the distinction between law and equity, and provided that there should be one form of action. See especially Rules 1 and 2.

QUESTIONS

Read the Rules Enabling Act, 28 U.S.C. § 2072, in the Supplement. Should the Federal Rules be considered to have the approval of Congress in the same sense as would a statute? *Cf.* 12 Wright & Miller, *Federal Practice and Procedure: Civil* § 3041 (1973) (the congressional history of Rule 71A). What are the advantages of court-made rules, as opposed to statutory procedural provisions such as those in the Field Code?

2. SOME OLD PROBLEMS PERSIST

Could it have been reasonably expected that the transition from the common-law system of procedure to the code system would represent a clean break with the past? Consider the following factors:

(a) The substantive law was supposed to remain unaltered, yet the substantive law had been intimately tied to the older mode of procedure. Moreover, certain procedural institutions—notably trial by jury—had acquired the character of substantive rights.

(b) The most fundamental aspects of procedure—such as the necessity of striking a balance between the function of pleading as setting the limits of the controversy and the function of trial as determining the true merits of the case —are not created by a particular system of procedure but are an integral part of an adjudicative process based upon a theory of party-presentation. Indeed it is rare that any system of procedure attempts by rigid rule to settle these issues definitively. Much will depend on the attitudes, experiences, and predispositions of those who are called upon to apply the rules.

(c) The problems presented by the change in procedure confronted a profession that had traditionally chosen precedent as its polestar, a profession comprised of men who might feel they had an interest in their established ways of proceeding and who in any event were trained in analysis under the older system. The judges who were called upon to interpret the new provisions were of course established members of this profession; indeed if the methods of judicial selection were effective, they were lawyers who had performed quite competently under the older procedure and they understandably may have been a little impatient with complaints that this procedure was replete with snares and absurdities.

Whatever the reasons, it is clear that many courts did not view the new codes as having been written on a clean slate. Even today concepts of the common-law system occasionally seem to assume a significant role in the decision of pleading and procedure questions. We will see more of this in the next Chapter. For the present we will look at one aspect of the perseverance of common-law notions—the "theory of the pleading" doctrine and related questions.

JONES v. WINSOR

Supreme Court of South Dakota, 1908.
22 S.D. 480, 118 N.W. 716.

CORSON, J. This is an appeal by the defendant from an order overruling his demurrer to the complaint.

It is alleged in the complaint, in substance: That on or about the 1st of April, 1907, the plaintiffs, being desirous of securing a franchise for a city railway system in the city of Sioux Falls, employed the defendant to act as an

attorney for them in securing or attempting to secure an ordinance from the city council granting the plaintiffs such license; that carrying out their purpose, * * * it became necessary for the plaintiffs to make a deposit with the city treasurer, and on said day the plaintiffs delivered to the defendant the sum of $2,500 to be by him deposited with the said treasurer of the city, and which money was so deposited * * *; that on or about the 4th day of April the defendant received a further sum of $130, which was to be used by the defendant for these plaintiffs in securing or attempting to secure the said franchise; that the said franchise which plaintiffs were attempting to secure from said city was not granted to these plaintiffs, and thereupon, about the 17th day of April, the city treasurer returned to the defendant the said sum of $2,500 "as money belonging to these plaintiffs and for their use and benefit"; that on or about the same day the said defendant rendered to these plaintiffs an account of all moneys received by him for and on account of these plaintiffs, with an itemized statement of all disbursements, and in connection therewith a pretended charge for his services or fee of $1,250, and with said account was a draft drawn in favor of the plaintiffs for $1,012.25; that the pretended charge of the defendant of the sum of $1,250 as shown upon said account and alleged to be for services rendered by him is unjust, unlawful, and fraudulent, and the reasonable value of the services rendered by the defendant was not and is not of the value of more than $250; that of the moneys so received by the defendant for and on behalf of these plaintiffs and for their use and benefit there remains in his hands the sum of $1,000, which he has refused and still refuses to pay over to these plaintiffs, although frequently requested so to do, and "he has wrongfully and fraudulently converted to his own use the said sum of $1,000"; that on or about the 10th day of September, 1907, the plaintiffs demanded of the said defendant payment * * * "but the said defendant then and there refused and still refuses to pay the same or any part thereof to the plaintiffs and has wrongfully converted the same to his own use." Wherefore "plaintiffs demand judgment against the said defendant for the sum of $1,000 and interest thereon from the 17th day of April, 1907, for the wrongful conversion of said property and for the costs of this action."
* * *

It is contended by the appellant that the complaint does not state facts sufficient to constitute a cause of action in trover or conversion, for the reason that the complaint nowhere alleges ownership by the plaintiffs of the property alleged to have been converted at the time the action was brought; nor does it allege ownership or possession of the property in the plaintiffs at the time it is alleged to have been converted which is absolutely essential in the form of action. Assuming that the complaint in this case was intended to state an action for the conversion of this money by the defendant, it is clearly insufficient in not alleging that the plaintiffs, at the time the defendant is charged with having converted it, were the owners or in possession of the money so alleged to have been converted. * * * But it is somewhat difficult to determine from the complaint whether the plaintiffs intended that their action should be for a tort or one ex contractu, as the complaint seems to have been framed with a double aspect. Taking a general view of the allegations of the complaint, it would seem that the pleaders intended to state a cause of action as for money had and received; but looking at the complaint in another aspect, and giving effect to some of the allegations therein, it would seem that the pleaders intended it as an action in conversion, in the nature of the old action of trover.

It is contended by the respondent, in support of the ruling of the court below upon the demurrer, that the action is to recover money had and received by the plaintiffs, and that the allegations contained in the complaint alleged [sic] the fraudulent conversion of the property, etc., may be treated as surplusage. Such a complaint, framed with a double aspect or to unite distinct and incongruous causes of actions, cannot be sustained on demurrer. While our Code has abolished forms of pleading, and only requires that the facts shall be stated in a plain and concise manner without unnecessary repetition, still the distinctions between actions as they formerly existed cannot be entirely ignored. In Pierce v. Carey, 37 Wis. 232, * * * Chief Justice Ryan, quotes with approval * * * Supervisors of Kewaunee County v. Decker, 30 Wis. 624, as follows: "Dixon, C. J. It would certainly be a most anomalous and hitherto unknown condition of the laws of pleading, were it established that the plaintiff in a civil action could file and serve a complaint, the particular nature and object of which no one could tell, but which might and should be held good, as a statement of two or three or more different and inconsistent causes of action, as one in tort, one upon money demand on contract, and one in equity, all combined or fused and moulded into one count or declaration, so that the defendant must await the accidents and events of trial, and until the plaintiff's proofs are all in, before being informed with any certainty or definiteness, what he was called upon to meet. The proposition that a complaint, or any single count of it, may be so framed with a double, treble, or any number of aspects looking to so many distinct and incongruous causes of action, in order to hit the exigencies of the plaintiff's case or any possible demands of his proofs at the trial, we must say, strikes us as something exceedingly novel in the rules of pleading. We do not think it is the law, and, unless the Legislature compels us by some new statutory regulation, shall hereafter be very slow to change this conclusion." The learned justice then proceeds in his opinion as follows: "Golden words, which should ever be present to the mind of every pleader under the Code, which was designed to substitute a plain and concise statement of causes of action, and of defenses, for the intricacies of pleading at common law. All that goes to the administration of justice should be definite and certain. * * * Simplicity, not uncertainty, is the object of the Code, and pleadings under it should be as certain in substance as they were before it—more certain in form, because freed from technical formality. * * * This distinction of actions in tort and on contract is as essential under our present practice as it ever was." * * *

As before stated, it is contended by the respondents that these allegations for conversion, etc., may be treated as surplusage, and the complaint held good as an action in assumpsit for money had and received; but in our opinion we would not be justified in holding that these allegations constitute mere surplusage and might be disregarded by the court.   To so hold would introduce into the law too much uncertainty and ambiguity in pleading which would have a tendency to mislead the courts and the opposing party.   A complaint should be framed upon the theory that it is either a complaint in tort or one ex contractu, and the two theories cannot be combined in one action; neither can an action at law and an action in equity be combined in one count in the same action. As was stated in the headnote in the case of Supervisors of Kewaunee County v. Decker, supra: "*   *   *   On demurrer to a complaint, or any count thereof, the court must determine what cause of action such complaint or count is designed to state, and then whether it states facts sufficient to constitute such a cause of action; and, if not, the demurrer must be sustained, though facts may be stated sufficient to show that plaintiff has a cause of action of a different character."

*   *   *

The order of the circuit court overruling the demurrer is reversed.

NOTES AND QUESTIONS

1.   Reread the provision of the Field Code that tells what a complaint shall contain, page 364–65, supra.   Is there language in that provision that lends support to the decision in the principal case?   What is the difference between Federal Rule 8(a) and the Field Code provision?

2.   Is it appropriate for a court to insist that plaintiff's complaint is based on a theory that is not supported by the alleged facts, as in *Jones v. Winsor*, especially when the facts are adequate to support a different theory?   Would your answer be different if the facts in the complaint were adequate to sustain either theory but the less apparent theory was the only one proved at trial?   Is the result in *Jones* consistent with Section 159 of the Field Code, p. 365, supra?   *Cf.* RIDDER v. WHITLOCK, 12 How.Pr. 208, 212 (N.Y.Sup.Ct.1856), in which the summons described the action as one in contract, but the complaint could be interpreted as sounding in either contract or tort; the court set aside the complaint for failure to conform with the summons, saying: "The plaintiffs should be held to this construction of their complaint by the old and familiar rule, that a pleading should be construed most strongly against the party whose pleading is brought in question."

3.   So far as the plaintiff's theory of his case means the legal position taken by his counsel—and this is generally its meaning—it would seem clear that this is not a part of the complaint.   This conclusion follows from the code ideal of stating the facts, not the law, the prayer for relief constituting no part of the cause of action.   If the plaintiff is to be expected to state only the past occurrences between the parties, and the court is then to grant him such relief as those occurrences justify, it should be immaterial that he called his action one of tort, whereas the court thought it was one of contract, or one in "equity," whereas the court thought it one "at law."

Clark, *Code Pleading* § 43, at 261 (2d ed. 1947).

———

CONAUGHTY v. NICHOLS, 42 N.Y. 83 (1870).   Plaintiff alleged that he had consigned goods to defendants for sale, that they had been sold for $690.82, and that after deducting the expenses of the sale there was due to plaintiff $618.43, that defendants had refused to pay this amount over to plaintiff and "have converted the same to their own use." After trial, plaintiff moved to amend the complaint by striking the allegation of conversion, but this motion was denied by the referee who then nonsuited plaintiff "on the ground that the cause of action stated in the complaint was for a tort, and the proof established a cause of action upon contract." The General Term reversed the judgment, and the Court of Appeals affirmed:

* * * If the words "and have converted the same to their own use" had been omitted in the complaint, it could not reasonably be contended, that the same was not adapted to the cause of action established by the evidence. The case, therefore, seems to be reduced to the proposition, whether the plaintiff, having alleged facts constituting a cause of action, and having sustained them by proof upon the trial, should have been nonsuited, because the pleading contained an allegation adapted to a complaint in an action *ex delicto*, and which was unnecessary to be stated or proved, to justify a recovery on contract. We are of opinion that no such rigid rule of construction in regard to pleading should prevail under the liberal system introduced by the Code.

* * * If the complaint in question had merely stated facts sufficient to authorize a recovery for a wrongful detention of the money, and upon the trial, the plaintiff had applied to amend by inserting facts appropriate to a cause of action on contract, and thereby changing the form and character of the action, the application should have been denied. That, however, was not the case, as the facts were fully stated, and the defendants apprized of what they were to meet upon the trial, and there was no pretense that they were surprised. If they chose to accept the complaint without moving to strike out any portion of it, or to compel the plaintiff to make it more definite, or to elect in regard to the form of action, they should not, upon the trial, have been allowed to prevent a recovery by the plaintiff of a judgment for the amount of his demand. * * * It is quite probable that the plaintiff intended, down to the trial, to recover against the defendants for a wrongful conversion of the proceeds of the sale of the property consigned to them, and doubtless the mistake should have been fatal but for the ample statement of facts contained in the complaint, which justified a recovery on contract for the amount of his demand. It does not follow that, because the parties go down to the trial upon a particular theory, which is not supported by the proof, the cause is to be dismissed, when there are facts alleged in the complaint, and sustained by the evidence, sufficient to justify a recovery upon a different theory or form of action. * * *

NOTES AND QUESTIONS

1. Is *Conaughty* consistent with *Jones v. Winsor?* "The reasoning of the Court in *Conaughty v. Nichols* that where the pleading is misleading the defendant should move to make it definite or to have the pleader elect between the possible theories, and that if he proceeds without doing so he is to be taken as fully understanding the pleading, seems very weak." Whittier, *The Theory of a Pleading,* 8 Colum.L.Rev. 523, 534 (1908). Why? If you were preparing a complaint in New York after *Conaughty,* what moral would you draw from the opinion in that case?

2. New York has varied in its approach to the theory-of-the-pleading doctrine. Early decisions that allowed considerable freedom to the pleader were brought up short in ROSS v. MATHER, 51 N.Y. 108 (1872), which held that if a complaint stated a cause of action for fraud, the action must fail if fraud was not proved, although the complaint contained allegations adequate to support an action for breach of warranty and those allegations were proved. See also Cohen v. City Co., 283 N.Y. 112, 27 N.E.2d 803 (1940); Walrath v. Hanover Fire Ins. Co., 216 N.Y. 220, 110 N.E. 426 (1915). A contrary trend seems to have been begun by DIEMER v. DIEMER, 8 N.Y.2d 206, 203 N.Y.S.2d 829, 168 N.E.2d 654 (1960), in which the Court of Appeals directed that an order of separation be entered on the ground of abandonment although the action for separation had been pleaded, tried, and appealed on the ground of cruel and inhuman treatment. The New York cases are explored in 3 Weinstein, Korn & Miller, *New York Civil Practice* ¶¶ 3013.05, 3017.06. See also Lane v. Mercury Record Corp., 21 A.D.2d 602, 252 N.Y.S.2d 1011 (1964), affirmed 18 N.Y.2d 889, 276 N.Y.S.2d 626, 223 N.E.2d 35 (1966). Examine Section 3013 of New York's Civil Practice Law and Rules, which appears in the Supplement in conjunction with the text of Federal Rule of Civil Procedure 8(a). Does the New York provision really abolish the theory-of-the-pleading doctrine? In particular does the requirement that the pleading give "the material elements of each cause of action or defense" contain the seed for a rebirth of the doctrine?

3. Actions in which the complaint speaks of fraud but contains the necessary elements of a cause of action for conversion or contract frequently have been the vehicle for a court's selection of the strict approach to the theory-of-the-pleading question. In addition to *Ross v. Mather,* Note 2, supra, see Neidefer v. Chastain, 71 Ind. 363 (1880), and Supervisors of Kewaunee Co. v. Decker, 30 Wis. 624 (1872), which is relied upon in *Jones v. Winsor.* See Albertsworth, *The Theory of the Pleadings in Code States,* 10 Calif.L.Rev. 202, 211 (1922); Whittier, Note 1, supra at 530.

4. England did not escape the theory-of-the-pleading problem. *Compare* Cooke v. Waring, 2 H. & C. 332, 159 Eng.Rep. 138 (Exch.1863), *with* Theyer v. Purnell, [1918] 2 K.B. 333.

INTERNATIONAL PHOTO RECORDING MACHINES, INC. v. MICROSTAT CORP.

Supreme Court of New York, Appellate Division, First Department, 1945.
269 App.Div. 485, 56 N.Y.S.2d 277.

COHN, Justice. Plaintiff by this action in equity sought to reform a written agreement between the parties alleging mutual mistake. After hearing the evidence the trial court decided that there had been no mistake and denied reformation. However, it construed the contract as written and held that under its terms plaintiff was entitled to a money judgment without the necessity of any reformation.   *   *   *   [D]efendant appeals.

      *   *   *

The business of defendant is the rental and sale of microfilm equipment and the photographic recording of business documents and other records. After preliminary negotiations, plaintiff, which owned and controlled certain patents   *   *   *, entered into a written agreement with defendant granting an exclusive license. The controversy is in connection with the royalty provisions of the agreement. In paragraph 2 of the contract, defendant Microstat covenanted to pay royalties upon the business done under its license from plaintiff International, at the rates therein specified. The contract then provided:

"3. Microstat covenants and agrees that the minimum royalties payable in each year during the life hereof shall be as follows:

For the first year, $5,000. For the second year, $7,500. For the third year, and each succeeding year during the life hereof, $10,000.

"In the event that the specific royalties payable, as per Paragraph 2 hereof, in any one year do not equal the minimum royalties as set forth above, Microstat shall have the right to pay the difference between the minimum royalties paid and the minimum royalties due, in cash, in order to keep this license in full force and effect.

      "   *   *   *

"12. In the event of any default by Microstat arising hereunder, International shall have the right to cancel this agreement upon sixty days' notice   *   *   *. Microstat shall also have the right to cancel this agreement upon sixty days' notice, by registered mail, to International at any time after the second year of the life hereof   *   *   *."

No royalties were actually earned. Defendant, however, paid the minimum royalties for the first year amounting to $5,000 and one installment (the annual payments were divided into twelve installments) of $625 on account of the second year, and then ceased making further payments.

Upon defendant's failure to pay the installments, plaintiff brought an action in the City Court of the City of New York to recover the sums unpaid on the theory that there was a covenant in the agreement to pay minimum rates in any event. That action was discontinued when defendant in its answer denied that there was such a covenant, and claimed that it was optional and not obligatory on its part to make the payments demanded. This action for reformation was thereupon instituted.

The complaint here alleges that it was the intention of the parties that the minimum royalties during the first two years were to become payable by defendant regardless of whether the specific royalties were earned; that by mutual mistake of the parties the agreement omitted so to provide; and that the agreement had been executed in the belief that such provision was embodied in its terms; that the minimum royalties of $7500 for the second year were payable in 12 monthly installments of $625, but that defendant failed and refused to pay the first three of these installments amounting to the sum of $1875. The complaint demands judgment: (1) "That the said agreement be reformed to express the true intent of the parties, by providing that the clause giving defendant the right to pay the difference between the minimum royalties paid and the minimum royalties due, in order to keep the agreement in force, apply only after the expiration of the second year of the agreement, and that the minimum royalties payable during the first two years of the agreement shall in any event be due and payable"; and (2) for the amounts which would be due and unpaid if such reformation were granted.

* * *

The trial court found that there had been no mutual mistake in the preparation and execution of the contract in suit; that it had been read over by the principals, consciously approved, and that it was worded exactly as the parties intended. These findings are fully sustained by the evidence. * * * The law is well settled that reformation may not be granted unless the case in support of it is of the clearest and most satisfactory character, nor may reformation be granted upon anything less than a certainty of error. * * * When the trial court ruled that there was no mutual mistake of fact and that hence there could be no reformation of the agreement, it passed upon the only issue presented by the pleadings.

In going beyond this, and in rendering a judgment in favor of plaintiff for the payments which it found to be due under the contract as written, we think the learned court erred. When it was found as a fact that there was no mutual mistake, the complaint should have been dismissed for want of equity. Upon the issues raised by the pleadings, the court had no concern with the construction or interpretation of the agreement as drawn, for that involved a wholly different cause of action from that set forth in the complaint. The weight of authority in this State is that where some ground of equitable jurisdiction is alleged in a complaint but fails of proof in its entire scope on the trial and it appears that there never was any substantial cause for equitable interference, the court will not retain the action and grant purely legal relief but will dismiss the complaint. Jackson v. Strong, 222 N.Y. 149, 153, 154, 118 N.E. 512, 513 * * *.

The familiar rule that when equity has obtained jurisdiction of the parties and the subject matter of the action, it may adapt the relief to the exigencies of the case does not apply here. "That rule applies when the general basis of fact upon which equitable relief was sought has been made out, but for some reason, it becomes impracticable to grant such relief, or where it would be insufficient; and not to a case like this, where it appears that there never was in fact any ground for equitable relief whatever, but the sole remedy was an action at law." Dudley v. Congregation Third Order St. Francis, 138 N.Y. at page 459, 34 N.E. at page 283.

The trial court assumed to determine the purely legal questions involved on the theory that the protection of the right to a jury trial was unnecessary in this case because there were no fact issues for a jury to decide. We are unable to concur in this view. Plaintiff in its complaint merely asked for reformation of the contract and for such moneys as would be due and unpaid if the reformation were granted. It did not plead a cause of action for damages at law under the contract as it was written. Had it done so, defendant would then have been afforded an opportunity of making answer to such a complaint and thereafter contesting the issues thus raised. If, as asserted by defendant, the contract is ambiguous, then evidence of the intent of the contracting parties must be heard and that issue of fact determined by a jury. * * * It is also argued that there may be a question as to due performance of the contract by plaintiff and that there may be other defenses or counterclaims available to defendant which were not presented by the pleadings or litigated upon the trial. * * *

For the foregoing reasons the judgment should be reversed with costs and the complaint dismissed with costs.

NOTES AND QUESTIONS

1. Is a theory-of-the-pleading requirement more justified or less justified when the alternative theories are legal and equitable than when both theories are legal? Is there a greater need for determining the theory of the litigation at the pleading stage when one of the possible theories is equitable? See pp. 806–26, infra.

2. Was defendant in *International Photo* prejudiced by the lower court's action? Do you believe defendant could justifiably or reasonably have failed to prepare to contest the issues discussed in the last paragraph of Justice Cohn's opinion? Should the court have dismissed the complaint without requiring defendant to show that it was prejudiced? What could plaintiff have done at the outset of the case to avoid the problem it later faced? The decision is discussed in Note, *Law and Equity in New York—Still Unmerged*, 55 Yale L.J. 826 (1946).

3. Would the court's disposition of *International Photo* have been proper under New York Civil Practice Law and Rules 4103, which is set out in the Supplement following Federal Rule 38? See 4 Weinstein, Korn & Miller, *New York Civil Practice* ¶¶ 4103.02, 4103.05–.06.

4. In discussing the statutory provision that "there shall be in this state * * * but one form of action * * * which shall be called a 'civil action,'" the Washington Supreme Court said:

> * * * This is a mandatory provision of the law, and a ready yielding of allegiance to this mandate on the part of the courts of the state will simplify legal proceedings and strip them of fictions and technicalities which find no place in the reformed procedure. This holding does not lead to the conclusion that all the distinctions between law and equity are abolished, or that equitable actions are not to be tried under the same rules under which they always have been tried. It simply means that it makes no difference what the action is termed, and that the relief sought must be granted according to the demands of the complaint if they are substantiated by proof; that an applicant for justice is not to be turned out of the temple of justice scourged with costs because he happens to come in at one door instead of another, and be compelled to enter that

other door to ask the same remedy at the hands of the same court. The court is the same, sitting at the same place, clothed with the same authority, and when once the applicant has gained legal access to the court through a statement of facts, which the law demands that the complaint shall be, he is entitled to just such relief as his complaint and his proof warrant; and in the trial of the cause, if it is discovered that the relief is equitable, the court will administer the equitable relief. If it becomes necessary in the trial of the cause to determine a purely legal right, the court, as it always has done, may call a jury to try out that question.

BROWN v. BALDWIN, 46 Wash. 106, 114, 89 P. 483, 486 (1907).

GARRITY v. STATE BOARD OF ADMINISTRATION OF EDUCATIONAL INSTITUTIONS

Supreme Court of Kansas, 1917.
99 Kan. 695, 162 P. 1167.

PORTER, J. The action was one, in the language of the learned judge of the district court, "to recover the value of an eighteen million year old lizard." The petition made the state board of administration of educational institutions the sole defendant, and was filed June 9, 1914. * * * A demurrer to the petition was sustained; plaintiff elected to stand upon the petition and appeals.

The petition charges that in July, 1911, the board of regents of the state university, by its assistant curator of mammals, wrongfully and without plaintiff's knowledge or consent, entered upon his farm in Wallace county and removed therefrom a large and valuable fossil, the property of plaintiff, and wrongfully converted it to the use and benefit of the board of regents and its successors, depositing the fossil in the museum of the university for exhibition and scientific purposes; that the fossil was of the value of $2,500, and plaintiff had received no compensation therefor. It is alleged that the board of administration is a board created by law for the government, management, and control of the university of Kansas, * * * and is the successor of the board of regents, subrogated to the rights, duties, and responsibilities of the board of regents, and subject to its obligations and liable for its debts and contracts. * * *

1. It is the defendants' contention that both the original and the amended petition were subject to demurrer because, if they stated a cause of action at all, it was barred by the statute of limitations; that the action is one sounding in tort, and therefore barred by the two-year statute * * *. On the other hand the plaintiff claims the right to waive the tort and recover upon an implied promise to pay what the fossil is worth. We think, if [the] petition stated a cause of action against defendants, it must be held that sufficient facts were stated to authorize plaintiff to waive the tort and rely upon an implied promise to pay the value of the property converted. * * *

The two-year statute of limitations was therefore no bar to the action.

*   *   *

3. The principal question raised by the appeal is whether the action can be maintained against the board of administration, the original defendant. Prior to 1913 the state university was managed and controlled by a board of regents which was a body corporate created by the Legislature. It went out of existence when the act of 1913 placed the state educational institutions in control of the state board of administration, which was not made a body corporate. The act   *   *   *   provided that the board shall manage and control the property of the educational institutions named, including the state university, and conferred upon the board power "to execute trusts or other obligations now or hereafter committed to any of the said institutions   *   *   *." The power "to execute trusts or other obligations now or hereafter committed to any of   *   *   *   said institutions" cannot be construed so as to make either the board of administration or its members liable for a tort committed by the board of regents; and the plaintiff cannot, by waiving the tort, make either the board or its members liable upon the theory of an implied promise.

*   *   *

The judgment is affirmed. All the Justices concurring.

NOTES AND QUESTIONS

1. Is *Garrity*, in either its statute-of-limitations aspect or its liability aspect, concerned with the theory of the pleading? In what way, if any, is the problem in *Garrity* different?

2. Why did the court hold that the action was in contract for purposes of the statute of limitations but in tort for purposes of deciding whether the Board was liable for the Regents' action?

3. Governments generally are immune from suit except as their immunity has been expressly waived by statute. Suits in contract are more commonly consented to than suits in tort. See 3 Davis, *Administrative Law Treatise* § 25.01 (1958). Under a statute consenting to suit in contract only, should a plaintiff be permitted to "waive" a tort and sue in "assumpsit"?

4. DANERI v. SOUTHERN CALIFORNIA R. CO., 122 Cal. 507, 508, 55 P. 243 (1898), was an action for damage to land occasioned by defendant's construction of a levee that deflected a river into a new channel across plaintiff's land. The California Supreme Court said:

> *   *   *   [I]t is to be determined whether the action is an action for trespass upon real property, in which case, having been brought within three years, the statute did not bar a recovery   *   *   *   or whether it was an action upon [another "liability, not founded on an instrument of writing"]   *   *   *   in which latter case, having been brought more than two years after the cause of action arose, it is barred. At common law such an action would not have been trespass, but an action on the case. While the forms of actions have been abolished in this state, yet, when our statute of limitations speaks of an action for trespass upon real property, for the meaning of the word "trespass," as thus used, we must go to the common law, and nowhere else.   *   *   *

But cf. Kentucky Dep't of Highways v. Ratliff, 392 S.W.2d 913, 15 A.L.R.3d 1225 (Ky.Ct.App.1965). See Annot., 15 A.L.R.3d 1228 (1967). In what respect is the rule applied in *Daneri* different from a theory-of-the-pleading requirement?

5. In a contract action, may a claim for money had and received based upon a conversion be brought as a counterclaim under a statute that provides that "in an action on contract, any other cause of action on contract" may be brought as a counterclaim? See Manhattan Egg Co. v. Seaboard Terminal & Refrig. Co., 137 Misc. 14, 242 N.Y.S. 189 (City Ct.N.Y.1929).

COCHRAN v. WHITESIDES

Supreme Court of Missouri, 1864.
34 Mo. 417.

DRYDEN, Judge, delivered the opinion of the court. This was an action commenced under the practice act of 1849, to recover damages for wrongfully entering and cutting timber on the land of the plaintiff. The evidence on the trial tended to show that at the time of the commission of the trespasses complained of, and for several years prior thereto, the defendant was in the actual possession of the land trespassed upon, claiming and holding the same adversely to the plaintiff. The court instructed as follows: "If the jury find that at the time of the commission of the alleged trespasses the plaintiff was not in the actual possession of the premises on which the trespasses were committed, and that the defendant was in the actual occupancy thereof, claiming the land adversely to the plaintiff, the plaintiff cannot recover in this action." The plaintiff then suffered a non-suit   *   *   *.

The action of trespass *quare clausum fregit* could be maintained at common law only where the plaintiff was in the possession of the close at the time of the commission of the trespass. It was an action for injury to the possession. If the injury was committed after ouster and while the premises were in the adverse possession of the wrongdoer, no action lay to redress such injury until the plaintiff first regained possession.   *   *   *

I think the law in this respect is unchanged by the practice act. That act abolished the distinction between actions, but did not give an action where none existed before. The point in this case is, that, in the condition of things at the time the suit was brought, the injury complained of was not then the subject of legal redress. The instruction was a correct exposition of the law as applicable to the case. If the plaintiff would recover damages for the alleged trespasses, let her bring her ejectment to regain possession; and in case she prevail, as an incident of that action she may recover as well damages for the waste and injury to the premises, as also the rents and profits.

    *   *   *   Let the judgment be affirmed.

Judge BAY concurs; Judge BAY dissents [sic].

NOTES AND QUESTIONS

1. To what extent is *Cochran* merely another narrow application of the theory-of-the-pleading doctrine? Is it an application of that doctrine at all? Is a more fundamental issue involved?

2. Was there an alternative in *Cochran* to nonsuiting plaintiff? Compare Federal Rules 18 and 54(c).

3. Might a court appropriately have regarded the philosophy of the code as a basis for eliminating what it considered to be hypertechnical restrictions on substantive rights? See Anthony v. Norton, 60 Kan. 341, 56 P. 529 (1899) (rejecting limitation of parent's recovery for seduction of daughter to loss of services); Cooper v. Seaverns, 81 Kan. 267, 105 P. 509 (1909) (words imputing unchastity to woman made actionable without proof of special damage).

CHAPTER 5

MODERN PLEADING

SECTION A. INTRODUCTION

In studying the rules of modern pleading practice, one should be aware that they ought to be considered on two levels. The first involves basic, generic problems unrelated to specific causes of action or defenses. The second deals with the precise technique of stating particular matters in different types of cases or under certain conditions.

This Chapter primarily is concerned with the first level and is designed to impart an understanding of the pleading process and the theoretical problems involved therein. Discussion of requirements of pleadings in particular situations generally is not helpful to such an understanding. Not only do the requirements vary among jurisdictions but they often depend on historical idiosyncracies and are prone to quick and dramatic change. Nevertheless there are a few specific pleading allegations, which because they arise so frequently, have been subject to special scrutiny by courts and legislatures and raise interesting and important questions of general pleading policy. These are included for discussion at pp. 427–43, infra.

MANWILL v. OYLER

Supreme Court of Utah, 1961.
11 Utah 2d 433, 361 P.2d 177.

CROCKETT, Justice. Defendants   *   *   *   challenge the denial of their motion to dismiss the plaintiff's complaint. The only issue presented is whether it states a cause of action against them.

Plaintiff alleged that during the years 1950, 1951, 1952 and 1953 he made payments on defendants' behalf aggregating $5,506.20 on a farm now occupied by the defendants; and that in the year 1954 he transferred to defendants a grazing permit worth $1,800 and 18 head of cattle worth $3,000. It is conceded that any action on those transactions would be barred by the statute of limitations. But the plaintiff further alleged that in July or August, 1956, the defendants orally agreed to pay said sums to him. After defendants filed a motion to dismiss, he amended to state that the oral promise to pay him

$5,506.20 occurred in October, 1957. The motion to dismiss was considered as directed to the complaint as amended. It was denied and they were given 15 days in which to answer. Instead of doing so, they * * * [appealed].
        * * *

The position the plaintiff essays is that the earlier payments he claims to have made for the defendants' benefit placed them under moral obligation to repay him, and that this constitutes valid consideration to make their 1957 oral promise a binding contract. The rule quite generally recognized is that a moral obligation by itself will not do so. Although some authorities appear to be otherwise, it will usually be found that there are special circumstances bolstering what is termed the moral obligation.

The difficulty we see with the doctrine is that if a mere moral, as distinguished from a legal, obligation were recognized as valid consideration for a contract, that would practically erode to the vanishing point the necessity for finding a consideration. This is so, first because in nearly all circumstances where a promise is made there is some moral aspect of the situation which provides the motivation for making the promise even if it is to make an outright gift. And second, if we are dealing with moral concepts, the making of a promise itself creates a moral obligation to perform it. It seems obvious that if a contract to be legally enforceable need be anything other than a naked promise, something more than mere moral consideration is necessary. The principle that in order for a contract to be valid and binding, each party must be bound to give some legal consideration to the other by conferring a benefit upon him or suffering a legal detriment at his request is firmly implanted in the roots of our law.

In urging that the moral consideration here present makes a binding contract, plaintiff places reliance on what is termed the "material benefit rule" as reflecting the trend of modern authority. The substance of that rule is that where the promisors (defendants) have received something from the promisee (plaintiff) of value in the form of money or other material benefits under such circumstances as to create a moral obligation to pay for what they received, and later promise to do so there is consideration for such promise. But even the authorities standing for that rule affirm that there must be something beyond a bare promise, as of an offered gift or gratuity. The circumstances must be such that it is reasonably to be supposed that the promisee (plaintiff) expected to be compensated in some way therefor.

Accepting that proposition for the sake of argument, the plaintiff has not set forth any of the facts surrounding the original transactions to show that there was any expectation that he would be compensated in this case. This may have been done advisedly because of the difficulty which would confront him: if the circumstances were such that the parties reasonably expected he was to be paid, there may have been an implied contract, which is now outlawed. Insofar as the statements in his complaint disclose, any benefits conferred on defendants would have been donative. Therefore, at the time of the alleged 1957 promise there could have existed nothing but a bare moral obligation to support the defendants' claimed oral promise to repay him. This alone would not constitute valid consideration to make a binding contract.

The conclusion we have reached finds support in the fact that by our statute the time in which an action may be brought is extended by an acknowledgement or promise to pay the same but it "must be in writing and signed by the party to be charged thereby." This affirmative provision, which has the effect of permitting an outlawed obligation to be renewed by a promise in writing, indicates an awareness and recognition of the well-established principle that an oral promise will not revive such an obligation.

Since the plaintiff has not alleged facts sufficient to make the alleged oral promise of 1957 a binding contract, it was error to deny the defendants' motion to dismiss.

Reversed with directions to dismiss the action. Costs to defendants (appellants).

NOTES AND QUESTIONS

1. Does the result in *Manwill* necessarily show that plaintiff's attorney was remiss in the initial research and evaluation of the case? Are there circumstances in which a lawyer may justifiably file suit despite the fact that existing case law would result in a decision against his client? Consider the effect a "no" answer would have on the development, expansion, and change of substantive law necessary to meet the requirements of a dynamic society. Also consider the extent to which the expense of filing an initial complaint plays an important role in law development.

2. How would this case have progressed if defendant had failed to challenge the sufficiency of plaintiff's complaint? Normally, a party waives all defenses and objections that are not raised in his pleadings. The failure to state a legal claim is one notable exception. Examine Federal Rule of Civil Procedure 12(h) (2) and the materials accompanying it in the Supplement. Why is that objection not waived as are other defenses? Should it be permitted even after the trial has taken place?

3. Could plaintiff's counsel in *Manwill* have avoided the decision merely by failing to allege whether the promise was oral or written? Section 430.10 (h) of the California Code of Civil Procedure expressly provides that in an action based on a contract defendant may challenge the complaint for failing to allege whether the contract was written or oral. Could plaintiff simply have claimed that the promise "was in exchange for a valuable consideration"? See Cook, *Statements of Fact in Pleading Under the Codes*, 21 Colum.L.Rev. 416 (1921) (as set out pp. 389–91, infra). What, if anything, prevented plaintiff's lawyer from alleging falsely that the contract was in writing? Do the rules of pleading tend to promote unscrupulous conduct by making it worthwhile?

4. Although a plaintiff may avoid a dismissal of the complaint by alleging facts for which there is no proof, this does not assure that the case will go to trial. Federal Rule 56(c), which is quite typical of the provisions in many states, provides for a summary judgment if a party introduces pleadings, depositions,

admissions, or affidavits showing there is no genuine issue of fact and that she is entitled to a judgment as a matter of law. See also *Alderman v. Baltimore & Ohio R. Co.*, p. 35, supra. Does such a rule obviate the need for a trial in any case in which one party has no factual basis to substantiate a claim or defense? Federal Rule 36 permits one party to request the opposing party to admit or deny under oath the truth of any relevant matters of fact in the case. If the fact is denied without good reason and the requesting party subsequently proves its truth, the latter may collect the reasonable expenses of proving the fact. How helpful is such a provision? Is it a sufficient penalty for a false denial?

MESSICK v. TURNAGE

Supreme Court of North Carolina, 1954.
240 N.C. 625, 83 S.E.2d 654.

In this action the plaintiff seeks to recover damages on account of injuries she received while a patron in defendant's moving picture theatre. The allegations in her complaint are in substance that she purchased a ticket and entered the theatre during a hard rain; that falling plaster and water behind her so frightened her that she involuntarily jumped from her seat, striking the metal part of the seat in front, causing her injury. The particular breach of duty on the part of the defendant which she alleges is actionable negligence is set out in the following words: "That the defendant failed to maintain a safe theatre and auditorium for plaintiff's enjoyment, in that the defendant knew or should have known by reasonable observation which was his duty, that said roof was leaking and in bad repair."

She further alleges somewhat indefinitely that this condition caused the plaster to give way. * * *

The defendant answered, denying negligence, and denying that the roof was leaking or in bad repair.

The evidence, in the light most favorable to the plaintiff, tended to show the theatre consisted of a main floor and a balcony which extended over the rear part of the main floor on either side and to the rear. A restroom on the level with the balcony floor was maintained for the patrons of the theatre. A valve in one of the fixtures in the restroom failed to close, causing water to spill out to the floor. This floor was of tile, sloping toward the center, and fitted with a drainpipe sufficient in size to carry all overflow. This pipe was covered with a grill. Cigarette butts and other debris had clogged the pipe. Water covered the floor to a depth sufficient to overflow a three-quarter-inch strip at the door. The balcony was covered with a carpet which soaked up the overflowing water. Seepage from the carpet through the floor of the balcony softened the plaster under the balcony. Suddenly this plaster gave way, and, to use plaintiff's own words, "I thought the whole balcony was coming down behind me, it made so much fuss. I did not know what was going on at the second when it happened, and it startled me so I hit my leg on the back of the seat." The plaintiff's evidence further tended to show the door to the restroom was closed. The sound of running water could not be heard from the outside. Water could not be discovered from the outside, except by examination or stepping on the carpet. At the close of plaintiff's evidence, motion for judgment of nonsuit was made and sustained. The plaintiff appealed.

* * *

HIGGINS, Justice. The negligence sufficiently pleaded in the complaint is to the effect that the defendant "knew or should have known * * * that said roof was leaking and in bad repair * * *." There is not a suggestion in the evidence that the roof was leaking and in bad repair. It was incumbent upon the plaintiff not only to prove negligence proximately causing her injury, but it was her duty to prove negligence substantially as alleged in her complaint. This she failed to do. Proof without allegation is as unavailing as allegation without proof. * * *

Affirmed.

NOTES AND QUESTIONS

1. Plaintiff in *Messick v. Turnage* was guilty of what is known technically as a "variance between the pleading and the proof." Is such a variance always the result of insufficient investigation by the attorney before attempting to draft a pleading? Could the problem in *Messick* have been avoided had plaintiff merely alleged defendant was negligent "in failing to maintain the theatre in a condition safe for patrons"?

2. What is the purpose of the variance rule as applied in *Messick*? Under what conditions should it be enforced? A number of jurisdictions have enacted statutory provisions to the effect that a variance shall be treated as immaterial unless it actually misled the adverse party at trial. Even if the opponent was misled, the trial judge may, in his discretion, permit the pleadings to be amended to conform to the evidence on terms that protect the adverse party's interests. Cal.Code Civ.Proc. § 469. Thus the court may grant a continuance for the purpose of gathering evidence on an issue not raised in the pleadings. However separate statutes distinguish a mere "variance" from a "failure of proof" when the action or defense proved differs from the pleading "in its entire scope and meaning." Cal.Code Civ.Proc. § 471. In the latter case no curative action is permitted. Was the trial court in *Messick* correct in treating the case as one involving a failure of proof?

Note that the action was dismissed at the close of plaintiff's case, before defendant was called upon to put in his evidence. Assuming that plaintiff's evidence, if believed, would have supported a verdict in her favor, what justification could there be at that stage of the trial for prohibiting an amendment to the complaint? Shouldn't the failure-of-proof rule be abandoned completely in favor of a provision that leaves to the trial judge the decision whether or not an amendment is justified in light of the prejudice to the adverse party? See Federal Rules 15(a) and 15(b).

Further discussion of the problems of variance and amendment appear later in this Chapter at pp. 482–97, infra.

SECTION B. THE NATURE AND FORM OF ALLEGATIONS

---

1. DETAIL REQUIRED UNDER THE CODES

Read South Carolina Code §§ 10–632, 10–642, which appear in the Supplement in conjunction with Federal Rules of Civil Procedure 8 and 12, respectively.

GILLISPIE v. GOODYEAR SERVICE STORES

Supreme Court of North Carolina, 1963.
258 N.C. 487, 128 S.E.2d 762.

The hearing below was on demurrers to the complaint.

Plaintiff alleges she and each of the four individual defendants are citizens and residents of Alamance County, North Carolina; that defendant Goodyear Tire & Rubber Company is a corporation doing business in North Carolina and having a place of business and store in Burlington, North Carolina; and that Goodyear Service Stores is a division of defendant Goodyear Tire & Rubber Company.

The remaining allegations of the complaint and the prayer for relief are as follows:

"4. On or about May 5, 1959, and May 6, 1959, the defendants, without cause or just excuse and maliciously came upon and trespassed upon the premises occupied by the plaintiff as a residence, and by the use of harsh and threatening language and physical force directed against the plaintiff assaulted the plaintiff and placed her in great fear, and humiliated and embarrassed her by subjecting her to public scorn and ridicule, and caused her to be seized and exhibited to the public as a prisoner, and to be confined in a public jail, all to her great humiliation, embarrassment and harm.

"5. By reason of the defendants' malicious and intentional assault against and humiliation of the plaintiff, the plaintiff was and has been damaged and injured in the amount of $25,000.00.

"6. The acts of the defendants as aforesaid were deliberate, malicious, and with the deliberate intention of harming the plaintiff, and the plaintiff is entitled to recover her actual damages as well as punitive damages from the defendants and each of them.

"THEREFORE, the plaintiff prays that she have and recover of the defendants the sum of $25,000.00 as damages and $10,000.-

00 in addition thereto as punitive damages, and that she have such other and further relief as may be just and proper."

* * *

BOBBITT, Justice.   * * *

Does the complaint state *facts* sufficient to constitute *any* cause of action?

A complaint must contain "(a) plain and concise statement of the facts constituting a cause of action * * *." G.S. § 1–122. "The cardinal requirement of this statute * * * is that the facts constituting a cause of action, rather than the conclusions of the pleader, must be set out in the complaint, so as to disclose the issuable facts determinative of the plaintiff's right to relief." Shives v. Sample, 238 N.C. 724, 79 S.E.2d 193. The cause of action consists of the facts alleged. * * * The statutory requirement is that a complaint must allege the material, essential and ultimate facts upon which plaintiff's right of action is based. * * * "The law is presumed to be known, but the facts to which the law is to be applied are not known until properly presented by the pleading and established by evidence." McIntosh, North Carolina Practice and Procedure, § 379.

The facts alleged, but not the pleader's legal conclusions, are deemed admitted when the sufficiency of the complaint is tested by demurrer. * * * Where the complaint merely alleges conclusions and not facts, it fails to state a cause of action and is demurrable. * * * However, it is well settled that a complaint must be fatally defective before it will be rejected as insufficient, and "if in any portion of it or to any extent it presents *facts* sufficient to constitute a cause of action the pleading will stand." (Our italics) Snotherly v. Jenrette, * * * 232 N.C. p. 608, 61 S.E.2d p. 711. * * *

When a complaint alleges defendant is indebted to plaintiff in a certain amount and such debt is due, but does not allege in what manner or for what cause defendant became indebted to plaintiff, it is demurrable for failure to state facts sufficient to constitute a cause of action. * * *

"In an action or defense based upon negligence, it is not sufficient to allege the mere happening of an event of an injurious nature and call it negligence on the part of the party sought to be charged. This is necessarily so because negligence is not a fact in itself, but is the legal result of certain facts. Therefore, the facts which constitute the negligence charged and also the facts which establish such negligence as the proximate cause, or as one of the proximate causes, of the injury must be alleged." Shives v. Sample, supra * * *.

Plaintiff alleges, in a single sentence, that defendant, "without cause or just excuse and maliciously," trespassed upon premises occupied by her as a residence, assaulted her and caused her to be seized and confined as a prisoner. The complaint states no facts upon which these legal conclusions may be predicated. Plaintiff's allegations do not disclose *what* occurred, *when* it occurred, *where* it occurred, *who* did *what*, the relationships between defendants and plaintiff or of defendants *inter se*, or any other factual data that might identify the occasion or describe the circumstances of the alleged wrongful conduct of defendants.

* * * When considered in the light most favorable to plaintiff, this complaint, in our opinion, falls short of minimum requirements.

In Stivers v. Baker, 10 Ky. 523, 9 S.W. 491, * * * the court, in opinion by Holt, J., points out that a statement of the facts constituting a cause of action "is not only necessary to enable the opposite party to form an issue, and to inform him of what his adversary intends to prove, but to enable the court to declare the law upon the facts stated. It cannot do so if a mere legal conclusion is stated. The term 'assault' has a legal meaning; as much so as the word 'trespass.'" * * *

The judgments sustaining the demurrers are affirmed on the ground the complaint does not state facts sufficient to constitute any cause of action. It would seem appropriate that plaintiff, in accordance with leave granted in the judgments from which she appealed, now file an amended complaint and therein allege the facts upon which she bases her right to recover.

Affirmed.

NOTES AND QUESTIONS

1. Is the court in *Gillispie* legitimately concerned with the inability of defendants to ascertain the claims against them in order that they might answer and prepare their defenses? Of what significance is the fact that in North Carolina one party can take a pretrial deposition of the opposing party in order to obtain information necessary to prepare a pleading and to obtain evidence for use at trial? Can it be said that the pleading in *Gillispie* is unsatisfactory because the trial judge will not know what evidence is or is not relevant?

2. To what extent might the court in *Gillispie* have been motivated by the notion that a detailed account of the facts might well show that plaintiff did not have a valid claim for relief? Is it significant that at the time of the *Gillispie* decision North Carolina did not have a provision for summary judgment? Has the North Carolina court simply followed a hard and fast line concerning the "fact" pleading requirement, quite forgetting its basic purpose as a device for pretrial communication?

3. Note the ultimate disposition in the *Gillispie* case. Suppose that plaintiff's amended complaint also is deficient. Will she be given leave to amend again? How should the right to amend affect the question of whether or not a pleading is or is not satisfactory?

———

McCAUGHEY v. SCHUETTE, 117 Cal. 223, 224–26, 48 P. 1088 (1897). Plaintiff alleged that he contracted to buy a piece of real estate from defendant in exchange for the cancellation of several of defendant's promissory notes held by plaintiff. Plaintiff further alleged that the notes were cancelled and the deed to the property delivered but that defendant had refused to yield physical possession of the property to plaintiff. Defendant demurred on the ground that the complaint failed to state a cause of action. The trial court overruled the demurrer and the case proceeded to trial at which a verdict was rendered for plaintiff. On appeal, the state supreme court reversed, adopting the following language from a lower appellate-court decision in the same case (46 P. 666):

It is a fundamental rule of our code pleading that ultimate and not probative facts are to be averred in a pleading. * * *

It will be observed that in the complaint in the present case there is no averment of seisin, or ownership, or possession, or right of possession, to the demanded premises, but the pleader contents himself with a statement of evidentiary facts, which, if proven at the trial, would authorize the court in finding the ultimate fact of ownership and right to possession in the plaintiff.

* * *

Such pleading wes [sic] bad at common law, and is none the less so under our code system.

To uphold such a pleading is to encourage prolixity and a wide departure from that definiteness, certainty, and perspicuity which it was one of the paramount objects sought to be enforced by the code system of pleading, and that, too, with no resultant effect, except to encumber the record with verbiage and enhance the cost of litigation.

NOTES AND QUESTIONS

1. "Quite commonly an allegation has been held bad as a statement of law only. The stating of evidence, while subject to criticism, is not so often held to render the pleading bad, since the court itself will draw the ultimate conclusion where it is the one necessarily following from the allegations made." Clark, *Code Pleading* § 38, at 228 (2d ed. 1947). When does the ultimate conclusion "necessarily follow"? In ROBINSON v. MEYER, 135 Conn. 691, 693–94, 68 A.2d 142, 143 (1949), the court, in upholding the pleading, stated:

The defendants filed an * * * answer in which they alleged facts adequate to establish title by adverse possession if they were proved to have existed for the required length of time. * * * [C]onsiderable evidence was introduced as to use and occupation of the disputed tract. * * * All the facts necessary to establish ouster and that [the] * * * deed was therefore void were alleged in the pleading. * * * Under these circumstances it was not necessary to plead the legal result, although that would have been proper and desirable.

Consider also O'REGAN v. SCHERMERHORN, 25 N.J.Misc. 1, 50 A.2d 10 (Sup.Ct.1946), in which the court refused to infer the defense of truth in a defamation suit when defendant alleged he believed the statement to be true and further alleged the facts on which that belief was based.

2. Should a party be able to plead an essential fact merely by referring to an exhibit in which the fact is stated? Consider ANDERSON v. CHAMBLISS, 199 Or. 400, 409, 262 P.2d 298, 302 (1953), in which the court refused to permit a lien notice attached to and referred to in the complaint to supply the necessary

allegation that the notice was filed within sixty days of completion of construction. The court said:

> An exhibit may be considered as a part of the pleading and in aid and explanation thereof; but annexing an exhibit to a pleading does not amount to an allegation that the statements contained therein are true. Of course, it is well settled that if there is any discrepancy between the averments of a pleading and the terms of a writing properly identified or attached to a statement of facts constituting a cause of action or a defense, the language of the exhibit will control in determining its legal effect. * * * However, an exhibit to a pleading cannot serve the purpose of supplying necessary and material averments.

See also Lion Secor Real Estate Co. v. Westgate Village Shopping Center, Inc., 117 Ohio App. 96, 191 N.E.2d 179 (1962).

Compare STANDARD REGISTER CO. v. GREENBERG, 120 Vt. 112, 116, 132 A.2d 174, 177 (1957).

> Inclusion of the exhibit as a part of the pleading does not appear to work any hardship on this defendant. Reference to the writing, coupled with its annexation to the complaint, brings the context of the agreement before the court as effectively as a recopy of the document verbatim, into the body of the complaint itself. * * * The rule permitting such method of pleading is accepted, with varying limitations, in numerous other jurisdictions. * * * And even by rigid rules of common law pleading, a writing became a part of a declaration by profert and oyer, to be considered on demurrer. * * * The written agreement of the defendant * * *, exhibited with the complaint, is to be considered in determining the sufficiency of the plaintiff's pleading.

Is the decision in *Anderson* preferable to that in *Greenberg*? Does Federal Rule 10(c), which makes a written instrument that is attached to a pleading as an exhibit "a part thereof for all purposes," raise any special problem in those situations in which the party is required to attest under oath to the truth of his pleading?

The exhibit in the *Greenberg* case was annexed to the complaint. Should it be possible to incorporate a document by reference only? *Compare* Legg v. Ford, 185 Cal.App.2d 534, 8 Cal.Rptr. 392 (2d Dist.1960), *and* Bradley v. Condon, 217 N.Y.S.2d 821 (Sup.Ct.1961), *with* Jeffrey Structures, Inc. v. Grimaldi, 186 Pa. Super. 437, 142 A.2d 378 (1958). Most jurisdictions permit incorporation by reference of other pleadings in the law suit. See, e. g., Ogier v. Pacific Oil & Gas Dev. Corp., 132 Cal.App.2d 496, 282 P.2d 574 (1st Dist.1955). *Contra*, Hill v. Hill Spinning Co., 244 N.C. 554, 94 S.E.2d 677 (1956).

COOK, STATEMENTS OF FACT IN PLEADING UNDER THE CODES, 21 Colum.L.Rev. 416, 416–19, 422 (1921):

In a recent case in New York [California Packing Corp. v. Kelly Storage & Distributing Co., 228 N.Y. 49, 126 N.E. 269 (1920)] the plaintiff alleged in his complaint that the promise for the breach of which he was suing was made in exchange for "a valuable consideration." The case went to the Court of Appeals upon the question whether this allegation is a "statement of fact" or a "conclusion of law." For many years prior to this decision the Appellate Division of the First Department had held this to be a "mere conclusion of law," whereas the Appellate Division of the Third Department regarded it as a "statement of fact." An examination of the authorities in other code jurisdictions reveals a conflict of authority. Under the common law system of pleading, however, there seems to have been substantial unanimity in holding the statement to be a "conclusion of law." In the case referred to, the Court of Appeals held the allegation "sufficient as 'a plain and concise statement' of the ultimate, principal and issuable fact of consideration."

The movement for "simplified procedure" began in this country about the middle of the last century. How comes it that after more than seventy years of discussion and judicial decision, a question of this kind can still be an open one? Why is it that eminent judges and lawyers took and still take opposite views upon this and similar questions? To answer these questions is the object of the present discussion. To do so we must begin with the provisions of the codes themselves.   *   *   *

These provisions at first sight seem simple, and probably the men who first drew them so believed. That the simplicity is not real, however, becomes clear when one reads the hundreds, not to say thousands, of decisions which have passed upon the question whether in a given case the pleader has "stated the facts" in an acceptable manner. In many cases he is told that he has pleaded "evidentiary facts" instead of the "facts constituting the cause of action"; in many others he is held to have stated merely "conclusions of law."

All this is matter of common knowledge. Where lies the root of the difficulty? Primarily, it is believed, in the assumption that the problem is a simple one, that there is some clear, easily drawn and scientific distinction between so-called "statements of evidentiary facts," "statements of fact," and "conclusions of law," whereas in truth there is none. In other words, as is so often the case, a failure to analyze carefully the meaning of the terms used and so to form clear views as to the concept for which they stand is the chief cause of the doubt and confusion.

When such an analysis is made, it will appear at once that there is no logical distinction between statements which are grouped by the courts under the phrases "statements of fact" and "conclusions of law." It will also be found that many, although by no means all, pleadings held bad because they are said to plead "evidence" rather than "the facts constituting the cause of action" or defense really do nevertheless "state" the operative facts which the pleader will have to prove at the trial, but in a form different from that to which courts and lawyers are accustomed to recognize as a proper method of pleading.
    *   *   *

The facts of life which compose the group of "operative facts" to which the law attaches legal consequences are always *specific* and not *generic*.   *   *   *   [I]n an action on the case for, let us say, negligently injuring the plaintiff by the operation of an automobile, the "operative" or "ultimate" facts proved at the trial will always be specific. It will appear that the defendant was driving a particular kind of automobile at some particular rate of speed, *etc., etc.* If now a plaintiff were to state the facts thus specifically in his complaint he would doubtless be told by the average court that he had "pleaded his evidence" and not the "facts constituting the cause of action." This would of course be erroneous. What is according to accepted notions the proper way to plead is merely a mode of stating the facts generically rather than specifically.

It must of course be recognized that at times a pleader really does err by "pleading evidence," i.e., by stating, generically or specifically, facts which do not form part of the group of operative facts, but are merely facts from which by some process of logical inference the existence of the operative facts can be inferred. More often, however, the "error" consists merely in pleading the operative facts more specifically than is usual.

So much for the cases involving the distinction between pleading "evidence" and "ultimate facts." Let us now examine "conclusions of law." The first thing noticed upon analysis is that a so-called "conclusion of law" is a generic statement which can be made only after some legal rule has been applied to some specific group of operative facts. Consider, for example, a statement in a pleading that "defendant owes plaintiff $500." Standing by itself in a pleading this is usually treated as a mere "conclusion of law." It can, however, be made only when one knows certain facts and also the applicable legal rule. It is, in fact, the conclusion of a logical argument: Whenever certain facts, a, b, c, *etc.,* exist, B (defendant) owes A (plaintiff) $500; facts a, b, c, *etc.,* exist; therefore B owes A $500. This being so, when the bare statement is made that "B owes A $500" we may, if we wish, regard it as a statement in generic form that all the facts necessary to create the legal duty to pay money described by the word "owe" are true as between A and B. In dealing, for example, with misrepresentation, such statements are more often than otherwise regarded in exactly this way. The same statement may, however, under proper circumstances be merely a statement as to the law applicable to facts given or known, and so be purely a statement of a "conclusion of law."

* * * How specific or how generic statements in a pleading may and must be can obviously not be settled by mere logic, but according to notions of fairness and convenience. The pleading should give the adversary and the court reasonable notice of the real nature of the claim or defense; nothing more should be required.

NOTES AND QUESTIONS

1. For other discussions of the problem of pleading "facts," see Clark, *Code Pleading* § 38, at 225–36 (2d ed. 1947); Cook, *"Facts" and "Statements of Fact,"* 4 U.Chi.L.Rev. 233 (1937); Gavit, *Legal Conclusions,* 16 Minn.L.Rev. 378 (1932); Morris, *Law and Fact,* 55 Harv.L.Rev. 1303 (1942); Wheaton, *Manner of Stating Cause of Action,* 20 Cornell L.Q. 185 (1935).

2. In ROBINSON v. BOARD OF COUNTY COMMISSIONERS, 262 Md. 342, 278 A.2d 71 (1971), plaintiff alleged that defendants "did then and there falsely, maliciously, and without just cause * * * arrest [plaintiff]

* * * on charge[s] of disorderly conduct and resisting arrest, * * * [they took him] to the police station where he was forceably imprisoned, kept, detained and restrained of his liberty * * * [but upon trial he] was acquitted * * *. [Defendants] well knew that the prosecution was false, groundless, and without probable cause * * *." The court held that this passage stated facts sufficient to constitute a cause of action. Compare this pleading with that in *Gillispie*. Is one of the pleadings more informative than the other? See also D'Auria v. Niemiec, 15 Misc.2d 449, 450, 182 N.Y.S.2d 378, 379 (Sup.Ct.1959), upholding as sufficient an allegation "That on or about July 1, 1956, on Amherst Street in the City of Buffalo, New York, the defendant assaulted, battered and beat plaintiff without any provocation or just cause."

3.   There are numerous modern examples of cases reaching conflicting results as to whether a specific allegation is or is not a conclusion of law rather than a statement of ultimate fact. *Compare*, for example, Roblyer v. Hoyt, 343 Mich. 431, 72 N.W.2d 126 (1955) (general allegation of "no probable cause" in action for malicious prosecution is conclusion of law), *with* Hardy v. Vial, 48 Cal.2d 577, 311 P.2d 494 (1957) (allegation of "no probable cause" is ultimate fact). For another interesting contrast, *compare* Holden v. Pioneer Broadcasting Co., 228 Or. 405, 365 P.2d 845 (1961) (general averment of "malice" in defamation suit is conclusion of law), *with* Boston Nutrition Soc'y v. Stare, 342 Mass. 439, 173 N.E. 2d 812 (1961) (general allegation of "malice" is proper). Finally, *compare* Howell v. Simon, 225 Ark. 535, 283 S.W.2d 680 (1955) (general averment that defendant acted within the scope of his employment held to be a conclusion of law), *with* Ledman v. Calvert Iron Works, Inc., 92 Ga.App. 733, 89 S.E.2d 832 (1955) (general allegation that defendant acted within the scope of his employment held to be an ultimate fact).

4.   To what extent do the problems in determining what are "facts" represent an inherent defect of the code system?

---

2.   DETAIL REQUIRED UNDER THE FEDERAL RULES

Read Federal Rules of Civil Procedure 8(a) and 12(b) in the Supplement.

DIOGUARDI v. DURNING

United States Circuit Court of Appeals, Second Circuit, 1944.
139 F.2d 774.

CLARK, Circuit Judge.   In his complaint, obviously home drawn, plaintiff attempts to assert a series of grievances against the Collector of Customs at the Port of New York growing out of his endeavors to import merchandise from Italy "of great value," consisting of bottles of "tonics." We may pass certain of his claims as either inadequate or inadequately stated and consider only these two: (1) that on the auction day, October 9, 1940, when defendant sold the merchandise at "public custom," "he sold my merchandise to another bidder with my price of $110, and not of his price of $120," and (2) "that three weeks before the sale, two cases, of 19 bottles each case, disappeared." Plaintiff does not make wholly clear how these goods came into the collector's hands, since he alleges compliance with the revenue laws; but he does say he made a claim for "refund of merchandise which was two-thirds paid in Milano, Italy," and that the collector denied the claim. These and other circumstances alleged indicate (what, indeed, plaintiff's brief asserts) that his original dispute was with his consignor as to whether anything more was due upon the merchandise, and that the collector, having held it for a year (presumably as unclaimed merchandise under 19 U.S.C.A. § 1491), then sold it, or such part of it as was left, at public auction. For his asserted injuries plaintiff claimed $5,000 damages, together with interest and costs, against the defendant individually and as collector. This complaint was dismissed by the District Court, with leave, however, to plaintiff to amend, on motion of the United States Attorney, appearing for the defendant, on the ground that it "fails to state facts sufficient to constitute a cause of action."

Thereupon plaintiff filed an amended complaint, wherein, with an obviously heightened conviction that he was being unjustly treated, he vigorously reiterates his claims, including those quoted above and now stated as that his "medicinal extracts" were given to the Springdale Distilling Company "with my betting [bidding?] price of $100: and not their price of $120," and "It isn't so easy to do away with two cases with 37 bottles of one quart. Being protected, they can take this chance." An earlier paragraph suggests that defendant had explained the loss of the two cases by "saying that they had leaked, which could never be true in the manner they were bottled." On defendant's motion for dismissal on the same ground as before, the court made a final judgment dismissing the complaint, and plaintiff now comes to us with increased volubility, if not clarity.

It would seem, however, that he has stated enough to withstand a mere formal motion, directed only to the face of the complaint, and that here is another instance of judicial haste which in the long run makes waste. Under the new rules of civil procedure, there is no pleading requirement of stating "facts sufficient to constitute a cause of action," but only that there be "a short and plain statement of the claim showing that the pleader is entitled to relief," * * * rule 8(a) * * *; and the motion for dismissal under Rule 12 (b) is for failure to state "a claim upon which relief can be granted." The District Court does not state why it concluded that the complaints showed no claim upon which relief could be granted; and the United States Attorney's brief before us does not help us, for it is limited to the prognostication—unfortunately ill founded so far as we are concerned—that "the most cursory examination" of them will show the correctness of the District Court's action.

We think that, however inartistically they may be stated, the plaintiff has disclosed his claims that the collector has converted or otherwise done away with two of his cases of medicinal tonics and has sold the rest in a manner incompatible with the public auction he had announced—and, indeed, required by 19 U.S.C.A. § 1491, above cited, and the Treasury Regulations promulgated under it, formerly 19 CFR 18.7–18.12, now 19 CFR 20.5, 8 Fed. Reg. 8407, 8408, June 19, 1943. As to this latter claim, it may be that the collector's only error is a failure to collect an additional ten dollars from the Springdale Distilling Company; but giving the plaintiff the benefit of reasonable intendments in his allegations (as we must on this motion), the claim appears to be in effect that he was actually the first bidder at the price for which they were sold, and hence was entitled to the merchandise. Of course, defendant did not need to move on the complaint alone; he could have disclosed the facts from his point of view, in advance of a trial if he chose, by asking for a pre-trial hearing or by moving for a summary judgment with supporting affidavits. But, as it stands, we do not see how the plaintiff may properly be deprived of his day in court to show what he obviously so firmly believes and what for present purposes defendant must be taken as admitting. * * *

On remand, the District Court may find substance in other claims asserted by plaintiff, which include a failure properly to catalogue the items (as the cited Regulations provide), or to allow plaintiff to buy at a discount from the catalogue price just before the auction sale (a claim whose basis is not apparent), and a violation of an agreement to deliver the merchandise to the plaintiff as soon as he paid for it, by stopping the payments. In view of plaintiff's limited ability to write and speak English, it will be difficult for the District Court to arrive at justice unless he consents to receive legal assistance in the presentation of his case. The record indicates that he refused further help from a lawyer suggested by the court, and his brief (which was a recital of facts, rather than an argument of law) shows distrust of a lawyer of standing at this bar. It is the plaintiff's privilege to decline all legal help, United States v. Mitchell, 2 Cir., 137 F.2d 1006, 1010, 1011; but we fear that he will be indeed ill advised to attempt to meet a motion for summary judgment or other similar presentation of the merits without competent advice and assistance.

Judgment is reversed and the action is remanded for further proceedings not inconsistent with this opinion.

NOTES AND QUESTIONS

1. The *Dioguardi* decision was sharply criticized in McCaskill, *The Modern Philosophy of Pleading: A Dialogue Outside the Shades,* 38 A.B.A.J. 123 (1952), and has been a focal point of opposition to the so-called liberal "notice-pleading" of the Federal Rules. How would the *Dioguardi* case have been decided in a jurisdiction that requires a statement of "facts constituting a cause of action"?

2. Since 1938 many states have adopted the federal pleading rules. One of the first states to do so, Colorado, added the following provision to its Rule 8(e) (1): "pleadings otherwise meeting the requirements of these rules shall not be considered objectionable for failure to state ultimate facts as distinguished from conclusions of law." What purpose does such a provision serve?

State courts have not always made the transition from pleading under the codes to pleading under the Federal Rules without difficulty. See, e. g., Walden, *The "New Rules" in New Mexico*, 25 F.R.D. 107, 108–11 (1960).

3. Does Federal Rule 8(a) have the effect of completely eliminating the requirement of detailed fact pleadings? Is *Dioguardi* typical or atypical? The Supreme Court in CONLEY v. GIBSON, 355 U.S. 41, 47–48, 78 S.Ct. 99, 103, 2 L.Ed.2d 80, 85 (1957), cited *Dioguardi* and gave its views as follows:

> * * * [T]he Federal Rules of Civil Procedure do not require a claimant to set out in detail the facts upon which he bases his claim. To the contrary, all the Rules require is "a short and plain statement of the claim" that will give the defendant fair notice of what the plaintiff's claim is and the grounds upon which it rests. The illustrative forms appended to the Rules plainly demonstrate this. Such simplified "notice pleading" is made possible by the liberal opportunity for discovery and the other pretrial procedures established by the Rules to disclose more precisely the basis of both claim and defense and to define more narrowly the disputed facts and issues.

Shortly thereafter Judge Clark made the following comment:

> * * * Some people love to say that all the rules require is fair notice, that pleading under the rules is only notice pleading. * * * Notice pleading is a beautiful nebulous thing. I ought not to say too much about it because there are two pretty good decisions of the Supreme Court that speak of notice pleading. One of the last was the *Conley* decision just this fall, where Justice Black for the Court speaks of modern pleading as being designed only to give fair notice. I don't use that expression—not that I object to it as such. I think it is something like the Golden Rule, which is a nice hopeful thing; but I can't find that it means much of anything and it isn't anything that we can use with any precision. What we require is a general statement of the case, and our best precedents are those that have been honored over the years, which shows that we haven't done anything really violent. We do not require detail. We require a general statement. How much? Well, the answer is made in what I think is probably the most important part of the rules so far as this particular topic is concerned, namely, the Forms. These are important because when you can't define you can at least draw pictures to show your meaning.

Clark, *Pleading Under the Federal Rules*, 12 Wyo.L.J. 177, 181 (1958).

4. Examples of the simplicity of pleading under Rule 8(a) are found in the Appendix of Forms, which are set out in the Supplement following the Federal Rules of Civil Procedure; in particular see Forms 9 and 11. Note that in 1946, Rule 84 was amended to state that the Forms were not mere guides but were themselves "sufficient under the rules." This change was intended to overcome the effect of WASHBURN v. MOORMAN MFG. CO., 25 F.Supp. 546 (S.D.Cal. 1938), in which it was held that a complaint failed to state a claim for relief despite the fact that it followed one of the forms.

5. It is important to note that even under the Federal Rules special provisions require a more detailed pleading of specific matters. For example, Federal Rule 9(b) requires that "in all averments of fraud or mistake, the circumstances constituting fraud or mistake shall be stated with particularity." See also the

language of Federal Rule 9(g) which requires items of special damage to be "specifically stated." Several "special" pleading rules are discussed on pp. 439–47, infra. See generally 5 Wright & Miller, *Federal Practice and Procedure: Civil* §§ 1291–1315 (1969).

LODGE 743, INTERNATIONAL ASSOCIATION OF MACHINISTS v. UNITED AIRCRAFT CORP.

United States District Court, District of Connecticut, 1962.
30 F.R.D. 142.

CLARIE, District Judge. The plaintiff in the above action is a labor organization, eligible to bring suit under the Labor Management Relations Act, 29 U.S.C.A. § 185; and brings this action for a declaratory judgment, specific performance, damages and other relief, arising out of a claimed violation of a strike settlement contract.

*   *   *

Pursuant to [Federal] Rule 12(e)   *   *   *   defendant has requested a more definite statement of the plaintiff's claim.   *   *   *

The allegations to which the motion is addressed are as follows:

"24. Plaintiff alleges that defendant breached the strike settlement contract by the following acts and conduct:

"(a) *   *   *

"(b) failing and refusing to supply to plaintiff information and material in defendant's possession relevant to defendant's administration of said contract although such information and material is necessary to police defendant's performance of its obligations thereunder;

"(c) failing and refusing to return registered strikers to their former jobs, although such jobs were available;

"(d) failing and refusing to recall registered strikers whose former jobs were not immediately available to other jobs for which they qualified;

"(e) failing and refusing to recall registered strikers for whom jobs were not immediately available, as jobs for which they qualified became available, before hiring new employees;

"(f) failing and refusing to restore to their former jobs, when said jobs became available, registered strikers who had been placed in inferior jobs;

"(g) failing and refusing to recall registered strikers prior to January 1, 1961, to jobs for which they qualified which defendant developed, or was required to have developed, prior to January 1, 1961;

"(h) failing and refusing to restore to registered strikers hired after January 1, 1961, their former or comparable jobs, their seniority and other rights and privileges."

The present motion of the defendant requests that the plaintiff be ordered to furnish a more definite statement of its claim under paragraph 24 of the complaint in respect to the following matters:

(1) That plaintiff identify and specify the nature of the information and material in defendant's possession relevant to defendant's administration of the contract, under sub-paragragh [sic] (b);

(2) that plaintiff identify by name the registered strikers referred to in sub-paragraph (c) and specify the jobs available to which they might have been returned;

(3) that plaintiff identify by name the registered strikers and specify the "other jobs" for which such strikers were qualified as claimed in sub-paragraph (d);

(4) that plaintiff identify by name the registered strikers which defendant failed or refused to recall, specify the jobs which became available for them and identify by name the new employees hired in their stead, under sub-paragraph (e);

(5) that plaintiff identify by name the registered strikers who were not restored to their former jobs, as they became available, but were placed in inferior jobs, as alleged in sub-paragraph (f);

(6) that plaintiff identify by name the registered strikers who were not recalled prior to January 1, 1961 to jobs which defendant developed or was required to have developed and define the meaning of the later phrase, under sub-paragraph (g);

(7) that plaintiff identify by name the registered strikers hired after January 1, 1961 whom the defendant failed or refused to restore to their former or comparable jobs, with specifications of such jobs and the rights and privileges of which it is claimed they were deprived.

It is the defendant's claim that the present form of the complaint is so vague and uncertain that it is unable to prepare a responsive pleading. It claims further that the two plants concerned employ several thousand employees, among which were approximately 2,000 registered strikers under the strike settlement agreement; and that it has no knowledge of having denied any individual reemployment in violation of the terms of said agreement.

The plaintiff contends that if the court grants the defendant's motion, it will be tantamount to a dismissal of their action. It is their claim that under the terms of the strike settlement agreement the company was contractually obligated to keep separate "preferred hiring lists" which it failed or refused to do; that the detailed information sought in their present motion is factual data which is only obtainable from the defendant company's personnel files. They claim further that if the court orders them to provide these details at this time, they will not be able to comply and will therefore be forced to withdraw their action or be subject to a dismissal of it.

general rule:
1) fair notice

2) no particulars
   needed when
   info knowledge w/i
   A's knowledge

" * * * [A]ll that Rule 8(a) requires of a complaint is that it indicate generally the type of litigation that is involved; and a generalized summary of the case that affords fair notice is sufficient.   *   *   *   The rule is that
a complaint does not require amplification by a bill of particulars where the information sought to be obtained by such devise [sic] is peculiarly within the
knowledge of the defendant."   Sunbeam Corp. v. Payless Drug Stores, 113
F.Supp. 31, 37 (N.D.Calif.1953).

"The overwhelming weight of authority is to the effect that a motion for
a bill of particulars or a motion for more definite statement of the claim should
not be granted if the complaint sets forth a cause of action with sufficient definiteness to enable the defendant to frame an answer.   Additional details that
the defendant needs in order to prepare for trial shall be obtained by discovery
after issue is joined."   Montgomery v. Kingsland, 83 U.S.App.D.C. 66, 166
F.2d 953, 955 (1948) [See Federal Rules 26–37]   *   *   *.

In the present case, however, the union has brought suit for and in behalf
of itself and an uncertain number of its members, under the Federal Labor
Management Relations Act, vaguely alleging that the defendant company has
failed or refused to rehire an indefinite number of its members in violation of
the strike settlement contract or that certain of the rehired strikers were not restored to jobs to which they were entitled.   These allegations might be applicable to a few or as many as 2,000 registered strikers.   It is the company's claim
that it has no information within its possession of any instance where those
allegations are applicable and is at a loss to prepare a proper defense.

The plaintiff-union contends that while it has substantial reason to believe the allegations of the complaint are true, it is not presently in a position
to name the union members to whom the allegations apply nor the jobs which
they claim have been unjustly and illegally filled and their members discriminated against.   Under such circumstances, no good purpose could be accomplished at this time by the defendant-corporation resorting to the use of interrogatories, in order to procure more definite specifications in this regard.

In a comparable situation involving litigation related to the illegal use of
inventions or trade secrets, where the defendant had filed interrogatories rather than a motion for more definite statement as was done in this case, the court
ordered, " * * * that the plaintiff not be required to answer any of the interrogatories   *   *   *   until 'its own discovery proceedings are completed.' "
Sperry Rand Corporation v. Rothlein, 288 F.2d 245 (2 Cir. 1961).

The motion of the defendant for more definite statement is granted as to
subsection (b), (c), (d), (e), (f), (g) and (h) of Paragraph 24 of the complaint, as is requested in paragraphs 1 through 7 of defendant's motion.
However, the plaintiff shall not be required to answer any part of said motion
until its own discovery proceedings are completed.   This order is without prejudice to the defendant to move for a modification of this ruling during the
course of the discovery proceedings by the plaintiff, if good cause appears.

NOTES AND QUESTIONS

1. In WEBB v. WEBB, 32 F.R.D. 615 (W.D.Mo.1963), defendant was charged with negligence in extracting a tooth and rendering postoperative care. He moved for a more definite statement to require plaintiff to specify the acts of negligence. The court denied the motion, pointing out that the complaint clearly was sufficient under Form 9. Does the *Webb* decision in any way subvert the policy of Federal Rule 12(e)? Is *Webb* consistent with *United Aircraft*? Why shouldn't a plaintiff be required to specify the elements of defendant's alleged negligence?

2. The proper function of the Federal Rule 12(e) motion for a more definite statement is better understood in light of its history. Read the commentary accompanying Federal Rule 12(e) in the Supplement and consider the amendments that have been made in the Rule since its original promulgation. What was the purpose of these changes? Is the decision in the principal case consistent with the policies underlying the amendments? Why shouldn't the Federal Rules contain a provision for a bill of particulars as an additional method of discovery? For a good general commentary on the history and application of Federal Rule 12(e), see Comment, *Federal Civil Procedure—Federal Rule 12(e): Motion for More Definite Statement—History, Operation and Efficacy*, 61 Mich.L.Rev. 1126 (1963). See also 5 Wright & Miller, *Federal Practice and Procedure: Civil* §§ 1374–79 (1969).

3. The problems raised by the motion for a more definite statement are not necessarily limited to jurisdictions that have adopted Federal-Rule type pleading. In most other jurisdictions defects of form, rather than of the legal sufficiency of the pleading, are challenged by a motion to make more definite and certain. See, e. g., Wis.Stat.Ann. § 263.43. In other jurisdictions there are, in addition to the general demurrer for failure to state a cause of action, separate "special" demurrers for ambiguity, uncertainty, or unintelligibility. See, e. g., Cal.Code Civ. Proc. § 430.10(g). Unlike the motion under Federal Rule 12(e), the availability of these devices does not rest on whether the moving party can prepare a responsive pleading. It often is unclear at what point a pleading, although subject to challenge for indefiniteness, nevertheless will be held sufficient to state a cause of action or defense. Such a determination may be significant in that the objection that a pleading fails to state facts sufficient to constitute a cause of action or defense can be raised at any time, whereas the defect of uncertainty is waived if not raised immediately. See, e. g., Cal.Code Civ.Proc. §§ 430.10, 430.80.

3. THE CONTINUING DEBATE ON THE ROLE OF PLEADINGS—PROPOSALS TO OBVIATE DEFICIENCIES

A. A RETURN TO CODE PLEADING

The uncertainty over the proper role of the pleadings in modern practice is far from settled. Although pleading rules similar to Federal Rule 8(a) have been widely adopted by the states, there are still a number of jurisdictions that prefer the code formulation, and from time to time recommendations are made that Rule 8(a) itself be amended to require a "statement of facts constituting a cause of action." These recommendations are based on the claim that so-called "notice pleading" encourages unfounded lawsuits filed by attorneys who have no prior need to scrutinize the facts of their cases to see if they justify litigation. Moreover, there is the fear that because the pleadings do not set forth all the factual issues, there is always a danger that one of the parties will be surprised at trial with an issue not previously seen and which that party is unprepared to meet. Although surprise can be eliminated by the widespread use of discovery, such usage often is costly and burdensome, if counsel is to be certain that all conceivable issues are uncovered. See Report of The Committee on Federal Practice of the State Bar of California to the Board of Governors, *Claim or Cause of Action*, 13 F.R.D. 253 (1951).

B. UTILIZATION OF THE PRETRIAL CONFERENCE

Not everyone who adversely criticizes the pleading philosophy of the Federal Rules advocates a return to the codes and to all of the evils of interpretation that would flow from such a development. Instead, a number of people take the position that no satisfactory system of pleadings has been or can be developed that would fully inform the court and the parties at the outset of the case precisely as to what matters will be at issue. Therefore it is suggested that the lawyers for the parties and the judge engage in a pretrial conference sometime after the case has been filed and the initial investigation completed, from which would emerge a pretrial order that supersedes the pleadings and sets forth in detail the precise issues to be determined at trial. See, e. g., Fee, *The Lost Horizon in Pleading Under the Federal Rules of Civil Procedure*, 48 Colum.L.Rev. 491 (1948). The pretrial conference is specifically authorized by Rule 16 of the Federal Rules and a number of comparable state provisions. Although only limited studies have been made comparing cases tried after a pretrial conference with those tried without such a conference, there is some evidence that a pretrial conference results in a more competent presentation of the case at trial and often results in the elimination of surprise. See Rosenberg, *The Pretrial Conference and Effective Justice* 68 (1964). For further discussion of the pretrial conference and the manner in which it is employed, see Chapter 9, infra.

C. THE USE OF OFFICIAL FORMS

A prime example of the uncertainty regarding the proper role of the pleadings is the New York pleading provision adopted in 1963, N.Y.C.P.L.R. 3013, which opens with the statement that the pleadings "shall be sufficiently particular to give the court and parties notice of the   * * *   transactions or occurrences, intended to be proved," but then goes on to require a statement of the "material elements of each cause of action or defense." As originally proposed the New York code would have required development of a number of official forms, akin to the forms accompanying the Federal Rules, to illustrate the precise detail required and to help avoid technical interpretations of the pleading provision.

Prior to the adoption of the new pleading provision Judge Clark commented on it as follows:

> In the light of   * * *   [experience with Federal Rule 8(a)] and against the New York background of hopeless confusion in "stating the facts," it is particularly discouraging to note the lack of firm approach to this basic issue shown by the New York reformers. In fact their suggestions seem so hesitant or blind that it is not possible to deduce just what is intended. Thus proposed Rule 26.5 makes the basic requirement that of "fair notice," that delusive term so attractive to text writers (perhaps since it can be made to mean all things to all men) but never yet a general rule of pleading for major courts. It is of course a pure abstraction, without content except as injected by the immediate user, worthy to stand with the abstractions which were so unfortunate a feature of the original Field Code. But at once we perceive an anomaly. The "notice" concept is normally employed to signify a rejection of both fact and issue pleading in favor of a system of unusual generality of expression. Yet apparently the intent here is just the opposite * * *. In terms [the language of the proposal] * * * goes beyond even the old fact pleading in New York. * * * Such conflict or vagueness makes the proposed illustrative forms of the utmost importance as a guide to a determination of rule intent; but as yet at least these forms have not appeared. Perhaps the draftsmen have not yet been able to settle upon their own meaning of these provisions.

Clark, *Two Decades of the Federal Civil Rules,* 58 Colum.L.Rev. 435, 450–51 (1958). Before New York enacted the Civil Practice Law and Rules, however, the reference to official forms was dropped and no forms were set forth in the new code. In a subsequent about face, Section 107 was added to the New York procedure code authorizing the preparation and promulgation of an Appendix of Official Forms by that state's Judicial Conference. A set of forms became effective in 1968.

D. ADOPTION OF SPECIAL RULES FOR CERTAIN TYPES OF CASES

An area of special concern has been the role of pleading in cases containing numerous complex factual issues, a prime example being antitrust suits in the federal courts. From time to time some federal judges have insisted that a separate, more rigorous standard of pleading should apply in these cases. See, e. g., BAIM & BLANK, INC. v. WARREN-CONNELLY CO., 19 F.R.D. 108, 109–10 (S.D.N.Y.1956):

> The modern "notice" theory of pleading is not sufficient when employed in a complaint under the anti-trust laws. It is all very well for Professor Moore to state that: "The modern philosophy concerning pleadings is that they do little more than indicate generally the type of litigation that is involved." [2A Moore, *Federal Practice* ¶ 8.03, at 1613 (2d ed.).] This will not do in this type of case. If a complaint contains nothing more than general allegations that defendants have violated various provisions of the anti-trust laws combined with a prayer for relief, such a pleading, as I have previously said, "becomes a springboard from which the parties dive off into an almost bottomless sea of interrogatories, depositions, and pre-trial proceedings on collateral issues, most of which may have little relationship to the true issue in the case." [New Dyckman Theatre Corp. v. Radio-Keith-Orpheum Corp., 16 F.R.D. 203, 206 (S.D.N.Y.1954).]

> For these reasons it is not practical in these cases to proceed as in a negligence case or in a simple commercial case. * * * The complaint should show the relationship of the parties, the specific acts complained of, and the relation of the acts to the damages claimed.

Decisions of this type have become increasingly rare, however, as court after court has specifically held that the so-called "big case" cannot receive special treatment since the Federal Rules do not provide for it. See, e. g., Walker Distrib. Co. v. Lucky Lager Brewing Co., 323 F.2d 1, 3 (9th Cir.1963); Nagler v. Admiral Corp., 248 F.2d 319 (2d Cir.1957). Should the Federal Rules be amended to require more detailed pleadings in antitrust and other complex actions? Given the variety of contexts in which difficult factual disputes may arise, what should such an amendment say? Should trial courts have discretion to require the pleading of extra detail in any case that involves complex factual issues?

For various views of the problem, see Report to the Judicial Conference of the United States, *Procedure in Antitrust and Other Protracted Cases,* 13 F. R.D. 62, 66–68 (1953); Clark, *Special Pleading in the "Big Case,"* 21 F.R.D. 45 (1958); Freund, *The Pleading and Pre-Trial of an Antitrust Claim,* 46 Cornell L.Q. 555 (1961); Recent Developments, 58 Colum.L.Rev. 408 (1958).

The need for special procedures to handle antitrust suits, class actions, and similar complex cases has not gone unheeded. In 1968 the Congress enacted 28 U.S.C. § 1407, to permit the transfer of related civil actions pending in different federal courts to a single district in order to permit coordinated or consolidated pretrial proceedings. The legislation established a Judicial Panel on Multidistrict Litigation to handle these matters. The Panel's Rules of Procedure plus a set of general procedures suggested for pretrial and trial of complex cases, which were compiled by a coordinating committee of federal judges and members of the bar, appears in the Manual for Complex Litigation, which periodically is revised and reissued. The suggested procedures do not deal with pleadings, but concentrate on techniques of discovery, pretrial conferences, and pretrial orders.

---

4.   ALTERNATIVE AND INCONSISTENT ALLEGATIONS

Read Federal Rule of Civil Procedure 8(e) (2) and the related materials in the Supplement.

PAVALON v. THOMAS HOLMES CORP.

Supreme Court of Wisconsin, 1964.
25 Wis.2d 540, 131 N.W.2d 331.

Action by plaintiff Wesley D. Pavalon against defendants The Thomas Holmes Corporation (formerly Sulray, Inc.); Seymour Fishman; and Golkin & Bomback, Inc. (formerly Golkin, Divine & Fishman, Inc.), to compel the defendants to re-purchase a $50,000 note and an accompanying stock warrant, the maker of which is the first named defendant under its former name of Sulray, Inc. For the purposes of brevity, defendants Fishman and Golkin & Bomback, Inc. frequently hereafter will be referred to as "defendant brokers."

* * * A summary of the material allegations pleaded as the first cause of action are: On or about January 2, 1962, defendant brokers "on their

own behalf or as agent" for Sulray sold to plaintiff in Wisconsin Sulray's $50,000 note together with a warrant to purchase common stock of Sulray. Defendant brokers, "acting in their own behalf or as agent for" Sulray used the United States mails to consummate the sale and to deliver the note and warrant to plaintiff in Wisconsin. At various times in December, 1961, defendant Fishman "on his own behalf or as agent for one or both of the two corporate defendants" solicited plaintiff to purchase the note and warrant by telephone calls made from Illinois to plaintiff in Wisconsin and by a written offering circular sent to plaintiff in Wisconsin by defendant brokers "acting on their own behalf or as agent" for Sulray. This offering circular contained some materially false statements and omitted to state certain other material facts. Each of defendants knew, or in the exercise of reasonable care, should have known of such omissions and of the untruth of such statements. The material facts were omitted and the untrue statements were made with intent to induce plaintiff to purchase the note and warrant. Plaintiff first learned of the untruth of such statements and the omission of such facts on April 25, 1963, and has demanded that defendants re-purchase the note and warrant.

 * * * [T]he circuit court overruled [Sulray's] * * * demurrer to the first cause of action * * *.

 CURRIE, Chief Justice. * * *

SUFFICIENCY OF FIRST CAUSE OF ACTION.

 If the defendant brokers in inducing and making the sale to plaintiff acted only on their own behalf and not as agents of appellant, the complaint spells out no cause of action against appellant. An allegation, therefore, that defendant brokers so acted as agents of appellant, or some other allegation which under the federal Securities Act would establish appellant's liability, is crucial to the first cause of action stating a cause of action against appellant. The complaint, however, contains no positive allegation that defendant brokers did so act as agents of appellant. The allegations with respect to agency are all phrased in the alternative and allege that defendant brokers acted either as agents or as principals. Under the authorities, allegations in the alternative are fatally defective. * * * The first cause of action of the complaint, therefore, fails to state a cause of action and it was error not to sustain the demurrer thereto.

 * * *

NOTES AND QUESTIONS

 1. In BISCHOFF v. HUSTISFORD STATE BANK, 195 Wis. 312, 218 N.W. 353 (1928), plaintiff alleged in two separate counts that he was entitled to recover under the terms of an existing contract, and that he was entitled to recover in rescission and restitution because the contract was void for fraud. The Wisconsin Supreme Court held that these inconsistent claims could be united in the complaint. To what extent are *Pavalon* and *Bischoff* reconcilable? In which case is the pleader's position most clearly stated? What would the results in these two cases have been had they been decided under the Federal Rules?

2.   As previously noted, see pp. 325–28, supra, under the original common-law rules, pleadings were designed to reduce every controversy to a single issue of law or fact.   Alternative and hypothetical allegations would have made the search for the single issue impossible and therefore they were forbidden.   See generally McDonald, *Alternative Pleading: I*, 48 Mich.L.Rev. 311 (1950).   Is there any justification today for a rule prohibiting alternative allegations?   To what extent does the availability of discovery, pretrial conference, and summary judgment affect your answer?

McCORMICK v. KOPMANN

Illinois Court of Appeals, Third District, 1959.
23 Ill.App.2d 189, 161 N.E.2d 720.

REYNOLDS, Presiding Justice.   On the evening of November 21, 1956, Lewis McCormick was killed on Main Street in Gifford, Illinois, when a truck being operated by defendant Lorence Kopmann collided with the automobile which McCormick was driving.

This action was brought by McCormick's widow   *   *   *.

Count I is brought by plaintiff as Administratrix of McCormick's Estate, against Kopmann, under the Illinois Wrongful Death Act.   *   *   *   It is charged that Kopmann negligently drove his truck across the center line of Main Street and collided with McCormick's automobile.   In paragraph 3 of Count I, plaintiff alleges:

> "That at the time of the occurrence herein described, and for a reasonable period of time preceding it, the said decedent was in the exercise of ordinary care for his own safety and that of his property."

Count IV is brought by plaintiff as Administratrix of McCormick's Estate, against the Huls, under the Illinois Dram Shop Act.   *   *   *   It is alleged that Anna Huls operated a dramshop in Penfield, Illinois;   that John and Mary Huls operated a dramshop in Gifford;   that on November 21, 1956 the Huls sold alcoholic beverages to McCormick which he consumed and which rendered him intoxicated;   and that "as a result of such intoxication" Mc-Cormick drove his automobile "in such a manner as to cause a collision with a truck" being driven by Kopmann on Main Street in Gifford.

Kopmann, defendant under Count I, moved to dismiss the complaint on the theory that the allegations of that Count I and Count IV were fatally repugnant and could not stand together, because McCormick could not be free from contributory negligence as alleged in Count I, if his intoxication caused the accident as alleged in Count IV.   Kopmann also urged that the allegation in Count IV that McCormick's intoxication was the proximate cause of his death, is a binding judicial admission which precludes an action under the Wrongful Death Act.   Kopmann's motion was denied.   He raised the same defenses in his answer.

*   *   *

The jury returned a verdict against Kopmann for $15,500 under Count I.

* * *

Kopmann has appealed. His first contention is that the trial court erred in denying his pre-trial motion to dismiss the complaint. Kopmann is correct in asserting that the complaint contains inconsistent allegations. The allegation of Count I that McCormick was free from contributory negligence, cannot be reconciled with the allegation of Count IV that McCormick's intoxication was the proximate cause of his death. Freedom from contributory negligence is a prerequisite to recovery under the Wrongful Death Act. * * *

[Section 43(2) of] * * * the Civil Practice Act expressly permits a plaintiff to plead inconsistent counts in the alternative, where he is genuinely in doubt as to what the facts are and what the evidence will show. The legal sufficiency of each count presents a separate question. It is not ground for dismissal that allegations in one count contradict those in an alternative count. These principles have been applied recently in cases similar to that at bar. * * *

Sound policy weighs in favor of alternative pleading, so that controversies may be settled and complete justice accomplished in a single action. * * * If the right is abused, as where the pleader has knowledge of the true facts (viz., he knows that the facts belie the alternative) pleading in the alternative is not justified. Thus in Church v. Adler, 350 Ill.App. 471 at page 483, 113 N.E.2d 327 at page 332, we said:

> "* * * alternative pleading is not permitted when in the nature of things the pleader must know which of the inconsistent averments is true and which is false. Plaintiff must know whether she will be sick, sore, lame and disordered for the rest of her life or whether on the contrary she has regained her health, as alleged in Count II. She must make up her mind which is the fact, and strike the inconsistent allegation from her pleading on remand."

There is nothing in the record before us to indicate that plaintiff knew in advance of the trial, that the averments of Count I, and not Count IV, were true. * * * Where, as in the Church case, the injured party is still living and able to recollect the events surrounding the accident, pleading in the alternative may not be justified, but where, as in the case at bar, the key witness is deceased, pleading alternative sets of facts is often the only feasible way to proceed. * * *

Kopmann's next argument is that the allegations of Count IV regarding McCormick's intoxication constitute binding judicial admissions. He contends that plaintiff's action against him should have been dismissed on the basis of the allegations in Count IV regarding McCormick's intoxication.

In 20 Am.Jur., Evidence, § 635, the author states (p. 538):

> "The rule in the majority of jurisdictions is that the admissions made by a pleader in one count or plea are not admissible against him on an issue raised by his denials or averments made in another count or plea. In other words, where inconsistent counts

or defenses are pleaded, the admissions in one of them cannot be used to destroy the effect of the other."

The author goes on to point out that in some few jurisdictions, statements in one count "are held admissible against the pleader on the issue raised by another." No Illinois case has been called to our attention to support this rule. The court below permitted Kopmann to read the allegations of Count IV as admissions.

We know of no case which supports the position Kopmann takes in this court, viz., that the admission is conclusively binding and is a ground for judgment notwithstanding the verdict. If this were the law, the provisions of the Civil Practice Act sanctioning pleading in the alternative, "regardless of consistency," would be a legal snare.

* * *

Alternative fact allegations made in good faith and based on genuine doubt are not admissions against interest so as to be admissible in evidence against the pleader. The pleader states the facts in the alternative because he is uncertain as to the true facts. Therefore, he is not "admitting" anything other than his uncertainty. An essential objective of alternative pleading is to relieve the pleader of the necessity and therefore the risk of making a binding choice, which is no more than to say that he is relieved of making an admission.

* * * Plaintiff pleaded alternative counts because she was uncertain as to what the true facts were. Even assuming she introduced proof to support all essential allegations of both Count I and Count IV, she was entitled to have all the evidence submitted to the trier of fact, and to have the jury decide where the truth lay. She was not foreclosed *ipso facto* from going to the jury under Count I, merely because she submitted proof, under Count IV, tending to prove that McCormick's intoxication proximately caused his death. If this were the rule, one who in good faith tried his case on alternative theories, pursuant to the authorization, if not the encouragement of Section 43, would run the risk of having his entire case dismissed. The provisions of the Civil Practice Act authorizing alternative pleading, necessarily contemplate that the pleader adduce proof in support of both sets of allegations or legal theories, leaving to the jury the determination of the facts.

* * *

What we have said is not to say that a plaintiff assumes no risks in adducing proof to support inconsistent counts. The proof in support of one inconsistent count necessarily tends to negate the proof under the other count and to have its effect upon the jury. While the fact alone of inconsistent evidence will not bar submission of the case to the jury, it may very well affect the matter of the weight of the evidence and warrant the granting of a new trial, even though, as we have held, it does not warrant *ipso facto* a directed verdict or judgment notwithstanding the verdict.

Kopmann argues that plaintiff should have been required to elect between her alternative counts before going to the jury. The doctrine known as "election of remedies" has no application to the case at bar. Here, either of two defendants may be liable to plaintiff, depending upon what the jury finds the facts to be. * * * Plaintiff need not choose between the alternative counts. Such a requirement would, to a large extent, nullify the salutary purposes of alternative pleading. Since she could bring actions against the defendants seriatim, or at the same time in separate suits, she is entitled to join them in a single action, introduce all her proof, and submit the entire case to the jury under appropriate instructions. * * *

Judgment affirmed.

NOTES AND QUESTIONS

1. WALLACE v. BOUNDS, 369 S.W.2d 138 (Mo.1963), was an action arising out of an automobile collision between defendant and plaintiff's intestate. Under Missouri law if the accident was the cause of death, plaintiff's exclusive remedy was under a wrongful-death statute. If, however, the accident was not the cause of death, recovery was exclusively under a survival statute allowing the personal representative of the decedent to pursue the action to the same extent that the latter could have done so had he been alive. Since the question of causation was a doubtful one, plaintiff joined claims under both statutes.

At the close of all the evidence, the trial court, on motion of defendant, required plaintiff to elect which of the two claims should be submitted to the jury. Verdict went for defendant, plaintiff appealed, and the state supreme court affirmed. Missouri Rule of Civil Procedure 55.12 (V.A.M.S. § 509.110) is identical to Federal Rule 8(e)(2) except that in the Missouri provision, the words "regardless of consistency" are omitted from the provision permitting a party to state "as many separate claims or defenses as he has." The appellate court made no mention of this difference, however, but simply characterized Rule 55.12 as a rule of pleading, which presumably meant that the court did not believe it had any relevance to the submission of causes to the jury, and held that it is error to submit inconsistent and contradictory theories of recovery to the trier of fact.

Is there any reason for preferring the result in *Wallace* to that in *McCormick?* Both Illinois and Missouri have extensive provisions for discovery, pretrial conference, and summary judgment. Does the availability of these procedures indicate that if an election between inconsistent factual claims is to be made, it should be accomplished before trial? What advantages are there to an early election? What disadvantages?

2. The so-called "election of remedies" doctrine, although referred to and sometimes relied upon in cases such as *Kopmann* and *Wallace,* is applied primarily to situations in which a person who has a choice between two substantive theories of recovery first takes steps to enforce rights under only one of the theories and later attempts to rely upon the alternative. From a pleading point of view the election problem is whether or not a plaintiff, by filing a claim based on one theory of relief, has by that act alone been precluded from later basing a claim upon an inconsistent theory. Consider the case in which plaintiff has fraudulently been induced to enter into a contract. Plaintiff may choose either to affirm the contract and sue for her rights under it, or to disaffirm the contract and sue for damages. If plaintiff files a suit for breach, should she be barred thereafter from disaffirmance? To what extent should the answer depend on the nature of the

contract and the unperformed obligations of plaintiff as well as defendant? Suppose plaintiff, prior to suit, wrote defendant a letter affirming the contract. Should plaintiff then be permitted to file a complaint based on disaffirmance?

Whether or not commencement of suit alone should constitute an election by plaintiff has been the subject of many conflicting decisions. See Annot., 6 A.L.R. 2d 10 (1949). Most commentators are clear that the answer should be in the negative. See, e. g., Clark, *Code Pleading* § 77 (2d ed. 1947); 3 Weinstein, Korn & Miller, *New York Civil Practice* ¶¶ 3002.01–.05. Isn't this a necessary result in any jurisdiction that permits plaintiffs to state alternative and inconsistent claims for relief in their complaints? The election-of-remedies doctrine is discussed further at pp. 1078–83, infra.

3. Suppose plaintiff is able, on a single set of alleged facts, to pursue two separate legal theories each of which would afford compensation at least in part for the same injury. See, for example, BRINK v. GRIFFITH, 65 Wash.2d 253, 396 P.2d 793 (1964), in which plaintiff sought damages for emotional distress and injury to reputation on alternative theories of defamation and invasion of privacy. Should a jury be allowed to render separate verdicts for plaintiff on each theory? How can the court prevent double recovery? Should an election before trial be required? Would such an election amount to nothing more than a return to the theory-of-the-pleadings doctrine? See pp. 367–79, supra.

When a plaintiff successfully sues two or more defendants each of whom is liable individually for the entire amount of the judgment, plaintiff may collect the judgment from any one or from all, but any recovery obtained from one will be set off when he proceeds against the others. Can this same technique be utilized to prevent double recovery when plaintiff successfully sues a single defendant on two separate theories?

THE SEPARATE-STATEMENT REQUIREMENT

Rules permitting parties to plead in the alternative usually are coupled with provisions requiring each separate cause of action or defense to be separately stated. See, e. g., Ill.Ann.Stat. ch. 110, §§ 33(2), 43(1).

Federal Rule of Civil Procedure 10(b) does not contain a formal separate-statement requirement, although the Rule does express the hope that "as far as practicable" each paragraph will be limited "to a statement of a single set of circumstances." The Rule also requires separation of claims founded on different transactions "whenever separation facilitates the clear presentation of the matters set forth." One commentator argues that this type of discretionary rule coupled with Rule 8(e), which permits inconsistent allegations in a single count, may be too liberal and may encourage confusion in pleading. He goes on to state:

> * * * If consistency promotes clarity, it is no great burden upon the plaintiff for him to state his separate grounds of recovery consistently. But if his position is clear, and it is obvious that the inconsistencies arise from an attempt to press alternative interpretations of the facts, little is to be gained by striking the pleading only to have it reformed in multiple counts asserting the same grounds of recovery.

McDonald, *Alternative Pleading in the United States: I*, 52 Colum.L.Rev. 443, 464 (1952). See also O'Donnell v. Elgin, J. & E. Ry., 338 U.S. 384, 70 S.Ct. 200, 94 L.Ed. 187 (1949). Is the code-system requirement of separate counts, each of which is consistent within itself, preferable to Federal Rule 10(b)?

When a party violates the separate-statement requirement, the usual corrective procedure is a motion to separate. See, e. g., Conn. Practice Book of 1951, 309 (Form 252); Trussell v. United Underwriters, Ltd., 228 F.Supp. 757, 777 (D.Colo.1964). But jurisdictions differ. In ERSPAMER v. OLIVER IRON MINING CO., 179 Minn. 475, 229 N.W. 583 (1930), the proper remedy was a motion to strike; in HEATH v. KIRKMAN, 240 N.C. 303, 82 S.E.2d 104 (1954), it was a demurrer. In any case the party will be allowed to amend his pleading to conform to the rules. If a plaintiff refuses to amend, should the case be dismissed? See Sawyer v. Sawyer, 181 Okl. 567, 75 P.2d 423 (1937) (dismissal proper).

---

5. PROVISIONS TO ENSURE TRUTHFUL ALLEGATIONS

Read Federal Rule of Civil Procedure 11 and the related materials in the Supplement.

SUROWITZ v. HILTON HOTELS CORP.

Supreme Court of the United States, 1966.
383 U.S. 363, 86 S.Ct. 845, 15 L.Ed.2d 807.

Certiorari to the United States Court of Appeals for the Seventh Circuit.

Mr. Justice BLACK delivered the opinion of the Court.

Petitioner, Dora Surowitz, a stockholder in Hilton Hotels Corporation, brought this action in a United States District Court on behalf of herself and other stockholders charging that the officers and directors of the corporation had defrauded it of several million dollars by illegal devices and schemes designed to cheat the corporation and enrich the individual defendants. The acts charged, if true, would constitute frauds of the grossest kind against the corporation, and would be in violation of the Securities Act of 1933, the Securities Exchange Act of 1934, and the Delaware General Corporation Law. * * * The [detailed] complaint [containing more than 60 printed pages] was signed by counsel for Mrs. Surowitz in compliance with Rule 11 of the Federal Rules of Civil Procedure which provides that "The signature of an attorney constitutes a certificate by him that he has read the pleading; that to the best of his knowledge, information, and belief there is good ground to support it; and that it is not interposed for delay." Also pursuant to Rule 23(b) [now Rule 23.1] of the Federal Rules, the complaint was verified by Mrs. Surowitz, the petitioner, who stated that some of the allegations in the complaint were true and that she "on information and belief" thought that all the other allegations were true.

So far as the language of the complaint and of Mrs. Surowitz's verification was concerned, both were in strict compliance with the provisions of Rule 23(b) which states that a shareholder's complaint in a secondary action must contain certain averments and be verified by the plaintiff. Notwithstanding the sufficiency of the complaint and verification under Rule 23(b), however, the court, without requiring defendants to file an answer and over petitioner's protest, granted defendants' motion to require Mrs. Surowitz to submit herself to an oral examination by the defendants' counsel. In this examination Mrs. Surowitz showed in her answers to questions that she did not understand the complaint at all, that she could not explain the statements made in the complaint, that she had a very small degree of knowledge as to what the lawsuit was about, that she did not know any of the defendants by name, that she did not know the nature of their alleged misconduct, and in fact that in signing the verification she had merely relied on what her son-in-law had explained to her about the facts in the case. On the basis of this examination, defendants moved to dismiss the complaint, alleging that "1. It is a sham pleading, and 2. Plaintiff, Dora Surowitz, is not a proper party plaintiff. * * *" In response, Mrs. Surowitz's lawyer, in an effort to cure whatever infirmity the court might possibly find in Mrs. Surowitz's verification in light of her deposition, filed two affidavits which shed much additional light on an extensive investigation which had preceded the filing of the complaint. Despite these affidavits the District Judge dismissed the case holding that Mrs. Surowitz's affidavit was "false," that being wholly false it was a nullity, that being a nullity it was as though no affidavit had been made in compliance with Rule 23, that being false the affidavit was a "sham" and Rule 23(b) required that he dismiss her case, and he did so, "with prejudice."

The Court of Appeals affirmed the District Court's dismissal * * * despite the fact that the charges made against the defendants were viewed as very serious and grave charges of fraud and that "many of the material allegations of the complaint are obviously true and cannot be refuted." 342 F.2d, at 607. We cannot agree with either of the courts below and reverse their judgments. * * *

Mrs. Surowitz, the plaintiff and petitioner here, is a Polish immigrant with a very limited English vocabulary and practically no formal education. For many years she has worked as a seamstress in New York where by reason of frugality she saved enough money to buy some thousands of dollars worth of stocks. She was of course not able to select stocks for herself with any degree of assurance of their value. Under these circumstances she had to receive advice and counsel and quite naturally she went to her son-in-law, Irving Brilliant. Mr. Brilliant had graduated from the Harvard Law School, possessed a master's degree in economics from Columbia University, was a professional investment advisor, and in addition to his degrees and his financial acumen, he wore a Phi Beta Kappa key. In 1957, six years before this litigation began, he bought some stock for his mother-in-law in the Hilton Hotels Corporation, paying a little more than $2,000 of her own money for it. * * *

About December 1962, Mrs. Surowitz received through the mails a notice from the Hilton Hotels Corporation announcing its plan to purchase a large amount of its own stock. Because she wanted it explained to her, she took the notice to Mr. Brilliant. Apparently disturbed by it, he straightway set out to make an investigation. Shortly thereafter he went to Chicago, Illinois, where Hilton Hotels has its home office and talked the matter over with Mr. Rockler. Mr. Brilliant and Mr. Rockler had been friends for many years. * * * The two decided to investigate further, and for a number of months both pursued whatever avenues of information that were open to them. By August of 1963 on the basis of their investigation, both of them had reached the conclusion [that defendants were engaged in a fraudulent scheme, and Mr. Brilliant explained this to Mrs. Surowitz.] * * *

* * * When, on the basis of this conversation, Mrs. Surowitz stated that she agreed that suit be filed in her name, Mr. Rockler prepared a formal complaint which he mailed to Mr. Brilliant. Mr. Brilliant then, according to both his affidavit and Mrs. Surowitz's testimony, read and explained the complaint to his mother-in-law before she verified it. Her limited education and her small knowledge about any of the English language, except the most ordinarily used words, probably is sufficient guarantee that the courts below were right in finding that she did not understand any of the legal relationships or comprehend any of the business transactions described in the complaint. She did know, however, that she had put over $2,000 of her hard-earned money into Hilton Hotels stock, that she was not getting her dividends, and that her son-in-law who had looked into the matter thought that something was wrong. She also knew that her son-in-law was qualified to help her and she trusted him. It is difficult to believe that anyone could be shocked or harmed in any way when, in the light of all these circumstances, Mrs. Surowitz verified the complaint, not on the basis of her own knowledge and understanding, but in the faith that her son-in-law had correctly advised her either that the statements in the complaint were true or to the best of his knowledge he believed them to be true.

* * * Rule 23(b) was not written in order to bar derivative suits. Unquestionably it was originally adopted and has served since in part as a means to discourage "strike suits" by people who might be interested in getting quick dollars by making charges without regard to their truth so as to coerce corporate managers to settle worthless claims in order to get rid of them. * * *

When the record of this case is reviewed in the light of the purpose of Rule 23(b)'s verification requirement, there emerges the plain, inescapable fact that this is not a strike suit or anything akin to it. Mrs. Surowitz was not interested in anything but her own investment made with her own money. Moreover, there is not one iota of evidence that Mr. Brilliant, her son-in-law and counselor, sought to do the corporation any injury in this litigation. In fact his purchases for the benefit of his family of more than $50,000 of securities in the corporation, including a $10,000 debenture, all made years before this suit was brought, manifest confidence in the corporation, not a desire to harm it in any way. The Court of Appeals in affirming the District Court's dismissal, however, indicated that whether Mrs. Surowitz and her counselors acted in good faith and whether the charges they made were truthful were irrelevant once Mrs. Surowitz demonstrated in her oral testimony that she knew nothing about the content of the suit. * * *

We cannot construe Rule 23 or any other one of the Federal Rules as compelling courts to summarily dismiss, without any answer or argument at all, cases like this where grave charges of fraud are shown by the record to be based on reasonable beliefs growing out of careful investigation. The basic purpose of the Federal Rules is to administer justice through fair trials, not through summary dismissals as necessary as they may be on occasion. These rules were designed in large part to get away from some of the old procedural booby traps which common-law pleaders could set to prevent unsophisticated litigants from ever having their day in court. If rules of procedure work as they should in an honest and fair judicial system, they not only permit, but should as nearly as possible guarantee that bona fide complaints be carried to an adjudication on the merits. Rule 23(b), like the other civil rules, was written to further, not defeat the ends of justice. The serious fraud charged here, which of course has not been proven, is clearly in that class of deceitful conduct which the federal securities laws were largely passed to prohibit and protect against. There is, moreover, not one word or one line of actual evidence in this record indicating that there has been any collusive conduct or trickery by those who filed this suit except through intimations and insinuations without any support from anything any witness has said. The dismissal of this case was error. It has now been practically three years since the complaint was filed and as yet none of the defendants have even been compelled to admit or deny the wrongdoings charged. They should be. The cause is reversed and remanded to the District Court for trial on the merits.

Reversed and remanded.

Mr. Justice HARLAN, concurring.

Rule 23(b) directs that in a derivative suit "the complaint shall be verified by oath" but nothing dictates that the verification be that of the plaintiff shareholder. * * * In the present circumstances, it seems to me the affidavit of Walter J. Rockler, counsel for Mrs. Surowitz, amounts to an adequate verification by counsel, which I think is permitted by a reasonable interpretation of the Rule at least in cases such as this. On this premise, I agree with the decision of the Court.

NOTES AND QUESTIONS

1. The *Surowitz* case is noted in 18 Stan.L.Rev. 1221 (1966). Why is a dismissal ever an appropriate way of enforcing the verification provision of Rule

23.1? Shouldn't plaintiff be prosecuted for the crime of perjury instead? Of what significance is it that any recovery in a suit under Rule 23.1 goes directly to the corporation, not to plaintiff? Suppose the statute of limitations on the claim runs just before the dismissal. What additional problems would this raise?

2. Why does Rule 23.1 require verification? Why doesn't the Rule 11 procedure suffice? Even in those jurisdictions in which fact pleadings do not have to be verified, there are certain exceptions. Some of the typical ones are: petitions for divorce (Ga.Code Ann. § 30–105; Iowa Code Ann. § 598.7; Kan. Stat.Ann. § 60–1604(a); Okl.Stat.Ann. tit. 12, § 1273), petitions to enjoin a nuisance (Okl.Stat.Ann. tit. 12, § 1397), and complaints to obtain support of an illegitimate child (Iowa Code Ann. § 675.13). What makes these actions sufficiently distinctive to require verification?

3. In Georgia, New York, and a number of other jurisdictions, it is, in most cases, up to plaintiff whether or not to verify. What is the rationale of this approach? Does this type of an option tend to legitimize false, unverified pleadings? In these jurisdictions if the complaint is verified, then the answer must be verified as well. Does this impose an unfair burden on a defendant who wishes, in good faith, to assert two factually inconsistent defenses? See BELL v. BROWN, 22 Cal. 671, 678 (1863):

> * * * The right to set up numerous defenses in a suit is equally as important to the defendant [when the answer is verified as when it is not] * * *. In many cases it would be a denial of justice if a defendant should be shut out from setting up several defenses.
>
> There is this difference, however, between verified and unverified pleadings, that if the truth of a fact is directly averred in any part of the former whether in a complaint or answer, and then in any other part of the same pleading, whether in the statement of several causes of action in the complaint, or separate defenses in the answer, the same fact is directly contradicted or denied, the person verifying it is guilty of perjury, for both cannot be true; and the averment which bears most strongly against the party so pleading will be taken as true upon the trial. * * *

To what extent is the decision in *Pavalon v. Thomas Holmes Corp.*, p. 403, supra, relevant or helpful in finding a sensible solution to the dilemma of a pleader whose choice between alternative positions ultimately will depend on a fact that he cannot ascertain conclusively prior to the time a verified pleading must be filed?

4. Because of Federal Rule 11, the burden of good-faith pleading falls upon the lawyers in the federal courts. To what extent must an attorney investigate the accuracy of a client's story before filing a complaint or answer? Does the imposition of a duty of good-faith pleading effectively answer critics who claim that modern federal pleading, with its de-emphasis of facts, leads to unfounded or speculative litigation? See McCaskill, *The Modern Philosophy of Pleading: A Dialogue Outside the Shades*, 38 A.B.A.J. 123, 126 (1952).

Is a motion to strike a pleading an appropriate means of enforcing an attorney's obligations under Rule 11? Would your answer be the same if the pleading states or could be amended to state, a good claim for relief or defense? See Bertucelli v. Carreras, 467 F.2d 214 (9th Cir.1972) (dismissal without leave to amend reversed). What other sanctions might be imposed? See generally 47 Va.L.Rev.

1434 (1961). In AMERICAN AUTO. ASS'N v. ROTHMAN, 104 F.Supp. 655 (E.D.N.Y.1952), the court found that the answer, signed by defendant's attorney, contained a counterclaim that the attorney knew to be based on false allegations. The court's sanction was to order its opinion condemning the attorney's action to be filed in the office of the clerk of the court and indexed against the name of the attorney, in order that the matter be of record "in the event that his professional conduct in any other connection shall become a subject of inquiry." Is such a reprimand more effective than might otherwise appear?

For a case in which an attorney was ordered disbarred for a wilful violation of his obligation under Rule 11, see In re Lavine, 126 F.Supp. 39 (S.D.Cal.1954), reversed on other grounds sub nom. In re Los Angeles County Pioneer Soc'y, 217 F.2d 190 (9th Cir.1954). In light of the place pleadings occupy in the federal pretrial picture, is disbarment too severe a penalty, even for a flagrant violation?

SECTION C. THE COMPLAINT

---

1. PLEADING JURISDICTION

Read Federal Rule of Civil Procedure 8(a) (1) in the Supplement.

GIANCANA v. JOHNSON, 335 F.2d 366, 371 (7th Cir.1964), certiorari denied 379 U.S. 1001, 85 S.Ct. 718, 13 L.Ed.2d 702 (1965). Plaintiff brought suit to enjoin defendant, a local FBI executive, from keeping plaintiff under constant FBI surveillance. Jurisdiction was based on the existence of a federal question under Section 1331 of Title 28. Plaintiff made no express allegation as to the jurisdictional sum but sought to uphold jurisdiction on the ground that "priceless rights" were involved. The trial court held that jurisdiction existed but the court of appeals reversed. Judge Swygert dissented:

> It is incongruous to hold that a formal allegation of the amount in controversy is necessary when personal liberties of the magnitude alleged in the complaint and found by the district court are involved. To require a dollar value to be specifically averred in these circumstances is to exalt form over substance.

> In my opinion the fact that there was no formal allegation of the requisite jurisdictional amount did not prevent the district court from assuming jurisdiction. The complaint alleged that defendant and his agents deprived plaintiff of the use of his home and that they violated his right of privacy and personal liberty. From these allegations the district court could infer, contrary to what the majority indicates, that the amount in controversy exceeded $10,000.

NOTES AND QUESTIONS

1.   Could plaintiff have avoided the problem merely by alleging specifically that more than $10,000 was in controversy? See, e. g., Stewart v. Shanahan, 277 F.2d 233 (8th Cir.1960) (allegation of jurisdictional amount need only be in good faith to avert dismissal). Review the materials on pp. 212–19, supra. What are the ingredients of an allegation of diversity-of-citizenship jurisdiction? Read 28 U.S.C. §§ 1331(b), 1332(b) in the Supplement. What is the purpose of these provisions? Should they apply to a monetary claim made in good faith? If a claim was not made in good faith, isn't the court required to dismiss the entire proceeding? See generally 5 Wright & Miller, *Federal Practice and Procedure: Civil* §§ 1205–14 (1969).

2.   In state courts plaintiffs normally are not required to allege specifically the basis of the court's jurisdiction. Why not?

---

2. PLEADING THE RIGHT TO RELIEF

Read Federal Rule of Civil Procedure 8(a) (2) in the Supplement.

A. STATING THE ESSENTIAL ELEMENTS

(i) Determining the Factors with Legal Significance

A proper complaint, whether governed by Federal Rule 8(a) or a code-pleading provision, must contain sufficient allegations to show that plaintiff has a right to relief. In order to determine precisely what allegations are required in a particular case, it is first necessary to isolate all those factors that have legal significance with respect to the claim to be alleged. For example, an action for slander will be successful, if, but only if:

1.   Defendant made a statement concerning plaintiff.

2.   The statement was published, that is, heard by a third party.

3.   Plaintiff suffered injury because of the statement.

4.   The statement was not true.

5.   The statement was not privileged, or even if the statement normally would be privileged, it was uttered maliciously and with the intent to injure plaintiff.

6.   Defendant has not paid plaintiff in settlement of the claim.

7.   No prior action has determined the same claim.

8.   The statute of limitations has not run.

The list of relevant factors actually is much longer, since there are a number of other possible defenses to the action that could be mentioned.

In pleading a claim for relief, whatever the nature of the action, plaintiff is not required to include every one of the relevant factors in his complaint; some are considered defenses to be raised by defendant in the answer. It is to the basic question of how courts and lawyers determine which factors are vital to the complaint and which are not that we now turn.

(ii) Allocating the Burden of Pleading Between Plaintiff and Defendant

EFFECT OF THE BURDEN OF PRODUCTION

The burden of pleading an issue usually is assigned to the party who has the burden of producing evidence on that issue at trial. Plaintiff has the burden of production on two types of issues. First, plaintiff must put forth evidence on certain matters basic to the action or he cannot prevail. In a slander action, for example, plaintiff must introduce evidence that the remarks were made, that they were published, and that he was injured thereby. If plaintiff rests his case without producing evidence on any one of these issues, the court will dismiss the action and enter judgment for defendant. Second, if, but only if, defendant establishes a defense, plaintiff will then have a second burden of production, this time to introduce evidence as to new facts that will avoid defendant's defense. For example, if defendant proves that allegedly slanderous statements were made to plaintiff's prospective employer under conditions that rendered the statements privileged, plaintiff must then carry the burden of producing evidence showing that the statements were made maliciously and solely with intent to injure plaintiff.

Plaintiff has the burden of pleading all matters of the first type in the complaint; that is, he is required to plead those matters on which he must introduce evidence at trial. The rationale for the rule is simple. If plaintiff cannot legitimately allege the existence of each of the basic elements of his claim, it may be assumed that he could not introduce evidence on them at trial. Since the action would have to be dismissed as soon as plaintiff rested his case, it would be an idle act to permit the trial to begin, and the action might as well be terminated at the pleading stage.

On the other hand, plaintiff normally does not have to plead matters on which defendant must introduce proof. If plaintiff were required to plead the nonexistence of every defense, not only would the pleading be long, complex, and fraught with danger for a plaintiff who omitted a remote possibility, but the pleadings would not reveal, in any direct way, precisely upon which defenses defendant actually intended to rely. By placing the burden of pleading defenses on defendant, the court and parties know exactly on which of the many possible defenses he intends to introduce evidence, thus making preparation for trial and work at trial more manageable. Obviously, plaintiff is not required to plead, in the original complaint, matters to avoid defenses, since he cannot tell which defenses will be raised until the answer is filed. In some jurisdictions plaintiff is required to set forth such matters of avoidance in a second pleading, which serves as a reply to the answer; in other jurisdictions the decision whether to require a reply is left to the trial court's discretion.

EFFECT OF OTHER CONSIDERATIONS

Aside from those matters upon which he must initially introduce evidence if he is to prevail, plaintiff, in the complaint, is sometimes required to plead the nonexistence of certain defenses upon which defendant has the burden of proof, although as we have seen, such a requirement is technically illogical. The reason for these special rules is sometimes historical and sometimes practical. Consider, for example, a case in which plaintiff sues defendant on an overdue note. Payment of a note traditionally has been considered a defense to be proved by defendant, who by virtue of having a receipt usually is in a better position to put in evidence on the issue. Nevertheless, plaintiff, as part of the claim, must allege nonpayment. Without such an allegation the complaint would really say nothing; it would simply set forth the existence of the note without mentioning the nature of the breach of its terms. To inform the court and defendant as to the basis of the complaint, an allegation of nonpayment is essential. It is only when a defense, such as payment, goes to the very heart of the action, so that plaintiff should, in order to state a claim, be required to face the issue and allege in good faith that such defense does not exist, that the burden of pleading and the burden of producing evidence need not coincide. Another example occurs in the slander context in which some courts consider the truth of the remarks an absolute defense. In some of these jurisdictions, although not all, falsity is thought to be so much a part of the basic action, that plaintiff must plead it, even though defendant has the burden of introducing evidence of truth.

Because of the technical imbalance in cases in which plaintiff must plead the nonexistence of a defense in order to state a claim, some courts require defendant to raise the defense specially in the answer, rather than by simply denying plaintiff's allegation, if defendant really intends to pursue it; otherwise the defense will be waived. Thus before such an issue actually is tried, it will be pleaded twice, once in the complaint and once in the answer.

Allocation of the pleading burden sometimes is complicated by rules or statutes that specifically set forth matters that are to be considered defenses and contained in the answer. See, e. g., Federal Rule of Civil Procedure 8(c). The enumerated matters usually are those that traditionally have been treated as defenses both as to the burden of pleading and the burden of proof. Not all jurisdictions have adhered to these traditional views, however. For example, contributory negligence historically was treated as a defense, but today, in a number of jurisdictions, plaintiff, in order to prevail in a negligence case, must prove his own due care. If the pleading rule in these jurisdictions deems the issue of plaintiff's negligence to be a defense, it creates a serious anomaly, since defendant must raise the issue even though plaintiff is required to prove it. Furthermore, since a defense is waived if defendant does not plead it, the failure of defendant to raise the matter in the answer would seem to obviate plaintiff's proof of the matter, thus thwarting the express policy of the jurisdiction requiring plaintiff to prove his own due care.

Fortunately those situations in which the burden of proof and burden of pleading do not coincide are few in number and usually are well known. By following approved pleading forms and precedents covering these odd cases, most attorneys handle such cases without incident.

For further discussion of the problems of allocating the burden of pleading, plus specific examples of the problems discussed above, see *Holliday v. Great Atlantic & Pacific Tea Co.*, p. 441, infra, and the Notes and Questions following it. See also Cleary, *Presuming and Pleading: An Essay on Juristic Immaturity*, 12 Stan.L.Rev. 5 (1959).

GARCIA v. HILTON HOTELS INTERNATIONAL, INC.

United States District Court, District of Puerto Rico, 1951.
97 F.Supp. 5.

ROBERTS, District Judge. The action here is for damages for defamation brought by plaintiff, a citizen and resident of Puerto Rico, against defendant, a Delaware corporation, in the District Court of Puerto Rico and removed to this Court by defendant corporation. The complaint sets forth two causes of action and the paragraphs considered herein are identical in each cause. Defendant has moved to dismiss the complaint for failure to state a claim upon which relief can be granted and, in the alternative, to strike Paragraphs 5, 6, 7 and 8 and for a more definite statement.

In supoprt [sic] of its motion to dismiss, defendant contends that no publication of the alleged slanderous statement is alleged and that the complaint, therefore, fails to state a cause of action. This contention will be considered first with respect to Paragraph 4 of the complaint, which reads as follows: "4. On August 22, 1950, the plaintiff was violently discharged by the defendant, being falsely and slanderously accused of being engaged in bringing women from outside the Hotel and introducing them into the rooms thereof for the purpose of developing prostitution in the Hotel and that such women brought by him from outside the Hotel and introduced therein carried on acts of prostitution in said Hotel."

* * *

The controlling question here, with respect to the motion to dismiss, is whether the allegations of Paragraph 4 of the complaint, state a claim upon which relief can be granted. An examination of the authorities is persuasive that is [sic] does. It is settled, with respect to motions to dismiss for insufficiency of statement, that the complaint is to be construed in the light most favorable to the plaintiff with all doubts resolved in his favor and the allegations accepted as true. If, when a complaint is so considered, it reasonably may be anticipated that plaintiff, on the basis of what has been alleged, could make out a case at trial entitling him to some relief, the complaint should not be dismissed. * * *

In the instant case, it is true that Paragraph 4, of the complaint, fails to state, in so many words, that there was a publication of the alleged slanderous utterance and, to that extent, the cause of action is defectively stated. However, it does not follow that the allegations do not state a claim upon which relief can be granted. It is alleged that plaintiff was "violently discharged" and was "falsely and slanderously accused" of procuring for prostitution. While in a technical sense, this language states a conclusion, it is clear that plaintiff used it intending to charge publication of the slanderous utterance and it would be unrealistic for defendant to claim that it does not so understand the allegations. See, Edelman v. Locker, D.C., 6 F.R.D. 272, 274. Clearly, under such allegations it reasonably may be conceived that plaintiff, upon trial, could adduce evidence tending to prove a publication. * * *

In further support of its motion to dismiss, defendant contends that the alleged slanderous utterance was conditionally privileged. Conceding that to be so does not require that a different conclusion be reached with respect to the motion to dismiss. Rule 12(b) requires that every defense in law or fact be asserted in a responsive pleading when one is required or permitted under the rules. The rule, however, enumerates certain defenses which may be asserted by motion to dismiss, all of which go to the jurisdiction except that of failure to state a claim upon which relief can be granted, rule 12(b) (6). And this latter defense may be asserted successfully by a motion prior to responsive pleading only when it appears to a certainty that plaintiff would be entitled to no relief under any state of fact which could be proved in support of the claim asserted by him. * * *

The conclusiveness of privilege as a defense depends upon whether the privilege involved is [sic] absolute or conditional. When the privilege involved is absolute, it constitutes a finally determinative or conclusive defense to an action based on the utterance. Consequently, when it appears from a complaint that absolute privilege exists, the defense of failure to state a claim properly may be asserted to accomplish a dismissal on motion under rule 12 (b). It is for the court to determine the existence of privilege and when absolute privilege is found, it constitutes an unassailable defense and, clearly, in such a case, the claim stated is one upon which relief cannot be granted.

But conditional privilege is not a conclusive defense to an action based on a slanderous utterance. It is but a qualified defense which may be lost to the defendant if plaintiff can prove abuse of the privilege or actual malice. * * * When from the allegations contained therein, a complaint indicates the availability of the defense of conditional privilege, it cannot be held therefrom as a matter of law, that there has been a failure to state a claim upon which relief can be granted, such as will warrant dismissal of the complaint on motion under rule 12(b)(6), for the factual question remains whether defendant abused the privilege or made the communication maliciously. * * *

As has been noted, on motion to dismiss for failure to state a claim, complaint must be construed in the light most favorable to plaintiff with all doubts resolved in his favor and the allegation taken as true. That being so, when allegations are sufficient to sustain the defense of conditional privilege they will be, generally, sufficient to permit the introduction of evidence tending to prove abuse of the privilege or actual malice. Save in some extraordinary situation, allegations which are adequate for the admission of evidence to prove the defense of qualified privilege are adequate for the admission of evidence to negative that defense. It appears from the complaint in the instant case that defendant is entitled to raise the defense of conditional privilege. But this defense may be lost to it if plaintiff proves abuse of the privilege or actual malice. And, clearly, plaintiff may introduce evidence under the allegations for the purpose of proving abuse of the privilege or actual malice. Therefore, it is concluded that defendant's motion to dismiss the complaint for failure to state a claim upon which relief can be granted should be denied.

The conclusion to deny defendant's motion to dismiss requires that consideration be given its alternative motion to strike Paragraphs 5, 6, 7 and 8 of the complaint. It is alleged in these paragraphs, in substance, that upon being discharged, plaintiff made claim with the Labor Department of Puerto Rico for severance pay and overtime as is provided for by law (Section 20, Organic Act of Labor Department of Puerto Rico, approved April 14, 1931); that during a hearing on such claim held by the Labor Department, defendant, falsely and slanderously, repeated its charge that plaintiff had been engaged in procuring for prostitution; and, that, after said hearing defendant had compromised plaintiff's claim for severance pay and overtime. As respects defendant's motion to strike, the controlling allegations are contained in Paragraph 7 of this complaint.

Section 4 of "An Act Authorizing Civil Actions to recover Damages for Libel and Slander", enacted by the Legislature of Puerto Rico and approved on February 19, 1902, (Code of Civil Procedure of Puerto Rico, Ed. 1933, page 309) provides in part as follows: "Section 4. A publication or communication shall not be held or deemed malicious when made in any legislative or judicial proceeding or in any other proceeding authorized by law. * * *"

The effect of the above quoted portions of the statute is to confer absolute privilege upon any communication made in any of the proceedings contemplated therein. If the hearing held by the Labor Department on plaintiff's claim for severance pay and overtime, referred to in Paragraph 7 of the complaint, is a proceeding within the meaning of the phrase "or any other proceeding authorized by law" as used in said Section 4 of the Act of February 19, 1902, the utterance was absolutely privileged and such privilege constitutes a conclusive defense in an action based on that utterance.

It appears that the hearing on plaintiff's claim by the Labor Department, referred to in Paragraph 7 of the complaint, is a proceeding "authorized by law" within the meaning of Section 4 of the Act of February 19, 1902. The Labor Department is authorized to hold such a hearing by Act No. 122 of the Legislature of Puerto Rico, approved April 27, 1949, which statute requires the Commissioner of Labor to enforce labor protecting laws. * * *

It appears, upon examination, that this Statute (Act No. 122) has for its purpose the protection of the welfare of the workman and the furtherance of the public good, and that when hearings are held pursuant to its terms it is necessary, if those purposes are to be effectuated, that those called upon to give evidence therein must be protected against liability, civil or criminal, for communications given in evidence at such hearings. And this without regard for the motives of the witness or the truth or falsity of his statements. For otherwise, the giving of full, free and honest testimony, essential to the enforcement of such laws, will be discouraged. Therefore, communications made by witnesses in the course of such hearings, should be absolutely privileged in the same manner and to like extent as those made in the course of a judicial proceeding.

* * *

Clearly, then, the utterance of the defendant made during the Labor Department hearing referred to in Paragraph 7 of the complaint was absolutely privileged and that Paragraph 7 is, therefore, redundant in that it fails to state a claim upon which relief can be granted. It appears then, that defendant's motion to strike Paragraphs 5, 6, 7 and 8 should be granted.

The parties have agreed on hearing in open court that Paragraph 9 of the complaint should be stricken. And this Court being of the opinion that Paragraphs 5, 6, 7 and 8 should be stricken as redundant, defendant's motion for a more definite statement need be considered only with respect to the allegations of Paragraph 4 of the complaint.

As has been noted herein, conditional privilege is an affirmative defense which properly should be raised by its assertion in a responsive pleading. Consequently, when it appears from a complaint that the defense of conditional privilege may be available to a defendant, the allegations thereof should be reasonably adequate to permit the preparation of a responsive pleading asserting such defense. But when, in an action for slander, the complaint fails to set out substantially the utterance alleged to have been slanderously made or the facts relied upon to establish a publication of such utterance, such omission constitutes vagueness such as is a ground for granting a motion for more definite statement within the contemplation of rule 12(e). Obviously, when such material allegations are insufficient, it would be unreasonable to require the defendant to prepare a responsive pleading without a more definite statement of the pertinent facts.

Considering the allegations of Paragraph 4 of the complaint, the defense of conditional privilege is indicated. However, the allegations suffer from vagueness with respect to the utterance alleged to have been slanderously made and the facts relied upon to establish a publication of the utterance. It is concluded that the defendant here is entitled to a more definite statement setting forth substantially the words alleged to have been slanderously uttered and the facts relied upon to establish a publication thereof.

Defendant's motion to dismiss the complaint for failure to state a claim upon which relief can be granted is denied. Defendant's motion to strike Paragraphs 5, 6, 7 and 8 of the complaint is granted. Defendant's motion for a more definite statement with respect to the matters prescribed in this opinion, is granted. Paragraph 9 of the complaint is ordered stricken. The decisions herein reached are hereby made applicable to the second cause of action set out in the complaint.

NOTES AND QUESTIONS

1. To what extent could plaintiff in *Garcia* have phrased the complaint to avoid the granting of defendant's motions? How should plaintiff alter the complaint to satisfy the court's order for a more definite statement? Can he merely eliminate some of the allegations that gave rise to the conditional privilege?

2. Suppose defendant's motion under Federal Rule 12(e) had been denied by the court. What other means might he have used to learn the details of the alleged defamatory publication? What advantage, if any, is there to a motion under Federal Rule 12(e) as opposed to these other means?

3. Assume plaintiff in *Garcia* had not included any facts in the complaint indicating either a conditional or absolute privilege. How could defendant have raised these issues? See Federal Rule 8(c). Since privilege is obviously a matter of defense, why should it be significant whether plaintiff raises it in the complaint? Shouldn't these matters simply be ignored unless defendant pursues them in the answer? See ELLIS v. BLACK DIAMOND COAL MINING CO., 265 Ala. 264, 90 So.2d 770 (1956): "Even though a complaint at law shows on its face that the cause of action is barred by the statute of limitations the defense of the statute cannot be taken by demurrer." Compare BAGGETT v. CHAVOUS, 107 Ga.App. 642, 131 S.E.2d 109 (1963) (involving the anticipated defense of accord and satisfaction in a contract action): " 'Ordinarily the plaintiff, in his petition, need not anticipate or negative a possible defense. Where, however, such defense is anticipated, it must be effectively avoided, or the complaint is bad.' " On what basis, if any, can *Ellis* and *Baggett* be reconciled? Would it be fair to say that the decision in *Garcia* is consistent with *Ellis* and inconsistent with *Baggett*?

4. In most jurisdictions the timeliness of an action can be challenged by demurrer when the fact that the statute of limitations has run appears on the face of the complaint. See, e. g., Marks v. McCune Constr. Co., 370 P.2d 560 (Okl.1962); Annot., 69 A.L.R.2d 300 (1958). If that fact does not appear on the face of the complaint, it must, of course, be pleaded as an affirmative defense or raised by a motion for summary judgment.

Suppose that the defect appears on the face of the complaint but defendant, rather than demur, raises the issue as an affirmative defense in the answer. Should the defense be held waived by the failure to demur? Many cases hold no. But see DIXON v. SCHOONOVER, 226 Or. 443, 359 P.2d 115 (1961), stating the rule in Oregon that defendant must demur or lose the defense. Can the application of the rule in *Dixon* be justified if it is confined to the statute-of-limitations defense and not extended to other defenses that appear on the face of plaintiff's complaint?

In WAGNER v. FAWCETT PUBLICATIONS, 307 F.2d 409, 412 (7th Cir.1962), certiorari denied 372 U.S. 909, 83 S.Ct. 723, 9 L.Ed.2d 718 (1963), defendants failed to raise the statute-of-limitations defense either by motion to dismiss or by answer. The trial court, however, on its own motion, found that the defense appeared on the face of the complaint and therefore dismissed the action. The court of appeals affirmed the decision on other grounds but stated that the trial judge had acted improperly since any defense not raised by motion or in the answer is waived under the provisions of Federal Rule 12(h). Was this statement incorrect in light of the exception in that Rule expressly permitting the defense that the complaint fails to state a claim for which relief may be granted to be raised at any time during trial?

OWENS GENERATOR CO. v. H. J. HEINZ CO.

United States District Court, Northern District of California, 1958.
23 F.R.D. 121.

WOLLENBERG, District Judge. Both parties construe the complaint as based on fraud. The complaint sets forth a long involved series of transactions which, although preliminary to, are unconnected with the alleged fraudulent act. Each defendant made a *motion to dismiss* the complaint (1) as the action is barred by the applicable California statute of limitations (Code of Civil Procedure, §§ 338, subd. 4, 343), and (2) for failure to state a cause of action.[a] For purposes of these motions it is only necessary to consider plaintiffs' allegation that they "have commenced this action within 3 years after discovery by them of the facts constituting the fraudulent conduct of the defendants * * *". Except for this sparse allegation, the complaint does not particularize the details of the discovery.

The applicable California substantive law concededly governs this diversity action. Erie Ry. Co. v. Tompkins, 1938 * * *. This Court must determine just what part, if any, of the California law stated in the following paragraph is substantive under the Guaranty Trust Co. of New York v. York * * * "outcome of the action" rule. Even though Federal Rule of Civil Procedure 8 (c), 28 U.S.C.A., provides that the statute of limitations is a matter of affirmative defense, such rule in case of conflict with the state substantive law must give way to the demands of Erie Ry. Co. v. Tompkins * * *. While the line delineating the usual substantive-procedure dichotomy is often difficult of ascertainment, it is especially so under the Guaranty Trust rule. Each term "implies different variables depending upon the particular problem for which it is used." Guaranty Trust Co. of New York v. York, 326 U.S. at page 108, 65 S.Ct. at page 1469. What is accepted as procedural under state law may often be substantive under Guaranty Trust Co. v. York, supra, and binding on a federal court.

As a *general rule*, the defense of the statute of limitations of a common law cause of action is procedural. The defendant must affirmatively plead such defense or it is waived. However, as an exception to the above general

---

[a] The California statute provides that an action based on fraud or mistake must be commenced within three years, except that "the cause of action in such case [is] not to be deemed to have accrued until the discovery, by the aggrieved party, of the facts constituting the fraud or mistake."

rule, when a plaintiff commences an action more than three years after the fraudulent conduct the California law requires him to affirmatively plead *discovery* of the fraud within three years of the commencement of the action as "an element of [his] right of action". Lady Washington Consolidated Co. v. Wood, 1896, 113 Cal. 482, 486, 45 P. 809, 810. Specifically, the plaintiff must plead (1) the time and circumstances of the discovery of the facts constituting the fraud and (2) that said acts were committed under such circumstances that plaintiff would not be presumed to have any knowledge of them.

* * *

In applying the above principles this Court concludes that for purposes of satisfying Guaranty Trust Co. v. York, supra, it is sufficient to withstand a motion to dismiss based on the statute of limitations if the plaintiff merely alleges *discovery* of the fraud within three years of the commencement of the action. To this extent Federal Rule of Civil Procedure 8(c) is inapplicable. The state rule requiring the plaintiff to plead the *facts* of the discovery is procedural; it is merely the manner of stating the claim and as such is governed by federal law. Thus, except to the extent already indicated, the California rule in question does not "significantly affect the result of a litigation in a federal court * * *" so as to be binding on this court. Guaranty Trust Co. v. York, 1945, 326 U.S. 99, 109, 65 S.Ct. 1464, 1470.

* * *

This determination then leads to the question of whether, as a matter of federal law, the complaint must set forth the *facts* of the discovery in order to withstand a motion to dismiss for "failure to state a claim upon which relife [sic] can be granted." F.R.C.P. 12(b) (6). There are cases in this Circuit indicating the complaint must state such facts. * * * However, these cases antedate Conley v. Gibson, 1957, 355 U.S. 41, 78 S.Ct. 99, 2 L.Ed.2d 80.

* * *

[That case held that "]The Federal Rules of Civil Procedure do not require a claimant to set out in detail the facts upon which he bases his claim." * * * The Rules have adopted *"notice pleading"*. * * * The plaintiff merely need set forth facts showing a "claim" justifying relief; he need not set forth a cause of action. Thus, the federal cases cited by defendants rejecting "notice pleading" have been superseded by Conley v. Gibson * * *.

In accordance with the above opinion, the Court orders that the motions to dismiss the complaint be, and the same are hereby denied.

NOTES AND QUESTIONS

1. In PALMER v. HOFFMAN, 318 U.S. 109, 117, 63 S.Ct. 477, 482, 87 L.Ed. 645, 651 (1943), a diversity-of-citizenship case involving negligence, the Supreme Court discussed the scope of application and effect of Federal Rule 8(c) as follows:

> Respondent [plaintiff] contends * * * that the charge [that defendant had the burden of proving contributory negligence] was correct because of the fact that Rule 8(c) of the Rules of Civil Procedure makes contributory negligence an affirmative defense. We do not agree. Rule

8(c) covers only the manner of pleading. The question of the burden of establishing contributory negligence is a question of local law which federal courts in diversity of citizenship cases * * * must apply.

Does this statement conflict with the *Owens* decision? Does a valid distinction exist between the burden of pleading and the burden of proof for purposes of whether state or federal law should apply in a diversity case? See Cleary, *Presuming and Pleading: An Essay on Juristic Immaturity,* 12 Stan.L.Rev. 5, 14–15 (1959):

> Determining what elements are relevant to a case and allocating them between the parties does not of necessity have to be done at any particular stage of litigation. These questions can be left suspended in mid-air like Mohammed's coffin until the very end of the case, when it can be decided what are the responsibilities of each party and whether he has discharged them. This is the practice followed in small claims cases. However, decision prior to trial helps to eliminate uncertainties and lends direction and assurance to preparation and presentation. This is one of the useful functions of pleadings. Unhappily, certain characteristics of the legal mind at times enter in to divorce the pleadings from the realities.
>
>   * * *
>
> A modern instance, arising from seeming unwillingness to admit a mistake, is *Palmer v. Hoffman.* Almost simultaneously, the Supreme Court of the United States had adopted the Federal Rules, in which contributory negligence was listed as an affirmative defense, and had decided that in diversity cases the federal courts were required to apply the substantive law of the state. Moreover, the allocation of the burden of proof was held a matter of substance. Now in some states contributory negligence is not an affirmative defense, and plaintiff must establish that he was in the exercise of ordinary care. What procedure, then, was to be followed by a federal court in a diversity case in one of these states? Instead of saying, "Sorry, gentlemen, we did not anticipate this situation, and the pleading rule will have to be changed," the court said, "Rule 8(c) covers only the manner of pleading. The question of the burden of establishing contributory negligence is a question of local law which federal courts in diversity of citizenship cases * * * must apply."

2. Does uncertainty as to whether Rule 8(c) or a conflicting state pleading rule governs in a federal action create a trap for an unwary litigant? See Federal Rules of Civil Procedure 8(d), 12(h). What steps should an attorney take to safeguard her client's interests?

3. Would the decision in *Owens* be any different if the case were to be decided today, after the Supreme Court decision in *Hanna v. Plumer,* p. 284, supra?

B. PROBLEMS OF PLEADING IN SPECIFIC CASES

(i) Conditions

Read Federal Rule of Civil Procedure 9(c) in the Supplement.

PARKINSON v. ROBERTS

Supreme Court of Wyoming, 1958.
78 Wyo. 478, 329 P.2d 823.

Mr. Justice PARKER delivered the opinion of the court.

This is a suit by a "buyer" of real estate to recover from the "seller" a down payment after the seller had allegedly refused to complete the transaction. The salient facts shown by the record are: On May 19, 1956, plaintiff, Harry A. Parkinson, signed a Standard Purchase Offer, Acceptance and Receipt, offering to buy some thirty-six acres of land for a total price of $32,500: $2,000, deposit; $7,400, cash upon delivery of acceptable warranty deed; balance, $23,100, installment note and mortgage. Defendants, Fred M. and Mildred A. Roberts, the owners of the property, accepted the offer, and D. L. Holcomb, Roberts' real estate agent, signed the instrument as having received the deposit from plaintiff. * * * On June 8 Roberts had his attorney prepare a deed, note, and mortgage; and on June 9 he took them to his agent to conclude the sale. When the agent voiced the view that under paragraph two of the purchase offer the buyer had until the first day of July to pay the money, Roberts took the deed, note, and mortgage to * * * [plaintiff's attorney] demanding payment. [The latter] * * * said that he had to get in touch with plaintiff, then out of town. * * * On June 12 defendants' attorney sent a registered letter to plaintiff notifying him of the termination of said purchase offer by reason of failure "to seasonably complete" its terms, and on June 13 plaintiff delivered to defendants' agent a cashier's check for $7,400 payable to the defendants. The agent discussed the matter with defendants' attorney and on June 14 contacted Roberts who refused the $7,400 payment and said that if plaintiff could pay him all cash he could complete the deal, otherwise not.

In essence the controversy arose over the different views of the date upon which the buyer was obligated to pay the $7,400. The defendants insist that when the deed was tendered by the sellers after title had been found merchantable the balance of down payment was due immediately and that nonpayment was a cause for termination of the contract and retention of the former down payment as liquidated damages. Plaintiff on the other hand contends that he had until July 1 to complete the down payment.

The trial court found generally for plaintiff and against defendants, entering judgment for the $2,000. From this judgment defendants have appealed, presenting nine specifications of error. These deal primarily with three points: (a) Plaintiff's petition was insufficient to constitute a cause of action and hence the introduction of evidence as well as the granting of a judgment was improper   *   *   *.

On the first point, defendants prior to the trial objected to the introduction of any evidence because of the insufficiency of the petition. To the same purpose defendants after plaintiff had rested, and again at the conclusion of all testimony in the case, moved for judgment on the ground of insufficiency of the petition. The court ruled adversely in each instance, and these rulings are here presented as error—it being the view of the defendants that plaintiff had failed to allege any breach of duty by defendants upon which to predicate plaintiff's recovery. To that end defendants urge that the following allegation of plaintiff's petition is a conclusion of law, "although the Plaintiff performed all the conditions upon his part to be kept and performed the Defendants did refuse to keep and perform all the conditions on their part   *   *   *." Similar criticism is applied to other allegations. Plaintiff insists that such statements in the petition are within the meaning of § 3–1413, W.C.S.1945, which reads as follows:

> "In pleading the performance of conditions precedent in a contract, it shall be sufficient to state that the party duly performed all the conditions on his part; and if such allegation be controverted, the party pleading must establish, on the trial, the facts showing such performance."

Defendants in their argument make no reference to our statute but cite general authorities which condemn pleadings relying upon allegations by legal conclusion. Such general statements are, of course, to be considered controlling only when there is no applicable statute; and accordingly, we review the pleadings here to have the situation in mind. Plaintiff's allegation that he "performed all the conditions" was positive and without qualification. True, he did not use the word "duly" provided by the statute, which some courts in the past have held to be requisite. It was, however, a much stronger statement than if the word "substantially" had been used as in the case of Lusk Lumber Co. v. Independent Producers Consolidated, 35 Wyo. 381, 249 P. 790; Id., 36 Wyo. 34, 252 P. 1029. In the light of the relaxation of pleading rules obviating technical niceties, we think a positive pleading of performance meets the conditions which were intended to be imposed when the statute was passed; and plaintiff was, therefore, not obligated to plead the details of his performance.

There is a further reason why the defendants should not be heard to complain at any deficiency in the petition because of an improper allegation of performance: Where a defendant has repudiated the contract in issue, an allegation of performance by the plaintiff is unnecessary.   *   *   *   In Smith v. Gorsuch, 36 Wyo. 430, 434, 256 P. 664, 665, we said, "If the acts of the defendant showed that he renounced the contract and did not consider himself bound by it, plaintiff had the right to treat the contract as at an end."   *   *   *   In the present case, defendants said that for good cause they had elected to terminate the purchase offer and no longer had any obligation under it. Plaintiff's petition by a reasonable interpretation leaves little doubt that he intended to allege repudiation on the part of the defendants. It would not be either equitable or in accordance with good pleading principles to require him to plead performance when defendants had insisted that performance was not possible.

* * *

NOTES AND QUESTIONS

1. Is there any justification for holding that the allegation "plaintiff performed all conditions on its part" is a conclusion of law rather than an ultimate fact?

A large number of states have provisions related to pleading conditions similar to that quoted in *Parkinson*. Is the purpose of these provisions merely to simplify plaintiff's pleading burden? If plaintiff must prove performance of every condition precedent why shouldn't plaintiff be required to plead performance in detail? Note that under this system a denial of a general allegation of performance is legitimate if defendant seeks to challenge performance of only one of a number of conditions. Yet such a denial seems to place all conditions in issue. Would plaintiff be better advised to plead performance of each condition separately in the hope that defendant would deny only those allegations the defendant wished to contest at trial, thus admitting the remaining allegations and substantially reducing the need for plaintiff's proof? Is there some other way of making the pleadings more effective?

2. In REICHHOLD CHEMS., INC. v. WELLS, 189 Misc. 188, 189, 70 N.Y.S.2d 805, 806 (Sup.Ct.1947), the court held:

> Rule 92 of the Rules of Civil Practice provides that, in pleading the performance of a condition precedent in a contract, it is no longer necessary to state the facts constituting performance, but that the plaintiff may state, in general terms, " * * * that he, or the party whom he represents, duly performed all the conditions of such contract on his part." * * * This rule, being in derogation of the common law, is to be strictly construed * * * and cannot be extended by construction. In other words, the Legislature will not be presumed to intend innovations upon the common law, and its enactments will not be extended, in directions contrary to the common law, further than is indicated by the express terms of the rule or by fair and reasonable implications from its nature or purpose or the language employed * * *. Accordingly, if the condition is one to be performed by a third party and not the plaintiff, or a party whom it represents, the complaint must state the facts constituting performance, as at common law.

Does this decision make sense from a practical point of view? The present New York provision, N.Y.C.P.L.R. 3015(a), is set out in the Supplement in conjunction with Federal Rule 9(a). Would the *Reichhold* case be decided in the same fashion under the present New York provision? Why?

3. Suppose a plaintiff, as in *Parkinson*, intends to prove an excuse for nonperformance but instead of alleging the excuse in the complaint relies solely on a general allegation of performance. Should plaintiff be permitted to prove the

excuse at trial? *Compare* Winter & Giordano Landscape Contracting Corp. v. Colaizzo, 17 Misc.2d 450, 191 N.Y.S.2d 565 (Sup.Ct.App.T.1959) (proof of excuse excluded), *with* Erskine v. Upham, 56 Cal.App.2d 235, 132 P.2d 219 (2d Dist.1942) (proof of excuse not prohibited).

4. A number of jurisdictions have provisions similar to that in *Parkinson* but with some significant variations. For example, see Missouri Rule of Civil Procedure 55.18, which accompanies the text of Federal Rule 9(c) in the Supplement. What additional advantages are obtained under the Missouri provision? See generally Prashker, *Pleading Performance of Conditions Precedent: New York and Federal Rules*, 13 St. John's L.Rev. 242, 269–77 (1939). In light of the liberal pleading requirements of Federal Rule of Civil Procedure 8(a) (2), is there any need for Rule 9(c)? In those jurisdictions with provisions similar to the one in Missouri is there justification for retaining any requirement whatsoever that plaintiff plead performance of conditions precedent?

5. All the special provisions discussed above deal only with conditions precedent as distinguished from conditions subsequent. The former must be complied with before a right to relief exists; therefore they are considered essential elements of plaintiff's case and she must sustain the burden of proof, even if plaintiff is absolved from the burden of pleading. On the other hand, a condition subsequent is one that cuts off an existing right to relief and therefore is considered a matter of defense to be pleaded and proved by defendant. Why aren't there special provisions for the method of pleading conditions subsequent? Unfortunately, the distinction between conditions precedent and subsequent is far from a clear one. See, e. g., 5 Williston, *Contracts* § 667A, at 148, 151–52 (3d ed. 1961):

> What are generally called conditions subsequent in contracts are so called with little propriety. They are in substance conditions precedent to a duty of immediate performance and are subsequent only in form.
>
> * * * Though the nomenclature of these conditions is fixed as "conditions subsequent," the name should not cause it to be forgotten that except for purposes of pleading and proof they are conditions precedent.

Does this help to explain why nearly every jurisdiction has a provision permitting a general allegation of performance of conditions precedent?

(ii) Common Counts

Reread *Abadie v. Carrillo,* p. 365, supra.

LEONI v. DELANY

California District Court of Appeal, First District, 1948.
83 Cal.App.2d 303, 188 P.2d 765.

JONES, Justice pro tem. This is an action to recover upon a creditor's claim against the estate of Baltasar Corral. The argument of the appellant upon the rehearing is addressed to the point that the claim is not sufficient to support the complaint and particularly the second cause of action thereof. In this respect it is urged that a contract unenforceable because it is not in writing is presented and that on this account the claim can not be made the basis of a cause of action in any form. The claim is for personal services rendered to the decedent during his lifetime, and which are alleged to be of the reasonable value of $5,000.

The plaintiff filed suit on April 20, 1944, seeking to recover in two counts. In the first count recovery is sought upon the theory of an express contract, and the second is upon a common count to recover the reasonable value of services rendered. The case was tried before a jury which found for the plaintiff in the sum of $4,000, and from the judgment entered on the verdict the defendant has appealed.

The claim recites: "That on or about the 3d day of December, 1940, claimant and decedent, in his lifetime, entered into an oral agreement that, in consideration of the promise of claimant to marry said decedent at a future date when legally entitled to do so, and in consideration of services rendered, and to be rendered by said claimant, said decedent promised and agreed that, instead of paying claimant in cash for said services current wages, he would leave to claimant all of his property as compensation for the performance of said services, and that he would make claimant the beneficiary of a life insurance policy on his life, in the principal sum of $5,000.00, designating said claimant as beneficiary; that said promises were reiterated and restated by said decedent many times thereafter and that in consideration of said promises, said claimant accepted said offer of marriage aforesaid and agreed to perform certain services on behalf of said decedent, consisting of housekeeping, nursing care and attention, and that said claimant entered upon the performance of said services on or about December 3, 1940, pursuant to said agreement, and performed the same continuously up to the time of the death of said decedent, which occurred about October 13, 1943, and that said services so performed are of the reasonable value of $5,000.00."

   * * *

In regard to the sufficiency of the complaint, it is argued that the first count alleges a contract which the law requires to be in writing, and, since it is not, it is unenforceable; that the second count is based upon the same state of facts, and the same claim, and therefore must fall with the first count.

In support of his position the appellant has cited Rose v. Ames, 53 Cal. App.2d 583 * * *, and Hays v. Temple, 23 Cal.App.2d 690 * * *. These cases hold that it is proper to sustain a general demurrer to a common count separately pleaded in a complaint where the recovery sought on such count is obviously based on the same set of facts specifically pleaded in another count but which other count fails to state a cause of action. In this respect there is a distinction between a count which fails to state facts sufficient to establish the existence of a contract and one which pleads a contract which is unenforceable because it is not in writing. It is the unenforceability of an otherwise valid contract which gives rise to the right of relief through the medium of a common count. The law contemplates that when one receives a benefit at the expense or detriment of another, he should compensate the latter to the extent of the reasonable value of the benefit received.   *   *   *   In the cases of Hays v. Temple and Rose v. Ames, supra, relied upon by the appellant, the common counts were based upon the same facts relied on by the plaintiffs to make out a contract.   In each case it was held that the count relied upon to establish the contract was fatally defective in that it failed to state sufficient facts to show a contractual relation, and that the common count based upon the same facts must also fall.   That is not the question involved here. Where a contract is merely unenforceable because within the purview of the statute of frauds, an action generally will lie upon a common count.

It is also a well established principle of law that where a person seeks to recover for services rendered and there is a fair and reasonable doubt as to whether he is entitled to recover upon an express or implied contract, he is entitled to plead a claim upon each and to recover according to the proof.   This right to state different causes of action to meet such phases of the evidence as may be fairly and reasonably anticipated is recognized in Wilson v. Smith, 61 Cal. 209, where the plaintiff was in doubt as to whether he was entitled to recover upon a common count for the reasonable value of services rendered or whether his rights were fixed by an express contract.   He pleaded two causes of action, one upon an express contract and the other upon a common count. The court permitted the case to go to the jury upon both counts, and a judgment for the plaintiff was affirmed on appeal.   *   *   *

In Ruble v. Richardson, 188 Cal. 150, 204 P. 572, 574, the plaintiff brought an action for the breach of an alleged contract of a decedent to make provision for plaintiff in her will for personal services rendered.   The claim of the plaintiff was rejected by the executor and she sued in two counts.   The first count was for a recovery upon an alleged breach of the contract, and the second upon a quantum meruit.   When the case came on for trial, quoting from the opinion, "Plaintiff thereupon offered to prove by competent testimony other than her own, under the second cause of action, the fact of the rendition of the services to the deceased and their reasonable value.   Defendant objected upon the ground that the second count of the amended complaint did not state facts sufficient to constitute a cause of action.   The objection was sustained, and the trial court refused to permit plaintiff to make any proof under the quantum meruit."   In commenting upon this ruling the court there said: "We think the trial court was in error in holding that the second count of the complaint did not state a cause of action.   *   *   *   As to the contention that the claim did not apprise the executor of the nature of the services rendered, there should be considerable liberality in construing the pleadings when the foundation thereof is a claim against an estate.   The facts stated therein should not be too strictly construed, for such a claim need not be drawn with the precision which would render a complaint good against a special demurrer, and its sufficiency is not to be tested by the rules of pleading.   *   *   * "

Where two causes of action are so pleaded the plaintiff is entitled to introduce evidence upon both causes of action and the decision as to which of them is sustained is a matter for the jury.   *   *   *   If one count is not affected by error and there is substantial evidence to support a verdict with respect to it, it is immaterial that there may have been errors committed in connection with another count or that there is not sufficient evidence to sustain a verdict as to such other count. * * * One count sustained by sufficient evidence and free from error is all that is required to support a verdict. The specifications of error which the appellant has made with reference to giving and the refusal to give certain instructions, all pertain to the first cause of action and are immaterial to the second count.

If there is substantial evidence to support the second count the judgment must stand. * * * The evidence produced by the plaintiff here contains no suggestion of improbability, and if it were opposed, which it is not, it is such probative force that it would create a substantial conflict. It appears ample to support the second count. * * *

The judgment appealed from is affirmed.

GOODELL, Justice. * * * I dissent:

* * * The contract pleaded was not only unenforceable because not in writing but was one wherein plaintiff promised to marry decedent "at a future date when legally entitled to do so." Indeed that promise was alleged to be part of the consideration for decedent's promises. At the time when these promises were exchanged the plaintiff was a married woman. She did not commence divorce proceedings against her husband until after decedent's death.

In Smith v. McPherson, 176 Cal. 144, 146, 167 P. 875 * * * the court said: "* * * It is unquestionably true that a promise given under such circumstances is against the manifest policy of the law, and therefore wholly void. * * *"

Such being the settled law on the subject, it was prejudicial error to instruct the jury that such a contract, based in part on the promise of a married woman to marry "at a future date when legally entitled to do so," was based on a legal consideration.

It should be observed, further, that the contract pleaded in the first count was likewise carried into the second, for the second count by reference pleaded the filing of the creditor's claim, which claim set forth the plaintiff's promise to marry decedent "at a future date when legally entitled to do so".

* * *

NOTES AND QUESTIONS

1. In WESTERN TITLE INS. & GUAR. CO. v. BARTOLACELLI, 124 Cal.App.2d 690, 693–95, 269 P.2d 165, 168 (1st Dist.1954), the court stated:

> * * * [R]espondents concede that the third cause of action properly pleads a cause of action not subject to demurrer. * * * But it is their theory that the underlying transaction is fully pleaded in the first cause of action, that those allegations disclose that appellant has no capacity to sue * * * and that the first count is therefore subject to a general demurrer. They argue that it is the law that, where the plaintiff

alleges in one count all of the underlying facts, and that count is subject to a demurrer, the other counts of the complaint based on the same facts, even though such count or counts standing alone would be immune from attack, are likewise subject to demurrer.

* * * [The cited] cases do not support the broad legal proposition urged by respondents. * * * [They] involve complaints where in one count all of the facts are alleged, and then a common count is pleaded. In that event if the fact count is demurrable, so is the cause of action predicated upon the common count. But that rule is limited to pleadings involving a common count. The general well settled rule is that if any count of a multicount complaint states a cause of action, it is error to sustain a demurrer to the complaint as a whole. Each count stands or falls upon its own allegations. * * * The rule based on the common count exception is predicated on the anomalous nature of the common count in our system of pleading. The common count states simply a conclusion of law and discloses none of the facts upon which it is predicated. * * * The exception involving a common count cannot be extended to cases where any one count pleads facts alleging a good cause of action.

Is the special rule regarding common counts sensible? How can a court be positive that a common count is based on "the same facts" as an express contract count? Can't a plaintiff always rely upon the reasoning in *Leoni* whenever the express count is demurrable?

2. In 1955 Illinois amended its code, Ill.Stat.Ann. ch. 110, § 33(1), to abolish the use of the common counts. See also Iowa Rule of Civil Procedure 67, which can be found in Volume 58 of the Iowa Code Annotated. Is this approach preferable to that taken by the California courts?

3. Under the federal pleading rules common counts are clearly appropriate. See Official Forms 5, 6, and 8, which appear in the Supplement.

(iii) Negligence

DAVIS v. AIKEN

Court of Appeals of Georgia, 1965.
111 Ga.App. 505, 142 S.E.2d 112.

PANNELL, Judge. * * * The petition, omitting the formal parts and the allegations relating to injuries and doctor's bills, etc., is as follows:

"That on June 9, 1962, and at all times hereinafter mentioned, defendants Aiken and Hardy operated for profit the Dallas Drag Strip in Paulding County, Georgia.

"* * * Defendants Aiken and Hardy would solicit the participation of various drivers of automobiles in the races conducted at said Dallas Drag Strip. *Said drivers would furnish their own automobiles.* Said defendants would charge admission fees for spectators to enter the premises controlled by them and view said automobile racing. No grandstands were provided for the benefit of such spectators but they would view the races from *positions* alongside said paved track or strip.

" *   *   *

"Prior to permitting automobiles to race at said Dallas Drag Strip defendants Aiken and Hardy made only a cursory inspection of the same, inspecting only brakes and steering mechanism of the vehicle to be raced. *   *   *

"At or about 10:00 o'clock P.M. on the date aforementioned, plaintiff was approximately one-third (⅓) to one-half (½) of the way from the beginning to the end of said track or strip. *He was standing twelve (12) feet to fifteen (15) feet from the pavement watching automobiles race.*

"As plaintiff watched said automobiles race, *a piece of metal, the exact nature of which is unknown to plaintiff but is well known to the defendant Lane, came off one of said automobiles owned and driven by the defendant Lane.* Said piece of metal came across the pavement and unpaved strip and struck plaintiff on his left leg, fracturing the same, causing plaintiff to suffer great pain and disabling him.

" *   *   *

"Said injuries and damage were not caused by any fault on the part of the plaintiff but were directly and proximately caused by the following acts of negligence on the part of the defendants Aiken and Hardy, their agents, servants, representatives and employees, as follows: (a) By failing to exercise ordinary care in keeping the premises of the Dallas Drag Strip safe for spectators. (b) By failing to exercise ordinary care in not placing adequate fences or barricades along the paved strip or track so that spectators at the Dallas Drag Strip *would not be injured by parts coming off of automobiles.* (c) By failing to give any warning to spectators at the Dallas Drag Strip that *parts of automobiles* were likely to come off said automobiles and strike spectators, in violation of the requirements of ordinary care and diligence. (d) By failing to make adequate inspection of vehicles to be raced at Dallas Drag Strip to determine if the vehicles were in good mechanical condition and free from danger to the public, in violation of the requirements of ordinary care and diligence. (e) In sponsoring and operating a *dangerous instrumentality* in a public and crowded place, in violation of the requirements of ordinary care and diligence.

"Said injuries and damage were not caused by any fault on the part of the plaintiff but were directly and proximately caused by the following acts of negligence on the part of the defendant Lane, as follows: (a) In constructing and operating a 'dragster' *which was likely to lose parts when racing,* in violation of the requirements of ordinary care and diligence. (b) In operating a dangerous instrumentality in a public and crowded place, in violation of the requirements of ordinary care and diligence. (c) In failing to make an adequate inspection of his 'dragster' prior to racing it on June 9, 1962, in violation of the requirements of ordinary care and diligence.

"These acts of negligence were the direct and proximate cause of the injuries to plaintiff and he could not have avoided the results of said negligence by the exercise of ordinary care after he had learned of the negligence."

* * * [Defendants] demurred to the petition on the ground that it set forth no cause of action against * * * them. * * * These demurrers were sustained by the trial judge, and the plaintiff has * * * [appealed].

* * * It is alleged in the petition that no grandstands were provided for spectators "but they would view the races from *positions* alongside" the drag strip. This allegation is ambiguous and does not definitely disclose whether or not the positions alongside the drag strip were designated by the defendant operators or not. Construing this allegation most strongly against the pleader, this allegation would indicate that, while there were no grandstands, positions alongside the drag strips were provided for spectators. The further allegation that the plaintiff was standing 12 or 15 feet from the pavement is not an allegation that he was in a position reserved for spectators. * * * The allegation that a piece of metal, the exact nature of which is unknown to plaintiff, came off one of said automobiles driven by the defendant Lane, is not an allegation that the automobile was defective, nor is the allegation that the automobile was homemade an allegation that the automobile was defective.

The allegations of negligence against the defendants who operated the drag strip will be taken up in their order: (a) by failing to exercise ordinary care in keeping the premises safe for spectators. There is no allegation of fact in the petition showing that the drag strip was not safe for spectators, where spectators were supposed to be; (b) by failing to place fences or barricades along the track so that spectators would not be injured by parts coming off automobiles. Again there are no allegations of fact showing that spectators in their proper place would be injured by parts coming off automobiles, nor are there any facts alleged showing that the defendants knew, or in the exercise of ordinary care should have known, that parts would come off the automobiles. The same holds true of allegation (c) of failure to warn spectators that parts of automobiles were likely to come off. As to allegation (d) relating to their failure to make adequate inspection of the cars to determine if the vehicles were in good mechanical condition, etc., there is no allegation that the car was defective or that an inspection of the car, the failure of which inspection is alleged to be negligence, would have disclosed the defect, if any. In the absence of such allegations, we must assume that it would not have disclosed the defect even if the car was defective. Under these circumstances, the failure to inspect, even though negligent, could not possibly be the proximate cause of the injury to plaintiff. The operators of the drag strip are charged with negligence in operating and sponsoring a dangerous instrumentality. There are no allegations that any dangerous instrumentality was being operated, nor would the facts alleged support such allegation if there were such.

The owner and driver of the car is charged with negligence in operating and constructing a dragster "which was likely to lose parts when racing." There is no allegation that the plaintiff was injured by any *parts* lost from the dragster, nor is it alleged that this defendant knew, or in the exercise of ordinary care, should have known, that the automobile was likely to lose parts when racing; and, further, the petition specifically alleges that it was a piece of metal, the nature of which was unknown. The owner and driver is also charged with operating a dangerous instrumentality in a public and crowded place. This is a bare conclusion and there are no facts alleged showing that the automobile operated by the defendant Lane was a *dangerous instrumentality*. Lane is also charged with failing to make an adequate inspection prior to racing his car. The facts alleged do not disclose that an inspection would have discovered the defect, if any. If the inspection would not have discovered the defect, then the failure to inspect cannot be the proximate cause of any injury to the plaintiff. The whole case depends upon the failure of the petition to allege that an inspection would have discovered the alleged and claimed defect. If an inspection would have failed to disclose such alleged defect to any of the defendants, then the negligence alleged against them could not have been the proximate cause of the injury to the plaintiff.

The pleader in the present case contends that under the doctrine of res ipsa loquitur these various deficiencies may be inferred from the allegations of the petition. This doctrine does not apply to pleadings; it is only a rule of evidence. * * * Defective pleadings cannot be aided by the maxim "res ipsa loquitur." * * * It is not enough to aver facts from which the ultimate fact may be inferred unless the evidentiary facts pleaded are such as to demand the inference of its existence. * * * Essential averments will not be construed into pleadings. * * *

Judgment affirmed.

EBERHARDT, Judge (concurring specially).

Since it appears from the allegations of the petition that plaintiff was in an unprotected area alongside the track when he was injured, it must be concluded, [that he] * * * assumed the risk of injury, and the trial court did not err in sustaining the * * * demurrer.

* * *

[A dissenting opinion by Chief Judge FELTON has been omitted.]

HALL, Judge (dissenting). * * * Since my first semester in law school I have always been under the impression that a general allegation of negligence was good as against general demurrer. Also, that as against a general demurrer, no particular form is required in alleging causal connection between the negligence charged and the injury and that, as a general rule it is sufficient to make a direct allegation that plaintiff's injury resulted from or was caused by such negligence. * * * I am surprised to learn from five of my associates that they do not understand this to be the law. This would also come as somewhat of a shock to Mr. Chitty, Blackstone and Lord Coke if they were still alive. I am sure they would be amazed at the liberality of common-law pleading in their day compared to our present system.

* * *

In the latter part of 1964, the State Bar of Georgia conducted a survey on the question of whether our rules of pleading and practice should be simplified. The vote was overwhelmingly in the affirmative (For 2565—Against 287). A bill is now pending before the Georgia General Assembly that will exhaustively modernize civil pleading and practice rules in the trial courts of this State. The keystone of these rules is that "All pleadings shall be so construed as to do substantial justice." They seek to assure an adjudication on the merits rather than on myopic technicalities of pleadings.

If anyone has any doubts as to the need of this proposed legislation, let him read the opinions in this case.

NOTE

Note that the court in *Davis v. Aiken* construed the allegations "most strongly against the pleader." What justification is there for such a position? Compare *Garcia v. Hilton Hotels Int'l, Inc.*, p. 419, supra and see Brown v. Western Ry. of Alabama, 338 U.S. 294, 70 S.Ct. 105, 94 L.Ed. 100 (1949), discussed at p. 314, supra.

———

ARMSTRONG v. WALLACE, 8 Cal.App.2d 429, 436–37, 47 P.2d 740, 743–44 (3d Dist.1935). Plaintiff commenced an action for medical malpractice against her doctor alleging that she suffered injuries as a result of the doctor's failure to remove a sponge from her body upon completion of an operation. Plaintiff sought to obtain an instruction based on the doctrine of *res ipsa loquitur*. Defendant objected on the ground that the doctrine is inapplicable when plaintiff attempts in her complaint to set forth the specific acts of negligence. The court permitted the instruction, stating as follows:

In Atkinson v. United Railroads, 71 Cal.App. 82, * * * after a study of the rule in various states, it was found that in some the rule is absolute that where specific acts of negligence are pleaded, the right to rely upon the presumption resulting from the doctrine of res ipsa loquitur is totally lost. In other states the rule has been adopted that plaintiff is not deprived of the benefit of such doctrine merely because he has made allegations of specific omissions of duty; and in other jurisdictions, and the court places California among them, a qualified rule has been adopted to the effect "that, where plaintiff makes specific allegations of negligence, he must rely for his recovery upon, and he is limited to, such specific acts of negligence, and cannot recover for any other negligent act, but he is not deprived of the benefit of the doctrine of res ipsa loquitur so far as those specific acts of negligence are concerned. In other words, it is held in substance that the allegation of specific acts of negligence, while not depriving plaintiff of the benefit of said doctrine, relieves the carrier from the burden of disproving or meeting any other negligent acts than those alleged, for the reason that, having specified the acts of negligence, plaintiff will be confined to them and not allowed to prove or to recover upon other causes than those alleged."

NOTES AND QUESTIONS

1. The confusion and conflict as to the applicability of the doctrine of *res ipsa loquitur* when the pleadings are said to contain general allegations of negligence, specific allegations of negligence, or both have been well documented and discussed. See, e. g., Niles, *Pleading Res Ipsa Loquitur,* 7 N.Y.U.L.Rev. 415 (1929); Comment, *The Effect of Specific Allegations on the Application of Res Ipsa Loquitur,* 27 Fordham L.Rev. 411 (1958); Annot., 79 A.L.R. 48 (1932); Annot., 160 A.L.R. 1450 (1946); Annot., 2 A.L.R.3d 1335 (1965). Compare the practice in England as set forth in Bennett v. Chemical Construction (6B) Ltd., 3 All Eng.Rep. 822 (Ct.App.1971), holding that the application of *res ipsa* relates only to the proof of negligence and not to pleading.

2. Under the language of *Davis v. Aiken,* is it possible for a plaintiff, who must rely on the *res ipsa* doctrine, to plead a valid cause of action in a Georgia court?

3. Read Delaware Superior Court Rule (Civil) 9(b), which accompanies Federal Rule 9(b) in the Supplement. Note that the two provisions are identical except for the Delaware Rule's reference to negligence. In addition, Delaware has adopted Federal Rule 8 without material alteration. Is Delaware's inclusion of "negligence" sound? For a decision minimizing the effect of the Delaware provision, see Phillips v. Delaware Power & Light Co., 194 A.2d 690, 694–98 (Del.Super.1963).

(iv) Fraud and Defamation

CONSUMERS TIME CREDIT, INC. v. REMARK CORP.

United States District Court, Eastern District of Pennsylvania, 1964.
227 F.Supp. 263.

KRAFT, District Judge. Consumer Time Credit, Inc. (Consumers) brought this action against six corporations and three individuals, asserting claims based, inter alia, upon an accounts receivable financing agreement between Consumers and Remark Corp. (Remark), one of the corporate defendants.

Plaintiff commenced its suit by writ of fraudulent debtor's attachment, pursuant to the Pennsylvania Rules of Civil Procedure, and attached bank accounts and other personal property of defendants Sara L. Bokser, Lewis Bokser and Lewis Bokser, Inc.

The case is before us on petitions to dissolve the attachments, which allege, in part, that the complaint fails to set forth ground for attachment.

* * *

Count 1 of the complaint states a claim against Remark alone, and alleges that by reason of sundry defaults, breaches of warranty, misrepresentations and other breaches of the accounts receivable financing agreement, the entire indebtedness owing by that defendant to plaintiff has matured and is now immediately due and payable.

Paragraph 5 of this Count avers:

"5. The defaults, breaches of warranty, misrepresentations and other violations of the terms and provisions of the aforesaid accounts receivable financing agreement, include, inter alia, the unlawful conversion and fraudulent diversion by defendant of merchandise and proceeds of at least 85 of the accounts receivable and/or chattel paper transactions assigned by defendant to plaintiff, constituting a conversion and diversion of approximately $45,000.00 worth of the collateral assigned to plaintiff as security."

* * *

Count 4 is directed against all defendants except Remark. Paragraph 13 of this Count is as follows:

"13. The defaults, breaches, misrepresentations and other violations of the accounts receivable financing agreement by Remark Corp., were made or done with the intent to defraud the plaintiff and such conduct was participated in and joined in by defendant, Lewis Bokser, defendant, Maurice Kramer and the other corporate defendants, who as guarantors and sureties of Remark Corp., and who by reason of substantial identity of directorship and principal control, acted in concert with Remark Corp., and its principals to conceal property from the plaintiff and to transfer property so as to place the same out of reach of the plaintiff. The property concealed or transferred, included not only property owned by Remark Corp., and/or the other defendants, but also property or proceeds thereof in which the plaintiff has a security interest pursuant to the provisions of the Pennsylvania Uniform Commercial Code."

In our view paragraphs 5 and 13, read together, sufficiently allege that Remark, at least, has concealed and transferred its property with intent to defraud the plaintiff. We agree with petitioners that the attachments can be sustained only if plaintiff has alleged that *petitioners* have concealed or transferred *their* property, or were about to, with the requisite intent. * * *

The complaint avers a concealment and transfer of property "with the intent to defraud the plaintiff." We think this is a sufficiently particular statement of "the circumstances constituting fraud," [as required by Rule 9(b)]. In Barron & Holtzoff, Federal Practice and Procedure, Rules Edition, Vol. 1A, § 302, p. 217, it is stated:

"There has been a tendency in some, though far from all, cases, to give Rule 9(b) an over-strict reading, which seemingly fails to take into account the general simplicity of pleadings contemplated by the rules. [See Form 13 in the Appendix following the Federal Rules.] * * *

As one court has correctly observed, in upholding such a simple allegation, the circumstances constituting the fraud could not have been pleaded with greater particularity without pleading evidence.

> "In view, too, of the further provision of Rule 9(b) that malice, intent, knowledge and other condition of mind may be averred generally, the sufficiency of a pleading must largely depend upon the nature of the case, the complexity or simplicity of the transaction or occurrence, the relationship of the parties and the determination of how much circumstantial detail is necessary to give notice to the adverse party and enable him to prepare a responsive pleading."

In view of the nature of the present case, and considerations, we believe that the complaint sufficiently apprises petitioners of the scope and character of plaintiff's claim.

HOLLIDAY v. GREAT ATLANTIC & PACIFIC TEA CO.

United States Court of Appeals, Eighth Circuit, 1958.
256 F.2d 297.

GARDNER, Chief Judge. This appeal is from a judgment for the defendant based upon a jury verdict in an action in which appellants as plaintiffs sought to recover damages upon three causes of action. We shall refer to appellants as plaintiffs.

[The action sought damages for false imprisonment, slander, and assault and battery. Plaintiffs, minors, charged that an employee of defendant had searched them and falsely accused them of shoplifting. In the first part of its opinion, the Court of Appeals rejected several challenges by plaintiff to the district court's rulings regarding the admissibility of certain evidence and its instruction withdrawing the question of punitive damages from the jury's consideration.]

* * *

It is finally urged that the court erred in directing a verdict for defendant on the issue of slander. Each plaintiff pleaded that:

> "* * * while plaintiffs were in defendant's store for the purposes aforesaid, the defendant, its agents, servants and employees did wrongfully, wantonly and maliciously spoke of and concerning the plaintiff certain defamatory and slanderous words, to-wit: that plaintiff had stolen some of defendant's merchandise, whereby plaintiff has been greatly injured in his good name and fame to his damage in the sum of $2,500.00 actual damages and by reason of the malicious and wanton acts and conduct of defendant, its agents, servants and employees, defendant should be required to pay plaintiff in addition to the actual damages aforesaid, punitive damages in the sum of $10,000.00."

In an action for slander or libel the words alleged to be defamatory must be pleaded and proved. It is also essential that it be alleged that the accusation was untrue. * * * In Fritschle v. Kettle River Co., 346 Mo. 196, 139 S. W.2d 948, * * * the Supreme Court of Missouri states the rule with reference to the sufficiency of the pleading and proof in an action for libel or slander as follows:

> "Because of plaintiff's failure to set out any words claimed to have been used and because of his failure to allege that the statement made was false, we hold that the trial court properly sustained defendants' demurrers."

The actual words allegedly used by defendant's employee are not set out but only plaintiffs' conclusion as to the import as to whatever words may have been used. It is to be observed too that it is not alleged that the allegedly defamatory words used were false.

* * * The judgment appealed from is * * * affirmed.

NOTES AND QUESTIONS

1. Are the decisions in *Consumers Time Credit* and *Holliday* in harmony with the spirit of the federal pleading rules? Are they consistent with one another? Compare *Garcia v. Hilton Hotels Int'l, Inc.*, p. 419, supra.

2. In CARROLL v. PARAMOUNT PICTURES, INC., 3 F.R.D. 95, 97 (S.D.N.Y.1942), the court held as follows:

> Defendant further complains that the alleged libelous matter upon which the plaintiff predicates his second cause of action has not been set forth in full in the complaint. Upon this motion to dismiss this cause of action every fair inference of the pleading must be taken in the pleader's favor. Here the vehicle of the alleged libel, a motion picture, militates against a detailed pleading of the libelous matter. Plaintiff's second cause of action appears to indict the entire motion picture in question as an inferior production and pleads that the imputation of its authorship to the plaintiff, an allegedly well-known and competent producer, constitutes a libel upon the plaintiff. The practical difficulty of specifying the alleged libelous material in a complaint based upon a libelous motion picture has been recognized in New York State courts. In Brown v. Paramount Publix Corp., 240 App.Div. 520, 270 N.Y.S. 544, the court held under similar circumstances that a plaintiff need only plead the ultimate and not the evidentiary facts. * * * Certainly as much, if not more, latitude is permissible under the Federal Rules of Civil Procedure which make simple and concise pleadings mandatory. Rule 8(e) (1) F.R.C.P. Libel is not one of the matters listed in Rule 9, F.R.C.P., of which all the averments "shall be stated with particularity."

Is this opinion consistent with those in *Holliday* and *Garcia*?

3. Many states have enacted statutes or promulgated rules governing pleading in fraud and defamation cases. The requirements as to pleading fraud are generally similar to those found in Federal Rule 9(b) and are designed to ensure more detailed allegations than might otherwise be required. See, e. g., N.Y.C.

P.L.R. 3016(b).   On the other hand, special statutes dealing with libel and slander are generally intended only to relax the requirement that the application of defamatory words to the plaintiff must be shown by detailed allegations. See, e. g., Missouri Rule of Civil Procedure 55.22.

4.   In almost all jurisdictions truth is a defense to an action for libel or slander.   Why then should plaintiff be required to plead that the allegations were false?   In FOWLER v. DONNELLY, 225 Or. 287, 358 P.2d 485 (1960), the court took the same position as did the court in *Holliday*:

> In the absence of special circumstances a defamatory publication, in order to be actionable, must be false * * *.   Accordingly, an averment of falsity is necessary to enable the complaint to state a cause of action.   * * *   Truth is a defense and must be alleged by the defendant * * *.   The defendant has the burden of establishing his plea of truth with evidence * * *.   The purpose of requiring parties to set forth their facts in their pleadings is to bring the facts to light.   By going through that process each party gains knowledge of the contentions of his adversary, and the result of their efforts provides the man on the bench, so far as the individual case is concerned, with something in the nature of a compass.   The sooner that each party states his position the greater is the service to the administration of justice which the exchange of pleadings can render.

> There is nothing novel in the requirement that a complaint in a libel action must allege falsity in order to set forth a cause of action and yet require that if the defendant relies upon truth as his defense he must allege and prove it, for we have a corresponding situation in some other types of action.   For example, a plaintiff who sues after maturity upon a debt which arose out of contract must allege nonpayment in order to enable his complaint to state a cause of action, but he need not offer evidence of non-payment.   Payment is an affirmative defense. If a defendant depends upon payment as his defense he must allege and prove it. * * *

One justice dissented as follows:

> * * *   It is conceded by the majority that it is defendant's burden to plead and prove truth as an affirmative defense.   What purpose is served, then, by requiring plaintiff to allege falsity? * * *   To insist upon such surplusage is to make a fetish out of technical procedure. It should not be necessary to allege in the complaint anything more than is necessary to apprise the defendant of the theory of plaintiff's cause of action.   Can it be seriously contended that defendant is not so apprised by a complaint which sets out the alleged defamatory words and charges that he wrote and published them "wilfully and maliciously intending to defame plaintiff; thereby holding plaintiff up to public scorn, contempt and ridicule all to plaintiff's general damage in the sum of $25,000"?   In what way would the addition of the word "falsity" to the above allegation aid the defendant in the preparation or prosecution of his defense?

C. PLEADING DAMAGES

ZIERVOGEL v. ROYAL PACKING CO.

St. Louis Court of Appeals, Missouri, 1949.
225 S.W.2d 798.

McCULLEN, Judge. This action was brought by respondent as plaintiff against appellant as defendant to recover damages for injuries plaintiff alleged she sustained as a result of a collision between an automobile driven by her and a motor vehicle (tractor-trailer, also referred to as truck) operated by defendant's employee. A trial before the court and a jury resulted in a verdict and judgment in favor of plaintiff against defendant in the sum of $2000.00. After an unavailing motion for a new trial defendant appealed.

Petition.

* * * Describing her injuries plaintiff alleged in her petition that "Plaintiff sustained injuries to her neck, back, spine and nervous system and was otherwise injured and her earning capacity has been permanently impaired."

* * *

For its first point defendant contends that the trial court erred in permitting plaintiff's counsel in his opening statement, over defendant's objection, to state to the jury that plaintiff's blood pressure had increased by the accident and in refusing to declare a mistrial on defendant's motion because of such statement and in permitting plaintiff to introduce evidence over defendant's objection of plaintiff's increased blood pressure and in refusing to declare a mistrial on defendant's motion because of the introduction of such evidence and also in permitting [plaintiff] over defendant's objection to present evidence of an injury to her shoulder. Defendant points out that plaintiff's petition does not allege that she was caused to develop high blood pressure or that such an existing condition was aggravated by the accident. Defendant further contends that the evidence does not establish that a continuing elevation in blood pressure is an inevitable or necessary result of the injuries averred and that the evidence of such condition was, therefore, inadmissible. In support of these contentions defendant cites a number of cases which apply the principle of law that before a plaintiff can recover for a physical condition claimed to have resulted from the negligence of another, such condition must be pleaded or the evidence must establish the condition as being the inevitable or necessary result of injuries which are particularly set out in the petition. The reason underlying such decisions is that it would be unjust to permit a plaintiff to take advantage of a defendant at the trial by presenting evidence of injuries of which the defendant did not have the kind of notice required by law, namely, through allegations in plaintiff's petition.

It is true the evidence in this case does show, as plaintiff contends, that defendant had actual notice before trial of plaintiff's increased blood pressure, which she claimed was a result of the collision, through a statement made by plaintiff to that effect to the Claim Agent of defendant's insurer and through an examination of plaintiff made by defendant's doctor, Dr. Leo A. Will, and reported by him to said Claim Agent as well as through plaintiff's deposition which was taken by defendant. However, we are of the opinion that although it cannot be said that defendant was "surprised" when plaintiff presented evidence at the trial relating to the condition of her blood pressure, defendant nevertheless had the right to object to such evidence on the ground that it related to "special damages" which were not pleaded in plaintiff's petition. Although defendant could not have claimed "surprise" upon the introduction of such evidence, it was not required to do so and its objections at the trial to such evidence in the absence of proper allegations thereon in plaintiff's petition should have been sustained. No such special damages were pleaded by plaintiff, nor did plaintiff ask leave to amend her petition to include such special damages which she could have done on such terms, at that stage of the proceedings, as the court should order. However, plaintiff did not amend her petition, nor ask leave to amend, and defendant had the right to object to the evidence in question.

* * * [Section 52 of the Civil Code] expressly provides: "When items of special damage are claimed, they shall be specifically stated." * * *

It has been held by our Supreme Court that a specific personal injury which is not the necessary or inevitable result of an injury alleged in the petition constitutes an element of "special damage" which must be specifically pleaded before evidence thereof is admissible. See State ex rel. Grisham v. Allen, 344 Mo. 66, 124 S.W.2d 1080. * * *

In the case at bar the only allegations in plaintiff's petition with respect to the injuries she suffered as the result of the collision were as follows: "Plaintiff sustained injuries to her neck, back, spine and nervous system and was otherwise injured and her earning capacity has been permanently impaired." It will be observed that not only is there no mention of increased blood pressure but no injuries are alleged from which it can reasonably be said that an increase in blood pressure was an inevitable or necessary result. Nor was there any evidence to show that the increased blood pressure was the necessary or inevitable result of the injuries alleged in the petition.

Plaintiff refers to form 10 of the Appendix of Illustrative Forms to the Federal Rules of Civil Procedure, 28 U.S.C.A., approved by the United States Supreme Court and argues that the allegation in her petition "and was otherwise injured" is in accord with said form 10 and that the trial court herein properly ruled that the allegations in her petition were sufficient to justify the admission of the evidence of plaintiff's increased blood pressure. Plaintiff's argument ignores Section 52, supra, of the new Civil Code which expressly requires "special damages" to be "specifically stated." We are not at liberty to ignore said section which we believe is conclusively determinative of the point under consideration.

* * *

What we have said herein with respect to the evidence of plaintiff's increase of blood pressure applies with equal force to the evidence of the injury to plaintiff's shoulder. In the absence of any allegation in plaintiff's petition relating to that injury, it was error for the court to admit such evidence.

* * *

On Motion for Rehearing or, in the Alternative, to Transfer to Supreme Court.

McCULLEN, Judge. Plaintiff has filed an extended motion for rehearing in which she earnestly argues that this court committed error in holding that the trial court erred in permitting plaintiff to introduce evidence of her high blood pressure when no such damage was pleaded in plaintiff's petition. * * *

It is contended by plaintiff that Section 52 of the Civil Code of Missouri, Mo.R.S.A. § 847.52, which provides that when "items of special damage" are claimed "they shall be specifically stated," having been copied verbatim from Rule 9(g) of the Federal Rules * * *, the "construction" given said rule 9(g) by the Federal Courts must be given to Section 52, supra.

* * *

In the lengthy argument of plaintiff she repeatedly refers to the "construction" given to Federal Rule 9(g) but nowhere is there cited any authority showing what such "construction" was in any kind of a case. * * * Plaintiff evidently has found no case in point on the facts of this case (just as we have found none) because, as we see it, the words of both Federal Rule 9(g) and the state statute, Section 52, supra, are so simple, plain and unambiguous that no one has ever heretofore contended in a court of last resort that a party could plead only "general" damages and recover for "special" damages.

* * *

[Motion denied.]

NOTES AND QUESTIONS

1. In EPHREM v. PHILLIPS, 99 So.2d 257, 260–61 (Fla.App.1st Dist. 1957), a case arising out of an auto accident, plaintiff, who alleged only that she was "painfully, seriously and permanently injured, bruised and lacerated in and throughout her head, body and limbs," sought and was permitted to collect damages for a required abortion. The court held:

> Within the allegations of the complaint it is clear that plaintiff might show any change in her physical condition due to the injuries sustained, and such was the abortion. Where only such damages as may be reasonably expected to follow an injury are claimed, no allegation of special damages is required. In personal injury actions proof that the plaintiff's pain and suffering resulted in and were aggravated by an abortion is

clearly admissible. So far as the abortion augments the physical injury, pain or suffering, then so far is it proper to be considered on the question of damages.

For the foregoing reasons we hold that a claim based upon pain and anguish, suffered as a consequence of injuries sustained from the negligent act of another, is not an item of special damages merely because such pain and anguish resulted in and was aggravated by an abortion.

Can *Ziervogel* and *Ephrem* be reconciled? Did plaintiff's lawyer in *Ziervogel* hurt his client's case by pleading too much? See THACKER v. WARD, 263 N.C. 594, 140 S.E.2d 23, certiorari denied 382 U.S. 865, 86 S.Ct. 134, 15 L.Ed.2d 104 (1965), in which the court refused to permit a plaintiff who had alleged physical injuries to his body and nervous system to collect damages for unpleaded psychological disturbances that resulted from the physical injuries but had an emotional, rather than a physical, basis.

2. Should medical bills incurred as a result of personal injuries be considered special damages requiring special pleading or should they be provable as a logical and necessary result of the injuries themselves? See Sossamon v. Nationwide Mut. Ins. Co., 243 S.C. 552, 135 S.E.2d 87 (1964), which held a general allegation of damages sufficient to permit proof of doctor and hospital bills. There are many cases that take a contrary view. For a general discussion of the authorities, see Annot., 98 A.L.R.2d 746 (1964).

Elements of special damages that must be pleaded if proof of them is to be allowed at trial also may appear in other types of actions. In contract actions, for example, special damages are those that would not normally be foreseen as the consequence of defendant's breach. Special damages can be recovered in contract actions from a defaulting party who was informed that they might result from a breach. See 5 Corbin, *Contracts* § 1007 (1964).

"Special Damages" in Contract.

3. Although the normal consequence of failing to plead special damages is being barred from proving them at trial, it is important to note that with regard to a few types of cases the existence of special damages is an integral part of the claim, and the failure to plead them renders the complaint subject to a demurrer or motion to dismiss. This is true, for example, in many slander actions in which the words are not considered actionable *per se.* See, e. g., Weiss v. Nippe, 5 A.D.2d 789, 170 N.Y.S.2d 642 (2d Dep't 1958). Should the degree of specificity required in pleading special damages be the same in all cases or should it depend on whether the special damages are simply added elements of injury or are an integral part of the claim? Does the fact that a distinction along these lines is drawn by the courts of the state in which the federal court is sitting have any relevance to a federal court's construction of Federal Rule 9(g)?

3. PRAYER FOR RELIEF

Read Federal Rules of Civil Procedure 8(a) (3) and 54(c) in the Supplement.

BAIL v. CUNNINGHAM BROTHERS, INC.

United States Court of Appeals, Seventh Circuit, 1971.
452 F.2d 182.

PELL, Circuit Judge. * * * The final contention raised by defendant on this appeal is that the judgment against defendant should be remitted from $135,000 to $85,000.

Plaintiff's original complaint sought damages in the amount of $100,-000. On the morning the trial was to begin, plaintiff presented a motion to amend the complaint requesting that the ad damnum clause in the complaint against defendant be increased from $100,000 to $250,000. The district judge denied this motion " * * * for the reason that the case is at issue, it is set for trial this date, and the defendant was not given notice of the filing of the motion."

The jury notwithstanding the complaint-contained limitation of $100,-000 returned a verdict for the higher figure of $150,000. In a post-trial motion Bail sought and was granted leave to amend the complaint by increasing the ad damnum clause to $150,000. Bail had received $15,000 from another defendant originally named in the complaint in return for "a covenant not to pursue." This payment had been set off, leaving the final judgment of $135,000. It has been said that the office of the ad damnum in a pleading is to fix the amount beyond which a party may not recover on the trial of his action. Gable v. Pathfinder Irrigation District, 159 Neb. 778, 68 N.W.2d 500, 506 (1955). However, an examination of the cases reveals that the rule thus enunciated, if indeed it still be a rule, has flexibility to the virtual point of nonexistence. Thus, in *Gable* the court pointed out that there was also a general rule that amendment may be made to a pleading which did not change the issues or affect the quantum of proof as to a material fact and that no good reason was apparent for not applying this privilege of amendment to the ad damnum clause. *Id*. at 506.

In the case before us, even though it is a diversity case, a matter of procedure is involved and governed, therefore, entirely by the federal rules. Riggs, Ferris & Geer v. Lillibridge, 316 F.2d 60, 62 (2d Cir. 1963).

* * *

There is substantial authority for the proposition that pursuant to Rule 54(c) a claimant may be awarded damages in excess of those demanded in his pleadings. * * *

Cunningham, however, contends that the authority is not all one way * * * [citing, inter alia,] the case of Wyman v. Morone, 33 A.D.2d 168, 306 N.Y.S.2d 115 (1969), to the effect that under New York law the granting of the motion to increase the amount sued for, after a jury has rendered its verdict, is an abuse of discretion. We, of course, in view of Rule 54 (c) are not in any way bound by the interpretation of this lower court of New York as to the law of that state but do observe that there apparently was some significance attached to the extended delay in moving to amend and in any event feel that the dissenting opinion in *Wyman* swims with the main current of judicial thinking in this particular area as opposed to the contrary movement of the majority opinion.

The difficulty, if any there be, posed here, however, lies in the fact that Bail attempted to amend the ad damnum clause in advance of trial and the right of amendment was denied by the court. In this respect the case would seem to be one of first impression as no case involving this exact factual situation has been brought to our attention. It appears to us that the motion to amend, even though on the morning of the trial, should have been granted. It not having been granted, our inquiry must be as to whether the normal rule prevailing under 54(c) should be varied. In our opinion, it should not be.

On oral argument, inquiry was directed to counsel for Cunningham as to how the conduct of the trial would have differed if the pretrial motion to amend had been granted. The thought was ventured that the attorneys might have tried the case differently, that they might have argued damages to the jury (which subject they conspicuously avoided in final argument) or they might have cross-examined more extensively. With hindsight, they may well think that they should have argued damages even if no post-trial amendment were to be permitted and the limitation on recovery were left at $100,000. In essence, however, we cannot see that the quantum of proof as to any material fact varied or that any change of issues resulted, or would have resulted, from an amendment of the ad damnum clause. Counsel competently and vigorously defended on the theory of no liability whatsoever, and we can find no basis for an assumption that $100,000 is such an insignificant amount that counsel somehow would try harder if they knew that the exposure might be $250,000.

No doubt if the ad damnum had sought some insignificant amount such as $1,000, the case would not have received the attention from trial counsel that it did. In the case before us, however, defense counsel were never confronted with an insignificant amount.

It perhaps is unfortunate that the district court did not permit the amendment as requested in advance of trial so as to eliminate the claim that the defendant somehow was prejudiced in relying on this. Finding, however, no real prejudice we will follow the rule generally prevailing to the effect that even though the party was not successful in demanding such relief in his pleadings, he was entitled thereto under the evidence. At least the jury thought that he was so entitled, and we find no basis for upsetting their determination irrespective of whether we would have reached this exact amount in assessing damages. Further, the district court who heard the evidence on a front line basis was satisfied that the amendment should be allowed on a post-trial motion.

Although Bail's counsel under the constraint of the court's ruling did confine his final argument to an amount within the unamended ad damnum clause, it is not entirely unreasonable to assume that he and his client would have been well satisfied with a verdict of $100,000 and, indeed, it does not stretch the imagination too far to conceive that a settlement could have been arrived at for less than that figure if the general practical pattern of settlements in personal injury cases had had any application here. Nevertheless, the case was not settled and inasmuch as the damages cannot be shown to be excessive, nor to have been dictated by passion and prejudice, the verdict will stand. While Cunningham finds some source of complaint in the fact that plaintiff's counsel himself argued less than $100,000 and while it may not now be much solace to Cunningham, nevertheless there was the trial advantage to the defense that plaintiff was precluded from arguing a larger sum.

What we have had to say with regard to the ad damnum clause is indicative of the anachronistic character of the clause. Indeed, there is a well publicized school of thought that it should be done away with altogether. * * * It is true that in some suits it is necessary to allege a jurisdictional amount, but ordinarily this is far less than the ad damnum prayer and can be gleaned in most instances from the pleadings and discovery procedures.

As a matter of fact in the case before us it appears from the record that the jury was in no way aware of the amount of the ad damnum in the complaint and, therefore, clearly their verdict did not reflect a conscious arrival at a figure in excess of the ad damnum.

* * *

Affirmed.

NOTES AND QUESTIONS

1. Is the damage prayer anachronistic as the court in *Bail* suggests? Should it be abolished? What problems would this create? Would elimination of the ad damnum clause have avoided the uncertainty upon which defendant in *Bail* based the claim of prejudice? Suppose the court had found defendant to have been unduly prejudiced by the trial court's refusal to grant plaintiff's pretrial amendment. In that case should the jury award have been reduced? What other remedy is available? See pp. 898–912, infra.

2. Note that under Federal Rule 54(c) relief is limited by the ad damnum clause in default cases. Why? See 10 Wright & Miller, *Federal Practice and Procedure: Civil* § 2663 (1973).

3. Why should courts ever permit relief to be granted that is different from or in excess of plaintiff's demand? The Iowa courts apparently never do. See STROMBERG v. CROWL, 257 Iowa 348, 353, 132 N.W.2d 462, 465 (1965):

> Plaintiffs' petition prays for $700, [plus interest] * * *.
> The judgment entered is for $715, the amount proved by plaintiffs, [plus interest] * * *.
>
> Plaintiffs admit they made some mistake in calculating the amount due them and their recovery cannot exceed the amount they requested.

The court then modified the judgment to permit recovery of $700.00 plus interest. See also Bower v. Certain-Teed Prods. Corp., 216 Ga. 646, 119 S.E.2d 5 (1961); McKelvie v. Hackney, 58 Wash. 2d 23, 34, 360 P.2d 746, 753 (1961).

4. How far does the mandate found in Federal Rule 54(c) go? Suppose a party claims a certain element of damage on the basis of proof at trial despite the fact that the pleadings contained no claim or indication of a claim that would permit such recovery? In CONVERTIBLE TOP REPLACEMENT CO. v. ARO MFG. CO., 312 F.2d 52, 58 (1st Cir.1962), modified on other grounds 377 U.S. 476, 84 S.Ct. 1526, 12 L.Ed.2d 457 (1964), in which plaintiff sued for patent infringement, defendant not only answered, alleging, *inter alia*, the defense of patent misuse, but also counterclaimed for a declaratory judgment that plaintiff had misused the patent. The trial court's finding against defendant on the issue of misuse was not challenged on appeal. Defendant argued, however, that having asserted a counterclaim it could recover, under Rule 54(c), any relief to which it was entitled, and that the record in the case showed that plaintiff had violated the federal antitrust laws, which permitted defendant to recover treble damages. The court denied the claim as follows:

> * * * The short answer to this contention is that Aro has never pleaded a cause of action under the antitrust laws.
>
> * * * [Rule 54(c)] does not authorize a grant of the relief requested. That Rule should be liberally construed to grant a prevailing party substantial justice. But it is not to be so liberally construed as to conflict with the requirement of Rule 8(a) * * *. There is no merit whatever in this appeal.

Is this decision sound? Is it merely a return to the generally discarded theory-of-the-pleadings doctrine? See pp. 367–79, supra.

5. In HANEY v. BURGIN, 106 N.H. 213, 208 A.2d 448 (1965), plaintiff originally brought suit for $15,000. After the first day of trial plaintiff was permitted to amend the complaint to request $25,000. Two days later, when defendant's sole witness strongly supported plaintiff's case, plaintiff was allowed to amend to pray for $50,000 damages. Subsequently the jury returned a verdict of $87,345. Plaintiff in order to receive the full amount of the verdict, once again was permitted to amend the prayer, this time to $100,000. The New Hampshire Supreme Court held that since defendant had not requested a continuance as a condition of granting any of the motions to amend, he could not have been prejudiced

and therefore there was no error. Does the use of amendment to permit full recovery in a jurisdiction that does not allow relief in excess of that requested in the
pleadings make more sense than the adoption of a provision like Federal Rule
54(c)?

6. The jurisdiction of inferior state tribunals often is limited as to the type
and amount of relief that can be awarded. See pp. 187–88, supra. For example,
a Minnesota Municipal Court may not entertain cases that request equitable relief
of any kind or in which more than $1000 is in controversy. Minn.Stat.Ann.
§§ 488.04(3), 488.05(1)(d). At the same time, however, many of these
inferior courts operate under rules similar to Federal Rule 54. See, e. g., Minn.
Municipal Court Rule of Civ.Proc. 54, which can be found in 27B Minn.Stat.
Ann.

Suppose a plaintiff prays for relief within an inferior court's jurisdictional
limits but introduces evidence clearly showing a right to relief in excess of that
which the court is permitted to award. Should plaintiff be held to have waived
the right to the excess relief or may a second action be commenced for the difference? Section 488.05(2) of the Minnesota Statutes provides:

> Whenever * * * it shall * * * appear that the municipal
> court is without jurisdiction in a cause pending therein, the fact shall be
> recorded, and the clerk shall transmit to the clerk of the district court a
> certified transcript of the record and all papers filed in the case. There-
> after the cause shall proceed to judgment in the district court as if it had
> there been commenced * * *.

Does this mean that the action must be tried all over again in the district court?
Is that fair to defendant who already has incurred the costs of an initial trial?

What if plaintiff obtains a verdict for an amount in excess of the court's jurisdictional maximum? Under the Minnesota statute should plaintiff be permitted
to waive the excess and preserve the verdict or must the case be transferred? A
very similar provision in California, Cal.Code Civ.Proc. § 396, specifically provides that if plaintiff's *demand* exceeds the jurisdictional maximum of the inferior
court "the excess may be *remitted* and the action may continue in the court where
it is pending." [Emphasis added.] *Cf.* Styblo v. McNeil, 317 Ill.App. 316, 45
N.E.2d 1011 (1st Dist.1943) (plaintiff permitted to preserve jurisdiction by waiving amount of jury verdict that exceeded court's maximum jurisdictional amount).
Should a waiver, if allowed, require the consent of defendant as well as of plaintiff? For a general discussion of jurisdictional amount problems, reread pp. 212–
19, supra.

SECTION D.   THE ANSWER

1.   DENIALS

Read Federal Rules of Civil Procedure 8(b) and 8(d) and the materials accompanying them in the Supplement.

CRUM, SCOPE OF THE GENERAL DENIAL, 27 No.Dak.L.Rev. 11, 11–12, 14, 21 (1951):

One portion of the law of pleading which it is submitted is ripe for re-examination consists of the rules which have grown up around the general denial permitted by the Field Code.   Based as it is upon the common law development of pleading which was very unusual in character, the general denial presents a serious obstacle toward the development of a clear and concise system of pleading which serves to notify both parties of the issues to be litigated.

The general denial is simply a pleading which denies every material allegation of the plaintiff's complaint.   In form it is ordinarily very brief and simple:

"For his answer to the complaint of the plaintiff herein, the defendant denies each and every allegation of the complaint."

Despite this superficial simplicity, however, the plea presents a series of complex and difficult problems.   Before considering the present status of the plea, it may be well to consider briefly the history which underlies it.

As it now exists, the general denial is the lineal descendant of the plea of the general issue permitted under the common law system of special pleading. Modern legal thinking recognizes pleading for what it actually is—a branch of the law of procedure which has as its chief object the furnishing of notice to the adversary party of the claims and defenses which it is proposed to present in a pending legal proceeding.   But at common law, pleading was regarded as being an end in itself instead of as a means to an end.

* * *   By simply pleading the general issue the common law pleaders found they could avoid the reefs awaiting them once they embarked on the sea of special pleading.   The popularity of the plea of the general issue with the common law pleaders may be in part explained on the theory that it was a practical method of simplifying a system of pleading which had grown too technical for successful application.

But a further explanation of the use of the general issue by the common law pleaders may be found.   The verbalistic precision of the common law courts had early led them to admit proof of practically any matter which went to show that the plaintiff did not have a right of recovery when the case came to trial. This was particularly true of the general issue when used in the actions of debt and assumpsit. So construed, the general issue was an ideal tactical weapon for a defendant. It permitted him to keep his adversary in the dark as to his defense until the last minute. * * *

Tested by its function in the system of pleading, it is doubtful whether any serious argument can be made that the general denial serves a useful purpose. The American Bar Association has listed the purposes of the pleadings as follows: (1) to serve as a formal basis for the judgment to be entered; (2) to separate issues of fact from questions of law; (3) to give litigants the advantage of the plea of res judicata if again molested; and (4) to notify the parties of the claims, defenses and cross demands of their adversaries.[49] Of these, the modern pleading systems tend to emphasize the fourth, or notice, function. Yet of all pleadings, surely the general denial does least to notify the adverse party of the defenses which it is proposed to introduce. Indeed, its main purpose is ordinarily to conceal the defenses to the plaintiff's action until the last possible moment. It has been pointed out that it is only in exceptional cases that a plea of the general denial can be considered truthful; in not one case in a thousand can one party deny in good faith every allegation of the other party's pleading.

ZIELINSKI v. PHILADELPHIA PIERS, INC.

United States District Court, Eastern District of Pennsylvania, 1956.
139 F.Supp. 408.

VAN DUSEN, District Judge. Plaintiff requests a ruling that, for the purposes of this case, the motor-driven fork lift operated by Sandy Johnson on February 9, 1953, was owned by defendant and that Sandy Johnson was its agent acting in the course of his employment on that date. The following facts are established by the pleadings, interrogatories, depositions and uncontradicted portions of affidavits:

1. Plaintiff filed his complaint on April 28, 1953, for personal injuries received on February 9, 1953, while working on Pier 96, Philadelphia, for J. A. McCarthy, as a result of a collision of two motor-driven fork lifts.

2. Paragraph 5 of this complaint stated that "a motor-driven vehicle known as a fork lift or chisel, owned, operated and controlled by the defendant, its agents, servants and employees, was so negligently and carelessly managed * * * that the same * * * did come into contact with the plaintiff causing him to sustain the injuries more fully hereinafter set forth."

3. The "First Defense" of the Answer stated "Defendant * * * (c) denies the averments of paragraph 5 * * *."

[49] 35 A. B. A. Rep. 614, 638–39 (1910), cited in Clark, Code Pleading 3 (2d ed. 1947).

4. The motor-driven vehicle known as a fork lift or chisel, which collided with the McCarthy fork lift on which plaintiff was riding, had on it the initials "P. P. I."

5. On February 10, 1953, Carload Contractors, Inc. made a report of this accident to its insurance company, whose policy No. CL 3964 insured Carload Contractors, Inc. against potential liability for the negligence of its employees contributing to a collision of the type described in paragraph 2 above.

6. By letter of April 29, 1953, the complaint served on defendant was forwarded to the above-mentioned insurance company. This letter read as follows:

"Gentlemen:

"   *   *   *

"We find that a fork lift truck operated by an employee of Carload Contractors, Inc. also insured by yourselves was involved in an accident with another chisel truck, which, was alleged, did cause injury to Frank Zielinski, and same was reported to you by Carload Contractors, Inc. at the time, and you assigned Claim Number OL 0153–94 to this claim.

"Should not this Complaint in Trespass be issued against Carload Contractors, Inc. and not Philadelphia Piers, Inc.?

"We forward for your handling."

7. Interrogatories * * * and the answers thereto, which were sworn to by defendant's General Manager on June 12, 1953, and filed on June 22, 1953, read as follows:

"1. State whether you have received any information of an injury sustained by the plaintiff on February 9, 1953, South Wharves. If so, state when and from whom you first received notice of such injury. A. We were first notified of this accident on or about February 9, 1953 by Thomas Wilson.

"2. State whether you caused an investigation to be made of the circumstances of said injury and if so, state who made such investigation and when it was made. A. We made a very brief investigation on February 9, 1953 and turned the matter over to (our insurance company) for further investigation.

"*   *   *"

8. At a deposition taken August 18, 1953, Sandy Johnson testified that he was the employee of defendant on February 9, 1953, and had been their employee for approximately fifteen years.

9. At a pre-trial conference held on September 27, 1955,[3] plaintiff first learned that over a year before February 9, 1953, the business of moving freight on piers in Philadelphia, formerly conducted by defendant, had been

---

[3] The applicable statute of limitations prevented any suit against Carload Contractors, Inc. after February 9, 1955, 12 P.S. § 34.

sold by it to Carload Contractors, Inc. and Sandy Johnson had been transferred to the payroll of this corporation without apparently realizing it, since the nature or location of his work had not changed.

* * *

11.   Defendant now admits that on February 9, 1953, it owned the fork lift in the custody of Sandy Johnson and that this fork lift was leased to Carload Contractors, Inc.   It is also admitted that the pier on which the accident occurred was leased by defendant.

12.   There is no indication of action by either party in bad faith and there is no proof of inaccurate statements being made with intent to deceive. Because defendant made a prompt investigation of the accident (see answers to Interrogatories 1, 2,   *   *   *), its insurance company has been representing the defendant since suit was brought, and this company insures Carload Contractors, Inc. also, requiring defendant to defend this suit, will not prejudice it.

Under these circumstances, and for the purposes of this action, it is ordered that the following shall be stated to the jury at the trial:

> "It is admitted that, on February 9, 1953, the towmotor or fork lift bearing the initials 'P. P. I.' was owned by defendant and that Sandy Johnson was a servant in the employ of defendant and doing its work on that date."

This ruling is based on the following principles:

1.   Under the circumstances of this case, the answer contains an ineffective denial of that part of paragraph 5 of the complaint which alleges that "a motor driven vehicle known as a fork lift or chisel (was) owned, operated and controlled by the defendant, its agents, servants and employees."   [See] F.R. Civ.P. 8(b)   *   *   *.

For example, it is quite clear that defendant does not deny the averment in paragraph 5 that the fork lift came into contact with plaintiff, since it admits,   *   *   *   that an investigation of an occurrence of the accident had been made and that a report dated February 10, 1953, was sent to its insurance company stating "While Frank Zielinski was riding on bumper of chisel and holding rope to secure cargo, the chisel truck collided with another chisel truck operated by Sandy Johnson causing injuries to Frank Zielinski's legs and hurt head of Sandy Johnson."   Compliance with the above-mentioned rule required that defendant file a more specific answer than a general denial.   A specific denial of parts of this paragraph and specific admission of other parts would have warned plaintiff that he had sued the wrong defendant.

* * *

Under circumstances where an improper and ineffective answer has been filed, the Pennsylvania courts have consistently held that an allegation of agency in the complaint requires a statement to the jury that agency is admitted where an attempt to amend the answer is made after the expiration of the period of limitation.   *   *   *   Although the undersigned has been able to find no federal court decisions on this point, he believes the principle of these Pennsylvania appellate court decisions may be considered in view of all the facts of this case, where jurisdiction is based on diversity of citizenship, the accident occurred in Pennsylvania, and the federal district court is sitting in Pennsylvania. * * *

2. Under the circumstances of this case, principles of equity require that defendant be estopped from denying agency because, otherwise, its inaccurate statements and statements in the record, which it knew (or had the means of knowing within its control) were inaccurate, will have deprived plaintiff of his right of action.

If Interrogatory 2 had been answered accurately by saying that employees of Carload Contractors, Inc. had turned the matter over to the insurance company, it seems clear that plaintiff would have realized his mistake. The fact that if Sandy Johnson had testified accurately, the plaintiff could have brought its action against the proper party defendant within the statutory period of limitations is also a factor to be considered, since defendant was represented at the deposition and received knowledge of the inaccurate testimony.

At least one appellate court has stated that the doctrine of equitable estoppel will be applied to prevent a party from taking advantage of the statute of limitations where the plaintiff has been misled by conduct of such party. See, Peters v. Public Service Corporation, 132 N.J.Eq. 500, 29 A.2d 189, 195 (1942). In that case, the court said, 29 A.2d at page 196:

> "Of course, defendants were under no duty to advise complainants' attorney of his error, other than by appropriate pleadings, but neither did defendants have a right, knowing of the mistake, to foster it by its acts of omission."

* * *

Since this is a pre-trial order, it may be modified at the trial if the trial judge determines from the facts which then appear that justice so requires.
* * *

NOTES AND QUESTIONS

1. To what extent is a federal trial judge justified in striking a general denial that appears to have been made in bad faith? In UNITED STATES v. LONG, 10 F.R.D. 443, 445 (D.Neb.1950), the court stated:

> * * * [U]pon his honor as a member of the bar of this court and in the face of * * * Rule 11, counsel for the defendant, by signing, serving and filing the answer—and now by the express statement of his brief—assures this court that his client intends to controvert "every allegation of the plaintiff's complaint," to borrow his own language. The court is compelled to accept those assurances as being tendered in good faith.

Compare BIGGS v. PUBLIC SERV. COORDINATED TRANSP., 280 F.2d 311, 313–14 (3d Cir.1960), a diversity-of-citizenship case, in which defendant generally denied plaintiff's jurisdictional allegations, including an express claim that defendant was a New Jersey corporation. The court stated:

> * * * We do not think that the able and experienced lawyer for the defendant should be put in the position of having to urge that his

general denial applied to the corporate citizenship of his client. Fed.R.
Civ.P. 11 * * *.

We cannot for a moment believe that defendant's counsel was denying in good faith that his client was a New Jersey corporation. We think
the only fair interpretation of the pleading in this case is that the denial
does not run to the allegation of defendant's citizenship. Therefore, that
allegation must be deemed to be admitted. Fed.R.Civ.P. 8(d).

See also Vrooman Floor Covering, Inc. v. Dorsey, 267 Minn. 318, 126 N.W.2d
377 (1964) (general denial raises no defenses when entered in bad faith).

2. In the *Biggs* case defendant, in addition to the general denial, had specifically denied the allegation that the amount in controversy exceeded the minimum
jurisdictional amount required in diversity cases. Does this help to explain the
decision? Should a defendant who joins general and special denials in the answer
be permitted to rely upon a general denial to put in issue those allegations by
plaintiff that have not been specially denied? See Fawcett v. Miller, 85 Ohio L.
Abs. 443, 172 N.E.2d 328 (Ct.App.1961) (failure of defendant to elect to rely
on a general denial results in admissions of all facts not specially denied); 18
Ohio St.L.J. 544 (1957). Suppose a defendant's answer couples a general denial
with specific admissions of facts alleged in the complaint. Should defendant be
permitted to elect to stand on the denial at trial, thus forcing plaintiff to prove
even those facts admitted? See Johnson v. School Dist. No. 3, 168 Neb. 547, 96
N.W.2d 623 (1959) (admissions take precedence over a general denial even though
admissions were made in connection with an affirmative defense).

3. In Green, *Restore the General Issue in Pleading*, 42 Ill.B.J. 302, 303
(1954), the author comments on Section 40 of the Illinois Practice Code as follows:

It is contrary to the true concept of American liberty that a citizen
shall stand convicted of any charge that is made against him unless he
denies it. Until the above Statute was passed, there was no presumption
that a defendant was guilty of any charge that might be alleged against
him, merely because he stood mute; until a prima facie case was established by proof, there was no presumption of any alleged wrong by him
committed, suffered or done. But that rule was reversed by this statute,
which provides that unless a charge is denied with specific definiteness,
the party charged is not only presumed guilty, but he must be adjudged
guilty merely if he fails to specifically deny the allegation.

Consequently the answer to a complaint in an ordinary personal injury case to comply literally with Section 40 of the Civil Practice Act is
longer than the complaint itself. The courts have evaded deciding
squarely the question of whether or not a general denial of the allegations
of a paragraph or a complaint is sufficient; the statute says it is not;
therefore, a careful pleader very properly worries about the sufficiency of
a general denial in an answer to the allegations of a complaint.

We should get the Illinois Legislature to return us to the observance
of the established American Doctrine that a mere charge of negligence,
misprison, malfeasance, or wilful injury, is not sufficient to convict a
citizen, instead of having him stand convicted merely because he may refuse or even neglect to specifically deny the charge.

The General Issue should be restored to common law pleading. The plaintiff should carry the burden of proof of his allegations, whether or not the defendant denies them.

Is this view justifiable?

4. To what extent should defendant be permitted to respond that "he neither admits nor denies" plaintiff's allegations? Should it make any difference whether or not a general denial is allowed? See Rahal v. Titus, 107 Ga.App. 844, 131 S.E.2d 659 (1963). In many jurisdictions statutes specifically prohibit "evasive denials." E. g., Ill.Stat.Ann. ch. 110, § 40(3). Compare the language of Federal Rule 8(b).

5. In California, if a complaint is verified, the answer not only must be verified but it cannot contain a general denial. See Cal.Code Civ.Proc. §§ 431.30(d), 446. What justification is there for such provisions?

OLIVER v. SWISS CLUB TELL

California District Court of Appeal, First District, 1963.
222 Cal.App.2d 528, 35 Cal.Rptr. 324.

MOLINARI, Justice. This is an appeal by plaintiffs from a summary judgment in favor of defendant "The Swiss Club Tell, an unincorporated association" [on the ground that it is nonexistent.] * * *

Plaintiffs filed no counteraffidavit. When the motion came on for hearing on September 5, 1961, plaintiffs did not appear, the motion for summary judgment was granted, and a judgment was entered pursuant thereto on September 15, 1961. * * *

Plaintiffs have devoted a considerable portion of their briefs to the assertion that the answer admits that the named defendant is an unincorporated association. The basis of this contention is that the denial in said answer, upon information and belief, of the allegation that defendant is an unincorporated association amounts to an admission of that allegation. This assertion is predicated upon the argument that the existence or nonexistence of defendant as an unincorporated association is a matter of public record and therefore not deniable upon information and belief. Accordingly, say plaintiffs, the allegation in the complaint stands undenied because no issue was tendered as to whether defendant is an unincorporated association. This is an allegation of fact which, say plaintiffs, is admitted in the answer and must be treated as admitted on appeal. * * * Although section 437 of the Code of Civil Procedure permits a denial in a nonpositive form based upon information and belief, or upon lack of information or belief, such denials are insufficient where the facts are presumptively within the knowledge of the defendant. * * * This rule is frequently applied to matters of public record. Accordingly, a denial upon information and belief, or for want of information or belief, of an alleged fact which may be ascertained from the inspection of a public record within reach of a defendant is insufficient to raise an issue, and such a denial constitutes an admission of the allegation of the complaint. * * *

Plaintiffs argue that defendant could have determined its existence or nonexistence as an unincorporated association by a perusal of the articles of incorporation of the Swiss Club Tell, Inc. If, as we have pointed out above, the unincorporated association was nonexistent, a purported answer on its behalf would be a nullity and the manner and extent of the denials therein would be of no moment. It is obvious that such a nonentity would be incapable of entertaining the claimed presumptive knowledge. We must, however, consider the arguments advanced by plaintiffs because the pleadings do not show on their face that defendant is nonexistent. Accordingly, our immediate inquiry is directed to whether the issue of the existence or nonexistence of the unincorporated association was properly tendered to the trial court for adjudication. Turning, then, to the question of presumptive knowledge, we fail to see how a perusal of the records showing the existence of a corporation known as the Swiss Club Tell, Inc., would establish the existence or nonexistence of The Swiss Club Tell, an unincorporated association, unless such records affirmatively show that such unincorporated association was merged in the corporation. Moreover, even though it could be said that an investigation of the public records showing the filing of the articles of incorporation of said corporation would lead one to facts which would establish the existence or nonexistence of the unincorporated association, *facts* so ascertained may be denied on information and belief or for lack of information or belief. While a defendant may not make a nonpositive denial of matters of public record, such denials are sufficient as to the facts relating or pertaining to recorded documents. * * *

A more persuasive argument, lightly touched upon by plaintiffs, is that, irrespective of any public record, a defendant ought to know whether or not it is an unincorporated association. The rule precluding the use of nonpositive denials, where matters are presumptively within the defendant's knowledge, has been applied to corporations as well as to natural persons. * * * It is evident that an unincorporated association has possession of its own records, an examination of which will disclose its status, and thus enable it to answer definitely an allegation that it is such an association. * * * Accordingly, in the instant case, the denial, purportedly based upon lack of information or belief, was to matters which would be within the actual knowledge of a defendant, and, as such, raises no issue and is in effect an admission of the truth of the allegation in the complaint "that defendant the Swiss Club Tell is an unincorporated association transacting business for the benefit of its members. * * *"

The said purported denial is defective for still another reason. The language of the denial is that "defendants do not have sufficient information to answer. * * *" Such a denial is insufficient and does not comply with section 437 of the Code of Civil Procedure, which provides in part: "If the defendant has no information or belief upon the subject sufficient to enable him to answer an allegation of the complaint, he may so state in his answer, and place his denial on that ground." * * *

Code

Under the state of the pleadings as they stood in the present case the existence of the "Swiss Club Tell, an unincorporated association," was purportedly admitted. It appears from the pretrial conference order, however, that the issue remained in the case for adjudication. Plaintiffs not only contended at the pretrial conference that "the Swiss Clubtel [sic] *is* an unincorporated association and has been regularly served" (emphasis added), but the pretrial conference order specifically provides that "issue has been joined by the parties named above but there remains open for adjudication the nature and capacity of the Defendants Swiss Clubtel [sic]." Implicit in this issue is the question of the existence or nonexistence of defendant as an unincorporated association. The pretrial conference order controls the subsequent course of the litigation and supersedes the pleadings where inconsistent with them unless modified at or before trial. * * * Upon this posture of the case, therefore, the existence of defendant as an unincorporated association was a fact which plaintiffs were required to prove as part of their cause of action and consequently was issuable.

In view of the conclusions herein reached by us that the motion for summary judgment should not have been granted, the judgment based thereon must be reversed. Defendant will therefore be restored as a party defendant in the action against whom the issues tendered by the pleadings will have to be tried, including the issue as to whether defendant exists as an entity.

* * *

NOTES AND QUESTIONS

1. What facts are "presumptively within the knowledge" of a defendant? To what extent should defendant be obligated to ascertain facts that are easily obtainable? For example, should a corporate enterprise be charged with knowledge of representations to customers made by several of its salesmen? Does the answer depend on the size and nature of the business? See Kayser v. Railway Express Agency, 54 N.Y.S.2d 623 (Sup.Ct.1945). Suppose plaintiff's complaint alleges facts that can be ascertained only by a detailed and costly search of defendant's records? Should defendant be required to discharge this burden prior to its answer? See Olin v. Town of North Hempstead, 194 N.Y.S.2d 979 (Sup.Ct.1959). To what extent is the response affected by the fact that under state rules defendant usually has at most 30 days in which to file an answer? See, e. g., Missouri Rule of Civil Procedure 55.27(a) (30 days); Or.Rev.Stat. § 15.040(3) (10 or 20 days); *cf.* Fed.Rule Civ.Proc. 12(a) (20 days).

2. In *Oliver* the court held, *inter alia*, that the purported denial was ineffective because it was improperly stated. Is there any justification for this holding? Did the form of the denial create any added opportunity for untruthful or evasive pleading?

WINGFOOT CALIFORNIA HOMES CO. v. VALLEY NAT. BANK, 80 Ariz. 133, 294 P.2d 370 (1956). Plaintiff sued to recover on a series of notes, each of which permitted plaintiff to obtain reasonable attorneys' fees for collection thereon. Accordingly plaintiff's complaint contained the following allegation (referred to as Paragraph VII), with respect to each of the notes: "That the sum of $150.00 is a reasonable sum to be allowed to the plaintiff as and for its attorneys' fees in this cause of action * * *." The answer merely stated that defendant "denies the allegations contained in Paragraphs VII * * *."

The plaintiff sought summary judgment on the ground that the pleading showed that no material issue of fact existed. The trial court granted the motion, awarding $100 for attorneys' fees regarding each of the notes. Defendant appealed on the ground that the denial put the matter of attorney's fees in issue. The Arizona Supreme Court upheld the decision below, stating:

> * * * [P]laintiff's argument was that this general denial that the reasonable value of attorneys' fees in each cause of action was $150, constituted a negative pregnant in that it admitted that any sum less than $150 was a reasonable sum. A negative pregnant with an admission may be defined as that form of denial which involves an affirmative implication favorable to the adversary. The general rule is that since a negative pregnant is a negative which implies an affirmative, it cannot be found in a general denial, because a general denial puts in issue every averment of the complaint which a plaintiff is required to prove to sustain his cause of action including jurisdiction. * * * But where the defendant merely denies that a debt or damage is the precise sum alleged by the plaintiff it is an admission of the value, debt or damage in a lesser amount. * * * The allegation concerning attorneys' fees is found in Paragraph VII of the complaint. The answer specifically denied Paragraph VII. This can only be interpreted to mean that defendants denied that $150 was a reasonable attorneys' fee in each cause of action for the services rendered for the plaintiff. * * * [E]mploying the use of a general specific denial as to Paragraph VII of the complaint does not invest the denial with any of the legal effects of a general denial to the entire complaint which, as above stated, is construed as denial of every allegation in the complaint. * * *

> * * * Defendants did not deny that an attorneys' fee in some amount less than $150 would be a reasonable fee for the services rendered. In fact such a denial would have indicated on its face a lack of good faith on the part of the defendants in filing such a pleading. The only effect of the denial is that they contend that the sum of $150 is not reasonable. Such a denial does not fairly meet the substance of the averment in the complaint relating to attorneys' fees. If it was defendants' intention to deny that the sum of $150 was an unreasonable [sic] fee in order to form an issue on the reasonableness thereof it was incumbent on them,

as above stated, to state in their pleadings the specific amount which they considered to be a maximum of the reasonable value thereof. * * *

One Justice dissented as follows:

> * * * The doctrine of negative pregnant is merely a specific application of the general rule that evasive and dilatory pleadings are defective. Thus if a plaintiff sets up a certain hypothesis in his pleading and defendant denies this is [sic] the same words used, including inconsequential and qualifying facts of the complaint, then the answer is considered evasive for the reason that defendant may just as logically be denying the inconsequential qualifying facts as the primary or material ones. Therefore to *punish* such evasiveness, the doctrine states that the denial will be considered as traversing only the immaterial and admitting the material issues of fact, and the denial (or negative) is spoken of as "pregnant with admission of the material issues."

> * * *

> The majority opinion concedes that a negative pregnant cannot be found in a broad general denial to an entire complaint. * * * They seem to concede that if defendant had generally denied the whole complaint, no negative pregnant would exist. Yet where precisely the same effect is created by a denial of all the allegations of a specific paragraph they shut their eyes to said effect and treat the denial as defective. I submit the same reasoning whereby no negative pregnant can be found in a general denial of the whole complaint applies to the denial herein, which as to paragraph VII operated as a general denial. * * *

NOTES AND QUESTIONS

1. For a later and somewhat different view of the negative-pregnant doctrine in Arizona, see Frank v. Solomon, 94 Ariz. 55, 381 P.2d 591 (1963) (amendment should be permitted to eliminate negative pregnant). Compare State v. Means, 71 Nev. 340, 291 P.2d 909 (1955).

2. In JANEWAY & CARPENDER v. LONG BEACH PAPER & PAINT CO., 190 Cal. 150, 211 P. 6 (1922), plaintiff alleged that defendant "made, executed, and delivered its contract for goods to the plaintiff." Defendant denied the allegation specifically, using the identical words of the complaint. The court held that this denial was evasive and therefore admitted the existence of a contract. What arguments can be made in support of the decision? What arguments against? This type of pleading defect is termed a "conjunctive denial." To what extent does it differ from a "negative pregnant"?

2. DENIALS VERSUS AFFIRMATIVE DEFENSES

Read Federal Rule of Civil Procedure 8(c) and the accompanying materials in the Supplement.

DENHAM v. CUDDEBACK

Supreme Court of Oregon, 1957.
210 Or. 485, 311 P.2d 1014.

WARNER, Justice. This is an action in trespass by the plaintiffs-appellants, Bert Denham and wife, against the defendant-respondent, Sol A. Cuddeback, to recover treble damages for cutting and removing timber from land alleged to be owned by plaintiffs. The jury found for defendant and from the judgment in favor of defendant, plaintiffs appeal.

* * *

Plaintiffs' complaint consists of two allegations: (1) that they are the owners of a particularly-described parcel of land, and (2) that the defendant cut and removed more than 65 M board feet of timber therefrom to their damage. The defendant, Cuddeback, answered by a general denial, only. Under this traverse, the defendant offered evidence of the defendant's ownership by adverse possession of the small timbered area in controversy.

The admission of this evidence under the circumstances is made the basis for plaintiffs' first assignment of error.

Plaintiffs contend that such evidence of ownership in the defendant amounts to an affirmative defense and, if available to defendant, must be so pleaded. * * *

The rule which permits defendant to controvert plaintiffs' allegation of ownership by the introduction of evidence under defendant's general denial showing title in defendant, although not universally applied, is an ancient one and long and firmly established in many jurisdictions. The fundamental reason being that both the act of trespass and the claim of title in plaintiffs are put in issue under a general denial and therefore any title in the defendant, whether freehold or possessory, is admissible in evidence. * * *

In Hill v. Bailey, 8 Mo.App. 85, the appellant plaintiffs' claim of title to certain lands was denied on the ground that the defendants had acquired an absolute title by operation of the statute of limitations. The appeal was on the ground that the evidence of defendant's title had been wrongly admitted under his general denial. Although the Hill case, supra, was not an action in trespass, the holding of the court is of pertinent interest here. The court in denying plaintiffs' contention, said, 8 Mo.App. at page 87:

"The plaintiffs insist that the finding and judgment were erroneous, because the answer did not set up the statute in defence. When the statute is relied on as a bar to the remedy merely, it must

be specially pleaded.   The rule is ancient, and needs no citation
of authorities to sustain it.   But where the title to real estate is in
question, the operation of the statute is found to have a higher range.
It is capable of conferring an absolute title.   Hence it has long
been held that a general denial of the plaintiff's title will suffice
for the admission of evidence of adverse possession for the statutory period; because this will not merely bar the remedy, but may
establish a title in the defendant which will conclusively negative
any ownership in the plaintiff.   In other words, it sustains and veri-
fies the denial of the plaintiff's title.   *   *   *   The rule is not
confined to actions of ejectment.   *   *   *"

*   *   *

Neither of the parties have [sic] brought to our attention any trespass
cases wherein this court has passed upon the precise question presented by appellants' assignment of error, nor has our own inquiry discovered any cases of
that character.

We are, however, persuaded that our many pronouncements defining the
function of a general denial in answer to the allegations of a complaint, and
what may or may not be offered in evidence thereunder, justify our holding
that in an action for trespass, the defendant can prove under his general denial,
title in himself, no matter how acquired, whether by deed, inheritance or adverse possession.

The defendant "has a right to give evidence under his denial controverting any fact necessary to be established by the plaintiff to authorize a recovery.
*   *   *   An allegation of title to or right to possession of the close is an element which plaintiff must necessarily establish if he would successfully recover.   *   *   *   Plaintiffs' allegation of ownership, then, was not only a material, but an essential, allegation.   By proving that title to the land was in a person other than the plaintiff, in this instance, in the defendant, it is obvious that
defendant has successfully controverted plaintiffs' allegation of ownership in
themselves.

The test frequently employed to determine what evidence is admissible
under a general denial is: Does the evidence tendered tend *to destroy* rather
than *avoid* the cause of action as alleged by the complaint?

Test to determine admissable evidence based on the denial

*   *   *   [W]e hold that evidence of the defendant's title or right to
possession was in this action admissible under defendant's general denial, having as it did the force and effect, if believed by the jury, of controverting or
destroying plaintiffs' allegation of title.

*   *   *

NOTES AND QUESTIONS

1.   Reread the materials regarding the allocation of the burden of pleading
at pp. 417–19, supra.

2.   Which, if any, of the following "defenses" to a claim of negligence should
be raised by a denial? Why?

(a) Plaintiff's injury was due to an "unavoidable accident." *Compare* Ashworth v. Morrison, 93 Ohio L.Abs. 503, 26 Ohio Op.2d 25, 196 N.E.2d 465 (Ct. App.1963) (unavoidable accident must be specially pleaded), *with* Fenton v. Aleshire, 238 Or. 24, 393 P.2d 217 (1964) (unavoidable accident not an affirmative defense).

(b) Plaintiff's injury was caused by an "Act of God." *Compare* Chesapeake & O. Ry. v. Carmichael, 298 Ky. 769, 184 S.W.2d 91 (1944) (Act of God not affirmative defense and provable under general denial of negligence), *with* Young v. Marlas, 243 Iowa 367, 376, 51 N.W.2d 443, 448 (1952) (Act of God affirmative defense).

(c) Defendant's conduct was occasioned by a "sudden emergency" not of his own making. *Compare* Fontana v. State Farm Mut. Auto. Ins. Co., 173 So.2d 284 (La.App.1965) (sudden emergency affirmative defense), *with* Grebloski v. Faux, 151 Conn. 712, 200 A.2d 486 (1964) (sudden emergency not affirmative defense).

Can any of these issues be distinguished from the issue of title in the *Denham* case? Is *Denham* consistent with *Ziervogel,* p. 444, supra?

3. To what extent does the question whether an issue may be raised by a denial rather than an affirmative pleading depend upon the substantive law of the jurisdiction? Michigan General Court Rule 111.7, as does Federal Rule 8(c), lists a number of specific defenses that must be pleaded affirmatively, including the "defense" of assumption of risk. The Supreme Court of Michigan, in FELGNER v. ANDERSON, 375 Mich. 23, 133 N.W.2d 136 (1965), redefined the doctrine of assumption of risk, holding that in cases in which applicable, it can serve only to show that defendant was not negligent in that he either owed no duty to plaintiff or did not breach a duty owed. The doctrine no longer can be used by defendant as an independent defense once negligence has been established. Does this substantive alteration of the doctrine render the pleading rule obsolete?

PAGE v. BRODOFF, 22 Conn.Supp. 282, 169 A.2d 901 (Super.Ct. 1961). Plaintiffs brought suit for testator's wrongful death allegedly caused during an operation when defendant surgeon negligently pierced testator's esophagus with an esophascope. Defendant generally denied the allegations of the complaint and in a separate "defense" affirmatively alleged that the injury occurred when testator's body "suddenly and unexpectedly moved." Plaintiff demurred on the ground that defendant's affirmative allegation did not constitute a defense. The court overruled the demurrer on the ground that the separate defense was no more than a special denial of negligence. The court went on to hold that the additional defense could not possibly prejudice plaintiff on the ground that a "defendant who voluntarily alleges a fact which could also have been proved under a simple denial presumably does so with the idea of making his defense appear to be stronger and more aggressive, and invites the court to charge that he has assumed the affirmative upon that particular issue."

NOTES AND QUESTIONS

1. When defendant, as in *Page*, affirmatively pleads facts inconsistent with those alleged by plaintiff, defendant is said to have made an "argumentative denial." Some courts have held that such a denial is ineffective. See Zwerling v. Annenberg, 38 Misc. 169, 77 N.Y.S. 275 (Sup.Ct.1902) (amendment permitted); Clark, *Code Pleading* § 92, at 591–92 (2d ed. 1947). Is there any justification for this position?

2. Most courts uphold argumentative denials. Some of them, however, hold, in accord with *Page,* that this type of pleading shifts the burden of proof from plaintiff to defendant as to the "issues" so pleaded. See Comment, *Effect of Unnecessary Affirmative Pleading upon the Burden of Proof,* 39 Yale L.J. 117 (1929); 4 U.Chi.L.Rev. 498 (1937). What is the rationale behind such a shift? Is the reason given in *Page* persuasive? What does the court in *Page* mean by the term "issue"? Is defendant now obliged to show he was not negligent or does he merely have the burden of establishing the fact of plaintiff's movement during the operation? If only the latter, won't the court find it difficult if not impossible to avoid conflicting instructions to the jury? See CAHILL BROS. v. CLEMENTINA CO., 208 Cal.App.2d 367, 384–86, 25 Cal.Rptr. 301, 311–12 (1st Dist.1962), in which the trial court properly instructed that plaintiff had the burden of proving defendant an independent contractor but went on erroneously to instruct that the burden was on defendant to prove its "defense" that defendant was a joint venturer with plaintiff rather than an independent contractor.

SECTION E. THE REPLY

Read Federal Rule of Civil Procedure 7(a) and the accompanying materials in the Supplement. Pay particular attention to Title 12, § 280 of the Oklahoma Statutes Annotated.

NOTES AND QUESTIONS

1. The two prevailing types of provisions governing use of the reply are represented by Federal Rule 7(a) and the Oklahoma statute, which treats as admitted all allegations of an affirmative defense unless they are denied in a reply. Even the Oklahoma statute, by cutting off or severely restricting pleadings at the reply stage, see Okl.Stat.Ann. tit. 12, § 263, departs significantly from the common-law practice, which required pleadings to continue back and forth between plaintiff and defendant until disputed issues were isolated.

Is Federal Rule 7(a), when read in conjunction with Rule 8(d), consistent with Federal Rule 8(b), which requires a defendant to answer plaintiff's allegations specifically?

2. Although the text of Federal Rule 7(a) expressly provides that a court may order plaintiff to reply to allegations other than counterclaims, judges have been reluctant to do so, at least in the absence of "a clear and convincing

factual showing of necessity or other extraordinary circumstances of a compelling nature." MOVIECOLOR LTD. v. EASTMAN KODAK CO., 24 F.R.D. 325, 326 (S.D.N.Y.1959). Why, given liberal discovery rules, should it ever be necessary to order a reply? *Cf.* Reynolds v. Needle, 132 F.2d 161 (D.C.Cir.1942) (summary judgment granted when plaintiff's complaint revealed affirmative defense and plaintiff failed to request leave to reply or otherwise attempt to avoid the defense).

BECKSTROM v. COASTWISE LINE, 13 F.R.D. 480, 482–83 (D. Alaska 1953), provides an interesting illustration of a tactical use of the reply. Under the terms of Federal Rule 38(b), a party who wishes a trial by jury of any issue must make a demand therefor not later than 10 days after the service of the *last pleading directed to such issue.* Defendants had answered plaintiff's complaint on August 22, alleging several affirmative defenses; on October 6 plaintiff moved for leave to reply and, at the same time, made his first demand for trial by jury.

> * * * Plaintiff has not shown a substantial reason for seeking permission to file a reply or for being *ordered* to do so. Accordingly, plaintiff's motion * * * must be denied.

> * * * [I]n the absence of a reply now denied, [defendant's answer] was the last pleading directed to the issues between the plaintiff and the defendants in this action. The demand for jury trial as of right must therefore be denied.

What would you have done to improve plaintiff's strategy in this case? Do you consider this a proper or ethical use of the pleadings? Demand for trial by jury is discussed further on pp. 840–45, infra.

3.   Allegations to which a reply is not permitted or required are considered avoided or denied and plaintiff may controvert them at trial. See Federal Rule 8(d); N.Y.C.P.L.R. 3018(a). Conversely, matters requiring a responsive pleading are taken as admitted if not denied in the reply or if a reply is not filed. See Federal Rule 8(d); Okl.Stat.Ann. tit. 12, § 306.

Suppose defendant's answer contains an allegation denominated a "counterclaim," but plaintiff believes it is properly an affirmative defense. Or suppose in a "new matter" jurisdiction, such as Oklahoma, plaintiff thinks defendant's "affirmative defense" could be raised by a simple denial. See Vevelstad v. Flynn, 230 F.2d 695, 703 (9th Cir.), certiorari denied 352 U.S. 827, 77 S.Ct. 40, 1 L.Ed.2d 49 (1956) ("a counterclaim" held to be really a denial not requiring reply); Sais v. City Elec. Co., 26 N.M. 66, 188 P. 1110 (1920) ("affirmative defense" that could have been raised by denial does not require responsive pleading). What if plaintiff does not reply and the court believes that the material in fact was a counterclaim? See Dyotherm Corp. v. Turbo Mach. Co., 39 F.R.D. 370 (E.D.Pa. 1966) (plaintiff granted 10 days to file reply after court ruled against its contention that defendant's answer was not a properly denominated counterclaim). Should the court always grant plaintiff some relief? See Federal Rule 8(c). Note that if plaintiff files a reply when not permitted or required to do so, it will not be disregarded to the extent it contains admissions against plaintiff's interest. E. g., Berger v. State Farm Mut. Auto. Ins. Co., 291 F.2d 666, 668 n. 1 (10th Cir.1961). Should a court thus look with disfavor on a plaintiff who mistakenly refuses to reply?

4. Common-law rules would not permit plaintiff to depart from a claim asserted in the complaint by asserting a new claim or theory in a reply. The departure rule occasionally has been applied under more modern pleading systems, particularly in cases in which a plaintiff, having alleged negligence in the complaint, raises the doctrine of last clear chance in the reply in order to overcome a plea of contributory negligence in the answer. See Leach, *Burden of Pleading—Guest Statute and Last Clear Chance,* 23 Ohio St.L.J. 423, 433 (1962). *Compare* Thayer v. Denver & R. G. R. R., 21 N.M. 330, 154 P. 691 (1916) (reply raising last clear chance sets up independent cause of action, thus a departure upon which plaintiff cannot recover), *with* Barnes v. Wright, 123 Colo. 462, 231 P.2d 794 (1951) (plaintiff should have raised last clear chance in her reply).

Liberal amendment rules have considerably lessened the impact of departure. But an occasional case manages to keep the doctrine alive. See Grobart v. Society for Establishing Useful Manufactures, 2 N.J. 136, 65 A.2d 833 (1949) (reply "in tort" not allowed because complaint sounded "in contract").

SECTION F. CHALLENGES TO THE PLEADINGS

---

1. THE NATURE AND FORM OF CHALLENGES

A. ATTACKING THE SUBSTANTIVE SUFFICIENCY OF A PLEADING

Read Federal Rules of Civil Procedure 12(b)(6), 12(c), and 12(f) and the accompanying material in the Supplement.

As should be apparent from the preceding material in this Chapter, any discussion of the sufficiency of the pleadings necessarily involves some consideration of the methods by which pleadings are attacked. The procedural system of every jurisdiction provides various techniques by which the substantive sufficiency of the pleadings may be challenged. A decision as to which device is appropriate depends upon the time of the challenge, the identity of the party making it, and the nature of the alleged defect. Weinstein & Korn, *Preliminary Motions in New York: A Critique,* 57 Colum.L.Rev. 526 (1957). At common law and under the codes, a complaint was, and still is, challenged by a general demurrer based on the ground that no cause of action has been stated. In some jurisdictions, similar techniques have been available but they have been given other names—e. g., motion to strike the complaint. See Parnell v. Nationwide Mut. Ins. Co., 263 N.C. 445, 139 S.E.2d 723 (1965). When the draftsmen of the Federal Rules decided to eliminate detailed factual pleading, they felt that continuing the use of the technical term "demurrer" might lead to confusion. Hence Rule 7(c) was included to "abolish" demurrers and Rule 12(b) (6) was devised to provide for a challenge on the ground that the complaint, or any count in it, failed to state a claim upon which relief could be granted.

The demurrer also has been the traditional method of challenging the substantive sufficiency of an answer or any subsequent pleading. When the Federal Rules originally were promulgated, they failed to provide expressly for a motion to dismiss an insufficient answer; the result was confusion regarding the appropriate way in which to assert such a challenge. An entire answer could be attacked by a motion under Rule 12(c) for a judgment on the pleadings, but there seemed to be no method whatsoever for challenging only a part of the answer. As a result, Rule 12(f) was amended in 1946 specifically to permit the striking of an insufficient defense.

The motion for judgment on the pleadings mentioned above has been adopted by many jurisdictions as an alternative to the demurrer. It usually is available to both plaintiffs and defendants. Typically, the motion can be made only after all pleadings are filed and will be granted only when the entire complaint or answer is insufficient. If an answer must be filed in advance, of what value is such a motion to defendant? Notice that under the Federal Rules defendant may challenge a complaint under Rule 12(b)(6) and Rule 12(c). Are there any tactical advantages for using one procedure rather than another?

Every jurisdiction provides that a demurrer or motion to dismiss may be directed toward a part as opposed to an entire pleading. Thus, if plaintiff pleads in several counts, only one of which is sufficient to state a claim for relief, defendant may eliminate the insufficient counts by demurrer. In many jurisdictions, however, the rules provide that a party must specify the causes or defenses he seeks to challenge. Suppose a party demurs generally to the entire complaint or answer, but one or several of the claims or defenses is good. Should the demurrer be overruled? If there are two defendants and the complaint states a valid claim against one but not against the other, should a demurrer by the latter specify that the challenge only goes to claims against him? See Kriger v. Industrial Rehabilitation Corp., 8 A.D.2d 29, 185 N.Y. S.2d 658 (1st Dep't 1959), affirmed 7 N.Y.2d 958, 198 N.Y.S.2d 611, 166 N.E.2d 189 (1960); Clark, *Code Pleading* § 79, at 509, 511–12 (2d ed. 1947); Ind.Rule Proc. 8(E)(3). Compare the problems of pleading negative pregnants and conjunctive denials, discussed at pp. 461–63, supra.

It is important to keep in mind the distinction between an attack on a pleading, which considers only the pleading itself, and a claim that a pleading, although sufficient on its face, is sham and cannot be supported by evidence. The latter challenge, which was prohibited at common law, is now permitted in many jurisdictions that have adopted summary judgment procedures similar to Federal Rule 56. These procedures are discussed in detail at pp. 744–61, infra.

There are two other exceptions to the rule prohibiting consideration of matters other than the challenged pleading itself. The first of these is the doctrine of judicial notice, which permits the court to read into any pleading facts so universally known and accepted that there is no reason to believe they can be refuted. The second is the principle that permits the court to scrutinize the challenging party's own pleadings to determine if they are sufficient or whether they supply missing allegations necessary to uphold the pleading under attack. Both of these exceptions are discussed below.

COLVIG v. RKO GENERAL, INC., 232 Cal.App.2d 56, 63–64, 42 Cal.Rptr. 473, 478 (1st Dist.1965). Plaintiff, a radio announcer, who had been fired by defendant, his employer, had insisted on enforcement of a union-contract provision requiring arbitration of employment disputes. The arbitration award ordered defendant to restore plaintiff to his position. Although defendant paid plaintiff's salary as it became due, it refused to permit plaintiff to broadcast over the airwaves. Plaintiff then brought suit alleging that defendant's action was in violation of the arbitration award. In the complaint, plaintiff failed to allege that the arbitration award had become enforceable through confirmation by an appropriate court. Defendant demurred on the ground that the complaint thus failed to state a valid claim. The trial court granted the demurrer without leave to amend and plaintiff appealed. The appellate court reversed, stating as follows:

> While the complaint does not, on its face, disclose that the subject award was confirmed in action No. 522575 in the same court, the court below was entitled to take judicial notice of such other action since it was appropriately drawn to its attention. Courts take judicial notice of the public and private official acts of the judicial departments in this State where such acts are appropriately drawn to the attention of the court taking such notice. * * * Accordingly, in considering the sufficiency of the complaint, the trial court was not restricted to the matters appearing on the face of the complaint, but was entitled to read into it all matters of which it took judicial notice. * * * It is also well settled that where facts judicially noticed are contrary to those alleged in the complaint, the former must be regarded as true. * * * A reviewing court, furthermore, "can properly take judicial notice of any matter of which the court of original jurisdiction may properly take notice." (Varcoe v. Lee, 180 Cal. 338, 343, 181 P. 223, 225 * * *.)

NOTES AND QUESTIONS

1. The broad scope of facts that may be encompassed by the doctrine of judicial notice is indicated by Rule 9 of the Uniform Rules of Evidence:

(1) Judicial notice shall be taken without request by a party, of the common law, constitutions and public statutes in force in every state, territory and jurisdiction of the United States, and of such specific facts and propositions of generalized knowledge as are so universally known that they cannot reasonably be the subject of dispute.

(2) Judicial notice may be taken without request by a party, of (a) private acts and resolutions of the Congress of the United States and of the legislature of this state, and duly enacted ordinances and duly published regulations of governmental subdivisions or agencies of this state, and (b) the laws of foreign countries, and (c) such facts as are so generally known or of such common notoriety within the territorial jurisdiction of the court that they cannot reasonably be the subject of dispute, and (d) specific facts and propositions of generalized knowledge which are capable of immediate and accurate determination by resort to easily accessible sources of indisputable accuracy.

(3) Judicial notice shall be taken of each matter specified in paragraph (2) of this rule if a party requests it and (a) furnishes the judge sufficient information to enable him properly to comply with the request and (b) has given each adverse party such notice as the judge may require to enable the adverse party to prepare to meet the request.

A number of states have enacted judicial-notice statutes patterned after Uniform Rule 9 and generally covering the same classes of matters. See, e. g., Cal. Evid. Code §§ 451–53; Kan.Stat.Ann. § 60–409; N.Y.C.P.L.R. 4511. Other jurisdictions restrict the doctrine and vary considerably in their determinations of what types of facts properly can be noticed. See, e. g., JAMES v. UNKNOWN TRUSTEES, 203 Okl. 312, 314, 220 P.2d 831, 833–34 (1950), in which the court refused to take judicial notice of another action previously brought in the same court by the same parties.

2. A major effect of the doctrine of judicial notice is to excuse the party having the burden of establishing a fact from the necessity of producing evidence of that fact. What are the considerations underlying the doctrine of judicial notice with respect to its application to matters of proof? Do these same considerations justify the extension of the doctrine to cover matters of pleading? Should the scope of judicial notice with respect to pleading depend upon the precise nature of the fact to be noticed? Reread Rule 9(3) of the Uniform Rules of Evidence. The general rule is that the pleadings will be read to encompass all matters that can be judicially noted, and some states have specifically so provided by statute. E. g., Okl.Stat.Ann. tit. 12, § 308 (1961). Note that the effect of this approach is that judicial notice can work to the detriment as well as to the benefit of a pleader.

3. Over the years considerable attention has been given to the judicial notice of "foreign" law. Generally, a state court will take judicial notice of the laws of its own state as well as of federal law, and a federal court will notice the law of all the states as well as the laws of the United States. But under the common-law rule

not only would neither the state nor federal courts take judicial notice of the law of foreign countries but a state court would not notice the law of its sister states. According to ancient dogma, these categories of "foreign" law presented issues of fact that were required to be pleaded and proved like any other issue of fact. In the absence of pleading or proof, the courts generally presumed that the foreign law was the same as their own, although some courts adopted the Draconian policy of dismissing the action.

Through legislation or court rule, many courts have expanded the concept of judicial notice to encompass foreign law. More recently there has been an attempt to solve the foreign-law problem by eliminating the common-law constrictions of formal pleading and proof without substituting the often evanescent notion of judicial notice. In addition, there has been general recognition that it is unrealistic to treat issues of foreign law as issues of fact. See, e. g., Federal Rule 44.1, which took effect on July 1, 1966; Uniform Interstate and International Procedure Act §§ 4.01–4.03. These new provisions recognize that issues of foreign law, which may entail considerable research, differ markedly from judicial notice of other matters that are known or easily ascertained. Under the more modern procedures, a party who intends to raise an issue of foreign law normally is required so to inform the court and the other parties in advance, either in the pleadings or by other written notice, and is permitted to present any type of proof of the content of that law. For a comprehensive discussion of the history of judicial notice of foreign law and an analysis of the modern approach under Federal Rule 44.1, see Miller, *Federal Rule 44.1 and the "Fact" Approach to Determining Foreign Law: Death Knell for a Die-Hard Doctrine*, 65 Mich.L.Rev. 615 (1967).

THE RELEVANCE OF THE CHALLENGING PARTY'S OWN PLEADING

1.   Suppose that a plaintiff alleges facts A, B, and C, which are insufficient, without the addition of fact D, to state a valid claim for relief. Defendant, however, in the answer, alleges fact D. What effect should this have on defendant's claim that plaintiff's complaint should be dismissed? At common law a demurrer always was ruled upon in light of the content of all the pleadings that had been filed, not simply the one to which it was addressed. Thus a defective complaint could be "cured" or "aided" by allegations made by either party in subsequent pleadings. See Clark, *Code Pleading* § 119, at 735–36 (2d ed. 1947). What was the rationale of this rule? Should this practice be continued under modern pleading rules, such as those found in the Federal Rules?

2.   At common law the rule that the decision on a demurrer took into consideration all pleadings on file had an additional impact. If the party who made the challenge also had filed an insufficient pleading, the challenge subjected that party to an adverse ruling regarding her own pleading. Thus, if a plaintiff demurred to an answer on the ground that it stated no defense, but

on examination plaintiff's complaint proved insufficient, the entire action would be dismissed. See Note 8, p. 324, supra. Hence, the demurrer acted as "a searcher of the record." To what extent is it justifiable to apply this concept under modern pleading rules? See Roberts v. Fuquay-Varina Tobacco Bd. of Trade, Inc., 223 F.Supp. 212 (E.D.N.C.1963), modified 332 F.2d 521 (4th Cir.1964) (summary judgment entered against moving party).

B. ATTACKING IMPROPER FORM AND OTHER IRREGULARITIES

Read Federal Rules of Civil Procedure 12(e) and 12(f) in the Supplement.

One problem regarding challenges to the form of the pleadings already has been considered in connection with the *United Aircraft* and *Garcia* cases, which dealt with motions for a more definite statement. See pp. 396–99, 419–23, supra. A somewhat different challenge to the form arises when a party has included "scandalous," "impertinent," or "irrelevant" matter in a pleading. Traditionally, the remedy afforded is a motion to strike. See, e. g., Federal Rule 12(f); N.Y.C.P.L.R. 3024(b). On occasion some parties have attempted to utilize this motion to destroy or undercut their opponents' statements of valid claims or defenses. As held in GATEWAY BOTTLING, INC. v. DAD'S ROOTBEER CO., 53 F.R.D. 585 (W.D.Pa. 1971):

> With respect to the complaint that the material is scandalous, the question is again whether it asserts a valid and good faith defense to plaintiff's claim. To strike material as scandalous it must be obviously false and unrelated to the subject matter of the action. * * * The facts here may be unpleasant for plaintiff to have on the record and they certainly contain charges of reprehensible conduct but the same is true of many facts of life which are entitled to be pleaded as relevant to a cause of action or defense. Such, for example, are the facts concerning a divorce for adultery. These may be scandalous and annoying and prejudicial to the accused party but plaintiff or defendant is certainly entitled to plead them.

Even when allegations are not related to the subject matter of the case, the general rule today is that they will not be stricken from a complaint unless their presence will prejudice the adverse party. See Atlantic City Elec. Co. v. General Elec. Co., 207 F.Supp. 620 (S.D.N.Y.1962). The common law and code motions to strike allegations because they were "sham," "frivolous," "irrelevant," "redundant," "repetitious," "unnecessary," "immaterial," or "impertinent" have been eliminated, which "reflects a basic judgment that nothing is gained in the way of speedy and accurate disposition of litigation by disputes over the formal propriety of the allegations in the pleadings." 3 Weinstein, Korn & Miller, *New York Civil Practice* ¶ 3024.01.

The question whether allegations really are prejudicial seems to turn on whether the contents of the pleadings will be disclosed to the jury. In some instances pleadings themselves can become part of the evidence in the case and then, of course, the jury will be able to see and use them. However, such usage is strictly limited by the rules of evidence and irrelevant or prejudicial matters in the pleadings will be excluded. Hines v. Bost, 224 S.W. 698 (Tex.Civ.App.1920). Courts are divided on whether and to what extent such disclosure is proper when the pleadings are not introduced as part of the evidence in the case. Annot., 89 A.L.R. 1260 (1934). What circumstances, if any, would justify a motion to strike redundant, impertinent, or scandalous material in a case tried before a judge or before a jury in a jurisdiction that does not permit the jury to see the pleadings? See Silver v. Queen's Hospital, 53 F.R.D. 223 (D.Haw.1971).

Yet another problem of form exists in cases in which an entire pleading is challenged, either because it was filed too late, or necessary court approval had not been obtained, or other rules or orders have not been satisfied. Traditionally, this type of defect is reached by a motion to strike the pleading or to dismiss the claims that it contains. See Buck v. Morrossis, 114 Cal.App.2d 461, 250 P.2d 270 (1952).

C. RAISING MATTERS OF ABATEMENT

Read Federal Rules of Civil Procedure 12(b)(1)–(5), 12(b)(7), 12 (d) and the accompanying materials in the Supplement.

Pleas in abatement do not involve the merits or demerits of plaintiff's right to relief, but challenge plaintiff's right to maintain the action in the particular court or against the named parties. The bases for these pleas are discussed in other chapters. See, for example, pp. 65–178, supra, regarding matters of personal jurisdiction and service of process, pp. 238–63, supra, regarding proper venue, pp. 502–65, infra, referring to joinder of parties and causes, and p. 319, supra, dealing with common-law pleading.

Jurisdictions differ as to the mode by which matters in abatement are to be raised. On occasion the defect will appear on the face of the complaint. Defects of this type often will be handled by demurrer or special motion, in much the same way as substantive defects that appear on the face of the pleading. See Cal.Code Civ.Proc. § 430.10. If the defect does not appear on the face of the complaint, then it often will be raised in the answer as an affirmative defense. See Cal.Code Civ.Proc. § 430.30(b). There are other methods of challenge, however, and one must look to local law to see what is appropriate in each instance. For example, in many courts the usual manner of attacking personal jurisdiction is by motion to quash service, see e. g., Ill.Stat.Ann. ch. 110, § 20, and improper venue often is raised by a motion to transfer the case to a proper court, see, e. g., Ill.Stat.Ann. c. 110, § 8.

Often the manner in which a matter of abatement is raised will ensure an immediate decision on it. This is true, for example, when the challenge is by demurrer or motion to quash. Even when the defect is raised as an affirmative defense in the answer, however, some provisions, such as Federal Rule of Civil Procedure 12(d), often will permit special adjudication before trial. Why is early adjudication of abatement matters desirable? Should it be mandatory or are there exceptions? See Cal.Code Civ.Proc. §§ 597, 597.5, which are set out in the Supplement. When should a trial court defer hearing of a matter of abatement under Federal Rule 12(d) until the trial? See Grace v. MacArthur, 170 F.Supp. 442, 447–48 (E.D.Ark.1959). If the decision on this type of matter requires the resolution of a disputed issue of fact, what kind of evidence should the parties be allowed to present? See Unicon Management Corp. v. Koppers Co., 38 F.R.D. 474 (S.D.N.Y. 1965). If one of the parties has a right to and has demanded a trial by jury, must the matter in abatement be submitted to a jury or is the court always free to decide such an issue itself?

---

2. CONSEQUENCES OF THE RULING ON THE CHALLENGE

No matter whether a motion attacking a pleading is granted or denied, the losing party normally will be faced with the alternative of continuing the action in the trial court or appealing the decision on the motion. If the jurisdiction in which the case is tried permits appeals of interlocutory orders, the choice will be easier; if an appeal is indicated, it may be taken without prejudice to a continuation of the case in the trial court should the appeal be unsuccessful. Most jurisdictions, however, limit appeals from orders that are not final judgments to special situations. See pp. 1001–04, infra. Therefore, in order to appeal a decision on a motion attacking a pleading, a party first must permit a final judgment to be entered against him. Before deciding to do so he must balance his chance of success on the appeal against what may be serious consequences should he lose. What justification is there for a rule prohibiting interlocutory appeals on pleading matters? Are there situations in which such a rule is inappropriate?

KRIGER v. INDUSTRIAL REHABILITATION CORP., 8 A.D.2d 29, 185 N.Y.S.2d 658 (1st Dep't 1959), affirmed 7 N.Y.2d 958, 189 N.Y.S.2d 611, 166 N.E.2d 189 (1960). Plaintiffs brought a contract action against the defendants, X and Y. X successfully challenged the sufficiency of the first complaint, which was dismissed with leave to amend. Plaintiffs' amended complaint was dismissed as insufficient as against both X and Y. Again leave to amend was granted, but plaintiffs elected to stand on their pleading. On appeal they challenged the first dismissal as well as the second. The court refused to consider the propriety of the first ruling on the ground that by filing an amended complaint plaintiffs waived their right to appeal. The court reversed the dismissal of the amended complaint on the ground that several of the counts stated valid causes of action. The court did uphold the dismissal of one cause of action that it found insufficient. Plaintiffs then sought leave to amend to restate this claim. · The appellate court refused, noting that plaintiffs had been given the option to amend by the trial court but had decided to appeal instead.

NOTES AND QUESTIONS

1. A party whose pleading is dismissed or stricken as insufficient or otherwise improper normally will have the option of amending the pleading to correct the defects. See, e. g., Bertucelli v. Carreras, 467 F.2d 214 (9th Cir.1972); Breier v. Northern California Bowling Proprietors' Ass'n, 316 F.2d 787 (9th Cir. 1963), p. 482, infra.

Suppose plaintiff alleges facts A, B, C, and D, which plaintiff believes state a claim for relief. The trial court, however, upholds a motion to dismiss on the ground that no valid claim is stated, but indicates that an amended complaint alleging A, B, C, and E would be sufficient. Plaintiff must now decide whether to amend or appeal. What considerations should dictate his course of action?

2. What justification, if any, is there for a rule holding that by filing an amendment a litigant waives any right to appeal the decision dismissing the original pleading? See BLAZER v. BLACK, 196 F.2d 139, 143–44 (10th Cir. 1952):

In some jurisdictions, where a pleader elects to plead over and files an amended statement of his claim, any error committed by the trial court in striking allegations from his former statement is waived. * * * Other jurisdictions, while adhering to the general rule, recognize an exception under which the pleader does not waive his right to challenge the ruling on a motion to strike which leaves a question of fact in the pleadings. * * * It has long been the rule of Federal practice * * * that while the pleader who amends or pleads over, waives his objections to the ruling of the court on indefiniteness, incompleteness or insufficiency, or mere technical defects in pleadings, he does not waive his exception to the ruling which strikes "a vital blow to a substantial part" of his cause of action.

Normally there are two methods of amendment. The pleader may file an amendment that details those matters that should be added to or eliminated from the original pleading or may file an entirely separate amended pleading that does not refer to the original. Should the form of the amendment be of any significance? In LEGGETT v. MONTGOMERY WARD & CO., 178 F.2d 436, 438 (10th Cir.1949), the court held:

> It is argued that the [trial] court erred in dismissing the original complaint in the case. The order dismissing the original complaint provided that plaintiff be allowed ten days within which to file an amended complaint. The amended complaint was complete within itself and did not refer to or adopt the original pleading. By filing the amended complaint in that form, plaintiff completely waived any error in the ruling relating to the original complaint.

3. In most jurisdictions an appellate court has discretionary power to remand a case to allow a party to amend a pleading even though it has affirmed an order of the trial court holding that pleading insufficient. What criteria should an appellate court apply in deciding whether or not to exercise this power? To what extent should the appellate court's decision to allow an amendment after appeal differ from the trial court's obligation to do so, if no appeal is taken? What weight should be given to the fact that the jurisdiction does or does not permit interlocutory appeals?

4. If a party whose challenge is overruled wishes to appeal immediately and an interlocutory appeal is not permissible, he must first allow a judgment to be entered against him. If the appeal is rejected, should the party be permitted to re-open the case and proceed to trial? See STATE ex rel. RANDOLPH v. HANCOCK CIRCUIT COURT, 243 Ind. 156, 160, 182 N.E.2d 248, 249 (1962): "The Court having overruled the demurrer of the State of Indiana * * * and having entered a rule requiring the State to plead over or to answer * * *, it must be considered that the State by not answering or pleading over * * * not only waived all issues as to the pleadings, but also admitted that the * * * petition stated a good cause of action as a matter of law." Are the considerations in this context any different from those in a case in which a demurrer has been sustained and plaintiff, having foregone the right to amend in favor of an appeal that proved unsuccessful, then seeks to have the appellate court remand to permit an amendment?

Since a litigant who is careful to preserve her rights by proper objection throughout the trial always may appeal from an adverse verdict based upon a cause of action or defense not recognized in the law, why should a lawyer ever elect to take an immediate appeal from a decision overruling a challenge to the pleadings? Note that even if the appeal is successful, the case normally will be remanded to permit the opponent to seek leave to amend the defective pleading.

3. TIMING OF THE CHALLENGE—WAIVER

Read Federal Rules of Civil Procedure 8(d), 12(d), 12(g), and 12(h) and the accompanying materials in the Supplement.

VAN VOORHIS v. DISTRICT OF COLUMBIA

United States District Court, District of Columbia, 1965.
240 F.Supp. 822.

TAMM, District Judge.

* * * The facts giving rise to this case, as stipulated by the parties in the pretrial statement, are as follows: On January 22, 1960, at about 3:49 p. m., an automobile owned by plaintiff John Van Voorhis and operated by his wife plaintiff Mildred Van Voorhis, was proceeding in a south-westerly direction along Michigan Avenue, NE., in the District of Columbia. At the intersection of Michigan Avenue and South Dakota Avenue, NE., Mrs. Van Voorhis' car was in a collision with a fire engine of the District of Columbia, which was responding to a fire alarm. The fire truck was travelling southeast on South Dakota Avenue.

As a result of that collision, the plaintiffs filed suit on September 8, 1961, against the District of Columbia "pursuant to the provisions of 'The District of Columbia Employee Non-Liability Act' (hereinafter referred to as "Act") Public Law 86–654; 74 Stat. 519, approved July 14, 1960," and effective thirty days later on August 14, 1960, nearly seven months after the date of this accident. The complaint alleges gross negligence on the part of the District's employee in his operation of the fire truck and claims damages for personal injuries to Mrs. Van Voorhis. Mr. Van Voorhis sues for loss of consortium of his wife.

In its answer to the complaint, the District's first defense is "that the complaint fails to state a claim against it upon which relief can be granted." On November 4, 1964, following the stipulation of facts in the pretrial statement, defendant asserted this defense in a motion to dismiss the complaint on the ground that the Act has no application to the facts of this case and, therefore, the District is entitled to the defense of governmental immunity.

Defendant's motion was argued before Judge Curran, who held on January 8, 1965, that the Act, which deprives the District of the defense of governmental immunity in suits of this nature, was intended to be applied retroactively as well as prospectively and as so applied to this case would not be unconstitutional. Judge Curran, therefore, denied the defendant's motion to dismiss.

The case then went to trial before a jury, which was unable to reach a decision on the merits of the plaintiffs' case. Defendant now reasserts its defense of governmental immunity in the form of the present motion for judgment in spite of the failure of the jury to reach a verdict.

At the outset, the Court is met with plaintiffs' argument in opposition to this motion "that Judge Curran's memorandum opinion is the law of the case on this point and whether or not the question was incorrectly decided is not for this Court, but can only be resolved by the Court of Appeals." The Court, however, is unable to accept that argument.

* * * [T]here is a sound reason for not applying the law of the case doctrine where the prior ruling was on a motion to dismiss under Rule 12(b)(6) * * *. The defense of failure to state a claim upon which relief can be granted cannot be waived and can be asserted at the trial on the merits and hence neither the defendant nor the trial court is concluded by a prior ruling on a motion to dismiss from reconsidering the questions previously raised. * * *

Perhaps the strongest factor influencing the Court's decision to reconsider this question, notwithstanding Judge Curran's opinion, is that the parties in this matter are presently faced with the possibility of retrying the case before another jury, after having undergone the fruitless time and expense of the first trial. Since the Court disagrees with Judge Curran's opinion, its decision will result in a final order being entered in the case, which can be appealed from, if so desired. In that way, the issue can be finally determined, and any unnecessary and wasteful litigation may be avoided.

* * *

NOTES AND QUESTIONS

1. In NELSON v. AMERICAN EMPLOYERS INS. CO., 262 Wis. 271, 274, 55 N.W.2d 13, 14 (1952), the court held that:

> * * * Successive demurrers on the same ground to the same pleading can not be permitted if pending actions are to be disposed of.
> * * * The defendants had their day in court and it was incumbent on them then to submit their complete argument in support of their position. The case can not be heard again because counsels' subsequent research convinces them that more might be said.

What, if anything, can be said to counter this argument?

2.   Does it make sense to allow a challenge to the substantive sufficiency of a pleading once the parties are actively engaged in trial? See Wis.Stat.Ann. § 263.19 in the Supplement.   See generally 5 Wright & Miller, *Federal Practice and Procedure: Civil* §§ 1390–97 (1969).   Under Rule 12(h)(2) when does "the trial on the merits" terminate?   Should the word "trial" be read only to embrace the period during which evidence is presented or should it be held to permit a party to raise for the first time on appeal the defense that the complaint does not state a right to relief?   See Black, Sivalls & Bryson, Inc. v. Shondell, 174 F.2d 587, 590–91 (8th Cir.1949) (issues held waived by failure to raise them in the court below).   Compare SOUTHARD v. SOUTHARD, 305 F.2d 730 (2d Cir.1962), in which the trial court dismissed plaintiff's action prior to trial on the ground that it had discretion to refuse jurisdiction.   The appellate court, without specifically ruling on the jurisdiction point, affirmed the judgment below on the ground that the complaint, on its face, showed that relief was barred by principles of res judicata, a defense that was raised for the first time on appeal.   See also Unruh v. Truck Ins. Exchange, 7 Cal.3d 616, 622, 102 Cal.Rptr. 815, 819, 498 P.2d 1063, 1067 (1972).   What relevance, if any, does Federal Rule 15 have to this subject?

3.   With few exceptions, challenges to the form of pleadings or of pleas in abatement will be waived unless raised at an early stage in the proceedings. Federal Rule 12(h)(1) is somewhat more lenient than many state rules that allow such matters to be raised only at the earliest available opportunity. See, e. g., Ostrowski v. Miller, 226 Cal.App.2d 79, 86, 37 Cal.Rptr. 790, 793 (1964); Texas Securities Corp. v. Peters, 463 S.W.2d 263 (Tex.Civ.App.1971).

Note that once defendant makes a motion under Rule 12(g) much of the flexibility allowed under Federal Rule 12(h)(1) is lost. Is this procedure too rigid? Should defendant have two opportunities to raise each Rule 12(b) defense, one by motion and the other by answer? Federal Rule 12(b) clearly states that a defendant, without waiving any rights, can join defenses on the merits with challenges to jurisdiction and venue. But should he be permitted to go further and join a counterclaim for affirmative relief? In BEAUNIT MILLS, INC. v. INDUSTRIAS REUNIDAS F. MATARAZZO, S.A., 23 F.R.D. 654 (S.D. N.Y.1959), the court held that by filing a counterclaim defendant waived its challenges to jurisdiction and venue. Is the decision a sound one? See 59 Colum.L.Rev. 1093 (1959). See also Ryan v. Glenn, 336 F.Supp. 555 (N.D. Miss.1971).

SECTION G. AMENDMENTS

1. IN GENERAL

Read Federal Rule of Civil Procedure 15(a) and the accompanying materials in the Supplement.

BREIER v. NORTHERN CALIFORNIA BOWLING PROPRIETORS' ASS'N

United States Court of Appeals, Ninth Circuit, 1963.
316 F.2d 787.

BROWNING, Circuit Judge. Appellants operate bowling establishments in the San Francisco Bay Area. Appellees are a number of appellants' competitors, plus five local associations of bowling establishment proprietors and the Bowling Proprietors' Association of America. Appellants brought separate actions against appellees under the Antitrust Acts (15 U.S.C.A. §§ 1 and 15) charging appellees with conspiring to fix prices for bowling in Northern California. It was alleged that appellees enforced their price-fixing agreement by excluding customers of non-cooperating bowling establishments from tournaments organized by appellees, thereby making it impossible for appellants and other non-cooperating bowling establishments to remain in business.

Appellees moved to dismiss the complaints for failure to state a claim upon which relief can be granted. The District Court concluded that the complaints failed to allege that the restraint was one upon commerce "among the several States" within the meaning of 15 U.S.C.A. § 1, and entered an order granting the motions * * *.

Appellants inquired whether the order was intended to preclude amendment of the complaints. The District Court responded that it thought the complaints "so inherently frail" that they were "not the subject of any amendment." Judgment was then entered denying leave to file amended complaints and dismissing the actions.

FRCP #15. We think appellants were entitled to file amended complaints as a matter of right. "A party may amend his pleading once as a matter of course at any time before a responsive pleading is served * * *." Rule 15(a), Fed.R. Civ.P. A motion to dismiss is not a "responsive pleading" within the meaning of the Rule. Neither the filing nor granting of such a motion before answer terminates the right to amend; an order of dismissal denying leave to amend at that stage is improper, and a motion for leave to amend (though unnecessary) must be granted if filed. * * *[1]

---

1 * * *
The entry of *judgment* dismissing the *action* has been held to terminate the right to amend without leave. * * *

Even if the question had been addressed to the Court's discretion, we think leave to amend should have been granted. The purpose of pleading under the Rules "is to facilitate a proper decision on the merits." Conley v. Gibson, 355 U.S. 41, 48, 78 S.Ct. 99, 2 L.Ed.2d 80 (1957). To this end, Rule 15 "was designed to facilitate the amendment of pleadings except where prejudice to the opposing party would result." United States v. Hougham, 364 U.S. 310, 316, 81 S.Ct. 13, 5 L.Ed.2d 8 (1960). "If the underlying facts or circumstances relied upon by a plaintiff may be a proper subject of relief, he ought to be afforded an opportunity to test his claim on the merits. In the absence of any apparent or declared reason—such as undue delay, bad faith or dilatory motive on the part of the movant, repeated failure to cure deficiencies by amendments previously allowed, undue prejudice to the opposing party by virtue of allowance of the amendment, futility of amendment, etc.—the leave sought should, as the rules require, be 'freely given.'" Foman v. Davis, 371 U.S. 178, 182, 83 S.Ct. 227, 9 L.Ed.2d 222 (1962).

Amendment except where prejudice

* * * As we have recently said, leave to amend should be allowed unless the complaint "cannot under any conceivable state of facts be amended to state a claim." Alexander v. Pacific Maritime Ass'n, 9th Cir., 1963, 314 F.2d 690. * * *

Amend. should be allowed unless inconceivable to amend.

There are references in the record to an impact upon interstate commerce in "equipment, appointments and furnishings" used in the construction and maintenance of bowling establishments, in bowling pins and balls used in the daily operation of these establishments, in balls, bags and shoes which they sell to bowlers, and upon an "interstate network of tournaments" organized and conducted by appellees from which appellants' customers are said to be excluded. It cannot be said with certainty that appellants will be unable to allege a relationship between appellees' conduct and commerce among the states sufficient to state a claim upon which relief can be granted under Section 1 of the Sherman Act. * * *

We * * * decline to speculate as to whether the amended complaints will be legally sufficient. It has been said that the sufficiency of an amended pleading ordinarily will not be considered on motion for leave to amend * * * and in any event it is inappropriate for an appellate court to evaluate possible amendments not yet considered by the court below. * * *

Reversed.

NOTES AND QUESTIONS

1. Is there any justification for a provision permitting an amendment without leave of court? *Compare* Fed.Rule Civ.Proc. 15(a), *with* N.Y.C.P.L.R. 3025 (a), which is set out in the Supplement, as to the length of time within which such an amendment is allowed. Does the decision in *Breier* indicate that cases may arise in which the New York rule would be preferable?

2. In STANLEY WORKS v. HAEGER POTTERIES, INC., 35 F.R.D. 551, 554 (N.D.Ill.1964), the court held that a copy of the proposed amendment need not be attached to the motion for leave to amend. Is this sound? Shouldn't the sufficiency of the amendment be a major factor in deciding whether or not

leave should be granted? See Blevins v. Mullan Contracting Co., 235 Md. 188, 194, 201 A.2d 348, 351–52 (1964), upholding a denial of leave to amend on the ground that plaintiff at trial was not likely to prevail on the amended claim.

3. To what extent should a party be permitted to amend to state facts directly contradictory to those set out in the original pleading? Should it make any difference whether the court has ruled that a complaint or answer is insufficient because of the original facts stated?

To what extent can the original pleading be amended if it was verified? In OWENS v. TRAVERSO, 125 Cal.App.2d 803, 271 P.2d 164 (1st Dist.1954), the court held that a verified complaint that was dismissed because the allegations revealed the existence of a valid defense could not successfully be amended by eliminating the defense, at least not without an explanation of why an amendment was justifiable.

4. How many chances to amend should a pleader be allowed before leave to amend is denied? In GAUTIER v. GENERAL TEL. CO., 234 Cal.App.2d 302, 310, 44 Cal.Rptr. 404, 409 (2d Dist.1965), the court upheld dismissal, without leave to amend, of plaintiff's fourth amended complaint on the ground that "the trial court could reasonably conclude that the complaint was incapable of being amended to state a cause of action." *Compare* Hambaugh v. Peoples, 75 N.M. 144, 401 P.2d 777 (1965) (denial of leave to amend a first amended complaint reversed), *with* Heart Disease Research Foundation v. General Motors Corp., 463 F.2d 98 (2d Cir.1972) (denial of leave to amend a first amended complaint affirmed). What factors should a court consider in making its decision in such a case?

---

2. THE VARIANCE PROBLEM

Read Federal Rule of Civil Procedure 15(b) and the accompanying materials in the Supplement.

STANDARD TITLE INS. CO. v. ROBERTS

United States Court of Appeals, Eighth Circuit, 1965.
349 F.2d 613.

REGISTER, District Judge. This is a suit on a written guaranty of a corporate note, such note being executed by the appellee, individually, at a time when he was the president and sole stockholder of the corporate debtor. Trial was had before The Honorable Richard M. Duncan, sitting without a jury.

*   *   *

The sole cause of action alleged in the amended complaint was based on a written guaranty. In his answer the appellee asserted, as a defense, in paragraph 4 thereof, that the note involved was secured by certain collateral (notes secured by deeds of trust and guaranteed by title insurance policies) and that appellant was required by law to exhaust such collateral before proceeding against the appellee, or that appellee was entitled to the benefit of the collateral and, in paragraph 5, that said note had been fully paid and discharged. Appellant's reply to appellee's answer consists of eight paragraphs: Paragraph 1 is a general denial; each of the other paragraphs states that it is in reply to paragraph 4 of the answer. All of the allegations contained in the reply are asserted to be the basis upon which appellee should be estopped from requiring appellant to exhaust or look to that portion of the collateral represented by the title insurance policies. In substance, appellant asserts in its reply that appellee was guilty of a specific act of fraud in knowingly and falsely representing to the appellant that said title insurance policies insured first deeds of trust upon land described therein (when in fact he knew or should have known said land was then subject to a prior and superior deed of trust) and, also, that appellee received $25,000 withdrawn from a certain bank account in violation of an existing understanding and thereby became unjustly enriched.

Upon the issues as thus framed by the pleadings, the case proceeded to trial. During the course of the trial, the prior deed of trust and note secured thereby were offered and received as exhibits, by stipulation, and the real estate contract which was partially satisfied by the giving of such prior deed of trust was received in evidence as an exhibit without objection. Direct and cross-examination of two of appellant's witnesses were related to these exhibits, (viz., that said prior deed of trust was, at the time of the transaction involved and for several months prior thereto, of public record); to the question of whether the prior note and deed of trust were, in fact, known to the policy-signing agent of the appellant; to the withdrawal of the sum of $25,000 from the bank, and the deposit thereof in the account of the Woodridge Corporation; and to the use to which said sum, or a portion thereof, was put.

* * * [T]he trial was completed on January 14, 1964. Appellee offered no evidence, but stood on * * * [a] motion for directed verdict. On March 2, 1964 appellant filed its Motion for Leave to Amend Amended Complaint, which amendment proposed to add the following paragraph to the Amended Complaint:

"8. Defendant (appellee) is legally obligated to indemnify plaintiffs (appellant) for their loss by reason of defendant's active negligence and misconduct in connection with said transactions, and for the further reason that defendant has made possible the loss sustained by plaintiffs."

Appellant contends the record establishes "that the issue of its right to indemnification from defendant was submitted and tried by the express and implied consent of the parties at the trial," and emphasizes that portion of the record relative to the admission of the exhibits heretofore referred to in support thereof.

We do not agree with such contention; a careful reading of the trial record discloses that the case was tried on the issues as they existed under the pleadings at the time of trial. The alleged claim of liability against appellee

was based solely on the written guarantee; to such alleged liability appellee
pleaded specific defenses, in his answer. Appellant's allegation in its reply,
with respect to alleged fraud and negligence on the part of appellee, was directed specifically to certain defenses pleaded in the answer, and was for the
expressed sole purpose of estopping appellee from claiming the benefit of such
defenses. Thus, the only issue as to alleged fraud and negligence arose from
the answer and reply thereto, and related exclusively to whether appellee
should be estopped from relying upon specific, pleaded defenses. The record
clearly reveals that the evidence concerning the prior deed of trust was relevant
and material to the specific issue raised by the reply and answer. The proffered amendment set forth a completely new cause of action, based on a wholly
different theory from that alleged in the amended complaint. The fact that
the evidence submitted and received at the trial, on the then existing issue
raised by the answer and reply, would have been relevant and admissible in the
trial of such new cause of action does not mean that the latter was tried by the
express or implied consent of the appellee.   *   *   *

> "The purpose of an amendment to conform to proof is to bring the
> pleadings in line with the actual issues upon which the case was
> tried; therefore an amendment after judgment is not permissible
> which brings in some entirely extrinsic issue or changes the theory
> on which the case was actually tried, even though there is evidence
> in the record—introduced as relevant to some other issue—which
> would support the amendment. This principle is sound, since it
> cannot be fairly said that there is any implied consent to try an is-
> sue where the parties do not squarely recognize it as an issue in the
> trial." [3 Moore, *Federal Practice* ¶ 15.13[2], at 991–92 (2d
> ed.)]. * * *

Appellant next contends that "Even if the Court should find that the issue of indemnification was not tried by the express or implied consent of the
parties under Rule 15(b)   *   *   *   the Court, nevertheless, abused its discretion in tacitly denying plaintiff's Motion for Leave to Amend Amended
Complaint because justice required that the amendment be allowed in this instance." Reliance is placed upon Rule 15(a).   *   *   *

In this case the proposed amendment was submitted, some two and one-
half years after the filing of the original complaint; one year and eleven
months after the filing of the amended complaint; and more than six weeks
after the trial had been completed and the case taken under advisement by the
trial court. It in effect would have introduced a new cause of action, based on
an entirely different theory than that upon which the case had been tried. The
tactics and strategy of the appellee at the trial were doubtless dictated by the
then existing state of the pleadings and record—as is indicated by the fact that,
following completion of the appellant's proof, the appellee stood on his motion for directed verdict. When the Motion to Amend was made the trial
court may have considered the necessity of a partial retrial, and the extent
thereof, in event the same be granted. If a cause of action existed against the
appellee in favor of the appellant upon the basis of tort, unjust enrichment, or

some other equitable basis, the same could be litigated by institution of a proper action. Appellant has, in our opinion, failed to demonstrate that, under the facts of this case, the trial court abused its discretion in tacitly denying the Motion to Amend.

* * *

Affirmed.

NOTES AND QUESTIONS

1. What justification is there, if any, for a rule that, despite the absence of prejudice to the adverse party, would prohibit any amendment introducing a new cause of action or defense? Should the rule be the same if the amendment is offered before or during trial rather than afterward? Reread *Messick v. Turnage*, p. 383, supra, and the notes following it.

2. Notice the tactical dilemma faced by a party when the opposition seeks to introduce evidence at trial on an issue that clearly is not within the pleadings. The litigant may object and keep the evidence out, but this will induce the other side to request, leave to amend, perhaps even to add an issue of which the party seeking amendment previously was not aware. On the other hand, a failure to object may be taken as implied consent to try the issue, thus permitting an amendment to conform to the proof. See Comment, 4 Wm. & Mary L.Rev. 74 (1963). Whenever a party fails to object in this situation a second dilemma must be faced —whether or not to produce evidence on the point in question.

Even a party who objects to the evidence may face further problems. Suppose the court erroneously holds that the original pleadings encompass the newly introduced issue? In HAYES v. RICHFIELD OIL CORP., 38 Cal.2d 375, 382, 240 P.2d 580, 584 (1952), the court held:

> A variance between the allegations of a pleading and the proof will not be deemed material unless it has actually misled the adverse party to his prejudice * * *. If anything, Richfield's continued insistence [throughout the trial] that the issue was not presented by the pleadings indicates that it was fully aware that the [trial] court's rulings would permit recovery under * * * [the new] theory. It does not appear that Richfield has been in any way prejudiced by the variance * * *.

3. The *Roberts* case was tried without a jury. What should be the effect of a jury trial on the availability of leave to amend during or after trial?

4. Was the trial court in *Roberts* justified in denying leave to amend under Federal Rule 15(a)? What are the factors to be considered by a court in exercising its discretion in such a case? Should the court look only to see if there has been material prejudice to the opposing party, such as the death of an eyewitness, or should it balance the alleged prejudice against the interests of the party who seeks the amendment? See generally Donnici, *The Amendment of Pleadings—A Study of the Operation of Judicial Discretion in the Federal Courts*, 37 So.Cal.L.Rev. 529 (1964).

3. AMENDMENTS AND THE STATUTE OF LIMITATIONS

A. AMENDMENTS TO THE CLAIM FOR RELIEF

Read Federal Rule of Civil Procedure 15(c) and the accompanying materials in the Supplement.

LEVEY v. NEWARK BETH ISRAEL HOSPITAL

Essex County Court, Law Division, New Jersey, 1952.
17 N.J.Super. 290, 85 A.2d 827.

COLIE, J. S. C. This is a motion to amend the complaint in a negligence action. The complaint alleged that in May 1948, while plaintiffs were employed in the defendant hospital, "there had been confined in said hospital a patient suffering from a disease known as infectious mononucleosis and a condition of the liver, which conditions the defendant knew or should have known were highly infectious * * *; that due and proper care and proper medical practice required that any patient so suffering should be isolated and so managed and guarded as to prevent the spreading of such infection * * *; that due and proper care was not taken by the defendant * * * and that as a result of such negligence * * * the plaintiff(s) contracted infectious mononucleosis complicated by hepatitis" and as a result became ill and sustained damages which they now seek to recover.

The amendment seeks recovery on the allegation above quoted and also upon an allegation that "the defendant was negligent in failing to properly diagnose (their) condition, and was thereafter negligent in the treatment accorded * * * after (the) true condition was discovered, which improper treatment included a failure to provide adequate rest and an adequate period for proper recuperation, before being ordered to return to duty."

The statute has run against the institution of a new suit and the question for decision is whether the amendment to the complaint which the plaintiffs now seek leave to file, states a new and different cause of action.

Rule 3:15–1 provides that "a party may amend his pleading only by leave of court * * *; and leave shall be freely given when justice so requires." The question of whether or not an amendment will be allowed after the running of the statute of limitations has been before the Supreme Court. In Russo v. Wright Aeronautical Corp., 1 N.J. 417, 64 A.2d 71, 72 (1949) it was said: " '* * * an entirely new and different cause of action cannot be introduced after the statute has tolled the action.' But it is equally well settled 'that an amendment will not, as a rule, be held to state a new cause of action, if the facts alleged show substantially the same wrong with respect to the same transaction, or if it is the same matter more fully or differently laid, or if the gist of the action or the subject of controversy remains the same.' (Citing cases.) ' "Gist" is the essential ground or object of the action in point of law, without which there would be no cause of action; the cause for which an action will lie; the ground or foundation of a suit, without which it would not be maintainable;   *   *   *'."

Thereafter, in Welsh v. Bd. of Ed. of Tewksbury Tp., 7 N.J.Super. 141, 72 A.2d 350, 352 (App.Div.1950) the court said: "It has been the firmly implanted rule that an entirely new and distinctly different cause of action cannot by means of an amendment of the pleadings be introduced after the statute has tolled the action. (Citing cases.)

"The existing liberality in permitting amendments is bestowed to prevent legalistic technicalities from impeding, or obstructing, the paramount aspiration to promote substantial justice in all litigious controversies. The present progressive judicial policy is not, however, intended to afford a refuge to languid and dilatory litigants.   *   *   *

"It would be supremely impracticable, if not pernicious, to condone a practice which would permit adventurous litigants by means of successive amendments to the pleadings in the original action to prosecute, *seriatim,* a procession of distinctly disparate causes of action and thus elude the statutory limitations of time.   *   *   *

"*   *   *   Where a statute of limitations is involved, unwarranted graciousness might well constitute an unjustifiable judiciable trespass upon the legislative field."

With these statements as criteria, the question becomes one of determining whether the "gist" of the original complaint and the sought-for amendment are the same. The plaintiffs urge that there is no substantial change in the nature of the claim and rely upon O'Shaughnessy v. Bayonne News, 154 A. 13, 14, 9 N.J.Misc. 345 (Cir.Ct.1931); Id., 109 N.J.L. 271, 160 A. 696 (E. & A. 1932): "So an amendment will not as a rule be held to state a new cause of action if the facts alleged show substantially the same wrong with respect to the same transaction, or if it is the same matter more fully or differently laid, or, if the gist of the action or the subject of controversy remains the same; and this is true although the form of liability asserted, or the alleged incidents of the transaction may be different. Technical rules will not be applied in determining whether the cause of actions stated in the original and amended pleadings are identical, since in a strict sense almost any amendment may be said to change the original cause of action. 49 C.J. 510, 511.

[margin note: Test for "change" in amendment]

"In a tort action an amendment may vary the statement of the original complaint as to the manner in which the plaintiff was injured, or as to the manner of the defendants' breach of duty, without necessarily setting up a new cause of action."

No entirely satisfactory definition of a cause of action has as yet been enunciated but a generally accepted definition is that a cause of action is "the fact or facts which establish or give rise to a right of action, the existence of which affords a party a right to judicial relief." 1 Am.Jur., Actions, p. 404.

[margin note: definition of a C/A]

Confusion arises from confounding the cause of action, that is, the invasion of the right of the plaintiff, on the one hand and on the other hand the damages that flow therefrom. If the plaintiffs establish that there was negligence from the failure to exercise reasonable precautions in isolating the patient with the infectious disease, presumably a cause of action arises. If they establish that there was negligence in diagnosis and treatment, it may well be that they have a cause of action therefor but that is a far cry from saying that the latter is not a new and different cause of action. Referring to the definition of "gist," quoted earlier in this opinion, it would be well to consider the fact that the plaintiffs might recover in an action based upon the sought-for amendment and not even assert the earlier ground set forth in the complaint. That such a result might readily follow, in the event that the amendment was allowed, seems to point up the fact that the second ground upon which plaintiffs seek to recover is both new and different. The evidence to support the two bases for recovery.would, or might, be entirely different. In the first action, the negligence might well be the failure of the management personnel of the hospital, whereas in the second cause of action, grounded upon erroneous or faulty diagnoses, presumably the negligence would be that of the doctors who attended plaintiffs. Parenthetically, the doctors might or might not be the agents of the hospital. It seems clear that what plaintiffs now seek is to set up a new and different cause of action after the statute has run. That they may not do and the motion to amend is denied.

[handwritten margin note: Holding.]

NOTES AND QUESTIONS

1. The general attitude of those courts that have applied Federal Rule 15(c) or one of its state counterparts is evidenced by the Supreme Court of Michigan in LaBAR v. COOPER, 376 Mich. 401, 405–06, 137 N.W.2d 136, 138 (1965):

GCR 118 is an adoption of Federal Rule 15. The purpose of its adoption is stated by Professor Hawkins and Jason Honigman, [Esq.] at 1 Michigan Court Rules Annotated, page 416:

"* * * The test is no longer conceptual, but rather functional. The amendment relates back to the date of the original pleading and, therefore, is not barred by limitations, whenever the claim or defense asserted in the amendment arose out of the conduct, transaction, or occurrence set forth or attempted to be set forth in the original pleading. *It is thus beside the point that the amendment introduces new facts, a new theory, or even a different cause of action, so long as it springs from the same transactional setting as that pleaded originally.* The new test satisfies the basic policy of the statute of limitations, because the transactional base of the claim must still be pleaded before the statute runs, thereby giving defendant notice within the statutory period that he must be prepared to defend against all claims for relief arising out of that transaction." (Emphasis supplied.)

[handwritten margin note: Same pleading if it arises from the same transactional setting.]

See also N.Y.C.P.L.R. 203(e); Scott v. Newsom, 74 N.M. 399, 394 P.2d 253 (1964); Keel v. Brown, 162 So.2d 321 (Fla.App.2d Dist.1964). On the other hand, a sizeable number of recent cases still reflect a restrictive view of the "relation back" doctrine. See, e. g., Nason v. Jones, 278 Ala. 532, 179 So.2d 281 (1965); Johnson v. Bar-Mour, Inc., 27 Wis.2d 271, 133 N.W.2d 748 (1965).

2. In PINKSTON v. LIEB, 48 Cal.App.2d 352, 354, 119 P.2d 1010, 1011 (2d Dist.1941), plaintiffs brought a slander action, alleging that defendant informed the police that plaintiffs were running a house of prostitution. Evidently plaintiffs originally were uncertain where and to which officers the statements were made, because at the trial, after the statute of limitations had run, plaintiffs amended their complaint in this regard. The court, in holding that the amendment did not relate back to the time the original pleadings were filed, stated as follows:

> * * * It needs no citation of authority to support the proposition that an allegation that defendant made slanderous remarks in the presence of certain specified persons at the Lincoln Heights Police Station on June 22, 1939, is an entirely separate and distinct cause of action from an allegation that he made similar statements in the presence of Carl W. Bittner and another police officer at or about No. 3018 Division Street, Los Angeles, on June 22, 1939. Proof of each of the allegations would have supported judgments on two separate and distinct causes of action. Recovery on one would not have constituted a bar to a recovery upon the other cause of action.

How would *Pinkston v. Lieb* have been decided under Federal Rule 15(c)? Would the *Levey* case have been decided the same way under Rule 15(c)? Examine the New Jersey amendment rule in the Supplement once again.

B. AMENDMENTS ADDING PARTIES

Reread Federal Rule of Civil Procedure 15(c) and those accompanying materials in the Supplement referring to the addition of new parties by amendment.

MARTZ v. MILLER BROTHERS CO.

United States District Court, District of Delaware, 1965.
244 F.Supp. 246.

CALEB M. WRIGHT, Chief Judge. * * *

On April 7, 1961, James W. Martz, Jr., suffered injuries when some cement and ceiling material fell while he was passing on a sidewalk adjacent to Miller Brothers' furniture store in Newark, Delaware. * * * The complaint was filed just two days before the statute of limitations ran on plaintiff's claim, and service of process was not effected until April 10, 1963, several days after the tolling of the statute. Indeed, plaintiff's attorney apparently had to act with some haste in order to commence this action in time because he was not apprised of the claim until a few days before the filing of the complaint.

On April 29, 1963 defendant moved for summary judgment on the ground that it did not own or operate the Newark store. Subsequently, an affidavit was filed in which Bruno E. dePolo, secretary of the defendant, stated on information and belief that the premises upon which plaintiff was injured were owned by Miller Brothers Company of Newark, a corporation separate and distinct from Miller Brothers Company.

There followed a period in which plaintiff's attorney sought through interrogatories and depositions to establish the true ownership of the Newark store. He found that the Newark store was, indeed, operated by Miller Brothers Company of Newark which was a separate corporation from Miller Brothers Company which operated a furniture store in Wilmington. He also discovered that the two stores had the same officers with the exception of the secretary. The secretary of Miller Brothers Company was dePolo and the secretary of Miller Brothers Company of Newark was Richard Miller. It was dePolo who was served with the summons and complaint in this action.

The result of the discovery was a motion by plaintiff seeking leave to amend his complaint to name Miller Brothers Company of Newark as defendant. This motion was filed December 1, 1964.

ISSUE

The two motions before the court—the motion for summary judgment and the motion for leave to amend—turn on one central question: whether the court will permit an amendment to the name of the defendant *which relates back to the time of the original complaint.* If the court were to find that the wrong corporation had indeed been named and refuse to permit an amendment, the statute of limitations will have run on plaintiff's claim. Thus, by determining whether or not plaintiff is entitled to an amendment which relates back to the time he filed his original complaint, the court will effectively protect or foreclose plaintiff's claim.

R/L

*   *   *   While an amendment may be made to correct a mistake in the name of a party, a new party may not be brought into an action once the statute of limitations has run because such an amendment amounts to a new and independent cause of action.   *   *   *   Because of this rule courts have come to analyze cases in which it is sought to substitute a party defendant in terms of "misnomer." If the amendment merely corrects a misdescription of the party intended to be sued for the purpose of proper identification, a misnomer is set to right. If, on the other hand, the amendment in effect brings in a new party, a new cause of action results and the amendment cannot relate back to the original complaint.

Unfortunately, the fruits of analysis in these terms have not been entirely satisfactory. "Even in theory the distinction between an amendment changing or correcting such mistakes in the names of the parties and an amendment aiming at the substitution of parties plaintiff or defendant is not free from difficulty, but in actual practice the line between the two types of amendments can hardly be drawn accurately.   *   *   *" 8 A.L.R.2d 6, 16 (1949).

With an eye to the facts in this case fully aware that leave to amend "shall be freely given where justice so requires," this court has extensively examined cases from this jurisdiction and others.   At the threshold a vexing question is met, i. e., is this matter one of substance or procedure?   If the matter be one of substance, the court must, of course, follow the Delaware decisions. * * * These decisions have followed a strict line refusing to permit amendments to relate back to the original pleading.   * * *

If, on the other hand, the question is one of procedure, the court may depart from the strict Delaware rule, should it see fit to do so.

It is far from clear whether, in a <u>diversity action</u>, a federal court is bound by the state rule on the question of relation back of amendments to pleadings. The cases are in conflict.   The majority hold that the <u>state law need not be followed</u>.   * * *

This court is in agreement with the majority point of view.   * * *

In the past, courts which have permitted relation back of amendments to the denomination of parties defendant after the running of the statute of limitations appear to have proceeded on one or more of three theories: (1) that neglect of the plaintiff or his attorney in suing the wrong party was excusable, (2) that defendant had misled plaintiff or "lulled" him into the feeling that he had sued the right defendant when he had not, or (3) that the party actually sued and the party whom plaintiff meant to sue had sufficient "identity of interest" or were so closely connected that notice to one should suffice to inform the other of a pending claim for relief.   This last category contains several subcategories.   Courts have found different reasons for sufficient identity of interest to allow substitution of one party for the other to relate back.   In some instances the connection is found in the form of a business enterprise; for example, where individual partners were sued, a later amendment to sue the partnership was allowed to relate back, and a partnership has been substituted for a corporate defendant.   In other instances the connection has been arrived at in terms of agency.   Persons served with process have been found to hold a position of trust in both the corporation or business enterprise sued and the one intended to be sued and courts have held service on the one sufficient to permit an amendment to relate back on the theory that the intended defendant received adequate notice through its agent.   Indeed, some courts have said that service on a wrongly-named corporation was actually service on the intended corporation although two separate, viable corporate entities existed * * *.

Other courts, however, have steadfastly refused to look beyond the existence of distinct corporate entities.   In a recent case, the Texas Court of Civil Appeals refused to substitute "Epps Super Market No. 2, Inc." for "Epps Super Market, Inc." despite the fact that both corporations had the same officers and legal counsel.   * * *

In the case before the court some element of each rationale for permitting relation back of amendments—excusable neglect, misleading by defendant, and adequate notice due to close relationship has been raised.

It has been implied that the attorney for the plaintiff did not have sufficient time to ascertain the correct defendant.   We are told that the case was presented to him only a few days before the statute of limitations expired on his client's claim. However, there is no assertion that plaintiff's attorney relied on any official record or consulted any authority other than his own knowledge in deciding upon which defendant to sue. * * * The court is not aware of what a diligent search on the part of plaintiff's counsel would have uncovered. But there is no assertion that any search whatever was undertaken. Nonetheless, given such short time to prepare, the court cannot hold that inadequate preparation must lead to a finding that counsel was negligent. Since counsel cannot be held negligent, the question of the excusability of his negligence can have no bearing here.

Plaintiff's attorney also asserts that he was misled into naming the wrong defendant. He points to such things as joint advertising by the Newark and Wilmington stores and joint telephone listings to establish this argument. However, in the majority of cases where courts have found that a defendant had misled an erstwhile plaintiff, the misleading acts have come after suit was commenced and have been motivated by the suit. * * *

[The court then analyzed Williams v. Pennsylvania R. Co., 91 F.Supp. 652 (D.Del.1950), in which plaintiff erroneously brought suit against E. J. Lavino and Company instead of against the Lavino Shipping Company. The officers of the two companies were largely identical and they were fully aware of plaintiff's error. Nevertheless, the named defendant filed an answer alleging a number of affirmative defenses and otherwise misled plaintiff into believing he had sued the appropriate defendant, until the statute of limitations on the claim had run. The court permitted the appropriate defendant to be joined by amendment despite the running of the statute.]

Finally, plaintiff maintains that the two corporations involved in this suit are so closely linked to one another that the service of his complaint upon Miller Brothers Company was, in effect, service upon Miller Brothers Company of Newark. It is this category, the category of identity of interest between parties with the attendant agency concept, in which the courts have most frequently granted relief to an erring plaintiff and permitted correction of "misnomers". The rationale for this approach is that the close relation between the party actually sued and the one intended assures that the intended defendant received notice of the plaintiff's claim and was not misled by the error. * * *

A procedure for determining when amendments to pleadings shall relate back based on notice to the intended defendant is the aim of Rule 15(c). A proposed amendment to the rule makes the notice feature more explicit. [The proposal referred to was adopted and became effective on July 1, 1966 and appears as part of the current version of Federal Rule 15(c).] * * *

Even if the law were as proposed, however, plaintiff's position would not be advanced. * * * The rule provides that the party to be substituted must receive notice of the action "within the period provided by law for commencing the action against him." Given the facts in this case, it is apparent that Miller Brothers Company of Newark had no notice until after the statute of limitations had run. One cannot have notice that a suit has been brought against him until he hears of it. Even if dePolo were found to be an agent of Miller Brothers Company of Newark, the fact remains that he had no notice of this suit until April 10, 1963, three days after the statute of limitations had run.

Thus, in this instance, under the proposed rule, we have the anomalous result that service on dePolo as an agent of Miller Brothers Company would properly commence a law suit although service on dePolo as an agent of Miller Brothers Company of Newark (should he be found to be an agent) would not.

* * * Under the facts of this case there are two possible avenues of approach. For one, the court could find dePolo the agent of Miller Brothers Company of Newark and hold service of the complaint on him sufficient to bring that corporation into court. But this position is untenable. DePolo was not an officer of Miller Brothers Company of Newark. He was not even a shareholder in that company. While cases are numerous in which courts have allowed service on an individual in one capacity to stand for service on him in a different capacity, there is no rational basis for such a result where the one served has no dual capacity. The court has searched in vain for a case holding sufficient service upon one not connected in any official capacity with the defendant to be sued.

The court is impressed with the reasoning that because of the business connection of the Miller Brothers stores, Miller Brothers Company of Newark was likely to hear of the claim against it. We are not blind to the fact that on reading the summons and complaint dePolo should have been aware of the import of the claim. Further, it is reasonable to assume that dePolo informed the proper parties of Martz's claim and of his mistake in bringing suit.

But the court cannot act on surmise or on its own investigations to determine adequacy of service. * * * Absent some recognized capacity in which to act, some connection cognizable in law, dePolo cannot be held the agent of Miller Brothers Company of Newark for purposes of service of process.

Nor can the court accept the second alternative presented, the argument that the two corporations are so closely linked that service on one is equal to service on the other. This argument requires that the two stores be regarded simply as enterprises of the Miller family. The court could then say that an employee of either store was ultimately beholden to the family and find service on dePolo sufficient to notify the family—hence any or all of its corporate extensions.

But such a piercing of the corporate veil does violence to the facts here. The officers of both corporations overlap, but they are not the same in each case. While the shareholders of each corporation are Millers, they are not always the same Millers. Nor is there evidence that where the same shareholders do participate in each company, their proportion of ownership in each is identical. Thus, one cannot say that any recovery to Martz would "come out of the same pocket." * * *

The fact that plaintiff missed the mark narrowly, that service on any officer of Miller Brothers Company other than dePolo would have also been service on an officer of Miller Brothers Company of Newark and that an officer of Miller Brothers Company of Newark did have notice shortly after dePolo was served, causes the court concern. But statutes of limitations are not approximate goals to be aimed at. They cannot be extended willy-nilly by the court as it might extend the time for a brief to be filed. They are rules of law. The court cannot substitute its own assumptions, or notions of fair play, or reluctance to see controversies decided upon technicalities, for the clear mandate of the law.

Holding:

Defendant's motion for summary judgment will be granted. Plaintiff's motion for leave to amend his complaint will be denied.

NOTES AND QUESTIONS

1. In STAUFFER v. ISALY DAIRY CO., 4 Ohio App.2d 15, 27, 211 N.E. 2d 72, 80 (1965), plaintiff originally named and served the Isaly Dairy Company of Pittsburgh, a different corporation than the proper defendant, the Isaly Dairy Company. The two corporations maintained the same address, the person who was served was an officer of both corporations, and plaintiff had no idea that more than one corporation existed. In holding that an amendment altering the name of the defendant related back to the time the original complaint was filed, the court stated: "[W]hen intermingled corporations have intermingled officers who conduct the business and management of such corporations in such a manner that the general public is under the impression that they are all one and the same corporation, we feel that these corporations should be bound by their representations."

Court disagrees: They had notice

2. In SKEEN v. SISTERS OF ST. JOSEPH, 194 Kan. 212, 398 P.2d 587 (1965), plaintiff originally brought suit against St. Joseph Hospital and Rehabilitation Center, a nonexistent entity. After the limitations period had run, plaintiff amended the complaint to sue the proper corporate defendant, the Sisters of St. Joseph of Wichita, Kansas. The court held that there was "such a dissimilarity in the named defendants" that the amendment did not relate back. Is this holding sound? In what way does the case differ from *Martz* and *Isaly*?

3. Suppose plaintiff brings an action against someone who has nothing to do with the claim whatsoever, but the proper defendant, upon hearing of the suit, enters an appearance for the purpose of fighting the case on the merits. Upon formal motion by plaintiff to substitute the proper defendant, should the latter be permitted to claim that the period of limitations has since run and the action is time barred? See Darling v. Flamm, 20 App.Div.2d 880, 248 N.Y.S.2d 839 (1st Dep't 1964) (defendant estopped from raising a statute of limitations defense).

4. A number of jurisdictions have sought by statute or rule to permit a change of party defendant after the limitations period has run, when the circumstances would make it just to do so.

(a) Federal Rule 15(c) is one example. Does the text of Rule 15(c) go far enough? Should it be amended to include cases such as *Martz* in which plaintiff's failure to join the proper defendant is reasonable under the circumstances? How sound is the requirement in Rule 15(c)(2)? Compare Ill.Stat.Ann. ch.

110, § 46(4)(d), which is in the Supplement. See generally 6 Wright & Miller, *Federal Practice and Procedure: Civil* §§ 1498–1502 (1971).

(b) The Illinois statute would be far-reaching except for the requirement in Section 46(4) (c), that service has to have been made. What cases does this eliminate? What purpose does that provision serve? Operation of the Illinois statute has been further limited by decisions as to the meaning of "inadvertent" in Section 46(4)(b). Unless plaintiff acts with dispatch to amend the complaint as soon as the error is discovered, the amendment will not relate back. Horan v. Brenner, 57 Ill.App.2d 83, 206 N.E.2d 488 (1st Dist. 1965). Is Federal Rule 15(c) deficient in not specifically providing a similar safeguard?

(c) Section 474 of the California Code of Civil Procedure is the most unique provision of all. In effect it provides that plaintiff may name as defendants any number of "John Does" against whom the statute of limitations will then cease to run on any causes of action stated against them. When plaintiff becomes aware that he has sued a wrong defendant or has failed to sue a proper defendant, he may then merely substitute the name of the new defendant for one of the John Doe-defendants and proceed with the case. Why isn't this the most sensible way in which to handle the relation-back problem? At least one federal court has taken the position that this practice is proper in the federal courts even in the absence of any statute or rule. Duisen v. Terrel, 332 F.Supp. 127 (W.D.Mo.1971). But wouldn't use of fictitious defendants be impossible in a federal diversity-of-citizenship action? See Fifty Associates v. Prudential Ins. Co., 446 F.2d 1187 (9th Cir.1970).

5. In STAGGERS v. OTTO GERDAU CO., 359 F.2d 292, 297 (2d Cir. 1966), the original plaintiff, an assignee of the claim, died prior to trial. Subsequently, and after the statute of limitations on the claim had run, an amendment substituted both the original plaintiff's administrator and the assignor of the claim as parties plaintiff. The trial court held that the amendment did not relate back to the time of the original complaint. The court of appeals reversed:

> No matter who the plaintiffs are, the "transactions" with which we
> are concerned are those which led to the establishment and breach of the
> * * * contracts * * * set forth in the "original pleading."
> There is no meaningful statute of limitations problem here; the claims of
> all potential plaintiffs relate back to the date of the original pleading.

Does this language go too far? Are there different considerations with regard to relation back of amendments when it is a plaintiff rather than a defendant who is added? Rules and statutes such as Federal Rule 15(c) usually are oriented solely toward joinder of new defendants. When a new plaintiff is joined after the limitations period has passed is it significant that the jurisdiction relies on a new cause-of-action theory rather than a same-transaction-or-occurrence rule in deciding generally whether amendments relate back? See Maxson v. McElhinney, 370 Pa. 622, 88 A.2d 747 (1952) (in wrongful-death action brought by deceased's widow who had no standing to sue, an amendment substituting deceased's personal representative would state a new cause of action and would not relate back). See also Brauer v. Republic Steel Corp., 460 F.2d 801 (10th Cir.1972) (amendment naming additional plaintiffs and adding new negligence claim after limitations period had run held to relate back to original claim for breach of warranty).

SECTION H. SUPPLEMENTAL PLEADINGS

Read Federal Rule of Civil Procedure 15(d) in the Supplement.

SLAVENBURG CORP. v. BOSTON INS. CO.

United States District Court, Southern District of New York, 1962.
30 F.R.D. 123.

EDELSTEIN, District Judge.   This is an action on an open marine insurance policy issued by defendant to plaintiff.   *   *   *   Plaintiff, claiming a financial interest in 118 Volkswagen automobiles, seeks to recover the insured value thereof in the sum of $169,548.11.   The automobiles were aboard the S.S. MONGABARRA which sank after a collision with another vessel.   It is plaintiff's claim that the open policy automatically insured the automobiles which were lost,   *   *   *   unless otherwise excluded by the policy.   Defendant contends that the policy provided automatic insurance only in respect of commodities and voyages mentioned in the rate schedule thereto, and that all other commodities and voyages, including the instant shipment, were accepted for insurance from time to time by special agreement, shipment by shipment.

    *   *   *   In the event that on the trial of this action plaintiff establishes that the policy was automatic with respect to coverage of Volkswagens, defendant has set up certain affirmative defenses based on the proposition that plaintiff was obliged to report and pay premiums with respect to all such shipments. In the amended answer, defendant has set up, as affirmative defenses, matter relating to three shipments which preceded the casualty and which defendant claims were not reported until after the casualty.   *   *   *   [D]efendant has pleaded its election to treat the policy as void from the date of each such breach.

    Subsequent to the filing of the amended answer, defendant learned that there had been other shipments of Volkswagens which plaintiff had not declared and for which no premiums were paid during the period that the policy was in force.   Defendant now moves   *   *   *   for leave to file a second amended answer setting up four additional affirmative defenses based upon a representative selection of unreported shipments.   Plaintiff opposes the motion on the ground that the matter sought to be pleaded is in the nature of a supplemental pleading, Rule 15(d), F.R.Civ.P., and not an amended pleading, Rule 15(a), F.R.Civ.P.   Plaintiff has no objection to permitting defendant to set forth the new defenses in a supplemental answer.

    Plaintiff argues that to permit defendant to set up these defenses by way of amendment would deprive it of a substantial claim.   It is plaintiff's contention that defendant knew or should have known, long before the present motion, that the grounds upon which it desires to declare a forfeiture of the policy existed. Plaintiff proposes, with the hope of invalidating the defense, to assert a claim that defendant thus waived its option to declare such a forfeiture. If the defenses are pleaded as amendments, then Rule 15(c) dealing with relation back of amendments would be applicable. Rule 15(c) F.R.Civ.P. applies only to Rule 15(a) and not to Rule 15(d). Plaintiff is concerned lest the defenses now sought to be pleaded will, if permitted as amendments, relate back and deprive it of the opportunity to assert its waiver argument. Since the merit of plaintiff's waiver argument is a matter properly left for the trial court, it will not be considered here. Defendant contends that the court should decide the motion for leave to amend without considering whether the amendment will relate back. In this it is correct. "The fact that Rule 15(c) makes provision for the relation back of amendments to the date of the original pleading, can not be put forward as a ground for denying leave. If this were not so, a rule with regard to amendments, intended to operate remedially, would operate to destroy the privilege of amendment at its source." Copeland Motor Co. v. General Motors Corp., 199 F.2d 566, 568 (5th Cir.1952) * * *. Thus, the issue to be decided here, unencumbered by the question of relation back, is simply whether the proposed pleading is properly an amended answer as urged by defendant, or a supplemenal [sic] answer as urged by plaintiff.

"An amended pleading is designed to include matters occurring before the filing of the bill, but either overlooked or not known at the time. * * * A supplemental pleading is designed to cover matters subsequently occurring but pertaining to the * * * original claim." Walder v. Paramount Publix Corp., 23 F.R.Serv. 15a.3, case 1 at 185 (S.D.N.Y. 1956) * * *. "An amended pleading pro tanto supersedes the pleading which it amends while a supplemental pleading stands with the original and adds to it some fact or facts happening after the filing of the pleading to which it is a supplement * * *." United States v. L. D. Caulk Co., 114 F. Supp. 939, 940 (D.Del.1953). * * *

It is true, as urged by defendant, that the underlying facts which make up the subject matter of the new affirmative defenses occurred prior to the filing of the answer. But in the context of this case, that alone is not dispositive. An examination of the four proposed defenses shows that defendant is in fact pleading a present act. * * * The proposed defenses are to the effect that no liability exists because the policy is null and void. But before the defense can come into being, the forfeiture must be declared by defendant. The language used in the proposed pleading is in the *present* tense. Thus, the proposed pleading does two things; it exercises the defendant's option to declare a forfeiture and it pleads the nullity of the policy as a defense to the action. In contrast, the affirmative defenses in the existing answer merely plead the defense in terms of a forfeiture which had been previously declared in a letter from defendant to plaintiff. Since the forfeiture which defendant now seeks to declare occurs after the filing of the answer, the proposed pleading does not qualify as an amended answer.

* * * [T]he motion which seeks to amend the answer to set up the affirmative defenses is denied. Defendant will be permitted to set up the affirmative defenses in a supplemental answer.

NOTES AND QUESTIONS

1. "The office of a supplemental complaint is to aid the cause of action already averred, not to enable the plaintiff to recover upon a cause of action which has accrued since the action was commenced." HALSTEAD v. HALSTEAD, 7 Misc. 23, 27 N.Y.S. 408 (C.P.1894). This passage was quoted with approval in Giglio v. Konold, 5 Ohio App.2d 250, 251, 214 N.E.2d 806, 808 (1965) (plaintiff cannot file supplemental complaint alleging defendants' refusal to obey trial court order pending appeal; proper step is to file new action for contempt). *Cf.* Wallace v. Hanover Ins. Co., 164 So.2d 111 (La.App.1964) (defendant cannot raise by supplemental pleading an affirmative defense of fraud when only defense relied upon in original answer was premature filing of claim). What reason, if any, is there for prohibiting a "new cause of action" in a supplemental pleading?

Compare the statement by the revisers of New York's supplemental pleadings statute, N.Y.C.P.L.R. 3025(b), which appears in the Supplement in conjunction with Federal Rule of Civil Procedure 15(d): "[This new section is] * * * intended to grant the widest possible discretion to the court in granting leave to serve supplemental pleadings and imposing terms, even if the pleader had no cause of action at the time of the original pleading but has subsequently acquired and stated one in a supplemental pleading." N. Y. Advisory Comm. on Practice & Procedure, *First Preliminary Rep.* 78 (1957). Taking its cue from the revisers' statement, the court in HERZOG v. HERZOG, 43 Misc.2d 1062, 252 N.Y.S.2d 704 (Sup.Ct.1964), permitted a wife suing for separation to add a cause of action for divorce based on alleged evidence that her husband had developed into an adulterer. The husband protested—unsuccessfully—that the supplemental complaint was being improperly used to obtain divorce jurisdiction over him in a suit that had begun as a simple separation action. Wasn't the court clearly unfair to Mr. Herzog? Does the New York rule go too far? The New York provision is further analyzed in 3 Weinstein, Korn & Miller, *New York Civil Practice* ¶¶ 3025.12, 3025.17–.25. The lower federal courts appear to be favoring the New York position. See, e. g., Vernay Laboratories, Inc. v. Industrial Electronic Rubber Co., 8 Fed.R.Serv.2d 33.319, Case 2 (N.D.Ohio 1964) (Federal Rule 15(d) permits additional infringement claims based on newer patent nearly identical to original patent). *But see* General Bronze Corp. v. Cupples Prods. Corp., 9 F.R.D. 269 (E.D.Mo.1949).

2. Suppose, rather than adding supplemental facts setting out a "new cause of action" to an already validly stated claim, a party seeks instead to add supplemental facts without which the original pleading is defective. Are the considerations relevant to the two situations the same? Federal Rule 15(d) provides that a supplemental pleading *may* be allowed "even though the original pleading is defective in its statement of a claim for relief or defense." Until 1963, when this provision was added, the federal courts were split as to whether curative supplemental pleadings should ever be allowed. *Compare* La Salle Nat. Bank v. 222 East Chestnut St. Corp., 267 F.2d 247, 252–53 (7th Cir.), certiorari denied 361 U.S. 836, 80 S.Ct. 88, 4 L.Ed.2d 77 (1959), *with* Friedman v. Typhoon Air Conditioning Co., 31 F.R.D. 287, 290 (E.D.N.Y.1962). Under what circumstances should a court deny leave to supplement a defective pleading? What relation, if any, does the 1963 amendment to Rule 15(d) have to the new-cause-of-action problem? See generally 6 Wright & Miller, *Federal Practice and Procedure: Civil* § 1505 (1971); 3 Moore, *Federal Practice* ¶ 15.16[2]–[3] (2d ed.).

3. "Although supplemental pleadings are treated in most respects as are amended pleadings, they are not permitted to relate back * * *." Note, *Federal Rule 15(c) and the Doctrine of Substantive Conformity*, 59 Colum.L.Rev. 648, 653–54 (1959). Compare the discussion in *Slavenburg*. Would this always be true? Consider, for example, the following case. On June 10, 1962, A files suit against B alleging that 10 days earlier A had supplied materials to B for which A had not yet paid. The action is based on a statute that stipulates that suit can be brought only after 90 days have elapsed since the date the materials were furnished; B moves to dismiss for lack of jurisdiction. A now seeks, on October 18, 1963, to file a supplemental complaint alleging that more than 90 days have elapsed and that B still has not paid. However, the statute also provides that no suit can be commenced after the expiration of one year after the day on which the materials were supplied. What argument would you make for A? For B?

In SECURITY INS. CO. v. UNITED STATES FOR THE USE OF HAYDIS, 338 F.2d 444, 445–46, 449 (9th Cir.1964), the court declared:

> This appeal presents one of those "neat" questions which delight legal technicians, but have nothing to do with the merits of the case. * * *

> Appellant's argument, in substance, is this: When the complaint was filed the plaintiff had no claim for relief because the ninety-day period * * * had not expired. When the supplement to the complaint was filed, more than one year from the pertinent date had expired. A supplemental complaint alleges new matter; therefore its allegations, unlike those of an amended complaint, or of an amendment to a complaint, do not relate back so as to remove the bar of the statute of limitations. Hence the action was barred by the one year limitation * * *. Moreover, say appellants, if the allegations of the supplemental complaint can be said to relate back, then under Rule 15(c), F.R.Civ.P. they must relate back to the time when the action was filed and at that time the plaintiff had no claim for relief. Consequently, the court was and remains without jurisdiction.

> Nothing but the most compelling authority * * * would induce us to stay on this legal merry-go-round.

> * * * [R]egardless of whether the supplement to the complaint filed in the present action be considered an amendment to the complaint or a supplemental complaint, we think that the doctrine of relation back can properly be applied to prevent the one-year provision of subdivision (b) from barring the action, but that we are not required to apply the doctrine of relation back so literally as to carry it to a time within the ninety-day period specified in subdivision (a), so as to prevent the maintenance of the action in the first place.

> If the supplement to the complaint be treated as filed under Rule 15 (d), we can apply the doctrine of relation back, even though that rule does not mention it * * *. If it be treated as an amendment, to which Rule 15(c) applies, then * * * [we should not] apply Rule 15(c) so literally as to defeat a decision on the merits.

Contra, Walton v. Kern County, 39 Cal.App.2d 32, 102 P.2d 531 (4th Dist.1940).

CHAPTER 6

JOINDER OF CLAIMS AND PARTIES: EXPANDING THE SCOPE OF THE CIVIL ACTION

In its simplest form, the paradigm of a lawsuit has a single plaintiff asserting a single cause of action against a single defendant. Although the equity courts were more flexible, the common-law courts, with their emphasis on the unitary civil action, rarely deviated from this model and developed rules relating to joinder along strict and formalistic lines. See generally Blume, *A Rational Theory for Joinder of Causes of Action and Defences, and for the Use of Counterclaims,* 26 Mich.L.Rev. 1 (1927); Sunderland, *Joinder of Actions,* 18 Mich.L.Rev. 571 (1920). As the complexity of society increased and more intricate disputes were generated, the need for obviating piecemeal litigation became widely recognized. The most obvious method of accomplishing this objective was by expanding the scope of civil actions by permitting the joinder of claims and parties. This Chapter will explore the various forms that this expansion has taken.

SECTION A. JOINDER OF CLAIMS BY PLAINTIFF

HARRIS v. AVERY

Supreme Court of Kansas, 1869.
5 Kansas 146.

VALENTINE, J. This action was brought in the court below by Avery * * *. The petition states two causes of action,—false imprisonment and slander,—and alleges that both arose out of the same transaction. Harris demurred to this petition, on the ground "that it appears on the face of the petition that several causes of action are improperly joined." The district court overruled the demurrer, and this ruling is assigned as error. The petition shows that the two causes of action are founded upon the following facts: Harris met Avery in the city of Fort Scott, and, in the presence of several other persons, called Avery a thief; said he had a stolen horse; took the horse from Avery, and kept the horse for four or five days; arrested Avery, and confined him in the county jail with felons four or five days. We think these facts, as detailed in the petition, constitute only one transaction, * * * and whether they constitute more than one cause of action, under our Code practice, may be questionable.   *   *   *   But as we have not been asked to decide the latter question, we will pass it over and treat the case as though the facts stated constitute two causes of action.

Section 89 of the Code (Comp.Laws, 138,) provides "that the plaintiff may unite several causes of action in the same petition, whether they be such as have heretofore been denominated legal or equitable, or both, when they are included in either one of the following classes: First, *the same transaction* or transactions connected with the same subject of action." This differs in many respects from the common-law rule. At common law, "where the same form of action may be adopted for several distinct injuries, the plaintiff may, in general, proceed for all in one action, though the several rights affected were derived from different titles," (1 Chit. Pl. 201; Tidd, Pr. 11;) and different forms of action may be united, "where the same plea may be pleaded and the same judgment given on all the counts of the declaration, or whenever the counts are of the same nature, and the same judgment is to be given on them, although the pleas be different." 1 Chit. Pl. 200.

Code [margin note]

In the action at bar, if Harris had arrested Avery on a warrant, which Harris had maliciously and without probable cause obtained from a court of competent jurisdiction, and had also converted the horse to his own use, then at common law Avery would have had three distinct causes of action, which he could unite in one suit: *First*, an action for the false imprisonment or malicious prosecution; *second*, an action of slander for the words spoken; and, *third*, an action of trover for the conversion of the horse. These may all be united in an action on the case,   *   *   *   trover being a species of case. Avery might, also, at common law unite with these causes of action as many other causes of action as he might have, for malicious prosecution, slander, trover, criminal conversation, nuisance, and other causes of action which may be sued in an action on the case, and although they each may have arisen out of a different transaction, and at a different time, and in a different place. But if Harris arrested Avery without any process—which was the fact in this case— and in an entirely irregular manner, then the two causes of action for false imprisonment and slander could not at common law be united, as the first would have to be sued in an action of trespass and the second in an action on the case, and it would make no difference whether they both arose out of the same transaction or not. Our Code has abolished all the common-law forms of action, and has established a system for the joinder of actions   *   *   *. It follows the rules of equity more closely than it does those of the common law, one object seeming to be to avoid the multiplicity of suits, and to settle in one action, as equity did, as far as practicable, the whole subject-matter of a controversy. Hence, the common law on this question is no criterion. It is probably true that the two causes of action for false imprisonment and slander cannot, under our Code, be united, unless both arise out of the same transaction, one being an injury to the person and the other being an injury to the character; but we do not know of any reason why they should not be united when both do arise out of the same transaction.   *   *   *

Rationale [margin note]

The order of the district court overruling the demurrer to the petition is affirmed.

Holding [margin note]

NOTES AND QUESTIONS

1. The typical code provision authorized joinder of claims when they fell within one of several statutory classes, which generally included the following:

(a) Contracts, express or implied;

(b) Injuries to the person;

(c) Injuries to character;

(d) Injuries to property;

(e) Actions to recover real property, with or without damages;

(f) Actions to recover chattels, with or without damages; and

(g) Actions arising out of the same transaction or transactions connected with the same subject of the action.

In what ways do these categories differ from the use of the common-law forms of action as guidelines for the joinder of claims? What is the logic of each of these classes? Is the code approach to joinder of claims as described in *Harris* any less formalistic than the common-law theory? Joinder at common law and under the codes is discussed in Clark, *Code Pleading* §§ 68–70 (2d ed. 1947); Blume, *A Rational Theory for Joinder of Causes of Action and Defences, and for the Use of Counterclaims*, 26 Mich.L.Rev. 1 (1927).

2. What objectives are served by permitting Avery to join the false imprisonment and slander actions? Are there any disadvantages? In SPORN v. HUDSON TRANSIT LINES, 265 App.Div. 360, 38 N.Y.S.2d 512 (1st Dep't 1942), the court had before it an attempt to join five causes of action for negligence resulting in personal injuries with one cause of action for malicious prosecution. It stated:

> The causes of action for negligence and for malicious prosecution are essentially different in nature; each type involves different rules of law; each requires different testimony to establish a case and each carries a different measure of damages. If a single jury were to try both types of action at the one time, there is a strong likelihood that confusion would exist in the minds of the jurors as to the rules of law to be applied to the respective actions and they would undoubtedly entertain much difficulty in applying the various parts of testimony introduced to the appropriate cause of action. There is nothing in common to be found in the two types of action.

> Moreover, it is clear that if these actions were tried together jurors might, quite naturally, engender a prejudice against the appellant in the negligence actions if the proof adduced in the malicious prosecution action were to show that, in causing the arrest of one of the respondents for reckless driving, there was, as alleged in the complaint, malice and want of probable cause. In such a situation it might well be that a jury would be unduly liberal in assessing damages under the causes of action in negligence and that they might visit upon appellant in those actions damages which were punitive rather than compensatory.

> In the interest of justice, we think there should be a severance. * * * The avoidance of a multiplicity of suits is much to be desired, but where, as here, the enforcement of such a rule might entail prejudice to

appellant's substantial rights and would tend to confuse the jury, the divergent causes of action should be severed.

Id. at 361–62, 38 N.Y.S.2d at 514. Would the result in *Sporn* have been different if the action had been brought in a federal court? Read Federal Rules 18 and 42. Does the availability of severance eliminate all of the objections to permitting unrestricted joinder of claims as an initial matter? To what extent does the court's power to sever claims prevent the system from achieving the objectives of a liberal joinder rule?

3. Note that Federal Rule 18 removes all obstacles to joinder of claims and permits the joinder of both legal and equitable actions; the only restriction on the claims that may be joined is imposed by subject matter jurisdiction requirements. But the Federal Rule only describes the claims that a plaintiff may assert against defendant; it does not require plaintiff to join claims in a single action. Some commentators have argued that there should be compulsory joinder of all related claims existing between the litigants. See Friedenthal, *Joinder of Claims, Counterclaims and Cross-Complaints: Suggested Revision of the California Provisions*, 23 Stan.L.Rev. 1, 11–17 (1970). Michigan's joinder provision, Michigan General Court Rule 203.1, which is in the Supplement following Federal Rule 18, is unusual in that it provides for the compulsory joinder of certain claims. See generally Honigman & Hawkins, *Michigan Court Rules Annotated*, Rule 203, Author's Comment; Meisenholder, *Joinder of Claims and Parties—The New Michigan Pre-Trial Procedural Rules—Models For Other States?*, 61 Mich.L.Rev. 1389, 1417 (1963).

4. Even though the joinder of claims by plaintiffs in the federal courts is permissive, the principles of res judicata, which prohibit the splitting of a cause of action into two or more lawsuits, often have the effect of compelling plaintiff to join all related claims. See generally Blume, *Required Joinder of Claims*, 45 Mich.L.Rev. 797 (1947). Thus, for example, if A and B are involved in an automobile accident in which A suffers both bodily injury and damage to her automobile, the risk of res judicata typically will lead A to join both claims in one action, although Federal Rule 18 does not require him to do so. See pp. 1063–71, infra.

SECTION B. ADDITION OF CLAIMS BY DEFENDANT

1. COUNTERCLAIMS

The counterclaim in its present form did not exist at common law, although it has well-recognized precursors in set-off and recoupment and in equity practice. The philosophy underlying set-off and recoupment was the common sense view that someone should not be compelled to pay one moment what he will be entitled to recover back the next. See generally Mc-

Connell, *The Doctrine of Recoupment in Federal Taxation*, 28 Va.L.Rev.
577 (1942). Judge Clark outlined the development and theory of set-off
and recoupment as follows:

> * * * At first * * * [recoupment] was limited to a
> showing of payment, or of former recovery. Later, recoupment
> was developed so as to allow a defendant to show for the purpose
> of reducing the plaintiff's recovery any facts arising out of the
> transaction sued upon or connected with the subject thereof, which
> facts might have founded an independent action in favor of the
> defendant against the plaintiff. * * * It was not necessary that
> the opposing claims be liquidated, or that they be of the same
> character; i.e., a claim in "tort" could be set off against one in
> "contract." It was essential, however, that the claims of both
> plaintiff and defendant involve the same "subject-matter," or arise
> out of the "same transaction" * * *.

> But where the defendant's claims arose out of a transaction
> different from that sued upon, the common-law recoupment was
> unavailable. The defendant, therefore, was compelled to bring a
> separate suit in order to satisfy his claim against the plaintiff.
> Equity, at an early date, relieved the defendant of this hardship by
> allowing a set-off of claims [growing out of a transaction differ-
> ent from the plaintiff's claim] * * *.

> Under the set-off * * *, it was necessary that the demands
> either be liquidated, or arise out of contract or judgment. It was
> necessary, also, that the demands be due the defendant in his own
> right against the plaintiff, or his assignor, and be not already barred
> by the statute of limitations * * *.

Clark, *Code Pleading* § 100, at 634–36 (2d ed. 1947). See also Waterman,
Set-Off, Recoupment and Counterclaim §§ 302–03 (2d ed. 1872). The
utility of the common-law recoupment and set-off practice was limited because in the former situation defendant was not permitted to recover affirmative relief; the claim could be used only to reduce or "net out" plaintiff's
recovery. In the case of set-off the claim had to be for a liquidated amount.

The movement for procedural reform in the mid-nineteenth century gave
passing attention to the problem of defendant's claims against plaintiff; the
original New York Field Code of 1848 made no provision for counterclaims.
Amendments in 1852 corrected this omission and permitted as a counterclaim:

1. A cause of action arising out of the contract or transaction
    set forth in the complaint, as the foundation of the plaintiff's
    claim, or connected with the subject of the action; and

2. In an action arising on contract, any other cause of action aris-
    ing on contract, and existing at the commencement of the ac-
    tion.

See Blume, *A Rational Theory for Joinder of Causes of Action and Defences,
and for the Use of Counterclaims*, 26 Mich.L.Rev. 1, 48 (1927). Did New

York's provision, which subsequently was adopted by a number of other states, create a new procedure or did it merely codify the existing recoupment and set-off practice?

The English Judicature Act of 1873 eliminated the historic limitations on defendant's ability to assert claims against plaintiff. Then, at the beginning of this century, a number of states amended their codes to adopt the English practice. Note that the text of Federal Rule 13(a) goes beyond the English and code practice by *requiring* defendant to assert certain claims. Why is this step desirable?

———

Read Federal Rules of Civil Procedure 13(a)–(f) and the accompanying material in the Supplement.

———

GREAT LAKES RUBBER CORP. v. HERBERT COOPER CO.

United States Court of Appeals, Third Circuit, 1961.
286 F.2d 631.

BIGGS, Chief Judge. This is an appeal from an order of the court below dismissing a counterclaim of Great Lakes Rubber Corporation (Great Lakes), made against Herbert Cooper Co., Inc. (Cooper), on the ground that the court lacked jurisdiction of the subject matter of the counterclaim. * * *

On May 12, 1959, Great Lakes filed an amended complaint naming Cooper as defendant. Jurisdiction was allegedly based on diversity. The allegations fall roughly into three groups. First, it was alleged that Howard Cooper and Joseph Herbert had been employed by Great Lakes * * * and that they left Great Lakes' employ taking with them certain information relating to the flexible rubber tubing manufactured by Great Lakes, and lists disclosing Great Lakes' customers; that shortly thereafter they, with others, founded Cooper; that Cooper competed for and obtained customers that were, until then, customers of Great Lakes; and, that Cooper's "offering to sell, and manufacturing and selling flexible tubing made and offered for sale with utilization of knowledge and information acquired while these men [Cooper and Herbert] were in a fiduciary relationship with plaintiff" constituted "acts of unfair competition and unfair business practices."

* * * [The second allegation was that Cooper had obtained government contracts for tubing of a type that would infringe on patents licensed to Great Lakes, and that Cooper had been able to submit the lowest bid for these contracts because it was not paying patent royalties. Great Lakes claimed that Cooper "is and has been in an unfair competitive position" because of its operations as an "unlicensed infringer."]

Third, it was alleged that Cooper implied to customers of Great Lakes that the quality of the tubing manufactured by Great Lakes was inferior; that Cooper represented to the United States Air Force that no validly patented ideas, processes or inventions held by others would be utilized in fulfilling its contracts for flexible tubing, that their representations were false; and, that these acts have damaged and imminently threaten Great Lakes' business operations.

Great Lakes referred to various contracts with the United States Army and Air Force which it alleged it had failed to obtain but which Cooper did obtain, and further specified an Air Force contract on which it was then being underbid by Cooper and which it would not obtain if Cooper's acts of "unfair competition" were not enjoined. Great Lakes asked for relief in the form of an injunction, an accounting for profits and an award of damages.

Cooper's counterclaim

On June 23, 1959, Cooper filed an answer to the amended complaint and a counterclaim which asserted that Great Lakes, Fred T. and Robert E. Roberts, * * * and various * * * companies and individuals "have been and still are * * * conspiring together and attempting both individually and in concert to restrain and monopolize interstate commerce" in violation of Sections 1 and 2 of the Sherman Act, 15 U.S.C.A. §§ 1 and 2. The conspiracy was alleged to include, without limitation, the making of false representations to certain of Cooper's material suppliers that they were guilty of contributory infringement when the conspirators knew that the supplied items were staple articles of commerce and could not be the basis of such liability.

The counterclaim also alleged, and this is of prime importance in the instant case, "the bringing of a series of unjustified lawsuits by the conspirators in bad faith and without color of right with the sole object of harassing and preventing defendant from competing in the manufacture and sale of flexible hose and thus eliminating defendant as a competitor, including this action [i. e., the action brought by the filing of the amended complaint by Great Lakes] * * *." The counterclaim asked treble damages, costs and attorneys' fees.

1) dismissal of Great Lake — failure of diversity

2) Cooper counterclaim becomes new claim.

↓

Great Lakes counter claims.

On July 2, 1959, Cooper moved to dismiss Great Lakes' amended complaint on the ground that there was no diversity of citizenship between the parties. By order dated December 9, 1959, the court granted Cooper's motion to dismiss. Jurisdiction of Cooper's counterclaim was retained on the ground that it had an independent basis of jurisdiction in that it asserted a claim arising under the laws of the United States. No appeal was taken from that order. * * *

On December 28, 1959, Great Lakes filed an answer and a counterclaim to Cooper's counterclaim. Great Lakes' counterclaim repeated in substance the allegations of its amended complaint. The counterclaim is distinguishable from the amended complaint only in that it is more specific and in that it * * * [contained further allegations of misconduct by Cooper].

On June 6, 1960, Cooper moved to dismiss the Great Lakes counterclaim on the ground that the court below lacked jurisdiction of the subject matter. In opposition to this motion Great Lakes contended that the court had ancillary jurisdiction of its counterclaim as a compulsory counterclaim arising out of the same transaction and occurrences that were the subject matter of Cooper's claim arising under the Federal antitrust laws. On May 5, 1960, the court granted Cooper's motion to dismiss on the ground that Great Lakes' counterclaim was not a compulsory counterclaim. This appeal followed.

A federal court has ancillary jurisdiction of the subject matter of a counterclaim if it arises out of the transaction or occurrence that is the subject matter of an opposing party's claim of which the court has jurisdiction. * * * Similarly, a counterclaim that arises out of the transaction or occurrence that is the subject matter of an opposing party's claim is a "compulsory counterclaim" within the meaning of Rule 13(a) of the Federal Rules of Civil Procedure. It is stated frequently that the determination of ancillary jurisdiction of a counterclaim in a federal court must turn on whether the counterclaim is compulsory within the meaning of Rule 13(a). Such a statement of the law relating to ancillary jurisdiction of counterclaims is not intended to suggest that Rule 13(a) extends the jurisdiction of the federal courts to entertain counterclaims for the Federal Rules of Civil Procedure cannot expand the jurisdiction of the United States courts. What is meant is that the issue of the existence of ancillary jurisdiction and the issue as to whether a counterclaim is compulsory are to be answered by the same test. It is not a coincidence that the same considerations that determine whether a counterclaim is compulsory decide also whether the court has ancillary jurisdiction to adjudicate it. The tests are the same because Rule 13(a) and the doctrine of ancillary jurisdiction are designed to abolish the same evil, viz., piecemeal litigation in the federal courts.

We have indicated that a counterclaim is compulsory if it bears a "logical relationship" to an opposing party's claim. Zion v. Sentry Safety Control Corp., 3 Cir., 1958, 258 F.2d 31. * * * The phrase "logical relationship" is given meaning by the purpose of the rule which it was designed to implement. Thus, a counterclaim is logically related to the opposing party's claim where separate trials on each of their respective claims would involve a substantial duplication of effort and time by the parties and the courts. Where multiple claims involve many of the same factual issues, or the same factual and legal issues, or where they are offshoots of the same basic controversy between the parties, fairness and considerations of convenience and of economy require that the counterclaimant be permitted to maintain his cause of action. Indeed the doctrine of *res judicata* compels the counterclaimant to assert his claim in the same suit for it would be barred if asserted separately, subsequently.

Cooper alleges that the claims originally asserted in Great Lakes' amended complaint, reiterated in substance in its counterclaim, are "unjustified" and were brought in "bad faith and without color of right with the sole object of harassing and preventing defendant [Cooper] from competing in the manufacture and sale of flexible hose." These are the only allegations set out by Cooper's counterclaim which demonstrate a relationship within the purview of Rule 13(a) to Great Lakes' amended complaint or counterclaim. But that they do demonstrate a relationship is unquestionable. It is clear that a determination that Cooper's claims that the claims asserted in Great Lakes' amended complaint and reiterated in substance in its counterclaim are harassing will entail an extensive airing of the facts and the law relating to Great Lakes' counterclaim. It follows that the court below was in error in dismissing Great Lakes' counterclaim on the ground that it was permissive. We hold that Great Lakes' counterclaim was a compulsory one within the meaning of Rule 13(a).

* * *

The judgment will be reversed and the cause will be remanded with the direction to proceed in accordance with this opinion.

NOTES AND QUESTIONS

1. The classic definition of "transaction" is found in MOORE v. NEW YORK COTTON EXCHANGE, 270 U.S. 593, 46 S.Ct. 367, 70 L.Ed. 750 (1926). Plaintiff, Moore, sought to compel defendant to install a price quotation ticker in plaintiff's place of business. Defendant counterclaimed for damages, alleging that although plaintiff had been denied permission to use quotations from defendant's exchange, plaintiff "was purloining them and giving them out." In the course of holding defendant's counterclaim compulsory under former Equity Rule 30, the court said:

> * * * "Transaction" is a word of flexible meaning. It may comprehend a series of many occurrences, depending not so much upon the immediateness of their connection as upon their logical relationship. The refusal to furnish the quotations is one of the links in the chain which constitutes the transaction upon which appellant here bases its cause of action. It is an important part of the transaction constituting the subject-matter of the counterclaim. It is the one circumstance without which neither party would have found it necessary to seek relief. Essential facts alleged by appellant enter into and constitute in part the cause of action set forth in the counterclaim. That they are not precisely identical, or that the counterclaim embraces additional allegations, as, for example, that appellant is unlawfully getting the quotations, does not matter. To hold otherwise would be to rob this branch of the rule of all serviceable meaning, since the facts relied upon by the plaintiff rarely, if ever, are in all particulars, the same as those constituting the defendant's counterclaim. * * *

Id. at 610, 46 S.Ct. at 371, 70 L.Ed. at 757.

In INTERNATIONAL UNION, UNITED AUTOMOBILE, AIRCRAFT & AGRICULTURAL IMPLEMENT WORKERS v. PIASECKI AIRCRAFT CORP., 241 F.Supp. 385 (D.Del.1965), the union brought suit against an employer for violation of a collective-bargaining agreement. Defendant counterclaimed for damages resulting from a strike by the union. The court said:

> * * * Thus, the complaint charges damages resulting to employees by reason of (1) Piasecki's alleged default in making contributions to the insurance program, (2) for the violation of seniority provisions of the contract, (3) lost wages, (4) lost union dues and (5) lost vacation benefits. On the other hand, the subject matter of the counterclaim is a common law tort action for damages * * *.

> While * * * there is a broad relationship between the two,
> nevertheless, the questions of fact relevant to alleged violence on the picket
> line are not common to the subject matter of the complaint and the two
> claims do not represent the "same basic controversy" envisioned by the
> reasoning of * * * [Great Lakes].

Id. at 389. Is the court's application of the principal case correct? See 6 Wright
& Miller, *Federal Practice and Procedure: Civil* § 1410 (1971). See also
GLOBE INDEM. CO. v. TEIXEIRA, 230 F.Supp. 444 (D.Haw.1963), in
which plaintiff insurance company joined the insured and the injured parties in a
declaratory-judgment action. Plaintiff disclaimed liability under the policy because at the time of the accident the insured was driving a car without the permission
of the owner. The injured defendants cross- and counterclaimed for damages. The
court held that the counterclaims did not arise from the same transaction or occurrence and were not compulsory because "the subject matter of the complaint herein is the liability or non-liability of plaintiff on the insurance policy," whereas "the
subject matter of the counterclaims is the negligence or non-negligence of defendant." Defendants' counterclaims were not even permitted to stand as permissive
because the insurance policy prohibited suits against the insurer until the amount of
the insured's liability had been established. Can the court refuse to entertain
a permissive counterclaim if there are independent jurisdictional grounds supporting it? When might the court wish to do so and what alternatives does the
court have to dismissing the counterclaim?

2. Assume that in a diversity action defendant has two counterclaims—one
permissive, one compulsory—neither of which is for an amount in excess of $10,-
000. Although the compulsory counterclaim is proper as part of the court's
ancillary jurisdiction, can its dollar value be aggregated with the permissive
counterclaim so that the latter also may be heard in the same suit? See McKnight
v. Halliburton Oil Well Cementing Co., 20 F.R.D. 563 (N.D.W.Va.1957), noted
in 44 Va.L.Rev. 251 (1958). Reconsider the material on aggregation on p. 219,
supra.

3. There is considerable disagreement as to the wisdom of the compulsory
counterclaim. Consider the following arguments:

> Compulsory counterclaim rules may at first blush appear harsh. On
> their face they are opposed to the dominant trend in procedure today
> which is to get away from penalizing a party's procedural errors by an ad-
> verse judgment against an otherwise meritorious claim. Yet such rules
> are an important part of the movement to end a multiplicity of litigation,
> and thus are in the interest of both litigants and the public. Since there is
> never any need for a party to incur the penalty for failure to counterclaim,
> and since there are ample remedies for the party who has so acted through
> inadvertence, the actual working of the rules has not been harsh. Their
> salutary effect has been had with comparatively little injustice * * *.

Wright, *Estoppel by Rule: The Compulsory Counterclaim Under Modern Pleading*,
38 Minn.L.Rev. 423, 465 (1954).

> * * * Certainly a rule of compulsion extended to every allowable
> counterclaim cannot be regarded as defensible. If a compulsory rule is
> ever justifiable it is only when the counterclaim operates by way of defense
> to the principal claim. Just as a defendant may not with impunity with-

draw a defense, so we may without violence to the traditional maxim deny him the right to withdraw a counterclaim if this in whole or part is of a defensive nature. * * *

Millar, *Civil Procedure of the Trial Court in Historical Perspective* 138 (1952). Is Professor Millar arguing for a return to common-law recoupment? Are there any strong arguments for going further than Professor Millar suggests by not making counterclaims compulsory under any circumstances?

The states have widely divergent attitudes toward compulsory counterclaims. The Minnesota compulsory-counterclaim rule, for example, is virtually identical to Federal Rule 13(a), except that the reference to "occurrence" is omitted from the rule, which has led that state's courts to read the rule restrictively. In HOUSE v. HANSON, 245 Minn. 466, 72 N.W.2d 874 (1955), the Minnesota Supreme Court held that "Rule 13.01 was approved by this court with the express understanding and intent that the omission therefrom of the word 'occurrence' would insure that tort counterclaims would not be compulsory."

Examine the text of the South Carolina counterclaim provision, which is set out in the Supplement. It seems to require the assertion of all counterclaims by defendant, whether or not they bear any relationship to plaintiff's claim. What are the disadvantages of requiring all counterclaims to be asserted? In other states that have similar language, however, the courts have construed "must" to mean "may." See Huether v. Baird, 62 N.D. 434, 244 N.W. 125 (1932); Diamond Ice & Storage Co. v. Klock Produce Co., 103 Wash. 369, 174 P. 435 (1918). Analyze the Michigan counterclaim rule, also in the Supplement. In what ways does it differ from Federal Rule 13 and the South Carolina statute? New York rejected any form of compulsory-counterclaim rule when it revised its procedural system in 1963. The reasons are stated in 3 Weinstein, Korn & Miller, *New York Civil Practice* ¶ 3019.12.

CONSEQUENCES OF FAILING TO PLEAD A COUNTERCLAIM

Rule 13(a) is silent as to the consequences of a failure to raise a compulsory counterclaim. It seems clear that an unasserted compulsory counterclaim cannot be raised in a subsequent suit in a federal court, although the courts differ as to the proper theory for reaching this conclusion. Some apply a res judicata theory; others use waiver; and yet another group relies on estoppel. See Scott, *Collateral Estoppel by Judgment*, 56 Harv.L.Rev. 1 (1942) (res judicata theory); Wright, *Estoppel by Rule: The Compulsory Counterclaim Under Modern Pleading*, 38 Minn.L.Rev. 423 (1954) (estoppel). Does it make any difference which theory is used?

Under what circumstances should the liberal amendment policy of Federal Rule 13(f) be used to permit the tardy assertion of a compulsory counterclaim? See Safeway Trails, Inc. v. Allentown & Reading Transit Co., 185 F.2d 918 (4th Cir.1950), in which leave to amend was granted when the excuse for failing to plead an omitted counterclaim was that defendant's lawyer had not read the federal rules! For a strict application of the barring effect of a failure to assert a compulsory counterclaim, see Keller v. Keklikian, 362 Mo. 919, 244 S.W.2d 1001 (1951). If the statute of limitations has run on a counterclaim between the filing of the original action and defendant's motion under Rule 13(f), so that the claim would be barred if asserted independently, does the filing of the counterclaim relate back to the filing of the original action under Rule 15(c)? Should the result depend on whether the counterclaim is compulsory or permissive?

Hypothesize an action in a federal court in which defendant fails to raise a compulsory counterclaim. Does the failure to bring the claim in federal court prevent defendant from raising it in a subsequent state-court action? What if defendant brings suit on the unasserted claim in a state court before the federal action is terminated? Should the state court hearing the alleged counterclaim grant a motion to dismiss based on the assertion that Federal Rule 13(a) barred the state action? What other action might it take? Should the federal court hearing plaintiff's suit restrain further proceedings in the state court?

> The answer * * * depends upon a determination of whether or not Congress intended in adopting Rule 13(a) to create another statutory exception to its policy of Federal Courts' non-interference with State Court actions. [See 28 U.S.C. § 2283.] Insofar as the effect of a party's failure to plead a compulsory counterclaim under said Rule in a Federal action is concerned the Congressional intent is clear—said party is thereafter barred from pleading same on the ground that it is res judicata. However, insofar as the effect of such failure on a State Court action is concerned the Congressional intent is not so clear; thus, in the absence of a clearer expression than is contained in Rule 13(a) we are unwilling to say that Congress, in adopting said Rule, intended to grant Federal Courts the authority to enjoin State Court actions * * *.

FANTECCHI v. GROSS, 158 F.Supp. 684, 687 (E.D.Pa.1957), appeal dismissed 255 F.2d 299 (3d Cir.1958). Are the considerations any different when the situation is reversed and the first action is brought in a state court in which a compulsory-counterclaim rule is in effect and the second case is in a federal court? Can plaintiff in the state proceeding ask the state court to enjoin the parties to a federal court action from litigating what should have been a compulsory counterclaim in the state court? Should the federal court grant a motion to dismiss? *Cf.* Donovan v. City of Dallas, 377 U.S. 408, 84 S.Ct. 1579, 12 L.Ed.2d 409 (1964). Should one state be required to give full faith and credit to another state's compulsory-counterclaim rule?

SOUTHERN CONSTRUCTION COMPANY v. PICKARD

United States Supreme Court, 1962.
371 U.S. 57, 83 S.Ct. 108, 9 L.Ed.2d 31.

PER CURIAM. Southern Construction Company, one of the petitioners here, was the prime contractor on contracts with the United States for the rehabilitation of certain barracks at Fort Campbell, Tennessee, and Fort Benning, Georgia. There were three contracts covering the Georgia project and one covering the Tennessee project. Pursuant to the provisions of the Miller Act, * * * 40 U.S.C.A. §§ 270a–270d, Southern furnished performance and payment bonds, with Continental Casualty Company, co-petitioner here, as surety. The plumbing and heating subcontractor on both projects was the respondent Samuel J. Pickard, doing business as Pickard Engineering Company. Pickard's primary supplier on both projects was the Atlas Supply Company.

In December 1955, Pickard's men left the Tennessee job before it was fully completed, and shortly thereafter left the Georgia project. Atlas, Pickard's supplier, claimed that $34,520 was due it for materials furnished on the Tennessee job and $104,000 for materials furnished on the Georgia project. Following a conference in August 1956 between Southern officials and representatives of Atlas, Southern paid Atlas $35,000 in exchange for a complete release of all liability of Southern on Pickard's accounts with respect to both the Georgia and Tennessee projects.

*   *   *

[Pickard then filed suit against Southern in district courts in both Georgia and Tennessee under the Miller Act for amounts due on the contracts. He was forced to bring two suits because the Act provides that an action can be brought only in the district in which the particular contract was to be performed. Defendant elected to assert its counterclaim for the amount paid Atlas in the Tennessee suit, the second of the two suits commenced. Pickard answered that the counterclaim was barred for failure to raise it in the first suit as a compulsory counterclaim.]

The District Court, in deciding that Pickard was not entitled to any recovery, allowed this $34,520 item as a credit against Pickard's claim, but on this point the Court of Appeals for the Sixth Circuit reversed. * * * It held that since there had been no allocation of the $35,000 payment as between the Georgia and Tennessee projects the item, under Rule 13(a) * * *, was a "potential compulsory counterclaim" in either of the two suits; that when the responsive pleading in the Georgia suit was filed the counterclaim was not the subject of any other pending action and was therefore "compulsory" in *that* suit; and, accordingly, that such counterclaim could not later be asserted in the present action. We granted certiorari to consider the applicability of Rule 13(a) in these unusual circumstances. * * *

We accept for present purposes the ruling below that the $35,000 payment had not been allocated as between the Tennessee and Georgia projects and that it therefore could have been asserted in either action. Nevertheless, we do not believe that Rule 13(a) operates to prohibit its use in the later Tennessee action. The requirement that counterclaims arising out of the same transaction or occurrence as the opposing party's claim "shall" be stated in the pleadings was designed to prevent multiplicity of actions and to achieve resolution in a single lawsuit of all disputes arising out of common matters. The Rule was particularly directed against one who failed to assert a counterclaim in one action and then instituted a second action in which that counterclaim became the basis of the complaint.   *   *   *

It is readily apparent that this policy has no application here. In this instance, the plaintiff-respondent, who originally sought to combine all his claims in a single suit, correctly concluded that he was required by statute to split those claims and to bring two separate actions in two different districts. The fragmentation of these claims, therefore, was compelled by federal law, and the primary defendant in both actions was thus for the first time confronted with the choice of which of the two pending suits should be resorted to for the assertion of a counterclaim common to both. Under these circumstances, we hold that Rule 13(a) did not compel this counterclaim to be made in whichever of the two suits the first responsive pleading was filed. Its assertion in the later suit, to which Southern, not without reason, considered it more appurtenant   *   *   *   by no means involved the circuity of action that Rule 13(a) was aimed at preventing. Accordingly, the judgment of the Court of Appeals insofar as it related to this counterclaim is reversed, and the case is remanded to that court for further proceedings consistent with this opinion.

*   *   *

NOTES AND QUESTIONS

1. Should the "common-law" exception to Rule 13(a) the Supreme Court invoked in *Pickard* be limited to the situation in which the governing substantive law requires plaintiff to bring related claims in separate districts?

2. Several exceptions to the compulsory-counterclaim rule are set out in the text of Rule 13(a) itself. Consider their relevance to the following situations.

(a) In UNION PAVING CO. v. DOWNER CORP., 276 F.2d 468 (9th Cir.1960), the court discussed the passage in Rule 13(a) providing that waiver will not result from the failure to assert a counterclaim that already is the subject of litigation pending in another court.

*   *   * The purpose of this exception is seemingly to prevent one party from compelling another to try his cause of action in a court not of the latter's choosing when the same cause of action is already the subject of pending litigation in another forum, one which was probably chosen by the owner of the cause of action concerned. The language of the exception clause in Rule 13(a)—"such a claim *need not* be so stated [as a counterclaim] if at the time the action was commenced the claim was the subject of another pending action"—seems clearly permissive. [The italics are ours.] The exception enables a party to escape the waiver rule if he has already begun his action in another forum of his own choosing. It does not preclude him from electing instead to counterclaim his cause of action in the instant case.

This conclusion is reinforced by the fact that under Rule 13(b) pending litigation on the same cause of action has no effect on the ability to plead a permissive counterclaim. Thus, under the district court's theory, a cause of action which did *not* arise out of the same transaction or occurrence as the main claim could be pleaded as a counterclaim under Rule 13(b) even though the counterclaim was the subject of another pending action; but a claim so closely connected with the main action that it would otherwise be a compulsory counterclaim subject to waiver under Rule 13(a) cannot be pleaded at all if it is the subject of another pending action.   Such a result is wholly unreasonable.   * * *

Id. at 270–71.

In BETHLEHEM STEEL CO. v. LYKES BROS., S.S. CO., 35 F.R.D. 344 (D.D.C.1964), the principle of the *Union Paving* case was applied to a situation in which the action that normally would be the subject of the compulsory counterclaim was pending before an administrative body (the Federal Maritime Board). Was this proper? If a party chooses to plead an excepted counterclaim under Rule 13(a) should it be treated as if it were compulsory or permissive for purposes of the waiver of the counterclaimant's objections to venue and personal jurisdiction?

(b) If defendant has a claim that arises out of the same transaction or occurrence as plaintiff's claim but can be brought only against plaintiff and a third person who is "indispensable" and over whom defendant cannot obtain jurisdiction, is assertion of the claim mandatory?

(c) Suppose that plaintiff obtains jurisdiction by attaching defendant's property. Defendant fails to appear and a default judgment is entered and enforced against the attached property. Subsequently, defendant brings an action that arose out of the same transaction or occurrence as plaintiff's original suit. The original plaintiff moves to dismiss the suit. What result?

(d) If five days after defendant serves her answer she becomes the assignee of a claim against plaintiff and if the assigned claim arose out of the same transaction or occurrence as plaintiff's claim against defendant, must defendant amend her answer and assert it? *Cf.* Federal Rule 13(e). What if the counterclaim is acquired during the trial?

(e) If defendant is sued in one capacity (e. g., as an administrator in an action based on the negligence of an intestate) and has a counterclaim in another capacity (e. g., as a beneficiary in a wrongful-death action) that arises out of the same transaction or occurrence, is it compulsory? See Newton v. Mitchell, 42 So.2d 53 (Fla.1949).

3.   Assume plaintiff commences an action within the appropriate statute of limitations and defendant has a compulsory counterclaim that would be barred by the statute of limitations if asserted in an independent action. Should the claim be permitted? See Nathan v. McKernan, 170 Neb. 1, 101 N.W.2d 756 (1960). Does it make any difference if defendant's claim was not time-barred when plaintiff commenced the suit but became so before defendant was required to answer? Assuming that the claim would be barred if asserted as a counterclaim, should it be permitted if it otherwise qualifies as a common-law recoupment or set-off? See American Law Institute, *Study of the Division of Jurisdiction Between State and Federal Courts*, Official Draft, 258 (1969).

4.   If defendant's answer contains a counterclaim, must plaintiff assert a compulsory counterclaim to defendant's counterclaim? Does it matter whether defendant's counterclaim is compulsory or permissive? Is a counterclaim to a counter-

claim likely to be so confusing that it will prevent the orderly disposition of the case? Would it make any difference if plaintiff amended the complaint to include the claim rather than asserting it as a counterclaim? See Millar, *Counterclaim Against Counterclaim*, 48 Nw.U.L.Rev. 671, 690 (1954).

---

2. CROSS-CLAIMS

Read Federal Rules of Civil Procedure 13(g) and (h) and the accompanying material in the Supplement.

LASA PER L'INDUSTRIA DEL MARMO SOCIETA PER AZIONI v. SOUTHERN BUILDERS, INC.

United States District Court, Western District of Tennessee, 1967.
45 F.R.D. 435, reversed United States Court of Appeals,
Sixth Circuit, 1969, 414 F.2d 143.

BAILEY BROWN, Chief Judge. Southern Builders, Inc. of Tennessee, City of Memphis and Continental Casualty Co. have moved to dismiss a cross-claim filed against them by Alexander Marble and Tile Co., a partnership. A. L. Aydelott and A. L. Aydelott and Associates, Inc. have filed a motion to dismiss a third party complaint filed against them by this same partnership. The contentions are that the cross-claim and third party complaint are not authorized by the Federal Rules of Civil Procedure. * * *

The original complaint was filed by an Italian corporation, referred to herein, for brevity, as "LASA." This complaint, as twice amended and supplemented, alleges in substance as follows. Southern Builders, a Tennessee corporation, as principal contractor, entered into a contract in 1962 with the City to build a city hall and under the contract obligated itself to the City to pay for all labor and materials. Southern Builders procured and furnished to the City a statutory performance and payment bond, with Continental Casualty as surety, under which Southern Builders obligated itself to the City to perform the contract and to pay for all labor and materials. Alexander Marble and Tile Co., a partnership, whose partners are Tennessee residents, together with Marble International, Inc., a Texas corporation, as joint venturers, entered into a subcontract with Southern Builders under which they were to supply all marble and anchoring devices and install the marble. Alexander then contracted with LASA to supply to it all of the marble for a contract price of $468,641.26, that the marble has been supplied as agreed, and that there is a balance due of $127,240.80. * * *
The City improperly released retainages to the principal contractor, Southern Builders. LASA therefore sues Alexander * * * Marble Interna-

tional, Southern Builders, Continental Casualty and the City for the alleged balance due.

To this original complaint Alexander (partnership and corporation) filed an answer and counterclaim * * * [in which] they contend that the actual net contract price for the marble was only $265,050.00; that, after LASA had failed to ship marble as agreed and had threatened to cease shipments, the price was then under duress increased, first to $336,030.00 and then to $370,686.90; that a total of $406,967.74 has actually been paid to LASA; that much of the marble that was shipped arrived late, was broken, or was of the wrong type; and that LASA had failed to ship all the marble it was obligated to ship. Alexander by this counterclaim sues LASA for overpayment of the contract price and for unliquidated damages for failure to ship marble as agreed.

To this original complaint, Continental Casualty and Southern Builders have filed answers and Southern Builders has filed a counterclaim. They aver that Southern Builders is obligated to pay only "just and valid" claims for labor and materials and that LASA has no such claim; aver that nothing is owed LASA for marble delivered and installed on this job; deny that the City improperly released any retainages; and aver that LASA failed to ship marble as agreed. Southern Builders by its counterclaim sues LASA for all damages to it because of LASA's failure to ship marble as agreed to Alexander.

Alexander (partnership) has filed a cross-claim against Southern Builders, Continental Casualty and the City * * * for a balance alleged to be due under its subcontract with Southern Builders.

In the same cross-claim, it is further averred that Southern Builders, under the insistence of the architect, A. L. Aydelott, hindered Alexander in the performance of the subcontract * * *. It is further averred that Southern Builders, under the insistence of Aydelott, wrongfully terminated the subcontract, forced Alexander off the job, and brought in another subcontractor which was allowed to finish the job not in accordance with the original specifications (as Alexander had sought) and at an inflated price. It is further averred that Southern Builders and Aydelott injured the business reputation of Alexander by publicly blaming Alexander for many ills not its fault and which were the fault of Southern Builders and Aydelott. Alexander, in this cross-claim, accordingly also sues only Southern Builders for unliquidated damages, actual and punitive.

Southern Builders and Continental Casualty have filed answers to Alexander's cross-claim against them, and Southern Builders has filed * * * cross-claims against Alexander for any amount it is held to be liable to LASA in the original action. Southern Builders further cross-claims against Alexander for unliquidated damages for not maintaining progress schedules, for faulty materials and workmanship, for overdrawing money pursuant to false project information, and failing generally to follow the specifications, the subcontract, and the general contract.

Alexander has also filed a third party complaint, which has been once amended, against A. L. Aydelott and Associates, Inc. and against Aydelott, individually, who is its principal officer (hereinafter collectively referred to as "Aydelott") alleging that they had the architectural contract with the City. * * * It is alleged that Aydelott negligently provided improper specifications and insisted they be followed; negligently failed to require Southern Builders to properly perform its work; wrongfully required Alexander to install marble in inclement weather; wilfully refused to approve Alexander's estimates for work done; wrongfully directed Southern Builders to terminate the subcontract, allowed the new subcontractor to follow different specifications, and approved payment to the new subcontractor at an inflated price; wrongfully misinterpreted the specifications and the subcontract; and wrongfully and maliciously injured Alexander's business reputation. Alexander sues in this amended third party complaint for unliquidated actual and punitive damages under the general law and, under a Tennessee statute, for treble damages for inducing Southern Builders to breach the subcontract.

* * *

In support of its right to file this cross-claim, Alexander relies on Rule 13(g) * * *.

In support of its right to file the third party complaint, Alexander relies on Rule 13(h) * * *.

In his brief and argument, Aydelott contends that the right to file a third party complaint is controlled by Rule 14, which deals with "Third Party Practice." Aydelott further argues that, since he could not be liable and it is not contended that he is liable to Alexander for all or any part of LASA's claim against Alexander, as is required by Rule 14, this third party complaint cannot be maintained against him. While Aydelott is technically correct, it is also true, as Alexander contends, that by the simple expedient of amending the third party complaint to style it as a cross-claim against an additional cross-defendant, Alexander could then rely on Rule 13(h). It was therefore agreed at argument that the Court should test the propriety of the filing of this third party complaint by treating it as a cross-claim against an additional party under Rule 13(h).

It should be noted that Rule 13(h) provides that the right to make an additional party a cross-defendant is governed by Rules 19 and 20. Alexander does not contend that Rule 19 would allow Alexander to make Aydelott an additional cross-defendant. Alexander does contend, however, that this is authorized by that part of Rule 20, which provides:

"* * * All persons may be joined in one action as defendants if there is asserted against them jointly, severally, or in the alternative, any right to relief in respect of or arising out of the same transaction, occurrence, or series of transactions or occurrences and if any question of law or fact common to all defendants will arise in the action."

It is Alexander's contention, in other words, that since Southern Builders et al. have been properly made cross-defendants and since its claims for relief against Aydelott arise out of the same transaction or occurrence or series of transactions or occurrences as its claims against Southern Builders et al., Rule 13(h) allows the joining of Aydelott as an additional cross-defendant. Alexander is correct in this contention, if, as it assumes, its claims against Southern Builders et al. are authorized by Rule 13(g). * * *

This brings us to the ultimate question, which is: does Alexander's cross-claim, or any part of it, arise out of the transaction or occurrence that is the subject matter of the original action of LASA or the two counterclaims against LASA?

The original action is to collect an alleged balance due on the contract price of marble sold and delivered by LASA to Alexander. Alexander's counterclaim against LASA is to collect an alleged overpayment for marble sold and delivered and for unliquidated damages for the alleged failure of LASA to supply marble as agreed. The counterclaim of Southern Builders against LASA is for unliquidated damages for alleged failure of LASA to supply marble to Alexander as agreed. On the other hand, Alexander's cross-claim against all cross-defendants is to collect an alleged balance due on its subcontract with Southern Builders, and its cross-claim against Southern Builders alone is for unliquidated damages, compensatory and punitive, for alleged hindrance of Alexander in the performance of its subcontract, for failure to make payments to it when due, for wrongful termination of the subcontract, and for injury to its business reputation.

* * *

Alexander argues that the same general contract, bond, and subcontract, and some of the same evidence which would be involved in the original action and the counterclaims therein would also be involved in that part of its cross-claim against Southern Builders et al. for the balance alleged to be due under the subcontract. It then goes on to relate the remainder of its cross-claim, against Southern Builders alone, including even that for injury to its business reputation, to its cross-claim for the balance due, thus by this claim relating all of its cross-claims to these other claims.

It seems absolutely clear to us that none of that part of Alexander's cross-claim which includes a claim for damages for hindrance in performance of the subcontract and for cancellation of the subcontract and for damage to its business reputation has any logical relation to the original action or the counterclaims therein. Furthermore, none or hardly any of the issues of fact or law relating to the original action or the counterclaims therein would be the same as those relating to this part of Alexander's cross-claim, nor would a judgment on the original action or the counterclaims therein bar a subsequent suit on this part of the cross-claim, nor would any or hardly any of the same evidence support or refute this part of the cross-claim and the other claims. The only claim asserted by Alexander in its cross-claim that even arguably, applying these tests, arises out of the same transaction or occurrence that is the subject matter of LASA's claim and the counter-claims against LASA is that part of Alexander's cross-claim for the al-leged balance due under the subcontract. * * * [I]t would be stretch-ing the "logical relation" test to its utmost limits to say that Alexander's claim for a balance due under its subcontract with Southern Builders is logi-cally related to LASA's claim as a supplier of marble for a balance due under its contract with Alexander or to the counterclaims against LASA for failure to supply marble to Alexander as agreed. We do not believe, in spite of the admonition of some courts that Rule 13(g) is to be liberally interpreted, that the rule was ever intended to go so far. We therefore conclude that the cross-claim filed by Alexander must be dismissed in its en-tirety.

Inasmuch as we have previously stated that the merit of the motion to dismiss the third party complaint (treated as a cross-claim) against Aydelott depends on whether or not the cross-claim against Southern Builders et al. is authorized by Rule 13(g), and since we herein do hold that the cross-claim filed by Alexander against Southern Builders et al. is not authorized by Rule 13(g), it follows that the third party complaint filed by Alexander against Aydelott should likewise be dismissed.

It further appears that the cross-claim filed by Southern Builders against Alexander for unliquidated damages for breach of the subcon-tract likewise does not arise out of the same transaction or occurrence that is the subject matter of the original action or the counterclaims therein. On the other hand, insofar as Southern Builders cross-claims against Alex-ander on the theory that Alexander would be liable to Southern Builders for any amount Southern Builders is held liable to LASA in the original ac-tion, the cross-claim is clearly authorized by Rule 13(g). While Alexander has not filed a motion to dismiss the cross-claim of Southern Builders against it, the very position taken and argument made by Southern Builders on the motion to dismiss Alexander's cross-claim is inconsistent with its right to maintain a cross-claim against Alexander for unliquidated damages for breach of the subcontract, and therefore on the Court's own motion we will dismiss this part of the cross-claim of Southern Builders.

* * *

NOTES AND QUESTIONS

1. The Sixth Circuit reversed the principal case, stating:

Our reading of the pleadings in this case convinces us that there is a "logical relationship" between the cross-claims (including the third party complaint against the architect) and the "transaction or occurrence" that is the subject matter of the complaint and the two pending counter-claims. Although different subcontracts are involved, along with the prime contract and specifications, all relate to the same project and to problems arising out of the marble used in the erection of the Memphis City Hall. The recurring question presented by the various pleadings is directed to the principal issue of who is responsible for the marble problems which arose on this job. Blame is sought to be placed upon plaintiff as furnisher of the marble, upon Alexander as subcontractor, upon the prime contractor and upon the architect. Many of the same or closely related factual and legal issues necessarily will be presented under the complaint, counterclaims and cross-claims in the resolution of these issues. It seems apparent that some of the same evidence will be required in the hearing on cross-claims and in the hearing or hearings with respect to the complaint and the two pending counterclaims.

414 F.2d 143, 147 (6th Cir.1969). Is this reasoning persuasive? Shouldn't the fact that different subcontracts were involved, which therefore necessarily meant that different transactions were before the court, be determinative? If the appellate court's analysis is correct, what ways other than dismissal could be employed to deal with the complexity of the litigation or to avoid confusion?

2. Note that the expression "same transaction or occurrence" is used in the Federal Rules in connection with both compulsory counterclaims and cross-claims. Should the two passages be construed in the same fashion? See Benson Mfg. Co. v. Bell Tel. Co., 35 F.R.D. 29, 33 (E.D.Pa.1964). Should a cross-claim arising from the "same transaction or occurrence" be barred if defendant fails to assert it, as would be true of a counterclaim? See Hathcock v. Mitchell, 277 Ala. 586, 173 So.2d 576 (1965). Are there any reasons for treating a cross-claim differently than a compulsory counterclaim? Should cross-claims be treated as within the ancillary jurisdiction of the federal courts?

In SEBO v. UNITED AIR LINES, INC., 10 F.R.D. 327 (S.D.N.Y.1950), plaintiff, whose decedent had been a passenger in an airplane that had crashed, joined United Air Lines and Douglas Aircraft as defendants—United for careless operation and maintenance and Douglas for careless construction and design. United cross-claimed against Douglas, alleging that United had discovered certain defects in the plane, that pursuant to certain warranties Douglas had undertaken to correct the defects, that United resumed use of the plane in reliance on Douglas' clearance, and that the crash occurred shortly thereafter. Should the cross-claim have been dismissed?

3. Some states have adopted a narrow definition of a transaction for cross-claim purposes. In LIEBHAUSER v. MILWAUKEE ELEC. RY. & LIGHT CO., 180 Wis. 468, 193 N.W. 522, 43 A.L.R. 870 (1923), plaintiff-passenger sued to recover for personal injuries allegedly sustained while a passenger on one of defendant-railway company's street cars when it collided with an automobile owned and driven by defendant Kroscher. Kroscher cross-claimed against the railway company alleging that the collision was due solely to the negligence of the company and seeking $150 for damages to his automobile. The Wisconsin cross-claim provision stated that "A defendant * * * may have affirmative relief against a codefendant * * * but in all such cases such relief must involve or in some manner affect the contract, transaction or property, which is the subject-

matter of the action." The court, construing that statute, dismissed the cross-claim, saying:

> Whether or not the defendant Kroscher may set up by way of cross-complaint a cause of action and demand affirmative relief against his co-defendant depends upon whether or not the relief which Kroscher asks involves the transaction which constitutes the subject-matter of plaintiff's action. * * * The subject-matter of the action, then, in this case is the plaintiff's right to have the defendants exercise the required degree of care in respect to her. Manifestly, the relief demanded by Kroscher in his cross-complaint against the company in no way involves or affects the plaintiff's main primary right. Kroscher's cause of action, if any he has, arose by reason of the failure of the company to exercise the required degree of care in respect to him, and it was entirely complete before plaintiff's cause of action arose. It cannot, therefore, be said logically that the relief demanded by Kroscher in his cross-complaint involves in any respect the transaction which is the subject-matter of the plaintiff's action or her main primary right.

> The mere fact that the two occurrences were nearly contemporaneous in time in no manner affects the question. * * *

> The statute does not say that one defendant may set up in a cross-complaint a cause of action against a codefendant arising out of the same transaction out of which the plaintiff's cause of action arose. He may do so only when the relief demanded involves the transaction which constitutes the subject-matter of the plaintiff's action. In this case the defendant Kroscher demands a money judgment against his codefendant. The granting of this relief to Kroscher does not in the slightest degree involve the act by which the plaintiff's main primary right was invaded, which is the subject-matter of her action. It will not diminish by a single cent the amount of her recovery. If she establish the allegations of her complaint, her rights will be in no way affected by the relief which may be granted to the defendant Kroscher. * * * Kroscher is suing for the invasion of one primary right, the plaintiff is suing for the invasion of an entirely distinct and different primary right, and the right of the defendant Kroscher to relief is wholly independent of the plaintiff's right, as much so as if the injuries complained of had risen upon a different day and at a different place. * * *

> A careful study of the matter * * * convinces us that the revisers intended to limit the cases where cross-complaints might be filed to those where the rights of the plaintiff were necessarily involved. Underlying this is a sound public policy. Plaintiff should have a right to bring her action and obtain an adjudication of her rights without being compelled to become a mere observer in a contest between two defendants which in no way whatever concerns her. In the present case it is conceivable that the plaintiff might establish without difficulty a right of recovery against both defendants, and be entitled to receive compensation for the injuries complained of, and yet the determination of her right might be compelled to await the issue of long litigation between the defendants, in which she was in no way concerned, and in

which the act by which her main primary right was invaded was in no way involved. There can be but one judgment in the action. To make the plaintiff's right to judgment dependent upon final adjudication of an independent controversy existing between the defendants is in effect to grant her the right to appeal to the courts upon a condition. This should not be. * * *

Id. at 473–74, 475–76, 481–82, 193 N.W. at 524–25, 525. Compare the reasoning of the *Liebhauser* case with Section 3019(b) of the New York Civil Practice Law, which is in the Supplement following Rule 13. In what ways do the two provisions differ? The New York statute is discussed in 3 Weinstein, Korn & Miller, *New York Civil Practice* ¶ 3019.14.

4. Can a party plaintiff cross-claim against a coplaintiff? If so, under what circumstances? In DANNER v. ANSKIS, 256 F.2d 123 (3d Cir.1958), the driver and passenger of one car sued the driver of a second car for damages arising out of a two-car collision. The passenger-plaintiff also attempted to cross-claim for her injuries against the driver-plaintiff. The trial court's dismissal of the cross-claim was affirmed:

> The purpose of Rule 13(g) is to permit a defendant to state as a cross-claim a claim against a co-defendant growing out of the same transaction or occurrence that is the subject matter of the original action * * *, and to permit a plaintiff against whom a defendant has filed a counterclaim to state as a cross-claim against a co-plaintiff a claim growing out of the transaction or occurrence that is the subject matter of the counterclaim. * * * This, we think, is the clear intent of the language of the rule. In other words, a cross-claim is intended to state a claim which is ancillary to a claim stated in a complaint or counterclaim which has previously been filed against the party stating the cross-claim. * * * Unless so limited the rule could have the effect of extending the jurisdiction of the district court to controversies not within the federal judicial power. * * * Accordingly, Rule 13(g) does not authorize a plaintiff to state as a cross-claim against a co-plaintiff a claim arising out of the transaction or occurrence which is also the subject matter of their common complaint against the defendant. * * *

Id. at 124. Is the court's approach to the question of cross-claims between coplaintiffs sound? How is the *Danner* court defining "transaction"?

5. In WASHINGTON BUILDING REALTY CORP. v. PEOPLES DRUG STORE, INC., 82 U.S.App.D.C. 119, 161 F.2d 879 (D.C.Cir.1947), the injured party joined Washington (lessor) and Peoples (lessee) in a suit for injuries suffered from an alleged failure to maintain a proper exit-way. Peoples cross-claimed against Washington, alleging the injury was due solely to Washington's negligence. In affirming the dismissal, the court said:

> * * * It is not alleged that the parties are jointly liable, as a result of which a claim for contribution would arise, nor that Peoples is only secondarily liable, as a result of which it would have a claim for indemnity, nor that there is a contract between Peoples and Washington Building Corporation which would entitle Peoples to complete indemnity. In short, in its cross-claim appellee has alleged only facts that constitute as

> to it a complete defense to the original tort action, and nothing constituting
> a claim against Washington Building Corporation.

Id. at 880. What should Peoples do once its cross-claim is denied? Would a slight difference in the pleadings have saved Peoples' cross-claim? See Bohn v. American Export Lines, 42 F.Supp. 228 (S.D.N.Y.1941).

6. In order to invoke Rule 13(h), defendant must be asserting a claim against someone who already is a party. Note that this differs from claims under Rule 14. In *LASA* the trial court treated defendant's attempt to interpose a Rule 14 claim as if it were a motion to bring in an additional cross-defendant under Rule 13(h). Isn't it true, therefore, that Rule 14 claims can be transformed into Rule 13(h) motions whenever defendant is able to assert a cross-claim against a party? Is there any tactical advantage in doing so? Are the additional party's rights any different if it is brought in under Rule 13(h) rather than Rule 14? See the discussion of Rule 14 at pp. 557–65, infra.

SECTION C. CLAIMS INVOLVING MULTIPLE PARTIES

The scope of a lawsuit can be expanded not only by proliferating the number of claims but also by increasing the number of participants in the action—a subject governed by the rules relating to joinder of parties. Joinder of parties differs from joinder of claims against a single party because in the former context the interests of persons other than the original parties must be considered. Before determining who *may* be made a party to a civil action, however, it is necessary to examine briefly the question of who *must* be made a party.

---

1. REAL PARTY IN INTEREST

The "real-party-in-interest" rule is based on the proposition that the party instituting a civil action should be the person to whom the substantive law ascribes a right to prosecute and secure a remedy for defendant's alleged misconduct. Historically, the "real party in interest" has always been required to bring the action but has not always been required to litigate in his own name. Since the common-law courts took cognizance only of legal rights, plaintiff had to be a person whose legal rights were affected by defendant's activities. Consequently, the holder of an equitable interest generally could sue at law only in the name of the person having legal title to the property involved in the dispute. For example, an assignee of a chose in action could not sue in his own name at law, although the action could be commenced in the name of the assignor. By comparison, the equity courts only required plaintiff to have a material interest in the suit, which enabled an assignee of a chose in action to recover in his own name in chancery. The merger of law and equity necessitated the elimination of this discrepancy in practice. In the case of the original New York Code of 1848, the framers, with the assignment situation in mind, formulated the requirement subsequently adopted by almost all the states and the Federal Rules—every action must be prosecuted in the name of the real party in interest. For further discussion, see Clark, *Code Pleading* § 22 (2d ed. 1947).

Care should be taken to distinguish the concepts of real party in interest, capacity to sue and be sued, and standing to sue. As embodied in Rule 17(a), the real-party-in-interest principle is a means to identify the person who possesses the right sought to be enforced and is a method to direct the court's attention to whether the plaintiff has a significant interest in the particular action. Capacity under Rules 17(b) and 17(c) deals with the situation in which a party who has the personal right to litigate in a federal court is not qualified to do so under the applicable law or is under some disability and needs assistance from the court, which typically takes the form of the appointment of a guardian ad litem. The requirement applies to all the parties to the suit and is not dependent on the character of the specific claim involved in the litigation. Thus, for example, a person may be the real party in interest and yet lack capacity to sue because he has become mentally incompetent or is an infant. Conversely, plaintiff may have capacity to sue under Rule 17(b), but have assigned all of his interest in the claim before the action was instituted and therefore no longer be the real party in interest. For a more detailed discussion of capacity to sue see 6 Wright & Miller, *Federal Practice and Procedure: Civil* §§ 1559–69 (1971).

A third problem of proper parties occurs in the realm of public law. When governmental action is attacked on the ground that it violates private rights or some constitutional principle, the courts have tended to analyze the question whether the challenger is a proper party plaintiff to assert the claim in terms of the judge-made doctrine of standing to sue—requiring that plaintiff be adversely affected by defendant's conduct—rather than according to real-party-in-interest or capacity principles. See Davis, *Standing: Taxpayers and Others*, 35 U.Chi.L.Rev. 601 (1968), and Jaffee, *The Citizen as a Litigant in Public Actions: The Non-Hohfeldian or Ideological Plaintiff*, 116 U.Pa.L.Rev. 1033 (1968). To the extent that standing is understood to mean that the litigant actually must be injured by the governmental action that is being assailed, it closely resembles the notion of real party in interest under Rule 17(a). However, several other elements of the standing doctrine clearly are unrelated to the simple real-party-in-interest test. One significant context in which the two concepts diverge is when for standing purposes plaintiff is required to show both that he has been adversely affected by the governmental conduct that is under attack and has suffered an injury to a legally protected right. When standing is defined in this fashion it may entail a preliminary consideration of the merits of the case and therefore is quite different from the real-party-in-interest notion.

Read Federal Rule of Civil Procedure 17(a) in the Supplement.

ELLIS CANNING CO. v. INTERNATIONAL HARVESTER CO.

Supreme Court of Kansas, 1953.
174 Kan. 357, 255 P.2d 658.

PARKER, Justice. * * *

In its petition plaintiff alleged that in furnishing service on its tractor defendant negligently started a fire in that vehicle resulting in damage amounting to $479.79; that plaintiff was insured in The Potomac Insurance Company against the loss, under a policy containing a subrogation clause; that it had been paid in full for the amount of its loss; and that it had commenced and was maintaining the action to recover such amount in its own name for the use and benefit of the insurance company.

Defendant's amended answer denied *seriatim* all acts of negligence * * *; admitted all allegations of that pleading respecting insurance, the amount of the loss, and the fact such loss had been fully paid by the insurance company; and then, in the third paragraph thereof, * * * alleged and charged, that since plaintiff was seeking to recover the amount paid to it by the insurer as full compensation for the loss of the tractor, the insurance company was the real party in interest and plaintiff had no legal right to maintain the action.

Plaintiff's motion to strike paragraph three of the answer and its demurrer to the same paragraph of that pleading * * * were overruled by the trial court. This appeal followed.

The appellant insists, the appellee concedes, and we agree, the sole question involved is whether the insured (appellant), after having been paid the full amount of its loss, is a real party in interest and legally entitled to maintain this action, for the use and benefit of the insurer, to recover such loss from the party (appellee), whose negligence is alleged to be responsible therefor. The question thus raised is not new in this jurisdiction and we frankly concede is one on which there is apparent conflict in our decisions.

Subject to certain exceptions, not here involved, our statute, G.S.1949, 60–401, requires that "Every action must be prosecuted in the name of the real party in interest." Given its common and accepted meaning, particularly where—as here—it must be conceded the appellant is no longer directly interested in the subject matter of the litigation, it would seem that, in and of itself, language of the statute would compel a negative answer to the question now under consideration. * * *

Notwithstanding, earlier decisions * * * holding that in the situation disclosed by the pleadings in the case at bar, the insurer is the real and only party in interest and must undertake the maintenance of the action for his reimbursement, it must and should be frankly admitted that in * * * [two decisions], as appellant contends, we held the insured might maintain the action in his own name for the use and benefit of the insurer. Be that as it may it must be conceded, that fully aware of the rule announced in those cases, we have repudiated what was there said and held with respect to such rule and now recognize and adhere to the doctrine that under the facts and circumstances disclosed by such pleadings an insured who has been fully paid for his loss is not the real party in interest * * * and hence cannot maintain an action to recover the amount of such loss in his own name for the use and benefit of the insurer. Conversely stated, the rule now recognized and applied is, that under the confronting conditions and circumstances the right of action against the alleged wrongdoer vests wholly in the insurer who * * * may, and indeed must, bring the action as the real and only party in interest if one is to be maintained. * * *

The judgment is affirmed.

NOTES AND QUESTIONS

1. What is the tactical objective of having the insured sue for defendant's negligence inasmuch as the former has been paid by the insurer? If the insured lost, should the insurer be permitted to bring a second suit claiming it was the real party in interest and thus was not bound by the prior judgment? Are any of the insured's "rights" or "interests" at stake? Must the real party in interest have a direct pecuniary interest in the outcome of the suit? Why should International Harvester be concerned about the identity of the plaintiff in this context? For a decision contrary to *Ellis*, see Anheuser-Busch, Inc. v. Starley, 28 Cal.2d 347, 170 P.2d 448, 166 A.L.R. 198 (1946). Would the real-party-in-interest defense have been available in *Ellis* if the loss from the fire had exceeded the amount of the policy or if the policy provided that the first $100 of loss was to be borne by the insured? Under these circumstances, should the insurer and the insured be required to prosecute the action jointly? See Pinewood Gin Co. v. Carolina Power & Light Co., 41 F.R.D. 221 (D.S.C.1966). Is the insurer the real party in interest if it simply lends the insured the amount due on the policy and the insured is required to pay it back only to the extent the insured obtains a recovery against defendant? Does it make any difference if such a loan-receipt arrangement is sanctioned by state law?

2. Is a federal district court in Kansas obliged to follow *Ellis* in diversity cases? See Hughey v. Aetna Cas. & Sur. Co., 32 F.R.D. 340 (D.Del.1963); Comment, *Diversity of Citizenship and the Real Party in Interest*, 4 U.C.L.A.L.Rev. 619 (1957). If the possibility of prejudice at trial is of concern, couldn't it be

eliminated by full disclosure of the insurance company's subrogation interest? Even if this were an effective technique, could a federal judge disclose this information in a diversity case in a state that prohibits the existence of insurance to be disclosed to the jury? Reconsider *Guaranty Trust Co. v. York*, p. 272, supra, and *Byrd v. Blue Ridge Elec. Coop., Inc.*, p. 278, supra. Would this procedure eliminate any need for a federal court to follow *Ellis*? See generally Kennedy, *Federal Rule 17 (a): Will the Real Party in Interest Please Stand?*, 51 Minn.L.Rev. 675, 715 (1967).

3. Since the citizenship of the real party in interest governs for purposes of diversity jurisdiction, the assignment of a claim or the appointment of a particular individual as administrator or guardian may determine the existence or nonexistence of jurisdiction. Section 1359 of the Judicial Code provides that a district court does not have jurisdiction of a civil action in which any party, by assignment or otherwise, has been improperly or collusively made or joined to *invoke* the jurisdiction of such court. Does the appointment of a nonresident administrator for the sole purpose of creating diversity fall within the prohibition? See McSparran v. Weist, 402 F.2d 867 (3d Cir.1968), certiorari denied 395 U.S. 903, 89 S.Ct. 1739, 23 L.Ed.2d 217 (1969). See also Comment, *Appointment of Non-Resident Administrators To Create Federal Diversity Jurisdiction*, 73 Yale L.J. 873 (1964). What if the assignment or appointment is made for the purpose of *defeating* federal jurisdiction? See Mecom v. Fitzsimmons Drilling Co., 284 U.S. 183, 52 S.Ct. 84, 76 L.Ed. 233 (1931); Bernblum v. Travelers' Ins. Co., 9 F.Supp. 34 (W.D.Mo.1934). Would it be sufficient to show that the assignment or appointment for purposes of collection is valid under state law to avoid the application of Section 1359? See Kramer v. Caribbean Mills, Inc., 394 U.S. 823, 89 S.Ct. 1487, 23 L.Ed.2d 9 (1969).

The American Law Institute has proposed the following statute:

> An executor, or an administrator, or any person representing the estate of a decedent or appointed pursuant to statute with authority to bring an action because of the death of a decedent shall be deemed to be a citizen only of the same State as the decedent; and a guardian, committee, or other like representative of an infant or incompetent shall be deemed to be a citizen only of the same State as the person represented.

ALI, *Study of the Division of Jurisdiction Between State and Federal Courts*, Official Draft, § 1301(b) (4) (1969). Is the ALI approach superior to Section 1359 in terms of minimizing the possibility that parties will attempt to manufacture diversity?

4. If the party designated in the original complaint is not the real party in interest, should a substitution of the proper party be given retroactive effect to the date of the original complaint for statute of limitations purposes? Should a motion for substitution be made under the provisions of Federal Rule 25(c), or does Rule 15(c) (2) adequately cover the situation? See Link Aviation, Inc. v. Downs, 117 U.S.App.D.C. 40, 325 F.2d 613 (D.C.Cir.1963). Federal Rule 17(a) was amended in 1966 to add the provision that no action shall be dismissed because it was not prosecuted in the name of the real party in interest until a reasonable time has been allowed for substitution. The Advisory Committee's Notes, which appear in the Supplement, specifically limit the application of this passage to cases in which

the proper party to sue is difficult to ascertain or when an excusable mistake has been made. Does the court have any discretion to refuse substitution? For example, if a suit originally is brought by John Doe against an airline for personal injuries arising out of an airline crash, should the court later allow the names of all the victims of the disaster to be substituted as the real parties in interest?

5. Various authorities have advocated the abolition of the real-party-in-interest concept. In Atkinson, *The Real Party In Interest Rule: A Plea For Its Abolition,* 32 N.Y.U.L.Rev. 926, 959–60 (1957), the author suggests:

> The * * * rule is * * * misleading and * * * does nothing except abolish the name suit. * * * Then too the name suit should be deemed abolished by the modern procedural systems where law and equity are united and fictions abolished. * * *
>
> The impression that some specific provision is necessary to indicate who may be a plaintiff is an aberration. If further proof of this is necessary it is demonstrated by the absence of any counterpart of the real party in interest rule in the case of defendants. * * *

New York, the originator of the real-party-in-interest rule, has abolished it. According to 2 Weinstein, Korn & Miller, *New York Civil Practice* ¶ 1004.01:

> * * * [I]t was unnecessary because (1) the law would be the same without any express rule, (2) it was an inept statement of an obvious principle of substantive law, (3) it misleadingly seemed to say that the action must be brought by the party to be benefited, and (4) the second part of [the former New York rule (which was similar to the second sentence of Federal Rule 17(a))] * * * was not an exception to the first part even though it was cast in the form of an exception.
>
> The question of who has a substantive right and whether that right has been violated to the extent that an action for redress may be brought is a matter of substantive not procedural law. Where a claim is, for example, assigned before the action is commenced, the assignor lacks any substantive right against the debtor which can be enforced. Analysis is impeded by attempting to treat the problem in terms of "real party in interest."

The judicial precedents bearing on who comes within the provisions of real-party-in-interest statutes are examined in Clark & Hutchins, *The Real Party In Interest,* 34 Yale L.J. 259 (1925), and Simes, *The Real Party In Interest,* 10 Ky.L.J. 60 (1922).

2. NECESSARY AND INDISPENSABLE PARTIES

Read Federal Rule of Civil Procedure 19 and the accompanying material in the Supplement.

BANK OF CALIFORNIA NAT. ASS'N v. SUPERIOR COURT

Supreme Court of California, 1940.
16 Cal.2d 516, 106 P.2d 879.

GIBSON, Chief Justice.   *   *   *

Sara M. Boyd   *   *   *   died testate in June, 1937, leaving an estate valued at about $225,000. On July 8, 1937,   *   *   *   her will was admitted to probate, and petitioner, Bank of California, was appointed executor. The will left individual legacies and bequests amounting to $60,000 to a large number of legatees,   *   *   *   some residing in other states and in foreign countries. Petitioner, St. Luke's Hospital, was named residuary legatee and devisee, and thereby received the bulk of the estate.

On October 14, 1937, Bertha M. Smedley, a niece and legatee, brought an action to enforce the provisions of an alleged contract by which decedent agreed to leave her entire estate to the plaintiff. The complaint named as parties defendant the executor and all of the beneficiaries under the will, and prayed for a decree adjudging that plaintiff is, by virtue of the agreement, the owner of the entire estate of the decedent after payment of debts and expenses. It was further prayed that plaintiff's title to the property be quieted   *   *   *.

Summons was served only upon petitioners, the executor and the residuary legatee. No other defendants were served, and none appeared.   *   *   *   [At trial] petitioners made a motion   *   *   *   for an order to bring in the other defendants, and to have summons issued and served upon them. The motion was made on the ground that all of the other defendants were "necessary and indispensable parties" to the action, and that the court could not proceed without them. The motion was denied by respondent court. Petitioners then applied for a writ of prohibition to restrain the trial until these other parties should be brought in.

In support of their application, petitioners point out that the complaint challenges the right of every legatee and devisee to share in the estate, and prays for an award of the entire property to plaintiff. It is contended that a trial and judgment without the absent defendants would adversely affect the rights of such parties, would result in a multiplicity of suits, and would subject the petitioning executor to inconvenience, expense and the burden of future litigation.

*   *   *   [T]he precise issue is   *   *   *   whether the absent defendants are not only proper parties but "indispensable parties" in the sense that service upon them or their appearance is essential to the jurisdiction of the court to proceed in the action.   *   *   *

At common law, joinder of plaintiffs was compulsory where the parties under the substantive law, were possessed of joint rights.   Joint promises under a contract, partners, and joint tenants were familiar examples.   Equity courts developed another theory of compulsory joinder, to carry out the policy of avoiding piecemeal litigation and multiplicity of suits.   Those persons necessary to a complete settlement of the controversy were usually required to be joined, in order that the entire matter might be concluded by a single suit.   Obviously, this theory of joinder covered many situations where the substantive rights were not joint, and accordingly joinder would not have been required in an action at law.   *   *   *   Generally speaking, the modern rule under the codes carries out the established equity doctrine.   Thus, section 389 of the Code of Civil Procedure states: "The court may determine any controversy between parties before it, when it can be done without prejudice to the rights of others, or by saving their rights; but when a complete determination of the controversy cannot be had without the presence of other parties, the court must then order them to be brought in   *   *   *."   Such statutes have been interpreted as declaratory of the equity rule and practice.   *   *   *

But the equity doctrine as developed by the courts is loose and ambiguous in its expression and uncertain in its application.   Sometimes it is stated as a mandatory rule, and at other times as a matter of discretion, designed to reach an equitable result if it is practicable to do so.   *   *   *   Bearing in mind the fundamental purpose of the doctrine, we should, in dealing with "necessary" and "indispensable" parties, be careful to avoid converting a discretionary power or a rule of fairness in procedure into an arbitrary and burdensome requirement which may thwart rather than accomplish justice.   These two terms have frequently been coupled together as if they have the same meaning; but there appears to be a sound distinction, both in theory and practice, between parties deemed "indispensable" and those considered merely "necessary."   As Professor Clark has remarked: "It has been objected that the terms 'necessary' and 'indispensable' convey the same idea.   *   *   *   But a distinction has been drawn.   While necessary parties are so interested in the controversy that they should normally be made parties in order to enable the court to do complete justice, yet if their interests are separable from the rest and particularly where their presence in the suit cannot be obtained, they are not indispensable parties.   The latter are those without whom the court cannot proceed."   Clark, Code Pleading, p. 245, note 21.   *   *   *

First, then, what parties are indispensable?   There may be some persons whose interests, rights, or duties will inevitably be affected by any decree which can be rendered in the action.   Typical are the situations where a number of persons have undetermined interests in the same property, or in a particular trust fund, and one of them seeks, in an action, to recover the whole, to fix his share, or to recover a portion claimed by him.   The other persons with similar interests are indispensable parties.   The reason is that a judgment in favor of one claimant for part of the property or fund would necessarily determine the amount or extent which remains available to the others. Hence, any judgment in the action would inevitably affect their rights. Thus, in an action by one creditor against assignees for the benefit of creditors, seeking an accounting and payment of his share of the assets, the other creditors were held indispensable * * * and in an action by plaintiff to enforce a trust, where he claimed the property in his own right, to the exclusion of another actual beneficiary, failure to join the latter was held fatal to the judgment. * * * Where, also, the plaintiff seeks some other type of affirmative relief which, if granted, would injure or affect the interests of a third person not joined that third person is an indispensable party. Thus, in an action by a lessor against a sublessee to forfeit a parent lease because of acts of the sublessee, the sublessors (original lessees) were indispensable parties, since a decree of forfeiture would deprive them of their lease. * * * And in a suit to cancel illegal registration of voters, all voters whose registration was challenged were indispensable parties. * * *

[margin note: Indispensable]

All of these persons are, of course, "necessary" parties, but the decisions show that they come within a special classification of necessary parties, to which the term "indispensable" seems appropriate. An attempt to adjudicate their rights without joinder is futile. Many cases go so far as to say that the court would have no jurisdiction to proceed without them, and that its purported judgment would be void and subject to collateral attack. The objection being so fundamental, it need not be raised by the parties themselves; the court may, of its own motion, dismiss the proceedings, or refuse to proceed, until these indispensable parties are brought in. * * *

The other classification includes persons who are interested in the sense that they might possibly be affected by the decision, or whose interests in the subject matter or transaction are such that it cannot be finally and completely settled without them; but nevertheless their interests are so separable that a decree may be rendered between the parties before the court without affecting those others. These latter may perhaps be "necessary" parties to a complete settlement of the entire controversy or transaction, but are not "indispensable" to any valid judgment in the particular case. They should normally be joined, and the court, following the equity rule, will usually require them to be joined, in order to carry out the policy of complete determination and avoidance of multiplicity of suits. But, since the rule itself is one of equity, it is limited and qualified by considerations of fairness, convenience, and practicability. Where, for example, it is impossible to find these other persons or impracticable to bring them in, the action may proceed as to those parties who are present.

[margin note: necessary]

* * *

With the foregoing distinctions in mind, the present action may be examined to determine whether the absent defendants are indispensable or only necessary parties. The nature of such an action has been frequently discussed by the courts. The probate court cannot, of course, take cognizance of the contract, and an equity court cannot compel the making of a will. Hence, there is

[margin note: Issue: are absent defendants indispensable or only necessary?]

no specific performance of the contract in the strict sense. But equity gives relief which is the equivalent of a specific performance. Though the estate may be probated and the property distributed accordingly, the court will, in an action by the promisee, impose a constructive trust upon any particular property in the hands of the individual distributee. * * *

The action in these cases is against the distributee personally, and not against the estate; and it is independent of the will and the probate proceeding. Each distributee is individually held as a constructive trustee solely of the property which came to him, and none is interested in the granting or denial of similar relief as to any other. Where there are a number of legatees and devisees, they would all appear to be "necessary" parties in the sense that the main issue, the validity of the testamentary disposition of the property of decedent, affects their property interests, and the entire matter, the disposition of all of the decedent's property, cannot be finally settled without a binding adjudication for or against every legatee or devisee. Hence, the court will usually order them served and brought in unless there is some good reason for not doing so. But the absent defendants in such a case are not indispensable parties. Unlike the situations discussed above, in which any judgment would necessarily affect the rights of the absent persons, the case here is one where plaintiff may litigate her claim against the appearing defendants alone and obtain a decree which binds them alone. The absent defendants, not being before the court, will not be bound by the judgment, whether favorable or unfavorable, and their property interests will not be affected.

* * *

Only brief mention need be made of the contention that the prosecution of the action against less than all of the distributees will cause inconvenience and multiplicity of suits to the injury of the executor. These are all matters within the discretion of the court to consider in connection with its policy to settle the entire controversy in one proceeding, if possible. * * *

We have refrained from discussing the question whether the lower court's denial of the motion to bring in the absent defendants was, under the circumstances, an abuse of discretion. If they were readily available and could have been brought in without serious difficulty, it may well be that the motion should have been granted. On the other hand, if, as is asserted by respondents, many reside outside the state or the country, great difficulty might be encountered in any attempt to bring them in, and the trial might be indefinitely delayed, to the detriment of the present parties. The fact that the interests of the absent defendants are trivial as compared with that of the residuary legatee, which received over seventy-five percent of the estate, is perhaps some indication of the reason why plaintiff chose to go to trial against the latter alone. All these considerations, however, were for the trial court in the first instance, and its determination, though reviewable in the proper manner, cannot be attacked on an application for writ of prohibition.

The alternative writ, heretofore issued, is discharged, and the peremptory writ is denied.

NOTES AND QUESTIONS

1. WARNER v. PACIFIC TEL. & TEL. CO., 121 Cal.App.2d 497, 263 P.2d 465 (2d Dist.Ct.App.1953), involved the following three successive telephone listings: (1) Warner, Caryl atty, 639 S Spring—TUkr 9171 Woodland Hills Office, 21042 Rios—DIamnd 85761; (2) Warner, Caryl Mrs. 1600 Westrly Ter—NOrmndy 22011; and (3) Warner, Caryl Mrs. Warner Caryl atty 21042 Rios Wdlnd Hills—DIamnd 85761. The "Mrs. Caryl Warner" in the second listing was the first wife of Caryl Warner; the "Mrs. Caryl Warner" in the third listing was Caryl Warner's wife at the time of the lawsuit. After the telephone company refused to delete or change the second listing, the present Mrs. Warner brought suit against the company for damages on the ground that the existing listings injured her reputation in the community and has caused her "emotional distress, humiliation, fear, vexation, annoyance, scorn and ridicule as to her marital status, rendering her sick, with recurrent asthma attacks, to her damage." Plaintiff also asserted that she owned the title "Mrs. Caryl Warner," that the name has acquired a secondary meaning by reason of the professional and social standing of Caryl Warner, that her prestige and dignity were being depreciated, that the telephone listings constitute an invasion of privacy because they depict plaintiff as a party to a bigamous marriage, and that the telephone company knew or should have known that its maintenance of the listings would cause damage to plaintiff. The telephone company demurred to plaintiff's third amended and supplemental complaint on the ground, *inter alia,* that plaintiff had failed to join an indispensable party—the first Mrs. Caryl Warner. In light of the *Bank of California* case, should the California Court of Appeals affirm or reverse the lower court's grant of the demurrer? Why? Is it relevant that the Pacific Telephone & Telegraph Company is a public service corporation that is bound to furnish its services to the public without discrimination?

2. Is the failure to join an indispensable party really a jurisdictional defect as the *Bank of California* case suggests? See Hazard, *Indispensable Party: The Historical Origin of a Procedural Phantom,* 61 Colum.L.Rev. 1254, 1255–56 (1961). In MALLOW v. HINDE, 25 U.S. (12 Wheat.) 193, 198, 6 L.Ed. 599, 600 (1827), the Supreme Court held that the action had to be dismissed for failure to join an indispensable party on the ground that "no court can adjudicate directly upon a person's right, without the party being actually or constructively before the court." Since under traditional res judicata and collateral estoppel principles only parties to an action are bound by the resulting judgment, what was the Supreme Court concerned about? Even though the absent party's rights cannot be formally adjudicated, in what ways might the absentee be affected? Do these factors justify an automatic dismissal of plaintiff's action? See generally Reed, *Compulsory Joinder of Parties in Civil Actions,* 55 Mich.L. Rev. 327 (1957). Courts have not refused to entertain a creditor's suit because a judgment against the debtor might impair his ability to pay creditors not before the court. Similarly, numerous persons may be prejudiced by the stare decisis effect of a decision, but it does not follow that they must be joined because the decision may be an adverse precedent. Of what relevance is the availability of intervention? See pp. 630–48, infra.

3. If the indispensable-party rule cannot be justified on the ground that the absentee's rights will be prejudiced by a judgment, are there other considerations

that might induce a court to refrain from adjudicating an action when an interested party is not present? Consider MAHR v. NORWICH UNION FIRE INS. SOC'Y, 127 N.Y. 452, 28 N.E. 391 (1891), in which plaintiff brought an action to restrain an insurance company from indemnifying the insured or his assignee. The policy had been issued to Bartlett and although delivered to plaintiff as collateral for a loan, it never was formally assigned. Thereafter Bartlett assigned the policy to Kelly, an Iowa resident, who had not been made a party to the action and could not be joined because he was beyond the jurisdiction of the New York courts. The insurance company moved to dismiss, claiming that Kelly was an indispensable party, but the trial court denied the motion. The Court of Appeals reversed expressing the fear that "payment or performance may be exacted as many times as there are separate claimants." In fact, Kelly had brought suit against the insurance company in an Iowa court. Even if the threat of an inconsistent decision is remote, shouldn't the threat of multiplicity be sufficient to excuse defendant from defending the action? See Petrogradsky M.K. Bank v. National City Bank, 253 N.Y. 23, 170 N.E. 479, certiorari denied 282 U.S. 878, 51 S.Ct. 82, 75 L.Ed. 775 (1930).

Is prejudice to defendant and the possibility of inconsistent adjudications only a factor to be weighed as part of a balancing of competing interests? Doesn't *Western Union Tel. Co. v. Pennsylvania*, p. 145, supra, elevate the threat of multiple liability to a constitutional level? Isn't nationwide service of process, as is now available under the Federal Interpleader Act, 28 U.S.C. § 2361, see pp. 616–29, infra, the most efficacious solution to the joinder of parties problem? Notice that a federal court can acquire jurisdiction over an absentee not within the state pursuant to any state long-arm statute, Rule 4(e), and that it also can serve persons brought in under Rule 19 if they are within 100 miles from the place where the action is commenced, whether or not the place of service is within the state in which the action is pending, Rule 4(f). Should the remaining territorial barriers be broken down?

4. SHIELDS v. BARROW, 58 U.S. (17 How.) 129, 15 L.Ed. 158 (1854), established the notion that parties could be classified as necessary or indispensable depending on the nature of their substantive rights ("joint" or "severable"). The consequences of this classification were extremely important. If an absent party who was not subject to the jurisdiction of the court or whose joinder would destroy the pre-existing diversity of citizenship was labelled indispensable, the entire action had to be dismissed. On the other hand, if the absentee merely was necessary, the court might exercise its discretion in determining whether or not to continue without that person. Because a plaintiff might have been deprived of any remedy if a party was found to be indispensable, courts often strained to avoid that conclusion. As might be suspected, this method had a debilitating effect on the standard for classification. See Note, *Multiparty Litigation: Proposed Changes in the Federal Rules,* 50 Iowa L.Rev. 1135 (1965); Comment, *Attacking the Party Problem,* 38 So.Cal.L.Rev. 80, 83 (1965).

PETTENGILL v. UNITED STATES, 253 F.Supp. 321 (N.D.Ill.1966), which was decided prior to the effective date of the 1966 amendment to Federal Rule 19, involved three separate tax refund actions, one brought by the administratrix and two by heirs of the deceased, to recover taxes erroneously collected from the decedent's estate. A third heir brought an individual refund action in a Florida District Court. The United States argued that all the heirs were required to join as indispensable parties in a single action. Plaintiffs had commenced separate actions because venue barred them from bringing suit in a single court and because there is no trial by jury in the Court of Claims, an alternative forum. If the court dismissed for lack of an indispensable party, a subsequent action would have been barred by the statute of limitations; if it did not, the Government would be put to the expense of defending separate actions. What factors should the court weigh in reaching its result and what should that result be?

5.   What should the result be when plaintiff, a citizen of Texas, sues defendant, a citizen of Arkansas, in a federal district court in Arkansas, and, on defendant's motion, the court requires that X, a citizen of Texas, be joined as a defendant in the action? See Calcote v. Texas Pac. Coal & Oil Co., 157 F.2d 216 (5th Cir.1946); Aetna Ins. Co. v. Busby, 87 F.Supp. 505 (N.D.Ala.1950); Osborne v. Campbell, 37 F.R.D. 339 (S.D.W.Va.1965). Is the concept of ancillary jurisdiction helpful here? See *Developments in the Law—Multiparty Litigation in the Federal Courts*, 71 Harv.L.Rev. 874, 992 (1958). Are the consequences of a dismissal significant if a state court is available to entertain the action? See Fouke v. Schenewerk, 197 F.2d 234 (5th Cir.1952).

6.   Reconsider the hypothetical concerning partial subrogation in Note 1 on p. 528, supra. In that context are the insured and the insurer necessary or indispensable parties? If one of the two refuses to join in an action, is there any way to make her a party? In INDEPENDENT WIRELESS TEL. CO. v. RADIO CORP. OF AMERICA, 269 U.S. 459, 46 S.Ct. 166, 70 L.Ed. 357 (1926), the owner of a patent refused to join with plaintiff, an exclusive licensee, in a suit to enjoin further infringement by defendant. The owner was not amenable to process and could not be made a party defendant. The court held that it was proper to treat the recalcitrant absentee as an "involuntary plaintiff" to secure "justice." What are the advantages of the technique employed in the *Independent Wireless* case? Its disadvantages? Commentary, *The Involuntary Plaintiff*, 4 F.R.Serv. 907 (1941).

7.   In KROESE v. GENERAL STEEL CASTINGS CORP., 179 F.2d 760, 15 A.L.R.2d 1117 (3d Cir.), certiorari denied 339 U.S. 983, 70 S.Ct. 1026, 94 L. Ed. 1386 (1950), suit was brought by a shareholder for the declaration of a dividend. Plaintiff did not serve a majority of the members of the board of directors of the corporation. Defendants argued that joinder of a majority was indispensable to the suit since in order to make the court's decree effective, if it decided that a dividend should be declared, the directors would have to be forced to act and this could be done only by binding them to the decree as parties. The court rejected this argument, stating:

> But how can the chancellor's action be made effective? To doubt its effectiveness is to doubt the power of a court wielded by a chancellor with legal imagination. It is certainly true that he cannot do anything to directors who are not subject to his jurisdiction. But he can do a great deal to the property of the corporate group which is within his jurisdiction. The Pennsylvania courts know how to sequester assets of foreign corporations when the case is such that this form of relief is appropriate and the federal courts are equally potent in this respect. If the formal act by the board of directors is necessary under the Delaware General Corporation Law to regularize the dividends to which shareholders are entitled, we cannot think that a receivership or sequestration of a foreign corporation's property will not produce the result.

Equity courts have known for a long time how to impose onerous alternatives at home to the performance of affirmative acts abroad as a means of getting those affirmative acts accomplished. In other words, if there is a corporate defendant properly subject to suit within the state and the plaintiff makes out a legal right against the corporation and the corporation has property within the state * * *, the chancellor can accomplish the result the plaintiff is entitled to have accomplished.

Id. at 764–65. Does this holding have any application outside the immediate context of forcing the payment of dividends? Is it indeed any different from simply ordering the corporation to pay dividends, and ignoring the directors? Should a court be able to control the conduct of persons not subject to its personal jurisdiction by seizing control of property they own within its jurisdiction?

PROVIDENT TRADESMENS BANK & TRUST CO. v. LUMBERMENS MUT. CAS. CO.

United States Supreme Court, 1968.
390 U.S. 102, 88 S.Ct. 733, 19 L.Ed.2d 936.

Certiorari to the Circuit Court of Appeals for the Third Circuit.

Mr. Justice HARLAN delivered the opinion of the Court. This controversy, involving in its present posture the dismissal of a declaratory judgment action for nonjoinder of an "indispensable" party, began nearly 10 years ago with a traffic accident. An automobile owned by Edward Dutcher, who was not present when the accident occurred, was being driven by Donald Cionci, to whom Dutcher had given the keys. John Lynch and John Harris were passengers. The automobile crossed the median strip of the highway and collided with a truck being driven by Thomas Smith. Cionci, Lynch, and Smith were killed and Harris was severely injured.

Three tort actions were brought. Provident Tradesmens Bank, the administrator of the estate of passenger Lynch and petitioner here, sued the estate of the driver, Cionci, in a diversity action. Smith's administratrix, and Harris in person, each brought a state-court action against the estate of Cionci, Dutcher, the owner, and the estate of Lynch. These Smith and Harris actions, for unknown reasons, have never gone to trial and are still pending. The Lynch action against Cionci's estate was settled for $50,000, which the estate of Cionci, being penniless, has never paid.

Dutcher, the owner of the automobile and a defendant in the as yet untried tort actions, had an automobile liability insurance policy with Lumbermens Mutual Casualty Company, a respondent here. That policy had an upper limit of $100,000 for all claims arising out of a single accident. This fund was potentially subject to two different sorts of claims by the tort plaintiffs. First, Dutcher himself might be held vicariously liable as Cionci's "principal"; the likelihood of such a judgment against Dutcher is a matter of considerable doubt and dispute. Second, the policy by its terms covered the direct liability of any person driving Dutcher's car with Dutcher's "permission."

The insurance company had declined, after notice, to defend in the tort action brought by Lynch's estate against the estate of Cionci, believing that Cionci had not had permission and hence was not covered by the policy. The facts allegedly were that Dutcher had entrusted his car to Cionci, but that Cionci had made a detour from the errand for which Dutcher allowed his car to be taken. The estate of Lynch, armed with its $50,000 liquidated claim against the estate of Cionci, brought the present diversity action for a declaration that Cionci's use of the car had been "with permission" of Dutcher. The only named defendants were the company and the estate of Cionci. The other two tort plaintiffs were joined as plaintiffs. Dutcher, a resident of the State of Pennsylvania as were all the plaintiffs, was not joined either as plaintiff or defendant. The failure to join him was not adverted to at the trial level.

The major question of law contested at trial was a state-law question. * * * The District Court * * * directed verdicts in favor of the two estates. * * * The jury * * * found that Cionci had had permission, and hence awarded a verdict to Harris also.

Lumbermens appealed the judgment to the Court of Appeals for the Third Circuit, raising various state-law questions.[1] The Court of Appeals, * * * did not reach any of these issues. Instead, after reargument *en banc*, it decided, 5–2, to reverse on two alternative grounds neither of which had been raised in the District Court or by the appellant.

The first of these grounds was that Dutcher was an indispensable party. The court held that the "adverse interests" that had rendered Dutcher incompetent to testify under the Pennsylvania Dead Man Rule also required him to be made a party. The court did not consider whether the fact that a verdict had already been rendered, without objection to the nonjoinder of Dutcher, affected the matter. Nor did it follow the provision of Rule 19 of the Federal Rules of Civil Procedure that findings of "indispensability" must be based on stated pragmatic considerations. It held, to the contrary, that the right of a person who "may be affected" by the judgment to be joined is a "substantive" right, unaffected by the federal rules; that a trial court "may not proceed" in the absence of such a person; and that since Dutcher could not be joined as a defendant without destroying diversity jurisdiction the action had to be dismissed.

* * * Concluding that the inflexible approach adopted by the Court of Appeals in this case exemplifies the kind of reasoning that the Rule was designed to avoid, we reverse.

---

[1] Appellants challenged the District Court's ruling on the Dead Man issue that Dutcher was incompetent to testify under Pennsylvania law against an estate if he had an adverse interest to that of the estate, the fairness of submitting the question as to Harris to a jury that had been directed to find in favor of the two estates whose position was factually indistinguishable, and certain instructions.

I.

* * *

We may assume, at the outset, that Dutcher falls within the category of persons who, under * * * [Rule 19] (a), should be "joined if feasible." The action was for an adjudication of the validity of certain claims against a fund. Dutcher, faced with the possibility of judgments against him, had an interest in having the fund preserved to cover that potential liability. Hence there existed, when this case went to trial, at least the possibility that a judgment might impede Dutcher's ability to protect his interest, or lead to later relitigation by him.

The optimum solution, an adjudication of the permission question that would be binding on all interested persons, was not "feasible," however, for Dutcher could not be made a defendant without destroying diversity. Hence the problem was the one to which Rule 19(b) appears to address itself: in the absence of a person who "should be joined if feasible," should the court dismiss the action or proceed without him? Since this problem emerged for the first time in the Court of Appeals, there were also two subsidiary questions. First, what was the effect, if any, of the failure of the defendants to raise the matter in the District Court? Second, what was the importance, if any, of the fact that a judgment, binding on the parties although not binding on Dutcher, had already been reached after extensive litigation? The three questions prove, on examination, to be interwoven.

Conclusion

We conclude, upon consideration of the record and applying the "equity and good conscience" test of Rule 19(b), that the Court of Appeals erred in not allowing the judgment to stand.

Rule 19(b) suggests four "interests" that must be examined in each case to determine whether, in equity and good conscience, the court should proceed without a party whose absence from the litigation is compelled. Each of these interests must, in this case, be viewed entirely from an appellate perspective since the matter of joinder was not considered in the trial court. First, the plaintiff has an interest in having a forum. Before the trial, the strength of this interest obviously depends upon whether a satisfactory alternative forum exists. On appeal, if the plaintiff has won, he has a strong additional interest in preserving his judgment. Second, the defendant may properly wish to avoid multiple litigation, or inconsistent relief, or sole responsibility for a liability he shares with another. After trial, however, if the defendant has failed to assert this interest, it is quite proper to consider it foreclosed.

Third, there is the interest of the outsider whom it would have been desirable to join. Of course, since the outsider is not before the court, he cannot be bound by the judgment rendered. This means, however, only that a judgment is not *res judicata* as to, or legally enforceable against, a nonparty. It obviously does not mean either (a) that a court may never issue a judgment that, in practice, affects a nonparty or (b) that (to the contrary) a court may always proceed without considering the potential effect on nonparties simply because they are not "bound" in the technical sense. Instead, as Rule 19(a) expresses it, the court must consider the extent to which the judgment may "as a practical matter impair or impede his ability to protect" his interest in the subject matter. When a case has reached the appeal stage the matter is more complex. The judgment appealed from may not in fact affect the interest of any outsider even though there existed, before trial, a possibility that a judgment affecting his interest would be rendered. When necessary, however, a court of appeals should, on its own initiative, take steps to protect the absent party, who of course had no opportunity to plead and prove his interest below.

Fourth, there remains the interest of the courts and the public in complete, consistent, and efficient settlement of controversies. We read the Rule's third criterion, whether the judgment issued in the absence of the nonjoined person will be "adequate," to refer to this public stake in settling disputes by wholes, whenever possible, for clearly the plaintiff, who himself chose both the forum and the parties defendant, will not be heard to complain about the sufficiency of the relief obtainable against them. After trial, considerations of efficiency of course include the fact that the time and expense of a trial have already been spent.

Rule 19(b) also directs a district court to consider the possibility of shaping relief to accommodate these four interests. Commentators had argued that greater attention should be paid to this potential solution to a joinder stymie, and the Rule now makes it explicit that a court should consider modification of a judgment as an alternative to dismissal. Needless to say, a court of appeals may also properly require suitable modification as a condition of affirmance.

Had the Court of Appeals applied Rule 19's criteria to the facts of the present case, it could hardly have reached the conclusion it did. We begin with the plaintiffs' viewpoint. It is difficult to decide at this stage whether they would have had an "adequate" remedy had the action been dismissed before trial for nonjoinder: we cannot here determine whether the plaintiffs could have brought the same action, against the same parties plus Dutcher, in a state court. After trial, however, the "adequacy" of this hypothetical alternative, from the plaintiffs' point of view, was obviously greatly diminished. Their interest in preserving a fully litigated judgment should be overborne only by rather greater opposing considerations than would be required at an earlier stage when the plaintiffs' only concern was for a federal rather than a state forum.

Opposing considerations in this case are hard to find. The defendants had no stake, either asserted or real, in the joinder of Dutcher. They showed no interest in joinder until the Court of Appeals took the matter into its own hands. This properly forecloses any interest of theirs, but for purposes of clarity we note that the insurance company, whose liability was limited to

$100,000, had or will have full opportunity to litigate each claim on that fund against the claimant involved. Its only concern with the absence of Dutcher was and is to obtain a windfall escape from its defeat at trial.

The interest of the outsider, Dutcher, is more difficult to reckon. The Court of Appeals, concluding that it should not follow Rule 19's command to determine whether, as a practical matter, the judgment impaired the non-party's ability to protect his rights, simply quoted the District Court's reasoning on the Dead Man issue as proof that Dutcher had a "right" to be joined:

> "The subject matter of this suit is the coverage of Lumbermens' policy issued to Dutcher. Depending upon the outcome of this trial, Dutcher may have the policy all to himself or he may have to share its coverage with the Cionci Estate, thereby extending the availability of the proceeds of the policy to satisfy verdicts and judgments in favor of the two Estate plaintiffs. Sharing the coverage of a policy of insurance with finite limits with another, and thereby making that policy available to claimants against that other person is immediately worth less than having the coverage of such policy available to Dutcher alone. By the outcome in the instant case, to the extent that the two Estate plaintiffs will have the proceeds of the policy available to them in their claims against Cionci's estate, Dutcher will lose a measure of protection. Conversely, to the extent that the proceeds of this policy are not available to the two Estate plaintiffs Dutcher will gain. * * * It is sufficient for the purpose of determining adversity [of interest] that it appears clearly that the measure of Dutcher's protection under this policy of insurance is dependent upon the outcome of this suit. That being so, Dutcher's interest in these proceedings is adverse to the interest of the two Estate plaintiffs, the parties who represent, on this record, the interests of the deceased persons in the matter in controversy." [11]

There is a logical error in the Court of Appeals' appropriation of this reasoning for its own quite different purposes: Dutcher had an "adverse" interest (sufficient to invoke the Dead Man Rule) because he would have been *benefited* *in favor of* the insurance company; the question before the Court of Appeals, however, was whether Dutcher was *harmed* by the judgment *against* the insurance company.

The two questions are not the same. If the three plaintiffs had lost to the insurance company on the permission issue, that loss would have ended the matter favorably to Dutcher. If, as has happened, the three plaintiffs obtain a judgment against the insurance company on the permission issue, Dutcher may still claim that as a nonparty he is not estopped by that judg-

[11] 218 F.Supp. 802, 805–806, quoted at 365 F.2d, at 805.

ment from relitigating the issue. At that point it might be argued that Dutcher should be bound by the previous decision because, although technically a nonparty, he had purposely bypassed an adequate opportunity to intervene. We do not now decide whether such an argument would be correct under the circumstances of this case. If, however, Dutcher is properly foreclosed by his failure to intervene in the present litigation, then the joinder issue considered in the Court of Appeals vanishes, for any rights of Dutcher's have been lost by his own inaction.

If Dutcher is not foreclosed by his failure to intervene below, then he is not "bound" by the judgment in favor of the insurance company and, in theory, he has not been harmed. There remains, however, the practical question whether Dutcher is likely to have any need and if so will have any opportunity, to relitigate. The only possible threat to him is that if the fund is used to pay judgments against Cionci the money may in fact have disappeared before Dutcher has an opportunity to assert his interest. Upon examination, we find this supposed threat neither large nor unavoidable.

The state-court actions against Dutcher had lain dormant for years at the pleading stage by the time the Court of Appeals acted. Petitioner asserts here that under the applicable Pennsylvania vicarious liability law there is virtually no chance of recovery against Dutcher. We do not accept this assertion as fact, but the matter could have been explored below. Furthermore, even in the event of tort judgments against Dutcher, it is unlikely that he will be prejudiced by the outcome here. The potential claimants against Dutcher himself are identical with the potential claimants against Cionci's estate. Should the claimants seek to collect from Dutcher personally, he may be able to raise the permission issue defensively, making it irrelevant that the actual monies paid from the fund may have disappeared: Dutcher can assert that Cionci did not have his permission and that therefore the payments made on Cionci's behalf out of Dutcher's insurance policy should properly be credited against Dutcher's own liability. Of course, when Dutcher raises this defense he may lose, either on the merits of the permission issue or on the ground that the issue is foreclosed by Dutcher's failure to intervene in the present case, but Dutcher will not have been prejudiced by the failure of the District Court here to order him joined.

If the Court of Appeals was unconvinced that the threat to Dutcher was trivial, it could nevertheless have avoided all difficulties by proper phrasing of the decree. The District Court, for unspecified reasons, had refused to order immediate payment on the Cionci judgment. Payment could have been withheld pending the suits against Dutcher and relitigation (if that became necessary) by him. In this Court, furthermore, counsel for petitioners represented orally that they, the tort plaintiffs, would accept a limitation of all claims to the amount of the insurance policy. Obviously such a compromise could have been reached below had the Court of Appeals been willing to abandon its rigid approach and seek ways to preserve what was, as to the parties, subject to the appellants' other contentions, a perfectly valid judgment.

The suggestion of potential relitigation of the question of "permission" raises the fourth "interest" at stake in joinder cases—efficiency. It might have been preferable, at the trial level, if there were a forum available in which both the company and Dutcher could have been made defendants, to dismiss the action and force the plaintiffs to go elsewhere. Even this preference would have been highly problematical, however, for the actual threat of relitigation by Dutcher depended on there being judgments against him and on the amount of the fund, which was not revealed to the District Court. By the time the case reached the Court of Appeals, however, the problematical preference on efficiency grounds had entirely disappeared: there was no reason then to throw away a valid judgment just because it did not theoretically settle the whole controversy.

II.

Application of Rule 19(b)'s "equity and good conscience" test for determining whether to proceed or dismiss would doubtless have led to a contrary result below. The Court of Appeals' reasons for disregarding the Rule remain to be examined. The majority of the court concluded that the Rule was inapplicable because "substantive" rights are involved, and substantive rights are not affected by the Federal Rules. Although the court did not articulate exactly what the substantive rights are, or what law determines them, we take it to have been making the following argument: (1) there is a category of persons called "indispensable parties"; (2) that category is defined by substantive law and the definition cannot be modified by rule; (3) the right of a person falling within that category to participate in the lawsuit in question is also a substantive matter, and is absolute.

With this we may contrast the position that is reflected in Rule 19. Whether a person is "indispensable," that is, whether a particular lawsuit must be dismissed in the absence of that person, can only be determined in the context of particular litigation. There is a large category, whose limits are not presently in question, of persons who, in the Rule's terminology, should be "joined if feasible," and who, in the older terminology, were called either necessary or indispensable parties. Assuming the existence of a person who should be joined if feasible, the only further question arises when joinder is not possible and the court must decide whether to dismiss or to proceed without him. To use the familiar but confusing terminology, the decision to proceed is a decision that the absent person is merely "necessary" while the decision to dismiss is a decision that he is "indispensable." The decision whether to dismiss (i. e., the decision whether the person missing is "indispensable") must be based on factors varying with the different cases, some such factors being substantive, some procedural, some compelling by themselves, and some subject to balancing against opposing interests. Rule 19 does not prevent the assertion of compelling substantive interests; it merely commands the courts to examine each controversy to make certain that the interests really exist. To say that a court "must" dismiss in the absence of an indispensable party and that it "cannot proceed" without him puts the matter the wrong way around: a court does not know whether a particular person is "indispensable" until it has examined the situation to determine whether it can proceed without him.

The Court of Appeals concluded, although it was the first court to hold, that the 19th century joinder cases in this Court created a federal, common-law, substantive right in a certain class of persons to be joined in the corresponding lawsuits. At the least, that was not the way the matter started. The joinder problem first arose in equity and in the earliest case giving rise to extended discussion the problem was the relatively simple one of the inefficiency of litigation involving only some of the interested persons. [Elmendorf v. Taylor, 23 U.S. (10 Wheat.) 152, 6 L.Ed. 289 (1825).]
* * *

Following this case there arose three cases, also in equity, that the Court of Appeals here held to have declared a "substantive" right to be joined. It is true that these cases involved what would now be called "substantive" rights. This substantive involvement of the absent person with the controversy before the Court was, however, in each case simply an inescapable fact of the situation presented to the Court for adjudication. The Court in each case left the outsider with no more "rights" than it had already found belonged to him. The question in each case was simply whether, given the substantive involvement of the outsider, it was proper to proceed to adjudicate as between the parties.

* * *

The most influential of the cases in which this Court considered the question whether to proceed or dismiss in the absence of an interested but not joinable outsider is Shields v. Barrow, 17 How. 130, 15 L.Ed. 158, referred to in the opinion below. There the Court attempted, perhaps unfortunately, to stage general definitions of those persons without whom litigation could or could not proceed. In the former category were placed

> "Persons having an interest in the controversy, and who ought to be made parties, in order that the court may act on that rule which requires it to decide on, and finally determine the entire controversy, and do complete justice, by adjusting all the rights involved in it. These persons are commonly termed necessary parties; but if their interests are separable from those of the parties before the court, so that the court can proceed to a decree, and do complete and final justice, without affecting other persons not before the court, the latter are not indispensable parties."

The persons in the latter category were

> "Persons who not only have an interest in the controversy, but an interest of such a nature that a final decree cannot be made without

either affecting that interest, or leaving the controversy in such a condition that its final termination may be wholly inconsistent with equity and good conscience."

These generalizations are still valid today, and they are consistent with the requirements of Rule 19, but they are not a substitute for the analysis required by that Rule. Indeed, the second *Shields* definition states, in rather different fashion, the criteria for decision announced in Rule 19(b). One basis for dismissal is prejudice to the rights of an absent party that *"cannot"* be avoided in issuance of a final decree. Alternatively, if the decree can be so written that it protects the interests of the absent persons, but as so written it leaves the controversy so situated that the outcome may be inconsistent with "equity and good conscience," the suit should be dismissed.

The majority of the Court of Appeals read Shields v. Barrow to say that a person whose interests "may be affected" by the decree of the court is an indispensable party, and that all indispensable parties have a "substantive right" to have suits dismissed in their absence. We are unable to read *Shields* as saying either. It dealt only with persons whose interests must, unavoidably, be affected by a decree and it said nothing about substantive rights. Rule 19(b), which the Court of Appeals dismissed as an ineffective attempt to change the substantive rights stated in *Shields,* is, on the contrary, a valid statement of the criteria for determining whether to proceed or dismiss in the forced absence of an interested person. It takes, for aught that now appears, adequate account of the very real, very substantive claims to fairness on the part of outsiders that may arise in some cases. This, however, simply is not such a case.

* * *

Judgment vacated and case remanded to Court of Appeals.

NOTES AND QUESTIONS

1. *Provident Tradesmens* interprets the amended version of Federal Rule 19, which was promulgated in 1966. Examine the Advisory Committee's Note to Rule 19, which is set out in the Supplement. What impact does the amendment have on the distinction between necessary and indispensable parties? What is the purpose of Rule 12(b) (7) given the amendment? For a negative appraisal of the amended text, see Fink, *Indispensable Parties and the Proposed Amendment to Federal Rule 19,* 74 Yale L.J. 403 (1965). See also Note, *Multiparty Litigation: Proposed Changes in the Federal Rules,* 50 Iowa L.Rev. 1135 (1965); Comment, *Attacking the Party Problem,* 38 So.Cal.L.Rev. 80 (1965).

2. What was the basis of the Court's finding in *Provident Tradesmens* with regard to prejudice for purposes of Rule 19(b) if Dutcher was not joined? Consider the following comments in an article written shortly after the Third Circuit decision dismissing the action and before the Supreme Court's decision.

* * * How has Dutcher been affected? The judgment declaring that Cionci was driving with permission does not bind Dutcher legally, since he was not a party. Dutcher is free to contest the point with all, including the insurer. Be it noted that although he testified in the action, Dutcher made no attempt to intervene; as the minority suggests, he might have reasonably preferred to stay out of the action. Whereas a judgment declaring Cionci to be an insured did not bind Dutcher, a judgment the other way would very likely have inured to Dutcher's benefit * * *.

Kaplan, *Continuing Work of the Civil Committee: 1966 Amendments of the Federal Rules of Civil Procedure (I)*, 81 Harv.L.Rev. 356, 373 (1967).

In what ways might the court shape relief in order to lessen any prejudice? Is the court free simply to grant a remedy other than the one originally requested— for example, by awarding money damages when specific performance might have a detrimental impact on the absentee? Of what importance is the availability of another forum in determining whether the action must be dismissed in the absence of someone whose joinder is not feasible?

3. What weight should be given to the various factors listed in Rule 19? Because there is no precise formula for determining whether a particular nonparty must be joined under Rule 19(a), the decision has to be made in light of the general policies of the rule. Can you articulate what those policies are? For example, what is the difference between the Rule 19(a) (1) standard that in the absence of the nonparty "complete relief cannot be accorded among those already parties," and the third factor listed in Rule 19(b), "whether a judgment rendered in the person's absence will be adequate"? The second test set out in Rule 19(a) focuses on the prejudicial effect of not joining the absentee. What type of prejudice must be shown to meet this requirement?

4. In HAAS v. JEFFERSON NATIONAL BANK OF MIAMI BEACH, 442 F.2d 394 (5th Cir.1971), plaintiff, a citizen of Ohio, sought an injunction directing defendant, a Florida bank, to issue certain shares of its common stock to him. Haas alleged an agreement with Glueck, also an Ohio citizen, under which they jointly purchased shares of the bank's stock; the certificates were issued in Glueck's name. Haas contended that Glueck had been requested to direct the bank to issue certificates reflecting plaintiff's ownership of some of the shares and that Glueck had done so. The bank responded by claiming that it refused to make the assignment because Glueck was indebted to the bank under a note that required him to "pledge, assign and transfer" to the bank any property owned by Glueck that came into the bank's possession. The district court ordered Glueck's joinder and then dismissed on the ground of incomplete diversity of citizenship. The Fifth Circuit affirmed in a comprehensive opinion by Judge Aldisert of the Third Circuit, who was sitting by designation. In agreeing with the lower court's determination that Glueck should be joined under Rule 19(a) the court said:

> [H]is presence is critical to the disposition of the important issues in the litigation. His evidence will either support the complaint or bolster the defense: it will affirm or refute Haas' claim to half ownership of the stock; it will substantiate or undercut Haas' contention that the Bank had knowledge of his alleged ownership interest; it will corroborate or compromise the Bank's contention that Glueck rescinded the transfer order; and it will be crucial to the determination of Glueck's obligation to the Bank under the promissory note. The essence of

Haas' action against the Bank is that it "unlawfully and recklessly seized, detained, [and] exercised improper dominion" over his shares in transferring and delivering them to the second bank as collateral for Glueck's loan. Thus, Glueck becomes more than a key witness whose testimony would be of inestimable value. Instead he emerges as an active participant in the alleged conversion of Haas' stock.

Applying the criterion of Rule 19(a) (2) (ii), we believe that Glueck's absence would expose the defendant Bank "to a substantial risk of incurring double, multiple, or otherwise inconsistent obligations by reason of his claimed interest." If Haas prevailed in this litigation in the absence of Glueck and were adjudicated owner of half of the stock, Glueck, not being bound by *res adjudicata,* could theoretically succeed in later litigation against the Bank in asserting ownership of the whole. In addition, a favorable resolution of Haas' claim against the Bank could, under (a) (2) (i), "as a practical matter impair or impede [the absent party's] ability to protect [his] interest" in all of the shares—an interest that is at least apparent since all of the stock was issued in Glueck's name.

Id. at 398.

Note that the court's main argument appears to be that Glueck's evidence is essential to establishing the claim against the bank. If that is the case, what justifies the court considering Glueck as a party rather than an important witness? How realistic is the court's concern that if not joined Glueck might later bring an action to establish sole ownership of the stock after the first suit has determined that Haas was entitled to half ownership? Wouldn't the judgment in *Haas* have some effect in a second action? Isn't it inconsistent for the court to hold that the Bank may be subject to multiple liability because Glueck could bring a separate suit and, at the same time, to conclude that Glueck's ability to protect his interest is impeded by the present suit? Aren't the tests for Rules 19(a) (2) (ii) and 19(a) (2) (i) contradictory and thus mutually exclusive?

5. Does the Court's decision in the *Provident Tradesmens* case automatically mean that a federal court need not apply state standards of indispensability in a diversity suit? In this connection reconsider the effect of *Hanna v. Plumer,* p. 284, supra. See also Note, *Federal Rules of Civil Procedure—Rule 19 and Indispensable Parties,* 65 Mich.L.Rev. 968 (1967). If state substantive law indicates that plaintiff does not have a particular right of action unless certain persons are joined, shouldn't a federal court sitting in diversity dismiss the action "in equity and good conscience" if those persons cannot be brought into the suit?

3.   PERMISSIVE JOINDER OF PARTIES

Read Federal Rules of Civil Procedure 20, 21, and 42(a) in the Supplement.

RYDER v. JEFFERSON HOTEL CO.

Supreme Court of South Carolina, 1922.
121 S.C. 72, 113 S.E. 474, 25 A.L.R. 739.

MARION, J.   The complaint in this action   * * *   alleges in substance that the plaintiff Charles A. Ryder and the plaintiff Edith C. Ryder are husband and wife; that [they] * * * became guests of the defendant Jefferson Hotel Company * * *;   that thereafter, during the night * * *, the defendant S. J. Bickley, acting as the servant and agent of the defendant Jefferson Hotel Company, roused the plaintiffs by rapping upon their room door, and in a rude and angry manner insulted the plaintiff Edith C. Ryder; that as a result of the insults * * * the plaintiffs were compelled to give up the accommodations due them and leave the said hotel, and were forced at midnight and at great inconvenience and uncertainty to seek another lodging place; that by reason of such high-handed, malicious, and willful conduct, on the part of the said hotel and its servant and agent, the plaintiffs were greatly injured in their reputations, credit, and business, and that the plaintiff Charles A. Ryder has suffered great loss of custom and has been deprived of great gains and profits * * *; and that * * * the plaintiffs have been damaged in the sum of $10,000.

Defendants separately demurred to the complaint upon the ground that it appeared upon the face thereof that several causes of action had been improperly united therein, for the reason that the several causes of action united do not affect all the parties to the action.   From an order overruling the demurrer, defendants appeal.

The sole question for determination is: Does the complaint contain two causes of action which may be joined in the same complaint?   It is apparent, as appellants suggest, that the complaint alleges a cause of action by Charles A. Ryder against the defendants for a personal tort—that is, for a breach of duty growing out of the relationship existing between the parties, to wit, innkeeper and guest—and also a cause of action by Edith C. Ryder against the defendants for a tortious breach of duty growing out of the same relationship.   It is also apparent that both of these alleged causes of action arose out of the same transaction, in the sense that the injury to each of the plaintiffs was caused by the same delict.   But appellants contend that it is equally apparent from the allegations of the complaint that the rights invaded and the injuries sustained are necessarily several, and that plaintiffs cannot maintain a joint action and recover joint damages therefor.   We think that contention must be sustained.

Section 218 of the Code of Procedure (1912), classifying the various causes of action which may be united in the same complaint, contains this proviso:

> "But the causes of action, so united, must all belong to one of these classes, and, except in actions for the foreclosure of mortgages, must affect all the parties to the action, and not require different places of trial, and must be separately stated."

The rule applicable is thus stated by Judge Pomeroy in his work on Code Remedies (4th Ed.) p. 215:

> "When a tort of a personal nature * * * is committed upon two or more, the right of action must, except in a very few special cases, be several. In order that a joint action may be possible, there must be some prior bond of legal union between the persons injured—such as partnership relation—of such a nature that the tort interferes with it, *and by virtue of that very interference* produces a wrong and consequent damage common to all. It is not every prior existing legal relation between the parties that will impress a joint character upon the injury and damage. Thus, if a husband and wife be libeled, or slandered, or beaten, although there is a close legal relation between the parties, it is not one which can be affected by such a wrong, and no joint cause of action will arise. * * * "

That the rights infringed and the injuries suffered by the two plaintiffs in the case at bar are several, and not joint, would not seem open to question. To illustrate: If the two plaintiffs, husband and wife, occupying the same berth in a sleeping car, had both been physically injured in a wreck of the train, it would scarcely be contended that they could properly bring a joint action for the damages sustained by each on account of the carrier's delict. The complaint here does not state a cause of action for injuries to the wife alone * * *. Neither is the husband's alleged cause of action based upon loss of consortium and expenses incurred on behalf of the wife. The wife's cause of action as alleged does not "affect" the husband, and the husband's cause of action does not "affect" the wife, in the sense that the Code of Procedure (section 218) requires that the causes of action joined in the same complaint "must affect all parties to the action." Neither has a legal interest in the pecuniary recovery of the other, and in contemplation of law there can be no joint and common damage to both resulting from a wrong which gives rise to separate and distinct rights personal to each. * * *

At common law it seems that even the husband's cause of action for the loss of the wife's services and companionship and expenses incurred by him on account of injury to the wife could not be joined with the cause of action for injuries personal to the wife. * * * In the case at bar not only are the parties plaintiff different, and the potential elements of damage recoverable by the parties different, but neither party has the right to sue for the benefit of the other * * *. We are therefore clearly of the opinion that there is no such joint right to enforce a common recovery as entitles the plaintiffs in the case at bar to join their several causes of action in the same complaint. * * *

The order of the circuit court is reversed.

GARY, C. J., and COTHRAN, J., concur.

FRASER, J. (dissenting). * * * The plaintiffs * * * were expelled from the hotel, under the allegation that they were not husband and wife. It was a denial of the joint relationship that caused the trouble.

It seems to me that the illustrations used are not appropriate to the case. When a husband and wife are injured in one railroad accident, the injuries are individual, and not joint. It seems to me that the case is somewhat like an injury to a copartnership. I do not think that it will be doubted that the copartnership can bring an action for injury to the copartnership, although the injury to the two copartners may not be the same. * * * In the joint action the other copartner may not be able to recover for the injury peculiar to himself; but the injury to the copartnership is a joint injury, and for this injury it may recover. Here the offense was against the husband and wife and affected their relation as husband and wife. This is manifestly a joint injury. * * *

For these reasons I dissent.

NOTES AND QUESTIONS

1. Doesn't *Ryder* emasculate the concept of permissive joinder by allowing joinder only when the parties are "united in interest" and presumably would be *compelled* to join? In this connection consider the court's reliance on Pomeroy's statement that "although there is a close legal relation between the parties, it is not one which can be *affected* by such a wrong and no joint cause of action will arise." (Emphasis added.) If the injury *affected* a relationship, wouldn't the parties to that relationship be classified as necessary or indispensable parties and be required to join? Is the joint-interest standard consistent with the objectives of permissive joinder?

The *Ryder* approach has been rejected in a substantial number of jurisdictions. See, e. g., Peters v. Bigelow, 137 Cal.App. 135, 30 P.2d 450 (3d Dist. 1934).

2. How would *Ryder* have been decided by a federal court? What are the factors that should be weighed under Rule 20 in deciding a permissive joinder question? Consider the following cases. In REKEWEG v. FEDERAL MUT. INS. CO., 27 F.R.D. 431 (N.D.Ind.1961), judgment affirmed 324 F.2d 150 (7th Cir.1963), certiorari denied 376 U.S. 943, 84 S.Ct. 798, 11 L.Ed.2d 767 (1964), the court permitted an injured plaintiff to join a claim against an insurance company and its agent for fraudulently inducing plaintiff's attorney to delay the filing of a personal injury claim until after the statute of limitations had run with a claim against plaintiff's attorney for negligent delay in bringing a timely action. But in SUN–X GLASS TINTING OF MID–WISCONSIN, INC. v. SUN–X INT'L, INC., 227 F.Supp. 365 (W.D.Wis.1964), an action for fraud in which eight distributors sought to join as plaintiffs against the company for which they agreed to act as distributors, the court found that there was no

single transaction or occurrence since the solicitation, negotiation, and execution of each distributor's contract was unrelated to any of the other contracts. Can these two cases be reconciled?

3.   In STATE ex rel. CAMPBELL v. JAMES, 263 S.W.2d 402 (Mo.1953), plaintiffs sought to join as defendants (1) persons who detonated dynamite and destroyed the plaintiff's property and (2) insurance companies who issued policies covering the property.   The court denied joinder under the Missouri permissive-joinder provision, which is identical to Federal Rule 20.

> * * *   In the suits here involved there is no connection or inter-dependence between the insurance contracts issued by the insurance com-panies and the cause of action in tort alleged against relators.   It is true that the cause of action plaintiffs have against each of the insurance com-panies and the causes of action they have against relators spring from the same event, to wit: the explosion, and, by coincidence, present common questions of law and fact, yet each cause of action arises out of a separate legal right, neither of which is dependent upon the other for its existence.

Id. at 408.   Are there any policy justifications for the result in *Campbell*?

In AKELY v. KINNICUTT, 238 N.Y. 466, 144 N.E. 682 (1924), one hun-dred ninety-three plaintiffs joined in an action alleging that they were induced to purchase shares of stock in a corporation by defendant's prospectus.   The question of fraud was common to all but separate questions relating to individual plaintiffs also were certain to arise—e. g., whether each plaintiff justifiably relied on the prospectus.   Defendant objected to joinder on the grounds that (1) the presence of separate questions outweighed the advantages of joinder and (2) the claims did not arise out of the same transaction.   The court upheld joinder because the fraud issue was fundamental and would involve more dispute and elicit more evidence than any other issue.   The court also held that there was but one transaction, stating:

> * * *   The transaction in respect of or out of which the cause of action arises is the purchase by plaintiff of his stock * * * and such purchases conducted by one plaintiff after another respectively plainly constitute a series of transactions within the meaning of the statute.   The purchase by plaintiff of his stock is not robbed of its character as a "trans-action" because * * * the transaction was not a dual one occurring between the plaintiff and the defendants, and the many purchases by plaintiffs respectively do not lose their character as a series of transactions because they occurred at different places and times extending through many months.

Id. at 474, 144 N.E. at 684.   Compare Goodman v. H. Hentz & Co., 265 F.Supp. 440 (N.D.Ill.1967).   Could plaintiffs in *Akely* have brought a class action un-der Federal Rule 23?   See pp. 571–81, *infra*.   What possible advantage would there be in bringing a class action under Rule 23, rather than joining the addi-tional parties under Rule 20(a)?

In LUCAS v. CITY OF JUNEAU, 15 Alaska 413, 127 F.Supp. 730 (1955), and STATE v. WEINSTEIN, 398 S.W.2d 41 (St. Louis Ct.App.1965), plaintiff's injuries were sustained through the negligence of A and were aggravated by the subsequent negligence of B, an ambulance driver, while taking plaintiff to the hos-pital.   In *Lucas*, the ambulance accident occurred eighteen days after the original injury to plaintiff.   In both cases, the court concluded that the ambulance trips were necessitated by the original accidents and permitted joinder.

In WATTS v. SMITH, 375 Mich. 120, 134 N.W.2d 194 (1965), plaintiff was a passenger in a car that was struck from the rear twice in one day—once when plaintiff and his driver were en route to work in the morning and again when they were returning home in the afternoon. Plaintiff attempted to join the drivers of the other cars in one action. Michigan General Court Rule 206.1 allows persons to be joined in one action as defendants (1) if there is asserted against them jointly, severally, or in the alternative, any right to relief in respect of or arising out of the same transaction, occurrence or series of transactions or occurrences, and if any question of law or fact common to all of them will arise in the action; or (2) if it appears that their presence in the action will promote the convenient administration of justice. Relying on the second provision, the Michigan court allowed joinder because separation of the causes would permit each defendant to argue that it was uncertain what injuries plaintiff sustained from each accident. Do you perceive any problems in permitting joinder in this case? See Note, *The Challenge of the Mass Trial*, 68 Harv.L.Rev. 1046 (1955).

4. Many of the tactical factors that must be considered before attempting to join multiple defendants are discussed in Friedenthal, *Whom to Sue—Multiple Defendants*, in 5 *Am.Jur. Trials* 1–25 (1966).

TANBRO FABRICS CORP. v. BEAUNIT MILLS, INC.

Supreme Court of New York, Appellate Division, First Department, 1957.
4 App.Div.2d 519, 167 N.Y.S.2d 387.

BREITEL, Justice. * * *

The underlying business dispute spawned three lawsuits. In the first action * * *, the seller, Beaunit, sought to recover the purchase price of goods sold and delivered to Tanbro. The Buyer, Tanbro, counterclaimed for breach of warranty for improper manufacture, as a result of which the goods were subject to "yarn slippage." The seller replied to the counterclaim by denying that the slippage was due to improper manufacture. A portion of the goods still being in the hands of the processor, Tanbro initiated another action * * *, in replevin, to recover these goods. The processor, Amity, counterclaimed for its charges and asserted its claim to the goods under an artisan's lien. In the exchanges that preceded and attended the bringing of these lawsuits, the buyer Tanbro received Beaunit's assertion that the yarn slippage was caused by the processor's improper handling, while with equal force the processor charged the same defect to Beaunit as a consequence of its improper manufacture.

At this juncture, Tanbro, the buyer, brought the third lawsuit * * * against Beaunit and Amity, charging the goods were defective because of yarn slippage and that such slippage was caused by either the seller, Beaunit, or alternatively the processor, Amity, or both. This is the main action before the court.

At Special Term, the buyer Tanbro moved to consolidate the three actions. Beaunit and Amity separately cross-moved to dismiss the complaint in the buyer's main action on the ground that there were prior actions pending between the parties with respect to the same cause of action. The motion to consolidate was denied and Beaunit's cross-motion to dismiss the complaint as against it was granted.

* * *

Both the seller and the processor resist consolidation. They do so on the ground that each had a separate and different relationship to the buyer, and that each was involved in a separate and independent contract. Therefore, they say, there is not involved the "same transaction or occurrence," nor any common question of law or fact to sustain either a joinder of parties or a consolidation of the actions. They stress that the buyer Tanbro wishes to pit against each other the seller and the processor on the issue of responsibility for the alleged defect, while the buyer sits back free from the obligation to prove a full case, as it would otherwise have to do in separate actions against the seller and the processor. The buyer, on the other hand, argues that what is identical to the cases are the goods and the defect, with the common question of who is responsible for the defect. The buyer concedes that it would have to prove the defect, and also prove that the defect must have been caused by either the seller or the processor or both of them; that, therefore, this involves a single transaction or occurrence and involves a common question of fact.

The controlling statute is Section 212 of the Civil Practice Act. * * * The portion pertinent to the joinder of defendants reads as follows:

"2.   All persons may be joined in one action as defendants if there is asserted against them jointly, severally, or in the alternative, any right to relief in respect of or arising out of the same transaction, occurrence, or series of transactions or occurrences and if any question of law or fact common to all of them would arise in the action.   *   *   * "

A reading of the section by itself would suggest little or no difficulty in permitting a joinder of parties in the buyer's main action or a consolidation of the three actions. However, the section has a history, which has created some confusion as to the meaning and application of the section.

The seller and the processor rely heavily on Ader v. Blau, 241 N.Y. 7, 148 N.E. 771, 41 A.L.R. 1216. The case arose under the predecessor statute permitting joinder * * *. In that case the plaintiff sought to join in one death action the person charged with having caused the accident resulting in the injuries ending in death and a treating physician who, it was charged, by his incompetence, was the cause of the decedent's death. The Court of Appeals * * * [held] that Section 258 of the Civil Practice Act, since repealed, albeit a restriction on joinder of causes of action in pleading, was a limiting factor in permitting joinder of parties. Applying the statute, it held the joinder impermissible.

In reaction to this decision   *   *   *   Section 258 was repealed in favor of a broad pleading section   *   *   *. In making the recommendation, the Judicial Council referred to the Ader case, supra, and the fact that the court had regarded the area of joinder of parties limited by the pleading restrictions of Section 258. It added, "Complete freedom should be allowed in the joinder of causes of action as in the joinder of parties, and it is submitted that the correct approach to the joinder both of parties and of causes of action is the English one: May the matters conveniently be tried together? The problem is to combine as many matters as possible to avoid multiplicity and at the same time not unduly complicate the litigation for the jury."

The full effect of the repealer of old Section 258 has, however, not been left to speculation. The Court of Appeals, in Great Northern Telegraph Company v. Yokohama Specie Bank, 297 N.Y. 135, 76 N.E.2d 117, discussed the question frontally. It held that the Ader case, supra, was a result of the pleading limitation contained in the old, and now repealed, Section 258. * * * And in the Great Northern case, itself, joinder was allowed plaintiff against the Superintendent of Banks for payments due plaintiff, on which claim the Superintendent was asserting as a bar a time limitation provided by statute, and a correspondent Bank, which plaintiff asserted owed a duty to plaintiff to file the claim promptly with the Superintendent of Banks, in the event that it should be held that the claim was barred by lapse of time.

Notably, in the Great Northern Telegraph case, and in the English cases relied upon therein, there were joined, as defendants, parties that owed to plaintiff obligations under independent and separate contracts and in independent and separate relationships. In none of the cases was the "same transaction or occurrence" construed to require an identity of duty and relationship. * * *

This then is the background for the present section 212 of the Civil Practice Act. It should be beyond argument, by now, that it is no longer a bar to joinder, and, by parallel reasoning, *a fortiori,* to consolidation, that there is not an identity of duty or contract upon which to assert alternative liability. It is still necessary, of course, that there be a finding that the alternative liability arises out of a common transaction or occurrence involving common questions of fact and law. But this is not a rigid test. It is to be applied with judgment and discretion, in the balancing of convenience and justice between the parties involved * * *. Indeed, the buyer's situation prompted Special Term to comment that the buyer, Tanbro, "is in the unenviable position of not knowing possibly which of its contracting parties is responsible and in separate actions may find itself confronted with defeat in each event though the product as finally delivered may be defective."

     * * *

The right of joinder and the privilege to obtain consolidation is always counterbalanced, of course, by the power of the court to grant a severance, or to deny a consolidation, if prejudice or injustice appear. In this case, the danger of separate trials, leading, perhaps, to an unjust and illogical result, is a possibility well worth avoiding. The buyer is entitled to a less hazardous adjudication of his dispute, so long as he is able to make out a prima facie case of alternative liability.

Accordingly, the order of Special Term insofar as it granted the cross motion to dismiss the complaint in the first described action as against the defendant Beaunit and denied the buyer Tanbro's motion to consolidate the three actions should be modified to deny the cross motion and to grant the motion to consolidate, and otherwise should be affirmed   * * *.

All concur.

NOTES AND QUESTIONS

1. Where one of two persons are [sic] liable but the plaintiff is not certain he can make out a case against either, the opportunity to join them as defendants is of great tactical importance. The court should not dismiss after the close of plaintiff's case merely because the plaintiff has not shown which of the two defendants is responsible if he has shown that one of them must have been. It is not unfair to require each of the defendants to assume the risk of a failure to show that he was not responsible. Some attorneys sometimes fail to recognize that evidence supplied by one co-defendant may be used against another to support the plaintiff's case. * * * Even if the court might feel that a prima facie case has not been made out against one of the co-defendants, it should at least reserve decision on the motion to dismiss until after the defendants rest.

2 Weinstein, Korn & Miller, *New York Civil Practice* ¶ 1002.08. See also 7 Wright & Miller, *Federal Practice and Procedure: Civil* § 1654 (1972).

In *Tanbro*, the buyer's motion was for consolidation. The court's opinion might convey the impression that the court assumed the New York standard for consolidation was identical to that for joinder. In fact, however, the New York consolidation provision is much broader than the New York joinder provision. The text of both have been set out in the Supplement—the former under Federal Rule 42(a) and the latter under Federal Rule 20. In comparing the Federal Rules with the New York provisions note that the Federal Rules also differentiate between joinder and consolidation. Can a discrepancy between the availability of joinder and consolidation be justified?

2. If the joinder of a party destroys the court's diversity-of-citizenship jurisdiction, must the court dismiss the action or may it drop the nondiverse party and proceed? See Horn v. Lockhart, 84 U.S. (17 Wall.) 570, 21 L.Ed. 657 (1873). Should it make any difference if joinder is sought by a plaintiff or a defendant? According to Federal Rule 19(a), certain enumerated persons are to be joined only when their presence will not destroy subject-matter jurisdiction. Does this mean that other persons who would merely be "proper" parties cannot be joined when it would result in a loss of jurisdiction? See Note, *Federal Rule 21—Federal Jurisdiction Preserved and Perfected*, 44 Iowa L.Rev. 193 (1958). Prior to the 1966 amendment of Rule 19(a), many courts allowed a party who was not indispensable to be added to an action removed from a state court, and, if the party was nondiverse, remanded the case to the state court. See Clark v. Safeway Stores, Inc., 117 F.Supp. 583 (W.D.Mo.1953); Cummings v. Riley Stoker Corp., 6 F.R.D. 5 (W. D.Mo.1946).

A further obstacle to joinder in diversity actions is the jurisdictional-amount requirement. Can plaintiffs aggregate their claims when they unite to assert an undivided interest in property against a defendant? See Phillips Petroleum Co.

v. Taylor, 115 F.2d 726 (5th Cir.1940), certiorari denied 313 U.S. 565, 61 S.Ct. 941, 85 L.Ed. 1524 (1941). Should the result be different when their claims are separate and distinct? See Snyder v. Harris, 394 U.S. 332, 89 S.Ct. 1053, 22 L.Ed.2d 319 (1969), which can be found at p. 587, infra. Can a plaintiff aggregate claims when they are asserted against more than one defendant? Should the answer depend upon the nature of the claims asserted? See Calvert Distillers Corp. v. Rosen, 115 F.Supp. 147 (N.D.Ill.1953). Some text writers have advocated that federal courts should accept jurisdiction over all claims arising out of one transaction when the plaintiff asserts at least one claim exceeding the jurisdictional amount. See 7 Wright & Miller, *Federal Practice and Procedure: Civil* § 1659 (1972), and Note, *The Federal Jurisdictional Amount Requirement and Joinder of Parties Under the Federal Rules of Civil Procedure*, 27 Ind.L.J. 199 (1952). Is this a proper context for the use of ancillary jurisdiction? *Compare* Manufacturers Cas. Ins. Co. v. Coker, 219 F.2d 631 (4th Cir.1955), *with* Eagle Star Ins. Co. v. Maltes, 313 F.2d 778 (5th Cir.1963).

3. For a history of American joinder rules, see Blume, *Free Joinder of Parties, Claims, and Counterclaims*, 2 F.R.D. 250 (1943), and Legislation, *Recent Trends in Joinder of Parties, Causes, and Counterclaims*, 37 Colum.L.Rev. 462 (1937). For a comparative view, see Millar, *The Joinder of Actions in Continental Civil Procedure*, 28 Ill.L.Rev. 26, 177 (1933).

SECTION D. IMPLEADER

Read Federal Rule of Civil Procedure 14 and the material accompanying it in the Supplement.

JEUB v. B/G FOODS, INC.

United States District Court, District of Minnesota, 1942.
2 F.R.D. 238.

NORDBYE, District Judge. The facts are briefly these: The complainants seek to recover damages from the defendant, B/G Foods, Inc., on the grounds that, in one of the restaurants operated by this defendant, they were served with certain ham which was contaminated, unwholesome, and deleterious to the health, causing complainants to become sick and distressed to their damage. * * * Prior to the service of the answer, on application of the defendant, an ex parte order was obtained, making Swift and Company a third-party defendant. The third-party complaint set forth that the ham served was canned "Swift Premium Ham", a product of Swift and Company, and purchased in a sealed can by B/G Foods the day preceding the serving of the ham to the complainants. It is asserted that B/G Foods was entirely free from any blame or negligence in connection therewith. It is further alleged in the third-party complaint that "if any of said ham was unwholesome, poisonous, deleterious or otherwise in any way unfit for human consumption, such condition was caused solely and entirely by negligence and carelessness and unlawful conduct on the part of Swift and Company." Further, that "Swift and Company is liable to indemnify and reimburse B/G Foods, Inc., for the whole amount of any recovery made by plaintiff, * * * against B/G Foods, Inc., on account of said ham being served to her in its food shop. * * *" Judgment is prayed that any recovery be against Swift and Company and not B/G Foods, Inc., and that B/G Foods, Inc., have judgment against Swift and Company for any and all sums which may be adjudged against B/G Foods, Inc., in favor of the plaintiff.

The motion to vacate the order is based on the showing that plaintiffs have not amended, and have refused to amend, their complaints to state any cause of action against Swift and Company. It is therefore the position of the third-party defendant that no relief can be granted against it in this proceeding; that [Federal] Rule 14 * * * is merely procedural and does not create any substantive rights; that no right of contribution or indemnity exists under the Minnesota law merely because a suit has been commenced; and that the party must have suffered some loss or paid more than his share of the loss before any rights will inure. It is pointed out that, as yet, the B/G Foods has suffered no loss and has made no payment growing out of the incident in question.

That the rights over and against Swift and Company, which B/G Foods may have by reason of any loss sustained by it, must be governed by the substantive laws of this State is entirely clear. The invoking of the third-party procedural practice must not do violence to the substantive rights of the parties. However, an acceleration or an expedition of the presentation of such rights does not conflict with any Minnesota law. [Federal] Rule 14 * * * permits the impleader of a party "who is or may be liable." The fact that an independent action for money recovery could not be brought at this time does not militate against B/G Foods' right to invoke a procedure which will determine rights of the parties concurrently with that of the basic proceeding, and if and when any loss has been sustained as to which Swift and Company is liable over, the laws of this State in regard thereto may be made effective. * * * Rule 14 is not restricted to the rights of indemnity or contribution which are presently enforcible * * *.

The apparent purpose of Rule 14 is to provide suitable machinery whereby the rights of all parties may be determined in one proceeding. Manifestly if Swift and Company is liable over to B/G Foods, Inc., for any or all damages sustained by reason of the tortious act alleged, no cogent reason is suggested why the original defendant should not avail itself of this rule. Otherwise, B/G Foods, Inc., would be required to await the outcome of the present suit, and then if plaintiffs recover, to institute an independent action for contribution or indemnity. The rule under consideration was promulgated to avoid this very circuity of proceeding. Neither is any good reason suggested why the determination of the entire controversy in one proceeding will prejudice the rights of any of the parties. Certainly, plaintiffs cannot complain. They have not availed themselves of the opportunity to join Swift and Company as a party defendant. To require the same jury to determine the controversy between the third-party plaintiff and third-party defendant will not harm or jeopardize their rights or position before these triers of fact. The rights of Swift and Company are likewise not prejudiced by being made a third-party defendant. If it is liable over, it is concerned with the payment by B/G Foods, Inc., of any loss or damage obtained by these plaintiffs. However, the recognition or preservation of that right presents no particular difficulty. Any judgment against it by way of contribution or indemnity may be stayed until the judgment in the original proceeding against the B/G Foods, Inc., is paid or satisfied. One jury impaneled to determine the entire controversy may not only save time and expense, but it is fair to assume that the ends of justice will be served by disposition of the entire matter through the facilities of one jury.   *   *   *

The motion, therefore, to vacate the order making Swift and Company a third-party defendant in each of the above-entitled cases, is denied. Swift and Company is hereby allowed twenty days after the filing of this order within which to file its answers herein.   *   *   *

NOTES AND QUESTIONS

1. In a diversity case in a state that adheres to the common-law rule prohibiting contribution among joint tortfeasors, must a federal court deny impleader of a joint tortfeasor? Note that in *Jeub* the applicable state law recognized a substantive right of action but merely failed to provide a procedural device for the acceleration or concurrent determination of the liability as part of the principal lawsuit. How might the court shape the relief on an accelerated or contingent claim to reflect the limitations of substantive state law?

2. What factors should the court consider in determining whether to allow a third-party defendant to be impleaded? May a defendant-insured in a negligence action implead the liability insurer under Rule 14 when the insurance policy contains either a "no action" clause or a provision to the effect that "nothing contained in this policy shall give any person or organization any right to join the company as a codefendant in any action against the insured to determine the latter's liability"?

3. In MISKELL v. W. T. COWN, INC., 10 F.R.D. 617 (E.D.Pa.1950), defendant moved to bring in a third party. Plaintiff opposed the motion on the ground that the third party was a sailor who might be unavailable at the time of trial or exempted from appearing under the Soldiers and Sailors Civil Relief Act. The court rejected plaintiff's arguments.

> The plaintiff's concern is, I believe, premature. For even though the motion to implead be granted, this Court has, under the Federal Rules, ample discretion to protect the plaintiff from prejudice and inconvenience. If, at the time of trial, the third party is not required to answer, the Court may order a separate trial between plaintiff and defendant under Rule 42(b) and, under Rule 54(b) enter a separate judgment. In this manner, not only may the plaintiff be protected but the defendant may also be protected against the necessity of filing a separate suit should the situation not require it.   *   *   *

Id. at 618.

In GOODHART v. UNITED STATES LINES CO., 26 F.R.D. 163 (S.D.N. Y.1960), plaintiff sued for personal injuries caused by defendant's employee. The court denied a motion to implead the employee:

> I feel safe in taking judicial notice of the fact that the operator of a hi-lo [defendant's employee] will not be financially able to indemnify defendant to any substantial extent. Defendant must have some other reason or reasons for seeking impleader. One of those reasons is that jurors will likely render a smaller verdict if they are required to find that an individual employee of defendant is ultimately responsible for its payment. Another is that the interest of the hi-lo operator in a verdict for his employer will be heightened. * * *

> In seeking the first result defendant, in effect, asks me to give it the advantage of the chance that the jury will proceed upon a false supposition that the hi-lo operator will pay the judgment. In seeking the second result defendant, in effect, asks me to help him threaten the hi-lo operator with the necessity of going through bankruptcy unless he testifies favorably to defendant. Neither of these pleas recommends itself to the court as a subject for exercise of the court's discretion. Such legitimate claim as defendant may have against the hi-lo operator is amply protected by defendant's right to bring a separate suit.

Id. at 164. Would permitting impleader but granting a motion for separate trials under Rule 42(b), as suggested in *Miskell*, have adequately protected plaintiff from possible prejudice? Are there any advantages to this procedure?

REVERE COPPER & BRASS, INC. v AETNA CAS. & SUR. CO., 426 F.2d 709, 715–17 (5th Cir.1970). Revere sued Aetna on a surety bond executed in connection with a construction contract, alleging that Fuller, the builder, had breached express and implied warranties and specific contract provisions, had been negligent, had made false representations, and had failed to complete its work within the prescribed time. It sought damages of $2,045,000. Aetna impleaded Fuller under Rule 14(a) claiming that the builder had agreed to indemnify Aetna for all losses sustained as a result of the suretyship. Fuller asserted a "counterclaim" against Revere seeking $1,328,880 based on the breach of certain express and implied warranties and for wanton and willful misconduct. Revere moved to dismiss Fuller's claim on the ground that there was no diversity of citizenship between Revere and Fuller; the district court held the claim to be within its ancillary jurisdiction. On appeal, the Fifth Circuit, after discussing the six reported district court decisions dealing with the question, affirmed, holding that the claim clearly fell within the core of aggregate facts upon which the original claim rested and thus was within the court's ancillary jurisdiction. Judge Morgan, speaking for the court, stated:

> It is easily seen that Fuller's claim arises out of the aggregate of operative facts which forms the basis of Revere's claim in such a way to put their logical relationship beyond doubt. The two claims are but two sides of the same coin. The construction was not completed before the time provided in the two contracts. If Revere is not responsible for the delay, as Fuller alleges, Fuller

must at least be guilty of breach of contract, not to mention the other allegations of fault in Revere's complaint. To paraphrase the Supreme Court in Moore v. New York Cotton Exchange, * * * [p. 510, supra]: so close is the connection between the case sought to be stated in Revere's complaint and that set up in Fuller's Rule 14(a) counterclaim that it only needs the failure of the former to establish the foundation for the latter.

Not only is the parallel between a Rule 14(a) counterclaim and a compulsory counterclaim under Rule 13(a) so close as to be persuasive on the question of ancillarity, the parallel between the instant case and cases dealing with the ability of an intervenor of right under Rule 24(a) to counterclaim against the original plaintiff without an independent basis of federal jurisdiction removes any substantial doubt. It is well established that a contractor who has agreed to indemnify his surety on a performance bond can intervene as a party defendant as of right in a suit on the performance bond against the surety and then assert his counterclaim against the plaintiff, even in the absence of an independent ground of federal jurisdiction. * * * It would be anomalous to hold that Fuller could have asserted its counterclaim against Revere free of any jurisdictional impediment if it had taken the initiative of intervening, and yet hold that since Fuller was brought into this action involuntarily as a third-party defendant, its counterclaim must satisfy the requirements of strict diversity and thus fail.

* * * Revere argues that since there must be an independent ground of jurisdiction to support the original plaintiff's claim against a third-party defendant, the same requirement must be met by the third-party defendant in asserting a counterclaim against the original plaintiff. Suffice it to say that the two situations are the converse of each other only superficially and that there are differences which militate against identical treatment. First of all, the plaintiff has the option of selecting the forum where he believes he can most effectively assert his claims, he has not been involuntarily brought to a forum, faced with the prospect of defending himself as best he can under the rules that forum provides, or defending himself not at all. Since a plaintiff could not initially join a non-diverse defendant, it is arguable he should not be allowed to do so indirectly by way of a fortuitous impleader. Moreover, there is the possibility, whether real or fanciful, of collusion between the plaintiff and an overly cooperative defendant impleading just the right third party. Whatever the merit or demerit of these reasons, they point to a sufficient difference to require that the application of ancillary jurisdiction to each type of claim must be decided separately. Consequently,

this decision is to be strictly limited to the precise question decided.

* * *

NOTES AND QUESTIONS

1. The *Revere* case is discussed in 59 Ky.L.J. 506 (1970); 1970 Wash.
U.L.O. 511: and 49 N.C.L.Rev. 503 (1971).

As pointed out in *Revere* it generally is held that a claim by the original
plaintiff against the third-party defendant arising out of the transaction or occurrence that is the subject matter of plaintiff's claim against the original defendant may be interposed only if it meets independent jurisdictional requirements.
Are the following arguments against that conclusion persuasive?

      * * * First, it is argued that plaintiff should not be allowed
to do indirectly what he cannot do directly. If, for example, there is no
diversity between plaintiff and the third-party defendant and the dispute between them does not involve a federal question, plaintiff could
not sue him in an independent action and should not be allowed to
assert a claim against him simply because he has been brought into the
action by defendant. But this argument ignores the fact that plaintiff
cannot determine whether the third-party defendant will be made a party
to the action. The bringing in of the third-party is determined by the
original defendant and recognizing ancillary jurisdiction in this context
would not encourage plaintiff to initiate actions in the hope that the
third-party defendant would be impleaded.

      The second objection to permitting ancillary jurisdiction is that the
third-party defendant may have been made a party to the action as a
result of collusion between plaintiff and defendant. The response to
this fear is that rather than totally rejecting the use of ancillary jurisdiction in the context of claims by the original plaintiff against the third-
party defendant, the courts should dismiss only those claims that the
third-party defendant can show have been asserted collusively. Also,
* * * the type of impleader most likely to occasion collusion between plaintiff and the third-party defendant was eliminated by the
1948 amendment to Rule 14(a). Defendant no longer can bring in a
third party solely on the basis that he is liable to plaintiff; he must be
able to assert a claim against the third-party on his own behalf. If he
asserts a valid third-party claim, presumably he will stand to benefit
thereby; his other motives for doing so and the fact that it works to
the benefit of plaintiff should not be relevant. Moreover, any claim
plaintiff may assert against the third party must arise out of the transaction or occurrence that already has been made the subject of the court's
jurisdiction and is between persons who have been made parties to the
action. Exercising ancillary jurisdiction in such a case therefore will
not increase the burden on the federal court appreciably and the possibility of reducing the overall burden on both the state and federal
courts will be enhanced.

6 Wright & Miller, *Federal Practice and Procedure: Civil* § 1444, at 230–32
(1971).

2. According to the existing case law the statutory venue limitations have
no application to Rule 14 claims even if they would require the third-party pro-

ceeding to be heard in another district had it been brought as an independent action. However, should jurisdiction and venue be treated the same or differently in the context of a claim by the third-party defendant against the original plaintiff? See *Developments in the Law—Multiparty Litigation in the Federal Courts,* 71 Harv.L.Rev. 874, 911–12 (1958). Reconsider the materials on ancillary jurisdiction on pp. 226–30, supra. See also Pennsylvania R.R. v. Erie Ave. Warehouse Co., 302 F.2d 843 (3d Cir. 1962).

3. Are there any limitations on the third-party defendant's ability to assert a claim against the third-party plaintiff? Against the original plaintiff? In HEINTZ & CO. v. PROVIDENT TRADESMENS BANK & TRUST CO., 30 F.R.D. 171 (E.D.Pa.1962), plaintiff alleged that defendant negligently permitted Kerr to open a bank account in plaintiff's name and to draw checks without plaintiff's permission. Defendant impleaded Kerr. Kerr then filed a claim against plaintiff for services rendered and materials furnished to plaintiff in connection with the establishment of a branch office managed by Kerr. The court found Kerr's claim within Rule 14 because it arose out of the same transaction as the original suit.

> * * * The only distinction between a counterclaim under Rule 13(a) and the sort of claim we have before us under Rule 14 is that defendant "must" plead his counterclaim under Rule 13(a) if it grows out of the same transaction or occurrence, whereas under Rule 14, the third party "may" plead his claim for relief. But this, we think, is a distinction without a difference. The ancillary nature of the claim is not to be determined by whether the pleader "must" or "may" assert it, but by its relation to the transaction that is the subject of the main suit.

Id. at 174. If the original plaintiff has a counterclaim arising out of the same transaction as the claim asserted by the third-party defendant, is it compulsory? Can the original plaintiff assert a permissive counterclaim against the third-party defendant?

Another problem in third-party practice is exemplified by NOLAND CO. v. GRAVER TANK & MFG. CO., 301 F.2d 43 (4th Cir.1962), which grew out of a suit originally brought by Ruscon Construction Company, a general contractor, against Noland, a subcontractor, for the difference between the cost of a water tank and the subcontractor's bid price. Noland's bid was based on estimates given to it by Graver, a water tank supplier. Noland impleaded Graver not only to obtain indemnity for his liability to Ruscon but also to recover $4,000 in contemplated profits. The district court allowed Noland only the indemnity. The Fourth Circuit framed the issue as:

> * * * [W]hether, under Rule 14, a third-party defendant, *once made a party to an action,* can be proceeded against by the third-party plaintiff upon a claim closely related to, yet different from and for an amount in excess of, the original plaintiff's claim asserted in the primary action. * * *

Id. at 49. The court then held:

> * * * In view of the ease with which disposition of all claims herein could be made in this one action, we conclude that Rule 14 should be construed to be sufficiently broad and flexible so as to permit the District Court, in the exercise of its sound discretion, to make such disposition.

Id. at 50. In a more recent Third Circuit opinion, SCHWAB v. ERIE LACKA-
WANNA R.R. CO., 438 F.2d 62 (3d Cir.1971), the court held that although it
would be improper to allow the third-party plaintiff to bring an additional claim
against the third-party defendant under Rule 14, the claim was proper under
Rule 18 and came within the ancillary jurisdiction of the court. Does it make
any difference under which rule the claim is asserted? Does it make any difference if the third-party plaintiff's additional claim does not have a close nexus
with the ancillary claim under Rule 14? See U.S. for Use of Payne v. United
Pacific Ins. Co., 472 F.2d 792 (9th Cir.1973).

HORTON v. CONTINENTAL CAN CO.

United States District Court, District of Nebraska, 1956.
19 F.R.D. 429.

[Horton was employed by Wade and Son, a construction contractor doing
work for Continental Can Company. He was injured while working on a me-
tallic scaffold owned by Continental but being used by Wade and Son in connection with its work for Continental. Wade and Son paid benefits to Horton
under the Nebraska Workmen's Compensation Law. Subsequently, Horton
instituted this action against Continental on the theory that the latter had negligently maintained the scaffold. Wade and Son was made a party defendant in
order to protect its right to subrogation in any judgment obtained against Continental to the extent of its earlier workmen's compensation payments. Continental denied negligence and sought, by third-party complaint, to assert that if
it was liable to Horton, that liability arose only by reason of the active negligence by one Elbert T. Culver, an iron workers crew foreman of Wade and
Son. The answer further asserted that Wade and Son, as Culver's employer
and master, was ultimately liable. In the first part of its opinion, the District
Court concluded that Elbert T. Culver could be made a third-party defendant
but, because of a technical defect in Continental's motion papers, a new third-
party complaint was necessary. The court then went on to discuss Continental's
attempt to make Wade and Son a third-party defendant.]

DELEHANT, Chief Judge.   *   *   *

In the context of the case the motion to bring in Wade and Son as a
third-party defendant presents a different question. Wade and Son is a party
to the action and has been from its institution. Upon the record it is a defendant. Continental argues with some force that it should be aligned as a
plaintiff along with Horton. But that point need not be determined.
Whether it is substantially a defendant or a plaintiff, Wade and Son is a party to the case. It has voluntarily appeared, and has served and filed its answer praying for judgment in its behalf in the sum of its compensation payments on account of plaintiff "out of any judgment rendered against the defendant, Continental Can Company, Inc., in favor of the plaintiff", and has
served and filed a designation of the place of trial.

In such a situation the pertinent language of Rule 14 needs to be re-called. * * * For the invocation of the rule it appears * * * to be required that the proposed additional defendant be not only one who is or may be liable to the moving defendant for all or part of plaintiff's claim against him, but, what is of present significance, also "a person not a party to the action". And it is obvious that Wade and Son is not such a person. Being already a party to the action, it appears to be quite unnecessary that it be now made a party under a new title or style. * * * Continental would seem already to possess resources in pleading appropriate for the assertion of its claim against Wade and Son. And resort to Rule 14, seemingly not available, ought also to be quite unnecessary. * * *

An order is, therefore, being made denying and overruling the motion in-sofar as it seeks to make Wade and Son a third-party defendant, but without prejudice to the right of Continental to assert its claim against Wade and Son by any other appropriate procedure, in respect of which the order does not make, or this memorandum suggest, any limitation.

* * *

NOTES AND QUESTIONS

1. The court in *Horton* states that Continental could assert its claim against Wade and Son other than under Rule 14. There are at least two possible proce-dures; what are they? One is dealt with in Sporia v. Pennsylvania Greyhound Lines, Inc., 143 F.2d 105 (3d Cir.1944). What difference does it make if Con-tinental's claim is brought under Rule 14 or by some "other appropriate proce-dure"? Does it make any sense to conclude that a third-party claim is proper as against Culver but not as against Wade and Son? What is the logic of Rule 13 (a), (b), and (g) permitting or requiring counterclaims and cross-claims to be as-serted against persons who already are parties and Rule 14(a) denying impleader in that context?

2. * * * This practice [impleader] has its roots in the common-law procedure of "vouching to warranty," whereby a person whose title to land has been attacked could notify his vendor of the attack if the latter had warranted the title. The vendor, whether or not he chose to participate, would then be bound by the prior determination in a subsequent suit by his vendee.

Developments in the Law—Multiparty Litigation in the Federal Courts, 71 Harv. L.Rev. 874, 907 (1958). In what ways does third-party practice under Federal Rule 14 differ from the common-law procedure of vouching to warranty? See Note 4 on p. 1136, infra. For a discussion of the "vouching-in" procedure, see Degnan & Barton, *Vouching to Quality Warranty: Case Law and Commercial Code,* 51 Calif.L.Rev. 471 (1963).

3. The states take a variety of different approaches to third-party practice. Indeed, the practice in a number of states is very different from that under Federal Rule 14. Many of the reasons for this difference in practice are described in Friedenthal, *The Expansion of Joinder in Cross-Complaints by the Erroneous In-terpretation of Section 442 of the California Code of Civil Procedure,* 51 Calif.L. Rev. 494 (1963).

CHAPTER 7

SPECIAL DEVICES FOR HANDLING DIS-
PUTES INVOLVING MULTIPLE
PARTIES

SECTION A. CLASS ACTIONS

Read Federal Rule of Civil Procedure 23 and the material accompanying it in the Supplement.

---

1. HISTORY AND PHILOSOPHY OF THE CLASS ACTION

The history of the class action can be traced to the English "bill of peace" in the Seventeenth Century. The "bill" was a procedural device utilized by the Courts of Chancery to allow an action to be brought by or against representative parties when (1) the number of persons involved was too large to permit joinder, (2) all the members of the group possessed a joint interest in the question being adjudicated, and (3) the named parties adequately represented the interests of those who were not present. If these three conditions were met, the judgment that ultimately was entered was binding on all the members of the represented group.

Although provisions for class actions modelled after the English procedure existed in various state codes and the Federal Equity Rules, Federal Rule 23, as originally adopted in 1938, represented the first attempt to provide for class actions in a mature form. Moreover, with the adoption of the Federal Rules the class action became available in both legal and equitable actions in the federal courts.

Original Rule 23 attempted to describe when a class action was proper in a highly conceptualized way. All class actions were divided into three categories and a particular suit was assigned to one classification or another depending on the character of the right being asserted. The differences among the various categories was important for determining questions such as whether jurisdictional requirements were met, the binding effect of a decree, and when the statute of limitations was tolled. Briefly, the categories were as follows. A so-called "true" class action was involved when the class members possessed joint and common interests in the subject matter of the action; a "hybrid" class action was present when several claims to the same property were being litigated; and what was described as a "spurious" class action existed when persons possessing independent interests joined together in the suit.

This structure proved to be confusing to apply, see 7 Wright & Miller, *Federal Practice and Procedure: Civil* § 1752 (1972), and in 1966 the Advisory Committee completely rewrote Rule 23 to substitute functional tests for the conceptual categories and to provide some procedural guidance for the courts with regard to handling class actions. The amendment also made clear that a judgment in a class action is binding on all class members, except in those cases in which the right to opt-out under Rule 23(c)(2) applies and has been exercised. The philosophy of the 1966 amendment was aptly described by the Reporter to the Advisory Committee when he said:

> * * * [The Advisory Committee] perceived, as lawyers had for a long time, that some litigious situations affecting numerous persons "naturally" or "necessarily" called for unitary adjudication. The problem was how to elaborate this insight while avoiding the pitfalls of abstract classification on the style of 1938. Approaching rule 23, then, in much the same spirit in which it was considering rule 19, the Committee strove to sort out the factual situations or patterns that had recurred in class actions and appeared with varying degrees of convincingness to justify treatment of the class *in solido*. The revised rule was written upon the framework thus revealed * * *.

Kaplan, *Continuing Work of the Civil Committee: 1966 Amendments of the Federal Rules of Civil Procedure (I)*, 81 Harv.L.Rev. 356, 386 (1967).

The increasing complexity and urbanization of modern American society has magnified tremendously the importance of the class action as a procedural device for resolving disputes affecting large numbers of persons. Some sense of its utility is suggested by the following excerpt from Judge Weinstein's opinion in DOLGOW v. ANDERSON, 43 F.R.D. 472 (E.D.N.Y.1968), a class action by four stockholders for damages, punitive damages, and rescission against a corporation and its principal officers and directors who allegedly manipulated stock prices by misleading investors:

> It is the duty of the federal courts to render private enforcement practicable. Other than the class action, the procedures available for handling proliferated litigation—joinder, intervention, consolidation, and the test case—cannot serve this function in a situation like the one presented here. These alternative devices pre-

suppose "a group of economically powerful parties who are obviously able and willing to take care of their own interests individually through individual suits or individual decisions about joinder or intervention." Frankel, Amended Rule 23 From A Judge's Point of View, 32 Antitrust L.J. 295, 298 (1966). * * *

The class action is particularly appropriate where those who have allegedly been injured "are in a poor position to seek legal redress, either because they do not know enough or because such redress is disproportionately expensive." Kalven and Rosenfield, The Contemporary Function of the Class Suit, 8 U.Chi.L.Rev. 684, 686 (1941). Its "historic mission" has been to "[take] care of the smaller guy." Statement of Professor Ben Kaplan, Reporter of the new Rules, quoted in Frankel, Amended Rule 23 From A Judge's Point of View, 32 Antitrust L.J. 295, 299 (1966). * * *

Subdivision (b)(3) lists as a factor in determining whether the class action is superior to other methods of litigating the controversy "the interest of members of the class in individually controlling the prosecution or defense of separate actions." Particularly apt in this case is the Advisory Committee's emphasis on the impracticality of individual suits where the claim of each prospective plaintiff is small. * * *

This comment applies with particular force to a case involving tens of thousands of small shareholders. As the S.E.C. amicus brief makes patently clear, "since the difficulty of proving a violation under the securities laws often is great and the injury to individual investors may not be sufficiently large to justify on an individual basis the investigative and litigation expense involved, a class action may be the only meaningful method by which private rights may be effectively enforced." * * *

The Rule 23 class action has much the same prophylactic function in the field of securities regulation that the shareholder derivative suit has in the area of general corporate law. In addition to seeking to compensate those directly injured, the federal securities laws are designed to deter corporate officials and insiders from engaging in the kind of machinations alleged to have taken place here. * * * By making real the threat of exposure and civil liability, the class action also serves to effectuate this objective. * * *

Those who criticize the class action on the grounds that it stirs up plaintiffs and serves only to provide fees for attorneys overlook the fact that we are not dealing with the traditional lawsuit which concerns primarily those litigants before the court.

> The public's concern with openness and honesty in public se-
> curities markets gives it an interest no less significant than that
> of particular plaintiffs and defendants.

Id. at 484–85, 487. And it has been argued that the class action has even
greater significance for consumers since they generally are in a less favorable position than stockholders to secure legal redress for the wrongs committed against them.

> Frequently numerous consumers are exposed to the same dubious
> practice by the same seller so that proof of the prevalence of the
> practice as to one consumer would provide proof for all. Indi-
> vidual actions by each of the defrauded consumers is often imprac-
> ticable because the amount of individual recovery would be insuf-
> ficient to justify bringing a separate action; thus an unscrupulous
> seller retains the benefits of its wrongful conduct. A class action
> by consumers produces several salutary by-products, including a
> therapeutic effect upon those sellers who indulge in fraudulent
> practices, aid to legitimate business enterprises by curtailing ille-
> gitimate competition, and avoidance to the judicial process of the
> burden of multiple litigation involving identical claims. *   *   *

Vasquez v. Superior Court of San Joaquin County, 4 Cal.3d 800, 808,
94 Cal.Rptr. 796, 800–01, 484 P.2d 964, 968–69 (1971).

The utility of the class action as a means of vindicating the rights of
small claimants has led to its increasing use by various social activist groups.
This phenomenon has led to criticism of the procedure from some quarters
on the ground that it imposes large burdens on the already overcrowded
courts, and is "a form of legalized blackmail." See Handler, *The Shift
from Substantive to Procedural Innovations in Antitrust Suits—The Twen-
ty-Third Annual Antitrust Review*, 71 Colum.L.Rev. 1, 9 (1971). See
also American College of Trial Lawyers Report and Recommendations of
the Special Committee on Rule 23 of the Federal Rules of Civil Procedure (1972). In recent years this counterattack has achieved some success. Class action treatment has been rejected in a number of cases on
various grounds, including unmanageability and the existence of dissimilar
interests within the class. Revision of the rule also has been proposed.

As might be expected, members of the business world have reacted
strongly in opposing the use of the class action by consumers and environ-
mentalists. In Carruth, *The "Legal Explosion" Has Left Business Shell-
Shocked*, Fortune 65 (April, 1973), the author explains some of their
fears.

> *   *   * "Everyone who deals with the public today is
> open to brand-new areas of litigation," says Abraham Pomerantz,
> the dean of the plaintiff's bar in class-action suits (although lately
> he has at times turned up as counsel for the defense). "This is
> driving many corporations to something bordering on hysteria.

The big problem for them today is not so much increasing legal expenses—it's the enormously increased legal *exposure*. That class suit really strikes at the pocketbook. In some cases the corporation's very existence is at stake."

On balance, the pressures to settle class actions are great. If the corporations lose, a court may award higher damages than they could have bargained for. Furthermore, the very fact of being assailed as a polluter, or price fixer, or discriminator can damage a company's reputation. The prospective damage to its public image was an important factor in American Standard's decision three years ago to pay $15 million in settlement of four antitrust class actions.

There are now pending in the federal district courts at least 1,000 class-action suits involving corporations, and the totals are still growing. * * *

Now a move is afoot in Congress * * * that would open up that possibility of broad attacks by consumers, and corporations eying the proposed legislation are naturally somewhat upset by it. Says a lawyer who is helping to frame the legislation: "These people are really scared. The ironic thing is that most consumers are still completely unaware of the possibilities for class action. One can only wonder what the situation will be when all the groups that can stand to benefit have marshaled their attack."

Id. at 66–67.

Despite the negative picture painted by the opponents of the class action, some commentators and judges have argued that the class action itself is not abusive. Consider the following arguments:

The * * * [argument] that class actions generally impose too heavy a burden on the federal courts, does not present great latitude for constructive discussion without the reliable kind of quantitative data not yet, in my opinion, available. * * *

My own view is that * * * increased availability of the courts to those with grievances as a result of providing lawyers for the poor and modifications of such doctrines as standing, mootness, abstention and justiciability, have provided a valuable escape valve, preventing explosive reactions during a period of boiling social change.

* * *

A particularly bothersome aspect of the class action is their strike suit aspect. * * * It exists in every individual litigation, and we all acknowledge and deal with it in settlements every day. The trial judge may, however, use his discretion to reduce the effect of possible abuse in these class actions, and when they are suitably controlled, the balance of possible abuse against social advantage, it seems to me, is tolerable.

* * *

In sum, we want to control, we want to prevent abuses. We do not want to really kill this little beastie. We do not want to so entangle it so that it cannot be used effectively. It does give us a more adequate tool for the deterrence of unlawful, socially destructive conduct through civil suits.

Weinstein, *Some Reflections on the "Abusiveness" of Class Actions,* 58 F.R.D. 299, 300, 302, 304 (1973).

2. REQUIREMENTS FOR BRINGING A CLASS ACTION

WEAVER v. PASADENA TOURNAMENT OF ROSES ASS'N, 32 Cal.2d 833, 198 P.2d 514 (1948). Four persons, on behalf of themselves and others similarly situated, brought a class action seeking a $100 statutory penalty for each member of the class for wrongful exclusion from the Rose Bowl football game on New Years Day, 1947. Plaintiffs alleged that defendant had publicly advertised that 7,500 tickets would go on sale on December 23, 1946; that plaintiffs and others lined up at the box office; that they were given stubs evidencing their places in line and entitling them to purchase two tickets each; that after 1500 tickets had been sold, defendant closed the box office and announced no more were available; that, in fact, additional tickets were available but were sold privately and in fraudulent disregard of the priority evidenced by the stubs. Defendant demurred for want of jurisdiction, claiming that the action was not a proper class action and that the amount in controversy was below the Superior Court's jurisdictional minimum. The Court sustained the demurrer. The Supreme Court of California affirmed:

* * * The causes of action of the several plaintiffs and the other unnamed aggrieved individuals are separate and distinct. The question, as to each individual plaintiff, is whether *he* "as a person over the age of twenty-one years" presented himself and demanded admittance to the game, whether *he* tendered the price of the ticket, and whether, as to *him*, the refusal of admission was wrongful under section 53 of the Civil Code, entitling him "to recover * * * his *actual damages*, and one hundred dollars in addition thereto." (* * * emphasis added.) Moreover, other independent factors of consideration arise in connection with the respective individual claims by reason of the provision that a "person under the influence of liquor, or who is guilty of boisterous conduct, or [who is] of lewd or immoral character, may be excluded from any such [public] place of amusement." (Civ.Code, § 53.) Thus, a decision favorable or adverse to these plaintiffs— or any one of them—could not determine the rights of any of the unnamed parties whom plaintiffs purport to represent. True, the plaintiffs, and perhaps others who waited in line and were refused tickets of admission, have an interest in a common question of law * * *. But the determination of such question in the present case would still leave to be litigated the right of any other person to recover on his statutory claim in the light of whether *he*, in reliance upon the advertised sale, stood in line, received an identification stub, was denied tickets before the promised 7,500 had been sold, presented himself at the Rose Bowl as a "sober, moral person," demanded admission, tendered the price, and was refused, entitling him "to recover * * * his actual damages" as well as the fixed statutory penalty of $100.

* * * In the present case there is no ascertainable class * * *. Rather, there is only a large number of individuals, each of whom may or may not have, or care to assert, a claim against the operators of the 1947 Rose Bowl Game for the alleged wrongful refusal of admission thereto. * * * Moreover, each claimant would have the independent right, under section 54 of said code, to litigate the question of his recovery of "actual damages" in addition to the $100 penalty imposed by the statute. While each would be "similarly situated" in that his cause of action arises under the same statute, his recovery would rest on a distinct premise correlative with varying proof as to the facts of his particular case. * * *

Id. at 838–40, 198 P.2d at 517–18.

NOTES AND QUESTIONS

1. One reason given in *Weaver* for denying the class suit was that defendant might have special or personal defenses against some of the persons allegedly injured by its conduct. How important should this factor be? How does Federal Rule 23 deal with the possibility that individual issues or defenses may be presented?

2. Is it relevant that in *Weaver* the identity of many of the persons allegedly injured probably was not ascertainable? To what extent would the ability to identify all of the members of the class be germane to determining whether a class action is proper?

DAAR v. YELLOW CAB CO., 57 Cal.Rptr. 198 (2d Dist.Ct.App.1967), was a suit by a taxicab customer for himself and all others similarly situated to recover excessive charges by the taxicab company over a four-year period. One part of the complaint dealt with fares paid with scrip issued to customers by the company. The company allegedly had records identifying the persons who purchased the scrip. The second part of the complaint contained a claim on behalf of those who used cash to pay for taxicab transportation. According to the court:

> In the case at bench there is no allegation that the improper overcharges found their way into any separate fund which can be impressed with a trust. Each taxicab user has a cause of action for money which, when reduced to judgment, will be collectible out of the defendant's property like any other money judgment.

Id. at 204. The court went on to note that the identity of the persons who had paid cash was unknown and that there was no effective way of giving them reasonable notice of the suit. Consequently, "the high probability that no substantial part of the recovery would even reach the real owners is itself a compelling reason for refusing to entertain the second cause of action as a class suit."

The California Supreme Court, in a lengthy opinion, reversed. 67 Cal.2d 695, 63 Cal.Rptr. 724, 433 P.2d 732 (1967). It initially determined that the class was ascertainable on the ground that the requisite "community of interest" among the members of the alleged class was present. As to the contention that the class action was improper because the identity of many of the members was unknown, the court stated:

> Defendant apparently fails to distinguish between the necessity of establishing the existence of an ascertainable class and the necessity of identifying the individual members of such class as a prerequisite to a class suit. If the existence of an ascertainable class has been shown, there is no need to identify its individual members in order to bind all members by the judgment. The fact that the class members are unidentifiable at this point will not preclude a complete determination of the issues affecting the class. Presumably an accounting in the suit at bench will determine the total amount of the alleged overcharges; any judgment will be binding on all the users of taxicabs within the prior four years. However, no one may recover his separate damages until he comes forward, identifies himself and proves the amount thereof.

Id. at 732, 433 P.2d at 740. Was *Weaver* overruled by *Daar* by implication? If a class action is appropriate in the *Daar* context, can you conceive of any situation in which a group of people who have been injured by the same person or conduct would not constitute a valid class? Is *Daar* consistent with DeBRE-MAECKER v. SHORT, 433 F.2d 733 (5th Cir.1970), in which class action treatment was denied to a suit brought on behalf of "residents of this State active in the 'peace movement' who have been harassed and intimidated * * *." Id. at 734.

3. In BARRETT v. KUNZIG, 331 F.Supp. 266 (M.D.Tenn.1971), a class action to enjoin the government's inspection of packages and briefcases carried into a United States courthouse was allowed to proceed on behalf of all the attorneys who practiced in the federal district court, but was denied on behalf of persons desiring to enter as spectators. Can *Barrett* be distinguished from *Daar*? Of what importance is the fact that in *DeBremaecker* determining who was a member of the class depended, at least in part, on the intent or state of mind of the particular individual rather than some objective fact or financial interest?

4. BAILEY v. PATTERSON, 323 F.2d 201, 203 (5th Cir.1963):

  * * * Plaintiffs alleged that defendants, acting under color of state law, policy, and custom, denied to plaintiffs and the class of all others similarly situated, their right to transportation service free from racial discrimination. * * * Plaintiffs sought to enjoin the enforcement of state and municipal segregation laws affecting common carriers, and to enjoin all defendants from maintaining racial segregation in any manner, by the use of signs or otherwise, on the carriers or in or around their terminals or other facilities anywhere in the state. Plaintiffs also sought to enjoin the municipal authorities from continuing to arrest, harass, intimidate, threaten or coerce plaintiffs or members of their class in the exercise of their federally protected rights.

Should this action be maintainable under Federal Rule 23? Can you define the class?

TECHNOGRAPH PRINTED CIRCUITS, LTD. v. METHODE ELECTRONICS, INC.

United States District Court, Northern District of Illinois, 1968.
285 F.Supp. 714.

BECKER, District Judge.

Background

  In the years 1958 to 1963, Technograph Printed Circuits, Ltd., and Technograph, Inc. (formerly Technograph Printed Electronics, Inc.), a corporation, instituted approximately 74 civil actions for patent infringement against approximately 80 manufacturers of electronic equipment in 18 different United States District Courts. In addition, there is one action pending in the United States Court of Claims instituted by the plaintiffs herein in which the United States is alleged to have participated in patent infringement. * * *

  The plaintiffs herein have commenced four actions in the Eastern Division of the Northern District of Illinois against the following defendants:

1. Methode Electronics, Inc. * * *;

2. General Telephone & Electronics Corporation and Automatic Electric Company * * *;

3. Webcor Electronics, Incorporated * * *; and

4. Croname, Incorporated * * *.

  The parties herein, by order of this Court, have filed amended pleadings. In these amended pleadings the plaintiffs seek to convert these actions into a [defendant] class action under new Civil Rule 23. * * *

Subdivision (a) of Rule 23

This Court finds from the records and files that all four of the initial prerequisites to maintaining a class action, set forth in subdivision (a) of Rule 23, exist in these cases.

* * * [T]he *Technograph* litigation is massive multidistrict litigation of national interest. Over 70 actions have been filed in 18 federal district courts and in the Court of Claims. In the amended pleadings of certain defendants it is stated that there are 240 alleged infringers of one or more of the Eisler patents. These allegations are not controverted by the plaintiffs. Furthermore, the parties have stated that there are or may be many more alleged infringers whose identity and location are unknown at this time. The known alleged infringers of one or more of the Eisler patents constitute a class so numerous that joinder of all members is impracticable, not only because of venue problems, but also because of the great number of such parties. * * * This Court further finds that joinder of all known members of this class would not only be impracticable [as required by Rule 23(a)(1)] but may be impossible.

The second prerequisite of subdivision (a) of Rule 23 is as follows:

"(2) there are questions of law or fact common to the class * * *"

The questions to be determined on the amended pleadings of the parties herein include questions of law or fact or both common to the class, namely, the (1) validity of one or more of the Eisler patents, (2) alleged procurement of one or more of the patents through fraud on the Patent Office, and (3) alleged misuse of the patents. In respect to these questions subclasses of the primary class will hereafter be defined under Rule 23(c)(4), and the orders hereafter to be entered herein shall so provide.

* * *

In respect to the plaintiffs' claims of infringement it is hereby concluded that the questions of infringement of one or more of the Eisler patents is not a "question of law or fact common to the class," and the claims of infringement will not be adjudicated as a class action unless otherwise hereafter ordered by the Court. The issues of infringement will be ordered to be the subject of a separate trial under Rule 42, F.R.Civ.P., and the trial thereof deferred until determination of the class action on the merits, unless otherwise hereafter ordered.

The third prerequisite of subdivision (a) of Rule 23 is as follows:

"(3) the claims or defenses of the representative parties are typical of the claims or defenses of the class * * *"

* * * Both Methode Electronics, Inc. and Croname, Inc. are claimed to have infringed, and in defense of the claims assert the alleged invalidity and misuse of, all three of the Eisler patents. Automatic Electric Company in defense alleges the invalidity and misuse of the two patents * * *

which it is claimed to have infringed. Webcor Electronics, Inc. asserts the invalidity and misuse of the one patent * * * for the infringement of which relief is claimed. The issues of invalidity and misuse of one or more of the patents in suit is also raised by the counterclaims of each of the defendants in counts under the Declaratory Judgment Act. The amended counterclaims raise the defense of invalidity and misuse on behalf of the other members of the class. In addition Methode asserts the unenforceability of the patents on grounds of laches and of the statute of limitations. Further, Methode, Automatic Electric, Webcor and Croname claim unenforceability of [one patent] * * *, alleging fraud on the United States Patent Office and misuse. Methode, Automatic Electric and Webcor combine these claims of unenforceability with a counterclaim for damages under the anti-trust laws. * * * From the pleadings and hearings herein it is found that the claims and defenses which have actually been raised by the parties representing the class and the subclasses to be defined hereafter are typical of the claims and defenses reasonably expected to be raised by the members of the class and of the subclasses to be defined hereafter.

The fourth prerequisite of subdivision (a) of Rule 23 is as follows:

"(4) the representative parties will fairly and adequately protect the interests of the class."

The interests of the defendants herein, as representatives of the class, in the outcome of the controversy is great. The four defendants are represented by able and determined counsel. Each defendant in representing itself will fairly and adequately represent the interests of the class and of any subclass of which it is a member. It is therefore found that parties defendant possess the means, skill and integrity necessary to protect fairly and adequately the interests of the class and of any subclass of which any of them is a member.

* * *

Subdivision (b) of Rule 23

Next the provisions of subdivision (b), under which class actions are maintainable, will be considered. In that connection it is hereby found that, in addition to satisfying all of the prerequisites of subdivision (a), these actions meet all of the provisions of subdivision (b). * * *

Subdivision (b)(1) and Clause (A) thereof provide:

"the prosecution of separate actions by or against individual members of the class would create a risk of * * * inconsistent or varying adjudications with respect to individual members of the class which would establish incompatible standards of conduct for the party opposing the class * * *."

The prosecution of separate actions by and against the individual members of the class and any subclasses thereof would create a risk of inconsistent adjudications on the common questions, namely invalidity, fraud on the United States Patent Office, and misuse, preventing the patentee from enforcing one or more of the patents against some alleged infringers while permitting enforcement thereof against others. As a result incompatible standards of conduct for the plaintiffs would be established. The presence in the counterclaims of prayers for declaratory judgments as well as for treble damages increases the risk that the adjudications in the separate actions of the rights, obligations and privileges of the patentee may be inconsistent and varying.

* * * The likelihood of varying adjudications in respect to claimed monopolies of the Eisler patents, and each of them, presents a real threat of incompatible adjudications which transcends the "possibility of incompatible adjudications" mentioned in the Advisory Committee Notes to Rule 23. Not only is this clear concerning the pending litigation and the defendants in these cases, but is apparent concerning the threatened litigation against the hundreds of alleged infringers who have been notified in writing of plaintiffs' claims including claims for damages for past, present and future alleged infringements of the defendants. These are additional cogent reasons for finding that the prosecution of separate actions by or against the individual members of the class would create the risk of varying adjudications with respect to individual members of the class which would establish incompatible standards of conduct for the party opposing the class, as required by Clause (A) of subdivision (b)(1).

* * * It is found that subdivision (b)(1) and Clause (B) thereof are applicable, because the prosecution of separate actions against individual members of the class and any subclasses thereof would create a risk of adjudications which would as a practical matter be dispositive of the interests of other members not parties to the adjudication, or substantially impair or impede their ability to protect their interests. Selected adjudications of the questions of invalidity, misuse and fraud on the United States Patent Office may be accorded great weight in industrial relations by comity between courts and may greatly impair and impede the ability of members of the class and any subclasses thereof who are not parties to this action to protect their interests. To the extent that such selected adjudications vary or are inconsistent the ability of those who are not parties to this action will be further impaired and impeded.

The disruption of industrial relations of the members of the class by threats and claims based upon the patent grants, and also upon the possibility of a final, favorable adjudication to plaintiffs in some competent court, as well as the great expense of defending these and other separate actions to the point of adjudication would substantially impair or impede the ability of members of the class to protect their interests.

The next provision of subdivision (b) of Rule 23 is (b)(2) * * *. It is found that by obtaining patents, notifying some alleged infringers of the patents, and threatening some of them with infringement suits unless they take licenses, and by bringing civil actions against some of them, the plaintiffs herein have acted on grounds generally applicable to the class and any subclasses thereof. Further plaintiffs' claims for relief against each defendant contain prayers for injunctions. Each defendant has amended its counterclaims to pray for declaratory and injunctive relief. These prayers are typical of the requests for relief usually made by patentees and alleged infringers in patent infringement actions. By these counterclaims final injunctive relief and declaratory relief with respect to the class as a whole has been made appropriate.

* * *

It is found that the questions of alleged invalidity, misuse and alleged fraud on the United States Patent Office are not only common to the members of the subclass mentioned above but are also predominant over any questions affecting only individual members of the class or the subclasses thereof [for purposes of qualifying the case under Rule 23(b)(3)].

It is further found that considering each of the four factors listed in Clauses (A), (B), (C) and (D) of subdivision (3) (described as "nonexhaustive" in the Advisory Committee's Comment), a class action is and will be superior to the other available methods for the fair and efficient adjudication of the questions common to the subclass. The advantages of a class action in this forum far outweigh the disadvantages to the subclass when all pertinent matters mentioned in subdivision (b)(3) of Rule 23 are considered.

With respect to Clause (A), the interests of members of the class (and of any subclass) in individually controlling the prosecution and defense of separate actions are slight when compared to the many benefits of adjudication of the common questions in a class action in this forum.

With respect to Clause (B), it appears that plaintiffs have commenced nearly 74 infringement actions in 19 different federal courts. Adjudication on the merits in other districts prior to the time of pretrial and trial proceedings on the merits in these cases will cause those defendants to be excluded from the (b)(3) subclass. Further, it does not appear that the individual case of a member of the (b)(3) subclass would be delayed or made more burdensome in another district if a class action is maintained here under subdivision (b)(3), nor would the plaintiffs, who are prosecuting over 25 suits, be delayed or hindered in securing an adjudication on their claimed rights. Plaintiffs' counsel are not convinced of this because of plaintiff's [sic] involvement in active litigation in the Court of Claims, California and in Illinois simultaneously. But plaintiffs instituted the litigation in these jurisdictions. The action taken here offers promise of preventing further simultaneous involvement in active litigation in other states. Furthermore the prospect of a fair and efficient disposition of this litigation offers many rewards to the plaintiffs and members of the class and all subclasses thereof. In respect to the Court of Claims litigation, efforts are well underway to co-ordinate the pretrial proceedings and discovery in this Court and in the Court of Claims so as to lessen the burden of all parties concerned. The common issues of the litigation already instituted against known members of the (b)(3) subclass are substantially the same. Therefore, the use of a class action device would not appear to alter materially the nature of pending and prospective actions.

Concerning Clause (C), the concentration of the litigation of the common questions in this forum in the North Central United States is desirable because a substantial number of actions is already pending therein, and because an efficient, fair and economical adjudication of the common questions can be accomplished in this forum. Such a concentration of the litigation is desirable in the interest of the class and any subclass now or hereafter defined.

Concerning Clause (D), the difficulties likely to be encountered in the management of a class action are not important when weighed against the benefits to the class, and any subclasses thereof, and to the administration of justice. An adjudication of the common questions in these actions treated as a class action will be effective to settle the common questions arising in these actions and in the potential claims against and defenses of over two hundred known and potentially many more unknown parties who may be alleged to have infringed one or more of three related patents. To process the pending litigation and most of the remaining active, inactive and the potential litigation by a large number of separate trials would "raise administrative difficulties far exceeding those present in this class action." Brennan v. Midwestern United Life Ins. Co. (N.D.Ind., 1966) 259 F.Supp. 673, 684.

In conclusion it is hereby determined that a class action under Rule 23 would achieve the objectives enumerated in the Notes of the Advisory Committee * * * namely:

"* * * economies of time, effort, and expense, and promote uniformity of decision as to persons similarly situated, without sacrificing procedural fairness or bringing about other undesirable results."

* * *

NOTES AND QUESTIONS

1. Decisions in state and federal courts have varied widely on the question of when a class is so numerous that joinder of all the members is impractical. See Citizens Banking Co. v. Monticello State Bank, 143 F.2d 261 (8th Cir.1944) (forty holders of collateral trust notes large enough to make joinder impractical); George v. Benjamin, 100 Wis. 622, 76 N.W. 619 (1898) (thirty-one does not constitute impracticability of joinder). What factors other than the size of the

class might the court consider in determining whether the joinder of all the parties is impracticable?

2. What is the difference between the requirement that there be common questions of law or fact in Rule 23(a) (2) and the requirement that the claims or defenses of the representative parties be typical in Rule 23(a) (3)? Isn't Rule 23(a) (2) superfluous in light of the inclusion in Rule 23(b) (3) of the prerequisite that common questions "predominate over any questions affecting only individual members"? What does "typical" in Rule 23(a) (3) mean? Need the representative's claims or defenses be coextensive with or substantially identical to those of the absent class members to meet this test? If the claims or defenses of the class members depend upon establishing different fact patterns, can Rule 23(a) (3) be satisfied? See State of Iowa v. Union Asphalt & Roadoils, Inc., 281 F.Supp. 391 (S.D.Iowa 1968), affirmed on other grounds 409 F.2d 1239 (8th Cir.1969). For example, can a group of Blacks or Women bring a class action based on discrimination in hiring when each potential plaintiff has different qualifications for a particular job or each member of the putative class applied for different jobs. See generally 7 Wright & Miller, *Federal Practice and Procedure: Civil* §§ 1763–64 (1972).

3. What factors did the court look at in *Technograph* to determine whether there was adequate representation? Are there any other considerations that the court might have deemed relevant? See pp. 582–86, infra.

4. If an action can be brought under more than one subdivision of Rule 23(b), as was true in *Technograph,* does it make any difference which subdivision is relied upon for purposes of determining the propriety of the class action? Does it have any effect on what type of notice should be given to members of the class? See Van Gemert v. Boeing Co., 259 F.Supp. 125 (S.D.N.Y.1966).

5. What is the difference between the standard employed in Rule 19 for determining what persons should be joined to insure a just adjudication of a dispute and that used in Rule 23(b) (1)? Would the requirements of Rule 23(b) (1) (A) be met if it is shown that separate judgments might oblige the opposing party to pay damages to some class members but not to others or to pay them differing amounts for the same injuries? Would the Rule 23(b) (1) (B) requirements be satisfied under the same circumstances?

6. What is the test for determining whether the opposing party has acted on grounds "generally applicable" to the class, as required by Rule 23(b) (2)? Would an action requesting an injunction against a defendant class alleging that its members are engaged in a conspiracy to monopolize trade by refusing to deal with plaintiff qualify under subdivision (b) (2)?

7. The class members in a Rule 23(b) (3) action typically are only loosely tied together by their interest in common questions of law or fact. What is the purpose of each of the two findings required to be made under that portion of the rule? Need the common questions be dispositive of the entire action in order for them to "predominate" over individual issues? Of what importance is the fact that damages typically will vary for each member of a Rule 23(b) (3) class? Isn't it true that the efficiency or economy of allowing a class action to be brought will be lost if separate damage trials must be held?

When determining whether "a class action is superior to other available methods for the fair and efficient adjudication of the controversy" as required by Rule 23(b)(3), what alternative "methods" might the court consider? See 7A Wright & Miller, *Federal Practice and Procedure: Civil* § 1779 (1972). Aren't individual actions utilizing the broad joinder of claims and parties rules always a viable means of providing relief?

Of what importance was the finding in *Technograph* that seventy-four other infringement actions had been commenced in nineteen different federal courts? Doesn't the allowance of a class action simply create one more action? Is there any similarity between the analysis employed in deciding whether the class-action forum represents an appropriate place to settle the controversy and that used in determining whether a transfer-of-venue motion should be granted under 28 U.S.C. § 1404(a)? What methods are provided in Rule 23 for facilitating any management difficulties that might arise in a Rule 23(b)(3) action? See the discussion of administering judicial relief at pp. 601–02, infra.

8. Federal Rule 23(c)(1) directs the court to determine whether the action should be allowed to proceed as a class action "as soon as practicable after the commencement" of the action. Why is it important for the court to make this determination at an early stage in the litigation?

9. Does the court have the authority to refuse to entertain a class action if all the requirements of Rule 23 are met? In RATNER v. CHEMICAL BANK NEW YORK TRUST CO., 54 F.R.D. 412 (S.D.N.Y.1972), plaintiff was seeking relief on behalf of 130,000 Master Charge card holders for alleged violations of the 1968 Truth in Lending Act based on defendant's failure to show a "nominal annual percentage rate" on its periodic statements reporting the outstanding balance. The statute provided for $100 minimum recovery, plus costs and attorney's fees, for defaults in the statutory obligation to inform the consumer. The district court denied class action treatment, stating:

> * * * [T]he proposed recovery of $100 each for some 130,000 class members would be a horrendous, possibly annihilating punishment, unrelated to any damage to the purported class or to any benefit to defendant, for what is at most a technical and debatable violation of the Truth in Lending Act. * * * [T]he allowance of this as a class action is essentially inconsistent with the specific remedy supplied by Congress and employed by plaintiff in this case.

Id. at 416.

3. DUE PROCESS CONSIDERATIONS

HANSBERRY v. LEE

Supreme Court of the United States, 1940.
311 U.S. 32, 61 S.Ct. 115, 85 L.Ed. 22.

[This suit was brought in an Illinois state court on behalf of a class of landowners to enforce a racially restrictive covenant involving land in the City of Chicago. The covenant provided that it was not effective unless signed by the "owners of 95 per centum of the frontage." Plaintiff alleged that Hansberry, a black, had purchased some of the restricted land from an owner who had signed the agreement and that suit was being brought to enjoin the sale as a breach of the covenant. He further alleged that the binding effect of the covenant had been established in an earlier Illinois state court action holding that 95 percent of all the landowners involved had signed the agreement. In response defendants pleaded that they were not bound by the res judicata effect of the earlier judgment as they had not been parties to that suit and were not successors in interest or in privity with any of the parties to that action. Thus they argued it would be a denial of due process to hold them to the first decree.

The Illinois Circuit Court held that the issue whether the covenant was valid was res judicata, even though it found that only about 54 percent of the owners actually had signed the agreement and that the previous judgment rested on a "false and fraudulent" stipulation of the parties. The Supreme Court of Illinois affirmed. It found that although the stipulation was untrue it was not fraudulent or collusive. The Illinois court then went on to conclude that the first action had been a "class" or "representative" suit, that as such it was binding on all the class members unless reversed or set aside on direct proceedings, and that Hansberry and the persons who had sold the land to him were members of the class represented in the first action and consequently were bound by the decree in that suit.]

Certiorari to the Supreme Court of the State of Illinois.

Mr. Justice STONE delivered the opinion of the Court.

* * *

* * * [W]hen the judgment of a state court, ascribing to the judgment of another court the binding force and effect of res judicata, is challenged for want of due process it becomes the duty of this Court to examine the course of procedure in both litigations to ascertain whether the litigant whose rights have thus been adjudicated has been afforded such notice and opportunity to be heard as are requisite to the due process which the Constitution prescribes. * * *

It is a principle of general application in Anglo-American jurisprudence that one is not bound by a judgment in personam in a litigation in which he is not designated as a party or to which he has not been made a party by service of process. Pennoyer v. Neff * * * [p. 65, supra]. A judgment rendered in such circumstances is not entitled to the full faith and credit which the Constitution and statute of the United States * * * prescribe * * and judicial action enforcing it against the person or property of the absent party is not that due process which the Fifth and Fourteenth Amendments requires. * * *

To these general rules there is a recognized exception that, to an extent not precisely defined by judicial opinion, the judgment in a "class" or "representative" suit, to which some members of the class are parties, may bind members of the class or those represented who were not made parties to it. * * *

The class suit was an invention of equity to enable it to proceed to a decree in suits where the number of those interested in the subject of the litigation is so great that their joinder as parties in conformity to the usual rules of procedure is impracticable. Courts are not infrequently called upon to proceed with causes in which the number of those interested in the litigation is so great as to make difficult or impossible the joinder of all because some are not within the jurisdiction or because their whereabouts is unknown or where if all were made parties to the suit its continued abatement by the death of some would prevent or unduly delay a decree. In such cases where the interests of those not joined are of the same class as the interests of those who are, and where it is considered that the latter fairly represent the former in the prosecution of the litigation of the issues in which all have a common interest, the court will proceed to a decree. * * *

It is evident that the considerations which may induce a court thus to proceed, despite a technical defect of parties, may differ from those which must be taken into account in determining whether the absent parties are bound by the decree or, if it is adjudged that they are, in ascertaining whether such an adjudication satisfies the requirements of due process and of full faith and credit. Nevertheless there is scope within the framework of the Constitution for holding in appropriate cases that a judgment rendered in a class suit is res judicata as to members of the class who are not formal parties to the suit. * * * With a proper regard for divergent local institutions and interests * * *, this Court is justified in saying that there has been a failure of due process only in those cases where it cannot be said that the procedure adopted, fairly insures the protection of the interests of absent parties who are to be bound by it. * * *

It is familiar doctrine of the federal courts that members of a class not present as parties to the litigation may be bound by the judgment where they are in fact adequately represented by parties who are present, or where they actually participate in the conduct of the litigation in which members of the class are present as parties * * * or where the interest of the members of the

class, some of whom are present as parties, is joint, or where for any other reason the relationship between the parties present and those who are absent is
such as legally to entitle the former to stand in judgment for the latter.
* * *

In all such cases, * * * we may assume for present purposes that
such procedure affords a protection to the parties who are represented though
absent, which would satisfy the requirements of due process and full faith and
credit. * * * Nor do we find it necessary for the decision of this case to
say that, when the only circumstance defining the class is that the determination of the rights of its members turns upon a single issue of fact or law, a state
could not constitutionally adopt a procedure whereby some of the members of
the class could stand in judgment for all, provided that the procedure were so
devised and applied as to insure that those present are of the same class as
those absent and that the litigation is so conducted as to insure the full and fair
consideration of the common issue. * * * We decide only that the
procedure and the course of litigation sustained here by the plea of res judicata
do not satisfy these requirements.

The restrictive agreement did not purport to create a joint obligation or
liability. If valid and effective its promises were the several obligations of the
signers and those claiming under them. The promises ran severally to every
other signer. It is plain that in such circumstances all those alleged to be
bound by the agreement would not constitute a single class in any litigation
brought to enforce it. Those who sought to secure its benefits by enforcing it
could not be said to be in the same class with or represent those whose interest
was in resisting performance, for the agreement by its terms imposes obligations and confers rights on the owner of each plot of land who signs it. If
those who thus seek to secure the benefits of the agreement were rightly regarded by the state Supreme Court as constituting a class, it is evident that
those signers or their successors who are interested in challenging the validity
of the agreement and resisting its performance are not of the same class in the
sense that their interests are identical so that any group who had elected to enforce rights conferred by the agreement could be said to be acting in the interest of any others who were free to deny its obligation.

Because of the dual and potentially conflicting interests of those who are
putative parties to the agreement in compelling or resisting its performance, it
is impossible to say, solely because they are parties to it, that any two of them
are of the same class. Nor without more, and with the due regard for the protection of the rights of absent parties which due process exacts, can some be
permitted to stand in judgment for all.

It is one thing to say that some members of a class may represent other
members in a litigation where the sole and common interest of the class in the
litigation, is either to assert a common right or to challenge an asserted obligation. * * * It is quite another to hold that all those who are free alternatively either to assert rights or to challenge them are of a single class, so that
any group merely because it is of the class so constituted, may be deemed adequately to represent any others of the class in litigating their interests in either

alternative.   Such a selection of representatives for purposes of litigation, whose substantial interests are not necessarily or even probably the same as those whom they are deemed to represent, does not afford that protection to absent parties which due process requires.   The doctrine of representation of absent parties in a class suit has not hitherto been thought to go so far.   *   *   *   Apart from the opportunities it would afford for the fraudulent and collusive sacrifice of the rights of absent parties, we think that the representation in this case no more satisfies the requirements of due process than a trial by a judicial officer who is in such situation that he may have an interest in the outcome of the litigation in conflict with that of the litigants. *   *   *

The plaintiffs in the   *   *   *   [first] case sought to compel performance of the agreement in behalf of themselves and all others similarly situated.   They did not designate the defendants in the suit as a class or seek any injunction or other relief against others than the named defendants, and the decree which was entered did not purport to bind others.   In seeking to enforce the agreement the plaintiffs in that suit were not representing the petitioners here whose substantial interest is in resisting performance. The defendants in the first suit were not treated by the pleadings or decree as representing others or as foreclosing by their defense the rights of others, and even though nominal defendants, it does not appear that their interest in defeating the contract outweighed their interest in establishing its validity.   For a court in this situation to ascribe to either the plaintiffs or defendants the performance of such functions on behalf of petitioners here, is to attribute to them a power that it cannot be said that they had assumed to exercise, and a responsibility which, in view of their dual interests it does not appear that they could rightly discharge.

Reversed.

NOTES AND QUESTIONS

1.   Does *Hansberry* mean that everyone in a class must agree with the acting plaintiffs before the class is deemed to be adequately represented?   Consider the following statement:

A class action should not be denied merely because every member of the class might not be enthusiastic about enforcing his rights.   Some landowners might have preferred to see their water or air polluted by a factory which employed them but equity recognized the right to bring class actions to stop the pollution;   some shareholders are the defendants accused of improprieties yet they sue themselves when a class action is brought;   and some negroes may want segregated schools but they are represented as a class in suits by others who do not.   The court need concern itself only with whether those members who are parties are interested enough to be forceful advocates and with whether there is reason to believe that a substantial portion of the class would agree with their representatives were they given a choice.   The refusal to recognize the adequacy of representation in *Hansberry v. Lee* seems based as much on the collusive and false stipulation in the prior case as on a fear that the plaintiffs did not represent the views of other members of the class. Moreover, subsequent developments in the law of restrictive covenants explain the *Hansberry* decision as one based on public policy against discrimination * * *.

Weinstein, *Revision of Procedure: Some Problems in Class Actions,* 9 Buffalo L.Rev. 433, 460 (1960). See also Coskery v. Roberts & Mander Corp., 97 F. Supp. 14 (E.D.Pa.), appeal dismissed 189 F.2d 234 (3d Cir.1951) (class action permitted when only 1600 shares of stock, which were owned by a single person, out of 330,000 outstanding shares, opposed action); Keeffe, Levy & Donovan, *Lee Defeats Ben Hur,* 33 Cornell L.Q. 327, 337–39, 342–49 (1948). Should a class action be allowed to proceed if the class members have conflicting rights in the subject matter of the action but are seeking to assert a common right against an interloper? If the court determines that a conflict exists or that one or more of the representatives have interests that are antagonistic to some of the class members, must it dismiss the action?

2. To what extent is the relationship between the size of the class or the size of the representatives' claims and the number of representatives relevant to the question of adequacy? See EPSTEIN v. WEISS, 50 F.R.D. 387 (E.D.La. 1970), an action brought by a husband and wife who had tendered 30 shares on behalf of a class of shareholders who had tendered 280,843 shares pursuant to the same tender offer, asserting a securities violation in the offer. How many of the shares in *Epstein* should the court require the representatives to own to insure that the class members were adequately represented?

3. When the class is a defendant, the representatives in effect are determined by plaintiff's selection of class members to sue. At a minimum, the court must be particularly careful in scrutinizing the adequacy of the representation and the quality of the notice of the action given the class members. But even so, can the constitutional requirements of due process ever be met when there is a defendant class? This problem is discussed in VanDercreek, *The "Is" and "Ought" of Class Actions Under Federal Rule 23,* 48 Iowa L.Rev. 273, 278 (1963). See also 7 Wright & Miller, *Federal Practice and Procedure: Civil* § 1770 (1972).

In UNITED STATES v. E. I. du PONT de NEMOURS & CO., 13 F.R.D. 98 (N.D.Ill.1952), the court held that an antitrust action could not be brought against a defendant class since any participation in a conspiracy to monopolize was individual and one defendant could not fairly present the personal defenses of each class member. But in UNITED STATES v. CANTRELL, 307 F.Supp. 259 (E.D.La.1969), the court held that the government properly could bring a Rule 23 action against a defendant class alleging racial discrimination in the operation of bars and cocktail lounges, provided that all the class members were fully apprised of the action. Can these two decisions be reconciled?

4. SUBJECT MATTER JURISDICTION PROBLEMS IN FEDERAL–COURT CLASS ACTIONS

SNYDER v. HARRIS

GAS SERVICE COMPANY v. COBURN

Supreme Court of the United States, 1970.
394 U.S. 332, 89 S.Ct. 1053, 22 L.Ed.2d 319.

Certiorari to the United States Court of Appeals for the Eighth Circuit and the United States Court of Appeals for the Tenth Circuit.

Mr. Justice BLACK delivered the opinion of the Court.

* * * The issue presented by these two cases is whether separate and distinct claims presented by and for various claimants in a class action may be added together to provide the $10,000 jurisdictional amount in controversy.

Each of these cases involves a single plaintiff suing on behalf of himself and "all others similarly situated." In No. 109, Mrs. Margaret E. Snyder, a shareholder of Missouri Fidelity Union Trust Life Insurance Company, brought suit against members of the company's board of directors alleging that they had sold their shares of the company's stock for an amount far in excess of its fair market value, that this excess represented payment to these particular directors to obtain complete control of the company, and that under Missouri law the excess should properly be distributed among all the shareholders of the company and not merely to a few of them. The suit was brought in the United States District Court for the Eastern District of Missouri, * * * diversity of citizenship being alleged as the basis for federal jurisdiction. Since petitioner's allegations showed that she sought for herself only $8,740 in damages, respondent moved to dismiss on the grounds that the matter in controversy did not exceed $10,000. Petitioner contended, however, that her claim should be aggregated with those of the other members of her class, approximately 4,000 shareholders of the company stock. If all 4,000 potential claims were aggregated, the amount in controversy would be approximately $1,-200,000. The District Court held that the claims could not thus be aggregated to meet the statutory test of jurisdiction and the Court of Appeals for the Eighth Circuit * * * affirmed * * *.

In No. 117, Otto R. Coburn, a resident of Kansas, brought suit in the United States District Court for the District of Kansas against the Gas Service Company, a corporation marketing natural gas in Kansas. Jurisdiction was predicated upon diversity of citizenship. The complaint alleged that the Gas Service Company had billed and illegally collected a city franchise tax from Coburn and others living outside city limits.   Coburn alleged damages to himself of only $7.81.   Styling his complaint as a class action, however, Coburn sought relief on behalf of approximately 18,000 other Gas Service Company customers living outside of cities.   The amount by which other members of the class had been overcharged was, and is, unknown, but the complaint alleged that the aggregation of all these claims would in any event exceed $10,000.   The District Court overruled the Gas Company's motion to dismiss for failure to satisfy the jurisdictional amount and, on interlocutory appeal, the Court of Appeals for the Tenth Circuit affirmed   *   *   *.   We granted certiorari to resolve the conflict between the position of the   *   *   *   Fifth and the Eighth Circuits and that of the   *   *   *   Tenth Circuit.

*   *   *   The traditional judicial interpretation under all of   *   *   * [the jurisdictional amount] statutes has been from the beginning that the separate and distinct claims of two or more plaintiffs cannot be aggregated in order to satisfy the jurisdictional amount requirement.   Aggregation has been permitted only (1) in cases in which a single plaintiff seeks to aggregate two or more of his own claims against a single defendant and (2) in cases in which two or more plaintiffs unite to enforce a single title or right in which they have a common and undivided interest.   It is contended, however, that the adoption of a 1966 amendment to Rule 23 effectuated a change in this jurisdictional doctrine.   Under old Rule 23, class actions were divided into three categories   *   *   *.   True class actions were those in which the rights of the different class members were common and undivided; in such cases aggregation was permitted.   Spurious class actions, on the other hand, were in essence merely a form of permissive joinder in which parties with separate and distinct claims were allowed to litigate those claims in a single suit simply because the different claims involved common questions of law or fact.   In such cases aggregation was not permitted: each plaintiff had to show that his individual claim exceeded the jurisdictional amount.   The 1966 amendment to Rule 23 replaced the old categories with a functional approach to class actions.   The new Rule establishes guidelines for the appropriateness of class actions, makes provision for giving notice to absent members, allows members of the class to remove themselves from the litigation and provides that the judgment will include all members of the class who have not requested exclusion.   In No. 117, Gas Service Company, the Court of Appeals for the Tenth Circuit held that these changes in Rule 23 changed the jurisdictional amount doctrine as well.   *   *   * The court held that because aggregation was permitted in some class actions, it must now be permitted in all class actions under the new Rule.   We disagree and conclude, as did the Courts of Appeal for the Fifth and Eighth Circuits, that the adoption of amended Rule 23 did not and could not have brought about this change in the scope of the congressionally enacted grant of jurisdiction to the district courts.

The doctrine that separate and distinct claims could not be aggregated was never, and is not now, based upon the categories of old Rule 23 or of any rule of procedure. That doctrine is based rather upon this Court's interpretation of the statutory phrase "matter in controversy." The interpretation of this phrase as precluding aggregation substantially predates the 1938 Federal Rules of Civil Procedure. In 1911 this Court said in Troy Bank v. G. A. Whitehead & Co.:

> "When two or more plaintiffs, having separate and distinct demands, unite for convenience and economy in a single suit, it is essential that the demand of each be of the requisite jurisdictional amount * * *." 222 U.S. 39, 40, 32 S.Ct. 9, 56 L.Ed. 81.

By 1916 this Court was able to say in Pinel v. Pinel, 240 U.S. 594, 36 S.Ct. 416, 60 L.Ed. 817, that it was "settled doctrine" that separate and distinct claims could not be aggregated to meet the required jurisdictional amount. In Clark v. Paul Gray, Inc., 306 U.S. 583, 59 S.Ct. 744, 83 L.Ed. 1001 (1939), this doctrine, which had first been declared in cases involving joinder of parties, was applied to class actions under the then recently passed Federal Rules. * * * Nothing in the amended Rule 23 changes this doctrine. The class action plaintiffs in the two cases before us argue that since the new Rule will include in the judgment all members of the class who do not ask to be out by a certain date, the "matter in controversy" now encompasses all the claims of the entire class. But it is equally true that where two or more plaintiffs join their claims under the joinder provisions of Rule 20, each and every joined plaintiff is bound by the judgment. And it was in joinder cases of this very kind that the doctrine that distinct claims could not be aggregated was originally enunciated. * * * The fact that judgments under class actions formerly classified as spurious may now have the same effect as claims brought under the joinder provisions is certainly no reason to treat them *differently* from joined actions for purposes of aggregation.

Any change in the Rules that did purport to effect a change in the definition of "matter in controversy" would clearly conflict with the command of Rule 82 that "[t]hese rules shall not be construed to extend or limit the jurisdiction of the United States district courts * * *." * * *

For the reasons set out above, we think that it is unmistakably clear that the 1966 changes in Rule 23 did not and could not have changed the interpretation of the statutory phrase "matter in controversy." It is urged, however, that this Court should now overrule its established statutory interpretation and hold that "matter in controversy" encompasses the aggregation of all claims that can be brought together in a single suit, regardless of whether any single plaintiff has a claim that exceeds the required jurisdictional amount. It is argued in behalf of this position that (1) the determination of whether claims are "separate and distinct" is a troublesome question that breeds uncertainty and needless litigation, and (2) the inability of parties to aggregate numerous small claims will prevent some important questions from being litigated in federal courts. And both of these factors, it is argued, will tend to undercut the attempt of the Judicial Conference to promulgate efficient and modernized class action procedures. We think that whatever the merit of these contentions, they are not sufficient to justify our abandonment of a judicial interpretation of congressional language that has stood for more than a century and a half.

It is linguistically possible, of course, to interpret the old congressional phrase "matter in controversy" as including all claims that can be joined or brought in a single suit through the class action device. But, beginning with the first Judiciary Act in 1789 Congress has placed a jurisdictional amount requirement on access to the federal courts in certain classes of cases, including diversity actions. The initial requirement was $500 and a series of increases have * * * finally placed the amount at $10,000. Congress has thus consistently amended the amount-in-controversy section and re-enacted the "matter-in-controversy" language without change of its jurisdictional effect against a background of judicial interpretation that has consistently interpreted that congressionally enacted phrase as not encompassing the aggregation of separate and distinct claims. This judicial interpretation has been uniform since at least the 1832 decision of this Court in Oliver v. Alexander, 6 Pet. 143, 8 L.Ed. 349. There are no doubt hazards and pitfalls involved in assuming that re-enactment of certain language by Congress always freezes the existing judicial interpretation of the statutes involved. Here, however, the settled judicial interpretation of "amount in controversy" was implicitly taken into account by the relevant congressional committees in determining, in 1958, the extent to which the jurisdictional amount should be raised. It is quite possible, if not probable, that Congress chose the increase to $10,000 rather than the proposed increases to $7,500 or $15,000 on the basis of workload estimates which clearly relied on the settled doctrine that separate and distinct claims could not be aggregated. * * *

To overrule the aggregation doctrine at this late date would run counter to the congressional purpose in steadily increasing through the years the jurisdictional amount requirement. That purpose was to check, to some degree, the rising caseload of the federal courts, especially with regard to the federal courts' diversity of citizenship jurisdiction. Any change in the doctrine of aggregation in class action cases under Rule 23 would inescapably have to be applied as well to the liberal joinder provisions of Rule 20 and to the joinder of claims provisions of Rule 18. The result would be to allow aggregation of practically any claims of any parties that for any reason happen to be brought together in a single action. This would seriously undercut the purpose of the jurisdictional amount requirement. The expansion of the federal caseload could be most noticeable in class actions brought on the basis of diversity of citizenship. Under current doctrine, if one member of a class is of diverse citizenship from the class' opponent, and no non-diverse members are named parties, the suit may be brought in federal court even though all other members of the class are citizens of the same State as the defendant and have nothing to fear from trying the lawsuit in the courts of their own State. * * *

Finally, it has been argued that unless the established aggregation principles are overturned, the functional advantages alleged to inhere in the new class action rule will be undercut by resort to the old forms. But the disadvantageous results are overemphasized, we think, since lower courts have developed largely workable standards for determining when claims are joint and common, and therefore entitled to be aggregated, and when they are separate and distinct and therefore not aggregable. Moreover, while the class action device serves a useful function across the entire range of legal questions, the jurisdictional amount requirement applies almost exclusively to controversies based upon diversity of citizenship. A large part of those matters involving federal questions can be brought, by way of class actions or otherwise, without regard to the amount in controversy. Suits involving issues of state law and brought on the basis of diversity of citizenship can often be most appropriately tried in state courts. The underlying claims in the two cases before us, for example, will be determined exclusively on the basis of Missouri and Kansas law, respectively. In No. 109, a separate suit litigating the underlying issues has already been filed in a Missouri state court. In No. 117, the residents of Kansas who contend that certain gas service charges are not authorized by Kansas law can bring a class action under Kansas procedures that are patterned on former Federal Rule 23. There is no compelling reason for this Court to overturn a settled interpretation of an important congressional statute in order to add to the burdens of an already overloaded federal court system. Nor can we overlook the fact that the Congress that permitted the Federal Rules to go into effect was assured before doing so that none of the Rules would either expand or contract the jurisdiction of federal courts. If there is a present need to expand the jurisdiction of those courts we cannot overlook the fact that the Constitution specifically vests that power in the Congress, not in the courts.

The judgment in No. 109 is Affirmed.

Affirmed.

The judgment in No. 117 is Reversed.

Reversed.

Mr. Justice FORTAS, with whom Mr. Justice DOUGLAS joins, dissenting.

The Court today refuses to conform the judge-made formula for computing the amount in controversy in class actions with the 1966 amendment to Rule 23 of the Federal Rules of Civil Procedure. The effect of this refusal is substantially to undermine a generally welcomed and long-needed reform in federal procedure.

Its impact will be noticeable not only in diversity of citizenship cases but also in important classes of federal question cases in which federal jurisdiction must be based on 28 U.S.C. § 1331, the general federal question provision, rather than on one of the specific grants of federal jurisdiction.

The artificial, awkward, and unworkable distinctions between "joint," "common," and "several" claims and between "true," "hybrid," and "spurious" class actions which the amendment of Rule 23 sought to terminate is now re-established in federal procedural law. Litigants, lawyers, and federal courts must now continue to be ensnared in their complexities in all cases where one or more of the coplaintiffs have a claim of less than the jurisdictional amount, usually $10,000.

It was precisely this morass that the 1966 amendment to Rule 23 sought to avoid. The amendment had as its purpose to give the Federal District Courts wider discretion as to the type of claims that could be joined in litigation. That amendment replaced the metaphysics of conceptual analysis of the "character of the right sought to be enforced" by a pragmatic, workable definition of when class actions might be maintained that is, when claims of various claimants might be aggregated in a class action, and it carefully provided procedures and safeguards to avoid unfairness.

* * * Now the Court, for reasons which in my opinion will not stand analysis, defeats the purpose of the amendment as applied to cases like those before us here and insists upon a perpetuation of distinctions which the profession had hoped would become only curiosities of the past.

The Court is led to this unfortunate result by its insistence upon regarding the method of computing the amount in controversy as embodied in an Act of Congress, as unaffected by the subsequent amendment of Rule 23, and as immune from judicial re-examination because any change would be an impermissible expansion of the jurisdiction of the courts. None of these premises is correct.

I.

Since the first Judiciary Act, Congress has included in certain grants of jurisdiction to the federal courts—notably the grants of jurisdiction based on diversity of citizenship and the later-established grant of a general jurisdiction to consider cases raising federal questions—a requirement that the "matter in controversy" exceed a stated amount of money. Congress has never expanded or explained the bare words of these successive jurisdictional amount statutes. Over the years the courts themselves have developed a detailed and complex set of rules for determining when the jurisdictional amount rquirements are met.

Among these rules is the proposition that multiple parties cannot aggregate their "separate and distinct" claims to reach the jurisdictional amount. * * * Applying that general principle to traditional property law concepts, the courts developed the more specialized rule that multiple parties who asserted very similar legal claims could not aggregate them to make up the jurisdictional amount if their interests, however similar in fact, were in legal theory "several," * * * but that such aggregation was permissible where the parties claimed undivided interests in a single "joint" right. * * *

This general aggregation rule, and its much later application to class actions, rest entirely on judicial decisions, not on any Act of Congress. There is certainly no reason the specific application of this body of federal decisional law to class actions should be immune from re-evaluation after a fundamental change in the structure of federal class actions has made its continuing application wholly anomalous.

* * *

The hearings and reports on the 1958 statute raising the jurisdictional amount from $3,000 to $10,000—which the majority fastens on as the adopting re-enactment—include not one word about the whole complex body of rules by which courts determine when the amount is at issue, much less any reference to the particular problem of aggregation of claims in class action cases. The majority speculates that it is "possible, if not probable," that Congress "implicitly" took into account the existing aggregation doctrines as applied to class action cases when it decided to raise the jurisdictional amount to $10,000 rather than some higher or lower amount. If we are to attribute to Congress any thoughts on this highly technical and specialized matter, it seems to me far more reasonable to assume that Congress was aware that the courts had been developing the interpretation of the jurisdictional amount requirement in class actions and would continue to do so after the 1958 amendments.

* * *

II.

Whatever the pre-1966 status of the aggregation doctrines in class action cases, the amendment of the Rules in that year permits and even requires a re-examination of the application of the doctrines to such cases. The fundamental change in the law of class actions effected by the new Rule 23 requires that prior subsidiary judicial doctrine developed for application to the old Rule be harmonized with the new procedural law. By Act of Congress, the Rules of Procedure, when promulgated according to the statutorily defined process, have the effect of law and supersede all prior laws in conflict with them. 28 U.S.C. § 2072 (1964 ed., Supp. III). Thus, even if the old aggregation doctrines were embodied in statute—as they are not—they could not stand if they conflicted with the New Rule.

The jurisdictional amount statutes require placing a value on the "matter in controversy" in a civil action. Once it is decided under the new Rule that an action may be maintained as a class action, it is the claim of the whole class and not the individual economic stakes of the separate members of the class which is the "matter in controversy." That this is so is perhaps most clearly indicated by the fact that the judgment in a class action properly maintained as such includes all members of the class. Rule 23(c)(3). This effect of the new Rule in broadening the scope of the "controversy" in a class action to include the combined interests of all the members of the class is illustrated by the facts of No. 117. That class action, if allowed to proceed, would, under the Rule, determine not merely whether the gas company wrongfully collected $7.81 in taxes from Mr. Coburn. It would also result in a judgment which, subject to the limits of due process, would determine—authoritatively and not merely as a matter of precedent—the status of the taxes collected from the 18,000 other people allegedly in the class Coburn seeks to represent. That being the case, it is hard to understand why the fact that the alleged claims are, in terms of the old Rule categories, "several" rather than "joint," means that the "matter in controversy" for jurisdictional amount purposes must be regarded as the $7.81 Mr. Coburn claims instead of the thousands of dollars of alleged overcharges of the whole class, the status of all of which would be determined by the judgment.

In past development of rules concerning the jurisdictional amount requirement, the courts have, properly, responded to changes in the procedural and substantive law. Now, confronted by an issue of the meaning of the jurisdictional amount requirement arising in the context of a new procedural law of class actions, we should continue to take account of such changes. We should not allow the judicial interpretation of the jurisdictional amount requirement to become petrified into forms which are products of, and appropriate to, another time. To do this would vitiate a significant part of the reform intended to be accomplished by the amendment of Rule 23. * * *

III.

Permitting aggregation in class action cases does not involve any violation of the principle, expressed in Rule 82 and inherent in the whole procedure for the promulgation and amendment of the Federal Rules, that the courts cannot by rule expand their own jurisdictions. While the Rules cannot change subject-matter jurisdiction, changes in the forms and practices of the federal courts through changes in the Rules frequently and necessarily will affect the occasions on which subject-matter jurisdiction is exercised because they will in some cases make a difference in what cases the federal courts will hear and who will be authoritatively bound by the judgment. For example, the development of the law of joinder and ancillary jurisdiction under the Federal Rules has influenced the "jurisdiction" of the federal courts in this broader sense. Indeed, the promulgation of the old Rule 23 provided a new means for resolving in a single federal litigation, based on diversity jurisdiction, the claims of all members of a class, even though some in the class were not of diverse citizenship from parties on the other side.

Similarly, the creation in a Rule having statutory effect of a new type of class action—one meeting the requirements of the new Rule as to suitability for class-wide resolution, although involving "several" interests of the members of the class—has changed the procedural context in which the subject-matter-jurisdiction statutes, like those referring to jurisdictional amount, are to be applied. * * *

For these reasons, I would measure the value of the "matter in controversy" in a class action found otherwise proper under the amended Rule 23 by the monetary value of the claim of the whole class.

NOTES AND QUESTIONS

1. The *Snyder* case is discussed in 22 Fla.L.Rev. 154 (1969); 83 Harv. L.Rev. 202 (1969); and 58 Ky.L.J. 403 (1970). See also 7 Wright & Miller, *Federal Practice and Procedure: Civil* § 1756 (1972). Prior to the 1966 amendments to Federal Rule 23 the general rule was that diversity of citizenship in a class action was determined by the citizenship of the named parties. Does *Snyder* change that rule?

2. In DIERKS v. THOMPSON, 414 F.2d 453 (1st Cir.1969), the court allowed the members of a plaintiff class to aggregate their claims in a suit by former employees to establish a trust fund against a corporate profit sharing plan. Arguably, of course, each employee could have been viewed as possessing an individual claim arising out of his separate contribution. According to Judge Aldrich: "Since plaintiffs, in one aspect, are seeking to establish a trust fund as distinguished from individual cash claims against the defendants, however, we are satisfied, * * * that this is a proper class suit." Id. at 456. The fact that some form of equitable relief is being sought does not mean that the class members necessarily will be found to have a common or undivided interest in the subject matter of the suit. In PORTRERO HILL COMMUNITY ACTION COMMITTEE v. HOUSING AUTHORITY OF THE CITY & COUNTY OF SAN FRANCISCO, 410 F.2d 974 (9th Cir.1969), the court denied aggregation in a suit by tenants in a federally financed low-cost housing project seeking a judgment directing the local authorities to improve the premises. Judge Duniway, speaking for the court, said:

> When we look to the facts of the present case, we find that plaintiffs have not shown any rights peculiar to the tenants of the Portrero Hill Project as a group. Rather their rights appear to arise only from the status of each as individual lessee of a portion of the project premises. Each project resident holds his own lease which confers benefits on the one hand and prescribes duties and obligations on the other, and these rights and obligations exist only between the single tenant and the Housing Authority. Accordingly, no "single right in which all have a common and undivided interest" has been shown, and the claims of the individual tenants cannot be aggregated.

Id. at 978. Would the decision in *Portrero* have been different if plaintiffs had sought to impress a constructive trust on a portion of their rents, which then would be used to improve their homes?

3. Given the Supreme Court's decision in *Snyder,* is a class action maintainable if the class representatives or at least one of them has a claim for more than the jurisdictional amount but the other class members do not? Consider the following argument:

> The rationale of the *Snyder* decision is inapplicable to the issue before us [whether if the representatives have sufficient jurisdictional claims the other class members may enter the suit under ancillary jurisdiction]. There is no "settled line of precedent" that every member of a Rule 23(b)(3) class must satisfy the amount in controversy requirement.

> * * * [W]ithin the last few years many federal courts have held that a court has discretion to adjudicate a jurisdictionally insufficient claim joined with a claim for more than $10,000 if the claims derive primarily from the same operative facts. * * *

> The other reason for the result in *Snyder*—to avoid a large increase in the workload of the federal courts—is also inapplicable to the present controversy. The four named plaintiffs here meet the jurisdictional requirements; a federal court must adjudicate their claims. The burden on the federal courts would not be substantially increased if the claims of the other class members were to be heard by the same court; the predominate questions of law or fact with regard to those claims must be common to all the claims or a class action could not be brought. * * *

ZAHN v. INTERNATIONAL PAPER CO., 469 F.2d 1033, 1038–39, (2d Cir.1972) (Timbers, J., dissenting). The Supreme Court, relying heavily on the rationale of *Snyder,* rejected these arguments and held that when members of a plaintiff class have separate and distinct claims, each member's claim must satisfy the jurisdictional amount requirement. —— U.S. ——, 94 S.Ct. 505, 38 L.Ed.2d 511 (1973). Note that in Jacobson v. Atlantic City Hospital, 392 F.2d 149 (3d Cir.1968), plaintiff was allowed to join claims for less than the jurisdictional amount against some defendants with claims in excess of that amount against other defendants. Is this distinguishable from the class-action situation?

4. Considerable attention has been given to the effect of the *Snyder* decision and it has been sharply criticized on the ground that it thwarts the basic purpose of the 1966 amendments.

> * * * [T]he analysis employed in the Snyder case is discouraging. The majority opinion by Justice Black, when it pulverizes the class to examine the interest of each named plaintiff, harks back to terminological distinctions that one would have thought inapposite to the new Rule; indeed Justice Black seems pro tanto to resurrect the 'spurious' action. The net effect of the decision is to disfavor the small fellow and thereby to defeat a main purpose of the Rule revision.

Kaplan, *A Prefatory Note, in The Class Action—A Symposium,* 10 B.C.Ind. & Com.L.Rev. 497, 498 (1969). The *Snyder* holding has been attacked by consumer advocates on the ground that, contrary to Mr. Justice Black's assertions, there are no effective state remedies or procedures available and the parties are left without any means of redress. See Starrs, *The Consumer Class Action,* 49 B.U.L.Rev. 209, 407 (1969) (two parts), for a detailed discussion of consumer class actions brought under state law. Thus there has been considerable pressure for federal legislation establishing a statutory consumer class action in which no jurisdictional amount would be required or for the overruling of *Snyder*.

5. Some attention has been given to means of avoiding or circumventing the aggregation problem. For example, is it possible for the state to bring an action on behalf of those of its citizens who purchased a defective product manufactured by defendant but none of whom have sustained individual damages in excess of $10,000? Would it make any difference if the state itself was a purchaser of the product and claimed damages in excess of the jurisdictional amount? See Comment, *Wrongs Without Remedy: The Concept of Parens Patriae Suits for Treble Damages Under the Antitrust Laws*, 43 S.Cal.L.Rev. 570 (1970). Could the state bring a traditional class action on behalf of its citizens, having them assign their claims to the state attorney general for purposes of litigation? See State of West Virginia v. Chas. Pfizer & Co., 440 F.2d 1079 (2d Cir.), certiorari denied 404 U.S. 871, 92 S.Ct. 81, 30 L.Ed.2d 115 (1971). See also Simburg, *State Protection of Economy and Environment*, 6 Colum.J. of Law & Soc. Prob. 411 (1970). See generally 7A Wright & Miller, *Federal Practice and Procedure: Civil* § 1782 (1972).

5. OTHER PROCEDURAL MATTERS

NOTICE

The requirement that some form of notice procedure be provided to inform class members of the pendency of the action is tied to the belief that it would be constitutionally impermissible to bind the absentees to a judgment entered in a Rule 23 action unless their interests were adequately protected so that functionally they have had their day in court. Notice serves to inform the absentees about the litigation so that they can take whatever steps they deem appropriate to make certain that their interests are represented. Reread *Mullane v. Central Hanover Bank & Trust Co.*, p. 115, supra. Rule 23(c)(2) provides for mandatory notice only in actions brought under Rule 23(b)(3); notice is discretionary for actions under Rule 23(b)(1) and (2) and may be given in those actions pursuant to Rule 23 (d)(2). Why is a distinction drawn between actions under Rule 23(b) (1) and (2) and those brought under Rule 23(b)(3)? Isn't notice constitutionally required in all class suits? See 7A Wright & Miller, *Federal Practice and Procedure: Civil* § 1786 (1972), and Comment, *Constitutional and Statutory Requirements of Notice Under Rule 23(c)(2)*, in *The Class Action—A Symposium*, 10 B.C.Ind. & Com.L.Rev. 571 (1969).

In JOHNSON v. CITY OF BATON ROUGE, LOUISIANA, 50 F.R.D. 295 (E.D.La.1970), four named plaintiffs, who were Black residents of a parish, brought a class action seeking to enjoin the recurrence of certain alleged incidents, which they characterized as examples of discriminatory police practices against Blacks. The court thought that publishing a notice of the action would pose an unnecessary risk of further disturbing the interracial relations in the community while contributing nothing to the resolution of the lawsuit and declined to order publication. What other factors might outweigh the need to give notice?

Note that the first sentence of Rule 23(c)(2) states that "the court shall direct * * * individual notice to all members who can be identified through reasonable effort." Once the court determines that the class members can be ascertained, does the rule really require that individual notice be sent to each of those members? Insisting upon individual notice occasionally would result in the suit being abandoned because of the financial burden it might impose. This situation was presented in EISEN v. CARLISLE & JACQUELIN, 52 F.R.D. 253 (S.D.N.Y.1971), an antitrust suit on behalf of approximately 3,750,000 odd-lot investors against the major odd-lot dealers on the New York Stock Exchange. The cost of individual notice was estimated at $400,000, which would have prevented plaintiffs from continuing the action. The district court devised a notice procedure that cost between $10,000 and $20,000. It ordered individual notice to be given to the member firms of the New York Stock Exchange, to commercial banks with large trust departments, to class members who had ten or more odd lot transactions during the period in question (about 2,000 persons), and to 5,000 individuals chosen randomly from the 2,000,000 identifiable persons in the class. In addition, notice was published in various major newspapers. After a preliminary hearing on the merits the trial court ruled that the defendants initially should bear 90 percent of the cost of giving notice since the plaintiff class was more than likely to prevail on its claim, 54 F.R.D. 565 (S.D.N.Y.1972). On appeal, the Second Circuit reversed, holding that individual notice was required by the explicit language of Rule 23(c)(2) and that if the notice would be so costly as to prevent plaintiffs from pursuing the litigation, then that indicated the suit was not manageable and should be dismissed as an improper class action. 479 F.2d 1005 (2d Cir.1973), certiorari granted —— U.S. ——, 94 S.Ct. 235, 38 L.Ed.2d 146 (1973). See Note, *Managing the Large Class Action: Eisen v. Carlisle & Jacquelin*, 87 Harv.L.Rev. 426 (1973); Note, *Notice, Mini-Hearings and Fluid Class Recovery: Some Reflections on Eisen v. Carlisle & Jacquelin and the Scope of Fed.R.Civ.P. 23*, 59 Iowa L.Rev. 252 (1973). Is this decision consistent with the purpose of class actions to permit the vindication of small claims? Isn't the approach taken by the district court in *Eisen* consistent with the standards set forth in *Mullane v. Central Hanover Bank & Trust Co.*, p. 115, supra? Are there any other ways of giving notice that can be utilized to reduce the burden on the class representatives that would be consistent with a literal reading of the rule?

The question of what should be included in the notice is a serious one since care must be taken to give the absent members a balanced picture of what the suit involves, as well as informing them of the possible litigation burdens that may be imposed if the suit is unsuccessful. Moreover, there has been great concern about preventing the notice from being used for claim solicitation. See 7A Wright & Miller, *Federal Practice and Procedure: Civil* §§ 1787–88 (1972).

SETTLEMENT

Rule 23(e) provides that a class action cannot be dismissed or compromised without court approval and that notice of any proposed dismissal or compromise must be given to all the class members. The purpose of these requirements is to protect the nonparty members from an unfair or unjust settlement by providing the absentees with the opportunity to contest the action should the representatives become fainthearted before the action is adjudicated. If the representatives reach a settlement before the court makes a finding under subdivision (c)(1) that the action properly is brought under Rule 23, is court approval and notice of the proposal to each of the class members necessary under Rule 23(e)? See Ace Heating & Plumbing Co. v. Crane Co., 453 F.2d 30 (3d Cir.1971).

The Second Circuit, in WEIGHT WATCHERS OF PHILADELPHIA, INC. v. WEIGHT WATCHERS INT'L, INC., 455 F.2d 770 (2d Cir.1972), has held that defendant may negotiate settlements with individual class members under judicial supervision prior to the determination that the action properly is brought under Rule 23 and that Rule 23(e) does not apply. However, these settlements would not affect the rights of any nonsettling class members. Judge Friendly, speaking for the court, noted that defendant's conduct could eliminate enough claims so that joinder of those remaining no longer would be impracticable, thereby destroying the class action. But he stated: "[W]e are unable to perceive any legal theory that would endow a plaintiff * * * with a right to prevent negotiation of settlements between the defendant and other potential members of the class who are of a mind to do this * * *." Id. at 773. Is this decision consistent with the purpose of Rule 23(e)? What difference does it make that defendant in *Weight Watchers* was attempting to negotiate with the individual unnamed members of the class rather than with the representative parties?

Consider the following comment in the Manual for Complex Litigation § 1.46 (1973 ed.):

> Another aspect of settlement of class actions which requires examination is the growing practice of forming tentative classes for the purposes of settlement. Such classes have been formed with court approved provisions for notice to members of the class informing them that they shall accept the settlement or opt out and be required or permitted to litigate their claims for relief. There is, to say the least, serious doubt that this practice is authorized by Rule 23 as amended, even if it is conceded that the courts are expected to develop new methods of employing the amended Rule 23.
>
>   *   *   *
>
> Several reasons support this conclusion. (1) Rule 23 does not authorize formation of tentative classes for the purpose of

settlement. (2) There can be no assurance that the class members will be adequately represented in the settlement negotiations until the findings which are condition precedent to the formation of a class are made by the court after an opportunity for an evidentiary hearing. Formation of a tentative class for the purpose of settlement with a requirement that the class member accept the settlement or opt out and litigate independently denies to the members of the class the opportunity to show the inadequacy of the representation of the class by the representative party or parties agreeing to the settlement and their counsel. (3) The appropriate membership of the class and the identity of the members cannot be determined in the absence of an opportunity for hearing and judicial findings of fact and conclusions of law. Nor can there be any assurance that the tentative class will be composed of interests which are not conflicting. Absent such findings and conclusions it will be impossible to determine how many members there are in a class, who they are, the aggregate of claims of each member in relation to the total claims of all members of the class and, therefore, the amount of money which will be payable to each member of the class. This information would seem to be essential to making any rational choice whether to remain in the class and accept the benefits of the settlements or to opt out. (4) In the absence of the development of the information relevant to liability, damages, and the expense of preparation for trial and of trial, there cannot be a fair recognition in settlement negotiations of the potential liability of the party or parties opposing the class and the potential damages that might be recovered for the class. (5) Formation of such a class preempts determination of the question of whether the claim for relief should be litigated for the members of the class or should be the subject of further pretrial preparation with a view toward securing a better settlement or a trial on the merits; and it also preempts the question of what parties and counsel should represent the tentative class since there must be an unofficially negotiated earlier settlement for the purpose of the tentative formation of the class. (6) The formation of a tentative class for the purpose of settlement denies to the class member the choice contemplated by amended Rule 23 to become a member of the proposed class for the purpose of litigation with adequate representation as a member of a litigating class. (7) Formation of such a class denies to a member of the class the right to appear in the action as a party and to maintain the position of a litigating party. (8) Formation of such a class results in a long delay in preparation of the case for trial of those parties who desire to litigate their claims for relief. (9) In the absence of reasonable discovery conducted on an adversary basis by counsel representing the class, it is impossible to determine whether the proposed settlement has any relation to the economic facts of life relevant to the case.

3. What factors should the court take into account when determining whether to approve a proposed settlement? How important is a finding that none of the other class members have intervened to oppose the settlement?

ATTORNEYS' FEES

Although there is no reference in Rule 23 to the power of the court to award attorneys' fees, the attorney for the successful representative parties typically will be awarded a fee. The rationale for this practice is that since his work on behalf of the representatives has conferred a benefit on all the class members, fairness demands that counsel be compensated out of the fund awarded them. In some contexts the fee is awarded pursuant to a specific statutory provision designed to provide an incentive for "private attorneys general." Traditionally the factor most relied upon in setting the amount of the fee has been the amount of benefit the lawsuit has produced. Because class-action settlements and recoveries generally are very substantial, this has led to awards that are extremely large and several courts have expressed concern that that class-action device may promote strike suits and bring bench and bar into disrepute. As one judge has warned: "[T]he attorneys who are taking advantage of class actions to obtain lucrative fees will find themselves vulnerable to the criticism expressed in the Italian proverb, 'A lawsuit is a fruit tree planted in a lawyer's garden.'" State of Illinois v. Harper & Row Publishers, Inc., 55 F.R.D. 221, 224 (N.D.Ill.1972). What factors other than the amount of recovery might the court consider in awarding attorneys' fees in a class action? See 7A Wright & Miller, *Federal Practice and Procedure: Civil* § 1803 (1972). See also Manual for Complex Litigation § 1.47 (1973 ed.). If an attorney's fee is to be awarded from a settlement fund and the representatives also have contingent fee arrangements with the attorney, how can the court equalize the fee burden between litigating and nonlitigating class members? See Lindy Bros. Builders, Inc. v. American Radiator & Standard Sanitary Corp., 487 F.2d 161 (3d Cir.1973). Can the court award an attorney's fee if the only relief awarded is an injunction?

ADMINISTERING JUDICIAL RELIEF

The award of relief to a plaintiff class that has brought suit successfully under Rule 23(b)(3) often presents some unusual difficulties because the members have been brought together by common questions of law or fact and considerations of convenience, and the damages they seek typically are individual in character and disparate in amount. As described by Judge

Weinstein in a speech to a Fifth Circuit Judicial Conference: "If this difficulty is ignored, then class action litigation seems little more than a lengthy, complicated search for an empty pot of gold at the end of the rainbow rather than a practical device for the fair resolution of disputes through the judicial process." Is the management problem in a class action any greater than it would be in a large multiparty antitrust suit? The court must determine not only the amount of each individual's damages but also how best to distribute the recovery among the class members in an efficient and inexpensive fashion without significantly impairing the fund. See Miller, *Problems in Administering Judicial Relief in Class Actions Under Federal Rule 23(b)(3),* 54 F.R.D. 501 (1972).

One possible approach is to try the damage issue once, arrive at a single damage award for the entire class, and then develop a means of dividing and distributing the lump sum among the class members. Any excess not distributed to the class might be applied to some socially desirable objective. For example, in STATE OF WEST VIRGINIA v. CHAS. PFIZER & CO., 440 F.2d 1079 (2d Cir.), certiorari denied 404 U.S. 871, 92 S.Ct. 81, 30 L.Ed.2d 115 (1971), a series of private antitrust class actions against drug companies, the court was faced with the problem of distributing a settlement of $100,000,000 to government entities, institutions, individual purchasers, wholesalers, and retailers. Although a detailed schedule was formulated for the settlement, the court noted that some individual purchasers never would present claims and suggested that the residue of the fund might be expended in ways that would prevent future conduct of the kind that gave rise to the *Pfizer* litigation. See Comment, *Damage Distribution in Class Actions: The Cy Pres Remedy,* 39 U.Chi.L.Rev. 448 (1972). But what if the case is not settled before trial? Can the lump sum approach be utilized without jeopardizing the class members' individual right to a jury trial of their damage claims? See Eisen v. Carlisle & Jacquelin, 479 F.2d 1005 (2d Cir.), certiorari granted —— U.S. ——, 94 S.Ct. 235, 38 L.Ed.2d 146 (1973).

Another example of judicial flexibility and creativity in handling the class recovery is DAAR v. YELLOW CAB CO., 67 Cal.2d 695, 63 Cal. Rptr. 724, 433 P.2d 732 (1967), which was discussed at pp. 572–73, supra. Faced with numerous class members who had no records of their dealings with defendant cab company and thus could not prove the amount of their damages, the court ordered defendant to lower its rates for a certain amount of time for the benefit of the public in general. Doesn't this amount to an award of punitive damages?

The court often will seek assistance from the parties by asking them to submit proposals for managing the damage distribution with a minimum of judicial supervision. By what other ways might the court relieve its administrative burdens and expedite the conclusion of the action?

BINDING EFFECT

Class actions provide an exception to the general rule that a judgment in an action binds only those persons who have been named as parties and served with process. A judgment entered in a class suit will be binding on all the class members, provided they have been adequately represented. This was not always the case. Prior to the 1966 amendment of Federal Rule 23 it was held that the effect of a judgment in a federal class action depended on the type of class action that was involved: a judgment in a "true" class action bound all the class members; a judgment in a "hybrid" suit bound all the class members with respect to their rights in the property that was the subject matter of the suit; and a judgment in a "spurious" class action bound only the parties before the court.

In UNION CARBIDE & CARBON CORP. v. NISLEY, 300 F.2d 561 (10th Cir.1961), petition for certiorari dismissed 371 U.S. 801, 83 S.Ct. 13, 9 L.Ed.2d 46 (1963), 36 miners brought a private action against two mining companies that allegedly monopolized or attempted to monopolize interstate trade in vanadium-bearing ore in the Colorado Plateau. The suit sought recovery for losses caused by defendants' alleged activities. The second count in the complaint took the form of a class action in which plaintiffs sought to recover for themselves and for a group of miners that had approximately 400 members. The jury returned separate verdicts in favor of the 36 plaintiffs and the unnamed plaintiffs. Following the verdicts, the court entered an order giving the unnamed miners six months in which to appear and file claims before a special master who was charged with the responsibility of determining the extent, if any, of each miner's damages in accordance with a prescribed per-pound formula. Toward the end of a lengthy opinion, the court dealt with the appellants' contention that the trial court's procedure erroneously authorized intervention by the unnamed plaintiffs after the rendition of a favorable verdict. The court dealt with what it termed to be "an unresolved question of procedural law, i. e., whether in a class action * * *, non-participating plaintiffs may intervene after determination of defendants' liability, to share in the fruits of a judgment obtained by their participating representatives." In the course of analyzing the practice under the pre-1966 version of Federal Rule 23(a), the court stated:

> One line of authority is to the effect that a 23(a)(3) class action is merely another joinder device, placed in the Federal Rules in order to obviate the jurisdictional requirements of complete diversity "where there are numerous persons who have claims or defenses that involve a common question of law or fact." * * * From this it has been reasoned that 23(a)(3) serves only this one purpose and, consequently, only those persons who are actually parties to the litigation are bound by or can share in a money judgment. * * *

Other courts, in cases where there has been an identifiable class, have allowed unnamed plaintiffs to intervene and share in the judgment obtained by their representatives, insofar as each is able to prove both membership in the class and damages. *   *   *

Undoubtedly this latter solution results in the more expeditious and efficient disposition of litigation and ought therefore to be favored. If, on the other hand, this type of class action was intended to have as its only function an adjunctive method of permissive joinder, there would be no logical reason for its being made a part of Rule 23 instead of another means of joinder under Rule 20. It is of no avail to say that 23(a)(3) is merely meant to obviate the requirements of complete diversity and thereby allow joinder by non-diverse parties in cases where there are numerous members of the class.   *   *   *   [W]e envisage it as having a broader purpose—to allow a final determination of common questions of law and fact.   *   *   *

It is likewise sophistic to argue that mutuality of estoppel operates to prevent the unnamed miners from intervening after rendition of the verdict. For one is not precluded from claiming the benefits of a favorable judgment to which he was not a named party, simply because he would not have been bound by an unfavorable judgment rendered against named parties who did not adequately represent his interests.   *   *   *   But, even so, whether these plaintiffs would have been bound by an unfavorable judgment is not decisive. The critical fact is that the court has yet to enter the final judgments, and mutuality of estoppel is therefore inapposite. Before any final judgment is rendered, all unnamed claimants will be present and required to prove their identity with the class who were damaged by force of defendants' unlawful acts. Defendants' liability and the extent thereof has been competently proven by the named plaintiffs and it would be grossly redundant to say that it must be proven again by the unnamed members of the represented class.   *   *   *

Id. at 588–89.

What is the effect of the 1966 amendment of Federal Rule 23 on *Nisely*? Why should class members in Rule 23(b)(3) actions have the privilege to opt out, if members in suits brought under the other provisions of Rule 23(b) do not? In order to control the course of the litigation and determine the scope of the action, some courts have required class members who intend to prove damages to file a proof-of-claim form at some stage in the action; if they fail to do so, they are not allowed to collect from any fund that might be recovered. How can this practice be reconciled with Rule 23(c)(2)(B), which provides that the notice to Rule 23(b)(3) class members should state that "the judgment, whether favorable or not, will include all members who do not request exclusion"? See Manual for Complex Litigation § 1.45 (1973 ed.).

Can an absent member of a successful plaintiff class take advantage of a judgment in a Rule 23 action when she was not formally notified of the action and had no opportunity to intervene or assure that her interests were adequatey represented? Consider the argument made in PASQUIER v. TARR, 318 F.Supp. 1350 (E.D.La.1970), that to allow the member to take advantage of such a judgment

> gives absent members of the class two bites at the apple at the expense of the defendant. For if a court rules on the merits in favor of the class, the absent members can reap the benefits of such a decision. But if the court should rule against the class on the merits, then * * * they can argue that they were not adequately represented.

Id. at 1354. Doesn't the fact that plaintiffs were successful in the first action indicate that they were adequately represented and that due process considerations have been satisfied? Schrader v. Selective Service System Local Bd. No. 76 of Wisconsin, 329 F.Supp. 966 (W.D.Wis.1971).

Is a class action judgment subject to collateral attack on the ground that the class was not adequately represented even though the court initially found that the action satisfied Rule 23(a)(4)? See Gonzales v. Cassidy, 474 F.2d 67 (5th Cir.1973); Note, *Collateral Attack on the Binding Effect of Class Action Judgments*, 87 Harv.L.Rev. 589 (1974).

SECTION B. INTERPLEADER

---

1. HISTORICAL LIMITATIONS ON THE USE OF INTERPLEADER

HANCOCK OIL CO. v. INDEPENDENT DISTRIBUTING CO.

Supreme Court of California, 1944.
24 Cal.2d 497, 150 P.2d 463.

EDMONDS, Justice. * * *

According to the complaint [filed by two corporate lessees of certain real property], in 1936 W. L. Hopkins and Gertrude Ann Hopkins, his wife, leased certain real property to Hancock Oil Company of California and R. R. Bush Oil Company. Landowner's royalties of approximately $1,500. have accrued. It is also alleged that in 1941, Independent Distributing Co., a copartnership composed of Merritt Bloxom, Eugene E. Olwell and Murray M. Olwell, brought an action asserting that W. L. Hopkins, Gertrude Ann Hopkins, and two persons sued by fictitious names, hold the real property described in the lease in trust for them. The relief sought in the suit of Independent Distributing Co. was an accounting of the rents of the land.

The copartnership and the copartners, together with W. L. Hopkins and Gertrude Ann Hopkins, H. James Hopkins and W. L. Hopkins, trustees of Wilbur T. Hopkins Trust, and H. James Hopkins and W. L. Hopkins, trustees of the H. James Hopkins Trust, are named as the defendants in the present suit, the charge of the complaint being that the copartnership and the copartners claim to be the owners of the land described in the lease and entitled to all of the landowner's royalties accrued and to accrue under that agreement. A further assertion of the complaint is that the defendants other than the copartnership and the copartners also claim the same royalties and by reason of these conflicting claims the lessees cannot safely determine to whom the rent should be paid.   *   *   *

To this complaint Merritt Bloxom, Eugene E. Olwell, Murray M. Olwell and Independent Distributing Co. filed an answer alleging that they are the owners of the property and entitled to all of the rents and profits from it. They also assert that the defendants named Hopkins are holding title to the property in trust for them. The defendants other than the copartners and the copartnership interposed a general demurrer and a special demurrer upon the ground of uncertainty. Each demurrer was sustained without leave to amend and the corporations' appeal is from the judgment which followed that order.

From an opinion of the trial judge, it appears that the demurrers were sustained upon the sole ground that a tenant may not question the title of his landlord at the date of the lease; accordingly, a suit by a tenant to interplead his landlord and one who claims the rent agreed to be paid in accordance with the terms of the lease by which he holds possession of the real property is in violation of this fundamental principle. The appellants assert that a suit in interpleader does not constitute a denial of the landlord's title but is simply a means by which the tenant may discharge his obligation to pay rent under the lease without becoming involved in the conflict between different claimants to the amount due and unpaid.   *   *   *

The common law bill of interpleader had four essential elements: (1) The same thing, debt, or duty must be claimed by both or all the parties against whom the relief is demanded; (2) all of the adverse titles or claims must be dependent, or be derived from a common source; (3) the one seeking the relief must not have nor claim any interest in the subject matter; and (4) he must have incurred no independent liability to either of the claimants. See 4 Pomeroy's Equity Jurisprudence, 5th Ed. 1941, § 1322, p. 906.

These requirements have been termed historical limitations upon this otherwise expeditious equitable proceeding   *   *   *   and in 1881 section 386 of the Code of Civil Procedure was amended to broaden the remedy. The statute   *   *   *   declares   *   *   *: "And whenever conflicting claims are or may be made upon a person for or relating to personal property, or the performance of an obligation, or any portion thereof, such person may bring an action against the conflicting claimants to compel them to interplead and litigate their several claims among themselves. The order of substitution may be made and the action of interpleader may be maintained, and the applicant or plaintiff be discharged from liability to all or any of the conflicting claimants, although their titles or claims have not a common origin, or are not identical, but are adverse to and independent of one another." The provision of this enactment, that interpleader lies "although their titles or claims have not a common origin * * * but are adverse to and independent of one another," directly abrogates the common law requirement that all the adverse titles or claims must be dependent or be derived from a common source, and it is therefore clear that privity between the conflicting claimants need not be shown to invoke the remedy under the code. * * *

Early in the history of interpleader, it was held that one who sought to maintain such a suit must show outstanding claims, identical in every respect and without the slightest degree of variation, to the same thing, debt or duty. In the case of conflicting claims to specific personal property, this rigid formalism did not seriously interfere with the effectiveness of the proceeding. But where, as is generally the situation modernly, the subject matter of the conflicting claims was an obligation, a debt or a duty, the requirement as to the identity of the defendant's demands very often prevented a stakeholder from using interpleader where he was doubly vexed with respect to one liability. For example, under the narrow rule of the common law, if one person claimed all of the fund held by a bank and another person asserted the right to only a portion of that fund, the bank could not secure a determination of its liability by means of the equitable proceeding. The Legislature has removed this restriction, yet the very rationale of interpleader compels the conclusion that the amendment does not allow the remedy where each of the claimants asserts the right to a different debt, claim or duty. If the conflicting claims are mutually exclusive, interpleader cannot be maintained, but the fact that an identical right is not asserted by each of the claimants does not preclude the use of the remedy. * * *

In the present case, the plaintiffs have alleged that each of the two groups against whom interpleader is sought claims the right to receive the rents and royalties reserved in the lease. If Independent Distributing Co. and the members of that copartnership should assert that they are entitled to the reasonable value of the use and occupation of the land leased to the plaintiffs, together with the mesne profits or damages for waste, the trial court would be required to deny the plaintiffs the right to interplead those parties with their lessors. Under such circumstances the claims of the parties would not relate to the same obligation. But as the appellants' complaint pleads that there are conflicting claims concerning their obligation to pay the rents and royalties reserved by the lease, the lessors and the third parties must answer and, if each of them agrees that his claim concerns the right to those rents and royalties, the lessees should be discharged from liability upon payment of their obligations under the lease.

As to the remaining common law principles governing a suit of inter-pleader, the appellants' complaint conforms with the requirement that the plaintiff in such a proceeding must stand in the position of a disinterested stakeholder. However, much of the present controversy centers about the last element which is specified as essential. Although the complaint discloses no obligation of the appellants other than under the lease, the respondents assert that the obligation to pay rent constitutes an independent liability and bars the remedy of interpleader.

 * * * The rule concerning independent liability is stated in Corpus Juris as follows: "Interpleader will not lie if the stakeholder has incurred some personal obligation to either of the claimants, independent of the title or the right to possession, because such claimant would in that event have a claim against him which could not be settled in a litigation with the other claimant." 33 C.J. 439. * * * The Supreme Court of Maine put the matter most convincingly when it said: "The mere fact that a contractual relation exists be-tween plaintiff and one of the defendants, under which the fund is required to be paid to such claimant, does not of itself defeat the right of interpleader. * * * If such were the law, it would be difficult to conceive of any set of facts which would enable a bank, a trustee, or other custodian of funds, or even a bailee, to maintain interpleader. The obligation referred to in the rule must be independent of the title or right of possession of the fund or property in question. * * *" First National Bank v. Reynolds, 127 Me. 340, 143 A. 266, 268, 60 A.L.R. 712. * * *

Although Professor Pomeroy declares that an independent liability "arises from the very nature of the original relation subsisting between" the landlord and tenant, he states that such a suit is proper whenever there is some privity between the claimant and the lessor, as, for example, when the relation of trus-tee and cestui que trust has been created between them. It seems, therefore, that the reason why the author asserts that the relationship of the landlord and tenant precludes interpleader by the tenant is not that, under the lease, there is an independent liability but because there is no privity between the landlord and the one joined with him as a defendant. * * *

From what has been said, then, it is clear that, in the present case, as ac-cording to the facts alleged in the complaint, the relations inter se of the re-spondents and the copartners are such that the decision will determine the lia-bility of the lessees to each of them, there is no independent liability which will bar the remedy of interpleader; accordingly the appellants' complaint is sufficient with respect to those of the four common law requirements for inter-pleader not abolished or modified by the amendment in 1881 to section 386 of the Code of Civil Procedure. * * *

[The court went on to consider the effect of the common law rule that a tenant may not dispute the title of his landlord at the time of the commence-ment of the relation.]

Notwithstanding the strict common law limitation on interpleader in landlord-tenant cases which is justified by an ancient rule of real property, the code provision concerning the remedy must be liberally construed. A remedial statute, its purpose is to avoid a multiplicity of suits and prevent vexatious litigation. * * *

* * * [I]n the absence of the right to interplead the landlord and the adverse claimant to the rent, the tenant is faced with the unfortunate alternative of forfeiting his lease or possibly paying twice. * * * And there is no action at law adequate to shield him from vexation by multiple litigation over the obligation for rent, against the risk of double liability upon the same obligation, and against insecurity of tenancy.

Furthermore, interpleader is not only of importance to the tenant; it is also of advantage to the third party claimant. If the tenant may not interplead his landlord and another under the common law rule, the third party must establish his right to rent in a separate action. During the progress of this litigation the tenant would pay the rents to the landlord. It is entirely conceivable that before judgment was rendered the tenant might become insolvent, leaving the third party without recourse, or because of financial difficulties overtaking the landlord, the tenant would be required to pay his obligation twice.

Unquestionably the landlord may suffer some disadvantage in being forced to defend a suit in interpleader. While the litigation continues the rent is withheld from him without interest. But the tenant may not maintain such a suit upon the mere pretext or suspicion of double vexation; he must allege facts showing a reasonable probability of double vexation. Without accurately appraising the rationale of interpleader, by some decisions this court has mentioned as an additional requirement that the plaintiff must allege facts showing a doubt as to which claimant he can safely pay. * * * However, to demand from a plaintiff that he express a doubt as to which adverse claimant he is liable is an admission that the basis upon which the right to interpleader rests is the avoidance of double liability. "The right to the remedy by interpleader is founded, however, not on the consideration that a man may be subjected to double liability, but on the fact that he is threatened with double vexation in respect to one liability." Pfister v. Wade, * * * 56 Cal. at page 47 * * *.

The complaint therefore states a cause of action against a general demurrer and denial of leave to amend was an abuse of discretion even if the special demurrer was well taken. * * *

The judgment is reversed.

[The dissenting opinion of Justice CARTER has been omitted.]

NOTES AND QUESTIONS

1. Does the fact that modern interpleader is a remodeling by the equity courts of the common-law writ of interpleader explain why its availability was limited prior to statutory modification? Re-examine the materials on equity in Chapter 4, pp. 355–60, supra.

2. The California Supreme Court states in *Hancock* that interpleader would have been denied if Independent Oil Company had asserted a claim for profits

and damages. In such a situation, the court reasoned, "the claims of the parties [Independent and Hopkins] would not relate to the same obligation." What does the court mean by "one obligation"? Consider the probable content of the allegations if Independent had asserted a claim for profits and damages and Hopkins had asserted a claim for the rents; would the claims have been mutually exclusive?

3. ALTON & PETERS v. MERRITT, 145 Minn. 426, 177 N.W. 770 (1920). Defendants, owners of certain real property, entered into a contract with plaintiffs, real-estate brokers, under which they agreed to pay plaintiffs a commission of $500 if they produced a purchaser ready, willing, and able to pay $200 per acre for defendants' land. Two weeks after the date of that contract, defendants entered into a similar contract with Sandlin, also a real-estate broker. Within the time stipulated in plaintiffs' contract, they presented to defendants a purchaser ready, willing, and able to buy the land at $200 per acre. At about the same time, Sandlin produced a different purchaser. Plaintiffs and Sandlin both claimed commissions. When plaintiffs brought suit to collect their commission, defendants sought to interplead Sandlin. The trial court's grant of the motion to interplead was reversed by the Minnesota Supreme Court. Was the appellate court's decision correct? Why? Would interpleader have been granted if the case had arisen in a jurisdiction adopting the *Hancock* approach? Would the result have been different if plaintiffs and Sandlin had found the same purchaser?

4. The typical interpleader suit has two stages. The first determines whether interpleader is proper; in it, the controversy is between the stakeholder on one side and all the claimants on the other. If interpleader is granted, the first stage ends with a decree allowing the stakeholder to withdraw from the case and enjoining the claimants from taking any further proceedings against the stakeholder. Before retiring, however, the stakeholder is required to deposit the money or property involved in the dispute with the court, generally less court costs and attorney's fees. In the second stage, the contest is among the claimants to determine their respective rights to the property or fund deposited in court. See McClintock, *Equity* § 188 (2d ed. 1948); 4 Pomeroy, *Equity Jurisprudence* § 1320 (5th ed. 1941).

5. PLAZA EXPRESS CO. v. GALLOWAY, 365 Mo. 166, 280 S.W.2d 17 (1955). Galloway commenced an action claiming $20,000 for personal injuries allegedly caused by the negligence of Plaza Express. When Galloway died, his administrator was substituted as a party plaintiff. Shortly before substitution, Galloway's widow brought a separate action for $15,000 against Plaza Express. According to Missouri law, a cause of action for personal injuries other than injuries resulting in death survives in the personal representative of the injured party, whereas a cause of action for wrongful death vests in the surviving spouse of the deceased. Plaza Express was allowed to interplead the administrator and the widow under a provision similar to the one found in Federal Rule of Civil Procedure 22(1). Would the same result have been reached if the action had been brought in a jurisdiction that follows the historical restrictions on interpleader? Would interpleader have been available if the case had been brought in California after the *Hancock* decision?

6. In PACKARD v. STEVENS, 58 N.J.Eq. 489, 46 A. 250 (Ct.Ch. 1899), a contractor made separate agreements with two subcontractors to fill an inlet with mud and sand to a level uniform with the surrounding ground. When the work was completed, the actual volume filled was one million cubic yards. But the

individual claims of the subcontractors, who had begun work on opposite sides of the inlet, totaled more than one million cubic yards; each demanded payment in accordance with his claim. The contractor was allowed to interplead the subcontractors. Were any of the historic requirements for interpleader lacking in this case?

7. The third requirement for interpleader mentioned in the *Hancock* case is that the party seeking interpleader must neither have nor claim any interest in the subject matter. The first case in which the requirement appeared, MITCHELL v. HAYNE, 2 Simons & Stuart 63 (Ct.Ch. 1824), cites no authority and gives no reasons for its adoption. Nevertheless, the requirement has been accepted by most American jurisdictions. See, e. g., Texas v. Florida, 306 U.S. 398, 406–07, 59 S.Ct. 563, 568, 83 L.Ed. 817, 825 (1939); Maxim v. Shotwell, 209 Mich. 79, 176 N.W. 414 (1920). For this requirement's early history, see Hazard & Moskovitz, *An Historical and Critical Analysis of Interpleader,* 52 Calif.L.Rev. 706, 744 (1964). At the time the *Hancock* case was decided, this requirement was still in full force in California. However, in 1951, Section 386 of California's Code of Civil Procedure, which is set out in the Supplement under Federal Rule 22, was amended to permit a defendant to interpose a claim to a portion of the property or money in dispute. Is there any reason why the right of an interested stakeholder to interplead apparently exists under the California statute only in favor of a defendant stakeholder? Can Section 386 be construed to give the same right to the plaintiff? See Note, *1951 Amendment to California Code of Civil Procedure Section 386,* 39 Calif.L.Rev. 591, 594 (1951). For a sharp attack on the no-interest-in-the-subject-matter requirement, see Chafee, *Modernizing Interpleader,* 30 Yale L.J. 814, 840–42 (1921).

8. The fourth historical requirement—that the stakeholder must not have incurred any independent liability with regard to the stake to either of the claimants—derived from the principle that the stakeholder should retire from the case once interpleader was allowed. By way of illustration, assume that a bailee who is subject to conflicting claims to the bailed article has expressly acknowledged one of the claimant's title to it. Interpleader could not be granted because a decision awarding ownership to the other claimant might not terminate the controversy concerning the bailed item; the losing claimant still might have a cause of action against the stakeholder based on the latter's acknowledgment of title and the stakeholder could not withdraw from the litigation at the end of the first stage of the suit. What underlies the principle that the stakeholder must be neutral, disinterested, and withdraw permanently from the suit when interpleader is allowed?

EX PARTE MERSEY DOCKS & HARBOUR BOARD, [1899] 1 Q.B. 546 (C.A.), involved a situation similar to the hypothetical. The court permitted interpleader and concluded that if the claimant with an independent cause of action regarding the stake lost as against the other claimant, he would be allowed to assert it against the bailee in a third stage of the same suit. Compare the hardship to the claimant of two contests, first with another claimant and then with the bailee, with the hardship to the bailee of two actions and a possible double recovery. Is the solution adopted in the *Mersey* case desirable? The status of this requirement in the federal courts is discussed in Note, *The Independent Liability Rule as a Bar to Interpleader in the Federal Courts,* 65 Yale L.J. 715 (1956). See also American Law Institute, *Study on the Division of Jurisdiction Between State and Federal Courts,* Official Draft, § 2361(b)(1969).

2. JURISDICTIONAL PROBLEMS

———

The historic territorial approach to jurisdiction over the person has raised a number of peculiar problems in the interpleader context. Occasionally, the stakeholder will not be able to obtain in personam jurisdiction over all of the claimants in any one state because of the limitations imposed by the due process clause of the Fourteenth Amendment. To overcome this difficulty, courts often have characterized interpleader as an in rem or quasi in rem proceeding and predicated jurisdiction on the presence of the stake within the territorial reach of the court. Assuming that this is a sound approach, should it make any difference that the stake is a debt rather than a chattel or a trust fund? In the case that follows, the Supreme Court was faced with the question of whether to treat a debt as an in rem or quasi in rem base for interpleader. Before proceeding, it might be advisable to review the materials in Chapter 2 on jurisdiction over the person and jurisdiction over property. In particular, reread *Harris v. Balk,* p. 107, supra.

———

NEW YORK LIFE INS. CO. v. DUNLEVY

Supreme Court of the United States, 1916.
241 U.S. 518, 36 S.Ct. 613, 60 L.Ed. 1140.

Certiorari to the Circuit Court of Appeals of the Ninth Circuit.

Mr. Justice McREYNOLDS delivered the opinion of the court:

Respondent, Effie J. Gould Dunlevy, instituted this suit in the superior court, Marin county, California, January 14, 1910, against petitioner and Joseph W. Gould, her father, to recover $2,479.70, the surrender value of a policy on his life which she claimed had been assigned to her in 1893, and both were duly served with process while in that state. It was removed to the United States district court, February 16, 1910, and there tried by the judge in May, 1912, a jury having been expressly waived. Judgment for amount claimed was affirmed by the Circuit Court of Appeals. * * *

The insurance company by an amended answer filed December 7, 1911, set up in defense * * * that Mrs. Dunlevy was concluded by certain judicial proceedings in Pennsylvania wherein it had been garnished and the policy had been adjudged to be the property of Gould. * * *

In 1907 Boggs & Buhl recovered a valid personal judgment by default, after domiciliary service, against Mrs. Dunlevy, in the common pleas court at Pittsburgh, where she then resided. During 1909, "the tontine dividend period" of the life policy having expired, the insurance company became liable for $2,479.70, and this sum was claimed both by Gould, a citizen of Pennsylvania, and his daughter, who had removed to California. In November, 1909, Boggs & Buhl caused issue of an execution attachment on their judgment, and both the insurance company and Gould were summoned as garnishees. He appeared, denied assignment of the policy, and claimed the full amount due thereon. On February 5, 1910,—after this suit was begun in California,—the company answered, admitted its indebtedness, set up the conflicting claims to the fund, and prayed to be advised as to its rights. At the same time it filed a petition asking for a rule upon the claimants to show cause why they should not interplead and thereby ascertain who was lawfully entitled to the proceeds, and, further, that it might be allowed to pay amount due into court for benefit of proper party. An order granted the requested rule, and directed that notice be given to Mrs. Dunlevy in California. This was done, but she made no answer and did not appear. Later the insurance company filed a second petition, and, upon leave obtained thereunder, paid $2,479.70 into court, March 21, 1910. All parties except Mrs. Dunlevy having appeared, a feigned issue was framed and tried to determine validity of alleged transfer of the policy. The jury found, October 1, 1910, there was no valid assignment, and thereupon, under an order of court, the fund was paid over to Gould.

Beyond doubt, without the necessity of further personal service of process upon Mrs. Dunlevy, the court of common pleas at Pittsburgh had ample power through garnishment proceedings to inquire whether she held a valid claim against the insurance company, and, if found to exist, then to condemn and appropriate it so far as necessary to discharge the original judgment. Although herself outside the limits of the state, such disposition of the property would have been binding on her. * * * But the interpleader initiated by the company was an altogether different matter. This was an attempt to bring about a final and conclusive adjudication of her personal rights, not merely to discover property and apply it to debts. And unless in contemplation of law she was before the court, and required to respond to that issue, its orders and judgments in respect thereto were not binding on her. Pennoyer v. Neff * * *.

Counsel maintain that having been duly summoned in the original suit instituted by Boggs & Buhl in 1907, and notwithstanding entry of final judgment therein, "Mrs. Dunlevy was in the Pennsylvania court and was bound by every order that court made, whether she remained within the jurisdiction of that court after it got jurisdiction over her person or not;" and hence, the argument is, "When the company paid the money into court where she was, it was just the same in legal effect as if it had paid it to her." This position is supposed to be supported by our opinion in Michigan Trust Co. v. Ferry, 228 U. S. 346, 57 L.Ed. 867, 33 S.Ct. 550, where it is said (p. 353): "If a judicial proceeding is begun with jurisdiction over the person of the party concerned, it is within the power of a state to bind him by every subsequent order in the cause. * * * This is true not only of ordinary actions, but of proceedings like the present. It is within the power of a state to make the whole administration of the estate a single proceeding, to provide that one who has undertaken it within the jurisdiction shall be subject to the order of the court in the matter until the administration is closed by distribution, and, on the same principle, that he shall be required to account for and distribute all that he receives, by the order of the probate court."

Of course the language quoted had reference to the existing circumstances, and must be construed accordingly. The judgment under consideration was fairly within the reasonable anticipation of the executor when he submitted himself to the probate court. But a wholly different and intolerable condition would result from acceptance of the theory that, after final judgment, a defendant remains in court and subject to whatsoever orders may be entered under title of the cause. * * * The interpleader proceedings were not essential concomitants of the original action by Boggs & Buhl against Dunlevy, but plainly collateral; and, when summoned to respond in that action, she was not required to anticipate them. * * *

The established general rule is that any personal judgment which a state court may render against one who did not voluntarily submit to its jurisdiction, and who is not a citizen of the state, nor served with process within its borders, no matter what the mode of service, is void, because the court had no jurisdiction over his person. * * *

We are of opinion that the proceedings in the Pennsylvania court constituted no bar to the action in California, and the judgment below is accordingly affirmed.

NOTES AND QUESTIONS

1. Partially in response to the *Dunlevy* decision, Congress passed the Federal Interpleader Act in 1917. The statute was successively broadened in 1926 and 1936 and was reconstituted in 1948 as part of the United States Judicial Code. It now appears as 28 U.S.C. §§ 1335, 1397, 2361. The present Interpleader Act manifests a congressional intent to avoid a repetition of the *Dunlevy* decision in an action arising in a federal court. For example, Section 1397 permits venue to be laid in any judicial district in which one or more of the claimants reside and Section 2361 permits nationwide service of process in order to reach all of the claimants. Further recognition of the interstate quality of interpleader and the need for the exercise of federal judicial power in this context is the provision in Section 1335 permitting the federal courts to assert jurisdiction when the stake is worth as little as $500. In light of the principles of federal jurisdiction explored in Chapters Two and Three, can the Federal Interpleader Act be challenged on constitutional grounds? The Federal Interpleader Acts are analyzed in a series of articles by the late Professor Chafee: *Interstate Interpleader,* 33 Yale L.J. 685 (1924); *Interpleader in the United States Courts,* 41 Yale L.J. 1134 (1932), 42 id. 41 (1932); *The Federal Interpleader Act of 1936,* 45 Yale L.J. 963, 1161 (1936); *Federal Interpleader Since the Act of 1936,* 49 Yale L.J. 377 (1940). The Federal Interpleader Act and interpleader under Federal Rule 22 are further discussed on pp. 616–29, infra.

2. Can *Dunlevy* be reconciled with *Harris v. Balk,* p. 107, supra? For a case reaching the same result as *Dunlevy,* see Hanna v. Stedman, 230 N.Y. 326, 130 N.E. 566 (1921). The *Dunlevy* result is defended in Chafee, *Interstate Interpleader,* 33 Yale L.J. 685, 712–14 (1924). In view of the extent to which state judicial power over nonresidents has been extended since the *Dunlevy* decision, would the Supreme Court limit the state's power over interpleader today as it did in *Dunlevy?* Which of the cases in Chapter 2 are relevant to this question? Do the "long-arm" or "single-act" statutes render the *Dunlevy* problem moot or is

there still some area in which federal interpleader can profitably function? Does the presence of the Federal Interpleader Act make it easier or harder for the Supreme Court to eliminate the *Dunlevy* limitation on state jurisdictional power? See von Mehren & Trautman, *Jurisdiction to Adjudicate: A Suggested Analysis,* 79 Harv.L.Rev. 1121, 1156–59 (1966). For a modern approach to *Dunlevy*, see *Developments in the Law—Multiparty Litigation in the Federal Courts,* 71 Harv. L.Rev. 874, 914–18 (1958).

3. Section 216 of the New York Civil Practice Law and Rules permits a stakeholder who has been sued by one claimant to apply to the court for permission to send notice of the action's pendency to another claimant who is not subject to the court's personal jurisdiction. The proceeding is then suspended and the nonresident may intervene within a year and ten days after the date the notice is sent. If the nonresident claimant does not appear within that period, the claim is barred in New York. The claim also may be barred in those states having "borrowing statutes" under which another jurisdiction's statutes of limitations are applied in certain situations rather than those of the forum. However, the stakeholder is not protected if the nonresident claimant asserts a right to the property in another jurisdiction before the statutory period has elapsed or in a jurisdiction that will not "borrow" New York's statute. Because of these risks, the New York Court of Appeals has held that the defendant stakeholder can challenge the claim of the resident claimants by asserting that title is held by a nonresident claimant. Solicitor v. Bankers Trust Co., 304 N.Y. 282, 107 N.E.2d 448 (1952). Are there any constitutional objections to the New York statute? For analyses of it, see Frumer, *On Revising the New York Interpleader Statutes,* 25 N.Y.U.L.Rev. 737 (1950); Note, *Statutory Notice to Non-resident Adverse Claimants to a Debt,* 37 Cornell L.Q. 533 (1952). See also 1 Weinstein, Korn & Miller, *New York Civil Practice* ¶¶ 216.01–.03.

4. ST. LOUIS S. W. RY. v. MEYER, 364 Mo. 1057, 272 S.W.2d 249 (1954), appeal dismissed 349 U.S. 942, 75 S.Ct. 871, 99 L.Ed. 1269 (1955). The board of directors of the St. Louis Southwestern Railway declared a cash dividend of $5 per share on both preferred and common stock and then declared a further dividend of $370,648. By resolution of the board, however, payment of this dividend was withheld because there was reasonable doubt as to the right of preferred stockholders to participate in dividends after a $5 dividend had been paid on all classes of stock in any one year. Because claims for a share in the fund were made by both common and preferred stockholders, the board deposited the $370,-648 into a special bank account and sought to interplead all the stockholders. The trial court granted interpleader and the company transferred the money into court. Service upon nonresident stockholders was made by publication under a statute that provided: "Service * * * by publication shall be allowed in all cases affecting a fund, will, trust estate, specific property, or any interest therein, or any res or status within the jurisdiction of the court. * * *" On appeal to the Supreme Court of Missouri, it was contended that there was no res and, therefore, service by publication was invalid and unauthorized. In upholding the jurisdiction of the trial court, the Supreme Court said:

> It may be that the sum of $370,648, set apart by resolution from the company's cash assets * * * is not, strictly speaking, a trust. * * *
> But it was segregated and set apart, deposited, initially, in a "special dividend account in trust" * * * and it is, undeniably, a "fund,"
> "specific property," or a "res" and, indisputably, was and is indeed, a

tangible thing "within the jurisdiction of the court" now and when this proceeding was instituted and plainly, within the meaning of the statute, authorized service by publication upon nonresident defendants.

Id. at 1069, 272 S.W.2d at 252–53. Can you reconcile this case with *Dunlevy*, keeping in mind the fact that in *Dunlevy* the disputed fund was also set apart and paid into court? Are there any constitutional objections to the result in *Meyer*?

5. In WESTERN UNION TEL. CO. v. PENNSYLVANIA, p. 145, supra, the Supreme Court stated:

> * * * [W]hen a state court's jurisdiction purports to be based, as here, on the presence of property within the State, the holder of such property is deprived of due process of law if he is compelled to relinquish it without assurance that he will not be held liable again in another jurisdiction or in a suit brought by a claimant who is not bound by the first judgment. * * *

368 U.S. at 75, 82 S.Ct. at 201, 7 L.Ed.2d at 142. If this statement is applicable to individual claims, as well as to a claim by the state to a particular fund, a court would have to dismiss a suit by a resident claimant against the stakeholder when there are potential nonresident claimants who cannot be brought within the jurisdiction of the court. Does this make it unwise to extend the *Western Union* doctrine to include private claims?

---

3. INTERPLEADER IN THE FEDERAL COURTS

Read 28 U.S.C. §§ 1335, 1397, 2361 and Federal Rule of Civil Procedure 22.

PAN AMERICAN FIRE & CAS. CO. v. REVERE

United States District Court, Eastern District of Louisiana, 1960.
188 F.Supp. 474.

WRIGHT, District Judge. On February 3, 1960, a   *   *   *   large tractor and trailer collided head-on with a bus carrying school children. The bus driver and three of the children were killed and 23 others were injured, some very seriously. A few moments later, compounding the disaster, another collision occurred between two cars following the bus. * * *

Alleging that three suits against it have already been filed and that numerous other claims have been made, the tractor's liability insurer has instituted this interpleader action, citing all potential claimants. It asks that they be enjoined from initiating legal proceedings elsewhere or further prosecuting the actions already filed and that they be directed to assert their claims in the present suit. Plaintiff has deposited a bond in the full amount of its policy limits, $100,000, and avers that "it has no interest" in these insurance proceeds, being merely "a disinterested stakeholder." On the other hand, the Company denies liability toward any and all claimants. This apparently contradictory position is explained by the statement of its counsel, incorporated in the record as an amendment to the complaint, that plaintiff "has no further claim" on the sum deposited with the court, but cannot technically admit "liability" since that would amount to a concession that its assured was negligent and expose him to a deficiency judgment.

The only question presented at this stage of the proceeding is whether, under the circumstances outlined, the remedy of interpleader is available to the insurer.   *   *   *

1. *Jurisdiction.*   *   *   *

[The court concluded that the jurisdictional amount and diversity requirements of the Interpleader Act and Federal Rule 22 had been satisfied.]

2. *Strict Interpleader or Bill in the Nature of Interpleader.*   Apparently of the opinion that the answer may affect the availability of the remedy sought here, the parties have debated the question whether this is a case for "true," "strict," or "pure" interpleader or whether the present facts support only an action "in the nature of interpleader."   The difference between the two is that in strict interpleader the plaintiff is a disinterested stakeholder while in the action in the nature of interpleader he is himself a claimant, whether directly or by denying the validity of some or all of the other claims.   State of Texas v. State of Florida, 306 U.S. 398, 406–407, 59 S.Ct. 563, 830, 83 L.Ed. 817. Thus, if the casualty insurer had brought in the claimants and said to them: "Gentlemen, I put before you the full amount of the policy which those of you who prove your claims must divide between you, but I deny that any of you is entitled to any portion of the fund and pray that all your demands be rejected and that the deposit be returned to me in due course," clearly this would not be a true interpleader but an action in the nature of interpleader.   The problem here is whether the allegation of disinterestedness already noted changes the character of the action to one of strict interpleader.   *   *   *

But does it matter how the action is characterized?   It would seem to make no difference since both Rule 22 and the Interpleader Act expressly provide for actions in the nature of interpleader as well as strict bills, the drafters in each case voicing their intent to erase the distinction.   But before so concluding, we must dispose of an old rule of equity that gave importance to the difference between "pure" and "impure" bills of interpleader.

3. *Special Equitable Ground for Bill in the Nature of Interpleader.* Though apparently known to the early common law, modern interpleader developed in the chancery courts and is today considered an equitable remedy. Hence, in theory at least, the resort to equity must be justified by the absence of an adequate remedy at law.   One might suppose that exposure to unnecessary vexation by a multiplicity of suits on the same obligation were a sufficient ground for equitable relief.   And so it is if the conditions of strict interpleader are met.   But, for reasons that no one bothered to explain, the rule was otherwise when the plaintiff was not a mere stakeholder.   It was laid down that a bill in the nature of interpleader would not lie unless supported by some special equity besides double vexation.   Thus, a suit like this one which has no in-

dependent equitable basis could not be maintained unless it could be characterized as a true bill of interpleader.

Though it was perhaps more honored in the breach than the observance, such was the rule. But, inherently weak, it could not long survive the liberalizing force of the Interpleader Act of 1936 and the Rules of Civil Procedure promulgated in 1938. Indeed, once the difference between strict bills and bills in the nature of interpleader was eliminated, there remained no basis for distinguishing the requirements and demanding special equities for the action in the nature of interpleader. Henceforth, it could be assumed that the prerequisites of interpleader were the same whether the plaintiff were interested or not, and that these conditions were spelled out in the written provisions. The point was forcibly made by Judge Chesnut whose celebrated opinion in John Hancock Mut. Life Ins. Co. v. Kegan, * * * [22 F.Supp. 326 (D.Md.1938)], noted the absurdity of distinguishing between the equities required for "pure" and "impure" interpleader and held that exposure to undue harassment by a multiplicity of suits was a sufficient ground to maintain a bill in the nature of interpleader. * * *

The present law, then, is that the only equitable ground necessary for interpleader, whether the plaintiff is a disinterested stakeholder or not, is exposure to double or multiple vexation. But, of course, this does not mean that every person threatened with a multiplicity of suits is entitled to interplead. The function of interpleader is to rescue a debtor from *undue* harassment when there are several claims made against the *same fund*. It is because the aggregate demands exceed the insurer's contractual obligation that the condition is here satisfied.

4. *Exposure to Multiple Liability.* Though the Interpleader Act makes no such requirement, Rule 22 apparently permits interpleader only if the claims "are such that the plaintiff is or may be exposed to double or multiple *liability*." (Emphasis added.) In theory at least, this is not necessarily the same thing as exposure to double or multiple *vexation* on a single obligation. There may be situations in which the debtor, though harassed by many suits on account of one transaction, is never in danger of being compelled to pay the same debt twice. Indeed, here, the argument is advanced that because it has fixed the limits of its liability in its policy, the insurer is not exposed to multiple liability no matter how many claims are filed, and, therefore, is not entitled to maintain interpleader, at least under the Rule.

But the requirement is not a strict one. * * * The key to the clause requiring exposure to "double or multiple liability" is in the words "may be." The danger need not be immediate; any possibility of having to pay more than is justly due, no matter how improbable or remote, will suffice. At least, it is settled that an insurer with limited contractual liability who faces claims in excess of his policy limits is "exposed" within the intendment of Rule 22, and we need go no further to find the requirement satisfied here.

5. *Adversity of Claimants.* In a somewhat overlapping objection, it is said that the present claims are not characterized by that "adversity" to one an-

other which is a prerequisite of interpleader. It is of course true that they are identical neither in origin nor in amount and that they are, in some degree at least, independent demands. But, despite the objection of purists who would retain the old doctrine of complete "mutual exclusiveness," both Rule 22 and the Interpleader Act now expressly provide that this is no bar to the remedy. On the other hand, there remains a requirement that the claimants be "adverse" in some way. The question is whether that requirement is met when, as here, the claimants, though in theory indifferent toward each other, are in fact competing for a fund which is not large enough to satisfy them all. The answer is clear. As Judge Thompson said in Fidelity & Deposit Co. of Maryland v. A. S. Reid & Co., D.C.E.D.Pa., 16 F.2d 502, 504: "In that situation it is to the interest of each claimant to reduce or defeat altogether the claim of every other claimant. * * * "

6. *Fault of Plaintiff. * * *

[The court here held that the plaintiff was not guilty of "unclean hands," which would have barred equitable relief.]

7. *Unliquidated Tort Claims as Justifying Interpleader.* Over and above the technical objections already disposed of, the argument is advanced that interpleader is not an appropriate method of adjudicating unliquidated tort claims. Such a bald proposition might be rejected summarily were it not for the startling fact that there appears to be no precedent in the federal courts for granting interpleader in the present situation. * * *

At the outset, it seems clear that interpleader will lie when there are several tort claimants who have obtained judgments which aggregate more than the amount of the policy.[34] Indeed, in that case it can make no difference whether the claims originated in tort or contract. Moreover, it is settled that interpleader is available to an insurer whose policy is insufficient to satisfy contract claims, though they have not been reduced to judgment.[35] Why, then, should the remedy be denied to a blameless insurer faced with excessive tort claims? Three reasons have been suggested: (1) As to quantum, at least, tort claims are more conjectural than contract claims; (2) since it is not directly liable to the claimants, the insurer's exposure as to tort claims is "remote" until they have been reduced to judgment; and (3) tort claims "are peculiarly appropriate for jury trial," which would have to be denied under the equitable practice of interpleader.

The effect of the first objection is only this: that it is more difficult in the case of tort claims to determine whether the aggregate will exceed the policy limits so as to render the claimants "adverse" and expose the insurer to "multiple liability." It may be that there are few cases in which this result can be reasonably anticipated, but, clearly, this is one of them.

---

34 See Klaber v. Maryland Casualty Company, [69 F.2d 934 (8th Cir.1934)] * * *, where it is implied that the remedy would be available in such a situation even under the 1926 Act, at least if bills in the nature of interpleader were authorized, as they now are.

35 See, e.g., Standard Surety & Casualty Co. of New York v. Baker, [105 F.2d 578 (8th Cir.1939)] * * *.

The second objection, though it forms the basis of the only reported decision denying interpleader to an automobile liability insurer,[36] is no better. Indeed, under the "may be exposed" clause of Rule 22 and the "may claim" clause of the Interpleader Act, it would not seem to matter how remote the danger might be. But, in any event, prematurity is no defense under the peculiar Louisiana law which allows a direct action against the automobile liability insurer.

8. *Jury Trial.* On the theory that the resort to equity defeats the right of trial by jury, it has been said that once interpleader is granted all issues in the case must be tried to the judge alone. There is, however, eminent authority to the contrary, including Judge Learned Hand,[41] Professor Chafee,[42] and Professor Moore,[43] who hold that legal issues arising in an interpleader action can be tried before a jury. Whatever may be the right solution in another case, here it seems clear that the questions of liability and damages ought to be put to a jury. * * * Nothing in Rule 22 or the Interpleader Act opposes such a procedure. Indeed, the provision of the Federal Rules which permits separate trial of distinct issues invites this solution. * * * Each claimant can be given a full opportunity to prove his case before a jury, reserving to the court only the task of apportioning the fund between those who are successful if the aggregate of the verdicts exceeds the amount of the insurance proceeds.

9. *Enjoining of Other Proceedings.* Usually interpleader will not be really effective unless all claimants are brought before the same court in one proceeding and restricted to that single forum in the assertion of their claims. * * * Immediately, the question arises whether Section 2283 of Title 28 of the Code presents an obstacle to enjoining state court proceedings.

As amended in 1948, that section prohibits a federal court from interfering with a pending state court action except in three situations: (1) Where such a course is "expressly authorized by Act of Congress"; (2) where the issuance of an injunction by the federal court is "necessary in aid of its jurisdiction"; and (3) where the court's action is required "to protect or effectuate its judgments." Clearly, the first exception is applicable to a suit brought under the Interpleader Act since that statute expressly empowers the court to enjoin the claimants "from instituting or prosecuting any proceeding in any State or United States court affecting the property, instrument or obligation involved in the interpleader action * * *." But the exception does not apply to an action under Rule 22, for the quoted provision authorizing stay orders is restricted to statutory interpleader. If state court proceedings can be enjoined when interpleader is brought under the Rule it must be by virtue of the second exception in Section 2283.

---

[36] American Indemnity Co. v. Hale, D.C.W.D.Mo., 71 F.Supp. 529, 533–534.

[41] See Sherman Nat. Bank of New York v. Shubert Theatrical Co., D.C.S.D.N.Y., 238 F.2d 225, 230–231, affirmed 2 Cir., 247 F. 256 * * * .

[42] Chafee, Federal Interpleader Since the Act of 1936, 49 Yale L.J. 377, 420.

[43] 3 Moore, Federal Practice, Para. 22.04(3), p. 3013.

The question whether the court entertaining a non-statutory interpleader suit may enjoin state court proceedings on the same issues on the theory that it is "necessary in aid of its jurisdiction" is not free from doubt. * * * But * * * every indication is that, regardless of the Interpleader Act, the power of a federal court to enjoin pending state court proceedings in a case like this one will be sustained. Certainly that result is desirable, if not indispensable. * * *

10. *Venue and Service of Process.* * * * [T]here are two procedural limitations on actions under the Rule which become important whenever the claimants are not all within the territorial jurisdiction of the district court. The first is that the only proper venue for the suit when the defendants do not all reside in the same state is the residence of the plaintiff; the second, that process cannot run beyond the boundaries of the state in which the court sits. These restrictions are of course waivable, but if objection is raised by the affected defendant, they usually form an absolute bar to the action. Thus, here, if Rule 22 alone were applicable, absent a waiver of venue by Wells [a passenger in one of the cars following the bus], the suit would have to be instituted at the plaintiff's domicile in Texas, and none of the defendants could be validly served unless they were found in that state.

But the situation is different when jurisdiction exists under the statute, for the Interpleader Act specially provides that the action may be commenced in any district where one defendant resides and that process will run throughout the United States. Unfortunately, these exceptional rules apply only to statutory interpleader. The present suit, then, is maintainable only under the Interpleader Act unless the Wisconsin defendant waives venue and voluntarily appears or is found in Louisiana.

11. *Conclusion.* * * * [T]he prayer for interpleader will be granted, without, however, discharging the plaintiff who is contractually bound to resist the demands. Injunctions will issue restraining all parties from further prosecuting any pending suits against plaintiff or its assured on account of the accident described, or from instituting like proceedings before this or any other court. All defendants will be required to enter their claims by way of answer in this action within thirty days from notice of this judgment. Thereafter, upon timely demand by any one of the parties, the court will order a joint jury trial of all the claims upon the issues of liability and damages. In the event the aggregate of the verdicts should exceed the amount of plaintiff's liability, the court reserves unto itself the task of apportioning the insurance proceeds in such manner as it deems just.

The motion to dismiss will be denied.

NOTES AND QUESTIONS

1. If an insurance company faced with the *Pan American* situation pays the full amount of the policy to certain claimants, either by way of settlement or in satisfaction of a judgment, can it defend later actions by unpaid claimants by argu-

ing that it has already exhausted the policy? To what extent is the answer to this question relevant in determining whether interpleader should be granted?

2. STEPHENSON v. BURDETT, 56 W.Va. 109, 117–18, 48 S.E. 846, 850 (1904):

> * * * The only material difference between the two kinds of bills, pointed out by the courts and the law writers is that, in a bill in the nature of a bill of interpleader, the plaintiff may show that he has an interest in the subject matter of the controversy between the defendants. Sometimes the statement of the nature of this bill is very general and somewhat indefinite. Thus, in Story's Eq. Pl. (10th Ed.) section 297b, it is said: "There are many cases where a bill, in the nature of a bill of interpleader, will lie by a party in interest to ascertain and establish his own rights, where there are other conflicting rights between third persons." * * * There is no suggestion * * * that there is any further departure from the principles governing a pure bill of interpleader. Must not the defendants claim the same thing from the plaintiff, according to the requirement in a pure bill of interpleader? Must not a relation of privity exist between the defendants? Can a tenant require his landlord to interplead with a third person claiming under a strange and hostile title? If the plaintiff show by his bill that he is in the attitude of a wrongdoer toward one of the defendants, may he require an interpleader? The language of a definition of a bill in the nature of a bill of interpleader, found in the books, does not answer any of these questions in the affirmative, or indicate that the principles governing a pure bill of interpleader are relaxed in any of these particulars. Nor do any of the decided cases countenance such a proposition.

3. In addition to the articles by Professor Chafee cited following the *Dunlevy* case, a useful discussion of federal interpleader is found in 7 Wright & Miller, *Federal Practice and Procedure: Civil* §§ 1701–21 (1972); *Developments in the Law—Multiparty Litigation in the Federal Courts,* 71 Harv.L.Rev. 874, 913–28 (1958). See also Ilsen & Sardell, *Interpleader in the Federal Courts,* 35 St. John's L.Rev. 1 (1960).

STATE FARM FIRE & CAS. CO. v. TASHIRE

Supreme Court of the United States, 1967.
386 U.S. 523, 87 S.Ct. 1199, 18 L.Ed.2d 270.

Certiorari to the United States Court of Appeals for the Ninth Circuit.

[This case arose out of a collision between a Greyhound bus and a pickup truck in Shasta County, California in September, 1964. Two of the bus passengers were killed and 33 others were injured, as were the bus driver, the driver of the truck, and its passenger. One of the dead and 10 of the injured passengers were Canadians; the rest of the individuals were citizens of five American states.

Four of the injured passengers filed suit in California state courts seeking damages in excess of $1,000,000 and naming as defendants: Greyhound Lines, Inc.; Nauta, the bus driver; Clark, the driver of the truck; and Glasgow, the truck passenger who apparently was its owner. Each of the individual defendants was a citizen of Oregon; Greyhound is a California corporation. Before the California cases came to trial and before any other suits were filed, petitioner, State Farm Fire & Casualty Company, an Illinois corporation, brought this action in the nature of interpleader in the United States District Court for the District of Oregon.

State Farm asserted that at the time of the collision it had in force an insurance policy covering Clark, the driver of the truck, for bodily injury liability up to $10,000 per person and $20,000 per occurrence. State Farm further asserted that the aggregate damages sought in actions already filed in California and other anticipated actions far exceeded the amount of its maximum liability under the policy. Accordingly, it paid into court the sum of $20,000 and asked the court (1) to require all claimants to establish their claims against Clark and his insurer in the Oregon proceeding and in no other action, and (2) to discharge State Farm from all further obligations under its policy. Alternatively, State Farm requested a decree that the insurer owed no duty to Clark and was not liable on the policy, and asked the court to refund the $20,000 deposit. State Farm joined as defendants Clark, Glasgow, Nauta, Greyhound, and each of the prospective claimants. Jurisdiction was predicated both upon the Federal Interpleader Act and general diversity of citizenship. Personal service was effected on each of the American defendants and registered mail was employed to give notice to the 11 Canadian claimants.

The Oregon district court issued an order requiring each of the defendants to show cause why he should not be restrained from filing or prosecuting any proceeding affecting the property or obligation involved in the interpleader action. In response, several of the defendants contended that the policy did cover the accident and advanced various arguments for the position that interpleader was inappropriate.

When a temporary injunction along the lines sought by State Farm issued, the respondents moved to dismiss and, in the alternative, sought a change of venue to the district in which the collision had occurred. After a hearing, the district court declined to dissolve the temporary injunction but continued the motion for a change of venue. Later, the temporary injunction was broadened so that all suits against Clark, State Farm, Greyhound, and Nauta had to be prosecuted in the interpleader proceeding.

On interlocutory appeal, the Ninth Circuit reversed on the ground that in states, such as Oregon, that do not permit a "direct action" against an insurance company until a judgment is obtained against the insured, State Farm could not invoke federal interpleader until the claims against the insured had been reduced to judgment. The court of appeals held that prior to that time claimants with unliquidated tort claims are not "claimants" within the meaning of Section 1335 of Title 28 and are not "persons having claims against the plaintiff" within the meaning of Federal Rule 22. The Ninth Circuit directed that the temporary injunction be dissolved and the action be dismissed. The Supreme Court granted certiorari.]

Mr. Justice FORTAS delivered the opinion of the Court.

* * *

I.

Before considering the issues presented by the petition for certiorari, we find it necessary to dispose of a question neither raised by the parties nor passed upon by the courts below. Since the matter concerns our jurisdiction, we raise it on our own motion. * * * The interpleader statute * * * has been uniformly construed to require only "minimal diversity," that is, diversity of citizenship between two or more claimants, without regard to the circumstance that other rival claimants may be co-citizens. The language of the statute, the legislative purpose broadly to remedy the problems posed by multiple claimants to a single fund, and the consistent judicial interpretation tacitly accepted by Congress, persuade us that the statute requires no more. There remains, however, the question whether such a statutory construction is consistent with Article III of our Constitution * * *. In Strawbridge v. Curtiss, 3 Cranch 267, 2 L.Ed. 435 (1806), this Court held that the diversity of citizenship statute required "complete diversity": where co-citizens appeared on both sides of a dispute, jurisdiction was lost. But Chief Justice Marshall there purported to construe only "The words of the act of Congress," not the Constitution itself. And in a variety of contexts this Court and the lower courts have concluded that Article III poses no obstacle to the legislative extension of federal jurisdiction, founded on diversity, so long as any two adverse parties are not co-citizens. Accordingly, we conclude that the present case is properly in the federal courts.

II.

We do not agree with the Court of Appeals that, in the absence of a state law or contractual provision for "direct action" suits against the insurance company, the company must wait until persons asserting claims against its insured have reduced those claims to judgment before seeking to invoke the benefits of federal interpleader. That may have been a tenable position under the 1926 [8] and 1936 interpleader statutes.[9] These statutes did not carry forward the language in the 1917 Act authorizing interpleader where adverse claimants "may claim" benefits as well as where they "are claiming" them.[10] In 1948, however, in the revision of the Judicial Code, the "may claim" language was restored.[11] Until the decision below, every court confronted by the question has

---

[8] 44 Stat. 416 (1926), which added casualty companies to the enumerated categories of plaintiffs able to bring interpleader, and provided for the enjoining of proceedings in other courts.

[9] 49 Stat. 1096 (1936), which authorized "bill[s] in the nature of interpleader," meaning those in which the plaintiff is not wholly disinterested with respect to the fund he has deposited in court. * * *

[10] 39 Stat. 929 (1917). See Klaber v. Maryland Cas. Co., 69 F.2d 934, 938–939, 106 A.L.R. 617 (C.A.8th Cir.1934), which held that the omission in the 1926 Act of the earlier statute's "may claim" language required the denial of interpleader in the face of unliquidated claims (alternative holding).

[11] * * * [I]t was widely assumed that restoration of the "may claim" language would have the effect of overruling the holding in Klaber, supra, that one may not invoke interpleader to protect against unliquidated claims. * * *

concluded that the 1948 revision removed whatever requirement there might previously have been that the insurance company wait until at least two claimants reduced their claims to judgments. The commentators are in accord.[13]

Considerations of judicial administration demonstrate the soundness of this view which, in any event, seems compelled by the language of the present statute, which is remedial and to be liberally construed. Were an insurance company required to await reduction of claims to judgment, the first claimant to obtain such a judgment or to negotiate a settlement might appropriate all or a disproportionate slice of the fund before his fellow claimants were able to establish their claims. The difficulties such a race to judgment pose for the insurer, and the unfairness which may result to some claimants, were among the principal evils the interpleader device was intended to remedy.

III.

The fact that State Farm had properly invoked the interpleader jurisdiction under § 1335 did not, however, entitle it to an order both enjoining prosecution of suits against it outside the confines of the interpleader proceeding and also extending such protection to its insured, the alleged tortfeasor. Still less was Greyhound Lines entitled to have that order expanded so as to protect itself and its driver, also alleged to be tortfeasors, from suits brought by its passengers in various state or federal courts. Here, the scope of the litigation, in terms of parties and claims, was vastly more extensive than the confines of the "fund," the deposited proceeds of the insurance policy. In these circumstances, the mere existence of such a fund cannot, by use of interpleader, be employed to accomplish purposes that exceed the needs of orderly contest with respect to the fund.

There are situations, of a type not present here, where the effect of interpleader is to confine the total litigation to a single forum and proceeding. One such case is where a stakeholder, faced with rival claims to the fund itself, acknowledges—or denies—his liability to one or the other of the claimants. In this situation, the fund itself is the target of the claimants. It marks the outer limits of the controversy. It is, therefore, reasonable and sensible that interpleader, in discharge of its office to protect the fund, should also protect the stakeholder from vexatious and multiple litigation. In this context, the suits sought to be enjoined are squarely within the language of 28 U.S.C. § 2361 * * *.

But the present case is another matter. Here, an accident has happened. Thirty-five passengers or their representatives have claims which they wish to press against a variety of defendants: the bus company, its driver, the owner of the truck, and the truck driver. The circumstance that one of the prospective defendants happens to have an insurance policy is a fortuitous event which should not of itself shape the nature of the ensuing litigation. * * * [A]n insurance company whose maximum interest in the case

---

[13] 3 Moore, Fed.Prac. ¶ 22.08, at 3024–3025; Keeton, Preferential Settlement of Liability-Insurance Claims, 70 Harv.L.Rev. 27, 41–42 (1956).

cannot exceed $20,000 and who in fact asserts that it has no interest at all, should not be allowed to determine that dozens of tort plaintiffs must be compelled to press their claims—even those claims which are not against the insured and which in no event could be satisfied out of the meager insurance fund—in a single forum of the insurance company's choosing. There is nothing in the statutory scheme, and very little in the judicial and academic commentary upon that scheme, which requires that the tail be allowed to wag the dog in this fashion.

State Farm's interest in this case   *   *   *   receives full vindication when the court restrains claimants from seeking to enforce against the insurance company any judgment obtained against its insured, except in the interpleader proceeding itself. To the extent that the District Court sought to control claimants' lawsuits against the insured and other alleged tortfeasors, it exceeded the powers granted to it by the statutory scheme.

We recognize, of course, that our view of interpleader means that it cannot be used to solve all the vexing problems of multiparty litigation arising out of a mass tort. But interpleader was never intended to perform such a function, to be an all-purpose "bill of peace." Had it been so intended, careful provision would necessarily have been made to insure that a party with little or no interest in the outcome of a complex controversy should not strip truly interested parties of substantial rights—such as the right to choose the forum in which to establish their claims, subject to generally applicable rules of jurisdiction, venue, service of process, removal, and change of venue. None of the legislative and academic sponsors of a modern federal interpleader device viewed their accomplishment as a "bill of peace," capable of sweeping dozens of lawsuits out of the various state and federal courts in which they were brought and into a single interpleader proceeding. And only in two reported instances has a federal interpleader court sought to control the underlying litigation against alleged tortfeasors as opposed to the allocation of a fund among successful tort plaintiffs. See Commercial Union Ins. Co. of New York v. Adams, 231 F.Supp. 860 (D.C.S.D.Ind.1964) (where there was virtually no objection and where all of the basic tort suits would in any event have been prosecuted in the forum state), and Pan American Fire & Cas. Co. v. Revere * * *.

In light of the evidence that federal interpleader was not intended to serve the function of a "bill of peace" in the context of multiparty litigation arising out of a mass tort, of the anomalous power which such a construction of the statute would give the stakeholder, and of the thrust of the statute and the purpose it was intended to serve, we hold that the interpleader statute did not authorize the injunction entered in the present case. Upon remand, the injunction is to be modified consistently with this opinion.

IV.

The judgment of the Court of Appeals is reversed, and the case is remanded to the United States District Court for proceedings consistent with this opinion.

* * *

[Mr. Justice DOUGLAS dissented on the ground that the litigants were not "claimants" to the fund as required by the Federal Interpleader Act. He pointed out that the insurance policy specifically provided that no action could be brought against the company until the insured's obligation was determined. Furthermore, he argued, both California and Oregon law did not permit a direct action against the insurer until after final judgment against the insured. The Justice also took issue with the majority's construction of the words "may claim" in the Federal Interpleader Act.]

NOTES AND QUESTIONS

1. In TREINIES v. SUNSHINE MINING CO., 308 U.S. 66, 60 S.Ct. 44, 84 L.Ed. 85 (1939), the Supreme Court held that a federal court could constitutionally assert jurisdiction under the Federal Interpleader Act despite the cocitizenship of the stakeholder and one of the claimants. In arriving at this conclusion, the Court said that the stakeholder's "disinterestedness as between the claimants and as to the property in dispute" was demonstrated by his deposit of the fund in court and his discharge, which left the dispute to be ironed out between the adverse claimants. Id. at 72, 60 S.Ct. at 48, 84 L.Ed. at 90. Was it realistic for the Court to regard the disinterested stakeholder as a nominal party for diversity purposes? Can you reconcile the Court's conclusion with the fact that under Federal Rule 22(1) jurisdiction is proper if there is diversity between the stakeholder and the claimants, even though there is no diversity between the claimants? But what if the stakeholder in *Treinies* had asserted a claim to the money? Would the requisite diversity have existed? In other words, should the Court's reasoning also extend to bills in the nature of a bill of interpleader? See Bierman v. Marcus, 140 F.Supp. 66, 70 (D.N.J.1956), reversed on other grounds 246 F.2d 200 (3d Cir.1957). *But cf.* Boice v. Boice, 135 F.2d 919, 920 (3d Cir.1943). Does *State Farm* answer this question?

2. Note that in the principal case, the stakeholder was a citizen of Illinois and defendants were citizens of California, Oregon, several other states, and Canada. A number of claimants were citizens either of the same state or Canada. Since *Treinies* only dealt with cocitizenship as between the stakeholder and a claimant, on what basis does the Supreme Court in *State Farm* cavalierly decide that cocitizenship between adverse claimants does not destroy diversity jurisdiction as long as there is "diversity between two or more of the claimants to the fund and between State Farm and all of the named defendants"? Would the result have been different in *State Farm* if there had not been diversity between State Farm and the named defendants as well as an absence of "complete diversity" among all of the claimants?

Perhaps the leading case on the subject of diversity in statutory interpleader actions prior to *State Farm* was HAYNES v. FELDER, 239 F.2d 868 (5th Cir.

1957), which involved a Texas stakeholder who brought interpleader against two rival sets of claimants consisting of a citizen of Texas on one side opposed by four joint claimants of whom three were citizens of Texas and one was a citizen of Tennessee. In an exhaustive and illuminating opinion, the Fifth Circuit held that sufficient diversity existed for purposes of the Federal Interpleader Act and seemingly adopted a test of "minimal diversity." In what ways is *State Farm* distinguishable from *Haynes?*

3. When an action has been brought against a stakeholder in a federal court, there is some authority permitting a stakeholder to file a bill of interpleader or a bill in the nature of a bill of interpleader against plaintiff and one or more of the claimants, regardless of the citizenship of the added claimants. If the resulting interpleader suit is considered ancillary to the suit against the stakeholder, it is immaterial that the stakeholder is a cocitizen with any of the added claimants or that these claimants are themselves cocitizens. See Sherman Nat. Bank v. Shubert Theatrical Co., 238 F. 225 (S.D.N.Y.1916), affirmed 247 F. 256 (2d Cir. 1917). For a discussion of ancillary jurisdiction and interpleader, see Chafee, *Interpleader in United States Courts,* 41 Yale L.J. 1134, 1145–60 (1931).

4. Consider the following situation. Decedent was a stockholder in both A and B Corporations. His stock certificates in these two corporations are in the hands of C–2, a broker, who contends that she bought the stock from decedent. C–1, decedent's executrix, says that decedent merely entrusted the stock certificates to C–2 for safekeeping. Each claimant requests that A Corporation recognize her as the owner of the stock. The corporation interpleads. In addition to responding to the interpleader, C–1's answer demands that C–2 hand over the stock in B Corporation. Ownership of both sets of certificates turns on precisely the same facts. If the interpleader suit is brought under the Federal Interpleader Act, should the court adjudicate the ownership of both the A and B stock? For an argument that an interpleader suit should permit litigation of claims between the claimants in an interpleader suit other than claims for the disputed fund, see Chafee, *Broadening the Second Stage of Interpleader,* 56 Harv.L.Rev. 541, 929 (1943).

But what about the statement in *Tashire* that: "[O]ur view of interpleader means that it cannot be used to solve all the vexing problems of multiparty litigation arising out of a mass tort." 386 U.S. at 535, 87 S.Ct. at 1206. Does this prohibit cross-claims between interpleader claimants, the assertion of an unrelated claim by a disinterested stakeholder against a claimant, and a counterclaim by a claimant against the stakeholder? See generally 7 Wright & Miller, *Federal Practice and Procedure: Civil* § 1715 (1972).

Assume that the interpleader suit concerning the A stock is brought in New York and that C–1 is a citizen of New York and C–2 is a citizen of Illinois and was personally served in that state under the Interpleader Act. If C–1 had started a separate action for the B stock, she would have had to travel to Illinois to try the suit because she could not have served C–2 with process in New York. Can the nationwide service of process permitted by the Interpleader Act be used to assert jurisdiction over the claims to the B stock by C–1 and C–2 in the suit involving the A stock? *Cf.* Moreno v. United States, 120 F.2d 128 (1st Cir.1941). See also Hagen v. Central Ave. Dairy, Inc., 180 F.2d 502 (9th Cir.1950). What if C–2 had been the first party to demand the B stock in her answer in the interpleader suit?

APPLICABLE LAW IN FEDERAL INTERPLEADER CASES

In GRIFFIN v. McCOACH, 313 U.S. 498, 61 S.Ct. 1023, 85 L.Ed. 1481 (1941), the Supreme Court held that in a statutory interpleader suit based on diversity jurisdiction a federal court is bound by the *Erie* doctrine to apply the conflict-of-law rules of the state in which it sits. The case was decided on the same day as *Klaxon Co. v. Stentor Elec. Mfg. Co.,* p. 296, Note 2, supra. Yet, in certain statutory interpleader actions, the courts of the forum state might never have been able to hear a comparable case due to Fourteenth-Amendment limitations on their personal jurisdiction. For a compelling argument that federal courts should develop their own conflicts rules when a federal act extends service of process beyond what is permitted a state by the Constitution, see *Developments in the Law— Multiparty Litigation in the Federal Courts,* 71 Harv.L.Rev. 874, 924–26 (1958). Are there any other arguments to suggest the inapplicability of *Erie* and *Klaxon* in statutory interpleader cases? The *Griffin* decision has been criticized in Cook, *The Federal Courts and the Conflict of Laws,* 36 Ill.L.Rev. 493, 507–15 (1942).

The American Law Institute has suggested the following principle for statutory interpleader cases. "Whenever State law supplies the rule of decision on an issue, the district court may make its own determination as to which State rule of decision is applicable." ALI, *Study of the Division of Jurisdiction Between State and Federal Courts,* Official Draft, § 2363(c) (1969).

Can a federal court grant interpleader under Federal Rule 22 when the state courts would deny interpleader because the stakeholder alleges a personal interest in the outcome of the case?

SECTION C. INTERVENTION

Read Federal Rule of Civil Procedure 24 in the Supplement.

BRUNE v. McDONALD

Supreme Court of Oregon, 1938.
158 Or. 364, 75 P.2d 10.

KELLY, Justice. * * *

It appears from the original complaint of plaintiff that on the 16th day of August defendant was driving his automobile, with plaintiff as his guest therein, * * * on the Mount Hood Loop Road, toward Hood river, and that, when in the vicinity of Van Horn, defendant drove his automobile off the highway, along the edge thereof, across a culvert, through a fence and into a tree, causing injuries to plaintiff.

To support the charge of gross negligence on defendant's part, plaintiff specifically alleged in her original complaint that defendant operated his automobile at an excessive rate of speed, failed to keep his automobile under control, failed to maintain a proper lookout, and failed and neglected to heed plaintiff's remonstrance against defendant's maintenance of such excessive speed. In said original complaint plaintiff also alleged that prior to said accident defendant had imbibed alcoholic liquor, and, in the face of plaintiff's positive opposition thereto, drank excessively of alcohol.

On the 19th day of December, 1936, an amended complaint was filed from which reference to defendant's use of alcohol was omitted.

On the 9th day of January, 1937, said Pacific Indemnity Company procured an order granting said company leave to file a complaint in intervention herein.

On the 15th day of January, 1937, said Pacific Indemnity Company filed its complaint in intervention, in which said company alleged * * * it insured defendant against loss by reason of the liability imposed by law upon him for damages on account of bodily injuries suffered or alleged to have been suffered by any person other than his employees as a result of the ownership, maintenance, or use for pleasure purposes of the automobile referred to in the amended complaint herein, subject to a limitation to the sum of $5,000 for bodily injuries sustained by any one person.

*   *   *

The intervener, in its complaint in intervention, alleges:

"* * *

"V. That prior to the trip during which said accident occurred plaintiff and defendant were and had been for a long time intimate friends and associates, frequently in the company of each other, and on frequent parties together, at which intoxicating liquors were consumed, and in the consumption of which both participated, and that plaintiff was well aware of the habits of defendant with respect to the use of intoxicating liquor.

"VI.   That on the afternoon of Sunday, August 16, 1936, plaintiff and defendant embarked upon a pleasure trip around the Mount Hood Loop Highway, taking with them a bottle of intoxicating liquor for consumption during the trip, and they did from time to time during said trip jointly participate in drinking said intoxicating liquor and at Government Camp on said highway jointly engaged in drinking other intoxicating liquor with other persons.

"VII.   That after said accident defendant gave to this intervenor several conflicting stories about the occurrences leading up to said accident, at first alleging that, while he was operating his automobile carefully and at a moderate speed, it was forced from the highway by another automobile, and then later that both plaintiff and defendant had consumed a considerable quantity of intoxicating liquor on the trip and that the accident occurred because of a momentary lapse of attention on his part while the automobile was being operated at a moderate speed; later plaintiff and defendant learned that there could be no recovery under said policy on such allegations and then connived and conspired with each other to mulct this intervenor of damages under said insurance policy and to that end jointly agreed that plaintiff should file an action against defendant for damages on account of her personal injuries and should allege that at the time of the accident defendant was grossly intoxicated and operating his automobile at a grossly high rate of speed and that defendant should represent to this intervenor that such charges were true and should deny to this intervenor that plaintiff participated in any of the drinking done on the trip, or knew that defendant was or was becoming intoxicated, thereby presenting an appearance of liability on the part of the defendant to plaintiff where none in truth and in fact existed, and with the intent of defrauding this intervenor of a substantial part of the face of said insurance policy.

"VIII.   That in pursuance of said conspiracy plaintiff caused a complaint to be filed in this cause wherein she made the charges heretofore referred to against defendant and defendant thereupon represented to intervenor that said charges were all true, and further represented that the plaintiff did not participate in the drinking of any liquor on said trip, that plaintiff was not aware that he was or was becoming intoxicated and was not aware of his habits respecting intoxicating liquor because of his peculiar ability and capacity to imbibe large quantities of intoxicating liquor without other persons being aware of the fact, all of which representations made by the defendant were false and known by him and by plaintiff to be false and were made in accordance with their joint agreement to deceive and defraud this intervenor.

"IX.   That by reason of the matters aforesaid said policy of insurance is void as to the accident in which plaintiff was injured and neither plaintiff nor defendant should be permitted to look to said policy in equity and in good conscience for any reimbursement or damages growing out of said accident; that plaintiff and defendant are planning to procure the entry of a judgment in favor of plaintiff and against defendant for a sum equal to the face of said policy but have agreed that plaintiff will look solely to this intervenor for the payment of said judgment and will make no attempt to collect any part of said judgment from defendant; that plaintiff will, unless restrained by this Court, procure a judgment to be entered against defendant and will then delay action on said policy of insurance until just prior to the expiration of the period of limitation applicable thereto, by which time the witnesses to establish the facts concerning said accident and said conspiracy of plaintiff and defendant, and the fraud perpetrated on defendant will have scattered and be unavailable.

"* * *"

The question here is whether said complaint in intervention states facts sufficient to warrant the court in granting the relief sought by the intervener, which is an injunction restraining the prosecution of plaintiff's cause of action until it can be determined whether defendant has breached the terms and conditions of said policy of insurance, as alleged by intervener.

The view usually expressed by the courts is that originally, in jurisdictions in which the common law prevailed, intervention was unknown except that it was in use to some extent in the ecclesiastical courts, and that apparently it is derived from the civil law. Therefore, in common-law jurisdictions intervention is usually regarded as of purely statutory origin. * * *

The generally accepted rule is that the right or interest which will authorize a third person to intervene must be of such a direct and immediate character that the intervener will either gain or lose by the direct legal operation of the judgment. * * *

It is obvious that the direct legal operation of the judgment in the case at bar would not cause intervener either to gain or lose anything.

It is equally apparent that the complaint in intervention herein tenders an entirely new and different issue from those of the complaint.

* * *

It will be noted that the intervener does not seek to interpose an answer to the complaint of plaintiff upon the merits of her alleged claim at law. Tested by a demurrer, the clause, "thereby presenting an appearance of liability on the part of the defendant to plaintiff where none in truth and in fact existed," does not constitute a statement of any defense to plaintiff's legal demand against defendant.

The relief sought by intervener is equitable. Intervener prays for an injunction restraining the further prosecution of plaintiff's action against defendant, until it can be determined whether the intervener would be liable to defendant upon its policy of insurance in case plaintiff should secure a judgment against defendant herein.

The reason assigned for seeking this relief is that by the time the judgment, if any, is procured by plaintiff against defendant, and proceedings are instituted to recover on intervener's policy, the intervener's witnesses to the alleged conspiracy will have become scattered and difficult, if not impossible, to procure, and that intervener will be confronted by a woman claimant whose femininity will render it much harder for intervener than if the same issue should be tried before plaintiff's claim against defendant has been adjudicated.

No case has been cited wherein such a procedure as intervener seeks to establish has been approved. The cases cited by intervener deal with sureties and with parties in interest who have been omitted in the original proceeding.

The policy of the courts generally has been to deal with the insurer in such a case as this as not being a party in interest and on the trial to guard against any willful reference to such insurer or to the fact that defendant is insured.

* * *

In giving effect to the allegations of the complaint in intervention we must assume that in case plaintiff prevails against defendant, the intervener will not be liable to defendant in any sum on that account. No liability on intervener's part could result in case defendant prevailed. We think that the supposed embarrassment which intervener alleges it will suffer by reason of the lapse of time necessary to determine this action at law, before the question of the validity or nonvalidity of intervener's policy of insurance can be presented, is not such an interest as the statute above quoted includes.

* * *

The controversy before the court, when the complaint in intervention was filed, was based upon a charge by plaintiff against defendant of gross negligence constituting the proximate cause of personal injury to plaintiff whereby plaintiff suffered damages in the amount demanded. It is obvious that this controversy may be completely determined without any reference, to intervener's policy of insurance. Certainly an invalid, void policy of insurance could not in any way affect the issues tendered in plaintiff's complaint.

* * *

We hold that no error was committed by the circuit court in sustaining plaintiff's demurrer to the complaint in intervention.

The judgment of the circuit court is affirmed.

———

KNAPP v. HANKINS, 106 F.Supp. 43, 47–48 (E.D.Ill.1952):

It is argued that the [insurance] Company may sit idly by and let the defendant employ counsel of his own choosing to defend the action. Under the terms of the policy defendant is obligated only to cooperate with the Company in defense of the suit. It would be unfair to require defendant to defend the case at his own expense if the policy is valid, even though he might subsequently recover such expenses from the Company; it would be equally unfair to require the Company to defend Hankins if the policy is void.

* * *

Lastly, the plaintiffs and the defendant contend that the intervention by the Company will introduce new issues in the controversy between plaintiffs and defendant and that the plaintiffs are not interested in the controversy between the Company and the defendant.

* * * The allowance of intervention in the suit will not change the issues between the plaintiffs and the defendant one iota, but before these issues are tried the Company and the defendant will be permitted to determine the validity of the policy. A separate trial will no doubt be had on the issues raised by the intervening petition.

WHARFF v. WHARFF, 244 Iowa 496, 502–03, 56 N.W.2d 1, 4–5 (1953). Plaintiff-husband brought a divorce action against defendant-wife. In his complaint plaintiff described certain real estate held under a tenancy in common by the parties and asked that each party be declared to have certain rights of ownership therein. In her answer, defendant alleged that the real estate had been purchased in part with money she held in trust for her children by a previous marriage. The children petitioned to intervene, claiming the existence of a trust agreement under which their mother, defendant, held the sum of $21,500 for them and part of which had been invested in the real estate in question. The intervention petition prayed for a trust to be impressed for the benefit of the children. The denial of plaintiff's motion to strike the petition of intervention was affirmed by the Supreme Court of Iowa, which said:

> * * * It is true that persons not parties to the litigation would not be bound by its result and might bring a separate action. But we think the rule that a multiplicity of suits will be avoided wherever possible has a direct application. It might also happen that if the plaintiff and defendant here should try out their action first, and intervenors be relegated to a separate suit, different and contradictory results would be reached. A division of the property of the original parties without the benefit of such evidence as the intervenors might produce could very well be inequitable, resulting, at the best, in an action to modify the divorce decree by the litigant whose rights were adversely affected by a later trial of the separate action to enforce a trust. * * *
> There seems every reason in policy why, if there are third parties claiming an interest in either the real or personal property, the entire matter should be decided at once. Such a course will do away with a multiplicity of suits and will enable the court to make orders concerning property rights and allowances with a full knowledge of the exact extent of the interests of the litigants. In the case at bar, if the court is not to be permitted to know the real interest of the plaintiff and defendant in the realty and personalty now owned by them, if this must be left to determination in a future and separate suit brought by the proposed intervenors, it will be greatly hampered in making a fair order. * * *

NOTES AND QUESTIONS

1. Is the statement in *Brune* that "the direct legal operation of the judgment * * * would not cause intervenor either to gain or lose anything" accurate? Does it mean that a party will be allowed to intervene only if the judgment will bind that party by principles of res judicata or collateral estoppel? Would the intervenors in *Wharff* have been affected by these doctrines had they not been allowed to intervene?

2. Consider the situation of a stakeholder subject to two conflicting claims to the fund he is holding. If the stakeholder prefers to defend an action brought by one claimant rather than use interpleader against both claimants, can the excluded claimant intervene in the other claimant's action? Would it make any difference if the excluded claimant could show that the stakeholder was not financially able to satisfy two judgments in the event that each claimant successfully prosecuted separate actions?

3. Should an alleged corespondent be permitted to intervene in a divorce suit in order to protect his or her reputation or to protect the public against fraud or collusion? See Leland v. Leland, 319 Ill. 426, 150 N.E. 270 (1925); Lickle v. Boone, 187 Md. 579, 51 A.2d 162, 170 A.L.R. 156 (1947).

4. The Oregon statute involved in *Brune* is a typical "liberal" intervention provision. A more restrictive provision is Section 2307.27 of the Ohio Revised Code, which appears in the Supplement following Federal Rule 24. Would intervention have been allowed in *Brune, Knapp,* and *Wharff* under the Ohio statute?

SMUCK v. HOBSON

United States Court of Appeals, District of Columbia Circuit, 1969.
132 U.S.App.D.C. 372, 408 F.2d 175.

[In Hobson v. Hansen, 269 F.Supp. 401 (D.D.C.1967), a class action brought on behalf of Black and poor children, the court found that the plaintiffs were being denied their constitutional rights to equal educational opportunities because the schools were being operated on a basis that was racially and economically discriminatory. The Board of Education voted not to appeal and ordered Dr. Carl Hansen, the Superintendent of Schools, not to appeal. Nonetheless, Dr. Hansen and Mr. Carl Smuck, one of the dissenting Board members filed notices of appeal. In addition motions to intervene were made in the district court and in the court of appeals by Dr. Hansen and twenty parents who said they "dissent from" the court's decision. The court of appeals decided to hold the direct appeals in abeyance and remanded the intervention motions for a hearing. The district court granted the motions to intervene, even though neither Hansen nor the parents had shown a substantial interest that could be protected only through intervention, "in order to give the court of appeals an opportunity to pass on the intervention questions raised here, and the questions to be raised by the appeal on the merits * * *." Hobson v. Hansen, 44 F.R.D. 18, 33 (D.D. C.1968). The court of appeals then considered the matter *en banc.*]

BAZELON, Chief Judge * * *. These appeals challenge the findings of the trial court that the Board of Education has in a variety of ways violated the Constitution in administering the District of Columbia schools. Among the facts that distinguish this case from the normal grist of appellate courts is the absence of the Board of Education as an appellant. Instead, the would-be appellants are Dr. Carl F. Hansen, the resigned superintendent of District schools, who appeals in his former official capacity and as an individual; Carl C. Smuck, a member of the Board of Education, who appeals in that capacity; and the parents of certain school children who have attempted to intervene in order to register on appeal their "dissent" from the order below.

* * * Whatever standing he might have possessed to appeal as a named defendant in the original suit * * * disappeared when Dr. Hansen left his official position. Presumably because he was aware of this, he subsequently moved to intervene under Rule 24(a) of the Rules of Civil Procedure in order to appeal as an individual. * * * The original decision was not a personal attack upon Dr. Hansen, nor did it bind him personally once he left office. And while it may or may not be true that but for the decision Dr. Hansen would still be Superintendent of Schools, the fact is that he did resign. He does not claim that a reversal or modification of the order by this Court would make his return to office likely. Consequently, the supposed impact of the decision upon his tenure is irrelevant insofar as an appeal is concerned, since a reversal would have no effect. Dr. Hansen thus has no "interest relating to the property or transaction which is the subject of the action" sufficient for Rule 24(a), and intervention is therefore unwarranted.

We also find that Mr. Smuck has no appealable interest as a member of the Board of Education. While he was in that capacity a named defendant, the Board of Education was undeniably the principal figure and could have been sued alone as a collective entity. Appellant Smuck had a fair opportunity to participate in its defense, and in the decision not to appeal. Having done so, he has no separate interest as an individual in the litigation. The order directs the board to take certain actions. But since its decisions are made by vote as a collective whole, there is no apparent way in which Smuck as an individual could violate the decree and thereby become subject to enforcement proceedings.

The motion to intervene by the parents presents a more difficult problem requiring a correspondingly more detailed examination of the requirements for intervention of right.

* * * The phrasing of Rule 24(a)(2) as amended parallels that of Rule 19(a)(2) concerning joinder. But the fact that the two rules are entwined does not imply that an "interest" for the purpose of one is precisely the same as for the other. The occasions upon which a petitioner should be allowed to intervene under Rule 24 are not necessarily limited to

those situations when the trial court should compel him to become a party under Rule 19. And while the division of Rule 24(a) and (b) into "Intervention of Right" and "Permissible Intervention" might superficially suggest that only the latter involves an exercise of discretion by the court, the contrary is clearly the case.

The effort to extract substance from the conclusory phrase "interest" or "legally protectable interest" is of limited promise. Parents unquestionably have a sufficient "interest" in the education of their children to justify the initiation of a lawsuit in appropriate circumstances, as indeed was the case for the plaintiff-appellee parents here. But in the context of intervention the question is not whether a lawsuit should be begun, but whether already initiated litigation should be extended to include additional parties. The 1966 amendments to Rule 24(a) have facilitated this, the true inquiry, by eliminating the temptation or need for tangential expeditions in search of "property" or someone "bound by a judgment." It would be unfortunate to allow the inquiry to be led once again astray by a myopic fixation upon "interest." Rather, as Judge Leventhal recently concluded for this Court, "[A] more instructive approach is to let our construction be guided by the policies behind the 'interest' requirement. * * * [T]he 'interest' test is primarily a practical guide to disposing of lawsuits by involving as many apparently concerned persons as is compatible with efficiency and due process." [12]

The decision whether intervention of right is warranted thus involves an accommodation between two potentially conflicting goals: to achieve judicial economies of scale by resolving related issues in a single lawsuit, and to prevent the single lawsuit from becoming fruitlessly complex or unending. Since this task will depend upon the contours of the particular controversy, general rules and past decisions cannot provide uniformly dependable guides. The Supreme Court, in its only full-dress examination of Rule 24(a) since the 1966 amendments, found that a gas distributor was entitled to intervention of right although its only "interest" was the economic harm it claimed would follow from an allegedly inadequate plan for divestiture approved by the Government in an antitrust proceeding.[14] While conceding that the Court's opinion granting intervention in Cascade Natural Gas Corp. v. El Paso Natural Gas Co. "is certainly susceptible of a very broad reading," the trial judge here would distinguish the decision on the ground that the petitioner "did show a strong direct economic interest, for the new company [to be created by divestiture] would be its sole supplier." [15] Yet while it is undoubtedly true that "*Cascade* should not be read as a carte

---

[12] Nuesse v. Camp, 128 U.S.App.D.C. 172, 385 F.2d 694, 700 (1967).

[14] Cascade Natural Gas Corp. v. El Paso Natural Gas Co., 386 U.S. 129, 132–136, 87 S.Ct. 932, 17 L.Ed.2d 814 (1967).

[15] 44 F.R.D. at 24–25.

blanche for intervention by anyone at any time," [16] there is no apparent reason why an "economic interest" should always be necessary to justify intervention. The goal of "disposing of lawsuits by involving as many apparently concerned persons as is compatible with efficiency and due process" may in certain circumstances be met by allowing parents whose only "interest" is the education of their children to intervene. In determining whether such circumstances are present, the first requirement of Rule 24(a)(2), that of an "interest" in the transaction, may be a less useful point of departure than the second and third requirements, that the applicant may be impeded in protecting his interest by the action and that his interest is not adequately represented by others.

This does not imply that the need for an "interest" in the controversy should or can be read out of the rule. But the requirement should be viewed as a prerequisite rather than relied upon as a determinative criterion for intervention. If barriers are needed to limit extension of the right to intervene, the criteria of practical harm to the applicant and the adequacy of representation by others are better suited to the task. If those requirements are met, the nature of his "interest" may play a role in determining the sort of intervention which should be allowed—whether, for example, he should be permitted to contest all issues, and whether he should enjoy all the prerogatives of a party litigant.

Both courts and legislatures have recognized as appropriate the concern for their children's welfare which the parents here seek to protect by intervention. While the artificiality of an appeal without the Board of Education cannot be ignored, neither can the importance of the constitutional issues decided below. The relevance of substantial and unsettled questions of law has been recognized in allowing intervention to perfect an appeal. And this Court has noted repeatedly, "obviously tailored to fit ordinary civil litigation, [the provisions of Rule 24] require other than literal application in atypical cases." [20] We conclude that the interests asserted by the intervenors are sufficient to justify an examination of whether the two remaining requirements for intervention are met.

* * *

[The court then determined that the disposition of the action might impair the applicants' ability to protect their interests if they were not allowed to intervene.]

---

[16] *Id.* The majority's splenetic displeasure with the substantive provisions of the divestiture plan approved by the Government and the trial court may have been an important factor in the liberal reading given Rule 24(a) in *Cascade.* * * *

[20] Textile Workers Union, etc. v. Allendale Co., 96 U.S.App.D.C. 401, 403, 226 F.2d 765, 767 (1955) (en banc), cert. denied, Allendale Co. v. Mitchell, 351 U.S. 909, 76 S.Ct. 699, 100 L.Ed. 1444 (1956), cited in Neusse v. Camp, 128 U.S.App.D.C. 172, 385 F.2d 694, 700 (1967).

The remaining requirement for intervention is that the applicant not be adequately represented by others. No question is raised here but that the Board of Education adequately represented the intervenors at the trial below; the issue rather is whether the parents were adequately represented by the school board's decision not to appeal. The presumed good faith of the board in reaching this decision is not conclusive. * * * As the conditional wording of Rule 24(a)(2) suggests in permitting intervention "unless the applicant's interest is adequately represented by existing parties," "the burden [is] on those opposing intervention to show the adequacy of the existing representation." In this case, the interests of the parents who wish to intervene in order to appeal do not coincide with those of the Board of Education. The school board represents all parents within the District. The intervening appellants may have more parochial interests centering upon the education of their own children. While they cannot of course ask the Board to favor their children unconstitutionally at the expense of others, they like other parents can seek the adoption of policies beneficial to their own children. Moreover, considerations of publicity, cost, and delay may not have the same weight for the parents as for the school board in the context of a decision to appeal. And the Board of Education, buffeted as it like other school boards is by conflicting public demands, may possibly have less interest in preserving its own untrammeled discretion than do the parents. It is not necessary to accuse the board of bad faith in deciding not to appeal or of a lack of vigor in defending the suit below in order to recognize that a restrictive court order may be a not wholly unwelcome haven.

The question of adequate representation when a motion is made for intervention to appeal is related to the question of whether the motion is timely. To a degree it may well be true that a "strong showing" is required to justify intervention after judgment. But by the same token a failure to appeal may be one factor in deciding whether representation by existing parties is adequate. As the opinion of the trial court in granting intervention demonstrates, the leading cases in which intervention has been permitted following a judgment tend to involve unique situations. The very absence of any precedent involving the same or even closely analogous facts requires a close examination of all the circumstances of this case. We conclude that the intervenor-appellants here have shown a sufficiently serious possibility that they were not adequately represented in the decision not to appeal.

Our holding that the appellants would be practically disadvantaged by a decision without appeal in this case and that they are not otherwise adequately represented necessitates a closer scrutiny of the precise nature of their interest and the scope of intervention that should accordingly be granted. The parents who seek to appeal do not come before this court to protect the good name of the Board of Education. Their interest is not to protect the board, or Dr. Hansen, from an unfair finding. Their asserted interest is rather the freedom of the school board—and particularly the new school board recently elected—to exercise the broadest discretion constitutionally permissible in deciding upon educational policies. Since this is so, their interest extends only to those parts of the order which can fairly be said to impose restraints upon the Board of Education. And because the school board is not a party to this appeal, review should be limited to those features of the order which limit the discretion of the old or new board.

* * *

[A partial concurring opinion by Judge McGOWAN and dissenting opinions by Judges DANAHER and BURGER are omitted.]

NOTES AND QUESTIONS

1. In addition to the reasons offered in *Smuck,* typical grounds for the assertion of inadequacy of representation for purposes of intervening as of right under Rule 24(a)(2) are: the applicant's interests are not represented at all, Gaines v. Dixie Carriers, Inc., 434 F.2d 52 (5th Cir.1970); the applicant and the attorney who supposedly represents his interest are antagonistic, United States v. C. M. Lane Lifeboat Co., 25 F.Supp. 410 (E.D.N.Y.1938), *but see* Stadin v. Union Elec. Co., 309 F.2d 912 (8th Cir.1962), certiorari denied 373 U.S. 915, 83 S.Ct. 1298, 10 L.Ed.2d 415 (1963); and there is collusion between the representative and the adverse parties, Park & Tilford, Inc. v. Schulte, 160 F.2d 984 (2d Cir.), certiorari denied 332 U.S. 761, 68 S.Ct. 64, 92 L.Ed.2d 347 (1947). See generally Shapiro, *Some Thoughts on Intervention Before Courts, Agencies and Arbitrators,* 81 Harv.L.Rev. 721 (1968).

It often is held that the United States adequately represents the public interest in antitrust suits and intervention in those cases is denied absent a clear showing to the contrary. Is this approach justifiable? How does the Department of Justice determine what the public interest is?

2. An example of a federal statute that permits intervention is Section 902 of the Civil Rights Act of 1964, 42 U.S.C. § 2000h–2, which gives the United States an unconditional right to intervene in actions seeking relief against a denial of equal protection of the laws under the Fourteenth Amendment on account of race, color, religion, or national origin. See Lemon v. Bossier Parish School Bd., 240 F.Supp. 709 (W.D.La.1965). Perhaps the single most important statutory provision permitting intervention by the United States is Section 2403 of the Judicial Code, which applies to actions involving the constitutionality of an act of Congress. This provision has even enabled the United States to intervene to show that a case should be decided on nonconstitutional grounds. See Smolowe v. Delendo Corp., 36 F.Supp. 790 (S.D.N.Y.1940), affirmed on other grounds 136 F.2d 231 (2d Cir.), certiorari denied 320 U.S. 751, 64 S.Ct. 56, 88 L.Ed. 446 (1943). The Government also has used it to show that the suit is collusive and there is no case or controversy before the court. See United States v. Johnson, 319 U.S. 302, 63 S.Ct. 1075, 87 L.Ed. 1413 (1943). See generally Note, *Federal Intervention in Private Actions Involving the Public Interest,* 65 Harv.L.Rev. 319 (1951). See 7A Wright & Miller, *Federal Practice and Procedure: Civil* § 1906 (1972), for a discussion of other statutes conferring an unconditional right to intervene. Can the United States intervene in nonconstitutional cases if it meets the requirements of Rule 24(a)(2) or Rule 24(b)(2)? See Berger, *Intervention by Pub-*

lic Agencies in Private Litigation in the Federal Courts, 50 Yale L.J. 65, 80–87 (1940).

3. Both Rule 24(a) and Rule 24(b) require that an application to intervene be "timely." As the court noted in *Smuck,* intervention after judgment will be allowed only in unique situations. One court has stated:

> The rationale which seems to underlie this general principle * * * is the assumption that allowing intervention after judgment will either (1) prejudice the rights of the existing parties to the litigation or (2) substantially interfere with the orderly processes of the court.

McDonald v. E. J. Lavino Co., 430 F.2d 1065, 1072 (5th Cir.1970).

What factors should the court consider when determining whether a motion to intervene is timely? Should a different standard be used for deciding the timeliness of motions to intervene permissively as opposed to motions to intervene as of right? If so, why?

4. If the applicant has a right to intervene under Rule 24(a), no independent basis for jurisdiction is required; the intervenor's claim is treated as ancillary to the main action. See Lenz v. Wagner, 240 F.2d 666 (5th Cir.1957). See also Frazer, *Ancillary Jurisdiction and the Joinder of Claims in the Federal Courts,* 33 F.R.D. 27, 43–45 (1963). For example, a party seeking to intervene as of right as a plaintiff in a diversity suit need not have different citizenship than defendant nor need the intervenor's claim satisfy the jurisdictional amount. In the past, however, the court dismissed the original action if the intervenor was an indispensable party to the original action and was a citizen of the same state as the adverse party. See Kentucky Nat. Gas Corp. v. Duggins, 165 F.2d 1011 (6th Cir. 1948). Has the 1966 amendment to Rule 19 affected this conclusion? Should the doctrine of ancillary jurisdiction also apply to cases of permissive intervention? See Durkin v. Pet Milk Co., 14 F.R.D. 374 (W.D.Ark.1953). *But see* Berman v. Herrick, 30 F.R.D. 9 (E.D.Pa.1962).

5. What if the applicant is attempting to intervene under Rule 24(b) in a class action? Should the fact that the judgment will be binding on all members of the class make any difference? Note that Rule 23(d) (2) and Rule 23(d) (3) contain references to intervention in class actions. Do these provisions establish an intervention standard for class actions that is different than Rule 24? If so, how is it different?

ATLANTIS DEVELOPMENT CORP. v. UNITED STATES

United States Court of Appeals, Fifth Circuit, 1967.
379 F.2d 818.

JOHN R. BROWN, Circuit Judge. This case involves a little bit of nearly everything—a little bit of oceanography, a little bit of marine biology, a little bit of the tidelands oil controversy, a little bit of international law, a little bit of latter day Marco Polo exploration. But these do not command our resolution since the little bits are here controlled by the less exciting bigger, if not big, problem of intervention. The District Court declined to permit mandatory intervention as a matter of right or to allow intervention as permissive. As is so often true, a ruling made to avoid delay, complications, or expense turns out to have generated more of its own. With the main case being stayed by the District Court pending this appeal, it is pretty safe to assume that the case would long have been decided on its merits (or lack of them) had intervention of either kind been allowed. And this seems especially unfortunate since it is difficult to believe that the presence of the attempted intervenor would have added much to the litigation. All of this becomes the more ironic, if not unfortunate, since the intervenor [1] and the Government sparring over why intervention ought or ought not to have been allowed, each try to persuade us the one was bound to win, the other lose on the merits which each proceeds to argue as though the parties were before or in the court. Adding to the problem, or perhaps more accurately aiding in the solution of it, are the mid-1966 amendments to the Federal Rules of Civil Procedure including specifically those relating to intervention. We reverse.

What the jousting is all about is the ownership in, or right to control the use, development of and building on a number of coral reefs or islands comprising Pacific Reef, Ajax Reef, Long Reef, an unnamed reef and Triumph Reef which the intervenor has called the "Atlantis Group" because of the name given them by Anderson, its predecessor in interest and the supposed discoverer. * * *

Just how or in what manner these reefs were "discovered" is so far unrevealed. Some time in 1962 William T. Anderson discovered the reefs apparently by conceiving the idea of occupying them through the construction of facilities for fishing club, marina, skin diving club, a hotel, and, perhaps as the chief lure, a gambling casino. Anderson made some sort of claim to it and with facilities unavailable to the adventurous explorers of the long past, he gave public notice of this in the United States and in England by newspaper advertisements in late 1962 and early 1963. These "rights" were acquired by Atlantis Development Corporation, Ltd., the proposed intervenor. Reflecting the desire manifested now by the persistent efforts to intervene to have legal rights ascertained in a peaceful fashion through established tribunals and not by self-help or the initiation of physical activities which would precipitate counter moves, physical or legal, or both, Atlantis (and predecessors) patiently sought permission from all governmental agencies, state and federal—just short of the United Nations—but to no avail.

* * * In December 1964 on learning that the defendants in the main case had formally sought a permit from the Engineers, Atlantis notified the Government of its claim to ownership of the islands and the threatened unauthorized actions by the defendants. This precipitated further communications with the Department of Justice with Atlantis importuning, apparently successfully, the Government to initiate the present action.

---

[1] Atlantis Development Corporation, Ltd., a Bahamian corporation, will be referred to interchangeably as either Atlantis or Intervenor.

It was against this background that the litigation commenced. The suit is brought by the United States against the main defendants.[5] The complaint was in two counts seeking injunctive relief. In the first the Government asserted that Triumph and Long Reefs are part of the bed of the Atlantic Ocean included in the Outer Continental Shelf subject to the jurisdiction, control and power of disposition of the United States. The action of the defendants (note 5, supra) in the erection of caissons on the reefs, the dredging of material from the seabed, and the depositing of the dredged material within the caissons without authorization was charged as constituting a trespass on government property. In the second count the Government alleged that the defendants were engaged in the erection of an artificial island or fixed structure on the Outer Continental Shelf in the vicinity of the reefs without a permit from the Secretary of the Army in violation of the Outer Continental Shelf Lands Act, 43 U.S.C.A. § 1333(f) and 33 U.S.C.A. § 403. * * *

Atlantis seeking intervention by proposed answer and cross-claim against the defendants admitted the jurisdiction of the District Court. It asserted that the United States has no territorial jurisdiction, dominion or ownership in or over the reefs and cannot therefore maintain the action for an injunction, and that conversely Atlantis has title to the property by discovery and occupation. In the cross-claim, Atlantis charged the defendants as trespassers against it. Appropriate relief was sought by the prayer.

The District Court without opinion declared in the order that intervenor "does not have such an interest in this cause as will justify its intervention, either as a matter of right or permissively." Leave was granted to appear amicus curiae.

We think without a doubt that under former F.R.Civ.P. 24(a), intervention as a matter of right was not compelled under (a) (2). The situation did not present one in which the intervenor "is or may be bound" by a decree rendered in his absence in the sense articulated most recently in Sam Fox [9] in terms of res judicata. Although not quite so clear, we also think it did not measure up to the notions loosely reflected in a case-by-case development under which, although res judicata was technically lacking, the decree is considered "binding" since in a very practical sense it would have an immediate operative effect upon the intervenor. In none of these cases was it suggested that if the only effect of the decree in intervenor's absence would be to raise the hurdle of stare decisis, this would amount to the absentee being bound as a practical matter.

This brings us squarely to the effect of the 1966 Amendments and the new F.R.Civ.P. 24(a). * * *

In assaying the new Rule, several things stand out. The first, as the Government acknowledges, is that this amounts to a legislative repeal of the rigid

[5] Acme General Contractors, Inc., and J. H. Coppedge Company, each Florida corporations, and Louis M. Ray, a resident of Dade County, Florida.

[9] Sam Fox Publishing Co. v. United States, 1961, 366 U.S. 683, 81 S.Ct. 1309, 6 L. Ed.2d 604.

Sam Fox * * * res judicata rule. But more important, the revision was a coordinated one to tie more closely together the related situations of joinder, F.R.Civ.P. 19, and class actions, F.R.Civ.P. 23.

As the Advisory Committee's notes reflect, there are competing interests at work in this area. On the one hand, there is the private suitor's interests in having his own lawsuit subject to no one else's direction or meddling. On the other hand, however, is the great public interest, especially in these explosive days of ever-increasing dockets, of having a disposition at a single time of as much of the controversy to as many of the parties as is fairly possible consistent with due process.

In these three Rules the Advisory Committee, unsatisfied with the former Rules which too frequently defined application in terms of rigid legal concepts such as joint, common ownership, res judicata, or the like, as well as court efforts in applying them, deliberately set out on a more pragmatic course. For the purposes of our problem, this course is reflected in the almost, if not quite, uniform language concerning a party who claims an interest relating to the subject of the action and is so situated that the disposition of the action may as a practical matter impair or impede his ability to protect that interest * * *

Although this is question-begging and is therefore not a real test, this approach shows that the question of whether an intervention as a matter of right exists often turns on the unstated question of whether joinder of the intervenor was called for under new Rule 19. Were this the controlling inquiry, we find ample basis here to answer it in the affirmative. Atlantis—having formally informed the Government in detail of its claim of ownership to the very reefs in suit, that the defendants were trespassing against it, and having successfully urged the Government to institute suit against the defendants—seems clearly to occupy the position of a party who ought to have been joined as a defendant under new Rule 19(a) (2) (i) * * *.

This interim conclusion is, of course, a rejection of the Government's approach made for this day, case, and time only that all new Rule 24(a) was to do was to abandon the rigidity of *Sam Fox* and codify the ameliorative exceptions * * * to escape the unfortunate consequences of a rule expressed in terms of the party being "bound," i. e., res judicata. Any such narrow approach is to deprecate the painstaking work of the Advisory Committee especially the deliberate efforts to dovetail F.R.Civ.P. 19, 24 and 23 together with two of them being radically rewritten.

When approached in this light, we think that both from the terms of new Rule 24(a) and its adoption of 19(a) (2) (i) intervention of right is called for here. Of course F.R.Civ.P. 24(a) (2) requires both the existence of an interest which may be impaired as a practical matter and an absence of adequate representation of the intervenor's interest by existing parties. There can be no difficulty here about the lack of representation. On the basis of the pleadings * * * Atlantis is without a friend in this litigation. The Government turns on the defendants and takes the same view both administratively and in its brief here toward Atlantis. The defendants, on the other hand, are claiming ownership in and the right to develop the very islands claimed by Atlantis.

Nor can there be any doubt that Atlantis "claims an interest relating to the property or transaction which is the subject of the action." The object of the suit is to assert the sovereign's exclusive dominion and control over two out of a group of islands publicly claimed by Atlantis. This identity with the very property at stake in the main case and with the particular transaction therein involved (the right to build structures with or without permission of the Corps of Engineers) is of exceptional importance. For 24(a) (2) is in the conjunctive requiring both an interest relating to the property or transaction and the practical harm if the party is absent. This sharply reduces the area in which stare decisis may, as we later discuss, supply the element of practical harm.

This brings us then to the question whether these papers reflect that in the absence of Atlantis, a disposition of the main suit may as a practical matter impair or impede its ability to protect that interest—its claim to ownership and the right to control, use and develop without hindrance from the Government, the Department of Defense, or other agencies. Certain things are clear. Foremost, of course, is the plain proposition that the judgment itself as between Government and defendants cannot have any direct, immediate effect upon the rights of Atlantis, not a party to it.

But in a very real and practical sense is not the trial of this lawsuit the trial of Atlantis' suit as well? Quite apart from the contest of Atlantis' claim of sovereignty vis-a-vis the Government resulting from its "discovery" and occupation of the reefs, there are at least two basic substantial legal questions directly at issue, but not yet resolved in any Court at any time between the Government and the defendants which are inescapably present in the claim of Atlantis against the Government. One is whether these coral reefs built up by accretion of marine biology are "submerged lands" under the Outer Continental Shelf Lands Act, 43 U.S.C.A. § 1331 et seq. The second basic question is whether, assuming both from the standpoint of geographical location and their nature they constitute "lands," does the sovereignty of the United States extend to them with respect to any purposes not included in or done for the protection of the "exploring for, developing, removing, and transporting * * *" natural resources therefrom, 43 U.S.C.A. § 1333(a) (1). Another, closely related, is whether the authority of the Secretary of the Army to prevent obstruction of navigation extended by § 1333(f) to "artificial islands and fixed structures," includes structures other than those "erected thereon for the purpose of exploring for, developing, removing, and transporting" mineral resources therefrom (§ 1333(a) (1) * * *).

The Government would avoid all of these problems by urging us to rule as a matter of law on the face of the moving papers that the intervenors could not possibly win on the trial of the intervention and consequently intervention should be denied. In support it asserts that the claim that the reefs are beyond the jurisdiction of the United States is self-defeating, and under the plain meaning of the Outer Continental Shelf Lands Act and the facts revealed from the Coast and Geodetic Chart of which we must take judicial knowledge as proof of all facts shown.

The first is at least contingently answered by § 1333(b) which invests jurisdiction in the United States District Court of the nearest adjacent state. As to the others, it is, of course, conceivable that there will be some instances in which the total lack of merit is so evident from the face of the moving papers that denial of the right of intervention rests upon a complete lack of a substantial claim. But it hardly comports with good administration, if not due process, to determine the merits of a claim asserted in a pleading seeking an adjudication through an adversary hearing by denying access to the court at all. * * *

If in its claim against the defendants in the main suit these questions are answered favorably to the Government's position, the claim of Atlantis for all practical purposes is worthless. That statement assumes, of course, that such holding is either approved or made by this Court after an appeal to it and thereafter it is either affirmed, or not taken for review, on certiorari. It also assumes that in the subsequent separate trial of the claim of Atlantis against the Government the prior decision would be followed as a matter of stare decisis. Do these assumptions have a realistic basis? Anyone familiar with the history of the Fifth Circuit could have but a single answer to that query. This Court, unlike some of our sister Circuit Courts who occasionally follow a different course, has long tried earnestly to follow the practice in which a decision announced by one panel of the Court is followed by all others until such time as it is reversed, either outright or by intervening decisions of the Supreme Court, or by the Court itself en banc. That means that if the defendants in the main action do not prevail upon these basic contentions which are part and parcel of the claim of Atlantis, the only way by which Atlantis can win is to secure a rehearing en banc with a successful overruling of the prior decision or, failing in either one or both of those efforts, a reversal of the earlier decision by the Supreme Court on certiorari. With the necessarily limited number of en banc hearings in this Circuit and with the small percentage of cases meriting certiorari, it is an understatement to characterize these prospects as formidable.

That is but a way of saying in a very graphic way that the failure to allow Atlantis an opportunity to advance its own theories both of law and fact in the trial (and appeal) of the pending case will if the disposition is favorable to the Government "as a practical matter impair or impede [its] ability to protect [its] interest." That is, to be sure, a determination by us that in the new language of 24(a) (2) stare decisis may now—unlike the former days under 24(a) (2)—supply that practical disadvantage which warrants intervention of right. It bears repeating, however, that this holding does not presage one requiring intervention of right in every conceivable circumstance where under the operation of the Circuit's stare decisis practice, the formidable nature of an en banc rehearing or the successful grant of a writ of certiorari, an earlier decision might afford a substantial obstacle. We are dealing here with a conjunction of a claim to and interest in the very property and the very transaction which is the subject of the main action. When those coincide, the Court before whom the potential parties in the second suit must come must itself take the intellectually straight forward, realistic view that the first decision will in all likelihood be the second and the third and the last one. Even the possibility that the decision might be overturned by en banc ruling or reversal on certiorari does not overcome its practical effect, not just as an obstacle, but as the forerunner of the actual outcome. * * *

Reversed.

NOTES AND QUESTIONS

1. Early commentary on the 1966 amendment to Federal Rule 24 appears in Cohn, *The New Federal Rules of Civil Procedure,* 54 Geo.L.J. 1204, 1229–32 (1966); Kaplan, *Continuing Work of the Civil Committee: 1966 Amendments of the Federal Rules of Civil Procedure (I),* 81 Harv.L.Rev. 356, 400–07 (1967).

2. In what ways other than those described in *Atlantis* does the amended text of Federal Rule 24 have the effect of liberalizing intervention as of right? Prior to 1966, one of the two conditions on intervention of right was a showing that the representation of the intervenor "is or may be inadequate." Under amended Rule 24(a) if the other conditions of that provision are satisfied intervention is of right unless it is shown that the applicant's interest is adequately represented. What is the effect of this change? Intervention classically has been viewed as having three functions: protection of nonparties, trial convenience, and protection of the original parties. In what ways has the balance among these three considerations been altered by the 1966 amendments?

3. In *Provident Tradesmen,* p. 538, supra, the Supreme Court indicated in dicta, that the failure to intervene as of right does not mean that the party necessarily would be bound by the judgment. Is this sound? Compare REICH v. UNITED STATES, 239 F.2d 134 (1st Cir.1956), certiorari denied 352 U.S. 1004, 77 S.Ct. 563, 1 L.Ed.2d 549 (1957). In an earlier proceeding the United States had obtained an injunction against the Wilhelm Reich Foundation, Wilhelm Reich, and Ilse Ollendorff under the Federal Food, Drug and Cosmetic Act restraining the defendants from introducing into interstate commerce or misbranding certain supposedly therapeutic devices known as "orgone energy accumulators." The named defendants did not contest the action and copies of the decree were served on the defendants and mailed to a number of duly licensed physicians who were known to have used orgone energy accumulators. Among the group of doctors was Dr. Michael Silvert who, with other doctors, sought to intervene. This motion was denied on the following grounds:

> * * * The original proceeding was an *in personam* action brought solely against three specifically designated persons for the purpose of enjoining them from manufacturing and distributing in interstate commerce orgone energy accumulators which were adulterated and misbranded within the meaning of the Food and Drug Act. * * *

> Since the applicants were not engaged in the manufacture and distribution in interstate commerce of orgone energy accumulators, nor were they in any respect legally associated with the named defendants, the named defendants were properly the only parties before this Court in the original proceeding. * * * Accordingly, persons who are not

parties to an injunction, nor in privity with them, and whose rights have not been adjudicated therein are not bound by a decree and cannot be held liable for acts done contrary thereto even though the decree assumes to bind them.

United States v. Wilhelm Reich Foundation, 17 F.R.D. 96, 101 (D.Me.), affirmed per curiam sub nom. Baker v. United States, 221 F.2d 957 (1st Cir.), certiorari denied 350 U.S. 842, 76 S.Ct. 82, 100 L.Ed.2d 750 (1955). The United States thereafter filed an information charging the Wilhelm Reich Foundation, Wilhelm Reich, and Michael Silvert with failing and refusing to obey the injunction and the district court specifically rejected Dr. Silvert's contention that he was not bound by the decree since he was not a defendant in the action arguing that it was clear that Dr. Silvert had knowledge of the decree because he was mailed a copy and even attempted to intervene.

CHAPTER 8

PRETRIAL DEVICES FOR OBTAINING INFORMATION: DEPOSITIONS AND DISCOVERY

SECTION A. THE GENERAL SCOPE OF DISCOVERY

Read Federal Rules of Civil Procedure 26(a), 26(b), 27(a)(1), and 32(a) and the accompanying materials in the Supplement.

The development of pretrial techniques for obtaining information has roughly paralleled the increasing complexity of litigation. Expansion of discovery also has provided a partial response to the call for new procedures to supplant, or at least augment, the pleadings, which have proven increasingly inadequate as a device for defining for the parties and the court the precise issues in controversy. The roots of discovery are found in early English equity practice, but the evolution of modern procedures did not begin until the merger of law and equity in the nineteenth century and progressed slowly until the adoption of the Federal Rules of Civil Procedure in 1938. Federal Rules 26 through 37, which are the basic discovery provisions, not only authorize the use of all the discovery techniques known at the time the rules were promulgated but they also increase greatly the scope of permissible inquiry. So attractive are these provisions that they have been adopted by a large majority of the states, including a number of states that have rejected the federal pleading rules.

Modern discovery has three major purposes. The first, and least controversial, is the preservation of relevant information that might not be available at trial. Basically, this objective relates to the testimony of witnesses who are aged or ill or who will be out of the jurisdiction at the time the trial commences. See Federal Rules 27 and 32(a). The earliest discovery procedures in the federal courts were designed primarily for this purpose. See *Developments in the Law—Discovery*, 74 Harv.L.Rev. 940, 949 (1961).

The second purpose is to ascertain and isolate those issues that actually are in controversy between the parties. There is little dispute that it is appropriate for one party to ask whether another party contests the existence or nonexistence of a fact that the pleadings formally have put in issue. See Federal Rule 36. However, it is not entirely clear precisely how far the discovery devices may be utilized to force a party to set out in detail his factual and legal contentions when the rules of pleading do not require that this be done. The same arguments for and against detailed pleadings as to the law and facts may be made with regard to the appropriate use and scope of discovery. See pp. 720–23, infra.

The final major purpose of discovery is to find out what testimony and other evidence is available on each of the disputed factual issues. Prior to discovery a party could ascertain these matters only through private investigation; if, for example, a witness refused to discuss a matter with a party, there was no way to learn the substance of that witness' testimony in advance of trial. As a result, cases often turned on the parties' relative access to the facts and their ability to keep certain facts secret until the trial.

To the extent that the person to be questioned is a known eyewitness to the event in controversy, there is little dispute over the propriety of discovery to ascertain what will be said at trial. But the matter is far more complex if a witness, who may be a party or an attorney, obtains evidence during the investigation of the case in preparation for trial. In this context there is a sharp division between those who favor broad discovery to obviate all traces of surprise and those who allege the need for privacy of investigation and development of evidence. Under one thesis it is argued that broad discovery will eliminate the advantage that a wealthy party enjoys over a poorer opponent, whereas others claim that such discovery will induce a lazy litigant to sit back while the opposing party investigates diligently and then by simple use of discovery to obtain all the fruits of that investigation.

The argument rages not only as to which witnesses may be questioned before trial, but what questions may be asked. For example, should a witness be interrogated not only as to what she would be permitted to say at trial but also as to other matters such as rumors and the like, which, although inadmissible in themselves, might lead to admissible evidence? In connection with this question, read the language of Federal Rule 26(b) (1) carefully and compare it with the rules for discovery set out in *Kelly v. Nationwide Mut. Ins. Co.*, the case following this Note.

Even if widespread discovery is assumed to be beneficial, however, a question still remains regarding the extent to which its benefits outweigh the increased expenditure of time and money that results from its use. Some discovery devices generally cost very little, but they are the least likely to produce highly significant information. On the other hand, those devices that are most apt to produce substantial results are costly since they require the participation and close supervision of the attorneys. Furthermore, all of the devices are susceptible of abuse, particularly by a wealthy litigant who may engage a less affluent opponent in so much discovery that it becomes cheaper to concede the case. The typical discovery system contains a number of provisions calling for judicial intercession to avoid abuse, but resort to these methods in itself involves some cost; moreover, the results of judicial involvement are not always satisfactory, since judges are reluctant to find that discovery that would be considered appropriate if both parties were of equal financial strength, is somehow improper if one of the parties has more limited resources than the other. Yet, if firm control cannot effectively be exercised, discovery ceases to be a means of promoting justice and becomes a tactical weapon for harassment. Because of the imperfections in discovery, many people believe that the scope of discovery should be curtailed at the outset to eliminate the opportunities for abuse, even though this might result in the loss of substantial benefits. In reading the materials that follow keep in mind the outlines of the philosophical dispute over the proper scope of discovery.

In 1970 a comprehensively revised set of federal discovery rules became effective. In large measure the purpose of the changes was to resolve inconsistent court interpretations that inevitably had occurred over the thirty-two year period since the rules had been promulgated. In some situations, however, the rules were altered to achieve certain policy objectives. In the materials that follow, a number of the significant 1970 changes are pinpointed for consideration and discussion. Analyze these changes both from a practical and a theoretical point of view. Consider whether, as a whole, the modified rules reflect any basic alteration in the discovery philosophy of the Federal Rules.

KELLY v. NATIONWIDE MUT. INS. CO.

Ohio Court of Common Pleas, Ashtabula County, 1963.
23 Ohio Op.2d 29, 188 N.E.2d 445.

PONTIUS, Judge. Plaintiff sued to recover damages to a motor vehicle under the terms of a comprehensive insurance policy, claiming that the damages arose because someone put sugar in the fuel tank of Plaintiff's truck "during the latter part of April, 1961." The Defendant denies that such an insurance policy was in effect on April 19, 1961 and otherwise its answer amounts to a general denial. To Defendant's answer was attached a list of forty-two interrogatories directed to Plaintiff. Plaintiff answered the interrogatories but Defendant moved to require more complete answers by Plaintiff.

The issue presented by Defendant's motion brings into question the proper use by a Defendant of interrogatories under R.C. § 2309.43, which reads as follows:

> "A party may annex to his pleading, other than a demurrer, interrogatories pertinent to the issue made in the pleadings, which interrogatories, if not demurred to, shall be plainly and fully answered under oath by the party to whom they are propounded, or if such party is a corporation, by the president, secretary, or other officer thereof, as the party propounding requires."

Although the old Common Law Bill in Equity for discovery has been largely supplanted in Ohio by this code section as well as R.C. § 2317.07, the question still remains as to whether some of the equitable principles are still in force. * * *

Defendant's answer sets up no affirmative defense. The Defendant therefore has assumed no burden of proof. The issue at first instance, at least, would seem to be narrowed to the question, may a defendant who has pleaded only a general denial attach to his answer and have answered by the plaintiff interrogatories which only pry into the evidence by which the plaintiff may sustain his own case, as distinguished from inquiring for ultimate facts within plaintiff's own knowledge which may be pertinent to the issue. In other words, does the Plaintiff have to reveal to the Defendant in advance of trial evidence which Plaintiff hopes to establish in support of his own case?

issue:

In some of the older cases in Ohio, trying to interpret this section (R.C. § 2309.43) there seems to have been established the principle that the general purpose of the discovery procedure was to aid a plaintiff in *establishing his case* or a defendant to *establish his defense*. * * * The proper use of interrogatories did not seem to extend to aiding an adversary to destroy his opponent's case. Ward v. Mutual Trucking Company, Ohio Com.Pl., 1 Ohio Supp. 42. In this case Judge Carpenter pointed out that the Ohio statute, which was passed in 1857, was very similar to the English Procedural Act passed in 1854 and quoted with approval at page 44 from the opinion in Whatley v. Crowder, 119 Rep. 645 as follows:

> "I think the interrogatories must be confined to matters which might be discovered by a bill of discovery in equity. I adopt the rule in the very terms used by Sir James Wigram (Wigram on Discovery, 261 (2nd Ed.): 'The right of a plaintiff in equity to the benefit of the defendant's oath, is limited to a discovery of such material facts as relate to the plaintiff's case—and does not extend to a discovery of the manner in which the defendant's case is to be established, or to evidence which relates exclusively to his case.' *You may inquire into all that is material to your own case, though it should be in common with that of your adversary; but you may not inquire into what is exclusively his case."* (Italics supplied.)
>   * * *

old equity view

Likewise, it has been held that interrogatories are not proper where the information sought is not within the personal knowledge of the other party and is not pertinent to an issue raised by the pleading of the inquirer. * * * It has been held that interrogatories are not proper where the answer calls for mere opinion of the party, * * * nor where the information sought is not within the personal knowledge of the party interrogated. * * *

In more recent cases it has been held that this statute and likewise its counterpart must be liberally construed and that interrogatories are proper if they are designed to seek information *pertinent to the action* as distinguished from being merely *pertinent to an issue* raised by the *pleading of the inquirer.* See Sloan v. S. S. Kresge Company, Ohio Com.Pl., 97 N.E.2d 238; * * * Feinstein v. Cleveland, 67 Ohio Law Abst. 518, "Interrogatories may seek information relevant to any *issue of the action* and to all sides of the case." (Italics supplied.)

Parenthetically, it also may be observed that this same philosophy is to prevail when the information is sought by way of deposition and the inspection and production of documents is sought under R.C. § 2317.32. * * * Many states have liberalized their statutory procedure, pointing toward, if not actually adopting, the very extreme liberal rules of discovery as provided by rules 26 through 37 of the Federal Rules of Civil Procedure. * * *

Certainly the Ohio statute of 1857, regardless of what interpretation may be put upon it, does not go as far nor is it as liberal as the Federal Rules of Practice, at least because two additional factors are present:—one, that the interrogatory must be pertinent to the issue made in the pleadings, and two, if admissible in evidence, the answer may be read by either party. (R.C. § 2309.45).

This Court is inclined to the more liberal and later construction of the Ohio statutes as disclosed by Sloan v. S. S. Kresge, rather than the older rule indicated in such cases as * * * Ward v. Mutual Trucking Company; and this Court holds to the view that interrogatories, whether filed with a pleading under favor of R.C. § 2309.43 or separately under R.C. § 2317.07, are proper when:

1. Relevant to an *issue in the action* as distinguished from merely being relevant, to an *issue in the pleading* of the inquirer,

2. They do not seek privileged information,

3. The information sought would also be admissible as evidence in the action.

The rule is limited, however, by the further rule that interrogatories may not seek discovery of the manner whereby the opponent's case is to be established nor evidence which relates exclusively to his case, nor to what his witnesses will testify.

In this Court's opinion, there is a marked distinction between records kept by a party in the regular course of his business operations and those amassed by him only after an incident has arisen out of which his lawsuit or defense arises. The former may be ordered produced, if pertinent to an issue in the action; the latter may not. * * *

With these rules in mind further inquiry directed toward the interrogatories of Defendant and answers by Plaintiff must be made.

The issue in the case as presented by the petition and the answer as distinguished from issues in only one pleading or the other would seem to be:

1. Did the Plaintiff hold a comprehensive insurance policy issued by the Defendant, which policy was in force in the latter part of April, 1961?

2. Did the policy cover a 1955 White tractor (owned by Plaintiff)?

3. Was sugar placed in the mechanism of this tractor?

4. Was the tractor damaged thereby and if so, to what extent?

Defendant's interrogatory number 2 calls upon Plaintiff to state whether she was the sole proprietor of a trucking business or whether same was a partnership or corporation at the time of Plaintiff's claim. This interrogatory has a direct bearing on the question of truck ownership and policy coverage. The Plaintiff's answer to the interrogatory is equivocal. The Plaintiff therefore will be directed to answer the interrogatory fully and completely, stating whether she owned the business as a sole proprietor or as a member of a partnership and if so, the other members thereof, or whether the business was incorporated.

Interrogatory number 6 calls for Plaintiff to state where the truck was at the time the sugar allegedly got into the mechanism of the truck. The answer given is "Don't personally know." Bearing in mind that previous interrogatories and answers thereto reveal the fact that the truck in question was under the care and custody of someone else other than Plaintiff, it would seem as though Plaintiff's answer to this interrogatory is full and complete. The motion with respect to interrogatory and answer number 6 is therefore overruled.

Interrogatories numbers 10, 12, and 15 through 33 all deal with matters arising at the time of or after Plaintiff's alleged claim arose. None deal with information or records maintained in the normal operation of Plaintiff's business. On the contrary, they call for information as to the manner in which the Plaintiff may attempt to establish her cause of action and do not countenance information presumably within Plaintiff's own personal knowledge. They call for information which Plaintiff may or may not be able to produce through testimony of witnesses upon trial. In other words, they call for hearsay or mere opinion evidence if Plaintiff's answer of "Don't personally know" is true. Certainly upon trial if Plaintiff were so inquired of and should so answer the same or similar interrogatories, she could not then be called upon to give her opinion or an answer which was obviously mere hearsay.

The same objection is true with interrogatories 36 and 37 and the answers given thereto; and likewise interrogatories 39 through 42 and Plaintiff's answers thereto. An additional objection to interrogatory number 42 exists, namely, assuming that a record of a test was made, it calls for the furnishing of information solely in support of Plaintiff's cause of action and obviously arises after the claim arose and in connection with Plaintiff's preparation for presentation of her claim and her lawsuit. This last mentioned objection is likewise true with many of the other interrogatories heretofore above covered.

Defendant's motion therefore will be overruled in all respects except with reference to the answer given by Plaintiff to interrogatory number 2, and Plaintiff is directed to file a complete answer as above indicated.

*   *   *

NOTES AND QUESTIONS

1. In 1970, seven years after *Kelly* was decided, Ohio adopted a set of discovery regulations almost identical with the Federal Rules. What purposes are served by extensive discovery under Rule 26 that are not served by the decision in *Kelly*? Are any particular groups of litigants, such as insurance companies or plaintiffs in negligence actions, favored or prejudiced by broad discovery? Note the limitations on the scope of discovery in Rule 26(b). Do they make the Rule too restrictive? In that connection, reconsider *Boldt v. Sanders*. p. 31, supra, which involved the Minnesota equivalent of Federal Rule 26. Are there certain categories or types of information not expressly mentioned in Rule 26 that should be beyond the scope of discovery or certain classes of litigation in which discovery should be prohibited or sharply curtailed?

2. In what ways can an open-ended discovery system be abused? To what extent are these abuses curbed by limiting the scope of discovery? Is there an alternative method of preventing abuse? See Federal Rules 26(c) and 30(d).

3. One major reason for permitting widespread discovery of the facts before trial is the elimination of surprise. Does full knowledge by one party of all the evidence to be presented by the opposing party lead to a better result at trial, or can justice sometimes be better served if a litigant is surprised by the evidence presented at trial. *Compare* Hawkins, *Discovery and Rule 34: What's So Wrong About Surprise?*, 39 A.B.A.J. 1075 (1953), *with* Holtzoff, *The Elimination of Surprise in Federal Practice,* 7 Vand.L.Rev. 576 (1954).

GRANT v. HUFF, 122 Ga.App. 783, 178 S.E.2d 734 (1970). Plaintiff, in a personal injury case, attempted to discover defendant's ability to pay a possible judgment by asking for information as to defendant's income, ownership of property, and the limits of a liability insurance policy. This inquiry was held improper on the ground that the information would not lead to admissible evidence at trial. In addition plaintiff sought discovery of the names and addresses of those witnesses defendant intended to use at the trial. This too was rejected on the ground that although plaintiff was entitled to discover who the eyewitnesses were, she was not entitled to know which witnesses defendant in fact would call to the stand.

NOTES AND QUESTIONS

1. (a) In what way would the decision in *Grant v. Huff* have been altered if Georgia had adopted Federal Rule 26(b) (2)? Over the years there has been considerable controversy regarding the discoverability of liability insurance. What are the competing arguments on this question? See the comments of the Advisory Committee on Rule 26(b) (2) set forth in the Supplement. See also the discussion in Cook v. Welty, 253 F.Supp. 875 (D.D.C.1966), in which the court said, "it is not to be doubted that information concerning liability insurance coverage and its extent is conducive to fair negotiations and to just settlements." Is this statement accurate in all contexts? When might the reverse be true? For a general review of the authorities, see 8 Wright & Miller, *Federal Practice and Procedure: Civil* § 2010 (1971).

(b) In STATE EX REL. KUBATZKY v. HOLT, 483 S.W.2d 799 (Mo. App.1972), a suit in which plaintiff sought punitive as well as compensatory damages, the court required defendant to answer a detailed set of interrogatories regarding his net worth. Can the decision be distinguished from *Grant v. Huff* and other cases in which permission to discover defendant's general financial status is refused?

(c) In ROY v. MONITOR–PATRIOT CO., 290 A.2d 207 (N.H.1972), plaintiff sued defendant newspaper for libel, due to the publication of an article written by columnist Drew Pearson. Under the applicable law, plaintiff could recover only by proving defendant acted maliciously. Prior to trial, plaintiff was permitted to discover the existence and nature of any agreement by which Pearson had promised to indemnify the paper for defamation actions that might result from publication of his columns. Should the discovery have been allowed? Of what consequence would it be that defendant intended to call Pearson to testify on its behalf? See also Maule Industries, Inc. v. Rountree, 264 So.2d 445 (Fla.App.1972).

2. What reasons justify the decision in *Grant v. Huff* refusing to permit discovery of the names of witnesses whom defendant intended to call at trial? Would it make a difference if the witnesses were scientific experts hired by defendant to aid in the preparation of the case? See Federal Rule 26(b) (4) (a), which is discussed in detail at pp. 712–15, infra.

LINDBERGER v. GENERAL MOTORS CORP.

United States District Court, Western District of Wisconsin, 1972.
56 F.R.D. 433.

JAMES E. DOYLE, District Judge. Plaintiff, Gordon C. Lindberger, a citizen of Wisconsin, filed a complaint against the defendants, General Motors Corporation and a division thereof, which are not citizens of Wisconsin. Plaintiff alleges that he suffered personal injuries proximately caused by the negligence of the defendants in manufacturing and designing a front end loader which was sold to the plaintiff's employer. * * *

Attorneys for the defendants have refused to answer interrogatories 23, 25 and 26, which were propounded by the plaintiffs pursuant to Rule 33, Fed.R.Civ.P. Plaintiffs have filed a motion to compel discovery.

Interrogatory 23 requests the defendants to state whether any changes have been made, and if so to describe such changes, subsequent to the date when the loader in question was produced, in either the design of the braking system or in the warning system for brake malfunctions. Interrogatory 25 requests the defendants to state how any such changes affect the utility of the loader. Interrogatory 26 requests the names of persons responsible for such design changes.

The defendants contend that the plaintiffs are not entitled to compel discovery because the subject matter of the disputed interrogatories is "privileged" and that consequently the standard of "relevancy" set out in Rule

26(b) * * * is inapplicable. The defendants' theory is that the evidence sought is "privileged" because of the rule of evidence which prohibits the admission of evidence at trial of subsequent remedial measures to establish negligence or culpability.

* * * The "privilege" which protects matter from discovery under * * * [Rule 26(b)] is the same as that applicable under the rules of evidence at a trial. United States v. Reynolds, 345 U.S. 1, 6, 73 S.Ct. 528, 97 L.Ed. 727 (1953) * * *. Furthermore, the party claiming the existence of the privilege has the burden of persuasion. * * * The defendants have not met this burden.

The defendants argue that the exclusion of evidence of subsequent measures is a "privilege" because this exclusion is based upon an external policy, promoting public safety by not discouraging subsequent repairs. Relying solely upon McCormick, Law of Evidence (1954), § 77, the defendants contend that any rule of exclusion, not looking to truth-finding at trial, but rather to an external policy, should be classified as a privilege.

[handwritten margin note: Δ's arg. remedial subsequent conduct is privileged]

I am not persuaded by defendants' arguments. Textwriters other than McCormick do not classify the doctrine of subsequent remedial conduct as a rule of privilege. * * * See Wright & Miller, Federal Practice & Procedure § 2016, p. 123, n. 57. Finally, it would seem that there is a substantial difference between the policy underlying the exclusion of evidence in the area of traditionally recognized privileges, e. g. the attorney-client privilege, the secret of state privilege, or the doctor-patient privilege, and in the "privilege" claimed in the instant case. Stringent protection is afforded to the traditional privileges because disclosure, in itself, even outside the trial of the case, may cause harm to the parties. But such harm would not result from disclosure in the instant case. It is disclosure at trial, where a jury may improperly draw an inference of negligence, which presents the danger to the defendants, and consequently to the public. For these reasons, I conclude that the defendants have not met their burden of persuasion.

The only remaining question is whether the subject-matter of the interrogatories falls within the scope of examination permitted under Rule 26 (b) * * *. [T]he plaintiff need not, at this stage of the proceedings, establish that the evidence sought would be admissible at trial. * * * It is clear that the information sought in the challenged interrogatories is relevant to the subject-matter of this action. The feasibility of the installation of a better brake system and of more adequate warning systems for brake malfunctions may be significant with respect to * * * [defendants' liability]. Furthermore, the knowledge of the defendants about the adequacy of the design of the loader as well as any information on this subject which may have been passed to the employer of the plaintiff may be relevant on the issues of negligence and contributory negligence.

[handwritten margin note: Held]

In conclusion, I find that the defendants' refusal to answer interrogatories 23, 25, and 26, is without justification. Accordingly, on the basis of the entire record herein, it is hereby ordered, pursuant to Rule 37 * * * that the defendants answer interrogatories 23, 25 and 26, within 30 days from the date of entry of this order.

NOTE

Claims as to what is or is not "relevant" within the meaning of Federal Rule 26(b) and its state counterparts have been as varied as the imaginations of the attorneys who practice under these rules. Consider the propriety of the following decisions:

(a) CORNET STORES v. SUPERIOR COURT, 108 Ariz. 84, 492 P.2d 1191 (1972). Plaintiff, a former manager of one of defendant's stores, sued for wrongful discharge, alleging that under his contract he could be fired only for misconduct, but that in fact he was fired because the contract called for higher pay than that received by the other managers. Plaintiff sought to discover the amount of pay that the other managers received. Defendant, who wished to keep its employee contracts confidential, objected that the inquiry was irrelevant since defendant was willing to stipulate that plaintiff had been the highest paid manager in its system. The court upheld discovery, stating:

> We think, however, that a party to litigation has the right to prove its case in the fashion it deems most satisfactory and may not be compelled by the court to accept an offer to stipulate, the effect of which may not have the same impact upon a jury as the evidence which establishes the fact.

(b) MUTUAL OF OMAHA INS. CO. v. GARRIGAN, 31 Ohio Misc. 1, 285 N.E.2d 395 (Ohio Common Pleas, Erie County, 1971). Plaintiff insurance company brought an action against the widow of its insured, asking for a declaration that the insured's death by carbon monoxide poisoning had not been accidental and hence was not covered by the policy. The company sought to discover the corpse, which would have required disinterment. The court refused, stating:

> While liberal discovery rules are to be encouraged and are generally accepted, it's questionable that they should be used to override the long standing common law and statutory limitations on disinterment. Historically, disinterment has been ordered in only rare instances and then only after the insurance company has presented evidence to show it is "reasonably certain that an examination may reveal something that will show fraud or mistake * * *." It is the opinion of this court that the plaintiffs have failed to meet that burden of proof. * * * Absent express statutory authorization, this court is not willing to extend the liberal discovery rules of Ohio into the grave.

(c) WILLIAMS v. THOMAS JEFFERSON UNIVERSITY, 16 Fed.R.Serv. 2d 444 (E.D.Pa.1972). Plaintiff, in a medical malpractice action involving abortion, sought to discover the names of women who had previously had abortions at defendant hospital. The stated purpose was to gather evidence to impeach testimony expected to be given by defendant doctor. Discovery was denied. The court said:

> In the abstract, abortion is discussed openly and with fervor. Nevertheless, it is an extremely personal thing to each woman who has had

an abortion. The consequences of allowing revelation and examination when considered in terms of family relationships and individual friendships could be disastrous to the subjects of an inquiry of the type plaintiff wants to make. A collateral attack for impeachment purposes does not weigh very heavily in a balancing of interests when opposed to such obvious reasons for privacy.

IN RE LEWIS

Court of Appeals of North Carolina, 1971.
11 N.C.App. 541, 181 S.E.2d 806.

This is a proceeding heard on a petition filed by James Ray Lewis and wife, Elizabeth Lewis, pursuant to G.S. § 1A–1, Rule 27(b), seeking to obtain an order to take the deposition of John McDowell, Director of the Forsyth County Department of Social Services, respondent, to obtain information to enable the petitioners to prepare a complaint. * * *

HEDRICK, Judge. G.S. § 1A–1, Rule 27(b), in pertinent part, provides:

"(b) Depositions before action for obtaining information to prepare a complaint.—

(1) Petition.—A person who expects to commence an action but who desires to obtain information from an expected adverse party or from any person for whose immediate benefit the expected action will be defended for the purpose of preparing a complaint may file a verified petition in the county where any expected adverse party resides or in the county where resides any person for whose immediate benefit the expected action will be defended.

* * *

The petition shall be entitled in the name of the petitioner and shall show (i) that the petitioner expects to commence an action cognizable in a court of this State, (ii) the names and addresses of the expected adverse parties, (iii) the nature and purpose of the expected action, (iv) the subject matter of the expected action and the petitioner's interest therein, (v) why the petitioner is unable to prepare a complaint with the information presently available, and (vi) that the petition is filed in good faith. The petition shall also designate with reasonable particularity the matters as to which information will be sought."

* * * Prior to the effective date of Rule 27(b), a party could not examine an adverse party for the purpose of obtaining information to prepare a complaint or other pleading until the action had been commenced by the issuance and service of summons. Under Rule 27(b), the petitioner is required to allege that the person to be examined is an "expected adverse party."

* * * No such allegation appears in the petition in the instant case. The petition shows on its face that the petitioners are not seeking information to enable them to prepare a complaint, but that they are seeking information for the purpose of determining whether they have a valid claim which they may or may not commence.

The petitioners allege: "[T]hat petitioners need further information from McDowell before a formal complaint against him and/or any complainant can be *filed,* * * * and without such information petitioners are unable to determine against whom their action should be brought." (Emphasis ours)

In this regard, the North Carolina Supreme Court, in Washington v. Safe Bus, Inc., 219 N.C. 856, p. 858, 15 S.E.2d 372, p. 373 (1941), said: "But the court will not permit a party to spread a dragnet for an adversary to gain facts upon which to sue him, or to harass him under the guise of a fair examination."

The petitioners allege generally that they have been wronged, embarrassed and damaged by an investigation conducted by the Forsyth County Department of Social Services, but they have not described the nature of any action they expect to commence, nor, as was said earlier, against whom they expect to bring any such action. It is essential under Rule 27(b) that the nature and purpose of any expected action be described in the petition in such detail as will enable the court to determine whether the information sought to be obtained from an expected adverse party is material and necessary to enable the petitioners to prepare their complaint.
* * *

It is our opinion that the petition in the instant case, when considered in the light of the requirements of Rule 27(b), is insufficient to support an order to examine the respondent to obtain information to enable the petitioners to prepare a complaint.

The * * * petition is dismissed.

NOTES AND QUESTIONS

1. Why shouldn't there be a specific provision permitting a prospective plaintiff to discover facts to aid in deciding whether or not a legal action is justified and in ascertaining against whom it should be brought? How could the concerns expressed in the *Lewis* case and the occasional need for broad pre-action discovery be accommodated? Compare N.Y.C.P.L.R. 3102(c): "Before an action is commenced, disclosure to aid in bringing an action, to preserve information or to aid in arbitration, may be obtained, but only by court order." For comment on the New York rule, see 3 Weinstein, Korn & Miller, *New York Civil Practice* ¶¶ 3102.11–.12.

Does a pre-action discovery provision have any practical effect when given a narrow interpretation, as in the *Lewis* case? Consider KEELY v. PRICE, 27 Cal. App.3d 209, 103 Cal.Rptr. 531 (2d Dist.1972), decided in California, which does not have a pre-action discovery rule. In *Keely* defendant successfully demurred to the complaint on the ground that it failed to state a cause of action. The appellate court upheld the demurrer, but reversed the trial court's denial of leave to amend, ordering that plaintiff be afforded sufficient time and opportunity for discovery to assist in making any amendment.

2.   The only Federal Rule permitting pre-action discovery is Rule 27, which provides that a person, with court approval, may take a deposition of himself or any other person for the purpose of perpetuating testimony for a contemplated action that cannot presently be brought.   The court must be satisfied that perpetuating the testimony may prevent a failure or delay of justice.   It has been held consistently that Rule 27 cannot be used as a means to determine whether a cause of action exists and, if so, against whom it should be brought.   See United States v. Local 14, International Union of Operating Engineers, 16 Fed. R.Serv.2d 111 (S.D.N.Y.1972);   In re Gurnsey, 223 F.Supp. 359 (D.D.C.1963). See 41 Texas L.Rev. 330 (1962).   What then is the purpose of the Rule?   Should the scope of a deposition before action be limited to evidence that would be material and admissible at trial or should its scope be the same as that allowed by Rule 26(b)?   See Martin v. Reynolds Metals Corp., 297 F.2d 49 (9th Cir.1961) (court refused to limit discovery to admissible evidence but left open the question whether the full scope of Rule 26(b) applies).

3.   To what extent do "relevancy" rules permit discovery solely to determine the existence of others who could be made parties to the action?   The issue arises in suits brought on behalf of a class, in which the active plaintiff seeks to establish the existence and scope of the alleged class.   Thus, in DIONNE v. SPRINGFIELD SCHOOL COMMITTEE, 15 Fed.R.Serv.2d 1265 (D.Mass.1972), the named plaintiff, who had been suspended from school for drinking alcoholic beverages, sought to obtain information as to the names of other students who had been suspended or dismissed and the reasons given therefor.   The court refused to require disclosure.   In doing so, it criticized the decision in Yaffe v. Powers, 454 F. 2d 1362 (1st Cir.1972), in which the court stated that plaintiff was entitled to utilize discovery to aid in opposing defendant's motion for a determination that a valid class did not exist.

SECTION B.   THE MECHANICS OF THE DISCOVERY DEVICES

1.   DEPOSITIONS

Study Federal Rules of Civil Procedure 26(d), 30, and 31 in the Supplement.

NOTES AND QUESTIONS

1.   The most important of the discovery devices is the oral deposition * * *.   It is the only significant discovery device which may be directed against any person, and is not confined to parties to the action. It is the only discovery device that permits examination and cross-ex-

amination of a live witness by counsel, where there is no opportunity to reflect and carefully shape the information given. Thus, despite its expense, it is the most valuable device if the deponent has important information.

* * *

Rule 31 specifies the procedure to be followed in taking depositions by written questions. This is an alternative to the taking of depositions by oral examination provided by Rule 30. * * *

Though Rule 31 appears to offer a saving in expense where the deposition is to be taken at some faroff place, its advantages are largely illusory.

Wright, *Federal Courts* §§ 84, 85, at 373, 379 (2d ed. 1970).

What are the advantages and disadvantages of written as compared with oral questioning? How likely is it that one party will invoke the opportunity to use written interrogatories under Federal Rule 30(c) in lieu of direct participation in an oral deposition conducted by the other parties in the case?

2. One of the most significant features of federal deposition procedure is that it is designed to function by private arrangement among the parties and without need for judicial intervention. Although the rules as to when, how, before whom, and on what notice as to time and place a deposition may be taken are spelled out in detail (see Federal Rules 28, 30, 31, and 32(d) respectively), Rule 29 permits the parties to stipulate in writing to take a deposition "before any person, at any time or place, upon any notice, and in any manner."

3. Judicial control over the course of a deposition in the federal courts is provided by Rules 26(c) and 30(d). Is this level of judicial involvement in the discovery process too limited, especially in light of the massive deposition practice that characterizes the "big" case? Is there any justification for the provisions in Rule 26(c) that permit the scope of the inquiry to be limited in advance? When one party is certain to ask improper questions of a deponent, should the attorney for the other party always ask the court for a limiting order under Rule 30(d)? Or, if the deponent will be cooperative, is it tactically better to have the witness refuse to answer the offending questions? Rule 37(a) specifies the procedure to be followed when the deponent refuses to answer. How onerous are the sanctions for a wrongful refusal?

4. Ever since modern discovery rules first appeared, courts have been faced with the situation in which the parties are vying to take the first deposition, each attempting to pin down the opponent or the opponent's key witness, before submitting himself or his own witnesses to the discovery process. Is there really a substantial advantage to deposing first? Does this advantage exist for an honest party as well as for an unscrupulous party who will deliberately color his testimony? See generally *Developments in the Law—Discovery*, 74 Harv.L.Rev. 940, 954–58 (1961), and review *Boldt v. Sanders*, p. 31, supra.

Prior to the adoption of Rule 26(d) in 1970, the federal courts generally had held that the party who first served a notice of a deposition was entitled to priority as to that deposition. This is still the situation in many states. See, e. g., N.Y.C.P.L.R. 3106.

The problem is complicated by the fact that in most of these jurisdictions plaintiff is prohibited, without leave of court, from serving a notice of deposition for a specific period of time in order to permit defendant to learn of the suit and employ counsel. *Cf.* Federal Rule 30(a). Leave of court normally has been permitted only under exceptional circumstances. Since there is no comparable restriction on defendant, he will receive priority merely by serving notice during the period plaintiff must wait.

Would elimination of plaintiff's waiting period eliminate the priority problem? If one party normally is to have priority if that party wants it, who should it be, plaintiff or defendant? Is there any satisfactory way to solve the priority question?

At the same time that Federal Rule 26(d) was adopted, Rules 30(a) and (b) were altered to include a number of related changes with regard to the timing of depositions. First, plaintiff's waiting period (30 days) was declared to run from the date defendant was served; formerly it ran from the date the complaint was filed with the clerk. Second, two significant qualifications were imposed: (1) the waiting period applies only until defendant formally seeks discovery; (2) if a plaintiff legitimately fears that a deponent is about to depart to a place where he cannot be served with process, plaintiff, upon stating the facts in the notice of deposition, can ignore the waiting period. Insofar as written depositions are concerned, Rule 31(a) has been altered to permit them by any party at any time after commencement of the action.

What evils were these alterations designed to correct? How effective do you think they are? Taken altogether do they end the priority problem? In its Note to Rule 26(d), the Advisory Committee states that a comprehensive study revealed that in only 16 per cent of the cases do defendants move for discovery within plaintiff's waiting period and that obviously in some of these cases priority is not a motive. Do these figures indicate that the amendments were unnecessary?

For extensive discussions of the priority problem see 8 Wright & Miller, *Federal Practice and Procedure: Civil* §§ 2045–47 (1970); *Developments in the Law—Discovery*, 74 Harv.L.Rev. 940, 954–58 (1961). See also Younger, *Priority of Pretrial Examination in the Federal Courts—A Comment*, 34 N.Y. U.L.Rev. 1271 (1959). The problem will be renewed in conjunction with *River Plate Corp. v. Forestal Land, Timber & Ry. Co.*, p. 689, infra.

———

Read Federal Rules of Civil Procedure 45(d), (e), and (f) in the Supplement.

———

COLLINS v. WAYLAND

United States Court of Appeals, Ninth Circuit, 1944.
139 F.2d 677.
Certiorari denied 322 U.S. 744, 64 S.Ct. 1151, 88 L.Ed. 1576.

MATHEWS, Circuit Judge. In the District Court of the United States for the District of Arizona, appellant, a citizen of Oregon, brought an action against appellees, citizens of Arizona, for damages in the sum of $21,000. Appellees answered. Thereafter, desiring to take the deposition of appellant upon oral examination, appellees gave notice as provided in Rule 30 * * * of the Federal Rules of Civil Procedure * * * as follows:

"You and each of you will please take notice that [appellees] will take the deposition of [appellant] upon oral examination as an adverse party before Louis L. Billar, a notary public in and for the County of Maricopa, State of Arizona, at the offices of Snell & Strouss [appellees' attorneys], 703 Heard Building, Phoenix, Arizona, at 10:00 o'clock A.M., Friday, the 20th day of November, 1942."

Appellant disregarded the notice. He did not appear before the officer who was to take his deposition, or at the place where his deposition was to be taken, on November 20, 1942, or at all. On December 4, 1942, appellees filed and served a verified motion stating these facts and praying the court to strike out appellant's complaint and enter a judgment by default against him, as provided in Rule 37(d) of the Federal Rules of Civil Procedure. After due notice, the court heard the motion and, on December 21, 1942, made the following order:

"It is ordered that [appellant] appear for the taking of his deposition at Phoenix, Arizona, January 11, 1943, at the offices of Messrs. Snell & Strouss, attorneys for [appellees]; otherwise this complaint herein will be dismissed."

Appellant disregarded the order. He did not appear for the taking of his deposition on January 11, 1943, or at all. On January 12, 1943, appellees moved the court to dismiss the action, as provided in Rule 37(d). After due notice, the court heard the motion, granted it and, on January 18, 1943, entered judgment dismissing the action. From that judgment this appeal is prosecuted.

The appeal is a frivolous one. The notice for taking appellant's deposition was a proper notice and was properly served. It is immaterial, if true, that no subpoena was served on appellant, for he was a party, and therefore no subpoena was necessary. Nor is it material that appellant's deposition was to be taken in the office of appellees' attorneys. The suggestion that, because appellant resided in Oregon, the District Court of the United States for the District of Arizona, whose jurisdiction he had invoked, could not require him to give a deposition in Arizona is untenable. If he wished to be relieved from going to Arizona, he could and should have sought such relief by "motion seasonably made," as provided in Rule [26(c)] * * *. Instead, he disregarded the notice and the court's order and wilfully failed to comply with either.

Judgment affirmed.

LESS v. TABER INSTRUMENT CORP.

United States District Court, Western District of New York, 1971.
53 F.R.D. 645.

CURTIN, District Judge. Teledyne, Inc., a non-party foreign corporation concededly doing business in this judicial district, was properly served by plaintiff with a subpoena commanding it to appear in this district for examination through "Henry E. Singleton, Chairman and Chief Executive Officer and * * * Edmund M. Kaufman, Assistant Secretary." Kaufman is no longer employed by Teledyne, and plaintiff concedes that his presence may not be compelled. Singleton, who is presently Chairman of Teledyne's Board of Directors and based at its Los Angeles, California, headquarters, was not personally served with a subpoena. The questions before the court are whether Singleton, a non-party director of a non-party corporation, may be required to submit to examination and, if so, shall he be so required and under what conditions.

Under the present discovery provisions of the Federal Rules of Civil Procedure, the deposition of a corporate party may be taken from a director named in the notice given to the corporation. The director need not be personally subpoenaed, and the corporation must produce him or risk the imposition of sanctions under Rule 37(d). * * * Teledyne argues that a different rule should apply to the director of a non-party corporation.

* * *

The Rules do not suggest that a different principle applies to discovery from a party corporation than applies to discovery from a non-party corporation. Rule 30(a), which governs the taking of depositions upon oral examination, does not distinguish between parties and non-parties; it simply provides that "any party may take the testimony of *any person, including a party,* by deposition upon oral examination." Fed.R.Civ.P. 30(a) (emphasis added). The provision that "[t]he attendance of witnesses may be compelled by subpoena as provided in Rule 45," Fed.R.Civ.P. 30(a), also connotes no operative distinction between parties and non-parties. The provision is merely intended to assure that the non-party whose testimony is sought submits to examination. There is no necessity for requiring service of a subpoena upon a party since adequate sanctions are provided in Rule 37 in the event that the party fails to respond to a notice to take a deposition.

* * * [A] non-party witness, even more than a party, must be protected against undue burden and expense. * * * Therefore, the court does not choose to depart from the ordinary rules that a mere witness will not be required to leave his residence and business and travel great distances for the convenience of the parties * * * and that the deposition of a corporation should be taken at its principal place of business. * * *

It is therefore the order of this court that the deposition upon oral examination of Henry E. Singleton be taken at the principal place of business of Teledyne, Inc. * * *.

NOTES AND QUESTIONS

1. Should the court in the *Less* case have discussed Federal Rule 30(b)(6)? Doesn't that provision clearly provide that a corporation has the right to choose who shall testify on its behalf? Are there reasons why the choice should be left to the corporation? See generally the Advisory Committee's Notes on the

1970 amendments to Rule 30, which appear in the Supplement. Even in the absence of a rule comparable to Rule 30(b) (6) some courts have held that the selection is to be made by the corporation, at least until it becomes apparent that the person chosen does not possess all the relevant facts known to the corporation. E. g., Abrams v. Vaughn & Bushnell Mfg. Co., 37 App.Div.2d 833, 325 N.Y.S.2d 976 (1971).

2. The party who gives notice of the taking of a deposition is not required to subpoena even a nonparty witness whose testimony is sought If no subpoena is issued, however, and the witness fails to attend, Federal Rule 30(g) (2) permits certain sanctions to be imposed upon the party who failed to use a subpoena. What tactical reasons might motivate a party to refrain from serving a subpoena on a witness? Note that under Rule 45(d) (2) if a witness refuses to cooperate, so that she must be subpoenaed, the deposition may have to be held in a district other than the one in which the case has been filed. Suppose the witness disobeys the subpoena. If she appears but refuses to answer questions properly put to her, the parties may seek assistance under Rule 37(a). According to Rule 37(a) (1) application for judicial assistance must be made to the court where the deposition is being held as opposed to the court where the action is filed. What is the purpose of this provision? Note that if the witness is a party, Rule 37(a) (1) permits either the court where the action is pending or the one where the deposition is being taken to issue orders relating to the deposition. Is there any reason for distinguishing between party and nonparty witnesses? See 62 Colum.L.Rev. 187 (1962).

3. Rule 37(d) provides special sanctions to be used against a party or "an officer, director, or managing agent of a party" who wilfully fails to appear to have a deposition taken. Why should these people be treated differently than other witnesses? Rule 37(d) does not apply to the ordinary employees of a party. Williams v. Lehigh Valley R.R., 19 F.R.D. 285 (S.D.N.Y.1956). Would it be wise to amend the rule to include all employees?

CARSON v. BURLINGTON NORTHERN INC., 52 F.R.D. 492 (D.Neb.1971). Plaintiff was injured when a steel press he was operating came down on his hand, allegedly due to defendant's negligence. Defendant moved to take plaintiff's deposition at the scene of the accident using video tape. Plaintiff objected that this procedure could only produce a staged, unnatural re-creation. The court granted the motion, holding that the 1970 amendment to Federal Rule 30(b)(4) specifically provided for video taping. The court, however, did hold that plaintiff would not be required to touch or operate the press; he only would be required to use a pointer to show the manner in which he operated the machine on the day of the accident.

NOTES AND QUESTIONS

1. Traditionally depositions have been recorded by stenographic means only. What are the advantages to be gained from audio and video tape-recorded depositions? See Lester v. Lester, 69 Misc.2d 528, 330 N.Y.S.2d 190 (1972);

Mich.Gen.Ct.Rules 302.7, 302.8; 8 Wright & Miller, *Federal Practice and Procedure: Civil* § 2115, at 426 (1970).

2. Does the use of tape-recorded depositions raise any special problems? Who should provide and be in charge of the recording equipment? Is there ever a need for more than one recording machine? See generally Marlboro Products Corp. v. North American Philips Corp., 55 F.R.D. 487 (S.D.N.Y.1972); Wescott v. Neeman, 55 F.R.D. 257 (D.Neb.1972).

---

2. INTERROGATORIES TO PARTIES

Read Federal Rule of Civil Procedure 33 in the Supplement.

IN RE MASTER KEY

United States District Court, District of Connecticut, 1971.
53 F.R.D. 87.

BLUMENFELD, District Judge.

I.

The interrogatory answers which are under attack are those filed by defendants Emhart Corporation and Eaton, Yale & Towne, Inc. For the *Facts* most part, they are the same. In response to Interrogatories Nos. 2, 3, 9, 27, 30, 31 and 46, Eaton has not given a specific answer, but has invoked Rule 33(c) Fed.R.Civ.P. "Option to Produce Business Records." Emhart has done the same in response to Interrogatories Nos. 5, 5(second), 6, 7, 8, 9, 10(b), 23, 31, 38, 43, 45 and 45(a).

A typical example is afforded by Emhart's answer to Interrogatory 5:

"5.   Did you enter into any agreement, contract, understanding, plan, or program, formal or informal, written or oral, with any of your distributors with respect to the allocation, division or assignment of customers, territories, and/or markets for the distribution or sale of master key systems and/or extensions to master key systems. If so, for each such agreement, contract, understanding, plan or program, give the following information:

(a) The distributor with whom it was entered into;

"(b) The date on which it was entered into;

"(c) If the agreement, contract, understanding, plan or program was oral, state the terms and provisions thereof;

"(d) If it is embodied or recorded in a document or documents, identify each such document;

"(e) Identify the individuals acting on your behalf and on behalf [of] each distributor; and

"(f) State the period for which the agreement, contract, understanding, plan or program was or is in effect.

"ANSWER

"5. If and to the extent that defendant entered into any agreement, contract, understanding, plan, or program, formal or informal, written or oral, with any of its distributors with respect to the subjects enumerated in this interrogatory, the information requested in this interrogatory is contained in defendant's files maintained at its Berlin, Connecticut, plant. Such files will be made available for inspection by counsel for plaintiff at the Berlin, Connecticut, plant in accordance with Rule 33(c) of the Federal Rules of Civil Procedure."

From the specific references by the defendants to Rule 33(c) in their responses and briefs, they unmistakably contend that their offer to make their files "available for inspection by counsel for the plaintiff" at the defendants' place of business constitutes a sufficient answer to the interrogatories.

II.

The basic fault with the challenged responses is that they leave the interrogating party to speculate whether an answer can be ascertained from an examination of the files. Thus, the question presented is whether Rule 33(c) permits a party from whom relevant information is being sought to respond by telling his interrogator where he may look for the answer without stating that the answer may be found there.

The fact that one use of the word "may" as defined in the dictionary is "be by chance" furnishes an arguably logical basis for the elliptical response of the defendants. But more than a dictionary is required to understand the meaning of "may" in Rule 33(c). * * * "May" has different shades of meaning; e. g. the dictionary notes that it is often used in the sense of "be competent" and that it is frequently substituted for the word *can* when used in this sense. * * *

It would be antipathetic to the spirit of the discovery rules to assume that the newly added Rule 33(c) was intended to diminish the duty of the parties to provide all information requested. Since a respondent is required to answer proper interrogatories, it is not plausible to assume that a response that an answer may (or may not) be found in its records, accompanied by an offer to permit their inspection is sufficient. This is little more than an offer to play the discredited game of blindman's buff [sic] at the threshold level of discovery. The challenged answers furnish no information whatever. Nor can the responses be read as stating that the defendants do not have or cannot obtain the information necessary to answer *failure to do so* the interrogatories. If a party cannot furnish information and details it may so state, under oath. *See* Riley v. United Air Lines, Inc., 32 F.R.D. 230, 233–34 (S.D.N.Y.1962) * * *.

I conclude that the option afforded by Rule 33(c) is not a procedural device for avoiding the duty to give information. It does not shift to the interrogating party the obligation to find out *whether* sought after information is ascertainable from the files tendered, but only permits a shift of the burden to dig it out once the respondents have specified the records from "where the answer" can be derived or ascertained. If the answers lie in the records of the defendants, they should say so; and, if, on the other side, they do not, they should say that. * * *   *R/L*

The defendants' answers to the interrogatories considered above are insufficient, and the defendants are * * * ordered to file further answers.

It is premature to decide now that the defendants may not invoke Rule 33(c) if it should later become applicable. Such a ruling must be deferred until, and if, it becomes necessary.

III.

Cryptic answers were given by Emhart to Interrogatory No. 11 relating (a) to whether it made any investigations and (b) if so, (1) the names of the persons interviewed; (2) the dates thereof; and (3) the existence of any memoranda relating thereto. The answer to (a) was "None except by counsel," and to the others: "not applicable." These answers are insufficient. Emhart is also directed to give full and complete answers to Interrogatories Nos. 11, 25 and 40.

IV.

The plaintiffs may submit to the court for later consideration affidavits in support of their request for an order that the defendants pay reasonable expenses incurred in obtaining this order.

NOTES AND QUESTIONS

1. Written interrogatories to parties are unusually well adapted for several particular purposes. Since interrogatories can be prepared by an attorney in his own office and at his leisure, thereby avoiding the expense of oral depositions and the time consumed therein, they may be very effectively employed where a thorough-going deposition is not necessary. * * * Illustrative of this type of use is the situation encountered in reference to an attempt to ascertain the names of persons having knowledge of relevant facts concerning the matter in litigation. In such a situation the only source of a better list of "witnesses" than the one possessed

by the interrogating party is the "adverse party," and, therefore, the logical source is amenable to the use of interrogatories under the rule. If the "adverse party" is a partnership association or corporation, one single interrogatory directed to the group covers the information in the hands of all members, agents, employees, etc. * * * If such information were sought by depositions of the individuals connected with the group, such depositions would cover only their own personal information. In many cases, this would necessitate the taking of numerous depositions and the costs incurred therewith, with no assurance that all persons who might have knowledge would be questioned.

Feirich & Feirich, *Interrogatories to Parties and Demands to Admit,* 1959 U.Ill. L.F. 733, 734. Did the adoption of Federal Rule 30(b) (6) in 1970 affect the validity of this statement? In what ways are written interrogatories under Rule 33 less effective than an oral examination under Rule 30? See 8 Wright & Miller, *Federal Practice and Procedure: Civil* § 2163 (1970); 4 Moore, *Federal Practice* ¶ 33.02 (2d ed.).

2. How extensive should the duty of investigation be under Rule 33(a)? Should a corporate party be charged with the responsibility of finding out what is known by each of its employees regardless of the size and nature of the business? Should the duty extend to information known to employees of subsidiary corporations that are not parties? See Sol. S. Turnoff Drug Distributors Inc. v. N.V. Nederlandsche Combinatie Voor Chemische Industrie, 55 F.R.D. 347 (E.D.Pa.1972). To what extent should the duty include former employees? In HENG HSIN CO. v. STERN, MORGENTHAU & CO., 20 Fed.R.Serv. 33.42, Case 2 (S.D.N.Y.1954), defendant failed to answer an interrogatory on the ground that the only employees who had knowledge of the facts had left defendant's employ between commencement of the action and service of the interrogatory. The court, in effect, ordered defendant to obtain the information or forfeit its right to present evidence on the issue in question: "Assuming, as I can, that defendant made for itself the best case it could, defendant permitted its employees to leave the employ without obtaining from them information necessary for the defense of pending litigation. This was either deliberate or negligent. In neither case should plaintiff bear the consequences." Does this decision impose an unfair burden on defendant?

The first sentence of Rule 33 can be construed as not requiring an individual party to make an investigation into matters that are outside that party's personal knowledge. Can a valid distinction be drawn between a corporation or association and an individual when the information sought is known to an employee or to the party's attorney. See *Hickman v. Taylor,* p. 700, infra, in which the Supreme Court said that a party cannot refuse to answer interrogatories merely because an attorney, rather than the party, knows the facts. Should the obligation to inquire extend beyond the party's employees and agents, perhaps to a spouse or other members of the party's immediate family?

3. Federal Rule 33(c) was added in 1970. It was derived from Section 2030(c) of the California Civil Procedure Code, which appears in the Supplement. The Federal Rule differs in that it adds the requirement that "the burden of deriving or ascertaining the answer" must be "substantially the same for the party serving the interrogatory as for the party served." What is the justification for this additional requirement? Is it too inflexible?

4. The original version of Federal Rule 33 expressly provided that a party had to obtain leave of court to serve more than one set of interrogatories on an opponent. In 1946 the leave requirement was eliminated. Is there any justification for a rule limiting the number of sets of interrogatories that can be served? Might there be more reason for such a provision in state as opposed to federal courts? The Minnesota version of Federal Rule 33 limits to 50 the number of interrogatories one party can serve on another party without leave of court. Is this more or less sensible than a restriction as to the number of sets of interrogatories?

5. Prior to the 1970 amendments of the discovery rules Federal Rule 33 only permitted interrogatories to be served on an adverse party. This requirement, which still exists in some states, was a source of confusion and controversy. Some courts held that parties were adverse only if the pleadings formally established an issue between them; others held that an actual conflict of interest was sufficient. *Compare* M.V.M., Inc. v. St. Paul Fire & Marine Ins. Co., 20 F.R.D 296 (S.D.N.Y.1957), *with* Gorman Rupp Industries, Inc. v. Superior Court, 20 Cal.App.3d 28, 97 Cal.Rptr. 377 (1971). See generally 8 Wright & Miller, *Federal Practice and Procedure: Civil* § 2171 (1970).

Is there any justification for prohibiting interrogatories between parties who are not adverse? Should Federal Rule 33 be further altered to permit service of interrogatories on nonparty witnesses? See *Developments in the Law—Discovery,* 74 Harv.L.Rev. 940, 1020–22 (1961).

6. Federal Rule 37 provides that a party who fails to answer interrogatories is exposed to the same sanctions as is a party who thwarts a deposition under Rule 30 or Rule 31. If the party served refuses to answer, the interrogating party has two possible routes to follow. The latter may obtain a court order under Rule 37(a) (2) requiring an answer, which, if not obeyed, may result in a variety of severe sanctions under Rule 37(b), or, if the failure to answer was wilful, the interrogating party may proceed under Rule 37(d) to obtain sanctions immediately.

---

3. REQUESTS TO ADMIT

Read Federal Rule of Civil Procedure 36 in the Supplement.

DeRYDER v. METROPOLITAN LIFE INS. CO.

Virginia Supreme Court of Appeals, 1965.
206 Va. 602, 145 S.E.2d 177.

SNEAD, Justice. On January 13, 1960, Jennie Mae Garner DeRyder, plaintiff, * * * filed a motion for judgment in * * * [an action alleging] *inter alia*, that plaintiff was the beneficiary of a certain policy of life insurance issued by defendant on the life of Leonard Joseph DeRyder, decedent, and that defendant had wrongfully paid the proceeds of the policy to someone other than plaintiff. *   *   *

A trial was had, and defendant moved the court to strike plaintiff's evidence at the conclusion thereof. The court stated that it would withhold its ruling on the motion. Whereupon, defendant offered no evidence, rested its case and renewed its motion to strike. Plaintiff's motion for summary judgment was overruled, and the court struck plaintiff's evidence and entered summary judgment for defendant. We granted plaintiff a writ of error.

The record discloses that Leonard Joseph DeRyder, the insured, died in Hampton, Virginia on November 17, 1958. At the time of his death an insurance policy was in effect upon his life in the sum of $5,000. This policy *   *   * provided that if, at the death of the insured, there was no designated beneficiary, the proceeds of the policy would be payable to the insured's widow. Decedent had not designated a beneficiary at the time of his death.

On December 1, 1958, Nannette O. DeRyder *   *   * filed a written claim with defendant for death benefits under the policy. On the application form Nannette stated that she and DeRyder were married on May 8, 1923, in Elizabeth City, North Carolina. She further stated that she and DeRyder had each been married only one time. All of these statements were subsequently proven to be false. Pursuant to the claim, defendant paid the $5,000 proceeds of the policy to Nannette as decedent's lawful widow. Sometime thereafter, Jennie DeRyder, the plaintiff, claimed that she was DeRyder's lawful widow and entitled to receive the proceeds of the policy. Upon defendant's refusal to honor her claim she instituted this action.

Jennie DeRyder testified *   *   * that she married [decedent] *   *   * on September 24, 1924 *   *   *. In 1930 DeRyder left Jennie and never lived with her again. *   *   *

Nannette DeRyder was called by plaintiff as an adverse witness. Her testimony may be summarized as follows: She first became acquainted with DeRyder at Norfolk, Virginia in 1919. In September, 1923, DeRyder went to New York where he remained until 1930. During his stay there (while living with Jennie) he mailed birthday, Christmas, and Easter cards to her. On March 29, 1927, she (Nannette) married Edward Wells in Norfolk. They separated in 1929, and in 1936 Wells died.

DeRyder returned to Norfolk in 1930 after leaving Jennie, and in May, 1933, three years before the death of Wells, he began living with Nannette. *   *   *

Nannette further testified that she and DeRyder were married on May 8, 1945 *   *   *. When asked why she falsely listed the date and place of the marriage as May 8, 1923, in Elizabeth City, North Carolina on the claim for death benefits she explained that DeRyder had told her to do so "for his children." *   *   *

In her assignments of error plaintiff contends that the court erred
*   *   *   in refusing to sustain her motion to strike certain answers made
by defendant in response to her request for admissions.

*   *   *   The record shows that before the case came to trial plaintiff
caused a written request for admissions to be served upon defendant pursuant
to Code, § 8–111.1.   Forty matters of fact were set forth in this request, and
defendant was asked to admit the truth of each statement.   Defendant filed a
response made under oath which admitted the truth of some of the statements
but as to a number of them the reply was in these words: "The fact requested
to be admitted is not within the knowledge of the defendant."   Written objections were also filed by defendant to two requests for admissions on the
ground that the requests were irrelevant.

Plaintiff subsequently filed a motion to strike those answers of defendant
which stated that the fact requested to be admitted was not within its knowledge.   She prayed that the court enter an order ruling either that the requests
"stand admitted" or that defendant be required to answer in accordance with
the statute.   The motion to strike was overruled, and by the same order the
court ruled that the requests for admissions to which defendant filed objections
and did not answer were irrelevant.   No error was assigned to the ruling on
objections.

*   *   *

Plaintiff argues that defendant's answers did not comply with the requirements of Code, § 8–111.1,   *   *   *   because they did not give the reasons why the matters could not be admitted.   She further argues that
*   *   *   Nannette DeRyder testified by way of discovery deposition as
to each of the facts requested to be admitted and that defendant had ample
time to investigate the truth of Nannette's testimony.

Defendant, on the other hand, contends that its answers to the requests for
admissions fully complied with the statute and denies that Nannette testified
in the discovery deposition "to each of the facts requested to be admitted."
Defendant points out a number of the requests for admissions which, it says,
were not testified to by Nannette nor within her knowledge.   In any event, the
discovery deposition was not made a part of the record in this case.

In General Accident Fire & Life Assurance Corp. v. Cohen, 203 Va. 810,
813, 127 S.E.2d 399, 401, we said:

> "The procedure dealing with requests for admissions is not to
> be used to cover the entire case and every item of evidence, but to
> force admissions of facts about which there is no real dispute.   (Cit-
> ing cases and authorities.)

> "The purpose of statutes and rules of procedure providing for
> admissions is to eliminate those facts which will not be disputed at
> the trial or about which there is no real controversy, to relieve the
> parties of the burden of proving them, to expedite the trial, and to
> facilitate a proper decision on the merits."   (Citing cases and au-
> thorities.)

The decisions are split as to whether a party should be required to admit or deny facts which are not within his knowledge. Some courts have held that a party is not compelled to admit or deny such facts. Other courts have ruled that where a proper request for admissions is made under Rule 36 of the Federal Rules * * * a party is required to answer even though he has no personal knowledge of the matter requested to be admitted, "if the means of information are reasonably within his power." A slight majority of the decisions supports the latter view, and we think that it represents the proper view in the light of the purpose of the rule and statute. * * *

It would unduly prolong this opinion and serve no useful purpose to discuss each of the 28 matters requested to be admitted to which defendant responded that the fact requested to be admitted was not within its knowledge. Suffice it to say that some of these requests required answers that were unknown to defendant but were within the knowledge of the decedent or plaintiff, or Nannette, who was not a party to this action. Plaintiff's requests for admissions Nos. 29 and 30 follow:

> "29. Plaintiff never filed a divorce suit or annulment suit against the decedent.

> "30. Decedent never filed a suit for divorce or annulment against plaintiff."

It is manifest that if defendant had been required to admit the truth of these matters it would have admitted the ultimate fact in issue, viz.: whether or not DeRyder's marriage to plaintiff had been dissolved by divorce, and there would have been no need for this litigation. "[I]t was not the intention of the legislature that § 8–111.1 was to be used to obtain admissions of controverted facts." General Accident Fire & Life Assurance Corp. v. Cohen, supra, 203 Va. at p. 813, 127 S.E.2d at p. 401.

Upon a reading of the requests for admissions in dispute we are convinced that it would have worked an undue hardship upon defendant to have required it to obtain the information it needed in order to admit or deny the requests. The "means of information" were not *reasonably* within its power. In effect, plaintiff was asking defendant to prove her case rather than to eliminate those facts which would not be disputed at the trial. Under the facts and circumstances of this case, defendant's response was sufficient.

We hold that the trial court was correct in refusing to strike defendant's answers.

For the reasons stated, the judgment appealed from is

Affirmed.

NOTES AND QUESTIONS

1. At the time the *DeRyder* case was decided, Section 8–111.1(a) of the Virginia Code and Federal Rule 36(a) were identical. The Federal Rule subsequently was amended in 1970, but the Virginia provision has not been modified.

Note the changes brought about by the 1970 amendments to Federal Rule 36, which are discussed in the Advisory Committee Notes accompanying Rule 36 in the Supplement. See also 8 Wright & Miller, *Federal Practice and Procedure: Civil* §§ 2254–57, 2261–63 (1970). How would the *DeRyder* case have been decided under the current federal provision?

2.   Although a number of jurisdictions have amended their rules to accord with the current version of Federal Rule 36, see, e. g., Ariz.R.Civ.P. 36; Fla.R. Civ.P. 1.370, other states have made no changes, despite restrictive interpretations by their courts. See HAROCHE v. HAROCHE, 38 App.Div.2d 957, 331 N.Y.S.2d 466 (1972), involving the duty of a father to pay for the services of an orthodontist for a child. The court held:

> The notice to admit sought the husband's admission of the necessity for and reasonableness of the dental treatment * * *. These issues were matters of expert opinion, not of fact, and were at the heart of the dispute between the parties. Accordingly, they were not a proper part of a request for admission * * *.

See also International Security Life Ins. Co. v. Maas, 458 S.W.2d 484 (Tex.Civ. App.1970), in which the court held improper a request to admit that plaintiff's illness began prior to the effective date of the health insurance policy issued by defendant.

Why do some courts appear so wary of requests to admit? Is there any justification for holding improper requests to admit facts that are "in controversy" or that are the ultimate facts in issue? How does one know whether a fact actually will be disputed at trial? Doesn't it make more sense to permit the request to admit to be made so that the responding party can deny it, if untrue? See Comment, *The Dilemma of Federal Rule 36*, 56 Nw.U.L.Rev. 679, 684–85 (1961). To what extent are problems regarding the scope of requests to admit obviated by the ability of a party to utilize interrogatories under a provision like Federal Rule 33?

3.   Under what circumstances is information not known to a party "readily obtainable by him"? When can it be said that a person "knows" that a fact is true and therefore is obligated to admit it? Suppose an individual sues a corporation for injuries sustained in a motor vehicle accident, allegedly caused by the negligent driving of defendant's employee? The employee, apparently the only eyewitness, when asked, states that she unlawfully went through a traffic signal. Must the corporate defendant, if requested to do so, admit the unlawful act, even though it suspects that its employee, motivated by compassion for the victim, might not be telling the truth? Suppose that ten impartial witnesses all tell the same story as the employee. Could defendant legitimately deny the request to admit on the theory that all of them could possibly be lying or mistaken? See generally Finman, *The Request for Admissions in Federal Civil Procedure*, 71 Yale L.J. 371, 404–09 (1962).

Note that it is well established under Rule 33 that a party has a duty to investigate to ascertain and disclose information that is not within its personal knowledge but reasonably within its power to obtain. Should the standards for investigation be as extensive under Rule 36?

4. If a responding party fails to reply to a set of requests to admit, the matters contained therein are deemed admitted. If, however, a party serves a sworn denial of the matters in the request to admit and at trial the matter is proved by the party requesting the admission, then Rule 37(c) provides that the latter may collect from the other party the reasonable expenses incurred in making the proof. How useful is this sanction? How can a party show that a given matter has been "proved"? Note that Rule 37(c) applies if the responding party in effect deliberately falsified an answer under oath. Shouldn't there be a more severe penalty in such a case?

5. In the *DeRyder* case plaintiff sought a court ruling either that the requests "stand admitted" or that defendant be required to make a more satisfactory answer. In 1970 a new last paragraph was added to Federal Rule 36(a) specifically allowing a motion to this effect; previously, some courts had rejected such a motion because there was no express authority for it. *Compare* United States v. New Orleans Chapter, Associated General Contractors of America, Inc., 41 F.R.D. 33 (E.D.La.1966), affirmed without opinion 396 U.S. 115, 90 S.Ct. 398, 24 L.Ed.2d 308 (1969) (court has no power to strike inadequate responses and deem requests admitted), *with* Heng Hsin Co. v. Stern, Morgenthau & Co., 20 Fed.R.Serv. 36a.52, Case 1 (S.D.N.Y.1954) (ordering responding party to give more satisfactory answers). Why is it necessary to provide for a court ruling that requests stand admitted? Isn't it enough that a failure to respond results in an admission and that an untruthful response permits sanctions under Rule 37(c)?

---

4. DISCOVERY AND PRODUCTION OF PROPERTY

Read Federal Rules of Civil Procedure 34 and 45(d) in the Supplement.

HART v. WOLFF

Supreme Court of Alaska, 1971.
489 P.2d 114.

CONNOR, Justice. Plaintiff Victor Hart has appealed from the dismissal of his complaint for failure to comply with an order to produce certain documents for defendant's inspection. * * *

facts:

On December 12, 1963, Hart filed suit against Wolff alleging that on two occasions Wolff had made statements defaming Hart. The statements concerned an alleged misappropriation of funds by Hart in the formation of Arctic Bowl, Inc., an Alaska corporation which Hart and Wolff, along with others, had organized in 1958 to operate a bowling alley in Fairbanks.

Wolff was vice-president of the corporation from 1958 until September 1959, when Metropolitan Mortgage and Securities Co., Inc., a Washington corporation, purchased a controlling interest in Arctic Bowl, Inc. Following this change in corporate control, Wolff ceased to be vice-president of the corporation. Hart, who had served as president in 1958 and 1959, remained with the corporation as a manager of the bowling alley.

* * *

Hart argues on appeal that the superior court could not properly order the production of records of Arctic Bowl, Inc., under Civil Rule 34, because the records were not in the possession, custody, or control of a party to the pending action. It is true that an order issued pursuant to Civil Rule 34 may be directed only against a party having possession, custody or control of the records. The order in question here was directed against Hart. Thus, the question which faces us is whether Hart had control over the records sought to be produced.

[margin: P: no possession or control of records]
[margin: P° arg]
[margin: issue:]

A prima facie case of control is all that need be established to justify issuance of an order under Civil Rule 34. Norman v. Young, 422 F.2d 470 (10th Cir. 1970) (construing Rule 34, F.R.Civ.P., which was then nearly identical to Alaska's Civil Rule 34) * * *. We believe that Wolff made a prima facie showing that Victor Hart had sufficient control over these records to justify the court's order of December 15, 1969.

[margin: ← only need prima facie case of control.]

The record in this case indicates that while Hart was no longer an officer of Arctic Bowl, Inc., at the time the motions to produce were made he was employed by that corporation in a position of authority and trust. Further, he was also employed during the same time by Metropolitan Mortgage, the controlling shareholder in Arctic Bowl, to handle Metropolitan's business affairs in Fairbanks.

[margin: Evidence of Hart's control]

This court in the past has favored liberal construction of the civil rules governing discovery. * * * While Rule 34 certainly has proper limits, the concept of "control" should not be given a hypertechnical construction that will undermine the policy favoring liberal pretrial discovery. As the United States Supreme Court stated in Societe Internationale Pour Participations Industrielles Et Commerciales S.A. v. Rogers, 357 U.S. 197, 206, 78 S.Ct. 1087, 1092, 2 L.Ed.2d 1255 (1958):

[margin: Rule 34 should be construed liberally]

> "Rule 34 [F.R.Civ.P.] is sufficiently flexible to be adapted to the exigencies of particular litigation. The propriety of the use to which it is put depends upon the circumstances of a given case * * *."

Thus, though Hart may not have had the authority to *force* Metropolitan to produce the records for Wolff's inspection, we believe the nature of Hart's relationships with Arctic Bowl and with Metropolitan Mortgage were such that the court could infer that he had some influence over Metropolitan with respect to Arctic Bowl, Inc., and could have used that influence to produce the records. In fact, following the issuance of the production order, at the hearing on the motion to strike, Hart himself testified that he imagined he did have some influence over Metropolitan.

[margin: Hart could have produced records. by his "influence"]

In opposition to defendant's motions to produce, Hart merely stated that he was not an officer or director of Arctic Bowl, Inc., and that he did not have the records in his possession, custody or control. At no time did he deny that he had a close employee-employer relationship with the corporation and with the corporation's major shareholder. We hold on this record that plaintiff failed to rebut the prima facie showing of control made by Wolff. The order to produce the records was, therefore, proper.

* * *

There is support in the record that plaintiff Victor Hart willfully refused to obey the December 15, 1969, order in that he himself testified that he made no efforts to produce the records of Arctic Bowl during the thirty days following that order. Nor did he make any satisfactory explanation to the court why they had not been produced. * * * In these circumstances, we cannot say that the superior court abused its discretion in dismissing plaintiff's complaint. The order is affirmed.

* * *

RABINOWITZ, Justice (concurring in part, dissenting in part).

* * * I find the record devoid of any factual basis for the majority's conclusion that Wolff made out a prima facie case of Hart's "possession, custody, or control" of Arctic Bowl's records. I cannot perceive any policy considerations, or precedential bases, for the majority's adoption of an "influence" test, either actual or potential, in substitution for the "possession, custody, or control" standards of Civil Rule 34. Nor can I agree that notions of "influence" and of liberal pretrial discovery policies furnish an adequate foundation for the discovery order and subsequent sanction which were entered.

* * *

One further comment. It strikes me as rather unusual that Wolff's battery of attorneys took approximately five years to obtain a decision on the Civil Rule 34 motion to require Hart to produce the records of Arctic Bowl, Inc. Equally extraordinary is the fact that Wolff's counsel never attempted to employ any other available discovery procedures, such as a subpoena duces tecum directed to a nonparty under Civil Rule 45(d)(1), to obtain the records of Arctic Bowl, Inc.

* * *

NOTES AND QUESTIONS

1. In *Societé Internationale v. Rogers*, quoted in *Hart v. Wolff*, plaintiff argued that it did not have "control" over documents it had been ordered to produce under Rule 34, because the production of the documents, which were in plaintiff's physical possession in Switzerland, would be in violation of the criminal laws of that country. The Supreme Court rejected the argument, stating that "Petitioner is in a most advantageous position to plead with its own sovereign for

relaxation of penal laws or for adoption of plans which will at the least achieve a significant measure of compliance with the production order * * *.''

Compare the decision in MUTUAL OF OMAHA INS. CO. v. GARRIGAN, 31 Ohio Misc. 1, 285 N.E.2d 395 (Ohio Common Pleas, Erie County, 1971), in which an insurance company brought a declaratory judgment action against the widow of its insured, alleging that the death of the insured by carbon monoxide poisoning was not accidental within the coverage of the policy. The company sought to inspect the corpse, which already had been buried. Under Ohio law, disinterment could be requested only by the deceased's next of kin, who were the children, not the widow. Accordingly, the court held that the widow did not have the requisite control required by Rule 34.

2.   Prior to the amendment of Federal Rule 34 in 1970, it provided for document discovery only on motion to the court granted upon a showing of good cause. Although many states have adopted the 1970 changes, some have retained the good cause requirement. *Compare* Ohio Civ.Proc.Rule 34(a) (good cause eliminated), *with* Utah Civ.Proc.Rule 34 (good cause retained). What justifications are there for the good-cause requirement? What advantages result from its elimination? See the Notes of the Advisory Committee accompanying the 1970 amendment to Federal Rule 34, which appear in the Supplement.

3.   Courts are divided on what constitutes a showing of good cause. On the one hand, there are a number of federal decisions rendered prior to the 1970 amendments in which the good-cause requirement was held satisfied by a showing that the requested documents were "relevant" within the meaning of Rule 26(b), provided that copies of the documents were not already in the hands of the party seeking discovery. See, e.g., Houdry Process Corp. v. Commonwealth Oil Refining Co., 24 F.R.D. 58 (S.D.N.Y.1959). On the other hand, most courts, both state and federal, have required a showing that the information sought is not available from another source. See, e.g., Guilford Nat. Bank v. Southern Ry., 297 F.2d 921, 923–25 (4th Cir.1962), certiorari denied 375 U.S. 985, 84 S.Ct. 518, 11 L.Ed.2d 473 (1964); Alseike v. Miller, 196 Kan. 547, 412 P.2d 1007 (1966).

4.   As the dissenting judge in *Hart v. Wolff* noted, items in the possession or control of a nonparty may be sought pursuant to Rule 45(d) (1). Under Rule 30(f) (1), and subject to the right of the witness to demand a court order under Rule 45(d) (1), any party has the right to inspect and copy any materials produced by a witness at a deposition. Should a court be able to go even further and, upon a showing of good cause, order possession of property to be turned over to an inquiring party? *Cf.* State ex rel. Crawford v. Moody, 477 S.W.2d 438 (Mo.App.1972), indicating "no," and giving as one reason the possibility that a party might fraudulently destroy the items so produced. Is this a valid reason?

If a nonparty witness objects to the inspection of items ordered to be produced, what showing should the discovering party be required to make to justify a court order under Rule 45(d) (1) permitting an inspection? Should the answer depend upon whether the jurisdiction does or does not retain the requirement of showing good cause under its counterpart of Rule 34? *Compare* Shepherd v. Castle, 20 F.R.D. 184, 189 (W.D.Mo.1957), *with* United States v. American Optical Co., 10 Fed.R.Serv.2d 26a.32, Case 1 (N.D.Cal.1966).

5. Discovery from nonparties under the rules is only permitted in connection with the taking of a deposition. In some circumstances in which a party seeks to inspect items in the hands of a nonparty, a deposition is useless. Why shouldn't Rule 45 be amended to provide for production of items for pretrial inspection without the artificial deposition requirement? N.Y.C.P.L.R. 3120(b) provides that "a person not a party may be directed by order to do whatever a party may be directed to do" with respect to production of documents or other items and also with respect to entry on land for the purpose of inspecting any object or operation thereon.

Federal Rule 34(c) was added in 1970 to make it clear that Rule 34 does not preclude independent proceedings for discovery under traditional equitable principles. According to the substantive equity provisions of at least some jurisdictions, such a proceeding could result in an order allowing a party to an action to enter the property of a nonparty for purposes of discovery. See the Advisory Committee Notes to the amendment adding Rule 34(c). Suppose that an equitable remedy is unavailable and that a party feels it must enter the property of a nonparty to inspect the premises or to view a large machine that cannot be removed to the lawyer's office during the course of a deposition. Is there any way under the current Federal Rules to obtain the necessary information? *Cf.* Carson v. Burlington Northern Inc., 52 F.R.D. 492 (D.Neb.1971), p. 666, supra.

———

COALITION OF BLACK LEADERSHIP v. DOORLEY, 349 F. Supp. 127 (D.R.I.1972). Plaintiffs brought a civil rights action against the city police department alleging that during the course of an arrest plaintiffs were beaten, kicked, and otherwise subject to harassment. At trial, defendant sought to introduce photographs of plaintiffs taken on the night of the arrest, presumably to show that there were no signs of physical abuse. Plaintiffs objected on the ground that defendants had failed to produce the photographs upon a request under Rule 34 asking for:

> All case records, incident reports, police log book entries and other related documents, memoranda, and reports regarding, involving, or referring to the arrests and jailing of * * * [plaintiffs].

The court held:

> Defendants, who had the photographs made pursuant to the arrests * * * attached to case files, produced the files but not the photographs. They argue that plaintiffs did not ask for photographs, so they were under no compulsion to produce them. I note that in Rule 34(a) * * * the term "documents" is expressly stated to include photographs. The photographs were within the scope of the discovery request. The failure to produce them would be sufficient to warrant their exclusion [at trial] under Fed.R.Civ.P. 37 * * *.

NOTE AND QUESTIONS

Rule 34(a) permits discovery of "designated documents." Was the court in *Coalition* too liberal regarding the designation requirement? Why shouldn't the designation be as precise as the circumstances permit? Should the party who seeks production have a duty to utilize other methods of discovery first, in order to learn what items exist in order that a precise designation can be made? For a general discussion of the varying degrees of specificity that have been required in the past, see Ronan, *Designation of Documents Under Rule 34*, 25 Ins.L.J. 313 (1958).

---

5. PHYSICAL AND MENTAL EXAMINATIONS

Read Federal Rule of Civil Procedure 35 in the Supplement.

SCHLAGENHAUF v. HOLDER

Supreme Court of the United States, 1964.
379 U.S. 104, 85 S.Ct. 234, 13 L.Ed.2d 152.

Certiorari to the United States Court of Appeals for the Seventh Circuit.

Mr. Justice GOLDBERG, delivered the opinion of the Court.

This case involves the validity and construction of Rule 35(a) of the Federal Rules of Civil Procedure as applied to the examination of a defendant in a negligence action. *   *   *

An action based on diversity of citizenship was brought in the District Court seeking damages arising from personal injuries suffered by passengers of a bus which collided with the rear of a tractor-trailer. The named defendants were The Greyhound Corporation, owner of the bus; petitioner, Robert L. Schlagenhauf, the bus driver; Contract Carriers, Inc., owner of the tractor; Joseph L. McCorkhill, driver of the tractor; and National Lead Company, owner of the trailer. Answers were filed by each of the defendants denying negligence.

Greyhound then cross-claimed against Contract Carriers and National Lead for damage to Greyhound's bus, alleging that the collision was due solely to their negligence in that the tractor-trailer was driven at an unreasonably low speed, had not remained in its lane, and was not equipped with proper rear lights. Contract Carriers filed an answer to this cross-claim denying its negligence and asserting "[t]hat the negligence of the driver of the *   *   * bus [petitioner Schlagenhauf] proximately caused and contributed to *   *   * Greyhound's damages."

*   *   *

Contract Carriers and National Lead then petitioned the District Court for an order directing petitioner Schlagenhauf to submit to both mental and physical examinations by one specialist in each of the following fields:

(1) Internal medicine;

(2) Ophthalmology;

(3) Neurology; and

(4) Psychiatry.

For the purpose of offering a choice to the District Court of one specialist in each field, the petition recommended two specialists in internal medicine, ophthalmology, and psychiatry, respectively, and three specialists in neurology —a total of nine physicians. The petition alleged that the mental and physical condition of Schlagenhauf was "in controversy" as it had been raised by Contract Carriers' answer to Greyhound's cross-claim. This was supported by a brief of legal authorities and an affidavit of Contract Carriers' attorney stating that Schlagenhauf had seen red lights 10 to 15 seconds before the accident, that another witness had seen the rear lights of the trailer from a distance of three-quarters to one-half mile, and that Schlagenhauf had been involved in a prior accident.

* * *

While disposition of this petition was pending, National Lead filed its answer to Greyhound's cross-claim and itself "cross-claimed" against Greyhound and Schlagenhauf for damage to its trailer. * * *

The District Court, on the basis of the petition filed by Contract Carriers, and without any hearing, ordered Schlagenhauf to submit to nine examinations —one by each of the recommended specialists—despite the fact that the petition clearly requested a total of only four examinations.

Petitioner applied for a writ of mandamus in the Court of Appeals against the respondent, the District Court Judge, seeking to have set aside the order requiring his mental and physical examinations. The Court of Appeals denied mandamus, one judge dissenting * * *.

We granted certiorari to review undecided questions concerning the validity and construction of Rule 35. * * *

Rule 35 on its face applies to all "parties," which under any normal reading would include a defendant. Petitioner contends, however, that the application of the Rule to a defendant would be an unconstitutional invasion of his privacy, or, at the least, be a modification of substantive rights existing prior to the adoption of the Federal Rules of Civil Procedure and thus beyond the congressional mandate of the Rules Enabling Act.

These same contentions were raised [and rejected] in Sibbach v. Wilson & Co., 312 U.S. 1, 61 S.Ct. 422, 85 L.Ed. 479, by a plaintiff in a negligence action who asserted a physical injury as a basis for recovery. * * * Petitioner does not challenge the holding in Sibbach as applied to plaintiffs. He contends, however, that it should not be extended to defendants. We can see no basis * * * for such a distinction. * * * Issues cannot be resolved by a doctrine of favoring one class of litigants over another.

We recognize that, insofar as reported cases show, this type of discovery in federal courts has been applied solely to plaintiffs, and that some early state cases seem to have proceeded on a theory that a plaintiff who seeks redress for injuries in a court of law thereby "waives" his right to claim the inviolability of his person.

* * * [The Court then rejected the "waiver" theory on the basis of language in the *Sibbach* case.] The chain of events leading to an ultimate determination on the merits begins with the injury of the plaintiff, an involuntary act on his part. Seeking court redress is just one step in this chain. If the plaintiff is prevented or deterred from this redress, the loss is thereby forced on him to the same extent as if the defendant were prevented or deterred from defending against the action.

* * *

Petitioner contends that even if Rule 35 is to be applied to defendants, which we have determined it must, nevertheless it should not be applied to him as he was not a party in relation to Contract Carriers and National Lead—the movants for the mental and physical examinations—at the time the examinations were sought. * * * While it is clear that the person to be examined must be a party to the case,[12] we are of the view that * * * Rule 35 only requires that the person to be examined be a party to the "action," not that he be an opposing party *vis-à-vis* the movant. There is no doubt that Schlagenhauf was a "party" to this "action" by virtue of the original complaint. * * * Insistence that the movant have filed a pleading against the person to be examined would have the undesirable result of an unnecessary proliferation of cross-claims and counterclaims and would not be in keeping with the aims of a liberal, nontechnical application of the Federal Rules. * * *

While the Court of Appeals held that petitioner was not a party *vis-à-vis* National Lead or Contract Carriers at the time the examinations were first sought, it went on to hold that he had become a party *vis-à-vis* National Lead by the time of a second order entered by the District Court and thus was a party within its rule. This second order, identical in all material respects with the first, was entered on the basis of supplementary petitions filed by National Lead and Contract Carriers. These petitions gave no new basis for the examinations, except for the allegation that petitioner's mental and physical condition had been additionally put in controversy by the National Lead answer and cross-claim, which had been filed subsequent to the first petition for examinations. Although the filing of the petition for mandamus intervened between these two orders, we accept, for purposes of this opinion, the determination of the Court of Appeals that this second order was the one before it and agree that petitioner was clearly a party at this juncture under any test.

[12] Although petitioner was an agent of Greyhound, he was himself a party to the action. He is to be distinguished from one who is not a party but is, for example, merely the agent of a party. * * * It is not now necessary to determine to what extent, if any, the term "party" includes one who is a "real party in interest" although not a named party to the action. Cf. Beach v. Beach, 72 App.D.C. 318, 114 F.2d 479, 131 A.L.R. 804.

Petitioner next contends that his mental or physical condition was not "in controversy" and "good cause" was not shown for the examinations, both as required by the express terms of Rule 35.

*   *   *

It is notable   *   *   *   that in none of the other discovery provisions is there a restriction that the matter be "in controversy," and only in Rule 34 is there Rule 35's requirement that the movant affirmatively demonstrate "good cause." [a]

This additional requirement of "good cause" was reviewed by Chief Judge Sobeloff in Guilford National Bank of Greensboro v. Southern Ry. Co., 297 F.2d 921, 924 (C.A.4th Cir.), in the following words:

"*   *   *

"Significantly, this freedom of action, afforded a party who resorts to depositions and interrogatories, is not granted to one proceeding under Rules 34 and 35. Instead, the court must decide as an initial matter, and in every case, whether the motion requesting production of documents or the making of a physical or mental examination adequately demonstrates good cause. The specific requirement of good cause would be meaningless if good cause could be sufficiently established by merely showing that the desired materials are relevant, for the relevancy standard has already been imposed by Rule 26(b). Thus, by adding the words   '*   *   * good cause   *   *   *,' the Rules indicate that there must be greater showing of need under Rules 34 and 35 than under the other discovery rules."

The courts of appeals in other cases have also recognized that Rule 34's good-cause requirement is not a mere formality, but is a plainly expressed limitation on the use of that Rule. This is obviously true as to the "in controversy" and "good cause" requirements of Rule 35. They are not met by mere conclusory allegations of the pleadings—nor by mere relevance to the case—but require an affirmative showing by the movant that each condition as to which the examination is sought is really and genuinely in controversy and that good cause exists for ordering each particular examination. Obviously, what may be good cause for one type of examination may not be so for another. The ability of the movant to obtain the desired information by other means is also relevant.

Rule 35, therefore, requires discriminating application by the trial judge, who must decide, as an initial matter in every case, whether the party requesting a mental or physical examination or examinations has adequately demonstrated the existence of the Rule's requirements of "in controversy" and "good cause," which requirements, as the Court of Appeals in this case itself recognized, are necessarily related. 321 F.2d, at 51. *   *   *

Of course, there are situations where the pleadings alone are sufficient to meet these requirements. A plaintiff in a negligence action who asserts men-

[a] The "good cause" requirement was eliminated from Rule 34 in 1970. See page 679, supra.

tal or physical injury   *   *   *   places that mental or physical injury clearly in controversy and provides the defendant with good cause for an examination to determine the existence and extent of such asserted injury. This   *   *   *   applies equally to a defendant who asserts his mental or ✓ physical condition as a defense to a claim, such as, for example, where insanity is asserted as a defense to a divorce action.   *   *   *

Here, however, Schlagenhauf did not assert his mental or physical condition either in support of or in defense of a claim. His condition was sought to be placed in issue by other parties. Thus, under the principles discussed above, Rule 35 required that these parties make an affirmative showing that petitioner's mental or physical condition was in controversy and that there was good cause for the examinations requested. This, the record plainly shows, they failed to do.

The only allegations in the pleadings relating to this subject were the general conclusory statement in Contract Carriers' answer to the cross-claim that "Schlagenhauf was not mentally or physically capable of operating" the bus at the time of the accident and the limited allegation in National Lead's cross-claim that, at the time of the accident, "the eyes and vision of   *   *   * Schlagenhauf was [sic] impaired and deficient."

The attorney's affidavit attached to the petition for the examinations provided:

> "That   *   *   *   Schlagenhauf, in his deposition   *   *   * admitted that he saw red lights for 10 to 15 seconds prior to a collision with a semi-tractor trailer unit and yet drove his vehicle on without reducing speed and without altering the course thereof.
>
> "The only eye-witness to this accident known to this affiant   *   *   *   testified that immediately prior to the impact between the bus and truck that he had also been approaching the truck from the rear and that he had clearly seen the lights of the truck for a distance of three-quarters to one-half mile to the rear thereof.
>
> " *   *   *   Schlagenhauf has admitted in his deposition   *   *   *   that he was involved in a [prior] similar type rear end collision.   *   *   *"

This record cannot support even the corrected order which required one examination in each of the four specialties of internal medicine, ophthalmology, neurology, and psychiatry. Nothing in the pleadings or affidavit would afford a basis for a belief that Schlagenhauf was suffering from a mental or neurological illness warranting wide-ranging psychiatric or neurological examinations. Nor is there anything stated justifying the broad internal medicine examination.

The only specific allegation made in support of the four examinations ordered was that the "eyes and vision" of Schlagenhauf were impaired. Considering this in conjunction with the affidavit, we would be hesitant to set aside a visual examination if it had been the only one ordered. However, as the case must be remanded to the District Court because of the other examinations or-

Only eye exam was pertinent to the issues of mental or physical condition of bus driver as put into controversy by D³' counterclaims

dered, it would be appropriate for the District Judge to reconsider also this order in light of the guidelines set forth in this opinion.

* * *

Accordingly, the judgment of the Court of Appeals is vacated and the case remanded to the District Court to reconsider the examination order in light of the guidelines herein formulated and for further proceedings in conformity with this opinion.

Vacated and remanded.

Mr. Justice BLACK, with whom Mr. Justice CLARK joins, concurring in part and dissenting in part.

* * *

In a collision case like this one, evidence concerning very bad eyesight or impaired mental or physical health which may affect the ability to drive is obviously of the highest relevance. It is equally obvious, I think, that when a vehicle continues down an open road and smashes into a truck in front of it although the truck is in plain sight and there is ample time and room to avoid collision, the chances are good that the driver has some physical, mental or moral defect. When such a thing happens twice, one is even more likely to ask, "What is the matter with that driver? Is he blind or crazy?" Plainly the allegations of the other parties were relevant and put the question of Schlagenhauf's health and vision "in controversy." * * *

Mr. Justice DOUGLAS, dissenting in part.

* * * When the defendant's doctors examine plaintiff, they are normally interested only in answering a single question: did plaintiff in fact sustain the specific injuries claimed? But plaintiff's doctors will naturally be inclined to go on a fishing expedition in search of *anything* which will tend to prove that the defendant was unfit to perform the acts which resulted in the plaintiff's injury. And a doctor for a fee can easily discover something wrong with any patient—a condition that in prejudiced medical eyes might have caused the accident. Once defendants are turned over to medical or psychiatric clinics for an analysis of their physical well-being and the condition of their psyche, the effective trial will be held there and not before the jury. There are no lawyers in those clinics to stop the doctor from probing this organ or that one, to halt a further inquiry, to object to a line of questioning. And there is no judge to sit as arbiter. The doctor or the psychiatrist has a holiday in the privacy of his office. The defendant is at the doctor's (or psychiatrist's) mercy; and his report may either overawe or confuse the jury and prevent a fair trial.

* * *

Neither the Court nor Congress up to today has determined that any person whose physical or mental condition is brought into question during some lawsuit must surrender his right to keep his person inviolate. Congress did, according to Sibbach, require a plaintiff to choose between his privacy and his purse; but before today it has not been thought that any other "party" had lost this historic immunity. Congress and this Court can authorize such a rule.

But a rule suited to purposes of discovery against defendants must be carefully drawn in light of the great potential of blackmail.

* * *

[Mr. Justice HARLAN's dissenting opinion is omitted.]

NOTES AND QUESTIONS

1. In 1970 Federal Rule 35(a) was amended to encompass persons "in the custody or under the legal control of a party." "Agents of a party" are not included in the Rule, although this had been recommended by the Advisory Committee in 1955. What reasons are there for not including agents? The 1970 amendment also redefined "physical condition" specifically to include blood type. For a general discussion of the need for the 1970 changes see Note, *Physical Examination of Non-Parties Under the Federal Rules of Civil Procedure,* 43 Iowa L.Rev. 375 (1958). See also 8 Wright & Miller, *Federal Practice and Procedure: Civil* §§ 2231–39 (1970).

2. N.Y.C.P.L.R. 3121 provides for physical examinations to be taken upon notice without a prior court order or showing of "good cause." Although in 1970 Federal Rule 34 was amended to eliminate the good-cause requirement as to discovery of documents and other items, the good-cause requirement in Rule 35 was retained. Is there more reason for a showing of good cause as a prerequisite when a physical examination is desired than there is when discovery of documents is sought?

3. The courts are called upon to exercise considerable discretion in determining the extent of the examination to be permitted, the place of the examination, see Annot., 71 A.L.R.2d 973 (1960), and the persons who may be present, see Annot., 64 A.L.R.2d 497 (1959). What justification is there for permitting the party to be examined to bring a lawyer and personal physician with him? What arguments can be made that these "outsiders" should not be permitted to attend?

LEWIN v. JACKSON, 108 Ariz. 27, 492 P.2d 406 (1972). Plaintiff sued for slander, alleging as damages the fact that she had been disinherited by her parents. Defendant sought to take the deposition of plaintiff's father, who had become incompetent and had been placed under the guardianship of plaintiff. Plaintiff objected, asking for a protective order under Rule 26(c) on the ground that her father was not physically or mentally able to give a deposition. The court stayed the deposition but ordered the father to undergo a medical examination for the purpose of determining whether or not he could be deposed. Plaintiff objected on the ground that Arizona Rule 35 (identical to Federal Rule 35) did not permit the examination in question. The court concluded that although the father was a person under the "custody" and "legal control of plaintiff," Rule 35 did not apply because the action had not been brought on his behalf. Nonetheless the court held the examination to be proper as part of the inherent power of a court "to assure itself not only that a witness' testimony will be accurate and lucid, but also that the act of testifying will not endanger the health of the proposed witness."

QUESTIONS

1. Is the court in *Lewin* correct in holding that the requested medical examination did not fall within the scope of Rule 35? Can the examination be justified as part of an order under Rule 26(c) controlling the course of a deposition? Should Rule 35 be considered the exclusive source of power by which a court can require a nonparty to submit to an examination?

2. How far does the inherent power invoked by the *Lewin* court extend? For example, can the court order a person who witnessed an event upon which the suit is based to submit to an eye examination to determine if that person can see well enough to be considered a competent witness at a deposition or at trial? If so, how effective is the limitation of Rule 35 to parties?

BENNING v. PHELPS, 249 F.2d 47 (2d Cir.1957). Prior to suit, plaintiff voluntarily submitted to a physical examination by defendant's physician. Thereafter plaintiff refused to submit to another examination and defendant moved the trial court to order plaintiff to do so. The court granted the motion and ordered defendant to provide plaintiff with a copy of the report of the examining physician. In compliance with the court's order, defendant delivered to plaintiff a copy of the physician's report, and then moved, under Rule 35(b)(1) to require plaintiff to give defendant the reports of plaintiff's doctors. The trial court denied the motion and the appellate court affirmed as follows:

> * * * [D]efendant is entitled to receive copies of the plaintiff's medical reports only if the plaintiff has previously requested and received copies of medical reports from the defendant. * * * Here the plaintiff received copies of the defendant's reports pursuant to an order of the court, and not pursuant to his own request. Since the trial court might properly have concluded that "good cause" had not been shown, * * * and hence might have refused to compel the plaintiff to submit to the second examination requested by the defendant, we cannot find that it erred in the condition which it placed upon its order.

In CHASTAIN v. EVENNOU, 35 F.R.D. 350 (D.Utah 1964), plaintiff voluntarily submitted to a physical examination by a physician designated by defendants, and plaintiff received a copy of the report in exchange for copies of certain reports by his own physicians. But plaintiff specifically withheld one physician's report, arguing that Rule 35(b) was inapplicable since no court-ordered examination had ever taken place. The court ordered production of the withheld report on the ground that the spirit of Rule 35 so demanded. What are the relevant considerations in determining the accuracy or inaccuracy of this decision?

NOTE AND QUESTIONS

Rule 35(b) (3) was added in 1970, in recognition of the fact that much discovery takes place by agreement of the parties without resort to court appearances. How far does this new provision go? Would it alter the result in *Benning v. Phelps?*

SECTION C. REALITIES OF DISCOVERY: TACTICS, HARASSMENT, AND UNDUE BURDENS

RIVER PLATE CORP. v. FORESTAL LAND, TIMBER & RY. CO.

United States District Court, Southern District of New York, 1960.
185 F.Supp. 832.

FREDERICK van PELT BRYAN, District Judge. This is a private anti-trust suit alleging a conspiracy to monopolize trade and commerce in quebracho and wattle extracts used in the tanning of leather, in violation of the Sherman, Clayton, and Wilson Tariff Acts, 15 U.S.C.A. §§ 1, 27, 44. Broad injunctive relief and damages in the sum of $3,600,000 are sought.

Plaintiff River Plate Corporation is a Delaware corporation. The fourteen defendants named include eight which appear to be residents of foreign countries. Service of process has been made on most of the domestic defendants. Plaintiff also claims to have effected service on The Forestal Land, Timber and Railway Co. Ltd., a United Kingdom corporation, (Forestal London) and La Forestal S.A. de Tierras Maderas y Explotaciones Commerciales e Industriales, an Argentine corporation, (Forestal Argentina) by serving defendants Barkey Importing Co. Inc. (Barkey), The Olson Importing Company, Inc. (Olson) in this district, and James M. Cavanaugh in New Jersey, as agents of these defendants. Defendant Protan S.R.L. (Protan), an Argentine entity claiming to be a limited partnership, is also claimed to have been served by service on defendants Barkey and Olson as its agents.

Defendants Forestal London, Forestal Argentina and Protan have moved, pursuant to Rule 12(b) * * * to quash service of process and to dismiss the complaint as to each of them on the grounds that they are not amenable to service of process here and that service was not effected on persons on whom service could be made on their behalf under Rule 4(d) * * * or authorized to receive service for them.

Plaintiff opposes these motions and has cross-moved to hold the motions in abeyance until it has had the benefit of discovery and has taken depositions here and abroad. Motions previously made by plaintiff for the issuance of letters rogatory to take depositions in England and Argentina are also now before me. In addition, plaintiff has served notices to take various depositions in this country which have not yet proceeded pending decision of the motions before me.

The first question is whether the motions to dismiss for lack of in personam jurisdiction over the two Forestal defendants and Protan should be determined on the merits at this time, or whether such motions should be held in abeyance pending the taking of depositions by plaintiff in an attempt to elicit facts to sustain jurisdiction. There is a subsidiary dispute as to whether such depositions, if allowed, should be confined to jurisdictional facts only or should also cover the merits. Defendants Olson and Barkey, concerning whom there is no jurisdictional question, contend that depositions of plaintiff on the merits which they have already noticed have priority and should be permitted to proceed without delay before plaintiff examines them.

The three defendants contesting jurisdiction contend that the affidavits and documents which they have submitted clearly establish that they are not inhabitants of nor may they be found in this district or in any district in the United States within the meaning of Section 12 of the Clayton Act, 15 U.S.C.A. § 22. They say that plaintiff has wholly failed to meet its burden of sustaining jurisdiction and that they have demonstrated that depositions would be fruitless on that subject.   *   *   *

I will not attempt to discuss in detail the voluminous affidavits before me, nor the checklist of facts which defendants say should be determinative of whether they can be found here. It may be noted, however, that the affidavit submitted by the plaintiff, liberally viewed, presents at least some facts which call into question what the defendants claim the facts to be with respect to their activities here within the last few years.

  *   *   *

The case at bar is not the usual case.

Here, the Forestal defendants candidly state that they have arranged their affairs so that they will not be "found" in the United States for purposes of suit. Changes in such arrangements were made after a prior anti-trust suit had been brought against them which was settled. The Forestal defendants carefully reworked their agreement with their distributors Barkey and Olson and with defendant Cavanaugh with the object of withdrawing from the jurisdiction, if, in fact, they were ever here. The agreements with Barkey and Olson now in force on their face indicate that these distributors are independent contractors who have no agency relationship with the Forestal companies or Protan, and that Cavanaugh has presently no direct relationship at all with the Forestal corporations. How different the relationships were prior to these changes in arrangements is by no means clear.

Plaintiff contends that depositions will establish that the formal arrangements do not show the present true relationship between Barkey, Olson and Cavanaugh and the Forestal defendants, and that a prior relationship subjecting defendants to jurisdiction persists. They contend further that concealment of such relationship is a part of the conspiracy to restrain commerce which is the gravamen of the complaint.

The Forestal defendants urge on the other hand that the best plaintiff has done up to now is to suggest that they may have been present here a year or two before service was attempted in this case. They point out that prior presence in the jurisdiction, standing by itself, will not ordinarily serve to sustain service of process and that corporate defendants are at liberty to withdraw from a jurisdiction if they so desire.

However, the fact that there may have been prior activities sufficient to constitute presence in the jurisdiction is at least an indication that a motion to dismiss for lack of jurisdiction should not be determined on affidavits alone, but that plaintiff should be afforded an opportunity to explore the question of whether such activities have in fact continued and whether the service is valid. * * *

Whether or not depositions should be permitted on such a motion as this is a matter of discretion, as the Forestal defendants readily concede. In my view under the facts and circumstances in this case discretion should be exercised so as to give plaintiff an opportunity to take depositions as to jurisdictional facts. * * * The decision of the motions made by the Forestal defendants will be held in abeyance pending the taking of such depositions.

There is less before me to support jurisdiction over the defendant Protan than over the Forestal defendants. Whether the defendant has shown sufficient [sic] to justify the taking of depositions on the jurisdictional question is not free from doubt. However, it appears that Protan concededly plays a part in the dealings between Forestal Argentina and Barkey. In view of this, and of the somewhat obscure relationships between those alleged to be a part of the Forestal complex of companies operating in many quarters of the globe, it would be unwise to determine the Protan motion to dismiss on jurisdictional grounds before the depositions on the jurisdictional question have been taken and the motions of the Forestal defendants are ready for decision. I will therefore, in the exercise of my discretion, also permit the taking of depositions on the question of jurisdiction over Protan and also hold the Protan motion to dismiss for want of jurisdiction in abeyance pending the completion of depositions.

The next question is the extent to which plaintiff will be permitted to go on such depositions.

Despite the earnest protestations of plaintiff that it should be permitted to examine the Forestal defendants, Protan, the American defendants and a number of witnesses on all phases of the case at this time, I am not persuaded that it should be allowed to do so. The threads upon which the plaintiff presently bases its claim of jurisdiction are slender against the Forestal defendants and even more slender against Protan. If the moving defendants are right in their claim that they are not to be "found" within the jurisdiction, it would be grossly unfair to subject them to examination as parties and to force them to disclose private and confidential material with respect to their business practices. Although the complaint alleges classic violations of the Anti-Trust Acts, if this court has no jurisdiction over the moving defendants they should not be placed in the position of being forced to disclose details of transactions which may be entirely lawful under foreign law.

Moreover, if jurisdiction is found to be lacking, the moving defendants would have been put to a heavy and entirely unjustifiable burden and expense, not only on the depositions taken of them as parties but on the depositions of the other defendants and of the proposed witnesses. The moving defendants would doubtless be forced for their own protection to participate in any general examination on the merits, a burden which would be quite unnecessary if the jurisdictional question were decided in their favor.

The plaintiff's plea that heavy burden and extra expense would be entailed if it were required to take one set of depositions on the question of jurisdiction and another set on the merits should jurisdiction be sustained, is far outweighed by the prejudice to the moving defendants which would result from enlarged examinations at this time. After all the burden is on the plaintiff to establish jurisdiction. * * * On the present record there is grave doubt as to whether plaintiff can sustain its burden. Confining such depositions to jurisdictional facts in cases like this is now common practice and such practice will be followed here. * * *

I consider that the issues as to jurisdiction have been defined by the voluminous papers submitted on these motions. These issues are confined to whether or not the Forestal defendants can be found here through their alleged agents Barkey, Olson and Cavanaugh and whether or not Protan can be found here through its alleged agents Barkey and Olson. The depositions will be strictly limited to such issues. The period of time to be covered will be limited to the three years immediately prior to February 4, 1960, the date when service is claimed to have been effected in this action. It is the relationship between the defendants and their respective alleged agents and any other activities which they carried on within the Southern District of New York in connection therewith during this period which is the subject matter of the examination, and nothing else.

I recognize that spelling out limits of the depositions is difficult and troublesome. Such limits will be appropriately defined in the letters rogatory to be issued pursuant to order of the court. The subject matter to be covered in the depositions to be taken by plaintiff in this country will be similarly limited in orders to be entered pursuant to this decision. Since counsel are more familiar with the problems likely to be encountered than the court can be, both sides will frame and submit such limitations and restrictions as they deem appropriate.

I have noted that defendants Barkey Importing Co. Inc. and Jacob A. Barkey, and The Olson Importing Company, Inc., the individual Olson defendants and the members of the Olson partnership have noticed depositions to be taken of the plaintiff prior to the depositions which the plaintiff now seeks to take. No motions were made by plaintiff to vacate or modify defendants' notices. Indeed, there is a stipulation between counsel for plaintiff and counsel for Barkey, approved by order of the court, specifically providing that their depositions shall proceed first. The right to priority of depositions is of considerable importance to these defendants, particularly since it is probable that some overlap between the question of jurisdiction and the merits will occur during the course of plaintiff's examinations. Moreover, these defendants assert that they can establish by such depositions that plaintiff is not entitled to maintain the action against them. I see no reason why they should lose the priority of examination to which they are entitled merely because plaintiff has become involved in a dispute as to jurisdiction with other defendants. The defendants not contesting jurisdiction who have served prior notices to take depositions of the plaintiff on the merits may proceed to do so at a date to be agreed upon by counsel or fixed by the court.

The depositions to be taken by the plaintiff of the defendants who have noticed deposition on the question of jurisdiction will not commence until after the completion of the defendants' depositions of the plaintiff. Counsel for the Forestal defendants and for Protan may attend such depositions if they so desire but shall not participate in them until their status as parties has been determined. They may, of course, take their own depositions of the plaintiff in due course if it should be found that the court has jurisdiction over them and that they are parties to the action.

When defendants' depositions of plaintiff are completed the depositions to be taken by the plaintiff of the defendants who do not contest jurisdiction will proceed within a reasonable time thereafter to be agreed upon by counsel or fixed by the court.

* * *

There remains the question as to the terms upon which the depositions under letters rogatory may be taken in England and Argentina. It seems to me impractical to have such depositions taken by written interrogatories as the Forestal defendants suggest. The depositions will be taken by oral examination under letters rogatory in accordance with the appropriate procedures upon such letters in England and Argentina.

Plaintiff urges that the moving defendants can be adequately represented by local counsel upon such examinations. This strikes me as naive to say the least. Counsel in Argentina, and even English counsel trained in the common law, would, I am sure, find our theories of jurisdiction elusive and jurisdiction is the subject matter of the examinations.

The moving defendants are entitled to be represented by American counsel at the taking of such depositions abroad as may affect them, and the plaintiff will be required to pay in advance the expenses of their attendance, including a reasonable counsel fee, the amount so paid to be a taxable cost in the event that plaintiff recovers the costs of the action. See Rule 4 of the Civil Rules of this Court. Since the two Forestal defendants have common representation they will be represented by one counsel both in England and in Argentina. The interests of Protan in Argentina may be quite different from those of the Forestal defendants and Protan will be allowed separate counsel there.   There is nothing to indicate that the interests of Protan will be involved in the depositions to be taken in England. Protan may attend the English examinations by counsel but I will not require that the plaintiff bear the expense of Protan's counsel on the examinations there.

Since the examinations abroad have been strictly limited to questions bearing on jurisdiction it does not seem necessary to require plaintiff to pay the expenses of counsel representing the American defendants on such examinations.   Of course, the American defendants may be represented at their own expense if they so desire.

Counsel for the moving defendants and the plaintiff will endeavor to agree upon a fair and reasonable sum to be paid in advance for expenses of counsel and counsel fees upon the foreign depositions.   If they are unable to agree they may submit to the court their respective views as to what reasonable expenses and counsel fees should be and the court will fix the amounts to be paid.

In order to afford the parties ample time to prepare the papers necessary to carry out this decision and to reach agreement on the question of counsel fees and expenses, such orders as are appropriate will be settled on 20 days' notice.

NOTES AND QUESTIONS

1.   Consider the relative positions of the parties in the *River Plate* case. What tactical considerations motivated the fight over the limits of the scope of discovery, the right of priority of examination, and the location of the examinations?   In what ways do the costs of pretrial litigation and the relative financial positions of plaintiff and defendant control a party's tactical decisions?   How might the addition of new Federal Rule 26(d), regarding priority of examination, affect the strategy?   See pp. 662–63, supra.

2.   Why didn't plaintiff in *River Plate* request that defendants' depositions be taken in New York, where the action was instituted?   See Fischer & Porter Co. v. Sheffield Corp., 31 F.R.D. 534 (D.Del.1962) (plaintiff ordered to take deposition at defendant's residence, rather than in forum state).   Suppose one of the Argentine defendants had served proper notice for taking plaintiff's deposition in Argentina.   Should plaintiff be able to secure an order changing the location of the deposition to New York?   If such an order is granted, should it be on condition that plaintiff pay the expenses of defendant's attorney in Argentina to come to New York to take the deposition?

3.   Many courts have said that when a plaintiff who lives in one jurisdiction files suit in another, that party must submit to oral examination in the forum state or may be given the option of paying the fees and expenses of defendant's attorney in taking the deposition at plaintiff's residence.   See, e. g., Sykes Int'l, Ltd. v. Pilch's Poultry Breeding Farms, Inc., 55 F.R.D. 138 (D.Conn.1972); Haviland & Co. v. Montgomery Ward & Co., 31 F.R.D. 578 (S.D.N.Y.1962). Under what circumstances should this general rule not be enforced?   See Forde

v. Urania Transp., Inc., 168 F.Supp. 240 (S.D.N.Y.1958). What justification is there for a rule that places the cost of attending a deposition of a nonparty on plaintiff? Why shouldn't the court place the cost on the party who most easily can afford it or on the party who requested the deposition? See Meredith v. Gavin, 51 F.R.D. 5 (W.D.Mo.1970).

4. Following the *River Plate* opinion the lawyers engaged in extensive negotiations to define the scope of examination and to fix the amounts to be advanced to defendants' attorneys for legal fees and travel and living expenses. An order ultimately issued limiting discovery "to the issues of whether or not defendant * * * can be found in the Southern District of New York through its alleged agents defendant Barkey and defendant Olson, or in the District of New Jersey through its alleged agent James M. Cavanaugh." The order further limited the scope of examination to "the relationships between defendant Forestal London and its alleged agents, and any activities which Forestal London carried on within the states of New York and New Jersey in connection therewith during the three years prior to February 4, 1960, and nothing else * * *." Forestal initially sought $300 per day for counsel fees and River Plate sought to limit the amount to $100 per day; the final order authorized the payment of $200 a day for ten days along with a $20 *per diem* and traveling expenses. A payment for legal fees and living expenses covering ten days ($2,200) and for traveling expenses was to be made in advance by plaintiff. The case was settled shortly after discovery commenced.

5. Wouldn't many of the practical problems of pretrial discovery be ameliorated by judicious use of recent technological innovations? For example, why couldn't a distant witness be examined via closed-circuit television? Wouldn't a kinescope or videotape of a deposition aid a court in deciding disputes over the propriety of particular questions or the sufficiency of certain answers? See *Carson v. Burlington Northern Inc.,* p. 666, supra. What other uses might be made of television during pretrial discovery? What about computers and xerography?

6. Read Federal Rule 28(b), which authorizes a number of different procedures for taking a deposition in a foreign country. Why are special provisions required for taking testimony in a foreign country and why are a variety of methods provided? See 8 Wright & Miller, *Federal Practice and Procedure: Civil* § 2083 (1970).

The ability to take testimony or secure discovery in foreign countries often requires cooperation between officials in the country whose court is seeking discovery and those in the country in which the examination will take place. In recent years Congress has enacted legislation to eliminate some of the serious deficiencies in our practices of international judicial cooperation and the Supreme Court has adjusted the Federal Rules in the areas of service of process (Rule 4(i)), pretrial discovery (Rule 28(b)), proof of records (Rule 44), and proof of foreign law (Rule 44.1). For a comprehensive analysis see Miller, *International Cooperation in Litigation Between the United States and Switzerland: Unilateral Procedural Accommodation in a Test Tube,* 49 Minn.L.Rev. 1069 (1965). See also Smit, *International Litigation Under the United States Code,* 65 Colum.L.Rev. 1015 (1965).

TRIANGLE MFG. CO. v. PARAMOUNT BAG MFG. CO.

United States District Court, Eastern District of New York, 1964.
35 F.R.D. 540.

ZAVATT, Chief Judge. The plaintiff herein, Triangle Mfg. Co., Inc. (hereinafter Triangle), alleges patent infringement and unfair competition by the defendants, Paramount Bag Mfg. Co., Inc., and Paramount Bag Co., Inc. (hereinafter Paramount). In substance, Triangle alleges that a shoe bag being marketed by Paramount infringes its patent in a similar bag, and that the sale of Paramount's product constitutes unfair competition and palming off. The case is now before this court on Triangle's motion, pursuant to Rule 33 of the Federal Rules of Civil Procedure, objecting to certain interrogatories propounded by Paramount. It is alleged generally that these interrogatories are "unduly burdensome, that much of the information constitutes business secrets such as customer lists, and that the information sought is neither relevant nor material."

The interrogatories in question are:

"1. With respect to the allegations of Paragraph 14 of the Amended Complaint that the Plaintiff has expended in excess of seventy thousand dollars ($70,000) to promote the sale of Plaintiff's bags:—

*   *   *

"(c) Set forth the places and dates of publication of each of such promotional activities."

"2. With respect to the allegation in Paragraph 15 of the Amended Complaint that in excess of two hundred thousand (200,000) of Plaintiff's bags have been sold:—

"a. Set forth the name and address of every vendee to whom such bags were sold;

"b. Set forth the number of bags sold to each such vendee;

"c. Set forth the dates of every such sale;

"d. Set forth the prices, discounts and allowances in respect of each such sale;

"e. Set forth the invoice numbers of any of every [sic] invoice covering each such sale;"

"5. With respect to the more than two hundred thousand (200,000) of Plaintiff's bags alleged in Paragraph 15 of the Amended Complaint to have been sold by the Plaintiff:—

"a. Describe all materials employed in the construction of such bags;

"b. Set forth the name and address of every person from whom such materials were bought;

"c. Set forth the quantity of materials referred to in item b of this interrogatory;

"d. Identify the invoices of the suppliers of the materials referred to in item b of this interrogatory;"

At the outset, this court cannot agree with Triangle's allegations that each of these interrogatories is irrelevant and, therefore, improper under Rule 33. The test of relevancy under this Rule is the same as that existing under Rule 26, i. e., that the "relevancy of interrogatories is to be determined by their relevancy to the proceedings and subject-matter and not relevancy to the issues in an action." Glick v. McKesson & Robbins, Inc., 10 F.R.D. 477, 479 (W.D.Mo. 1950). * * * It is readily apparent that each of these interrogatories falls within these bounds of propriety. Interrogatory No. 1(c) merely seeks information as to a matter alleged in the complaint, i. e., the use of advertisements to create a "secondary meaning" for Triangle's product. Paramount, faced with the task of attempting to disprove the allegation of "secondary meaning," is entitled to the dates and places of publication of the advertisements upon which the allegation is, in part, based. The same reasoning applies with equal force to interrogatories No. 2(a) through 2(e). * * * Interrogatories No. 5(a) through 5(d) are not as squarely on point as are the others, but, nonetheless, are relevant to the question of "secondary meaning." * * *

Notwithstanding the relevancy of these interrogatories, the court is disposed to sustain these objections on the ground that the required answers would place an unnecessary burden upon the plaintiff. Although "[i]nconvenience and burden are always the lot of a party to whom interrogatories are propounded," Leonia Amusement Corp. v. Loew's, Inc., 18 F.R.D. 503, 505 (S.D.N.Y.1955), there must necessarily be limits beyond which a party should not be required to go; this is particularly true when, as in the instant case, there exists a reasonable alternative to the discovery method employed by the inquiring party. Each of the interrogatories propounded by Paramount can be answered only by an extensive compilation of data contained in Triangle's records. As to the information sought by interrogatory 1(c), Triangle states in its moving papers that "a cataloguing of the places and dates of such promotional activities would fill a book and would take six months of office time to compile." Although this claim may be somewhat exaggerated, it seems clear that such a compilation would require an inordinate amount of time and effort and that the answers to the other interrogatories would require an equal, if not greater, expenditure. Under these circumstances, and since an order pursuant to Rule 34 would properly lie for the production of these records, it seems only fair that the party seeking such information be required to bear the burden of extracting and collating it. * * * The plaintiff's motion objecting to these interrogatories shall, therefore, be granted, and an order entered, pursuant to Rule 34, for the discovery and inspection of the relevant records from which Paramount can extract the information which it seeks.

It is the opinion of the court, however, that such an order must be accompanied by a protective order * * * [under Rule 26(c)]. Plaintiff has objected, and properly so, to the divulgence of certain information pertaining to its customers and sources of supply. While there is no absolute privilege protecting such information, * * * this court is most reluctant to make it available to a competitor such as Paramount. * * * It would seem, there-fore, that the proper procedure would involve the selection of an impartial third person, to be paid by Paramount but acceptable to each party, who will examine Triangle's records with regard to the information sought in inter-rogatories 2(a) through 2(e) and 5(a) through 5(d). * * * This third person will tabulate the information pertaining to Triangle's customers and sources of supply in such a manner as to give Paramount the maximum amount of information while at the same time maintaining the secrecy of the actual suppliers and customers. The identity of this third person, as well as the precise nature and scope of these tabulations, are to be agreed upon by the parties and incorporated, in detail, into the order to be submitted herein. Since the information sought by interrogatory No. 1(c) can in no way be regarded as a trade secret, inspection of the records pertinent thereto shall proceed without any protective order.

* * *

If the parties are unable to agree, on or before July 15, 1964, upon said impartial third person, they shall report their disagreement to the court on July 15, 1964, at 10 A.M. and thereupon the court will select an impartial third person.

Settle an order consistent herewith on or before July 15, 1964.

NOTES AND QUESTIONS

1. To what extent should a party be entitled to object to discovery on the ground that the interrogating party already has obtained information on the issue in question? Should the courts be amenable to motions that would limit the number of persons to be deposed if the same information is sought from each? See HOGAN v. ULTRONIC SYSTEMS CORP., 8 Fed.R.Serv.2d 45b.31, Case 1 (S.D.N.Y.1964), in which the court granted a limiting order with the caveat that if at a later time the examining party could show "some real necessity therefor," additional witnesses could be deposed. To what extent should the court grant a protective order on the basis that the volume of discovery sought is overwhelming, for example, when thousands of business documents are requested? See Morgan Smith Automotive Prods., Inc. v. General Motors Corp., 54 F.R.D. 19 (E.D.Pa. 1971).

2. Note that the trial court may control the tone of discovery proceedings as well as their physical details. See HARLEM RIVER CONSUMERS COOP-ERATIVE, INC. v. ASSOCIATED GROCERS OF HARLEM, INC., 54 F.R.D. 551 (S.D.N.Y.1972), in which plaintiff took photographs of defendants' attor-neys who had gathered at plaintiff's headquarters to examine documents pursuant to a request under Federal Rule 34. The court ordered the photographs sup-pressed, stating

The federal rules envision that discovery will be conducted by skill-ed gentlemen of the bar, without wrangling and without the intervention of the court. The vision is an unreal dream. Regrettably, hostility, and bitterness are more the rule than the exception in unsupervised discovery proceedings. * * * The ultimate curtailment of abuse requires the constant vigilance of the bench and bar to insure that any conduct threatening the orderly progress of discovery proceedings is nipped in the bud, lest the efficacy of modern discovery proceedings be destroyed.

* * *

There can be no question that defense counsel were understandably annoyed by the taking of photographs without their consent, for some extraneous purpose. That the taking of photographs detracts from the required calm and serene atmosphere essential to the administration of justice is recognized by General Rule 36 of this court, which prohibits the taking of photographs in the courthouse and its environs.

3. Is it appropriate for a trial court to issue a protective order that otherwise might be proper but has been sought by a party for the purpose of securing a tactical advantage? See MILSEN CO. v. SOUTHLAND CORP., 16 Fed.R. Serv.2d 110 (N.D.Ill.1972), in which defendant gave notice of the depositions of a number of coplaintiffs and then sought an order under Federal Rule 26(c)(5) prohibiting each plaintiff from attending any deposition other than its own. Defendant sought the order to ensure that each deponent would give an independent recollection of the facts without being influenced by what any other plaintiff had said. The order was granted except that each plaintiff was held free to attend any deposition subsequent to its own.

Read Federal Rule of Civil Procedure 26(e) and the accompanying Advisory Committee's comments in the Supplement.

THE DUTY TO SUPPLEMENT RESPONSES

Rule 26(e), adopted in 1970, was designed to eliminate inconsistent decisions regarding the existence and scope of the duty to update discovery answers. Note that the rule is not all-encompassing. What information obtained subsequent to the original responses is not covered by it? How should the word "knows" in subdivision (e)(2) be interpreted? See 8 Wright & Miller, *Federal Practice and Procedure: Civil* § 2049, at 323 (1970).

Why should there be any duty to supplement answers given in the course of discovery? Doesn't this duty constitute an undue burden on a responding party? Why isn't it enough that the discovering party simply can send a later set of interrogatories or engage in discovery immediately before trial if it wants up-to-date replies from another party? Would it be wise to limit the duty to the giving of names of any newly discovered witnesses? See *Developments in the Law—Discovery*, 74 Harv.L.Rev. 940, 961–63 (1961). Some jurisdictions that have not adopted a regulation on the matter have limited the duty to interrogatories that themselves call for an updating of the answers whenever further relevant information is obtained by the responding party. See Northwestern Mutual Ins. Co. v. Stromme, 4 Wash.App. 85, 479 P.2d 554 (1971). Does it make any sense to put control of supplementation into the hands of the discovering party? See Gorsha v. Commercial Transport Corp., 38 F.R.D. 188 (E.D.La.1965) (prior to 1970 there was no duty to supplement even when interrogatories themselves called for continuing answers). Should the duty to supplement responses continue until and even during trial? See Everett v. Morrison, 478 S.W.2d 312 (Mo.1972) (party must disclose identity of witness discovered after trial was in progress).

What is the appropriate sanction for a breach of a duty to supplement answers? Most courts merely have prohibited the admission of the undisclosed evidence or prohibited the undisclosed witnesses from giving testimony. The language of Rule 37 does not seem to permit this sanction. Should it? See Note, *Proposed 1967 Amendments to the Federal Discovery Rules*, 68 Colum.L.Rev. 271, 293 (1968). Since Rule 26(e) also says nothing regarding the matter, courts must justify the imposition of sanctions on their inherent powers of control over the discovery process. See 8 Wright & Miller, *Federal Practice and Procedure: Civil* § 2050 (1970).

SECTION D.   SPECIAL PROBLEMS REGARDING THE SCOPE OF DISCOVERY

---

1.   MATERIALS PREPARED IN ANTICIPATION OF TRIAL

Read Federal Rule of Civil Procedure 26(b)(3) and the accompanying materials in the Supplement.

HICKMAN v. TAYLOR

Supreme Court of the United States, 1947.
329 U.S. 495, 67 S.Ct. 385, 91 L.Ed. 451.

Certiorari to the Circuit Court of Appeals for the Third Circuit.

Mr. Justice MURPHY delivered the opinion of the Court. This case presents an important problem under the Federal Rules   *   *   *   as to the extent to which a party may inquire into oral and written statements of witnesses, or other information, secured by an adverse party's counsel in the course of preparation for possible litigation after a claim has arisen. Examination into a person's files and records, including those resulting from the professional activities of an attorney, must be judged with care. It is not without reason that various safeguards have been established to preclude unwarranted excursions into the privacy of a man's work.   At the same time, public policy supports reasonable and necessary inquiries.   Properly to balance these competing interests is a delicate and difficult task.

On February 7, 1943, the tug "J. M. Taylor" sank while engaged in helping to tow a car float of the Baltimore & Ohio Railroad across the Delaware River at Philadelphia.   The accident was apparently unusual in nature, the cause of it still being unknown.   Five of the nine crew members were drowned.   Three days later the tug owners and the underwriters employed a law firm, of which respondent Fortenbaugh is a member, to defend them against potential suits by representatives of the deceased crew members and to sue the railroad for damages to the tug.

A public hearing was held on March 4, 1943, before the United States Steamboat Inspectors, at which the four survivors were examined.   This testimony was recorded and made available to all interested parties.   Shortly thereafter, Fortenbaugh privately interviewed the survivors and took statements from them with an eye toward the anticipated litigation; the survivors signed these statements on March 29.   Fortenbaugh also interviewed other persons believed to have some information relating to the accident and in some cases he made memoranda of what they told him.   At the time when Fortenbaugh secured the statements of the survivors, representatives of two of the deceased crew members had been in communication with him.   Ultimately claims were presented by representatives of all five of the deceased; four of the claims, however, were settled without litigation.   The fifth claimant, petitioner herein, brought suit in a federal court under the Jones Act on November 26, 1943, naming as defendants the two tug owners, individually and as partners, and the railroad.

[margin note: attorney took W's statements w/eye toward litigation; they were signed.]

[margin note: memos of some other persons w/ info were made]

[margin note: eventually all surviving families did bring suit.]

One year later, petitioner filed 39 interrogatories directed to the tug owners.   The 38th interrogatory read: "State whether any statements of the members of the crews of the Tugs 'J. M. Taylor' and 'Philadelphia' or of any other vessel were taken in connection with the towing of the car float and the sinking of the Tug 'John M. Taylor'.   Attach hereto exact copies of all such statements if in writing, and if oral, set forth in detail the exact provisions of any such oral statements or reports."

[margin note: P's att. via interr. sought to gain info as to these statements.]

Supplemental interrogatories asked whether any oral or written statements, records, reports or other memoranda had been made concerning any matter relative to the towing operation, the sinking of the tug, the salvaging and repair of the tug, and the death of the deceased.   If the answer was in the affirmative, the tug owners were then requested to set forth the nature of all such records, reports, statements or other memoranda.

The tug owners, through Fortenbaugh, answered all of the interrogatories except No. 38 and the supplemental ones just described.   While admitting that statements of the survivors had been taken, they declined to summarize or set forth the contents.   They did so on the ground that such requests called "for privileged matter obtained in preparation for litigation" and constituted "an attempt to obtain indirectly counsel's private files."   It was claimed that answering these requests "would involve practically turning over not only the complete files, but also the telephone records and, almost, the thoughts of counsel."

In connection with the hearing on these objections, Fortenbaugh made a written statement and gave an informal oral deposition explaining the circumstances under which he had taken the statements. But he was not expressly asked in the deposition to produce the statements. The District Court for the Eastern District of Pennsylvania, sitting en banc, held that the requested matters were not privileged. 4 F.R.D. 479. The court then decreed that the tug owners and Fortenbaugh, as counsel and agent for the tug owners forthwith "Answer Plaintiff's 38th interrogatory and supplemental interrogatories; produce all written statements of witnesses obtained by Mr. Fortenbaugh, as counsel and agent for Defendants; state in substance any fact concerning this case which Defendants learned through oral statements made by witnesses to Mr. Fortenbaugh whether or not included in his private memoranda and produce Mr. Fortenbaugh's memoranda containing statements of fact by witnesses or to submit these memoranda to the Court for determination of those portions which should be revealed to Plaintiff." Upon their refusal, the court adjudged them in contempt and ordered them imprisoned until they complied.

[margin note: Dist. Ct. ordered release of info.]

The Third Circuit Court of Appeals, also sitting en banc, reversed the judgment of the District Court. 153 F.2d 212. It held that the information here sought was part of the "work product of the lawyer" and hence privileged from discovery under the Federal Rules of Civil Procedure. The importance of the problem, which has engendered a great divergence of views among district courts, led us to grant certiorari. * * *

[margin note: reverse]

There is an initial question as to which of the deposition-discovery rules is involved in this case. Petitioner, in filing his interrogatories, thought that he was proceeding under Rule 33.

* * *   [I]t does not appear from the record that petitioner filed a motion under Rule 34 for a court order directing the production of the documents in question. Indeed, such an order could not have been entered as to Fortenbaugh since Rule 34, like Rule 33, is limited to parties to the proceeding, thereby excluding their counsel or agents.

Thus to the extent that petitioner was seeking the production of the memoranda and statements gathered by Fortenbaugh in the course of his activities as counsel, petitioner misconceived his remedy. Rule 33 did not permit him to obtain such memoranda and statements as adjuncts to the interrogatories addressed to the individual tug owners. A party clearly cannot refuse to answer interrogatories on the ground that the information sought is solely within the knowledge of his attorney. But that is not this case. Here production was sought of documents prepared by a party's attorney after the claim has arisen. Rule 33 does not make provision for such production, even when sought in connection with permissible interrogatories. Moreover, since petitioner was also foreclosed from securing them through an order under Rule 34, his only

[margin note: only Rule 34 allows for discovery of documents + Rule 33 as used won't allow such doc's to be merely attached to interrogatories.]

recourse was to take Fortenbaugh's deposition under Rule 26 and to attempt to force Fortenbaugh to produce the materials by use of a subpoena *duces tecum* — "bring w/ you" in accordance with Rule 45. * * * But despite petitioner's faulty choice of action, the District Court entered an order, apparently under Rule 34, commanding the tug owners and Fortenbaugh, as their agent and counsel, to produce the materials in question. Their refusal led to the anomalous result of holding the tug owners in contempt for failure to produce that which was in the possession of their counsel and of holding Fortenbaugh in contempt for failure to produce that which he could not be compelled to produce under either Rule 33 or Rule 34.

But under the circumstances we deem it unnecessary and unwise to rest our decision upon this procedural irregularity, an irregularity which is not strongly urged upon us and which was disregarded in the two courts below. * * * [T]he basic question at stake is whether any of those devices may be used to inquire into materials collected by an adverse party's counsel in the course of preparation for possible litigation. The fact that the petitioner may have used the wrong method does not destroy the main thrust of his attempt. * * * [I]n the present circumstances, for the purposes of this decision, the procedural irregularity is not material. * * *

In urging that he has a right to inquire into the materials secured and prepared by Fortenbaugh, petitioner emphasizes that the deposition-discovery portions of the Federal Rules of Civil Procedure are designed to enable the parties to discover the true facts and to compel their disclosure wherever they may be found. It is said that inquiry may be made under these rules, epitomized by Rule 26, as to any relevant matter which is not privileged; and since the discovery provisions are to be applied as broadly and liberally as possible, the privilege limitation must be restricted to its narrowest bounds. On the premise that the attorney-client privilege is the one involved in this case, petitioner argues that it must be strictly confined to confidential communications made by a client to his attorney. And since the materials here in issue were secured by Fortenbaugh from third persons rather than from his clients, the tug owners, the conclusion is reached that these materials are proper subjects for discovery under Rule 26.

As additional support for this result, petitioner claims that to prohibit discovery under these circumstances would give a corporate defendant a tremendous advantage in a suit by an individual plaintiff. Thus in a suit by an injured employee against a railroad or in a suit by an insured person against an insurance company the corporate defendant could pull a dark veil of secrecy over all the pertinent facts it can collect after the claim arises merely on the assertion that such facts were gathered by its large staff of attorneys and claim agents. At the same time, the individual plaintiff, who often has direct knowledge of the matter in issue and has no counsel until some time after his claim arises could be compelled to disclose all the intimate details of his case. By endowing with immunity from disclosure all that a lawyer discovers in the course of his duties, it is said, the rights of individual litigants in such cases are drained of vitality and the lawsuit becomes more of a battle of deception than a search for truth.

But framing the problem in terms of assisting individual plaintiffs in their suits against corporate defendants is unsatisfactory. Discovery concededly may work to the disadvantage as well as to the advantage of individual plaintiffs. Discovery, in other words, is not a one-way proposition. It is available in all types of cases at the behest of any party, individual or corporate, plaintiff or defendant. The problem thus far transcends the situation confronting this petitioner. And we must view that problem in light of the limitless situations where the particular kind of discovery sought by petitioner might be used.

We agree, of course, that the deposition-discovery rules are to be accorded a broad and liberal treatment. No longer can the time-honored cry of "fishing expedition" serve to preclude a party from inquiring into the facts underlying his opponent's case. Mutual knowledge of all the relevant facts gathered by both parties is essential to proper litigation. To that end, either party may compel the other to disgorge whatever facts he has in his possession. The deposition-discovery procedure simply advances the stage at which the disclosure can be compelled from the time of trial to the period preceding it, thus reducing the possibility of surprise. But discovery, like all matters of procedure, has ultimate and necessary boundaries. As indicated by Rules 30(b) and (d) and 31(d), limitations inevitably arise when it can be shown that the examination is being conducted in bad faith or in such a manner as to annoy, embarrass or oppress the person subject to the inquiry. And as Rule 26(b) provides, further limitations come into existence when the inquiry touches upon the irrelevant or encroaches upon the recognized domains of privilege.

We also agree that the memoranda, statements and mental impressions in issue in this case fall outside the scope of the attorney-client privilege and hence are not protected from discovery on that basis. * * *

But the impropriety of invoking that privilege does not provide an answer to the problem before us. Petitioner has made more than an ordinary request for relevant, non-privileged facts in the possession of his adversaries or their counsel. He has sought discovery as of right of oral and written statements of witnesses whose identity is well known and whose availability to petitioner appears unimpaired. He has sought production of these matters after making the most searching inquiries of his opponents as to the circumstances surrounding the fatal accident, which inquiries were sworn to have been answered to the best of their information and belief. Interrogatories were directed toward all the events prior to, during and subsequent to the sinking of the tug. Full and honest answers to such broad inquiries would necessarily have included all pertinent information gleaned by Fortenbaugh through his interviews with the witnesses. Petitioner makes no suggestion, and we cannot assume, that the tug owners or Fortenbaugh were incomplete or dishonest in the framing of their answers. In addition, petitioner was free to examine the public testimony of the witnesses taken before the United States Steamboat Inspectors. We are thus dealing with an attempt to secure the production of written statements and mental impressions contained in the files and the mind of the attorney Fortenbaugh without any showing of necessity or any indication or claim that denial of such production would unduly prejudice the preparation of petitioner's case or cause him any hardship or injustice. For aught that appears, the essence of what petitioner seeks either has been revealed to him already through the interrogatories or is readily available to him direct from the witnesses for the asking.

* * *

In our opinion, neither Rule 26 nor any other rule dealing with discovery contemplates production under such circumstances. That is not because the subject matter is privileged or irrelevant, as those concepts are used in these rules. Here is simply an attempt, without purported necessity or justification, to secure written statements, private memoranda and personal recollections prepared or formed by an adverse party's counsel in the course of his legal duties. As such, it falls outside the arena of discovery and contravenes the public policy underlying the orderly prosecution and defense of legal claims. Not even the most liberal of discovery theories can justify unwarranted inquiries into the files and the mental impressions of an attorney.

Historically, a lawyer is an officer of the court and is bound to work for the advancement of justice while faithfully protecting the rightful interests of his clients. In performing his various duties, however, it is essential that a lawyer work with a certain degree of privacy, free from unnecessary intrusion by opposing parties and their counsel. Proper preparation of a client's case demands that he assemble information, sift what he considers to be the relevant from the irrelevant facts, prepare his legal theories and plan his strategy without undue and needless interference. That is the historical and the necessary way in which lawyers act within the framework of our system of jurisprudence to promote justice and to protect their clients' interests. This work is reflected, of course, in interviews, statements, memoranda, correspondence, briefs, mental impressions, personal beliefs, and countless other tangible and intangible ways—aptly though roughly termed by the Circuit Court of Appeals in this case [153 F.2d 212, 223] as the "Work product of the lawyer." Were such materials open to opposing counsel on mere demand, much of what is now put down in writing would remain unwritten. An attorney's thoughts, heretofore inviolate, would not be his own. Inefficiency, unfairness and sharp practices would inevitably develop in the giving of legal advice and in the preparation of cases for trial. The effect on the legal profession would be demoralizing. And the interests of the clients and the cause of justice would be poorly served.

We do not mean to say that all written materials obtained or prepared by an adversary's counsel with an eye toward litigation are necessarily free from discovery in all cases. Where relevant and non-privileged facts remain hidden in an attorney's file and where production of those facts is essential to the preparation of one's case, discovery may properly be had. Such written statements and documents might, under certain circumstances, be admissible in evidence or give clues as to the existence or location of relevant facts. Or they might be useful for purposes of impeachment or corroboration. And production might be justified where the witnesses are no longer available or can be reached only with difficulty. Were production of written statements and documents to be precluded under such circumstances, the liberal ideals of the deposition-discovery portions of the Federal Rules of Civil Procedure would be stripped of much of their meaning. But the general policy against invading the privacy of an attorney's course of preparation is so well recognized and so essential to an orderly working of our system of legal procedure that a burden rests on the one who would invade that privacy to establish adequate reasons to justify production through a subpoena or court order. That burden, we believe, is necessarily implicit in the rules as now constituted.

Rule 30(b), as presently written, gives the trial judge the requisite discretion to make a judgment as to whether discovery should be allowed as to written statements secured from witnesses. But in the instant case there was no room for that discretion to operate in favor of the petitioner. No attempt was made to establish any reason why Fortenbaugh should be forced to produce the written statements. There was only a naked, general demand for these materials as of right and a finding by the District Court that no recognizable privilege was involved. That was insufficient to justify discovery under these circumstances and the court should have sustained the refusal of the tug owners and Fortenbaugh to produce.

But as to oral statements made by witnesses to Fortenbaugh, whether presently in the form of his mental impressions or memoranda, we do not believe that any showing of necessity can be made under the circumstances of this case so as to justify production. Under ordinary conditions, forcing an attorney to repeat or write out all that witnesses have told him and to deliver the account to his adversary gives rise to grave dangers of inaccuracy and untrustworthiness. No legitimate purpose is served by such production. The practice forces the attorney to testify as to what he remembers or what he saw fit to write down regarding witnesses' remarks. Such testimony could not qualify as evidence; and to use it for impeachment or corroborative purposes would make the attorney much less an officer of the court and much more an ordinary witness. The standards of the profession would thereby suffer.

Denial of production of this nature does not mean that any material, non-privileged facts can be hidden from the petitioner in this case. He need not be unduly hindered in the preparation of his case, in the discovery of facts or in his anticipation of his opponents' position. Searching interrogatories directed to Fortenbaugh and the tug owners, production of written documents and statements upon a proper showing and direct interviews with the witnesses themselves all serve to reveal the facts in Fortenbaugh's possession to the fullest possible extent consistent with public policy. Petitioner's counsel frankly admits that he wants the oral statements only to help prepare himself to examine witnesses and to make sure that he has overlooked nothing. That is insufficient under the circumstances to permit him an exception to the policy underlying the privacy of Fortenbaugh's professional activities. If there should be a rare situation justifying production of these matters, petitioner's case is not of that type.

We fully appreciate the wide-spread controversy among the members of the legal profession over the problem raised by this case. It is a problem that rests on what has been one of the most hazy frontiers of the discovery process. But until some rule or statute definitely prescribes otherwise, we are not justified in permitting discovery in a situation of this nature as a matter of unqualified right. When Rule 26 and the other discovery rules were adopted, this Court and the members of the bar in general certainly did not believe or contemplate that all the files and mental processes of lawyers were thereby opened to the free scrutiny of their adversaries. And we refuse to interpret the rules at this time so as to reach so harsh and unwarranted a result.

We therefore affirm the judgment of the Circuit Court of Appeals.

Affirmed.

Mr. Justice JACKSON, concurring.

* * *

To consider first the most extreme aspect of the requirement in litigation here, we find it calls upon counsel, if he has had any conversations with any of the crews of the vessels in question or of any other, to "set forth in detail the exact provision of any such oral statements or reports." Thus the demand is not for the production of a transcript in existence but calls for the creation of a written statement not in being. But the statement by counsel of what a witness told him is not evidence when written. Plaintiff could not introduce it to prove his case. What, then, is the purpose sought to be served by demanding this of adverse counsel?

Counsel for the petitioner candidly said on argument that he wanted this information to help prepare himself to examine witnesses, to make sure he overlooked nothing. He bases his claim to it in his brief on the view that the Rules were to do away with the old situation where a law suit developed into "a battle of wits between counsel." But a common law trial is and always should be an adversary proceeding. Discovery was hardly intended to enable a learned profession to perform its functions either without wits or on wits borrowed from the adversary.

The real purpose and the probable effect of the practice ordered by the district court would be to put trials on a level even lower than a "battle of wits." I can conceive of no practice more demoralizing to the Bar than to require a lawyer to write out and deliver to his adversary an account of what witnesses have told him. Even if his recollection were perfect, the statement would be his language permeated with his inferences. Every one who has tried it knows that it is almost impossible so fairly to record the expressions and emphasis of a witness that when he testifies in the environment of the court and under the influence of the leading question there will not be departures in some respects. Whenever the testimony of the witness would differ from the "exact" statement the lawyer had delivered, the lawyer's statement would be whipped out to impeach the witness. Counsel producing his adversary's "inexact" statement could lose nothing by saying, "Here is a contradiction, gentlemen of the jury. I do not know whether it is my adversary or his witness who is not telling the truth, but one is not." Of course, if this practice were adopted, that scene would be repeated over and over again. The lawyer who delivers such statements often would find himself branded a deceiver afraid to take the stand to support his own version of the witness's conversation with him, or else he will have to go on the stand to defend his own credibility—perhaps against that of his chief witness, or possibly even his client.

Every lawyer dislikes to take the witness stand and will do so only for grave reasons. This is partly because it is not his role; he is almost invariably a poor witness. But he steps out of professional character to do it. He regrets it; the profession discourages it. But the practice advocated here is one which would force him to be a witness, not as to what he has seen or done but as to other witnesses' stories, and not because he wants to do so but in self-defense.

And what is the lawyer to do who has interviewed one whom he believes to be a biased, lying or hostile witness to get his unfavorable statements and know what to meet? He must record and deliver such statements even though he would not vouch for the credibility of the witness by calling him. Perhaps the other side would not want to call him either, but the attorney is open to the charge of suppressing evidence at the trial if he fails to call such a hostile witness even though he never regarded him as reliable or truthful.

Having been supplied the names of the witnesses, petitioner's lawyer gives no reason why he cannot interview them himself. If an employee-witness refuses to tell his story, he, too, may be examined under the Rules. He may be compelled on discovery as fully as on the trial to disclose his version of the facts. But that is his own disclosure—it can be used to impeach him if he contradicts it and such a deposition is not useful to promote an unseemly disagreement between the witness and the counsel in the case.

It is true that the literal language of the Rules would admit of an interpretation that would sustain the district court's order. * * * But all such procedural measures have a background of custom and practice which was assumed by those who wrote and should be by those who apply them. * * * Certainly nothing in the tradition or practice of discovery up to the time of these Rules would have suggested that they would authorize such a practice as here proposed.

The question remains as to signed statements or those written by witnesses. Such statements are not evidence for the defendant. Palmer v. Hoffman, 318 U.S. 109, 63 S.Ct. 477. Nor should I think they ordinarily could be evidence for the plaintiff. But such a statement might be useful for impeachment of the witness who signed it, if he is called and if he departs from the statement. There might be circumstances, too, where impossibility or difficulty of access to the witness or his refusal to respond to requests for information or other facts would show that the interests of justice require that such statements be made available. Production of such statements are governed by Rule 34 and on "Showing good cause therefor" the court may order their inspection, copying or photographing. No such application has here been made; the demand is made on the basis of right, not on showing of cause.

I agree to the affirmance of the judgment of the Circuit Court of Appeals which reversed the district court.

Mr. Justice FRANKFURTER joins in this opinion.

NOTES AND QUESTIONS

1. The *Hickman* decision left open a number of fundamental questions as to its scope. (1) Should the work-product doctrine apply to information obtained by someone other than the attorney—for example, a claims agent, a private investigator, or even the client—who then hands the information to the attorney? (2) Should the doctrine apply to information obtained prior to instigation of litigation—for example, during routine accident investigations—which is then given to the attorney for purposes of an action? (3) Should work-product encompass more than witness' statements, for example, the names of eyewitnesses that were obtained by an attorney only through considerable ingenuity and expense? (4) Should protection be limited to discovery of documents, or should it encompass all methods of discovery? (5) To what extent should a showing of need overcome normal work-product protection? Are there some matters that should be protected in any case? Are there some matters that should be disclosed as a matter of course?

These questions have been the subject of a considerable number of comments, debates, and judicial decisions in state as well as federal courts. See generally Taine, *Discovery of Trial Preparations in the Federal Courts,* 50 Colum.L. Rev. 1026 (1950); Tolman, *Discovery Under the Federal Rules: Production of Documents and the Work Product of the Lawyer,* 58 Colum.L.Rev. 498 (1958); *Developments in the Law—Discovery,* 74 Harv.L.Rev. 940, 1027–46 (1961); Comment, *The Work Product Doctrine in the State Courts,* 62 Mich.L.Rev. 1199 (1964).

2. In 1970, Federal Rule 26(b) (3) was added specifically to deal with the discovery of work product. Prior to the adoption of Rule 26(b) (3) many of the states that had adopted federal discovery rules already had added special provisions to deal with work-product and related problems. These provisions vary from state to state. See Friedenthal, *Discovery and Use of an Adverse Party's Expert Information,* 14 Stan.L.Rev. 455, 474–79 (1962). *Compare* Federal Rule 26(b)(3), *with* N.Y.C.P.L.R. 3101, *and* Minnesota Rule of Civil Procedure 26.02, both of which accompany Federal Rule 26 in the Supplement.

3. How many of the problems listed in Note 1, above, does Rule 26(b) (3) solve?

(a) Courts have split on the question whether and when Rule 26(b) (3) covers documents containing the results of a party's investigations made prior to hiring an attorney or the initiation of litigation. An example of a case in which discovery was permitted is THOMAS ORGAN CO. v. JADRANSKA SLOBODNA PLOVIDBA, 54 F.R.D. 367 (N.D.Ill.1972), involving a claim for damaged goods. Some seven months prior to the time plaintiff hired an attorney, its insurer conducted an investigation of the facts regarding the loss. The court held that the report of the investigation was made in the ordinary course of business and not for litigation, noting that in the vast majority of situations involving insurance claims, matters are settled without litigation. But discovery was denied in ALMAGUER v. CHICAGO, R. I. & PAC. R.R., 55 F.R.D. 147 (D.Neb.1972), in which a railroad employee brought suit against his employer for injuries incurred on the job. Plaintiff was not allowed to obtain a copy of a statement of an eyewitness taken by defendant's claims agent two months before plaintiff had employed a lawyer. The court said that whenever a railroad employee claims to have been injured on the job "the expectation of litigation * * * is a reasonable assumption."

Should the determination whether a report written prior to any legal action is discoverable be decided in terms of the likelihood that a lawsuit ultimately would be filed? See Abel Investment Co. v. United States, 53 F.R.D. 485, 489 (D.Neb.1971) (Internal Revenue Service field agent reports regarding plaintiff's tax liabilities held to be routine, and hence discoverable, since only a few such reports result in litigation).

(b) Rule 26(b) (3) refers only to "discovery of documents and tangible things." May a party ask by way of interrogatory what a specific document says? See PETERSON v. UNITED STATES, 52 F.R.D. 317, 320 (S.D.Ill.1971): "It is clear to this court that discovery of a detailed description of the contents of documents through interrogatories is equivalent to discovery of the documents themselves. The discovery sought by plaintiff through the interrogatories is therefore covered by rule 26(b) (3)." Is the court correct? Suppose plaintiff merely asked a question regarding a relevant fact, the answer to which was known to defendant only through documents uncovered by investigations of his attorney. Would such a question fall within the scope of the rule? Should it? Should work product encompass the names of eyewitnesses uncovered by an attorney or her client during pretrial investigation? Would it make a difference if a party seeks only the names of the witnesses the opposing party will call at trial? See *Grant v. Huff,* p. 655, supra. For a general discussion of the distinction between "documents and tangible things" and facts learned from them, see 8 Wright & Miller, *Federal Practice and Procedure: Civil* § 2023, at 194 (1970).

(c) Rule 26(b) (3) allows discovery of material otherwise protected "only upon a showing that the party seeking discovery has substantial need of the materials in the preparation of the case and that he is unable without undue hardship to obtain the substantial equivalent of the materials by other means." In SNEAD v. AMERICAN EXPORT-ISBRANDTSEN LINES, INC., 59 F.R.D. 148, 151 (E.D.Pa.1973), plaintiff, who had brought suit to recover for personal injuries moved for a court order requiring defendant to answer interrogatories as to whether defendant had possession of any secret motion pictures taken of plaintiff that would tend to bear on the scope of plaintiff's injuries. The court held as follows:

> Every need to provide information must be balanced against the need to withhold it. The need to know is but the converse of the need to keep secret. The only time there will be a substantial need to know about surveillance pictures will be in those instances where there would be a major discrepancy between the testimony the plaintiff will give and that which the films would seem to portray. By the same token this would be the only instance where there is a substantial need to withhold that information from plaintiff's counsel. If the discrepancy would be the result of the plaintiff's untruthfulness, the substantial need for his

counsel to know of the variance can hardly justify making the information available to him. On the other hand, if the discrepancy would result from misleading photography, the necessary background information should be made available to the plaintiff's attorney so the fraud can be exposed. It goes without saying that the means to impeach should not be the exclusive property of the defense. Any rule to be formulated, therefore, must balance the conflicting interests of the plaintiff against the conflicting interests of the defendant and protect both insofar as it is possible to do so. * * *

I conclude these purposes can best be achieved by requiring the defense to disclose the existence of surveillance films or be barred from showing them at trial. If the defense has films and decides it wants to use them, they should be exhibited to the plaintiff and his counsel. * * *

Before any of these disclosures, however, the defense must be given an opportunity to depose the plaintiff fully as to his injuries, their effects, and his present disabilities. Once his testimony is memorialized in deposition, any variation he may make at trial to conform to the surveillance films can be used to impeach his credibility, and his knowledge at deposition that the films may exist should have a salutary effect on any tendency to be expansive. At the same time, if the plaintiff believes that the films seem to give a false impression, he can then obtain the necessary data to serve as a basis for cross-examination.

Isn't it true that whenever a document or other item is to be introduced into evidence by one party the requisite need for discovery will be satisfied at least for the purposes of determining whether such an item has been forged, distorted, or altered in some way?

(d) Rule 26(b) (3) excludes from protection a party's own prior statement concerning the action. Why? See the Advisory Committee's Notes on Rule 26(b) (3) set out in the Supplement. The rule also permits a nonparty witness to obtain a copy of his statement upon request. Are the reasons for allowing a witness to obtain his own statement the same for a nonparty as they are for a party? Can friendship between the witness and one of the parties play a major role in determining whether discovery takes place under the present rule?

(e) Rule 26(b) (3) states that the court shall "protect against" disclosure of the mental impressions, conclusions, and opinions of an attorney or other representative of a party. Should this be read as an absolute prohibition on discovery? See Minnesota Rule of Civil Procedure 26.02. Don't statements of witnesses, particularly when given in response to an attorney's questions, often reveal the attorney's mental impressions and opinions? Note that Federal Rules 33(b) and 36(c) specifically allow discovery of opinions and contentions that relate to facts or applications of law to fact.

2. EXPERT INFORMATION

Read Federal Rule of Civil Procedure 26(b)(4) and the Advisory Committee's comments on it, which appear in the Supplement.

PERRY v. W. S. DARLEY & CO.

United States District Court, Eastern District of Wisconsin, 1971.
54 F.R.D. 278.

MYRON L. GORDON, District Judge. The plaintiff Robert Perry, a volunteer fireman, seeks damages for injuries allegedly sustained when he was struck by a fire truck as he attempted to activate a pump manufactured and installed on the truck by the defendant. The defendant has moved for an order compelling disclosure of the names of certain experts who examined the truck and pump shortly after the accident; the refusal to disclose the names occurred during the oral deposition of Ward Johnson, an employee of the workmen's compensation carrier for the fire department for which Mr. Perry works.

Counsel for the plaintiffs objected to disclosure of the experts' names on the basis that such information "constitutes both privileged communication and work product." However, the defendant argues in its brief that the experts are potential witnesses who "have knowledge of relevant facts" and that it is entitled, pursuant to Rule 26(b)(1), to the "identity and location of persons having knowledge of any discoverable matter."

The plaintiffs state that

"It should be noted that the [defendant's] question did not seek the disclosure of the identity of experts which plaintiffs expect to call as witnesses upon the trial, which disclosure is explicitly required by the July 1, 1970, amendment to the Federal Rules. Federal Rule 26(b)(4)(A). However, significantly, no similar requirement is made for the disclosure of identity of experts not retained or specially employed for purposes of testifying at trial. See Rule 26(b)(4)(B)."

Some courts recently have refused to adopt the position taken in earlier cases in which discovery of facts known by an expert was allowed but discovery of the expert's opinions and conclusions was refused. In United States v. Meyer, 398 F.2d 66, 73 (9th Cir. 1968), the court stated:

"No fact-opinion distinction is found in the discovery rules; Rule 26(b) extends discovery broadly to 'any matter, not privileged, which is relevant to the subject matter involved in the pending action.' In 1946 the Supreme Court rejected a proposal to amend the rules to restrict discovery of writings reflecting the conclusions of experts. The nearly contemporaneous use of the word 'fact' in certain passages in the opinion in Hickman v. Taylor, 329 U.S. [495] at 507–508, 67 S.Ct. 385, 91 L.Ed. 451, cannot be taken as an implicit adoption of the rejected limitation."

See also 8 Wright & Miller, Federal Practice and Procedure: Civil § 2029, at 247 (1970).

In addition, the Advisory Committee note to Rule 26(b)(4) states, in part:

"It should be noted that the subdivision does not address itself to the expert whose information was not acquired in preparation for trial but rather because he was an actor or viewer with respect to transactions or occurrences that are part of the subject matter of the lawsuit. Such an expert should be treated as an ordinary witness." 48 F.R.D. 487, 503 (1970).

The plaintiffs concede, as stated above, that they have a duty to disclose the identity of any expert whom they expect to call as a witness at the trial. As to experts who have been engaged "in anticipation of litigation or preparation for trial," however, the plaintiffs point to the provisions of Rule 26(b)(4)(B) to the effect that, when such experts are "not expected to be called as * * * [witnesses] * * * at trial," facts known or opinions held by them are discoverable

"* * * only as provided in Rule 35(b) or upon a showing of exceptional circumstances under which it is impracticable for the party seeking discovery to obtain facts or opinions on the same subject by other means."

No means are provided by Rule 26(b) by which it may be determined that an expert is a person whom a party expects to call as a witness at trial. However, Rule 26(e) provides, in part * * * [that a party must supplement its discovery responses with regard to]

"* * * the identity of each person expected to be called as an expert witness at trial, the subject matter on which he is expected to testify, and the substance of his testimony."

Furthermore, the final pretrial order regularly used by this court requires each party to provide the "names and addresses of each side's prospective expert witnesses, together with a narrative statement of each such expert's background and experience."

Rule 26(b)(4)(B) makes no distinction between the identity of an expert and facts known or opinions held by him, although it is stated in 8 Wright & Miller, Federal Practice and Procedure: Civil § 2032, at 255 (1970), that, "Apparently one party can find out the names of experts specially retained by another party who are not to be called." However, in an affidavit attached to the defendant's motion, the attorney for the defendant states that, because the experts viewed the fire truck well before the commencement of the present action, "this in and of itself is sufficient cause to require the plaintiff to turn over not only the names of the expert or experts but the reports of said expert or experts."

Held

In my opinion, no showing of "exceptional circumstances" has been made by the defendant in the case at bar, nor is there any evidence to indicate that the experts were actors or viewers "with respect to [the] transactions or occurrences that are part of the subject matter of the lawsuit." Rule 26 (b)(4) imposes a more rigorous standard upon the discovery of facts known and opinions held by an expert than is imposed with regard to other witnesses; I am not persuaded that such standard should be relaxed in the present case with regard to the identity of the experts who viewed the fire truck shortly after the accident.

Therefore, it is ordered that the defendant's motion for an order compelling answers to certain questions propounded to Ward Johnson be and hereby is denied.

NOTES AND QUESTIONS

1. What basis is there for the distinction between discovery from those experts who will testify at trial and those who will not? See Note, *Proposed 1967 Amendments to the Federal Discovery Rules,* 68 Colum.L.Rev. 271, 282 (1968). Can a party neutralize local experts likely to be unfavorable to its case by employing them without any intention of calling them to testify? See Note, *Discovery of Expert Information,* 47 N.C.L.Rev. 401, 406 (1969).

2. Federal Rule 26(b) (4) (A) (i) provides for limited discovery regarding information of experts who will be called to testify. How extensive must the opposing party's answers be under this provision? See WILSON v. RESNICK, 51 F.R.D. 510 (E.D.Pa.1970):

> * * * [P]laintiff served interrogatories on defendant, requesting that he state the identity of his expert witnesses, the subject matter on which they were expected to testify, the substance of the facts and opinions to which they were expected to testify and a summary of the grounds for each opinion. Defendant responded that Dr. Blaker was one of his expert witnesses; that he would testify on the question of whether plaintiff was treated in accordance with good, sound medical practice; that as to plaintiff's condition, it appears that reinnervation is occurring; that any residual complaint would be more annoying than anything else; that there is no functional disability; that the care and treatment by Dr. Resnick was in accordance with good, sound medical practice. Plaintiff contends that these answers are sketchy and conclusory and not in keeping with the letter and spirit of the Amended Federal Rules of Civil Procedure.

The court held that the answers were sufficient. Do you agree with the court's conclusion? Compare Rupp v. Vock & Weiderhold, Inc., 52 F.R.D. 111 (N.D. Ohio 1971). Under what circumstances will discovery under 26(b) (4) (A) (ii) be permitted? What justification is there for Rule 26(b) (4) (C) regarding the payment of fees and expenses?

3. Rule 26(b) (4) (B) permits discovery of facts and opinions from an expert employed in anticipation of trial and who will not be called to testify, but only upon a showing of special circumstances. What circumstances justify discovery under this provision? See Wasmuth v. Hinds-Toomey Auto Corp., 39 App.Div.2d 723, 331 N.Y.S.2d 804 (1972). Assuming that special circumstances are not shown, is there any good reason for requiring discovery of the identity of experts? Should one party be prohibited even from interviewing a willing expert employed by the opposition? If not, will it give an unfair advantage to wealthy litigants who can afford private investigators to find out the experts' names?

4. State provisions regarding discovery of expert information vary considerably. For example, Minnesota Rule of Civil Procedure 26.02 and N.Y.C.P. L.R. 3101(d), both of which accompany Rule 26 in the Supplement, appear more restrictive than Federal Rule 26(b) (4). On the other hand a much different approach is taken in New Jersey Civil Practice Rule 4:10–2(d), which provides that a party not only must identify experts who will testify and summarize the nature of their testimony but must also produce copies of any reports the experts have submitted. Furthermore, the New Jersey rule goes on to provide: "unless the court orders otherwise * * * [such an expert] may be deposed as to his opinions at a time and place convenient for him."

---

3. NOMINAL PARTIES—CLASS ACTIONS

BRENNAN v. MIDWESTERN UNITED LIFE INS. CO.

United States Court of Appeals, Seventh Circuit, 1971.
450 F.2d 999.
Certiorari denied 405 U.S. 921, 92 S.Ct. 957, 30 L.Ed.2d 792.

SWYGERT, Chief Judge. The issue on this appeal is whether in a class action under Rule 23, * * * those identifiable absent members of the representative plaintiff's class who received notice of the pendency of the suit and neither elected to be excluded nor entered an appearance may be required to submit to discovery under Rules 33 and 34, * * * on pain of dismissal of their claims with prejudice for failure to respond. This issue arises out of the denial of appellants' (hereinafter designated "movants") motion under Rule 60(b), * * * which asserted that the dismissal of their claims and those of all others similarly situated for noncompliance with a discovery order was void under clause (4) of Rule 60(b) or should have been set aside under residual clause (6) of that rule.

Shortly after a determination that the suit should be maintained as a class action * * * the district court, on October 12, 1966, caused a notice, pursuant to Rule 23(c)(2), * * * to be sent to all prospective members of the class, including movants. The notice described the nature of the action and informed those to whom the notice was sent that they could elect to be excluded from the action or to remain in the class and be represented either by counsel for the named plaintiff or by an attorney of their own choosing. Approximately 600 persons received the notice; of these, 535 became class members by not executing and returning the form (included with the notice) indicating their desire to be excluded. On January 4, 1967 the district court directed that the members of the class be notified of its order of that date setting a deadline of March 1, 1967 for the appearance of counsel of the class members' own choosing, but repeating what was said in the original notice, that such appearance was not necessary and, absent obtaining their own counsel, the interests of the class members would be represented by counsel for the named plaintiff. Prior to this order, Midwestern had filed requests under Rules 33 and 34 * * * for production of certain documents and records and for answers to interrogatories by the named plaintiff and each member of her class. On December 22, 1966 the court granted the motion to produce, directing compliance by March 1, 1967, and also instructed counsel for the named plaintiff and the defendant to agree on the form of the interrogatories to be submitted.

On January 12, 1967, at the district court's direction, counsel for the named plaintiff mailed to each class member, including movants, copies of the January 4 order, the order to produce documents, and the agreed-upon interrogatories. Plaintiff's counsel also prepared and mailed a memorandum describing the discovery proceedings, explaining the reason for the interrogatories and the production of documents, specifically mentioning the March 1 deadline for compliance, and encouraging each class member to seek the advice and help of his own lawyer, if he had one, or to request assistance from plaintiff's counsel.

* * *

At a pre-trial conference, held on April 17, 1967, the court directed counsel for the named plaintiff to prepare a list of those who had not yet answered the interrogatories or produced the documents. The judge stated that he would dismiss with prejudice the claims of such persons unless they responded within twenty days. On May 4, 1967, plaintiff's counsel wrote those, including movants, who had not complied with the discovery orders, explaining the consequences of their noncompliance. * * *

On June 7, 1967 the district court ordered the unresponsive members of the class, including movants, to show cause on or before July 14, 1967 why their claims should not be dismissed with prejudice for failure to answer the interrogatories. On June 9 counsel for the named plaintiff sent to all who had not responded copies of the show-cause order together with a letter * * * [which read in part, "We] would hate for you to lose your share of the recovery merely because you have failed to answer the Interrogatories in accordance with Federal Court procedure."

The July 14 deadline passed; and on August 9, 1967 Midwestern filed its motion to dismiss with prejudice the claims of those class members, including the movants, who had failed to respond either to the interrogatories or to the show-cause order. On August 17, 1967 the court granted the motion and dismissed the claims with prejudice.

The * * * action was tried in January 1968 and judgment was entered on June 26, 1968. Determination of the individual claims of the class members was referred to a special master. On September 29, 1969 this court affirmed the judgment of the district court. On March 11, 1970 the movants filed their motion to set aside the August 17, 1967 order dismissing their claims. Notice of the motion was given to all those similarly situated, informing them that they would be represented by movants' counsel unless they wished to be represented by counsel of their own choosing and that the court's ruling would be binding on them. Following a hearing, the court denied the motion; from that ruling this appeal was taken.

* * * Movants contend that absent class members are not "parties" to a suit and are consequently not subject to the "party" discovery procedures provided by Rules 33 and 34 * * *. Movants argue that Rule 23 * * * contemplates an adversary contest involving only the representative member of a class, with all other members of the class being permitted passively to wait the outcome of the principal suit, and that it is inconsistent with the purpose of Rule 23 to require any affirmative action from absent class members before the conclusion of the representative suit. While the question is a difficult one and there is some merit in movants' arguments, we hold that absent class members may, under certain circumstances, be required to submit to discovery under Rules 33 and 34 and that the sanctions of Rule 37 are available to compel compliance with such discovery orders.[2]

* * * We do not believe there is any real inconsistency between Rule 23's general policy of permitting absent class members to remain outside the principal action and our holding that in appropriate cases absent class members may be required to submit to discovery. It is true that an absent class member is given a "free ride" under Rule 23 and has no duty to actively engage in the prosecution of the action. Yet the absent class member's interests are identical with those of the named plaintiff and his rights and liabilities are adjudicated in the principal suit. If discovery from the absent member is necessary or helpful to the proper presentation and correct adjudication of the principal suit, we see no reason why it should not be allowed so long as adequate precautionary measures are taken to insure that

---

[2] Movants have argued that the dismissal of their claims under Rule 37 was an unduly harsh sanction and constituted an abuse of discretion. Movants ignored repeated requests that they comply with the discovery orders. Under the facts of this case, dismissal was warranted. Movants apparently contend that an appropriate sanction for a class member's failure to respond to discovery would be exclusion from the class. We agree that in many cases that would be an appropriate remedy. * * * As we have stated, however, the district judge did not abuse his discretion in imposing on movants the more severe sanction of dismissal of their claims.

the absent member is not misled or confused. While absent class members should not be required to submit to discovery as a matter of course, if the trial judge determines that justice to all parties requires that absent parties furnish certain information, we believe that he has the power to authorize the use of the Rules 33 and 34 discovery procedures.

The record shows that the district judge had valid reasons from the standpoint of preparing the case for trial for ordering the discovery in this case. The requests were not designed solely to determine the identity and amount of the class members' claims, but were also directed at obtaining information relating to certain defenses raised by Midwestern in the principal trial. Counsel for the named plaintiff admitted that the information sought by Midwestern was relevant to its claim that it was not liable to the class. Moreover, movants impliedly concede that the discovery was proper by their argument that Midwestern could have proceeded with its pretrial discovery under Rules 30 and 31 * * * to which the sanctions of Rule 45 * * * are applicable. Finally, there is nothing in the record to suggest that the discovery procedures were used as a tactic to take undue advantage of the class members or as a stratagem to reduce the number of claimants.

Movants argue, with some persuasiveness, that the initial notice under Rule 23(c)(2) which informed the class members that, unless they indicated a desire to be excluded, they would be included in the action which the named plaintiff and her counsel would prosecute on their behalf is inconsistent with a subsequent requirement that the absent class members furnish discovery information. Movants contend that the initial notice implied that class members could remain passive throughout the principal proceeding, and that consequently a subsequent requirement that a class member take some affirmative action is not only likely to create confusion in his mind but contradicts the implied understanding by which he elected to participate in the suit. The initial notice, however, in no way suggested that subsequent directions from the court could be ignored * * *. Moreover, even if movants had an initial impression that no action on their part was required to join the class and thereby participate in a recovery, if any, that impression should have been completely dispelled by the subsequent orders of the court and the efforts of counsel for the named plaintiff to get a response to those orders.

*   *   *

The order denying the motion to set aside the dismissals of the claims of movants and those similarly situated is affirmed.

STEVENS, Circuit Judge (dissenting).

Movants were not parties to the litigation in which the district court purported to adjudicate their rights. They were not involuntary parties because they were not served with process. None of them became voluntary parties by entering an appearance or taking any other affirmative action.

*   *   *

Unlike the other class members movants were unwilling or unable to respond to the discovery orders. In my opinion, they had a right to request exclusion from the class as an alternative to responding; they were never advised of any such right, and no such request was made on their behalf. They had no representative in court to advocate protection of their separate interests, whatever they may have been, in not divulging the requested information. Yet it is those separate interests which led to the entry of a judgment against them.

* * *

I respectfully dissent.

NOTES AND QUESTIONS

1. The *Brennan* decision is noted in 1971 Duke L.J. 1007; 40 Fordham L.Rev. 1969 (1972); 40 U.Cinn.L.Rev. 842 (1971). What is the basis for the court's statement that "absent class members should not be required to submit to discovery as a matter of course"? Why, if an absent member is a "party" within the meaning of the discovery rule, shouldn't the burden be on the member objecting to discovery to obtain a protective order? See SOUTHERN CALIFORNIA EDISON CO. v. SUPERIOR COURT, 7 Cal.3d 832, 103 Cal.Rptr. 709, 500 P.2d 621 (1972), in which the court refused to hold that protection exists as a matter of course. In this case, which involved a class of approximately 1500 plaintiffs, defendant sought to take depositions of some of the unnamed members of plaintiff class. Defendant did not subpoena the deponents, however, arguing that notice to the named plaintiffs' attorney is all that is required to take a party's deposition. The court agreed with defendant, but only in the absence of a protective order. The court held that since the class was loosely knit and since defendant had as much knowledge of the absent member's whereabouts as did the attorney for the named plaintiffs, it was unfair to put the burden of finding each deponent on the named plaintiffs. Therefore, the notices to take depositions were quashed subject to service of subpoenas by deponent. Does this decision make sense? Why shouldn't a party who brings a class action be "responsible" for the class? In the *Edison* case plaintiff had been unable to find many of the unnamed plaintiffs whose depositions were sought and some who were found refused to attend. Defendant gave notice that it would move to dismiss all those plaintiffs from the action under Rule 37(d). It also gave notice that it would continue to demand the depositions of other unnamed plaintiffs and to dismiss claims of those who failed to appear. To what extent should defendant's motive be considered in deciding whether a protective order is proper?

2. At least one federal court has flatly rejected the holding in *Brennan* that unnamed members of the class are parties. Wainwright v. Kraftco Corp., 54 F.R.D. 532 (N.D.Ga.1972). Another court rejected such discovery on the ground that, in the particular case, the burden of discovery far outweighed the value of the information sought. Gardner v. Awards Marketing Corp., 55 F.R.D. 460 (D.Utah 1972).

4. CONTENTIONS AND CONCLUSIONS

ZINSKY v. NEW YORK CENT. R.R.

United States District Court, Northern District of Ohio, 1964.
9 Fed.R.Serv.2d 33.342, Case 3.

JONES, KALBFLEISCH and GREEN, District Judges.　*　*　*

Each of these actions was brought under the Federal Employers Liability
Act, 45 U.S.C. § 51, to recover for alleged personal injuries.

In each of the complaints the general nature of the plaintiff's employment is alleged, and it is then alleged that,

"all or part of plaintiff's duties were in the furtherance of interstate
commerce, or directly, closely and substantially affecting such commerce."

Thereafter, the grounds of negligence, the damages alleged to have been sustained, and the prayer for recovery are set out.

The portions of defendant's answers relevant to these motions are substantially the same. Defendant has, in each case, admitted the allegation as to
the general nature of plaintiff's employment. Each answer contains an affirmative allegation that the plaintiff was himself negligent, and each concludes
with the following allegation:

"further answering defendant denies each and every, all and singu-
lar, the allegations of plaintiff's complaint contained, not herein
specifically admitted to be true."

In none of the answers is the allegation by plaintiffs concerning interstate
commerce admitted to be true.

Interrogatories have been propounded by plaintiffs to defendant in each
action, among which certain basically identical questions appear. Defendant
has objected to two common interrogatories, contending that the answers require the drawing of legal conclusions.

The first interrogatory objected to　*　*　*　is substantially as follows:

(a) Was plaintiff following the usual customs, rules and practices
in performing his work [at the time of the injury complained
of]

(b) If the answer to the preceding part (a) is in the negative,
then state specifically what customs, rules or practices plain-

tiff disregarded in performing his work [at the time of the injury complained of]

The court believes that this interrogatory relates to the factual circumstances surrounding plaintiff's conduct at the time of his injury, as such facts may be known to defendant, and is aimed at exploring defendant's claim of negligence on the part of plaintiff.

While the answer to this interrogatory may well require the drawing of a conclusion, or expression of an opinion or contention by defendant, it is as to a matter of fact rather than law.

An interrogatory calling for a factual inference or conclusion is proper, whereas an interrogatory calling for a legal conclusion is objectionable. United States v. Selby, 25 F.R.D. 12 (N.D.Ohio, 1960); Dusek v. United Air Lines, 9 F.R.D. 326 (N.D.Ohio, 1949).

It is the distinction between a factual conclusion and a legal conclusion that differentiates this interrogatory from the second one objected to by defendant.

* * * It reads as follows:

At the time of the accident, was the plaintiff engaged in duties which were in furtherance of interstate commerce or which directly and substantially affected interstate commerce?

This interrogatory calls upon the defendant to assume a state of facts as to the plaintiff's duties, analyze those facts and state an opinion as to whether those facts support the conclusion that the plaintiff was engaged in interstate commerce.

On the face of the pleadings in these actions the general nature of the plaintiffs' employment is not in issue. Only the conclusion pled by plaintiffs that such employment was in the furtherance of interstate commerce has been put in issue by defendant's denial of all matter not otherwise admitted to be true in the answers.

In an FELA action, when the essential facts with regard to a plaintiff's employment are not in dispute, the question of interstate commerce is deemed to be one of law for the court to determine. * * *

Therefore, at this point it appears that plaintiffs, under the interrogatory as it is presently phrased, are asking defendant to make a legal analysis of one of the factual issues in these cases. As was said in United States v. Selby, supra,

"The assertion and discussion of legal theories, and the classification of facts in support thereof, should be by the lawyers at trial and in whatever pre-trial procedures the court may require." (At p. 14.)

It is for the foregoing reason that this interrogatory, in its present form, is not proper.

* * * [I]t appears to the court that the denials of interstate commerce are pro forma denials, and serve little purpose. * * *

If the defendant is not willing to admit this issue, then plaintiffs are entitled to full discovery, within the limitations of the Federal Rules, in order to
determine what facts are known to defendant relevant thereto. Such discovery, however, does not include interrogatories calling for legal conclusions.

* * *

NOTES AND QUESTIONS

1. The *Zinsky* case was decided prior to the 1970 amendment to Federal
Rule 33, which added the second paragraph of Rule 33(b). Read the Advisory
Committee's Note on Rule 33(b) in the Supplement. Would *Zinsky* have been
decided any differently under the amended rule? Compare JOSEPH v. NOR-
MAN'S HEALTH CLUB, INC., 336 F.Supp. 307, 319 (E.D.Mo.1971), in which
the court upheld an interrogatory asking whether one defendant had ever assigned
any promissory notes to another. In overruling an objection that the interrogatory
called for a legal conclusion, the court held:

> The final sentence of Rule 33(b) added by amendment in 1970,
> * * * does not authorize interrogatories calling for legal conclu-
> sions as such. * * * [T]he only kind of interrogatory that is ob-
> jectionable without more as a legal conclusion is one that extends to
> "legal issues unrelated to the facts of the case."

What is a legal conclusion unrelated to the facts of the case? Does it encompass
the cases upon which a party intends to rely? See Fishermen & Merchants Bank
v. Burin, 11 F.R.D. 142 (S.D.Cal.1951). Consider ROGERS v. TRI-STATE MA-
TERIALS CORP., 51 F.R.D. 234, 246 (N.D.W.Va.1970), in which defendant
sought to discover any "presumption of law or fact" upon which plaintiff intended
to rely. The court upheld the interrogatory as follows:

> Plaintiff may not be schooled on the meaning of the term "res ipsa
> loquitur" but counsel, largely responsible for preparation of answers
> to interrogatories, will be able to explain that a state of facts may speak
> for itself under certain circumstances.

Compare Estate of May v. Zorman, 5 Wash.App. 368, 487 P.2d 270 (1971) (defendants held not required to answer questions asking whether their conduct was
negligent).

2. To what extent should a party's ability to discover the contentions of an
adversary be affected by federal decisions upholding as a sufficient pleading under Rule 8 any statement that possibly can be read to state a valid claim for relief
or a defense? See pp. 392–96, supra. For example, in a negligence case in
which only general allegations of negligence have been made, is it proper to inquire as to the specific acts or omissions upon which the allegations are based?
An inquiry of this type was upheld in *Rogers v. Tri-State Material Corp.*, quoted in
Note 1 above.

3. For an interesting discussion of the use of discovery to ascertain an adverse party's contentions, see James, *The Revival of Bills of Particulars under the
Federal Rules,* 71 Harv.L.Rev. 1473, 1481–83 (1958). As the author states:

> The real objection to requiring detailed statements of contentions is
> that they tie a party down in such a way that he may be deprived of his
> substantive rights. This is so because even astute counsel are unable

always to forecast the vicissitudes of litigation. Time and again some evidence, or some combination of evidence, will emerge for the first time on trial, or will be perceived in its full significance for the first time on trial by the party concerned, or by the tribunal.

* * *

Administrative efficiency will, to be sure, be promoted by the narrowing of issues, at least if they stay narrow. * * * If, however, the pleader has failed to specify some particular contention which would have been within the compass of a generalized pleading and which finds unexpected support or appreciation at trial, then the court is frequently put in a dilemma: It must either refuse to decide the case on the true facts and applicable law, or it must disrupt administrative efficiency to allow a continuance. Either resolution of the dilemma represents an evil.

How does the duty to update discovery under Federal Rule 26(e) affect the argument that a party may be too closely bound by his responses?

4. The 1970 amendments also added a provision to Federal Rule 36(a) extending the scope of requests to admit to matters "that relate to statements or opinions of fact or of the application of law to fact." See the Advisory Committee's Notes on Rule 36 in the Supplement. Are the considerations regarding the scope of requests to admit the same as those regarding interrogatories? Why should the changes as to conclusions appear only in Rules 33 and 36 and not in Rule 26(b)?

SECTION E. USE OF DISCOVERY AT TRIAL

Read Federal Rules of Civil Procedure 32, 36(b), and 30(e) in the Supplement.

RICHMOND v. BROOKS

United States Court of Appeals, Second Circuit, 1955.
227 F.2d 490.

CLARK, Chief Judge. Plaintiff, residing with her present husband in California, brought suit in the New York Supreme Court against defendant, her former husband, now divorced and a resident of New York, to collect loans she had made to him. It also appears—although the court below held it immaterial—that she conducts a business in Beverly Hills, California, in merchandising women's used garments, known as "Gowns of the Stars." Defendant removed the action to the district court below and the case went to trial to a jury some three and a half years later after the taking of various depositions of the defendant in New York and the plaintiff in California, the latter by interrogatories and cross interrogatories. At the trial plaintiff offered her deposition as her proof, but the court refused to receive it and later dismissed her action for failure of proof, refusing to grant her motion for a mistrial and for adjournment. Her appeal challenges these rulings.

Rat. for dismissal

In excluding the deposition the trial judge held that the defendant was entitled to require the presence of the plaintiff as a part of her case and the opportunity to cross-examine her before the jury. Certain cases cited to him as differently construing [what is now Federal Rule 32(a)] * * *, the governing rule, he distinguished as applying only to a *defendant's* proof. See, e. g., Weiss v. Weiner, D.C.Md., 10 F.R.D. 387; Van Sciver v. Rothensies, 3 Cir., 122 F.2d 697, 699 * * *.

F.R. [32(a)] * * * is quite clear in its terms, which apply without exception equally to plaintiffs and defendants. * * *

In * * * Hyam v. American Export Lines, 2 Cir., 213 F.2d 221 * * *, libellant, a resident of Bombay, India, sued in the court below for cargo damage on a shipment carried by respondent from Philadelphia to Bombay; and the parties were at issue preliminarily as to whether libellant's deposition in Bombay should be taken by written interrogatories, as he sought, or by "open commission," with the entire cost thereof paid by him, as sought by the respondent. The district court's solution was to deny the libellant's application and to order him to appear for oral examination in New York. When he failed to comply, his action was dismissed. We reversed, suggesting

Ct: reverse:

the "unusually and seriously burdensome" character of the requirement made below and finding error of law on the part of the district judge in failing to exercise discretion to accord the protection invoked by libellant pursuant to [what is now Federal Rule 26(c)] * * * and in proceeding erroneously on the theory that the respondent had the right to have the suing party in New York for oral examination. We said, * * * 213 F.2d 221, 223: "The federal courts are open to foreign suitors as to others, and procedural rules are not to be construed in such fashion as to impose conditions on litigants which in their practical effect amount to a denial of jurisdiction."

Applying this principle as a touchstone, we can find no occasion to add something to the rule which is not there and which effectually distorts its purpose and utility. The tactical burden assumed by the plaintiff in proceeding to trial in her absence, to which the first judge below called attention, is likely to limit frequent resort to this course; but a suitor not able to afford a New York trip should not be denied all remedy here. There is nothing in the general law to demand such a result. * * *

The defendant relies further on the limiting provision of F.R. [32(a) (3)(B)], * * * *viz.,* "unless it appears that the absence of the witness was procured by the party offering the deposition"; and he points out that the plaintiff was in New York City with her husband during the Christmas holidays some two weeks prior to the start of the trial on January 17, 1955. The district court did not consider this issue, rejecting as immaterial plaintiff's business interests in California; and hence we have no finding as to it. But no reason is apparent to justify a requirement that plaintiff must live in New York City—of course expensively, since that is the only mode of life there—awaiting the uncertain call of a case for trial or be penalized for a normal Christmas trip.   *   *   *

It is suggested, as in 4 Moore's Federal Practice 1195–1197 (2d Ed. 1950), that the "unless" clause just quoted may present an issue of construction as to whether the "absence" in question is from the territory embraced within the 100-mile radius or is from the trial itself, and that only the former interpretation (which is favored) permits a California resident as such to use his own deposition. Perhaps too much is made of this assumed dichotomy; it is not apparent why in this carefully defined context absence from the trial should not be tested for the validity of the excuse on the same principles as absence from the territory. Be that as it may, the language used, referring to different stages of trial *or hearing*, and obviously pointing back to the defining clause which sets forth the basic reasons for admissibility, makes it quite clear that the former is meant.

*   *   *

Reversed and remanded.

NOTES AND QUESTIONS

1. The principal case is noted in 69 Harv.L.Rev. 1503 (1956); 4 U.C.L.A. L.Rev. 150 (1956). The court in COLONIAL REALTY CORP. v. BRUNS-WICK CORP., 337 F.Supp. 546 (S.D.N.Y.1971), questioned whether the *Brooks* decision ought to apply automatically to a case in which plaintiff showed no hardship whatever and in which her credibility was a vital factor. Does Rule 32(a) provide the trial court with any discretion in such a case?

2. Suppose plaintiff in *Brooks* had sought to introduce her answers to a set of interrogatories served on her by defendant. In CALLAWAY v. PERDUE, 238 Ark. 652, 658–59, 385 S.W.2d 4, 8–9 (1964), the court stated that the answers were "self-serving declarations," and were inadmissible under the rules of evidence. In what ways do answers to interrogatories differ from the transcript of a deposition for purposes of using them at trial under Federal Rule 32(a)?

Suppose that a party, pursuant to its duty to update responses under Federal Rule 26(e), sends a supplementary set of answers much more favorable to itself than the original replies to deposition questions. May the adverse party introduce the original replies at trial? The court in MANGUAL v. PRUDENTIAL LINES, INC., 53 F.R.D. 301 (E.D.Pa.1971), held "yes," in accordance with normal evidence rules, which allow an adverse party to utilize any statement of its opponent. The court in *Mangual* went on to hold, however, that the party who made the responses was entitled to put in its subsequent answers, arguing that this was consistent with the policy of Rule 32(a)(4) providing that if only part of a deposition is introduced, the court, in the interests of justice, may order other portions to be introduced as well. Is the court's analogy a sound one?

3. Rule 36(b) was altered in 1970 to make clear that admissions under that Rule are conclusive for purposes of the pending action unless the court, on motion, permits the admission to be withdrawn or amended. Prior to the change a few courts had held that an admission was merely an item of evidence that could be rebutted at trial. See generally Finman, *The Request for Admissions in Federal Civil Procedure*, 71 Yale L.J. 371, 421–22 (1962). Does the language of Rule 36(b) too narrowly restrict the scope of the court's discretion to permit withdrawal or amendment of admissions?

4. Federal Rule 33 contains no provision comparable to Rule 36(b). Does this mean that an interrogatory will not be binding at trial? How does Federal Rule 26(e), which deals with the duty to supplement responses, affect your answer? See pp. 699–700, supra.

5. Florida Rule of Civil Procedure 1.330(a) is identical to Federal Rule 32(a) with one exception, which is spelled out in Rule 1.390 as follows:

> The testimony of an expert or skilled witness may be taken at any time before the trial in accordance with the rules for taking depositions and may be used at trial, regardless of the place of residence of the witness or whether he is within the distance prescribed by Rule 1.330(a) (3). No special form of notice need be given that the deposition will be used for trial.

What is the purpose of this rule? Should Federal Rule 32(a) be amended to include a similar provision? See also Mich.Gen.Ct.Rules 302.7, 302.8.

SECTION F. SANCTIONS

Read Federal Rule of Civil Procedure 37 in the Supplement.

KETCHIKAN COLD STORAGE CO. v. STATE OF ALASKA

Supreme Court of Alaska, 1971.
491 P.2d 143.

ERWIN, Justice. The state took certain land in Ketchikan, Alaska, by eminent domain for a street widening project. The property in question consisted of a 25-foot wide strip, which included a portion of a five-story cold storage building. The state deposited $191,725 with the superior court as estimated just compensation for the taking which occurred on December 15, 1966. The case was tried at Ketchikan in July of 1969.

* * *

I. THE ESTABLISHMENT-PRECLUSION ORDER

In July of 1968 the state served two interrogatories on the owner. These asked the owner to state in detail, for the years 1954 to 1967, inclusive, its revenues and income from the operation at the property, and its operating, maintenance, and depreciation expenses. The owner was also asked to supply the description, nature, custody, and location of all records reflecting such information.

On September 23, 1968, the state moved to compel answers to the interrogatories. An opposition to the interrogatories was filed October 2, 1968, in which the owner objected to the discovery on the grounds that evidence of profits of a business is inadmissible in a condemnation action, and that the information requested by the interrogatories could not reasonably lead to admissible evidence. After a hearing, the court ordered that the interrogatories be answered within 30 days after service of the order. The order of the court was dated October 15, 1968. Appellant did not comply with the order of the court. On February 25, 1969, the state moved for an order which would establish as proven that from 1954 to 1962 the income from the owner's operations followed a declining trend, while expenses did not proportionately decline; that from 1963 to 1967 expenses exceeded income, resulting in a net loss for each year; and that the aggregate operating expenses related to operating revenues and income over the entire period from 1954 to 1967 showed a total net loss. The state also moved for an order requiring the owner to pay the expenses incurred in obtaining the discovery orders.

Δ's refusal to discovery

P moved for order to establish record of business

On March 14, 1969, the court denied the motion to establish facts, because the owner was about to file answers to the interrogatories. At the same time the court ordered payment of certain costs and attorney's fees. It also found that the refusal by the owner to answer the interrogatories was initially without substantial justification, and that the owner failed and refused to comply within a reasonable time with the court's order of October 15, 1968. Answers to the interrogatories were filed March 19, 1969.

On April 4, 1969, the state again moved that certain facts concerning operating revenues and income, set out above, be considered established. The state claimed that the answers to the interrogatories filed by the owner were inadequate. Although the answers disclose the gross revenues received from sale of fish, and detail the operating expenses of the plant, they omit the cost of procuring the fish. Therefore, it is not possible to determine profit or loss from an examination of the answers to the interrogatories. After a hearing, the court on April 24, 1969, modified its previous order and held that the facts requested by the state should be considered established and that the owner should be precluded from introducing evidence controverting such facts.

P moves to establish facts of case

The question presented is whether, absent a finding of wilful failure by appellant to comply with the initial discovery order of October 15, 1968, the establishment-preclusion order should be upheld. We have concluded that it should not.

ISSUE

effects of
establishment-
preclusion
order

When a party refuses to comply with a discovery order, Civil Rule 37(b) provides the court with a flexible list of sanctions. One of the most severe sanctions is the establishment-preclusion order. When facts at issue in a controversy are established against one of the parties, he is precluded from introducing testimony to refute the points taken to be established. Thus, in effect, the party has been denied his right to trial on the merits to the extent that matters of fact have been rendered incontestable. The sanction is especially severe when the establishment-preclusion order goes to an issue which is central to the determination of the case. In the present case the jury was instructed that it could consider the cold storage plant's history of declining profits, established by court order, in determining the highest and best use of the condemned property. All other valuation evidence was excluded from the jury's consideration. It is difficult to conceive how the jury had any choice other than to find that the highest and best use of the condemned property was not as a cold storage plant when the only evidence of valuation before them was the declining economic history of the plant as established by court order. Thus, the establishment-preclusion order had a direct bearing on the critical issue determined by the jury: the highest and best use of the property.

* * *

The purpose of the Rule 37 sanctions is to effectuate the discovery process. The discovery rules have replaced common law pleading as the means of clarifying issues prior to trial. This permits the factual and legal issues to be brought into specific focus at an early time. It also may lead to settlement or early termination of lawsuits. Discovery has been quite successful in achieving these goals, and we must not condone any attempt to avoid the process. We cannot, however, allow a procedural rule to frustrate the major purpose of Rule 37, and in fact all the rules of civil procedure, which is to ensure that an individual may have a just determination of his case upon the merits.

The United States Supreme Court has stated that federal provisions similar to those of Civil Rule 37 must be read in light of the fifth amendment's guarantee that no person shall be deprived of property without due process of law. Societe Internationale Pour Participations Industrielles Et Commerciales, S. A. v. Rogers, 357 U.S. 197, 209, 78 S.Ct. 1087, 2 L.Ed.2d 1255, 1262 (1958). * * * We have concluded that an establishment-preclusion order which prevents full adjudication of a case on its merits is so drastic a sanction that it should be employed only upon the clearest showing that such a course is required.

Sanction:
establishment-
preclusion order
should be used
only on "clear
showing that it is
required"

↓

wilful failure to
comply, where order
relates to central issue of
the case.

Although Rule 37 does not in terms require a showing of wilfulness before any of its sanctions come into play, we will not sustain an establishment-preclusion order relating to a central issue in a case absent a showing of wilful failure to comply. * * * Our approach is in line with a number of cases which have found that the establishment-preclusion order is only appropriate in exceptional situations.

In our opinion the record does not show a wilful refusal on appellant's part to comply with the lower court's production order of October 15, 1968. The only evidence of wilful nondisclosure was appellant's delay in making discovery, and the unsupported allegations of opposing counsel that the purpose of the delay was to thwart the discovery process. Lacking the element of wilful noncompliance, the trial court under Rule 37 should not have entered an establishment-preclusion order in this case.

* * *

II. THE COST BILL

The court assessed against appellant the state's costs of $7,238.37 in obtaining the discovery order and the subsequent costs of $10,671.29 in enforcing that order. We find the lower court's assessment of the state's costs in obtaining the discovery order improper under Rule 37(a). The assessment of the state's costs in enforcing the order is, however, a proper sanction under Rule 37(b) for appellant's failure to comply with the discovery order.

A. *Costs in Obtaining the Discovery Order.*

A court can only require a refusing party to pay for the other party's costs in obtaining a discovery order when the former's refusal is "without substantial justification." It is not the purpose of Rule 37 to punish a party who innocently and reasonably resists discovery. * * *

After reviewing the record in this case we have concluded that the appellant's initial refusal of discovery was not without substantial justification. * * *

There is substantial authority that "evidence of the profits of a business conducted upon land taken for the public use is not admissible in proceedings for the determination of the compensation which the owner of the land shall receive." However, the trial court apparently found, and we agree, that this cold storage facility comes within an exception to this general rule permitting evidence of income from unique commercial property. Therefore, the lower court was entirely correct in granting the state's motion for a discovery order. In light of the great weight of authority disallowing evidence of business income from a commercial property in an eminent domain proceeding, however, we find that appellant's initial resistance of the state's efforts to discover the profits of the cold storage plant had substantial justification. Therefore, to tax appellants with the state's costs in obtaining the discovery order constituted a clear abuse of discretion.

B. *Costs as a Sanction for Failure to Comply with the Discovery Order.*

We uphold the trial court's assessment of the state's costs in seeking enforcement of the October 15 discovery order.

After the October court order, appellant was no longer entitled to resist the state's discovery efforts. However, appellant did not provide appellee with the requested information. The state was forced to bring appellant into court once again on March 14, 1969, to demand compliance with the discovery order. Appellant offered no excuse for the lengthy delay but promised to provide the answers to the state's interrogatories immediately. When the long-awaited answers were examined, they were incomplete and the state appeared in court once again to protest on April 18, 1969.

We have held that the severe sanction of an establishment-preclusion order was not justified in this case. But this type of costly tardiness and lack of cooperation with the discovery process does justify the imposition of sanctions under Rule 37(b). That rule permits the court, in its discretion, to enter "such orders in regard to the refusal as are just." The court chose in this instance to make appellant bear the full brunt of the state's costs in enforcing the October 15 discovery order. Absent a clear abuse, we will not interfere with the court's broad discretion in this area.

* * *

The case is reversed and remanded for further proceedings in accordance with this opinion.

NOTES AND QUESTIONS

1. Federal Rule 37 gives the court broad powers to impose sanctions against a party that fails to comply with the discovery requirements. Note that sanctions against a party can be imposed under Rule 37(b)(2) or 37(d). Why are there two separate provisions? How do they differ? Should Rule 37(d) permit sanctions only if a defaulting party has acted willfully? See Sapiro v. Hartford Fire Ins. Co., 452 F.2d 215 (7th Cir.1971), indicating that wilfullness is required before sanctions can be imposed under Rule 37(d) and reversing a default judgment on the ground that this drastic remedy normally is improper for delay in answering interrogatories, even though the delay is a serious one. See also Vac-Air, Inc. v. John Mohr & Sons, Inc., 471 F.2d 231 (7th Cir.1973), overturning as too harsh a default judgment for plaintiff under Rule 37(d) when defendant delayed serving answers to interrogatories until after plaintiff's motion for sanctions was filed.

Is there any reason to impose sanctions under Rule 37(b) without a showing of willful disregard of discovery orders? Courts generally seem more willing to impose severe sanctions when a violation of a court order is involved. *Compare* Seanor v. Bair Transport Co. of Delaware, Inc., 54 F.R.D. 35 (E.D.Pa.1971) (violation of court order resulted in entry of default), *with* Balistrieri v. Holtzman, 55 F.R.D. 470 (E.D.Wis.1972) (dismissal held improper when no court order involved). *But see* Leonard Brothers Trucking Co. v. Crymes Transports, Inc., 124 Ga.App. 341, 183 S.E.2d 773 (1971) (violation of court order cannot justify default judgment in absence of express finding that default was willful).

2. Note that Federal Rule 37(b)(2)(D), which permits a party who deliberately disobeys a court order to be held in contempt and hence imprisoned

or fined, specifically excludes cases in which a party refuses to submit to a physical or mental examination. Why?

3. Federal Rule 37(c) spells out the sanction available when a party falsely denies a request to admit under Rule 36. How potent is this sanction? See Bradshaw v. Thompson, 454 F.2d 75 (6th Cir.), certiorari denied 409 U.S. 878, 93 S.Ct. 130, 34 L.Ed.2d 131 (1972), in which plaintiff won a judgment of $13,323.27, and defendant was ordered to pay an additional $4,026.37 under Rule 37(c).

Is the granting of a motion under Rule 36(a) deeming matters to be admitted a more satisfactory way of imposing sanctions for violations of Rule 36? In BALISTRIERI v. HOLTZMAN, 55 F.R.D. 470 (E.D.Wis.1972), the court refused a motion to treat matters as admitted when the opposing party had failed to respond to requests to admit. The court held that under the rule these matters were automatically treated as having been admitted and thus the motion was unnecessary. Is there justification for this motion even when no response has been received?

4. In IN RE MACK, 330 F.Supp. 737 (S.D.Tex.1970), a seaman filed a petition to obtain past wages that the government claimed were forfeited because the seaman had willfully deserted his ship. The government sent to the seaman at his last known address a set of requests to admit but they never were received. The court held that the seaman had a duty to keep the court apprised of his current whereabouts. Therefore the requests were deemed admitted and on that basis default judgment was entered for the government. Does this determination amount to a taking of the seaman's property without due process? See Note, *Proposed 1967 Amendments to the Federal Discovery Rules,* 68 Colum.L.Rev. 271, 291–96 (1968).

The United States Supreme Court in *Societé Internationale v. Rogers,* cited in the *Ketchikan* case, addressed itself to the constitutional limitations on discovery sanctions as follows:

> The provisions of Rule 37 which are here involved must be read in light of the provisions of the Fifth Amendment that no person shall be deprived of property without due process of law, and more particularly against the opinions of this Court in Hovey v. Elliott, 167 U.S. 409, 17 S.Ct. 841, 42 L.Ed. 215, and Hammond Packing Co. v. State of Arkansas, 212 U.S. 322, 29 S.Ct. 370, 53 L.Ed. 530. These decisions establish that there are constitutional limitations upon the power of courts, even in aid of their own valid processes, to dismiss an action without affording a party the opportunity for a hearing on the merits of his cause. * * *
>
> In Hovey v. Elliott, supra, it was held that due process was denied a defendant whose answer was struck, thereby leading to a decree *pro confesso* without a hearing on the merits, because of his refusal to obey a court order pertinent to the suit. This holding was substantially modified by Hammond Packing Co. v. State of Arkansas, supra, where the Court ruled that a state court, consistently with the Due Process Clause of the Fourteenth Amendment, could strike the answer of and render a default judgment against a defendant who refused to produce documents in accordance with a pretrial order. The Hovey case was distinguished on grounds that the defendant there was denied his right to

defend "as a mere punishment"; due process was found preserved in Hammond on the reasoning that the State simply utilized a permissible presumption that the refusal to produce material evidence " * * * was but an admission of the want of merit in the asserted defense." 212 U.S. at pages 350–351, 29 S.Ct. at page 380. But the Court took care to emphasize that the defendant had not been penalized " * * * for a failure to do that which it may not have been in its power to do." All the State had required "was a *bona fide* effort to comply with an order * * *, and therefore any reasonable showing of an inability to comply would have satisfied the requirements * * *" of the order. 212 U.S. at page 347, 29 S.Ct. at page 378.

These two decisions leave open the question whether Fifth Amendment due process is violated by the striking of a complaint because of a plaintiff's inability, despite good-faith efforts, to comply with a pretrial production order. The presumption utilized by the Court in the Hammond case might well falter under such circumstances. * * * Certainly substantial constitutional questions are provoked by such action. * * *

* * * [W]e think that Rule 37 should not be construed to authorize dismissal of this complaint because of petitioner's noncompliance with a pretrial production order when it has been established that failure to comply has been due to inability, and not to willfulness, bad faith, or any fault of petitioner.

See generally 8 Wright & Miller, *Federal Practice and Procedure: Civil* § 2283 (1970).

CHAPTER 9

THE PRETRIAL CONFERENCE

Read Federal Rule of Civil Procedure 16 and the material accompanying it in the Supplement.

In studying the following materials on the pretrial conference, it is important to note that there are two quite different views as to its proper purpose. The first, which already has been mentioned in connection with pleading, see pp. 400–01, supra, is that the conference is a method of preparing for and shaping the contours of the trial; at the conference, the contentions of the parties are at last set forth precisely and a variety of details, including those enumerated in Rule 16, are determined in an effort to ensure a more meaningful trial. The second view, held most often by judges in areas where there is a substantial backlog of cases awaiting adjudication, is that the pretrial conference primarily is a means of obtaining settlements or otherwise disposing of cases without trial.

These views are not necessarily incompatible. Often when lawyers for opposing parties meet face to face to prepare for a difficult and costly trial, they soon realize that many of the formally contested issues can be eliminated or that the most sensible solution is an out-of-court compromise of the entire dispute. In any event, the court's attitude toward the purpose of pretrial determines the way in which the conference will be handled. In those jurisdictions in which settlement is the prime target, pretrial is likely to be mandatory. There may even be a separate "settlement conference" ordered in cases in which the court feels that a settlement might be reached if the parties were forced to direct their attention solely to that subject. During such a conference the judge will push each party to make concessions, argue with attorneys who appear stubborn, and conceivably even suggest reprisals if they insist on going to trial. It often is difficult to withstand such pressures, particularly if the pretrial judge, as is the case in some courts, also will preside at the trial of the case.

In courts in which trial preparation is the prime reason for pretrial conference, the atmosphere usually will be more relaxed. The court may actively attempt to obtain agreements on various matters but it will be less likely to push the parties to points beyond which they truly wish to go. In such jurisdictions pretrial normally will take place only when the case involves complex issues or when a considerable amount of evidence or a lengthy trial is expected. Mandatory conferences for simple cases would be a waste of time.

The extent to which the pretrial conference actually can accomplish the various goals sought to be obtained is as yet unclear. One thoughtful, though limited, study indicates that the pretrial conference does not result in a greater number of settled cases or even a shortening of trial time. The chief value seems to be that pretried cases are somewhat better prepared and presented by the attorneys and thus, in some unquantifiable way, may lead to "juster" results. See Rosenberg, *The Pretrial Conference and Effective Justice* 67–70 (1964). For a contrary view, see Levin & Wooley, *Dispatch and Delay* 63–66 (1961). Also unclear is the effectiveness of the pretrial conference as compared with other possible pretrial regulatory procedures, such as the appointment of masters, or the use of several pretrial control devices in the same case. See generally Zavatt, *The Use of Masters in Aid of the Court in Interlocutory Proceedings*, 22 F.R.D. 283 (1958). Some of the other techniques are described at pp. 771–78, infra.

FORM NOTICE OF PRETRIAL CONFERENCE

United States District Court, Southern District Indiana.
37 F.R.D. 311–12 (1965).

UNITED STATES DISTRICT COURT

Southern District of Indiana

CIVIL NO. ——————

NOTICE OF PRE-TRIAL CONFERENCE AND ORDER EXPEDITING TRIAL

The above case is hereby assigned for pre-trial conference pursuant to Rule 16, F.R.C.P., at Room ————, United States Courthouse, ————, Indiana, on ————, 19—, at ——— o'clock —M.

The parties through counsel are ORDERED to do each of the following things, where applicable, prior to such date, unless the time fixed be extended for good cause shown by affidavit:

(1) Meet with each other in order to exchange lists containing the names and addresses of all witnesses expected to be relied upon at trial, other than witnesses intended to be used solely for the purpose of impeachment or rebuttal, within ——— days from the date of receipt hereof. The names and addresses of witnesses discovered subsequent to such exchange of lists shall be furnished to opposing counsel forthwith upon discovery.

(2) Complete all discovery, including physical examinations.

(3) Display to each other all items intended to be offered as exhibits, and all items supporting claims for special damages, whether admissible as exhibits or not (i.e., copies of income tax returns, repair bills, etc.).

(4) Enter into a written stipulation, stipulating to the fullest possible extent the issues, undisputed facts, authenticity and admissibility of exhibits, and any and all other matters which will expedite the trial of the cause by reducing formal proof. SUCH WRITTEN STIPULATION WILL BE PRESENTED TO THE COURT AT TIME OF THE CONFERENCE. Failure to present such a stipulation will be construed to indicate that counsel have not met in compliance with this direction, unless otherwise explained to the Court's satisfaction.

(5) Make a good faith effort to settle the case.

Each party should be represented at the conference by the attorney who expects to try the case. Pending motions, if not ruled upon sooner, will be disposed of at the conference.

ALL OF WHICH IS CONSIDERED AND ORDERED This ———— day of ————, 19—.

_____

United States District Judge

NOTES AND QUESTIONS

1. What is the underlying purpose and justification for each of the following requirements in the Notice of Pretrial Conference set out above? (1) The parties must complete all discovery prior to the conference. (2) The parties must enter into a written pre-pretrial stipulation regarding the facts, authenticity and admissibility of exhibits, and other matters. (3) The attorneys must meet with each other to exchange lists containing the names and addresses of all witnesses. (4) The parties must be represented at the conference by the attorney who expects to try the case, rather than someone else in the law office. To what extent do these elements of the pretrial conference procedure in the Southern District of Indiana simply proliferate the pretrial process? Are any of these elements of the Form Notice justifiable under the text of Federal Rule 16? Are any of them inconsistent with the philosophy of *Hickman v. Taylor*, p. 700, supra?

2. See generally Becker, *A Modern, Efficient Use of the Bar and Other Parajudicial Personnel in Pretrial of Ordinary Civil Actions*, 53 F.R.D. 159 (1971); Kincaid, *A Judge's Handbook of Pre-Trial Procedure*, 17 F.R.D. 437 (1955); Kuykendall, *Pre-Trial Conference: A Dissent from the Bar*, 45 Va.L. Rev. 147 (1959); Thode, *The Case for the Pretrial Conference in Texas*, 35 Texas L.Rev. 372 (1957).

————

PADOVANI v. BRUCHHAUSEN

United States Court of Appeals, Second Circuit, 1961.
293 F.2d 546.

CLARK, Circuit Judge. This is a petition for a writ of mandamus directing Chief Judge Bruchhausen to vacate, reverse, or modify an order of preclusion he has made against the introduction of certain testimony or reliance on certain theories of law in the trial of an action brought by the present petitioner and now pending in the district court. The action is one for negligence and breach of warranty against Liggett & Myers Tobacco Company, wherein the plaintiff claims damages for a cancer of the larynx alleged to have occurred as a result of smoking cigarettes manufactured by the defendant.

* * * [D]efendant moved for an order directing pre-trial proceedings under F.R. 16, and the court * * * granted the motion. * * * But the hearing was not held because Judge Bruchhausen, the trial-part judge, acting on defendant's motion, ordered "a complete pre-trial statement," in accordance with the defendant's notice, by a time stated, with time also set for an answer by defendant. The plaintiff's statement when received was adjudged insufficient on defendant's motion, and the court ordered the plaintiff to file a new statement supplying the deficiencies asserted by defendant. This procedure was repeated a second and then a third time, * * * until eventually the court granted the defendant's motion for preclusion. * * *

The order * * * specifically precludes the plaintiff from offering at trial (1) any evidence of lay witnesses except the plaintiff and his wife; (2) any expert testimony; (3) any exhibits except three named (of a medical nature dealing with plaintiff's alleged treatment some years ago); (4) any evidence of damages, with four exceptions (a hospital and two doctors' bills, plus "pain and suffering"); and (5) any evidence "on the issue of liability in either negligence or breach of warranty." It appears to be conceded, as well as clear, that these preclusions remove all basis for proof by the plaintiff of his claim and that the trial now ordered can have only one outcome, namely, judgment for the defendant.

This case has given us the utmost concern. We realize that to make pretrial procedure effective appellate interference with trial court discretion must be kept to a minimum; and we are apprised of the devoted efforts of this court to meet a mounting burden of congestion with all weapons it can command, including notably those afforded by F.R. 16. Nevertheless, we do have an overriding responsibility to see that justice is done between litigants before the court. * * * Hence we are constrained to conclude that we must grant the petition for the several reasons we shall now indicate.

First is the anomalous and even self-defeating character of the order itself. It does not in form deny the jury trial sought by the plaintiff, but it does so in substance. While it avoids the clear-cut issue sought by plaintiff in his alternative request for outright dismissal (as a basis for appeal) yet it leaves a trial necessarily abortive in nature. There must be better ways to vindicate pre-trial orders than by superfluous and hopeless trials which can be only burdensome to the litigants and the court.

Second is the drastic nature of the penalty inflicted upon a litigant for what at most is an error or dereliction of his lawyer [in failing] * * * to comply with the court's requirements as to pre-trial. Further, there has here been not so much outright default on counsel's part as a debatably inadequate compliance—an issue in itself of some legal difficulty, as we shall presently indicate. It would seem hardly likely under these circumstances that the lay plaintiff could know or comprehend the doom about to be visited upon him, not his counsel, in time to avert it if, indeed, that were in any way possible.

Finally there is the form and content of the pre-trial procedure adopted here. And here we are constrained to conclude—with reluctance because of the extensive planning below, but with conviction of the need if pre-trial is to retain utility—that the course here followed not only is unauthorized, but is at odds with the purpose and intent of F.R. 16. That rule calls for a *conference* of counsel with the court to *prepare* for, not to avert, trial, leading to an order which shall recite the "agreements made by the parties as to any of the matters considered." It is subordinate and conciliatory, rather than compulsive, in character. Nothing in the rule affords basis for clubbing the parties into admissions they do not willingly make; but it is a way of advancing the trial ultimately to be had by setting forth the points on which the parties are agreed after a conference directed by a trained judge.

Here, however, the procedure was a kind of pre-pre-trial pleading—and special pleading at that—before hearing or conference was ever reached. So the successive orders and repleadings correspond to the motions and orders for a more definite statement of old pleading days, with more than a little of the futility therein so usual. * * *

This is shown vividly by the nature of the disclosures sought by the defendant and approved by the court. They were of two kinds: a demand for further particularity in the statement of the claim and a demand for the witnesses and exhibits to be offered by the plaintiff. So on the first point, defendant's original demand, which the judge incorporated in his order, was that the plaintiff state (1) "the facts of this case," identifying those admitted by the parties and those put in issue by the pleadings; (2) "plaintiff's legal theory or theories of recovery"; (3) what facts plaintiff intends to prove in support of each theory; and (4) the details of plaintiff's damage. On the second, the plaintiff was required (5) to list all proposed exhibits; (6) the names and addresses of all expert witnesses, together with their field of specialization and the substance of their testimony; (7) the names and addresses of all lay witnesses and the substance of their testimony; and (8) whether he intended to seek further relief or discovery, and if so, what. And the demand for the pleading of a legal theory became ever more insistent as the proceedings continued, so that at the end the defendant was seeking information as to detailed claims of law enumerated in several typewritten pages. Yet if there is any characteristic of the federal rules (and indeed of code pleading generally) which is well settled, it is that a plaintiff pleads facts and not law and that the law is to be applied by the court. * * *

The other branch of the preclusion order excluding lay and expert testimony and exhibits which the plaintiff's statement shows to be relevant to the issues appears to be an attempt to shorten what may well be a lengthy trial. The plaintiff * * * listed what does appear to be an excess of witnesses * * *. If at trial an excess of witnesses is presented, the trial judge may take steps to expedite the hearing; it may be doubtful if much can be done in advance of trial to that end. * * * As a matter of fact the courts have been sharply divided on the question whether a party can be forced to disclose his prospective witnesses in advance of trial, with the majority view apparently in the negative. We are not disposed, however, to rule that a court in a pre-trial conference may not inquire of counsel as to his then plans as to the calling of witnesses, including the hiring of experts. Such a direct inquiry is likely to elicit more specific information than will be found in detailed written statements. But in no event at this pre-trial stage should witnesses be excluded because of mere numbers, without reference to the relevancy of their testimony.

* * *

The benefits to courts and litigants from carefully conducted pre-trial proceedings are now well known and widely acclaimed. But these are not to be achieved automatically; they require the diligent efforts of both court and counsel working in earnest co-operation to a common purpose. For success the leadership, direction, and stimulus of the judge are vital. True, he needs unusual qualities of tact, persistence, and patience to instruct lawyers in trial ways unlike the state practice to which they are accustomed, to still the emotional animosities of counsel who have allowed themselves to become too closely identified with their clients' causes, and generally to lead the parties and their attorneys to the frank and unforced concessions which alone justify the procedure. If a judge is not prepared to give the time and effort thus required for successful pre-trial, it would seem that he should avail himself of the discretion still accorded him under F.R. 16 of not engaging in the attempt. But if he does undertake it and carry it through in the spirit of the rule, it is, as experience is now continually demonstrating, one of the most rewarding accomplishments to which a federal judge can aspire. He will deserve and receive public plaudits for his efficient dispatch of the public business; but even more, he will receive the grateful thanks of counsel and litigants for better justice more shortly and efficiently obtained. We suggest that with a new start and a fresh determination to co-operate, the parties and the court may well achieve wonders in this very case.

While we thus urge a return to the original purpose of the pre-trial conference, yet it may be desirable out of caution to note what we do not decide. Thus we do not hold that an order of preclusion may never be appropriate; indeed, it is one of the sanctions for discovery orders provided in F.R. 37(b) (2), though its use to preclude an entire case is unusual. Nor do we hold that a district judge may not request a pre-trial memorandum or statement from a party to assist him in formulating a pre-trial order showing the admissions and concessions of the parties and the issues remaining to be tried. But a requirement of successive repleadings to force a plaintiff against his will to limit his case beyond the issues he has tendered in his complaint is contrary to the basic principles of the federal rules. * * * The petition must therefore be granted * * *.

DAWSON, District Judge (dissenting in part and concurring in part).

I concur in so much of Judge Clark's opinion as grants the motion for a writ of mandamus vacating the preclusion order　*　*　*　because the directions issued by Judge Bruchhausen during the course of pre-trial hearings were not set forth with definiteness and precision and the plaintiff may perhaps have been in doubt as to what he was supposed to do　*　*　*.

Where I disagree is with the body of Judge Clark's opinion which purports to limit, not alone in this case but in all other cases, the procedure which a pre-trial may take. Thus Judge Clark seems to indicate that a court may not, in a pre-trial conference, direct the parties to submit written statements setting forth the facts the parties will seek to prove at the trial and the legal theory or theories on which they will attempt to predicate a recovery.　*　*　*

Judge Clark has apparently confused pre-trial problems with the problems of pleading. He is still carrying the torch for "notice pleading" as contrasted with more elaborate and particularized pleadings, but that battle is now long over. We are not here concerned with pleadings but with pre-trial statements to be filed long after the pleadings are closed.

However, in supporting the cause of notice pleading, Judge Clark himself has said, although briefly, that when details are lacking in a complaint they may be obtained in pre-trial. 21 F.R.D. at page 52. Now he says that they cannot be compelled to be provided in written statements.

But how are the facts and issues to be particularized? The way was well explained by Judge William E. Smith of New Jersey　*　*　*　(23 F.R.D. 414):

> "The success of the initial pre-trial conference will depend upon two factors, to wit, adequate preparation and cooperation. A basis for discussion may be laid in advance of the conference if counsel for the litigants are required to file with the Court written preliminary statements in which they shall particularize both the factual and legal issues. These statements should not be made a part of the pleadings. We are of the opinion that oral statements made at the pre-trial conference are inadequate because they do not permit the trial judge to limit the scope of discussion.

> "The plaintiff should be required to file with the trial judge a concise but comprehensive statement of the factual issues. This statement should not be couched in the usually verbose language of the complaint; the surplusage frequently found in the complaint should be eliminated. The defendant should be required to file a counterstatement of the factual issues but only if these issues as stated by the plaintiff are disputed. There should be incorporated in each of the preliminary statements a particularization of the legal issues, supported, if feasible, by citations of only the principal authorities.　*　*　*"

The inference in Judge Clark's opinion is that such procedure is not permissible. This will render pre-trial largely useless. His approach presupposes that we must wait until the trial is in progress before we ascertain what particular facts are in issue and what legal theories are relied upon by the parties.

And what is a judge to do if a party fails to comply with the order of the court [regarding pretrial?] * * *

The preclusion order in this case did, in effect, prevent the plaintiff from presenting any evidence at the trial which could lead to a recovery by the plaintiff. Plaintiff's inattention to the directions of the court may have justified this procedure. I am perfectly willing, however, to give the plaintiff a second try since the directions of Judge Bruchhausen were not made with definiteness and precision. I am not willing to accept the premise that if directions are made with definiteness and precision and then ignored by the plaintiff he may not be precluded from offering evidence at the trial * * *.

NOTES AND QUESTIONS

1. Is there something wrong with a procedural system that does not require the legal contentions of an adverse party to appear in the pleadings and will not permit them to be obtained through discovery, see *Zinsky v. New York Cent. R.R.,* p. 720, supra, or at a pretrial conference? Shouldn't there be some method by which legal as well as factual issues can be isolated and formulated prior to trial?

2. Suppose at a pretrial conference one party refuses formally to assent to the elimination of issues about which the parties are in fact in agreement. May the court itself, under Rule 16, issue a pretrial order eliminating these issues? In LIFE MUSIC, INC. v. EDELSTEIN, 309 F.2d 242, 243 (2d Cir.1962), the court held:

> * * * Although Rule 16 could have been more felicitously phrased in this regard, we cannot believe it was meant to circumscribe the judge as narrowly as petitioner urges. The Rule clearly authorizes the judge to seek a simplification of the issues and requires the attorneys to make a good faith effort to aid him. It could hardly have been intended that if, as a result of all this, the judge finds that the parties are really in accord, he may not issue an order defining their "agreement" simply because one of them refuses a formal manifestation of assent. Although "agreement" usually connotes a voluntary undertaking of two or more parties, this is not its only meaning. * * * A scholar may write that two of his fellows are in agreement, although each, cherishing some nuance of expression, loudly denies it. By the same token the judge may find that the parties are in "agreement" as to issues, even though they challenge his formulation.

3. What is the effect of *Padovani* on the effectiveness of the Form Notice of Pretrial Conference set out on pp. 734–35, supra? See also Glisan v. Kurth, 153 Colo. 102, 384 P.2d 946 (1963).

4. When, if ever, should the same judge who will hear the case at trial also conduct the pretrial conference? Should the conference be held in open court or in chambers? Various aspects of the pretrial conference procedure are discussed in

Wright, *Federal Courts* § 91, at 399–402 (2d ed. 1970); Clark, *Objectives of Pre-Trial Procedure,* 17 Ohio St.L.J. 163 (1956); Winters, *The Pre-Pre-Trial Conference Without the Judge in Federal District Courts,* 37 Neb.L.Rev. 449 (1958); *Handbook for Effective Pretrial Procedure,* 37 F.R.D. 255 (1964). See generally 36 Temple L.Q. 101 (1962).

5.　Suppose an attorney fails to attend a pretrial conference. What sanctions may a trial judge apply? In LINK v. WABASH R. R., 370 U.S. 626, 82 S.Ct. 1386, 8 L.Ed.2d 734 (1962), the trial court dismissed plaintiff's action two hours after his counsel did not arrive. That decision was approved by the Supreme Court by a 4 to 3 vote. The majority was careful to point out that the dismissal below had not been based solely on the failure of counsel to arrive at the particular conference but also on his pattern of delaying tactics throughout the case. Should Federal Rule 16 be amended to include a set of sanctions identical to those in Rule 37(b)? See Comment, *Dismissal for Failure to Attend a Pretrial Conference and the Use of Sanctions at Preparatory Stages of Litigation,* 72 Yale L.J. 819 (1963); 58 Nw.U.L.Rev. 130 (1963). See also Heisman v. Giordano, 343 F.Supp. 1258 (E.D.Pa.1972), dismissing plaintiff's case for repeated failure to file a pretrial memorandum as required by the court's rules and specifically ordered by the federal magistrate.

———

PACIFIC INDEMNITY CO. v. BROWARD COUNTY, 465 F.2d 99 (5th Cir. 1972). Airmotive filed a cross-claim against its codefendant, the county, for damages due to the loss of an airplane. Under applicable law Airmotive was required to plead and prove that it had filed a timely claim with the board of county commissioners. In its cross-claim Airmotive did include such an allegation, which the county denied. Thereafter, however, neither of the parties alluded to the matter, it was not listed in the pretrial order as an issue for trial, and no evidence was presented on it. The jury awarded Airmotive a verdict of $150,000. The trial court set the verdict aside and entered judgment for the county on the ground that Airmotive had failed to prove that it had filed its claim with the county board, a vital element of its case. Airmotive appealed, arguing that the pretrial order superseded the pleadings and therefore the county had waived the issue. The appellate court affirmed, stating:

> The failure to indicate in the pre-trial order that an issue remains to be resolved at trial usually precludes the offer of proof on the issue at trial—to the detriment of the party who has the burden to prove the issue. This common-sense rule has been followed where the plaintiff pleads a theory of recovery in his complaint, but fails to preserve the theory in the pre-trial order, * * * and where the defendant pleads a number of affirmative defenses which he fails to preserve during pre-trial * * *. In this manner the pre-trial order permits the parties and the court to prepare for trial with the assurance that they know what issues they must be ready to meet.

In the present case Airmotive had the burden to prove as part of its cause of action against the County that the statutory notice had been given as alleged. When the question was not admitted nor preserved for trial in the pre-trial order the County had grounds for a technical objection in the event Airmotive attempted to prove notice at trial. However the court in the exercise of its discretion to prevent manifest injustice under Rule 16 * * * could have amended the pre-trial order during trial to permit proof on the question. Alternatively, the court could have ordered a limited new trial under Rule 59 * * * where, as in these circumstances, the issue was in good faith overlooked by all concerned. But to hold, as Airmotive contends, that the County waived statutory notice because the County failed to remind Airmotive in the pre-trial stipulation that Airmotive still had to prove that it had given the County notice would strain the logic of our adversarial system and would destroy much of the usefulness of a pre-trial order as a device to reduce and limit issues at trial.

NOTES AND QUESTIONS

1. The appellate court in *Pacific Indemnity* did not discuss Federal Rule 51, although it is clear from the opinion that neither party had asked for an instruction on the "forgotten issue." Would appellant have been better advised to rely on Rule 51 rather than on the pretrial order?

2. The pretrial order normally does supersede the pleadings. Not only may the order eliminate matters originally raised but it may supply new issues not included within the original pleadings. See United States v. Hougham, 364 U.S. 310, 315–16, 81 S.Ct. 13, 17–18, 5 L.Ed.2d 8, 14 (1960). Of course, the order may be modified in much the same way and under the same conditions as the pleadings may be amended. See GLOBE INDEM. CO. v. CAPITAL INS. & SUR. CO., 352 F.2d 236, 239 (9th Cir.1965), in which the court stated:

> * * * Granted, a pre-trial order should not lightly be modified, nevertheless a court should be liberal in allowing amendments where no substantial injury will be done the opposing party, the failure to allow the amendment might result in a grave injustice to the moving party, and the inconvenience to the court is relatively slight.

See also Monod v. Futura, Inc., 415 F.2d 1170, 1174 (10th Cir.1969) (Federal Rule 15(b) applies to issues excluded in the pretrial order but tried by consent); Sherman v. United States, 462 F.2d 577 (5th Cir.1972) (denial of amendment to pretrial order reversed as abuse of discretion when no prejudice would result).

THE ROLE OF THE PRETRIAL CONFERENCE IN COMPLEX LITIGATION

Ever since the 1950's judges, particularly federal judges, have been concerned about the management of the increasing number of complex cases and situations in which a series of related lawsuits are brought in more than one court.　Trial of these cases requires careful planning if they are to be handled with any degree of efficiency and without deterring the prompt adjudication of the other litigation on the court's docket.　The challenge posed by complex cases has been heightened by liberalization of the rules permitting class actions, see pp. 566–71, supra, and the increased use of the courts to enforce consumer rights, environmental protection laws, and other measures involving social policy.　Although class suits perform the desirable function of permitting access to courts by many who could not afford to sue alone, they have created serious problems of court administration.

In the late 1960's a committee of federal judges, known as the Co-ordinating Committee for Multiple Litigation of the United States District Courts, together with legal scholars and representatives of the bar, drafted a manual of suggested procedures for dealing with the so-called "big case." This Manual for Complex and Multidistrict Litigation (the 1973 edition of which is titled Manual for Complex Litigation) suggests a series of four pretrial conferences; the first to assume control of the case and to handle preliminary matters such as pleading and the joinder of parties and claims, the second to plan discovery, the third to control the discovery process and provide for pretrial briefs, and the last to plan the details of the trial.　The Manual recognizes that these procedures must be altered to fit the needs of each case.　Thus, the Manual reflects the belief of experienced judges that a series of pretrial conferences can play a vital role in the proper handling of class actions and other large cases.　See generally 6 Wright & Miller, *Federal Practice and Procedure: Civil* § 1530 (1971).　Indeed, one appellate court, upon reversal of a judgment in a complex antitrust case, "advised" the trial judge on remand to hold pretrial conferences to avoid the waste of time that occurred throughout the first trial because no conferences had been held.　Elder-Beerman Stores v. Federated Department Stores, Inc., 459 F.2d 138, 150–51, 161, 164 (6th Cir.1972).

The ultimate success of the Manual's suggested procedures for large or complex litigation depends on the willingness of the courts to accept responsibility for the management of these cases and to be innovative in the exercise of their powers.　But there may be unanticipated, and possibly undesirable, side effects to this movement toward judicial management of lawsuits that warrant careful scrutiny.　For example, to what extent should the system permit trial judges to exercise discretion with regard to pretrial matters when, because of the interlocutory and ad hoc character of the conduct, their decisions largely will be unreviewable?　And how will the adversary system be affected by the fostering of active judicial intervention in the processing of litigation?　Will the role of the lawyer be limited or enhanced?

CHAPTER 10

ADJUDICATION WITHOUT TRIAL OR BY SPECIAL PROCEEDING

SECTION A. ATTACKING THE TRUTH OF THE PLEADINGS—SUMMARY JUDGMENT

THE "SPEAKING DEMURRER"

Under traditional rules, a demurrer or equivalent challenge could be determined only upon the face of the complaint. The so-called "speaking demurrer," one in which the challenging party added outside information to show that a cause of action or defense could not be proved, was not permitted. What was the rationale for this rule?

Many jurisdictions have recognized, however, that there are instances in which, although it appears from the pleadings that a genuine dispute exists, it can be shown that there is no material factual disagreement between the parties, and a trial would be a waste of time. Hence these jurisdictions have found ways to permit a "speaking demurrer" in appropriate cases. Originally this was done through judicial determinations that courts have "inherent power" to strike "sham" pleadings.

The difficulty with this approach was that it was at least partially based upon a fiction and became subject to considerable uncertainty and abuse. Is a "sham" pleading one that states a claim or defense that cannot be proved at trial, or one that was filed in bad faith? What kind of evidence is acceptable to expose a sham pleading? How much evidence is required before a case can be dismissed? Can a decision be rendered only on a portion of the case? These and similar questions have led most jurisdictions to adopt a formal procedure to permit immediate disposition of part or all of an alleged claim or defense that the facts clearly do or do not substantiate. The procedure that has evolved usually is referred to as a motion for summary judgment. See, e. g., Federal Rule 56. See generally Baumann, *Evolution of the Summary Judgment Procedure*, 31 Ind.L.J. 329 (1956); Korn & Paley, *Survey of Summary Judgment, Judgment on the Pleadings and Related Pre-Trial Procedures*, 42 Cornell L.Q. 483 (1957).

In many modern systems, the formalistic distinctions between a demurrer and summary judgment—between "speaking" and "nonspeaking" motions— have been blurred. For example, Federal Rules 12(b) (6) and 12(c) both provide that in the event that matters beyond the face of the pleading are submitted on behalf of the motion, the court may treat the motion as one for summary judgment. Does this provision make sense? Note that Rule 12(f) does not permit a motion to strike an insufficient defense to be treated as a motion for summary judgment. Should it be amended to do so? See N.Y.C.P.L.R. 3211(b), (c).

———

Read Federal Rule of Civil Procedure 56 and the accompanying materials in the Supplement.

———

LUNDEEN v. CORDNER

United States Court of Appeals, Eighth Circuit, 1966.
354 F.2d 401.

GIBSON, Circuit Judge. * * *

Appellant, plaintiff below, (hereinafter referred to as plaintiff) is a former wife of one Joseph Cordner, deceased. During their marriage two children were born, Maureen Joan Cordner and Michael Joseph Cordner. Prior to the time of his death Joseph Cordner was working in Libya. Mr. Cordner's employer Socony Mobil Oil Company, Inc. (Socony) carried a group life insurance contract with Metropolitan Life Insurance Company, (Metropolitan) under which Mr. Cordner as the insured had in 1956 designated his children, Maureen and Michael, as equal beneficiaries. In 1958 Joseph Cordner, having been divorced by plaintiff, married intervener, France Jeanne Cordner. In April 1960 a child was born of this second marriage. On October 3, 1962 Joseph Cordner died. During all periods above mentioned Mr. Cordner was in the employ of Socony stationed in Libya. The insurance policy and the annuity were in effect and due proof of loss was made. The contest for the proceeds arises between adverse claimants; the original designated beneficiaries, Maureen Joan and Michael Joseph Cordner; and France Jeanne Cordner, the second wife of assured, and Northwestern, as Trustee under the Last Will and Testament of Joseph F. Cordner, deceased.

On November 5, 1963, plaintiff as guardian and on behalf of her two children Maureen and Michael Cordner, the named beneficiaries, sued the insurer, Metropolitan, to recover the proceeds of the policy. Metropolitan answered that there were adverse claims to the policy benefits. Thereafter, Northwestern as the Trustee under the Last Will and Testament of the deceased, Joseph Cordner, was interpleaded as an additional defendant. Appellee, France J. Cordner, then intervened in the action. Both intervener and Northwestern allege that sometime in 1961 the decedent effected a change of beneficiaries [in favor of intervener]. * * *

It is clear that the first two children of decedent, Maureen and Michael, are the named beneficiaries. However, it is asserted that Joseph Cordner did everything within his power to effect a change of beneficiaries as alleged by intervener. Intervener presented affidavits and exhibits in support of her position and moved for summary judgment. The motion was granted and plaintiff contests this ruling on the ground that a summary judgment is not proper at this point in the litigation and that there remains a genuine issue on a material fact. It is now our task to determine if the summary judgment was properly granted.

* * * Plaintiff accepts as controlling the general rule of law that an insured's attempt to change his beneficiary will be given effect if all that remains to be done is a ministerial duty on the part of the insurer. * * *

Therefore, if deceased completed all the necessary steps required of him to change the beneficiary in his policy, intervener would be entitled to judgment. Furthermore, if intervener can demonstrate this fact so clearly that there is no longer a genuine issue of fact, summary judgment may be properly granted under provisions of Rule 56(c) of the Fed.R.Civ.P. * * *

We are of the opinion that the affidavits and exhibits introduced by intervener clearly and undeniably indicate that deceased made a change in his policy's beneficiaries. First, it appears that after deceased's marriage in 1958 to intervener he amended his group hospitalization and employee savings plan to include intervener. Furthermore, certain correspondence conclusively indicates that a change in the life insurance was actually made.

Mr. Iten, an employee of Socony in Libya, whose duties included administration of company benefit plans, * * * prepared a letter to the New York office, dated April 19, 1961, stating that Joseph Cordner desired information as to who were his present beneficiaries under the company benefit plans and that Mr. Cordner had married for a second time and was not certain whether he had changed his beneficiary. * * *

Mr. Iten was transferred from Libya shortly thereafter and his duties were assumed by Mr. Burks. Burks by affidavit stated that early in 1961 Mr. Cordner came to him with a request to change his beneficiaries; that Burks issued the necessary forms to Cordner and gave him instructions on how to complete the forms, at which time Cordner produced a copy of his Will made in North Dakota while vacationing from Libya in 1960. They discussed the form of beneficiary designation which might be appropriate under the terms of the Will. Mr. Cordner personally completed the forms, endorsed the beneficiary changes he wished to make on the back of each form, signed the forms in Burks' presence, (the latter acting as a witness to the signature) and then left the completed forms with Burks for transmittal. Since Burks was unfamiliar with the type of beneficiary changes endorsed on the forms he made a thermofax copy of Cordner's Will and sent this reproduction together with the completed change of beneficiary forms to the New York office in a letter dated May 11, 1961, which letter in part reads as follows:

"Please review the enclosed employee change of beneficiary forms and advise us if this designation is acceptable under the plan."

The Home Office responded by stating in a letter dated June 1, 1961:

"We are processing the Change of Beneficiary forms completed by the above employee [J. F. Cordner] and forwarded to us.

* * * We see no reason why the designation will not be acceptable."

Mr. Burks in his earlier affidavit of March 30, 1963 states that to the best of his recollection the change of beneficiary requested by Cordner was as follows:

> " 'One-fourth of the proceeds to my wife France Jeanne Cordner and the balance to the Northwestern National Bank of Minneapolis, Minneapolis, Minnesota in trust for the uses and purposes set forth in my Last Will and Testament.' "

Burks in his second affidavit prepared for the purpose of the summary judgment proceeding confirmed the factual statements in his earlier affidavit and detailed the discussion and the procedures employed in the requested change of beneficiary by Cordner. He further stated that since the New York office had the Certificate for endorsement and since the Home Office stated in its letter of June 1, 1961 that they were processing the change of beneficiary forms he had no reason to believe that the processing of the changes had not proceeded to completion in the normal course. He was in the New York office at the time when a search of the files was made for the change of beneficiary forms, which, of course, they were unable to locate. When he returned to Tripoli, with instructions from the New York office to continue the search and to forward to New York all company papers having to do with Mr. Cordner's employment, he found a copy of a letter addressed to Cordner by his attorney suggesting the form of beneficiary designation required to effect the provisions of his Will. Burks then recalled that Mr. Cordner had referred to this same letter when discussing beneficiary changes in 1961 and that Cordner had used the suggested language in completing his change of beneficiary forms. After stating that he cannot restate from memory the text of the changes, he said that "I can and do reconfirm, upon my own direct knowledge and positive recollection that beneficiary changes so made by Joseph Franklin Cordner were in the form suggested by his attorney's letter and quoted verbatim from that letter in my prior affidavit."

Further correspondence indicates that the change of beneficiary forms were forwarded to the employer's Annuity and Insurance Department. A search of the department, however, never uncovered the form or the exact language used therein. It also appears by affidavit that all of the above related correspondence was properly identified and was prepared, mailed, received and kept as part of the business records of the company.

Plaintiff presents no counter evidence nor in any way indicates that intervener's evidence is not worthy of belief. Therefore, we believe there is no genuine issue of fact on this point. It is clear that Joseph Cordner actually made a change in the beneficiaries of his life insurance policy.

However, to entitle intervener to summary judgment, it must not only be clear that a change was made, but the wording of that change must be shown beyond any reasonable and genuine dispute. This point, too, was well covered in intervener's supporting papers.

* * *

From the affidavit of the attorney concerning the discussion of deceased's desires, from the letter written by the attorney explaining how the beneficiaries should be changed to effectuate these desires, and from the wording of the Last Will and Testament it is clear that Joseph Cordner intended to change the beneficiaries of his insurance policy by giving one-fourth to intervener and the balance to Northwestern in trust. We can presume that this intent remained with Mr. Cordner during the intervening ten months between the Will's execution and the date of the beneficiary change. * * *

However, in addition to this presumption we have the uncontested affidavits of a non-interested third party who was in a position to be aware of the actual wording of the change. The affiant, Mr. Harold Burks, was a fellow employee of Mr. Cordner in Libya, and supervised Mr. Cordner in filling out the required change of beneficiary forms. Mr. Burks is probably the only person that was in a position to be aware of the wording of the document. His affidavits are entitled to considerable weight in determining the merits of a summary judgment motion, especially where there is no indication of any counter-evidence. Moreover, Mr. Burks' assistance in processing the change in beneficiary was done in the regular course of business of Socony, and pursuant to his assigned duties. It has been held that the clear affidavits from the only persons in a position to be aware of a factual situation can well serve as the basis for a summary judgment. Dyer v. MacDougall, 201 F.2d 265 (2 Cir. 1952).

* * *

So, in support of intervener's claim there is undisputed proof that Mr. Cordner had manifested an intent to give intervener one-fourth of his insurance proceeds with the balance going into the trust established by his Will. It is likewise clear beyond any shadow of doubt that Mr. Cordner subsequently made a change in his insurance beneficiaries. The logical conclusion is clear. He made the change in accordance with his prior expressed intent. This presumption is supported by the two affidavits of Mr. Burks which recite from direct and positive recollection that the beneficiary changes were copied from Mr. Cordner's letter from his attorney and were in form exactly as alleged by intervener.

In response to the overwhelming documentary evidence supported by affidavits all of which consistently showed that Cordner had requested a change of beneficiary in accordance with his lawyer's letter and his own Last Will and Testament, the plaintiff submitted her own counter-affidavit to the effect that Mr. Cordner was very much interested in the welfare of his first two children (the named beneficiaries) and was aware of the future financial difficulties they would face. No further information was offered. The Court, therefore, was not presented with a situation where it was asked to weigh conflicting affidavits. The problem was only, did the affidavits and exhibits of intervener sustain the necessary burden in order to allow a summary judgment? The trial court felt the burden was sustained, and from the above related facts we agree with the trial court's conclusion. * * *

We are of the opinion that if this information were presented at trial, intervener would be entitled to a directed verdict in her favor, and it has been said that if the information presented entitles one to a directed verdict, a summary judgment is in order.   *   *   *   Intervener having made a sufficient showing, it then rests upon the plaintiff to specify at least some evidence which could be produced at trial.   *   *   *   Plaintiff apparently is of the opinion that, since she makes a prima facie case by merely introducing the Certificate showing her children as designated beneficiaries, she is entitled to a trial on the issue of (1) whether any change of beneficiary was made, and (2) if so, what changes were actually made.   This we do not feel is a correct view of the law.

The counter-affidavit of the plaintiff does not meet the issues raised and supported by the intervener.   This leaves no genuine issue as to any material fact, and presents a predicate for a summary judgment under Rule 56(c), Fed. R.Civ.P.

*   *   *

The real gravamen of plaintiff's objection is not that there is conflicting evidence but rather that the summary judgment rests upon the affidavits of Harold Burks.   His testimony being so vital to intervener's cause, it is asserted that the case should proceed to trial in order that the demeanor of the witness could be observed and his testimony subjected to the test of cross-examination.

In passing on this contention it might be well to make four preliminary observations.   First, affiant Burks appears to be an unbiased witness.   He has no financial or personal interest in the outcome of this litigation.   Second, there is no doubt but what his testimony is competent both in regard to his mental capacity and his being in a position to directly observe the facts related in his affidavits.   Third, his participation in the change of beneficiaries was in the regular course of his duties with Socony.   Finally, both affidavits are positive, internally consistent, unequivocal, and in full accord with the documentary exhibits.   Therefore, even though cross-examination is a trial right which must be carefully protected, in this case, unlike many others there is no obvious advantage to be gained from a cross-examination.   If there were, a summary judgment might arguably be improper.   But where there is no indication that the affiant was biased, dishonest, mistaken, unaware or unsure of the facts, the cases declaring that cross-examination is necessary when one of the above is present, have no application here.   There being no positive showing that this witness's testimony could be impeached or that he might have additional testimony valuable to plaintiff, summary judgment was properly granted.   The opposing party cannot as a matter of course force a trial merely in order to cross-examine such an affiant, nor must the Court deny the motion for summary judgment on the basis of a vague supposition that something might turn up at the trial.   *   *   *

There is absolutely no showing that a trial would produce any different or additional evidence.   It appears that Burks is now stationed in Singapore, far beyond the subpoena powers of the trial court. Neither party would be able to compel his attendance before the trial court. Since this witness is out of the jurisdiction, any of the parties, on the other hand, would be free to introduce Burks' testimony by use of a deposition. Therefore, in all likelihood Burks would never have to appear in open court. What would plaintiff have to gain by forcing a trial under these circumstances? We feel very little, if anything. A full trial would not give plaintiff an opportunity to cross-examine Burks in open court, nor would it unveil his demeanor to the trier of fact.

In the event of a trial plaintiff would only be free to obtain Burks' sworn testimony by deposition or upon written interrogatories pursuant to Rule 28(b) or Rule 31, Fed.R.Civ.P. and by 28 U.S.C.A. § 1783(a) (1). Plaintiff, however, was free to take this action even prior to the present motion for summary judgment but chose not to do so. When the motion for summary judgment was presented, plaintiff, if she felt Burks had information valuable to her cause, was again free to move for a delay in judgment and secure Burks' deposition. Again plaintiff took no action. Apparently plaintiff felt she had nothing to gain by a deposition, yet under the circumstances of this case that is probably the most she could expect even if this case went to trial. Therefore, we do not feel that plaintiff is in a position at this time to force a trial. A trial would not secure Burks' presence, it would only force the taking of his deposition, a course previously open to plaintiff which she elected not to pursue.

* * *

The position declaring that a party opposed to a summary judgment based upon affidavits must assume some initiative in showing that a factual issue actually exists is perfectly sound in the light of Rule 56, Fed.R.Civ.P., which specifically allows the use of affidavits in summary judgment proceedings. For if plaintiff's position is correct that an affiant's credibility is always an issue for the trial court, then the granting of a summary judgment would be virtually impossible when it is based in any way upon an affidavit. Rule 56 would be nullified by the prevailing party's use of one affidavit and the bald objection by the opposing party to the affiant's credibility. The reference in this rule to "affidavits" would therefore be of no effect.

This does not mean that an affiant's credibility cannot properly be put in issue by a litigant, but in doing so specific facts must be properly produced. At this point the 1963 amendment to Rule 56(e) comes into play requiring the opposing party to respond or suffer the fate of a summary judgment, if otherwise appropriate. Plaintiff failed to respond to the adequate and substantial showing of intervener, so the trial court properly granted the summary judgment. Keeping in mind that the purpose of the summary judgment is to avoid useless trials, from the circumstances of this case we believe a trial would indeed be a useless waste of time and expense to the parties as well as a needless inconvenience to the Court.

* * *

Judgment affirmed.

NOTES AND QUESTIONS

1. Of what consequence is it that the intervenor would, at trial, have had the burden of persuading the trier of fact that it was more probable than not that decedent had changed the names of the beneficiaries? Did the appellate court erroneously assume that the burden was on plaintiff to show that the beneficiaries had not been changed? If so, should the decision below have been reversed?

Consider the paragraph in Cal.Code Civ.Proc. § 437c, which is set out in the Supplement, dealing with matters of credibility and lack of an opportunity for cross-examination. What is the objective of this paragraph? Should it be added to Federal Rule 56?

In DYER v. MacDOUGALL, 201 F.2d 265, 268–69 (2d Cir.1952), plaintiff brought suit for slander; defendant was granted summary judgment on the basis of the affidavits of all the persons present when the slanderous statements allegedly had been made. All of the affidavits denied plaintiff's allegations. The appellate court affirmed:

> * * * [I]f the cause went to trial, the plaintiff would have no witnesses by whom he could prove the slanders alleged * * * except the two defendants, * * * and they would all deny that the slanders had been uttered. On such a showing how could he escape a directed verdict? It is true that the carriage, behavior, bearing, manner and appearance of a witness—in short, his "demeanor"—is a part of the evidence. The words used are by no means all that we rely on in making up our minds about the truth of a question that arises in our ordinary affairs, and it is abundantly settled that a jury is as little confined to them as we are. They may, and indeed they should, take into consideration the whole nexus of sense impressions which they get from a witness. This we have again and again declared, and have rested our affirmance of findings of fact of a judge, or of a jury, on the hypothesis that this part of the evidence may have turned the scale. Moreover, such evidence may satisfy the tribunal, not only that the witness' testimony is not true, but that the truth is the opposite of his story; for the denial of one, who has a motive to deny, may be uttered with such hesitation, discomfort, arrogance or defiance, as to give assurance that he is fabricating, and that, if he is, there is no alternative but to assume the truth of what he denies.

> Nevertheless, although it is therefore true that in strict theory a party having the affirmative might succeed in convincing a jury of the truth of his allegations in spite of the fact that all the witnesses denied them, we think it plain that a verdict would nevertheless have to be directed against him. This is owing to the fact that otherwise in such cases there could not be an effective appeal from the judge's disposition of a motion for a directed verdict. He, who has seen and heard the "demeanor" evidence, may have been right or wrong in thinking that it gave rational support to a verdict; yet, since that evidence has disappeared, it will be impossible for an appellate court to say which he was. Thus, he would become the final arbiter in all cases where the evidence of witnesses present in court might be determinative.

2. The last two sentences of Rule 56(e) were added in 1963. According to the Advisory Committee on the Federal Rules, the change was designed to overcome a line of cases, chiefly in the Third Circuit, holding that a party against whom summary judgment was sought could successfully defeat the motion without

filing affidavits if "well pleaded" averments in the nonmovant's pleadings contradicted the moving party's affidavits on a material issue of fact. Judicial Conference of the United States, *Report of Proposed Amendments to Certain Rules of Civil Procedure for the United States District Courts,* 31 F.R.D. 621, 648 (1962); Wright, *Rule 56(e): A Case Study on the Need for Amending the Federal Rules,* 69 Harv.L.Rev. 839 (1956); Note, *Summary Judgment Under Federal Rule of Civil Procedure 56—A Need for a Clarifying Amendment,* 48 Iowa L.Rev. 453 (1963). Does this mean that the question of which party has the burden of persuasion is eliminated as a factor in deciding whether summary judgment is appropriate? See generally Louis, *Federal Summary Judgment Doctrine: A Critical Analysis,* 83 Yale L.J. 745 (1974).

Why should averments in the pleadings be disregarded when they contradict an opposing party's affidavits? Should it make any difference if such averments are contained in a pleading that has been verified by the party on whose behalf it was filed?

3. Does the fact that plaintiff in *Lundeen* failed to take the deposition of Burks under Federal Rule 31, by itself, justify the decision in the case? Is the same true of the failure to proceed under Rule 28?

4. General discussions of summary judgment can be found in Divilbiss, *Summary Judgments in Missouri—Some Disturbing Aberrations,* 32 Mo.L.Rev. 29 (1965); Forkosch, *Summary Judgment in Automobile Negligence Cases: A Procedural Analysis and Suggestions,* 53 Cornell L.Rev. 814 (1968); Guiher, *Summary Judgments—Tactical Problem of the Trial Lawyer,* 48 Va.L.Rev. 1263 (1962); Zack, *California Summary Judgment: The Need for Legislative Reform,* 59 Calif.L.Rev. 439 (1971); Comment, *Summary Judgment—Rule 56,* 51 Nw. U.L.Rev. 370 (1956).

CROSS v. UNITED STATES

United States Court of Appeals, Second Circuit, 1964.
336 F.2d 431.

MOORE, Circuit Judge: In this income tax refund suit, plaintiffs-appellees claim that they were entitled to a deduction of $1,300 on their joint return for the year 1954 because of expenses incurred by Professor Ephraim Cross in connection with his summer travel to various Mediterranean and European countries. Upon appellees' motion for summary judgment, the district court, whose examination of the facts included the affidavits of several professors tending to indicate the desirability of foreign travel for a teacher of languages as well as the pre-trial deposition of Professor Cross, concluded that there was no genuine issue as to any material fact, and granted appellees' motion. * * * The Government opposed the summary judgment procedure, claiming a right to cross-examine appellees as to the nature of their expenses and the educational benefits allegedly sought and also to cross-examine the affiant professors. On this appeal the only issue is whether there are triable issues of fact which render the award of summary judgment erroneous.

In 1954 Professor Cross was an Assistant Professor at City College in New York where he taught French, Spanish and romance linguistics (described by him as the study of the development of Latin into the romance languages, the study of the various dialects and the historic stages of those dialects). He, his wife and a pet dog sailed from New York on June 30, 1954 aboard a French freighter. The ship put in briefly in Portugal, Morocco, Tangiers, Oran, Algiers, Naples and Genoa and appellees spent a day or so in each place. When the freighter arrived at Marseilles, twenty-one days after leaving New York, appellees separated. Mrs. Cross joined a friend and continued touring while Professor Cross and their pet dog travelled to Paris. Although he did not pursue a formal course of study or engage in research, Professor Cross did visit schools, courts of law, churches, book publishers, theaters, motion pictures, restaurants, cafes and other places of amusement, read newspapers, listen to radio broadcasts, converse with students and teachers and attend political meetings. He rejoined his wife in this country on September 23, 1954 after his return aboard a French passenger liner.

Section 162(a), Int.Rev.Code of 1954 permits a deduction for "all the ordinary and necessary expenses paid or incurred   *   *   *   in carrying on any trade or business   *   *   *." The Regulations promulgated under that section, Treas. Reg. 1.162–5, state:

"Expenses for education—(a) Expenditures made by a taxpayer for his education are deductible if they are for education (including research activities) undertaken primarily for the purpose of:

"(1) Maintaining or improving skills required by the taxpayer in his employment or trade or business,   *   *   *

*   *   *   *   *   *   *   *   *   *

"Whether or not education is of the type referred to in subparagraph (1) of this paragraph shall be determined upon the basis of all the facts of each case. If it is customary for other established members of the taxpayer's trade or business to undertake such education, the taxpayer will ordinarily be considered to have undertaken this education for the purposes described in subparagraph (1) of this paragraph.

*   *   *   *   *   *   *   *   *   *

"(c) In general, a taxpayer's expenditures for travel (including travel while on sabbatical leave) as a form of education shall be considered as primarily personal in nature and therefore not deductible."

Appellees claim, and the district court held, that all of Professor Cross's expenses are deductible. Professor Cross asserted in his deposition, which was taken for discovery purposes and did not include cross-examination,

"My purpose [in making the trip] was to maintain my contacts with my foreign languages for the purpose of maintaining and improving my skill as a linguist and teacher of languages, and to make my general teaching more effective, and to extend my contacts with foreign culture which I have to teach in connection with my teaching of foreign languages per se, and this can be done effectively and properly only by going into a foreign language area."

The Government disputes this explanation. It contends that all or at least part of Professor Cross's travel was a vacation and thus a personal living expense for which a deduction is not allowed under Section 162 * * *. Moreover, the Government challenges the amount of the claimed deduction and questions whether any portion of that sum was expended on behalf of Mrs. Cross.

We believe that summary judgment was improvidently granted and that the Government is entitled to a trial at which all the circumstances may be developed for the consideration of the trier of fact. Rule 56(c), Fed.R.Civ.P. permits summary judgment only where "there is no genuine issue as to any material fact," a state of affairs not normally encountered where the problem is whether expenses are ordinary and necessary in carrying on a taxpayer's trade or business. * * * Before travelling expenses can be allowed as deductible, there must be a factual determination of what parts, if any, are to be attributed to vacation travel or to educational advancement.

The essentially factual character of the issue is particularly apparent here, where the ultimate facts were warmly contested. While there was no dispute that Professor Cross was a teacher of languages and that he travelled abroad, many of the facts remain largely within his own knowledge and the Government should have the opportunity to test his credibility on cross-examination. Summary judgment is particularly inappropriate where "the inferences which the parties seek to have drawn deal with questions of motive, intent and subjective feelings and reactions." Empire Electronics Co. v. United States, 311 F. 2d 175, 180 (2d Cir. 1962) * * *. " 'A judge may not, on a motion for summary judgment, draw fact inferences. * * * Such inferences may be drawn only on a trial.' " Bragen v. Hudson County News Co., 278 F.2d 615, 618 (3d Cir. 1960). While we have recently emphasized that ordinarily the bare allegations of the pleadings, unsupported by specific evidentiary data, will not alone defeat a motion for summary judgment, Dressler v. M/V Sandpiper, 331 F.2d 130 (2d Cir. 1964), this principle does not justify summary relief where, as here, the disputed questions of fact turn exclusively on the credibility of movants' witnesses.

To the teacher of modern languages, particularly in a country far removed from the European continent, it is highly important that his linguistic ear be retuned as frequently as possible to the ways in which a foreign language is expressed. Moreover, a thorough familiarity with the current social, political and cultural climate of a country properly may be regarded as a prerequisite to effective classroom presentation of its language. * * *

On the other hand, a mere pleasure trip through various countries by a professor who has some fluency with the language of each country might well not fall within the deductible category. * * *

Who can doubt that the alert American trial lawyer as a part of a summer vacation might not profit greatly by spending some time at the Old Bailey listening to British barristers exhibit their skills. The surgeon, too, might be benefitted in his profession by observing some delicate operation conducted by a European surgeon of renown. Yet it is questionable whether such tangible evidences of constant interest in one's profession entitle a taxpayer to deduct all his summer vacation expenses.

In addition to determining whether the trip was devoted in whole or in part to educational advancement, the trier of the facts will have to ascertain such amounts as are to be attributed to such purpose. Were the preliminary twenty-one days prior to the Marseilles landing all part of an educational program? What part, if any, was allocable to Mrs. Cross? What charges were incurred by the dog? Although probably *de minimis*, the Treasury frequently watches every penny and might not be generously inclined even though the dog were a French poodle.

The district court reasoned that summary judgment should be granted because the Government did not adduce facts to refute Professor Cross's claims as to the purpose of his trip, and that the Government had an opportunity to cross-examine when taking his deposition. The "right to use depositions for discovery * * * does not mean that they are to supplant the right to call and examine the adverse party * * * before the jury. * * * '[W]e cannot very well overestimate the importance of having the witness examined and cross-examined in presence of the court and jury.' " Arnstein v. Porter, 154 F.2d 464, 470 (2d Cir. 1946). By the same process, Professor Cross will have an opportunity to show with greater particularity that his more modern approach to the problem of linguistic improvement is far superior to the old-fashioned classroom lecture method.

Reversed and remanded for trial.

NOTES AND QUESTIONS

1. The *Cross* case is noted with approval in 53 Geo.L.J. 502 (1965). Can the case be reconciled with *Lundeen*? Didn't the court in *Cross* blatantly ignore the express language of Federal Rule 56(e)? Why wasn't the Government at least required to cross-examine Professor Cross at the deposition as to the truth of his assertions? In this regard consider the following excerpt from the opinion of the Supreme Court in ADICKES v. S. H. KRESS & CO., 398 U.S. 144, 159–60, 90 S.Ct. 1598, 1609–10, 26 L.Ed.2d 142, 155–56 (1970), in which the Court overturned a summary judgment for respondent:

Pointing to Rule 56(e), as amended in 1963, respondent argues that it was incumbent on petitioner to come forward with an affidavit properly asserting the presence of [facts] * * * to avoid summary judgment. Respondent notes in this regard that none of the materials upon which petitioner relied met the requirements of Rule 56(e).

This argument does not withstand scrutiny, however, for both the commentary on and background of the 1963 amendment conclusively show that it was not intended to modify the burden of the moving party under Rule 56(c) to show initially the absence of a genuine issue concerning any material fact. The Advisory Committee note on the amendment states that the changes were not designed to "affect the ordinary standards applicable to the summary judgment." And, in a comment directed specifically to a contention like respondent's, the Committee stated that "[w]here the evidentiary matter in support of the motion does not establish the absence of a genuine issue, summary judgment must be denied *even if no opposing evidentiary matter is presented."* Because respondent did not meet its initial burden of establishing [facts that would justify summary judgment] * * *, petitioner here was not required to come forward with suitable opposing affidavits.

2. What did the court in *Cross* mean when it stated that the trial judge was not entitled to "draw fact inferences"? Could more than a single inference be drawn from the facts presented by plaintiff through affidavits and deposition? For an interesting discussion as to whether matters of inference and credibility are questions of fact for summary judgment purposes, see Note, *Summary Judgment Under Federal Rule of Civil Procedure 56—A Need for a Clarifying Amendment,* 48 Iowa L.Rev. 453, 461–63, 468–69 (1963). *Cf.* pp. 938–48, infra.

WHALEY v. FOWLER

California District Court of Appeal, First District, 1957.
152 Cal.App.2d 379, 313 P.2d 97.

BRAY, Justice. In this action for alleged malpractice against defendant Sisters' Hospital, a corporation, and defendant physicians, the superior court entered an order dismissing the complaint as against said corporation and granted summary judgment in its favor. Plaintiff appeals therefrom.

* * *

The complaint alleged that defendants and each of them so carelessly and negligently attended and treated plaintiff for compound fractures of the left tibia and fibula as to cause osteomyelitis to develop in plaintiff's left leg, and that as a proximate result of said treatment plaintiff suffered the amputation of that leg below the knee. Defendant hospital's answer denied the material allegations of the complaint. Defendant hospital filed a motion for order dismissing the complaint and for summary judgment pursuant to section 437c, Code of Civil Procedure, on the ground that the action had no merit. Some 16 affidavits used in another proceeding were filed by reference in support of the motion. Two counter affidavits were filed.

* * *

In a proceeding under section 437c, Code of Civil Procedure, issue finding rather than issue determination is the pivot upon which the summary judgment law turns. * * * Whether an issue of fact exists is to be determined from the affidavits which have been filed. * * * If any doubt exists whether summary judgment should be granted, it should be resolved against the moving party. * * *

With these rules in mind let us examine the affidavits, first, those of defendant hospital, the moving party. The administrator and medical record custodian of the hospital averred that its records accurately recorded the treatment given patients, factual and medical information concerning their condition, any incident or occurrence affecting the patient's condition, and any accidental event occurring in connection with the patient's hospitalization and treatment. The record of the hospitalization and treatment of plaintiff contains no report or reference to any accidental occurrence or event affecting his physical welfare or condition.   It is the practice to report any such incident to the administrator and none concerning plaintiff has been received.

Norma Gintert, graduate and registered nurse, surgical nurse, assisted defendant Fowler in surgical procedures upon plaintiff during the latter's treatment at the hospital on four different occasions.   She has had 4½ years training and experience in surgical nursing procedure and is familiar with the standard of practice in surgical nursing procedure in the Santa Cruz area. (The hospital is located in Santa Cruz.)   Her actions and those of the other nurses assisting Dr. Fowler at these operations were in conformity with the standard of practice in the vicinity.   No accident or injury occurred to the patient during any of these operations.   At no time has she been employed by Dr. Fowler.   He is not employed by the hospital but is an independent orthopedic surgeon accredited to the hospital.   A similar affidavit was made by the "surgical supervisor and circulating for operative procedures" nurse, who was present at each of the operations.   Twelve registered nurses made affidavits to the effect that they cared for plaintiff as floor nurses during their respective tours of duty while he was in the hospital.   They administered drugs, medicines and treatment prescribed by Dr. Fowler, following orders directly. While under their care no accident or injury occurred which directly or indirectly affected plaintiff or his condition.   Each is familiar with the standards of nursing practice in the area.   The nursing care administered by the particular affiant and by the other nurses when observed by the affiant was in accordance with the standard practice.   None of the affiants had ever been employed by either Dr. Jacobson or Dr. Fowler.   Each nurse followed the specific orders of these doctors in respect to prescribed care and treatment of plaintiff, but in other matters followed the standard of nursing practiced in the area and the instructions and orders of the hospital.

Plaintiff filed two counter affidavits.   The affidavit of plaintiff's attorney states that he is familiar with the facts of the action, and if sworn as a witness could testify thereto;   that he has studied the hospital records and charts of plaintiff in connection with the accident described in the complaint;   that he took the deposition of defendant Fowler;   that defendant hospital is sued as a defendant because the negligence of its agents or employees caused plaintiff's personal injuries;   that an infection developed in plaintiff's left leg while he was a patient at the hospital;   that said infection was uncontrolled;   that the facts established by the hospital records and Fowler deposition disclose that the hospital is jointly negligent with defendant Fowler.

Obviously, this affidavit states no facts, merely hearsay and conclusions of law.   Neither the hospital records nor the deposition of defendant Fowler was before the court.   Said affidavit is of no value in determining whether there were issuable questions of *fact*.   *   *   *

Plaintiff's affidavit, after stating that the hospital is sued because of the negligence of its agents or employees that proximately contributed to plaintiff's injuries, states that he was a patient at the hospital from January 12, 1954, to September 28;   that during said period an infection developed in his left leg; that it was uncontrolled and that as a direct result thereof, it was necessary to amputate his leg; that the agents and/or employees of the hospital were careless and negligent in treatment of him in that said infection remained uncontrolled, and in that they failed to take necessary preventive measures to control said infection.

* * *

In McComsey v. Leaf, * * * 36 Cal.App.2d 132, 97 P.2d 242, the court reviews a number of authorities and determines that the rule on motions for summary judgments is that counter affidavits may state ultimate facts and conclusions of law and need not be composed wholly of evidentiary facts, and that to warrant a summary judgment there must be a failure on the part of the party defending against the motion to satisfy the court that there is any basis for his claim. * * * Concerning conclusions of fact and law in counter affidavits the court in Eagle Oil & Ref. Co. v. Prentice, supra, 19 Cal.2d 553, 561, 122 P.2d 264, 268, said: "Plaintiff asserts that defendant's affidavits contain nothing but conclusions of fact and law and are thus insufficient. As we have seen it is not necessary that the averments be rigidly restricted to evidentiary matter. It may be that some of the allegations or statements are somewhat in the nature of conclusions, but we are satisfied that facts within the knowledge of the affiants and to which they are competent to testify, are set forth with sufficient particularity, and from which it appears that a bona fide defense to the action exists. This is especially true when we are mindful of the rule of liberal construction applicable to cases of this character."

With these rules in mind let us examine plaintiff's affidavit. First, there is the averment that plaintiff's injuries were due to the hospital's negligence in not controlling the infection. This, in view of the authorities above cited, raises an issue of fact. Secondly, plaintiff avers as facts that an infection developed and that it was uncontrolled. Even a layman can testify to the fact that an infection developed in a member of his body and that it was uncontrolled. * * * It must be remembered that on this type of motion the case is not to be tried. The sole question to be determined is whether or not there are issuable questions of fact.

Plaintiff says that the infection in his leg remained uncontrolled and was the cause of the amputation. Defendant's affidavits did not deny that the infection was the cause of the amputation, and thereby it would appear that it was uncontrolled. The real issue is whether that fact was due to negligence of the nurses or any of them as the hospital's liability would only arise in such case. The nurses' affidavits categorically state that whatever they did was in accordance with good practice. Plaintiff, a layman, says, in effect, that it was not—it was negligently done. Defendant concedes that conclusions of fact and of law may considered upon a motion for summary judgment, but contends that the conclusion of fact, negligence, stated by plaintiff cannot be considered because as a layman he is not competent to come to that conclusion. In view of the admitted facts here, namely, the fact that the infection remained uncontrolled and necessitated the amputation, plus plaintiff's observation of the care or lack of care given him, together with the rule that his affidavit must be liberally construed   *   *   *, we feel that plaintiff's conclusion, although a layman's may be considered upon this type of motion.   As to the basic question, negligence, we feel " ' *   *   * *It never could have been, or in justice ought to have been, the intention of those who framed our Practice Act and rules thereunder that the decision of such a serious question as this should be flung off on a motion for summary judgment.   *   *   *'* "   (McComsey v. Leaf, supra, 36 Cal.App.2d at page 137, 97 P.2d at page 245.)   It must be remembered that on this type of motion plaintiff is not required to prove defendant's negligence.   He is only required to show that an issue of fact exists. "The summary judgment statute was not intended nor can it be used as a substitute for existing methods in the trial of issues of fact."   If there is any "doubt as to the propriety of the motion, courts should, without hesitancy, deny the same."   Travelers Indemnity Co. v. McIntosh, 112 Cal.App.2d 177, 182, 245 P.2d 1065, 1068   *   *   *.

In view of our decision, we deem it unnecessary to determine whether or not the facts alleged in plaintiff's affidavits raise the issue of res ipsa loquitur.

The judgment is reversed.

NOTES AND QUESTIONS

1.   Reread *Alderman v. Baltimore & O. R. Co.*, p. 35, supra, and compare that opinion with those in *Lundeen, Cross,* and *Whaley.*   To what extent does the determination whether or not an issue of fact exists depend upon the nature of the applicable substantive law?

2.   Examine the language of Federal Rule 56(e) and Cal.Code Civ.Proc. § 437c, which accompanies the text of the Federal Rule in the Supplement, dealing with the character and content of the affidavits required to support or oppose a summary-judgment motion.   Should a federal court, in ruling upon a summary-judgment motion, be required to disregard completely all affidavits containing only hearsay or other matters to which the affiant would not be permitted to testify at trial?

Suppose A and B were killed in an automobile accident, and A's executor brings suit against B's executor alleging wrongful death.   Plaintiff moves for summary judgment on the basis of a deposition of an impartial eyewitness who testified that B drove through a red light.   Defendant counters with an affidavit of a police officer who avers that at the scene, shortly after the accident, another impartial eyewitness, now deceased, informed the officer that it was A rather than B who had disobeyed the traffic signal.   Should any attention be paid to defendant's affidavit?   Should a different test be applied to affidavits on a summary-judgment motion in a case that will be tried by a court than in one that will be heard by a jury?

At trial evidence subject to exclusion normally is admitted unless the opposing party raises an objection to it.   Should the same be true of an improper affidavit or other paper filed in a summary-judgment proceeding?   See Klingman v. National Indem. Co., 317 F.2d 850, 854 (7th Cir.1963) (if no objection is made, the court may consider the affidavit); Zack, *California Summary Judg-*

ment: The Need for Legislative Reform, 59 Calif.L.Rev. 439, 466–68, 480–83 (1971).

3.   Assume that a party presents the affidavit of a witness who, if subpoenaed at trial, could refuse to testify because of a special evidentiary privilege.   Should the affidavit be required to aver that the privilege has been waived in order to "show affirmatively that the affiant is competent to testify" within the meaning of Rule 56(e)?   See Banco de Espana v. Federal Reserve Bank, 114 F.2d 438, 445 (2d Cir.1940).

4.   Suppose a party responding to a motion for summary judgment violates Federal Rule 56(c) by filing affidavits on the day of the hearing.   What if the court ignores the affidavits and grants summary judgment against the respondent?   In BEAUFORT CONCRETE CO. v. ATLANTIC STATES CONSTR. CO., 384 U.S. 1004, 86 S.Ct. 1908, 16 L.Ed.2d 1018 (1966), the Supreme Court denied a petition for certiorari in such a case.   Mr. Justice Black dissented:

> I find it entirely at odds with a fair system of trying lawsuits to throw out a litigant's case because his lawyer for negligence or some other reason fails by less than 24 hours to satisfy one of the many procedural time limits.   From the beginning to the end of a lawsuit a lawyer must meet a host of time limits for filing papers.   Surely a judge should not have discretion to enter final judgment at will every time a slight lapse occurs which may delay for half a day or so the service of one of a multitude of papers that must be served during the trial and appeal of a lawsuit.

> * * *   Procedural paper requirements should never stand as a series of dangerous hazards to the achievement of justice through a fair trial on the merits.

Id. at 1005–06, 86 S.Ct. at 1909–10, 16 L.Ed.2d at 1019–20.

5.   Suppose it is clear from the affidavit that summary judgment should be entered against the movant.   Should it be granted?   Courts throughout the country are divided.   If such a disposition is to be permitted, what conditions should be imposed before it is granted?   See generally Note, *The Propriety of Rendering a Summary Judgment in Favor of a Non-Movant Under Wyoming and Federal Rules of Civil Procedure,* 19 Wyo.L.J. 65 (1964); Annot., 48 A.L.R.2d 1188 (1956).   Compare the right of a court to sustain a demurrer against the moving party.   See pp. 473–74, supra.

6.   Note that one party, by filing a motion for summary judgment may force the opposing party to reveal the substance of the witnesses' testimony.   Is there any tactical advantage to obtaining discovery through summary judgment rather than by way of the discovery provisions themselves?   Is there anything wrong in permitting parties to utilize summary judgment for discovery purposes?   Is there any way to prevent them from doing so?

PARTIAL SUMMARY JUDGMENT

Rules and statutes permitting summary judgment normally provide that in circumstances in which judgment cannot be granted on the entire action, the court at least may withdraw from trial those aspects of the case that are established in the summary-judgment proceeding. See, e. g., Federal Rule 56(d). Furthermore, in a substantial number of jurisdictions the trial court may enter judgment with regard to any single claim that has been fully determined. See, e. g., Federal Rule 54(b). A major question remains, however, whether a party may secure the entry of summary judgment as to part of a claim that has not been fully adjudicated. For example, if plaintiff salesperson alleges that defendant employer owes him five items of back salary, and plaintiff conclusively establishes a right to two of those items, should plaintiff be entitled to a judgment on the amount of the two items in order to collect immediately from defendant? Do Federal Rules 56(a) and 56(b) answer the problem? A number of federal courts have denied relief by reading Rule 56(a) in light of Rule 54(b) or Rule 56(d). What justification, if any, exists for these decisions? See 10 Wright & Miller, *Federal Practice and Procedure: Civil* § 2737, at 680–81 (1973); 6 Moore, *Federal Practice* ¶ 56.20 (2d ed.); Comment, *Partial Summary Judgments Under Rule 56(a)*, 32 U.Chi.L.Rev. 816 (1965).

SECTION B.   UNCONTESTED ADJUDICATION AND TERMINATION OF SUIT

1. DEFAULT JUDGMENT

Read Federal Rule of Civil Procedure 55 and the accompanying materials in the Supplement.

COULAS v. SMITH

Supreme Court of Arizona, 1964.
96 Ariz. 325, 395 P.2d 527.

UDALL, Chief Justice. This is an appeal from an order of the Superior Court of Pima County, denying a motion to set aside a judgment entered against the appellant.

* * *

The plaintiff filed a complaint against the defendant and cross-claimant on two counts. The first count was for $669.32 on an open account. The second count was on a promissory note upon which $3,666.67 was alleged to be due. The cross-claimant answered individually by his attorney and denied any liability to the plaintiff on either count and thereafter filed a cross-claim against the defendant in which he sought judgment against the defendant for any sums or amounts which the plaintiff may obtain against him by virtue of the judgment; for the sum of $4,000 on a debt alleged to be owed by the defendant to him, and $500 attorney's fees. The defendant appeared individually by his attorneys and answered the complaint of the plaintiff, answered the cross-claim of the cross-claimant, and counterclaimed against the plaintiff, seeking damages in the sum of $18,000. The plaintiff replied to the defendant's counterclaim.

On July 11, 1958, the lower court made an order setting the case for trial on October 10, 1958. All counsel were notified by the clerk of the court. On October 6, 1958, counsel for the plaintiff and counsel for the cross-claimant stipulated that the trial be set for December 10, 1958. The lower court ordered that the prior trial date be vacated and the case be reset for trial on December 10, 1958. All counsel were regularly notified by the clerk of the new trial setting. The defendant's counsel was not present before the court on October 6, 1958, and did not participate in the stipulation vacating the original trial setting and resetting the case for trial on December 10, 1958. The defendant and defendant's counsel deny ever receiving any notice from the clerk concerning the new trial date.

On December 10, 1958, the new trial date, the case came on regularly to be heard. The defendant did not appear either in person or by counsel. The court made the following minute entry during the course of the trial:

"*   *   *

"The plaintiff Smith and the defendant Bray announce ready for trial.

"William J. Bray is sworn, cross-examined, and examined.

"Plaintiff's Exhibit 1, being a promissory note in the sum of $4,000.00 dated February 14, 1955, is marked for identification and admitted in evidence.

"Nicholas Coulas having failed to appear at this time either in person or by counsel, and it further appearing that this case was previously set for trial both as to the issues framed by the complaint and answer thereto of the defendant Nicholas Coulas and as to the cross-claim filed by the defendant William J. Bray, Jr., against the defendant Nicholas Coulas,

"IT IS HEREBY ORDERED that the default of the said defendant Nicholas Coulas be entered as to said complaint and as to said cross-claim and the court proceeding to hear evidence pertaining to said complaint and cross-claim and being fully advised in the premises,

"IT IS THEREFORE ORDERED that judgment is hereby rendered   *   *   *   against the defendant Nicholas Coulas   *   *   *."

The plaintiff obtained judgment against the defendant on both counts and against the cross-claimant as to count two (the promissory note). The cross-claimant obtained judgment against the defendant on the promissory note. The judgment was entered on December 11, 1958.

On October 29, 1960, nearly two years later, the defendant filed a motion to set aside and vacate the judgment. The trial court denied this motion. * * *

The defendant subsequently filed this appeal.

The defendant contends that the "default" judgment entered against him was void, since he did not receive 3 days' notice of the application for judgment by default pursuant to Rule 55(b) of the Arizona Rules of Civil Procedure * * *. The defendant's contention would be valid if the judgment below was a judgment by default. A default judgment obtains when a defendant fails to plead or otherwise defend. Rule 55. If he has made an appearance in the case, he must be given 3 days' notice of application for judgment by default. * * *

However, the defendant's contention is invalid here since the judgment below was not a default judgment. It should be noted that the defendant did plead to the merits. He answered the complaint and filed a counterclaim. He then failed to appear at the trial in person or by counsel. The trial proceeded, evidence was heard, and a judgment on the merits of the plaintiff's and counter-claimant's claims was entered. The judgment was not by default within the meaning of Rule 55. Therefore Rule 55(b) with its 3-day notice requirement is not applicable. In fact, the trial court would have erred if a default was entered, since the case was at issue. Bass v. Hoagland, 172 F.2d 205 (5th Cir.1949), cert. denied, 338 U.S. 816, 70 S.Ct. 57, 94 L.Ed. 494 (1949) * * *.

The following language is from Bass v. Hoagland * * * concerning the applicability of Rule 55:

> "Rule 55(a) authorizes the clerk to enter a default 'When a party against whom a judgment for affirmative relief is sought has failed to plead or otherwise defend as provided by these rules.' This does not require that to escape default the defendant must not only file a sufficient answer to the merits, but must also have a lawyer or be present in court when the case is called for a trial. The words 'otherwise defend' refer to attacks on the service, or motions to dismiss, or for better particulars, and the like, which may prevent default without presently pleading to the merits. *When Bass by his attorney filed a denial of the plaintiff's case neither the clerk nor the judge could enter a default against him. The burden of proof was put on the plaintiff in any trial. When neither Bass nor his attorney appeared at the trial, no default was generated*; the case was not confessed. The plaintiff might proceed, but he would have to prove his case." 172 F.2d p. 210 (emphasis added).

And note this language from Klein v. Rappaport, * * * [90 A.2d 834 (D.C.Mun.Ct.1952)]:

> "A more serious question is whether the trial court could properly enter a judgment by default on the then state of the record. It must be remembered that defendant had not defaulted in pleading. She had filed an answer and a counterclaim. Plaintiff having replied to the counterclaim, the case was at issue not only on the original claim but on the counterclaim as well. With the litigation in that posture and the judge having decided that there should be no further continuance, he should have proceeded to take proof and enter judgment on the merits. It was not proper to enter a judgment by default. *Absence of a defendant when a case is called for trial after it is at issue does not warrant a judgment against him by default,* but a trial or hearing on the issues is necessary and the judgment which follows is based on the proof adduced. * * *

The defendant relies heavily on the case of Phoenix Metals Corporation v. Roth * * * on page 109 of 79 Ariz., on page 647 of 284 P.2d:

> "Under the provisions of this rule [Rule 55], no judgment by default may be entered against a defendant who has appeared—as by timely filing an answer—unless he is given notice of the application for judgment."

To the extent the above language implies that a default judgment is proper where a defendant has answered to the merits, it is incorrect. The peculiar fact situation in that case made the above language somewhat misleading. * * * [T]he defendant had filed an answer in fact, but through clerical error the answer was attached to the wrong file and thus it appeared that the defendant had failed to answer and upon application to the clerk the default was erroneously entered and judgment granted thereon. This court held that judgment wholly void. It should therefore be stated that once an answer on the merits is filed and the case is at issue, a default judgment is not proper, and if the defendant fails to appear at the trial a judgment on the merits may be entered against him upon proper proof.

                    * * *

The contention of the defendant that he did not receive notice of the new trial date is not substantiated by the minutes. The record indicates that the clerk of the superior court notified all counsel of all of the orders and judgment pursuant to Rule 77(h), Arizona Rules of Civil Procedure. It is well settled that in the absence of a showing to the contrary a public officer, such as the clerk of the court in this case, is presumed to have performed the duty imposed upon him by law. * * * In addition, if the defendant's counsel did not receive the notice of the change of the trial date to December 10, 1958, he certainly would have learned of the change in the trial date when he appeared for trial on the earlier date, October 10, 1958.

Since the judgment of the lower court is merely voidable, at most, Rule 60(c) of the Arizona Rules of Civil Procedure prevents the defendant from attacking the judgment more than six months after it was entered. The defendant attempted to attack the judgment nearly two years after it was entered. * * * The lower court properly denied defendant's motion to set aside and vacate the judgment.

Judgment affirmed.

NOTES AND QUESTIONS

1. In *Bass v. Hoagland,* which is relied upon in *Coulas,* a default judgment was rendered in favor of plaintiff after defendant's counsel, who had filed an answer, had withdrawn from the case. The judgment recited that defendant had been informed of the withdrawal. Defendant did not appeal but collaterally attacked the judgment when enforcement was sought against him in another jurisdiction. Defendant claimed that he did not know of the counsel's withdrawal from the case and was not aware that the adverse judgment had been rendered. A majority of the Fifth Circuit held that, since an answer had been filed, defendant was not in default under Rule 55, that the entry of judgment without trial by jury, which had been demanded, was a violation of the due-process clause of the Fifth Amendment, and that the judgment was void. The court indicated that even if the case fell within Rule 55, the failure to give notice under Rule 55(b) (2) might render the judgment void, although in that event no jury trial would be required. The dissenting judge took the position that defendant, by not attending trial, was in default, no jury trial was required and therefore the decision was not void and not subject to collateral attack. The case is discussed in 62 Harv.L.Rev. 1400 (1949) and 59 Yale L.J. 345 (1950).

2. Federal Rule 54(c) provides that a plaintiff may recover all the relief to which he is entitled except that plaintiff is limited to the amount prayed for in the case of a default judgment. Suppose at trial in *Coulas v. Smith* plaintiff's evidence showed that defendant was liable for $10,000, although only $4,000 had been claimed. Would the court have been justified in awarding plaintiff the full amount?

3. What activities of a defendant, short of a formal challenge to the jurisdiction or the pleadings, constitute an "appearance" within the meaning of Federal Rule 55(b)(2)? In RHODES v. RHODES, 3 Mich.App. 396, 142 N.W. 2d 508 (1966), plaintiff, in a divorce action, obtained a default judgment against defendant without giving the notice required by Michigan General Court Rule 520.2(2), which is analogous to Federal Rule 55(b)(2). Defendant claimed that by signing a property settlement agreement and stipulating that it be incorporated in the divorce judgment, he "appeared" in the action. The court held that defendant had not shown that these acts were intended to constitute an "appearance" and refused to set aside the judgment.

4. Federal Rule 55(c) distinguishes between the setting aside of an "entry of default" ("for any good cause shown") and the setting aside of a "judgment by default" ("in accordance with Rule 60(b)").

* * * [T]he clerk or the court may enter a default upon the application of the nondefaulting party. The entry simply is an official recognition of the fact that one party is in default * * *.

In sharp contrast, a final default judgment is not possible against a party in default until the measure of recovery has been ascertained, which typically requires a hearing, in which the defaulting party may participate * * *.

* * * Not surprisingly, the federal courts are willing to grant relief from a default entry more readily and with a lesser showing than they are in the case of a default judgment.

10 Wright & Miller, *Federal Practice and Procedure: Civil* § 2692 (1973).

It is important to recognize that although relief-from-judgment rules do not distinguish between default and other judgments, the courts, in exercising discretion, are far more willing to set aside default judgments in order that cases may be decided on their merits. This is particularly true when the default is due to the carelessness of counsel. See, e. g., Hutton v. Fisher, 359 F.2d 913 (3d Cir. 1966). It is exceedingly rare in such a case that an appellate court will find that a trial court has abused its discretion in setting aside a default judgment. Nevertheless such decisions are reached from time to time. See, e. g., Benjamin v. Dalmo Mfg. Co., 31 Cal.2d 523, 190 P.2d 593 (1948). For a general discussion of the power to set aside judgments, see pp. 912–24, infra. Why shouldn't the default judgment be left unopened and the losing party be remitted to a negligence action against a careless attorney?

5. A special type of default judgment is one that is imposed on a party, who has appeared and contested the matters at issue but has wilfully violated the rules of procedure or disobeyed an order of the court. Such a "penalty" is invoked normally against parties who are defending claims; if the complaining party is guilty of comparable violations, the most typical remedy is to dismiss the case with prejudice. See, e. g., Federal Rule 41(b). The penalty default most frequently is rendered in cases in which a defending party wilfully refuses to comply with orders for pretrial discovery. Federal Rules 37(b)(2)(C) and 37(d) and their state counterparts specifically permit default judgments in these situations. See Riverside Casino Corp. v. J. W. Brewer Co., 80 Nev. 135, 390 P.2d 232 (1964); Isenberger v. Schumann, 415 Pa. 217, 203 A.2d 136 (1964). Do "penalty" defaults fall within the scope of Federal Rule 55? See Wilver v. Fisher, 387 F.2d 66 (10th Cir.1967) (notice provisions of Rule 55(b)(2) apply to default under Rule 37). Are "penalty" defaults subject to the limitation on recovery in Federal Rule 54(c)? In TRANS WORLD AIRLINES, INC. v. HUGHES, 32 F.R.D. 604, 607–08 (S.D.N.Y.1963), modified 332 F.2d 602 (2d Cir.1964), certiorari dismissed 380 U.S. 248, 85 S.Ct. 934, 13 L.Ed.2d 817 (1965),[a] the court, after granting plaintiff's motion for entry of a default judgment on the ground of defendant's failure to produce the owner of 100% of its stock for a deposition, held:

That branch of the [plaintiff's] motion seeking to increase the *ad damnum* clause from $105,000,000 to $135,000,000 is granted. This is

[a] The subsequent history of this case is discussed in Note 2, pp. 767–68, infra.

not a case where a party has defaulted in appearance. Here issue was joined and adversary proceedings continued in the pretrial stages of this litigation. The damages originally asserted were unliquidated and TWA is entitled to recover for whatever damage it can show it suffered. Furthermore, Toolco [a defendant] will be represented at the hearings necessary to assess damages under rule 55(b) (2).

Compare Fong v. United States, 300 F.2d 400, 412–13 (9th Cir.), certiorari denied 370 U.S. 938, 82 S.Ct. 1584, 8 L.Ed.2d 807 (1962). Suppose TWA's suit had been on a contract and the damages were for a liquidated sum that plaintiff had erroneously understated in its complaint. Would the result have been different?

———

C & H TRANSP. CO. v. WRIGHT, 396 S.W.2d 443 (Tex.Civ.App. 1965). Plaintiff brought suit against a former employer, alleging that the latter erroneously had deducted the sum of $470.55 from the amount due plaintiff upon termination of the employment. Defendant did not answer or appear and a default judgment was entered. Defendant then appealed on the ground that the complaint failed to allege a cause of action. The court reversed, holding that a default judgment must be supported by a statement of a cause of action in the complaint and that plaintiff's complaint was insufficient because it contained mere conclusions of law.

NOTES AND QUESTIONS

1. Suppose defendant in *Wright* had not appealed but instead had challenged the judgment collaterally after it had become final. Should relief have been granted? Should it make a difference if the defective complaint clearly cannot be remedied by an amendment? See Comment, *Attacking a Judgment in California on the Grounds that the Complaint Failed to State a Cause of Action,* 1 U.C.L.A. L.Rev. 195 (1954); 36 Texas L.Rev. 243 (1957); 49 Mich.L.Rev. 446 (1951).

2. In *Trans World Airlines v. Hughes,* Note 5, p. 766, supra, after the Supreme Court dismissed certiorari, the case was referred by the district court to a master for a determination of damages. In the hearing on the confirmation of the master's report, defendants sought to establish "as a matter of law that facts essential to establish * * * violations [of the antitrust laws], although alleged in the complaint, are in fact untrue and could not have been proved by TWA at trial." The district court rejected this effort:

> * * * TWA did not have to present any evidence to support the well-pleaded allegations of the complaint, and defendants may not offer evidence to controvert such allegations. That opportunity was forfeited by defendants as a result of the default.

> Defendants may show, however, that an allegation is not well pleaded, but only in very narrow, exceptional circumstances [as when] allegations * * * are contrary to facts of which the court will take judicial notice.

Trans World Airlines v. Hughes, 308 F.Supp. 679, 683 (S.D.N.Y.1969), affirmed 449 F.2d 51 (2d Cir.1971). The Supreme Court reversed on the ground that defendants' actions were immune from the antitrust laws under 49 U.S.C. §§ 1378, 1384, because they were under the regulatory control of the Civil Aeronautics Board; the Court held that it was not precluded from considering this issue by its earlier dismissal of certiorari, because there had been no final judgment at that time. Hughes Tool Co. v. Trans World Airlines, 409 U.S. 363, 93 S.Ct. 647, 34 L.Ed.2d 577 (1973).

---

2. OTHER MEANS OF TERMINATION WITHOUT PLENARY TRIAL

A. VOLUNTARY DISMISSAL

Read Federal Rule of Civil Procedure 41(a) and the accompanying materials in the Supplement.

DAVIS v. McLAUGHLIN, 326 F.2d 881 (9th Cir.), certiorari denied 379 U.S. 833, 85 S.Ct. 64, 13 L.Ed.2d 41 (1964). Plaintiffs' action was filed on December 8, 1961. Between that date and March 9, 1962, both plaintiffs and defendant engaged in discovery. Defendant took a deposition of one of the plaintiffs and plaintiffs served a set of interrogatories on defendant. On June 15, 1962, defendant filed a motion to dismiss or for a more definite statement. Before a hearing on this motion could be held, plaintiffs filed a notice of voluntary dismissal under Federal Rule 41(a)(1). The trial court, pursuant to a counter-motion by defendant, held that the only basis for a voluntary dismissal was Rule 41(a)(2). The court granted the dismissal but stated that it would be without prejudice only on condition that plaintiffs paid $4,967.25 to defendant to defray expenses. Plaintiffs refused payment and sought to revive the case but the trial court ordered the action dismissed with prejudice. The appellate court affirmed but failed to set out clearly the basis for its decision.

NOTES AND QUESTIONS

1. At common law plaintiff was permitted to dismiss a case voluntarily and without prejudice to refiling the action at a later date at any time prior to judgment. Today the right to dismiss voluntarily generally is governed by a rule or statute that typically permits a dismissal before "trial" or "commencement" of trial. These provisions have raised many problems of interpretation regarding the meaning of the words "trial" and "commencement." A few courts have held that "before trial" means at any time prior to submission to the jury or court for decision. See generally Annot., 1 A.L.R.3d 711 (1965). What justification is there for this construction?

As is made clear by *Davis v. McLaughlin,* Federal Rule 41(a) (1) is subject to problems of interpretation. Why was plaintiffs' notice of dismissal not timely in that case? Would the decision have been clearer if defendant had attached the deposition of plaintiff to defendant's motion to dismiss? See pp. 744–45, supra.

2. Are the requirements of Federal Rule 41(a) (1) too rigid? At what point should plaintiff's absolute right to dismiss be terminated?

3. Suppose that after a full trial in a federal court plaintiff realizes that her evidence is insufficient and that she cannot prevail. May she resort to Rule 41(a) (2) for relief? What considerations would be likely to sway the court on this question? May the trial court refuse to allow the dismissal altogether or does the court merely have power to govern the conditions upon which dismissal is permitted? See Alamance Indus., Inc. v. Filene's, 291 F.2d 142 (1st Cir.), certiorari denied 368 U.S. 831, 82 S.Ct. 53, 7 L.Ed.2d 33 (1961). For comprehensive discussions of judicial discretion under Rule 41(a) (2), see Note, *Exercise of Discretion in Permitting Dismissals Without Prejudice Under Federal Rule 41(a),* 54 Colum.L.Rev. 616 (1954); Note, *Voluntary Dismissal by Order of Court— Federal Rule of Civil Procedure 41(a) (2) and Judicial Discretion,* 48 Notre Dame Law. 446 (1972). Under Rule 41(a) (1) any dismissal is with prejudice if plaintiff previously has dismissed the same action. Should this restriction apply as well when the second dismissal is sought under Rule 41(a) (2)? See American Cyanamid Co. v. McGhee, 317 F.2d 295 (5th Cir.1963).

B.   DISMISSAL FOR FAILURE TO PROSECUTE

Courts long have been regarded as possessing inherent discretionary power to dismiss an action if the plaintiff does not proceed to trial with "due diligence." Exactly when this power should be invoked has been a matter about which judges have disagreed. Should simple delay by plaintiff be sufficient to justify dismissal, or should prejudice to defendant also be required? In MESSENGER v. UNITED STATES, 231 F.2d 328, 331 (2d Cir.1956), the court said: "The operative condition of the Rule is lack of due diligence on the part of the plaintiff—not a showing by the defendant that it will be prejudiced by denial of its motion. * * * It may well be that the latter factor may be considered by the court, especially in cases of moderate or excusable neglect, in the formulation of its discretionary ruling." Does this standard make sense? Does it have any practical utility as a guide for the trial judge? What is its effect on appellate-court review of the trial court's exercise of discretion?

Some jurisdictions control dismissals for want of prosecution by statute. Thus California permits dismissal only after the passage of two years from the filing of the complaint, but makes dismissal mandatory when five years have elapsed. Cal.Code Civ.Proc. § 583. What justification, if any, is there for this statutory arrangement? Is it superior to a system that leaves the decision solely within the court's discretion? Compare Indiana Rule of Trial Procedure 1–4C, which permits dismissal "when no action has been taken in a civil case for a period of sixty [60] days." See also N.Y.C.P.L.R. 3216. In view of the fact that, by definition, cases in which there is a failure to prosecute are not consuming judicial time or energy, why is a formal dismissal procedure necessary?

C. JUDICIALLY ASSISTED SETTLEMENT

(i) Consent Judgment

If the parties reach a settlement out of court, they may want to embody their agreement in a final judgment in order to make the agreement readily provable in another jurisdiction and to give it res judicata effect as a bar to further litigation. Consent judgments (also termed judgments by *stipulation* or *confession*) have the same binding effect as any other judgment, and can be set aside only in the same way. See Federal Rule 60. Unlike an ordinary judgment, a consent judgment is not based upon a record that can be searched to ascertain the scope and operation of the judgment if it should be challenged or become relevant in subsequent litigation. Therefore, the consent decree, as is true of any contract, must be drawn with extreme care if future legal difficulties are to be avoided. See Artvale, Inc. v. Rugby Fabrics Corp., 303 F.2d 283 (2d Cir.1962).

(ii) Offer of Judgment and Deposit in Court

In order to encourage and facilitate settlement, many jurisdictions have adopted provisions under which a defendant may make an offer to allow judgment to be taken against him for a specified amount of money or an identified piece of property. See, e. g., Federal Rule 68; N.Y.C.P.L.R. 3221. See also King, *Thumbs in the Dike: Procedures to Contain the Flood of Personal Injury Litigation,* 39 Fordham L.Rev. 223, 231–44 (1970). To make the offer of judgment more tempting, defendant may be permitted to pay the sum into court, thus assuring plaintiff the judgment not only will be collectible but collectible without costs of formal execution. See N.Y.C.P.L.R. 3219. A similar type of permission may be available to a defendant who wishes to settle the matter of damages but does not wish to concede liability.

Defendant may make the offer contingent on a finding of responsibility at trial.   See N.Y.C.P.L.R. 3220.

Invariably these provisions contain a clause providing that in the event the offer is not accepted and plaintiff fails to obtain a more favorable judgment at trial, plaintiff must pay the costs of trial from the time of the offer, and, under some rules, defendant's necessary expenses in fighting the case. See, e. g., Federal Rule 68; N.Y.C.P.L.R. 3219.   What justification is there for such a clause?   Is it fair to plaintiff?

SECTION C.   TECHNIQUES FOR STREAMLINED ADJUDICATION AND CALENDAR CONTROL

1.   THE NATURE OF THE NEED

In many areas in the United States, courts have not been able to cope with an ever-increasing amount of judicial business.   In some courts there is as much as a five-year wait between the time certain types of cases are filed and the time they are tried.   It is important to note that there are two types of delay, the first due to the unwillingness or inability of attorneys to prepare the case for trial, and the second due to the unwillingness or inability of courts to handle the cases as soon as the participants are ready.   There is little question that this second type of delay should be eliminated, or at least reduced as much as possible.   The public is entitled to prompt trials and prompt decisions.   It is somewhat less clear to what extent the legal system is obliged to seek the elimination of the first type of delay.   If a court can immediately process all cases presented to it for trial or other action, why isn't that the extent of its responsibility?   What duty does a court have to ride herd on attorneys who procrastinate, especially when neither side seems to object to the pace?   Why shouldn't the clients be obliged to provide the missing momentum?

The answers to these questions depend upon one's view of the ultimate goal of the judicial system and of the legal profession generally.   If the aim of the system is the prompt and final resolution of all legal problems, unjustified delay, even when due to the litigant's own attorney, is intolerable.   Any system that permits long periods of inactivity or the protraction of pretrial procedures not only is inefficient in terms of the time dimension but undoubtedly is inefficient from the perspective of the private and public expenditures that are devoted to dispute resolution.

Moreover, it is important to recognize that a majority of cases filed in the courts are never tried.   In many of these cases the lawyers for both sides do not even contemplate trial; they know that the case will be compromised at some point along the way. Yet without some mechanism to force the attorney's hand, these cases can drag on and on. Lawyers usually find their time consumed by knowledgeable clients with important litigation. It is the affairs of the less affluent client, who often has a difficult case, albeit one vital to her well being, that are put aside. And it is just such a client who puts complete trust in the attorney and often has no idea what steps she might take to protect her interests if the lawyer fails to do so. The small personal injury case involving $3,000 may be a trivial matter to a lawyer but it may be of tremendous importance to the client who is pressed to pay large medical bills.

Finally, it is important to note that delay is not the only administrative problem with which the courts must deal. Even if every court was able to keep its calendar current many litigants would still be deterred from prosecuting legitimate claims due to the high costs of litigation. All too often, the costs of filing suit plus an attorney's fee will exceed the amount sought from the defendant. In seeking ways to reduce or eliminate costs in minor cases, consideration must be given to the fact that such measures will increase the amount of litigation, which in turn will worsen the problems of congestion and ultimately increase the cost to society of maintaining a judicial system. Thus new methods not only must be inexpensive, they must be highly efficient in expediting adjudication.

For an excellent analysis of the problems of congestion and techniques for eliminating it, see Levin & Woolley, *Dispatch and Delay* (1961). See also Zeisel, Kalven & Buchholz, *Delay in the Court* (1959); Miller, *A Program For the Elimination of the Hardships of Litigation Delay*, 27 Ohio St.L.J. 402 (1966); Oglesby & Gallas, *Court Administration—A New Profession: A Role for Universities*, 10 Am.Bus.Law J. 1 (1972).

---

2. MEASURES TO SPEED PREPARATION OF CASES FOR TRIAL

The power of a court to dismiss a case for lack of prosecution is the traditional means of pushing the attorneys to resolve the dispute or ready the case for trial. As previously seen state provisions vary considerably. Review the California and Indiana rules, discussed on pp. 769–70, supra, and compare Federal Rule 41(b). How effective do you think these measures are as calendar control devices?

An increasing number of courts, to the extent they have the power to do so, have promulgated local rules to prevent lawyers from allowing their cases to become stale. See, e. g., Local Rule 13(d) of the United States District Court for the District of Columbia, which provides a means of preparing formal charges of misconduct against an attorney who has been derelict in the duty to prosecute a client's case. Is this threat of disciplinary action an appropriate way to avoid undue delay in the courts?

---

3. METHODS FOR SPEEDING ADJUDICATION OF CASES READY FOR TRIAL AND FOR LOWERING COSTS

A. BY-PASSING THE SYSTEM—SETTLEMENT AND ARBITRATION

Lawyers and clients frustrated by unreasonable delay in obtaining a trial date may go outside the court system to solve their problems. Often this simply means accepting a settlement that is not based upon a realistic evaluation of one's case, but is a forced concession due only to the inefficiency and costliness of the judicial process. Obviously, forced settlements often are unjust to the party whose case is sound but who cannot afford to wait for the dispensation of justice or who cannot survive a war of attrition waged by a wealthier adversary.

A somewhat different solution is the voluntary submission of the controversy to binding arbitration, a device that has been used increasingly in recent years, particularly in commercial disputes. Nearly every jurisdiction today has a statute sanctioning arbitration and providing for judicial enforcement of the award. See generally Sarpy, *Arbitration as a Means of Reducing Court Congestion,* 41 Notre Dame Law. 182 (1965). Arbitration has its drawbacks, however. An arbitrator is not a judge. He does not operate under rules of court. The arbitrator's decision is expected to be and usually is a form of compromise of the parties' claims. He is not strictly bound to follow legal rules as applied in a court of law and predictability of outcome is difficult. It is doubtful if voluntary arbitration will soon become an effective answer to dockets overcrowded with personal injury litigation. See King, *Thumbs in the Dike: Procedures to Contain the Flood of Personal Injury Litigation,* 39 Fordham L.Rev. 223, 247 (1970).

B. IMPROVING THE EXISTING SYSTEM

Historically, courts have been administered by the judges themselves, usually without the time, experience, or staff to do an adequate job in the face of mounting caseloads. As a result there has been an increasing awareness of the need to place court administration under the control of professional management personnel who are familiar with modern techniques and equipment and who will drastically revise current inefficient methods of operation. A few jurisdictions already have moved in that direction and more are certain to follow in the near future. See generally Friesen, Gallas & Gallas, *Managing the Courts* (1971); Oglesby & Gallas, *Court Administration—A New Profession: A Role for Universities,* 10 Am.Bus.Law J. 1 (1972).

One major stumbling block to administrative reform is the inability of some state courts to obtain increased funds to make the necessary alterations. May the courts compel the executive and legislative branches to provide adequate funds for the operation of the judicial system? See Commonwealth ex rel. Carroll v. Tate, 442 Pa. 45, 274 N.E.2d 193 (1971). It has been suggested that the inability to obtain needed funds is itself in large part due to the inefficiency of current court management regarding budgetary and fiscal matters. See Hazard, McNamara & Sentilles, *Court Finance and Unitary Budgeting,* 81 Yale L.J. 1286 (1972). It is obvious that the long range remedy for problems of court delay is to overhaul and streamline judicial operations and provide additional personnel if needed. In the meantime, however, there are a number of things that can be done to help remedy existing difficulties.

The first and simplest method is to maximize the effective use of the time of the judges already in office. Thus, if one judicial district is in desperate need of assistance, it should be able to borrow a judge from a neighboring area that does not have a similar problem. Moreover, within a district available judges should be assigned various tasks with an eye toward optimum efficiency. Thus it may be sound to assign one or more judges to handle nothing but the pretrial matters in all routine cases so that the remaining judges can handle the trials themselves without interruption. On the other hand, the rules should be flexible enough to permit assignment of one judge to handle all the aspects of a large complex case, because that judge's cumulative and intimate knowledge of the details will expedite both the pretrial and trial phases of the litigation.

A second method of improving the system is insistence upon full cooperation between the attorneys and the courts. When the lawyers say they are ready for trial, the courts should be able to set trial dates, satisfactory to the parties, and insist that the parties appear on those dates. On the other hand, the lawyers should be able to rely on the courts' ability to maintain its schedules and on their not altering the assigned dates at the last minute.

A third means of increasing efficiency is the use of the pretrial conference to narrow the issues, limit the witnesses, and generally provide for a more orderly trial. As was pointed out in Chapter Nine, p. 734, supra, however, it is not clear to what extent the pretrial conference leads to shorter trials or otherwise eliminates delay.

A fourth method of speeding adjudication is use of the bifurcated or separate trial. In many personal injury cases the issue of damages consumes most of the trial time and litigation funds since it involves detailed examination of expert medical witnesses. If a separate trial as to liability is held first, much time and cost can be eliminated in those cases in which defendant is exonerated. The method of handling pleas in abatement, which probably is the most common utilization of the bifurcated trial, has been discussed previously. See p. 476, supra. What dangers, if any, are there in the use of a bifurcated trial in personal injury actions? See Doutre v. Niec, 2 Mich.App. 88, 138 N.W.2d 501 (1965), p. 910, infra. Does such a trial tend to favor one party over the other? Would it be sensible to utilize the same jury to decide damages once liability has been established? For a general discussion of the problems of separate trial, see Committee on State Courts of Superior Jurisdiction, *Separate Trial of the Issues of Liability and Damages in Personal Injury Actions*, 20 Record of N.Y.C.B.A. 659 (1965); Weinstein, *Routine Bifurcation of Jury Negligence Trials: An Example of the Questionable Use of Rule Making Power*, 14 Vand.L.Rev. 830 (1961); Zeisel & Callahan, *Split Trials and Time Saving: A Statistical Analysis*, 76 Harv.L.Rev. 1606 (1963).

Finally, much of the existing delay could be avoided if trial by jury were eliminated or curtailed. There is no doubt that jury trials take far more time than do court trials, both in terms of preparation and actual trial. See Chapter Eleven, pp. 796–97, infra. In courts that have separate jury and nonjury calendars, the latter may be nearly current while the former is years behind. In those cases in which trial by jury is a constitutional or statutory right, see pp. 797–831, infra, the courts can do no more than encourage waiver of jury trial by making nonjury trial as attractive as possible. Statistics should be published to demonstrate that a litigant is not likely to fare differently before a jury than before a judge, and when significant differences exist between decisions of judges and juries, methods should be sought to eliminate the differential. It may be wise, for example, to provide trial by panels of judges to neutralize the fear that a single judge may be swayed by a particular latent bias.

C.   UTILIZING SPECIALIZED PROCEDURES

(i) Small-Claims Courts

A significant development in a number of jurisdictions is the so-called small-claims court in which cases, trivial in amount, can be disposed of with considerable dispatch and at almost no cost to the litigants. In California, for example, where the small-claims court is conducted by a trial judge, the litigants must appear themselves, without counsel. The proceedings are informal from the outset. There is no pleading as such, merely a one-sentence statement of the claim. The total cost of going to trial is only a few dollars and the court's jurisdiction extends to controversies involving as much as $500. Trial nearly always is set within a month following the date the claim is filed. Plaintiff, of course, has an option of filing suit in small-claims court or in the regular trial court. By going to small-claims court plaintiff waives any right to jury trial and the right to appeal the decision. A dissatisfied defendant may obtain a trial de novo in a regular court and may demand a jury. Rarely, however, does a defendant find it worthwhile to do so. See generally Cal.Code Civ.Proc. §§ 117–117q; Comment, *The California Small Claims Court*, 52 Calif.L.Rev. 876 (1964).

(ii) Compulsory Arbitration

Somewhat related to small-claims procedures is Pennsylvania's compulsory arbitration law. 5 Pa.Stat. § 30. Plaintiffs in all actions involving less than $10,000 in the larger counties, $5,000 in the smaller, may be compelled by court rule to bring their cases before a panel of arbitrators. Any litigant who is unhappy with the award may, however, upon payment of the arbitration fees, obtain a trial de novo in the courts. This procedure, which is inexpensive to the litigants, has been widely acclaimed and appears to have been quite successful. Nevertheless, it has the same drawbacks as does voluntary arbitration and these undoubtedly would be compounded if the compulsory law were to be extended to complex litigation involving large claims. See generally King, *Thumbs in the Dike: Procedures to Contain the Flood of Personal Injury Litigation*, 39 Fordham L.Rev. 223, 225, 244 (1970); Rosenberg & Schubin, *Trial by Lawyer: Compulsory Arbitration of Small Claims in Pennsylvania,* 74 Harv.L.Rev. 448 (1961); Legislation, 113 U.Pa.L.Rev. 1117 (1965).

(iii) Simplified Procedure Acts

For a number of years New York has had on its books a "Simplified Procedure" Act under which parties may agree to submit their case, regardless of type, without formal pleadings, for a speedy decision. See N.Y.C.P.L.R. 3031–3037. The submission may occur after the dispute arises or it may be a part of a contract that subsequently becomes a focal point of dispute. Thus, the Simplified Procedure has many of the attributes of "judicial arbitration."

The process is further speeded by treating the submission of the case to the Simplified Procedure as a waiver of jury trial and the technical rules of evidence.   See generally 3 Weinstein, Korn & Miller, *New York Civil Practice* ¶¶ 3031.01–3037.02.

The Simplified Procedure Act has a significant drawback.   Unlike the small-claims court or compulsory arbitration, both parties must agree to the procedure before it is operative.   It is true that there is no trial de novo once a decision is made but the success of small-claims courts and compulsory arbitration measures stems mostly from the fact that the impetus for the trial de novo is usually lacking.   This may be due in large part, however, to the fact that only small claims are involved.   Nonetheless, it is not surprising that few disputes have thus far been referred to New York's Simplified Procedure for resolution.

(iv) Separate Tribunals for Specific Types of Actions

A solution to the problem of congestion as yet relatively unexplored is the adoption of special courts or agencies to adjudicate specific types of cases based upon the subject matter involved.   Stereotyped procedures and personnel with special expertise regarding the law may be utilized to dispose speedily of various types of cases that would be significantly delayed if the standard methods of adjudication were used.   The use of special proceedings and tribunals is far from a new idea.   For example, many jurisdictions always have had special courts or divisions to handle probate matters.   In some of these courts the procedures are so well defined that many noncontested matters are handled by mail, without a single court appearance.

Perhaps the most significant use of special tribunals is in the area of workmen's compensation.   In many jurisdictions the adjudication of these claims is handled by hearing examiners under the control of a commission, totally outside the scope of the trial courts.   Such a procedure may bypass (and perhaps infringe upon) the constitutional right to jury trial, thus eliminating much of the cause of court congestion.   See James, *Civil Procedure* § 8.1, at 338–39 (1965).   In recent years, it frequently has been proposed that all automobile negligence cases be transferred to a special administrative tribunal. Unfortunately, most of these proposals also involve an alteration of the substantive law and fall prey to the criticism that they confuse substantive doctrine with procedural efficiency.   The fact remains, however, that, given the substantive law, if an administrative board can provide a prompter adjudication, with no loss in the quality of decision, the courts should be by-passed. See Blum & Kalven, *Public Law Perspectives On a Private Law Problem— Auto Compensation Plans*, 31 U.Chi.L.Rev. 641, 713–16 (1964).   Compare Green, *Basic Protection and Court Congestion*, 52 A.B.A.J. 926 (1966).

(v) Masters and Auditors

In many jurisdictions the courts are empowered to employ quasi-judicial officers to make initial determinations of many matters that normally are decided by a judge or jury. Such officers, usually referred to as masters or auditors, operate in the same way as do judges in small-claims courts or arbiters under compulsory arbitration laws. They may not be as limited, however, with regard to the size and nature of cases that they may handle. Furthermore, although a party may challenge the findings of such an officer, and obtain a trial by judge or jury, the master's decision is not totally disregarded. The official's findings may be considered binding in nonjury suits unless "clearly erroneous," and even in jury cases, the findings may be introduced into evidence for the jurors' consideration. At least in one context it has been shown that the routine use of special officers in state courts has resulted in the speedy, efficient disposition of litigation with a corresponding reduction in the backlog of cases for trial. See Rosenberg & Chanin, *Auditors in Massachusetts as Antidotes for Delayed Civil Courts*, 110 U.Pa.L.Rev. 27 (1961).

In the federal courts the appointment of masters is regulated by Rule 53. The rule, by its terms and through judicial interpretation, makes clear that such appointments are not favored and should be made only when deemed essential. The power to appoint masters is more limited in nonjury cases because a master's findings have a greater degree of finality than in jury cases in which the findings merely become part of the evidence. See generally 9 Wright & Miller, *Federal Practice and Procedure: Civil* §§ 2601–15 (1971); Kaufman, *Masters in the Federal Courts: Rule 53*, 58 Colum.L.Rev. 452 (1958). Reluctance to broaden the use of masters may be justified on the ground that frequently they lead to more protracted and costly litigation. A master who is appointed to handle a single case may be engaged in active law practice and can devote only a portion of time to her judicial duties. Moreover, whatever the master's findings, they must be analyzed by the court, if not by a jury, thereby causing further delay. Finally, the fees of the master, which may be very high, are borne by the parties, and not by the general public as are judicial salaries. See generally Note, 65 Yale L.J. 1057 (1956).

Masters probably can be used most efficiently to decide pretrial motions and to hold pretrial conferences. Assistance of this type takes some work pressure off the judges and allows them to concentrate on conducting trials, without many of the drawbacks that may occur when the master sits as a substitute for a judge at trial. The cost to each litigant normally will be nominal and the need for review will be strictly limited. Use of masters to decide pretrial matters has been a highly successful aspect of English practice for a number of years. See generally Zavatt, *The Use of Masters in Aid of the Court in Interlocutory Proceedings*, 22 F.R.D. 283 (1958).

CHAPTER 11
TRIAL

SECTION A. THE NATURE OF THE TRIAL PROCESS

---

1. SETTING THE CASE FOR TRIAL

In theory a case should automatically be tried once the pleadings are filed, discovery completed, settlement explored and rejected, and all pretrial motions decided. Normally, however, trial will not take place until one of the parties takes affirmative action to have the case placed on the appropriate trial calendar and the court disposes of all the cases previously placed on that calendar. As has been pointed out earlier, see pp. 771–72, supra, the wait can be a long one, often as much as four or five years when the case is to be tried before a jury.

The technique for placing a case on a waiting list for trial will vary from jurisdiction to jurisdiction. Generally it requires only a simple motion. But how is it possible to set a trial date in advance? Is it possible to know when the previous case assigned to a trial judge will be completed so that he and his courtroom will be available? How can one be certain that the lawyers will be free of other pressing obligations, or that crucial witnesses will not be indisposed? The answer, of course, is that there is no such certainty. Any scheduled trial date is at best tentative and is likely to be postponed a number of times.

The jockeying by the courts and the lawyers to bring a case to trial is an art. When sloppily done, it can lead to last minute alterations and result in unused courtrooms, unreasonable delays, and great logjams of cases waiting for trial. Even with the most careful and conscientious cooperation between court and counsel there may be difficulty. Ideally, if the court finds its own schedule altered so that the originally selected date for trial cannot be adhered to, it will inform the parties as far in advance as possible to enable them to readjust their schedules. Similarly, when a lawyer for one of the parties recognizes that a date for trial conflicts with another and more pressing obligation, that attorney will inform the court in advance to obtain a change in schedule. Adjustment usually is feasible for most lawyers who spend relatively little time

779

in active trial practice. But for an attorney who spends the bulk of his time in litigation, accommodation is most difficult, since a change in the trial date for one case probably will raise a conflict with a trial date for another.

Perhaps courts should require every trial attorney to have a sufficient staff to ensure that some lawyer in the firm will be available to handle a case whenever it is called. Rule 14(d) of the local rules of the district court in the District of Columbia provides:

> Engagement by an Attorney in another court (except the Supreme Court of the United States and the United States Court of Appeals for the District of Columbia Circuit) or in any division of this court, will not be ground to postpone the trial of another case if such attorney is counsel of record in more than twenty-five cases in this court, whether pending in the criminal division or on the general civil calendar, unless it be a civil case and consent of opposing parties is given.

Is this provision fair to the attorney or to the clients who have confided in him and relied on his expertise? See Gorman, *Excessive Delay in the Courts,* 21 Cleve.State L.Rev. 118 (1972).

Should modern management techniques and systems theory be applied to rationalize the flow of business through the courts? What risks might there be? Of what assistance might computers be to judicial administration? See Adams, *The Move Toward Modern Data Management in the Courts,* 23 U.Fla.L.Rev. 217 (1971); Commentary, *Court Administration: The Newest Profession,* 10 Duq.L.Rev. 220 (1971).

---

2. TRIAL BY JUDGE VERSUS TRIAL BY JURY

As will be discussed in Section B of this Chapter, see pp. 794–855, infra, the right to trial by jury is limited; the scope of the right usually is based upon a constitutional provision, augmented to some extent by statute. Unless the right is invoked properly by one of the parties, the case will be decided by the trial judge sitting alone, as are cases in which the right does not exist. In many jurisdictions the judge has the power in a nonjury case or when a jury-trial right is waived to impanel an advisory jury whose verdict the court has discretion either to embrace or ignore. See, e. g., Federal Rule 39(c).

A. TACTICAL CONSIDERATIONS IN DECIDING BETWEEN TRIAL BY JUDGE OR JURY

(i) Institutional Factors

Even when an attorney feels that a client's chances of winning on the merits are the same whether the case is tried by judge or by jury, there may be a decided tactical advantage in choosing one form of trial over another. Suppose, for example, that plaintiff in a personal-injury action is in serious financial difficulty. Obviously she will want to pursue the fastest litigation route possible in order to obtain a recovery at an early date. In many jurisdictions there is a substantial backlog of cases on the jury-trial calendar and a long wait is inevitable, whereas the judge-trial calendar is practically current and the case may be heard within a few months. If the suit has been brought in a jurisdiction in which this type of imbalance between the jury and nonjury calendars exists, plaintiff probably will waive the jury. On the other hand, a defendant, who knows plaintiff's plight will demand a jury trial hoping to force plaintiff into a quick settlement favorable to defendant.

P's position and effects of time

Similar considerations exist when time may ameliorate the extent of plaintiff's injuries. For example, if a young unmarried girl is seriously injured in an accident so that her physician will testify that there is a chance she may never be able to have children, a substantial verdict is likely. But she will be awarded far less if her case is not heard for a number of years and she has married and had a family in the interim. In cases of serious injury defendant usually has little to lose and much to gain by delay, except when the injuries are of a degenerative nature.

Also significant is the difference in cost between a jury and nonjury trial. On the average, a jury trial takes considerably more time than does a court trial. Jurors must be selected and instructed, more witnesses are called to testify, final arguments are longer, and more recesses are required. The result usually is higher counsel fees, more extensive payments to experts, and increased trial costs in the form of fees for jurors and witnesses. Although the latter fees often ultimately will be paid by the losing party, jury trial increases the financial gamble by a party who is uncertain as to his chances for success.

Cost

(ii) Psychological Factors

When is a jury more likely to give a favorable verdict than a judge? Are there substantial differences between judge and jury attitudes on questions of liability? On measuring damages? Every trial lawyer has a number of personal theories regarding these matters. Only a few empiric studies have been made and they are limited in scope. The available evidence indicates, however, that the similarities between judge and jury cases tend to outweigh the differences. As to the question of liability, statistics indicate that the judge and jury would agree in upwards of 80 percent of the cases. On the other hand, juries do seem to have a greater tendency to find against corporate and government defendants both as to liability and the amount of awards. See Broeder, *The University of Chicago Jury Project*, 38 Neb.L.Rev. 744, 750–51 (1959). *But see* Bledsoe, *Jury or Nonjury Trial—A Defense Viewpoint*, in 5 *Am.Jur. Trials* 123, 129, 139 (1966) (amount of jury awards on the average do not exceed awards by judges).

In making the choice between judge and jury a lawyer has much more to go on in the context of a particular case than these generalized comparisons between judge and jury trials. An attorney will consider the nature of the case, the characteristics of the parties and the witnesses, the passions that may surround the trial, the type of jurors who are likely to be chosen, and the background and predilections of the trial judge, if the judge's identity is known in advance, which often is not the case. Each of these factors is important in deciding whether the judge or the jury is most likely to identify with and be sympathetic to a lawyer's client.

Finally, the decision to demand a jury may depend on counsel's assessment of whether he is more effective in a judge or jury trial. In presenting a case to jurors the attorney must be a showman; he must be entertaining or their attention will wander; he must know how to excite their interest so that presentation of crucial testimony appears as a triumphant climax; and he must establish rapport with each and every juror, taking pains not to antagonize any of them by his actions or his appearance. By contrast, a lawyer in a nonjury trial need not concentrate heavily on the form of presentation since the judge will look for and pick out the significant aspects of the testimony even if they are not presented dramatically.

Rarely during the course of a jury case will an attorney have any clear sense of his success or failure in convincing the jury. He only can follow the planned presentation and hope that it was properly conceived. A sudden shift of tactics or a change of emphasis will tend to confuse and alienate the jurors. On the other hand, in a nonjury case, the judge, through statements during conferences, questions from the bench, and rulings on minor points, is constantly supplying the lawyers with clues as to her impressions of the case and the testimony. A sensitive attorney, upon detecting that things are not going well, may be able to salvage the case by changing the focus or direction of the testimony. For an interesting discussion of the different levels of involvement in the trial process as between the judge, sitting as a trier of fact, and the jury, see Wolf, *Trial by Jury: A Sociological Analysis*, 1966 Wis.L. Rev. 820.

3. THE SELECTION OF "FAVORABLE" JURORS

The first step in a jury trial is the selection of the jurors. The mechanics of selection are treated in detail in Section B of this Chapter. See pp. 845–55, infra. For present purposes it is sufficient to note that the attorneys have some control over the type of person who is chosen, since, in addition to the power to eliminate all persons who are in fact biased, each attorney may reject a small number of prospective jurors peremptorily, merely because counsel believes they will tend to react unfavorably to the client's case.

The process of trying to choose people who will make favorable jurors is extremely complex. Not only is it important to assess the way in which each individual juror is likely to view the case, but it also is necessary to analyze what effect each juror may have on the others during the course of deliberations. For example, one study indicates that as to issues involving scientific or technical information, a juror who has some relevant expertise wields considerable influence over the other jurors and often may control the verdict. Broeder, *Occupational Expertise and Bias As Affecting Juror Behavior: A Preliminary Look*, 40 N.Y.U.L.Rev. 1079 (1965). See also Bevan, Albert, Loiseaux, Mayfield & Wright, *Jury Behavior As a Function of the Prestige of the Foreman and the Nature of His Leadership*, 7 J.Pub.L. 419 (1958).

As a general rule a lawyer will seek jurors who will identify and sympathize with his client. Practically speaking, however, the lawyer only can guess at who they are, since he cannot possibly be aware of all of an individual juror's biases and hostilities. Consider, for example, a case brought by a young mother for the wrongful death of her husband. One would think that her attorney would be overjoyed if the jury contained a woman who also had been widowed and left with small children to raise. But the lawyer would not be pleased to learn that the juror in question, after a short period of mourning, had happily remarried, since that would greatly affect her attitude as to the proper amount of damages. Even if the juror had not remarried, her presence would be less desirable if her own marriage had been so unhappy that she preferred her present status. See generally Broeder, *Plaintiff's Family Status as Affecting Jury Behavior: Some Tentative Insights*, 14 J. Pub.L. 131 (1965).

4. THE SCOPE AND ORDER OF TRIAL

A. JURY CASES

Although the courts invariably have discretion to determine the order of trial, they usually do not deviate from standard practice, which is as follows:

1. Plaintiff's opening statement
2. Defendant's opening statement
3. Plaintiff's presentation of direct evidence
4. Defendant's presentation of direct evidence
5. Plaintiff's presentation of rebuttal evidence
6. Defendant's presentation of rebuttal evidence
7. Opening final argument by plaintiff
8. Defendant's final argument
9. Closing final argument by plaintiff
10. Giving instructions to the jury.

B. NONJURY CASES

Although generally jury and nonjury cases are handled in the same way, there are a number of significant differences in scope. For example, the court often will dispense with the opening statement and the closing argument, and, of course, there is never a need to give instructions. Some jurisdictions provide that an attorney has an absolute right to argue, even in nonjury cases. Rarely will such a right be exercised, however, if the judge, as is often the situation, makes clear that she believes an argument to be unnecessary.

----

5. TACTICAL CONSIDERATIONS REGARDING THE OPENING STATEMENT

Normally a case begins with plaintiff's opening statement. In the rare situation in which defendant has the burden of proof on *all* issues, such as when defendant admits plaintiff's allegations and goes to trial solely on his own affirmative defenses, the position of the parties is reversed throughout the trial and defendant has the right to open. Most lawyers regard the right to deliver the opening statement as so important that when they represent plaintiff they include some allegations in the complaint that defendant must deny in order to preserve the right. The reasons for viewing the right to open as substantial are fairly obvious. At the outset of the case the jurors are fresh, attentive, and impressionable. A carefully constructed statement laying out plaintiff's case in positive, coherent fashion can convince the jurors that plaintiff's version of the facts is the correct one, which will force defendant to fight an uphill battle to offset plaintiff's initial advantage. On experimental studies of the advantages in order of argument and proof, see Walker, Thibaut, and Andreoli, *Order of Presentation at Trial*, 82 Yale L.J. 216 (1972). See also Lawson, *Order of Presentation as a Factor in Jury Presentation*, 56 Ky.L.J. 523 (1968).

At common law defendant did not make his opening statement until plaintiff had presented the affirmative case. Today, in most jurisdictions, however, defendant has the option of making an opening statement immediately after plaintiff has done so. Most trial lawyers recommend that defendant open at the earliest opportunity. If defendant waits, the initial impression created by plaintiff's opening statement may be so fortified by the opening evidence that the case is lost by the time defendant begins presenting the opposing evidence. Defendant may be able to neutralize plaintiff's initial advantage if the former immediately sets out a contrary version of the facts. For an opposite view, see Stramondo & Goodspeed, *Defendant's Presentation*, 57 Mass.L.Q. 179 (1972), in which the authors take the position that defendant's opening argument is more effective when it refutes plaintiff's evidence.

One of the most difficult tactical questions regarding the opening argument is whether or not a party should avoid mentioning an important issue or a dramatic piece of evidence in the hope of gaining an advantage through surprise. With the availability of modern discovery techniques, it has become increasingly difficult to surprise one's opponent; moreover opposing counsel, by raising and disposing of the issue in his own opening argument, will insulate the jury from a dramatic shock. Nevertheless, with some items of evidence the less said about them in advance, the greater their impact. This occurs, for example, in cases in which defendant suddenly displays a movie of plaintiff, allegedly crippled for life as a result of defendant's negligence, playing tennis on the day before trial. However, since most items of evidence are not of such caliber, it generally is considered unsound to keep them secret, for to do so weakens the effectiveness of the opening statement and gives significant advantage to the opposition. For some interesting views on the tactics and style of opening argument, see Fuchsberg, *Opening Statements—Plaintiff's View*, in 5 Am.Jur. Trials 285 (1966); Hobson, *Selection of the Jury, Opening Statements and Closing Arguments*, 32 Neb.L.

Rev. 302 (1952); Stern, *Opening Statements—Defense View*, in 5 *Am.Jur. Trials* 305 (1966).

Just as an attorney's opening statement may advance a client's cause, it also may reveal fatal flaws in the claim or defense. If this occurs, in most jurisdictions the opposing party may move immediately for the entry of a judgment. The theory of this motion is the same as the philosophy underlying the demurrer and summary judgment—the court is not required to try a case once it becomes clear that one of the parties *must* prevail. See generally 4 Weinstein, Korn & Miller, *New York Civil Practice* ¶ 4016.14; Annot., 5 A.L.R.3d 405 (1966).

6. THE PRESENTATION OF EVIDENCE

A. THE PROBLEMS OF ADMISSIBILITY

The admissibility of evidence at trial is determined by a large and complex set of rules, the most important of which are discussed in Section C of this Chapter. See pp. 856–66, infra. Each lawyer must plan carefully and in advance of trial to make certain that the evidence considered to be important will be accepted. Often, if an item of evidence cannot be admitted under one rule, it can come in under another. Moreover, except in rare circumstances, no proffered item of evidence will be excluded unless the opposing party objects to its introduction. As a result an attorney often will offer otherwise inadmissible evidence in the hope that it will not be challenged. A lawyer must be careful, however, not to do this unsuccessfully too often as it may antagonize the judge or jury. Similarly, in many circumstances the opposing party will be well advised not to challenge inadmissible evidence that is not seriously prejudicial. An attorney who constantly objects may antagonize the jury by appearing to be an obstructionist. Even if the objections are sustained, the jurors may begin to believe something is being hidden from them, and will assume that the answers, had they been permitted, would have been unfavorable to the lawyer's client.

In some situations even the most diligent attorney is powerless to keep inadmissible, highly prejudicial statements from the jurors. For example, a witness simply may blurt out such a statement voluntarily without having been asked a question pertaining to it. In such cases the court has a choice. It may admonish the jury not to consider the evidence or it may declare a mistrial. In the latter case the jury is dismissed and the trial must begin anew before an entirely different panel. Obviously such drastic action is taken only when the error is severely prejudicial. Yet, is it realistic to expect jurors to ignore completely something they have heard and are told to forget?

B. THE TECHNIQUE OF PRESENTATION

Much has been written concerning the way in which evidence should be presented. Most of this commentary can be distilled into one basic observation: the better the preparation before trial, the better the presentation.

Usually most evidence is presented at trial through the examination and cross-examination of witnesses. A party should call witnesses in a logical order so that the jury will know, at every step of the way, what part of the case is being explored. Usually the most important witnesses are called first to put the jurors in a favorable frame of mind. The testimony of less important witnesses will then be understood by the jury as backing and fortifying that party's version of the facts. There are, of course, many factors that interfere with a planned presentation. First, the opposition, through cross-examination, will attempt to upset the pattern not only by raising questions as to the witnesses' accuracy but also by injecting new considerations that tend to confuse the jurors. Second, a party who wishes to stay on the good side of witnesses, particularly experts, may be forced to accommodate their interests by calling them when it is convenient for them to testify rather than at the most logical point in the trial. Finally, no matter how fine the preparation, every trial produces a number of surprises to which the lawyer must react immediately. If, for example, during cross-examination of an opposition witness, the interrogating attorney receives a surprise favorable response, he must press forward on the issue immediately, before the witness and the opposing attorney have the time and opportunity to soften the impact by planning an explanation.

Cross-examination is a potent trial weapon. With it a clever attorney can raise doubts concerning the accuracy of even the most accomplished and prepared witness, let alone an unsophisticated witness who actually is trying to cover up the facts. Consider, for example, the effect on the trier of fact of the following exchange from an actual cross-examination of a woman as reported in *Saturday Review*, August 19, 1967, p. 12, col. 2:

Q: Did you ever stay all night with this man in New York?

A: I refuse to answer that question.

Q: Did you ever stay all night with this man in Chicago?

A: I refuse to answer that question.

Q: Did you ever stay all night with this man in Miami?

A: No.

There are two ways to minimize the effects of cross-examination. The first is to make certain that the witness is clear as to the story and is telling the truth. This requires the attorney and the witness to go over the facts in detail shortly before the trial begins. Even after this precaution the excitement of the trial may so unnerve the witness that he forgets even the most basic facts. Consider the following actual exchange (with the names changed), again as reported in *Saturday Review*, August 19, 1967, p. 12, col. 2:

Q: What is your brother-in-law's name?

A: Borofkin.

Q: What's his first name?

A: I can't remember.

Q: He's been your brother-in-law for forty-five years and you can't remember his first name?

A: No, I tell you I'm too excited! (Rising from the witness chair and pointing to Borofkin.) Nathan, for God's sake tell them your first name!

The second method of limiting the effectiveness of cross-examination is for the attorney on direct examination to raise and dispense with any matter that might cast doubt on a witness' veracity if it were raised for the first time on cross-examination. For example, in most jurisdictions an attorney may impugn the credibility of an opposition witness by introducing evidence showing that the witness previously has been convicted of a felony. If the fact that the witness had once been convicted of a felony is raised at the very beginning of his testimony by the attorney who called him, the jury will tend to think of the witness as a person willing to suffer embarrassment to tell the truth; but if the matter is first raised on cross-examination, the jurors may tend to consider the witness a person who is trying to hide important facts. For a detailed treatment of tactical considerations in the presentation of evidence, see generally Keeton, *Trial Tactics and Methods* (2d ed. 1973).

C. THE ROLE OF THE TRIAL JUDGE IN THE PRESENTATION OF EVIDENCE

Suppose that an attorney's presentation of a case appears inadequate. To what extent should the trial judge take over the trial by interrogating the witness herself and perhaps by calling new witnesses she believes should be heard? Does it make a difference if the case is before a jury? These questions raise some fundamental considerations regarding the role of the trial judge: Is the court a mere umpire who must stand aloof except when called upon to make decisions or a participant with the right to supervise the conduct of the trial to help ensure a just result?

Although there is general agreement that judges do have some power to call and interrogate witnesses, there is considerable controversy as to the extent of the power. For example, in some jurisdictions it has been held that a case may be reversed if the trial judge frequently interrupts counsel's presentation or engages in extensive examination of the witnesses. See Laub, *Trial and Submission of a Case From a Judge's Standpoint,* 34 Temple L.Q. 1, 5–6 (1960). In other jurisdictions, however, the power apparently is unlimited and the only question is how it is to be exercised. See Gitelson & Gitelson, *A Trial Judge's Credo Must Include His Affirmative Duty to be an Instrumentality of Justice,* 7 Santa Clara Law. 7 (1966).

In recent years judges generally have tended to increase their active participation in the trial process. It even has been suggested that they *must* take a hand when the failure to do so will result in a miscarriage of justice, see Note, 58 Yale L.J. 183 (1948), but as yet judgments have not been reversed on this ground.

D. THE POWER OF JURORS TO QUESTION WITNESSES

What if a juror is dissatisfied with the evidence? Should he be permitted to ask a witness questions that were not asked by the attorneys? Would it be feasible, tactically, for an attorney to object to the question if it called for inadmissible evidence? Is there some means by which this latter problem could be avoided? See generally 44 Iowa L.Rev. 604 (1959).

7. THE CLOSING ARGUMENT

A. THE NATURE OF THE ARGUMENT

Closing argument is important because it is the only time when the attorneys can organize the evidence in the case for the trier of fact in a coherent fashion, without interruption, and when the logical implications of the evidence can be spelled out in detail.

Normally, final argument is in three parts, with plaintiff having the benefit of speaking both first and last. If, however, the only issues in the case are those upon which defendant has the burden of proof, the roles of the parties are reversed and defendant speaks first and last. Often the court will limit the amount of time available to each party. See Annot., 3 A.L.R.3d 1341 (1965). Whether or not such limits are imposed, the arguments should be brief, concise, sincere, easily understood, and emphasize the vital points of the case. See Sisson, *The Closing Argument*, 57 Mass.L.Q. 319 (1972).

B. PROPER VERSUS IMPROPER ARGUMENT

A proper argument is one that follows the facts of the case as supported by the evidence or inferences that properly can be drawn from the evidence. An argument is improper when it is based upon matters not in evidence; appeals to passion or racial or religious prejudice; contains references to the financial ability of the parties or includes remarks as to whether defendant is insured against the claimed liability; requests that the jurors treat the attorney's client as they would wish to be treated were they in the party's position; and distorts the evidence in order to arrive at unjustified inferences. In practice lawyers are permitted considerable leeway in argument with limitations being imposed only in certain easily defined circumstances. Opposing counsel will be reluctant to challenge an improper argument for fear of appearing weak, particularly if there is any chance that the challenge will not be upheld by the trial judge. At the same time many courts have been hesitant to interfere on their own motion, unless the argument gets completely out of hand. Is there any justification for such judicial reluctance? Shouldn't judges take a more active role in preventing abuse of the trial process? See Rinehart, *Final Argument*, 28 F.R.D. 235 (1960).

It often is difficult to detect an improper argument that is introduced subtly. Consider, for example, a case in which plaintiff, injured in a hit-run auto collision, is attempting to prove that defendant was the driver of the other car. Plaintiff's only evidence is that the accident occurred on Sunday and that the other car involved belonged to a neighbor of defendant who had permitted defendant to borrow it every Sunday for several months prior to the collision. In trying to convince the jury of the importance of this circumstantial evidence, plaintiff's attorney might say: "Suppose I were to tell you that defendant's fresh fingerprints were found on the steering wheel of the car shortly after the accident and that defendant's sweater was found near the accident. Surely there would be no doubt in your minds after that as to who was driving, even though no one saw defendant." Obviously such an argument, though proper on its face, should not be permitted since members of the jury might well believe that the fingerprints and the sweater were indeed found at the scene, although nothing in the evidence so indicates. For an excellent discussion of this and other similar problems of improper argument, see Levin & Levy, *Persuading the Jury with Facts Not in Evidence: The Fiction-Science Spectrum*, 105 U.Pa.L.Rev. 139 (1956).

8. INSTRUCTIONS TO THE JURY

Before it retires to deliberate and decide, the court instructs the jury as to the law to be applied and the manner in which it is to reach a decision.   The most significant legal controversy regarding the proper sequence of this phase of a jury trial is whether the instructions should come *before* or *after* the final arguments by counsel.   In most jurisdictions the courts take the position that the judge, as the impartial umpire in the case, should have the last word in order that partisan appeals by counsel will be tempered by a dispassionate statement of the law to be applied.   Those who favor instructions prior to argument ask: "How can any rational argument be made if the jurors have not yet been told about the law they must apply?"   Can this question be satisfactorily answered?   Note that it also might be argued that the jury cannot properly understand the opening statements of counsel or evaluate evidence as it is introduced unless they have prior knowledge of the legal significance of the facts presented.   Why then are the instructions not given by the court at the beginning rather than at the end of trial?   Would it make sense to give two sets of instructions, one at the beginning of trial and the other at the end?

Normally the court requires the attorneys to submit proposed instructions at some point during the trial, usually after the evidence has been completed. The court then determines which of these instructions to give and which of its own to add.   Under the rules of most jurisdictions a party cannot appeal the failure to give an instruction that he did not request or the giving of an erroneous instruction to which he made no immediate objection.   See, e. g., Federal Rule 51.   What is the purpose of rules such as these?   Why should an instruction be requested or challenged prior to the time the jury commences its deliberations?   Review *Alexander v. Kramer Bros. Freight Lines, Inc.*, p. 39, supra.

From a tactical point of view, the drafting of proposed instructions poses a serious dilemma.   On the one hand, every attorney wants a set of instructions that is as favorable to his client as possible.   On the other hand, the more slanted the instructions proposed, the less likely they are to be given and the more probable the judge will be antagonized by them since they will be of little assistance.   Moreover, there is always the danger that the judge will accept an instruction so prejudicial that a judgment based upon it will be reversed on appeal.   This not only is against the interests of the client but also harms the reputation of the attorney in the eyes of the trial judge who will hesitate to trust the attorney in future cases.   See generally Powers, *Requests for Instructions*, 28 F.R.D. 239 (1960).   Even if the instructions are favorable in substance, they will be totally ignored if they are so long and technical that the jurors cannot understand them.   Thus an attorney often is wise to seek a simple, favorable instruction on a point, even though a more complex charge might be framed in much more favorable terms.

9. SUBMISSION OF THE CASE TO THE JURY

After final arguments are completed and the instructions given, the jurors are placed in the custody of a bailiff or similar court official who guards them during deliberations. It is the bailiff's duty to make certain that the jurors remain together and have no contact with other persons except by court order.

In some cases the jurors will find it difficult to agree on a verdict. If this is due to uncertainty as to the content of the instructions, they may ask the court to reread the instructions, and, if necessary, to augment them. See, e. g., *Diniero v. United States Lines Co.,* p. 42, supra. If the major difficulty is due to disagreement as to what one or more of the witnesses said, the jurors may request that the testimony of those witnesses be read to them. See Annot., 50 A.L.R.2d 176 (1956). Whenever the jury reenters the courtroom, whether for further instructions or for the reading of testimony, it is wise to notify both parties and their attorneys in advance. Otherwise the verdict may be subject to reversal on appeal. What is the purpose of a rule requiring notice? How rigidly should it be enforced? For a general review of the cases on this point, see Annot., 84 A.L.R. 220 (1933).

Suppose after lengthy deliberations the jurors still are unable to agree. How long may they be kept in session? At what point does a court abuse its discretion by forcing them to continue their discussions? See Annot., 164 A.L.R. 1265 (1946). When a court does order an end to a session, must it then dismiss the jury and order a new trial? If not, must the jurors be locked up, free from all contact with outsiders, or should they be allowed to go home until such time as they are ordered to reassemble? See *Kramer v. Kister,* p. 893, infra; Annot., 77 A.L.R.2d 1086 (1961), for a detailed discussion of these matters.

At some point, of course, if the jurors continue to be unable to agree, they will have to be discharged and a mistrial declared. Courts are extremely reluctant to discharge a jury without its having reached a verdict because of the cost and delay of a new trial. Thus, as already noted, see Note 5, pp. 45–46, supra, a court often will urge a stalemated jury to make a further attempt to arrive at a verdict. Although many jurisdictions still require the traditional unanimous jury verdict, a substantial number have tried to cut down the number of stalemates by permitting a verdict to be based on something less than unanimity in civil cases. See, e. g., Cal.Code Civ.Proc. § 618 (three-fourths of jurors must agree); Mich.Gen.Ct.Rule 512.1 (five-sixths of jurors must agree). In Minnesota a less than unanimous verdict is permitted after the jury has deliberated for a certain length of time. Minn. Stat.Ann. § 546.17. Is there any reason why the requirement of unanimity should not be universally abolished? See Comment, *The Case for the Re-*

tention of the Unanimous Civil Jury, 15 De Paul L.Rev. 403, 405–06 (1966).[a]

In some cases the jury is able to arrive at a verdict almost immediately. Indeed, it may be possible for the jurors to agree without even leaving the jury box. Should a verdict in a complex case ever be subject to attack because it was rendered quickly? Invariably, the courts have said "no." See Annot., 91 A.L.R.2d 1220 (1963). Why should this be so?

---

10. DELIVERY OF THE VERDICT

The verdict of a jury is delivered by the foreman in open court. Traditionally the verdict was announced orally. Today, however, most juries render written verdicts on forms provided by the court. Once the verdict is formally announced or read by the judge or his clerk, any of the parties may demand that each of the jurors be polled to determine whether or not the verdict in fact has been agreed upon by the required number of jurors. This simply entails each of the jurors being asked whether the verdict as read reflects his or her decision. In many jurisdictions a poll is a matter of right; in others it is within the court's discretion to grant or deny. Under what circumstances would a court be inclined not to allow jurors to be polled if one of the parties so demanded? See generally Annot., 71 A.L.R.2d 640 (1960).

Suppose a poll reveals that the announced verdict was improperly arrived at or does not reflect the views of the jurors. Should the court dismiss the action and order a new trial? In most cases the court will send the jury back for further deliberations. Is there any danger that resubmission of the case to the jury might be prejudicial to one of the parties?

Sometimes the jury will reach a verdict that is improper on its face. For example, the jury might render a verdict for defendant even though it has been instructed to find for plaintiff and confine its deliberations to the amount of damages. Again, the court will have to decide whether to send the jury back for more discussion or to order a new trial. What factors should the court consider in making its determination?

---

a Although the criminal jury-trial guaranty of the Sixth Amendment to the United States Constitution has been held applicable to the states under the Fourteenth Amendment, Duncan v. Louisiana, 391 U.S. 145, 88 S.Ct. 1444, 20 L.Ed.2d 491 (1968), the Supreme Court has upheld the use of less-than-unanimous jury verdicts in state criminal trials. Johnson v. Louisiana, 406 U.S. 356, 92 S.Ct. 1620, 32 L.Ed. 2d 152 (1972); Apodaca v. Oregon, 406 U.S. 404, 92 S.Ct. 1628, 32 L.Ed.2d 184 (1972). What impact these decisions may have on the federal courts in criminal or civil matters remains unanswered. Compare the course of developments in the size of the jury, pp. 831–33, infra.

11. CHALLENGES TO THE VERDICT; ENTRY OF JUDGMENT

In the usual case when a verdict is in proper form, the trial judge or clerk will enter judgment in accordance with it. Before this is done, however, the parties will be given an opportunity to challenge the verdict on the basis of errors committed during the trial or on the ground that the evidence does not support it. The nature of these challenges and the consequences of a successful challenge are discussed in detail in Section F of this Chapter. See pp. 898–912, 948–56, infra. Serious errors not corrected at the trial-court level, of course, will lead to a reversal of a judgment on appeal. Why then is it necessary to give the trial judge a prior opportunity to upset the verdict? In actuality, the power of the trial judge to upset a verdict exceeds that of an appellate court to grant a reversal. Why should this be the case?

SECTION B. TRIAL BY JURY

---

1. THE INSTITUTION OF TRIAL BY JURY

During its formative period the jury was an activist group that not only judged the evidence but acquired much of it through its own investigation. An example of this drawn from twelfth century English history is the "jury" used to compile the famous Domesday Book, which contained an inventory of William the Conqueror's realm. The Domesday "jury" viewed the land and formed its own judgments without using witnesses. Today, of course, the jury is a passive, disinterested body that renders its decisions on the basis of the information placed before it.

The revered status of jury trial at common law is evidenced by Blackstone's statement that the right "has been, and I trust ever will be, looked upon as the glory of the English law * * * and * * * that it is the most transcendent privilege which any subject can enjoy or wish for, that he not be affected either in his property, his liberty, or his person, but by unanimous consent of twelve of his neighbors and equals." 3 Blackstone, *Commentaries* *378. Sir Winston Churchill expressed a similar view: "The jury system has come to stand for all we mean by English justice, because so long as a case has to be scrutinised by twelve honest men, defendant and plaintiff alike have a safeguard from arbitrary perversion of the law." 1 *A History of the*

English-Speaking Peoples 219 (1956).   Yet, in modern English practice, the jury is used comparatively infrequently.

In this country the jury system has been eulogized by the United States Supreme Court on many occasions.   For example, in SIOUX CITY & P. R.R. v. STOUT, 84 U.S. (17 Wall.) 657, 664, 21 L.Ed. 745, 749 (1873), the Court commented:

> * * *   Twelve men of the average of the community, comprising men of education and men of little education, men of learning and men whose learning consists only in what they have themselves seen and heard, the merchant, the mechanic, the farmer, the laborer; these sit together, consult, apply their separate experience of the affairs of life to the facts proven, and draw a unanimous conclusion.   This average judgment thus given it is the great effort of the law to obtain.   It is assumed that twelve men know more of the common affairs of life than does one man, that they can draw wiser and safer conclusions from admitted facts thus occurring than can a single judge.

More recently, the jury-trial institution has come under increasing attack because it seems "expensive and dilatory—perhaps anachronistic."   James, *Trial by Jury and the New Federal Rules of Civil Procedure*, 45 Yale L.J. 1022, 1026 (1936).   A fairly typical frontal assault appears in Peck, *Do Juries Delay Justice?*, 18 F.R.D. 455, 458–60 (1956):

> The plain fact is that the trial process designed for and inherited from the rural society of several centuries ago is not suited to handling the enormous volume of civil litigation resulting from the high speed, complexity and congestion of modern city living and the automobile age.   Indeed, we have been saved from a complete break-down of court services only by the fact that 95 per cent of the cases eventually get settled.   But because settlements often are not made until the eve of trial, settlements as well as trials are delayed by the length of time it takes for a case to reach trial.
>
> * * *
>
> Said G. K. Chesterton, "I would trust twelve ordinary men, but I cannot trust one ordinary man."   Perhaps this is a practical expression of the philosophy of the jury system.   We certainly want to hold to jury trials in serious criminal cases, but should we slavishly adhere to jury trials in all civil cases?   We can maintain the system for civil cases, and perhaps it is worth while, but we must understand the consequences, count the cost, note the alternatives and then deliberately decide what is in the public interest.

Perhaps the most outspoken critic of jury trial during the century has been the late Judge Jerome N. Frank of the Second Circuit.   His opinion of the institution is illustrated by the following passage from his book *Law and the Modern Mind* 180–81 (1930):

> The [jurors] * * * are hopelessly incompetent as fact-finders. It is possible, by training, to improve the ability of our judges to pass upon facts more objectively. But no one can be fatuous enough to believe that the entire community can be so educated that a crowd of twelve men chosen at random can do, even moderately well, what painstaking judges now find it difficult to do. * * * The jury makes the orderly administration of justice virtually impossible.

An excellent summary of Judge Frank's views is found in Paul, *Jerome Frank's Views on Trial by Jury*, 22 Mo.L.Rev. 28 (1957). More recent studies of the value of jury trial are O'Connell, *Jury Trials in Civil Cases*, 58 Ill.Bar J. 796 (1970), and Note, *With Love in Their Hearts but Reform on Their Minds: How Trial Judges View the Civil Jury*, 4 Colum.J.L. & Soc. Prob. 178 (1968).

One of the primary criticisms of the jury system is that it increases the time required for trial. One estimate is that jury-tried cases are on the average about forty percent longer than judge-tried cases, Zeisel, Kalven & Buchholz, *Delay in the Court* 71–81 (1959), and another commentator suggests that jury trials may run as much as three times longer than court trials. Hazard, *Book Review*, 48 Calif.L.Rev. 360, 369–70 (1960). In light of these statistics, the authors of *Delay in the Court* propose the abolition of jury trial in certain actions and efforts to induce jury waivers in others. See also Zeisel & Callahan, *Split Trials and Time Saving: A Statistical Analysis*, 76 Harv. L.Rev. 1606 (1963), which suggests that trials can be shortened by approximately twenty percent by conducting separate trials on jury and nonjury issues. What difficulties are presented by this suggestion? See pp. 806–26, infra. What is the justification for expending so much of the resources of our judicial system on jury trials? In this connection, consider the following remarks from Wolf, *Trial by Jury: A Sociological Analysis*, 1966 Wis.L.Rev. 820, 830:

> The presence of the jury is * * * an outlet [for the criticism to which the judiciary is "unusually susceptible"] and finds its counterpart in another social mechanism—the introduction of a stranger into a dispute to resolve it. Initially, in a nonjury case, the judge may stand in this relationship to the litigants; but as the trial progresses, he becomes a personalized being to them. Moreover, the judge has a definite interest in seeing a just result achieved, and this compels him, within limits, to become an active participant. The jury never achieves this status. It enters as a stranger and leaves as a stranger.

> * * * History alone should never suffice as the sole reason for retaining the anachronistic and useless. But before con-

signing to limbo an institution as venerable as the jury, the law should be quite certain what it is that is being thrown away.

As you study the remainder of this Section try to formulate judgments on the following questions: To what extent is the jury-trial institution an anachronism? Can we reform it to make it work more effectively in the twentieth century or should we eliminate it entirely? Have the courts been overly concerned with preserving jury trial even though it has been shown to be cumbersome and uneconomical? If we abandon jury trial, what other devices and procedures are available that might provide a more modern but democratic substitute? Why is it that even opponents of the civil jury simply assume, as does Justice Peck, that jury trial must be preserved in "serious criminal cases"? Is jury trial less of an anachronism in criminal than in civil cases? Does it serve any function in the criminal-law context that it doesn't on the civil-law side?

Excellent historical material on the jury can be found in 1 Holdsworth, *A History of English Law* 298–350 (3d ed. 1922); 1 Pollock & Maitland, *The History of English Law* 138–49 (2d ed. 1911); 2 *id.* 616–32, 641–59. See also Thayer, *The Jury and Its Development*, 5 Harv.L.Rev. 249, 295, 357 (1892), substantially reprinted in *A Preliminary Treatise on Evidence at the Common Law* 47–182 (1898). For discussions of civil jury trial in other countries, see Devlin, *Trial by Jury* (3d imp. 1966); Smith, *Civil Jury Trial: A Scottish Assessment*, 50 Va.L.Rev. 1076 (1964).

---

2. THE NATURE OF THE RIGHT TO TRIAL BY JURY

A. SOURCES OF THE RIGHT

Examine the Seventh Amendment to the United States Constitution and the state jury-trial guarantees set out in the Supplement. In what ways are they substantively different from each other? What reasons underlie these differences?

p.124

DAMSKY v. ZAVATT

United States Court of Appeals, Second Circuit, 1961.
289 F.2d 46.

FRIENDLY, Circuit Judge. * * *

The complaint of the United States asserts "This is a civil action to enforce federal tax liens on real property, and to obtain judgment for unpaid federal taxes" * * *. It alleges the making of assessments and the filing of notice of tax liens for 1946, 1947 and 1955 against Bernard [Damsky], for 1945 and 1946 against [his wife] Ollie, and for 1948, 1949, 1952 and 1953 against Bernard and Ollie jointly. The complaint further alleges that * * * Ollie owned two parcels of real estate in Brooklyn and that * * * Ollie conveyed one parcel to defendant Birns and the other to defendant Franz with intent to hinder, delay or defraud creditors or, in the alternative, without a fair consideration, Ollie then being or being rendered insolvent. * * * The United States prayed that the court adjudge Bernard and Ollie liable for the various taxes, penalties and interest assessed, plus interest; determine that the United States has valid tax liens on the real properties prior to any liens, claims and interests of the defendants or, in the alternative, determine that the real properties were transferred in fraud of creditors and set such transfers aside; and decree a sale of the real properties and distribution of the proceeds to the United States in satisfaction of its tax liens.

Petitioners answered and made a timely demand for a jury trial. This the government moved to strike. Judge Zavatt granted the government's motion; the petition for mandamus followed.

* * * The pertinent * * * [sections of the Internal Revenue Code] make no specific provision for or against jury trial. * * * If a jury demand includes issues as to which a party is not entitled to a jury trial, the court ought not to strike the demand altogether but should limit it to the issues on which a jury trial was properly sought, F.R.Civ.Proc. 39(a) (2).

* * * The considerations pertinent to various claims in the complaint differ; hence it will be necessary to examine these separately. It will be convenient to take first * * * the claims as to which we think jury trial was required; next discuss * * * those as to which it clearly was not; and end * * * with the claims we deem most debatable. If some of the discussion that follows may seem to reek unduly of the study, a sufficient answer is that the Seventh Amendment, like other provisions of the Bill of Rights, "is derived from history," Mr. Justice Frankfurter dissenting in Green v. United States, 1957, 355 U.S. 184, 199, 78 S.Ct. 221, 230, 2 L.Ed.2d 199, and we must turn to history to give it content and meaning.

I. *The claims asserted solely against Bernard.*

As to so much of the complaint as sought a judgment against Bernard for taxes, penalties and interest for which he was solely liable, the action was for a money judgment and nothing more. * * *

Study of the history of the Court of Exchequer shows that, under the common law of England in 1791, an action by the Crown to recover a judgment for taxes was a suit at common law in which the right of jury trial existed. This was the result of a long evolution.

The Exchequer of the twelfth century was "a compound institution, in part a judicial tribunal, in part a financial bureau." 1 Pollock & Maitland, The History of English Law (2d ed. 1889), 191–93.   *   *   *

By the end of the thirteenth century "the judicial side of the department was beginning to be more definitely separated from the administrative side," Holdsworth, [A History of English Law]   *   *   *   at 232; the Exchequer had become not merely an executive department but a revenue court trying cases brought by the King to collect his debts, Plucknett, A Concise History of the Common Law (5th ed. 1956) 159–60. *   *   *

By the time of Lord Coke the Exchequer was established as a third court of common law   *   *   *. Its business in part was to adjudicate with respect to "lands, rents, franchises, hereditaments, debts, duties, accounts, goods, chattels, and other profits, and benefits whatsoever due to the king." [IV Institutes 112]   *   *   *. Blackstone's description of the Exchequer in the following century is similar, 3 Commentaries, 43–45; in addition to its administrative functions, the King sued there "to adjust and recover his revenue   *   *   * as the withholding and non-payment thereof is an injury to his *jura fiscalia.*"

     *   *   *

Whether there was a right to jury trial in the informations of debt in the Exchequer seems not to have been explicitly discussed, probably because no one had any doubt about it. For the practice in the Exchequer was essentially that of the common law. Plucknett, supra, at 160 cites a Parliament roll of 1376 authorizing wager of law in the Exchequer, in cases where the King was not a party, on the modern-sounding ground "that jury trial was to the great damage of the people and the impoverishment of the jurors and caused much delay," Rot. Part ii, 337 no. 92. That a jury was used in such actions at the time most directly relevant to our problem is shown by [a]   *   *   * case from 35 Geo. III,   *   *   * the report of which recites "A verdict having been given for the crown." Moreover, there was a clear distinction between the "English information," which was in the nature of a bill in equity, and the "information of debt," which was an action at law. See United States v. Lyman, C.C.D.Mass.1818, 26 Fed.Cas. page 1024, No. 15,647 (Story, J.), which recognized the King's power to sue in debt for his taxes. The action of debt was one of the common-law forms of action; and in common-law actions there was a right to trial by jury.

In the colonies and the young states, "the process of distress [was] in nearly or quite universal use for the collection of taxes," Murray's Lessee v. Hoboken Land and Improvement Co., 1855, 18 How. 272, 278, 15 L.Ed. 372. That means of enforcement was likewise provided in the Federal Act of 1798 imposing a direct tax on dwelling houses, land and slaves, 1 Stat. 597, 600. Other federal statutes   *   *   * assured collection by means of bonds and forfeitures.   *   *   * Because of the comprehensive scheme of remedies thus provided, the issue of the Government's power to sue in debt for the tax itself seldom arose. But when it did, the power was upheld, and the trial was to a jury, at common law. * * *

In summary, in 1791 an action of debt lay in England for the collection of taxes, such an action has always lain in the federal courts even apart from statute, and nothing in I.R.C. § 6502, providing that any seasonably assessed tax "may be collected by levy or by a proceeding in court," or in any other relevant statute, suggests that the "proceeding in court" was to be otherwise than the historic one. The claim against Bernard for his separate taxes is thus a suit at common law within the Seventh Amendment, for the right to jury trial exists in actions by the United States where it would in a similar action between private parties. * * *

No different conclusion is warranted because of the statement of Chief Justice Taft in Wickwire v. Reinecke, 1927, 275 U.S. 101, 105–106, 48 S.Ct. 43, 45, 72 L.Ed. 184, that:

> "It is within the undoubted power of Congress to provide any reasonable system for the collection of taxes and the recovery of them when illegal, without a jury trial—if only the injunction against the taking of property without due process of law in the method of collection and protection of the taxpayer is satisfied. * * *"

Wickwire v. Reinecke was not an action by the Government to collect taxes; it was an action by a taxpayer against a collector for their recovery, in which a jury trial had been had. The quoted sentence followed an explanation that "the right of the petitioner to a jury in such a case is not to be found in the Seventh Amendment to the Constitution but merely arises by implication from the provisions of § 3226, Revised Statutes, which has reference to a suit at law"—an implication no plainer than that from I.R.C. §§ 6502 and 7401. * * *

However, we need not here decide whether Congress could constitutionally provide for an action *in personam* to secure a judgment for taxes without a jury trial. Clear indication of an intention to do this would be required, yet nothing in the statutes is indicative of this. No basis for discerning an intent by Congress to limit the rights of taxpayers to jury trials in actions to collect taxes brought against them by the United States can be found in Congress' action in 1954, c. 648, § 2(a), 68 Stat. 589, amending 28 U.S.C. § 2402 to grant taxpayers that right when they sue the United States in the district court for a refund under 28 U.S.C. § 1346(a) (1); if any inference could be drawn, it would be to the contrary. * * *

II. *The prayers for establishment of the tax liens against Ollie's real property and sale of the property to satisfy them.*

At the opposite extreme from the claims against Bernard just considered lies so much of the complaint as seeks to establish the validity of the tax liens against Ollie's real properties and the sale of the properties to satisfy them.

[handwritten left margin: Bernard entitled to trial by jury.]

Mr. Justice Story pointed out in Parsons v. Bedford, 1830, 3 Pet. 433, 446–447, 7 L.Ed. 732, that in view of the use of the phrase "all cases in law and equity" in Article III of the Constitution and the historic practice "that courts of equity use the trial by jury only in extraordinary cases, to inform the conscience of the court," the natural conclusion from the reference to suits at common law in the Seventh Amendment is "that this distinction was present to the minds of the framers of the amendment" and that they did not intend the amendment to apply to proceedings "where equitable rights alone were recognized, and equitable remedies were administered."

Foreclosure of the mortgagor's equity of redemption was an established head of equity jurisdiction well before 1791 * * * and this necessarily embraced the determination of the amount and validity of the mortgage debt.

Ollie =
No jury trial for
courts of equity.

* * * The more modern method of foreclosure through decree of sale, provided for United States tax liens by I.R.C. § 7403, is sufficiently akin to the historic equity practice to preclude successful contention for a right to jury trial with respect to the ascertainment of the amount of the tax lien as against taxpayer's property and enforcement of the lien by sale. * * *

III. *The prayer that the conveyances to Birns and Franz be disregarded.*

An action by a judgment creditor or a trustee in bankruptcy to set aside a fraudulent conveyance has long been cognizable in equity * * *. Hence the Seventh Amendment is inapplicable to such a claim * * * even though determination of the suit may involve the validity of the judgment as well as the circumstances of the conveyance. * * *

[A] tax assessment * * * has at least sufficient kinship to a judgment * * * that Congress, consistently with the Seventh Amendment, may extend to the United States the same rights to sue in equity to set aside a fraudulent conveyance that were held in 1791 by judgment creditors under the Statute of Elizabeth, 13 Eliz. 1, c. 5 (1571); and we read I.R.C. § 7403(c) as manifesting an intent to do precisely that. * * *

IV. *The claim for a personal judgment against Ollie.*

We shall first consider this problem as it would stand if the real properties were still in Ollie's name and then see whether any different conclusions are required because they are not.

Decisions and texts contain countless statements that, when the colonies separated from England, courts of chancery were without power to render a judgment for any deficiency that might remain unsatisfied after judicial sale of the mortgaged premises * * *. It was repeatedly stated that the procedure in England was to obtain a foreclosure of the equity of redemption in chancery and, either at the same time or thereafter, to bring a separate action at law to obtain judgment for any deficiency * * *. In any such action a defendant would, of course, be entitled to a jury trial. As a result of the absence of British precedents for a deficiency judgment in equity, it was held in New York and other states that there could be no deficiency judgment in a foreclosure suit * * *. Consequently several states enacted statutes authorizing the entry of money judgments in fore-closure actions * * * and the courts generally held no jury was required in trials under these statutes * * *. In the federal courts, the Supreme Court held equity had no power to enter a deficiency judgment * * *; then it immediately promulgated a rule of court authorizing such a judg-ment * * * and federal equity courts began granting it in foreclosure suits, without jury trial. * * *

How this practice was to be reconciled with the doctrine applied in both federal and state courts, that equity was not to be expanded beyond its estab-lished boundaries so as to curtail constitutionally guaranteed rights of jury trial, received little attention until the remarkable opinion of Judge Botts in the New Mexico case of Young v. Vail, [29 N.M. 324, 222 P. 912, 34 A.L.R. 980 (1924)] * * *. In England, before the statute of 15 & 16 Vict., C. 86, § 48 (1852), a suit to foreclose was not a suit to have a judicial sale; it was simply a suit to establish the rights of the parties in a parcel of land, by "strict fore-closure." * * * Since there was no sale, there was no determination of a deficiency to be made; title was declared in the mortgagee, and that was that. Therefore, there was no occasion for the chancery to consider whether it had power to enter deficiency judgments; and the absence of authority to that ef-fect does not indicate a lack of power. * * * Since the issue of equity's power to enter a deficiency judgment in a suit to foreclose by sale was thus un-decided by British precedents, reasoned Judge Botts, it should be resolved by general principles of equity jurisprudence. That meant application of the cleanup doctrine to avoid multiple litigation; and that, in turn, meant a de-ficiency judgment in equity. * * *

We find this reasoning completely persuasive. Hence Ollie would not be entitled to a jury trial as to her personal liability if the properties were still in her name * * *.

The argument that a different result is required here would be as follows: Ollie would be entitled to a jury trial of her personal liability, for the same rea-sons as Bernard has been held to be, were it not that the *in personam* judgment is incidental to foreclosure of the tax liens and sale of property. However, there can be no foreclosure or sale unless the alleged fraudulent conveyances are set aside, and it is impossible to tell now whether they will be. Hence, would run the argument, her jury demand should not be stricken as regards the issue of her personal liability * * * or, in the alternative, decision on the status of the jury demand in this respect should be deferred until the fraudu-lent conveyance claims have been determined.

Held| We disagree. The right to a jury trial depends on the nature of the relief sought, not on what may ultimately be secured * * *.

V. *The claim for a personal judgment against Bernard on his joint liabili-ty with Ollie.*

Modern texts state that a third party liable as co-maker or endorser of a secured obligation may be joined in an action to foreclose a mortgage, although he owns no interest in the property. * * *

* * * The reason for the absence of eighteenth century English authority for equity's entering a deficiency judgment against a joint obligor on a mortgage foreclosure is as likely to be the accident that the question would not arise in strict foreclosure as a view that the equity clean-up doctrine ought not be extended so far * * *. The readiness of American courts to permit equity to enter deficiency judgments against parties other than the mortgagor after the enactment of authorizing legislation, despite constitutional protection of jury trial, is strong evidence that such judgments were not beyond the true scope of equity's power in 1791, exactly as is the similar readiness to enter deficiency judgments against the mortgagors themselves. * * *

Accordingly the petition for mandamus is granted with respect to the claims asserted solely against Bernard Damsky and is otherwise denied.

CLARK, Circuit Judge (dissenting in part).

I dissent from so much of the opinion and judgment as grants a jury trial on the peripheral tax claims asserted solely against Bernard Damsky. In accordance with the precedents, as well as reason and policy, I find the question to be one purely of statutory intent, not of constitutional right. And since Congress—which has shown an ability to speak clearly on the issue when it so chooses—has conspicuously refrained from stating a requirement of trial by jury in this area of tax collection, I would hold Judge Zavatt correct in denying all jury trial demands in his decision below * * *.

The very careful and learned research by my brother Friendly into the history of the English Court of Exchequer beginning with the twelfth century serves in its fascinating, if uncertain, detail to highlight the artificiality of the chain of reasoning by which this restriction on twentieth century tax collection is discovered. The nub of the decision is the ruling that there is a constitutional right to a jury in the taxing area thus delimited. * * *

To reach the conclusion that the Seventh Amendment does restrict tax gathering in this one limited area * * * my brothers must resort to a technique which I must concede is not uncommon to lawyers, but which I do suggest would seem strange to any but lawyers. For first they must attach to this single form of claim an inapt label, namely, that of the writ of debt, and next, having made this venture in nomenclature and having further found on somewhat uncertain history that the writ always required a jury, they must hold that the name draws the action irrevocably into the constitutional aegis. I believe each of these steps to be quite unreal and unjustified. The modern all-inclusive civil action under the federal rules does not look like the old writ of debt, as set forth, say, in Chitty; and the attempt so to confine its broad terms seems to me at variance with the obvious intent of Congress to provide the widest remedial actions possible for tax collection. And even if by a strain upon history we now give it this limited name, that does not change the fact that the action is one *by the sovereign to collect its taxes* where the claim that a jury trial is constitutionally required has been authoritatively held "unfounded."

The result seems, therefore, to be one of logistic bootstrap lifting; it justifies my brothers' apology that their discussion "may seem to reek unduly of the study" or, I would add, "if not of the museum."

Of course American lawyers and judges have found the jury of immense value in assuming the burden of adjudicating troublesome issues of fact, notably in criminal and in negligence cases. But it is not showing care for the jury to force it into classes of claims where the right is dubious and the use inconvenient and burdensome. The present strain on juries in the cases where it is most needed is such that true believers should pause before they push it too far. The delays and court congestion of the jury calendars are a source of increasing tension, the long waits and infrequent sittings are a burden to the conscientious juror and lead him increasingly to avoid service, and Congress is regularly objecting to what it considers the undue cost of juries and cutting the appropriations therefor. And the actual inconvenience to adjudication by a rigid rule such as here announced is obvious. The claims made against Bernard, who has no property upon which the levy may be made, presumably are the least important of any before the court; and he was doubtless included both to foreclose any possible interest he might have in his wife's property and to prevent his later assertion of *res judicata* against other claims. And yet the very lack of substantial value to his case gives him alone a constitutional right of trial by jury and the power to condition and shape the entire litigation. * * *

NOTES AND QUESTIONS

1. The significance of the Seventh Amendment's reference to "suits at common law" is described in PARSONS v. BEDFORD, 28 U.S. (3 Pet.) 433, 447, 7 L.Ed. 732, 737 (1830), as follows:

> * * * [By "common law," the framers of the Constitution meant] suits in which legal rights were to be ascertained and determined, in contradistinction to those where equitable rights alone were recognized, and equitable remedies were administered; or where, as in the admiralty, a mixture of public law, and of maritime law and equity, was often found in the same suit. Probably, there were few, if any, states in the Union, in which some new legal remedies, differing from the old common-law forms, were not in use; but in which, however, the trial by jury intervened, and the general regulations in other respects were according to the course of the common law. * * * In a just sense, the amendment then may well be construed to embrace all suits, which are not of equity and admiralty jurisdiction, whatever may be the peculiar form which they may assume to settle legal rights. * * *

See Henderson, *The Background of the Seventh Amendment*, 80 Harv.L.Rev. 289 (1966). Does the "suits at common law" limitation make any sense now that law and equity have been merged? Consider this question in connection with *Beacon Theatres, Inc. v. Westover*, p. 807, infra.

Under existing constitutional doctrine, the Seventh Amendment does not generally apply to proceedings in state courts. See Walker v. Sauvinet, 92 U.S. 90, 23 L.Ed. 678 (1876). Yet the Supreme Court has held that other parts of the

Bill of Rights, such as the freedom of speech and expression in the First Amendment, the protection against searches and seizures in the Fourth Amendment, and the privilege against self-incrimination in the Fifth Amendment apply to the states. In what ways does the Seventh Amendment differ from these provisions? What are the arguments for applying the federal jury-trial guarantee to state-court actions? Are there any state-court actions in which a Seventh Amendment or "federal" jury trial is required at the present time? Reconsider the materials on federal law in the state courts on pp. 309–14, supra.

> 2. If "common law" in 1791 was understood by the framers of the seventh amendment as a process, rather than as a set of perpetually static rules, then one must ask whether, with the passage of time, the historical test has caused the amendment to diverge from the original conception. * * * During the centuries of their coexistence, the jurisdiction of the law courts and the chancellor * * * were subject to an unstatic process of accretion and erosion. * * * What remains constant over the history of this process, however, is the tendency toward expansion and enrichment of the remedies provided by the law courts. * * *

> If future development was contemplated—and if it is correct to view that development as largely one of the expansion of the remedies available at "common law"—then it would seem to follow that the "common law" of the seventh amendment was intended to have a changing meaning over time.

Wolfram, *The Constitutional History of the Seventh Amendment*, 57 Minn.L. Rev. 639, 738, 744 (1973). If the framers of the amendment understood "common law" as a process in which the remedies available in common-law courts would increase, is it likely that they viewed the right of jury trial as one that would expand or one that would contract?

3. In APPLICATION OF SMITH, 381 Pa. 223, 230, 112 A.2d 625, 629 (1955), the Pennsylvania Supreme Court upheld the constitutionality of a statute that provided for compulsory arbitration in certain circumstances. The Court said that a statute would not be an unconstitutional restriction on jury trial unless it

> closes the courts to litigants and makes the decision of the arbitrators the final determination of the rights of the parties; therefore there is no denial of the right of trial by jury if the statute preserves that right to each of the parties by the allowance of an appeal from the decision of the arbitrators or other tribunal. * * *

See also Capitol Traction Co. v. Hof, 174 U.S. 1, 19 S.Ct. 580, 43 L.Ed. 873 (1899). There are other inhibitions on securing a jury trial that have been held not to violate the constitutional mandate. For example, a party who requests a jury trial can be required to pay jury fees that ultimately are taxable as costs against the party who loses the action. What if the indexing or docketing fee for a jury trial is higher than the comparable fee for a nonjury trial? See Klein, *Jury Fees and Compensation of Jurors in the State Courts*, 26 F.R.D. 539 (1960).

4. McELRATH v. UNITED STATES, 102 U.S. 426, 440, 26 L.Ed. 189, 192 (1880), held that suits against the Government in the Court of Claims are not controlled by the Seventh Amendment because they are not suits at common law within its true meaning. "The government cannot be sued, except with its own

consent. It can declare in what court it may be sued, and prescribe the forms of pleading and the rules of practice to be observed in such suits." Is the conclusion of the Court in *McElrath* consistent with the spirit of the jury-trial guarantee? If McElrath had not sued the Government but the Government had initiated suit against him, would he then have had a right to jury trial on any legal issues that might have been raised? Absent any provision in the statute authorizing suit against the Government as to whether there is a right to jury trial, the legislative history is controlling. See United States v. Pfitsch, 256 U.S. 547, 41 S.Ct. 569, 65 L.Ed. 1084 (1921) (action under Lever and War Risk Insurance Acts held to be part of district court's general jurisdiction over actions at law and trial by jury held an incident thereto). See also Uarte v. United States, 7 F.R.D. 705 (S.D. Cal.1948).

B. THE EFFECT OF THE MERGER OF LAW AND EQUITY

Review the materials on pp. 350–79, supra.

Long before merger, equity developed the clean-up doctrine as a partial response to the problems of the bifurcation of law and equity. Under this doctrine, once an equity court obtained jurisdiction of a suit primarily of an equitable character, the court could decide any incidental legal issues that arose in the course of the litigation.

Sound considerations of policy lay behind * * * [the] "clean-up" rule, considerations which loom large and real against the background of two entirely independent systems of trial courts. The plaintiff entitled to both legal and equitable remedies needed relief from the burden of two days in court. Even worse was the plight of the litigant who had legitimately but vainly sought the chancellor's aid. The statute of limitations threatened him with total loss of remedy on an admittedly valid claim. It was the more dangerous a choice when crowded dockets and cumbersome procedure made the equitable process less than speedy. In any event, the dangers of a wrong choice of forum involved delay and all-consuming expense of litigation.

Here then was plaintiff's dilemma: to turn first to law might, as a simple matter of res judicata, lose him the more-desired chancellor's remedy; to turn to equity would often invite decision by an unpredictable conscience and perhaps the loss of all remedy. Equities had to be weighed on an imprecise balance and hardships measured by a rule the fine divisions of which were often known only to the chancellor himself. Small wonder then that the clean-up rule, the disposition of incidental questions legal in nature, was often applied even where all equitable relief was denied.

The cost of this efficiency was, however, substantial, for it involved the denial of trial by jury on all legal issues so adjudicated. In some situations this price was considered too heavy to pay for the trial convenience achieved. In others, where equity viewed a plaintiff's conduct as sufficiently reprehensible, the chancellor was pleased not to afford him aid by rapid disposition of a remaining issue.

Levin, *Equitable Clean-up and the Jury: A Suggested Orientation*, 100 U.Pa. L.Rev. 320, 320–21 (1951).

Although the codes and the Federal Rules abolish the procedural distinctions between law and equity and substitute a single form of action, they do not abrogate the differences between the substantive and remedial rules of the two systems. See pp. 360–79, supra. Undoubtedly the greatest obstacle to complete unification of law and equity has been the presence of a jury-trial right in actions that would have been triable in a law court under the bifurcated system. Indeed, Professor Chafee, in an unpublished lecture, characterized jury trial as "the sword in the bed that prevents the complete fusion of law and equity." In many ways merger actually has complicated the application of the jury-trial right because a party now may enter a single court with both legal and equitable claims. See generally Note, *The Right to Jury Trial Under Merged Procedures*, 65 Harv.L.Rev. 453 (1952). The problem of defining the contours of the right and the significance of the clean-up doctrine in these "mixed" actions, especially when the legal and the equitable claims overlap, has proven to be of considerable complexity. It is to this question that we now turn.

(i) Jury Trial in the Federal Courts

BEACON THEATRES, INC. v. WESTOVER

Supreme Court of the United States, 1959.
359 U.S. 500, 79 S.Ct. 948, 3 L.Ed.2d 988.

Certiorari to the United States Court of Appeals for the Ninth Circuit.

Mr. Justice BLACK delivered the opinion of the Court.

Petitioner, Beacon Theatres, Inc., sought by mandamus to require a district judge in the Southern District of California to vacate certain orders alleged to deprive it of a jury trial of issues arising in a suit brought against it by Fox West Coast Theatres, Inc. The Court of Appeals for the Ninth Circuit refused the writ, holding that the trial judge had acted within his proper discretion in denying petitioner's request for a jury. * * *

Fox had asked for declaratory relief against Beacon alleging a controversy arising under the Sherman Antitrust Act, 26 Stat. 209, as amended, 15 U.S.C.

§§ 1, 2, and under the Clayton Act, 38 Stat. 731, 15 U.S.C. § 15, which authorizes suits for treble damages against Sherman Act violators. According to the
complaint Fox operates a movie theatre in San Bernardino, California, and has
long been exhibiting films under contracts with movie distributors. These contracts grant it the exclusive right to show "first run" pictures in the "San Bernardino competitive area" and provide for "clearance"—a period of time during which no other theatre can exhibit the same pictures. After building a
drive-in theatre about 11 miles from San Bernardino, Beacon notified Fox
that it considered contracts barring simultaneous exhibitions of first-run
films in the two theatres to be overt acts in violation of the antitrust laws.
Fox's complaint alleged that this notification, together with threats of
treble damage suits against Fox and its distributors, gave rise to "duress
and coercion" which deprived Fox of a valuable property right, the right
to negotiate for exclusive first-run contracts. Unless Beacon was restrained, the complaint continued, irreparable harm would result. Accordingly, while its pleading was styled a "Complaint for Declaratory Relief," Fox
prayed both for a declaration that a grant of clearance between the Fox and
Beacon theatres is reasonable and not in violation of the antitrust laws, and for
an injunction, pending final resolution of the litigation, to prevent Beacon
from instituting any action under the antitrust laws against Fox and its distributors arising out of the controversy alleged in the complaint. Beacon filed an
answer, a counterclaim against Fox, and a cross-claim against an exhibitor who
had intervened. These denied the threats and asserted that there was no substantial competition between the two theatres, that the clearances granted were
therefore unreasonable, and that a conspiracy existed between Fox and its distributors to manipulate contracts and clearances so as to restrain trade and monopolize first-run pictures in violation of the antitrust laws. Treble damages
were asked.

Beacon demanded a jury trial of the factual issues in the case as provided
by Federal Rule   *   *   *   38(b). The District Court, however, viewed the
issues raised by the "Complaint for Declaratory Relief," including the question
of competition between the two theatres, as essentially equitable. Acting under the purported authority of Rules 42(b) and 57, it directed that these issues
be tried to the court before jury determination of the validity of the charges of
antitrust violations made in the counterclaim and cross-claim. A common issue of the "Complaint for Declaratory Relief," the counterclaim, and the
cross-claim was the reasonableness of the clearances granted to Fox, which depended, in part, on the existence of competition between the two theatres.
Thus the effect of the action of the District Court could be, as the Court of Appeals believed, "to limit the petitioner's opportunity fully to try to a jury every
issue which has a bearing upon its treble damage suit," for determination of
the issue of clearances by the judge might "operate either by way of res judicata or collateral estoppel so as to conclude both parties with respect thereto at
the subsequent trial of the treble damage claim."   *   *   *

The District Court's finding that the Complaint for Declaratory Relief
presented basically equitable issues draws no support from the Declaratory

Judgment Act, 28 U.S.C. §§ 2201, 2202; Fed.Rules Civ.Proc. 57. * * *
That statute, while allowing prospective defendants to sue to establish
their nonliability, specifically preserves the right to jury trial for both
parties. It follows that if Beacon would have been entitled to a jury trial in a
treble damage suit against Fox it cannot be deprived of that right merely because Fox took advantage of the availability of declaratory relief to sue Beacon
first. Since the right to trial by jury applies to treble damage suits under the
antitrust laws, and is, in fact, an essential part of the congressional plan for
making competition rather than monopoly the rule of trade * * *, the
Sherman and Clayton Act issues * * * were essentially jury questions.

Decl. Judgement Act preserves right to jury trial

Nevertheless the Court of Appeals * * * held that the question of
whether a right to jury trial existed was to be judged by Fox's complaint read as
a whole. In addition to seeking a declaratory judgment, the court said, Fox's
complaint can be read as making out a valid plea for injunctive relief, thus stating a claim traditionally cognizable in equity. A party who is entitled to maintain a suit in equity for an injunction, said the court, may have all the issues in
his suit determined by the judge without a jury regardless of whether legal
rights are involved. The court then rejected the argument that equitable relief, traditionally available only when legal remedies are inadequate, was rendered unnecessary in this case by the filing of the counterclaim and cross-claim
which presented all the issues necessary to a determination of the right to injunctive relief. Relying on American Life Ins. Co. v. Stewart, 300 U.S. 203,
215, 57 S.Ct. 377, 380, 81 L.Ed. 605, decided before the enactment of the
Federal Rules * * *, it invoked the principle that a court sitting in equity
could retain jurisdiction even though later a legal remedy became available.
In such instances the equity court had discretion to enjoin the later lawsuit in
order to allow the whole dispute to be determined in one case in one court.
Reasoning by analogy, the Court of Appeals held it was not an abuse of discretion for the district judge, acting under Federal Rule * * * 42(b), to
try the equitable cause first even though this might, through collateral estoppel, prevent a full jury trial of the counterclaim and cross-claim which were as
effectively stopped as by an equity injunction.[6]

Ct. of Appeals complaint stated a claim upon which equitable relief could be granted

Beacon takes issue with the holding of the Court of Appeals that the complaint stated a claim upon which equitable relief could be granted. As initially
filed the complaint alleged that threats of lawsuits by petitioner against Fox
and its distributors were causing irreparable harm to Fox's business relationships. The prayer for relief, however, made no mention of the threats but
asked only that pending litigation of the claim for declaratory judgment, Beacon be enjoined from beginning any lawsuits under the antitrust laws against
Fox and its distributors arising out of the controversy alleged in the complaint.

---

[6] 252 F.2d at page 874. In Ettelson v. Metropolitan Life Ins. Co., 317 U.S. 188,
192, 63 S.Ct. 163, 164, 87 L.Ed. 176, this Court recognized that orders enabling equitable causes to be tried before legal ones had the same effect as injunctions. In City
of Morgantown, W. Va. v. Royal Ins. Co., 337 U.S. 254, 69 S.Ct. 1067, 93 L.Ed. 1347,
the Court denied at least some such orders the status of injunctions for the purposes
of appealability. It did not, of course, imply that when the orders came to be reviewed they would be examined any less strictly than injunctions. * * *

Evidently of the opinion that this prayer did not state a good claim for equitable relief, the Court of Appeals construed it to include a request for an injunction against threats of lawsuits. * * * But this fact does not solve our problem. Assuming that the pleadings can be construed to support such a request and assuming additionally that the complaint can be read as alleging the kind of harassment by a multiplicity of lawsuits which would *traditionally* have justified equity to take jurisdiction and settle the case in one suit, we are nevertheless of the opinion that, under the Declaratory Judgment Act and the Federal Rules * * *, neither claim can justify denying Beacon a trial by jury of all the issues in the antitrust controversy.

The basis of injunctive relief in the federal courts has always been irreparable harm and inadequacy of legal remedies. At least as much is required to justify a trial court in using its discretion under the Federal Rules to allow claims of equitable origins to be tried ahead of legal ones, since this has the same effect as an equitable injunction of the legal claims. And it is immaterial, in judging if that discretion is properly employed, that before the Federal Rules and the Declaratory Judgment Act were passed, courts of equity, exercising a jurisdiction separate from courts of law, were, in some cases, allowed to enjoin subsequent legal actions between the same parties involving the same controversy. This was because the subsequent legal action, though providing an opportunity to try the case to a jury, might not protect the right of the equity plaintiff to a fair and orderly adjudication of the controversy. * * * Under such circumstances the legal remedy could quite naturally be deemed inadequate. Inadequacy of remedy and irreparable harm * * * today must be determined, not by precedents decided under discarded procedures, but in the light of the remedies now made available by the Declaratory Judgment Act and the Federal Rules.

Viewed in this manner, the use of discretion by the trial court under Rule 42(b) to deprive Beacon of a full jury trial on its counterclaim and cross-claim, as well as on Fox's plea for declaratory relief, cannot be justified. Under the Federal Rules the same court may try both legal and equitable causes in the same action. * * *

Thus any defenses, equitable or legal, Fox may have to charges of antitrust violations can be raised either in its suit for declaratory relief or in answer to Beacon's counterclaim. On proper showing, harassment by threats of other suits, or other suits actually brought, involving the issues being tried in this case, could be temporarily enjoined pending the outcome of this litigation. Whatever permanent injunctive relief Fox might be entitled to on the basis of the decision in this case could, of course, be given by the court after the jury renders its verdict. In this way the issues between these parties could be settled in one suit giving Beacon a full jury trial of every antitrust issue. * * * By contrast, the holding of the court below while granting Fox no additional protection unless the avoidance of jury trial be considered as such, would compel Beacon to split his antitrust case, trying part to a judge and part to a jury. Such a result, which involves the postponement and subordination of Fox's own legal claim for declaratory relief as well as of the counterclaim which Beacon was compelled by the Federal Rules to bring is not permissible.

Our decision is consistent with the plan of the Federal Rules and the Declaratory Judgment Act to effect substantial procedural reform while retaining a distinction between jury and nonjury issues and leaving substantive rights unchanged. Since in the federal courts equity has always acted only when legal remedies were inadequate, the expansion of adequate legal remedies provided by the Declaratory Judgment Act and the Federal Rules necessarily affects the scope of equity. Thus, the justification for equity's deciding legal issues once it obtains jurisdiction, and refusing to dismiss a case, merely because subsequently a legal remedy becomes available, must be re-evaluated in the light of the liberal joinder provisions of the Federal Rules which allow legal and equitable causes to be brought and resolved in one civil action. Similarly the need for, and therefore, the availability of such equitable remedies as Bills of Peace, *Quia Timet* and Injunction must be reconsidered in view of the existence of the Declaratory Judgment Act as well as the liberal joinder provision of the Rules. * * *

If there should be cases where the availability of declaratory judgment or joinder in one suit of legal and equitable causes would not in all respects protect the plaintiff seeking equitable relief from irreparable harm while affording a jury trial in the legal cause, the trial court will necessarily have to use its discretion in deciding whether the legal or equitable cause should be tried first. Since the right to jury trial is a constitutional one, however, while no similar requirement protects trials by the court,[17] that discretion is very narrowly limited and must, wherever possible, be exercised to preserve jury trial. * * * [O]nly under the most imperative circumstances, circumstances which in view of the flexible procedures of the Federal Rules we cannot now anticipate, can the right to a jury trial of legal issues be lost through prior determination of equitable claims. See Leimer v. Woods, 8 Cir., 196 F.2d 828, 833–836. As we have shown, this is far from being such a case.

                    * * *

The judgment of the Court of Appeals is reversed.

Reversed.

Mr. Justice FRANKFURTER took no part in the consideration or decision of this case.

Mr. Justice STEWART, with whom Mr. Justice HARLAN and Mr. Justice WHITTAKER concur, dissenting.

                    * * *

I.

The Court suggests that "the expansion of adequate legal remedies provided by the Declaratory Judgment Act * * * necessarily affects the scope of equity." Does the Court mean to say that the mere availability

---

[17] See Hurwitz v. Hurwitz, 78 U.S.App.D.C. 66, 136 F.2d 796, 798–799, 148 A.L.R. 226; cf. The Genesee Chief v. Fitzhugh, 12 How. 443, 459–460, 13 L.Ed. 1058.

of an action for a declaratory judgment operates to furnish "an adequate remedy at law" so as to deprive a court of equity of the power to act? That novel line of reasoning is at least implied in the Court's opinion. But the Declaratory Judgment Act did not "expand" the substantive law. That Act merely provided a new statutory remedy, neither legal nor equitable, but available in the areas of both equity and law. When declaratory relief is sought, the right to trial by jury depends upon the basic context in which the issues are presented. * * * If the basic issues in an action for declaratory relief are of a kind traditionally cognizable in equity, e. g., a suit for cancellation of a written instrument, the declaratory judgment is not a "remedy at law." If, on the other hand, the issues arise in a context traditionally cognizable at common law, the right to a jury trial of course remains unimpaired, even though the only relief demanded is a declaratory judgment.

Thus, if in this case the complaint had asked merely for a judgment declaring that the plaintiff's specified manner of business dealings with distributors and other exhibitors did not render it liable to Beacon under the antitrust laws, this would have been simply a "juxtaposition of parties" case in which Beacon could have demanded a jury trial. But the complaint * * * presented issues of exclusively equitable cognizance, going well beyond a mere defense to any subsequent action at law. Fox sought from the court protection against Beacon's allegedly unlawful interference with its business relationships —protection which this Court seems to recognize might not have been afforded by a declaratory judgment, unsupplemented by equitable relief. The availability of a declaratory judgment did not, therefore, operate to confer upon Beacon the right to trial by jury with respect to the issues raised by the complaint.

II.

* * * [T]he Court holds, quite apart from its reliance upon the Declaratory Judgment Act, that Beacon by filing its counterclaim and cross-claim acquired a right to trial by jury of issues which otherwise would have been properly triable to the court. Support for this position is found in the principle that, "in the federal courts equity has always acted only when legal remedies were inadequate. * * *" Yet that principle is not employed in its traditional sense as a limitation upon the exercise of power by a court of equity. This is apparent in the Court's recognition that the allegations of the complaint entitled Fox to equitable relief—relief to which Fox would not have been entitled if it had had an adequate remedy at law. Instead, the principle is employed today to mean that because it is possible under the counterclaim to have a jury trial of the factual issue of substantial competition, that issue must be tried by a jury, even though the issue was primarily presented in the original claim for equitable relief. This is a marked departure from long-settled principles.

It has been an established rule "that equitable jurisdiction existing at the filing of a bill is not destroyed because an adequate legal remedy may have become available thereafter." [8] American Life Ins. Co. v. Stewart * * *. It has also been long settled that the District Court in its discretion may order the trial of a suit in equity in advance of an action at law between the same parties, even if there is a factual issue common to both. * * *

III.

The Court today sweeps away these basic principles as "precedents decided under discarded procedures." It suggests that the Federal Rules of Civil Procedure have somehow worked an "expansion of adequate legal remedies" so as to oust the District Courts of equitable jurisdiction, as well as to deprive them of their traditional power to control their own dockets. But obviously the Federal Rules could not and did not "expand" the substantive law one whit.

Like the Declaratory Judgment Act, the Federal Rules preserve inviolate the right to trial by jury in actions historically cognizable at common law, as under the Constitution they must. They do not create a right of trial by jury where that right "does not exist under the Constitution or statutes of the United States." Rule 39(a). Since Beacon's counterclaim was compulsory under the Rules, see Rule 13(a), it is apparent that by filing it Beacon could not be held to have waived its jury rights. * * * But neither can the counterclaim be held to have transformed Fox's original complaint into an action at law. * * *

The Rules make possible the trial of legal and equitable claims in the same proceeding, but they expressly affirm the power of a trial judge to determine the order in which claims shall be heard. Rule 42(b). Certainly the Federal Rules were not intended to undermine the basic structure of equity jurisprudence, developed over the centuries and explicitly recognized in the United States Constitution.

For these reasons I think the petition for a writ of mandamus should have been dismissed.

NOTES AND QUESTIONS

1. Does *Beacon Theatres* mean the demise of the clean-up doctrine? Is the case in conflict with the historical test for jury trial employed in *Damsky? Compare* Savings Bank v. Santaniello, 130 Conn. 206, 33 A.2d 126 (1943) (clean-up doctrine applied to defendant's set-off in a suit for strict foreclosure of a mortgage), *with* Swofford v. B & W, Inc., 336 F.2d 406, 411 (5th Cir.1964) (clean-up doctrine repudiated; "to continue the past practice is to convert an administrative rule into a jurisdictional one so as to deprive the parties of a jury on what is basically a money claim for damages").

---

[8] The suggestion by the Court that "This was because the subsequent legal action, though providing an opportunity to try the case to a jury, might not protect the right of the equity plaintiff to a fair and orderly adjudication of the controversy" is plainly inconsistent with many of the cases in which the rule has been applied. * * *

2. The majority in *Beacon Theatres* adopted the test for determining the existence of a jury-trial right employed in LEIMER v. WOODS, 196 F.2d 828 (8th Cir.1952). In that case Woods sought an injunction, restitution, and damages. The Eighth Circuit reversed the district court's conclusion that there was no right of jury trial on the damage issue.

> * * * [W]here joinder has been made of co-ordinate equitable and legal causes of action and some of such causes of action, as here, involve a common, controlling issue of fact, on which there normally is a right to a jury trial as to the legal cause of action, the question ordinarily should be deferentially allowed to be determined by a jury, rather than for the court, without some special reason or impelling circumstance in the situation, to undertake to foreclose it as a matter of res judicata by designedly proceeding to make a previous disposition of the equity cause of action.

Id. at 834. Does *Beacon Theatres* expand upon the *Leimer* test or simply restate it?

In FRASER v. GEIST, 1 F.R.D. 267 (E.D.Pa.1940), the court stated: "The decision as to whether or not the plaintiff is entitled to a jury trial as 'of right' must rest upon a prior determination as to whether the action, in its essence, is one at law or equity." See also Ring v. Spina, 166 F.2d 546 (2d Cir.), certiorari denied 335 U.S. 813, 69 S.Ct. 30, 93 L.Ed. 368 (1948) (complaint for damages and injunction under Sherman Anti-Trust Act held "basically legal" and jury trial granted). Criticism of the "basic nature of the issue" test is found in Note, *The Effect of the Merger of Law and Equity on the Right of the Jury Trial in Federal Courts*, 36 Geo.L.J. 666 (1948).

A third pre-*Beacon Theatres* test is illustrated by TANIMURA v. UNITED STATES, 195 F.2d 329 (9th Cir.1952), a suit to enjoin the violation of rent regulations and for treble damages. The lower court held that the claims for an injunction against further violation and restitution of overpayments were equitable and to be tried first without a jury. The Ninth Circuit affirmed stating that the district court had discretion to determine whether the equitable issues or the legal issues should take precedence.

3. Consider the relevance of *Beacon Theatres* to the jury-trial right in the following situations.

(a) An action in which plaintiff seeks redress for a single wrong but asks for both legal and equitable relief. An example would be a copyright infringement action in which damages for past infringement (legal) and injunctive relief against future infringement (equitable) are sought. See Bruckman v. Hollzer, 152 F.2d 730 (9th Cir.1946).

(b) A situation in which plaintiff is entitled to either legal or equitable relief but not both. For example, a breach of contract action in which plaintiff sues for specific performance or damages in the alternative. If plaintiff demands a jury, will the resolution of the question depend on which relief he prefers and on the extent of the common issues? See Ford v. C. E. Wilson & Co., 30 F.Supp. 163 (D.Conn.1939), affirmed 129 F.2d 614 (2d Cir.1942). If defendant demands a jury trial and plaintiff opposes it, does this mean that plaintiff prefers equitable relief?

(c) A case in which a legal counterclaim is asserted against a claim for equitable relief or an equitable counterclaim is asserted against a legal claim. Should the permissive or compulsory nature of the counterclaim be relevant in determining whether there is a jury-trial right? *Compare* Bendix Aviation Corp. v. Glass, 81 F.Supp. 645 (E.D.Pa.1948), *with* Liberty Oil Co. v. Condon Nat. Bank, 260 U.S. 235, 43 S.Ct. 118, 67 L.Ed. 232 (1922).

For an excellent analysis of many *Beacon Theatres* problems, see McCoid, *Procedural Reform and the Right to Jury Trial,* 116 U.Pa.L.Rev. 1 (1967).

4. Because of the crowded condition of jury dockets in many parts of the country, application of the *Beacon Theatres* decision may delay the adjudication of cases that would progress more rapidly on a nonjury docket. The delay may cause commercial injury to the litigants. For example, in the *Beacon Theatres* context some parties might hesitate to deal with Fox pending the outcome of the litigation, thereby adversely affecting Fox's commercial relationships during this period. This problem is partially alleviated by Rule 57, which permits the trial court to advance all declaratory-judgment actions on the calendar for speedy determination. Can the procedure in Federal Rule 42(b) be used to mitigate some of the detrimental effects of the litigation on the parties?

———

DAIRY QUEEN, INC. v. WOOD, 369 U.S. 469, 82 S.Ct. 894, 8 L.Ed. 2d 44 (1962), arose out of a licensing agreement entered into by respondents, owners of the trademark "DAIRY QUEEN," under which petitioner agreed to pay $150,000 for the exclusive right to use that trademark in certain parts of Pennsylvania. The contract provided for a small initial payment with the remaining payments to be made at the rate of 50% of all amounts received by petitioner on sales and franchises to deal with the trademark; minimum annual payments were to be made regardless of petitioner's receipts. In August 1960, respondents wrote petitioner a letter in which they claimed that the latter had committed "a material breach of that contract" by defaulting on the contract's payment provisions and notified petitioner that the contract would be terminated unless the claimed default was remedied immediately. When petitioner continued to deal with the trademark, respondents brought an action for breach of contract praying for: (1) temporary and permanent injunctions to restrain petitioner from any future use of or dealing in the franchise and the trademark; (2) an accounting to determine the exact amount of money owed by petitioner and a judgment for that amount; and (3) an injunction pending an accounting to prevent petitioner from collecting any money from "Dairy Queen" stores in the territory.

The Eastern District of Pennsylvania granted a motion to strike petitioner's demand for a jury trial on the alternative grounds that either the action was "purely equitable" or, if not purely equitable, the legal issues were "incidental" to equitable issues, and, in either case, no right to trial by jury existed. The Third Circuit refused to mandamus the district judge to vacate this order. The Supreme Court reversed.

The Court first disposed of the district court's conclusion that there is no right to jury trial on legal issues that are "incidental" to equitable issues.

* * * The holding in Beacon Theatres * * * applies whether the trial judge chooses to characterize the legal issues presented as "incidental" to equitable issues or not. Consequently, in a case such as this where there cannot even be a contention of such "imperative circumstances," Beacon Theatres requires that any legal issues for which a trial by jury is timely and properly demanded be submitted to a jury. * * *

Id. at 472–73, 82 S.Ct. at 897, 8 L.Ed.2d at 48.

As to the lower court's conclusion that the action was "purely equitable," the Court said:

* * * The most natural construction of the respondents' claim for a money judgment would seem to be that it is a claim that they are entitled to recover whatever was owed them under the contract as of the date of its purported termination plus damages for infringement of their trademark since that date. * * * As an action on a debt allegedly due under a contract, it would be difficult to conceive of an action of a more traditionally legal character. And as an action for damages based upon a charge of trademark infringement, it would be no less subject to cognizance by a court of law.

The respondents' contention that this money claim is "purely equitable" is based primarily upon the fact that their complaint is cast in terms of an "accounting," rather than in terms of an action for "debt" or "damages." But the constitutional right to trial by jury cannot be made to depend upon the choice of words used in the pleadings. The necessary prerequisite to the right to maintain a suit for an equitable accounting, like all other equitable remedies, is, as we pointed out in Beacon Theatres, the absence of an adequate remedy at law. Consequently, in order to maintain such a suit on a cause of action cognizable at law, as this one is, the plaintiff must be able to show that the "accounts between the parties" are of such a "complicated nature" that only a court of equity can satisfactorily unravel them. In view of the powers given to District Courts by Federal Rule * * * 53(b) to appoint masters to assist the jury in those exceptional cases where the legal issues are too complicated for the jury adequately to handle alone, the burden of such a showing is considerably increased and it will indeed be a rare case in which it can be met. * * * A jury, under proper instructions from the court, could readily determine the recovery, if any, to be had here, whether the theory finally settled upon is that of breach of contract, that of trademark infringement, or any combination of the two. * * *

Id. at 476–79, 82 S.Ct. at 899–900, 8 L.Ed.2d at 50–52.

KATCHEN v. LANDY, 382 U.S. 323, 86 S.Ct. 467, 15 L.Ed.2d 391 (1966). Petitioner filed two claims in bankruptcy for sums allegedly due him *facts* from an insolvent corporation. The trustee in bankruptcy responded by asserting that certain payments from corporate assets to petitioner and others were "voidable preferences" under the Bankruptcy Act and could be recouped by the trustee in summary bankruptcy proceedings. Despite petitioner's objections, judgment was rendered for the trustee on the preferences and it was ordered that petitioner's claims remain unpaid until after the judgment in favor of the trustee had been satisfied. The Court of Appeals affirmed.

In the Supreme Court, petitioner argued that a creditor who has received a preference can hold the property under a substantial adverse claim without filing a claim in the bankruptcy proceeding, thereby forcing the trustee to recover the preference by a plenary action under Section 60 of the Act, 11 U.S.C. § 96; in such a plenary action the creditor could demand a jury trial. Petitioner also contended that the situation is the same when a creditor files a claim and the trustee not only objects to its allowance but also demands surrender of the preference; petitioner's theory was that the Bankruptcy Act does not give the bankruptcy court summary jurisdiction to order preferences surrendered; petitioner contended that if it did, it would violate the Seventh Amendment.

After an extensive analysis of the "structure and purpose" of the Bankruptcy Act, the Court held that the Act does confer summary jurisdiction to compel a claimant to surrender preferences. As to the jury-trial issue, the Court said:

> * * * [A]lthough petitioner might be entitled to a jury trial on the issue of preference if he presented no claim in the bankruptcy proceeding and awaited a federal plenary action by the trustee * * *, when the same issue arises as part of the process of allowance and disallowance of claims, it is triable in equity. The Bankruptcy Act, * * * converts the creditor's legal claim into an equitable claim to a pro rata share of the *res* * * *, a share which can neither be determined nor allowed until the creditor disgorges the alleged voidable preference he has already received. * * * As bankruptcy courts have summary jurisdiction to adjudicate controversies relating to property over which they have actual or constructive possession * * * and as the proceedings of bankruptcy courts are inherently proceedings in equity * * * there is no Seventh Amendment right to a jury trial for determination of objections to claims * * *.

Petitioner's final reliance is on the doctrine of Beacon Theatres v. Westover * * * and Dairy Queen v. Wood * * *.

The argument here is that the same issues—whether the creditor has received a preference and, if so, its amount—may be presented either as equitable issues in the bankruptcy court or as legal issues in a plenary suit and that the bankruptcy court should stay its own proceedings and direct the bankruptcy trustee to commence a plenary suit so as to preserve petitioner's right to a jury trial. * * *

[P]etitioner's argument would require that in every case where a § 57g objection [b] is interposed and a jury trial is demanded the proceedings on allowance of claims must be suspended and a plenary suit initiated, with all the delay and expense that course would entail. Such a result is not consistent with the equitable purposes of the Bankruptcy Act nor with the rule of Beacon Theatres and Dairy Queen * * *. In neither Beacon Theatres nor Dairy Queen was there involved a specific statutory scheme contemplating the prompt trial of a disputed claim without the intervention of a jury. We think Congress intended the trustee's § 57g objection to be summarily determined * * *. Both Beacon Theatres and Dairy Queen recognize that there might be situations in which the Court could proceed to resolve the equitable claim first even though the results might be dispositive of the issues involved in the legal claim. * * *

Id. at 336–40, 86 S.Ct. at 476–78, 15 L.Ed.2d at 401–03. Mr. Justice Black and Mr. Justice Douglas dissented for the reasons stated in the dissenting opinion of Judge Phillips in the Court of Appeals. 336 F.2d 535, 540 (10th Cir.1964).

QUESTIONS

In what ways does *Dairy Queen* clarify or go beyond the *Beacon Theatres* decision? Is *Katchen* a retreat from *Beacon Theatres* and *Dairy Queen*? Compare the Supreme Court's decision in FITZGERALD v. UNITED STATES LINES CO., 374 U.S. 16, 83 S.Ct. 1646, 10 L.Ed.2d 720 (1963), that a Jones Act claim, which is under the aegis of a statutory jury-trial right, and a maintenance-and-cure claim, which traditionally has been a nonjury admiralty question, arising out of a single occurrence had to be tried together before a jury. Should the Court have reached that result?

ROSS v. BERNHARD, 396 U.S. 531, 90 S.Ct. 733, 24 L.Ed.2d 729 (1970). Plaintiffs brought a derivative suit in federal court against the directors of a closed-end investment company of which they were shareholders and joined the company's brokers, alleging that the company had been charged excessive brokerage fees. Plaintiffs' demand for jury trial,

[b] Section 57g of the Bankruptcy Act forbids the allowance of a claim when the creditor receives or acquires a preference that is void or voidable under the Act if he does not surrender the preference.

granted by the trial court but set aside by the Second Circuit, was upheld by the Supreme Court in a five-to-three decision:

The common law refused * * * to permit stockholders to call corporate managers to account in actions at law. * * * Early in the 19th century, equity provided relief both in this country and in England. * * * The remedy made available in equity was the derivative suit, viewed in this country as a suit to enforce a *corporate* cause of action against officers, directors, and third parties. As elaborated in the cases, one precondition for the suit was a valid claim on which the corporation could have sued; another was that the corporation itself had refused to proceed after suitable demand, unless excused by extraordinary conditions. Thus the dual nature of the stockholder's action: first, the plaintiff's right to sue on behalf of the corporation and, second, the merits of the corporation's claim itself.

Derivative suits posed no Seventh Amendment problems where the action against the directors and third parties would have been by a bill in equity had the corporation brought the suit. Our concern is with cases based upon a legal claim of the corporation against directors or third parties. Does the trial of such claims at the suit of a stockholder and without a jury violate the Seventh Amendment?

* * * The heart of the action is the corporate claim. If it presents a legal issue, one entitling the corporation to a jury trial under the Seventh Amendment, the right to a jury is not forfeited merely because the stockholder's right to sue must first be adjudicated as an equitable issue triable to the court. *Beacon* and *Dairy Queen* require no less.

If under older procedures, now discarded, a court of equity could properly try the legal claims of the corporation presented in a derivative suit, it was because irreparable injury was threatened and no remedy at law existed as long as the stockholder was without standing to sue and the corporation itself refused to pursue its own remedies. * * *

* * * Actions are no longer brought as actions at law or suits in equity. Under the Rules there is only one action—a "civil action"—in which all claims may be joined and all remedies are available. Purely procedural impediments to the presentation of any issue by any party, based on the difference between law and equity, were destroyed. In a civil action presenting a stockholder's derivative claim, the court after passing upon the plaintiff's right to sue on behalf of the corporation is now able to try the corporate claim for damages with the aid of a jury. * * * The "expansion of adequate legal remedies provided by * * * the Federal

Rules necessarily affects the scope of equity." Beacon Theatres, Inc. v. Westover, 359 U.S., at 509.

Thus, for example, before-merger class actions were largely a device of equity, and there was no right to a jury even on issues that might, under other circumstances, have been tried to a jury. * * * [I]t now seems settled in the lower federal courts that class action plaintiffs may obtain a jury trial on any legal issues they present. * * *

Mr. Justice Stewart, dissenting, responded:

* * * Since, as the Court concedes, a shareholder's derivative suit could be brought only in equity, it would seem to me to follow by the most elementary logic that in such suits there is no constitutional right to trial by jury. * * *

[T]he Court's effort to force the facts of this case into the mold of *Beacon Theatres* and *Dairy Queen* simply does not succeed. Those cases involved a combination of historically separable suits, one in law and one in equity. * * *

But the present case is not one involving traditionally equitable claims by one party, and traditionally legal claims by the other. Nor is it a suit in which the plaintiff is asserting a combination of legal and equitable claims. For, as we have seen, a derivative suit has always been conceived of as a single, unitary, equitable cause of action. It is for this reason, and not because of "procedural impediments," that the courts of equity did not transfer derivative suits to the law side. * * *

If history is to be so cavalierly dismissed, the derivative suit can, of course, be artificially broken down into separable elements. But so then can any traditionally equitable cause of action, and the logic of the Court's position would lead to the virtual elimination of all equity jurisdiction. An equitable suit for an injunction, for instance, often involves issues of fact which, if damages had been sought, would have been triable to a jury. Does this mean that in a suit asking only for injunctive relief these factual issues *must* be tried to the jury, with the judge left to decide only whether, given the jury's findings, an injunction is the appropriate remedy? * * *

Id. at 534–35, 539–41, 544, 549–50, 90 S.Ct. at 736, 738–39, 741, 743–44, 24 L.Ed.2d at 733–34, 736–37, 739, 742.

NOTES AND QUESTIONS

1. SIMLER v. CONNER, 372 U.S. 221, 222, 83 S.Ct. 609, 610–11, 9 L.Ed. 2d 691, 693 (1963):

* * * The federal policy favoring jury trials is of historic and continuing strength. * * * Only through a holding that the jury-trial right is to be determined according to federal law can the uni-

formity in its exercise which is demanded by the Seventh Amendment be achieved. In diversity cases, of course, the substantive dimension of the claim asserted finds its source in state law, * * * but the characterization of that state-created claim as legal or equitable for purposes of whether a right to jury trial is indicated must be made by recourse to federal law.

Review *Byrd v. Blue Ridge Elec. Coop., Inc.,* p. 278, supra.

2. Is there a constitutional right to a nonjury trial on issues that historically were considered equitable and therefore were tried by the chancellor? What is the significance of the statement in *Beacon Theatres* that "the right to jury trial is a constitutional one * * * while no similar requirement protects trials by the court." In MICHAELSON v. UNITED STATES ex rel. CHICAGO, ST. P., M. & O. RY. CO., 291 F. 940, 946 (7th Cir.1923), the court remarked that "Congress cannot constitutionally deprive the parties in an equity court of the right of trial by the chancellor." The Supreme Court reversed, 266 U.S. 42, 45 S.Ct. 18, 69 L.Ed. 162 (1924), on other grounds and simply acknowledged the importance of the question.

Courts in at least seven states—Michigan, Wisconsin, Montana, New Jersey, South Carolina, South Dakota, and Utah—have declared that there is a constitutional right to a nonjury trial. The judicial reasoning is described in Van Hecke, *Trial by Jury in Equity Cases,* 31 N.C.L.Rev. 157, 173 (1953), as follows:

> The courts which have asserted that there is a constitutional right in equity cases to a trial of the facts by the judge alone, appear to have been motivated by (a) tradition, (b) respect for the chancellor's professional skill as a trier of facts, (c) a consciousness that the need for a court of equity had arisen in part from the limitation that jury trial had imposed upon the adequacy of various common-law actions, (d) an over-literal application of state constitutional provisions relating to the structure of state courts, (e) unsympathetic reaction to early legislative attempts to fuse the administration of law and equity into one procedural system, and (f) an uninformed fear of how jury trial would work in equity cases.

Are any of these reasons of sufficient magnitude to counter the policy in favor of jury trials apparent in *Byrd, Beacon Theatres,* and *Dairy Queen?* See generally Note, *The Right to Nonjury Trial,* 74 Harv.L.Rev. 1176 (1961).

(ii) Jury Trial in the State Courts

In Georgia, North Carolina, Tennessee, and Texas, there is a right to jury trial in equity cases, which eliminates the problem presented by *Beacon Theatres* and *Dairy Queen.* See generally Van Hecke, *Trial by Jury in Equity Cases,* 31 N.C.L.Rev. 157 (1953). In most states that have merged law and equity, however, issues similar to those in the federal courts have arisen since the adoption of the codes.

The Commissioners who prepared the original New York Code of Civil Procedure (1848) were aware of the problem presented by abolishing the distinction between law and equity at a time when the state constitution continued to guarantee "trial by jury in all cases in which it has been heretofore used." [c] But they may have underestimated the difficulty. Not content to leave the issue solely one of constitutional interpretation as it has been in the federal courts, they attempted to solve it by specific provisions:

§ 208. Whenever, in an action for the recovery of money only, or of specific real or personal property, there shall be an issue of fact, it must be tried by a jury, unless a jury trial be waived * * *.

§ 209. Every other issue is triable by the court, which, however, may order the whole issue, or any specific question of fact involved therein, to be tried by a jury * * *.

These provisions were copied in a great many states. But "in most jurisdictions * * * the courts, while occasionally giving the statute some weight, have regarded it generally as merely restating the law-equity dichotomy, and have proceeded to make their determination on historical grounds." Note, *The Right to Jury Trial under Merged Procedures,* 65 Harv.L.Rev. 453, 454 (1952). In civil actions in which damages alone are sought, there has been little difficulty in finding that a jury is required, and of course in traditional equity cases, such as those involving trusts or injunctions, no jury has been allowed. In most states, there has been a reluctance to allow a mixed form of trial, with some issues being tried by the court and some by a jury. When there have been "legal" and "equitable" issues in the same case, the tendency has been to find one or the other the "predominant" concern and try the case accordingly. Perhaps most frequently the decision has been to find the case "predominantly" equitable, with jury trial denied on the "legal" issues on the grounds that they are "incidental," or that a jury trial is waived by joining a legal claim in an equitable action. Id. at 454–55.

The Supreme Court's decisions in *Beacon Theatres* and *Dairy Queen* have not had a broad impact on the state courts, and in the state cases in which those decisions have been discussed, the reception has been mixed. *Compare* Adams v. Citizens Bank, 248 So.2d 682 (Fla.Dist.Ct.App.1971), *with* Phoenix Mut. Life Ins. Co. v. Conway, 11 N.Y.2d 367, 229 N.Y.S.2d 740, 183 N.E.2d 754 (1962).

---

[c] This language appeared in the New York Constitutions of 1777, 1821, 1846, and 1894. Because it was interpreted to mean that each successive constitution guaranteed jury trial in any case to which it had been extended by the legislature since the adoption of the preceding constitution, it was changed in the constitution of 1938 to guarantee jury trial only "in all cases in which it has heretofore been guaranteed by constitutional provision." See 4 Weinstein, Korn & Miller, *New York Civil Practice* ¶¶ 4101.07–.08.

HIATT v. YERGIN

Indiana Court of Appeals, Second District, 1972.
—— Ind.App. ——, 284 N.E.2d 834.

[Plaintiffs alleged that they had simultaneously entered into two contracts with defendants. Under the first contract, plaintiffs agreed to sell their one-half interest in Henry County Beverage Company to defendants; under the second contract, defendants agreed to resell the interest to plaintiffs under the same terms if plaintiffs were unable to obtain a Federal Basic Permit and state Alcoholic Beverage Commission approval for their operation of another liquor distributorship. Plaintiffs further alleged that they had performed the first contract and the conditions precedent to the second contract, but that defendants had refused their demand for reconveyance of the Henry County Company stock. They claimed $500,000 damages for the withholding of the stock, and also demanded an accounting for the period during which the stock was withheld. Finally they alleged that they would sustain irreparable injury unless defendants were compelled to return the stock.

[Plaintiffs demanded "trial by jury of the action herein and the issues formed on the pleadings herein." The trial court denied the motion, and after a trial found that plaintiffs had not used due diligence in seeking the permit for the operation of the second distributorship, and that they had not applied for the necessary permits for the retransfer of the Henry County Company stock. "If the specific performance requested * * * was granted," said the court, "an operating business would be closed, causing irreparable harm to the owner of the other [half-interest]." The trial court entered judgment against plaintiffs.]

BUCHANAN, Judge.

* * * It is our opinion that the trial court did not err in overruling Hiatt's request for a trial by jury because Rules TR. 38(A) and (C) deny a party a jury trial if the cause is of exclusive equitable jurisdiction; the main theory of this cause is equitable.

* * *

Rules TR. 38 and 39 of the Indiana Rules of Trial Procedure respectively govern Jury Trial of Right and Trial by Jury or by the Court. Pertinent parts of each provide:

"Trial Rule 38
"*Jury trial of right*

"(A) *Causes triable by court and by jury. Issues of law and issues of fact in causes* that prior to the eighteenth day of June, 1852, were of exclusive equitable jurisdiction shall be tried by the court; issues of fact *in all other causes* shall be triable as the same are now triable. In case of the *joinder of causes of action* or de-

fenses which, prior to said date, were of exclusive equitable jurisdiction with *causes of action* or defenses which prior to said date
were designated as actions at law and triable by jury—the former
shall be triable by the court, and the latter by a jury, unless waived;
the trial of both may be at the same time or at different times, as
the court may direct.

  * * * * * * * *

  "(C) *Same: Specification of issues.* In his demand a party
may specify the *issues* which he wishes so tried; otherwise he shall
be deemed to have demanded trial by jury for all *issues* triable as
of right by jury. * * *

  The emphasis supplied to the above excerpted portions exhibits to us a
semantic cloud hovering over the repeated use of the word "issues" in Rules
TR. 38(C) and 39(A)(1) and (2). "Issues" do not exist in a vacuum;
they result from factual allegations in civil actions consisting of one or more
claims which may or may not be triable by jury because they are "of exclusive equitable jurisdiction." While Rule TR. 38(A) concerns itself with
issues in "causes" and "causes of action," subsections (B) and (C) and Rule
TR. 39(A)(2) speak only of "issues" which a party may demand be tried
by jury. At first blush, it appears that it is "issues" rather than "causes"
which determine a party's right to a jury trial. This is not our construction
of these Rules.

  We thus conclude that * * * a party's right to trial by jury depends
upon the nature of the claim(s) stated and not upon the issues that may arise
within such claim(s). * * *

  [O]ur courts have had little difficulty in determining when a party
is entitled to a jury trial as a matter of right, if the cause was either
exclusively equitable or exclusively legal, or even if there was a joinder of
equitable causes of action with legal causes of action. Reichert v. Krass,
(1895) 13 Ind.App. 348, 40 N.E. 706 (foreclosure of a mechanic's lien
and matters contained in a counterclaim for damages on breach of contract
found to be an exclusively equitable proceeding); * * * Towns v. Smith,
(1888) 115 Ind. 480, 16 N.E. 811 (creditor's bill to set aside and cancel a
fraudulent conveyance with additional relief seeking to recover a personal
judgment on a promissory note deemed an exclusively equitable action);
* * * Fish v. Prudential Ins. Co., (1947) 225 Ind. 448, 75 N.E.2d 57
(action to rescind and cancel a life insurance policy with a cross-complaint
for full recovery on the policy found to be an essentially equitable cause of
action).

  * * *

  We now turn to the Indiana precedents specifically determining the
right to jury trial in causes where one or more of the issues of fact are of
exclusive equitable jurisdiction and others are not. The cases are confusing.

However, the tendency to deny jury trial in these circumstances is a common thread that runs through most of them.

Typical is Towns v. Smith, *supra,* where the court announced as early as 1888 that *"if any essential part of a cause* is exclusively of equitable cognizance, the *whole* is drawn into equity" (emphasis supplied) and tried without a jury. * * *

In further support of the proposition that the whole is drawn into equity when any essential part of a cause is exclusively equitable, is this language in Carmichael v. Adams, * * * [91 Ind. 526 (1883)]:

> *"The court, having acquired jurisdiction of * * * a suit in equity * * * was not bound to dissect the suit into separate members,* and try each separately, one member as a matter of law, and the other as a matter of equity, but had a right to *treat the case as a unity,* and as one of exclusive equitable jurisdiction.
> * * *

> "It would lead to confusion and injustice to direct separate trials in such cases. Should a jury find there was no right to recover on the [legal cause of action], and the court adjudge that there was a right to recover on the [equitable cause of action], there would then be a conflict not easily overcome. To be sure, the court might set aside the verdict and grant a new trial, but this, after all, would leave the control with the court, and it might just as well be there in the first instance." (Emphasis supplied.)
> * * *

We think the foregoing exposition of Indiana law and our commentary on the historical dilemma point the way to a solution of whether Hiatt is entitled to a jury trial in this case. Before doing so, we must scatter one more cloud, a federal one this time.

The repetitious use of the word "issues" in Rule TR. 38(C) * * * lends credence to holdings of the United States Supreme Court to the effect that the existence of an issue, not of equitable jurisdiction, even though incidental, in a cause that is otherwise equitable in character requires a jury trial of such issue and, further, that the legal issue must be tried first. Beacon Theatres, Inc. v. Westover * * *; Dairy Queen, Inc. v. Wood * * *. When these cases were decided, the Federal Rules of Civil Procedure contained provisions substantially similar to our Rules * * *.

As the Seventh Amendment to the United States Constitution applies only to civil trials in federal courts, the states are free to develop their own body of law concerning the right to trial by jury in civil matters.

The dissent in Beacon Theatres v. Westover, *supra,* provides [an additional] reason why we should reject the majority holding that as long as there is any incidental issue of fact not equitable in character for which a jury trial has been demanded, it must be submitted to the jury. The three dissenters potently argued that to adopt the majority view was to "undermine the basic structure of equity jurisprudence, developed over the centuries." * * *

The dissenters expressed the prophetic fear that to adopt the majority approach results in clogging of court calendars with frivolous or dilatory demands for jury trials and leads to administrative impasse. Rules of procedure should not oust equity of "Jurisprudence developed over the centuries and explicitly recognized in the U. S. Constitution * * * The court today sweeps away these basic principles * * *"

Hardly an inviting approach for Indiana to adopt.

* * * [W]e turn to Hiatt's one paragraph Complaint to see if he was improperly denied a jury trial.

An overview of the pleadings indicates a blending of issues of fact predominately of equitable jurisdiction with others not of such character so that the cause is in the nature of a bill in equity.

The choice of the pleader was to plead breach of contract and out of that same transaction or set of circumstances, allege substantive facts the primary object of which was equitable relief. The main theory outlined by the facts pleaded is not for damages, but for specific performance of the agreement(s) between Hiatt and Yergin with an attendant accounting and an injunction as to the manner of the future operation of the Henry County Beverage Company * * *.

* * * While the amount of damages sought, *i. e.*, $500,000.00, is not inconsequential, the recovery of damages appears to be incidental to the main theory of the action. We note that Hiatt's last allegation is that the "Plaintiffs [Hiatt] are without an adequate remedy at law."

The decision of the trial court is therefore affirmed.

[Concurring opinion of WHITE, P. J., is omitted.]

C. STATUTORY ACTIONS

ROGERS v. LOETHER

United States Court of Appeals, Seventh Circuit, 1972.
467 F.2d 1110.

STEVENS, Circuit Judge. The question presented is whether appellant was entitled to a jury trial in an action for compensatory and punitive damages brought under § 812 of the Civil Rights Act of 1968, 42 U.S.C. § 3612.[1]

In her complaint, plaintiff alleged that the three defendants had refused to rent her an apartment because of her race. She requested injunctive relief restraining defendants from renting the apartment to anyone else, money damages for her actual losses, punitive damages of $1,000, and attorney's fees.

The district court, after an extended hearing, entered a preliminary injunction. Subsequently, with plaintiff's consent, the injunction was dissolved; thereafter only plaintiff's claims for compensatory and punitive damages and attorney's fees remained. Defendants' request for a jury trial of those issues was denied * * *. After trial, the court found that plaintiff had suffered no actual damages but assessed punitive damages of $250; the prayer for attorney's fees was denied.

* * *

The district court held that a jury trial was not required by the Seventh Amendment or by a fair interpretation of the statute.

* * *

Our study of the issue persuades us that (1) the constitutional right to trial by jury applies in at least some judicial proceedings to enforce rights created by statute; (2) this action for damages is "in the nature of a suit at common law"; (3) the nature of the claim is "legal" within the test identified in Ross v. Bernhard * * *; (4) the right to a jury trial may not be denied on the ground that the damage claim is incidental to a claim for equitable relief; (5) cases involving an award of back pay pursuant to the 1964 Act are inapplicable; and finally (6) in view of our grave doubts as to the constitutionality of a denial of the right to a jury trial and the failure of Congress expressly to indicate that the traditional procedure for litigating damage claims should not be followed, the statute should be construed to authorize trial by jury. Accordingly, we have decided to reverse.

Findings of Ct.

I.

The Seventh Amendment preserves the substance of the right to a jury trial which existed under English common law when the amendment was adopted. It has never been suggested that the application of the amendment is narrowly confined to such common law writs as might be enforceable in a federal court. On the contrary, since the bulk of the civil litigation in the

---

[1] Section 812 provides, in part:

* * *

"(c) The court may grant as relief, as it deems appropriate, any permanent or temporary injunction, temporary restraining order, or other order, and may award to the plaintiff actual damages and not more than $1,000 punitive damages, together with court costs and reasonable attorney fees in the case of a prevailing plaintiff: *Provided,* That the said plaintiff in the opinion of the court is not financially able to assume said attorney's fees." * * *

federal judicial system involves the assertion of a federal right derived either from an act of Congress or the Constitution itself, necessarily the principal significance of the Seventh Amendment has been in such cases. It is perfectly clear that the fact that a litigant is asserting a statutory right does not deprive him or his adversary of the protection of the amendment. 7ᵗʰ.

* * *

N. L. R. B. v. Jones & Laughlin Steel Corp., 301 U.S. 1, 48–49, 57 S.Ct. 615, 81 L.Ed. 893, does not hold—as is sometimes assumed—that no jury trial is required in a cause of action created by statute since any such action would have been unknown to the common law and therefore beyond the reach of the Seventh Amendment. The *Jones & Laughlin* opinion expressly recognizes that the amendment is applicable not only to a suit at common law, but also to a judicial proceeding "in the nature of such a suit." The distinction drawn in the opinion is not between substantive rights derived from the common law as opposed to those created by statute; it is the difference between a proceeding "in the nature of a suit at common law" and a "statutory proceeding."

Jury Trial applicable in 1) suit at CL; 2) "in the nature of such a suit.

* * * The procedure approved by *Jones & Laughlin* was, of course, fundamentally different from a common law trial. It was administrative rather than judicial and did not invoke the original jurisdiction of a court in determining factual issues or fashioning a remedy. The initial case was not "tried" in a court of law or equity; it was "tried" in a separate *proceeding* created by statute.

Here there is no statutory *proceeding*. The statute authorizes a "civil action" in the courts of the United States. * * * The issue we must consider, therefore, is whether an action for damages authorized by the Civil Rights Act of 1968 is, in the language of *Jones & Laughlin*, "in the nature of a suit at common law."

II.

There are three reasons why this action is the kind of case which is appropriately described as in the nature of a suit at common law.

3 reasons suit is "in nature of suit at CL" (Historical)

First, the tribunal whose jurisdiction is invoked is a court created pursuant to Article III of the Constitution. * * * In all respects—at least all except the right to a jury trial if our appraisal of that right is not correct —it is clear that the procedure to be followed in this case is precisely that which is applicable to suits at common law which are tried in the federal judicial system.

Second, the remedy sought, including both compensatory and punitive damages, is the relief most typical of an action at law. * * *

Finally, the nature of the substantive right asserted, although not specifically recognized at common law, is analogous to common law rights. An English innkeeper who refused, without justification, to rent lodgings to a traveler was apparently liable in an action at law triable to a jury. Refusing to rent an apartment on the false ground that an applicant is an unfit tenant, when race is the real motivation, is a species of defamation; libel and slander, of course, are common law causes of action. Discrimination might involve mental distress or other emotional harm, and the developing common law of torts recognizes a cause of action for the intentional infliction of emotional harm.

We therefore conclude that a suit for damages for discrimination in the sale or rental of housing facilities is sufficiently analogous to a suit at common law to be appropriately characterized as a "legal" claim triable to a jury.

Conclusion: discrim. suit is "legal" claim.

III.

Although the full implications of the Supreme Court's decision in Ross v. Bernhard * * * have yet to be determined, it is clear that mere analogy to history may not be sufficient to define the scope of the Seventh Amendment. * * *

[T]he Court identified <u>history as only one of three criteria</u> that should be considered in determining the "legal" nature of an issue. The other two were: "<u>second, the remedy sought</u>; and, <u>third, the practical abilities and limitations of juries.</u>" Indeed, not only did the Court identify these two additional criteria; it also implied, without expressly stating, that history may be a less reliable guide than the other two. We have already concluded that under an historical analysis a jury trial is required in the present case; we proceed to consider the other two criteria.

* * * The relief sought was actual damages and punitive damages. Both the <u>determination of the amount</u> which <u>would adequately compensate</u> a litigant for an unliquidated claim and the punitive element of the award are <u>appropriate for jury</u> determination. * * *

damage determ. appropriate for jury

The "practical abilities and limitations of juries" obviously present no obstacle to their determination of the issues presented in these civil rights cases. Typically, the facts are not complex and decision turns on appraisals of credibility and motive. Certainly such matters are far more suitable for jury determination than complicated commercial issues that routinely arise in derivative and antitrust litigation. * * *

IV.

The *Jones & Laughlin* holding that the Seventh Amendment is inapplicable to an N.L.R.B. proceeding terminating in the entry of an order directing reinstatement and awarding back pay was supported not only by the Court's characterization of the proceeding as statutory, but also by reference to chancery practice in which damages could be awarded as an element of complete equitable relief. In this case the district court also regarded the relief authorized by the 1968 Act as primarily equitable and considered it appropriate to award damages as incident to such relief.

As the case developed, the defendant's right to demand a jury was not determined until after plaintiff's claim for equitable relief had been abandoned. Nevertheless, we share the district court's view that the right to a jury trial in this kind of case may properly be tested by the character of the relief requested in plaintiff's complaint. Our decision is not predicated on the special circumstance that only the damage claims remained when defendant's demand for a jury was denied.

* * *

It would appear that *Beacon* and *Dairy Queen* have mandated that once any claim for money damages is made, the legal issue—whether defendant breached a duty owed plaintiff for which defendant is liable in damages —must be tried to a jury whether or not there exists an equitable claim to which the damage claim might once have been considered "incidental." * * *

V.

Since the district court relied on several cases holding that in an employee's suit for reinstatement and back pay under Title VII of the Civil Rights Act of 1964, the employer is not entitled to a jury trial, we should briefly indicate why we think the reasoning of those cases is inapplicable here.

First, insofar as the cases hold that back pay is a legal remedy which may be recovered as incidental to equitable relief, we believe they cannot stand in the face of *Beacon* and *Dairy Queen*.

Second, to the extent that they hold, relying on N. L. R. B. v. Jones & Laughlin Steel Corp. * * *, that a jury trial is not required because the right vindicated is a statutory right, we reject the conclusion because it fails to differentiate between a statutory proceeding and the enforcement of a statutory right in an ordinary "civil action" in the courts.

Third, an acceptable rationale for awarding back pay in a non-jury judicial proceeding is consistent with our analysis of the damage claims asserted in this case. It is not unreasonable to regard an award of back pay as an appropriate exercise of a chancellor's power to require restitution. Restitution is clearly an equitable remedy. * * * The retention of "wages" which would have been paid but for the statutory violation (of improper discharge) might well be considered "ill-gotten gains"; ultimate payment restores the situation to that which would have existed had the statute not been violated.

The payment of compensatory damages in a housing discrimination case, however, is not a return to plaintiff of something which defendant illegally obtained or retained; it is a payment in money for those losses— tangible and intangible—which plaintiff has suffered by reason of a breach of duty by defendant. Such damages, as opposed to rent overcharges, unpaid overtime wages, or back pay, cannot properly be termed restitution.

* * *

Reversed and remanded.

NOTES AND QUESTIONS

1. The Supreme Court affirmed the instant case in a unanimous decision on February 20, 1974. Curtis v. Loether, 415 U.S. 189 (1974). The opinion by Mr. Justice Marshall rests on essentially the same analysis as that of the Seventh Circuit. The Court of Appeals opinion is discussed in Note, *Congressional Provision for Nonjury Trial under the Seventh Amendment*, 83 Yale L.J. 401 (1973).

2. The principal case referred to in the opinion as denying jury trial in actions for reinstatement with back pay under Title VII is Johnson v. Georgia Highway Express, Inc., 417 F.2d 1122 (5th Cir.1969). To the same effect, in districts outside the Fifth Circuit, are cases from federal courts in Connecticut, Maryland, Massachusetts, and Virginia. See cases cited in Ochoa v. American Oil Co., 338 F.Supp. 914, 923 n.6 (S.D.Tex.1972), a scholarly opinion that quarrels with the ruling of the Fifth Circuit in *Johnson,* although adhering to it. See also Note, *The Right to Jury Trial under Title VII,* 37 U.Chi.L.Rev. 167 (1969).

In LAWTON v. NIGHTINGALE, 345 F.Supp. 683, 684 (N.D.Ohio 1972), the court held that there was no right to jury trial in an action for damages under 42 U.S.C. § 1983, the Civil Rights Act of 1871, because it is a statutory action, and because: "If a jury could be resorted to in actions brought under this statute, the very evil the statute is designed to prevent would often be attained. The person seeking to vindicate an unpopular right could never succeed before a jury drawn from a populace mainly opposed to his views."

3. Is there a limit to the power of a legislature to avoid the jury-trial guarantee by creating statutory actions in place of common-law actions and providing administrative tribunals for their adjudication, as has been done in the case of workmen's compensation? Could the legislature provide that ordinary personal injury actions be decided by such a tribunal? See Opinion of the Justices, 87 N.H. 492, 179 A. 344, 110 A.L.R. 819 (1933); Brown, *Administrative Commissions and the Judicial Power,* 19 Minn.L.Rev. 261 (1935); Note, *Application of Constitutional Guarantees of Jury Trial to the Administrative Process,* 56 Harv.L. Rev. 282 (1942).

D. THE SIX–MEMBER JURY

In PATTON v. UNITED STATES, 281 U.S. 276, 288, 50 S.Ct. 253, 254, 74 L.Ed. 854, 858 (1930), a criminal case, the Court said that the words "trial by jury"

> includes all the essential elements as they were recognized in this country and England when the Constitution was adopted * * *. Those elements were: (1) That the jury should consist of twelve men, neither more nor less; (2) that the trial should be in the presence and under the superintendence of a judge having power to instruct them as to the law and advise them in respect of the facts; and (3) that the verdict should be unanimous.

But in WILLIAMS v. FLORIDA, 399 U.S. 78, 90 S.Ct. 1893, 26 L.Ed.2d 446 (1970), the Court held that a state might constitutionally use a jury with six (or perhaps fewer) members in a criminal case. Because the Court had held in DUNCAN v. LOUISIANA, 391 U.S. 145, 88 S.Ct. 1444, 20 L.Ed.2d 491 (1968), that the Sixth Amendment guarantee of jury trial in criminal cases applied to the states through "incorporation" in the Fourteenth Amendment, the result in *Williams* required the Court to recognize that such a jury would also satisfy the constitutional guarantee in federal criminal cases, a recognition it made explicit.[d]

Seizing upon the holding in *Williams* and transferring it to the civil-jury guarantee in the Seventh Amendment, numerous federal district courts through their Rule 83 power to make local rules have provided that ordinary civil actions shall be tried by six-member juries only.

———

COLGROVE v. BATTIN, 413 U.S. 149, 93 S.Ct. 2448, 37 L.Ed.2d 522 (1973). Petitioner sought mandamus to compel a federal district judge to impanel a twelve-member jury, notwithstanding Local Rule 13 (d)(1) of the District Court for the District of Montana, which provided for a six-member jury in all civil cases. Petitioner argued that the Local Rule violated the Seventh Amendment, the Enabling Act, 28 U.S.C. § 2072, and Federal Rule 48. The Court of Appeals denied mandamus, and the Supreme Court affirmed, five to four:

> * * * [T]he historical setting in which the Seventh Amendment was adopted highlighted a controversy that was generated not by concern for preservation of jury characteristics at common law but by fear that the civil jury itself would be abolished unless protected in express words. * * *

> * * * We can only conclude, therefore, that by referring to the "common law," the Framers of the Seventh Amendment were concerned with preserving the *right* of trial by jury in civil cases where it existed at common law, rather than the various incidents of trial by jury. In short, what was said in *Williams* with respect to the criminal jury is equally applicable here: constitutional history reveals no intention on the part of the Framers "to equate the constitutional and common-law characteristics of the jury." * * *

d "The decision evinces, I think, a recognition that the 'incorporationist' view * * * which underlay *Duncan* * * * must be tempered to allow the States more elbow room in ordering their own criminal systems. With that much I agree. But to accomplish this by diluting constitutional protections within the federal system itself is something to which I cannot possibly subscribe. Tempering the rigor of *Duncan* should be done forthrightly, by facing up to the fact that at least in this area the 'incorporation' doctrine does not fit well with our federal structure, and by the same token that *Duncan* was wrongly decided." Williams v. Florida, 399 U.S. 78, 118, 90 S.Ct. 1893, 1915, 26 L.Ed.2d 446, 464 (1970) (Harlan, J., concurring).

* * * In *Williams*, we rejected the notion that "the reliability of the jury as a factfinder . . . [is] a function of
its size," * * * and nothing has been suggested to lead us to
alter that conclusion. * * *

* * * Significantly, our determination that there was "no
discernible difference between the results reached by the two dif-
ferent-sized juries," * * * drew largely upon the results of
studies of the operations of juries of six in civil cases. * * *
Thus, while we express no view as to whether any number less
than six would suffice, we conclude that a jury of six satisfies
the Seventh Amendment's guarantee of trial by jury in civil cases.
Id. at 152, 155–56, 157, 158–60, 93 S.Ct. at 2450, 2452, 2453–54, 37 L.Ed.
2d at 526, 528, 529, 530–31.

The Court further found that the Montana Local Rule did not violate
the Enabling Act, since it concluded that the Congress in saying that the
rules "shall preserve the right of trial by jury as at common law and as
declared by the Seventh Amendment" had not intended to go beyond the
Seventh Amendment guarantee itself. Finally, it held that the Local Rule
was not in conflict with Federal Rule 48, saying that the latter was only
concerned with numbers stipulated by the parties, and was inapplicable
when a number was imposed regardless of the parties' consent.

NOTE

The majority and dissenting opinions in *Colgrove* cite a number of studies
of the six-member jury, including Devitt, *The Six-Man Jury in the Federal Court,*
53 F.R.D. 273 (1971), and Zeisel, *And Then There Were None: The Diminution of the Federal Jury,* 38 U.Chi.L.Rev. 710 (1970), which are two excellent
presentations of opposing views.

---

3. THE PROVINCE OF JUDGE AND JURY

SLOCUM v. NEW YORK LIFE INS. CO., 228 U.S. 364, 382, 33 S.Ct.
523, 530, 57 L.Ed. 879, 888 (1912), p. 957, infra:

In the trial by jury * * * both the court and the jury are essential
factors. To the former is committed a power of direction and superinten-
dence, and to the latter the ultimate determination of the issues of fact. Only
through the cooperation of the two, each acting within its appropriate sphere,
can the constitutional right be satisfied. And so, to dispense with either, or to
permit one to disregard the province of the other, is to impinge on that right.

JERKE v. DELMONT STATE BANK, 54 S.D. 446, 456–59, 223 N.W.
585, 589–90 (1929):

* * * We frequently see the phrase, "It is for the jury to say what
the facts are." Historically speaking, this may have been true in the sixteenth

century, but it has long since ceased to be true. The power and right and duty of the jury is not "to *say* what the facts are," but to adjudge and determine what the facts are by the usual and ordinary intellectual processes; that is, by applying the thinking faculties of their minds to the evidence received and the presumptions existing in the case, if any, and thereby forming an opinion or judgment.   *   *   *

Jurors do not determine all questions of ultimate fact, even in jury cases. They determine the existence or nonexistence of those facts, and those only, with reference to the existence of which the judgment of reasonable men might differ as a result of the application of their intellectual faculties to the evidence. If the proof offered by the party having the burden in support of the existence of ultimate issuable facts is so meager that a reasonable mind could not therefrom arrive at the existence of such ultimate fact, there is nothing for the jury, and the judge not only may, but should, direct a verdict against the party having the burden of proof.e   *   *   *

WEINER, THE CIVIL JURY AND THE LAW–FACT DISTINCTION, 54 Calif.L.Rev. 1867, 1867–68 (1966):

The categories of "questions of law" and "questions of fact" have been the traditional touchstones by which courts have purported to allocate decision-making between judge and jury.   *   *   *   Many statutes in effect today echo   *   *   *   [the] dichotomy, utilizing the law and fact terminology to identify the respective provinces of the judge and the jurors in a civil case. None of these statutes, however, attempts to define what is meant by a question of law or a question of fact. Nor have the courts shown any inclination to fashion definitions which can serve as useful guidelines. Indeed, when faced with a dispute as to whether a specific issue should be resolved by the judge or the jury, the typical appellate opinion today does no more than label the question as one of law or of fact, perhaps citing some authorities which are equally devoid of any more detailed consideration of the point.   *   *   *   A question of law or a question of fact is a mere synonym for a judge question or a jury question.

DOBSON v. MASONITE CORP.

United States Court of Appeals, Fifth Circuit, 1966.
359 F.2d 921.

HUTCHESON, Circuit Judge: *   *   *

Masonite desired to rid its Mississippi lands   *   *   *   of all oak timber and undesirable and unwanted species of tree. In March, 1963, Dobson

---

e There is substantial evidence that during the colonial period and the first part of the nineteenth century the jury determined questions of law in some jurisdictions and that the law-fact dichotomy was a later development. See Scott, *Trial by Jury and the Reform of Civil Procedure*, 31 Harv.L.Rev. 669, 675–78 (1918); Note, *The Changing Role of the Jury in the Nineteenth Century*, 74 Yale L.J. 170 (1964).

orally agreed to undertake cutting operations on Masonite's lands. Neither party disputes the existence of the oral agreement; nor is there any real quarrel regarding the basic terms of the agreement. Under the contract Dobson was (1) to cut all oak * * *; (2) to have complete control over the entire cutting operation and the timber cut; (3) to sell so much of the cut timber as he could; and (4) to pay Masonite initially twelve dollars, and subsequently ten dollars, per thousand log feet of oak actually sold, and to retain all amounts received in excess thereof as compensation for his services. Dobson incurred rather heavy expenditures in preparing for operations, found buyers for much of the oak to be cut, and commenced clearing the lands.

During the period in question the stumpage value of oak was approximately twenty dollars per thousand log feet; thus by selecting and selling the merchantable oak from that which he cut, Dobson was able to realize profits from his operations. Dobson continued clearing operations from March, 1963, to December, 1963, at which time Masonite unilaterally terminated the agreement and ordered Dobson to discontinue his operations. Dobson during this time cleared 4,000 acres of land, and realized a net profit, after all expenses, including payments to Masonite, of $9,383.02.

This suit was initiated by Dobson to recover the amount of net profits he would have realized had he been permitted to complete the clearing of Masonite's lands. Dobson interpreted the contract as one for services; he argued that the agreement was for clearing the land of unwanted oak trees. Masonite denied liability, interpreting the contract as one for the sale of standing timber, and invoking the Mississippi Statute of Frauds to bar Dobson's claim. At the close of the evidence Masonite moved for a directed verdict. The court denied this motion and submitted the case to the jury on special interrogatories inquiring (1) whether the contract was for services or for the sale of timber; and (2) whether the agreement could have been completed within the permissible period under the Statute of Frauds. The jury answered the interrogatories in favor of Dobson and assessed damages at $26,500.

Masonite then moved for judgment notwithstanding the verdict under Fed.R.Civ.P. 50(b). The district court sustained this motion, stating that only "the legal analysis and legal effect of that done" was in question, ruling that as a matter of law Dobson by virtue of the contract acquired an interest in standing timber, and holding that recovery under the contract was therefore barred by the Statute of Frauds.

The district court quite properly observed that under the Mississippi Statute of Frauds, an oral contract for the sale of standing timber is unenforceable. * * * Counsel for Dobson is also correct in his statement of Mississippi law; an agreement for services in cutting and clearing land of timber is not within the Statute. * * *

But this [is] of little assistance in determining *which type* of contract—sales or service—was here involved. This calls for an interpretation of the agreement between the parties to determine what they meant by the terms of that agreement. Interpretation is always a question of fact. * * * As a question of fact, this issue was properly presented to, and determined by, the jury; and unless there was no evidence which, if believed, would authorize the jury's conclusions, they must stand. * * *

Plainly what the parties meant by the language of the contract was uncertain and at the heart of this controversy; just as plainly, this was the very issue presented to the jury through special interrogatories. On the record before us, there is certainly ample evidence from which the jury could conclude that the contract between Dobson and Masonite was for the rendition of services, rather than for the sale of standing timber. In drawing the ultimate conclusion as to the meaning of the parties, we believe the jury was fulfilling its traditional function as the finder of the facts. * * *

The district court, apparently because there was no dispute regarding the existence of the oral contract or its terms, felt that only a legal question, what was the legal effect of the contract, was involved. But "legal effect" is the result of applying rules of law to the facts; necessarily this determination must await a determination of all the facts. And, as we have stated, deciding what is the meaning of the contract is a question of fact.

* * *

Reversed and remanded with directions.

NOTES AND QUESTIONS

1. In RANKIN v. FIDELITY TRUST & SAFE DEPOSIT CO., 189 U.S. 242, 23 S.Ct. 553, 47 L.Ed. 792 (1903), the existence or nonexistence of a contract depended upon the effect given to a series of letters that were contradictory in many respects. The Supreme Court held that the question whether a contract existed was for the jury subject to the court's instruction. In HOLTMAN v. BUTTERFIELD, 51 Cal.App. 89, 196 P. 85 (1st Dist.1921), plaintiff alleged that an undisputed unambiguous letter constituted a contract. The court held that there being no contradictory evidence, the question was for the court. Can the two cases be harmonized? Is either case inconsistent with *Dobson*? In what way is it relevant that in *Dobson* the contract is oral? What difficulties in differentiating questions of law from questions of fact do these cases suggest? See generally 3 Corbin, *Contracts* § 554, at 222–23 (1960).

2. * * * The statement that jurors are the judges of the facts and the weight of evidence must be qualified by a recognition of the admitted powers of the court (1) to find in certain cases the existence or nonexistence of facts as a necessary basis for the determination of the competency of proffered witnesses or written evidence; (2) under certain circumstances to direct a nonsuit or particular verdict at the close of plaintiff's or defendant's evidence, or at the close of all the evidence; (3) to charge or instruct the jury on the facts in the Federal courts and some state courts; and (4) to set aside the verdict of the jury for error of law, or if contrary to the manifest weight of the evidence; and (a) to grant a new trial, or (b) condition the overruling of a new trial upon the

entry of a remittitur or (c) to enter a judgment contrary to and notwithstanding the verdict.

Busch, *Law and Tactics in Jury Trials* 238 (1949). Many of these powers will be
discussed later in Parts E and F of this Chapter.

3. To what extent should the categorization of a particular issue as one of
fact or law depend on whether the question should be decided with reference to
a fixed standard that applies to all members of the community impartially or
as an ad hoc matter in particular cases? When an issue is classified as one
of "law," the rule binds litigants in subsequent cases. Of course, the crucial
question is when is the need for a precise legal standard sufficient to justify withdrawing the matter from the jury? In many contexts the answer
depends on whether the system has accumulated enough experience on the
issue to justify announcing a standard that will be binding in future cases. Another basis for differentiation is whether the issue involves a sensitive area that
warrants a "popular" or "communal" judgment. Consider, for example, the case
of a prosecution of a publisher for distributing an allegedly obscene book.
Shouldn't the decision to give the question of obscenity to a judge or a jury depend on whether the need for certainty on that issue outweighs the desirability of a
judgment by the community as reflected by several juries passing on the question
in different locales? Shifting to another context, should the interpretation of the
words of an unambiguous contract be left to the jury or to the court? In that connection, re-examine *Dobson, Rankin,* and *Holtman.* What about the issue of
negligence? Consider the following passage from Holmes, *The Common Law*
123–26 (1881).

> When a case arises in which the standard of conduct, pure and
> simple, is submitted to the jury * * * the court, not entertaining any
> clear views of public policy applicable to the matter, derives the rule to
> be applied from daily experience, as it has been agreed that the great body
> of the law of tort has been derived. But the court further feels that it
> is not itself possessed of sufficient practical experience to lay down the
> rule intelligently. It conceives that twelve men taken from the practical
> part of the community can aid its judgment. Therefore it aids its con-
> science by taking the opinion of the jury.

> But supposing a state of facts often repeated in practice, is it to be
> imagined that the court is to go on leaving the standard to the jury for-
> ever? Is it not manifest, on the contrary, that if the jury is, on the whole,
> as fair a tribunal as it is represented to be the lesson which can be got
> from that source will be learned? Either the court will find that the fair
> teaching of experience is that the conduct complained of usually is or is
> not blameworthy, and therefore, unless explained, is or is not a ground of
> liability; or it will find the jury oscillating to and fro, and will see the
> necessity of making up its mind for itself. * * *

> If this be the proper conclusion in plain cases, further consequences
> ensue. Facts do not often exactly repeat themselves * * *. A judge
> who has long sat at *nisi prius* ought gradually to acquire a fund of ex-
> perience which enables him to represent the common sense of the com-
> munity in ordinary instances far better than an average jury. He should
> be able to lead and to instruct them in detail, even where he thinks it
> desirable, on the whole, to take their opinion. Furthermore, the sphere

in which he is able to rule without taking their opinion at all should be continually growing.

It has often been said, that negligence is pure matter of fact, or that, after the court has declared the evidence to be such that negligence *may* be inferred from it, the jury are always to decide whether the inference shall be drawn. But it is believed that the courts, when they lay down this broad proposition, are thinking of cases where the conduct to be passed upon is not proved directly, and the main or only question is what that conduct was, not what standard shall be applied to it after it is established.

Most cases which go to the jury on a ruling that there is evidence from which they may find negligence, do not go to them principally on account of a doubt as to the standard, but of a doubt as to the conduct. Take the case where the fact in proof is an event such as the dropping of a brick from a railway bridge over a highway upon the plaintiff, the fact must be inferred that the dropping was due, not to a sudden operation of weather, but to a gradual falling out of repair which it was physically possible for the defendant to have prevented, before there can be any question as to the standard of conduct.

* * * It will be seen that in each of these well-known cases the court assumed a rule which would make the defendant liable if his conduct was such as the evidence tended to prove. When there is no question as to the conduct established by the evidence, * * * the jury have, sometimes at least, been told in effect that if they believed the evidence, the defendant was liable.

The principal argument that is urged in favor of the view that a more extended function belongs to the jury as matter of right, is the necessity of continually conforming our standards to experience. No doubt the general foundation of legal liability in blameworthiness, as determined by the existing average standards of the community, should always be kept in mind, for the purpose of keeping such concrete rules as from time to time may be laid down conformable to daily life. * * * But these considerations only lead to the conclusion that precedents should be overruled when they become inconsistent with present conditions * * *. On the other hand, it is very desirable to know as nearly as we can the standard by which we shall be judged at a given moment, and, moreover, the standards for a very large part of human conduct do not vary from century to century.

4. Juries frequently have been accused of invading the province of the judge by ignoring his instructions, fabricating their own rules of law, and applying them to the facts. E. g., Frank, *Courts on Trial* 110–11 (1949). Consider the situations described in the following excerpt in terms of whether the jury really is abusing its function:

In tort actions, especially negligence cases, where the jury functions at its best, it knocks off many rough edges of the law. Although the law may state that a plaintiff who has been guilty of contributory negligence, no matter how slight, cannot recover, the general verdict has often times refused to leave the plaintiff remediless. There is considerable evidence that juries are now making defendants in Federal Employers' Liability and Jones Act cases absolutely liable for injury; and this is probably also true as to defendants in motor accident cases, especially where the defendant is a common carrier.   In theory this is a sorry way to correct the law of contributory negligence or to extend the law of absolute liability, but practice cannot always wait upon the proper development of legal theories. * * *   Legislatures and courts are often laggards in the process of synchronization.   Jury legislation narrows the length of time required for synchronization.   It is akin to a private bill. * * *

5 Moore, *Federal Practice* ¶ 38.02[1], at 15–17 (2d ed.).   See also James, *Functions of Judge and Jury in Negligence Cases,* 58 Yale L.J. 667 (1949); Kalven, *The Dignity of the Civil Jury,* 50 Va.L.Rev. 1055, 1062–68 (1964).   Does the fact that the law often lags behind social reality justify the jury stepping outside its historical bounds and "taking the law into its own hands"?   Isn't the jury's invasion of the court's province and its knocking "off many rough edges of the law" likely to inhibit change in the law by making legislative and judicial innovation "unnecessary"?

5.   To what extent does our willingness to permit juries to modify the legal rules described by the judge depend on the particular substantive issues and the parties involved in the case?   *Compare* Scheflin, *Jury Nullification: The Right to Say No,* 45 So.Cal.L.Rev. 168 (1972), *and* Note, *Jury Nullification: The Forgotten Right,* 7 New Eng.L.Rev. 105 (1971), *with* Lawton v. Nightingale, Note 2, p. 831, supra.   Should the jury have a different degree of freedom in criminal cases than in civil cases, especially in light of the fact that a verdict of acquittal in a criminal case cannot be set aside?   Consider the following passage from Professor Howe's review of Kalven & Zeisel, *The American Jury,* in *Scientific American,* vol. 215, pp. 295, 298, Sept., 1966.

* * *   As the study shows, juries commonly tend to disregard a fundamental axiom of our jurisprudence that the only parties to litigation in the criminal law are the state and the defendant.   Thanks to this sloppy indifference, many jurors allow the contributory negligence or the viciousness of the victim of the crime to enter into their weighing of the culpability of the defendant.   In other words, the jurors confound the clear distinction between the civil and the criminal law and look on the action charged to the defendant as a tort rather than a crime. "The cases," we are told, "show a bootlegging of tort concepts of contributory negligence and assumption of risk into the criminal law."

* * *   Many will ask the same question James Fenimore Cooper asked more than a century ago: In a society that has been foolish enough to establish an elective judiciary and wise enough to make judicial tenure subject to good behavior, does a jury serve any more useful purpose than that of a symbol of freedom?   On Patriot's Day we celebrate the fortitude of the juries that set William Penn and John Peter Zenger free.   On what days shall we celebrate the courage of those solid yeoman who, in our own day, saw fit to let * * * [those accused of killing] Medgar Evers, Mrs. Viola Liuzzo and Jonathan Daniels go free?   There are surely occasions on which one is tempted to suggest that the time has come to amend our constitutions so as to allow the abolition of the jury even in criminal cases. * * *

Before that happens, however, I hope that someone will undertake a study no less extensive than the Chicago-Ford jury project to determine whether or not our judges are to be trusted with the power that would be theirs were they to go it alone. I confess *The American Jury* seems infected by an excessive respect for the vision, wisdom and integrity of American judges. I have too often heard practicing lawyers from our large cities insist that the one reason—and that a compelling one—for preserving jury trial is that it is our best safeguard against the corruption of judges.

Doesn't the fact that it is very rare for a jury verdict to be overturned despite certain acts of "misconduct" or even when it appears to be against the weight of the evidence demonstrate that our judicial system is fully prepared to allow, and often encourages, the jury to manipulate the legal standards offered by the trial judge? In this connection, reread *Texas Employers' Ins. Ass'n v. Price,* p. 47, supra, and *Lavender v. Kurn,* p. 51, supra; reconsider this question again in connection with the material on jury misconduct on pp. 886–94, infra.

---

4. DEMAND AND WAIVER OF TRIAL BY JURY

SEGAL v. AMERICAN CAS. CO.

United States District Court, District of Maryland, 1966.
250 F.Supp. 936.

NORTHROP, District Judge. This case involves defendants' motion to strike plaintiffs' demand for a jury trial. * * *

In essence, plaintiffs claim that they are entitled to a jury trial, notwithstanding the fact that this action was removed from the Circuit Court of Worcester County on April 3, 1963, that the answer was filed on November 25, 1964, and that a demand for a jury trial in this court was not made until June 29, 1965. The demand, urge the plaintiffs, was filed for the sole purpose of informing the court and counsel for the defendants that plaintiffs did not consent to trial without a jury. Thus, they claim that they would be entitled to a jury trial even in the absence of the June 1965 demand.

* * *

It is the contention of plaintiffs that the time limitations of Rule 38(b) are not applicable in this case, inasmuch as Rule 81(c) removes the necessity for a demand when no demand would have been necessary, under state law, in the court from which the case was removed. * * *

I

Plaintiffs claim that "state law" did not require that a demand for jury trial be made in the Circuit Court for Worcester County, and that, therefore, they were not required to demand a jury trial in this court, but were entitled to trial by jury without demand. This claim must be rejected.

Section 2 of Rule VII of the court from which this case was removed reads as follows:

"On the Saturday of the second week preceding each jury term at 10 o'clock A.M., there shall be a preliminary call by the clerk of cases on the civil docket appearing on the trial calendar. As each case is called the litigants, in proper person or by attorneys, will indicate by proper order whether the respective cases will be tried or continued at the first available trial date under these rules, *and if to be tried whether a jury will be required.* * * * The election of a jury at the preliminary call shall be final for the next ensuing jury session of the court unless the parties shall agree and the court consent otherwise, or unless the case shall be settled, continued or removed by order of court. * * * " (Emphasis added.)

In the Circuit Court for Worcester County, if a request for a jury trial is not made at the preliminary call of the docket, a jury trial cannot be had. Thus, by rule of the court, if the party seeking trial by jury does not signify this election, his case is not tried before a jury. This procedure in Worcester County is different from that in certain other counties in the state of Maryland; in these other counties, the filing of a case on the law side of the court automatically results in the setting of the case for jury trial, with no further action being required of the litigants. The issue, then, is whether the rule of court in Worcester County is "state law in the court from which the case is removed." This court concludes that it is.

* * *

The rule in the Circuit Court for Worcester County is not contrary to or conflicting with any statute or any rule of the Maryland Court of Appeals. Nor does the rule contravene section 6 of Article XV of the Maryland Constitution, preserving the *right* to jury trial. Rather, the local rule, like the corresponding federal rules, merely states the manner in which the *right* to a jury trial must be *exercised.* The local rule, having the force and effect of law, * * * is "state law" within the meaning of Federal Rule 81(c).

II

* * *

Admittedly, at the time of removal this case was in the early stages. The time for the preliminary call of the docket in the state court, and, therefore, the time at which an election for a jury trial would have to be made, were a long way off. This situation is similar to that in McRae v. Arabian American Oil Co., 34 F.R.D. 513 (S.D.N.Y.1964). There, state law required a demand for a jury trial at a stage in the proceedings subsequent to the stage reached by the time of removal. The plaintiffs in that case claimed that since, at the stage reached by the time of removal, they were not required to make formal demand for a jury trial, Rule 81(c) obviated the necessity for a demand after removal. * * * [T]he court replied:

" * * * The answer to that contention is that the plain language of the amendment does not so provide; it merely obviates the necessity of a demand after removal in the absence of *any* state requirement for a demand." 34 F.R.D. at 515. [Emphasis added.]

This court agrees with the reasoning of the *McRae* case and concludes ~~that under Rule 81(c) a party seeking a jury must, after removal, make a for-~~ mal demand for a jury trial if, in the court from which the case was removed, he would have had to take some action to exercise his right to a jury trial. This court finds, as did the court in *McRae*, that the necessity for a demand after removal is obviated only where the case automatically would have been set for jury trial in the court from which removed, without the necessity for any action on the part of the party desiring jury trial. * * *

Since the benefits of Rule 81(c) are not available to plaintiffs in this case, the successful exercise of their right to trial by jury depends upon their compliance with the provisions of Rule 38(b). Inasmuch as the demand in the present case was not made until many months after removal and after the answer had been filed, those time limitations have not been met. Plaintiffs, therefore, are not entitled to claim trial by jury as of right.

III

Although this court, in the exercise of its discretion under Rule 39(b), might allow a jury trial notwithstanding the lateness of the demand, it declines to do so.

In Washington County Ins. Co. v. Wilkinson, 19 F.R.D. 177, 178–179 (D.Md.1956), also involving an appeal to the court's discretion where the demand for jury trial had not been timely made, Judge Chesnut remarked:

"In my opinion the determining factor in such cases should be whether, despite the failure to comply with the rule, the nature of the case is such that one or the other of the parties is likely to be really prejudiced by the failure to have a jury trial. Where the issues are predominantly factual rather than legal there is more reason for the liberal exercise of the discretion to grant a jury trial. * * *

"There is still another consideration to be weighed. * * * I think rule 38 providing for the waiver of a jury trial unless specifically demanded within the time mentioned, is an illustration of the general policy of interpretation announced in rule 1. It is a matter of common experience that in civil cases, particularly those of a contractual nature, a nonjury trial can fairly and properly be concluded in substantially less time than is usually required in a jury case. And it should also not be overlooked that, especially where there is a considerable number of cases pending on the docket ready for trial, the time unnecessarily consumed in the trial of a particular case delays the trial of subsequent cases. And it is also to be remembered that needlessly longer trials usually involve more expense to litigants and to the government which freely provides the courts for the litigants."

On similar grounds, this court declines to exercise its discretion to grant a jury trial:

1. There are ten similar cases pending, each arising from the same storm in Ocean City and each involving a similar clause in the insurance policies.

2.   In nine of the ten similar cases, as in this one, the demand for a jury trial was made a number of months after removal and after the filing of the answer.

3.   In a case tried earlier, involving the same storm and the same contractual clause, a jury trial consumed two weeks; there is no indication that any of the pending cases would take less time if tried before a jury.

4.   The docket of this court is overcrowded, as is the case with most courts today.

5.   The expert testimony in each of these cases will be lengthy and complex. * * *

6.   The court can see no possible prejudice which would result from a trial before the court without a jury.

7.   There will be much less expense for all parties if the cases are tried without a jury.

Therefore, the motion to strike plaintiffs' demand for a jury trial is granted. * * *

NOTES AND QUESTIONS

1.   The "discretion" given the district court by Federal Rule 39(b) to permit a jury trial despite the absence of a demand is exercised sparingly. E. g., Canister Co. v. National Can Corp., 8 F.R.D. 408, 409 (D.Del.1948) (the fact that the equitable relief originally sought with legal relief no longer was available was not a basis for exercising discretion when plaintiff failed to ask for a jury trial for over five years). Is the negligence of an attorney in failing to demand jury trial a proper ground for exercising discretion to grant an untimely demand? See Supplies, Inc. v. Aetna Cas. & Sur. Co., 18 F.R.D. 226 (W.D.Pa.1955); Krussman v. Omaha Woodmen Life Ins. Soc'y, 2 F.R.D. 3 (D.Idaho 1941). Rather than deny a party a jury trial, shouldn't the attorney be punished in a way that does not adversely affect the client? How can this be done?

Does the following passage from BECKSTROM v. COASTWISE LINE, 13 F.R.D. 480, 483 (D.Alaska 1953), explain the restrictive application of Rule 39(b)?

> * * * For more than two years past, the Court has uniformly denied such requests by reason of the volume of litigation—more than 850 cases a year—coming before this Court for determination. This is more than three times the average number of cases per judge in the 86 * * * District Courts of the United States. The granting of trials by jury in such cases, where demand is not seasonably made, inevitably results in further delay and consequent further "denial of justice" to other litigants, who are presumed to have equally meritorious causes. Until an additional judge is authorized and appointed for this Division the practice will be adhered to. * * *

Is the attitude expressed in *Beckstrom* consistent with this country's commitment to jury trial? Should a constitutional right be used as a pawn in a struggle for more adequately staffed courts?

2.   Isn't requiring a demand before assigning a case to the jury docket inconsistent with the notion that the jury-trial right is a fundamental incident of

our system?   Indeed, are automatic waiver provisions constitutional?   In AETNA
INS. CO. v. KENNEDY, 301 U.S. 389, 57 S.Ct. 809, 81 L.Ed. 1177 (1937), the
Court said "as the right of jury trial is fundamental courts indulge every reasonable presumption against waiver."   Nonetheless, the constitutionality of waiver
provisions has been upheld.   See Wilson v. Corning Glass Works, 195 F.2d 825
(9th Cir.1952); Oliver v. Herron, 106 Ala. 639, 17 So. 387 (1895).

The early code provisions relating to jury trial required an express waiver
or a failure to perform certain procedural acts before a party lost his jury-trial
right.   Practice under these provisions became cumbersome and the affirmative
demand procedure came into vogue, although a few states still require an express
waiver.   See generally Clark, *Code Pleading* § 17 (2d ed. 1947); 4 Weinstein,
Korn & Miller, *New York Civil Practice* ¶¶ 4102.01–.22.   Courts in many states
that have rules patterned after the Federal Rules appear to be more lenient than
the federal courts in exercising discretion to relieve a party's failure to make a
timely demand.   See, e. g., Wood v. Warriner, 62 So.2d 728 (Fla.1953) (jury
demand granted even though plaintiff did not request jury until the first day
of trial).   *But see* Bloch v. Bentfield, 1 Ariz.App. 412, 403 P.2d 559 (1965)
(waiver by failure to appear at trial).

Should a contractual waiver of jury trial be honored?   See N.Y. Real Property
Law § 259–c.   What policies are relevant to this question?   If these clauses are
valid, does the waiver bind persons who become parties to the contract after its
execution?   Suppose the waiver is challenged because of fraud or on some other
basis; is there a right to jury trial on the issues raised by the challenge?   See
generally Annot., 73 A.L.R.2d 1332 (1960).

3.   In BERESLAVSKY v. CAFFEY, 161 F.2d 499 (2d Cir.), certiorari denied 332 U.S. 770, 68 S.Ct. 82, 92 L.Ed. 355 (1947), plaintiff sought
an injunction against patent infringement.   Subsequently he amended the complaint by striking the request for equitable relief and asking for money damages.
The court held that plaintiff was entitled to trial by jury even though the Rule
38(b) time period had expired.   The court reasoned that although the original
complaint carried no right to jury trial, a later amendment changing the claim
from equitable to legal relief renewed the right and gave plaintiff an additional
ten days to demand a jury.   The demand period was not extended in ALCOA
S.S. CO. v. RYAN, 211 F.2d 576 (2d Cir.1954), apparently because plaintiff's
claim under certain insurance policies remained substantially the same after the
amendment, which simply eliminated allegations requesting rescission of an agreement canceling the policies.   Does anything turn on whether the party who seeks
a jury trial is the same party who amended the pleadings?   If plaintiff in *Alcoa*
felt that a jury trial on the issues in the amended complaint was tactically important, could it have obtained it by taking a voluntary dismissal under Federal Rule
41, reinstituting the suit, and making a new demand for jury trial?   *Cf.* Noonan
v. Cunard S.S. Co., 375 F.2d 69 (2d Cir.1967).

4.   In LOCAL 783, ALLIED INDUSTRIAL WORKERS v. GENERAL
ELECTRIC CO., 471 F.2d 751 (6th Cir.), certiorari denied —— U.S. ——, 94
S.Ct. 120, 38 L.Ed.2d 55 (1973), plaintiff, who originally had asked only for
injunctive relief, filed a motion to amend the complaint by adding a legal claim
for damages nine months after the original claim and only eight days before
trial.   The court of appeals held that the trial judge had erred in permitting the
amendment only on the condition that jury trial be waived.

What should a court do when an amendment is sought to change a claim for legal relief, on which jury trial has been demanded, to a claim for equitable relief? In ruling on the motion to amend, should the court take into account that a loss of jury trial may be entailed? A seaman injured by the negligence of his employer may bring suit under the Jones Act, 46 U.S.C. § 688, on the law side of the court with a right of jury trial or in admiralty without a jury. Federal Rule 9(h) provides that a complaint in a case that can be brought at law or in admiralty may contain "a statement identifying the claim as an admiralty or maritime claim for the purpose of Rule * * * 38(e)," and that the "amendment of a pleading to add or withdraw an identifying statement is governed by the principles of Rule 15." In JOHNSON v. PENROD DRILLING CO., 469 F.2d 897 (1972), rehearing en banc granted 478 F.2d 1208 (5th Cir.1973), it was held that the trial judge erred in allowing plaintiffs to withdraw their claim to jury trial by amending their complaints to identify them as admiralty claims without the consent of defendant.

---

5. SELECTION AND COMPOSITION OF THE JURY

FLOWERS v. FLOWERS

Court of Civil Appeals of Texas, 1965.
397 S.W.2d 121.

CHAPMAN, Justice. The subject matter of this suit involves a question of the disqualification of a juror in a child custody contest tried to a jury * * *.

This case was tried in a town and county of very small population where the record shows many members of the jury panel had heard what they referred to as gossip or rumors concerning the case. The parties to the suit are Billie Charlene Flowers, plaintiff below, the mother; and R. A. Flowers, Jr., the father. The victims of the unfortunate broken home are three little girls ranging in ages from two to ten at the time of the filing of divorce by their mother in January 1964.

* * *

The jurors were told on voir dire examination that the evidence would show that plaintiff drank some socially and on one or two occasions had consumed alcoholic beverages to excess. They were questioned as to whether that fact standing alone would prejudice them against her as a fit and proper person to have custody of the children.

The record preserved upon examination of Mrs. Schmidt as a prospective juror shows that she first testified she was well acquainted with the Flowers family, belonged to the same Baptist church they did in the little town of Miami, and that she had no opinion formed in the case at all. Then when counsel said to her the evidence will show "that Billie does drink upon social occasions with the crowd at a dance, or something of that sort, she would have a highball or cocktail, and it will show on one occasion that she had too much, or two times had too much, what is your attitude—," she answered:

"A.   I am against drinking in any manner, any kind.

Q.   Any way or any fashion at all?

A.   Any type.

Q.   Mrs. Schmidt, that would definitely affect your judgment in the case wouldn't it?

A.   If the evidence was true.

Q.   Could you enter the—you would take a seat as a juror with a positive feeling that any drinking whatsoever is wrong, and it is bad so far as the mother of these little girls is concerned,—

A.   Anybody else.

Q.   If the evidence shows Billie has had one drink or two—drinks at a social occasion, you would hold that against her?

A.   I don't approve."

The court then took over the examination and asked her a number of questions, one of which was:

"Q.   Well, are you saying by that, Mrs. Schmidt, that you wouldn't grant either party to this law suit custody of their children if they drank?

A.   I am."

The court then turned to leading questions to the juror as to her attitude about passing upon whether the mother was a fit person to have the custody of the girls, saying:

"Q.   Dependent upon the testimony you hear in a trial; the mere fact that she got drunk a few times and threw a conniption fit or something, you wouldn't hold that against her and think she wasn't—

A.   Not especially."

The court then overruled the challenge of the juror for cause.

The record also shows by affidavit of a lady juror panelist who sat next to Mrs. Schmidt during voir dire examination that Mrs. Schmidt stated "* * *   she felt sorry for R. A. Flowers, Jr. and that you had to admire a man that would go on to Sunday School and church after what had happened to him." Mrs. Philpot's affidavit also affirmed that Mrs. Schmidt made a statement to one of the other prospective jurors sitting next to her before the jury was selected that Billie Flowers had run off and left R. A. Flowers, Jr. once before and that both of such statements were made before she was selected and sworn to serve as a juror.

At both the motion for mistrial and motion for new trial based partly upon the proceedings just related, the court declined to hear Mrs. Philpot's tendered testimony as a witness in support of her affidavit.   Upon the hearing of the motion for new trial Mrs. Flowers' attorney testified there were eleven jurors, including Mrs. Schmidt, who were undesirable to the plaintiff and that if Mrs. Schmidt on voir dire had correctly stated her attitude reflected by Mrs. Philpot's affidavit, they would have exercised a peremptory challenge as to her rather than as to some other juror. * * *

Article 2134, Vernon's Ann.Tex.Civ.St., provides as one of the disqualifications: "Any person who has a bias or prejudice in favor of or against either of the parties."

This disqualification for bias or prejudice extends not only to the parties personally, but also to the subject matter of the litigation. * * * Compton v. Henrie, Tex., 364 S.W.2d 179.

In defining the terms "bias" and "prejudice" as used in Article 2134 our Supreme Court in the HENRIE case just cited has said:

"Bias, in its usual meaning, is an inclination toward one side of an issue rather than to the other, but to disqualify, it must appear that the state of mind of the juror leads to the natural inference that he will not or did not act with impartiality. Prejudice is more easily defined for it means pre-judgment, and consequently embraces bias; the converse is not true. The establishment of such a state of mind would disqualify Fugate from serving on this jury as a matter of law. * * *

Mrs. Schmidt's statements indicate to us both bias and prejudice factually and such a prejudgment of the case as to indicate she could not have acted with impartiality. If we are correct in this factual conclusion then under the authorities just cited her disqualification is not a matter of discretion with the trial court but a matter of law. * * *

Even if we are in error in our pronouncements in the preceding paragraphs, it cannot be gainsaid that the record shows bias and prejudice on the part of Mrs. Schmidt toward plaintiff and toward her alcoholic consumption her attorney admitted would be shown before the examination of the jury on voir dire. From the viewpoint of this writer, such feelings on the part of Mrs. Schmidt are to her credit even if it did disqualify her as a juror. But even if under the facts of this case bias or prejudice was a fact to be determined by the trial court, those feelings having been clearly established, her answer of "Yes, sir" to a leading question to the effect that she would be able to decide the case on the evidence submitted, should be disregarded. * * * In any event we believe the court abused its discretion in refusing to hold the juror disqualified.

      *   *   *

The judgment of the trial court is reversed and remanded for a new trial.

NOTES AND QUESTIONS

1. What are the respective advantages and disadvantages of permitting *voir dire* to be conducted by the trial court or by counsel? Note that Federal Rule

47(a) leaves the entire matter to the trial judge's discretion. Some states have held that the judge may conduct the entire examination subject to suggestions from counsel. Others have held it error not to allow each juror to be examined by counsel prior to the exercise of challenges. See Oden v. State, 166 Neb. 729, 90 N.W.2d 356 (1958). See generally 4 Weinstein, Korn & Miller, *New York Civil Practice* ¶¶ 4107.01–.06.

2. How far can an attorney go in relating the *voir dire* examination to the lawsuit that the jury will hear? Can the lawyer state hypothetical questions based on the actual facts of the case or ask how the juror would apply certain legal principles to those facts? See Note, *Voir Dire—Prevention of Prejudicial Questioning,* 50 Minn.L.Rev. 1088 (1966). In SMITH v. NICKELS, 390 S.W.2d 578, 582–83 (Mo.1965), the court said:

> From the reported cases, it can be concluded * * * that counsel is given great latitude in seeking out any bias or prejudice. No difficulty is created by interrogation seeking to reveal a "present state of mind," or * * * establishing some basis for anticipating the reaction of the prospective juror to the immediate issues involved. However, when the inquiry includes questions phrased or framed in such manner that they require the one answering to speculate on his own reaction to such an extent that he tends to feel obligated to react in that manner, prejudice can be created. * * *
>
> Do the questions at issue exceed the limits of proper *voir dire?* They first ask the veniremen to assume defendant Nickels has shown an absence of negligence on his part, and then respond to: " * * * would any of you hesitate to find in favor of my client?" An elementary thought could be that error is impossible for after the assumption of no negligence, their duty would be to find in his favor. * * * It is possible the inquiry was made in such manner that no prejudgments were made. * * * Conceivably instances may arise when questions are objectionable by reason of considerations divorced from the actual words employed, as for example where by intonation, expression or emphasis, connotations not normally implicit in the words may be inspired. The words here used are susceptible to such abuse by experienced trial counsel. As known to anyone having actually participated in jury trials, the prejudicial effect, if any, may not be reflected in the printed record. * * *

3. Should a juror's relationship with an insurance company be a proper subject for inquiry by plaintiff's counsel on *voir dire?* What about her willingness to be fair in assessing damages even though she knows defendant is insured? Can you suggest a method of eliciting a juror's attitudes toward insurance without informing that juror of its relevance to the particular case? See generally Vetter, *Voir Dire II—Liability Insurance,* 29 Mo.L.Rev. 305 (1964); Comment, *Liability Insurance and the Jury Trial,* 7 St. Louis U.L.J. 111 (1962). For a colorful debate on the question of insurance and *voir dire,* read the four opinions in Fosness v. Panagos, 376 Mich. 485, 138 N.W.2d 380 (1966).

4. Challenges to individual jurors—sometimes called challenges to the polls—are of two kinds: for cause and peremptory. Challenges for cause permit a prospective juror to be rejected when partiality can be shown. Peremptory

challenges permit rejection of jurors without any statement of reason and usually are based on an assumed partiality that may not be susceptible of proof. Challenges to the composition and selection of the entire panel—frequently called challenges to the array—are the subject of *Thiel v. Southern Pac. Co.,* the next case.

The number of peremptory challenges allowed each side varies among the states. The general range is from two to six. In the federal courts each side is permitted three. See 28 U.S.C. § 1870. Should the number be increased if there are multiple parties on one or both sides? Since the number of peremptory challenges is limited, they usually are carefully husbanded. See generally Busch, *Law and Tactics in Jury Trials* 208 (1949). The use of the peremptory challenge is discussed generally in Kennelly, *Jury Selection in a Civil Case,* 1965 Trial Law. Guide 87, and Davis & Wiley, *49 Thoughts on Jury Selection,* 1965 Trial Law. Guide 351. Various psychological factors relevant to the exercise of peremptory challenges are described in Kalven, *The Jury, the Law, and the Personal Injury Damage Award,* 19 Ohio St.L.J. 158 (1958).

An unlimited number of challenges for cause are permitted each party. These challenges are determined by the trial judge, although some states have experimented with so-called "triers"—independent officials who have the responsibility of determining challenges for cause. On what grounds should a juror be challenged for cause? Can the judge disqualify a prospective juror on the court's own motion or must he wait for a motion from one of the parties? See generally Busch, op.cit. supra at 140. May jurors be interrogated as to possible racial, religious, economic, or political prejudice? Compare the following from Comment, *The Right of Peremptory Challenge,* 24 U.Chi.L.Rev. 751, 762 (1957):

> * * * [C]ourts may well be reluctant to sustain challenges for cause based on these grounds; a holding that race, religion, and nationality are legally acceptable causes for challenge would give too explicit a sanction to a type of discrimination elsewhere disapproved by the law. The peremptory challenge has avoided the necessity for such holdings; in the cases found, challenges based on the race, religion, or nationality of veniremen seem to have always been peremptory. * * *

See also People v. Roxborough, 307 Mich. 575, 12 N.W.2d 466 (1943); Comment, *Fair Jury Selection Procedures,* 75 Yale L.J. 322 (1965). Is it relevant that the plaintiff or defendant is an individual or an organization espousing an unpopular viewpoint or cause? What if plaintiff or defendant merely happens to be a member of a group of this type? See Casey v. Roman Catholic Archbishop of Baltimore, 217 Md. 595, 143 A.2d 627 (1958).

THIEL v. SOUTHERN PAC. CO.

Supreme Court of the United States, 1946.
328 U.S. 217, 66 S.Ct. 984, 90 L.Ed. 1181.

Certiorari to the Circuit Court of Appeals for the Ninth Circuit.

Mr. Justice MURPHY delivered the opinion of the Court.

Petitioner, a passenger, jumped out of the window of a moving train operated by the respondent * * *. He filed a complaint in a California state court to recover damages, alleging that the respondent's agents knew that he was "out of his normal mind" and should not be accepted as a passenger or else should be guarded and that, having accepted him as a passenger, they left him unguarded and failed to stop the train before he finally fell to the ground. At respondent's request the case was removed to the federal district court at San Francisco on the ground of diversity of citizenship, respondent being a Kentucky corporation. * * *

After demanding a jury trial, petitioner moved to strike out the entire jury panel, alleging inter alia that "mostly business executives or those having the employer's viewpoint are purposely selected on said panel, thus giving a majority representation to one class or occupation and discriminating against other occupations and classes, particularly the employees and those in the poorer classes who constitute, by far, the great majority of citizens eligible for jury service." * * * [T]he motion was denied. Petitioner then attempted to withdraw his demand for a jury trial but the respondent refused to consent. A jury of twelve was chosen. Petitioner thereupon challenged these jurors upon the same grounds previously urged in relation to the entire jury panel and upon the further ground that six of the twelve jurors were closely affiliated and connected with the respondent. The court denied this challenge. The trial proceeded and the jury returned a verdict for the respondent.

Petitioner renewed his objections in his motion to set aside the verdict or, in the alternative, to grant a new trial. In denying this motion the court orally found that five of the twelve jurors "belong more closely and intimately with the working man and employee class than they do with any other class" and that they might be expected to be "sympathetic with the experiences in life, the affairs of life, and with the economic views, of people who belong to the working or employee class." The Ninth Circuit Court of Appeals affirmed * * *.

The American tradition of trial by jury, considered in connection with either criminal or civil proceedings, necessarily contemplates an impartial jury drawn from a cross-section of the community. * * * This does not mean, of course, that every jury must contain representatives of all the economic, social, religious, racial, political and geographical groups of the community; frequently such complete representation would be impossible. But it does mean that prospective jurors shall be selected by court officials without systematic and intentional exclusion of any of these groups. Recognition must be given to the fact that those eligible for jury service are to be found in every stratum of society. Jury competence is an individual rather than a group or class matter. That fact lies at the very heart of the jury system. To disregard it is to open the door to class distinctions and discriminations which are abhorrent to the democratic ideals of trial by jury.

The choice of the means by which unlawful distinctions and discriminations are to be avoided rests largely in the sound discretion of the trial courts and their officers. * * *

The undisputed evidence in this case demonstrates a failure to abide by the proper rules and principles of jury selection. Both the clerk of the court and the jury commissioner testified that they deliberately and intentionally excluded from the jury lists all persons who work for a daily wage. They generally used the city directory as the source of names of prospective jurors. In the words of the clerk, "If I see in the directory the name of John Jones and it says he is a longshoreman, I do not put his name in, because I have found by experience that that man will not serve as a juror, and I will not get people who will qualify. The minute that a juror is called into court on a venire and says he is working for $10 a day and cannot afford to work for four, the Judge has never made one of those men serve, and so in order to avoid putting names of people in who I know won't become jurors in the court, won't qualify as jurors in this court, I do leave them out. * * *" The jury commissioner corroborated this testimony, adding that he purposely excluded "all the iron craft, bricklayers, carpenters, and machinists" because in the past "those men came into court and offered that [financial hardship] as an excuse, and the judge usually let them go." The evidence indicated, however, that laborers who were paid weekly or monthly wages were placed on the jury lists, as well as the wives of daily wage earners.

It was further admitted that business men and their wives constituted at least 50% of the jury lists, although both the clerk and the commissioner denied that they consciously chose according to wealth or occupation. Thus the admitted discrimination was limited to those who worked for a daily wage, many of whom might suffer financial loss by serving on juries at the rate of $4 a day and would be excused for that reason.

This exclusion of all those who earn a daily wage cannot be justified by federal or state law. * * * A juror, to be competent, need only be a citizen of the United States over the age of 21, a resident of the state and county for one year preceding selection, possessed of his natural faculties and of ordinary intelligence and not decrepit, and possessed of sufficient knowledge of the English language. California Code of Civil Procedure, § 198. * * *

Moreover, the general principles underlying proper jury selection clearly outlaw the exclusion practiced in this instance. Jury competence is not limited to those who earn their livelihood on other than a daily basis. One who is paid $3 a day may be as fully competent as one who is paid $30 a week or $300 a month. * * * Wage earners, including those who are paid by the day, constitute a very substantial portion of the community, a portion that cannot be intentionally and systematically excluded in whole or in part without doing violence to the democratic nature of the jury system. Were we to sanction an exclusion of this nature we would encourage whatever desires those responsible for the selection of jury panels may have to discriminate against persons of low economic and social status. We would breathe life into any latent tendencies to establish the jury as the instrument of the economically and socially privileged. That we refuse to do.

It is clear that a federal judge would be justified in excusing a daily wage earner for whom jury service would entail an undue financial hardship. But that fact cannot support the complete exclusion of all daily wage earners regardless of whether there is actual hardship involved. Here there was no effort, no intention, to determine in advance which individual members of the daily wage earning class would suffer an undue hardship by serving on a jury at the rate of $4 a day. All were systematically and automatically excluded. In this connection it should be noted that the mere fact that a person earns more than $4 a day would not serve as an excuse. Jury service is a duty as well as a privilege of citizenship; it is a duty that cannot be shirked on a plea of inconvenience or decreased earning power. Only when the financial embarrassment is such as to impose a real burden and hardship does a valid excuse of this nature appear. Thus a blanket exclusion of all daily wage earners, however well-intentioned and however justified by prior actions of trial judges, must be counted among those tendencies which undermine and weaken the institution of jury trial.   *   *   *

It follows that we cannot sanction the method by which the jury panel was formed in this case. The trial court should have granted petitioner's motion to strike the panel. That conclusion requires us to reverse the judgment below in the exercise of our power of supervision over the administration of justice in the federal courts.   *   *   *   On that basis it becomes unnecessary to determine whether the petitioner was in any way prejudiced by the wrongful exclusion or whether he was one of the excluded class.   *   *   *   It is likewise immaterial that the jury which actually decided the factual issue in the case was found to contain at least five members of the laboring class. The evil lies in the admitted wholesale exclusion of a large class of wage earners in disregard of the high standards of jury selection. To reassert those standards, to guard against the subtle undermining of the jury system, requires a new trial by a jury drawn from a panel properly and fairly chosen.

Reversed.

Mr. Justice JACKSON took no part in the consideration or decision of this case.

Mr. Justice FRANKFURTER, with whom Mr. Justice REED concurs, dissenting.

*   *   *   [I]t is not suggested that the jury was selected so as to bring property prejudice into play in relation to this specific case or type of case, nor is there the basis for contending that the trial judge allowed the selective process to be manipulated in favor of the particular defendant.   *   *   *   Neither is it claimed that the district judges for the Northern District of California, with the approval of the circuit judges, designed racial, religious, social, or economic discrimination to influence the makeup of jury panels, or that such unfair influence infused the selection of the panel, or was reflected in those who were chosen as jurors in this case. Nor is there any suggestion that the method of selecting the jury in this case was an innovation. What is challenged is a long standing practice adopted in order to deal with the special hardship which jury service entails for workers paid by the day. What is challenged, in short, is not a covert attempt to benefit the propertied but a practice designed, wisely

or unwisely, to relieve the economically least secure from the financial burden which jury service involves under existing circumstances.

No constitutional issue is at stake. The problem is one of judicial administration. * * *

Trial by jury presupposes a jury drawn from a pool broadly representative of the community as well as impartial in a specific case. Since the color of a man's skin is unrelated to his fitness as a juror, negroes cannot be excluded from jury service because they are negroes. * * * A group may be excluded for reasons that are relevant not to their fitness but to competing considerations of public interest, as is true of the exclusion of doctors, ministers, lawyers, and the like. * * * But the broad representative character of the jury should be maintained, partly as assurance of a diffused impartiality and partly because sharing in the administration of justice is a phase of civic responsibility. * * *

It is difficult to believe that this judgment would have been reversed if the trial judge had excused, one by one, all those wage earners whom the jury commissioner, acting on the practice of trial judges of San Francisco, excluded. For it will hardly be contended that the absence of such daily wage earners from the jury panel removed a group who would act otherwise than workers paid by the week or the wives of the daily wage earners themselves. * * *

No doubt, in view of the changes in the composition and distribution of our population and the growth of metropolitan areas, a reexamination is due of the operation of the jury system in the federal courts. * * * The object is to devise a system that is fairly representative of our variegated population, exacts the obligation of citizenship to share in the administration of justice without operating too harshly upon any section of the community, and is duly regardful of the public interest in matters outside the jury system. This means that the many factors entering into the manner of selection, with appropriate qualifications and exemptions, the length of service and the basis of compensation must be properly balanced. These are essentially problems in administration calling for appropriate standards flexibly adjusted.

* * *

The Court now deals by adjudication with one phase of an organic problem and does so by nullifying a judgment which, on the record, was wholly unaffected by difficulties inherent in a situation that calls for comprehensive treatment, both legislative and administrative. * * * To reverse a judgment free from intrinsic infirmity and perhaps to put in question other judgments based on verdicts that resulted from the same method of selecting juries, reminds too much of burning the barn in order to roast the pig.

I would affirm the judgment.

NOTES AND QUESTIONS

1. Read 28 U.S.C. §§ 1861–1866 in the Supplement. The *Report of the Committee on the Operation of the Jury System of the Judicial Conference of the United States,* on which the present federal jury-selection statute is based, appears

in 42 F.R.D. 353 (1967). An extended discussion of various earlier methods of selecting federal jury panels is found in Dow v. Carnegie-Illinois Steel Corp., 224 F.2d 414 (3d Cir.1955).

How representative of the community is a federal jury in view of the substantial classes of people who are exempt or may be exempted under Section 1863(6) or who may be excused under Section 1863(5)? See Mills, *A Statistical Profile of Jurors in a U.S. District Court*, 1969 Law & Social Order 329. For other studies of jury selection, see Kairys, *Juror Selection: The Law, A Mathematical Method of Analysis, and a Case Study*, 10 Am.Crim.L.Rev. 771 (1972); Note, *Economic Discrimination in Jury Selection*, 1970 Law & Social Order 474. On selection of jurors in state courts, see the survey of state statutory provisions in Vanderbilt, *Minimum Standards of Judicial Administration* 162 (1949), and Comment, *Jury Selection in California*, 5 Stan.L.Rev. 247 (1953).

2. A number of different methods are used to select names for jury lists. The person responsible for compiling the list (usually called the jury commissioner) may pick names from his own knowledge, rely on names referred by others, use telephone and city directories, voter lists, census reports, property-tax lists, club lists, or other sources.

The "key number" system, which is based on the voter registration list, is a recommended method of compiling a jury list. Under it, the commissioner calculates the number of jurors needed for the year, draws names, and sends questionnaires to those whose names are drawn. Prospective jurors are then examined and if finally selected their names are placed in a box for weekly drawing. The term of service usually is two weeks. See *Key Number System Guarantees Competent Juries*, 25 J.Am.Jud.Soc'y 27 (1941).

The so-called "key man" system consists of sending a letter to certain select individuals with a "high sense of civic responsibility" and asking them "to furnish a stated number of prospective jurors 'with a good reputation for honesty and morality, with sufficient education to understand the problems involved in a lawsuit and who are worthy representatives of your county and favor proper enforcement of the law.' * * * The key-men are requested to include in their lists, so far as reasonably practicable, women, Negroes, and other representatives of all economic or social classes, and from every walk of life." Wicker, *Jury Panels In Federal Courts*, 22 Tenn.L.Rev. 203, 212–13 (1952).

Does it make any difference how the names for jury lists are selected? How much discretion should the jury commissioner have in making up jury lists? Would any of the methods mentioned above discriminate against any class or groups? Would there be any advantage in having a uniform system for the selection of jury lists for all federal courts? For the states?

3. Qualifications for jury service vary from state to state and include such factors as citizenship, local residence, ownership of property, health, and payment of taxes. Until 1948, jurors in the federal courts were required to qualify under the standard of the state in which the court sat. In that year an amendment altered this practice and, in conjunction with amendments in 1957 and 1968, has effectively eliminated conformity to state practice.

4. The special or "blue ribbon" jury, which is composed of people who are specially selected because of their above-average intelligence, is an attempt to meet the contention that the ordinary juror is incompetent to deal with the complex problems of modern litigation. In FAY v. NEW YORK, 332 U.S. 261, 67 S.Ct. 1613, 91 L.Ed. 2043 (1947), the Supreme Court upheld the constitutionality of a New York statute that gave the trial court discretion to empanel a "blue ribbon" jury upon application of either party. Would the Supreme Court uphold a federal statute that provided for "blue ribbon" juries in federal courts? Are "blue ribbon" juries consistent with the Seventh Amendment or the idea that a person should be "judged by peers" or by a group that represents a cross-section of society? See generally Baker, *In Defense of the "Blue Ribbon" Jury,* 35 Iowa L.Rev. 409 (1950).

5. The use of questionnaires, personal interviews, and psychological tests has been suggested for ascertaining the competence of prospective jurors. A number of approaches are evaluated in A.B.A. Sec.Jud.Admin., *The Improvement of the Administration of Justice* 67 (3d ed. 1952); Redmount, *Psychological Tests for Selecting Jurors,* 5 Kan.L.Rev. 391 (1957); Comment, *Jury-Pretrial Selection— Suggested Improvements,* 56 Mich.L.Rev. 954 (1958). To what extent is the following passage from Note, *Psychological Tests and Standards of Competence for Selecting Jurors,* 65 Yale L.J. 531, 541 (1956), wishful thinking:

> * * * A more competent jury may force a change in the tactics of advocacy, so that attorneys will put greater emphasis on rational rather than emotional appeals. Parties may also be dissuaded from taking weak cases to court in the hope of achieving an unjustified result. Exclusionary rules of evidence, evolved to protect litigants from inept juries, can be liberalized. Juries held in higher esteem will restore respect for the right of trial by jury, and even, perhaps, for jury duty.

Wouldn't psychological testing of jurors result in the erosion of our traditional views of jury composition? Would they be permissible under *Thiel?*

6. Women cannot be systematically excluded from federal jury lists. The value of women on the jury is summarized by Mr. Justice Douglas in BALLARD v. UNITED STATES, 329 U.S. 187, 193–94, 67 S.Ct. 261, 264, 91 L.Ed. 181, 186 (1946):

> * * * The truth is that the two sexes are not fungible; a community made up exclusively of one is different from a community composed of both; the subtle interplay of influence one on the other is among the imponderables. To insulate the courtroom from either may not in a given case make an iota of difference. Yet a flavor, a distinct quality is lost if either sex is excluded. The exclusion of one may indeed make the jury less representative of the community than would be true if an economic or racial group were excluded.

Isn't Mr. Justice Douglas' reasoning applicable to any defined societal group? What if all women had the option to excuse themselves and consistently declined to serve on juries? Would this render the jury system objectionable?

SECTION C. THE LAW OF EVIDENCE

1. THE NATURE AND PURPOSES OF EVIDENCE

The law of evidence is concerned with one of the most complex undertakings in the entire litigation process—the reconstruction of past events in an effort to arrive at "the truth." Truth is not sought in an absolute sense; in a civil case, for example, the existence or nonexistence of a fact usually need only be shown to be "more probable than not." Even so, the task of finding truth is difficult, in large part because the adversary nature of the trial process effectively discourages the presentation of evidence in a scientific manner under laboratory conditions. Instead, each attorney attempts to construct the strongest possible case in favor of his client, with tactics and personalities often determining which items of evidence are presented and stressed and which items are omitted or de-emphasized. The search for truth is weakened further by the fact that evidence presented is not analyzed and appraised by experts, especially in a jury case; so that emotion or "hunch" may play a large part in the evaluation of evidence and the ultimate decision.

One may ask why the law does not embrace a more efficient system—one that takes advantage of modern advances in medicine, science, and engineering. Why, for example, shouldn't factual determinations be made by a panel of scientific experts who employ "truth sera," hypnosis, psychoanalysis, and similar techniques to question every person who might have relevant knowledge? Why, in an age of high-speed analog and digital computers, aren't we gathering, analyzing, and making judgments about information electronically rather than by archaic and imprecise manual methods? What would be wrong with using such procedures in the judicial process? In Sweden, experts at assessing the testimony of others may be called to give their views of the evidence. See Trankell, *Reliability of Evidence* (1972); Trankell, *Was Lars Sexually Assaulted?*, 56 J. Abnormal & Soc. Psychology 385 (1958). What should be the criteria for a satisfactory system of arriving at "truth"? See generally Weinstein, *Some Difficulties in Devising Rules for Determining Truth in Judicial Trials*, 66 Colum.L.Rev. 223 (1966); Wright, *Procedural Reform: Its Limitations and its Future*, 1 Ga.L.Rev. 563, 582–85 (1967).

Within the framework of the current system of trial, an elaborate set of rules has been devised to control the presentation of evidence. Generally speaking, the rules have three basic purposes: (1) to avoid prejudicing the trier of fact by prohibiting presentation of evidence that is inherently unreliable, (2) to expedite trial by eliminating worthless evidence, and (3) to protect the privacy of individuals when social policy places a higher value on that privacy than it does on learning the truth for purposes of litigation. Those rules that are designed to avoid prejudice are aimed primarily, if not solely, at jurors. Thus, they generally are ignored in nonjury litigation, although technically there is but one law of evidence and it is applicable in all cases. See Note 4, pp. 903–04, infra; Davis, *An Approach to Rules of Evidence for Non-Jury Cases*, 50 A.B.A.J. 723 (1964). Does it make sense to keep evidence from the jury that may help it to reach a sound decision, on the ground that the jury may misuse the evidence? Why can't we rely on jurors to weigh each item of evidence in light of its inherent weaknesses?

Some of the major aspects of evidence law are discussed in the material that follows, although the analysis is far from exhaustive. The function of this description is to demonstrate generally the types of problems lawyers face in attempting to prove their cases. Since the law of evidence is best understood in the context of the factual issues in a particular dispute, we shall consider the subject in light of the following situation:

> Plaintiff, Patsy, has filed suit for slander alleging that she was falsely branded a prostitute by Dolly, defendant. As the case goes to trial there are three matters in dispute: (1) Is the Hill Club, where Patsy admits she lives, a house of prostitution; (2) if the answer to (1) is "yes," is Patsy merely a boarder at the club, unaware of the activities around her; and (3) if Dolly's alleged statement is false and Patsy is entitled to collect, what is the extent of the damage to her reputation?

---

2. RELEVANCY

An item of evidence will not be admitted unless it has some logical connection with an issue sought to be proved. Suppose, for example, that in our hypothetical, Dolly's attorney calls a witness to testify solely that Patsy had leased a room at the Hill Club. Although such evidence would tend to prove that Patsy did live at the Hill Club, that fact has been admitted; it is not an issue in the case and unless the evidence is relevant for some other purpose, it should be excluded.

Not all questions of relevancy are quite that easy, however. Suppose, for example, that a witness is called to testify that Patsy is friendly with Marie who lives at the Hill Club and who has been arrested and convicted of prostitution three times within the past eight months. What inferences can be drawn from this testimony regarding Patsy's behavior? Does the mere fact that Marie lives at the Hill Club tend to establish that it is a brothel? Does Patsy's association with Marie lead to the conclusion that Patsy shares the same occupation? Isn't it equally possible that Patsy is a religious or social missionary who cultivated a friendship with Marie in an effort to "save her soul"? If so, should the evidence be excluded as irrelevant because it does not, of itseif, tend to prove or disprove the existence of a fact in issue?

In answering the latter question consider the impact of exclusion on the ability of an attorney, in this case Dolly's attorney, to build a case for her client. Isn't it necessary to define evidence as irrelevant only if it could not, either by itself or in association with other evidence, show the existence or nonexistence of a fact in dispute? See McCormick, *Evidence* § 185 (2d ed. 1972). Doesn't this mean that most evidence will be considered relevant? Is that desirable? Indeed, why are the courts even concerned with the exclusion of irrelevant evidence? After all, the trier of fact is asked to do many difficult tasks: choose among competing inferences, analyze credibility, reject perjury, and apply difficult legal rules, to name just a few. Why is it too much to ask that the trier also disregard evidence that can have no logical bearing on the decision?

Even if evidence is logically probative of a material fact, it still may be excluded as not being "legally" relevant for other reasons. Thus, Uniform Rule of Evidence 45 provides:

> * * * [T]he judge may in his discretion exclude evidence if he finds that its probative value is substantially outweighed by the risk that its admission will (a) necessitate undue consumption of time, or (b) create substantial danger of undue prejudice or of confusing the issues or of misleading the jury, or (c) unfairly and harmfully surprise a party who has not had reasonable opportunity to anticipate that such evidence would be offered.

What are the justifications for such a rule? How should it be applied? Suppose, for example, that in our hypothetical suit seven of the twelve jurors are nonunion workers in a factory owned and operated by Smythe, who, to the surprise of everyone, takes the witness stand to testify that he owns the Hill Club. Should the court exclude as unduly prejudicial Smythe's testimony that he personally supervised operation of the Club and, as an honest citizen, would never permit its use as a house of prostitution?

---

3. HEARSAY

One of the basic rules of evidence is the rejection of hearsay testimony. Generally speaking, hearsay may be defined as the repetition (or description) by a witness of an out-of-court statement (or writing or action) by another person (or occasionally by the witness himself) regarding the existence of a fact in issue when the statement is sought to be used to prove that fact. See Proposed Federal Rules of Evidence 801–802. The deficiency of hearsay testimony is the inability to test the credibility of the out-of-court declarant.

For example, suppose that Dolly's attorney, in an attempt to prove that the Hill Club is a house of prostitution, calls as a witness an undercover detective to testify that upon entering a local taxi, the driver said: "If you want some action, I'll take you to the Hill Club. It's the only place in town the police allow prostitutes to operate unmolested." Before cavalierly permitting such testimony, shouldn't we be concerned as to the source of the cab driver's information and the possibility that he might have been mistaken or lying? Is it clear exactly what was meant by the words "operate unmolested"? Obviously it would be much more satisfactory if the driver were called to testify so that he could be examined and cross-examined. But why should the availability of a better source render the testimony of the detective inadmissible? Unless it is totally unreliable, why don't we trust the trier of fact to evaluate the detective's testimony in light of its inherent weaknesses?

Sometimes it is difficult to determine whether evidence is or is not hearsay. Suppose, for example, that our undercover detective testified he had shared his taxicab with plaintiff, Patsy, and that when the driver made his statement she replied, "That's the place I'm headed for. Let's go." Note that these facts may impart new significance to the words of the taxicab driver; they may now be important merely because they were uttered without regard to their truth; if so, they would no longer be hearsay. Why should this be true? If we permit the detective to testify that the driver's statement was made in Patsy's presence, however, how do we avoid the danger that the trier of fact may not only consider the statement for purposes of determining whether it was made but also as an indication of the truth of its content? Often a court will counsel a jury to consider evidence only for a certain purpose. How effective is such an instruction? Does this practice cast doubt on the validity of the basic rule excluding hearsay?

---

4. EXCEPTIONS TO THE HEARSAY RULE

The rule excluding hearsay testimony is riddled with formal exceptions, which, generally speaking, are based (1) on the fact that there are special circumstances tending to make a particular item of hearsay reliable and (2) on the fact that the evidence is likely to be of importance. In analyzing a few of the more significant exceptions set out below, consider the extent to which they cast doubt on the validity of the hearsay rule itself.

A. ADMISSIONS OF A PARTY

———

Suppose a witness is called to testify that our plaintiff, Patsy, said that "she is one of the fun-girls at the Hill Club." Such relevant out-of-court statements by a party universally are admitted when presented by an opposing party, even though technically they may fall within the definition of hearsay. Why? Isn't witness repetition of a party's out-of-court statement subject to the same hearsay dangers as the statement of a nonparty? Is there any significance to the fact that a party is able to testify in his or her own behalf but a nonparty may be unavailable as a witness?

———

B. DECLARATIONS AGAINST INTEREST

———

Suppose our undercover detective is prepared to testify that the cab driver confessed that he was a panderer who procured customers for Patsy. Should this evidence be admitted? Is it significant that pandering is a criminal act? In some jurisdictions the driver's statement would be excluded and in others it would be admitted in evidence as an exception to the hearsay rule; usually an exception to the hearsay rule is recognized only if the statement would be against the pecuniary interests of the cab driver, for example, if he admitted that he owed Patsy money collected on her behalf. Does a distinction between pecuniary and penal interests make any sense? Suppose that Jones, a well respected member of the community and a family man, tells the detective that he knows Patsy is a prostitute because he has been one of her clients. Should this statement be admissible? Testimony concerning declarations against interest is allowed only if the declarant is unavailable to testify in person.

———

C. SPONTANEOUS AND CONTEMPORANEOUS STATEMENTS

———

Suppose a young lady in search of a room enters the Hill Club only to emerge a few minutes later, screaming: "Good gracious, it's full of prostitutes; they thought I was one!" Should a passerby be permitted to testify as to what she said? Courts usually admit a hearsay statement made spontaneously under emotional stress. Why?

What difference, if any, should it make if the statement was made by the young lady to a police officer some twenty minutes after the event? Suppose that upon entering the Hill Club and seeing that it was a brothel, she had calmly borrowed the Club phone and informed the police of the illegal activities? A few courts, at least, would permit the police officer who received the call to relate her dispassionate description of the ongoing events.

D. WRITTEN RECORDS

Suppose that our plaintiff, Patsy, claims that she has been attending college every evening during the hours when the Hill Club allegedly opens its doors for its "business activities." In order to prove her whereabouts Patsy seeks to introduce the school attendance records, which reveal that she has not missed a class for two years. These records consist of the absentee lists filed by each of her teachers at the conclusion of each class. The school secretary who keeps the records testifies as to the routine by which they are prepared and filed, but, of course, he cannot vouch for their accuracy. In effect, the records are statements of Patsy's teachers and are hearsay.

Courts permit the introduction of such routine business reports, however, when they are made soon after the events detailed by a person having first-hand knowledge, and when there is no reason to suspect that the reports are inaccurate. Is such an exception justifiable? Recognize that if it were not permitted, Patsy would be required to call her teachers to testify as to the attendance records. Assuming the teachers are available to testify, how likely are they to remember the extent to which Patsy was or was not present over the two-year period? The law recognizes the inability of individuals to recall such details. Therefore, if a witness testifies that he cannot remember a certain event, but presents a written account, which he made shortly after the event, that account may be admitted, even if it is not a business record; of course, there must be no reason to suspect that the account is inaccurate.

---

5. PRIVILEGE

The rules regarding privilege have been mentioned briefly in connection with the materials on pretrial discovery, see pp. 656–59, supra. They differ markedly from other evidence rules in that they are not designed to aid the trier of fact to reach a just decision with dispatch. Instead they are designed to withhold valid, nonprejudicial evidence for reasons of external policy.

Assume, for example, that in the hypothetical case our defendant, Dolly, informs her attorney that she has no information whatsoever to support her public statements that plaintiff is a prostitute. May defendant's attorney be called as a witness to testify as to this admission by the client?   The answer is "no."   Statements made by a client to an attorney for the purpose of obtaining legal advice are privileged, and cannot be revealed without the client's consent.   What justification is there for this rule?   In many jurisdictions, although not all, there is a privilege for statements made by a patient to a medical doctor for purposes of receiving treatment.   There are similar privileges for statements made by one spouse to another and by a penitent to his priest during confession.   Are all of these privileges justifiable? Should privileges be extended to cover confidential statements made to accountants, investment counselors, bankers, newsmen, and close relatives such as parents or children? †

What if the taxicab driver is called to the witness stand and asked whether or not he is a panderer?   The law clearly provides that a witness need not answer any question that might tend to incriminate him of illegal activities. Note the significant difference between this type of privilege and that which protects confidential communications.   In this context we are not merely prohibiting one person from revealing second-hand information received in confidence from another; instead we are allowing an individual with direct, first-hand knowledge, to remain silent.   How can such a rule be justified? Note that the privilege against self-incrimination is not the same thing as the right of a defendant in a criminal case to refuse to take the witness stand.   A litigant in a civil action cannot refuse to testify, even though the testimony will be detrimental to the party's interests, unless it can be shown that the testimony might lead to a criminal conviction.

---

6.   RELIABILITY OF DOCUMENTARY EVIDENCE

Suppose that plaintiff, Patsy, in order to show the damages she has suffered, offers into evidence a letter purportedly from the dean of a local law school, rejecting her application for admission on the ground that there is a serious question whether she is of good character.   Before the letter will be admitted, Patsy must make some showing that it is genuine.   See Proposed Federal Rules of Evidence 901.   This may be done in a number of ways: by calling the dean himself; by calling someone who can testify that the signature is, in fact, that of the dean; or by showing that the letter was in response to a letter sent to the dean.   What reason is there for a

---

† Many civil-law jurisdictions have extremely broad evidentiary privileges and render a number of groups of potential witnesses incompetent to testify.   See generally Miller, *International Cooperation in Litigation Between the United States and Switzerland: Unilateral Procedural Accommodation in a Test Tube*, 49 Minn.L.Rev. 1069, 1092–93 (1965).

rule requiring a preliminary showing of validity before the evidence is admitted? If the letter is admitted and the opposing party believes it to be a forgery, that party is free to introduce evidence to that effect, in order to convince the trier of fact to disregard the letter. Isn't the opposing party's right to challenge the letter a sufficient safeguard against fraudulent evidence?

What if Patsy attempts to introduce a copy of the dean's letter rather than the original? The so-called best-evidence rule requires that a party either furnish the original of a document or an explanation as to why the original is unavailable. The fact that the original is lost or destroyed is enough to permit the copy to be introduced but only if it can be authenticated as a true copy of a genuine original.

Note that analogous problems of authentication exist with regard to other types of nontestimonial evidence. Suppose, for example, that defendant wishes to introduce a motion picture allegedly taken of activities in the Hill Club. Defendant must call to the witness stand the photographer who took the pictures and the people who had custody of the film thereafter to testify that the pictures were not faked or altered prior to trial.

7. RELIABILITY OF ORAL TESTIMONY

A. COMPETENCY OF WITNESSES

What if defendant calls as a witness a four-year-old child to testify as to activities allegedly observed on the grounds of the Hill Club, which is adjacent to the child's home? What possible damages or risks do you see in permitting a small child to testify? Would it make any difference if the child were testifying on a less sensitive subject? How do the problems differ if the witness is a physically handicapped or mentally ill adult?

The law does not exclude the relevant testimony of any person who has the capacity to observe and remember the matters on which that person testifies, the ability to communicate this knowledge, and an understanding of the obligation to tell the truth. When any of these factors are in doubt, it is up to the trial judge, by preliminary examination of the witness, to determine whether the witness can meet these requirements.

B.   OPINION

As a general proposition, a witness is not permitted to include opinions in his testimony. Thus a person would not be allowed to conclude, "From what I've seen of the Hill Club, the way people go in and out at all hours of the night, and the noise, in my opinion it's a house of prostitution." What is the reason for this rule? Is testimony of this type unreliable? As one might suspect, the line between fact and opinion hardly is clear cut. By way of example, is it improper for a witness to testify that he often sees plaintiff emerge from the Hill Club in a "drunken stupor"? Could the statement be framed in a different way so as to avoid any claim that it contained opinion? Is it helpful to the trier of fact if the witness is permitted to give such an opinion?

The major exception to the proscription against opinions involves the expert witness who is called for the express purpose of rendering an opinion. Why is the exception justified? What kind of opinions should the expert be permitted to give? If, for example, Patsy is examined by a gynecologist, undoubtedly she could testify as to whether in her opinion Patsy had ever engaged in acts of sexual intercourse. Could she go on to testify that Patsy had done so frequently? Could the doctor give an opinion as to whether Patsy was a prostitute? Should the court permit Patsy's psychiatrist to testify that she is psychologically incapable of sexual activity?

C.   FORM OF EXAMINATION

Suppose defendant's attorney, in our hypothetical case, begins her examination of a witness with the following question: "Isn't it true that just three weeks ago, at 10 p.m., you entered the Hill Club, asked the desk clerk for a girl, paid $25, were directed to a small room containing a bed, waited for a short period until plaintiff in this case entered the room, and then engaged in an act of sexual intercourse with her?" This is referred to as a "leading question" and normally is improper for use on direct examination. Why? However, if the witness is the opposing party or any other witness who is hostile to the interests of the examining attorney's client, the attorney may then resort to leading questions. Furthermore, such questions universally are permitted on cross-examination. What justifications are there for these exceptions? Shouldn't the proper form of the question depend on the nature of the evidence sought to be elicited? For example, wouldn't the use of leading questions be appropriate and save a great deal of time in obtaining routine information such as the name, address, and occupation of the witness?

8.   IMPEACHMENT

There are many ways by which an attorney can overcome unfavorable testimony.   The lawyer may present new evidence to contradict what has been said, may cross-examine unfavorable witnesses and force them to change their original testimony, and, finally, may show that the unfavorable witnesses are unreliable and hence not to be believed.

Assume that Patsy's attorney is faced with the task of discrediting the taxicab driver's testimony that Patsy was a prostitute for whom he procured customers.   Her attorney will be permitted to introduce into evidence a prior statement made to a detective by the driver that the latter had known Patsy all her life and that she was of high moral character.   Note, however, that in most courts the statement may be used only to impugn the driver's credibility; it is normally considered improper to introduce it to prove the truth of the statement because this would violate the hearsay rule.   Does this make any sense when the statement is introduced during cross-examination of the driver who is present to explain exactly what he meant by the prior statement?   Should there be a special exception to the hearsay rule to cover this situation?

A witness' reliability also may be weakened by showing that the witness is biased.   For example, Patsy's attorney would be permitted to introduce evidence showing that the taxicab driver had become extremely angry with her when she rejected his advances.   Or the attorney might show that the driver was in the part-time employ of Dolly, our hypothetical defendant.

A final method of impeachment is through the use of character evidence. Basically there are three permissible methods of attacking a witness' character. First, in most, but not all, jurisdictions a witness may be asked questions on cross-examination regarding personal associations and history.   The courts tend to keep tight control over such questioning, limiting it to important witnesses and to matters that have a direct relationship to their reliability at the present time.   Second, as has previously been pointed out, see p. 788, supra, an attorney may bring out on cross-examination that the witness has previously been convicted of a serious crime, at least if the conviction was fairly recent.   Finally, an attorney may impeach a witness by calling another person who will testify that he is aware of the witness' reputation for truth and veracity in the community in which the witness lives, and that it is bad.   Is there any ground upon which this method of attack can be justified?   Does application of such a rule make more sense in some communities than in others?

9. JURISDICTIONAL VARIATIONS

In attempting to evaluate the law of evidence several things should be remembered. First, the foregoing review of the basic rules of evidence is skeletal and far from complete. Second, every jurisdiction has its own evidence rules and there are marked differences among them, although serious efforts are being made to bring some degree of uniformity to the subject. See, e. g., Uniform Rules of Evidence. Finally, the law of evidence has been changing radically and rapidly in an effort to eliminate archaic rules based on assumptions shown to be erroneous by modern behavioral and scientific study.

One final point should be noted. Federal Rule 43 is designed to govern the admission of evidence in the federal courts. Read the rule carefully. Note the extent to which it embraces state law under Rule 43(a). Would it be desirable to have a uniform set of evidence rules for all federal courts? See Degnan, *The Law of Federal Evidence Reform*, 76 Harv.L. Rev. 275 (1962); Note, *The Admissibility of Evidence Under Federal Rule 43(a)*, 48 Va.L.Rev. 939, 958 (1962). The United States Supreme Court, in November, 1972, formally approved a set of rules, entitled Rules of Evidence for United States Courts and Magistrates. They were to take effect July 1, 1973. Pursuant to the requirement of the Rules Enabling Act, 28 U.S.C. § 2072, these rules were referred to the Congress and normally would have become effective within 90 days unless the Congress took contrary action. Because some of the proposed rules were controversial, particularly those relating to privileges, the Congress immediately enacted Pub.L.No. 93–12, 93rd Cong., 1st Sess., March 30, 1973, barring the rules from taking effect until they expressly have been approved by the Congress. On February 6, 1974, the House of Representatives passed a rewritten, and less controversial, set of evidence rules. The Senate must act before the end of 1974 session of the Congress or the legislation will die. The House measure would deny the Supreme Court any power to create, abolish, or modify any evidentiary privilege through its rulemaking power without affirmative congressional action.[f1]

If the new federal rules ultimately are approved, will their application in diversity-of-citizenship cases raise serious problems when the federal and state rules differ materially? See Comment, *Federal Rule 43(a): The Scope of Admissibility of Evidence and the Implications of the Erie Doctrine*, 62 Colum.L.Rev. 1049 (1962).

[f1] Congress enacted the Federal Rules of Evidence in Public Law 93–595, and they became effective on January 2, 1975.

SECTION D. THE BURDEN OF PROOF: PRODUCTION AND PERSUASION

KNOWLES v. GILCHRIST CO.

Supreme Judicial Court of Massachusetts, 1972.
—— Mass. ——, 289 N.E.2d 879.

TAURO, Chief Justice. The plaintiff (bailor) in an action of tort and contract in the Municipal Court against the defendant Gilchrist Company (bailee) seeks to recover damages for loss of certain articles of furniture in the bailee's possession pursuant to an agreement by the bailee to reupholster and return furniture to the bailor. [It was agreed that the furniture was destroyed by fire while in the bailee's possession.] There was a finding for the bailor in the amount of $800. * * * The Appellate Division vacated the Municipal Court's finding for the bailor and ordered judgment for the bailee. The bailor appeals.

The Appellate Division rested its decision on the basis of our cases which have held that the bailor has the burden of proving by a fair preponderance of the evidence that the bailee broke the bailment contract by its negligence in caring for the goods. * * * Well established case authority in Massachusetts and in most other States has followed this rule despite the obvious problems in situations where, because the property was in the bailee's exclusive possession, the bailor has no knowledge of or access to the facts concerning its loss.

Originally, Massachusetts case law made a distinction between tort and contract actions in deciding where the burden of proof would be fixed. In Cass v. Boston & Lowell R. R., 14 Allen 448 (1867), the plaintiff bailor brought a contract action against a warehouseman to recover for the bailee's failure to return the goods entrusted to it. This court held that when the bailor alleged and proved that the bailee had received the bailor's property and failed to deliver it upon timely demand, the bailee had the burden of proving that the goods had been lost without any fault on its part. The pleadings were held to be decisive on the issue of burden of proof. * * * Since the bailor had sued in *contract*, he had not alleged that the bailee was negligent. The *Cass* opinion placed the burden of proving the absence of negligence on the party who alleged it in its pleadings, namely, the bailee. This line of reasoning led the court to conclude that the burden of proof lies on the *bailor* in tort actions because the bailor must allege negligence in his pleadings. * * *

Thus, the majority opinion in the *Cass* case created a rule predicated on the art of pleading. * * *

       * * *

Chief Justice Bigelow in his dissenting opinion in the *Cass* case also relied on a pleading rationale to allocate the burden of proof. His position was that ultimately the plaintiff bailor had to show a want of due care on the bailee's part to prove that the bailee breached his contract. * * *

Just twenty years later, this court adopted Chief Justice Bigelow's dissent as the law and in effect overruled the *Cass* case in [Willet v. Rich, 142 Mass. 356, 7 N.E. 776 (1886)]. * * * Thus, the *Willett* case established the rule, which is followed by most other jurisdictions, that the bailor has the burden of proving the bailee's negligence, regardless of whether the bailor's action sounds in tort or contract.

* * * Under this rule, since the bailor has the burden of proving the bailee's negligence, the bailee can simply plead impossibility as a defence, introduce evidence of a fire and rest as the bailee did in the instant case, even though the bailee may be the only party with access to the facts surrounding the loss.

In response to the obvious inequities and difficulties created by fixing the burden of proof on the bailor, recent decisions by State and Federal courts have held that the bailor can establish an inference or presumption of negligence merely by showing a bailment and failure to deliver by the bailee. Once the bailor makes this showing, the burden of *production* shifts to the bailee to go forward with evidence to rebut this presumption. * * * The United States Supreme Court adopted this procedure for proof of negligence in Commercial Molasses Corp. v. New York Tank Barge Corp., 314 U.S. 104, 62 S.Ct. 156, 86 L.Ed. 89. The court noted * * * "Since the bailee in general is in a better position than the bailor to know the cause of the loss and to show that it was one [not] involving the bailee's liability, the law lays on him the duty to come forward with the information available to him. * * * It does not cause the burden of proof to shift, and if the bailee does go forward with evidence enough to raise doubts as to the validity of the inference [of negligence on the bailee's part], which the trier of fact is unable to resolve, the bailor does not sustain the burden of persuasion which upon the whole evidence remains upon him, where it rested at the start."

This court followed the Supreme Court's lead in Bean v. Security Fur Storage Warehouse, Inc., 344 Mass. 674, 184 N.E.2d 64. * * *

* * * [I]t appears that our cases have adopted the rule followed by a majority of the States that the bailee may satisfy his burden of production and rebut the presumption of negligence arising from his failure to return goods entrusted to him by proof of loss arising from a fire or other extraordinary event. * * *

The irrational result of this holding is that evidence of a fire is sufficient evidence of due care on the bailee's part to overcome the bailor's inference of negligence. Moreover, it leaves the bailor in the same position of having to produce evidence of the bailee's negligence although it may have no access to such information. The imposition of such a minimal burden of production on the bailee defeats the rule's basic purpose because the bailee can simply note that a theft or a fire of unknown origin made delivery of the bailed goods impossible and rest his case.

Realizing the obvious defects of such a rule, many State courts have recently imposed a more stringent burden of production on the bailee. The Alaska Supreme Court's decision in Harris v. Deveau, 385 P.2d 283, reflects this modern trend in bailment cases. * * * "[T]he bailee must not only prove that the damage or loss occurred by reason of theft, fire or other cause beyond his control, but produce further evidence in explanation of the actual damage or loss which would indicate exercise of care on his part in the protection of the property. * * * He should disclose, to the extent that he is able, the manner in which the damage or loss occurred, the facts and circumstances attending such damage or loss and the precautions taken to prevent it." * * *

However, we feel that defining the bailee's burden of production in this manner resolves only in part the problem created by fixing the ultimate risk of nonpersuasion (or burden of proof by a fair preponderance of the evidence) on the bailor. A stringent burden of production on the bailee mitigates but does not cure the evil of imposing the burden of proof (or persuasion) on the party who has little or no access to the facts surrounding the loss or damage of the bailed property. * * * This essential unfairness is even more pronounced in cases, like the instant one, where the bailor is a consumer. The consumer's unfamiliarity with the bailee's trade practices and commercial customs *aggravates* the difficult task that all bailors face in trying to rebut the inference of due care which the bailee has created by selecting the most favorable facts from all the information exclusively available to him.

* * * As we have already noted, this court has justified placing the burden of proof on the bailor by relying on a pleading rationale. * * * The obvious problem with this rule is that it begs the essential question, which party should bear the *ultimate* burden of proving that the bailee was negligent. Until the burden of proof has been allocated to one of the parties, the fact of negligence is no less essential to one side than the other. Moreover, the fact that the bailor may have to affirmatively plead negligence does not justify placing the burden of proof on him. * * *

Since negligence is the determinative issue in the ordinary bailment case, the burden of proof should rest on the party who is in the best position to determine what actually happened to the goods and what safeguards existed both before and after the precipitating event that destroyed or damaged the bailed property. Clearly, the bailee has greater access to the information needed to show negligence or due care.

* * *

Therefore, we hold that once the bailor proves delivery of the property to the bailee in good condition and the failure to redeliver upon timely demand, the burden of proof is irrevocably fixed upon the bailee to prove by a fair preponderance of the evidence that he has exercised due care to prevent the property's loss or destruction. * * *

The order of the Appellate Division is reversed. * * *

[Opinion of BRAUCHER, J., dissenting in part, is omitted.]

NOTES AND QUESTIONS

1. In a jury case, who decides whether the burden of production on a particular issue has been met, the judge or the jury? What happens if a party fails to meet the burden of production?

2. Under the decision in *Knowles,* will a plaintiff in a similar case have any burden of production? Will plaintiff have the burden of persuasion on any issue? Describe the course of the trial in terms of the burden of production. What would have been the course of the trial before *Knowles?* What will the jury be told about the burden of persuasion after *Knowles?*

3. In civil cases, the burden of persuasion usually is defined as requiring proof by a preponderance of the evidence, with the additional caution that this does not mean simply the volume of the evidence or the number of witnesses. In some civil cases, particularly those involving allegations of fraud, many courts impose a heavier burden of persuasion—"proof by clear and convincing evidence." In criminal cases, "proof beyond a reasonable doubt" is constitutionally required. In re Winship, 397 U.S. 358, 90 S.Ct. 1068, 25 L.Ed.2d 368 (1970). See generally McCormick, *Evidence* §§ 339–41 (2d ed.1972). Can the jury's degree of certainty on a particular point meaningfully be divided into these three categories?

SECTION E.   INSTRUCTIONS AND VERDICTS

1.   INSTRUCTIONS

Read Federal Rule of Civil Procedure 51 and the accompanying materials in the Supplement. Note in particular Ga.Code Ann. § 70–207.

GRIFFIN v. CITY OF CINCINNATI

Court of Appeals of Ohio, Hamilton County, 1952.
92 Ohio App. 492, 111 N.E.2d 31.

PER CURIAM. On March 3, 1949, at about 7 p.m., the plaintiff, a man 37 years of age and in good health, approached the intersection of Sycamore and Eighth streets in the city of Cincinnati, going eastwardly on the north sidewalk of Eighth street. He was walking at a "normal pace," and, as he neared the intersection, he did not glance down at the sidewalk, but constantly looked straight ahead. * * * The sidewalk was constructed of concrete blocks and on a line with the north building line of Eighth street and about the middle of the Sycamore street sidewalk an offset of about one and one-half inches existed and a small section of one of the blocks was missing, making a shallow depression of undetermined depth. The plaintiff did not see either the offset or the depression before he fell while in the act of turning to go north on Sycamore street. It was either the offset or the depression, or both, that caused him to fall. His foot caught on this defect in the sidewalk.

* * * The jury found for the plaintiff. * * *

It is urged * * * that the court erred in the giving and refusal of certain special charges.

The court refused to give this special charge, requested by defendant:

> "If you find from the evidence that the plaintiff was guilty of negligence in failing to look where he walked at the time and place as alleged in the petition filed herein, and if you find that such negligence was a proximate cause of and directly contributed in the slightest degree to the accident, you must bring a verdict for the defendant, the city of Cincinnati, even though you find that the defendant was guilty of a violation of its statutory duty."

It is urged in support of this refusal that the special charge assumed that the plaintiff failed to look where he was walking. Authorities are cited to sustain this position holding that a charge which assumes a controverted fact is an invasion of the province of the jury and is erroneous. There is no doubt about that rule. Its inapplicability here results from the fact that the fact assumed was not controverted. The plaintiff testified that he did not look. He, of course, was bound by his own testimony. The only issuable fact left, therefore, was whether such failure constituted negligence * * *. We hold that the special charge was a correct statement of the law applicable to the controverted facts and that the court erred in refusing to give it.

But it is urged that no prejudice resulted because of the giving of other special charges at defendant's request. We have examined the special charges relating to the duty of the plaintiff and find that none of them submitted to the jury the specific issue of whether the admitted failure to devote at least some of his sense of vision to the sidewalk upon which he was walking was a failure to exercise reasonable care—whether it was negligence.

We, therefore, conclude that the failure to give the special charge was prejudicial.

At the plaintiff's request, the court gave this special charge:

> "The court charges you that, if you find that the sidewalk in question was not in a state of repair at the time plaintiff fell and that this condition existed for a time sufficient to have given the

city of Cincinnati constructive notice of its condition, then it was the duty of the city to notify the abutting property owner to repair it and if said property owner failed to do so within a reasonable time it was the duty of the city to make the repairs and to recover the costs thereof from such property owner."

The defendant excepted to the giving of this charge, and now assigns this as error.

The duty of the abutting property owner was entirely irrelevant to the issues in this case between a pedestrian on the sidewalk and the municipality. Whether it was the duty of the municipality to notify the property owner was immaterial. This irrelevant and immaterial issue was coupled with a positive vice in the charge that gave the municipality more than a reasonable time to repair the sidewalk. It permitted the municipality to notify the property owner to repair and then wait a reasonable time for him to repair the defect before proceeding to perform its duty. This gave the municipality more than a reasonable time after notice of the existence of the defect. While part of the charge was favorable to defendant and part unfavorable, we are of the opinion it was prejudicial error to give this charge.

* * *

Judgment reversed.

ROSS, Judge (dissenting). I cannot agree that the court committed error in refusing the special instruction, requested by the defendant, quoted in the opinion of the majority.

Here is a cleverly designed pitfall for the jury. It is true that the trained legal mind is able to dissect the language employed and arrive at the conclusion that the jury is not told that failure to look is negligence as a matter of law, but the average layman would so construe such instruction and the court properly refused it. It is more than apparent that the attention of the jury was intended to be directed to the words, "guilty of negligence in failing to look where he walked."

Technically, and from a pure academic standpoint, the words, "if you find from the evidence," may be said to stabilize the charge as correct. In this particular case, where as stated in the opinion of the majority "the plaintiff's attention was more dispersed while turning than it would have been while walking in a straight line with his view unobstructed in any way by the abutting building," the jury should be presented an instruction which in no way may be construed to state that failure to look directly at a defect in the sidewalk is negligence, and that is exactly what a jury of laymen would infer from the charge refused, although that is not what is actually stated.

I think that this special instruction should receive the definite disapproval of the court, and that in no case should it be given. It contains a correct statement of law which will always mislead the jury into a misapprehension of what is the applicable rule.

* * *

Now as to the special instruction given by the court, quoted in the majority opinion, requested by the plaintiff, and objected to by the defendant:

The "vice" in this instruction * * * is one of which the plaintiff might have complained, but certainly the city may not complain * * *.

The instruction did deal with matters extraneous to the issues involved. But was the jury misled to the prejudice of the defendant? * * *

I think the judgment should be affirmed.

NOTES AND QUESTIONS

1.   Assuming that the dissenting judge in *Griffin* is correct in deciding that the instruction refused below was improper in form (and that the other challenged instruction was not prejudicial), does it necessarily follow that the judgment below should be affirmed?   To what extent would Federal Rule 51 bear on the answer if the case had been brought in a federal court?   Reread pp. 38–41, supra.   See TURNER CONSTR. CO. v. HOULIHAN, 240 F.2d 435, 439 (1st Cir.1957):

> The first sentence of Rule 51 permits, but does not require, the filing of requests for instructions.   If none are filed, the court must nevertheless charge the jury on the broad general fundamental rules of law applicable to the principal issues of fact in the case. * * * If, however, counsel want the jury instructed specifically on particular matters, requests for such instructions must be filed.

Compare OUILLE v. SALIBA, 246 Miss. 365, 368–69, 149 So.2d 468, 469 (1963), stating the law in Mississippi: "Appellant did not request any instructions in accordance with the counterclaim * * *.   If appellant desired instructions on her counterclaim, she should have requested them.   The judge cannot instruct the jury on his own motion."

What is the duty of the court to instruct under Section 70–207(c) of the Georgia Code?   If there is to be a positive duty on the court to give proper instructions, regardless of the aid of counsel, how far should that duty go?   In North Carolina, apparently, it is not enough that the judge charge generally on the issues involved; the court must go further and relate the law to the evidence that has been introduced.   What dangers do you see in such a rule?   For a general discussion of the problems that arise when the court has a positive duty to instruct the jury, see Paschal, *A Plea for a Return to Rule 51 of the Federal Rules of Civil Procedure in North Carolina*, 36 N.C.L.Rev. 1 (1957).

2.   Suppose defendant in *Griffin* had failed to challenge the alleged erroneous instruction.   Section 647 of the California Code of Civil Procedure provides that an aggrieved party, although barred from objecting to the omission of an instruction that counsel failed to request, may challenge for the first time on appeal an erroneous instruction that in fact was given.   Compare California's approach with Section 70–207(c) of the Georgia Code.   What justification, if any, is there for these special provisions?   Would it be more sensible to be lenient with an attorney who fails to request a vital instruction than with one who sits back and permits an erroneous instruction to be given?   *Compare* Turner Constr. Co. v. Houlihan, quoted in Note 1, supra, *with* Crespo v. Fireman's Fund Indem. Co., 318 F.2d 174 (9th Cir.1963) (even "plain error" will not justify an attack on an instruction not challenged at trial).   See WIRTZ v. INTERNATIONAL HARVESTER CO., 331 F.2d 462 (5th Cir.), certiorari denied 379 U.S.

845, 85 S.Ct. 36, 13 L.Ed.2d 50 (1964), in which the court reversed a judgment on the ground that a vital instruction, not challenged below, clearly was incorrect. The appellate court stated that *both* parties have a duty to ensure that important instructions are properly phrased, not just the party who would be injured if the improper instruction were to be given.

3. Why shouldn't instructions be the sole responsibility of the trial judge? Federal Rule 51 and its state counterparts usually are justified on the ground that a court should be told of its errors and omissions in time to correct them in order to avoid the costs and delays of a new trial. Is there some other reason? Note that Rule 51 requires the trial judge to inform the lawyers prior to their closing arguments as to what instructions will be given. What purpose does this serve?

Doesn't rigid application of rules requiring a party to object to erroneous or omitted instructions simply result in decisions, erroneous as a matter of law, that cannot successfully be appealed? Are such rules consistent with provisions allowing a complaint to be challenged at any time for failure to state a claim, see pp. 479–81, supra, or with cases setting aside default judgments based on such complaints, see p. 767, supra?

4. Rule 51 spells out the manner and timing in which requests for instructions and objections are to be made. Why should requests for instructions be made in writing? Note that objections are to be made before the jury retires but out of its hearing. What purposes do these provisions serve?

Formal objections are not required under most modern procedural rules. See, e. g., Federal Rule 46. All that is necessary is that the complaining party make clear the nature of the error. It is not sufficient, however, for a party simply to make a general objection to an instruction without pointing out the specific defect. See RATAY v. LINCOLN NAT. LIFE INS. CO., 378 F.2d 209 (3d Cir.1967), in which the court admonishes trial judges who have permitted and even encouraged use of general objections to the instructions. Why should an appellate court be so concerned about the format of an objection? Is there any argument in favor of permitting general objections? See generally 16 Buffalo L.Rev. 415 (1967).

5. What if a trial court erroneously gives or refuses an instruction? Does this necessarily mean that the decision must be reversed? Suppose, for example, in the *Griffin* case the trial court had given an instruction, correct in form and substance, regarding the general duty of plaintiffs with respect to contributory negligence. Should this render harmless the failure to give a requested instruction relating directly to the evidence in the case? Or suppose the issue of whether plaintiff had looked where he was walking had been in dispute. Does the *Griffin* decision make it clear that the trial court would then have been reversed had it given the special instruction? Would it make any difference if prior to giving such a special instruction, the trial court had charged the jury that one of the issues to be decided was whether plaintiff had looked where he was going and properly had placed the burden of proof of that issue on plaintiff? See Peterson v. Brune, 273 S.W.2d 278, 284 (Mo.1954) (incorrect instruction harmless when all instructions, read together, are not misleading).

6. Lawyers and judges always will be seriously concerned with the precise wording of jury instructions as long as technical inaccuracies may lead to reversal on appeal. The irony is that many jurors do not even understand the basic aspects of the instructions, let alone the fine distinctions that often are

drawn. Part of the problem is due to the manner in which the instructions are given. All too often the judge reads the instructions in disjointed fashion in a nearly inaudible monotone using technical terms without any regard for the fact that the statements are incomprehensible. Much of this evil could be corrected if trial judges made an effort to improve the way in which they deliver the charge. See Devitt, *Ten Practical Suggestions About Federal Jury Instructions*, 38 F.R.D. 75 (1965). But even then, it is a great deal to ask of a juror, even in a simple case, to grasp the fine points of the applicable law. As already discussed, see Notes 4 and 5, pp. 838–40, supra, the value of the jury may lie in the fact that it does not, and is not expected to, apply the law in strict fashion. If this is true, would it not be possible to eliminate instructions or at least limit them to a short generalized statement? Is preservation of appellate review of the technical wording of jury instructions necessary to the proper development and growth of the law?

7. In recent years there has been a strong tendency for courts and lawyers to resort to the use of standard or "pattern" instructions. In a number of jurisdictions such instructions have been developed by courts and judges to cover a wide variety of common legal issues. What advantages and disadvantages are there to the use of standard instructions? Should use of such instructions be required? See Ill.Stat.Ann.c. 110A, § 239.

8. For an interesting discussion of the problems of giving accurate and meaningful instructions plus an example of an entire set of instructions, see Smith, *Effective Instructions to the Federal Jury in Civil Cases—A Consideration in Microcosm*, 18 Syracuse L.Rev. 559 (1967). See also Devitt & Blackmar, *Federal Jury Practice and Instructions* §§ 8.01–.05 (1970); White, *Some Approaches to the Instructional Problem*, 40 Neb.L.Rev. 413 (1961).

———

NUNLEY v. PETTWAY OIL CO., 346 F.2d 95 (6th Cir.1965). Plaintiff brought suit for personal injuries received when a truck fell off a grease rack in a gas station. The jury found plaintiff to be a licensee rather than an invitee at the time of the accident, and, applying the applicable law, the court entered judgment for defendant. On appeal plaintiff contended that the court had improperly commented to the jury on the licensee-invitee question. During their initial deliberations the jurors were unable to agree on this issue, whereupon the judge called them into the courtroom and urged them to try to arrive at a decision as follows:

> Now, the jury of course is the sole and exclusive judge of the facts in this lawsuit. It is appropriate that the Court in an effort to be possibly of some help to the jury may comment upon the evidence. I refrain from doing that and have refrained until this time from doing it in this case. However, in an effort to be of some possible assistance to you I think that I should under these circumstances make some comment upon the evidence upon this issue of invitee-licensee. I want you to understand, however, that in making these comments that you are not in any degree, in any respect, obligated to receive or accept or agree with what I may say. It is your

duty to accept what I say with regard to the law in the case, but it is not your duty to accept any comment that I may make or any evaluation that I may make or conclusion that I might reach on the evidence. That is solely your responsibility and solely your duty. *But, with that understanding, it is the opinion of the Court in this case that, from all the evidence upon the issue of invitee or licensee, that the evidence will establish that at the time and place of the accident the plaintiff was a licensee and not an invitee.* Now, I say that just for the purpose, as I say, of possibly being of some help to you, but I want you to understand that in making that comment you are not obligated whatsoever to accept that comment as your comment or as your opinion in the case, because it is your job and your responsibility to resolve that issue. I only make that with the thought and the hope that it may be of some possible assistance to you. At any rate, I want to ask you once again to retire and consider your verdict and see if you cannot come to some agreement, some verdict that will reflect the views of all of the jurors.   *   *   *

Id. at 98. The court of appeals reversed, stating:

> We recognize that the right of a District Judge to comment on the evidence is firmly established in the federal system. See Quercia v. United States, 289 U.S. 466, 53 S.Ct. 698, 77 L.Ed. 1321 (1933)   *   *   *.
>
> Nonetheless, we believe that under the circumstances enumerated, the trial judge's opinion on the licensee-invitee issue was an opinion on an ultimate fact question peculiarly for jury consideration and amounted to an instructed verdict as to defendant Pettway Oil Company.
>
> In Quercia v. United States, supra, Chief Justice Hughes commented:
>
>> "This privilege of the judge to comment on the facts has its inherent limitations. His discretion is not arbitrary and uncontrolled, but judicial, to be exercised in conformity with the standards governing the judicial office. In commenting upon testimony he may not assume the role of a witness. He may analyze and dissect the evidence, but he may not either distort it or add to it. His privilege of comment in order to give appropriate assistance to the jury is too important to be left without safeguards against abuses.
>>
>>   " *   *   *
>>
>> "Nor do we think that the error was cured by the statement of the trial judge that his opinion of the evidence was not binding on the jury and that if they did not agree with it they should find the defendant not guilty. His definite and concrete assertion of fact, which he had made with all the

persuasiveness of judicial utterance, as to the basis of his opinion, was not withdrawn. * * * "

Id. at 98–99.

NOTES AND QUESTIONS

1. In *Quercia,* a *criminal* case, the trial court had charged the jury as follows:

> And now I am going to tell you what I think of the defendant's testimony. You may have noticed, Mr. Foreman and gentlemen, that he wiped his hands during his testimony. It is rather a curious thing, but that is almost always an indication of lying. Why it should be so we don't know, but that is the fact. I think that every single word that man said, except when he agreed with the Government's testimony, was a lie.
>
> Now, that opinion is an opinion of evidence and is not binding on you, and if you don't agree with it, it is your duty to find him not guilty.

Is the court in *Nunley* justified in relying on *Quercia?* Aren't there substantial differences between the two cases?

2. In light of the decision in *Nunley,* what is the meaning of the court's statement: "We recognize that the right of a District Judge to comment on the evidence is firmly established in the federal system"? The trial judge's common-law power to comment on the evidence, as retained in a minority of jurisdictions, includes the power to express an opinion regarding both evidentiary issues and the credibility of witnesses. See Lukowsky, *The Constitutional Right of Litigants to Have the State Trial Judge Comment Upon the Evidence,* 55 Ky.L.J. 121 (1966). For an example of the broad exercise of the power in a criminal case, see People v. Schwenkner, 191 Cal.App.2d 46, 12 Cal.Rptr. 408 (4th Dist.1961).

3. Those federal decisions that appear to limit the common-law practice are in line with limitations in a majority of states, which take two basic forms: (1) the trial judge is confined to a statement of the applicable law and deprived of power even to mention the evidence (see Colorado Rule of Civil Procedure 51), or (2) the court is limited to presenting an impartial summary of the evidence (see, e. g., Belk v. Schweizer, 268 N.C. 50, 149 S.E.2d 565 (1966)). It has been suggested that the latter approach is not feasible. Wright, *Instructions to the Jury: Summary Without Comment,* 1954 Wash.U.L.Q. 177. Why?

4. The *Nunley* opinion emphasizes that the judge's comment was on an "ultimate fact question." The Fifth Circuit holds that comments are proper on "evidentiary matters," but not on "ultimate factual issues." Travelers Ins. Co. v. Ryan, 416 F.2d 362, 364 (5th Cir.1969). Is there any sound basis for this distinction?

5. What are the arguments for and against allowance of a broad judicial power to comment on the evidence? See Lukowsky, supra; Stone, *Instructions to Juries: A Survey of the General Field,* 26 Wash.U.L.Q. 455 (1941). Professor Wigmore passionately advocated restoration of the broad power, and severely criticized the federal approach exemplified in *Quercia.* 9 Wigmore, *Evidence* § 2551 n. 7 (3d ed. 1940).

6. Jurisdiction in the *Nunley* case was based on diversity of citizenship. Suppose that the law of the state permits the trial judge to express an opinion as to whether the evidence is sufficient to establish the ultimate facts in the case. To what extent is the federal court bound by the state practice? See *Byrd v. Blue Ridge Rural Elec. Coop.*, p. 278, supra.

PERMITTING INSTRUCTIONS TO BE TAKEN INTO THE JURY ROOM

1. A substantial number of state and federal courts either require or permit written instructions to be taken into the jury room. See California Law Revision Commission, *Recommendation and Study Relating to Taking Instructions into the Jury Room*, pp. C–15–C–17 (1956) (Tabular Summary of the Law of Other States). The Study speaks about the merits of these provisions as follows:

> Much can be said, it is believed, for giving a copy of the instructions to the jury, either as a matter of routine or upon the request of a party or of the jury. The instructions are intended to guide the jury's deliberations. Yet, even in a relatively simple case they are usually lengthy and complex. It is hardly reasonable to suppose that the jury, composed as it is of persons unfamiliar with either law or legal language and having heard the instructions but once as given orally by the court, will be able to remember them in detail as it ponders the matters committed to it for decision.

See generally Cunningham, *Should Instructions Go Into the Jury Room?*, 33 Calif.St.B.J. 278 (1958); Katz, *Reinstructing the Jury by Tape Recording*, 41 J.Am.Jud.Soc'y 148 (1958); Note, *The Availability of Written Instructions to the Jury in Indiana*, 33 Ind.L.J. 96 (1957).

2. Are there any effective arguments against allowing the jury to possess the written instructions during its deliberations? What effect does the possession of written instructions have on the focus of the jury's discussion? Does possession of written instructions tend to affect the amount of influence some jurors have on the rest of the panel? *Cf.* James, *Status and Competence of Jurors*, 64 Am.J.Sociology 563, 563–70 (1959).

3. In many jurisdictions jurors are permitted and even encouraged to take notes throughout the trial for use during the deliberations. See State ex rel. Dept. of Highways v. Lehman, 462 P.2d 649 (Okl.1969), 7 Tulsa L.Rev. 56 (1970); Annot., 14 A.L.R.3d 831 (1967). Does this obviate any need for written instructions? Is there any reason why note-taking should not be permitted?

2. THE FORM OF THE VERDICT

———

Read Federal Rule of Civil Procedure 49 in the Supplement.

———

The traditional form of the jury decision, used almost exclusively in the great majority of courts, is the general verdict. No matter how complex the case and how long and involved the instructions were, all a jury need do to render a general verdict is to announce which party wins, and, if it is plaintiff, the amount that should be recovered. This type of verdict has two major deficiencies. First, there is no way to tell how the jurors decided specific issues, which, in turn, can result in the unnecessary retrial of the entire case. For example, suppose a defendant raises a number of defenses, any one of which, if established, would require a verdict for defendant. Then the court, in an otherwise faultless charge, erroneously instructs the jury on one of these defenses in a manner detrimental to plaintiff, after which the jury finds for defendant. On appeal the court will be required to reverse since it has no way of telling whether the verdict was based solely on the tainted defense. If, however, the jury had been required to render a verdict on each one of the defenses, the court would know at once the bases of the jury decision and whether the error in the instruction was harmless. See, e. g., Castilleja v. Southern Pacific Co., 445 F.2d 183 (5th Cir.1971). The second major drawback to the general verdict is the fact that there is no way of knowing whether the jury actually focused its attention on every major aspect of the case as required by the instructions, or whether it ignored the instructions altogether and rendered a decision based solely on sentiment, public opinion, bias, or similar emotion.

To avoid these objections, many writers have advocated use of the special verdict, which requires the jury to answer a series of questions regarding each facet of the case. For example, in Frank, *Courts on Trial* 141–42 (1950), the following argument is advanced:

> A special verdict would seem to do away with some of the most objectionable features of trial by jury. The division of functions between jury and judge is apparently assured, the one attending to the facts alone, the other to the legal rules alone. The jury seems, by this device, to be shorn of its power to ignore the rules or to make rules to suit itself. As one court said, special verdicts "dispel * * * the darkness visible of general verdicts." The finding of facts, says Sunderland, "is much better done by means of the special verdict. Every advantage which the jury is popularly supposed to have over the [judge] as a trier of facts is retained, with

the very great additional advantage that the analysis and separation of the facts in the case which the court and the attorney must
necessarily effect in employing the special verdict, materially reduce the chance of error. It is easy to make mistakes in dealing at
large with aggregates of facts. The special verdict compels detailed consideration. But above all it enables the public, the parties
and the court to see what the jury has really done * * *. The
morale of the jury also is aided by throwing off the cloak of secrecy, for only through publicity is there developed the proper feeling
of responsibility in public servants. So far, then, as the facts go,
they can be much more effectively, conveniently, and usefully tried
by abandoning the general verdict * * *. The special verdict is
devised for the express purpose of escaping the sham of false
appearances." [Sunderland, *Verdicts General and Special*, 29
Yale L.J. 253 (1920).]

   * * * It is suggested, too, that a special verdict "searches
the conscience of the individual juror, as a general verdict does not,"
because "such are the contradictions in human nature that many
a man who will unite in a general verdict for a large and unwarranted sum of money will shrink from a specific finding against his
judgment of right and wrong." [Clementson, *Special Verdicts
and Special Findings by Juries* 15 (1905).]

This view has been strongly opposed on the ground that the special verdict improperly subverts the fundamental nature of the jury decision. See 5
Moore, *Federal Practice* ¶ 49.05, at 2217 (2d ed.):

   * * * [T]he general verdict, at times, achieves a triumph
of justice over law. The jury is not, nor should it become, a scientific fact finding body. Its chief value is that it applies the "law,"
oftentimes a body of technical and refined theoretical principles
and sometimes edged with harshness, in an earthy fashion that comports with "justice" as conceived by the masses, for whom after all
the law is mainly meant to serve. The general verdict is the answer from the man in the street. If on occasion the trial judge
thinks the jury should be quizzed about its overall judgment as
evidenced by the general verdict, this can be done by interrogatories
accompanying the general verdict. But if there is sufficient evidence to get by a motion for directed verdict, then the problem is
usually best solved by an overall, common judgment of the jurors—
the general verdict.

And see the statement of Mr. Justice Black and Mr. Justice Douglas issued in
connection with the 1963 amendment of Rule 49, 374 U.S. 865, 867–68, 83
S.Ct. 43, 44–45 (1963):

   * * * Rule 49 should be repealed. * * * Such devices are used to impair or wholly take away the power of a jury

to render a general verdict.   One of the ancient, fundamental reasons for having general jury verdicts was to preserve the right of trial by jury as an indispensable part of a free government.   Many of the most famous constitutional controversies in England revolved around litigants' insistence, particularly in seditious libel cases, that a jury had the right to render a general verdict without being compelled to return a number of subsidiary findings to support its general verdict.   Some English jurors had to go to jail because they insisted upon their right to render general verdicts over the repeated commands of tyrannical judges not to do so.   Rule 49 is but another means utilized by courts to weaken the constitutional power of juries and to vest judges with more power to decide cases according to their own judgments.

See also 9 Wright & Miller, *Federal Practice and Procedure: Civil* § 2505 (1971).

———

NOLLENBERGER v. UNITED AIR LINES, INC.

United States District Court, Southern District of California, 1963.
216 F.Supp. 734.
Vacated 335 F.2d 379 (9th Cir.).
Certiorari dismissed 379 U.S. 951, 85 S.Ct. 452, 13 L.Ed.2d 549 (1964).

HALL, Chief Judge.   [This is a wrongful-death action in which the jury, pursuant to Rule 49(b), rendered a general verdict accompanied by interrogatories.   The plaintiffs allege that the answers to the interrogatories are inconsistent with the general verdict.   They request that the court either submit additional interrogatories to the jury, or calculate the verdict on the basis of the answers to the questions given, or grant a new trial.]

* * *

The first task of the Court is to determine whether or not the Findings of Fact in the answers, given by the jury to the special interrogatories, are consistent with each other and whether one or more, if consistent with each other, are inconsistent with the general verdict fixing the total sum of damages to the plaintiffs resulting from the death of the decedent.   And in doing so, Gallick v. Baltimore & Ohio R. R. Co., 372 U.S. 108, 83 S.Ct. 659, 9 L.Ed.2d 618 (1963), "it is the duty of the courts to attempt to harmonize the answers, if it is possible under a fair reading of them * * *."

The text of the special verdict on damages in the Nollenberger case is as follows:

"We, the Jury in the above entitled case, unanimously find as follows:

QUESTIONS	ANSWERS

1. Which one of the following named persons, viz.: William Edward Nollenberger, 45 years of age on April 21, 1958; Catherine B. Nollenberger, his widow, age 47 on April 21, 1958; William Edward Nollenberger, Jr., son, age 20 on April 21, 1958; Lawrence P. Nollenberger, son, age 11 on April 21, 1958; had the shortest life expectancy?

Wm. E. Nollenberger
(Name)

2. How many years was that life expectancy on April 21, 1958?

25
(Total number of years)

3. How many years was decedent's work and earning expectancy from and after April 21, 1958?

15 yrs
(Total number of years)

4. From and after April 21, 1958, what total sum of money do you find the decedent would have earned during the period of his work and earning expectancy stated in your answer to No. 3 above?

$235,210
(Total)

5. From and after the end of his work and earning expectancy, and during the remainder of his life, if any such remained, what total sum of money do you find decedent would have received as a result of his government employment?

$100,200
(Total sum)

6. What is the total reasonable value of services susceptible of being furnished by others which you find it was reasonably probable that decedent would have provided under my instructions to you to the plaintiffs during his lifetime?

$25,000
(Total value)

7. What percentage of his annual earnings, had he lived, from and after April 21, 1958, would have been used by decedent for his own personal expenses which were eliminated by his death?

25%
(Percentage of annual earnings)

QUESTIONS	ANSWERS
8. What percentage of his income would be paid as annual income tax had he lived after April 21, 1958?	15%
9. What percentage of the income from the award will be paid by plaintiffs as income tax?	11%
10. In determining the present reasonable value of services as defined in No. 6 above, what annual rate of inflation, if any, do you find should be allowed?	1%
11. What discount rate should be applied in arriving at the total sum of general damages?	4% (Discount rate)
12. What sum of money do you find plaintiffs' general damages to be which you assess against Defendant United Air Lines?	$114,655.00

DATED: At Los Angeles, California, January 16, 1963.

S/   Burford A. Reynold
Foreman"

The answers to the Special Interrogatories No. 1 to No. 11 are plainly consistent with each other and are amply supported by the evidence.

But, in repeated efforts to "harmonize" and "reconcile" the answers to the 11 special interrogatories with the general verdict of $114,655.00, I have been unable to do so. And hence I must and do conclude that they are not harmonious or reconcilable.

While Rule 49(b) * * * under such circumstances permits, as one of three alternatives, the Court to re-submit the matter to the jury for further consideration, the plaintiffs desire the Court to go further and to submit additional interrogatories * * *. [H]ad it been the intention to permit *additional interrogatories* to be submitted *after* the general verdict and answers to the special interrogatories submitted with the verdict, the rule would have so provided, and the rule would not have contained the restrictive language of the second sentence of Rule 49(b) that the Court "* * * shall direct the jury both to make written answers and to render a general verdict," or the language in the fourth sentence of Rule 49(b) (applicable here) that the Court, as one alternative, "* * * may return the jury for *further consideration of its answers and verdict.*"

It could be argued from the portion of the rule last quoted that if that procedure were followed the jury could change both its answers and general verdict, or only the answers and not the general verdict. * * * That such action by the jury was not intended by the Rule is evidenced from the citation in the note to Rule 49 by the Advisory Committee of the case of Victor-American Fuel Co. v. Peccarich (C.C.A.1913) 209 F. 568, cert. den. 232 U.S. 727, 34 S.Ct. 603, 58 L.Ed. 817. In that case the Court stated, at page 571: "* * * these special findings must control when they clearly compel a different judgment from that which would follow the general verdict" * * *.

I conclude (1) that the findings of fact of the jury in answer to special interrogatories control over the general verdict; (2) that it is not within the power of the court under F.R.Civ.P. 49(b) to submit additional interrogatories after the jury has returned its verdict answering special interrogatories and at the same time returned a general verdict; (3) that in * * * Nollenberger * * * the answers to the special interrogatories are consistent with each other and inconsistent with and cannot be reconciled or harmonized with the general verdict; (4) that before granting a new trial, it is the duty of the Court to make calculations from the special interrogatories, and enter a judgment thereon. Which latter, I shall now do.

[The court then calculated the damages at $171,702.00 and entered judgment for that amount.]

* * *

NOTES AND QUESTIONS

1. In overturning the *Nollenberger* decision, the court of appeals held as follows (335 F.2d 379, 407–09):

> The district court stated that after repeated efforts, by mathematical calculation, to harmonize and reconcile the answers to the eleven special interrogatories with the general verdict, no harmony resulted. This may be so. But nothing in the law compelled the jury to calculate its damage awards according to a fixed mathematical formula using only the factors contained in the eleven special findings. * * *

> The jury was admonished to award damages in accordance with all the instructions of the court. No party specifies as error the giving of any of the instructions set forth in the margin.[43]

> * * * Suffice it to say that the answers to the eleven special interrogatories do not exhaust all of the factors of damage included within the instructions, and therefore no square conflict exists between the answers and the general verdict. We are not called upon to consider

---

43 * * *

"You should award the plaintiffs herein such sum as, *under all of the circumstances of the case, may be fair and just compensation* for the pecuniary loss which the [widow and child(ren)] have suffered by reason of the death of [decedent].
" * * *

"In weighing these matters, you may consider * * * *the disposition of the deceased, whether it was kindly, affectionate or otherwise; whether or not he showed an inclination to contribute to the support of the plaintiffs or any of them;* the earning capacity of the deceased; and *such other facts shown by the evidence as throw light upon the pecuniary value of the support, society, care, comfort and protection* other than the loss of consortium between husband and wife, which the plaintiffs reasonably might have expected to receive from the deceased had he lived. * * *" (Emphasis added.)

either whether the jury should not have been permitted to consider one or more of the italicized factors or whether the damage awards manifest such passion or prejudice as would render them inadequate. We hold that the court's utilization of the provisions of Rule 49(b) did not render proper its increase of damages in accordance with mathematical computations based upon the special findings.

2. Is the appellate-court decision in *Nollenberger* realistic? If so, what possible justification was there for the trial court's decision to present the jury with special interrogatories? The appellate court gave plaintiff the option of accepting the jury's general verdict or of having the case returned to the trial court for a ruling on plaintiff's motion for a new trial. Should the court of appeals itself have decided whether there should be a new trial in the event that plaintiff decided not to accept the jury award?

3. Just how far should a court go in attempting to reconcile a jury's answers to specific interrogatories, either among themselves or with a general verdict? In BROWN v. DALE, 395 S.W.2d 677, 679–80 (Tex.Civ.App.1965), the crucial issue was contributory negligence. In interrogatories 6 and 7, the court asked the jury whether "immediately before the accident" plaintiff had failed to maintain a proper lookout and, if so, whether this failure was a proximate cause of the accident. Both questions were answered affirmatively. In interrogatories 10 and 11 the court asked whether "at the time and on the occasion in question," plaintiff failed to see that he could proceed with safety and, if so, whether or not this constituted negligence. The jury responded by saying plaintiff had failed to see the danger, but specifically found that such failure was not negligent. The court, in upholding a verdict for defendant, stated as follows:

> The first premise we wish to state is that it is the duty of the trial court to reconcile conflicts in the findings of the jury if reasonably possible from the issues in question and the facts pertaining thereto. * * *

> We believe the issues under discussion may be reconciled in that No. 6 inquires of that period *immediately* before the accident. * * *

> Special Issue No. 10 does not pinpoint the time to *immediately* before the accident but is less definite in its inquiry; simply placing it at the time and on the occasion in question.

> * * * It requires no citation of authority to say that one properly submitted issue on contributory negligence with an affirmative answer as to both negligence and proximate cause found against the plaintiff, when supported by probative evidence, makes other separate, distinct and unrelated contributory negligence questions immaterial where there is rendered a take-nothing judgment.

4. Reread and reconsider the materials on pp. 42–45, supra. Do the difficulties faced by courts that utilize special-verdict forms indicate an inherent weakness in the jury-trial system?

5. For a comprehensive discussion of Federal Rule 49, see Comment, *Special Verdicts: Rule 49 of the Federal Rules of Civil Procedure*, 74 Yale L.J. 483 (1965). For other discussions of special forms of verdict, see Note, *The Case for Interrogatories Accompanying a General Verdict*, 52 Ky.L.J. 852 (1964); Annot., 6 A.L.R.3d 438 (1966).

3. JURY MISCONDUCT AND THE INTEGRITY
OF THE VERDICT

IMPEACHMENT OF THE VERDICT USING JUROR'S TESTIMONY

The general rule that jurors' affidavits cannot be utilized to attack the verdict already has been noted. See p. 50, supra. The rule's validity has vigorously been challenged. For example in SOPP v. SMITH, 59 Cal.2d 12, 27 Cal.Rptr. 593, 377 P.2d 649 (1963), an auto accident case, a motion for new trial was based on affidavits of several jurors stating that during the trial they had visited the scene of the accident personally to check driver visibility, road conditions, and distances about which testimony had been produced. The California Supreme Court upheld a denial of a new trial on the ground that the affidavits were inadmissible. Justice Peters dissented:

> The majority, following the rule of stare decisis, adhere to a court created doctrine first announced by Judge Mansfield in Vaise v. Delaval, 1 Term R. 11, 99 Eng.Rep. 944 (K.B.1785). That rule is that affidavits of jurors may not be used to impeach their verdict.

> * * * At least 12 jurisdictions, by judicial decision, have [followed the lead of Iowa in modifying] * * * the strict Mansfield rule. * * *

> The Iowa rule is based upon the distinction between extrinsic or overt acts which may be corroborated or disproved, such as access to improper matter or an illegal method of reaching a verdict, and intrinsic matters which "inhere in the verdict itself" and hence are known only to the individual juror, such as misunderstanding or prejudice. Because matters which "inhere" in the verdict, including the thought processes and motives of the juror in reaching his decision, are not readily capable of being either corroborated or disproved they should be excluded.

> * * *

> In spite of the fact that the legal scholars in this field are practically unanimous in their opinion that the Iowa rule is sound, it must be conceded that the majority of the states still adhere to the Mansfield rule. The reason for this has been several times noted. Justice Learned Hand stated it as follows: " * * * judges again and again repeat the consecrated rubric which has so confused the subject; it offers an easy escape from embarrassing choices." (Jorgensen v. York Ice Machinery Corp., * * * (2nd Cir.1947) 160 F.2d 432, 435, cert. denied, 332 U.S. 764, 68 S.Ct. 69, 92 L.Ed. 349.) * * *

Generally speaking, * * * the courts cite one or more of the following reasons for continuing to invoke the strict rule of exclusion: (1) The need for stability of verdicts; (2) the need to protect jurors from fraud and harassment by disappointed litigants; (3) the desire to prevent prolonged litigation; (4) the need to prevent verdicts from being set aside because of the subsequent doubts or change of attitude by a juror; (5) the concept of the sanctity of the jury room.

Wigmore has completely demolished these arguments (8 Wigmore on Evidence (McNaughton rev. 1961) § 2353, pp. 697–699). In 47 Colum.L.Rev. 1373, 1375, it is stated * * * "It is anomalous that the best and usually the only evidence of which the case admits should be excluded [citation]. The objection that admission of this evidence would allow undue tampering with jurors is greatly exaggerated; courts in early decisions before the rule was adopted were apparently not troubled by fear of excessive jury corruption [citations]. The argument that uncertainty of jury verdicts would result from a more liberal rule of admissibility is misdirected since the acceptance of jurors' testimony does not mean that any jury irregularity warrants a new trial, but only that such evidence may be considered in determining whether or not a new trial is required [citation]. The real problem, therefore, is substantive rather than procedural; namely, what kind of jury misbehavior should be considered grounds for reversal."

The fear that under the Iowa rule a juror might have doubts about his verdict and subsequently seek to upset it by an affidavit on motion for new trial is unfounded. This is so because a juror's testimony or affidavit is and should be admissible only when it concerns overt acts. Furthermore, admissibility of the evidence does not a fortiori mean reversal—prejudice must be proved. (See e. g., 10 Hastings L.J. 319 and 13 Hastings L.J. 415.)

* * * The trial court held, as a matter of law, that the affidavits of the offending jurors could not be considered by it. Such testimony was obviously the best evidence available on the issue. Had the wife of one of the offending jurors who accompanied him while he made the improper measurements filed the affidavit to the effect that she had observed her husband, such affidavit would admittedly have been admissible. * * * Yet here where it is admitted that misconduct occurred, the majority say that even though such misconduct may have deprived the plaintiff of a fair trial we will not permit him to show that by the affidavit of the very man that committed the overt act that constituted the misconduct. This is logically absurd. * * *

Id. at 15–20, 27 Cal.Rptr. at 595–98, 377 P.2d at 651–54.

NOTES AND QUESTIONS

1. See Note, *Impeachment of Jury Verdicts,* 53 Marq.L.Rev. 258 (1970); Note, *Invasion of Jury Deliberations,* 23 Baylor L.Rev. 445 (1970); Note, *Impeachment of Jury Verdicts by Jurors: A Proposal,* 1969 U.Ill.L.Forum 388.

2. Suppose the jurors agree upon a verdict but through the mistake of the jury foreman, judge, or court clerk a different verdict is entered. Should affidavits of jurors be admissible to correct the error? Is this "impeachment" within the meaning of the common law? If so, would the case fall within the exceptions permitted by the Iowa rule?

In an action to recover an automobile from a person who claimed to be a bona fide purchaser for value, the jury in a special verdict answered that defendant had purchased the automobile in good faith, but answered "No" to a question whether defendant had obtained it for "new value." After the verdict was taken and the jury was dismissed, eight jurors filed an affidavit that the answer to the second question was intended to be "Yes." The Wisconsin Supreme Court overruled an earlier case recognizing an exception to the no-impeachment rule when there was an alleged error in recordation of the verdict and ordered that the verdict stand as originally received. FORD MOTOR CREDIT CO. v. AMODT, 29 Wis. 441, 139 N.W.2d 6 (1966).

May affidavits be used when a verdict for plaintiff was rendered, but the amount of damages found was omitted? See Hodgkins v. Mead, 119 N.Y. 166, 23 N.E. 559 (1890).

3. Rule 606(b) of the Proposed Federal Rules of Evidence provides:

Inquiry into validity of verdict or indictment. Upon an inquiry into the validity of a verdict or indictment, a juror may not testify as to any matter or statement occurring during the course of the jury's deliberations or to the effect of anything upon his or any other juror's mind or emotions as influencing him to assent to or dissent from the verdict or indictment or concerning his mental processes in connection therewith, except that a juror may testify on the question whether extraneous prejudicial information was improperly brought to the jury's attention or whether any outside influence was improperly brought to bear upon any juror. Nor may his affidavit or evidence of any statement by him concerning a matter about which he would be precluded from testifying be received.

HUKLE v. KIMBLE

Supreme Court of Kansas, 1952.
172 Kan. 630, 243 P.2d 225.

SMITH, Justice. This was an action for damages alleged to have been sustained when plaintiff was caught between a truck driven by one of defendants and a pillar in the driveway of an elevator where plaintiff was employed. Judgment was for the plaintiff. Defendants have appealed.

* * *

Defendants * * * argue that the trial court erred in overruling their motion for a new trial. One of the grounds of this motion was misconduct of the jury. On the hearing of the motion for a new trial testimony of various members of the jury was heard on the question of whether the verdict was a quotient verdict. One of the jurors testified as follows:

"Q. Without giving any of the other deliberations—in other words, without telling what was in your mind—I would like to ask you how this verdict was arrived at, the amount of this verdict? A. Mr. Brann was the foreman of the jury and he asked that—or suggested that if the—there was a judgment, which he thought there should be, if we would all put down an amount on a piece of paper, which we did, then someone in the group added it up and divided it by 12 and arrived at the $5,208.33, and then Mr. Brann said, 'Is there anyone that feels this is an unfair amount? Is this the amount that all of us wish, if you don't feel that way why speak up now,' and we all agreed that that would be the amount that we felt was right.

"Q. And there had been something said before the quotient was taken, before you divided by 12 to do that to arrive at a verdict? A. I think so. I think it was. I think it was agreed that, before we wrote down those amounts that that would be the fair way, if one person said one amount and someone else said something higher and not knowing any better way, we agreed that an average would be right, and we discussed the average after we took it." The foreman of the jury testified as follows:

"Q. You have heard the testimony of these two other jurors? A. Yes, sir.

"Q. Is that what occurred there at the time? A. That is correct.

"Q. Do you have anything to add to it at all? A. I don't know as there is anything I could add. I thought it was fair and square.

"Q. You suggested that you add their respective figures together and then divide the sum by 12 and that that would be adopted as the verdict; is that right? A. Well, yes."

Plaintiff realizes the potency of this evidence and seeks to counteract it by claiming that on cross-examination these jurors testified that they were asked after the quotient had been reached whether they believed the amount to be fair and all the jury members said it was. The fact remains, however, that the evidence is uncontradicted, that the jury members all agreed that the quotient would be the verdict and it was. * * * The result is the trial court erred in overruling the defendant's motion for a new trial.

NOTES AND QUESTIONS

1.   What is improper about the way in which the jury reached its decision in *Hukle?* Is the quotient verdict as evil as deciding a case by flipping a coin? Would it be of significance if the jurors had taken a quotient verdict before deliberating the question of liability?   What difference, if any, would it have made had the jury, after arriving at the quotient figure, discussed at length its propriety in light of the evidence?   For an extensive general discussion of the problems of quotient verdicts, see Annot., 8 A.L.R.3d 335 (1966).

2.   There are many forms of jury misconduct, some of which were discussed in Chapter One, see pp. 46–50, supra. See generally Comment, *Impeachment of Jury Verdicts,* 25 U.Chi.L.Rev. 360, 366–72 (1958). Often the question is not whether the conduct was improper but whether the error is so serious that the verdict must be overturned.   Assuming that a trial court has before it the following sets of facts, what rulings should it make on motions for a new trial?

(a) The jury, after deliberation, was deadlocked seven to five for defendant, but because, during trial, one juror had learned of the death of a son and wished to return home, the jurors agreed to abide by the vote of the majority, and therefore, without further discussion, rendered a verdict for defendant. See Jorgensen v. York Ice Mach. Corp., 160 F.2d 432 (2d Cir.), certiorari denied 332 U.S. 764, 68 S.Ct. 69, 92 L.Ed. 349 (1947).   Suppose the jury, although properly instructed, erroneously believed that a majority verdict was all that was necessary? *Cf.* Hoffman v. French, Ltd., 394 S.W.2d 259, 266 (Tex.Civ.App.1965).

(b) On voir dire in a personal-injury action, the prospective jurors had been asked whether they had ever had any claims arising from the alleged negligence of another person.   Four members of the panel had asserted such claims, and they had been paid cash settlements without filing suit.   Nonetheless they remained silent, believing the question to relate only to actual lawsuits.   These four were not challenged and thus sat on the jury that rendered a verdict for plaintiff. *Compare* Photostat Corp. v. Ball, 338 F.2d 783 (10th Cir.1964) (denial of new trial reversed), *with* Derr v. St. Louis Pub. Serv. Co., 399 S.W.2d 241 (Mo.App.1965) (denial of new trial affirmed).   Suppose the jurors had understood the question but nevertheless concealed the fact of their prior claims. Should the motives of the jurors bear on the question? See Beggs v. Universal C. I. T. Credit Corp., 387 S.W.2d 499 (Mo. 1965) (denial of new trial reversed).

(c) After the case was submitted to the jury and the jury deliberated for more than an hour without reaching a verdict the bailiff, on instruction of the court, took the jurors to lunch in a local hotel and supplied them with alcoholic beverages in moderate amounts.   Shortly thereafter the jurors returned to the court and after a half hour of deliberation, rendered a verdict. See Kealoha v. Tanaka, 45 Hawaii 457, 370 P.2d 468 (1962) (denial of new trial affirmed by 3–2 decision).   What difference would it make if one juror had become intoxicated? See generally Annot., 6 A.L.R.3d 934 (1966).

(d) During a court recess plaintiff entered an elevator containing three jurors on their way to lunch.   The plaintiff initiated a friendly conversation with one of the jurors regarding the fact that some of plaintiff's relatives lived in the area where the juror owned and operated a drugstore.   The conversation was short and nothing was said about the case. See United States v. Harry Barfield Co., 359 F. 2d 120 (5th Cir.1966) (denial of new trial reversed by a 2 to 1 decision).

There are many cases in which jurors have been charged with misconduct for holding unauthorized conversations concerning the case. See Annot., 62 A.L.R.2d 298 (1958) (contact with a party to the case or his attorney); Annot., 52 A.L.R. 2d 182 (1957) (contact with witnesses); Annot., 41 A.L.R.2d 288 (1955) (contact with judges, court officials, and attendants); Annot., 64 A.L.R.2d 158 (1959) (contact with outsiders generally). Most of the decisions turn on the nature of the conversation regarding the case and the extent to which the juror might have been influenced in his decision. Does it make sense conclusively to presume prejudice in contexts such as *United States v. Harry Barfield Co.*, above? Should every contact between a juror and a party or attorney, or between a juror and a witness, be considered prejudicial? See generally Note, *Communications Between Parties and Jurors may be Irrebuttably Prejudicial as a Matter of Law*, 4 Houston L.Rev. 583 (1966).

ROBB v. JOHN C. HICKEY, INC.

Circuit Court of New Jersey, Morris County, 1941.
19 N.J.Misc. 455, 20 A.2d 707.

LEYDEN, Judge. The issues presented by the pleadings were the negligence of the defendants and the contributory negligence of the plaintiff's decedent. The jury was instructed concerning the applicable principles of law, in the course of which it was pointed out that if contributory negligence upon the part of the plaintiff's decedent had been established, the comparative degrees of the negligence of the parties was immaterial.

The jury returned a verdict in the absence of the judge and it was recorded at the clerk's desk as follows: "The jury finds that there was negligence on the part of both parties involved—The evidence shown is that the defendant was more negligent than the plaintiff—We therefore recommend an award of $2,000.00 to the plaintiff Clyde J. Robb and against the defendants John C. Hickey, Inc., a New Jersey Corporation and Roger W. King."

Both parties are dissatisfied with the verdict; the plaintiff with its substance and the defendants with its form. Plaintiff has a rule to set aside the verdict upon the ground that it is ambiguous, inconsistent, inadequate and contrary to the charge of the court. Defendants, upon notice, move to mould the verdict into one in favor of the defendants and against the plaintiff, urging that it is merely informal and the intent of the jury to find for the defendants is clearly indicated * * *.

It is true that a verdict must be responsive to the issues and recommendations of the jury dehors the issues submitted by the court, such as the suggestion of the equal division of another fund between the parties * * * or the amount claimed in the suit be donated to the American Red Cross * * * or each party (plaintiff being unsuccessful) pay his own cost * * * or of leniency in a criminal case * * * may be treated as surplusage and properly disregarded.

However, such is not the situation in the instant case. Here the verdict finds both parties guilty of negligence, erroneously compares the degrees of their negligence and recommends an award of $2,000 in favor of the plaintiff and against both defendants. What then did the jury agree upon and intend? Did it find in favor of the defendants as is legally indicated by the first sentence, or in favor of plaintiff in the sum of $2,000 as is clearly indicated by the last sentence? The recommendation of an award to the plaintiff is pertinent to the issues, for basically the liability of defendants to plaintiff in damages was in question. It cannot be treated as surplusage and disregarded. Reading the verdict as a whole, it is self-contradictory, inconsistent and ambiguous. One is left to conjecture and surmise as to the real purpose of the jury. It is defective in substance, not merely in form.

The court may, in fact should, mould an informal verdict to render it formal, effective and to coincide with the substance of the verdict as agreed upon and intended by the jury, but this power is only exercised where the real purpose and intent of the jury clearly, sufficiently and convincingly appears. * * * Where, as here, the verdict is uncertain or ambiguous, it cannot be moulded. The court will not substitute its verdict in place thereof. * * *

This leads to the denial of defendants' motion to mould and is also dispositive of the plaintiff's rule. The latter will be made absolute and a new trial granted.

NOTES AND QUESTIONS

1. Why is the verdict in *Robb* different from a verdict that recommends that the amount claimed be donated to the American Red Cross? Can't a strong argument be made in favor of a new trial in the latter situation?

2. Suppose plaintiff brings suit for injuries suffered in an accident allegedly due to defendant's negligence. The jury renders a verdict in favor of plaintiff but assesses damages at zero, although it is clear from the evidence that plaintiff has been badly hurt. May the judge enter judgment on the verdict? See Wingerter v. Maryland Cas. Co., 313 F.2d 754 (5th Cir.1963), and Pitcher v. Rogers, 259 F.Supp. 412 (N.D.Miss.1966), in which the courts answered "yes." Can these decisions be reconciled with *Robb*? To what extent does the answer depend upon the nature of the evidence regarding the causation of damages? There are a number of decisions holding that such a verdict cannot stand. See, e. g., Bushey v. French, 171 Neb. 809, 108 N.W.2d 237 (1961).

3. How far should a trial court go in attempting to ascertain the "true intent" of the jury in order to be able to "mould" a verdict? Should the court be permitted to ask the jurors what they intended? Why shouldn't all but the clearest cases be returned for a new trial? *Compare* Hanolt v. Mlakar, 421 Pa. 136, 218 A.2d 750 (1966), *with* Gilday v. Hauchwit, 91 N.J.Super. 233, 219 A. 2d 873 (App.Div.1966). Is there any way to avoid the costs and delays of a new trial if the verdict cannot be moulded?

KRAMER v. KISTER, 187 Pa. 227, 233–36, 40 A. 1008, 1008–10 (1898). [The jury agreed to a sealed verdict and separated. When the verdict was opened the next morning, one juror dissented from it; the jury was sent out again and returned shortly with the same verdict, which was entered.]

* * * At common law the jury were kept together from the time they were sworn, as is still the general rule in criminal cases involving life. After they had retired to consider their verdict, they were kept without food, drink, fire, or light until they agreed; and Blackstone says, "It has been held that, if the jurors do not agree in their verdict before the judges are about to leave the town, though they are not to be threatened or imprisoned, the judges are not bound to wait for them, but may carry them round the circuit, from town to town, in a cart." 3 Bl.Comm. 376. From the manner of this mention, it is to be inferred that this latter practice was at least unusual in Blackstone's day; and he says expressly that the deprivation of food, fire, and light was subject to the indulgence of the court. * * * With the prolongation of trials in the more complicated issues of modern times, and especially with the amelioration of manners, the treatment of jurors has gradually become less harsh, and changes of practice have been made in their relief. It is no longer the custom to keep them together and secluded during the whole trial, though I apprehend that the judge may do so in any case where public excitement or other exceptional reason may make it advisable, in the interest of the proper administration of justice, to do so * * *. After the retirement of the jury to consider their verdict, this indulgence terminates, and they are kept together and apart from others until verdict rendered. But, if the adjournment of the court is to such time or under such circumstances as seem likely to lead to serious inconvenience to the jurors, the practice of allowing them to seal a verdict grew up. * * * When a juror dissents from a sealed verdict, there is a necessary choice of evils,— a mistrial, or a verdict finally delivered under circumstances that justly subject it to suspicion of coercion or improper influences. * * * If the dissenting juror was honest in his declaration that he had not agreed to the first verdict, except because he thought he was obliged to, then his agreement to the second without having been instructed as to his rights cannot be freed from a well-founded appearance of coercion. If, on the other hand, the second verdict had been for the defendant, contrary to the first, the inference could hardly have been escaped that the change was produced by new evidence, or information illegally acquired by the dissenting juror, or by even more reprehensible means. The only safe way out of such a situation is to treat it as a mistrial, and discharge the jury. * * *

NOTES AND QUESTIONS

1. Note that very few jurisdictions today require jurors constantly to remain together once the case has been submitted to them. See Annot., 77 A.L.R. 2d 1086 (1961). Before allowing the jurors to separate, however, the court

normally will warn them not to discuss the case with anyone outside the jury room and not to inspect sites referred to in the testimony or otherwise to obtain evidence. See Steckler, *Management of the Jury,* 28 F.R.D. 190, 191 (1960). What effect should the failure to give such cautionary instructions have on the validity of the verdict?

2. Do you agree with the reasoning of the court in *Kramer* as to why the resubmission was improper? To what extent does the case turn upon the time at which the resubmission was made? Suppose, for example, that the original verdict had been an oral one, rendered at the end of the deliberations. Would an immediate resubmission have been justifiable? If so, in light of modern practice permitting jurors to separate during their deliberations, isn't *Kramer* outmoded? See Annot., 164 A.L.R. 1265, 1276–79 (1946).

To what extent should the validity of resubmission depend upon whether the jury has been discharged from the case? Suppose the error in the verdict is first noticed after such a discharge but while the jurors are still present in the courtroom? See generally Annot., 66 A.L.R. 536 (1930).

3. To what extent may a court resubmit a verdict for defects other than the lack of unanimity or a proper majority?

(a) Suppose, for example, the error is one that the court could correct itself by moulding a proper verdict. Wouldn't it be preferable to resubmit the case to the jury? See Gilday v. Hauchwit, 91 N.J.Super. 233, 219 A.2d 873 (App.Div. 1966).

(b) What if the error was similar to that in *Robb v. John C. Hickey, Inc.* in which the court held that it could not correct the verdict itself. Would a resubmission to the jury have been improper? See Sigel v. Boston & Me. R. R., 107 N.H. 8, 216 A.2d 794 (1966) (resubmission held appropriate). Isn't resubmission always preferable to a new trial?

---

4. FINDINGS AND CONCLUSIONS IN NONJURY CASES

Read Federal Rule of Civil Procedure 52 in the Supplement.

ROBERTS v. ROSS

United States Court of Appeals, Third Circuit, 1965.
344 F.2d 747.

MARIS, Circuit Judge. The plaintiff, Herbert J. Roberts, appeals from a judgment entered in the District Court of the Virgin Islands dismissing his action brought to recover the sum of $3,087.50 which he alleged the defendant Norman M. Ross, Jr. promised to pay him for services rendered in producing a buyer for a dwelling house which the defendant had built in St. Thomas. The defendant answered, denying any such promise and, subsequently, with leave of court, he filed an amended answer in which he interposed the special defense of the Statute of Frauds.

* * *

On December 30, 1963, the trial judge entered an order stating that he had found for the defendant on the issues presented and directing counsel for the defendant within 10 days to file proposed findings of fact, conclusions of law and draft of judgment.   Counsel for the plaintiff was given leave within 10 days thereafter to file objections thereto, which he did.   On January 14, 1964 the findings of fact, conclusions of law, and judgment prepared and filed by counsel for the defendant were signed by the trial judge without change.   It was concluded as a matter of law that "plaintiff has failed to prove by a preponderance of the evidence that the sale of said property by the defendant was procured through the agency of plaintiff," and that "in any event, said alleged promise not being in writing is within the Statute of Frauds."   The plaintiff appealed from the judgment entered thereon dismissing his complaint.

* * *

The defendant   * * *   argues that   * * *   the plaintiff failed to prove the alleged agreement by a preponderance of the evidence, and the trial judge was accordingly justified in concluding that any discussion relating to compensating plaintiff for alleged sale of the property was at most the offer of a gratuity on the part of the defendant not specifically enforceable for indefiniteness.   The fallacy in defendant's argument is that the trial judge failed to make any such findings.   There is no finding as to whether the defendant agreed to pay the plaintiff a commission for producing a customer for the sale of the property—a question which was the crucial issue in the case.   And there is no support in the record for the conclusion as a matter of law that "plaintiff has failed to prove by a preponderance of the evidence that the sale of said property by the defendant was procured through the agency of plaintiff."   For it was undisputed that the plaintiff brought [the buyer]   * * *   to the property and introduced him to the defendant as a prospective purchaser.   Perhaps the term "agency" in the quoted conclusion is intended to mean that the plaintiff, in doing so, did not act as agent for the defendant, thus possibly implying that the defendant did not agree to pay plaintiff a commission if he producd [sic] a buyer for the property.   The trial judge's conclusion is, however, so inadequate as to afford this court no indication of the legal standard under which the evidence was considered.

This Court has had occasion to point out that Rule 52(a) of the Federal Rules of Civil Procedure requires the trier of the facts to find the facts specially and state his conclusions of law thereon with clarity.   The findings of fact and conclusions of law must be sufficient to indicate the bases of the trial judge's decision.   * * *   The findings and conclusions in the present case do not meet this requirement.

Moreover we have observed in this case and in a number of others which have been brought here from the district court for review that the judge of the court has followed the practice of announcing his decision for the plaintiff or the defendant substantially in the form of a general verdict, either in a written order or by communication to counsel, and of thereupon directing counsel for the prevailing party to prepare and submit findings of fact, conclusions of law and a form of judgment. The trial judge's order has not been accompanied by an opinion setting out, even summarily, the facts and legal conclusions which have brought him to his decision. Obviously the judge must have dealt with the questions of fact and law involved in the case in the course of the reasoning by which he has reached his ultimate conclusion, even though his reasoning has not been articulated and put on paper. But counsel who is called upon to articulate and write out the findings and conclusions must do so without any knowledge of the fact findings and reasoning processes through which the judge has actually gone in reaching his decision.

We strongly disapprove this practice. For it not only imposes a well-nigh impossible task upon counsel but also flies in the face of the spirit and purpose, if not the letter, of Rule 52(a). The purpose of that rule is to require the trial judge to formulate and articulate his findings of fact and conclusions of law in the course of his consideration and determination of the case and as a part of his decision making process, so that he himself may be satisfied that he has dealt fully and properly with all the issues in the case before he decides it and so that the parties involved and this court on appeal may be fully informed as to the bases of his decision when it is made. Findings and conclusions prepared ex post facto by counsel, even though signed by the judge, do not serve adequately the function contemplated by the rule. At most they provide the judge with an opportunity to reconsider the bases of his original decision but without affording the parties any information as to what those bases were or which of them are being reconsidered. At worst they are likely to convict the judge of error because, as here, they are inadequate to support his decision or because, as we have observed in other cases, they are loaded down with argumentative over-detailed partisan matter much of which is likely to be of doubtful validity or even wholly without support in the record.

* * * We * * * do not * * * mean to suggest that a trial judge should not have the right to invite counsel for both parties to submit to him proposed findings of fact and conclusions of law, accompanied by briefs if he desires them, to assist him in formulating his own findings and conclusions and reaching his decision. In the process of studying the facts and the law, findings and conclusions formulated and proposed by the parties may be most helpful to the judge in sharpening the issues and may serve a very useful purpose in aiding him in drafting his own findings and conclusions. In most cases it will appear that many of the findings proposed by one or the other of the parties are fully supported by the evidence, are directed to material matters and may be adopted verbatim and it may even be that in some cases the findings and conclusions proposed by a party will be so carefully and objectively prepared that they may all properly be adopted by the trial judge without change. But it should be remembered that findings and conclusions prepared by a party and adopted by the trial judge without change are likely to be looked at by the appellate court more narrowly and given less weight on review than if they are the work product of the judge himself or at least bear evidence that he has given them careful study and revision. For the latter procedure would assure the appellate court, as Judge Wis-

dom pointed out in Louis Dreyfus & Cie. v. Panama Canal Company, 5 Cir., 1962, 298 F.2d 733, 738, "that the trial judge did indeed consider all the factual questions thoroughly and would guarantee that each word in the finding is impartially chosen." It has been the general practice of the district judges of the Third Circuit in the past under Rule 52(a) to formulate their findings of fact and conclusions of law in the course of and as a part of their decision-making process and to articulate and file them at the time of announcing the decision, either in an opinion if filed at that time or in a separate document. For the reasons set out in this opinion we strongly approve this practice and direct it to be followed in the future by the court below.

* * *

The judgment of the district court will be vacated and the cause remanded for further proceedings not inconsistent with this opinion.

NOTES AND QUESTIONS

1. *Roberts v. Ross* is noted in 51 Cornell L.Q. 567 (1966), in which it is noted that on remand, the trial court, without a new hearing, reversed its earlier decision, and entered judgment for the party against whom it ruled initially. Compare HETEROCHEMICAL CORP. v. UNITED STATES RUBBER CO., 368 F.2d 169, 172 (7th Cir.1966):

> After post-trial briefing and oral arguments, the district court invited findings and conclusions from both parties and ordered an exchange of the proposals. * * * The court thereafter adopted the proposals of United States Rubber.

> This court has termed the adoption of proposed findings a "practical and wise custom," in view of the obligation of a prevailing party to assist a busy court. In re Woodmar Realty Co., 307 F.2d 591, 594 (7th Cir. 1962). This is particularly true in a case where the evidence is highly technical, so long as the trial court's procedure is fair to both parties and the findings reveal insight and understanding of the basic issue. * * * In view of the district court's procedure in adopting findings of fact and conclusions of law, we are not persuaded that they were "mechanically adopted"; nor can we agree that they do not reveal insight and understanding of the basic issue. * * * The district court was within its discretion in deciding not to construct its own findings and conclusions with respect to highly technical matters. * * *

2. In LEIGHTON v. ONE WILLIAM STREET FUND, INC., 343 F.2d 565, 567 (2d Cir.1965), the court discussed Federal Rule 52(a) as follows:

> The purpose of Rule 52(a), as it is applied to a non-jury case, is usually stated to be three-fold: (1) to aid the appellate court by affording it a clear understanding of the ground or the basis of the decision of the trial court; (2) to make definite just what is decided by the case to enable the application of *res judicata* and estoppel principles to subsequent decisions; and (3) to evoke care on the part of the trial judge in ascertaining the facts.

Which of the listed purposes of Rule 52(a) do you find most important?

3. To what extent is an appellate court able finally to dispose of a case in which the trial court has omitted a special finding on a material fact? See Note, *The Effect of an Omitted Special Finding of Fact,* 33 Ind.L.J. 273 (1958).

4. Suppose in an action without a jury, in which the amount of damages depends solely upon the estimates of a number of expert witnesses, the trial judge arrives at a finding as to damages by totalling all the estimates and dividing the sum by the number of experts. Should this finding be set aside on appeal as a "quotient verdict"? In FOSTER v. CITY OF AUGUSTA, 174 Kan. 324, 331, 256 P.2d 121, 126 (1953), the court upheld the finding as follows:

> * * * We cannot presume from the mere fact that the trial judge averaged the damage testimony in the course of determining the amount of his judgment, that he violated his judicial duties and failed to consider the evidence in accordance with his duty. The presumption is to the contrary, i. e., that in the absence of anything affirmatively appearing to the contrary, it must be presumed that the trial court disposed of each and every issue, both of law and of fact, submitted to it in the case giving due consideration to the evidence, and that his action was regular and in accordance with the law. * * *
>
> It is a rule of this court that whether a verdict was or was not a quotient verdict is a question of fact for the trial court to determine * * * and the judgment having been entered and approved by the trial court in the instant case, this court will not disturb the judgment on that account.

Do you approve of the court's reasoning? Can the case be reconciled with *Hukle v. Kimble,* p. 888, supra?

SECTION F. ATTACKS ON VERDICTS AND JUDGMENTS

1. CHALLENGING ERRORS AND MISCONDUCT: NEW TRIAL

A. THE NATURE AND THE SCOPE OF THE POWER TO GRANT A NEW TRIAL

Read Federal Rule of Civil Procedure 59 and the accompanying materials in the Supplement. Note particularly the grounds for new trial listed in Minnesota Rule of Civil Procedure 59.01.

MAGNANI v. TROGI

Appellate Court of Illinois, Second District, 1966.
70 Ill.App.2d 216, 218 N.E.2d 21.

CORYN, Presiding Justice. * * *

Plaintiff's complaint states two separate causes of action. In Count I she seeks recovery of $30,000.00, as Administratrix, for the wrongful death of her decedent, pursuant to the Wrongful Death Act (Ill.Rev.Stats., ch. 70, §§ 1 & 2). By the second count of the complaint she seeks reimbursement, in her individual capacity, for medical and funeral expenses necessarily incurred by her as the result of the injury and death to her husband, pursuant to the Family Expense Statute (Ill.Rev.Stats., ch. 68, § 15).

The Wrongful Death Act provides that any recovery thereunder shall be distributed by the court in which the cause was heard to the widow and next of kin of the decedent, in proportion, as determined by the trial court, "that the percentage of dependency of each such person upon the deceased person bears to the sum of the percentages of dependency of all such persons upon the deceased person." Here, any award of the jury, for a wrongful death, would be apportioned by the trial court to the widow and minor son of decedent. There would be no apportionment of any award made under the provisions of the Family Expense Statute.

* * *

In the instant case, there can be no doubt that the recovery sought under each count of plaintiff's complaint was based on separate causes of action, that is, one action for wrongful death, and the other under the Family Expense Statute. Unfortunately, neither party to this suit tendered separate forms of verdict for each of these counts. Rather, a single form of verdict was submitted by the court to the jury without objection from plaintiff or defendant. Using this form the jury returned the following verdict: "We, the jury, find in favor of the plaintiff and against the defendant. We assess the damages in the sum of $19,000.00." The trial judge, in his memorandum of opinion allowing a new trial, properly expressed the dilemma this verdict created for him by stating: "In the case at bar, there were two counts. Does the single verdict all apply to just one count, or to both counts? It might be that the verdict was all for the wrongful death action, and non-liability as to the medical expense cause of action." After making this observation, the trial judge then concluded that the verdict must be set aside and a new trial ordered as to both the liability and damage aspects of the case. Although other points have been raised in this appeal, we believe the determinative issue to be whether the trial judge, when faced with this situation, abused his discretion by granting a new trial.

The purpose of vesting the trial judge with power to grant a new trial is to permit him, before losing jurisdiction of the case, to correct errors that he or the jury might have made during the course of the trial. Courts of review have repeatedly stated that they will not disturb the decision of a trial court on a motion for new trial unless a clear abuse of discretion is affirmatively shown. The reason for this rule is that the trial court has had the opportunity to consider the conduct of the trial as a whole, and therefore is in a superior position to consider the effects of errors which occurred, the fairness of the trial to all parties, and whether substantial justice was accomplished. * * * Greater latitude is allowed a trial court in granting a new trial than in denying a new trial. * * *

Plaintiff argues that defendant has waived his right to complain of the form of verdict because he did not object to the giving of this form to the jury, but raised the issue for the first time in his post-trial motion. In most instances this would be a valid argument. Here, however, because of the single form of verdict, the jury's determination of liability and damages on each of the two causes of action was not made known. It appears that the jury found liability against the defendant on the wrongful death action, but any conclusion about what the jury's verdict was regarding liability on the family expense action is pure conjecture. Also, the language of the verdict returned gives no indication of the jury's determination as to what portion of the total verdict of $19,000.00 it attributed to damages for wrongful death, and what portion, if any, to damages for medical and funeral expenses. The determination of liability and damages, in the first instance, is to be made by the jury.

The jury returned its verdict on December 21, 1962, and the defendant filed his post-trial motion on January 15, 1963, thereby raising this issue for the first time. It was impossible, then, for the court to re-assemble the jury and instruct them to correct the error in the form of verdict. * * * We are not holding, by this opinion, that the failure to submit to the jury separate forms of verdict in cases involving multiple causes of action should, in every instance, result in the granting of a new trial, but rather, that in the situation presented here it was not an abuse of discretion for the trial judge to grant a new trial.

The order of the Circuit Court of Lake County, granting defendant's motion for new trial, vacating and setting aside the verdict and judgment, and denying defendant's motion for judgment notwithstanding the verdict, is affirmed.

Affirmed.

STOUDER, Justice (dissenting). I do not agree with the opinion of the majority. The record before us clearly shows that Plaintiff waived any individual interest in the verdict. The verdict, then being within the range of the evidence and the law, any possible dilemma facing the trial court was thereby solved.

As was succinctly stated in Hall v. Chicago and Northwestern Ry. Company, 349 Ill.App. 175, 110 N.E.2d 654 "We are not unmindful of the rule and cases which hold that the trial judge is allowed broad discretion in granting motions for a new trial, and that his actions will not be reversed on appeal except in cases of clear abuse of such discretion; but this rule, like all others, has its limitations. A judge is not empowered to set aside a verdict in any case simply because he does not agree with it.   *   *   * "   In the instant case the trial court's granting of a new trial was based upon a finding that the forms of verdict submitted to the jury were improper.   It therefore should be our duty to examine the propriety of this finding in order to determine the limits which were self-imposed upon the discretion of the trial court.

Upon thorough examination of the record before us I am unable to find that Defendant made any objection to the forms of verdict at the conference on instructions or at any time prior to his post-trial motion.   *   *   *   Defendant's failure to object to the forms at the proper time as well as his later failure to show that he was in fact prejudiced compels me in the instant case to find that the trial court's finding was erroneous and Defendant's motion for a new trial should have been denied.

*   *   *

Read Federal Rule of Civil Procedure 61 and Colorado Rules of Civil Procedure 59(f) and 59(h), which accompany Federal Rule 59 in the Supplement.

THE RANGE OF THE TRIAL COURT'S DISCRETION

1. Errors or acts of misconduct committed during the course of a trial may be categorized as follows: (i) those that would result in reversal if the case were to be appealed; (ii) those that may have had an impact on the verdict, but which would not justify reversal on appeal, and (iii) those that did not significantly affect the outcome.   Obviously errors that do not have any impact on the decision are harmless and it would be an abuse of discretion for the trial court to predicate a new trial on them.   On the other hand, errors that would justify reversal on appeal would seem to demand remedial measures at the trial level.   A judge should not force a litigant to pay the costs of prosecuting an appeal as well as the costs of the new trial to which he is entitled.

2. Theoretically, it is only with regard to errors that affect the result in the case but would not lead to reversal on appeal that the trial court has discretion to decide whether or not a new trial is appropriate.   As a practical matter, however, the unlimited power of the trial court with regard to the granting of new trials is far greater than it might otherwise seem to be.   First, an aggrieved litigant may decide to stand or fall on the motion for new trial since the case simply may not be worth the added cost of an appeal or the litigant may not have sufficient funds to continue fighting.   Second, in many jurisdictions, the grant of a new trial, not being a final judgment, cannot be appealed. See pp. 954–56, infra.   Thus the cost of a new trial will have to be absorbed before an appeal is even possible.   Third, the very question of what constitutes reversible error on appeal often is affected by the ruling of the trial judge on the motion for new trial.   In those jurisdictions in which a motion for a new trial is a prerequisite for appeal, see, e. g., Martin v. Opdyke Agency, 156 Colo. 316, 398 P.2d 971 (1965) (applying Colorado Rule 59(f)); Evans v. Wil-

kerson, 419 P.2d 275 (Okl.1966), the denial of a new trial certainly will influence the appellate court in deciding whether the error is harmless for purposes of appeal if the effect of the error in question can better be determined by the trial judge. Even when a motion for a new trial is not required, and when, theoretically, the appellate court should not penalize a litigant for having so moved, knowledge that the trial judge has rejected the alleged error as harmless may have an impact on the appellate-court decision. Finally, in some jurisdictions, the trial judge may grant a new trial without specifying or without actually relying on any precise grounds. Obviously this narrows the scope of review of such decisions.

———

GINSBERG v. WILLIAMS, 270 Minn. 474, 135 N.W.2d 213 (1965). Plaintiff brought suit for damages received in an automobile accident. The jury rendered a verdict for defendant and plaintiff moved for a new trial. The court granted the motion "in the interests of justice," giving no other basis for its ruling. Defendant sought a writ of prohibition to restrain enforcement of the ruling, claiming that the trial court is empowered to grant a new trial only for one of the grounds specifically set forth in Rule 59.01 of the Minnesota Rules of Civil Procedure. The Minnesota Supreme Court granted the writ, holding as follows:

> * * * The causes enumerated in Rule 59.01 are so comprehensive that they include every conceivable reason for which a new trial ought to be ordered. Those causes requiring the exercise of discretion, such as 59.01(1) (irregularities depriving the moving party of a fair trial) and 59.01(8) (insufficiency of the evidence), vest the broadest possible discretionary power in the trial court. To permit granting a new trial "in the interests of justice" would invite an arbitrary exercise of power over which appellate review is not now available. Even if it were, it would be difficult to fashion any effective rules to control arbitrary action since the basis for such an order would necessarily be subjective, varying from judge to judge. Further, each of the causes enumerated is designed to promote justice and prevent injustice. It is one thing to order a new trial "on the ground that on the evidence substantial justice has not been done" or in the interest of justice on the ground that the evidence does not justify the verdict, and quite another thing to order a new trial simply "in the interests of justice." It is difficult to conceive how such a general ground would add anything to the grounds enumerated in our rules unless it is desirable to restore the common-law power of granting a new trial when the judge is personally dissatisfied with the verdict.

Id. at 483–84, 135 N.W.2d at 220.

NOTES AND QUESTIONS

1. In COPPO v. VAN WIERINGEN, 36 Wash.2d 120, 123–24, 217 P.2d 294, 297 (1950), the court stated:

> One of the reasons assigned by the trial judge in the instant cases for granting new trials is that "substantial justice has not been done." The statutes which enumerate the grounds on which new trials may be granted * * * make no mention of such a ground for a new trial; but we have always upheld the right of the trial judge to grant a new trial when he is convinced that substantial justice has not been done, on the theory that it is an exercise of the trial court's inherent power. * * *

> Actually, of course, when a trial judge says that "substantial justice has not been done," he is stating a conclusion for which there must be a reason or reasons. * * * The reason we have barred any review of an order granting a new trial based on this conclusion * * * was expressed by the supreme court of Wisconsin in the case of McLimans v. City of Lancaster, 57 Wis. 297, 15 N.W. 194, 195: "The judge before whom the cause was tried heard the testimony, observed the appearance and bearing of the witnesses and their manner of testifying, and was much better qualified to pass upon the credibility and weight of their testimony than this court can be. *There are many comparatively trifling appearances and incidents, lights and shadows, which are not preserved in the record, which may well have affected the mind of the judge as well as the jury in forming opinions of the weight of the evidence, the character and credibility of the witnesses, and of the very right and justice of the case.* These considerations cannot be ignored in determining whether the judge exercised a reasonable discretion or abused his discretion in granting or refusing a motion for a new trial."   (Italics ours.)

For subsequent developments in Washington, see Knecht v. Marzano, 65 Wash.2d 290, 396 P.2d 782 (1964); Trautman, *Serving Substantial Justice—A Dilemma*, 40 Wash.L.Rev. 270 (1965).

2. Suppose a party moves for a new trial based on a number of specific errors, no one of which alone would be sufficiently prejudicial to justify a new trial. May the court under *Ginsberg v. Williams* grant the motion on the ground that all of the errors, taken together, deprived the losing party of a fair trial? *Cf.* Walker v. Holiday Lanes, Inc., 196 Kan. 513, 413 P.2d 63 (1966); Miller v. Staton, 64 Wash.2d 837, 394 P.2d 799 (1964).

3. To what extent does the decision in *Ginsberg* provide significant appellate-court control over "arbitrary exercise" of power by the trial judge? Isn't the exercise of discretion by the trial court necessarily based on subjective considerations not appearing in the record and, hence, not subject to review? What more can the exercise of discretion mean than that the trial judge can decide that errors, trivial in appearance, have, because of "lights and shadows which are not preserved in the record," resulted in manifest injustice to the party seeking a new trial?

4. Under what circumstances, if any, should errors or misconduct during trial justify a new trial in a nonjury case? In the much quoted opinion in

BUILDERS STEEL CO. v. COMMISSIONER, 179 F.2d 377, 379 (8th Cir. 1950), the court said:

> In the trial of a nonjury case, it is virtually impossible for a trial judge to commit reversible error by receiving incompetent evidence, whether objected to or not. An appellate court will not reverse a judgment in a nonjury case because of the admission of incompetent evidence, unless all of the competent evidence is insufficient to support the judgment or unless it affirmatively appears that the incompetent evidence induced the court to make an essential finding which would not otherwise have been made. * * * On the other hand, a trial judge who, in the trial of a nonjury case, attempts to make strict rulings on the admissibility of evidence, can easily get his decision reversed by excluding evidence which is objected to, but which, on review, the appellate court believes should have been admitted. In the case of Donnelly Garment Co. v. National Labor Relations Board, 8 Cir., 123 F.2d 215, 224, we stated our views upon this subject as follows: "* * * We think that experience has demonstrated that in a trial or hearing where no jury is present, more time is ordinarily lost in listening to arguments as to the admissibility of evidence and in considering offers of proof than would be consumed in taking the evidence proffered, and that, even if the trier of facts, by making close rulings upon the admissibility of evidence, does save himself some time, that saving will be more than offset by the time consumed by the reviewing court in considering the propriety of his rulings and by the consequent delay in the final determination of the controversy. One who is capable of ruling accurately upon the admissibility of evidence is equally capable of sifting it accurately after it has been received, and, since he will base his findings upon the evidence which he regards as competent, material and convincing, he cannot be injured by the presence in the record of testimony which he does not consider competent or material. Lawyers and judges frequently differ as to the admissibility of evidence, and it occasionally happens that a reviewing court regards as admissible evidence which was rejected by the judge, special master, or trial examiner. If the record on review contains not only all evidence which was clearly admissible, but also all evidence of doubtful admissibility, the court which is called upon to review the case can usually make an end of it, whereas if evidence was excluded which that court regards as having been admissible, a new trial or rehearing cannot be avoided. * * *"

Is the attitude of the court proper? To what extent should the court's reasoning apply to errors other than the improper admission of evidence?

B.   THE POWER TO GRANT CONDITIONAL AND PARTIAL NEW TRIALS

FISCH v. MANGER

Supreme Court of New Jersey, 1957.
24 N.J. 66, 130 A.2d 815.

JACOBS, J.   The plaintiff suffered serious injuries in an automobile accident and, after trial, received a jury verdict in the sum of $3,000. He applied for a new trial because of the inadequacy of the verdict but his application was denied when the defendants consented that the damages awarded to the plaintiff be increased to the sum of $7,500. The plaintiff appealed and we thereafter certified on our own motion.

*   *   *

The plaintiff's actual expenditures to doctors and nurses and for drugs and hospitalization exceeded $2,200. And although he received most of his normal earnings despite his temporary incapacity, there was a loss of wages approximating $620. While the jury's verdict of $3,000 just about took care of the plaintiff's actual monetary losses, it awarded substantially nothing for his suffering and permanent injuries. Its gross inadequacy was recognized by the trial judge who pointed out that "there was no dispute but that the plaintiff suffered excruciating pain, and was rendered totally helpless for a considerable period of time." On June 28, 1956 the trial judge wrote to the parties advising that unless the defendants filed a consent in writing that the verdict be increased from $3,000 to $7,500, "then the verdict heretofore rendered will be set aside and a new trial granted limited to damages only." The consent was filed by the defendants and on June 30, 1956 a formal order was entered dismissing the plaintiff's motion for a new trial.   *   *   *

The first point which he urges in support of his appeal is that once the trial court had concluded that the damages awarded by the verdict were inadequate it had no legal power whatever to condition the grant of a new trial upon the defendants' failure to consent to a prescribed increase in the verdict. *   *   *   Much has appeared in the law reviews in support of the practices of *remittitur* and *additur* as enlightened aids in securing substantial justice between the parties without the burdensome costs, delays and harassments of new trials. See Carlin, *"Remittiturs* and *Additurs,"* 49 W.Va.L.Q. 1 (1942); Note, "Correction of Damage Verdicts by *Remittitur* and *Additur,"* 44 Yale L.J. 318 (1934)   *   *   *. The term *remittitur* is used to describe an order denying the defendant's application for new trial on condition that the plaintiff consent to a specified reduction in the jury's award, whereas the term *additur* is used to describe an order denying the plaintiff's application for a new trial on condition that the defendant consent to a specified increase in the jury's award. While it is now recognized that the two practices are logically and realistically indistinguishable, *remittiturs* have been recognized almost everywhere, whereas *additurs* are still outlawed in some, though by no means all, of the states.
*   *   *

The English precedents prior to the American Revolution are somewhat obscure and they are discussed in the majority and minority opinions in Dimick v. Schiedt, 293 U.S. 474, 55 S.Ct. 296, 302, 79 L.Ed. 603 (1935). There Justice Sutherland, speaking for a majority of five (with Justice Stone, joined by Chief Justice Hughes and Justices Brandeis and Cardozo, dissenting) held that although *remittitur* is permissible in the federal courts, *additur* is prohibited by * * * the Seventh Amendment * * *. In Belt v. Lawes (1884), 12 Q.B. 356, the court sustained the denial of a new trial upon the plaintiff's consent to accept a lesser amount than that awarded by the jury; on appeal, Brett, M. R. not only approved the practice followed below but suggested that the court would also have power "to say that the damages given are too small, but that if the defendant will agree to their being increased to such a sum as may be stated, a new trial shall be refused." * * * In the later case of Watt v. Watt (1905), A.C. 115 the court took an opposite position and rejected the view that a court could condition a denial of a new trial on the plaintiff's acceptance of a reduced verdict. * * * However, Justice Sutherland in the Dimick case did not follow the result in the Watt case and declined to upset the *remittitur* practice, first approved by Justice Story in Blunt v. Little, 3 Fed.Cas.No. 1,578 (C.C.Mass.1822), and since reaffirmed in many federal decisions. * * *

In his dissenting opinion in the Dimick case, Justice Stone pointed out that the Seventh Amendment was concerned with substance rather than form and that the Supreme Court had often declined to construe it as perpetuating in changeless form the minutiae of trial practice as it existed in the English courts in 1791; he referred to the many jury procedures unknown to the common law but now well established in federal practice; he considered wholly impersuasive the suggested differentiation between the settled *remittitur* practice which the majority continued and the *additur* practice which it rejected; and he concluded with the following remarks * * *:

> "To me it seems an indefensible anachronism for the law to reject the like principle of decision, in reviewing on appeal denials of motions for new trial, where the plaintiff has consented to decrease the judgment or the defendant has consented to increase it by the proper amount, or to apply it in the one case and reject it in the other. It is difficult to see upon what principle the denial of a motion for a new trial, which for centuries has been regarded as so much a matter of discretion that it is not disturbed when its only support may be a bad or inadequate reason, may nevertheless be set aside on appeal when it is supported by a good one: That the defendant has bound himself to pay an increased amount of damages which the court judicially knows is within the limits of a proper verdict."

The majority opinion in Dimick has been the subject of much criticism and it is doubtful whether the Supreme Court would still subscribe to it; [g] in

---

[g] *But see* Novak v. Gramm, 469 F.2d 430 (8th Cir.1972).

any event, the Seventh Amendment differs somewhat from our constitutional provision and has no application to proceedings in our state courts. * * * We must look primarily to our own history and precedents in ascertaining whether the highly desirable practices of *remittitur* and *additur* may be adhered to in our State * * *.

The *remittitur* practice has been recognized in New Jersey since early days. * * * [In 1917] the Court of Errors and Appeals had occasion to deal with a negligence case in which the practice of *additur* had been invoked. * * * Chancellor Walker, speaking for the entire court, had this to say ([Gaffney v. Illingsworth,] 90 N.J.L. at page 492, 101 A. at page 243):

> "The power of the court in granting a new trial upon the ground that the damages are *excessive*, upon terms that a new trial shall be had unless the plaintiff will accept a certain sum named, less than that awarded by a verdict, is too well established to be questioned. It would seem to follow, by parity of reasoning, that when a new trial is granted because the damages are inadequate, the court may impose like terms, that is, terms to the effect that if the defeated party will pay a certain sum, greater than that awarded by the verdict, the rule will be discharged, subject, doubtless, to the power of an appellate court to vacate any such terms when they appear to be an abuse of discretion. * * * "

* * *

Shortly after the adoption of the 1947 Constitution our courts had occasion to deal anew with the practices of *remittitur* and *additur*. In Esposito v. Lazar * * * [2 N.J. 257, 66 A.2d 172 (1949)] the jury returned a verdict for plaintiff in the sum of $1,200; the trial court found the damages inadequate and ordered a new trial limited to damages unless the defendant consented to increasing the award to $3,500. The defendant refused and on retrial the jury awarded $3,000. On appeal, this court, in an opinion by Justice Ackerson, approvingly cited Gaffney v. Illingsworth, supra, and expressly recognized that a trial court has discretionary power to deny a new trial upon the plaintiff's consent to accept a reduced amount or upon the defendant's consent to pay a larger amount. See 2 N.J. at page 259, 66 A.2d at page 173. It held, however, that in the case before it the new trial should not have been limited to damages because the original jury verdict appeared to represent a compromise finding on the issue of liability. * * *

In the light of all of the foregoing, we are satisfied that the practices of *remittitur* and *additur* violate none of our constitutional interdictions and, if fairly invoked, serve the laudable purpose of avoiding a further trial where substantial justice may be attained on the basis of the original trial. * * * Accordingly, we reject the first point urged by the plaintiff and come now to his meritorious contention that, in any event, the prescribed increase to $7,500 was "grossly inadequate and should be set aside." * * * In the instant matter, we believe that the trial judge had a mistaken notion of the evidence which led to his prescribing the scanty sum of $7,500. He stated that the plaintiff was not entitled to a "great sum, because he certainly did have a back condition before this accident occurred"; but the evidence in the record points to the view that whatever "back condition" the plaintiff had as a result of the 1950 accident had cleared up and had no relation to the very severe injuries resulting from the 1953 accident. Under these highly special circumstances, we believe that the trial court's action should not be permitted to stand and that the interests of justice will best be served by permitting a second jury to pass on the issue of damages. The separable issue of liability was clearly and properly decided against the defendants; under the evidence it could hardly have been determined otherwise and need not be submitted for redetermination.   *   *   *

Reversed, with direction for a new trial on the issue of damages.

HEHER, J. (concurring in result).   *   *   *

As is shown by Justice Sutherland's analysis of the case history in Dimick v. Schiedt   *   *   *, there was no power in the English courts at the time of the adoption of the New Jersey Constitution of 1776 to increase, either abso·lutely or conditionally, the damages fixed by a jury in a case such as this. *   *   *

*   *   * Justice Sutherland concluded, and with unquestionable authority, that "while there was some practice to the contrary in respect of *decreasing* damages, the established practice and the rule of the common law, as it existed in England at the time of the adoption of the Constitution, forbade the court to *increase* the amount of damages awarded by a jury in actions such as that here under consideration." He observed that "this court in a very special sense is charged with the duty of construing and upholding the Constitution; and in the discharge of that important duty, it ever must be alert to see that a doubtful precedent [involving *remittitur*] be not extended by mere analogy to a different case if the result will be to weaken or subvert what it conceives to be a principle of the fundamental law of the land"; and that "the power to conditionally increase the verdict of a jury does not follow as a necessary corollary from the power to conditionally decrease it," since in the case of a conditional *remittitur* "a jury has already awarded a sum in excess of that fixed by the court as a basis for a *remittitur*, which at least finds some support in the early English practice, while in the second case, no jury has ever passed on the increased amount, and the practice has no precedent according to the rules of the common law."

The "controlling distinction between the power of the court and that of the jury," said Justice Sutherland, "is that the former is the power to determine the law and the latter to determine the facts," and while the *remittitur* practice in the case of an excessive verdict "is not without plausible support in the view that what remains is included in the verdict along with the unlawful excess,— in the sense that it has been found by the jury,—and that the *remittitur* has the effect of merely lopping off an excrescence," yet where an inadequate verdict is increased by the court there is a "bald addition of something which in no sense can be said to be included in the verdict," and if that be done with the consent of the defendant alone, the plaintiff is compelled to forego his "constitutional right to the verdict of a jury and accept 'an assessment partly made by a jury which has acted improperly, and partly by a tribunal which has no power to assess.' "

* * *

There can be no doubt that the *additur* practice sanctioned here contravenes the essence of the common-law right of trial by jury at the time of the adoption of the 1776 Constitution, then and ever since a basic right under the law of England; and this is the very substance of our own constitutional guaranty. * * *

POWERS v. ALLSTATE INS. CO., 10 Wis.2d 78, 102 N.W.2d 393 (1960). Plaintiff received a jury award for permanent injuries in the amount of $5,000. The award was excessive and called for a remittitur. The question before the state supreme court was what standard should determine the amount to which the damages should be reduced. The court noted that since its decision in HEIMLICH v. TABOR, 123 Wis. 565, 102 N.W. 10 (1905), Wisconsin judges had been required to set damages at the lowest amount that a reasonable jury could have awarded. This rule was contrary to the practice in most jurisdictions, in which "the courts follow the practice of allowing the plaintiff the option of avoiding a new trial by remission of the excess above an amount which the court considers reasonable." The court went on to point out that the Wisconsin rule tended to limit the effectiveness of the remittitur practice.

> * * * We are firmly of the opinion that if the plaintiff were granted the option of accepting a reasonable amount as determined by the trial or appellate court, instead of the least amount that an unprejudiced jury properly instructed might award, the number of instances in which the plaintiff would be likely to refuse such option and elect a new trial would be greatly reduced.

The court then specifically overruled *Heimlich* and adopted the standard rule.

NOTES AND QUESTIONS

1. Should a trial court have discretion to set a reasonable remittitur figure somewhere between the highest and lowest possible verdicts? Would it make more sense to require, as the alternative to a new trial, the highest amount an unprejudiced jury could properly have awarded plaintiff?

2. Suppose the federal courts had adopted the rule in the *Heimlich* case, which was overruled in *Powers*. Would application of an analogous rule to additur have permitted its use without violation of the Seventh Amendment?

3. In an action under the Federal Employers Liability Act, 45 U.S.C. § 51, the California Supreme Court held that the trial court could order an additur.

Jehl v. Southern Pacific Co., 66 Cal.2d 821, 59 Cal.Rep. 276, 427 P.2d 988 (1967). In light of *Dimick,* is this holding consistent with *Dice* v. *Akron, Canton & Youngstown R.R.,* p. 309, supra?

4.   If defendant appeals from a judgment for plaintiff, who has consented to a remittitur, may plaintiff cross-appeal on the ground that the verdict should not have been reduced? See Jangula v. Klocek, 284 Minn. 477, 170 N.W.2d 587 (1969), 54 Minn.L.Rev. 1096 (1970).

DOUTRE v. NIEC

Michigan Court of Appeals, 1965.
2 Mich.App. 88, 138 N.W.2d 501.

T. G. KAVANAGH, Judge.   Defendants operate a beauty shop in Flint. On April 19, 1962 plaintiff was given a bleach and color treatment by defendants without a pretreatment patch test. Plaintiff received head and facial injuries as a result of the treatment and sued for damages.

During the trial defendants were not allowed to testify as to the standard of care observed by beauty shops in the Flint area when administering such treatment. The jury awarded plaintiff $10,000. Defendants filed a motion for a new trial. Such motion was granted and a new trial ordered but limited to the question of liability.

Both parties appeal.

The plaintiff alleges error in granting the new trial as to liability on the theory that the court was correct in the first place when he ruled at the trial that the proffered testimony on the standard of care was not admissible. The defendants allege the court erred in limiting the new trial to the issue of liability on the theory that the questions of liability and damages are so closely intertwined that they should be tried together.

As to the plaintiff's claim we find little merit. His objection is based on the theory that the defendants could know of the practices of the trade in Flint only by hearsay. This is not supported by the record.

The record shows that one of the defendants had been in the business for 24 years and the other for 14 years; they had attended conventions of beauticians and observed their practices and said they were abreast of the practices of other beauticians in Genesee County.

We agree with the trial court's last ruling that these witnesses should have been allowed to testify and that to exclude their testimony was error requiring a new trial. Such testimony is admissible because no one is held to a higher standard of care than the average in the industry.   *   *   *

The limitation of the trial to the issue of liability only poses a more difficult problem.

It has long been recognized that the questions of liability and damages are so closely intertwined that they may not usually be separated. The only excep-

tion the Michigan Supreme Court has so far recognized is in the case wherein "liability is clear" a retrial of the issue of damage alone may be permitted.
* * *

In this case the court reiterated its position that despite the court rule authorizing it (GCR 1963, 527.1), limited new trials are not favored.

No compelling reason moves us to extend the rule.

The trial judge's opinion states: "This ruling (on the evidentiary question) may have materially influenced the jury on the liability issue. It could not, however, by any stretch of the imagination have affected the issue of damages." This bespeaks an assurance we do not share.

In the case before us the damages are not liquidated and the liability was determined pursuant to a trial in which an admitted error touching on liability was committed.

Under these circumstances it seems to us that justice requires that the jury which determines the liability or lack of it should have the responsibility for measuring any damages.

The trial court's order for a new trial shall be extended to all of the issues.

Costs are awarded defendants.

NOTES AND QUESTIONS

1. Compare the dissenting opinion of Judge Freedman in HUTTON v. FISHER, 359 F.2d 913, 920 (3d Cir. 1966):

> * * * [A]s a matter of practical justice the damage verdict should not be permitted to stand where the question of liability is to be retried. It is the great and saving virtue of the jury system in accident cases that it permits laymen guided by the courts on questions of law to work out in a worldly way an accommodation between the strict requirements of law and their everyday view of justice. That a defendant therefore suffers disadvantage when a trial is limited to damages and liability is conceded is a fact of life, acknowledged everywhere but in courtrooms. * * * The limitation of a new trial by excluding some of the issues decided is exceptional, and the power to grant a partial new trial must be "exercised with caution." Geffen v. Winer, 100 U.S.App.D.C. 286, 244 F.2d 375, 376 (1947). A retrial of liability will be less than the full relief the defendants are entitled to have, for its effect will be insulated from the damage question into which it ordinarily percolates.

2. In LARIMER v. PLATTE, 243 Iowa 1167, 53 N.W.2d 262 (1952), in which plaintiff's decedent was killed in a motor-vehicle collision, plaintiff sought damages for wrongful death and defendant counterclaimed for damage to his vehicle and the loss of its use during repair. Based on stipulation of the parties, the court instructed the jury that if it found for defendant on the counterclaim, it must find damages for repairs in the amount of $2205.49. In addition the jury was instructed it could find damages for loss of use not to exceed $600. The jury found for defendant and awarded him $600. Plaintiff's motion for a new trial was overruled on the ground that only defendant was prejudiced by the

jury verdict. On appeal the court reversed and granted a new trial on the counterclaim. Plaintiff also requested a new trial on his claim for wrongful death. Should the request have been granted?

3. To what extent should the court in deciding whether to grant a partial new trial consider the extra cost to the court and the parties of a new trial on all of the issues? See pp. 775, supra.

C. THE POWER TO SET ASIDE A JUDGMENT ON GROUNDS DISCOVERED AFTER IT WAS RENDERED

Read Federal Rule of Civil Procedure 60 in the Supplement.

(i) Mistake and Excusable Neglect—Timeliness of Requests for New Trial

---

HULSON v. ATCHISON, TOPEKA & SANTA FE RY.

United States Court of Appeals, Seventh Circuit, 1961.
289 F.2d 726.
Certiorari denied 368 U.S. 835, 82 S.Ct. 61, 7 L.Ed.2d 36.

HASTINGS, Chief Judge. This is an action for damages alleged to have resulted from personal injuries sustained in an accident on December 22, 1957.

Edward T. Hulson and Walter A. Christensen (plaintiffs) were employed by the United States Post Office as postal transportation clerks. On December 22, 1957, together with other clerks, they began their work at 9:10 o'clock a. m. inside a railroad car, half of which was constructed and designed as a railway post office, while such car was standing on a track at the Kansas City, Missouri terminal. This car was moved from that location and coupled with other cars of The Atchison, Topeka and Santa Fe Railway Company (defendant) as a part of defendant's train No. 12. About noon that day while defendant was engaged in a switching operation wherein certain cars of this train were being moved, plaintiffs were injured as a result of being thrown against various parts of the inside of the car in which they were working.

Plaintiffs commenced this action by filing a complaint against defendant in the Circuit Court of Cook County, Illinois. * * * Defendant removed the cause to the United States District Court for the Northern District of Illinois, Eastern Division, on diversity grounds.

Defendant answered denying generally the allegations in the complaint. The cause was set for trial on the sole issue of liability. * * *

On June 7, 1960, after the close of all the evidence, plaintiffs moved for a directed verdict.   The motion was denied at that time.

On June 7, 1960, the jury returned a verdict finding defendant "not guilty" as to both plaintiffs.   On the same day judgment was entered on the verdict against plaintiffs and favorable to defendant.

On June 16, 1960, plaintiffs served on defendant and filed with the clerk of the district court a written notice that they would appear before the trial court on June 17, 1960 and present a motion (copy of which was attached) praying that the plaintiffs be "granted a reasonable time *to amend their motion for a new trial* by making specific objections to specific instructions."   (Emphasis added.)   An affidavit was attached to the motion by plaintiffs' counsel in which counsel stated that he had been diligent in his efforts to secure a transcript of the jury instructions and that it would be impossible to set out the specific instructions to which he objected and to state the objections thereto "unless the Court sees fit to permit him to amend his Motion for a new trial within a reasonable time."   At that time no motion for a new trial had been filed by plaintiffs.

On June 17, 1960, counsel for all parties were present in court, and plaintiffs' attorney orally moved the court for an order extending the time in which to file plaintiffs' motion for a new trial.   Plaintiffs' counsel stated that defendant's counsel had no objection to the motion.   At that time the following colloquy took place between the court and counsel in open court:

*   *   *   *   *   *   *   *   *   *

"The Court: * * *   Would you be available later this afternoon?

"Mr. Patterson [plaintiffs' attorney]: Yes, Your Honor, but counsel has no objection.   I am merely asking for an extension of time in which to file my motion for a New Trial.

"The Court: All right, if that is all you are asking, why the motion is granted.

"Mr. Patterson: You will extend the time for what period, your Honor?

*   *   *   *   *   *   *   *   *   *

"Mr. Svolos [defendant's attorney]: There is only one thing I would like to point out to the Court; I will be gone for the next two months.   I will be out on the West Coast.   It would be impossible for me to argue this orally this summer."

On the same day the court entered the following order:

"On motion of plaintiffs, time to file motion for judgment notwithstanding the verdict or, in the alternative, for a new trial extended for a period of ten days, briefs to follow."

On June 27, 1960, for the first time, plaintiffs filed their motion for judgment notwithstanding the verdict, or in the alternative, for a new trial. The motion set out eight grounds for entry of a judgment n. o. v. and twenty-four grounds for granting a new trial.   *   *   *

On July 15, 1960, defendant filed its written motion to strike plaintiffs' motion for judgment n. o. v., or in the alternative, for a new trial. The ground for this motion to strike was that plaintiffs' motion was not filed within the time and limits prescribed by Rule 50(b) and Rule 59(b), (d) and (e) of the Federal Rules * * *. It was further stated that the trial court was prohibited from enlarging the time in which to file such motion by the provisions of Rule 6(b). * * *

On August 23, 1960, plaintiffs filed their motion for relief under Rule 60(b). Following briefs addressed to this latter motion, on September 7, 1960, the trial court entered an order granting defendant's motion to strike plaintiffs' motion for judgment n. o. v., or in the alternative, for a new trial; and such motion was stricken. In a memorandum opinion filed on September 13, 1960 the trial court held that it could not grant relief to plaintiffs under Rule 60(b).

Plaintiffs filed their notice of appeal on October 4, 1960 stating that they were appealing from:

"1. The judgment on the verdict finding the defendant not guilty, entered in this action on June 7, 1960;

"2. The order denying the plaintiffs' motion for a directed verdict at the close of all of the evidence, entered in this action on June 7, 1960;

"3. The order extending for a period of 10 days the time to file a motion for judgment notwithstanding the verdict, or in the alternative, for a new trial, entered in this action on June 17, 1960;

"4. The order allowing the defendant's motion to strike the motion of the plaintiffs for judgment notwithstanding the verdict or in the alternative for a new trial, and striking the plaintiffs' said motion, entered in this action on September 7, 1960."

Defendant moved in this court "to dismiss paragraphs 1, 2 and 3 of the [above] notice of appeal," and we ordered the motion continued without prejudice and to be taken with the case on its merits as to the above paragraph 4.

We shall first consider defendant's motion to dismiss this appeal as to paragraphs 1, 2 and 3 in the notice of appeal.

As applied to this case, under Rule 73(a) plaintiffs were permitted to take an appeal within "30 days from the entry of the judgment appealed from." [h] The jury verdict was received and judgment entered thereon finding defendant not guilty on June 7, 1960. The notice of appeal was filed on October 4, 1960.

Under Rule 50(b) plaintiffs were required to move for motion for judgment n. o. v. "[w]ithin 10 days after the reception of a verdict * * *."

[h] Federal Rule of Civil Procedure 73(a), which was in effect at the time *Hulson* was decided, provided that the 30 day period runs from the time of entry of judgment unless a "timely" motion under Rule 50(b), Rule 52(b), or Rule 59 is made, in which case the period runs from the date of the ruling on the motion. See Federal Rule of Appellate Procedure 4(a).

Plaintiffs' said motion was not filed until June 27, 1960, or 20 days thereafter.

Under Rule 59(b) "[a] motion for a new trial shall be served not later than 10 days after the entry of the judgment"; under subsection (d) the trial court of its own initiative may order a new trial for any reason for which it might have granted a new trial on motion of a party "[n]ot later than 10 days after entry of judgment"; and under subsection (e) "[a] motion to alter or amend the judgment shall be served not later than 10 days after entry of the judgment." Judgment was entered on June 7, 1960, and plaintiffs' motion in question was not served until June 27, 1960.

Under Rule 6(b) the trial court "may not extend the time for taking any action under rules * * * 50(b), * * * 59(b), (d) and (e), 60(b), and 73(a) and (g), except to the extent and under the conditions stated in them."

Thus, it is quite clear that plaintiffs' motion for judgment n. o. v. was not made within 10 days after the reception of the verdict and is not within the limitation imposed by Rule 50(b). Under such circumstances "the rule forbids the trial judge or an appellate court to enter such a judgment." Johnson v. New York, N. H. & H. R. Co., 1952, 344 U.S. 48, 50, 73 S.Ct. 125, 127, 97 L.Ed. 77 * * *.

Further, Rule 59(b), (d) and (e) prohibits a trial court from granting a motion for a new trial made after the expiration of 10 days after entry of judgment. * * *. If the motion for new trial is untimely, the trial court has no choice but to deny the motion; and *the tardy motion will not toll the time for taking an appeal.* * * *

The 10 day limit for filing a motion for new trial fixed in Rule 59(b) cannot be enlarged under Rule 6(b), except as provided in subsection (c) of Rule 59, and such exception has no application to the situation before us here. * * *

In order to avoid the application of the foregoing rules, plaintiffs urge this court to treat the motion for extension "to amend their motion for a new trial," served on June 16, 1960, as a motion for a new trial. The trial court did not err in rejecting this contention. Plaintiffs' motion "cannot be measured by its unexpressed intention or wants." It "should be treated as nothing but what it actually was," one to amend a motion for a new trial which was not on file and was never timely filed. * * *

In light of the foregoing, we hold that defendant's motion to dismiss this appeal as to paragraphs 1, 2 and 3 of the notice of appeal must be sustained for lack of jurisdiction, pursuant to Rules 73(a) and 6(b).

The question raised in paragraph 4 of the notice of appeal and the denial of relief under Rule 60(b) is properly before us. This concerns the appeal from the order of the district court entered on September 7, 1960. * * *

Plaintiffs point to the fact that defendant's counsel agreed to the extension of time for filing their motion for judgment n. o. v., or in the alternative, for a new trial and thereby, in effect, waived plaintiffs' failure to comply with the rules. However, it is quite clear that counsel cannot waive the strict requirements of the rules. *   *   *

Plaintiffs candidly admit that they were mistaken in understanding the requirements of the rules, but urge that counsel for all parties and the trial court in good faith believed at the time that granting the extension of time was proper and permissible under the rules. Ignorance of the rules resulting in an agreement for an unauthorized extension of time cannot serve to furnish grounds for relief under Rule 60(b), under the facts before us in this appeal.

Plaintiffs rely heavily on the following statement made by the district court in its memorandum opinion:

> "It is with a great deal of reluctance that I arrive at the conclusion that defendant's motion to strike must be allowed. There is considerable merit in plaintiffs' motion for a new trial and if the Court had jurisdiction, I would set aside the verdict and the judgment entered thereon, and allow the plaintiffs a new trial on the ground that the verdict was against the overwhelming weight of the evidence *   *   *."

*   *   *

We think the statement made by Judge Maris in John E. Smith's Sons Co. v. Lattimer Foundry & Mach. Co., 3 Cir., 1956, 239 F.2d 815, 817–818, is dispositive of the issue raised under Rule 60(b):

> " *   *   * Conceding that under appropriate circumstances the district court may entertain under Rule 60(b) a motion for a new trial which is untimely under Rule 59(b) it is perfectly plain that it may do so only if a showing is made which complies with the requirements of that rule, clause (1) of which requires a showing of 'mistake, inadvertence, surprise, or excusable neglect' and clause (6) a showing of 'any other reason justifying relief from the operation of the judgment.' As we pointed out in Federal Deposit Insurance Corp. v. Alker, 3 Cir., 1956, 234 F.2d 113, 117, Rule 60(b) provides for extraordinary relief and may only be invoked upon a showing of exceptional circumstances. Here, however, as the district court has pointed out in its opinion, the defendant's motion for the application of Rule 60(b) contained no allegations whatever which would support the granting of relief under that rule.
>
> "Since the motion for a new trial was untimely served under Rule 59(b) and no showing was made of exceptional circumstances calling for extraordinary relief under Rule 60(b) the district court did not err in striking the motion."

We hold the trial court did not err in striking plaintiffs' motion for judgment n. o. v., or in the alternative, for a new trial, and in denying plaintiffs relief under Rule 60(b).

* * *

Appeal dismissed in part and affirmed in part.

NOTES AND QUESTIONS

1.   In THOMPSON v. IMMIGRATION & NATURALIZATION SERV., 375 U.S. 384, 84 S.Ct. 397, 11 L.Ed.2d 404 (1964), petitioner's motion for new trial was served 12 days after entry of judgment but only 10 days from receipt of notice of entry of judgment by his lawyers who had not been in court when the judgment was entered.   Respondent raised no objection as to the timeliness of the motion and the trial court specifically declared it to have been made "in ample time."   The motion was denied on the merits and petitioner appealed.   Under Federal Rule 73 the appeal was timely if the period for filing was measured from the date of the denial of the motion but not timely if measured from the date of the entry of judgment.   The Supreme Court held (5 to 4) that petitioner was entitled to rely upon the trial court's statement that the new-trial motion was timely and, therefore, the appeal also was timely.

To what extent does *Thompson* cast doubt on the rigid application of the 10-day time limit in Rule 59(b)?   Does the case indicate that *Hulson* is incorrect in holding that plaintiff was not entitled to relief under clauses (1) and (6) of Rule 60(b)?

2.   (a) Under Federal Rule 7(b) a motion in the federal courts normally must be in writing and state the grounds on which it is based.   Suppose a party serves a timely motion for new trial but fails to specify a ground upon which he intends to rely.   May he amend his motion subsequent to the 10-day period?   Although there is some authority to the contrary, a large majority of cases have held "no."   See 6A Moore, *Federal Practice* ¶ 59.09[2] (2d ed.); 5 Wright & Miller, *Federal Practice and Procedure: Civil* § 1195 (1969).   What justification is there for a rigid application of the time limit?

(b) Rule 59(d) provides that a court may order a new trial on its own initiative, but again, there is a 10-day limit.   Suppose a party serves a timely motion but fails to include as a ground an error that the court believes should result in a new trial.   May the court order a new trial on such a ground subsequent to the 10 day period?   Prior to the 1966 amendment to Federal Rule 59(d) the answer was generally held to be "no."   The amendment, adding what is now the second sentence of that Rule, was designed specifically to give the trial courts such power.   See Steinberg v. Indemnity Ins. Co., 36 F.R.D. 253 (E.D.La.1964).   As a practical matter doesn't this amendment take the sting out of the rule that a party cannot amend a motion once the 10-day period has elapsed?

(c) Note that the time limit in Rule 59(b) is geared to the time a motion is served on the parties rather than to the time the motion is filed with the court. The only provision as to filing is contained in Rule 5(d) requiring a motion to be filed within a reasonable time after service.   If the motion was served within the 10-day limit it should make no difference if the filing took place within a reasonable time thereafter.   See Claybrook Drilling Co. v. Divanco, Inc., 336 F.2d 697

(10th Cir.1964). Suppose a motion is filed within the 10-day period but served thereafter? Should it be dismissed? See Sutherland v. Fitzgerald, 291 F.2d 846 (10th Cir.1961).

3. The decision in *Hulson* raises the question of what type of cases do fall within the scope of Rule 60(b) (1). In almost every instance they involve situations in which a party was prevented from obtaining any trial whatsoever, such as a default judgment, see Rooks v. American Brass Co., 263 F.2d 166 (6th Cir. 1959) (defendant's illness prevented a proper defense), an erroneous stipulation by counsel that resulted in a summary judgment against the client, see Griffin v. Kennedy, 344 F.2d 198 (D.C.Cir.1965), or a dismissal for failure of plaintiff to prosecute the action, see Leong v. Railroad Transfer Serv., Inc., 302 F.2d 555 (7th Cir.1962). Should the rule specifically be limited to such matters of default? Rule 5015(a) (1) of the New York Civil Practice Law and Rules, which is the counterpart of Federal Rule 60(b) (1), provides for relief only on the basis of "excusable default." See 5 Weinstein, Korn & Miller, *New York Civil Practice* ¶¶ 5015.04–.05. That the courts generally disfavor default judgments and readily set them aside is abundantly clear. In such cases it is often said that the errors of counsel should not be attributed to clients. See, e. g., Mieszkowski v. Norville, 61 Ill.App.2d 289, 209 N.E.2d 358 (2d Dist.1965). Why should the rule be any different when the errors are committed during or after a hearing on the merits?

4. The proper scope of Rule 60(b) (6) has been the subject of considerable litigation. It frequently has been held that the Rule must have been intended to cover only matters outside the scope of Rules 60(b) (1)–(5). E. g., Costa v. Chapkines, 316 F.2d 541 (2d Cir.1963); Federal Deposit Ins. Corp. v. Alker, 30 F.R. D. 527, 532 (E.D.Pa.1962), affirmed 316 F.2d 236 (3d Cir.), certiorari denied 375 U.S. 880, 84 S.Ct. 150, 11 L.Ed.2d 111 (1963). Otherwise the specific time limits on motions under Rules 60(b) (1), (2), and (3) would be meaningless. But it is the existence of these very limits that have pressured many courts, in the interests of justice, to find that errors ostensibly falling within Rules 60(b) (1), (2), or (3), are somehow so special that they come within Rule 60(b) (6) and hence are not subject to a specific time limitation. See 58 Mich.L.Rev. 793 (1960); Note, *Federal Rules 52(a) and 60(b)—A Chinese Puzzle*, 21 Sw.L.J. 339, 346–47 & nn. 52–53 (1967); Note, *Federal Rule 60(b): Relief from Civil Judgments*, 61 Yale L.J. 76, 82–84 (1952). Can a strained interpretation of Rule 60(b) be justified by the fact that otherwise few if any cases would fall within Rule 60(b) (6)? See United States v. Karahalias, 205 F.2d 331, 333 (2d Cir. 1953). See generally 11 Wright & Miller, *Federal Practice and Procedure: Civil* § 2864 (1973).

Note that although Rule 60(b) (6) (and Rules 60(b) (4) and (5)) has no specific time limitation, the motion still must be made within a reasonable time. Is a motion under Rules 60(b) (1), (2), or (3) always timely as long as it is filed within the one-year period? See Di Vito v. Fidelity & Deposit Co., 361 F.2d 936, 939 (7th Cir.1966) (failure to move within four and one-half months from discovery of fraud held to bar relief); Schildhaus v. Moe, 335 F.2d 529, 531 (2d Cir.1964) (motion filed within 8 months held untimely).

(ii) Newly Discovered Evidence; Fraud

PATRICK v. SEDWICK, 413 P.2d 169 (Alaska 1966).   Plaintiff brought an action for medical malpractice, alleging permanent physical injuries.   The case was tried in October 1961 without a jury.   In February 1962 the trial judge rendered findings on the issues of liability.   These findings were subject to a lengthy appeal and it was not until more than two years later that the appellate court directed the trial court to enter findings for plaintiff on all issues of liability and to proceed to determine damages.   The trial judge fixed the amount of damages on the basis of the evidence that had been presented at the trial and entered judgment on January 12, 1965.   On January 22, 1965, defendant moved for a new trial on the ground that in 1963 a Dr. Robert Lewy had devised a new treatment that would ameliorate plaintiff's injuries and therefore should reduce his damages.   The trial court denied the motion. The judge rejected the significance of the new treatment since there was no assurance that any improvement it might bring would be permanent.

The appellate court affirmed the denial of a new trial with the following explanation:

> * * * [A] motion for new trial on the grounds of newly discovered evidence must meet the following requirements before it [can] * * * be granted:
>
> > (1) must be such as would probably change the result on a new trial; (2) must have been discovered since the trial; (3) must be of such a nature that it could not have been discovered before trial by due diligence; (4) must be material; (5) must not be merely cumulative or impeaching.
>
> In addition to the foregoing requirements, it is established that for any evidence to come within the category of "newly discovered" such evidence must relate to facts which were in existence at the time of the trial. * * *
>
> We hold, under the authorities referred to, that the trial court did not abuse its discretion in denying appellee's motion for a new trial on the grounds of newly discovered evidence.   It is clear from the record that Dr. Lewy's discovery of the Teflon technique did not occur until a considerable period of time had elapsed after the case was tried in October 1961.   Thus, the Lewy technique was not in existence at the time the trial took place and under the above authorities would not qualify as newly discovered evidence.

Id. at 177.

NOTES AND QUESTIONS

1. In KROCK v. ELECTRIC MOTOR & REPAIR CO., 339 F.2d 73 (1st Cir.1964), plaintiff alleged that defendant was guilty of a breach of contract in failing to deliver a number of second-hand electric motors. At trial plaintiff's evidence of lost profits consisted of the uncorroborated testimony of its principal officer that he had contracted to resell the motors to a number of customers all over the country. After verdict for plaintiff, defendant moved for a new trial on the basis of evidence, newly discovered, that the witness had lied. Plaintiff argued that had defendant properly utilized discovery he would have been able to learn before trial the substance of the officer's testimony and hence, by further investigation, also could have uncovered any impeaching evidence. The trial court denied the motion. The appellate court, in dictum, adversely criticized the trial court's decision on the ground that defendant had no "general duty to ascertain suchever evidence as plaintiff might offer by way of damages for failure to deliver a quantity of goods." Is this view sound? Is it consistent with the opinion in *Patrick v. Sedwick?* Compare United States Fidelity & Guar. Co. v. Lawrenson, 34 F.R.D. 121 (D.Md.), affirmed 334 F.2d 464 (4th Cir.), certiorari denied 379 U.S. 869, 85 S.Ct. 141, 13 L.Ed.2d 71 (1964).

2. Suppose a plaintiff obtains damages based on testimony that her injuries will prevent her from bearing children. Shortly thereafter plaintiff becomes pregnant and delivers a normal, healthy child. Should the trial court grant a motion by defendant to reopen the case? *Cf.* Anshutz v. Louisville R. Co., 152 Ky. 741, 154 S.W. 13 (1913). See generally Annot., 31 A.L.R.2d 1236 (1953).

3. To what extent, if any, should Rule 60(b) permit a case to be reopened for consideration of a change in the applicable law? In TITLE v. UNITED STATES, 263 F.2d 28, 31 (9th Cir.), certiorari denied 359 U.S. 989, 79 S.Ct. 1118, 3 L.Ed.2d 978 (1959), appellant sought to set aside a judgment of denaturalization on the ground that some two years thereafter the United States Supreme Court, in a different case, interpreted the immigration act in such a way as to demonstrate that the original decision in *Title* was erroneous. Appellant relied on Rules 60(b) (4) and (5). The trial court denied the motions and the court of appeals affirmed: "Rule 60(b) was not intended to provide relief for error on the part of the court or to afford a substitute for appeal. * * * Nor is a change in the judicial view of applicable law after a final judgment sufficient basis for vacating such judgment entered before announcement of the change." See also Berryhill v. United States, 199 F.2d 217 (6th Cir.1952); Loucke v. United States, 21 F.R.D. 305 (S.D.N.Y.1957); Comment, 44 Iowa L.Rev. 574 (1959).

What does Rule 60(b) (5) mean when it allows relief from a judgment when "a prior judgment upon which it is based has been reversed or otherwise vacated"? See Jackson v. Jackson, 276 F.2d 501 (D.C.Cir.), certiorari denied 364 U.S. 849, 81 S.Ct. 94, 5 L.Ed.2d 73 (1960).

SMITH v. GREAT LAKES AIRLINES, INC., 242 Cal.App.2d 23, 51 Cal.Rptr. 1 (2d Dist.1966). The airline originally brought an action for breach of contract against Smith, the current plaintiff. The airline claimed that it had purchased a plane from Smith; that Smith promised to turn over documents showing that the plane had been overhauled pursuant to the regulations of the Civil Aeronautics Administration; that Smith failed to produce the necessary documents; and that, as a result, the airline was required by the C. A.A. to make a major overhaul. At trial, an official of the C.A.A. testified that the required major overhaul had been completed. As a result, the airline was awarded substantial damages.

This action was instituted by Smith to set aside the original decision on the ground of fraud. Smith contended that in fact a major overhaul was neither required nor made. Allegedly, the government official who testified had conspired with the airline to perjure himself. Smith had not challenged the substance of this testimony at the trial, but had relied on the official status of the witness.

The trial judge sustained a demurrer to Smith's complaint and Smith appealed. The appellate court affirmed on the ground that the fraud alleged was "intrinsic," and that an action can be set aside only on the basis of "extrinsic" fraud. Extrinsic fraud was defined as that which prevents a litigant from making a claim or defense, for example, when one party fraudulently induces the opposing party not to file suit until the statute of limitations has become a bar. On the other hand, intrinsic fraud was said to be that which the trial itself is designed to discover, that is, which witnesses are lying. The court held that Smith should have been ready to meet all the issues in the case, and could not set the decision aside because he had not been prepared.

NOTES AND QUESTIONS

1. The current attitude in the federal courts is demonstrated by the opinion in PEACOCK RECORDS, INC. v. CHECKER RECORDS, INC., 365 F.2d 145, 147 (7th Cir.1966), certiorari denied 385 U.S. 1003, 87 S.Ct. 707, 17 L.Ed.2d 542 (1967), in which the court reversed as an abuse of discretion a denial of a motion under Rule 60(b):

> * * * We hold that where it appears that perjured testimony may have played some part in influencing the court to render a judgment, the perjury will not be *weighed,* on a motion to set aside the judgment. This seems self evident. * * * [If the judgment was obtained in part by the use of perjury] then it was clearly the duty of the district court to set aside the judgment, because poison had permeated the fountain of justice.

2. In BROWN v. PENNSYLVANIA R. CO., 282 F.2d 522 (3d Cir.1960), certiorari denied 365 U.S. 818, 81 S.Ct. 690, 5 L.Ed.2d 696 (1961), plaintiff brought suit under the Federal Employers' Liability Act against the railroad, his employer. Plaintiff's doctor testified that plaintiff's condition was such as to make it increasingly difficult if not impossible for him to work in the future. Defendant's medical witnesses testified that plaintiff had fully recovered from any injuries received in the accident. A verdict was rendered for plaintiff, but in an amount less than had been sought. Shortly after the trial, defendant discharged plaintiff, relying on the testimony given by plaintiff's doc-

tor at the trial. Plaintiff moved for a new trial on damages under Rule 60(b)
(3). The motion was denied and the appellate court affirmed. Is the decision
sound? Is it consistent with the *Peacock Records* case?

3. Note that Rule 60(b) distinguishes between fraud perpetrated by one
party on an opponent and fraud on the court. What is the reason for the
distinction? What effect does it have? In HAZEL-ATLAS GLASS CO. v.
HARTFORD-EMPIRE CO., 322 U.S. 238, 245–46, 64 S.Ct. 997, 1001, 88
L.Ed. 1250, 1255–56 (1944), plaintiff brought an action in the court of appeals to set aside a judgment rendered against it some nine years earlier. The
first action had turned on the validity of a patent held by defendant. Both the
issuance of that patent by the Patent Office and the determination of its validity
by the federal court of appeals in the prior action had been affected by an article
offered by defendant, ostensibly written by a disinterested expert, but actually
prepared by defendant's own officials, to the effect that the machine under
patent was a "revolutionary device." One of the attorneys who presented defendant's case in the first action also had participated in the scheme to prepare
and publish the fraudulent article. The court of appeals refused to set aside
the judgment; the Supreme Court reversed:

> Every element of the fraud here disclosed demands the exercise
> of the historic power of equity to set aside fraudulently begotten judg-
> ments. This is not simply a case of a judgment obtained with the aid
> of a witness who, on the basis of after-discovered evidence, is believed
> possibly to have been guilty of perjury. Here, even if we consider
> nothing but Hartford's sworn admissions, we find a deliberately planned
> and carefully executed scheme to defraud not only the Patent Office but
> the Circuit Court of Appeals. * * *

> The Circuit Court did not hold that Hartford's fraud fell short
> of that which prompts equitable intervention, but thought Hazel had
> not exercised proper diligence in uncovering the fraud and that this
> should stand in the way of its obtaining relief. We cannot easily under-
> stand how, under the admitted facts, Hazel should have been expected
> to do more than it did to uncover the fraud. But even if Hazel did
> not exercise the highest degree of diligence, Hartford's fraud cannot
> be condoned for that reason alone. This matter does not concern only
> private parties. There are issues of great moment to the public in a
> patent suit. * * * Furthermore, tampering with the administration
> of justice in the manner indisputably shown here involves far more than
> an injury to a single litigant. It is a wrong against the institutions set
> up to protect and safeguard the public, institutions in which fraud can-
> not complacently be tolerated consistently with the good order of society.
> Surely it cannot be that preservation of the integrity of the judicial proc-
> ess must always wait upon the diligence of litigants. The public welfare
> demands that the agencies of public justice be not so impotent that they
> must always be mute and helpless victims of deception and fraud.

Does *Hazel-Atlas* stand for the proposition that a court on its own motion may
set aside a judgment obtained by fraud on the court? Was it proper for the
Court to find that there had been a fraud on the lower court? See Toscano v.
Commissioner of Internal Revenue, 441 F.2d 930 (9th Cir.1971); Hawkins
v. Lindsley, 327 F.2d 356, 359 (2d Cir.1964); Lockwood v. Bowles, 46 F.R.D.

625, 632 (D.D.C.1969). If so, wouldn't ordinary perjury also qualify? Should the notion of fraud on the court apply only to situations such as bribery or corruption of a member of the court or jury?

4. Many jurisdictions, including the federal courts under Rule 60(b), permit an independent action in equity to set aside a judgment, which is discussed after these notes. As seen in *Smith v. Great Lakes Airlines, Inc.,* fraud is one of the substantive grounds upon which relief may be granted in such an action. Can the distinction between extrinsic and intrinsic fraud be justified when the judgment is attacked collaterally in a separate action as opposed to being attacked directly under a Rule 60(b) type motion? Did the acts of the defendants in the *Hazel-Atlas* case qualify as extrinsic fraud? The majority did not discuss the issue; Mr. Justice Roberts, in a dissenting opinion, stated that the fraud was extrinsic. 322 U.S. at 261 n. 18, 64 S.Ct. at 1009 n. 18, 88 L.Ed. at 1264 n. 18.

Suppose that instead of putting forth false information, a party merely conceals facts of which she has direct knowledge that would have a definite bearing on the outcome of the case. Does this constitute fraud? If so, is it extrinsic? See Buice v. T. & B. Builders, Inc., 219 Ga. 259, 132 S.E.2d 784 (1963); Jennings v. Bridgeford, 403 S.W.2d 289 (Tenn.1966).

5. For a general discussion of the provision in Federal Rule 60(b) regarding fraud, see Note, *Attacking Fraudulently Obtained Judgments in the Federal Courts,* 48 Iowa L.Rev. 398 (1963). See also 11 Wright & Miller, *Federal Practice and Procedure: Civil* §§ 2860–61 (1973).

(iii) The Independent Action to Obtain Relief from a Prior Judgment

---

1. Federal Rule 60(b) expressly preserves the right of the trial court to entertain an independent action to relieve a party from a prior judgment. What conceivable justification is there for retaining this procedure? Shouldn't Rules 60(b) (1)–(6) be read to cover all possible grounds? Can an independent action be anything more than a method of avoiding the time limits set out in Rule 60(b)? See CAPUTO v. GLOBE INDEM CO., 41 F.R.D. 239 (E.D.Pa.1966), in which the court held that the denial of relief under Rule 60(b) (1) because the motion was filed more than a year after judgment did not bar an independent action to set the judgment aside on the same grounds that had been alleged on the motion. Compare LOCKLIN v. SWITZER BROS., INC., 335 F.2d 331 (7th Cir.1964), certiorari denied 379 U.S. 962, 85 S.Ct. 652, 13 L.Ed.2d 557 (1965), in which plaintiff filed a separate action in the Northern District of Illinois to set aside a judgment rendered in a federal court in California. Previously, plaintiff had made a timely but unsuccessful motion in the latter court under Rule 60(b) to set aside its judgment, advancing the same grounds subsequently alleged in the independent action. The Seventh Circuit affirmed a denial of relief on the ground that the prior decision under Rule 60(b) barred relief

in an independent action by way of res judicata. It rejected an argument based on California state decisions that a denial of a post-trial motion should not bar a later independent action to set aside the judgment on the same grounds.

2. In the *Locklin* case the independent action was brought in a jurisdiction other than the one in which the judgment was rendered and the court accepted the case, although it denied relief. Is there any argument that would justify refusal by the second court to accept jurisdiction? See LAPIN v. SHULTON, INC., 333 F.2d 169 (9th Cir.), certiorari denied 379 U.S. 904, 85 S.Ct. 193, 13 L.Ed.2d 177 (1964), which "remanded" the parties for relief to the court issuing the initial judgment. Compare Bankers Mortgage Co. v. United States, 423 F.2d 73 (5th Cir.), certiorari denied 399 U.S. 927, 90 S.Ct. 2242, 26 L.Ed.2d 793 (1970). There is ancillary jurisdiction over an independent action brought in the court that entered the initial judgment. Crosby v. Mills, 413 F.2d 1273 (10th Cir.1970).

3. Suppose a party brings an action in a federal court, based on diversity-of-citizenship jurisdiction, to set aside a judgment rendered in a state court. If the state itself would provide a means of challenging the judgment, should the federal court refuse to hear the case? If the federal court does hear the case, what law should apply in determining whether relief is appropriate? See Comment, *Judgments: Fraud as a Basis for Relief in Federal Courts from Final State Court Judgments,* 1964 Duke L.J. 109.

---

2. TESTING THE SUFFICIENCY OF THE EVIDENCE: DIRECTED VERDICTS, JUDGMENTS NOTWITHSTANDING THE VERDICT, AND NEW TRIALS

A. THE CONSTITUTIONAL ISSUES

GALLOWAY v. UNITED STATES

Supreme Court of the United States, 1943.
319 U.S. 372, 63 S.Ct. 1077, 87 L.Ed. 1458.

Certiorari to the United States Circuit Court of Appeals for the Ninth Circuit.

Mr. Justice RUTLEDGE delivered the opinion of the Court.

Petitioner seeks benefits for total and permanent disability by reason of insanity he claims existed May 31, 1919. On that day his policy of yearly renewable term insurance lapsed for nonpayment of premium.

* * * At the close of all the evidence the District Court granted the Government's motion for a directed verdict. Judgment was entered accordingly. The Circuit Court of Appeals affirmed. * * * Both courts held the evidence legally insufficient to sustain a verdict for petitioner. He says this was erroneous and, in effect, deprived him of trial by jury, contrary to the Seventh Amendment.

* * *

I.

Certain facts are undisputed. Petitioner worked as a longshoreman in Philadelphia and elsewhere prior to enlistment in the Army November 1, 1917. He became a cook in a machine gun battalion. His unit arrived in France in April, 1918. He served actively until September 24. From then to the following January he was in a hospital with influenza. He then returned to active duty. He came back to the United States, and received honorable discharge April 29, 1919. He enlisted in the Navy January 15, 1920, and was discharged for bad conduct in July. The following December he again enlisted in the Army and served until May, 1922, when he deserted. Thereafter he was carried on the Army records as a deserter.

In 1930 began a series of medical examinations by Veterans' Bureau physicians. On May 19 that year his condition was diagnosed as "Moron, low grade; observation, dementia praecox, simple type." In November, 1931, further examination gave the diagnosis, "Psychosis with other diseases or conditions (organic disease of the central nervous system—type undetermined)." In July, 1934, still another examination was made, with diagnosis: "Psychosis-manic and depressive insanity incompetent * * *."

Petitioner concededly is now totally and permanently disabled by reason of insanity and has been for some time prior to institution of this suit. It is conceded also that he was sound in mind and body until he arrived in France in April, 1918.

The theory of his case is that the strain of active service abroad brought on an immediate change, which was the beginning of a mental breakdown that has grown worse continuously through all the later years. Essential in this is the view it had become a total and permanent disability not later than May 31, 1919.

[Petitioner's evidence was as follows: Two witnesses who had served with him in France testified to conduct on petitioner's part there that evinced a disturbed mind. A boyhood friend, one O'Neill, testified that in 1919 petitioner "was a wreck compared to what he was before he went away; * * * [his] mind was evidently unbalanced." A chaplain testified that he had observed a Private Galloway in an Army mental ward in 1920 who appeared insane; his identification of petitioner, however, was less than positive. Petitioner's naval commanding officer deposed that petitioner had caused trouble by disobedience and absence without leave, and his Army commanding officer in 1921 deposed that he was sometimes "one of the very best soldiers," and at other times undependable, that he had alternate periods of gaiety and depression, talked incoherently at times, but seemed to get along well with other soldiers. A physician who first saw petitioner shortly before trial testified as to his conclusion, based upon his own observation as well as the other testimony and petitioner's documentary medical history, that petitioner was born with an inherent instability, that he had "gone to pieces" in France, and that he was insane at all times subsequent to July 1918.]

II.

* * *

But if the record is taken to show that some form of mental disability existed in 1930, which later became total and permanent, petitioner's problem remains to demonstrate by more than speculative inference that this condition itself began on or before May 31, 1919 and continuously existed or progressed through the intervening years to 1930.

To show origin before the crucial date, he gives evidence of two abnormal incidents occurring while he was in France, one creating the disturbance before he came near the fighting front, the other yelling that the Germans were coming when he was on guard duty at the Marne. There is no other evidence of abnormal behavior during his entire service of more than a year abroad.

* * *

O'Neill's testimony apparently takes no account of petitioner's having spent 101 days in a hospital in France with influenza just before he came home. But, given the utmost credence, as is required, it does no more than show that petitioner was subject to alternating periods of gaiety and depression for some indefinite period after his return, extending perhaps as late as 1922. But because of its vagueness as to time, dates, frequency of opportunity for observation, and specific incident, O'Neill's testimony concerning the period from 1922 to 1925 is hardly more than speculative.

We have then the two incidents in France followed by O'Neill's testimony of petitioner's changed condition in 1919 and its continuance to 1922.[11] There is also the testimony of Commander Platt and Lt. Col. James E. Matthews as to his service in the Navy and the Army, respectively, during 1920–1922. Neither thought petitioner was insane or that his conduct indicated insanity. Then follows a chasm of eight years. * * *

This period was eight years of continuous insanity, according to the inference petitioner would be allowed to have drawn. If so, he should have no

---

11 Chaplain Mathews' testimony would be highly probative of insanity existing early in 1920, if petitioner were sufficiently identified as its subject. However, the bare inference of identity which might otherwise be drawn from the mere identity of names cannot be made reasonably in view of its overwhelming contradiction by other evidence presented by petitioner and the failure to produce records from Fort MacArthur Hospital or the Army or from persons who knew the fact that petitioner had been there at any time. The omission eloquently testifies in a manner which no inference could overcome that petitioner never was there. The chaplain's testimony therefore should have been stricken, had the case gone to the jury, and petitioner can derive no aid from it here.

* * *

need of inference.   Insanity so long and continuously sustained does not hide itself from the eyes and ears of witnesses.   The assiduity which produced the evidence of two "crazy" incidents during a year and a half in France should produce one during eight years or, for that matter, five years in the United States.

Inference is capable of bridging many gaps.   But not, in these circumstances, one so wide and deep as this.   Knowledge of petitioner's activities and behavior from 1922 or 1925 to 1930 was peculiarly within his ken and that of his wife, who has litigated this cause in his and presumably, though indirectly, in her own behalf.   His was the burden to show continuous disability.   What he did in this time, or did not do, was vital to his case.   Apart from the mere fact of his marriage, the record is blank for five years and almost blank for eight.   For all that appears, he may have worked full time and continuously for five and perhaps for eight, with only a possible single interruption.

No favorable inference can be drawn from the omission.   It was not one of oversight or inability to secure proof.   That is shown by the thoroughness with which the record was prepared for all other periods, before and after this one, and by the fact petitioner's wife, though she married him during the period and was available, did not testify.   The only reasonable conclusion is that petitioner, or those who acted for him, deliberately chose, for reasons no doubt considered sufficient (and which we do not criticize, since such matters including tactical ones, are for the judgment of counsel) to present no evidence or perhaps to withhold evidence readily available concerning this long interval, and to trust to the genius of expert medical inference and judicial laxity to bridge this canyon.

In the circumstances exhibited, the former is not equal to the feat, and the latter will not permit it.   No case has been cited and none has been found in which inference, however expert, has been permitted to make so broad a leap and take the place of evidence which, according to all reason, must have been at hand.   To allow this would permit the substitution of inference, tenuous at best, not merely for evidence absent because impossible or difficult to secure, but for evidence disclosed to be available and not produced.   This would substitute speculation for proof.   Furthermore, the inference would be more plausible perhaps if the evidence of insanity as of May, 1919, were stronger than it is, such for instance as Chaplain Mathews' testimony would have furnished if it could be taken as applying to petitioner.   But, on this record, the evidence of insanity as of that time is thin at best, if it can be regarded as at all more than speculative.

Beyond this, there   is   nothing to   show   totality   or   permanence.
*   *   *

III.

What has been said disposes of the case as the parties have made it.   For that reason perhaps nothing more need be said.   But objection has been advanced that, in some manner not wholly clear, the directed verdict practice offends the Seventh Amendment.

It may be noted, first, that the Amendment has no application of its own force to this case. The suit is one to enforce a monetary claim against the United States. It hardly can be maintained that under the common law in 1791 jury trial was a matter of right for persons asserting claims against the sovereign. Whatever force the Amendment has therefore is derived because Congress * * * has made it applicable. Even so, the objection made on the score of its requirements is untenable.

If the intention is to claim generally that the Amendment deprives the federal courts of power to direct a verdict for insufficiency of evidence, the short answer is the contention has been foreclosed by repeated decisions made here consistently for nearly a century. More recently the practice has been approved explicitly in the promulgation of the Federal Rules of Civil Procedure. * * * The objection therefore comes too late.

Furthermore, the argument from history is not convincing. It is not that "the rules of the common law" in 1791 deprived trial courts of power to withdraw cases from the jury, because not made out, or appellate courts of power to review such determinations. The jury was not absolute master of fact in 1791. Then as now courts excluded evidence for irrelevancy and relevant proof for other reasons. The argument concedes they weighed the evidence, not only piecemeal but *in toto* for submission to the jury, by at least two procedures, the demurrer to the evidence and the motion for a new trial. The objection is not therefore to the basic thing, which is the power of the court to withhold cases from the jury or set aside the verdict for insufficiency of the evidence. It is rather to incidental or collateral effects, namely, that the directed verdict as now administered differs from both those procedures because, on the one hand, allegedly higher standards of proof are required and, on the other, different consequences follow as to further maintenance of the litigation. Apart from the standards of proof, the argument appears to urge that in 1791, a litigant could challenge his opponent's evidence, either by the demurrer, which when determined ended the litigation, or by motion for a new trial which if successful, gave the adversary another chance to prove his case; and therefore the Amendment excluded any challenge to which one or the other of these consequences does not attach.

The Amendment did not bind the federal courts to the exact procedural incidents or details of jury trial according to the common law in 1791, any more than it tied them to the common-law system of pleading or the specific rules of evidence then prevailing. Nor were "the rules of the common law" then prevalent, including those relating to the procedure by which the judge regulated the jury's role on questions of fact, crystalized in a fixed and immutable system. On the contrary, they were constantly changing and developing during the late eighteenth and early nineteenth centuries.[23] In 1791 this

---

[23] E. g., during the eighteenth and nineteenth centuries, the nonsuit was being transformed in practice from a device by which a plaintiff voluntarily discontinued his action in order to try again another day into a procedure by which a defendant could put in issue the sufficiency of the plaintiff's evidence to go to the jury, differing from the directed verdict in that respect only in form. * * * The nonsuit, of

process already had resulted in widely divergent common-law rules on procedural matters among the states, and between them and England. * * *

This difficulty, no doubt, accounts for the amorphous character of the objection now advanced, which insists, not that any single one of the features criticized, but that the cumulative total or the alternative effect of all, was embodied in the Amendment. The more logical conclusion, we think, and the one which both history and the previous decisions here support, is that the Amendment was designed to preserve the basic institution of jury trial in only its most fundamental elements, not the great mass of procedural forms and details, varying even then so widely among common-law jurisdictions.

Apart from the uncertainty and the variety of conclusion which follows from an effort at purely historical accuracy, the consequences flowing from the view asserted are sufficient to refute it. It may be doubted that the Amendment requires challenge to an opponent's case to be made without reference to the merits of one's own and at the price of all opportunity to have it considered. On the other hand, there is equal room for disbelieving it compels endless repetition of litigation and unlimited chance, by education gained at the opposing party's expense, for perfecting a case at other trials. The essential inconsistency of these alternatives would seem sufficient to refute that either or both, to the exclusion of all others, received constitutional sanctity by the Amendment's force. The first alternative, drawn from the demurrer to the evidence, attributes to the Amendment the effect of forcing one admission because another and an entirely different one is made,[28] and thereby compels conclusion of the litigation once and for all. The true effect of imposing such a risk would not be to guarantee the plaintiff a jury trial. It would be rather to deprive the defendant (or the plaintiff if he were the challenger) of that right; or, if not that, then of the right to challenge the legal sufficiency of the

course, differed in consequence from the directed verdict, for it left the plaintiff free to try again. * * *

Similarly the demurrer to the evidence practice was not static during this period as a comparison of Cocksedge v. Fanshaw, 1779, 1 Doug. 118, with Gibson v. Hunter, 1793, 2 H.Bl. 187, and the American practice on the demurrer to the evidence reveals * * *. Nor was the conception of directing a verdict entirely unknown to the eighteenth century common law. * * * While there is no reason to believe that the notion at that time even approximated in character the present directed verdict, the cases serve further to show the plastic and developing character of these procedural devices during the eighteenth and nineteenth centuries.

[28] By conceding the full scope of an opponent's evidence and asserting its insufficiency in law, which is one thing, the challenger must be taken * * * also to admit he has no case, if the other's evidence is found legally sufficient, which is quite another thing. In effect, one must stake his case, not upon its own merit on the facts, but on the chance he may be right in regarding his opponent's as wanting in probative content. If he takes the gamble and loses, he pays with his own case, * * * without opportunity for the jury to consider it. To force this choice and yet deny that afforded by the directed verdict would be to imbed in the Constitution the hypertechnicality of common-law pleading and procedure in their heyday. * * *

opposing case. The Amendment was not framed or adopted to deprive either party of either right. It is impartial in its guaranty of both. To posit assertion of one upon sacrifice of the other would dilute and distort the full protection intended. The admitted validity of the practice on the motion for a new trial goes far to demonstrate this.[29] It negatives any idea that the challenge must be made at such a risk as the demurrer imposed. As for the other alternative, it is not urged that the Amendment guarantees another trial whenever challenge to the sufficiency of evidence is sustained. * * * That argument, in turn, is precluded by the practice on demurrer to the evidence.

Each of the classical modes of challenge, therefore, disproves the notion that the characteristic feature of the other, for effect upon continuing the litigation, became a part of the Seventh Amendment's guaranty to the exclusion of all others. * * * Alternatives so contradictory give room, not for the inference that one or the other is required, but rather for the view that neither is essential.

Finally, the objection appears to be directed generally at the standards of proof judges have required for submission of evidence to the jury. But standards, contrary to the objection's assumption, cannot be framed wholesale for the great variety of situations in respect to which the question arises. * * * The matter is essentially one to be worked out in particular situations and for particular types of cases. Whatever may be the general formulation, the essential requirement is that mere speculation be not allowed to do duty for probative facts, after making due allowance for all reasonably possible inferences favoring the party whose case is attacked. The mere difference in labels used to describe this standard * * * cannot amount to a departure from "the rules of the common law" which the Amendment requires to be followed. * * *

Judged by this requirement, or by any standard other than sheer speculation, we are unable to conclude that one whose burden, by the nature of his claim, is to show continuing and total disability for nearly twenty years supplies the essential proof of continuity when he wholly omits to show his whereabouts, activities or condition for five years, although the record discloses evidence must have been available, and, further, throws no light upon three additional years, except for one vaguely described and dated visit to his former home. * * * The words "total and permanent" are the statute's, not our own. They mean something more than incipient or occasional disability. We hardly need add that we give full credence to all of the testimony. But that cannot cure its inherent vagueness or supply essential elements omitted or withheld.

---

[29] Under that practice the moving party receives the benefit of jury evaluation of his own case and of challenge to his opponent's for insufficiency. If he loses on the challenge, the litigation is ended. But this is not because, in making it, he is forced to admit his own is insufficient. It is rather for the reasons that the court finds the opposite party's evidence is legally sufficient and the jury has found it outweighs his own. There is thus no forced surrender of one right from assertion of another.

On the other hand, if the challenger wins, there is another trial. But this is because he has sought it, not because the Amendment guarantees it.

Accordingly, the judgment is

Affirmed.

Mr. Justice BLACK, with whom Mr. Justice DOUGLAS and Mr. Justice MURPHY concur, dissenting.

*   *   *

The Court here re-examines testimony offered in a common law suit, weighs conflicting evidence, and holds that the litigant may never take this case to a jury.   *   *   *   Today's decision marks a continuation of the gradual process of judicial erosion which in one hundred fifty years has slowly worn away a major portion of the essential guarantee of the Seventh Amendment.

I.

Alexander Hamilton in The Federalist emphasized his loyalty to the jury system in civil cases and declared that jury verdicts should be re-examined, if at all, only "by a second jury, either by remanding the cause to the court below for a second trial of the fact, or by directing an issue immediately out of the Supreme Court."

*   *   *   The first Congress expected the Seventh Amendment to meet the objections of men like Patrick Henry to the Constitution itself.   Henry, speaking in the Virginia Constitutional Convention, had expressed the general conviction of the people of the Thirteen States when he said, "*   *   *   We are told that we are to part with that trial by jury with which our ancestors secured their lives and property.   *   *   *   I hope we shall never be induced, by such arguments, to part with that excellent mode of trial.   No appeal can now be made as to fact in common law suits.   *The unanimous verdict of impartial men cannot be reversed."*   *   *   *

In 1789, juries occupied the principal place in the administration of justice.   They were frequently in both criminal and civil cases the arbiters not only of fact but of law.   Less than three years after the ratification of the Seventh Amendment, this Court called a jury in a civil case brought under our original jurisdiction.   There was no disagreement as to the facts of the case. Chief Justice Jay, charging the jury for a unanimous Court, three of whose members had sat in the Constitutional Convention, said: "For as, on the one hand, it is presumed, that juries are the best judges of facts; it is, on the other hand, presumable, that the court[s] are the best judges of law.   But still, both objects are lawfully within your power of decision."   State of Georgia v. Brailsford, 3 Dall. 1, 4, 1 L.Ed. 483.   *   *   *

The principal method by which judges prevented cases from going to the jury in the Seventeenth and Eighteenth Centuries was by the demurrer to the evidence.   *   *   *   This practice fell into disuse in England in 1793, Gibson v. Hunter, 2 H.Bl. 187, and in the United States federal courts in 1826, Fowle v. Alexandria, 11 Wheat. 320, 6 L.Ed. 484.   The power of federal judges to comment to the jury on the evidence gave them additional influence.

* * * The right of involuntary nonsuit of a plaintiff, which might have been used to expand judicial power at jury expense was at first denied federal courts. * * *

As Hamilton had declared in The Federalist, the basic judicial control of the jury function was in the court's power to order a new trial. In 1830, this Court said: "The only modes known to the common law to re-examine such facts, are the granting of a new trial by the court where the issue was tried, or to which the record was properly returnable; or the award of a venire facias de novo, by an appellate court, for some error of law which intervened in the proceedings." Parsons v. Bedford, * * * 3 Pet. at page 448, 7 L.Ed. 732. * * *

A long step toward the determination of fact by judges instead of by juries was the invention of the directed verdict.[11] In 1850, what seems to have been the first directed verdict case considered by this Court, Parks v. Ross, 11 How. 362, 374, 13 L.Ed. 730, was presented for decision. The Court held that the directed verdict serves the same purpose as the demurrer to the evidence, and that since there was "no evidence whatever" on the critical issue in the case, the directed verdict was approved. The decision was an innovation, a departure from the traditional rule restated only fifteen years before in Greenleaf v. Birth, 1835, 9 Pet. 292, 299, 9 L.Ed. 132, in which this Court had said: "Where there is no evidence tending to prove a particular fact, the court[s] are bound so to instruct the jury, when requested; but they cannot legally give any instruction which shall take from the jury the right of weighing the evidence and determining what effect it shall have."

This new device contained potentialities for judicial control of the jury which had not existed in the demurrer to the evidence. In the first place, demurring to the evidence was risky business, for in so doing the party not only admitted the truth of all the testimony against him but also all reasonable inferences which might be drawn from it; and upon joinder in demurrer the case was withdrawn from the jury while the court proceeded to give final judgment either for or against the demurrant. * * * Imposition of this risk was no mere technicality; for by making withdrawal of a case from the jury dangerous to the moving litigant's cause, the early law went far to assure that facts would never be examined except by a jury. * * * The litigant not only takes no risk by a motion for a directed verdict, but in making such a motion gives himself two opportunities to avoid the jury's decision; for under the federal variant of judgment notwithstanding the verdict, the judge may reserve

---

[11] I do not mean to minimize other forms of judicial control. In a summary of important techniques of judicial domination of the jury, Thayer lists the following: control by the requirement of a "reasonable judgment"—i. e., one satisfactory to the judge; control of the rules of "presumption" * * * ; the control of the "definition of language"; the control of rules of practice, and forms of pleading ("It is remarkable how judges and legislatures in this country are unconsciously travelling back towards the old result of controlling the jury, by requiring special verdicts and answers to specific questions. * * *"); the control of "mixed questions of law and fact"; the control of factual decisions by appellate courts. Thayer on Evidence (1898 ed.) p. 208 et seq.

opinion on the motion for a directed verdict and then give judgment for the moving party after the jury was formally found against him.   In the second place, under the directed verdict practice the courts soon abandoned the "admission of all facts and reasonable inferences" standard referred to, and created the so-called "substantial evidence" rule which permitted directed verdicts even though there was far more evidence in the case than a plaintiff would have needed to withstand a demurrer.

The substantial evidence rule did not spring into existence immediately upon the adoption of the directed verdict device.   For a few more years federal judges held to the traditional rule that juries might pass finally on facts if there was "any evidence" to support a party's contention.   The rule that a case must go to the jury unless there was "no evidence" was completely repudiated in Schuylkill and Dauphin Improvement Co. v. Munson, 1871, 14 Wall. 442, 447, 448, 20 L.Ed. 867, upon which the Court today relies in part.   There the Court declared that "some" evidence was not enough—there must be evidence sufficiently persuasive to the judge so that he thinks "a jury can properly proceed."   The traditional rule was given an ugly name, "the scintilla rule", to hasten its demise.   *   *   *   The same transition from jury supremacy to jury subordination through judicial decisions took place in State courts.

Later cases permitted the development of added judicial control.   *   *   *   [J]ury verdicts on disputed facts have been set aside or directed verdicts authorized so regularly as to make the practice commonplace while the motion for directed verdict itself has become routine.   *   *   *   Today the Court comes dangerously close to weighing the credibility of a witness and rejecting his testimony because the majority do not believe it.

*   *   *

The call for the true application of the Seventh Amendment is not to words, but to the spirit of honest desire to see that Constitutional right preserved.   Either the judge or the jury must decide facts and to the extent that we take this responsibility, we lessen the jury function.   Our duty to preserve this one of the Bill of Rights may be peculiarly difficult, for here it is our own power which we must restrain.   *   *   *   As for myself, I believe that a verdict should be directed, if at all, only when, without weighing the credibility of the witnesses, there is in the evidence no room whatever for honest difference of opinion over the factual issue in controversy.   *   *   *

II.

*   *   *   It is undisputed that the petitioner's health was sound in 1918, and it is evidently conceded that he was disabled at least since 1930. When in the intervening period, did the disability take place?

*   *   *   There is substantial testimony from which reasonable men might conclude that the petitioner was insane from the date claimed.

Two witnesses testify as to the petitioner's mental irresponsibility while he was in France.   *   *   *   The Court disposes of this testimony, which obviously indicates some degree of mental unbalance, by saying no more than that it "does not prove he was insane." No reason is given, nor can I imagine any, why a jury should not be entitled to consider this evidence and draw its own conclusions.

* * * The Court analyzes O'Neill's testimony for internal consistency, criticizes his failure to remember the details of his association with the petitioner fifteen years before his appearance in this case, and concludes that O'Neill's evidence shows no more than that "petitioner was subject to alternating periods of gaiety and depression for some indefinite period." This extreme emotional instability is an accepted symptom of the disease from which the petitioner suffers. If he exhibited the same symptoms in 1922, it is, at the minimum, probable that the condition has been continuous since an origin during the war. O'Neill's testimony coupled with the petitioner's present condition presents precisely the type of question which a jury should resolve.

* * * The testimony of his Commanding Officer while he was in the Army, Col. Matthews, is that the petitioner had "periods of gaiety and exhilaration" and was then "depressed as if he had had a hangover"; that petitioner tried to create disturbances and dissatisfy the men; that he suffered from a belief that he was being treated unfairly; and that generally his actions "were not those of a normal man". The Colonel was not a doctor and might well not have recognized insanity had he seen it; as it was, he concluded that the petitioner was an alcoholic and a narcotic addict. However, the officer was unable, upon repeated investigations, to discover any actual use of narcotics. A jury fitting this information into the general pattern of the testimony might well have been driven to the conclusion that the petitioner was insane at the time the Colonel had him under observation.

All of this evidence, if believed, showed a man healthy and normal before he went to the war suffering for several years after he came back from a disease which had the symptoms attributed to schizophrenia and who was insane from 1930 until his trial. Under these circumstances, I think that the physician's testimony of total and permanent disability by reason of continuous insanity from 1918 to 1938 was reasonable. The fact that there was no direct testimony for a period of five years, while it might be the basis of fair argument to the jury by the government, does not, as the Court seems to believe, create a presumption against the petitioner so strong that his case must be excluded from the jury entirely. Even if during these five years the petitioner was spasmodically employed, we could not conclude that he was not totally and permanently disabled. * * * It is not doubted that schizophrenia is permanent even though there may be a momentary appearance of recovery.

* * *

This case graphically illustrates the injustice resulting from permitting judges to direct verdicts instead of requiring them to await a jury decision and then, if necessary, allow a new trial. The chief reason given for approving a directed verdict against this petitioner is that no evidence except expert medical testimony was offered for a five to eight year period. Perhaps, now that the petitioner knows he has insufficient evidence to satisfy a judge even though he may have enough to satisfy a jury, he would be able to fill this time gap to meet any judge's demand.   *   *   *   If, as the Court believes, insufficient evidence has been offered to sustain a jury verdict for the petitioner, we should at least authorize a new trial.   *   *   *

NOTES AND QUESTIONS

1.   Traditional rules, still followed today in some jurisdictions, require a party to assume a risk in order to move for a directed verdict.   What policy is served by a rule requiring entry of judgment against a party whose motion is denied?   Or by a rule to the effect that before moving for a directed verdict at the end of plaintiff's case, defendant must waive the right to produce evidence if the motion fails?   *Cf.* Morley v. Liverpool & London & Globe Ins. Co., 85 Mich. 210, 48 N.W. 502 (1891); Bartholomew v. Impastato, 12 So.2d 700 (La.Ct.App. Orleans 1943).   Or by providing that if plaintiff and defendant both move for a directed verdict at the close of the evidence, they waive the right to jury trial in the event that both motions are denied?   See Bunch v. Davidson, 242 Or. 635, 409 P.2d 910 (1966), overruled Godell v. Johnson, 244 Or. 587, 418 P.2d 505 (1966); Share v. Coats, 29 S.D. 603, 137 N.W. 402 (1912) (motion by both parties for directed verdict constitutes waiver in absence of request to the contrary before jury returns verdict as directed by the judge); Annot., 68 A.L.R.2d 300 (1959).   To what extent are the policies underlying such rules dictated by the same considerations that support jury trial? Are these rules consistent with rules and decisions in other areas of procedure that have reduced the part played by formal requirements and technical errors? How does Federal Rule 50 treat these questions?

2.   On the demurrer to the evidence, see Thayer, *A Preliminary Treatise on Evidence at the Common Law* 234–39 (1898); Comment, *Trial Practice— Demurrer Upon Evidence as a Device for Taking a Case from the Jury,* 44 Mich.L.Rev. 468 (1945).

3.   What do you think of the following argument as addressed to a case such as *Galloway?*

> It seems to me that in this case the strongest argument in favor of submitting the cause to the jury is the widely divergent views among the members of this court, not only as to the conclusions which may properly be drawn from the testimony, but as to the testimony itself. If the judges of this court so differ in the proportion of four to three, can it be said that there is but one inference to be drawn, or that different minds may not honestly draw different conclusions?   If the minds of the members of this court may so honestly differ, why may not the minds of jurors just as honestly differ?   The logical deduction from the opinion of the court is that minority judges, and jurors generally, either do not have rational minds, or that they may not honestly reach a conclusion differing from the majority.

NUCCI v. COLORADO & S. RY. CO., 63 Colo. 582, 602, 169 P. 273, 281 (1917) (dissenting opinion).

4.   Reread *Lavender v. Kurn*, p. 51, supra.   Is that case consistent with *Galloway?*   What factor do you believe the majority in *Galloway* found most significant in reaching its conclusion?   Was there a comparable factor in *Lavender?* Should a jury be permitted to infer a fact necessary to the case from the failure

of a party to testify or present evidence on the issue? Should it make a difference whether that party has the burden of persuasion on that issue?

———

HERRON v. SOUTHERN PAC. CO., 283 U.S. 91, 51 S.Ct. 383, 75 L. Ed. 857 (1931). The Arizona Constitution, Article 18, Section 5, provides that the defenses of contributory negligence and assumption of risk "shall, in all cases whatsoever, be a question of fact and shall, at all times, be left to the jury." Does this provision prevent a federal court in Arizona, hearing a diversity case, from directing a verdict for defendant on the ground that as a matter of law plaintiff was guilty of contributory negligence? Mr. Chief Justice Hughes, writing for the Supreme Court, said it does not.

It does not appear to be insisted by the appellant, and it could not be maintained, that this constitutional provision must be followed by the federal courts by virtue of the Conformity Act * * *. The state, without violating the requirements of due process, may provide such a rule for its own courts, * * * but, in view of its nature and effect, the rule cannot be regarded as one that relates merely to practice or to a "form" or "mode of proceeding." The provision "cuts deep into the right, observed at common law, by which a defendant can obtain a decision by the court upon a proven state of facts." Atchison, Topeka & Santa Fé Railway Company v. Spencer (C.C.A.) 20 F.2d 714, 718. * * *

Nor is the * * * [Rules of Decision Act] applicable, * * *. The controlling principle governing the decision of the present question is that, state laws cannot alter the essential character or function of a federal court. The function of the trial judge in a federal court is not in any sense a local matter, and state statutes which would interfere with the appropriate performance of that function are not binding upon the federal court * * *.

In a trial by jury in a federal court, the judge is not a mere moderator, but is the governor of the trial for the purpose of assuring its proper conduct and of determining questions of law. This discharge of the judicial function as at common law is an essential factor in the process for which the Federal Constitution provides. * * *

Id. at 93, 51 S.Ct. at 384, 75 L.Ed. at 859.

NOTES AND QUESTIONS

1. Would the issue in the *Herron* case have been decided differently after *Erie R.R. Co. v. Tompkins,* p. 265, supra? Why?

2. Could the Congress deprive the federal courts of the power to direct verdicts on the issue of contributory negligence in a case based upon a state cause of action? In a case based upon a federal cause of action? Does the latter question present a different issue than would be posed if the Congress abolished the defense of contributory negligence in a federal cause of action?

In KILEY v. CHICAGO, M. & ST. P. RY., 138 Wis. 215, 225, 119 N.W. 309, 314 (1909), the Wisconsin Supreme Court, presented with a challenge to a state statute directing that certain questions of negligence and contributory negligence be left to the jury, said:

> It is contended that the Legislature intended to deprive the courts of their judicial functions, * * * and to confer such functions on juries * * *. The powers conferred on courts and juries by these constitutional provisions were well defined in the established system of jurisprudence in this country at the time of their adoption. This court interpreted these constitutional provisions as conferring on court and jury those well-defined powers as they existed, and had been repeatedly exercised by court and jury, under the common law. * * * Under the system of law as it then existed it devolved on the court to determine the legal sufficiency of the evidence tending to prove a fact; and, when the court had judicially ascertained that the evidence adduced tended to establish the constituent facts of the matter at issue, it then devolved on the jury to determine whether, upon the evidence, the fact was satisfactorily proven. The powers of the court and jury in the administration of the law in these respects were distinct and well defined at the time of the adoption of our Constitution, and became vested in the court and jury by its provisions. They cannot be abrogated or modified by legislative action (to the extent of impairing, in any degree, the judicial power). * * *

> Did the Legislature intend * * * to confer judicial power, vested in the court, on the jury? It declares: "In all cases under this act the question of negligence and contributory negligence shall be for the jury." In their general sense the words are but a declaration of the law as it exists, namely, that when the court has found that there is legal evidence tending to show negligence or contributory negligence, it is for the jury to determine from the evidence adduced whether negligence or contributory negligence exists. This interpretation of the provision does not make a change in the law * * *.

3.   The constitutional provision involved in the *Herron* case has not escaped restrictive interpretation by the courts of Arizona. See, e. g., Franco v. Vakares, 35 Ariz. 309, 277 P. 812 (1929) ("independent" negligence of plaintiff required directed verdict for defendant); Sax v. Kopelman, 96 Ariz. 394, 396 P.2d 17 (1964) (directed verdict *for* plaintiff on issue of contributory negligence required when no evidence of contributory negligence introduced).

B. STANDARDS FOR THE DIRECTED VERDICT AND JUDGMENT NOTWITHSTANDING THE VERDICT

———

Read Federal Rule of Civil Procedure 50 in the Supplement.

———

DENMAN v. SPAIN

Supreme Court of Mississippi, 1961.
242 Miss. 431, 135 So.2d 195.

LEE, Presiding Justice. Betty Denman, a minor, * * * sued * * * [the] executrix of the estate of Joseph A. Ross, deceased, to recover damages for personal injuries sustained by her, allegedly resulting from the negligence of the decedent in the operation of an automobile. The issue was submitted to a jury on the evidence for the plaintiff—no evidence being offered for the defendant—and there was a verdict and judgment for the plaintiff in the sum of $5,000. However, on motion of the defendant, a judgment *non obstante veredicto* * * * was sustained and entered. From that action, the plaintiff has appealed.

* * *

The appellant contends that the evidence offered by her, together with the reasonable inferences therefrom, was sufficient to make an issue for the jury as to whether the alleged negligence of the deceased driver, Ross, proximately caused or contributed to the collision and the consequent damage * * *.

A careful scrutiny and analysis of the evidence is therefore necessary:

Sunday, March 23, 1958, was a rainy, foggy day. About six o'clock that afternoon, at dusk, Mrs. Eva B. Denman, accompanied by her granddaughter, Betty, the plaintiff, was driving her Ford car southward on U. S. Highway 49E. At that time, Joseph A. Ross, accompanied by Miss Euna Tanner and Mrs. J. L. Haining, was driving his Plymouth car northward on said highway. Just south of the Town of Sumner, the cars collided. Mrs. Denman, Miss Tanner and Ross were killed. Betty, nearly seven years of age at the time, and Mrs. Haining were injured. Neither had any recollection of what had happened at the time of the collision. * * *

Plaintiff's father, Stuart Denman, who went to the scene shortly after the collision, described the situation substantially as follows: The Ford car was about seven yards off the paved surface on the east side in a bar pit "heading back towards the railroad track, which is in an easterly direction." The engine and transmission were on the opposite side of the road, out of the car and about fifty yards apart. The Plymouth was also on the east side, facing west, about fifteen yards north of the Ford.

No proof was offered as to skid marks, or other evidence to show the point of contact between these two vehicles. Eleven photographs of the dam-

aged Plymouth, taken from various positions, and thirteen pictures of the damaged Ford, also taken from various positions, other than being mute evidence
of a terrible tragedy, depict no reasonable or plausible explanation as to why
this collision occurred, or who was responsible for it.   Three other photographs portraying the topography of this immediate area, afford no excuse
whatever for such grievous human error.

Over objection by the defendant, John Barnett testified that he was driving a Dodge pickup north of highway 49E on his way to Tutwiler; that he was
traveling at a speed of fifty or fifty-five miles per hour; that the Plymouth,
which was in the wreck, passed him about three-fourths of a mile south of
where the collision occurred, going at a speed of about seventy miles per hour;
that when it passed, it got back in its lane, and neither wavered nor wobbled
thereafter; that he followed and observed it for a distance of forty or fifty
yards, and that it stayed in its proper lane as long as he saw it.   Although another car was on the road ahead of him, he could have seen as far as the
place of the accident except for the rain and fog.

Over objection by the defendant, Hal Buckley, a Negro man, testified
that he was also traveling north on 49E on his way to Tutwiler at a speed of
forty to fifty miles per hour.   About two hundred yards south of the place
where the collision occurred, a light green Plymouth, which he later saw at the
scene of the accident, passed him at a speed of seventy-five or eighty miles an
hour.   He could see its taillights after it passed, and "he was just steady going;
he wasn't doing no slowing up."   He saw it until it ran into the other car.   On
cross-examination, he said that, after this car passed him, it got back on its side
of the road, drove straight, and he did not notice that it ever went back over
the center.   Also on cross-examination, in an effort at impeachment, a part of
the transcript in the other trial, [i] containing this question and answer, was
read to him as follows: "What do you estimate the speed of that car was
when it passed you—the one that was going the same direction that you
were?," and the answer was: "Well, I don't have no idea."   When he was
asked why he made this difference in his testimony, he hesitated and replied, "I didn't give no sorta idea how fast he was going?"   He then admitted that when the car passed him, it got back on its side and drove straight
ahead, and that he could see the accident, but he could not tell anything
about it or on which side of the road it happened.   He also did not notice
the other car, which came from the other direction.

Since Barnett did not see the car any more after it had gone forty or fifty
yards beyond him, and his knowledge of speed was based on what he saw
about three-fourths of a mile south of the place where the collision occurred,
this evidence was inadmissible * * *.   On the contrary, since Buckley testified the speed of this car, when it passed him, was seventy-five to eighty
miles an hour and that it did not slow down in the remaining distance of two

---

[i] Plaintiff had separately sued the estate of her grandmother.   Trial in that case
resulted in a directed verdict for defendant, which was affirmed.   Denman v. Denman, 242 Miss. 59, 134 So.2d 457 (1961).

hundred yards before the collision, such evidence was competent and admissible * * *. The attempted impeachment went to its credibility and not its admissibility.

From this evidence, the plaintiff reasons that the jury could, and did, find that the Ross car was being operated, under inclement weather conditions, at an unlawful and negligent rate of speed, and that, if Ross had had his car under adequate and proper control, in all probability the collision could have been avoided. She voices the opinion that the physical facts, including the pictures of the wrecked vehicles, indicated that the Ford car was probably across the highway at an angle of perhaps forty-five degrees at the time of the collision.

But the testimony of Buckley showed only that the Plymouth was being operated at an excessive and negligent rate of speed. It otherwise showed that the car was in its proper lane. He did not notice it go over the center at any time, but it was driven straight down the road. No eyewitness claimed to have seen what happened. There was no evidence to indicate the place in the road where the vehicles came in contact with each other. There was no showing as to the speed of the Ford, whether fast or slow; or as to whether it was traveling on the right or wrong side of the road; or as to whether it slid or was suddenly driven to the wrong side of the road into the path of the Plymouth. The cars were so badly damaged that the pictures afford no reasonable explanation as to what person or persons were legally responsible for their condition. In other words, just how and why this grievous tragedy occurred is completely shrouded in mystery.

The burden was on the plaintiff to prove by a preponderance of the evidence, not only that the operator of the Plymouth was guilty of negligence but also that such negligence proximately caused or contributed to the collision and consequent damage. By the use of metaphysical learning, speculation and conjecture, one may reach several possible conclusions as to how the accident occurred. However such conclusions could only be classed as possibilities; and this Court has many times held that verdicts cannot be based on possibilities. At all events, there is no sound or reasonable basis upon which a jury or this Court can say that the plaintiff met that burden.

The judgment must be affirmed.

Affirmed.

NOTES AND QUESTIONS

1. At this point I am going to say something which you may find very shocking. [The judge] * * * is supposed to submit an issue to the jury if, as the judges say, the jury can decide reasonably either way. But to say that I can decide an issue of fact reasonably either way is to say, I submit, that I cannot, by the exercise of reason, decide the question. That means that the issue which we typically submit to juries is an issue which the jury cannot decide by the exercise of its reason.

The decision of an issue of fact in cases of closely balanced probabilities, therefore, must, in the nature of things, be an emotional rather than a rational act * * *.

Michael, *The Basic Rules of Pleading,* 5 Record of N.Y.C.B.A. 175, 199–200 (1950). Do you agree with Professor Michael? What is the relevance of this comment to the opinion in the *Denman* case?

2. Do you believe a jury could properly have found for plaintiff in the *Denman* case? What inferences would have to be drawn from the evidence to reach such a conclusion? How would you support the proposition that these inferences could reasonably be found to be stronger than other inferences that would not lead to a verdict for plaintiff?

3. Is the *Denman* case contrary to *Lavender v. Kurn,* p. 51, supra? In PLANTERS MFG. CO. v. PROTECTION MUT. INS. CO., 380 F.2d 869 (5th Cir.1967), the court of appeals concluded that the two cases are inconsistent, and thus had to confront squarely the question whether a state standard for directing a verdict is controlling under *Erie,* a question the United States Supreme Court has found unnecessary to answer in two cases that raised it. Dick v. New York Life Ins. Co., 359 U.S. 437, 79 S.Ct. 921, 3 L.Ed.2d 935 (1959), and Mercer v. Theriot, 377 U.S. 152, 84 S.Ct. 1157, 12 L.Ed.2d 206 (1964). How should the question be resolved? It has been argued that while "federal courts may appropriately follow their own standards * * * with respect to at least most of the problems surrounding jury evaluation of witness credibility * * * problems of jury freedom with respect to drawing inferences from the evidence and applying the law to the facts * * * should almost invariably be referred to state standards." Cooper, *Directions for Directed Verdicts: A Compass for Federal Courts,* 55 Minn.L.Rev. 903, 975–76 (1971). *But cf.* 9 Wright & Miller, *Federal Practice and Procedure: Civil* § 2303 (1971).

4. Cases like *Denman,* which involve head-on vehicular collisions, present a difficult problem with regard to the control of jury verdicts. The circumstances of these collisions ordinarily suggest that at least one driver was negligent but may not indicate which driver it was, and direct evidence often is lacking because all witnesses are dead. See Annot., 77 A.L.R.2d 580 (1961). Can you suggest a solution to the problem?

KIRCHER v. ATCHISON, T. & S. F. RY. CO., 32 Cal.2d 176, 195 P.2d 427 (1948). Plaintiff sued for the loss of a hand, which had been run over by defendant's train. According to plaintiff's evidence, he had stumbled in a hole on a station platform thirteen feet west of the west rail of the track, pitched forward, striking his head against a standing car on the track, and fallen under the train that then moved; the hand was severed on the east rail. The railroad's evidence was that plaintiff had been on the east side of the train, where he should not have been, and had stumbled on a cross-tie. A judgment for plaintiff was affirmed. Justice Carter, for the court, said:

> * * * In the light of all the circumstances * * * it cannot be held as a matter of law, that plaintiff's version was such as to contravene the laws of nature, or as to render the jury's acceptance of it unreasonable. * * * Although he stated quite frankly that he was unable to explain with certainty the manner in

which his left hand came to be placed on the east rail * * *,
the jury had before it evidence indicating that * * * there was
a hole in the depot platform * * * and the ultimate fact that
defendant's train ran over his hand at the time and place in question.   In these circumstances the jury was not compelled to find
against him because he could not with certainty relate the exact
manner in which his left hand came to be on the east rail.   It could
reasonably have inferred that his failure to explain this circumstance was due to the fact that in the critical few minutes he was
under the train he was unconscious, or substantially so, from the
blow on his head as the outcome of stepping into the hole.

Id. at 184, 195 P.2d at 433.

Justice Traynor, dissenting, said:

It is my opinion that although the accident as described by
plaintiff is not outside the realm of possibility, his version, which
is that of an interested and impeached witness, involves so extraordinary and improbable a sequence of events that without corroboration it does not warrant belief by a reasonable jury.

Id. at 189, 195 P.2d at 436.

NOTES AND QUESTIONS

1.   Does the *Kircher* case present the same kind of issue as the *Denman*
case?

2.   Should a verdict ever be directed for the party having the burden of
producing evidence on an issue when the evidence in that party's favor is testimonial rather than documentary?   *Compare* Alexander v. Tingle, 181 Md. 464,
30 A.2d 737 (1943), *with* New England Mut. Life Ins. Co. v. Huckins, 127 Fla.
540, 173 So. 696 (1937).   Why does this question differ from the question of directing a verdict for a party who is not the proponent?   See Ferdinand v.
Agricultural Ins. Co., 22 N.J. 482, 126 A.2d 323, 62 A.L.R.2d 1179 (1956);
Note, *The Power of the Court to Determine Witness Credibility: A Problem in
Directing a Verdict for the Proponent of the Evidence,* 107 U.Pa.L.Rev. 217
(1958); Annot., 62 A.L.R.2d 1191 (1958).

On the general question of the jury's power to disregard uncontradicted and
disinterested testimony, as well as on the question of what constitutes "interest,"
see the excellent discussion in Cooper, *Directions for Directed Verdicts: A Compass for Federal Courts,* 55 Minn.L.Rev. 903, 930–47 (1971), which concludes
that a majority of courts properly deny the jury this power.

3.   As previously noted, see pp. 358–59, supra, hearsay evidence is excluded on objection because it is not regarded as a reliable basis for a jury's
decision.   If hearsay evidence comes in without objection, and the party against
whom that evidence militates subsequently moves for a directed verdict, should
the hearsay evidence be taken into account in determining whether there is
sufficient evidence to support a jury verdict for the other party?   See Annot.,
79 A.L.R.2d 890, 914–19 (1961).

ROGERS v. MISSOURI PACIFIC R.R.

Supreme Court of the United States, 1957.
352 U.S. 500, 77 S.Ct. 443, 1 L.Ed.2d 493.

Certiorari to the Supreme Court of Missouri.

Mr. Justice BRENNAN delivered the opinion of the Court.

A jury in the Circuit Court of St. Louis awarded damages to the petitioner in this action under the Federal Employers' Liability Act. The Supreme Court of Missouri reversed upon the ground that the petitioner's evidence did not support the finding of respondent's liability.   *   *   *

Petitioner was a laborer in a section gang, working on July 17, 1951, along a portion of respondent's double-track line which, near Garner, Arkansas, runs generally north and south. The tracks are on ballast topping the surface of a dirt "dump" with sloping sides, and there is a path about a yard wide bordering each side of the surface between the crest of the slope and the edge of the ballast. Weeds and vegetation, killed chemically preparatory to burning them off, covered the paths and slopes. Petitioner's foreman assigned him to burn off the weeds and vegetation—the first time he was given that task in the two months he had worked for the respondent. He testified that it was customary to burn off such vegetation with a flame thrower operated from a car running on the tracks. Railroad witnesses testified, however, that the respondent discontinued the use of flame throwers at least a year earlier because the fires started by them sometimes spread beyond the railroad right of way.

Petitioner was supplied with a crude hand torch and was instructed to burn off the weeds and vegetation along the west path and for two or three feet down the west slope. The events leading to his mishap occurred after he proceeded with the work to a point within thirty to thirty-five yards of a culvert adjoining the path.

Petitioner testified, without contradiction, that the foreman instructed him and other members of the section gang to stop what they were doing when a train passed and to take positions off the tracks and ties to observe the journals of the passing train for hot boxes. The instructions were explicit not to go on either of the tracks or to stand on or near the ends of the ties when a train was passing on a far track. This was a safety precaution because "the sound of one train would deaden the sound of another one that possibly would come from the other way."

On this day, petitioner heard the whistle of a train which was approaching from behind him on the east track. He promptly "quit firing" and ran north to a place on the path near the mentioned culvert. He was standing a few feet from the culvert observing the train for hotboxes when he became enveloped in smoke and flames. The passing train had fanned the flames of the burning vegetation and weeds, carrying the fire to the vegetation around his position. He threw his arm over his face, retreated quickly back on the culvert and slipped and fell from the top of the culvert, suffering the serious injuries for which he sought damages in this suit.

*   *   *

We think that the evidence was sufficient to support the jury finding for the petitioner. The testimony that the burning off of weeds and vegetation was ordinarily done with flame throwers from cars on the tracks and not, as here, by a workman on foot using a crude hand torch, when that evidence is considered with the uncontradicted testimony that the petitioner was where he was on this narrow path atop the dirt "dump" in furtherance of explicit orders * * *, supplied ample support for a jury finding that respondent's negligence played a part in the petitioner's injury. These were probative facts from which the jury could find that respondent was or should have been aware of conditions which created a likelihood that petitioner, in performing the duties required of him, would suffer just such an injury as he did. Common experience teaches both that a passing train will fan the flames of a fire, and that a person suddenly enveloped in flames and smoke will instinctively react by retreating from the danger and in the process pay scant heed to other dangers which may imperil him. In this view, it was an irrelevant consideration whether the immediate reason for his slipping off the culvert was the presence of gravel negligently allowed by respondent to remain on the surface, or was some cause not identified from the evidence.

The Missouri Supreme Court based its reversal upon its finding of an alleged admission by the petitioner that he knew it was his primary duty to watch the fire. From that premise the Missouri court reasoned that petitioner was inattentive to the fire and that the emergency which confronted him "was an emergency brought about by himself." It said that if, as petitioner testified, the immediate cause of his fall was that loose gravel on the surface of the culvert rolled out from under him, yet it was his inattention to the fire which caused it to spread and obliged petitioner "to move blindly away and fall," and this was "something extraordinary, unrelated to, and disconnected from the incline of the gravel at the culvert."

We interpret the foregoing to mean that the Missouri court found as a matter of law that the petitioner's conduct was the sole cause of his mishap. But when the petitioner agreed that his primary duty was to watch the fire he did not also say that he was relieved of the duty to stop to watch a passing train for hotboxes. Indeed, no witness testified that the instruction was countermanded. At best, uncertainty as to the fact arises from the petitioner's testimony, and in that circumstance not the court, but the jury, was the tribunal to determine the fact.

We may assume that the jury could properly have reached the court's conclusion. But, as the probative facts also supported with reason the verdict favorable to the petitioner, the decision was exclusively for the jury to make. The jury was instructed to return a verdict for the respondent if it was found that negligence of the petitioner was the sole cause of his mishap. We must take it that the verdict was obedient to the trial judge's charge and that the jury found that such was not the case but that petitioner's injury resulted at least in part from the respondent's negligence.

The opinion may also be read as basing the reversal on another ground, namely, that it appeared to the court that the petitioner's conduct was at least as probable a cause for his mishap as any negligence of the respondent, and that in such case there was no case for the jury. But that would mean that there is no jury question in actions under this statute, although the employee's proofs support with reason a verdict in his favor, unless the judge can say that the jury may exclude the idea that his injury was due to causes with which the defendant was not connected, or, stated another way, unless his proofs are so strong that the jury, on grounds of probability, may exclude a conclusion favorable to the defendant. That is not the governing principle defining the proof which requires a submission to the jury in these cases. The Missouri court's opinion implies its view that this is the governing standard by saying that the proofs must show that "the injury would not have occurred but for the negligence" of his employer, and that "[t]he test of whether there is causal connection is that, absent the negligent act the injury would not have occurred." * * *

Under this statute the test of a jury case is simply whether the proofs justify with reason the conclusion that employer negligence played any part, even the slightest, in producing the injury or death for which damages are sought. It does not matter that, from the evidence, the jury may also with reason, on grounds of probability, attribute the result to other causes, including the employee's contributory negligence. Judicial appraisal of the proofs to determine whether a jury question is presented is narrowly limited to the single inquiry whether, with reason, the conclusion may be drawn that negligence of the employer played any part at all in the injury or death. Judges are to fix their sights primarily to make that appraisal and, if that test is met, are bound to find that a case for the jury is made out whether or not the evidence allows the jury a choice of other probabilities. The statute expressly imposes liability upon the employer to pay damages for injury or death due "in whole or *in part*" to its negligence. (Emphasis added.)

* * *

The Congress when adopting the law was particularly concerned that the issues whether there was employer fault and whether that fault played any part in the injury or death of the employee should be decided by the jury whenever fair-minded men could reach these conclusions on the evidence. Originally, judicial administration of the 1908 Act substantially limited the cases in which employees were allowed a jury determination. That was because the courts developed concepts of assumption of risk and of the coverage of the law, which defeated employee claims as a matter of law. Congress corrected this by the 1939 amendments and removed the fetters which hobbled the full play of the basic congressional intention to leave to the fact-finding function of the jury the decision of the primary question raised in these cases—whether employer fault played any part in the employee's mishap. * * *

The judgment is reversed. * * *

Mr. Justice BURTON concurs in the result.

Mr. Justice REED would affirm the judgment of the Supreme Court of Missouri.

[Dissenting opinions of Mr. Justice FRANKFURTER and Mr. Justice HARLAN are omitted.]

NOTES AND QUESTIONS

1. Is the nature of the issue that the Court said should have been left to the jury in *Rogers* different from that in *Lavender, Denman,* and *Kircher?* If so, is the difference significant to the formulation of a standard? Might a directed verdict be more readily sustained on one type of issue than the other?

2. A municipal ordinance permitted an authorized emergency vehicle to proceed past a stop signal or exceed the speed limit, "when the driver of such vehicle sounds a siren, bell or exhaust whistle to the extent reasonably necessary." A police car in rush-hour traffic, on call to a robbery then in progress, proceeded at excessive speed through a red light, and struck plaintiff. In LO CICERO v. COLUMBIA CAS. CO., 268 F.2d 440 (5th Cir.), certiorari denied 361 U.S. 917, 80 S.Ct. 261, 4 L.Ed.2d 187 (1959), the court held that the jury should have been instructed that the policeman was negligent as a matter of law in failing to sound the siren. Is this distinguishable from directing a verdict on the issue of negligence when no statute is involved? *Cf.* pp. 837–38, supra.

3. Compare and evaluate the following statements:

(a) [Nonsuit, directed verdict, and dismissal] * * * invoke the concept of the sufficiency of the evidence. There has been some controversy over the questions of whether credibility may be considered on some or all of these motions and whether a judge may properly direct a verdict wherever he would set aside an opposite one. There may, to be sure, be some shadings in the application of the sufficiency test for the different devices, and among different jurisdictions. And there may once have been wider variations in the test applied. But by and large the sufficiency test * * * is used pretty uniformly in this country when any of these devices is invoked, and the doctrinal differences referred to are largely battles of words.

So far as credibility goes, *all* courts consider it on a motion for directed verdict to the minimum degree of determining whether testimony is capable of belief by reasonable men or is incredible as a matter of law. * * * The real differences, for the most part, are in the willingness to find contradiction with physical facts or some other basis for declaring evidence incredible as matter of law. * * * Some courts call the problem described in this paragraph one of credibility, others do not.

* * *

The motions for nonsuit, directed verdict, or dismissal test not only the factual aspect but also the evaluative aspect of the concept of sufficiency. Here greater differences are probably found in the availability of one of these motions than in the matter of credibility. * * *

Also, there is probably more variation among decisions concerning the legitimacy of inferences from circumstantial evidence than concerning credibility. * * *

James, *Sufficiency of the Evidence and Jury-Control Devices Available Before Verdict,* 47 Va.L.Rev. 218, 232–35 (1961). See also James, *Civil Procedure* § 7.13 (1965).

(b) The question is thus presented, in determining * * * [the] sufficiency of evidence to go to the jury, whether there are any detailed *tests to control or to guide the judge* in his ruling.

The ruling will, in truth, depend entirely on the nature of the evidence offered in the case in hand; and it is seldom possible that a ruling can serve as a precedent. It has been ruled, for instance, that to show a 'scienter' of a horse's unmanageable disposition, a single instance of its having run away is, though admissible, not sufficient evidence for the jury; mere identity of name has been thought both sufficient and insufficient evidence of identity of person; but even these can hardly be taken as fixed precedents. There is no virtue in any form of words.

9 Wigmore, *Evidence* § 2494, at 296 (3d ed. 1940).

(c) [I]n non-FELA federal cases * * * the formulation of the test of sufficiency of evidence is substantially different. * * * [T]he court should consider all of the evidence—not just that evidence which supports the non-mover's case—but in the light and with all reasonable inferences most favorable to the party opposed to the motion. If the facts and inferences point so strongly and overwhelmingly in favor of one party that the Court believes that reasonable men could not arrive at a contrary verdict, granting of the motions is proper. On the other hand, if there is substantial evidence opposed to the motions, that is, evidence of such quality and weight that reasonable and fair-minded men in the exercise of impartial judgment might reach different conclusions, the motions should be denied, and the case submitted to the jury.

BOEING CO. v. SHIPMAN, 411 F.2d 365, 373–74 (5th Cir.1969) (en banc).

(d) * * * Our function is not to weigh the evidence factually as the jury does. It is to decide whether plaintiff's case, as made, was strong enough for us to allow the jury to consider it. To do this we must apply some standard. But we cannot weigh plaintiff's case against defendants'. Less than preponderance is sufficient. How much less is hard to state abstractly. Commonly the * * * [evidence] weighed, to stand, is required to be substantial, more than a scintilla, such as a reasonable man might believe. All these are just different ways of saying that less than preponderance is required, but the evidence should not be so thin that it would be dangerous for the jury to consider it.

The danger to be guarded against is a too obvious and gross miscarriage of justice, a departure too far from established lines of liability. Facts are primarily within the jury's function. Hence it must be given wide latitude, or trial by jury becomes trial by court. But the jury is not absolute in the realm of fact. Like judges, jurors have weaknesses of emotion and judgment. Unlike judges, they seldom have a background of decision experience against which to check them. Our tradition supplies this through judicial controls. Exclusion of evidence is one. When one side's case is thin, determining its "legal sufficiency" is another. This really means weighing it factually, not for conviction, but for doubt as to the outcome. The verdict sustained therefore represents the jurors' conviction that it is right, and the judge's that it may be right.

CHRISTIE v. CALLAHAN, 124 F.2d 825, 826–27 (D.C.Cir.1941) (Judge, later Mr. Justice, Rutledge).

(e) In this jurisdiction, unlike in some others, there need be only a scintilla of evidence to require reference of the issue raised thereby to the jury for decision. If there is "a mere 'gleam,' 'glimmer,' 'spark,' 'the least particle,' 'the smallest trace'—'a scintilla' " afforded from the evidence to sustain the issue, the court in duty bound must submit the question to the jury.

BARBER v. STEPHENSON, 260 Ala. 151, 156, 69 So.2d 251, 255–56 (1953).

4. Mr. Justice Frankfurter dissented in the *Rogers* case on the ground that certiorari had been "improvidently granted"; the justice declined to express himself on the merits. The case is one of many in which he argued that the Supreme Court should not take time to review cases in which the only issue was the sufficiency of the evidence to take a case to the jury. See pp. 1057–59, infra.

C. NEW TRIAL BECAUSE THE VERDICT IS AGAINST THE WEIGHT OF THE EVIDENCE

AETNA CASUALTY & SURETY CO. v. YEATTS

United States Circuit Court of Appeals, Fourth Circuit, 1941.
122 F.2d 350.

PARKER, Circuit Judge. This is the second appeal in a suit originally instituted to obtain a declaratory judgment with respect to the coverage of a policy of indemnity insurance. * * * The company denied liability on the ground that the defendant Yeatts was engaged in the performance of a criminal abortion at the time he incurred the liability for which the recovery was had against him, and that such liability was expressly excluded from the coverage of the policy. The question as to whether the defendant Yeatts was engaged in such criminal conduct was submitted to the jury, and from verdict and judgment in his favor the plaintiff brings this appeal.

There was testimony below from which the jury would have been amply justified in finding in favor of the plaintiff insurance company on the issue submitted; but the defendant himself was examined as a witness and, if his testimony is believed, he was guilty of no criminal act. No motion for directed verdict was made by the plaintiff, nor was the sufficiency of the evidence to sustain a finding in favor of the defendant challenged in any other way before verdict. After verdict, plaintiff moved for judgment non obstante veredicto and also for a new trial, on the ground that the verdict was contrary to the credible evidence in the case * * *.

Even if a motion for directed verdict had been made by plaintiff, it is clear that same should have been denied as should also, any motion for judgment non obstante veredicto based thereon * * *.

The motion to set aside the verdict and grant a new trial was a matter of federal procedure, governed by Rule * * * 59 and not subject in any way to the rules of state practice. On such a motion it is the duty of the judge to set aside the verdict and grant a new trial, if he is of opinion that the verdict is against the clear weight of the evidence, or is based upon evidence which is false, or will result in a miscarriage of justice, even though there may be substantial evidence which would prevent the direction of a verdict. The exercise of this power is not in derogation of the right of trial by jury but is one of the historic safeguards of that right. * * * The matter was well put by Mr. Justice Mitchell, speaking for the Supreme Court of Pennsylvania in Smith v. Times Publishing Co., * * * [178 Pa. 481, 36 A. 298], as follows: "The authority of the common pleas in the control and revision of excessive verdicts through the means of new trials was firmly settled in England before the foundation of this colony, and has always existed here without challenge under any of our constitutions. It is a power to examine the whole case on the law and the evidence, with a view to securing a result, not merely legal, but also not manifestly against justice,—a power exercised in pursuance of a sound judicial discretion, *without which the jury system would be a capricious and intolerable tyranny,* which no people could long endure. This court has had occasion more than once recently to say that it was *a power the courts ought to exercise unflinchingly.*" (Italics supplied).

In the same case, Mr. Justice Williams, in a concurring opinion, traces the history of the exercise of this power and sums up his conclusion as follows:
"* * *

"As early * * * as 1665, the courts at Westminster did precisely what we have done in this case, and for the same reason. The right of trial by jury was not then supposed to give to a successful party the right to insist on an advantage due to the mistake or the willful misconduct of the jury, no matter how grossly unjust and oppressive the result might be; but the supervisory control of the court in banc, sitting as a court of review, was promptly exercised to relieve against the miscarriage of justice. The exercise of this power was then thought to be in aid of trial by jury. * * *"

In 1757, Lord Mansfield in Bright v. Eynon, * * * [1 Burrows 390] had this to say with respect to the exercise of the power:

"Trials by jury in civil causes, could not subsist now without a power, *somewhere,* to grant new trials. * * * There are numberless *causes* of false verdicts, *without* corruption or bad intention of the jurors. They may have heard too much of the matter before the trial; and imbibed prejudices without knowing it. The cause may be intricate: the examination may be so long as to distract and confound their attention. Most general verdicts include *legal consequences* as well as propositions of fact: in drawing these consequences the jury may mistake, and infer directly contrary to law. The parties may be *surprised* by a case falsely made at the trial, which they had no reason to expect, and therefore could not come prepared to answer. If *unjust* verdicts obtained under these and a thousand like circumstances, were to be conclusive for ever, the determination of civil property, in this method of trial would be very precarious and unsatisfactory. It is absolutely *necessary to justice,* that there should, upon many occasions, be opportunities of *reconsidering* the cause by a new trial."

* * *

The distinction between the rules to be followed in granting a new trial and directing a verdict were stated by us with some care in Garrison v. United States, 4 Cir., 62 F.2d 41, 42, * * * as follows: "Where there is substantial evidence in support of plaintiff's case, the judge may not direct a verdict against him, even though he may not believe his evidence or may think that the weight of the evidence is on the other side; for, under the constitutional guaranty of trial by jury, it is for the jury to weigh the evidence and pass upon its credibility. He may, however, set aside a verdict supported by substantial evidence where in his opinion it is contrary to the clear weight of the evidence, or is based upon evidence which is false; for, even though the evidence be sufficient to preclude the direction of a verdict, it is still his duty to exercise his power over the proceedings before him to prevent a miscarriage of justice. * * *"

It is equally well settled, however, that the granting or refusing of a new trial is a matter of resting in the sound discretion of the trial judge, and that his action thereon is not reviewable upon appeal, save in the most exceptional circumstances. * * * The rule and the reason therefor is thus stated by Mr. Justice Brandeis in Fairmont Glass Works v. Cub Fork Coal Co., * * * [287 U.S. 474, 53 S.Ct. 254, 77 L.Ed. 439]: "The rule that this Court will not review the action of a federal trial court in granting or denying a motion for a new trial for error of fact has been settled by a long and unbroken line of decisions * * *. The rule precludes likewise a review of such action by a Circuit Court of Appeals. Its early formulation by this Court was influenced by the mandate of the Judiciary Act of 1789, which provided in section 22 that there should be 'no reversal in either (circuit or Supreme) court on such writ of error * * * for any error in fact.' Sometimes the rule has been rested on that part of the Seventh Amendment which provides that 'no fact tried by a jury, shall be otherwise reexamined in any court of the United States than according to the rules of the common law'. More frequently the reason given for the denial of review is that the granting or refusing of a motion for a new trial is a matter within the discretion of the trial court."

While an examination of the record has led us to the conclusion that the trial judge might very properly have granted the motion for new trial, we cannot say that his denial of the motion amounted to an abuse of discretion on his part or that there are present any of the special circumstances which would subject his action to review by this court. The judgment appealed from will accordingly be affirmed.

Affirmed.

NOTES AND QUESTIONS

1. Under Federal Rule 50(b), a party may move for judgment notwithstanding the verdict and in the alternative may move for a new trial on the ground that the jury's verdict is against the weight of the evidence; under Federal Rule 50(c), the district court judge must rule on both parts of the motion. If the judge can see no reasonable basis on which the jury's verdict can be supported and therefore orders judgment notwithstanding the verdict, does it follow that the court must find the verdict against the weight of the evidence and order a new trial in the alternative, which automatically would take effect if the grant of the judgment notwithstanding the verdict is reversed, or does the Rule 50(c) procedure confront the judge with a "dilemma"? See Momand v. Universal Film Exchange, Inc., 72 F.Supp. 469 (D.Mass.1947).

In MARSH v. ILLINOIS CENT. R. CO., 175 F.2d 498, 500 (5th Cir.1949), the district judge had granted judgment notwithstanding the verdict, but had denied an alternative motion for new trial, saying: "It is my judgment that the evidence was insufficient to go to the jury, but if I am wrong in that, then I do not think a new trial should be granted as there were no other errors of law." The court of appeals reversed:

> * * * While it is not our function to weigh the evidence, we do agree with the trial judge's first expressed opinion that the weight of the evidence is "overwhelmingly against the plaintiff". But we do not agree that the grant of a judgment notwithstanding the verdict was therefore justified. There was evidence of the appellant, not very explicit or positive, which if believed might authorize a jury to conclude he was hurt in the manner he claims. Because the trial judge does not believe it, because of appellant's own contradictions and conduct and of opposing evidence which seem to overwhelm it, is not ground for a judgment notwithstanding the verdict, and we must reverse that judgment. * * *

> But it is ground for the trial judge to grant a new trial, though the trial was free of other error. He has in strong terms disapproved the verdict as contrary to the evidence * * *. We have reversed the entering of a final judgment, but it is evident that the new trial ought to be granted and would have been except for the misconception that absence of other error prevented it. The full discretion vested in the trial judge not having been exercised, we will remand the case with direction to the judge to grant a new trial * * * if he continues to think the verdict to be against the overwhelming weight of the evidence.

2. In cases such as *Lavender v. Kurn,* p. 51, supra, and *Denman v. Spain,* p. 938, supra, when there is a lack of proof of what happened rather than a conflict of proof, would the grant of a new trial be any more appropriate than the direction of a verdict? In McCLAM v. NEW YORK LIFE INS. CO., 9 F.Supp. 415, 415–16 (E.D.S.C.1935), suit was brought for the proceeds of an insurance policy; plaintiff claimed death was accidental; defendant claimed it was suicide. The court, in granting a new trial, said:

> * * * Following Tabor v. Mutual Life Insurance Company [13 F.2d 765 (4th Cir.1926)] I reluctantly submitted the case to the jury. * * * The insured died from a gunshot wound concededly inflicted by his own hand (that is, without other human intervention), either acci-

dentally or with suicidal intent. If the jury be better qualified to pass upon this question than the court, as is stated in the Tabor Case, of what weight is the court's opinion in passing upon motion for a new trial? The jury was an average jury from all parts of the district, and may come within the definition "fair and impartial" as used by Judge Waddill. The conscience of the court was nevertheless shocked by the verdict; which, though rendered within a comparatively short time, was delayed sufficiently to indicate that there was a difference of opinion among the jurors. While the case went to the jury on the presumption against suicide under the Tabor Case, there was nothing more than the presumption to support plaintiff's allegation of accidental death. In the absence of any proof of accident other than surmise, such proof as definitely tended to show self-destruction or suicide was of much more weight. * * *

The court regrets that this order is not subject to review. The Tabor opinion should be either modified or carried out to its logical conclusion. The trial judge should know whether the principle extends to relief of his duty to grant a new trial, otherwise indicated, where the verdict of the jury is based upon its view of the question of suicide or accident.

3. In DYER v. MacDOUGALL, 201 F.2d 265, 271 (2d Cir.1952), Judge Frank, concurring, said:

* * * The well-settled rule is that, in passing on a motion for a directed verdict, the trial judge always must utterly disregard his own views of witnesses' credibility, and therefore of their demeanor; that he believes or disbelieves some of the testimony is irrelevant. When asked to direct a verdict for the defendant, the judge must assume that, if he lets the case go to the jury, the jurymen will believe all evidence— including "demeanor evidence"—favorable to the plaintiff. In other words, the judge must not deprive plaintiff of any advantage that plaintiff might derive from having the jury pass upon the oral testimony. Indeed, the important difference between a trial judge's power on a motion for a new trial and on a motion for a directed verdict is precisely that on a new-trial motion he may base his action on his belief or disbelief in some of the witnesses, while on a directed-verdict motion he may not.

Compare BOWDITCH v. BOSTON, 101 U.S. 16, 18, 25 L.Ed. 980, 980–81 (1880): "It is now a settled rule in the courts of the United States that whenever, in the trial of a civil case, it is clear that the state of the evidence is such as not to warrant a verdict for a party, and that if such a verdict were rendered the other party would be entitled to a new trial, it is the right and duty of the judge to direct the jury to find according to the views of the court." The *Bowditch* case is but one of many with language of this kind. For an excellent discussion of the standards for granting a directed verdict and a new trial on the weight of the evidence, see the scholarly opinion of Judge (later Mr. Justice) Lurton, in MT. ADAMS & E. P. INCLINED RY. v. LOWERY, 74 F. 463 (6th Cir.1896).

4. On the unreviewability of orders denying new trials, see Taylor v. Washington Terminal Co., 133 U.S.App.D.C. 110, 409 F.2d 145, 148 (D.C.Cir.), certiorari denied 396 U.S. 835, 90 S.Ct. 93, 24 L.Ed.2d 85 (1969); Wright, *The*

Doubtful Omniscience of Appellate Courts, 41 Minn.L.Rev. 751, 758–63 (1957); p. 1050–51, infra. On the circumstances in which an order granting a new trial may be reviewed, see pp. 954–56, infra.

5. Suppose a verdict has been set aside and a new trial granted. If the jury in the second trial returns a verdict similar to the one rendered in the first action, may the court again order a new trial on the ground that the verdict is against the weight of the evidence? *Compare* Palmer v. Miller, 60 F.Supp. 710 (W.D.Mo.1945) (yes), *with* Mo.Rev.Stat. (V.A.M.S.) § 510.330, which appears in the Supplement following Federal Rule 59. See 6A Moore, *Federal Practice* ¶ 59.08[5], at 3816–17 (2d ed.): "While there is probably no fixed limit at common law upon the number of new trials which the trial court may grant, solely because the verdict is against the weight of the evidence, the trial court must, nevertheless, realize that the successive grants of a new trial, on that ground, cannot be limitless without violating the constitutional right of jury trial."

DYER v. HASTINGS, 87 Ohio App. 147, 149–50, 94 N.E.2d 213, 215 (Ct.App. Hardin Co. 1950):

No judgment may be vacated or set aside and new trial granted upon the ground that the verdict is against the weight of the evidence except as a matter of law; and a judgment will not be vacated or set aside and a new trial granted upon such ground where the verdict is supported by competent, substantial and apparently credible evidence which goes to all the essential elements of the case.   *   *   *

In formulating this rule the word, "substantial," modifying the word, "evidence," is used in the sense of "constituting more than a scintilla of," and the word, "apparently," as used to modify the word "credible," is used to indicate that the court does not undertake to judge the credibility of the evidence, but only to judge whether it has the semblance of credibility.

The evidence in the instant case is in direct and sharp conflict on many essential elements of the case and is such that a verdict for either party would be supported by competent, substantial and apparently credible evidence.

In this situation it was the sole function of the jury to determine the credibility of the evidence, which it did by returning a verdict in favor of the defendant.

IN RE GREEN'S ESTATE, 25 Cal.2d 535, 542–43, 154 P.2d 692, 695–96 (1944):

It is next contended by contestant that the court erred in granting proponent's motion for a new trial on the ground "that the evidence as a whole was insufficient as a matter of law to support a verdict for respondents."

The rules of law applicable to an appeal from an order of the trial court granting a motion for a new trial on the ground of the insufficiency of the evidence are well settled and, as stated in one of our most recent decisions, are as follows: " * * * When the motion is granted, as here, for insufficiency of the evidence, it is only in rare cases showing abuse of discretion that an appellate court will interfere because the trial judge must weigh all the evidence and determine the just conclusion to be drawn therefrom. * * * It cannot be held that a trial court has abused its discretion where there is a conflict in the evidence or where there is any evidence which would support a judgment in favor of the moving party." Hames v. Rust, 14 Cal. 2d 119, 123, 124, 92 P.2d 1010, 1012.

* * *

We may not agree with the determination reached by the trial judge or with any of his conclusions. That is not the question before us. It is his duty to weigh the evidence and to pass upon any and all conflicts existing therein. * * * If after such an examination of the evidence he concludes that it is insufficient to support the verdict, his duty is to grant the motion and a reviewing court may not set aside his conclusion unless a showing of abuse of discretion is made out by appellant. * * * As we have seen, if there is any substantial evidence in the case supporting the trial court's action, then we should not interfere with its order granting said motion.

NOTES AND QUESTIONS

1. As for equating the test for directing a verdict to that for setting aside a verdict and granting a new trial, the matter is complicated by the wide range among the tests used in different jurisdictions for setting a verdict aside. * * * [T]he equation is more nearly valid in some jurisdictions than it is in others, but the differences are rather because of variations in the new trial test than because of any variation in the directed verdict test.

James, *Sufficiency of the Evidence and Jury-Control Devices Available Before Verdict*, 47 Va.L.Rev. 218, 233–34 (1961). See also James, *Civil Procedure* § 7.13, at 286 (1965).

2. It is difficult to ascertain the standard for granting a new trial in a particular jurisdiction and to compare it with the standard applied in another jurisdiction because of peculiarities regarding the appealability, reviewability, and scope of review of a decision on a motion for a new trial. In many jurisdictions the grant of a new trial may be unappealable because it is not a "final order"; even if appealable, a grant or denial of the motion may not be disturbed on appeal except upon a showing of an abuse of discretion by the trial court, which is rarely found. The result is that the new-trial standard actually is formulated and controlled by trial, not appellate courts; inasmuch as the standard is shaped by courts whose opinions are infrequently reported and therefore will not provide a guideline for other courts, or provide a body of precedent, the standard may vary widely from case to case.

In GREEN v. ACACIA MUT. LIFE INS. CO., 156 Ohio St. 1, 100 N.E.2d 211 (1951), the Ohio Supreme Court held unconstitutional the statute under which the Ohio Court of Appeals in *Dyer v. Hastings* had reviewed the grant of a new trial, because it conferred authority on the Ohio Courts of Appeals to review non-final judgments.   In AID INVESTMENT & DISCOUNT, INC. v. YOUNKIN, 66 Ohio L.Abs. 514, 118 N.E.2d 183 (Ct.App. Franklin Co. 1951), another court of appeals, reviewing a grant of a new trial, held that by reason of *Green* it could reverse only if it found an abuse of discretion, and, that, although it regarded the trial court's order as erroneous it could not say it was an abuse of discretion.   Do *Green* and *Younkin* affect the standard for granting a new trial in Ohio announced in *Dyer v. Hastings?*

3.   In *In re Green's Estate* is the California Supreme Court discussing a standard for granting the motion for a new trial or a standard for reviewing the grant of the motion?

LIND v. SCHENLEY INDUSTRIES, INC., 278 F.2d 79, 90–91 (3d Cir.), certiorari denied 364 U.S. 835, 81 S.Ct. 58, 5 L.Ed.2d 60 (1960).   A jury verdict for plaintiff had been set aside, and judgment n.o.v. ordered for defendant as well as a new trial in the event the judgment for defendant should be reversed.   The Court of Appeals, en banc (5–2), held that the trial court erred both in granting judgment n.o.v. and in granting the new trial:

> * * * [T]here is no consensus of opinion as to the exact standards to be used by a trial court in granting a new trial and * * * the criteria to be employed by an appellate tribunal charged with reviewing the trial judge's decision in this respect are equally indefinite.   New trials granted because (1) a jury verdict is against the weight of the evidence may be sharply distinguished from (2) new trials ordered for other reasons: for example, evidence improperly admitted, prejudicial statements by counsel, an improper charge to the jury or newly discovered evidence. * * * In the latter instances something occurred in the course of the trial which resulted or which may have resulted in the jury receiving a distorted, incorrect, or an incomplete view of the operative facts, or some undesirable element obtruded itself into the proceedings creating a condition whereby the giving of a just verdict was rendered difficult or impossible. * * * Under these conditions there is no usurpation by the court of the prime function of the jury as the trier of the facts and the trial judge necessarily must be allowed wide discretion in granting or refusing a new trial.
>
> But where no undesirable or pernicious element has occurred or been introduced into the trial and the trial judge nonetheless grants a new trial on the ground that the verdict was against the weight of the evidence, the trial judge in negating the jury's verdict has, to some extent at least, substituted his judgment of the facts and the credibility of the witnesses for that of the jury. * * * It then becomes the duty of the appellate tribunal to exercise a

closer degree of scrutiny and supervision than is the case where a
new trial is granted because of some undesirable or pernicious
influence obtruding into the trial.   *   *   *

Where a trial is long and complicated and deals with a subject
matter not lying within the ordinary knowledge of jurors a verdict
should be scrutinized more closely by the trial judge than is necessary where the litigation deals with material which is familiar
and simple, the evidence relating to ordinary commercial practices.
An example of subject matter unfamiliar to a layman would be a
case requiring a jury to pass upon the nature of an alleged newly
discovered organic compound in an infringement action.   *   *   *
A prime example of subject matter lying well within the comprehension of jurors is presented by the circumstances at bar.

The subject matter of the litigation before us is simple and
easily comprehended by any intelligent layman.   The jury's main
function was to determine the veracity of the witnesses: i. e. what
testimony should be believed.   If Lind's testimony and that of
Mrs. Kennan, Kaufman's secretary, was deemed credible, Lind
presented a convincing, indeed an overwhelming case.   We must
conclude that the jury did believe this testimony and that the court
below substituted its judgment for that of the jury on this issue
and thereby abused its legal discretion.

NOTES

1.   In DAILY v. TIMMER, 292 F.2d 824 (3d Cir.1961), the court of appeals "dismissed for lack of jurisdiction" an appeal from an order granting a new
trial, distinguishing *Lind* on the ground that "this Court, in that case, had jurisdiction because there was an appeal from a judgment N.O.V.," and the "new
trial action was incidental to the main point."

2.   In DUNCAN v. DUNCAN, 377 F.2d 49 (6th Cir.1967), after a verdict for defendant, the trial court, on plaintiff's motion, ordered a new trial,
which resulted in a verdict for the plaintiff.   On appeal from the judgment in
the second trial, the court of appeals held that the grant of the new trial was an
abuse of discretion and ordered the entry of judgment for defendant.

D. JUDGMENT NOTWITHSTANDING THE VERDICT IN THE FEDERAL COURTS—A PROCEDURAL MUDDLE

———

Read Federal Rules of Civil Procedure 50(b), (c), and (d) and the accompanying material in the Supplement.

———

SLOCUM v. NEW YORK LIFE INSURANCE CO.

Supreme Court of the United States, 1913.
228 U.S. 364, 33 S.Ct. 523, 57 L.Ed. 879.

Certiorari to the United States Circuit Court of Appeals for the Third Circuit.

Mr. Justice VAN DEVANTER delivered the opinion of the court.

* * * The case made by the evidence, in that view of it which is most favorable to the plaintiff, was as follows: [Defendant insurer issued a policy of life insurance to plaintiff's decedent on November 27, 1899; death occurred December 31, 1907. The annual premium due November 27, 1907, was not paid, but on the last day of the grace period, December 27, plaintiff paid a portion of it in cash and received a note, to be signed by the decedent, for the balance; plaintiff told the agent that her husband was ill and might not be able to sign the note for several days and was told to mail the note as soon as she could. Decedent died before signing the note. Plaintiff brought suit on the policy in a federal circuit court; defendant's motion for a directed verdict at the close of the evidence was denied. The jury returned a verdict for plaintiff. In accordance with Pennsylvania practice, defendant moved for judgment notwithstanding the verdict which was also denied. On writ of error, the circuit court of appeals reversed the judgment for plaintiff with instructions to sustain the motion for judgment n. o. v. "on the ground that the evidence did not legally admit of the conclusion that the policy was a subsisting contract of insurance at the date of the insured's death."] * * *

We are * * * of opinion that the evidence did not admit of a finding that the policy was in force at the time of the insured's death, and therefore that the circuit court should have granted the company's request that a verdict in its favor be directed. As that request was denied, the circuit court of appeals did not err in reversing the judgment.

It becomes necessary, therefore, to consider whether that court should have directed a new trial instead of a judgment on the evidence contrary to the verdict.

* * * [T]he circuit court of appeals directed a judgment for one party when the verdict was for the other, and did this on the theory, not that the judgment was required by the state of the pleadings, but that it was warranted by the evidence. It will be perceived, therefore, that the court * * * did not order a new trial, but assumed to pass finally upon the issues of fact presented by the pleadings and to direct a judgment accordingly. If this was an infraction of the 7th Amendment, it matters not that it was in conformity with the state statute, or with the practice thereunder in the courts of the state, for neither the statute nor the practice could be followed in opposition to the Amendment, which, although not applicable to proceedings in the courts of the several states, is controlling in the Federal courts.

* * *

In Parsons v. Bedford, 3 Pet. 433, 7 L.Ed. 732, decided in 1830, [Mr. Justice Story] * * * [analyzing] the clause * * * "no fact tried by a jury shall be otherwise re-examined in any court of the United States, than according to the rules of the common law," * * * [stated] (pp. 447, 448): "This is a prohibition to the courts of the United States to re-examine any facts tried by a jury in any other manner. The only modes known to the common law to re-examine such facts are the granting of a new trial by the court where the issue was tried, or to which the record was properly returnable; or the award of a venire facias de novo, by an appellate court, for some error of law which intervened in the proceedings."

* * * [It is] plain, first, that the action of the circuit court of appeals in setting aside the verdict and assuming to pass upon the issues of fact, and to direct a judgment accordingly, must be tested by the rules of the common law; second, that while under those rules that court could set aside the verdict for error of law in the proceedings in the circuit court, and order a new trial, it could not itself determine the facts; and, third, that when the verdict was set aside there arose the same right of trial by jury as in the first instance. How, then, can it be said that there was not an infraction of the 7th Amendment? When the verdict was set aside the issues of fact were left undetermined, and until they should be determined anew no judgment on the merits could be given. The new determination, according to the rules of the common law, could be had only through a new trial, with the same right to a jury as before. Disregarding those rules, the circuit court of appeals itself determined the facts, without a new trial. Thus, it assumed a power it did not possess, and cut off the plaintiff's right to have the facts settled by the verdict of a jury.

While it is true * * * that the evidence produced at the trial was not sufficient to sustain a verdict for the plaintiff, and that the circuit court erred in refusing so to instruct the jury, this does not militate against the conclusion just stated. According to the rules of the common law, such an error, like other errors of law affecting a verdict, could be corrected on writ of error only by ordering a new trial. * * * And this procedure was regarded as of real value, because, in addition to fully recognizing that right, it afforded an opportunity for adducing further evidence rightly conducing to a solution of the issues.

*   *   *   [W]hile it is the province of the court to aid the jury in the right discharge of their duty, even to the extent of directing their verdict where the insufficiency or conclusive character of the evidence warrants such a direction, the court cannot dispense with a verdict, or disregard one when given, and itself pass on the issues of fact. In other words, the constitutional guaranty operates to require that the issues be settled by the verdict of a jury, unless the right thereto be waived. *   *   *

*   *   *   At the trial the defendant requested that a verdict in its favor be directed, and had the court indicated its purpose to do that, it would have been open to the plaintiff, under the then prevailing practice, to take a voluntary nonsuit, which would have enabled her to make a fuller and better presentation of her case, if the facts permitted, at another trial in a new suit. *   *   *

The judgment of the Circuit Court of Appeals is accordingly modified by eliminating the direction to enter judgment for the defendant notwithstanding the verdict, and by substituting a direction for a new trial.

Mr. Justice HUGHES, dissenting:

I concur in the decision of the court so far as it holds that the circuit court of appeals was right in reversing the judgment; but I am unable to agree with the conclusion that the circuit court of appeals was bound to order a new trial *   *   *.

The serious and far-reaching consequences of this decision are manifest. Not only does it overturn the established practice of the Federal courts in Pennsylvania in applying, under the conformity act, the provisions of the state law, but it erects an impassable barrier—unless the Constitution be amended —to action by Congress along the same line for the purpose of remedying the mischief of repeated trials, and of thus diminishing in a highly important degree the delays and expense of litigation. It cannot be gainsaid that such a conclusion is not to be reached unless the constitutional provision compels it. I cannot see that it does compel it.

*   *   *   [W]herein has any matter of fact tried by a jury been re-examined? Concededly, there was no fact to be tried by a jury; the case as made was barren of any such fact; and there being none, there has been no re-examination of it. How can it be said that the circuit court of appeals has determined the facts or has passed upon issues of fact? Whether there was any evidence for the jury was a question of law. The trial court, in wrongly deciding it, did not convert it into a question of fact; it was not altered by the verdict, but remained the same in its nature,—a question for the determination of the court. That, it seems to me, is the substance of the matter, and all else is form and procedure. *   *   *   [I]t is not a matter withdrawn from legislative control by the constitutional provision for trial by jury, which is concerned with the settlement of disputes of fact, and not with the determination of legal questions, or with the consequences, which should ensue when that determination is decisive of the right of recovery on the case made.

* * *

The dominating idea, in overturning the practice below, seems to be that at common law, if there was an issue of fact upon the pleadings, the plaintiff was entitled to have a verdict taken in any event; that is, if he did not voluntarily take a nonsuit, it was essential that a verdict be rendered, notwithstanding that upon the evidence there was no question of fact for the jury.

* * *

It is not a new thing that a party should be able to challenge the legal sufficiency of the evidence adduced against him, and call upon the court to answer the question of law whether, upon the facts shown, there should be a recovery, nor is it a new thing that when he does so the court should give judgment without the intervention of the jury, and if the trial court errs in its ruling upon the law, the reviewing court should set the matter right and order the proper judgment to be entered.

This was accomplished by demurring to the evidence.   *   *   *

If, on a demurrer to the evidence, judgment was given for one party when it should have been given for the other, the error was corrected in the appellate tribunal by directing the proper judgment.   It is now said, in referring to this practice, that this was because the error was confined to the judgment, and did not reach the facts as ascertained and shown in the demurrer.   But what was the error?   What was the basis of the judgment, and upon what ground was it reversed and the proper judgment directed?   The facts, by the proceeding on the demurrer, were made a part of the record, and the question of the legal sufficiency of the evidence was thus one of law arising upon the record.   The court dealt with the question of law, that is, with the legal insufficiency of the evidence, and directed judgment which, as matter of law, followed the case made.

* * *

It is said that there was a *voluntary* joinder in demurrer. * * * Whether a demurrer should be allowed was the initial question for the trial court; but if the case was one where it was proper to allow the demurrer, and it was duly taken and allowed, the other party was not entitled to stand on his evidence and go to the jury.   Let it be assumed that he could take a nonsuit; but this is not to say that by refusing to join in the demurrer he had the right to have his case, although insufficient in law for that purpose, submitted to the decision of the jury.   Of course, if there were some defect or variance which he believed he could remedy, it would be natural for him to withdraw his case; but if he had proved all he could possibly prove, there would be no reason for a withdrawal unless he was willing to abandon the litigation.   If he did not desire to do this, but wished to proceed, insisting upon the legal sufficiency of the evidence to which the demurrer was taken, he had to join in it.
* * *

This is all, as it seems to me, that the Pennsylvania practice comes to. Had the old practice obtained, and had there been a demurrer to the evidence in this case, this court, in view of its holding that the "evidence did not admit of a finding that the policy was in force at the time of the insured's death," must necessarily have concluded that the demurrer was well taken; that the trial court would have been justified in directing judgment for the defendant without submitting the case to the jury; and that if it had not decided the question correctly, the appellate court could so decide it and direct the entry of that judgment. The rest of the matter was simply the exercise of caution to avoid unnecessary litigation by taking the verdict of the jury so that it might be available if it appeared that the case was one for the jury.

*   *   *

It is said, however, that a new trial affords opportunity to a plaintiff to better his case by presenting evidence which may not have been available before. But we are not dealing with an application for a new trial upon the ground of newly discovered evidence, or with the principles controlling an application of that sort. We are concerned with the question whether a party has a constitutional right to another trial, simply because the trial court erred in its determination of a question of law which was decisive of the case made. Had the trial court done what this court says it should have done, it would have directed a verdict for the defendant; and if the jury, simply following the instruction of the trial court, had so found, final judgment would have been entered and no new trial would now be granted. Still the jury would not have passed upon any question of fact, but would simply have obeyed the judge. The opportunity to better the case on a second trial would probably be as welcome, but it would not be accorded. I am unable to see any basis for a constitutional distinction which raises a constitutional right to another trial in the one case and not in the other.

*   *   *

I am authorized to say that Mr. Justice HOLMES, Mr. Justice LURTON, and Mr. Justice PITNEY concur in this dissent.

NOTES AND QUESTIONS

1. Under the Federal Rules, does a plaintiff have a right to a voluntary nonsuit that would allow the action to be recommenced? See Wall v. Connecticut Mut. Life Ins. Co., 2 F.R.D. 244 (S.D.Ga.1941). See pp. 768–69, supra.

2. How do the Federal Rules provide for the case in which a jury refuses to return a verdict as directed? Is this procedure consistent with the majority opinion in *Slocum?*

BALTIMORE & CAROLINA LINE, INC. v. REDMAN, 295 U.S. 654, 656, 658–60, 55 S.Ct. 890, 891–93, 79 L.Ed. 1636, 1637–40 (1935) (opinion by Mr. Justice Van Devanter):

This was an action in a federal court in New York to recover damages for personal injuries allegedly sustained by the plaintiff through the defendant's negligence. The issues were tried before the court and a jury. At conclusion of the evidence, the defendant moved for a dismissal of the complaint because the evidence was insufficient to support a verdict for the plaintiff, and also moved for a directed verdict in its favor on the same ground. The court reserved its decision on both motions, submitted the case to the jury subject to its opinion on the questions reserved, and received from the jury a verdict for the plaintiff. No objection was made to the reservation or this mode of proceeding. Thereafter the court held the evidence sufficient and the motions ill grounded, and accordingly entered a judgment for the plaintiff on the verdict.

The defendant appealed to the Circuit Court of Appeals, which held the evidence insufficient and reversed the judgment with a direction for a new trial. The defendant urged that the direction be for a dismissal of the complaint. But the Court of Appeals ruled that under our decision in Slocum v. New York Life Insurance Company the direction must be for a new trial. * * *

A very different situation [from *Slocum*] is disclosed in the present case. The trial court expressly reserved its ruling on the defendant's motions to dismiss and for a directed verdict, both of which were based on the asserted insufficiency of the evidence to support a verdict for the plaintiff. Whether the evidence was sufficient or otherwise was a question of law to be resolved by the court. The verdict for the plaintiff was taken pending the court's rulings on the motions and subject to those rulings. No objection was made to the reservation or this mode of proceeding, and they must be regarded as having the tacit consent of the parties. * * *

At common law there was a well-established practice of reserving questions of law arising during trials by jury and of taking verdicts subject to the ultimate ruling on the questions reserved; and under this practice the reservation carried with it authority to make such ultimate disposition of the case as might be made essential by the ruling under the reservation, such as nonsuiting the plaintiff where he had obtained a verdict, entering a verdict or judgment for one party where the jury had given a verdict to the other, or making other essential adjustments.

Fragmentary references to the origin and basis of the practice indicate that it came to be supported on the theory that it gave better opportunity for considered rulings, made new trials less frequent, and commanded such general approval that parties litigant assented to its application as a matter of course. But whatever may have been its origin or theoretical basis, it undoubtedly was well established when the Seventh Amendment was adopted, and therefore must be regarded as a part of the common-law rules to which resort must be had in testing and measuring the right of trial by jury as preserved and protected by that amendment.

NOTES AND QUESTIONS

1. How critical is the fact, emphasized by the Court, that plaintiff in the *Redman* case did not object to the reservation of the decision on the motion for a directed verdict? Does Federal Rule 50(b) require the nonmoving party's consent?

2. In *Lo Cicero v. Columbia Cas. Co.*, p. 946, supra, plaintiff had not asked that the jury be charged that the policeman was guilty of negligence as a matter of law in failing to sound a siren nor did plaintiff object to the failure so to charge. Although the jury returned a verdict for defendant, the court of appeals reversed, holding that the policeman was negligent as a matter of law, and remanded the case for a determination of the issues of proximate cause, contributory negligence, and last clear chance. Is this result consistent with the requirement that before judgment n.o.v. can be entered for a party, by a trial or an appellate court, the party must have moved for a directed verdict? Is that requirement inapplicable to any ruling that forecloses jury determination of a factual issue that does not by itself dispose of the entire claim?

3. If defendant moves for a directed verdict at the close of plaintiff's case, may defendant, without renewing the directed-verdict motion, move for judgment n.o.v. after verdict? May defendant seek a new trial by raising the denial of the earlier motion as error on appeal? *Cf.* Union Pac. Ry. v. Daniels, 152 U.S. 684, 14 S.Ct. 756, 38 L.Ed. 597 (1894). Are your answers to these questions related to the doctrine that defendant may not move for a directed verdict without resting his case? See Columbia & P. S. R. R. v. Hawthorne, 144 U.S. 202, 12 S.Ct. 591, 36 L.Ed. 405 (1892).

NEELY v. MARTIN K. EBY CONSTRUCTION CO.

Supreme Court of the United States, 1967.
386 U.S. 317, 87 S.Ct. 1072, 18 L.Ed.2d 75.

Certiorari to the United States Court of Appeals for the Tenth Circuit.

Mr. Justice WHITE delivered the opinion of the Court.

Petitioner brought this diversity action in the United States District Court for the District of Colorado alleging that respondent's negligent construction, maintenance, and supervision of a scaffold platform used in the construction of a missile silo near Elizabeth, Colorado, had proximately caused her father's fatal plunge from the platform during the course of his employment as Night Silo Captain for   *   *   *   an engineering firm engaged in the construction of a missile launcher system in the silo. At the close of the petitioner's evidence and again at the close of all the evidence, respondent moved for a directed verdict. The trial judge denied both motions and submitted the case to a jury, which returned a verdict for petitioner for $25,000.

Respondent then moved for judgment notwithstanding the jury's verdict or, in the alternative, for a new trial * * *. The trial court denied the motions and entered judgment for petitioner on the jury's verdict. * * *

The Court of Appeals held that the evidence at trial was insufficient to establish either negligence by respondent or proximate cause and reversed the judgment of the District Court "with instructions to dismiss the action." * * * [P]etitioner then sought a writ of certiorari, presenting the question whether the Court of Appeals could, consistent with the 1963 amendments to Rule 50 * * * and with the Seventh Amendment's guarantee of a right to jury trial, direct the trial court to dismiss the action. Our order allowing certiorari directed the parties' attention to whether Rule 50(d) and our decisions in Cone v. West Virginia Pulp & Paper Co., 330 U.S. 212, 67 S.Ct. 752, 91 L.Ed. 849; Globe Liquor Co. v. San Roman, 332 U.S. 571, 68 S.Ct. 246, 92 L.Ed. 177; and Weade v. Dichmann, Wright & Pugh, Inc., 337 U.S. 801, 69 S.Ct. 1326, 93 L.Ed. 1704, permit this disposition by a court of appeals despite Rule 50(c) (2), which gives a party whose jury verdict is set aside by a trial court 10 days in which to invoke the trial court's discretion to order a new trial.[3] We affirm.

* * *

The question here is whether the Court of Appeals, after reversing the denial of a defendant's Rule 50(b) motion for judgment notwithstanding the verdict, may itself order dismissal or direct entry of judgment for defendant. As far as the Seventh Amendment's right to jury trial is concerned, there is no greater restriction on the province of the jury when an appellate court enters judgment n. o. v. than when a trial court does; consequently, there is no constitutional bar to an appellate court granting judgment n. o. v.

* * * Federal Rules 50(c) and 50(d) * * * were added to Rule 50 in 1963 to clarify the proper practice under this Rule. Though Rule 50(d) is more pertinent to the facts of this case, it is useful to examine these interrelated provisions together. * * * As the Advisory Committee's Note to Rule 50(c) makes clear, Rule 50(c) (1) contemplates that the appellate court will review on appeal both the grant of judgment n. o. v. and, if necessary, the trial court's conditional disposition of the motion for new trial. This review necessarily includes the power to grant or to deny a new trial in appropriate cases.

Rule 50(d) is applicable to cases such as this one where the trial court has denied a motion for judgment n. o. v. Rule 50(d) expressly preserves to the party who prevailed in the district court the right to urge that the court of appeals grant a new trial should the jury's verdict be set aside on appeal. Rule 50(d) also emphasizes that "nothing in the rule precludes" the court of appeals "from determining that the appellee is entitled to a new trial, or from

---

3 * * * In view of the question presented by petitioner and our order granting certiorari, we do not consider whether the Court of Appeals correctly held that petitioner's evidence of negligence and proximate cause was insufficient to go to the jury.

directing the trial court to determine whether a new trial shall be granted."
Quite properly, this Rule recognizes that the appellate court may prefer that
the trial judge pass first upon the appellee's new trial suggestion. Nevertheless, consideration of the new trial question "in the first instance" is lodged
with the court of appeals.   *   *   *

Rule 50(c) (2)   *   *   *   is on its face inapplicable to the situation
presented here. That Rule regulates the verdict winner's opportunity to move
for a new trial if the *trial court* has granted a Rule 50(b) motion for judgment
n. o. v. In this case, the trial court denied judgment n. o. v. and respondent
appealed. Jurisdiction over the case then passed to the Court of Appeals, and
petitioner's right to seek a new trial in the trial court after her jury verdict was
set aside became dependent upon the disposition by the Court of Appeals under Rule 50(d).

*   *   *   In Cone v. West Virginia Pulp & Paper Co., supra, the defendant moved for directed verdict, but the trial judge sent the case to the jury.
After a jury verdict for the plaintiff, the trial court denied defendant's motion
for a new trial. On appeal, the Court of Appeals reversed and ordered the entry of judgment n. o. v. This Court reversed the Court of Appeals on the
ground that the defendant had not moved for judgment n. o. v. in the trial
court, but only for a new trial, and consequently the Court of Appeals was precluded from directing any disposition other than a new trial.   *   *   *   In
Johnson v. New York, N. H. & H. R. R., 344 U.S. 48, 73 S.Ct. 125, 97 L.Ed.
77, this Court held that a verdict loser's motion to "set aside" the jury's verdict
did not comply with Rule 50(b)'s requirement of a timely motion for judgment n. o. v. and therefore that the Court of Appeals could not direct entry of
judgment n. o. v. And in Weade v. Dichmann, Wright & Pugh, Inc., supra,
where a proper motion for judgment n. o. v. was made and denied in the trial
court, we modified a Court of Appeals decision directing entry of judgment n.
o. v. because there were "suggestions in the complaint and evidence" of an alternative theory of liability which had not been passed upon by the jury and
therefore which might justify the grant of a new trial.   *   *   *

The opinions in the above cases make it clear that an appellate court may
not order judgment n. o. v. where the verdict loser has failed strictly to comply
with the procedural requirements of Rule 50(b), or where the record reveals a
new trial issue which has not been resolved. Part of the Court's concern has
been to protect the rights of the party whose jury verdict has been set aside on
appeal and who may have valid grounds for a new trial, some or all of which
should be passed upon by the district court, rather than the court of appeals,
because of the trial judge's first-hand knowledge of witnesses, testimony, and
issues—because of his "feel" for the overall case. These are very valid concerns to which the court of appeals should be constantly alert. Where a defendant moves for n. o. v. in the trial court, the plaintiff may present, in connection with that motion or with a separate motion after n. o. v. is granted, his
grounds for a new trial or voluntary nonsuit. Clearly, where he retains his
verdict in the trial court and the defendant appeals, plaintiff should have the
opportunity which 50(d) affords him to press those same or different grounds

in the court of appeals. And obviously judgment for defendant-appellant should not be ordered where the plaintiff-appellee urges grounds for a nonsuit or new trial which should more appropriately be addressed to the trial court.

But these considerations do not justify an ironclad rule that the court of appeals should never order dismissal or judgment for defendant when the plaintiff's verdict has been set aside on appeal. Such a rule would not serve the purpose of Rule 50 to speed litigation and to avoid unnecessary retrials. * * *

There are, on the one hand, situations where the defendant's grounds for setting aside the jury's verdict raise questions of subject matter jurisdiction or dispositive issues of law which, if resolved in defendant's favor, must necessarily terminate the litigation. * * *

On the other hand, where the court of appeals sets aside the jury's verdict because the evidence was insufficient to send the case to the jury, it is not so clear that the litigation should be terminated. Although many of the plaintiff-appellee's possible grounds for a new trial, such as inadequacy of the verdict, will not survive a decision that the case should not have gone to the jury in the first place, there remain important considerations which may entitle him to a new trial. The erroneous exclusion of evidence which would have strengthened his case is an important possibility. Another is that the trial court itself caused the insufficiency in plaintiff-appellee's case by erroneously placing too high a burden of proof on him at trial. But issues like these are issues of law with which the courts of appeals regularly and characteristically must deal. The district court in all likelihood has already ruled on these questions in the course of the trial and, in any event, has no special advantage or competence in dealing with them. They are precisely the kind of issues that the losing defendant below may bring to the court of appeals without ever moving for a new trial in the district court. * * *

A plaintiff whose jury verdict is set aside by the trial court on defendant's n. o. v. motion may ask the trial judge to grant a voluntary nonsuit to give plaintiff another chance to fill a gap in his proof. * * * The plaintiff-appellee should have this same opportunity when his verdict is set aside on appeal. Undoubtedly, in many cases this question will call for an exercise of the trial court's discretion. However, there is no substantial reason why the appellee should not present the matter to the court of appeals, which can if necessary remand the case to permit initial consideration by the district court.

* * *

In our view, therefore, Rule 50(d) makes express and adequate provision for the opportunity—which the plaintiff-appellee had without this rule—to present his grounds for a new trial in the event his verdict is set aside by the court of appeals. If he does so in his brief—or in a petition for rehearing if the court of appeals has directed entry of judgment for appellant—the court of appeals may make final disposition of the issues presented, except those which in its informed discretion should be reserved for the trial court. If appellee presents no new trial issues in his brief or in a petition for rehearing, the court of appeals may, in any event, order a new trial on its own motion or refer the question to the district court, based on factors encountered in its own review of the case.   *   *   *

In the case before us, petitioner won a verdict in the District Court which survived respondent's n. o. v. motion.   In the Court of Appeals the issue was the sufficiency of the evidence and that court set aside the verdict.   Petitioner, as appellee, suggested no grounds for a new trial in the event her judgment was reversed, nor did she petition for rehearing in the Court of Appeals, even though that court had directed a dismissal of her case.   Neither was it suggested that the record was insufficient to present any new trial issues or that any other reason required a remand to the District Court.   Indeed, in her brief in the Court of Appeals, petitioner stated, "this law suit was fairly tried and the jury was properly instructed."   It was, of course, incumbent on the Court of Appeals to consider the new trial question in the light of its own experience with the case.   But we will not assume that the court ignored its duty in this respect, although it would have been better had its opinion expressly dealt with the new trial question.

*   *   *

Affirmed.

Mr. Justice DOUGLAS and Mr. Justice FORTAS, while agreeing with the Court's construction of Rule 50, would reverse the judgment because in their view the evidence of negligence and proximate cause was sufficient to go to the jury.

Mr. Justice BLACK, dissenting.

I dissent from the Court's decision in this case for three reasons: First, I think the evidence in this case was clearly sufficient to go to the jury on the issues of both negligence and proximate cause.   Second, I think that under our prior decisions and Rule 50, a court of appeals, in reversing a trial court's refusal to enter judgment n. o. v. on the ground of insufficiency of the evidence, is entirely powerless to order the trial court to dismiss the case, thus depriving the verdict winner of any opportunity to present a motion for new trial to the trial judge who is thoroughly familiar with the case.   Third, even if a court of appeals has that power, I find it manifestly unfair to affirm the Court of Appeals' judgment here without giving this petitioner a chance to present her grounds for a new trial to the Court of Appeals as the Court today for the first time holds she must.

*   *   *

Since the adoption of Rule 50, our cases have consistently and emphatically preserved the right of a litigant whose judgment—whether it be a judgment entered on the verdict or judgment n. o. v.—is set aside to invoke the discretion of the trial court in ruling on a motion for new trial.   The first of these cases was Montgomery Ward & Co. v. Duncan, 311 U.S. 243, 61 S.Ct. 189, 85 L.Ed. 147, where the trial judge, unlike here, granted the defendant's motion for judgment n. o. v., but in doing so failed to rule on his alternative motion for a new trial.   The Court of Appeals reversed the trial court's grant of judgment n. o. v. to the defendant and remanded the case with directions to enter judgment on the verdict for the plaintiff. * * * Holding that the trial judge should have initially ruled on this alternative motion, this Court remanded the case to the trial judge for the purpose of passing on that motion. In explaining this result the Court said:

> "The rule contemplates that either party to the action is entitled to the trial judge's decision on both motions, if both are presented. * * *"
> * * *

This issue of whether a new trial is justified after a verdict is set aside either by a trial or an appellate court is a new issue which it was not necessary to decide in the original trial. It is a factual issue and that the trial court is the more appropriate tribunal to determine it has been almost universally accepted by both federal and state courts throughout the years. * * * Appellate tribunals are not equipped to try factual issues as trial courts are. A trial judge who has heard the evidence in the original case has a vast store of information and knowledge about it that the appellate court cannot get from a cold, printed record. Thus, as we said in *Cone*, the trial judge can base the broad discretion granted him in determining factual issues of a new trial on his own knowledge of the evidence and the issues "in a perspective peculiarly available to him alone." * * *

NOTES AND QUESTIONS

1. Reread Note 1, p. 951, supra. If the trial judge denies defendant's alternative motions for judgment n.o.v. and new trial, and the court of appeals finds that the lower court should have granted judgment n.o.v., but remands in order to permit the trial judge to consider a motion for a new trial by plaintiff, will the trial judge be confronted by a dilemma similar to the one described in the earlier Note?

2. In *Johnson v. New York, N. H. & H. R. Co.*, discussed in the *Neely* case, defendant's lawyer moved "to set aside the verdict on the ground that it is contrary to the law and contrary to the evidence and contrary to the weight of the evidence and excessive." The motion was denied, but the court of appeals directed that judgment n.o.v. for defendant be entered. The Supreme Court reversed, holding that the court of appeals could not order such a judgment in the absence of a motion for judgment n.o.v. after the return of the jury verdict and that the motion defendant's lawyer made could not be considered to constitute such a motion.

If a motion for directed verdict is made and denied, and the jury returns a verdict for the nonmoving party, may the trial court grant judgment n.o.v. for the party who asked for the directed verdict even if that party makes no motion for one? Should it make any difference how long after the verdict the court acts? Should it make any difference whether the trial judge has "expressly" reserved decision on the motion for a directed verdict? See First Safe Deposit Nat. Bank

v. Western Union Tel. Co., 337 F.2d 743 (1st Cir.1964); Shaw v. Edward Hines Lumber Co., 249 F.2d 434 (7th Cir.1957).

    3.   If a motion for a directed verdict is made and denied, and subsequent to the verdict a motion for judgment n.o.v. is made but a new trial is not requested, may the trial court, if it denies the judgment n.o.v., grant a new trial more than ten days after the judgment? See Jackson v. Wilson Trucking Corp., 243 F.2d 212 (D.C.Cir.1957), 71 Harv.L.Rev. 552 (1958). See pp. 912–18, supra.

CHAPTER 12

SECURING AND ENFORCING JUDGMENTS

The commencement of a lawsuit or, for that matter, even the entry of a judgment, does not necessarily mean that plaintiff actually will secure the objectives of the action. A victorious plaintiff's ability to collect a judgment—depends primarily on defendant's capacity and willingness to pay at the time the award is made and secondarily on the effectiveness of the court's judgment enforcement procedures in the event the judgment debtor is capable of paying but is being recalcitrant. For example, plaintiff's efforts may be frustrated if defendant has become insolvent during the litigation or has secreted his assets or fraudulently conveyed them to third persons. In short, the arduous litigation process often proves to be a preliminary to the equally protracted travail of collecting the award.

The attempts to enforce a libel judgment against a New York Congressman, the late Adam Clayton Powell, illustrate some of the problems that often face a judgment creditor. In the case of Powell, the creditor was Mrs. Ethel James whose efforts to claim her due are a study in the breakdown of the enforcement process. Mrs. James originally was awarded a $46,000 libel judgment in April, 1963 and that judgment was affirmed by the New York Court of Appeals in July, 1964. Employing a number of tactics, including transfers of property to relatives and invocations of congressional immunity from arrest and process, Powell avoided collection for 32 months. His maneuvers frustrated Mrs. James' attempts to discover Powell's assets in New York and Puerto Rico and resulted in her bringing suit against the Congressman again, basing her claim on the little used common-law tort of evasion of a judgment. After Powell failed to appear for examination in the second suit, his answer was stricken and compensatory damages were set at $75,000 and punitive damages were assessed at $500,000. These were reduced to $56,000 and $100,000 respectively in James v. Powell, 26 App. Div.2d 525, 270 N.Y.S.2d 789 (1st Dep't 1966). Pursuit of Powell continued into 1967, but so did his appeals and in early March, 1967, the New York Court of Appeals reversed the verdict in the evasion-of-judgment suit because Puerto Rican law should have been applied to the compensatory damage claim and New York law, which governed the remainder of the claim, apparently did not permit punitive damages under the circumstances of the case. 19 N.Y.2d 249, 279 N.Y.S.2d 10, 225 N.E.2d 741 (1967). Thus, Mrs. James was left with the original libel judgment and a cause of action under Puerto Rican law. See "No Home in the House," *Time*, March 10, 1967.

At one point Powell was paying off Mrs. James' libel judgment through the proceeds from a long-playing album, "Keep the Faith, Baby," part of which was recorded live at his Caribbean island retreat on Bimini. Mrs. James, apparently disillusioned by the entire episode, decided there must be a better way to make a living than collecting judgments. She followed Powell's example and recorded an album of her own. Fittingly, in some eyes at least, one number on that album exclaims:

> There was once a man
>   who said that he
> Would like to retire to Bimini,
> But that was before he
>   broke the law,
> And now the people are going
>   haw-haw-haw.

Who had the last laugh is not clear, but it certainly was not the courts. Other reports of the pursuit of the Congressman include, "Hooking a Catfish," *Newsweek*, December 27, 1965; "Man May Come and Man May Go (But Powell Goes on Forever)," *National Review*, June 29, 1965; and "Monstrous Mackerel," *Time*, December 24, 1965.

SECTION A. METHODS OF SECURING THE JUDGMENT—PROVISIONAL REMEDIES

Most states attempt to maximize a plaintiff's chances for collecting the judgment ultimately secured by providing a series of security devices that operate during the action. These so-called "provisional" remedies primarily are creatures of statute and their character and effectiveness vary considerably from state to state. Thus, in a creditor-oriented state, it is not surprising to find that provisional remedies generally are available in almost all actions, whereas in a debtor-oriented jurisdiction they will be restricted to particular types of actions and be subjected to a variety of procedural restrictions. By virtue of Federal Rule 64, a federal court may use the provisional remedies available to the courts of the state in which it is sitting to the extent the state remedies are not inconsistent with any other federal rule or statute.

Articles 60 through 65 of New York's Civil Practice Law and Rules provide a claimant with the remedies of attachment and garnishment of property and debts, injunction, receivership, civil arrest, and notice of pendency. Since New York's provisional-remedies scheme is one of the most fully developed systems in the United States, the description that follows will use it as a model. For a general discussion of provisional remedies, see Millar, *Civil Procedure of the Trial Court in Historical Perspective* 481–515 (1952). Federal practice is described in 11 Wright & Miller, *Federal Practice and Procedure: Civil* §§ 2931–36 (1973); 7 Moore, *Federal Practice* ¶¶ 64.01–.10 (2d ed.). On the practice in particular states, see, e. g., 7 Weinstein, Korn & Miller, *New York Civil Practice* ¶¶ 6001.01–6515.07; Johnson, *Attachment and Sequestration: Provisional Remedies Under the Louisiana Code of Civil Procedure,* 38 Tul.L.Rev. 1 (1963).

Although the need to provide creditors with expeditious remedies against recalcitrant debtors seems clear, there is no doubt that from time to time some of the provisional remedies have been used as a bludgeon to collect money that occasionally was not actually due plaintiff. In a series of cases that began in 1969 with Sniadach v. Family Finance Corp., 395 U.S. 337, 89 S.Ct. 1820, 23 L.Ed.2d 349 (1969), described below, the United States Supreme Court has significantly modified the availability of pretrial "provisional" remedies. The Court's decisions have been based on the theory that any interference with the property of a defendant prior to an adjudication of the merits of plaintiff's claim is an unconstitutional invasion of defendant's rights. See generally Countryman, *The Bill of Rights and the Bill Collector,* 15 Ariz.L.Rev. 521 (1973). Accordingly, in considering the material that follows, the reader must constantly be aware of these dramatic shifts in judicial thinking about provisional remedies.

---

1. ATTACHMENT

The use of attachment for securing jurisdiction in rem or quasi in rem when the court cannot acquire jurisdiction over the person of the defendant was examined in Chapter Two. See pp. 106–13, supra. Attachment also is valuable as a provisional remedy because it prevents defendant from selling or otherwise disposing of any real or personal property that has been taken into the custody of the attaching officer. Since attachment deprives defendant of the use and enjoyment of property long before liability is established (and, of course, in many cases no liability will be found), most jurisdictions limit its availability to certain classes of actions. Further limitations on the remedy's availability have resulted from restrictive judicial construction of attachment statutes. See, e. g., Arcturus Mfg. Corp. v. Superior Court, 223 Cal. App.2d 187, 35 Cal.Rptr. 502 (2d Dist.1963). How can the remedy of attachment be harmonized with our traditional notion that plaintiff's right to relief depends upon his establishment of the elements of his claim?

The procedure for invoking the remedy of prejudgment garnishment has been significantly affected by the Supreme Court's decision in SNIADACH v. FAMILY FINANCE CORP., 395 U.S. 337, 89 S.Ct. 1820, 23

L.Ed.2d 349 (1969), which held that the Wisconsin prejudgment garnishment procedure violated constitutional principles of due process. Under that state's procedure, a summons was issued at the request of the creditor's lawyer and the lawyer served the garnishee to set in motion machinery by which the debtor's wages were frozen during the period before the trial of the main suit without any opportunity on the part of the wage earner to be heard or to tender any defense that might exist. The Court, after reaffirming the principle of *Mullane v. Central Hanover Bank & Trust Co.,* p. 115, supra, said:

> A prejudgment garnishment of the Wisconsin type is a taking which may impose tremendous hardship on wage earners with families to support. Until a recent act of Congress, * * * which forbids discharge of employees on the ground that their wages have been garnished, garnishment often meant the loss of a job. Over and beyond that was the great drain on family income.
> * * *
> Apart from those collateral consequences, it appears that in Wisconsin the statutory exemption granted the wage earner is "generally insufficient to support the debtor for any one week."
>
> The result is that a prejudgment garnishment of the Wisconsin type may as a practical matter drive a wage-earning family to the wall. Where the taking of one's property is so obvious, it needs no extended argument to conclude that absent notice and a prior hearing * * * this prejudgment garnishment procedure violates the fundamental principles of due process.

Id. at 340–42, 89 S.Ct. at 1822, 23 L.Ed.2d at 353, 354. Mr. Justice Black dissented on the ground that the Court, in effect, was striking down Wisconsin's garnishment law simply because the majority felt that it was bad state policy.

Initially, the effect of the *Sniadach* reasoning on other provisional remedies was unclear. However, in FUENTES v. SHEVIN, 407 U.S. 67, 92 S.Ct. 1983, 32 L.Ed.2d 556 (1972), which appears at p. 123, supra, the Court held unconstitutional state statutes that provided for the replevin of chattels without a prior opportunity to be heard. State courts applying *Sniadach* also have invalidated prejudgment garnishment of accounts receivable without notice and a statute permitting the issuance of a prejudgment writ of immediate possession by a landlord pending a hearing on the merits. See generally Kennedy, *Due Process Limitations on Creditor's Remedies: Some Reflections on Sniadach v. Family Finance Corp.,* 19 Am.U.L.Rev. 158 (1970); McDonnell, *Sniadach, The Replevin Cases and Self-Help Repossession—Due Process Tokenism?,* 14 B.C.Ind. & Comm.L.Rev. 437 (1973); and Note, *Procedural Due Process—The Prior Hearing Rule and the Demise of Ex Parte Remedies,* 53 B.U.L.Rev. 41

(1973). As you proceed through this Chapter consider whether the various remedies discussed are valid in light of *Sniadach* and *Fuentes.*

New York's attachment statute, N.Y.C.P.L.R. 6201, permits attachment when plaintiff can show that defendant has departed from or is about to depart from the state or is keeping himself concealed within the state and defendant's conduct appears to be motivated by a desire either to defraud creditors or to avoid service of process. The New York statute also permits attachment in actions against foreign corporations and in certain cases involving fraud. In contrast to the New York approach, some states provide that attachment is available in all contract actions, whether against residents or nonresidents, and in any action against a nonresident. What is the logic behind the distinction between the treatment accorded residents and nonresidents?

All nonexempt tangible and intangible property in which defendant has a recognizable interest is subject to attachment for purposes of securing the enforcement of the prospective judgment. New York permits the attachment of income, whether already earned or to be earned in the future, claims under insurance policies, bank accounts, and assignable choses in action and judgments. Certain property is exempt from attachment in order to permit defendant to maintain his standard of living during the pendency of the action. The elaborate, and somewhat archaic, New York exemptions are set out in N.Y.C.P. L.R. 5205–5206. See also pp. 982–89, infra.

When property of or a debt owed to defendant is in the hands of a third person, that person (the garnishee) may be prohibited from selling, assigning, or interfering with any property in which defendant has an interest or from paying or discharging any debt except as directed by the sheriff or a court order. The garnishee also may be ordered to turn the property or proceeds of the debt over to the court at the conclusion of the action for application to the final judgment.

Even if the statutory requirements for attachment are met and even if plaintiff is willing to post a bond to protect defendant, the court still has discretion to deny the remedy if it believes that the harm to defendant outweighs the risk that plaintiff's judgment will be unenforceable. Thus when the value of the property sought to be attached is significantly greater than defendant's potential liability or when the property is part of an ongoing business, the remedy may be denied. See generally Gray v. American Sur. Co., 129 Cal.App.2d 471, 277 P.2d 436 (3d Dist.1954).

The mechanics of attachment are relatively simple. A writ of attachment is directed to the appropriate law-enforcement officer, usually the sheriff, who serves the writ on defendant and seizes property equal in value to the amount set forth in the writ. The attachment remains in force for a limited period— usually until the action is concluded or for a fixed period long enough to permit the final determination of plaintiff's claim. In cases of hardship or special circumstances, the court may alter the length of time the attachment remains in force. See Arcturus Mfg. Corp. v. Superior Court, supra. For further information on the remedy of attachment, see Cohen, *Attachment of Property Fraudulently Transferred in New York: The Influence of Abstractions on the Rights of Creditors*, 49 Colum.L.Rev. 501 (1949); Note, *Garnishment in Kentucky—Some Defects*, 45 Ky.L.J. 322 (1956).

---

2. PRELIMINARY INJUNCTIONS AND TEMPORARY RESTRAINING ORDERS

A preliminary injunction is available when defendant is acting or threatening to act in a manner that would irreparably injure plaintiff or render the judgment in the action ineffectual. Since a preliminary injunction is granted before there has been a trial on the merits and it often has the same effect as the ultimate relief requested by plaintiff, it may have an extremely adverse impact on defendant; as a result, the courts use preliminary injunctions only in the most appealing and necessary circumstances. Moreover, because of the "extraordinary" character of the remedy, the moving party traditionally has been required to show that none of the less drastic provisional remedies provides an adequate alternative. For example, in CRAMOND v. AFL-CIO, 267 Minn. 229, 126 N.W.2d 252 (1964), plaintiff sought equitable relief and damages to correct his wrongful removal from office in a labor union. The court required plaintiff to demonstrate that there was no alternative to a preliminary injunction and that final relief would be ineffective unless a temporary injunction was issued against a scheduled election. According to the court, the grant or denial of a preliminary injunction depends upon a balancing of the relative harm to each party. Is this balancing technique objectionable because it amounts to a trial on the merits and thus is wasteful of judicial time? Are there ways of avoiding this duplication. See Federal Rule 65(a). See generally 11 Wright & Miller, *Federal Practice and Procedure: Civil* §§ 2947–50 (1973).

When plaintiff believes that immediate relief is essential, most states will entertain an application for a temporary restraining order (T.R.O.), which will issue upon a showing that irreparable harm will occur absent the order. Unlike the preliminary injunction, an application for a restraining order usually is made ex parte since time considerations do not permit the giving of formal notice. Because of a concern over the potential unfairness of ex parte proceedings, a number of special conditions, such as those set out in Federal Rule 65(b), usually are imposed when notice is not given to all parties. See 11 Wright & Miller, *Federal Practice and Procedure: Civil* §§ 2951–53 (1973). Are temporary restraining orders consistent with the *Sniadach* requirements of notice and an opportunity to defend? To what extent does the imposition of special conditions such as those described in Rule 65(b) satisfy due process considerations? A temporary restraining order generally will remain effective only for a relatively brief period or until a hearing is held on plaintiff's request for a preliminary injunction. See generally Curtis v. Tozer, 374 S.W.2d 557 (Mo.App. 1964).

Despite the judicial hesitancy in issuing preliminary injunctions and temporary restraining orders, these remedies are among the most useful weapons in the procedural arsenal. Injunctions are extremely flexible and can be molded to restrain or compel the performance of a wide variety of acts. Because the primary purpose of these orders is to preserve the status quo pending a full hearing on the merits, they usually will be negative or prohibitory in character and restrain defendant from acting in a particular fashion. On the other hand, when property must be maintained or a course of conduct continued in order to preserve the status quo or prevent irreparable injury, the court will not hestitate in granting a request that defendant continue certain activities or honor a given standard of care. Such an order generally is referred to as mandatory or affirmative. Many jurisdictions insist upon a greater showing of need on a request for this type of order than they do when a negative or prohibitory order is sought. See, e. g., Braswell v. Malone, 262 Ala. 323, 78 So.2d 631 (1955). Can you think of any reasons for this disparity in treatment?

In addition to the requirement that defendant's conduct violate plaintiff's rights and tend to render the ultimate judgment ineffectual, the act to be restrained must affect the subject matter of the action. Thus, a preliminary injunction or temporary restraining order relating to defendant's conduct is unavailable in an ordinary tort or contract action for money damages, since money is not considered the "subject" of the action. See generally Eastern Rock Products, Inc. v. Natanson, 239 App.Div. 529, 269 N.Y.S. 435 (3d Dep't 1933). As to the notion that defendant must be endangering the effectiveness of the final judgment, see, e. g., Maine Products Co. v. Alexander, 115 App.Div. 109, 112, 114, 100 N.Y.S. 709, 711, 712 (1st Dep't 1906) (three cases).

Even if plaintiff demonstrates a need for a preliminary injunction or temporary restraining order, the remedy will not necessarily be granted. The court's discretion will be exercised in light of the same principles of equity that influence a judicial determination as to whether a permanent injunction should issue. These factors include the availability of an adequate legal remedy, the difficulties of administering and enforcing the order, whether the injunction will prove effective, the possibility of irreparable harm, and whether the applicant has "unclean hands" or is guilty of laches.

Preliminary injunctions and temporary restraining orders usually bind only the parties to the action, their agents and servants, and anyone acting in collusion with or for the benefit of a party. In determining who is bound by the order, a great deal of caution is exercised to insure that anyone affected by the injunction has had a day in court and that the freedom of individual action and the right to voice personal opinions are not impaired simply because that person is a member of a group or unincorporated organization that has been enjoined by the court. Many courts inquire into the association's control over its members as an aid in determining whether or not individual members should be bound by an order issued against the group.

A problem that presents a particularly difficult question is whether a preliminary injunction or temporary restraining order should be used to prohibit parties from commencing or continuing an action in another court or from enforcing a judgment issued by another court. The problem becomes bound up with questions of jurisdiction and conflict of laws when a state court is asked to enjoin the parties from proceeding in an action pending in another state or in a federal court. For an illustration, see MERRITT-CHAPMAN & SCOTT CORP. v. MUTUAL BENEFIT LIFE INS. CO., 237 App.Div. 70, 73, 260 N.Y.S. 374, 378 (1st Dep't 1932), in which the court said it would not interfere with an action in another court "unless it has clear priority of jurisdiction, or exceptional circumstances are shown to exist which require such drastic remedy." See McClintock, *Equity* § 37 (2d ed. 1948); 7 Weinstein, Korn & Miller, *New York Civil Practice* ¶ 6301.27. What factors are relevant to the question whether a federal court should enjoin parties from proceeding in a state court? See Moore, *Conflict of Jurisdiction*, 23 La.L.Rev. 29 (1962). Are the considerations different when a state-court order purports to direct the parties not to proceed in a federal court? See Donovan v. City of Dallas, 377 U.S. 408, 84 S.Ct. 1579, 12 L.Ed.2d 409 (1964).

---

3. RECEIVERSHIP

Because the remedy originated in equity and therefore can be characterized as "extraordinary," a number of courts refuse to appoint a receiver to act as a custodian or manager of disputed property pendente lite whenever the movant is shown to have an adequate remedy at law or an alternative remedy. See, e. g., State ex rel. Larry C. Iverson, Inc. v. District Court, 146 Mont. 362, 406 P.2d 828 (1965). Even today, however, this hesitancy is both understandable and appropriate since in many instances the remedy will deprive defendant of the control and enjoyment of property without a hearing on the merits or because of the high cost of a receivership.

Defendant's actual or potential insolvency is the primary reason for the appointment of a receiver. Another appropriate use of the remedy is to preserve property pending litigation when there is a substantial danger that the property will be removed from the state, lost, materially injured, or destroyed. See, e. g., Cafadaris v. Bulow, 138 Misc. 301, 244 N.Y.S. 600 (Sup.Ct.1930) (receiver appointed when immigration visa of person in possession of property about to expire). See also Gunther v. Gunther, 283 S.W.2d 826 (Tex.Civ. App.1955) (court stated that receivership may be used when it is incidental to an injunction or *lis pendens*).

In most states only plaintiff can secure the appointment of a receiver and the receivership extends only to property actually involved in the litigation. New York, however, gives its courts the power to appoint a receiver upon the motion of any person having an "apparent interest" in the property. N.Y. C.P.L.R. 6401. What possible justification is there for such a provision? New York practice also requires any person who moves for the appointment of a receiver to be joined as a party, thereby permitting the movant to protect her interest in the property in the previously commenced action; of course, this practice occasionally may prove burdensome to the person seeking the appointment of the receiver. See 7 Weinstein, Korn & Miller, *New York Civil Practice* ¶ 6401.13. Doesn't this unnecessarily complicate and proliferate the litigation?

A temporary receiver must be disinterested and owes primary allegiance to the appointing court and not to the parties or the person who sought the appointment. Because of this status, virtually all of a receiver's official acts are subject to the approval of the appointing court. As a result, a person dealing with a receiver does so at his peril in the sense that the appointing court may refuse to ratify a transaction entered into by the receiver. What other qualities should a receiver possess? See, e. g., Cohen v. Hechtman, 187 Misc. 994, 66 N.Y.S.2d 305 (Sup.Ct.1946).

A temporary receiver's powers are found in the statute or rule authorizing the appointment or in the court order naming the receiver. He usually is required to take possession of the property as soon as possible after the appointing order has been entered. In VANDER VORSTE v. NORTHWESTERN NAT. BANK, 81 S.D. 566, 138 N.W.2d 411 (1965), the basic obligation of a receiver is described as the duty of preserving and protecting the property and assets of the estate that have been placed in protective custody. Although the receiver is not given title to the property, he generally is given the responsibility of managing or disposing of the property and the power to take any action necessary to maintain or improve it. See, e. g., Knickerbocker Fed. Sav. & Loan Ass'n v. 531 E. 144th St., Inc., 39 Misc.2d 23, 240 N.Y.S.2d 112 (Sup.Ct.1963).

In order to prevent dereliction in the performance of his duties, a temporary receiver normally is required to execute and file an undertaking before any official duties are initiated. The undertaking protects the integrity of the court and the litigants by guaranteeing that injuries caused by any defalcation by the receiver can be indemnified.

The appointment of receivers in the federal courts is governed by Federal Rule 66. A receiver's function typically is to take control of property that is involved in or is likely to become involved in litigation and to preserve it pending the final disposition of the suit. Section 959(b) of Title

28 of the United States Code defines the receiver's substantive rights, duties, and liabilities. See 12 Wright & Miller, *Federal Practice and Procedure: Civil* §§ 2981–86 (1973), for a discussion of federal receivers.

---

4. CIVIL ARREST

The provisional remedy of civil arrest had its genesis in the common-law practice of commencing an action by taking into custody and imprisoning defendant until judgment was rendered or bail was posted. Although incarceration effectively prevented defendant from rendering the potential judgment unenforceable, its Draconian quality made it a frequent source of abuse. The debtor's prison strikingly portrayed by Dickens in the *Pickwick Papers* illustrates the unpleasant consequences of the remedy. Consequently, courts and legislatures have sharply restricted the availability of civil arrest in most jurisdictions.[a] For an historical discussion of the development and use of civil arrest see Freedman, *Imprisonment for Debt*, 2 Temple L.Q. 330 (1928).

The availability of civil arrest varies widely from state to state. Some state constitutions (Mississippi Const., Art. III, § 30 and Texas Const., Art. 1, § 18) prohibit imprisonment for debt and thus render civil arrest unavailable; a number of states simply have not enacted legislation authorizing civil arrest, although their constitutions would not prohibit use of the remedy. Other states allow civil arrest only in limited types of actions, such as New York, which permits the remedy only in actions based on fraud, deceit, and conversion, and then only if the person to be arrested is not a woman.[b] New York also authorizes civil arrest when "plaintiff has demanded and would be entitled to a judgment or order requiring the performance of an act, the neglect or refusal to perform which would be punishable by the court as a contempt" and defendant is a nonresident of New York or there is a substantial danger that she is about to leave the state and her departure would render the prospective judgment or order ineffectual. N.Y.C.P.L.R. 6101. An interesting tabulation of the actions in which civil arrest is available in the several states appears in Study, *Grounds for Civil Arrest and Body Execution, Third Preliminary Report of the Advisory Committee on Practice and Procedure*, N.Y. Leg.Doc.No. 17, p. 797 (1959).

Even when civil arrest has been authorized by statute, certain public policy exemptions generally limit its application. For example, the New York courts

[a] One of the most incisive critiques of civil arrests was penned by Charles Evans Hughes, later Chief Justice of the United States Supreme Court, in *Arrest and Imprisonment on Civil Process*, 28 N.Y. State Bar Ass'n Rep. 151 (1905).

[b] Civil arrest is available in many states in actions involving extremely violent or cruel batteries and other "malicious torts." See generally Shatz v. Paul, 7 Ill.App. 2d 223, 129 N.E.2d 348 (1st Dist.1955), which contains an excellent historical discussion of the use of arrest.

have exempted all public servants from civil arrest. See Family Fin. Corp. v. Starke, 36 N.Y.S.2d 858 (Sup.Ct.1942). States granting immunity from service of process to nonresident witnesses also generally extend that immunity to cover civil arrest.

A motion for civil arrest is addressed to the court's discretion, which, in view of the severity of the remedy, is exercised with a great degree of caution. This is exemplified by the following statement from SUMMERS v. DISTRICT COURT, 68 Nev. 99, 227 P.2d 201 (1951):

> The legislative authorization of such a remedy based upon probability is an extraordinary grant of power to the courts and carries with it extraordinary judicial responsibilities. The extensive discretion so granted assumes the highest of judicial wisdom and, accordingly, demands the highest degree of consideration in its exercise.

Furthermore, plaintiff usually must file an "undertaking" guaranteeing the payment of any legal costs and damages that defendant may sustain if the arrest proves to have been wrongful. The undertaking protects defendant and insures that those thinking about invoking the remedy will "look before they leap."

An arrested defendant will be released if bail is posted in an amount designated by the court; the bail then serves as security for any judgment plaintiff ultimately may recover. Bail usually is set high enough to cover the prospective judgment, although the court will avoid setting bail at a figure that makes it impossible for defendant to secure his release. See People v. Tweed, 5 Hun. 382 (1st Dep't), appeal dismissed 63 N.Y. 202 (1875). But for a grievous example of the possible consequences of civil arrest, see In re Harris, 69 Cal.2d 486, 72 Cal.Rep. 340, 446 P.2d 148 (1968).

---

5.   NOTICE OF PENDENCY

Although not strictly a provisional remedy, the notice of pendency is included in this discussion because of its similarity to the four provisional remedies already described. The genesis of the notice of pendency is found in the common-law doctrine of *lis pendens*, which sought to guarantee the effectiveness of a judgment in an action involving specific tangible property by charging any purchaser or encumbrancer of the property with knowledge that an action involving it had been instituted. Thus, at common law a prospective purchaser or encumbrancer not only had to check all of the conveyance records to be certain of the vendor's good title but also had to investigate whether the vendor was involved in any pending litigation that might affect the property —often a practical impossibility. Today, this burdensome aspect of the *lis pendens* doctrine generally has been restricted by statute. See, e. g., Picerne v.

Redd, 72 R.I. 4, 47 A.2d 906 (1946). For a history of the common-law procedure, see Bennett, *Lis Pendens* (1887).

The statutory notice of pendency is designed to protect prospective purchasers and encumbrancers by requiring plaintiff to file a notice of the litigation before the protection of constructive notice can be claimed. Thus, if plaintiff fails to file a notice of pendency and properly index it, he will not be protected against a purchaser or encumbrancer who does not have actual knowledge of the litigation involving the property. In some states, such as New York, notice of pendency statutes apply only to real property, which may mean that the harsher *lis pendens* doctrine is still applicable to actions involving personalty. More likely, the common-law practice has been eliminated by negative implication.

Statutory notice of pendency differs from other provisional remedies because it usually does not involve judicial discretion; the right to file a notice is absolute in any litigation falling within the classes enumerated in the notice-of-pendency statute. The only question on which the court must exercise its judgment usually is whether the action affects real property. Obviously, however, the court's power over this issue can be used to restrict or contract the availability of the remedy considerably. See the discussion in Braunston v. Anchorage Woods, Inc., 10 N.Y.2d 302, 222 N.Y.S.2d 316, 178 N.E.2d 717 (1961). Why shouldn't the courts be able to handle notice-of-pendency applications on a discretionary basis?

---

6. A POSTSCRIPT

Despite their obvious practical importance to the proper functioning of a judicial system, little effort has been devoted to the rationalization of provisional remedies and their integration into the total procedural picture. Indeed many practitioners are ill-informed as to the availability and operation of provisional remedies in their jurisdiction and often miss an opportunity to protect their clients against debilitating and frustrating post-judgment enforcement procedures. What better evidence of the second-class treatment accorded the subject of provisional remedies is there than the cavalier incorporation of state provisional-remedy practice by Federal Rule 64 and the reference to federal receivership practice "heretofore followed" in Rule 66? With the goals and the structure of federal procedure as a background, see if you can formulate a comprehensive provisional-remedies rule for the federal courts; make certain that it will be consistent with contemporary notions of due process as set forth in the United States Supreme Court cases described on pages 972–74, supra. Would you employ New York's compartmentalization approach to provisional remedies or do you think that a single unifying and workable theme can be verbalized and put into the form of a rule? In what ways are the availability or unavailability of post-judgment enforcement techniques relevant to framing a provisional-remedies rule? Reconsider this question after studying the remaining materials in this Chapter.

SECTION B. METHODS OF COLLECTING AND ENFORCING THE JUDGMENT

1. EXECUTION

GRIGGS v. MILLER

Supreme Court of Missouri, 1963.
374 S.W.2d 119.

WALTER H. BOHLING, Special Commissioner. Bill Griggs, on January 19, 1961, sued W. A. Brookshire in ejectment for the possession of a 322 acre farm in Boone County, Missouri, and for damages for withholding possession. Plaintiff had purchased the farm for $20,600 on January 16, 1961, at a public sale under a general execution against defendant. * * * Defendant filed an answer and counterclaim. Defendant's answer was a general denial, and his counterclaim sought to set aside the sheriff's execution sale and deed. Glen Powell, who as Sheriff of Boone County conducted said sale and was grantor in said deed, was made a third-party defendant upon the application of defendant. The cause was considered and treated by the parties and the court "as one of 'equitable cognizance.' " The court found the issues for the plaintiff and against the defendant on plaintiff's petition; for the plaintiff and the third-party defendant on defendant's counterclaim; and that plaintiff was entitled to $2,483.24 damages by reason of defendant's withholding of possession of said farm from January 18, 1961, to November 15, 1961, the date of said judgment and decree, and that plaintiff recover $250 per month from and after November 15, 1961, for so long as defendant withheld possession from plaintiff. Defendant Brookshire, after filing his notice of appeal, was incarcerated in the Missouri Penitentiary. Chapter 460 and § 222.010. * * * Thereafter, upon application of plaintiff Griggs, George C. Miller was appointed trustee of the Estate of W. A. Brookshire, and substituted as a party litigant for said Brookshire.

* * *

A suit to set aside a prior execution sale and sheriff's deed of defendant's 322 acre farm is reported under the style of W. A. Brookshire v. Glenn Powell * * *; said Powell being the sheriff conducting said sale and the other named defendants being the purchasers thereat.

Ray Crouch recovered a judgment against W. A. Brookshire, defendant, in the Circuit Court of Henry County, Missouri, on July 15, 1959, for $1,966.-69. Said judgment was affirmed on December 5, 1960, in Crouch v. Brookshire, Mo.App., 341 S.W.2d 336. The right to an execution follows immediately upon the rendition of a judgment. * * * No supersedeas bond was given to stay an execution. * * * A general execution was issued on said judgment to the Sheriff of Boone County on December 10, 1960. The Sheriff levied on defendant's 322 acre farm December 14, 1960, filed a notice of his levy in the office of the Recorder of Deeds of Boone County, and advertised and sold said real estate at public sale on January 16, 1961.

Dorothy Contestible, Administratrix of the Estate of Ralph Burton Collings, Deceased, recovered a judgment of $17,000 against William Albert Brookshire, defendant, in a wrongful death action in the Circuit Court of Audrain County, Missouri, on July 29, 1960. A general execution issued on said $17,000 judgment to the Sheriff of Boone County on December 23, 1960. This execution was mailed to Mrs. Contestible's attorneys in Columbia and was delivered to Sheriff Powell January 10, 1961. He levied upon defendant's 322 acres under said execution on January 11, 1961.

Defendant contends it was error to sell his 322 acre farm without attempting to make the judgment debt, interest and costs out of a portion of said farm.

Our Civil Rules contemplate that a judgment debtor is to be afforded reasonable protection in levying on and selling his property under execution. Civil Rule 76.21 (§ 513.095) provides in effect that if a judgment debtor gives the officer a list of his property sufficient to satisfy the execution, "the officer shall levy upon the property, and no other, if in his opinion it is sufficient; if not, then upon such additional property as shall be sufficient."

Civil Rule 76.24 (§ 513.210) provides: "When an execution shall be levied upon real estate, the officer levying the same shall divide such property, if susceptible of division, and sell so much thereof as will be sufficient to satisfy such execution, unless the debtor in the execution shall desire the whole of any tract or lot of land to be sold together, in which case it shall be sold accordingly."

And Rule 76.25 (§ 513.100) provides: "The person whose goods, chattels and real estate are taken in execution may elect what part thereof shall be first sold; and if he shall deliver to the officer having charge thereof a statement, in writing, of such election, three days before the day appointed for the sale, stating specifically what goods, chattels and real estate he desires to be first sold, and so on, until the execution be satisfied, the officer shall proceed according to such election, until sufficient money shall be made to satisfy the amount in the execution specified and costs."

It is stated in 21 Am.Jur., Execution, § 380, that an execution is not "leviable upon all the debtor's property, but only upon sufficient property owned by the debtor within the jurisdiction to satisfy the debt, interest, and costs"; and, while the officer is left to his own judgment, he "must exercise the care and discretion which a reasonably prudent man would exercise under like conditions and circumstances." And, with respect to the property to be sold when more than enough to satisfy the debt is seized, it is stated in § 384: "The general rule is that the execution officer may make a division of the property, if that is practicable, and sell only so much of it as is necessary to satisfy the debt." * * * A failure to divide real estate and sell only enough to satisfy the execution was considered an abuse of discretion in State ex rel. Koeln v. Sanders, 326 Mo. 76, 30 S.W.2d 986 [1], and a constructive fraud in Queen City Inv. Co. v. Kreider, Mo., 31 S.W.2d 1002, 1005 [10].

As stated by the trial court, plaintiff's testimony placed the value of defendant's 322 acres at $50,000 while defendant contended it was much higher, approximately $90,000.

* * *

Defendant wrote Sheriff Powell under date of January 11, 1961, re the Crouch judgment, levy and sale, stating, among other things, that his land was worth in excess of $100 an acre; and: "I am restricting the amount which you can sell to the northeast 40 acres of said tract of land. This land is clear. There is no mortgage or encumbrance of any kind against it."

Defendant protested the execution sale to those assembled for the sale and stated in effect that the judgment involved had been obtained in Henry County and the case was on appeal and the judgment was not final; that: "After the judgment becomes final it will be paid"; that Crouch had in his possession cattle belonging to defendant worth $10,000 against which there was no lien; that "I have notified the sheriff that this farm is clear of any mortgages whatsoever; that it is worth approximately $50,000.00; that one forty acre sold would be more than adequate. I have pointed out the forty acres * * * to be sold"; that he was certain the $17,000 judgment against him in the Contestible case would be reversed; that a supersedeas bond would be given; that this sale would be illegal and whoever bought the farm would buy a law suit. (The Contestible judgment, however, was affirmed January 8, 1962, in Contestible v. Brookshire, Mo., 355 S.W.2d 36.)

Sheriff Powell, who had been sheriff for about twenty years, admitted 40 acres of defendant's farm "might have been" worth far in excess of $2,000. Asked why he had not told defendant the 40 acres would not be sufficient, he would take 80 acres, Sheriff Powell answered: "I didn't intend to take 80 acres." He testified he had levied on and held three or four execution sales of defendant's 322 acre farm. He stated he did not know it was illegal to sell $50,000 worth of property to satisfy a $2,000 judgment; and there was testimony he had levied on the 322 acres to collect a $13.00 judgment, and to collect a $600 judgment. He stated "I checked the record and there was several thousand dollars" against all of the farm, and that is why "I levied on all of it." He also stated "I never checked the records." He did not levy on personal property because "It was much easier to do it this way." He knew defendant had stocks in various corporations and had more than 200 head of Hereford cattle on the farm; that they might have sold for at least $200 a head on the market and as registered cattle would have brought more, and that 20 head of the cattle "might have" been sufficient to more than pay the Crouch judgment, interest and costs.

Ray Crouch, the judgment creditor, testified he wanted to and asked his attorney to levy on defendant's farm, and that he knew defendant had collateral * * * to take care of the Crouch judgment. Sheriff Powell testified that Crouch had told him defendant had deposited sufficient collateral with the Hartford Insurance Company to take care of the Crouch judgment.

* * *

A sheriff conducting an execution sale is the agent of the property owner and the judgment creditor, and his duty is to protect the interests of both and to see that the property is not sacrificed. * * * Forced sales of property usually do not bring full value.

Sheriff Powell's advertisement of the sale of defendant's 322 acre farm was to "sell all of said real estate or as much thereof as *it* be necessary to pay the judgment of $1,966.69," in the Henry County Circuit Court, which, with interest and costs, amounted to $2,308.16 on the day of sale.

Defendant's farm was never advertised for sale under the Audrain County (Contestible) execution. Defendant first knew of the levy on his farm under the $17,000 Audrain County judgment about 30 minutes before its sale under the Crouch judgment. Sheriff Powell testified that he sold under the Henry County, and not under the Audrain County, execution.

Defendant's 322 acres was not divided for the purpose of selling but was sold as a whole to plaintiff for $20,600.00. The only bidders were Ed Orr, one of the attorneys for Mrs. Contestible, and Ralph Alexander, a bondsman and attorney for the sheriff. Plaintiff Griggs testified he heard the farm would bring enough to satisfy the two judgments about 15 or 20 minutes before the sale; that about 5 or 10 minutes before it was sold he decided to buy it because "it didn't bring any more than it did," and that he asked Mr. Alexander to bid for him. * * *

It is not questioned but that this 322 acre farm, consisting of approximately eight forties, could have been offered for sale in parcels. Rule 76.24 (§ 513.210) contemplates that the officer "divide such property, if susceptible of division, and sell so much thereof as will be sufficient to satisfy such execution." This was not done, and we hold that it should have been so divided. In Brookshire v. Powell, Mo., 335 S.W.2d 176, 181, the disparity between the market value of this farm and a bid of $2,300 was considered so great as to require setting aside that execution sale and sheriff's deed. In the case at bar the Henry County judgment, interest and costs amounted to $2,308.16; and for that amount under said execution and the constructive levy of the Audrain County execution, but without an advertisement for sale under Rule 76.36, supra, under said Audrain County execution, it is sought to justify this forced sale for $20,600 of property valued at about $46,000. This record calls for the result reached in Brookshire v. Powell * * *.

Defendant is entitled to relief upon doing equity. * * * Accordingly, if defendant will, within thirty days, deposit in this court, for the use and benefit of those entitled thereto, the sum of $20,600 with interest at the rate of 6% per annum from the date of sale until the same is paid, the decree appealed from will be reversed and the cause remanded with directions to cancel the sheriff's sale and the sheriff's deed to plaintiff made pursuant thereto; otherwise the decree will stand affirmed. In either event the costs are assessed against the estate of defendant Brookshire.

PER CURIAM. The foregoing opinion by BOHLING, Special Commissioner, is adopted as the opinion of the court.

All of the Judges concur.

[The court's opinion on a motion to modify and for a rehearing and the court's supplemental opinion are omitted.]

NOTES AND QUESTIONS

1.   Execution is the traditional method of enforcing a money judgment. In contemplating the effectiveness of the device, consider the following questions. What is the territorial reach of an execution? In what order should various types of property be levied upon and sold by the officer to whom the execution is delivered? How is the judgment debtor effectively prevented from disposing of the property after the executing officer has levied upon it? How long does an execution remain effective? How are priorities determined as between competing executions? Use of the execution in particular situations and the interrelationship between execution and other judgment-enforcement devices are discussed in Heiserman, *Procedures Available for Implementation of a Judgment in Iowa,* 42 Iowa L.Rev. 265 (1957); King, *The Enforcement of Money Judgments in California,* 11 So.Cal.L.Rev. 224 (1938). For further information, see the articles in the symposium on judgment enforcement in 42 Iowa L.Rev. 151–284 (1957) and the five articles in 1951 U.Ill.L.F. 1–120 (1951).

2.   The text of Federal Rule 69 and the cases decided under it indicate that the procedures of the state in which the federal court is sitting are to be followed in enforcing federal-court judgments. See United States v. Hackett, 123 F.Supp. 106 (W.D.Mo.1954). Is this incorporation of state practice appropriate? Does it mean that executions on federal judgments are handled by state sheriffs rather than United States marshals? Is the identity of the executing officer of any moment? By way of exception to the use of state practice, Rule 69 provides that "any statute of the United States governs to the extent that it is applicable." In addition, a judgment creditor who wishes to examine the judgment debtor or any other person as to the debtor's assets may proceed under either state supplementary proceeding practice or under the Federal Rules relating to depositions and discovery. See generally Bank of America Nat. Trust & Sav. Ass'n v. Bair, 34 F. Supp. 857 (D.Mont.1939), affirmed 112 F.2d 247 (9th Cir.), certiorari denied 311 U.S. 684, 61 S.Ct. 61, 85 L.Ed. 441 (1940); 11 Wright & Miller, *Federal Practice and Procedure: Civil* §§ 3011–15 (1973).

3.   State law generally exempts part or all of the judgment debtor's income and real and personal property from enforcement procedures such as execution and

garnishment. See generally Abrahams & Feldman, *The Exemption of Wages from Garnishment: Some Comparisons and Comments*, 3 De Paul L.Rev. 153 (1954). The percentage of income exempted from execution varies from little or nothing to a high of ninety percent. What accounts for this disparity? An excellent critique of garnishment appears in Brunn, *Wage Garnishment in California: A Study and Recommendations*, 53 Calif.L.Rev. 1214 (1965). After an analysis of the existing garnishment pattern, the author concludes

> The time when a family had few, if any, debts except perhaps a home purchase mortgage may be remembered nostalgically, but it has passed. The years following the end of World War II saw the development of what might be called the American way of debt. * * * Consumer credit has become a major industry and consumer debt consumes a major slice of many a family's income. Repayment of installment debt alone equalled fourteen per cent of disposable personal income in 1964. * * * Total consumer credit repayments are probably running at a level close to twenty per cent of disposable personal income and well over twenty per cent of employees' earnings.

> Individual debt, not so long ago discouraged and regarded with suspicion, is now encouraged. More than encouraged, debt today is merchandised as intensively and skillfully as any commodity, notwithstanding occasional pious reminders to "never borrow money needlessly." The communications media that touch a family's life constantly urge it to buy on "easy" terms, to open charge accounts with "nominal" monthly service charges, to get a new car at "bank" terms, to travel now and pay later—whether the family can afford it or not. * * *

> Even with sales managers named Jesse James, one may grant that the contribution of consumer credit to the economy and to the standard of living of many families is substantial. But when personal debt is no longer unusual, no longer a sign of improvidence, when debt has instead become a mass production, hard-sell item that citizens are widely encouraged to "buy," one may doubt the continued appropriateness of a device such as wage garnishment. * * * Today this harsh remedy, humiliating at best, disastrous to the debtor and his family at worst, seems far less justifiable than in an age when personal debt was uncommon and disfavored. It is time that our attitude toward wage garnishment—which is, after all, a drastic form of intervention by government on behalf of creditors—caught up with our attitude toward debt.

>   * * *

> Collection agencies find wage garnishment a useful tool, not only because of the debtor's earnings actually reached by levies, but because the threat of garnishment encourages the debtor to make payments. Whether one views this effect as persuasive or coercive depends to some extent on one's point of view. In any event, the encouragement is due to the debtor's fear that he will lose his job if there are more garnishments. The fear is real. Discharges because of repeated wage levies are not uncommon. Employers dislike the added work and expense brought by levies and often limit the number of levies they will permit without

discharge. Labor organizations have apparently not been able to bargain effectively on this issue.[c]

The employee who is threatened with discharge, and who cannot pay, sometimes chooses bankruptcy as a means of saving his job. The expansion of consumer credit in the postwar years has been accompanied by a sharp rise in bankruptcies, particularly in nonbusiness bankruptcies. Bankruptcy rates tend to be lower in states that do not permit wage garnishment or that sharply restrict its use. * * *

Wage garnishment is costly. Its immediate costs include official fees—chargeable to debtors—expense to employers, and the community's subsidy of the garnishment process. There are other costs in terms of distress and economic hardship when the family whose earnings are garnished spirals into bankruptcy or unemployment. And there are losses to creditors from garnishment-triggered no-asset bankruptcies. Hardship is not limited to bankruptcy and unemployment; a debtor who avoids both is faced with a * * * wage exemption, [in] an amount that in the great bulk of cases is grossly inadequate.

Wage garnishment does not produce benefits to match these disadvantages. There is no evidence that the granting of credit depends on the availability of this tool. Economic data, even data supplied by collection agencies, show that the ratio of installment credit to retail trade is as high in states that do not permit garnishment as in states that do. The data show further that a state's volume of retail trade and its level of per capita income is unrelated to garnishment laws. * * * Further, collection data show that several states with a ninety per cent wage exemption have higher percentage recoveries by collection agencies than California [which has a fifty per cent wage exemption]. [d]

Id. at 1243–47.

A 1970 amendment to the Consumer Credit Protection Act of 1968 establishes a nationwide limit on the amount of an employee's wages that are subject to garnishment and affords an employee some protection against being discharged as a result of garnishment. 15 U.S.C. §§ 1673–1674 (Supp.1973).

Real and personal-property exemptions from execution usually are defined by statute on an item-by-item basis rather than by percentage of property value. The failure to revise these statutes over long periods of time has led to some incredibly out-dated provisions. By way of illustration, see the lists of property exempted from execution by Section 5205 (personal) and Section 5206 (real) of New York's Civil Practice Law and Rules. In some in-

---

[c] New York has attempted to solve this problem by statute. See N.Y.C.P.L.R. 5252.

Since the publication of the article in text California has enacted a statute preventing an employee from being discharged because his wages have been garnished. See Cal.Stats.1971, Ch. 1607.

[d] California is reviewing its garnishment statutes with a view toward comprehensively revising them. See Recommendation Relating to Attachment, Garnishment, and Exemptions from Execution: Employees' Earnings Protection Law (November 1971), reprinted in 10 Cal.L.Rev. Comm'n Reports 701 (1971).

stances the result of a failure to revise these statutes is far from amusing. For example, New York exempts from execution a lot of land that is being used as a residence by a householder or a woman, but only up to a value of $2,000. N.Y.C. P.L.R. 5206(a). Until recently, the exemption was limited to $1,000. If the purpose of homestead exemptions is to permit the judgment debtor and family to maintain a minimum standard of living, this exemption is woefully inadequate. See Dean, *Economic Relations Between Husband and Wife in New York,* 41 Cornell L.Q. 175, 213–14 (1956). See generally 6 Weinstein, Korn & Miller, *New York Civil Practice* ¶¶ 5205.01–5206.29.

Since one of the primary purposes of exemption statutes is to protect the judgment debtor's dependents against an overzealous judgment holder, nearly every state provides that the exemptions do not apply when the attaching creditor is the spouse or a dependent of the debtor. See Fischer v. Fischer, 13 N.J. 162, 98 A.2d 568 (1953). In SCHLAEFER v. SCHLAEFER, 112 F.2d 177, 185 (D.C.Cir.1940), the court said:

> * * * [T]he usual purpose of exemption is to relieve the person exempted from the pressure of claims hostile to his dependents' essential needs as well as his own personal ones, not to relieve him of familial obligations and destroy what may be the family's last and only security, short of public relief. * * *

4.   In an attempt to reduce the cost of enforcing a spouse's duty of support, the National Conference of Commissioners on Uniform State Laws has adopted the Uniform Reciprocal Enforcement of Support Act §§ 1–33, 9C Uniform Laws Annotated 5 (1967). In a Prefatory Note, the Act's operation is described as follows:

> Sections 9 to 24 cover details of what is known as the two-state proceeding. In the past, the greatest difficulty in enforcing support where the parties are in different states has been the expense of travel to a distant state to litigate the rights of the destitute obligee. Under this Act this expense can be reduced to filing fees plus a few postage stamps. In a nutshell, this two-state proceeding is as follows: It opens with an action (Section 9) which normally will be commenced in the state where the family has been deserted (the initiating state). A very simplified petition is filed (Section 10). The judge looks it over to decide whether the facts show the existence of a duty of support and if they do he sends the petition and a copy of this Act to a court of the responding state to which the husband has fled or in which he has property (Section 13). That court will take the steps necessary to obtain jurisdiction of the husband or his property, will hold a hearing (Section 17) and if the court finds that a duty of support exists, it may order the defendant to furnish support (Section 20) and will transmit a copy of its order to the court in the initiating state (Section 21). To enforce compliance with its orders the court may subject the defendant to such terms and conditions as it may deem proper, may require him to furnish bond or make periodic payments or, in case of refusal, may punish him for contempt (Section 22). It has the duty to transmit to the initiating court any payments it receives and upon request to furnish a certified statement of those payments (Section 23). The initiating court must receive and disburse these payments (Section 24).

Would this type of a system cure some of the deficiencies in the existing procedures for collecting a judgment by execution or garnishment?

2. SUPPLEMENTARY PROCEEDINGS

COHEN, COLLECTION OF MONEY JUDGMENTS IN NEW YORK: SUPPLEMENTARY PROCEEDINGS, 35 Colum.L.Rev. 1007, 1012–14, 1030–34 (1935):

* * * [S]upplementary proceedings existed at common law, although under a different trade name. After the return of execution unsatisfied a creditor was empowered to proceed in equity by way of a judgment creditor's bill for two primary purposes: (a) to reach "equitable" assets beyond the scope of legal execution, and (b) to uncover property owned by the judgment debtor but deviously concealed and "transferred."

The judgment creditor's suit fitted itself into a finely grooved routine in its course through the court of chancery. * * * [U]pon the service of the bill and subpoena on the judgment debtor two courses were open. The debtor could contest the bill, in which case the creditor would proceed with his injunction, have a receiver appointed and the case would run its course to a decree. Or the debtor could, instead of answering, follow the chancery rule which arose as the former procedure became formalized, and deliver to the creditor a consent to the entry of an order "taking the bill as confessed," appointing a receiver, and making a reference to take the examination. Upon such consent the case was referred to a master, and the debtor ordered "to assign, transfer and deliver" to the receiver "all his property, equitable interests, things in action and effects." Thereupon the usual examination followed.

* * *

Thus the net result of the judgment creditor's bill was an examination of the debtor, a disclosure by him of his property, and the assignment thereof under order of the court to a receiver who acted as the agent of the court in converting the judgment debtor's property into currency, rendering it applicable to the payment of the original claim. * * * [T]he creditor's bill finally became a highly formalized procedure which, although available to almost every judgment creditor, involved him in Jarndyce's disease. In their labors to provide a new and simpler scheme for judgment collection the [New York] Code Commissioners devised a practice which was expressly intended to be a substitute for the old creditors' bill: the "supplementary proceedings."

There would be an examination of the judgment debtor. This might disclose: (a) debts due to the judgment debtor, (b) tangible personal property of the judgment debtor in his own possession or in the possession of a third party, (c) real property owned by the judgment debtor. Real property could be reached by execution. For third party debtors there was devised the third party order, and for tangible personal property in the hands of the debtor or third persons there was created an order directing such property to be applied in satisfaction of the judgment. * * * In addition, * * * the Code Commissioners provided that the judge could appoint a receiver of the property of the judgment debtor.

* * *

The effectiveness of the remedy granted by way of supplementary proceedings depends in large part upon the efficiency with which the instrument may be used to discover property of the debtor and have it applied upon the judgment. Conceivably the proceeding may be so broad as to permit all issues as to title to be adjudicated therein with finality. That this has not happened in most Code states is one of the prime causes of the ineffectiveness of the modern judgment collection system. Under the [New York] Field-Throop Code, and under the [New York] Civil Practice Act, the examination is not a trial. It merely affords the creditor an opportunity to question the debtor in an attempt to discover assets.

At the outset the creditor is faced with the problem of obtaining personal service of the order on the debtor. In plenary suits jurisdiction may be obtained by substitution upon debtors who evade service, but no similar provision is available in supplementary proceedings, although these constitute a new proceeding and would seem analogous to a plenary suit. Should the judgment debtor desire to dodge service the creditor can do little but spend time and money trying to catch him. * * *

Having obtained service the creditor will find that the court facilities afforded for the examination are quite meagre. The debtor is not examined in the presence of the Court, nor is the testimony officially transcribed. * * * The * * * statute provides that upon the consent of the debtor or his attorney the examination may be taken before a notary public or commissioner of deeds at any place mutually agreeable to the parties. And it also specifies, in what may be a helpful reform, that the Appellate Division may assign official referees to preside at examinations, although it is to be regretted that the statute did not incorporate the reform * * * that the examination be held immediately after the trial and before the justice then presiding.

* * * Where there is no official supervision, constant disputes arise as to the scope of the examination and the accuracy with which it was transcribed. This tends to hamper the investigation and affords evasive debtors opportunities to change their testimony. Thus the absence of satisfactory judicial facilities, at least in New York City, often results in defeating creditors' efforts at collection.

This situation has been aggravated by some judicially evolved rules defining the creditor's rights. After examining the debtor the creditor naturally desires to adjourn the examination so that he may have an opportunity to investigate the debtor's testimony. Prior to the new statute, such adjournments were denied as a matter of right, and rested solely in the consent of the debtor or the discretion of the justice at Special Term. Moreover the creditor was denied the power to investigate the debtor's books and records. He could subpoena them, but he could not examine them; they could be used solely to "refresh" the debtor's recollection.

The current reforms have attempted to remedy some of these difficulties. Reexaminations of the debtor at stated intervals are permitted. In certain cases the creditor may examine witnesses within six months after the debtor's examination has been closed. * * * And finally, perjury is now punishable as a contempt. However, since the statute predicates the applicability of this sanction upon the "materiality" of the testimony in question, the effectiveness of this sanction will rest largely upon what the court feels is "material" evidence.

These, however, are minor matters. As it stands today the examination merely affords the creditor an opportunity to discover that the debtor's assets do not belong to him, but to his wife and kindred, and that they were transferred to pay long standing obligations to the spouse, as to which no records exist. The scope of the examination is not such as to permit a trial of title; whenever a question of title is raised, the dispute may not be settled within the supplementary proceeding. For any real relief the creditor must start a separate action to set aside transfers obviously made to prevent judgment collection.

NOTES AND QUESTIONS

1. New York extensively revised the supplementary procedures described in the quoted passage in 1935. See Cohen, *Collection of Money Judgments: Experimentation with Supplementary Proceedings,* 36 Colum.L.Rev. 1061 (1936), which outlines these changes and comments on the practice in many other states. New York's judgment-collection procedures were revamped again in 1963. Present New York practice is described in Volume Six of Weinstein, Korn & Miller, *New York Civil Practice.* Because modernization of enforcement procedures generally has lagged throughout the country, the excerpt from the Cohen article provides a good statement of the supplementary proceedings presently in force in many states.

2. Should supplementary proceedings be treated as a separate action or merely an adjunct to the action in which the judgment was recovered? On this question *compare* Arnold v. National Union of Marine Cooks & Stewards Ass'n, 44 Wash. 2d 183, 257 P.2d 629 (1953) (part of main action), *with* Riley v. Fatt, 47 So.2d 769 (Fla.1950) (separate action). What turns on the answer to this question?

3. Suppose A recovers a judgment from B and during supplementary proceedings B claims that C is in possession of property belonging to B. When A attempts to have the property applied to the judgment, C contests B's interest. How is the dispute between B and C as to the ownership of the property to be determined? If the supplementary proceeding is under the control of a judge, can the court determine the dispute between B and C and, if it finds in B's favor, apply the property to the satisfaction of A's judgment. What objections are there to the judge making such a determination? *Compare* Letz v. Letz, 123 Mont. 494, 215 P.2d 534 (1950), *with* Mewes v. Jacobson, 70 Idaho 427, 220 P.2d 681 (1950). In THOMAS v. THOMAS, 192 Cal.App.2d 771, 13 Cal. Rptr. 872 (2d Dist.1961), defendant's former wife brought an action for support payments and tried to reach defendant's pension installments. What effect might a good-faith denial by defendant's employer of any indebtedness to the employee have on the original trial-court's jurisdiction to determine whether the ex-wife had any right in future installments? In *Thomas,* defendant's employer contended that it was a denial of due process to proceed with the supplementary proceeding and that an independent action was necessary. How should that question have been resolved?

4.   When a judgment is reversed on appeal, what is the status of the enforcement proceedings already undertaken? Is the prevailing party liable for damages caused by the attempt to enforce the judgment? In HARP v. BROOKSHIRE, 197 Ky. 794, 248 S.W. 177 (1923), H sued B for a declaration that he had a right of way over B's farm. H obtained a temporary injunction to prevent B from interfering with the claimed right of way. The trial court held that H had no right of way and dissolved the injunction. During the pendency of H's appeal, B refused to let H cross the land. The lower court's decision ultimately was reversed and H's right of way upheld. In a subsequent suit by H for damages caused by B's excluding him from the land, the court held that although a party generally is not liable for the consequences of acts performed in obedience to a judgment that later is reversed, B would be held liable since the acts were not directly or expressly authorized by the judgment. But didn't the trial court's decision effectively declare B's ownership of the land and give him the right to control access to it? How could B have protected himself pending H's appeal? See generally Gordon, *Effect of Reversal of Judgments on Acts Done Between Pronouncement and Reversal*, 74 L.Q.Rev. 517 (1958).

----

3.   CONTEMPT AND BODY EXECUTION

REEVES v. CROWNSHIELD

Court of Appeals of New York, 1937.
274 N.Y. 74, 8 N.E.2d 283.

FINCH, Judge.   The uncollectibility of money judgments has ever been a subject of concern to bench and bar. A large part of the statute law of this state is designed to enable a judgment creditor to obtain satisfaction upon his money judgment. That a large percentage of these money judgments have remained uncollectible has been confirmed by statistical surveys. Johns Hopkins University Institute of Law, Survey of Litigation in New York (1931). Many debtors who were in a position to pay have evaded their legal obligations by unlawful and technical means. Discontent with this situation resulted in agitation for reform in collection procedure.   *   *   *   Finally, in 1935, upon the recommendation of the Judicial Council, a law was enacted creating a new mode of enforcing the payment of judgments.   *   *   *

Section 793 of the Civil Practice Act [currently N.Y.C.P.L.R. 5226] now provides that, in addition to the garnishee provisions of the old law, the court may make an order directing a judgment debtor to make payments in installments out of the income which he receives. Such orders must be made upon notice to the judgment debtor and after he has had an opportunity to show inability to pay, and with due regard to the reasonable requirements of the judgment debtor and his family, as well as of payments required to be made by him to other creditors. Section 801 of the Civil Practice Act [now found in N.Y.C.P.L.R. 5251] provides that refusal to pay after such an order of the court is punishable as a contempt.   *   *   *

This new procedure was invoked against the appellant, in an attempt to collect a judgment for approximately $400. The examination in supplementary proceedings disclosed that he was employed by the Federal Government as a steamship inspector at a salary of $230 per month, less a small pension deduction. He has no children, and the whereabouts of his wife are unknown. Aside from $48 a month paid as rent and his living expenses, he has no financial obligations. The court ordered the appellant to pay installments of $20 per month until the judgment was satisfied. Upon his failure to pay, he was held in contempt and fined the sum of $20, commitment being provided for in default of payment.

An appeal was taken directly to this court from the City Court of New York City on the ground that a constitutional question was involved.

* * *

The judgment debtor challenges the constitutionality of section 793 and section 801 on the ground that in effect they provide for imprisonment for debt. It is admitted that neither the State nor the Federal Constitutions contain provisions expressly prohibiting imprisonment for debt, and that the statutory provision forbidding imprisonment for debt found in section 21 of the New York Civil Rights Law excepts cases otherwise specially prescribed by law. It is asserted, however, that imprisonment for debt is barred by the due process clauses of the State and Federal Constitutions (Const.N.Y. art. 1, § 6; Const.U.S. Amend. 14). No cases so holding are cited * * *. Whatever doubt there may exist as to whether imprisonment for debt without regard to ability to pay may be treated as a deprivation of liberty without due process of law * * *, there can be no doubt that imprisonment for failure to obey an order of a court to make payment out of income, which order is made with due regard to the needs of the debtor and his family, is not violative of the due process clause.

* * *

In the case at bar the judgment debtor has not complained that the order directing the payment of $20 per month is unjust, inequitable, or harsh. His position is an arbitrary refusal to pay. It is based upon the ground that the courts are powerless to compel him to pay out of his income an amount fixed after deducting the sum necessary for his reasonable needs.

The Legislature has seen fit to provide a creditor with a direct remedy for the collection of his just debts. A refusal to recognize such an order by the judgment debtor entitles the creditor to move to have him punished for contempt. Without this right, there would be no power in the court to enforce its order. To compel the judgment debtor to obey the order of the court is not imprisonment for debt, but only imprisonment for disobedience of an order with which he is able to comply. His refusal is contumacious conduct, the same as a refusal to obey any other lawful order of the court.

It also is asserted that the application of this law to the appellant is unconstitutional, since it interferes with the operation of a federal instrumentality. To sustain this contention, reference is made to the cases declaring State laws taxing the salaries of federal officers unconstitutional. * * * Analysis shows that these cases are not in point. The true basis for declaring a state tax on the salaries of federal officers unconstitutional is that since the Federal Government presumably finds it necessary to pay its officers a salary based upon the value of their services, the state should not be permitted to tax the salaries thereby reducing the compensation and making it necessary for the Federal Government to increase the salaries paid by it.

* * *

It is true that the wages of a federal employee cannot be garnisheed, but once his wage has been paid to him a state is not prohibited from ordering him to apply a portion of such income towards the payment of his just debts. The moment the salary is received it becomes a part of the general income of the owner. If he should therewith purchase property the property could be taken under execution for the payment of a judgment against the owner. No reason appears for exempting the income while still held as money and not exempting it when it has been converted into property. * * *

It follows that the orders appealed from should be affirmed, with costs.

* * *

Orders affirmed.

NOTES AND QUESTIONS

1. Compare the principal case with PEOPLE ex rel. SARLAY v. POPE, 230 App.Div. 649, 650, 246 N.Y.S. 414, 416 (3d Dep't 1930), in which the court said that the "imprisonment of the defendants until the payment of a fine in the amount of the judgment recovered in the contract action would be, in effect, imprisonment for a civil debt." In the absence of an express constitutional provision forbidding imprisonment for debt, is there any theory under which it can be held unconstitutional? If contempt or body execution is aimed at the recalcitrant or dilatory judgment debtor, how is the good faith, but penniless, debtor protected against being caught in the contempt trap? Is it sufficient simply to require that the judgment debtor's failure be "wilful" in order to punish for contempt? See generally Note, *Present Status of Execution Against the Body of the Judgment Debtor*, 42 Iowa L.Rev. 306 (1957), which outlines the history of body execution and the statutory provisions in the various states.

2. What are the differences between body execution and contempt? Should courts in jurisdictions that have prohibited or severely limited body execution use contempt proceedings to circumvent the restrictions on body execution? See Note, *Present Status of Execution Against the Body of the Judgment Debtor*, Note 1, supra. See also the distinctions between contempt and body execution drawn in Zeitinger v. Mitchell, 244 S.W.2d 91 (Mo.1951).

3. Doesn't the *Reeves* case suggest that the problems that frequently arise during supplementary proceedings could be cured by an order to disclose all hidden or undiscovered assets reinforced by the contempt sanction? How would the court determine whether or not the judgment debtor is telling the truth when he claims to have no leviable property? What types of post-judgment defaults other than the one involved in *Reeves* properly are punishable by contempt? See generally 6 Weinstein, Korn & Miller, *New York Civil Practice* ¶¶ 5251.10–.21.

4. LIENS AND PRIORITIES

MATTER OF FORNABAI

United States District Court, District of New Jersey, 1964.
227 F.Supp. 928.

SHAW, District Judge.   This matter comes before the Court * * * on Petition for Review of an order by the Referee in Bankruptcy. The order of the Referee in Bankruptcy dated June 4, 1963 determined that two judgment liens were entitled to priority in satisfaction over tax liens of the United States of America out of a real estate fund being administered by the Court.

The pertinent facts may be recited briefly as follows: On May 2, 1962 Nicholas Fornabai individually and doing business as Fornaby Equipment Co. was adjudicated a bankrupt in a Chapter XI proceeding.   The realty of the bankrupt was sold and valid liens against the realty transferred to the proceeds of the sale.   The amount thereof held by the Trustee in Bankruptcy is insufficient for full satisfaction of all valid liens.

* * *   The lien of the United States is for taxes assessed against the bankrupt pursuant to provisions of the Internal Revenue Code of 1954. Truck Equipment Corporation recovered a judgment in the Superior Court of New Jersey against the bankrupt on December 8, 1960.   The amount is $13,-716.85 plus interest.   Pak-Mor Manufacturing Co. recovered its judgment against the bankrupt in the United States District Court for the District of New Jersey on March 10, 1961.   The amount of this judgment is $18,199.61 plus interest.   Both judgments were docketed as of the dates of recovery thereof.   The United States filed notice of tax liens against the bankrupt.   * * *

The precise question presented is whether the liens of the two judgment creditors above mentioned were perfected in the sense that they became choate liens on the realty of the bankrupt prior to the date when the United States filed its notice of tax liens.   If so, the judgment liens are entitled to priority.

A judgment docketed in the Superior Court of New Jersey is a lien upon all real estate of the judgment debtor located within the State of New Jersey from the date the judgment is docketed.   N.J.S.A. 2A:16-1. * * *

By federal statute it is provided with respect to judgments of the United States District Court that:

"Every judgment rendered by a district court within a State shall be a lien on the property located in such State in the same manner, to the same extent and under the same conditions as a judgment of a court of general jurisdiction in such State, and shall cease to be a lien in the same manner and time. * * * "   28 U.S.C.A. § 1962.

Taxes assessed against a taxpayer pursuant to the provisions of the Internal Revenue Code of 1954 become liens in favor of the United States upon all property and rights to property belonging to the taxpayer.   26 U.S.C.A. §

6321. But the lien for taxes is not valid "as against any mortgagee, pledgee, purchaser, or *judgment creditor* until notice thereof has been filed." (Emphasis supplied.) 26 U.S.C.A. § 6323. As noted above, the earliest date on which the Government filed notice of a tax lien was April 10, 1961.

Federal law determines which secured creditors are judgment creditors for purposes of protection under Section 6323.   *   *   *

In the case of United States v. Gilbert Associates, Inc., [345 U.S. 361, 73 S.Ct. 701, 97 L.Ed. 1071 (1953)]   *   *   *   the Supreme Court stated:

"*   *   *

"A cardinal principle of Congress in its tax scheme is uniformity, as far as may be. Therefore, a 'judgment creditor' should have the same application in all the states. In this instance, we think Congress used the words 'judgment creditor' in § 3672 [now 26 U.S.C. A. § 6323] in the usual, conventional sense of a judgment of a court of record, since all states have such courts."

The priority of a lien created by state law over a tax lien of the federal government depends on the time it attached to the property in question and became choate. It is perfected to the point of being a choate lien "when the identity of the lienor, the property subject to the lien, and the amount of the lien are established." United States v. Pioneer American Insurance Co., 374 U.S. 84, 88, 89, 83 S.Ct. 1651, 1655, 10 L.Ed.2d 770 (1963).

Each of the judgments here were recovered in a court of record and docketed therein. The identity of each judgment lienor, the property subject to the judgment lien and the amount thereof has been established. Nevertheless, the Government contends that neither of the judgments imposed a choate lien upon realty of the bankrupt because neither of the judgment creditors caused a writ of execution to issue against the real estate of the bankrupt. In support of its argument, the Government cites N.J.S.A. 2A:17–39   *   *   *. [The cited statute gives the purchaser of real property good title as against a judgment creditor who has not issued an execution against the property.]

The effect and purpose of the above cited statutory provision is misconstrued. A writ of execution on a judgment does not create the lien; it is merely the procedural means by which the judgment creditor obtains satisfaction out of the proceeds of the sale of realty.   *   *   *

It is clear from the language of the statutory provision upon which the Government relies, and the judicial interpretation of it over many years that its provisions were intended to apply only to priority inter se among those holding liens by judgment or recognizance and that it has no effect in the determination of priority of lien holders other than those mentioned. It creates an exception to the Common Law rule of "the first in time is the first in right," in favor of a subsequent judgment creditor who has issued execution on the judgment and the reason for the exception is clearly stated in the statute. In the early case of Clement v. Kaighn, 15 N.J.Eq. 47 (Chancery 1862), the Court stated that a judgment shall bind the lands of a defendant from the time of actual entry of the judgment on the record of the Court, but that the purpose of the statutory exception among judgment creditors was to give a junior judgment creditor whose execution was first sued out the "proper effect and fruits thereof." * * *

It would be manifestly inequitable if a senior judgment creditor were permitted to stand by while a junior judgment creditor incurred the expense in issuance of a writ of execution, levy upon, and sale of lands of a defendant, and then step in to share first in the proceeds. This would deny the junior lien holder who proceeded with diligence "the proper effect and fruits thereof." It was this inequity in procedural enforcement affecting judgment creditors and liens attaching by recognizance that the State Legislature recognized and sought to correct. Application of the provisions of the statute to priority status of liens other than those existing by virtue of judgment or recognizance would rest upon an interpretation which the plain language of the statutory provision does not support and one which finds no sanction by weight of judicial precedent in the state courts.

There is no rational basis upon which the Government can equate its tax lien in this instance with a judgment lien or recognizance for purposes of claiming the benefit of the provisions of N.J.S.A. 2A:17–39. Its position might be analogous to that of a judgment creditor who had issued execution on a judgment, if it had been *first* to take action to enforce the tax lien against realty of the taxpayer pursuant to the provisions of Title 26 U.S.C.A. § 7403. But that is not the case here. The mere filing of its notice of tax lien without further action to subject property of the taxpayer to payment of the tax liability, does not give the Government a status analogous to that of a judgment creditor who has issued a writ of execution to satisfy a judgment. Accordingly, as between the Government holding a tax lien by virtue of assessment and notice filed and a judgment creditor who has not issued a writ of execution, the common law rule of "the first in time is the first in right," is the applicable rule. * * *

Moreover, it might be stated as a matter of practical observation, that if the provisions of 26 U.S.C.A. § 6323 in favor of prior judgment creditors were to have no application until the property in question was in the process of sale to satisfy a judgment, the limited effect thereof on judgment liens generally would render the intended benefits sterile. This indeed would be a narrow interpretation of a remedial statute with emphasis upon local procedures to enforce satisfaction of a lien rather than upon the substantive right created by the lien.

* * * A judgment entered in the Superior Court of New Jersey is a lien upon all real estate within the jurisdiction of the court from the date of entry thereof. * * * The judgment creates the substantive right of lien, not the writ of execution.

Accordingly, the determination by order of the Referee in Bankruptcy that the two judgment creditors have priority of lien over the federal tax liens is affirmed. An appropriate order in accordance herewith will be submitted.

NOTES AND QUESTIONS

1.   Lien and priority-of-lien problems are among the most complex in the law of judgment enforcement. The traditional "lien" situation involves the judgment creditor's right to a particular piece of property as against the judgment debtor or someone claiming under the latter, such as an assignee or purchaser of the property. The judgment creditor's rights against a transferee are based on the purchaser's or assignee's having actual or constructive notice of the creditor's rights in the property. Questions of "priority of liens," as in the *Fornabai* case, involve a dispute between two or more judgment creditors over the debtor's property. As a general rule, the rights of one creditor *vis à vis* another are based on the equitable principle of "diligence," which seeks to prevent a creditor from refraining from enforcing a judgment while maintaining priority of lien. What factors should determine whether one judgment creditor is more "diligent" than another?

Because courts often confuse "priority-of-lien" and "lien" situations, the line between the two has been somewhat obscured. The New York practice is analyzed in 6 Weinstein, Korn & Miller, *New York Civil Practice* ¶ 5202.02. The terminology is further analyzed in Distler & Schubin, *Enforcement Priorities and Liens: The New York Judgment Creditor's Rights in Personal Property,* 60 Colum.L.Rev. 458 (1960). For illustrations of some of the many problems that arise in this context, see Burroughs, *The Choate Lien Doctrine,* 1963 Duke L.J. 449; Comment, *Priorities of Creditors Under Judgment Creditor's Bills,* 42 Yale L.J. 919 (1933).

2.   Section 5202 of New York's Civil Practice Law and Rules expressly provides that an execution creditor's rights in the judgment debtor's personal property are superior to those of anyone who acquires an interest after the delivery of an execution to a sheriff except: (1) transferees who acquire the debt or property for fair consideration before levy and (2) transferees who acquire the debt or property, when it is not capable of delivery, for fair consideration after it was levied upon but without knowledge of the levy. What are the purposes of these two exceptions? See 6 Weinstein, Korn & Miller, *New York Civil Practice* ¶¶ 5202.19–.21. The judgment creditor's lien remains in effect as long as the execution is in force but once it expires the judgment creditor's lien terminates and the transfer of any property that was not actually levied upon under the execution made while the execution was in force will be effective as against the judgment creditor.

3.   An execution creditor can lose her lien or priority of lien if she allows the execution to become "dormant," which permits the rights of a diligent creditor to be advanced over those of a creditor who is not pursuing the enforcement of a claim. A classic definition of dormancy is found in EXCELSIOR NEEDLE CO. v. GLOBE CYCLE WORKS, 48 App.Div. 304, 310, 62 N.Y.S. 538, 541 (4th Dep't 1900):

> The law * * * seems to be settled that any direction by the execution creditor to the sheriff, which suspends the lien or delays the enforcement of the levy, renders the execution dormant against subsequent creditors or *bona fide* purchasers. However veiled may be the direction; however much it may be founded on a humane desire to protect the debtor; if it is tantamount to a mandate or instruction to the sheriff to

withhold the execution of his process during the interim that he accedes to this demand, the levy ceases to be effective. That doctrine rests on public policy and is necessary to prevent fraud and it should receive a fairly rigorous enforcement.

What justification is there for the dormancy doctrine? Should a judgment creditor's execution or attachment become dormant when he directs the sheriff not to levy out of a hope that the judgment debtor will become financially stable if the property and business are not disturbed and the latter is not besieged by creditors?

CHAPTER 13
APPELLATE REVIEW

SECTION A. THE PRINCIPLE OF FINALITY

---

1. THE BASIC CONCEPT

CRICK, THE FINAL JUDGMENT AS A BASIS FOR APPEAL, 41
Yale L.J. 539, 541–43, 545–48, 550 (1932):

From very early times in England the method whereby a litigant came
into the king's court and attacked a decision rendered in a feudal or manorial
court was the complaint of false judgment. It was early decided, however,
that the king's courts could not be charged with a false judgment, and the
means whereby the King's Bench corrected errors in the other common law
courts was by writ of error, the method destined to survive in many jurisdictions to our own day. The common law decisions involving writ of error are
clearly the origin of our rule that only final judgments are appealable. The
real factors in the establishment of this practice must go back to the very beginning of the history of the writ of error, and it is impossible at this time to give
more than an explanation which is merely plausible.

* * * The matter seems to be connected in some way with the "record" by which the proceedings in the lower court are made known to the King's
Bench, for counsel in [John de Ralegh's Case, Y.B. 17 Ed. 3 (R.S.) 234
(1343)] * * * says, "You have no warrant to try this record for the
record is not fully here, because the case is still pending in another Court.
* * * It is impossible that on one and the same original writ there should
be two records in different courts." * * *

If we combine with this conception of the record, the fact that a proceeding on a writ of error seems to have been regarded as a new action, and not
merely a continuation of the suit in the inferior court, we see how it may have
been that the record could not be sent up until the suit below had been completed. Suing out a writ of error before final judgment would result in two
actions in different courts, to the procedure of each of which the formal record
was essential. To remove it while the case was pending below "would disturb
the proceedings" there, while the reviewing court could not proceed until it
was informed of what had happened below.

* * *

Taking Blackstone's time as a convenient point of departure, we find that the course of litigation in a simple case in equity went something as follows.

The pleadings having been filed and the parties at issue upon the facts, the evidence was taken down in writing and the case set for hearing before the chancellor or the Master of the Rolls. There the evidence was read and such orders made from time to time as might be necessary. When everything had been heard the decree was pronounced. Generally it was merely interlocutory, but eventually the final decree was made and the rights of the parties completely adjudicated.

We see, then, that there were three types of pronouncements made during the course of a case. First, orders, second, interlocutory decrees, and third, final decrees. Unlike the common law, however, which as we have seen, required a case to go to final judgment before the decisions of the court might be questioned, equity gave relief from all three types of pronouncements. * * *

Thus we see that equity practice never knew the rule of the common law that only final judgments were appealable. Not only could interlocutory decrees be taken to the House of Lords, but also those decisions which had not even attained the dignity of decrees, that is, orders. As to the reason for this, we may tentatively assign two factors. First, appeals to the House of Lords from the Lord Chancellor were established comparatively late in legal history. * * * During the intervening centuries, therefore, a given case had its beginning and ending in the same court, and the only method by which a decision could be altered was by rehearing before the chancellor. * * *

When the House of Lords finally asserted appellate jurisdiction over proceedings in chancery, therefore, it found a system whereby the chancellor passed on all decrees issued, as well as on interlocutory orders, and we need not be surprised that appeals were taken to the Lords from interlocutory decrees because in chancery there was no particular magic in a final decree. * * *

Second, when we consider the character of litigation handled in chancery we see how much more convenient it was to review intermediate decisions as the case progressed. * * * [M]uch of its litigation was of a complicated type unsuited to the more simple common law forms of action. There was a much greater use of subordinate officials than in the common law courts, and the requirement of documentation of evidence introduced difficulties unknown to the King's courts. In equity, judgments were not compelled to follow stereotyped forms, and this made possible dealing with the case by as many orders, decrees, and modifications of the same as were necessary in the particular case. Thus, equity had a more elastic procedure, and also required a less rigid practice on appeal to review the many and varied steps taken below.

When we pass to the American scene we are at once confronted with confusion. * * * However, two main trends seem to have characterized the process.

First, there has been a general tendency to take the common law rule that error lay only after final judgment and to apply it to equity procedure. Second, hampered by this restriction in both law and equity, the courts have gone through elaborate logical exercises in order to escape from the strict application of the restriction   *   *   *.

Another factor which may have had some effect was the failure to keep distinct the practice of law and equity, particularly on appeal. Very commonly one appellate court was established to hear appeals in both law and equity, and in some states, at least, the common law writ of error was the method of appeal in equity cases as well as at law.   *   *   *

NOTE

In McLISH v. ROFF, 141 U.S. 661, 12 S.Ct. 118, 35 L.Ed. 893 (1891), error was brought under the act creating the circuit courts of appeals, 26 Stat. 826 (1891), to review the overruling of a demurrer to the trial-court's jurisdiction. The statute did not contain an express requirement of finality, but the Supreme Court dismissed the writ on the ground that the very word "appeal," through usage, had come to mean the process by which a trial court's *final* judgment was brought before an appellate court for review.

———

Read 28 U.S.C. § 1291 in the Supplement.

———

JETCO ELECTRONICS INDUSTRIES, INC. v. GARDINER, 473 F.2d 1228 (5th Cir.1973). Plaintiff Jetco filed suit against three defendants, ETL, Gardiner, and Gardiner Electronics. The trial court granted ETL's motion to dismiss for lack of personal jurisdiction and for failure to state a claim for relief, and an appeal was taken from that order. Several months after the order involving ETL, the trial court entered a second order disposing of Jetco's claims against Gardiner and Gardiner Electronics. On ETL's motion to dismiss the appeal, the court of appeals held as follows:

> The March order dismissing appellants' suit against ETL   *   *   *   said nothing about appellants' rights as against the other two defendants, Gardiner and Gardiner Electronics   *   *   *. That order is thus not a final judgment   *   *   *. Nor was the later order entering an agreed judgment disposing of appellants' claim against Gardiner and Gardiner Electronics a final judgment [since]   *   *   *   it did not adjudicate appellants' rights as against ETL. Nevertheless, these two orders, considered together, terminated this litigation just as effectively as would have been the case had the district judge gone through the motions of entering a single order formally reciting the substance of the earlier two orders. Mindful of the Supreme Court's command that practical, not technical, considerations are to govern the application of prin-

ciples of finality   *   *   *   we decline appellee's invitation to exalt form over substance by dismissing this appeal. We hold that the March order dismissing appellants' suit against ETL is, under the circumstances of this case, within our appellate jurisdiction.   *   *   *

Id. at 1231.

NOTES AND QUESTIONS

1. The question whether a court may hear an appeal—with its constituent issues of finality, timeliness, and mode—is almost without exception viewed as involving "jurisdiction over the subject matter." E. g., Collins v. Miller, 252 U.S. 364, 40 S.Ct. 347, 64 L.Ed. 616 (1920); United States v. Girault, 52 U.S. (11 How.) 22, 13 L.Ed. 587 (1850). All the doctrinal overtones of that concept are present. For example, a lower appellate-court's decision will be reversed for lack of appellate jurisdiction and the appeal will be ordered dismissed even though the issue of the propriety of the appeal was not raised in the lower court; the parties may not waive the requirements for an appeal; neither the trial nor appellate court can supply the defects or depart from the rigid rules of law regarding appeals. What are the reasons for this approach? Are the same dangers present when an appellate court conducts a premature review as when a trial court hears a cause that is not within its competence? The rigidity of the traditional view is cogently criticized in 6 Moore, *Federal Practice* ¶ 54.43 (2d ed.).

2. Does the *Jetco* decision represent a departure from the traditional approach discussed in Note 1 above? Does your answer depend on whether the trial court's second order, dismissing the case against Gardiner and Gardiner Electronics, was rendered prior to the time Jetco's appeal was filed? Compare Oak Constr. Co. v. Huron Cement Co., 475 F.2d 1220 (6th Cir.1973) (subsequent trial court action cannot save appeal that was inappropriate at the time it was filed). Should Jetco be free to file a separate appeal challenging the court's second order?

---

2. THE NEW YORK APPROACH

Read N.Y.C.P.L.R. 5701, which is found in the Supplement following 28 U.S.C. § 1292.

PEART v. PEART, 48 Hun (N.Y.) 79 (Sup.Ct. 5th Dep't 1888). Defendant's motion to require plaintiff to make her complaint more definite and certain was denied, and defendant appealed. A motion to dismiss the appeal was denied:

> The order is appealable. It is definitely settled so far as this court is concerned, that orders made at a Special Term involving questions as to the form of the pleadings and whether they contain irrelevant, redundant or scandalous matter, or are so indefinite and uncertain that the precise meaning or application of an allegation

therein is not apparent, may be reviewed by this court on appeal, and if any error has been committed it may be corrected.

KORN, CIVIL JURISDICTION OF THE NEW YORK COURT OF APPEALS AND APPELLATE DIVISIONS, 16 Buffalo L. Rev. 307, 330, 332 (1967):

It is generally recognized that this broad authority for appeal as of right from almost every kind of intermediate determination is a prime source of delay and expense in litigation and imposes an undue burden on the Appellate Divisions. Nevertheless, the proposal of the CPLR revisers to eliminate the broad catch-all language met with substantial opposition from some segments of the bar. The result was a compromise limited only to orders on motions to require a more definite statement or to strike scandalous or prejudicial matter in a pleading; as to these CPLR 5701(b) now requires permission to appeal.

* * *

Today * * * it is well known that there is hardly a question of practice that cannot be appealed; and, if a matter is said to be addressed to the court's discretion or favor, this may mean a more limited scope of review but will rarely affect appealability. Appeals on practice matters are legion, ranging far and wide over questions of venue, parties, consolidation and joint trial, pleading and pre-trial disclosure. The only meaningful method of inquiry as to the content of the present standards is to examine the types of orders that have been held *not* to involve some part of the merits or affect a substantial right.[a]

BROWN v. GOLDEN, 6 A.D.2d 766, 174 N.Y.S.2d 75 (4th Dep't 1958). The court held plaintiff could not appeal from two discovery orders. One justice dissented:

(1) The plaintiffs, upon the advice of their attorney, refused to answer questions upon the examination before trial seeking to elicit the names and addresses of doctors who had treated the plaintiff's wife on various occasions, prior to, and after, the treatment by the defendant physician, which is the basis of the present malpractice action. The plaintiffs' counsel maintained that the disclosure of the information sought would violate the plaintiffs' privilege * * *. Nevertheless, the Special Term directed the plaintiffs to answer the questions. * * *

The order appealed from, in my opinion, "affects a substantial right" of the plaintiffs and is therefore appealable * * *.

The plaintiffs had no way of protecting their position except by refusing to answer. If they had answered the questions and dis-

----

[a] See also 7 Weinstein, Korn & Miller, *New York Civil Practice* ¶¶ 5701.03–.06.

closed the information and it was later determined that their privilege had been violated, it would be too late to remedy the situation. The disclosure, once made, could not be recalled.

The overriding of a claim of privilege presents a very different question from that presented by the overruling of an objection to a question upon the ground that it was irrelevant or that it was outside the scope of the examination. In such a case, it is arguable that no harm is done by requiring the party to answer the question, subject to a final determination of the propriety of the question at the trial. * * *

It has been suggested that the remedy of the party or witness whose claim of privilege is overruled is to refuse to answer the question despite the direction of the court and to await contempt proceedings and then to appeal from the order adjudging him in contempt. This suggestion, it seems to me, exalts form over substance. There would be nothing of substance in the record upon an appeal from an order adjudging the plaintiffs in contempt which is not before us in the present record. * * *

Furthermore, the plaintiffs ought not to be placed in the position of being required to defy the court and to run the risk of being punished for contempt in order to raise, in good faith, the question of a privilege of nondisclosure. * * *

(2) The part of the order denying the plaintiffs' motion to compel the defendant to answer * * * questions [about the medical practices followed] stands upon a somewhat different footing. * * *

By denying the plaintiffs' motion to compel the defendant to answer, the Special Term order in effect limited the scope of the examination before trial. If the order had done this in express terms, it concededly would have been appealable. This court and other departments of the Appellate Division hear appeals from orders fixing the scope of examination before trial at practically every term. * * * Indeed, if an order limiting the scope of an examination before trial were held to be nonappealable, the purpose of the provisions of the practice in this regard might well be frustrated. The purpose of examination before trial is to enable the party to prepare for trial and, if the scope of the examination is erroneously limited, the opportunity to prepare adequately is gone forever.

* * *

Ample precedent for the entertaining of this appeal may also be found in the uniform line of cases holding that orders allowing or disallowing specific questions, upon the settlement of interrogatories, are appealable. * * *

NOTES AND QUESTIONS

1. What are the advantages of freely allowing appeals from interlocutory orders? The disadvantages? Is it better to resolve the question of allowing an interlocutory appeal by weighing these advantages and disadvantages against each other in the abstract or by considering them as they apply in each case? See generally Crick, *The Final Judgment as a Basis for Appeal,* 41 Yale L.J. 539 (1932); Note, *Appealability in the Federal Courts,* 75 Harv.L.Rev. 351 (1961).

2. In refusing to allow an appeal from an interlocutory order, we may avoid an unnecessary appellate hearing; in allowing an appeal, we may avoid an unnecessary trial, either by disposing of the case at that stage or by correcting in advance of trial an error that might otherwise require a new trial. Is there any basis for supposing that the appellate hearing is more likely to prove unnecessary than the trial? Is it relevant that the trial judge, hopefully, will be correct in his rulings more often than he is wrong?

Even if we assume that a reversal of the trial court's order by the appellate court is as probable as its affirmance and we also take into consideration that trial may demand more time of lawyers and judges than an appeal, does it follow that interlocutory appeals should be freely allowed? Consider the effect of the following factors. (1) In the course of a single lawsuit there may be many interlocutory orders from which one of the parties would like to appeal; thus, if finality is required, several appeals may be saved for every trial that would be saved under the other approach. (2) Not every reversal of an interlocutory order will terminate the case without trial. What, for example, would have been the effect of a reversal in *Brown v. Golden?* (3) The number of appellate courts cannot be increased as readily as can the number of trial courts in order to take care of heavier calendars. There will be a serious problem as long as it is the function of appellate courts not only to review trial-court decisions but to establish and maintain a degree of uniformity in the law.

The debate over the relative merits of a final-judgment rule and an interlocutory-appeal system is intertwined with the larger problem of court congestion at the appellate level. The attention given to crowding at the trial level has obscured the fact that a comparable problem exists in many reviewing courts. The problems of one court have been detailed in Wright, *The Overloaded Fifth Circuit: A Crisis in Judicial Administration,* 42 Texas L.Rev. 949 (1964). Professor Wright's article discusses the following methods for reducing the backlog of cases in the Fifth Circuit:

1. The most extensive assignment of judges who are not fully occupied to sit with busier courts.

2. Increased use of per curiam opinions.

3. Additional law clerks and secretarial help for the judges.

4. Curtailment, or abolition, of diversity jurisdiction.

5. Appeal as of right only when a particular amount is in controversy.

6. Refusal of interlocutory appeals.

7. Creation of specialized courts to review decisions of administrative agencies, and to hear other specialized areas of litigation.

8. Limitation of the scope of review to errors of law, rather than factual matters.

What are the advantages and disadvantages of each of these suggestions? Why not simply add more judges to the Fifth Circuit? Another enlightening analysis of delay in the appellate courts is found in Hazard, *After the Trial Court—The Realities of Appellate Review,* in *The Courts, the Public, and the Law Explosion* 60–84 (Jones ed. 1965). Other deficiencies in the appellate system are discussed in Sunderland, *A Simplified System of Appellate Procedure,* 17 Tenn.L.Rev. 651 (1943); Willcox, Karlen & Roemer, *Justice Lost—By What Appellate Papers Cost,* 33 N.Y.U.L.Rev. 934 (1958). An interesting account of practice in one of the United States Courts of Appeals appears in Note, *The Second Circuit: Federal Judicial Administration in Microcosm,* 63 Colum.L.Rev. 874 (1963).

3. Appeals are expensive. See Willcox, Karlen & Roemer, Note 2, supra; Note, *Cost of Appeal,* 27 Mont.L.Rev. 49 (1965). Preparation of the necessary briefs and records demands a substantial amount of the lawyer's time, and duplication of these documents is costly, although some progress has been made in recent years by reducing the need to reproduce certain parts of the record and by using cheaper processes than printing for duplicating records and briefs. Substantial travelling costs often are involved because an appellate court usually is not as proximate to the attorneys as is the trial court. Because of expense and the delay caused by congestion, the availability of appeal often presents a tactical opportunity to one of the parties. Is there any effective sanction against the use of appeal for purely tactical reasons? See Kamine, *Frivolous Appeals,* 47 Calif.St. B.J. 307 (1972). In what ways might modern communications and duplication technology reduce the cost of appeals?

4. Should the avoidance of extra expense, delay, and needless hearings be the only consideration in deciding whether to permit appeals from interlocutory orders? Is the trial judge's independence and discretion threatened by too frequent a review? Is a party who has been ordered to answer questions in a deposition interested in obtaining immediate review solely in order to save time or money?

3. MODIFICATIONS AND DEPARTURES FROM THE FINAL-JUDGMENT RULE IN THE FEDERAL COURTS

A. AMELIORATION OF THE BASIC CONCEPT

(i) Cases involving multiple claims or parties

Read Federal Rule of Civil Procedure 54(b) in the Supplement, with the accompanying material.

SEARS, ROEBUCK & CO. v. MACKEY

Supreme Court of the United States, 1956.
351 U.S. 427, 76 S.Ct. 895, 100 L.Ed. 1297.

Certiorari to the United States Court of Appeals for the Seventh Circuit.

Mr. Justice BURTON delivered the opinion of the Court.

This action, presenting multiple claims for relief, was brought by Mackey and another in the United States District Court for the Northern District of Illinois, Eastern Division, in 1953. The court expressly directed that judgment be entered for the defendant, Sears, Roebuck & Co., on two, but less than all, of the claims presented. It also expressly determined that there was no just reason for delay in making the entry. After Mackey's notice of appeal from that judgment to the Court of Appeals for the Seventh Circuit, Sears, Roebuck & Co. moved to dismiss the appeal for lack of appellate jurisdiction. The Court of Appeals upheld its jurisdiction and denied the motion   *   *   *. Because of the importance of the issue in determining appellate jurisdiction and because of a conflict of judicial views on the subject, we granted certiorari.   *   *   *   For the reasons hereafter stated, we sustain the Court of Appeals and its appellate jurisdiction.

*   *   *

The complaint contains six counts. We disregard the fifth because it has been abandoned and the sixth because it duplicates others.   *   *   *   The appeal before us is from a judgment striking out Counts I and II without disturbing Counts III and IV, and the question presented is whether such a judgment is presently appealable   *   *   *.

In Count I, Mackey, a citizen of Illinois, and Time Saver Tools, Inc., an Illinois corporation owned by Mackey, are the original plaintiffs *   *   *. Mackey charges Sears with conduct violating the Sherman Antitrust Act in a manner prejudicial to three of Mackey's commercial ventures

* * *. His first charge is unlawful destruction by Sears, since 1949, of the market for nursery lamps manufactured by General Metalcraft Company, a corporation wholly owned by Mackey. * * * His second charge is unlawful interference by Sears, in 1952, with Mackey's contract to sell, on commission, certain tools and other products of the Vascoloy-Ramet Corporation * * *. His third charge is unlawful destruction by Sears, in 1952, of the market for a new type of carbide-tipped lathe bit and for other articles manufactured by Time Saver Tools, Inc. * * *. Mackey combines such charges with allegations that Sears has used its great size to monopolize commerce and restrain competition in these fields. He asks for damages and equitable relief.

In Count II, Mackey * * * incorporates the allegations of Count I as to the Metalcraft transactions and asks for $250,000 damages for Sears' wilful destruction of the business of Metalcraft, plus $50,000 for Mackey's loss on obligations guaranteed by him.

In Count III, Mackey seeks $75,000 in a common-law proceeding against Sears for unlawfully inducing a breach of his Vascoloy commission contract.

In Count IV, Time Saver seeks $200,000 in a common-law proceeding against Sears for unlawfully destroying Time Saver's business by unfair competition and patent infringement.

The jurisdiction of the Court of Appeals to entertain Mackey's appeal from the District Court's judgment depends upon 28 U.S.C. § 1291 * * *.

* * * The controversy before us arises solely because, in this multiple claims action, the District Court has dismissed the claims stated in Counts I and II, but has left unadjudicated those stated in Counts III and IV.

Before the adoption of the Federal Rules * * *, such a situation was generally regarded as leaving the appellate court without jurisdiction of an attempted appeal. It was thought that, although the judgment was a final decision on the respective claims in Counts I and II, it obviously was not a final decision of the whole case, and there was no authority for treating anything less than the whole case as a judicial unit for purposes of appeal. This construction of the judicial unit was developed from the common law which had dealt with litigation generally less complicated than much of that of today.

With the Federal Rules * * *, there came an increased opportunity for the liberal joinder of claims in multiple claims actions. This, in turn, demonstrated a need for relaxing the restrictions upon what should be treated as a judicial unit for purposes of appellate jurisdiction. Sound judicial administration did not require relaxation of the standard of finality in the disposition of the individual adjudicated claims for the purpose of their appealability. It did, however, demonstrate that, at least in multiple claims actions, some final decisions, on less than all of the claims, should be appealable without waiting for a final decision on *all* of the claims. Largely to meet this need, in 1939, Rule 54(b) was promulgated in its original form * * *.

It gave limited relief. The courts interpreted it as not relaxing the requirement of a "final decision" on each individual claim as the basis for an appeal, but as authorizing a limited relaxation of the former general practice that, in multiple claims actions, *all* the claims had to be finally decided before an appeal could be entertained from a final decision upon any of them. Thus, original Rule 54(b) modified the single judicial unit theory but left unimpaired the statutory concept of finality prescribed by § 1291. However, it was soon found to be inherently difficult to determine by any automatic standard of unity which of several multiple claims were sufficiently separable from others to qualify for this relaxation of the unitary principle in favor of their appealability. The result was that the jurisdictional time for taking an appeal from a final decision on less than all of the claims in a multiple claims action in some instances expired earlier than was foreseen by the losing party. It thus became prudent to take immediate appeals in all cases of doubtful appealability and the volume of appellate proceedings was undesirably increased.

Largely to overcome this difficulty, Rule 54(b) was amended, in 1946, to take effect in 1948.   *   *   *

"(b) Judgment Upon Multiple Claims. *When more than one claim for relief is presented in an action*, whether as a claim, counterclaim, cross-claim, or third-party claim, *the court may direct the entry of a final judgment upon one or more but less than all of the claims only upon an express determination that there is no just reason for delay and upon an express direction for the entry of judgment.*   *   *   * (Emphasis supplied.)

In this form, it does not relax the finality required of each decision, as an individual claim, to render it appealable, but it does provide a practical means of permitting an appeal to be taken from one or more final decisions on individual claims, in multiple claims actions, without waiting for final decisions to be rendered on *all* the claims in the case.   *   *   *

To meet the demonstrated need for flexibility, the District Court is used as a "dispatcher." It is permitted to determine, in the first instance, the appropriate *time when each "final decision"* upon "one or more but less than all" of the claims in a multiple claims action is ready for appeal. This arrangement already has lent welcome certainty to the appellate procedure. Its "negative effect" has met with uniform approval. The effect so referred to is the rule's specific requirement that for "one or more but less than all" multiple claims to become appealable, the District Court must make both "an express determination that there is no just reason for delay" and "an express direction for the entry of judgment." A party adversely affected by a final decision thus knows that his time for appeal will *not* run against him until this certification has been made.

*   *   *

In the case before us, there is no doubt that each of the claims dismissed is a "claim for relief" within the meaning of Rule 54(b), or that their dismissal constitutes a "final decision" on individual claims. Also, it cannot well be argued that the claims stated in Counts I and II are so inherently inseparable from, or closely related to, those stated in Counts III and IV that the District

Court has abused its discretion in certifying that there exists no just reason for delay. They certainly *can* be decided independently of each other.

Petitioner contends that amended Rule 54(b) attempts to make an unauthorized extension of § 1291. We disagree. It could readily be argued here that the claims stated in Counts I and II are sufficiently independent of those stated in Counts III and IV to satisfy the requirements of Rule 54(b) even in its original form.   *   *   *

While it thus might be possible to hold that in this case the Court of Appeals had jurisdiction under original Rule 54(b), there at least would be room for argument on the issue of whether the decided claims were separate and independent from those still pending in the District Court. Thus the instant case affords an excellent illustration of the value of the amended rule which was designed to overcome that difficulty. Assuming that the requirements of the original rule are not met in this case, we nevertheless are enabled to recognize the present appellate jurisdiction of the Court of Appeals under the amended rule. The District Court *cannot*, in the exercise of its discretion, treat as "final" that which is not "final" within the meaning of § 1291. But the District Court *may*, by the exercise of its discretion in the interest of sound judicial administration, release for appeal final decisions upon one or more, but less than all, claims in multiple claims actions. The timing of such a release is, with good reason, vested by the rule primarily in the discretion of the District Court as the one most likely to be familiar with the case and with any justifiable reasons for delay.   *   *   *

Rule 54(b), in its original form, thus may be said to have modified the single judicial unit practice which had been developed by court decisions. *   *   *

Rule 54(b), in its amended form, is a comparable exercise of the rule-making authority of this Court. It does not supersede any statute controlling appellate jurisdiction. It scrupulously recognizes the statutory requirement of a "final decision" under § 1291 as a basic requirement for an appeal to the Court of Appeals. It merely administers that requirement in a practical manner in multiple claims actions and does so by rule instead of by judicial decision. By its negative effect, it operates to restrict in a valid manner the number of appeals in multiple claims actions.

We reach a like conclusion as to the validity of the amended rule where the District Court acts affirmatively and thus assists in properly timing the release of final decisions in multiple claims actions. The amended rule adapts the single judicial unit theory so that it better meets the current needs of judicial administration. Just as Rule 54(b), in its original form, resulted in the release of some decisions on claims in multiple claims actions before they otherwise would have been released, so amended Rule 54(b) now makes possible the release of more of such decisions subject to judicial supervision. The amended rule preserves the historic federal policy against piecemeal appeals in many cases more effectively than did the original rule.

*   *   *

Affirmed.

[On the same day it decided *Mackey*, the Supreme Court in COLD MET-AL PROCESS CO. v. UNITED ENGINEERING & FOUNDRY CO., 351 U. S. 445, 76 S.Ct. 904, 100 L.Ed. 1311 (1956), held that an appeal by defendant was appropriate under Section 1291 and Rule 54(b) even though a counterclaim arising out of the same transaction had not yet been decided.]

Mr. Justice FRANKFURTER, whom Mr. Justice HARLAN joins, concurring in * * * [*Mackey*] and dissenting in * * * [*Cold Metal*].

* * *

The opinion in Cold Metal declares that 28 U.S.C. § 1291 remains unimpaired but surely that section does not remain what it was before these opinions were written. Rule 54(b) is apparently the transforming cause. The Court could have said that Rule 54(b), promulgated under congressional authority and having the force of statute, has qualified 28 U.S.C. § 1291. It does not say so. The Court could have said that it rejects the reasoning of the decisions in which this Court for over a century has interpreted § 1291 as expressing a hostility toward piecemeal appeals. It does not say so. The Court could have said that Rule 54(b)'s requirement of a certificate from a district judge means that the district judges alone determine the content of finality. The Court does not say that either.

The Court does indicate that what has been the core of the doctrine of finality as applied to multiple claims litigation—that only that part of a litigation which is separate from, and independent of, the remainder of the litigation can be appealed before the completion of the entire litigation—is no longer to be applied as a standard, or at least as an exclusive standard, for deciding what is final for purposes of § 1291. The Court does not, however, indicate what standards the district courts and the courts of appeals are now to apply in determining when a decision is final. It leaves this problem in the first instance to the district courts, subject to review by the courts of appeals for an abuse of discretion. In other instances where a district court's ruling can be upset only for an abuse of its discretion, the scope of review is necessarily narrow. Here, in regard to the present problem, what is to come under review is a newly modified requirement of finality. But the requirement continues to be based upon a statute * * * and that statute defines and constricts the jurisdiction of the courts of appeals. Therefore the issue of compliance with this congressional command would, I should suppose, cast upon the courts of appeals a duty of independent judgment broader than is implied by the usual flavor of the phrase "abuse of discretion."

For me, the propositions emerging from analysis of the relationship of Rule 54(b) to 28 U.S.C. § 1291 are clear.

1. 28 U.S.C. § 1291 is left intact by Rule 54(b). * * *

2. 28 U.S.C. § 1291 is not a technical rule in a game. It expresses not only a deeply rooted but a wisely sanctioned principle against piecemeal appeals governing litigation in the federal courts. * * * The great importance of this characteristic feature of the federal judicial system * * *

is made luminously manifest by considering the evils where, as in New York, piecemeal reviews are allowed.

3. * * * What have been called exceptions are not exceptions at all in the sense of inroads on the principle. They have not qualified the core, that is, that there should be no premature, intermediate appeal.

* * *

4. The expansion by the Federal Rules of the allowable content of a proceeding and the range of a litigation inevitably enlarged the occasions for severing one aspect or portion of a litigation from what remains under the traditional test of a "final decision." On the basis of prior cases, we held that it was not a departure from the policy against piecemeal appeals to permit an appeal with respect to that part of a multiple claims litigation based on a set of facts separate and independent from the facts on which the remainder of the litigation was based. * * *

The principles which this Court has heretofore enunciated over a long course of decisions under § 1291 furnish ready guides for deciding the appealability of the certified parts of the litigation in the two cases now before the Court. Count II in Sears, Roebuck and Co. v. Mackey, is appealable since the transactions and occurrences involved in it do not involve any of those embraced in Counts III and IV. Count I involves at least two transactions which are also the subject matter of Counts III and IV but is appealable under § 1292(1) as an interlocutory order denying an injunction. In Cold Metal * * * the counterclaim, even if not compulsory, is based in substantial part on the transactions involved in the main litigation and hence not appealable.

* * *

NOTES AND QUESTIONS

1. Why did the Supreme Court indicate in *Mackey* that Rule 54(b) would be an unauthorized rule if it extended the scope of 28 U.S.C. § 1291? Reread 28 U.S.C. § 2072 in the Supplement.

2. How does the Supreme Court's reading of amended Rule 54(b) in the paragraph beginning "In this form" differ from the reading it says the federal courts gave to the original Rule? Does the Court adhere to this reading of the amended Rule in the later stages of its opinion? How does the amended Rule "make possible the release of more of such decisions," as the Court says it does in the last paragraph of its opinion? Why does the Court say the amended Rule "operates to restrict in a valid manner the number of appeals in multiple claims actions"?

3. Is the purpose of Rule 54(b) the same as that underlying 28 U.S.C. § 1292(b), which allows interlocutory appeals at the joint discretion of the district judge and the court of appeals? Will the appeal of separate claims speed up or delay the final resolution of the entire case?

4. If the trial judge determines that there is no reason for delay and orders judgment entered on a separate claim, and no immediate appeal is taken from that order, may the judgment on the separate claim be attacked on an appeal from the

final judgment on the entire case? *Cf. Dickinson v. Petroleum Conversion Corp.,* p. 1036, infra. May the propriety of entering judgment on the separate claim be challenged at that time?

5. If the trial judge, in accordance with Rule 54(b), directs entry of judgment on a separate claim that "certainly *can* be decided independently," may the court of appeals nonetheless refuse to hear the appeal? In PANICHELLA v. PENNSYLVANIA R. R., 252 F.2d 452 (3d Cir.1958), the court held that the district judge had abused his discretion in directing the separate entry of judgment against defendant on his claim against an impleaded third party, because (1) the whole matter would be moot if defendant prevailed against plaintiff, (2) the legal effect of the same release was in question both on the third-party claim and the principal claim and thus would have to be determined twice by the court of appeals if this appeal were allowed, and (3) the claimed advantage of allowing the appeal —that the two claims could be tried together if the appeal were successful—would necessitate delaying the trial of the principal claim. Does the fact that a third-party claim was involved affect the weight to be given the court's third point?

6. In UNITED STATES v. CROWE, POPE & LAND ENTERPRISES, INC., 474 F.2d 200 (5th Cir.1973), the federal government brought suit to enjoin defendant from polluting a section of the Chattahoochee River. Federal statutes permitted relief only if the government could show either that the river was itself navigable or that it was a tributary of a navigable river. At a preliminary stage of the proceedings the trial court made a finding that the river was not navigable, leaving open the tributary question. The government sought to appeal the finding on the ground that it constituted a final decision on one of the government's claims. The court dismissed the appeal stating that the action did not involve separate claims but only a single claim with different legal theories. Was the court correct in its analysis? How useful is a distinction between "claims" and "theories" in determining whether or not a decision is appealable under Rule 54(b)? See 10 Wright & Miller, *Federal Practice and Procedure: Civil* § 2657 (1973).

(ii) Decisions involving "collateral orders"

COHEN v. BENEFICIAL INDUSTRIAL LOAN CORP., 337 U.S. 541, 69 S.Ct. 1221, 93 L.Ed. 1528 (1949). Plaintiff brought a shareholder's derivative suit in a New Jersey federal court. The district court denied defendants' motion to require plaintiff to post security for costs pursuant to a New Jersey statute, holding the statute inapplicable to an action in a federal court. The circuit court of appeals reversed, and the Supreme Court affirmed that decision. It addressed itself to the question of appealability in the following passage:

> * * * Appeal gives the upper court a power of review, not one of intervention. So long as the matter remains open, unfinished or inconclusive, there may be no intrusion by appeal.

But the District Court's action upon this application was concluded and closed and its decision final in that sense before the appeal was taken.

Nor does the statute permit appeals, even from fully consummated decisions, where they are but steps towards final judgment in which they will merge. The purpose is to combine in one review all stages of the proceeding that effectively may be reviewed and corrected if and when final judgment results. But this order of the District Court did not make any step toward final disposition of the merits of the case and will not be merged in final judgment. When that time comes, it will be too late effectively to review the present order and the rights conferred by the statute, if it is applicable, will have been lost, probably irreparably. We conclude that the matters embraced in the decision appealed from are not of such an interlocutory nature as to affect, or to be affected by, decision of the merits of this case.

This decision appears to fall in that small class which finally determine claims of right separable from, and collateral to, rights asserted in the action, too important to be denied review and too independent of the cause itself to require that appellate consideration be deferred until the whole case is adjudicated. The Court has long given this provision of the statute this practical rather than a technical construction. * * *

We hold this order appealable because it is a final disposition of a claimed right which is not an ingredient of the cause of action and does not require consideration with it. * * * Here it is the right to security that presents a serious and unsettled question. If the right were admitted or clear and the order involved only an exercise of discretion as to the amount of security, a matter the statute makes subject to reconsideration from time to time, appealability would present a different question.

Id. at 545, 69 S.Ct. at 1225, 93 L.Ed. at 1536.

NOTES AND QUESTIONS

1. In UNITED STATES v. RYAN, 402 U.S. 423, 91 S.Ct. 1580, 29 L.Ed. 2d 85 (1971), and COBBLEDICK v. UNITED STATES, 309 U.S. 323, 60 S. Ct. 540, 84 L.Ed. 783 (1940), petitioners had moved unsuccessfully in the district court to quash subpoenas directing them to appear and produce documents before a grand jury. In each case the Supreme Court held that the court of appeals was required to dismiss the appeal from the district court order. According to the Supreme Court, if petitioners disobeyed the order and were found in contempt, their situation would become "so severed from the main proceeding as to permit an appeal." The Court distinguished PERLMAN v. UNITED STATES, 247 U.S. 7, 38 S.Ct. 417, 62 L.Ed. 950 (1918), in which an appeal was allowed from an order denying a motion to prohibit turning over to a grand jury property already in the custody of the court, on the ground that the person making the mo-

tion in that case was otherwise "powerless to avert the mischief of the order." Are the cases really distinguishable? Consider the fact that a grand jury proceeding has no defined litigants and that it renders no "final judgments" in the same sense as does a court.

In NIXON v. SIRICA, 487 F.2d 700, 707 n. 21 (D.C.Cir.1973), in which the President of the United States had been ordered to produce certain tape recordings for examination by a federal district judge, the court of appeals, although permitting review by a petition for a writ of mandamus, see p. 1028, infra, said that an appeal would lie under the doctrine of the *Perlman* case, because "in the case of the President, contempt of a judicial order * * * would be a course unseemly at best." See also United States v. Nixon, 418 U.S. 683, 94 S.Ct. 3090, 41 L.Ed.2d 260 (1974).

2. May a person always obtain review of an interlocutory order by disobeying it and being found in contempt? In what type of case might even this Spartan tactic be unavailable? When it is available, is this method of obtaining review an adequate or rational substitute for allowing an appeal from the interlocutory order in the first place? *Hickman v. Taylor,* p. 700, supra, was a case in which review was obtained of an interlocutory discovery order through disobedience and contempt. In that case, defendants and their lawyer were found in criminal contempt, and an appeal was allowed. Had they been found in civil contempt—i. e., if the contempt citation were intended only to coerce compliance with the order and not to punish their disobedience of it—the lawyer, but not defendants themselves, would have been able to appeal because an adjudication of civil contempt is not regarded as a final order as to the parties. See Fox v. Capital Co., 299 U.S. 105, 57 S.Ct. 57, 81 L.Ed. 67 (1936). See also Fenton v. Walling, 139 F.2d 608 (9th Cir.1943).

3. Would the orders in *Ryan* and *Cobbledick* have been appealable in New York? Would a discretionary appeal be available under 28 U.S.C. § 1292(b) to test a discovery order in a federal court? See pp. 1029–31, infra.

FORGAY v. CONRAD, 47 U.S. (6 How.) 201, 203, 12 L.Ed. 404, 405 (1848). The trial court, upon finding that a fraudulent conveyance had been made, ordered property delivered to an assignee in bankruptcy and directed an accounting before a master. The order to deliver was held appealable even before the conclusion of the accounting because of the irreparable injury that might be sustained if the property were disposed of by the assignee in bankruptcy while the accounting was in progress. Chief Justice Taney said: "Undoubtedly, [the decree] * * * is not final, in the strict, technical sense of that term. But this court has not heretofore understood the words 'final decrees' in this strict and technical sense, but has given to them a more liberal, and, as we think, a more reasonable construction, and one more consonant to the intention of the legislature." See also Altschuler v. Altschuler, 399 Ill. 559, 78 N.E.2d 225, 3 A.L.R.2d 333 (1948); Annot., 3 A.L.R.2d 342 (1949).

BROWN SHOE CO. v. UNITED STATES, 370 U.S. 294, 82 S.Ct. 1502, 8 L.Ed.2d 510 (1962). The district court found defendant had violated the antitrust laws and directed divestiture of a subsidiary, but it had reserved its ruling on a specific plan of divestiture. On a direct appeal by the Shoe Company under the Expediting Act, 15 U.S.C. § 29, the Supreme Court held the divestiture decree was sufficiently final to be appealable even though a specific plan had not been formulated. Its own past practice, said the Court, had been to hear such appeals in antitrust cases; the substantive aspects of the case had been fully determined and to delay decision on the merits would chill the "careful, and often extended, negotiation and formulation" of the final divestiture order.

_____

NOTES AND QUESTIONS

1. Should an appeal from an order such as those in *Cohen, Forgay,* and *Brown* be subject to the requirements of Rule 54(b)? See 10 Wright & Miller, *Federal Practice and Procedure: Civil* § 2658, at 67–75 (1973). See also Comment, *The Collateral Order Doctrine in California,* 15 Hast.L.J. 105 (1963).

2. In which of the cases thus far considered would it be practical for the proceedings in the lower court to continue while the appeal was being determined? Is this factor relevant to the decision whether to allow appeal? See Note, *Appealability in the Federal Courts,* 75 Harv.L.Rev. 351, 365 (1961).

3. Does the *Brown Shoe* decision reflect the operation of the same considerations that Crick found to have been influential in the history of appeals in English equity? See p. 1002, supra.

_____

(iii) Non-final Decisions Having Irremediable Consequences

_____

GILLESPIE v. UNITED STATES STEEL CORP.

Supreme Court of the United States, 1964.
379 U.S. 148, 85 S.Ct. 308, 13 L.Ed.2d 199.

Certiorari to the United States Court of Appeals for the Sixth Circuit.

Mr. Justice BLACK delivered the opinion of the Court.

The petitioner, administratrix of the estate of her son Daniel Gillespie, brought this action in federal court against the respondent shipowner-employer to recover damages for Gillespie's death, which was alleged to have occurred when he fell and was drowned while working as a seaman on respondent's ship docked in Ohio. She claimed a right to recover for the benefit of herself and of the decedent's dependent brother and sisters under the Jones Act, which subjects employers to liability if by negligence they cause a seaman's injury or death. She also claimed a right of recovery under the Ohio wrongful death statute because the vessel allegedly was not seaworthy as required by the "general maritime law." The complaint in addition sought damages for Gillespie's pain and suffering before he died, based on the Jones Act and the general maritime law, causes of action which petitioner said survived Gillespie's death by force of the Jones Act itself and the Ohio survival statute, respectively. The District Judge, holding that the Jones Act supplied the exclusive remedy, on motion of respondent struck all parts of the complaint which referred to the Ohio statutes or to unseaworthiness. He also struck all reference to recovery for the benefit of the brother and sisters of the decedent, who respondent had argued were not beneficiaries entitled to recovery under the Jones Act while their mother was living.

Petitioner immediately appealed to the Court of Appeals. Respondent moved to dismiss the appeal on the ground that the ruling appealed from was not a "final" decision of the District Court   *   *   *.   Thereupon petitioner administratrix, this time joined by the brother and sisters, filed in the Court of Appeals a petition for mandamus or other appropriate writ commanding the District Judge to vacate his original order and enter a new one   *   *   *. Without definitely deciding whether mandamus would have been appropriate in this case or deciding the "close" question of appealability, the Court of Appeals proceeded to determine the controversy "on the merits as though it were submitted on an appeal"; this the court said it felt free to do since its resolution of the merits did not prejudice respondent in any way, because it sustained respondent's contentions by denying the petition for mandamus and affirming the District Court's order.   *   *   *

In this Court respondent joins petitioner in urging us to hold that 28 U.S.C. § 1291 does not require us to dismiss this case   *   *   *.   We agree. *   *   *   [A]s this Court often has pointed out, a decision "final" within the meaning of § 1291 does not necessarily mean the last order possible to be made in a case.   *   *   *   It is true that the review of this case by the Court of Appeals could be called "piecemeal"; but it does not appear that the inconvenience and cost of trying this case will be greater because the Court of Appeals decided the issues raised instead of compelling the parties to go to trial with them unanswered.   *   *   *   And it seems clear now that the case is before us that the eventual costs, as all the parties recognize, will certainly be less if we now pass on the questions presented here rather than send the case back with those issues undecided. Moreover, delay of perhaps a number of years in having the brother's and sisters' rights determined might work a great injustice on them, since the claims for recovery for their benefit have been effectively cut off so long as the District Judge's ruling stands. And while their claims are not formally severable so as to make the court's order unquestionably appealable as to them,   *   *   * there certainly is ample reason to view their claims as severable in deciding the issue of finality, particularly since the brother and sisters were separate parties in the petition for extraordinary relief.   *   *   *   Furthermore, in United States v. General Motors Corp., 323 U.S. 373, 377, 65 S.Ct. 357, 359, 89 L.Ed. 311, this Court contrary to its usual practice reviewed a trial court's refusal to permit proof of certain items of damages in a case not yet fully tried, because the ruling was "fundamental to the further conduct of the case." * * * We think that the questions presented here are equally "fundamental to the further conduct of the case." It is true that if the District Judge had certified the case to the Court of Appeals under 28 U. S.C. § 1292(b), the appeal unquestionably would have been proper; in light of the circumstances we believe that the Court of Appeals properly implemented the same policy Congress sought to promote in § 1292(b) by treating this obviously marginal case as final and appealable * * *.

[The opinion of Mr. Justice GOLDBERG, concurring in part and dissenting in part, is omitted.]

Mr. Justice HARLAN, dissenting.

* * * The Court substantially affirms the judgment of the Court of Appeals and the parties are remanded to a trial on the merits, but only after they have incurred needless delay and expense in consequence of the loose practices sanctioned by the Court of Appeals and in turn by this Court. This case thus presents a striking example of the vice inherent in a system which permits piecemeal litigation of the issues in a lawsuit.

* * * The justifications given by the Court for tolerating the lower court's departure from the requirements of § 1291 are, with all respect, unsatisfactory.

1. The Court relies on the discretionary right of a district court to certify an interlocutory order to the court of appeals under § 1292(b) when the "order involves a controlling question of law," but the District Court in its discretion—and rightly it turns out—did not make such a certification in this case, and the Court of Appeals, equally correctly in my judgment, refused to order it to do so. * * *

2. Cohen v. Beneficial Industrial Loan Corp. * * * does not support a different result. * * * It is clear in this case that had petitioner proceeded to trial and won on her Jones Act claim, her asserted cause of action for unseaworthiness would have merged in the judgment. * * * Conversely, her claim would have been preserved for appeal had she lost on her Jones Act claim. Surely the assertion that petitioner is entitled to submit her unseaworthiness theory to the jury is not collateral to rights asserted in her action * * *.

3. Finally, the Court's suggestion that "it seems clear now that the case is before us that the eventual costs, as all the parties recognize, will certainly be less if we now pass on the questions presented here rather than send the case back with those issues undecided," * * * furnishes no excuse for avoidance of the finality rule. Essentially such a position would justify review here of any case decided by a court of appeals whenever this Court, as it did in this instance, erroneously grants certiorari and permits counsel to brief and argue the case on the merits. That, I believe, is neither good law nor sound judicial administration.

* * *

[A memorandum by Mr. Justice STEWART is omitted.]

EISEN v. CARLISLE & JACQUELIN, 370 F.2d 119, 120 (2d Cir. 1966). Plaintiff Eisen brought suit on behalf of himself and all odd-lot purchasers and sellers on the New York Stock Exchange, alleging that defendants, the two major "odd-lot" dealers on the Exchange had conspired to monopolize odd-lot trading in violation of the antitrust laws. The trial court granted defendant's motion to dismiss the class action, leaving only Eisen's individual $70 claim before the court. Eisen's appeal from the trial court order was upheld by the Second Circuit,[b] which, after quoting extensively from *Gillespie,* stated:

> * * * The alternatives are to appeal now or to end the lawsuit for all practical purposes. * * * We can safely assume that no lawyer of competence is going to undertake this complex and costly case to recover $70 for Mr. Eisen. * * * If the appeal is dismissed, not only will Eisen's claims never be adjudicated, but no appellate court will be given the chance to decide if this class action was proper under the newly amended Rule 23.

> There are, therefore, most compelling reasons to deny this motion to dismiss the appeal * * *.

> Dismissal of the class action in the present case, however, will irreparably harm Eisen and all others similarly situated, for, as we have already noted, it will for all practical purposes terminate the litigation. Where the effect of a district court's order, if not reviewed, is the death knell of the action, review should be allowed.
> * * *

NOTES AND QUESTIONS

1. Is the thrust of the decisions in *Gillespie* and *Eisen* simply to adopt a system of discretionary appeals of nonfinal orders? Can this position be squared with the enactment in 1958 of 28 U.S.C. § 1292(b), allowing discretionary appeals from interlocutory orders in limited situations or with the 1946 amendment of Rule 54(b)?

2. Is there any difference in the considerations that underlay *Cohen, Forgay,* and *Brown* and those that supported *Gillespie* and *Eisen?* Is there a class of collateral orders that should be appealable even if no other factor, such as hardship, is involved? If not, does the concept of collateral orders have any independent significance?

3. A number of federal courts of appeals have flatly rejected the "death knell" theory of *Eisen.* See, e. g., King v. Kansas City Southern Industries, Inc., 479 F.2d 1259 (7th Cir.1973); Hackett v. General Host Corp., 455 F.2d 618 (3d Cir.), certiorari denied 407 U.S. 925, 92 S.Ct. 2460, 32 L.Ed.2d 812 (1972). The *Hackett* case is discussed in 25 Vand.L.Rev. 911 (1972) and 17 Vill.L.Rev. 962 (1972).

4. Courts that have accepted the "death knell" theory nonetheless have dismissed appeals from denials of class actions unless the remaining claims of the named plaintiffs are so small that it is clear the suit cannot be continued. See,

---

[b] For subsequent developments in the case with regard to the class action, see p. 598, supra.

e. g., Gosa v. Securities Investment Co., 449 F.2d 1330 (5th Cir.1971) (appeal dismissed when individual claim was for $3,322.20).

Apparently the Second Circuit has adopted a rule-of-thumb, generally allowing appeals only when the individual claims fall below $10,000. See 7A Wright & Miller, *Federal Practice and Procedure: Civil* § 1802 (1972). Do determinations of appealability based solely on the size of plaintiffs' individual claims give too little weight to the dangers of delay emphasized in *Gillespie?* The court in *Gosa* indicated its willingness to consider the costs of the litigation and plaintiff's resources. Should the court also consider other factors such as the intensity of a plaintiff's feeling about the justice of the action and plaintiff's willingness to press forward in spite of the cost? Should it make any difference that plaintiff has access to a legal-aid office whose policy is to carry forward litigation that a party could not otherwise afford?

5. If appeals had not been taken in *Forgay, Brown Shoe, Gillespie,* or *Eisen* at the stage at which they were in fact taken, would the matters decided in those cases have been foreclosed from consideration on later appeals from the ultimate judgment? See Durkin v. Mason & Dixon Lines, Inc., 202 F.2d 425 (6th Cir. 1953) (time for appeal ran from date of order denying one claim and granting recovery on a second, although district court reserved decision on computation of recovery).

CATES v. LTV AEROSPACE CORP., 480 F.2d 620, 622 (5th Cir. 1973). Plaintiff, in a civil action, obtained a subpoena ordering the Department of the Navy, which was not a party to the suit, to produce documents. On appeal from an order enforcing the subpoena, the court of appeals said:

> Initially it should be noted that discovery orders are generally not appealable. * * * However, discovery orders may be appealable when executive privilege is involved and the executive or governmental agency is not a party to the lawsuit. * * * The theory of allowing an appeal rests on the proposition that forced disclosure would irretrievably breach the claim of privilege and render an appeal from final judgment meaningless; hence, the exception.

NOTES AND QUESTIONS

1. The court in *Cates* did not cite either *United States v. Ryan* or *Cobbledick v. United States,* which are discussed in Note 1, p. 1016, supra. Can one distinguish *Cates* on the ground that it involves only a civil proceeding while *Ryan* and *Cobbledick* involved grand jury investigations into criminal matters?

2. Can a valid distinction be drawn between an action in which a discovery order is directed to a party and *Cates* in which it was directed to a nonparty? See GIALDE v. TIME, INC., 480 F.2d 1295 (8th Cir.1973), in which the trial court ordered defendant's employee, a newsman, to reveal confidential sources of information. *Defendant* immediately appealed the order, although no sanctions had been taken either against defendant or the employee. The appeal was dis-

missed. Dissenting in part, one judge cited a large number of decisions that had permitted review of similar orders noting that the courts "expressly or implicitly reject the notion that an acceptable alternative to immediate appellate review is to hazard a contempt citation and then to seek review if one is found in contempt."

B.　AVOIDANCE OR EVASION OF THE BASIC CONCEPT—MANDAMUS

Read 28 U.S.C. § 1651(a) in the Supplement.

LA BUY v. HOWES LEATHER CO.

Supreme Court of the United States, 1957.
352 U.S. 249, 77 S.Ct. 309, 1 L.Ed.2d 290.

Certiorari to the United States Court of Appeals for the Seventh Circuit.

Mr. Justice CLARK delivered the opinion of the Court.

These two consolidated cases present a question of the power of the Courts of Appeals to issue writs of mandamus to compel a District Judge to vacate his orders entered under Rule 53(b) * * * referring antitrust cases for trial before a master. The petitioner, a United States District Judge * * *, contends that the Courts of Appeals have no such power and that, even if they did, these cases were not appropriate ones for its exercise. The Court of Appeals for the Seventh Circuit has decided unanimously that it has such power and, by a divided court, that the circumstances surrounding the references by the petitioner required it to issue the mandamus about which he complains. * * *

History of the Litigation.—These petitions for mandamus * * * arose from two antitrust actions instituted in the District Court in 1950. Rohlfing involves 87 plaintiffs * * * [and] six named defendants * * *. Shaffer involves six plaintiffs * * * and six defendants * * *.

The record indicates that the cases had been burdensome to the petitioner. In Rohlfing alone, 27 pages of the record are devoted to docket entries reflecting that petitioner had conducted many hearings on preliminary pleas and motions. * * * It is reasonable to conclude that much time would have been saved at the trial had petitioner heard the case because of his familiarity with the litigation.

* * * The cases were called on February 23, 1955, on a motion to reset them for trial. * * * The petitioner announced that "it has taken a

long time to get this case at issue. I remember hearing more motions, I think, in this case than any case I have ever sat on in this court." The plaintiffs estimated that the trial would take six weeks, whereupon petitioner stated he did not know when he could try the case "if it is going to take this long." He asked if the parties could agree "to have a Master hear" it. The parties ignored this query and at a conference in chambers the next day petitioner entered the orders of reference *sua sponte*. The orders declared that the court was "confronted with an extremely congested calendar" and that "exception [*sic*] conditions exist for this reason" requiring the references. The cases were referred to the master "to take evidence and to report the same to this Court, together with his findings of fact and conclusions of law." * * *

Upon petitioner's refusal to vacate the references, these mandamus actions were filed in the Court of Appeals seeking the issuance of writs ordering petitioner to do so. These applications were grounded on 28 U.S.C. § 1651(a), the All Writs Act. * * * Declaring that the references amounted to * * * "a refusal on his [petitioner's] part, as a judge, to try the causes in due course," the Court of Appeals concluded that "in view of the extraordinary nature of these causes" the references must be vacated "if we find that the orders were beyond the court's power under the pertinent rule." * * * And, it being so found, the writs issued under the authority of the All Writs Act. * * *

The Power of the Courts of Appeals.—Petitioner contends that the power of the Courts of Appeals does not extend to the issuance of writs of mandamus to review interlocutory orders except in those cases where the review of the case on appeal after final judgment would be frustrated. * * * The question of naked power has long been settled by this Court. As late as Roche v. Evaporated Milk Association, 1943, 319 U.S. 21, 25, 63 S.Ct. 938, 941, 87 L.Ed. 1185, Mr. Chief Justice Stone reviewed the decisions and, in considering the power of Courts of Appeals to issue writs of mandamus, the Court held that "the common-law writs, like equitable remedies, may be granted or withheld in the sound discretion of the court." * * * Since the Court of Appeals could at some stage of the antitrust proceedings entertain appeals in these cases, it has power in proper circumstances, as here, to issue writs of mandamus reaching them. * * *

The Discretionary Use of the Writs.—It appears from the docket entries to which we heretofore referred that the petitioner was well informed as to the nature of the antitrust litigation * * *. Nevertheless, he referred both suits to a master on the general issue. Furthermore, neither the existence of the alleged conspiracy nor the question of liability *vel non* had been determined in either case. These issues, as well as the damages, if any, and the question concerning the issuance of an injunction, were likewise included in the references. Under all of the circumstances, we believe the Court of Appeals was justified in finding the orders of reference were an abuse of the petitioner's power under Rule 53(b). They amounted to little less than an abdication of the judicial function depriving the parties of a trial before the court on the basic issues involved in the litigation.

The use of masters is "to aid judges in the performance of specific judicial duties, as they may arise in the progress of a cause," Ex parte Peterson, 1920, 253 U.S. 300, 312, 40 S.Ct. 543, 547, 64 L.Ed. 919, and not to displace the court. The exceptional circumstances here warrant the use of the extraordinary remedy of mandamus.   *   *   *

It is also contended that the Seventh Circuit has erroneously construed the All Writs Act as "conferring on it a 'roving commission' to supervise interlocutory orders of the District Courts in advance of final decision." Our examination of its opinions in this regard leads us to the conclusion that the Court of Appeals has exercised commendable self-restraint. It is true that mandamus should be resorted to only in extreme cases, since it places trial judges in the anomalous position of being litigants without counsel other than uncompensated volunteers. However, there is an end of patience and it clearly appears that the Court of Appeals has [since 1938]   *   *   *   admonished the trial judges of the Seventh Circuit that the practice of making references "does not commend itself" and "*   *   *   should seldom be made, and if at all only when unusual circumstances exist."   *   *   *   Still the Court of Appeals did not disturb the reference practice by reversal or mandamus until this case was decided in October 1955.   *   *   *   The record does not show to what extent references are made by the full bench of the District Court in the Northern District; however, it does reveal that petitioner has referred 11 cases to masters in the past 6 years. But even "a little cloud may bring a flood's downpour" if we approve the practice here indulged, particularly in the face of presently congested dockets, increased filings, and more extended trials.   *   *   *   [B]e that as it may, congestion in itself is not such an exceptional circumstance as to warrant a reference to a master. If such were the test, present congestion would make references the rule rather than the exception. Petitioner realizes this, for in addition to calendar congestion he alleges that the cases referred had unusual complexity of issues of both fact and law. But most litigation in the antitrust field is complex. It does not follow that antitrust litigants are not entitled to a trial before a court. On the contrary, we believe that this is an impelling reason for trial before a regular, experienced trial judge rather than before a temporary substitute appointed on an *ad hoc* basis and ordinarily not experienced in judicial work.   *   *   *   We agree that the detailed accounting required in order to determine the damages suffered by each plaintiff might be referred to a master after the court has determined the over-all liability of defendants, provided the circumstances indicate that the use of the court's time is not warranted in receiving the proof and making the tabulation.

*   *   *

Affirmed.

Mr. Justice BRENNAN, with whom Mr. Justice FRANKFURTER, Mr. Justice BURTON and Mr. Justice HARLAN join, dissenting.

*   *   *   The case before the Court of Appeals was "not a case where a court has exceeded or refused to exercise its jurisdiction   *   *   *." Rule

53(b)   *   *   *   vested Judge La Buy with discretionary power to make a reference if he found, and he did, that "some exceptional condition" required the reference.   *   *   *   If Judge La Buy erred in finding that there was an "exceptional condition" requiring the reference or did not give proper weight to the caveat of the Rule that a "reference to a master shall be the exception and not the rule," that was mere error "in ruling on matters within [the District Court's] jurisdiction."   *   *   *

But, regrettable as is this Court's approval of what I consider to be a clear departure by the Court of Appeals from the settled principles governing the issuance of the extraordinary writs, what this Court says in reaching its result is reason for particularly grave concern.   I think this Court has today seriously undermined the long-standing statutory policy against piecemeal appeals.   My brethren say: "Since the Court of Appeals could at some stage of the antitrust proceedings entertain appeals in these cases, it has power in proper circumstances, as here, to issue writs of mandamus reaching them.   *   *   *"   I understand this to mean that proper circumstances are present for the issuance of a writ in this case because, if the litigants are not now heard, the Court of Appeals will not have an opportunity to relieve them of the burden of the added expense and delay of decision alleged to be the consequence of the reference.   But that bridge was crossed by this Court in Roche   *   *   *.

What this Court is saying, therefore, is that the All Writs Act confers an independent appellate power in the Courts of Appeals to review interlocutory orders.   I have always understood the law to be precisely to the contrary. *   *   *

The power of the Courts of Appeals to issue extraordinary writs stems from § 14 of the Judiciary Act of 1789.   Chief Judge Magruder, in In re Josephson, 1 Cir., 218 F.2d 174, provides us with an invaluable history of this power and of the judicial development of its scope.   He demonstrates most persuasively that "[t]he all writs section does not confer an independent appellate power; the power is strictly of an auxiliary nature, in aid of a jurisdiction granted in some other provision of law   *   *   *."

The focal question posed for a Court of Appeals by a petition for the issuance of a writ is whether the action of the District Court tends to frustrate or impede the ultimate exercise by the Court of Appeals of its appellate jurisdiction granted in some other provision of the law.   The answer is clearly in the affirmative where, for example, the order of the District Court transfers a cause to a District Court of another circuit for decision.   That was Josephson, where   *   *   *   "the effect of the order is that the district judge has declined to proceed with the determination of a case which could eventually come to this court by appeal from a 'final decision'."   *   *   *   In contrast, a District Court order denying a transfer would not come under the umbrella of power under the All Writs Act, since retention of the cause by the District Court can hardly thwart or tend to defeat the power of the Court of Appeals to review that order after final decision of the case.   *   *   *

The view now taken by this Court that the All Writs Act confers an independent appellate power, although not so broad as "to authorize the indiscriminate use of prerogative writs as a means of reviewing interlocutory orders," in effect engrafts upon federal appellate procedure a standard of interlocutory review never embraced by the Congress throughout our history, although it is written into the English Judicature Act and is followed in varying degrees in some of the States. That standard allows interlocutory appeals by leave of the appellate court. * * *

NOTES AND QUESTIONS

1. In SCHLAGENHAUF v. HOLDER, 379 U.S. 104, 85 S.Ct. 234, 13 L.Ed.2d 152 (1964), the substantive aspects of which are set out at p. 681, supra, the Court upheld the use of mandamus to review an order requiring a defendant to submit to physical and mental examination:

> It is, of course, well settled that the writ is not to be used as a substitute for appeal * * * even though hardship may result from delay and perhaps unnecessary trial * * *. The writ is appropriately issued, however, when there is "usurpation of judicial power" or a clear abuse of discretion * * *.
>
> [T]he challenged order * * * appears to be the first of its kind in any reported decision in the federal courts under Rule 35 * * *.
>
> * * * It is thus appropriate for us to determine on the merits the issues presented and to formulate the necessary guidelines in this area. * * *
>
> This is not to say, however, that following the setting of guidelines in this opinion, any future allegation that the District Court was in error in applying these guidelines to a particular case makes mandamus an appropriate remedy.

Id. at 110–12, 85 S.Ct. at 238–39, 13 L.Ed.2d at 156–60.

Do the decisions in *LaBuy* and *Schlagenhauf* give sufficient guidance as to when mandamus is an appropriate means of review? Note that both cases involve significant problems regarding application of the Federal Rules. It has been suggested that the *LaBuy* holding might "possibly be limited to issues of judicial administration which have broad significance beyond the particular case." Note, *Appealability in the Federal Courts,* 75 Harv.L.Rev. 351, 377 (1961). Compare WILL v. UNITED STATES, 389 U.S. 90, 88 S.Ct. 269, 19 L.Ed.2d 305 (1967), a criminal case in which the Government sought mandamus to overturn a district court order granting discovery for the defendant. The court of appeals granted the writ. The Supreme Court reversed, stating that the facts did not reveal an extraordinary situation for which the writs must be reserved; there was no showing that the district judge had engaged in a pattern of conduct as had occurred in *LaBuy*. The Court did not discuss the fact that without mandamus the Government cannot obtain guidance on discovery matters since it cannot appeal an acquittal. Since the court of appeals had already heard the case and granted the writ, wouldn't the Court's reasoning in *Gillespie v. United States Steel Corp.,* p. 1018, supra, have justified its reviewing the merits in *Will?*

Several cases in earlier Chapters were lodged in appellate courts by mandamus. See, e. g., *Hoffman v. Blaski*, p. 255, supra; *Dairy Queen, Inc. v. Wood*, p. 815, supra. Why was review by mandamus appropriate in each of these cases? Cf. *Boldt v. Sanders*, p. 31, supra (prohibition).

2. In LYONS v. WESTINGHOUSE ELEC. CORP., 222 F.2d 184 (2d Cir.), certiorari denied 350 U.S. 825, 76 S.Ct. 52, 100 L.Ed. 737 (1955), the district judge had stayed an antitrust case pending the determination of a related state-court action. The court of appeals held that if a state judgment would have a collateral estoppel effect on the federal action, it would not,

> literally speaking, end the jurisdiction of the district court; but it will do so in substance, if it is an estoppel at all, for it will conclude any further consideration of the existence of the conspiracy, and on that all else depends. For this reason, we hold * * * that the question whether a final judgment will be an estoppel so nearly touches the jurisdiction of the district court, as to make it proper for us to entertain the petition for mandamus.[c]

Id. at 186.

In light of the court's holding on the merits that the state-court judgment "can have no effect upon the decision of the action at bar," was the court justified in directing the district court to vacate the stay? What would the court have directed if it had ruled the other way on the merits? The court of appeals did not in fact issue a writ of mandamus. Its order reads: "Writ of mandamus to go thirty days after the filing of this opinion * * * unless [the stay] * * * has been vacated theretofore." Such conditional orders are common in mandamus cases. Why?

In RADIO CORP. OF AMERICA v. IGOE, 217 F.2d 218 (7th Cir.1954), certiorari denied 348 U.S. 973, 75 S.Ct. 533, 99 L.Ed. 758 (1955), on facts resembling those in *Lyons,* the court denied mandamus to review the denial of a stay. Is this situation distinguishable from that in *Lyons?*

———

NIXON v. SIRICA, 487 F.2d 700, 707 (D.C.Cir.1973). A district judge ordered the President of the United States to produce certain tape recordings for the judge's inspection prior to a determination whether the recordings were subject to a grand jury subpoena. The President petitioned for a writ of mandamus, and the court of appeals, although denying the petition on the merits, held that it was an appropriate mode of review:

> From the viewpoint of mandamus * * * the central question that the President raises—whether the District Court exceeded its authority in ordering an *in camera* inspection of the tapes—is essentially jurisdictional. It is, too, a jurisdictional problem of "first impression" involving a "basic, undecided ques-

---

[c] The collateral-estoppel aspects of the *Lyons* case are dealt with at pp. 1117–20, supra. See also Note 2, p. 1035, infra.

tion." And if indeed the only avenue of direct appellate review open to the President requires that he first disobey the court's order, appeal seems to be "a clearly inadequate remedy." These circumstances * * * warrant the exercise * * * of our review power under the All Writs Act, particularly in light of the great public interest in prompt resolution of the issues * * *.

See also on the appealability of the order involved in this case, p. 1017, supra.

C. DISPLACEMENT OF THE BASIC CONCEPT— DISCRETIONARY APPEALS

Read 28 U.S.C. § 1292(b) in the Supplement.

ATLANTIC CITY ELEC. CO. v. GENERAL ELEC. CO.

United States Court of Appeals, Second Circuit, 1964.
337 F.2d 844.

PER CURIAM. The district court has certified pursuant to section 1292(b) * * * that its order, sustaining objections to interrogatories designed to discover whether damages were actually sustained by plaintiffs who may have shifted such damages, if any, to their customers of electricity, involves a controlling question of law in these litigations and that there is substantial ground for differences of opinion. * * *

In sustaining the objections to the interrogatories posed, the district court has, in effect, foreclosed defendants from pre-trial discovery of facts relating to a defense that plaintiffs have "passed-on" to their customers any damages incurred by plaintiffs and hence are not entitled to recover to the extent that defendants can prove such passing-on.

Upon this application for leave to appeal it would not be appropriate to isolate and endeavor to decide before an appeal from any final judgment this particular question of law. Pre-trial leave to appeal applications must be decided against the background of the entire case. Many important questions of law will undoubtedly arise in these cases but the problem now confronting us is the feasibility and advisability of trying to decide this particular question in advance of trial.

If pre-trial discovery were allowed as defendants request it could easily develop into a multitude of full scale rate cases which could dwarf in time and testimony the already extensive pre-trial proceedings. If the district court is in error * * * defendants will have full opportunity in the event of an adverse judgment, if based in whole or in part upon this error, to have it corrected upon appeal together with any other errors which may be urged. It is doubtful that any discoveries or hearings required to establish the extent of any damages, if the passing-on-doctrine applies, would be more burdensome then than now. Since defendants' rights to this defense are not being taken away or prejudiced on any ultimate appeal by denial of the pre-trial appeal now sought, we believe that the ultimate disposition of these cases would be delayed rather than advanced by granting this application.

Application denied.

NOTES AND QUESTIONS

1. In COMMONWEALTH EDISON CO. v. ALLIS CHALMERS MFG. CO., 335 F.2d 203 (7th Cir.1964), having accepted an appeal under Section 1292 (b) on the same issue involved in the principal case, the Seventh Circuit held that the passing-on defense was not available, and hence affirmed an order sustaining objections to similar interrogatories. Which of the courts of appeals followed the sounder procedure? Should the Second Circuit have ruled differently if the district judge had directed plaintiffs to answer the interrogatories? See generally Note, *The Final Judgment Rule and Appellate Review of Discovery Orders in Nebraska,* 35 Neb.L.Rev. 469 (1956).

Suppose the trial court in *Atlantic City Elec. Co.* had ruled directly on the applicability of the passing-on defense. Would the court of appeals have had less justification for rejecting the appeal? Compare Obron v. Union Camp Corp., 477 F.2d 542 (6th Cir.1973) (allowing appeal).

2. Is Section 1292(b) a solution to the type of problem raised in *Ryan* or *Cobbledick,* p. 1016, supra? In UNITED STATES v. WOODBURY, 263 F.2d 784 (9th Cir.1959), the court declined to review an order granting discovery even though the district court had ordered defendant's answer and counterclaim stricken if it did not comply. But in GROOVER, CHRISTIE & MERRITT v. Lo-BIANCO, 336 F.2d 969, 973–74 (D.C.Cir.1964), a malpractice action, the court allowed an appeal from an order granting discovery of a letter by defendant to an insurer, detailing defendant's investigation of the case. The court then reversed, finding that "good cause" had not been adequately established under Rule 34, and directed the trial judge to make further findings and to consider whether the letter was privileged under *Hickman v. Taylor,* p. 700, supra. Judge Wright dissented vigorously, stating: "This case is a graphic illustration of the mischief that results when [Section 1292(b)] * * * is misused. * * * And rather than advance the ultimate termination of this litigation, the dilatory tactics * * * including this interlocutory appeal, have already been the cause of significant delay." Compare Judge Clark, dissenting, in MATTHIES v. SEYMOUR MFG. CO., 271 F.2d 740 (2d Cir.1959), certiorari denied 361 U.S. 962, 80 S.Ct. 591, 4 L.Ed.2d 544 (1960): "In passing I might note that this seems to me another illustration of the unfortunate tendency of the new interlocutory appeals statute * * * to overemphasize strict pleading and in so doing to throw our procedure out of line with the liberal spirit fostered by the civil rules." Why should Section 1292(b) have this effect? *Cf.* Clark, *Special Problems in Drafting and Interpreting Procedural Codes and Rules,* 3 Vand.L.Rev. 493, 498 (1950).

3. Would Section 1292(b) be a satisfactory device in *LaBuy* or *Lyons?* See Lear Siegler, Inc. v. Adkins, 330 F.2d 595 (9th Cir.1964). Should the court of appeals be given power to hear appeals from orders fulfilling the requirements described in Section 1292(b) without the certificate of the district judge? Compare Leasco Data Processing Equip. Corp. v. Maxwell, 468 F.2d 1326, 1344 (2d Cir.1972) (court of appeals cannot order trial court to issue certificate).

4. Should a court use Section 1292(b) as a basis for reviewing an order setting the amount of security required of a shareholder in a case such as *Cohen v. Beneficial Industrial Loan Co.,* p. 1015, supra? See Phelps v. Burnham, 327 F. 2d 812 (2d Cir.1964).

5. The courts of appeals have not been markedly hospitable to interlocutory appeals under Section 1292(b). Decisions during the 1950's placing strong emphasis on the exceptional nature of the relief, e. g., In re Heddendorf, 263 F.2d 887 (1st Cir.1959); Milbert v. Bison Labs, Inc., 260 F.2d 431 (3d Cir.1958), have not lost their precedential force. In the fiscal year 1966, the courts of appeals considered 68 applications and allowed only 36; in subsequent years the figures were 80 and 41 (1967); 122 and 58 (1968); 105 and 64 (1969). In 1970, both figures increased markedly: 290 applications considered, and 225 allowed. Annual Report of the Director of the Administrative Office of the United States Courts, 1966, p. 160; id. 1967, p. 191; id. 1968, p. 185; id. 1969, p. 195; id. 1970, p. 221. More recent reports have not included these figures.

6. In NICKERT v. PUGET SOUND TUG & BARGE CO., 480 F.2d 1039 (9th Cir.1973), a wrongful death case, one defendant, A, cross-claimed for indemnity against another defendant, B. Prior to trial on the cross-complaint, the trial court granted a "partial summary judgment" for B stating that if at trial it were to be found that A had negligently contributed to the wrongful death, indemnity would not be permitted. The trial judge thereupon issued a certificate under Section 1292(b)(2) allowing A to appeal. The court of appeals admitted that the issue was important and controversial, but nevertheless dismissed the appeal stating:

> * * * The trial court's announcement of its opinion on this question of law * * * is nothing more * * * than an hypothetical, advisory opinion. It is subject to revision or reversal at any time by the trial judge to the point where a definitive action has been taken on the question; for examples, an instruction to the jury, or the adoption of a conclusion of law in a trial to the court. Similarly, an announcement by this Court of its opinion of the trial judge's tentative opinion would be purely advisory * * *.

Id. at 1041.

Do you agree with the appellate court's decision? Does it undercut the policy upon which Section 1292(b) is based? Is it consistent with Rule 56(a) which permits partial summary judgment?

D. AN HISTORICAL FOOTNOTE TO THE BASIC
CONCEPT—INJUNCTIONS

Read 28 U.S.C. § 1292(a) (1) and Federal Rules of Civil Procedure 65(a) and (b) in the Supplement.

SMITH v. VULCAN IRON WORKS, 165 U.S. 518, 525, 17 S.Ct. 407, 410, 41 L.Ed. 810, 812 (1897):

The manifest intent of this provision, read in the light of the previous practice in the courts of the United States, contrasted with the practice in courts of equity of the highest authority elsewhere, appears to this court to have been, not only to permit the defendant to obtain immediate relief from an injunction, the continuance of which throughout the progress of the cause might seriously affect his interests, but also to save both parties from the expense of further litigation, should the appellate court be of opinion that the plaintiff was not entitled to an injunction because his bill had no equity to support it.

NOTES AND QUESTIONS

1. Is the Supreme Court's ruling that an appeal under the predecessor of Section 1292(a) (1) allows the reviewing court to consider not only the question whether the injunction should have been issued, but the merits of the whole case, supported by the traditional doctrines regarding the character of equitable relief? Review pp. 806–07, supra.

2. What are the reasons for allowing appeals from interlocutory orders granting or refusing injunctions? Do these reasons apply to orders granting or denying preliminary, as opposed to permanent, injunctions? Could these reasons be served as well by relegating the parties to discretionary appeals under Section 1292(b)?

3. Is the grant or denial of a temporary restraining order appealable under Section 1292(a) (1)? See Grant v. United States, 282 F.2d 165 (2d Cir.1960). In close cases it may be difficult to tell the difference between a preliminary injunction and a temporary restraining order. See Connell v. Dulien Steel Products, Inc., 240 F.2d 414 (5th Cir.1957), 71 Harv.L.Rev. 550 (1958) (28-day temporary restraining order). Are the differences between preliminary injunctions and temporary restraining orders relevant to the question whether appeal should be permitted in the case of the former and not permitted in the case of the latter?

In UNITED STATES v. WOOD, 295 F.2d 772 (5th Cir.1961), certiorari denied 369 U.S. 850, 82 S.Ct. 933, 8 L.Ed.2d 9 (1962), a Black who was active in voter registration in Mississippi was arrested for disturbing the peace and ordered to trial in fifteen days. Two days before trial, the United States, moving under 42 U.S.C. § 1971 and alleging that the prosecution would intimidate Blacks in the exercise of their voting rights, brought suit to restrain the criminal action. A temporary restraining order was denied and the Government appealed. The court of appeals held that it had jurisdiction under Section 1291. Inasmuch as the case would quickly become moot if the restraining order was not issued, the court said, its denial was "a final disposition of the * * * claimed right. * * * [T]o call this de facto dismissal a nonappealable interlocutory order is to preclude review altogether."

BALTIMORE CONTRACTORS, INC. v. BODINGER

Supreme Court of the United States, 1955.
348 U.S. 176, 75 S.Ct. 249, 99 L.Ed. 233.

Certiorari to the United States Court of Appeals for the Second Circuit.

Mr. Justice REED delivered the opinion of the Court.

* * *

This equitable action was brought in a state court for an accounting of the profits of a joint venture * * * and was removed to a federal district court on the basis of diversity of citizenship. * * *

The petitioner moved for a stay of the action pursuant to § 3 of the United States Arbitration Act, 9 U.S.C. § 3, * * * which authorizes a stay by a federal court when an issue is "referable to arbitration under an agreement in writing for such arbitration." The District Court refused the stay on the ground that the agreement between the parties did not constitute an agreement to arbitrate. The court apparently construed the * * * provision as limited to mathematical disputes. Petitioner appealed to the Court of Appeals for the Second Circuit. * * * On respondent's motion the Court of Appeals dismissed the appeal * * *. Certiorari was sought on the following question:

> "Whether in an action for an *accounting* an interlocutory order denying a stay under Section 3 of the United States Arbitration Act should be regarded as a denial of an injunction from which an appeal lies."

* * *

The trial court's interpretation of the quoted contract clause and its order denying a stay could not be called a final decision under § 1291. * * * Appealability here turns on whether the District Court's refusal to stay this trial for arbitration was the refusal of an "injunction" under § 1292.

* * *

A series of decisions of this Court has developed the rationale for determining the appealability of such an interlocutory order as this under § 1292 and its predecessors. The appealability of routine interlocutory injunctive orders raised few questions. * * * It was when stays of proceedings, in distinction to injunctions, were appealed that the issue of jurisdiction became sharp. In Enelow v. New York Life Ins. Co., 293 U.S. 379, 55 S.Ct. 310, 79 L.Ed. 440, a case arising when federal courts had actions at law and proceedings in equity, a complaint at common law on a life insurance policy was met by an answer alleging fraud in the policy's procurement with a prayer for its cancellation and a motion to try the equitable issue first. The motion was granted, and jurisdiction on appeal from that order was approved on this reasoning:

> "The power to stay proceedings in another court appertains distinctively to equity in the enforcement of equitable principles, and the grant or refusal of such a stay by a court of equity of proceedings at law is a grant or refusal of an injunction within the meaning of § 129 [§ 1292]. And, in this aspect, it makes no difference that the two cases, the suit in equity for an injunction and the action at law in which proceedings are stayed, are both pending in the same court, in view of the established distinction between 'proceedings at law and proceedings in equity in the national courts and between the powers of those courts when sitting as courts of law and when sitting as courts of equity.' * * * "

After the adoption of the one form of action * * * we reiterated this ruling in a like case. Ettelson v. Metropolitan Ins. Co., 317 U.S. 188, 63 S.Ct. 163, 164, 87 L.Ed. 176. We said a stay of the complaint until disposition of the fraud issue "is as effective * * * as an injunction * * *. The statute looks to the substantial effect of the order made."

The point was made in the Enelow case that power to stay mere steps within the framework of the litigation before a court differs as to appealability from an injunction prohibiting proceedings in another court. This distinction was applied in City of Morgantown v. Royal Ins. Co., 337 U.S. 254, 69 S.Ct. 1067, 93 L.Ed. 1347. There the insurance company brought a suit for reformation of the contract. The insured counterclaimed, seeking to enforce the contract as written, and demanded a jury trial; the company moved to strike the demand; the court granted the motion and set the case for trial to the court without a jury. The insured appealed and the Court of Appeals dismissed the appeal. We affirmed, holding that the Enelow rule did not apply; that since this was an equitable proceeding with a counter claim to enforce the policy, the decision to hear the reformation issue first without a jury was only a decision as to how to try the case, and therefore was not an interlocutory order in the nature of an injunction. To the argument that the importance of a jury trial justified treating the order of trial as an interlocutory injunction, we answered:

> "Many interlocutory orders are equally important, and may determine the outcome of the litigation, but they are not for that reason converted into injunctions." * * *

The Morgantown case controls here. Whether the District Court was right or wrong in its ruling that the contract provision did not require arbitration proceedings, it was simply a ruling in the only suit pending, actual or fictional. It was a mere order and not an injunction as that word is understood through the Enelow and the Ettelson cases as a stay through equitable principles of a common-law action. * * *

Affirmed.

Mr. Justice BURTON concurs in the judgment of the Court.

Mr. Justice BLACK, with whom Mr. Justice DOUGLAS concurs, dissenting.

I think the District Court's order denying a stay is appealable because it is (1) "final" within the meaning of 28 U.S.C. § 1291, and (2) a refusal to grant an interlocutory injunction within the meaning of § 1292. As the Court admits, a collateral issue may be so severable and unrelated to central trial issues that a judgment on the collateral issue is considered "final" and appealable under § 1291, even though other important issues are left undecided. Given this common sense meaning § 1291 authorizes the present appeal. For certainly decision of whether a judicial rather than an arbitration tribunal shall hear and determine this accounting controversy is logically and practically severable from the factual and legal issues crucial to determination of the merits of the controversy. And this Court has held that § 1292 makes all stay orders appealable that have the substantial effect of interlocutory injunction orders. * * * The refusal to stay here had that effect. * * *

NOTES AND QUESTIONS

1. In light of the other devices through which interlocutory review may be sought, should appeal automatically be available when a trial court makes an order that can be characterized as an injunction only by analogy to the way in which equity formerly imposed its will on the courts of law? If the trial judge's decision as to the sequence in which issues should be tried is to be reviewable at all, does it make sense, inasmuch as law and equity have been merged, to distinguish between *Ettelson* and *City of Morgantown*? Is the specific problem presented in those two cases reduced in significance by the Supreme Court's subsequent decisions in *Beacon Theatres, Inc. v. Westover*, p. 807, supra and *Dairy Queen, Inc. v. Wood*, p. 815, supra?

2. In *Lyons v. Westinghouse Elec. Corp.*, p. 1028, supra, an action at law, the court of appeals held (2–1) that the stay granted by the district judge was not an appealable injunction, but was simply a ruling that " 'a court of law, as well as a court of equity, may grant in a cause pending before it by virtue of its inherent power to control the progress of the cause,' " quoting from the *Enelow* opinion. Was the court correct in light of SHANFEROKE COAL & SUPPLY CORP. v. WESTCHESTER SERV. CORP., 293 U.S. 449, 55 S.Ct. 313, 79 L.Ed. 583 (1935), which followed *Enelow* and was distinguished in *Baltimore Contractors,* and in which the Supreme Court held that the denial of a stay in a common-law action until after arbitration was a denial of an injunction for appeal purposes?

3. Does Section 1292(a) (1) apply to an order denying a motion for summary judgment in an action in which a permanent injunction is sought? This question, which had plagued the courts of appeals for years, was resolved in SWITZERLAND CHEESE ASS'N, INC. v. E. HORNE'S MARKET, INC., 385 U.S. 23, 25, 87 S.Ct. 193, 195, 17 L.Ed.2d 23, 25 (1966):

> * * * [T]he denial of a motion for summary judgment because of unresolved issues of fact does not settle or even tentatively decide anything about the merits of the claim. It is strictly a pre-trial order that decides only one thing—that the case should go to trial. Orders that in

no way touch on the merits of the claim but only relate to pre-trial procedures are not in our view "interlocutory" within the meaning of § 1292 (a) (1). We see no other way to protect the integrity of the congressional policy against piecemeal appeals.

See also Goldstein v. Cox, 396 U.S. 471, 90 S.Ct. 671, 24 L.Ed.2d 663 (1970).

4. If an appeal is not taken from an interlocutory order that is made appealable by Section 1292(a) (1), are matters adjudged therein foreclosed on an appeal from the final judgment? See Victor Talking Mach. Co. v. George, 105 F.2d 697 (3d Cir.), certiorari denied 308 U.S. 611, 60 S.Ct. 176, 84 L.Ed. 511 (1939).

5. A somewhat premature report of the interment of the policy against piecemeal appeal appears in Frank, *Requiem for the Final Judgment Rule,* 45 Texas L.Rev. 292 (1966).

SECTION B. TIMELINESS

Read Federal Rules of Civil Procedure 6(b), 54, 55, 58, 59(b), and 79(a), and Federal Rules of Appellate Procedure 3 and 4(a) in the Supplement.

DICKINSON v. PETROLEUM CONVERSION CORP., 338 U.S. 507, 70 S.Ct. 322, 94 L.Ed. 299 (1950). Dickinson sued Lloyd to impress an equitable lien upon stock of the Petroleum Conversion Corporation that was in Lloyd's name. Certain shareholders intervened against both Dickinson and Lloyd, claiming that the stock in question had been fraudulently issued, and the Corporation also intervened making the same claim. On April 10, 1947, a decree was entered dismissing all of Dickinson's claims, dismissing all of the Corporation's claims except that to a part of the stock, and ordering judgment for the other intervenors against Dickinson and Lloyd for $174,620.56; further proceedings to ascertain the individual amounts of recovery were ordered. From this decree the Corporation took no appeal.

On August 3, 1948, a "final decree" was entered that apportioned the recovery among the claimants. It made no decision as to any issue involving the Corporation and in no way changed the 1947 decree. The Corporation appealed from the final decree. The Supreme Court held that the 1947 decree had been final as to the Corporation, "that its failure to appeal therefrom forfeits its right of review," and its "attempt to review the earlier decree by appealing from the later one is ineffective."

The liberalization of our practice to allow more issues and parties to be joined in one action and to expand the privilege of intervention by those not originally parties has increased the danger of hardship and denial of justice through delay if each issue must await the determination of all issues as to all parties before a final judgment can be had.   *   *   *

We have held that an order denying intervention to a person having an absolute right to intervene is final and appealable. Brotherhood of Railroad Trainmen v. Baltimore & Ohio R. Co., 331 U.S. 519, 67 S.Ct. 1387, 91 L.Ed. 1646 * * *. When the application for intervention is denied, the would-be intervenor is foreclosed from further action in the case and its proceedings cannot affect him nor can he affect them. As the court below observed, it is hard to see why the exclusion of an intervenor from the case should be less final when it is based upon the evidence than when it is based upon pleadings. In either case, the lawsuit is all over so far as the intervenor is concerned.

When its claims were dismissed by the decree of April 1947, any grievance that Petroleum Conversion Corporation had was fully matured. At that point Petroleum was out of the case. The decree was not tentative, informal nor incomplete as to it; and the case was concluded and closed as to its counterclaims. * * * What the court reserved was essentially supervisory jurisdiction over the distribution among the class of the recovery awarded the intervenors as the class' representatives. * * * Petroleum no longer had any concern with these questions and, however they were resolved, Petroleum could not possibly have been affected. * * *

Mr. Justice BLACK dissented:

I see no practical reason why the Court of Appeals should not have been free to review the respondent's challenge to the 1948 decree without regard to appealability of the 1947 decree. A rational system of jurisprudence should not attach inexorable consequences to failure to guess right on a legal question for the solution of which neither statutes nor court opinions have provided even a reasonably certain guide. * * *

Id. at 511, 513–15, 517, 70 S.Ct. at 324, 325, 327, 94 L.Ed. at 302, 303–04, 305.

NOTES AND QUESTIONS

1. At the time the *Dickinson* case arose, it was governed by Rule 54(b) as it read before the 1948 amendment. See Note on Amendments to Rule 54(b) in the Supplement. Would the 1947 order have been appealable if there had been no provision such as Rule 54(b)? If so, would the Rule as amended in 1948 have changed the outcome of the case if it had been in effect at the time of the order? Would the 1961 amendment to the Rule have made any difference? Is the "express direction" provision of Rule 54(b) applicable to orders that would be appealable even if the Rule were not in force? See Notes and Questions, p. 1014, supra.

2. In *Dickinson* the judges who decided the case in the court of appeals were of the opinion that the 1947 order had been appealable. Nonetheless, they felt compelled by an earlier decision in the same circuit to hold that it had not been appealable. Consider the dilemma that the corporation's lawyers might have found themselves in had they chosen to try to appeal the 1947 decree. In this connection, is it significant that the Supreme Court stated that it granted certiorari because of the intra-circuit conflict?

3. Strict compliance with time limits in taking appeals is treated by the courts as a matter of very great importance. Why should this be so? What provisions in the Federal Rules illustrate this concern?

UNITED STATES v. F. & M. SCHAEFER BREWING CO.

Supreme Court of the United States, 1958.
356 U.S. 227, 78 S.Ct. 674, 2 L.Ed.2d 721, 73 A.L.R.2d 235.

Certiorari to the United States Court of Appeals for the Second Circuit.

Mr. Justice WHITTAKER delivered the opinion of the Court.

* * * Respondent sued the Government for $7,189.57, alleged to have been illegally assessed and collected from it as federal stamp taxes, and for interest thereon from the date of payment. After issue was joined, respondent moved for summary judgment. The district judge, after hearing the motion filed an opinion on April 14, 1955 * * * in which, after finding that respondent had paid stamp taxes to the Government in the amount of $7,012.50 and interest in the amount of $177.07, but making no finding of the date or dates of payment, he referred to an earlier decision of the same legal question by his colleague * * * and concluded, saying: "I am in agreement with Judge Leibell's analysis and, accordingly, the plaintiff's motion is granted." Thereupon, the clerk made the following notation in the civil docket: "April 14, 1955. Rayfiel, J. Decision rendered on motion for summary judgment. Motion granted. See opinion on file."

Thereafter, on May 24, 1955, counsel for *respondent* presented to the judge, and the latter signed and filed, a formal document captioned "Judgment," which referred to the motion and the hearing of it and to the "opinion" of April 14, and then,

> "Ordered, adjudged and decreed that the plaintiff, The F. & M. Schaefer Brewing Co., recover of the defendant, United States of America, the sum of $7189.57 and interest thereon from February 19, 1954 in the amount of $542.80, together with costs as taxed by the Clerk of the Court in the sum of $37, aggregating the sum of $7769.37, and that plaintiff have judgment against defendant therefor."

On the same day the clerk stamped the document "Judgment Rendered: Dated: May 24th, 1955," and made the following notation in the civil docket:

> "May 24, 1955. Rayfiel, J. Judgment filed and docketed against defendant in the sum of $7,189.57 with interest of $542.80

together with costs $37 amounting in all to $7,769.37. Bill of Costs attached to judgment."

On July 21, 1955, the Government filed its notice of appeal from the order "entered in this action on May 25th, 1955 * * *." Thereafter, respondent moved to dismiss the appeal upon the ground that the opinion of April 14 constituted the "judgment," that the clerk's entry of that date constituted "entry of the judgment," and that the appeal was not taken within 60 days from the "entry of the judgment," as required by Rule 73(a). The Court of Appeals, holding that the opinion of April 14 was a "decisive and complete act of adjudication," and that the notation made by the clerk in the civil docket on that date constituted "entry of the judgment" within the meaning of Rule 58 and adequately disclosed the "substance" of the judgment as required by Rule 79(a), sustained the motion and dismissed the appeal as untimely. * * *

At the outset the Government contends that practical considerations— namely, certainty as to what judicial pronouncements are intended to be final judgments in order to avoid both premature and untimely appeals, to render certain the date of judgment liens, and to enable the procurement of writs of execution, transcripts and certified copies of judgments—require that a judgment be contained in a separate document so labeled, and urges us so to hold. Whatever may be the practical needs in these respects, the answer is that no present statute or rule so requires, as the Government concedes, and the decisional law seems settled that "[n]o form of words * * * is necessary to evince [the] rendition [of a judgment]." United States v. Hark, 320 U.S. 531, 534, 64 S.Ct. 359, 361, 88 L.Ed. 290. * * *

While an opinion may embody a *final decision*, the question whether it does so depends upon whether the judge has or has not clearly declared his intention in this respect in his opinion. Therefore, when, as here, the action is for money only * * * it is necessary to determine whether the language of the opinion embodies the essential elements of a judgment for money and clearly evidences the judge's intention that it shall be his final act in the case. If it does so, it constitutes his final judgment and, under Rule 58, it "directs that a party recover [a sum of] money," and, "upon receipt by [the clerk] of the [opinion]," requires him to "enter judgment forthwith" against the party found liable for the amount awarded, which is to be done by making a brief "notation of [the] judgment in the civil docket [showing the substance of the judgment of the court] as provided by Rule 79(a)." When all of these elements clearly appear final judgment has been both pronounced and entered, and the time to appeal starts to run under the provisions of Rule 73(a). And as correctly held by the Court of Appeals, the later filing and entry of a more formal judgment could not constitute a second final judgment in the case nor extend the time to appeal. * * *

But, on the other hand, if the opinion leaves doubtful whether the judge intended it to be his final act in the case—and, in an action for money, failure to determine either expressly or by reference the amount to be awarded is strong evidence of such lack of intention—one cannot say that it "directs that a party recover [a sum of] money"; * * * nor can one say that the clerk's "notation * * * in the civil docket"—if it sets forth no more substance than is contained or directed in the opinion, and being only a ministerial act * * * it may do no more—"show[s] * * * the substance of [a] judgment" of the court * * *.

But respondent argues, as the Court of Appeals held, that the opinion stated the amount of money illegally collected from respondent and, therefore, adequately determined the amount awarded, and that inasmuch as the clerk's entry incorporated the opinion by reference, it, too, adequately stated the amount of the judgment. This contention might well be accepted were it not for the fact that the action also sought recovery of interest on the amount paid by respondent from the date of payment to the date of judgment, and for the fact that the opinion does not state the date or dates of payment and, hence, did not state facts necessary to compute the amount of interest to be included in the judgment. * * * In an effort to counter the effect of these omissions, respondent states that a search of the record, which it urges we should make, would show that the Government's answer admitted the date of payment, and thus would furnish the information necessary to compute the amount of interest to be included in the judgment. * * * This argument cannot be accepted under the facts here for the reason that Rule 79(a) expressly requires that the clerk's entry "shall show * * * the substance of [the] judgment of the court * * *." Surely the amount of a judgment for money is a vital part of its substance. To hold that one must search the whole record to determine the amount, or the facts necessary to compute the amount, of a final judgment for money would be to ignore the quoted provision of Rule 79(a).

In these circumstances, the rule declared by this Court in the Hark case * * * is exactly apposite and controlling.

"Where, as here, a formal judgment is signed by the judge, this is *prima facie* the decision or judgment rather than a statement in an opinion or a docket entry. * * * The judge was conscious, as we are, that he was without power to extend the time for appeal. He entered a formal order of record. We are unwilling to assume that he deemed this an empty form or that he acted from a purpose indirectly to extend the appeal time, which he could not do overtly. * * *"

The actions of all concerned—of the judge in not stating in his opinion the amount, or means for determining the amount, of the judgment; of the clerk in not stating the amount of the judgment in his notation on the civil docket; of counsel for the Government in not appealing from the "opinion"; of counsel for respondent in preparing and presenting to the judge a formal "judgment" on May 24; and, finally, of the judge himself in signing and filing the formal "judgment" on the latter date—clearly show that none of them understood the opinion to be the judge's final act or to constitute his final judgment in the case. * * *

Reversed.

Mr. Justice HARLAN, dissenting.

The effort which has gone into this case has at least ended happily from the point of view of preserving the integrity of those provisions of the Federal Rules of Civil Procedure bearing on the timeliness of appeals. The Court's opinion, and the dissent of Mr. Justice Frankfurter which I have joined, are at one on the basic issue, namely, that entry of a formal judgment is not necessary to start the time for appeal running, and also agree that the determinative question in any given case is whether the District Court intended its décision on the merits to be a final disposition of the matter. * * *

[The dissenting opinion of Mr. Justice FRANKFURTER, joined by Mr. Justice HARLAN, is omitted.]

NOTES AND QUESTIONS

1. Read the Advisory Committee's 1963 Notes to Rule 58 in the Supplement. Do the changes made in 1963 substantially ameliorate the problem presented by *Schaefer?* In FOILES v. UNITED STATES, 465 F.2d 163, 168 (7th Cir.1972), the court of appeals held that "when the jury verdict is clear and unequivocal, setting forth a general verdict with reference to the sole question of liability and where nothing remains to be decided and when no opinion or memorandum is written, as is the situation described in clause (1) of Rule 58, there is no requirement for a separate document to start the time limits for appeal running." The Supreme Court reversed sub nom. United States v. Indrelunas, 411 U.S. 216, 93 S.Ct. 1562, 36 L.Ed.2d 202 (1973). Should the trial judge be required to direct the entry of a judgment expressly? What changes in Rule 58 short of that might be made?

2. Judgment for plaintiff was entered July 6, 1954. Defendant timely moved for a new trial, and its motion was denied August 24, 1954. Defendant filed a notice of appeal on September 17, 1954, "from the order entered * * * on August 24, 1954." The court of appeals dismissed the appeal, holding that the order denying a new trial was not appealable, and that the notice could not serve as a notice of appeal from the judgment, even though such a notice would have been timely. The Supreme Court reversed. STATE FARM MUT. AUTO. INS. CO. v. PALMER, 350 U.S. 944, 76 S.Ct. 321, 100 L.Ed. 823 (1956), reversing 225 F.2d 876 (9th Cir.1955). See also Comment, *Ad Hoc Relief for Untimely Appeals,* 65 Colum.L.Rev. 97 (1965). Review *Thompson v. Immigration & Naturalization Serv.,* p. 917, supra.

3. In some states separate appeals lie from the judgment and an order denying a motion for new trial. See, e. g., Minn.R.Civ.App.Proc. 103.03, which is in the Supplement following 28 U.S.C. § 1292. The time for each appeal typically is different, and each raises certain issues not raised by the other. See Note, *Scope of Review in Minnesota and its Dependence upon the Form of Appeal Taken,* 41 Minn.L.Rev. 110 (1956). Under provisions of this type, an appeal from either the judgment or the order cannot be treated as an appeal from the other.

SECTION C. THE AMBIT OF REVIEW

1. ISSUES SUBJECT TO REVIEW

ELECTRICAL FITTINGS CORP. v. THOMAS & BETTS CO.

Supreme Court of the United States, 1939.
307 U.S. 241, 59 S.Ct. 860, 83 L.Ed. 1263.

Certiorari to United States Circuit Court of Appeals for the Second Circuit.

Mr. Justice ROBERTS delivered the opinion of the Court.

This was a suit in equity by the respondents for alleged infringement of a patent. The District Court held claim 1 valid but not infringed and claim 2 invalid. Instead of dismissing the bill without more, it entered a decree adjudging claim 1 valid but dismissing the bill for failure to prove infringement.

The respondents did not appeal, but filed in the Patent Office a disclaimer of claim 2. The petitioners appealed to the Circuit Court of Appeals from so much of the decree as adjudicated claim 1 valid. The appeal was dismissed on the ground that the petitioners had been awarded all the relief to which they were entitled, the litigation having finally terminated in their favor. The court was of opinion that the decree would not bind the petitioners in subsequent suits on the issue of the validity of claim 1.

* * *

A party may not appeal from a judgment or decree in his favor, for the purpose of obtaining a review of findings he deems erroneous which are not necessary to support the decree. But here the decree itself purports to adjudge the validity of claim 1, and though the adjudication was immaterial to the disposition of the cause, it stands as an adjudication of one of the issues litigated. We think the petitioners were entitled to have this portion of the decree eliminated, and that the Circuit Court of Appeals had jurisdiction, * * * to entertain the appeal, not for the purpose of passing on the merits, but to direct the reformation of the decree.

* * *

Reversed and remanded.

NOTES AND QUESTIONS

1. NEW YORK TEL. CO. v. MALTBIE, 291 U.S. 645, 54 S.Ct. 443, 78 L.Ed. 1041, 1042 (1934) (per curiam):

The District Court * * * permanently enjoined, as confiscatory, the enforcement of the rate orders which are the subject of this suit. The injunction is unqualified. Appellant, having obtained this relief, is not entitled to prosecute an appeal from the decree in its favor, for the purpose of reviewing the portions of the decree fixing the value of appellant's property as of the years 1924, 1926, and 1928, and the rate of return to be allowed. The matters set forth in these portions of the decree are not to be regarded as res judicata in relation to subsequent legislative action by the Public Service Commission in fixing rates for the future or in any judicial proceeding relating to such rates.

2. Would the decree in *Electrical Fittings* have been res judicata of the validity of claim 1 of the patent? Why else might petitioners in that case have been concerned about the decree? The Declaratory Judgment Act, 28 U.S.C. §§ 2201–2202, was not in force at the time of the *Electrical Fittings* decision. Had it been, might it have been possible to treat the district court's decree as a declaratory judgment with respect to claim 1 and consider it as having been entered under the authority of Rule 54(c)?

3. In PARTMAR CORP. v. PARAMOUNT PICTURES THEATRES CORP., 347 U.S. 89, 74 S.Ct. 414, 98 L.Ed. 532 (1954), plaintiff leased its theater to, and entered into a franchise agreement with, defendant; the lease was to be terminable at plaintiff's option if the franchise agreement were terminated. Plaintiff sued to regain possession of the theater, alleging that it was entitled to terminate the lease because the franchise agreement was invalid under the antitrust laws; defendant counterclaimed for damages under the antitrust laws. The trial court denied plaintiff's claim, holding that the franchise agreements were not invalid because no conspiracy in violation of the antitrust laws had been established; it also dismissed the counterclaims. Defendant appealed from the dismissal of its counterclaims, and the Supreme Court held that the trial court's finding of no conspiracy on plaintiff's claim operated as collateral estoppel on the issue. See p. 1113, infra. Could defendant have appealed from the judgment in its favor on plaintiff's claim? Mr. Justice Reed, for the majority, said:

> While Partmar did not appeal, it might have. The finding and conclusion of law * * * were essential to the determination of Paramount's claim for possession of the theatre. Paramount's position * * * was that the agreements were invalid under the federal antitrust statutes as the product of an illegal conspiracy. It is only when a finding of law or fact is not necessary for a decree that the prevailing party may not appeal and the finding does not form the basis for collateral estoppel. * * *. See New York Telephone Co. v. Maltbie * * *. Electrical Fittings Corp. v. Thomas & Betts Co. * * * stated the practice negatively. "A party may not appeal * * * findings * * * not necessary to support the decree."

Id. at 99 n.6, 74 S.Ct. at 420 n.6, 98 L.Ed. at 541 n.6. Mr. Chief Justice Warren, dissenting, argued:

> * * * Petitioner, as the successful party in the eviction suit, could not appeal the District Court's finding that there was no evidence of conspiracy. * * * The adverse finding was not included in the Court's decree, as in Electrical Fittings Corp. * * * Because of this inability to appeal, the finding cannot bind petitioner in a subsequent action between the parties based upon a different cause of action. * * *

The Court's opinion * * * concedes that inability to appeal precludes a subsequent application of collateral estoppel, but contends that petitioner could have appealed here because the trial court's finding in the eviction suit (as to the absence of proof of conspiracy) was material to the decree in the eviction suit. The Court's opinion cites no case, in this Court or any other, holding that a successful party can appeal findings which are not inserted as part of the decree. Indeed, the opinion overlooks the very holdings of this Court on which it relies for support.

Id. at 109 n.8, 74 S.Ct. at 425 n.8, 98 L.Ed. at 546 n.8.

STANDARD ACC. INS. CO. v. ROBERTS

United States Circuit Court of Appeals, Eighth Circuit, 1942.
132 F.2d 794.

STONE, Circuit Judge. The Standard Accident Insurance Company issued its liability policy to Herbert Roberts. Thereafter, personal injury judgments were secured against Roberts by Clyde, Pearl, George Willie and Forest Wayne Primm. Thereafter, the Standard filed this action against Roberts and the Primms to obtain a declaratory judgment that it was not liable to them on the above policy. The trial court found that the cause of the injuries to the Primms was not within the coverage of the policy but determined that the Standard, "with full knowledge of the date, place and circumstances of the injuries" had assumed and retained control of the investigation and defense of the damage suit under such circumstances that it was estopped from denying liability thereon to the detriment and prejudice of Roberts. This is an appeal by the Standard from the judgment dismissing its petition.

Appellant presents three points: (1) that there was no liability under the policy and liability cannot be extended by estoppel; (2) that no estoppel was proven; (3) that insured was not prejudiced by the acts and conduct of Standard.

Appellees contest the above points and, in addition, urge: (1) that the policy should have been reformed to express the intention of the parties thereto; (2) that the court should have allowed reasonable attorney fees and the statutory penalty; (3) that the policy covered the accident causing the injuries to the Primms. Appellant urges that none of these three additional matters presented by appellees is open here because appellees took no cross-appeal. In this situation as to contentions of the parties, it is necessary to determine just what contentions are examinable here.

Since appellees' contentions as to reformation of the policy and as to allowance of attorney fees and penalty seek to change or to add to the relief accorded by the judgment which was in their favor, they can raise here such issues only by a cross-appeal. * * * On the other hand, the contention that the policy covered the accident seeks only to sustain the judgment for a reason presented at the trial and determined adversely to appellees. The recovery is upon the policy; and it is no more than a change of reason for such recovery, whether it be under the terms of the policy or because of an estoppel to question the applicability of the terms. In such situations the rule is that "a respondent or an appellee may urge any matter appearing in the record in support of a judgment". Le Tulle v. Scofield, 308 U.S. 415, 421, 60 S.Ct. 313, 316, 84 L.Ed. 355. * * * Therefore, appellees may, in support of the decree, urge here this ground that the policy covers the accident.

* * *

NOTES AND QUESTIONS

1. Read Federal Rule of Appellate Procedure 4(a) in the Supplement. Why is a party permitted to file a notice of appeal within 14 days after another party has noted an appeal?

2. Plaintiff's decedent was hired by a contractor to work on defendant railroad's roadbed. Plaintiff brought an action for decedent's death against the railroad in a state court, relying on the Federal Employers' Liability Act and on common-law negligence; the railroad brought a third-party claim against the contractor for indemnity. The trial court held that FELA was not applicable because decedent was not a servant of the railroad and also that the contractor was not liable to the railroad; it submitted the case against the railroad to the jury on common-law negligence, and the jury found for the railroad on the ground of contributory negligence, which is not a defense in an FELA action. Plaintiff appealed, posting an appeal bond in favor of both the railroad and the contractor, but the railroad did not perfect an appeal against the contractor. The Texas Court of Civil Appeals affirmed the judgment, but the United States Supreme Court reversed, holding the FELA applicable. On remand, the Texas Court of Civil Appeals, in BAKER v. TEXAS & P. RY., 326 S.W.2d 639, 640 (1959), held that because the "liability vel non of [the contractor] * * * on the Railroad's cross-action centers upon the facts, which will be rehashed even in greater detail than before * * * the situation, in our opinion, justif[ies] a reversal of cause in its entirety." Compare Whitehead v. American Sec. & Trust Co., 285 F.2d 282 (D.C.Cir.1960).

What is the effect of a reversal upon a party who took no part in an appeal at all? See In re Barnett, 124 F.2d 1005 (2d Cir.1941).

WARD v. TAGGART

Supreme Court of California, 1959.
51 Cal.2d 736, 336 P.2d 534.

TRAYNOR, Justice. At plaintiff * * * Ward's request * * * Thomsen, a real estate broker, undertook to look for properties that might be of interest to Ward for purchase. During a conversation about unrelated matters, defendant Marshall W. Taggart, a real estate broker, told Thomsen that as exclusive agent for Sunset Oil Company he had several acres of land in Los Angeles County for sale. Thomsen said that he had a client who might be interested in acquiring this property. When Thomsen mentioned to Taggart that another broker named Dawson had a "For Sale" sign on the property, Taggart replied that Sunset had taken the listing away from Dawson. With Ward's authorization Thomsen submitted an offer on his behalf to Taggart of $4,000 an acre. Taggart promised to take the offer to Sunset. Taggart later told Thomsen that Sunset had refused the offer and would not take less for the property than $5,000 an acre, one-half in cash. Thomsen conveyed this information to Ward, who directed Thomsen to make an offer on those terms. * * * At Taggart's direction, Thomsen inserted in the offer a provision for payment by Sunset of a ten per cent commission, which Taggart and Thomsen agreed to divide equally. * * * Subsequently, Taggart told Thomsen that Sunset had accepted Ward's offer and presented to him proposed escrow instructions naming Taggart's business associate, defendant H. M. Jordan, as seller acting for Taggart. Taggart stated that his designation as principal would enable him to "clear up the Dawson exclusive listing" as well as certain blanket mortgages on the property. * * * When Ward asked why Jordan was to be the payee of the notes and the beneficiary of the trust deeds, Thomsen replied that Taggart had said the arrangement was prompted by certain tax and other problems of the Sunset Oil Company and that the trust deeds would be turned over to Sunset after the escrow. Plaintiffs paid $360,246 for the 72.0492 acres conveyed to them.

Plaintiffs did not learn until after they had purchased the property that Taggart had never been given a listing by Sunset and that he had never presented to Sunset and never intended to present plaintiffs' offers of $4,000 and $5,000 per acre. Instead, he presented his own offer of $4,000 per acre, which Sunset accepted. He falsely represented to plaintiffs that the least Sunset would take for the property was $5,000 per acre, because he intended to purchase the property from Sunset himself and resell it to plaintiffs at a profit of $1,000 per acre. All the reasons he gave for the unusual handling of the sale were fabrications. * * * All of the money he used to pay Sunset the purchase price came from the Ward escrow.

Plaintiffs brought an action in tort charging fraud on the part of Taggart and Jordan. The case was tried without a jury, and the court entered judgment against both defendants for $72,049.20 compensatory damages, and against Taggart for $36,000 exemplary damages. * * *

Defendants contend that the judgment must be reversed on the ground that, there can be no recovery in a tort action for fraud without proof of the actual or "out-of-pocket" losses sustained by the plaintiff and that in the present case there was no evidence that the property was worth less than plaintiffs paid for it. * * * Although, as defendants admit, the evidence is clearly sufficient to support the finding of fraud, the only evidence submitted on the issue of damages was that the property was worth at least $5,000 per acre, the price plaintiffs paid for it. Since there was no proof that plaintiffs suffered "out-of-pocket" loss, there can be no recovery in tort for fraud. * * *

Plaintiffs contend, however, that their recovery is not limited to actual damages, on the ground that section 3343 [of the California Civil Code] does not apply to a tort action to recover secret profits. * * * In the present case, however, there is no evidence of an agency or other fiduciary relationship between plaintiffs and defendant Taggart or defendant Jordan. Plaintiffs dealt at arms length with Taggart through their agent Thomsen. * * * There is no evidence of any prior dealings between the parties or any acquaintanceship or special relationship that would create a fiduciary duty of defendants to plaintiffs. In the absence of a fiduciary relationship, recovery in a tort action for fraud is limited to the actual damages suffered by the plaintiff. * * *

Even though Taggart was not plaintiff's agent, the public policy of this state does not permit one to "take advantage of his own wrong" * * * and the law provides a quasi-contractual remedy to prevent one from being unjustly enriched at the expense of another. * * * As a real estate broker, Taggart had the duty to be honest and truthful in his dealings. * * * Through fraudulent misrepresentations he received money that plaintiffs would otherwise have had. Thus, Taggart is an involuntary trustee for the benefit of plaintiffs on the secret profit of $1,000 per acre that he made from his dealings with them.

Although this theory of recovery was not advanced by plaintiffs in the trial court, it is settled that a change in theory is permitted on appeal when "a question of law only is presented on the facts appearing in the record * * *." Panopulos v. Maderis, 47 Cal.2d 337, 341, 303 P.2d 738, 741 * * *. The general rule confining the parties upon appeal to the theory advanced below is based on the rationale that the opposing party should not be required to defend for the first time on appeal against a new theory that "contemplates a factual situation the consequences of which are open to controversy and were not put in issue or presented at the trial." * * * Such is not the case here. Although the facts pleaded and proved by plaintiffs do not sustain the judgment on the theory of tort, they are sufficient to uphold recovery under the quasi-contractual theory of unjust enrichment since that theory does not contemplate any factual situation different from that established by the evidence in the trial court. Defendants were given ample opportunity to present their version of the transaction involved, and the issue of whether or not their actions constituted fraud was decided adversely to them by the trial court.

Accordingly, the judgment for $72,092.20, representing the $1,000 per acre secret profit, against defendant Taggart must be affirmed. The judgment against defendant Jordan, however, must be reversed. Although she permitted her name to be used in the dual escrows, she did not share in the illicit profit that Taggart obtained. One cannot be held to be a constructive trustee of something he has not acquired.

* * *

[The opinion of Justice SCHAUER, concurring in part and dissenting in part, is omitted.]

NOTES AND QUESTIONS

1. If the Supreme Court of California had not found a quasi-contractual remedy available, and plaintiffs had shown evidence, not offered at trial, of

facts, not raised at trial, supporting the existence of a fiduciary relationship between Taggart and himself, what result should have been reached by the court? Read Cal.Code Civ.Proc. § 909 in the Supplement. "Probably the most significant practical characteristic of this California exception is its sparing use, especially in situations where the additional evidence aims at reversal of the judgment instead of affirmance." Louisell & Degnan, *Rehearing in American Appellate Courts,* 44 Calif.L.Rev. 627, 629 n.8 (1956).

2. Plaintiff brought an action for payments due on a subscription for two burial crypts. At the close of plaintiff's case, defendant moved for judgment on the ground that plaintiff had not shown that the mausoleum was constructed in accordance with the plans and specifications; the trial court denied plaintiff permission to reopen the case to supply the missing proof, and granted defendant's motion. On appeal, the Supreme Court of Arizona found that the refusal to permit plaintiff to reopen had been an abuse of discretion. At that point, should defendant have been permitted to raise for the first time plaintiff's failure to allege and prove that he was a licensed real-estate broker as required by law? See Bowman v. Hall, 83 Ariz. 56, 316 P.2d 484 (1957). See generally Millar, *New Allegation and Proof on Appeal in Anglo-American Civil Procedure,* 47 Nw. U.L.Rev. 427 (1952); Pound, *New Evidence in the Appellate Court,* 56 Harv.L. Rev. 1313 (1943).

2. SCOPE OF REVIEW OF FACTS

CORCORAN v. CITY OF CHICAGO

Supreme Court of Illinois, 1940.
373 Ill. 567, 27 N.E.2d 451.

MURPHY, Justice. John F. Corcoran * * * began a suit * * * against the city of Chicago * * * to recover damages for personal injuries alleged to have been caused by the negligent acts of the defendant. The cause was tried with a jury and resulted in a verdict for the plaintiff for $5,000. A motion for new trial was overruled and judgment entered on the verdict. On appeal, the Appellate Court for the First District reversed the judgment and remanded the cause for another trial. The plaintiff filed a motion in the Appellate Court asking that the remanding part of the order be stricken. * * * The motion was granted * * *.

The negligence charged was that defendant had carelessly and negligently permitted certain streets to be and remain in an unsafe condition for travel * * *. The evidence was conflicting. The Appellate Court found the verdict was against the manifest weight of the evidence and reversed the judgment for that reason.

It is conceded the power which the Appellate Court assumed to exercise in reviewing the evidence and setting aside the verdict is found in section

92(3b) of the Civil Practice Act * * * which provides that Appellate Courts may review "error of fact, in that the judgment, decree or order appealed from is not sustained by the evidence or is against the weight of the evidence." Plaintiff's position is that such provision, as applied to facts found by a jury upon conflicting evidence, as in the instant case, is unconstitutional, in that the findings of the Appellate Court * * * take from him the right to a trial by jury as guaranteed by section 5 of article 2 of the Constitution * * *.

* * *

Prior to 1837, the law of this state was that the granting or refusal of a motion for a new trial rested in the sound discretion of the trial court and the ruling thereon could not be urged as error in the court of review. * * * In 1837, an act was passed which provided "exceptions taken to opinions or decisions of circuit court overruling motions in arrest of judgment, motions for new trials and for continuance of causes shall hereafter be allowed and the party excepting may assign for error any opinion so excepted to, any usage to the contrary notwithstanding." The substance of the act * * * has been the statutory law of this state since 1837.

* * *

The effect of the operation of the statute was considered in Chicago & Rock Island Railroad Co. v. McKean, 40 Ill. 218, a case where the trial court had overruled a motion for new trial and error was assigned on such ruling. Mr. Justice Breese, speaking for the court, said: "This brings before us all the evidence in the case, and on the force to which it is entitled, we are required to pronounce. By the common law, and the practice under it which prevailed for ages, the refusal to grant a new trial could not be assigned as error. * * * The policy of this legislative enactment has been, and may well be questioned, as it brings before a tribunal, other than a jury, that which, in the institution of trial by jury, was for their determination alone, that is, the facts of a case. An appellate court was, before the passage of that act, judge of the law only * * *. The old and honored maxim once was, 'the judges respond to the law, the jury to the facts,' but now, by this innovation, the judges of an appellate court have as much power over the facts as the jury had in the first instance, for it is undeniable this court may set aside a verdict if the facts fail to satisfy it of its propriety. * * *"

Plaintiff contends that on all questions of fact where the evidence is conflicting the verdict of the jury can not be set aside as being against the weight of the evidence except by the court that tried the case, and asserts that such was the practice at common law. * * *

At an early date in the development of the common law the courts were centered at Westminster. A suit was instituted by filing it in the court at that place. When it was ready for trial it was sent to the county where the cause of action arose. Jurors were summoned to appear in such county and the King commissioned one of the judges of the court at Westminster to try the case. These courts came to be known as courts of assize and nisi prius. The judge at nisi prius presided at the trial, received the verdict and returned the record with the verdict and the proceedings attached in the form of a postea to the court at Westminster.   *   *   *   Thereafter, the record was reviewed by the court en banc at Westminster and judgment entered.   Motions for new trial were made to the court at Westminster.   *   *   *   At an early time the nisi prius judge certified his approval or dissatisfaction with the result of the verdict and it became a guide for the courts sitting en banc in Westminster. *   *   *   The certificate of the nisi prius judge was not controlling *   *   *.

There are statements in some of the later cases which support plaintiff's contention that at common law the power to award a new trial on the grounds the verdict was against the weight of the evidence, rested solely in the trial court.   Such statements seem to be partially based on the theory that the trial judge saw and heard the witnesses testify and was for that reason in a better position to consider the evidence than the judges of a court of review who had not had such opportunity.   As has been noted, at the early common law, motions for a new trial were addressed to the court at Westminster and not to the judge who presided at the trial.   The judges of Westminster acted only on the record before them and, as Blackstone said, "it was clearly held that whatever matter was of force to avoid a verdict ought to be returned upon the postea." The judge at nisi prius was a member of the court at Westminster.   The function of that court was to review the record and proceedings returned to it and determine whether judgment should be entered.   *   *   *   The judges of the court at Westminster had no opportunity of seeing the witnesses or hearing them testify.   The credibility and weight of the evidence was determined from the records and proceedings before them.

From the authorities cited and others which have been examined, we conclude that there was a practice at common law which authorized courts exercising appellate jurisdiction to set aside verdicts on the grounds the findings of fact were not supported by the evidence.   *   *   *

Judgment affirmed.

NOTES AND QUESTIONS

1.   For a scholarly criticism of the principal case, see Weisbrod, *Limitations on Trial by Jury in Illinois,* 19 Chi.-Kent L.Rev. 91 (1940).   See generally Clark & Stone, *Review of Findings of Fact,* 4 U.Chi.L.Rev. 190 (1937).   The English practice is described in Goodhart, *Appeals on Questions of Fact,* 71 L.Q.Rev. 402 (1955).

2.   In 1957, Professor Charles Alan Wright stated "that, so far as I can find, there is not a single case in which a federal appellate court has ever reversed and ordered a new trial on the ground that the trial court did abuse its discretion in denying a motion [for a new trial on the weight of the evidence] *   *   *." Wright, *The Doubtful Omniscience of Appellate Courts,* 41 Minn.L. Rev. 751, 760 (1957).   At the time he was criticizing a dictum of the Court of Appeals for the District of Columbia Circuit claiming the existence of the power to reverse; but, he observed, "today's dictum claiming extended power for appellate courts is frequently the prelude to tomorrow's holding to that effect." Id. at 763.

Subsequently at least one court of appeals has acted as he prophesied. Georgia-Pac. Corp. v. United States, 264 F.2d 161 (5th Cir.1959). Is there a significant difference between an appellate court's reversing a trial court's order denying a new trial and an appellate court's ordering a new trial because the trial court has erroneously denied a motion for a directed verdict as in *Slocum v. New York Life Ins. Co.,* p. 957, supra? Is there really a difference between reversing an order denying a new trial and reversing an order granting a new trial as in *Lind v. Schenley Industries, Inc.,* p. 955, supra?

3. The power to reverse denials of new trials on the ground that the verdict is excessive or to condition affirmance upon a remittitur is now asserted by most of the courts of appeals, after "seemingly endless controversy," and despite the extremely strong doubts thrown on the subject by Mr. Justice Brandeis' opinion in FAIRMOUNT GLASS WORKS v. CUB FORK COAL CO., 287 U.S. 474, 53 S.Ct. 252, 77 L.Ed. 439 (1933). See also the exhaustive opinion of Judge Medina in Dagnello v. Long Island R.R., 289 F.2d 797 (2d Cir.1961). Why should this power be more commonly found than the power discussed in Note 2?

ORVIS v. HIGGINS

United States Court of Appeals, Second Circuit, 1950.
180 F.2d 537.
Certiorari denied 340 U.S. 810, 71 S.Ct. 37, 95 L.Ed. 595.

FRANK, Circuit Judge. [This was an action for refund of federal estate taxes. Deceased husband and his wife each had set up a trust in 1934 in which the other received a life interest. If these trusts were set up independently, the husband's estate was not chargeable with any estate tax on the property that was in the trust created by the wife. If the trusts were set up by mutual agreement, however, each trust being in consideration of the other, then the trust set up by the wife would be treated as a trust set up by the husband, and since the deceased received a life income from the trust, the value of that trust would be taxable to the estate. The trial judge had found that the trusts were set up independently.]

In opinions holding that the findings of trial judges were not "clearly erroneous" within the meaning of Rule 52(a), * * * we have often stressed the importance of a trial judge's advantage over us when he saw and heard the witnesses as they testified. We have pointed out our inability to appraise the cogency of demeanor evidence, lost to us because it cannot be captured in the witness' words as recorded on paper. In so holding, we may perhaps, at times, have overlooked distinctions described in United States v. United States Gypsum Co., 333 U.S. 364, 394–396, 68 S.Ct. 525, 542, 92 L.Ed. 746.

There the Court made it clear that Rule 52(a) merely adopted the equity practice then prevailing in the federal courts. The Court said a finding of a trial court, if it be by a judge, "is 'clearly erroneous' when although there is evidence to support it, the reviewing court on the entire evidence is left with the definite and firm conviction that a mistake has been committed." * * *

In the light of the Gypsum case, we may make approximate gradations as follows: We must sustain a general or a special jury verdict when there is some evidence which the jury might have believed, and when a reasonable inference from that evidence will support the verdict, regardless of whether that evidence is oral or by deposition. In the case of findings by an administrative agency, the usual rule is substantially the same as that in the case of a jury, the findings being treated like a special verdict. Where a trial judge sits without a jury, the rule varies with the character of the evidence: (a) If he decides a fact issue on written evidence alone, we are as able as he to determine credibility, and so we may disregard his finding. (b) Where the evidence is partly oral and the balance is written or deals with undisputed facts, then we may ignore the trial judge's finding and substitute our own, (1) if the written evidence or some undisputed fact renders the credibility of the oral testimony extremely doubtful, or (2) if the trial judge's finding must rest exclusively on the written evidence or the undisputed facts, so that his evaluation of credibility has no significance. (c) But where the evidence supporting his finding as to any fact issue is entirely oral testimony, we may disturb that finding only in the most unusual circumstances.

It follows that evidence sufficient to support a jury verdict or an administrative finding may not suffice to support a trial judge's finding. So in the instant case, perhaps, on the record evidence, we might have affirmed a jury's verdict or an administrative agency's finding in plaintiff's favor. That, however, we need not decide. For here the finding is that of a trial judge, and the evidence consists in large part of facts neither side disputes, in circumstances such that the trial judge's evaluation of credibility becomes unimportant. In short, for reasons we shall state, the undisputed facts are such that we have a "definite and firm conviction" that the trial judge was mistaken in finding that Orvis and Mrs. Orvis "each pursued an independent course" in creating the 1934 trusts, and that no reciprocity was intended. We therefore hold that finding "clearly erroneous," and hold, rather, that each of those trusts was made in consideration of the other.

In so holding we assume that, because of the "evanescent factor which cannot come before us"—i. e., the demeanor of the witnesses—the trial judge fully believed everything they said. Even so, there is nothing in the testimony which in any manner offsets what we believe to be the virtually irresistible inference drawn from the undisputed facts. To offset that inference, the trial judge relied on no positive testimony that Mr. and Mrs. Orvis acted independently but relied merely on negative testimony as to the absence of an expressed intention to act reciprocally, i. e., that "no witness even intimated that the decedent acted with Mrs. Orvis' intention in mind or she with his." But those same witnesses, unequivocally and without contradiction by any other witnesses, testified to the following facts which we think can lead to but one reasonable conclusion: Mr. Orvis, in the Fall of 1934, spoke to his son, Warner, about creating a trust. Subsequently, in November 1934, Mrs. Orvis also spoke to Warner about creating a trust. He told his mother that Mr. Orvis had been looking into the subject of trusts and had already talked to his lawyer, Merritt, about his own proposed trust.   Mr. Orvis thereafter talked to his wife about her proposed trust.   On the advice of Warner, Mrs. Orvis also consulted Merritt, concerning her trust, in November, at the Orvis apartment; Mr. Orvis was then in the apartment, and may "have stepped into the room * * * and stayed for a minute."   There was not, Merrill [sic] testified, "any secretiveness by her" with respect to her intention to create a trust.   The only testimony on which the trial judge relied, or could have relied, to counterbalance the foregoing is that of Mr. Merritt as to the reasons respectively given to him by husband and wife for the creation of their respective trusts.   Not only were those respective reasons strikingly similar but none of them sufficed or purported to explain why each of the trusts set up a life estate;   nor did the expression of those reasons at all negative the existence of an intent to make the trusts reciprocal.   The finding of an absence of such an intention must, then, depend not on an inference drawn from anything positive in the testimony concerning statements of intention made by Mr. and Mrs. Orvis, but on an inference from their conduct.   And that inference, in turn, must rest on a belief in the purely chance concurrence of several events, although the coincidental occurrence of those events would ordinarily be highly improbable.   Such a belief ought not to be the foundation of a trial judge's finding on a fact issue, in favor of that side having (like plaintiffs here) the burden of proof as to that issue, unless the purely chance character of those events is positively confirmed by clear evidence.   There is no such confirmatory evidence here.

* * *

Reversed and remanded.

CHASE, Circuit Judge (dissenting).   * * *

This is a typical instance for the application of Civil Rule 52(a).   Though trial judges may at times be mistaken as to facts, appellate judges are not always omniscient.

I would affirm.

NOTES AND QUESTIONS

1.   Consider the following views:

(a) "There is no logical reason for placing the findings of fact of a trial judge upon a substantially lower level of conclusiveness than the fact findings of a jury of laymen, or those of an administrative agency * * *.   The existence of any doubt as to whether the trial court or this Court is the ultimate trier of fact issues in nonjury cases is, we think, detrimental to the orderly administration of justice, impairs the confidence of litigants and the public in the decisions of the district courts, and multiplies the number of appeals in such cases."   PENDERGRASS v. NEW YORK LIFE INS. CO., 181 F.2d 136, 138 (8th Cir.1950).

(b) "[E]ven where the question is what finding of fact should be made on the basis of documentary evidence, the trial judge has the advantage of having made the initial sifting of the entire record and of having put it into logical sequence, while the appellate court has lawyers before it picking out bits and pieces of the record to attack or defend a particular finding."   Wright, *The Doubtful Omniscience of Appellate Courts*, 41 Minn.L.Rev. 751, 782 (1957).

(c) "[R]eversal by a higher court is not proof justice is thereby better done. There is no doubt that if there were a super-Supreme Court, a substantial proportion of our reversals of state courts would also be reversed. We are not final because we are infallible, but we are infallible only because we are final." Mr. Justice Jackson, concurring, in BROWN v. ALLEN, 344 U.S. 443, 540, 73 S.Ct. 397, 427, 97 L.Ed. 469, 533 (1953).

2. Reread *Hicks v. United States*, p. 56, supra. Consider the following:

> Taking a cautious view of the propriety of directed verdicts in negligence cases tried to juries, appellate courts have warned, "Our ideas as to what would be proper care vary according to temperament, knowledge, and experience. A party should not be held to the peculiar notions of the judge as to what would be ordinary care." Curiously, most courts have failed to apply these observations to the nonjury trial. Using orthodox terminology, it makes sense to label the reasonable man standard a "question of fact" in the jury case, but a "question of law" in the nonjury case. In the nonjury negligence case, the appellate court, not the trial judge, should be analogized to the jury. * * * [O]nce the facts have been found without clear error, the group of judges on the appellate court is better qualified to decide the issue of negligence than is the trial judge acting alone, according to the teaching of jury cases.

Weiner, *The Civil Nonjury Trial and the Law-Fact Distinction*, 55 Calif.L.Rev. 1020, 1033 (1967).

SECTION D. THE VIEW AT THE TOP—COURTS ABOVE APPELLATE COURTS

Read 28 U.S.C. §§ 1251–1254, 1257, in the Supplement and all the accompanying material.

---

1. REVIEW AS OF RIGHT

In the federal-court system and in the judicial structure of about one-third of the states, intermediate appellate courts are interposed between the trial courts of general jurisdiction and the highest court. The principal purpose in creating intermediate appellate courts has been to relieve the pressure of burgeoning appellate litigation on the highest court, leaving that tribunal free to concentrate on deciding important and novel questions of law and on maintaining uniformity in the law applied by the lower courts. To achieve this purpose fully, two conditions must be met. Most appeals must begin and end in the intermediate appellate courts, but the possibility of review by the highest court must be open in every case.

Both conditions would be satisfied if the intermediate courts heard every appeal in the first instance and the highest court had complete discretion to review the decisions of those courts. But no American system seems to have fully adopted this approach. In every state that has intermediate appellate courts, as well as in the federal courts, some matters are reviewable directly by the highest court, and, in most systems, some matters, decided in the first instance by the intermediate courts, are appealable as of right to the highest court. The systems differ markedly, however, both in the extent to which the intermediate appellate courts are by-passed and the amount of discretion given to the highest court to choose the cases it hears.

NOTES AND QUESTIONS

1. Compare the provisions for direct appeal to the Supreme Court of California, the Supreme Court of Georgia, and the Court of Appeals of New York that are set out in the Supplement following 28 U.S.C. § 1254. What is the reason for each of these provisions? Which set of state provisions seems most appropriate?

Before the Constitution of California was amended in 1966, the provision for the direct-appeal jurisdiction of the Supreme Court was quite similar to that in Georgia. Under the authority of Article VI, Section 4c of the earlier California Constitution, which gave the Supreme Court the power now found in Section 12, however, the Supreme Court transferred many of its direct appeals to the district courts of appeals for decision.

2. In what cases do direct appeals lie to the Supreme Court of the United States from the decisions of district courts under 28 U.S.C. §§ 1252, 1253? Is direct appeal more or less appropriate in the federal-court system than in that of a state? What problems are presented by direct appeal in complex suits, such as Government antitrust actions? See Brown Shoe Co. v. United States, 370 U.S. 294, 355, 364, 82 S.Ct. 1502, 1541, 1546, 8 L.Ed.2d 510, 557, 562 (1962) (criticisms by Mr. Justice Clark and Mr. Justice Harlan). The Supreme Court has the power in those cases in which certiorari would lie to take up a case as soon as it is docketed in the court of appeals and before that court considers it, but the power is very rarely exercised. See, e. g., Youngstown Sheet & Tube Co. v. Sawyer, 343 U.S. 937, 72 S.Ct. 775, 96 L.Ed. 1345 (1952). Do the state courts mentioned in Note 1, supra, possess comparable authority?

3. A significant drawback of a provision for direct appeal is the confusion that may exist as to whether a particular case falls within the provision and as to the appropriate disposition of such case if it is appealed to the wrong court. A peculiarly snarled manifestation of the problem in the federal courts arises in the context of three-judge district courts because of the conjunction of 28 U.S.C. § 1253 and 28 U.S.C. § 2281. Read both of these statutes in the Supplement. In a case in which a United States district judge erroneously had refused to convene a three-judge district court, does the court of appeals have jurisdiction to remand the case for determination by a three-judge court, or is the only remedy a petition for mandamus in the United States Supreme Court? See Idlewild Bon Voyage Liquor Corp. v. Epstein, 370 U.S. 713, 82 S.Ct. 1294, 8 L.Ed.2d 794 (1962); Cancel v. Wyman, 441 F.2d 553 (2d Cir.1971); Wright, Federal Courts § 50 (2d ed. 1970).

4. Compare the allotment of discretionary and obligatory jurisdiction in the Supreme Court of California, the Court of Appeals of New York, and the Supreme Court of the United States. Which of these courts appears to have the most discretion in selecting the cases it will hear? Which has the least? Note particularly the text of N.Y.C.P.L.R. 5601(a). Article VI, Section 7(1) of the New York Constitution provides that there shall be an appeal of right to the Court of Appeals in the situation covered by Section 5601(a), unless the legislature otherwise directs. Does it seem necessary to provide a right to review in this situation? Is there any comparable federal provision? How do the guidelines laid down in Supreme Court Rule 19(1), which is set out in the Supplement, compare with the New York provision? Do the different provisions for obligatory and discretionary review in the California Supreme Court and the New York Court of Appeals suggest that the functions of the two courts are not entirely comparable?

5. In many cases in which there seems to be obligatory review in the Supreme Court of the United States, the obligation is somewhat illusory. For example, in cases that come up under Section 1257(2), the Court consistently has maintained that it has jurisdiction only if there is a "substantial federal question." Zucht v. King, 260 U.S. 174, 43 S.Ct. 24, 67 L.Ed. 194 (1922). See also Note, *Summary Disposition of Supreme Court Appeals: The Significance of Limited Discretion and a Theory of Limited Precedent*, 52 B.U.L.Rev. 373 (1972). Thus, when a state statute is challenged and upheld in the state court against a claim of invalidity under the United States Constitution, the Supreme Court, if it regards the federal claim as remote or well-settled in favor of the statute, will dismiss the appeal rather than affirm. The federal claim also must have been timely and properly raised and preserved. The most important restriction on Supreme Court review of state-court decisions of federal claims—whether review is sought by appeal or certiorari—is that the judgment necessarily must turn on the federal question and that it not rest upon an independent state ground.

A good example is FOX FILM CORP. v. MULLER, 296 U.S. 207, 56 S.Ct. 183, 80 L.Ed. 158 (1935). Plaintiff sued its licensee for breach of contract in a state court; the licensee defended on the ground that the contract was invalid under the antitrust laws. In an earlier case involving a substantially identical contract with another licensee, the United States Supreme Court had held that a provision requiring arbitration violated the antitrust laws. In the *Muller* case, the state court held that the contract was invalid, and that in any event the arbitration clause was nonseverable so that the whole contract was rendered invalid by it. Plaintiff sought review of the ruling that the contract violated the antitrust laws, but the Supreme Court dismissed, saying:

> Whether the provisions of a contract are nonseverable, so that if one be held invalid the others must fall with it, is clearly a question of general and not of federal law. The invalidity of the arbitration clause which the present contracts embody is conceded. * * * In that situation, the primary question to be determined by the court below was whether the concededly invalid clause was separable from the other provisions of the contract. The ruling of the state Supreme Court that it was not, is sufficient to conclude the case without regard to the determination, if, in fact, any was made, in respect of the federal question. It follows that the non-federal ground is adequate to sustain the judgment.

Id. at 210, 56 S.Ct. at 184, 80 L.Ed. at 160.

In *Muller*, the state court's judgment, based upon a state ground, had the same effect that it would have had if it had sustained the claim of a federal right. Should the Supreme Court's power be different when the effect of the state court's judgment is to defeat the claim of a federal right? See Sandalow, *Henry v. Mississippi and the Adequate State Ground: Proposals for a Revised Doctrine,* 1965 Sup.Ct.Rev. 187. Should it make any difference whether the state ground is substantive or procedural? See Henry v. Mississippi, 379 U.S. 443, 85 S.Ct. 564, 13 L.Ed.2d 408 (1965). See generally Wright, *Federal Courts* § 107 (2d ed. 1970).

6. For a discussion of the extent to which the jurisdiction of a state's highest court should be made obligatory, see Joint Committee on Michigan Procedural Revision, *Judicial Administration at the Appellate Level—Michigan* 24–35 (1959); Institute of Judicial Administration, *Intermediate Appellate Courts,* Rep. No. 2–U29, 5–8 (1954). See generally Curran & Sunderland, *The Organization and Operation of Courts of Review,* in *Third Report of the Judicial Council of Michigan* 51, 152–204 (1933).

7. Appeals from courts of inferior jurisdiction, such as justice-of-the-peace courts, probate courts, and municipal courts, frequently lie to the trial courts of general jurisdiction. The organization of inferior courts differs so widely from state to state that few generalizations can be drawn. Typically, however, the jurisdictional provisions call for a de novo hearing in the court of general jurisdiction and, in the case of very small claims, make the determination of the latter court final and unreviewable. See p. 775, supra.

---

2. DISCRETIONARY REVIEW

Review 28 U.S.C. §§ 1254(1), 1257(3).

DICK v. NEW YORK LIFE INS. CO., 359 U.S. 437, 448, 79 S.Ct. 921, 928, 3 L.Ed.2d 935, 943 (1959). Mr. Justice FRANKFURTER, dissenting:

Establishment of intermediate appellate courts in 1891 was designed by Congress to relieve the overburdened docket of the Court. The Circuit Courts of Appeals were to be equal in dignity to the Supreme Courts of the several States. The essential purpose of the Evarts Act was to enable the Supreme Court to discharge its indispensable functions in our federal system by relieving it of the duty of adjudication in cases that are important only to the litigants. The legislative history of the Evarts Act demonstrates that it was clear in 1891, no less than today that litigation allowed to be brought into the federal courts solely on the basis of diversity of citizenship is rarely of moment except to the parties. The Act provided, therefore, that in diversity cases "the judgments or decrees of the circuit courts of appeals shall be final." In a provision which Senator Evarts referred to as a "weakness" in the Act, this Court was given the discretionary power to grant certiorari in these cases, to be exercised if some question of general interest, outside the limited scope of an ordinary diversity litigation, was also involved.

* * *

Time and again in the years immediately following the passage of the Evarts Act this Court stated that it was only in cases of "gravity and general importance" or "to secure uniformity of decision" that the certiorari power should be exercised. * * *

These considerations have led the Court in scores of cases to dismiss the writ of certiorari even after oral argument when it became manifest that the writ was granted under a misapprehension of the true issues. * * *

To strengthen further this Court's control over its docket and to avoid review of cases which in the main raise only factual controversies, Congress in 1916 made cases arising under the Federal Employers' Liability Act * * * final in the Courts of Appeals, reviewable by this Court only when required by the guiding standards for exercising its certiorari jurisdiction. The Senate Report which accompanied this bill to the floor of the Senate suggested that this change would allow the Supreme Court more time for "expeditious determination of those [cases] having real substance."

In 1925 Congress enacted the "Judges' Bill," called such because it was drafted by a committee of this Court composed of Van Devanter, McReynolds, and Sutherland, JJ. At the hearings on the bill these Justices and Mr. Chief Justice Taft explained the bill and also the Court's past practice in respecting the limitations of its certiorari jurisdiction. These authoritative expositions and assurances to Congress, on the basis of which Congress sharply restricted the Court's obligatory jurisdiction, admit of no doubt, contain no ambiguity. Mr. Chief Justice Taft said:

"No litigant is entitled to more than two chances, namely, to the original trial and to a review, and the intermediate courts of review are provided for that purpose. When a case goes beyond that, it is not primarily to preserve the rights of the litigants. The Supreme Court's function is for the purpose of expounding and stabilizing principles of law for the benefit of the people of the country, passing upon constitutional questions and other important questions of law for the public benefit. It is to preserve uniformity of decision among the intermediate courts of appeal."

The House Report, in recommending to the House of Representatives passage of the bill, stated the matter succinctly:

"The problem is whether the time and attention and energy of the court shall be devoted to matters of large public concern, or whether they shall be consumed by matters of less concern, without especial general interest, and only because the litigant wants to have the court of last resort pass upon his right." * * *

Questions of fact have traditionally been deemed to be the kind of questions which ought not to be recanvassed here unless they are entangled in the proper determination of constitutional or other important legal issues. * * * The proper use of the discretionary certiorari jurisdiction was on a later occasion thus expounded by Mr. Chief Justice Hughes:

"Records are replete with testimony and evidence of facts. But the questions on certiorari are questions of law. * * * It is only when the facts are interwoven with the questions of law which we should review that the evidence must be examined and then only to the extent that it is necessary to decide the questions of law.   *   *   * ”

———

HARRIS v. PENNSYLVANIA R. R., 361 U.S. 15, 17–19, 80 S.Ct. 22, 24–25, 4 L.Ed.2d 1, 3–4 (1959). Mr. Justice DOUGLAS, concurring:

It is suggested that the Court has consumed too much of its time in reviewing these FELA cases. An examination of the 33 cases in which the Court has granted certiorari during the period [1949–1959] * * * reveals that 16 of these cases were summarily reversed without oral argument and without full opinions. Only 17 cases were argued during this period of more than a decade and, of these, 5 were disposed of by brief *per curiam* opinions. Only 12 cases in over 10 years were argued, briefed and disposed of with full opinions by the Court. We have granted certiorari in these cases on an average of less than 3 per year and have given plenary consideration to slightly more than 1 per year. Wastage of our time is therefore a false issue.

The difference between the majority and minority of the Court in our treatment of FELA cases concerns the degree of vigilance we should exercise in safeguarding the jury trial—guaranteed by the Seventh Amendment and part and parcel of the remedy under this Federal Act when suit is brought in state courts. * * * Whether that right has been impaired in a particular instance often produces a contrariety of views. Yet the practice of the Court in allowing four out of nine votes to control the certiorari docket is well established and of long duration. Without it, the vast discretion which Congress allowed us in granting or denying certiorari might not be tolerable. Every member of the Court has known instances where he has strongly protested the action of the minority in bringing a case or type of case here for adjudication. He may then feel that there are more important and pressing matters to which the Court should give its attention. That is, however, a price we pay for keeping our promise to Congress [3] to let the vote of four Justices bring up any case here on certiorari.

———

[3] The "rule of four" was given as one of the reasons why the Congress thought that the increase of our discretionary jurisdiction was warranted. The House Report stated:

"Lest it should be thought that the increase of discretionary jurisdiction might impair the administration of justice and lead to partial hearings and not secure a decision by the whole court, it is proper to call attention to the very thorough and complete system by which discretionary jurisdiction is exercised. * * *   Mr. Justice Van Devanter tells the whole story:

" * * * The party aggrieved by the decision of the circuit court of appeals and seeking a further review in the Supreme Court is required to present to it a petition and accompanying brief. * * * The petition and brief are required to be served on the other party, and time is given for the presentation of an opposing brief. When this has been done copies * * * are distributed among the members of the

NOTES AND QUESTIONS

1. The procedure followed by the Supreme Court in the disposition of petitions for certiorari, as well as its other business, is discussed in [Mr. Justice] Clark, *The Supreme Court Conference,* 19 F.R.D. 303 (1957); Leiman, *The Rule of Four,* 57 Colum.L.Rev. 975 (1957). See generally Note, *Supreme Court Certiorari Policy in Cases Arising Under the FELA,* 69 Harv.L.Rev. 1441 (1956).

2. The merits of the consistent practice of the Supreme Court to grant certiorari when there is a split between two federal courts of appeals on the legal question involved—or rather whether it is the Court's consistent practice—is debated in Roehner & Roehner, *Certiorari—What is a Conflict Between Circuits?,* 20 U. Chi.L.Rev. 656 (1953), and Stern, *Denial of Certiorari Despite a Conflict,* 66 Harv.L.Rev. 465 (1953).

3. *Compare* United States Supreme Court Rule 19(1), *with* California Appellate Rule 29, both of which are set out in the Supplement following 28 U.S.C. § 1254. What considerations should govern the highest court of a state in deciding whether to hear a case within its discretionary jurisdiction? See 7 Weinstein, Korn & Miller, *New York Civil Practice* ¶ 5602.04; Cuomo, *The New York Court of Appeals: A Practical Perspective,* 34 St. John's L.Rev. 197, 201 (1960); Poulos & Varner, *Review of Intermediate Appellate Court Decisions in California,* 15 Hastings L.J. 11, 15 (1963). Should these considerations be any different from those followed by the Supreme Court of the United States in ruling on a petition for a writ of certiorari?

Supreme Court, and each judge examines them and prepares a memorandum or note indicating his view of what should be done.

" 'In conference * * * each judge states his views * * *; any difference in opinion is discussed and then a vote is taken. I explain this at some length because it seems to be thought outside that the cases are referred to particular judges, as, for instance, that those coming from a particular circuit are referred to the justice assigned to that circuit, and that he reports on them, and the others accept his report.

" '* * * We always grant the petition when as many as four think that it should be granted and sometimes when as many as three think that way. We proceed upon the theory that, if that number out of the nine are impressed with the thought that the case is one that ought to be heard and decided by us, the petition should be granted.' " H.R.Rep. No. 1075, 68th Cong., 2d Sess., p. 3.

CHAPTER 14

THE BINDING EFFECT OF DECISIONS: RES JUDICATA, COLLATERAL ESTOPPEL, AND LAW OF THE CASE

———

"Courts can only do their best to determine the truth on the basis of the evidence, and the first lesson one must learn on the subject of res judicata is that judicial findings must not be confused with absolute truth." B. Currie, *Mutuality of Collateral Estoppel: Limits of the* Bernhard *Doctrine*, 9 Stan.L. Rev. 281, 315 (1957).

———

SECTION A. THE EFFECT OF ADJUDICATION UPON THE CAUSE OF ACTION INVOLVED

———

CLEARY, RES JUDICATA REEXAMINED, 57 Yale L.J. 339, 342–44 (1948):

* * * The rule * * * [of res judicata] falls into two divisions: (a) what was in fact determined in the former action, and (b) what might have been determined in the former action.

The first part of the rule, involving the ascertainment of what was in fact determined in the former action, presents no great difficulty, either practical or theoretical. Courts embark daily upon such inquiries when the question is one of what is usually called estoppel by verdict, or to use a newer phraseology, "collateral estoppel by judgment" * * *. Here we find the courts limiting the rule most scrupulously to what was in fact litigated and decided in the former proceeding * * *. The inquiry is factual and common-sense. The might-have-beens are left strictly out of the picture.

When we come to the second part of the rule, dealing with what might have been litigated in the former action, however, we leave the workaday world and enter into a wondrous realm of words, where results are obtained not by grubbing out facts but by the application of incantations which change pumpkins into coaches and one man's property into another's. The incantations are the various definitions of what constitutes a cause of

1061

action. If the cause of action in the second action was a part of the cause of action in the first action, plaintiff cannot recover. * * *

The problem essentially is one of splitting up the underlying situation which gives rise to litigation, and using the pieces to build more than one lawsuit. The splitting may be as to the theory of recovery; it may be along arithmetical lines; or it may involve the relief given.

Splitting as to theory of recovery occurs when plaintiff in his first action adopts one rule of substantive law, supported by an appropriate selection of the facts comprising the underlying situation out of which the litigation arose, while in his second action he changes his rule of substantive law or his selection of appropriate facts, or both, although the underlying situation remains the same. For example: In a personal injury case, plaintiff sues first for one kind of negligence, and in his second action on a theory of willful wanton misconduct, or for a different kind of negligence, the same accident being involved in each case.

What may be called "arithmetical" splitting occurs when plaintiff, more or less arbitrarily according to the circumstances, selects certain elements of damages for his first action and others for his second action, all having some basic connection. Examples are: * * * More than one action based on the conversion or destruction of various items of property by one wrongful act. * * *

Splitting of relief occurs when plaintiff fails to ask for or obtain in his first action all the relief to which he might have been entitled, and brings another action for additional relief. Examples are: In an action for the possession of real property plaintiff obtains a judgment for possession, but fails to obtain a decree requiring defendant to remove an obstruction of such nature that the sheriff cannot be compelled to remove it. In a subsequent proceeding plaintiff seeks a decree compelling defendant to remove the obstruction. * * *

1. MERGER

A. CAUSE OF ACTION AS A CLAIM

RUSH v. CITY OF MAPLE HEIGHTS

Supreme Court of Ohio, 1958.
167 Ohio St. 221, 147 N.E.2d 599.
Certiorari denied 358 U.S. 814, 79 S.Ct. 21, 3 L.Ed.2d 57.

Q: why bring 2 suits?

[Plaintiff was injured in a fall from a motorcycle. She brought an action in the Municipal Court of Cleveland for damage to her personal property; that court found that defendant city was negligent in maintaining its street and that this negligence was the proximate of plaintiff's damages, which were fixed at $100. Defendant appealed and the judgment was affirmed by the Ohio Court of Appeals and Supreme Court. Plaintiff also brought this action in the Court of Common Pleas of Cuyahoga County for personal injuries she incurred in the same accident; her motion to set trial on the issue of damages alone was granted on the ground that the issue of negligence was res judicata because of the Municipal Court action; judgment was entered on a verdict for $12,000, and the Court of Appeals affirmed.]

HERBERT, Judge. The eighth error assigned by the defendant is that "the trial and appellate courts committed error in permitting plaintiff to split her cause of action * * *."

In the case of Vasu v. Kohlers, Inc., 145 Ohio St. 321, 61 N.E.2d 707, 709, 166 A.L.R. 855, plaintiff operating an automobile came into collision with defendant's truck, in which collision he suffered personal injuries and also damage to his automobile. At the time of collision, plaintiff had coverage of a $50 deductible collision policy on his automobile. The insurance company paid the plaintiff a sum covering the damage to his automobile, whereupon, in accordance with a provision of the policy, the plaintiff assigned to the insurer his claim for such damage.

In February 1942, the insurance company commenced an action * * * against Kohlers, Inc., * * * to recoup the money paid by it to cover the damage to Vasu's automobile.

In August 1942, Vasu commenced an action in the same court against Kohlers, Inc., to recover for personal injuries which he suffered in the same collision.

In March 1943, in the insurance company's action, a verdict was rendered in favor of the defendant, followed by judgment.

Two months later an amended answer was filed in the Vasu case, setting out as a bar to the action * * * the judgment rendered in favor of defendant in the insurance company case. A motion to strike that defense * * * [was] sustained * * *. A trial of the action resulted in a verdict for plaintiff, upon which judgment was entered.

On appeal to the Court of Appeals the defendant claimed that the Court of Common Pleas erred in sustaining plaintiff's motion to strike from the defendant's answer the defense of *res judicata* claimed to have arisen by reason of the judgment in favor of the defendant in the action by the insurance company.

The Court of Appeals reversed the judgment of the Court of Common Pleas and entered final judgment in favor of defendant.

This court reversed the judgment of the Court of Appeals, holding in the syllabus, in part, as follows:

" * * *

Vasu Case

* ["4. Injuries to both person and property suffered by the same person as a result of the same wrongful act are infringements of different rights and give rise to distinct causes of action, with the result that the recovery or denial of recovery of compensation for damages to the property is no bar to an action subsequently prosecuted for the personal injury, unless by an adverse judgment in the first action issues are determined against the plaintiff which operate as an estoppel against him in the second action.

" * * *

"6. Where an injury to person and to property through a single wrongful act causes a prior contract of indemnity and subrogation as to the injury to property, to come into operation for the benefit of the person injured, the indemnitor may prosecute a separate action against the party causing such injury for reimbursement for indemnity monies paid under such contract.

"7. Parties in privy, in the sense that they are bound by a judgment, are those who acquired an interest in the subject matter after the beginning of the action or the rendition of the judgment; and if their title or interest attached before that fact, they are not bound unless made parties.

"8. A grantor or assignor is not bound, as to third persons, by any judgment which such third persons may obtain against his grantee or assignee adjudicating the title to or claim for the interest transferred unless he participated in the action in such manner as to become, in effect, a party."

* * * The sixth, seventh and eighth paragraphs deal with the factual situation which existed in the Vasu case, i. e., a prior contract of indemnity and subrogation. Although, as discussed *infra*, it was not actually necessary to the determination of the issue in that case, attention centers on the fourth paragraph.

* * * [Subsequent] cases, distinguishing and explaining the Vasu case, have not changed the rule established in paragraph four of the syllabus * * *.

* However, it is contended here that that rule is in conflict with the great weight of authority in this country and has caused vexatious litigation. * * *

Upon examination of decisions of courts of last resort, we find that the majority rule is followed in the following cases in each of which the action was between the person suffering injury and the person committing the tort, and where insurers were not involved, as in the case here. * * * [The court cited cases from 20 states forming the majority and 5 states forming the minority.]

The reasoning behind the majority rule seems to be well stated in the case of Mobile & Ohio Rd. Co. v. Matthews * * * [115 Tenn. 172, 91 S.W. 194 (1906)], as follows:

"The negligent action of the plaintiff in error constituted but one tort. The injuries to the person and property of the defendant in error were the several results and effects of one wrongful act. A single tort can be the basis of but one action. It is not improper to declare in different counts for damages to the person and property when both result from the same tort, and it is the better practice to do so where there is any difference in the measure of damages, and all the damages sustained must be sued for in one suit. This is necessary to prevent multiplicity of suits, burdensome expense, and delays to plaintiffs, and vexatious litigation against defendants. * * * "

(margin note: Both injuries arise from a single tort)

The minority rule would seem to stem from the English case of Brunsden v. Humphrey (1884), 14 Q.B. 141. The facts in that case are set forth in the opinion in the Vasu case * * * concluding with the statement:

(margin note: Cound: only 5 states)

"The Master of the Rolls, in his opinion, stated that the test is 'whether the same sort of evidence would prove the plaintiff's case in the two actions,' and that, in the action relating to the cab, 'it would be necessary to give evidence of the damage done to the plaintiff's vehicle. In the present action it would be necessary to give evidence of the bodily injury occasioned to the plaintiff, and of the sufferings which he has undergone, and for this purpose to call medical witnesses. This one test shows that the causes of action as to the damage done to the plaintiff's cab, and as to the injury occasioned to the plaintiff's person, are distinct.' "

(margin note: Separates personal and property injury into separate torts)

The fallacy of the reasoning in the English court is best portrayed in the dissenting opinion of Lord Coleridge, as follows:

" * * * [I]t seems to me a subtlety not warranted by law to hold that a man cannot bring two actions, if he is injured in his arm and in his leg, but can bring two, if besides his arm and leg being injured, his trousers which contain his leg, and his coat-sleeve which contains his arm, have been torn."

There appears to be no valid reason in these days of code pleading to adhere to the old English rule as to distinctions between injuries to the person and damages to the person's property resulting from a single tort. It would seem that the minority rule is bottomed on the proposition that the right of bodily security is fundamentally different from the right of security of property and, also, that, in actions predicated upon a negligent act, damages are a necessary element of each independent cause of action and no recovery may be had unless and until actual consequential damages are shown.

Whether or not injuries to both person and property resulting from the same wrongful act are to be treated as injuries to separate rights or as separate items of damage,   *   *   *   a plaintiff may maintain only one action to en- *
force his rights existing at the time such action is commenced.

The decision of the question actually in issue in the Vasu case is found in paragraphs six, seven and eight of the syllabus, as it is quite apparent from the facts there that the first judgment, claimed to be *res judicata* in Vasu's action against the defendant, was rendered against Vasu's insurer in an action initiated by it after having paid Vasu for the damages to his automobile.
*   *   *

Upon further examination of the cases from other jurisdictions, it appears that in those instances where the courts have held to the majority rule, a separation of causes of action is almost universally recognized where an insurer has acquired by an assignment or by subrogation the right to recover for money it has advanced to pay for property damage.

*   *   *

Holding   In the light of the foregoing, it is the view of this court that the so-called
* majority rule conforms much more properly to modern practice, and that the rule declared in the fourth paragraph of the syllabus in the Vasu case, on a point not actually at issue therein, should not be followed.

*   *   *

Judgment reversed and final judgment for defendant.

STEWART, Judge (concurring).   *   *   *   If it had been necessary [in *Vasu*] to decide the question whether a single tort gives rise to two causes of action as to the one injured by such tort, I would be reluctant to disturb that holding.   However, neither the discussion in the Vasu case as to whether a single or double cause of action arises from one tort nor the language of the fourth paragraph of the syllabus was necessary to decide the issue presented in the case, and obviously both such language and such paragraph are obiter dicta and, therefore, are not as persuasive an authority as if they had been appropriate to the question presented.

*   *   *

ZIMMERMAN, Judge (dissenting).   I am not unalterably opposed to upsetting prior decisions of this court where changing conditions and the lessons of experience clearly indicate the desirability of such course, but, where those considerations do not obtain, established law should remain undisturbed in order to insure a stability on which the lower courts and the legal profession generally may rely with some degree of confidence.

*   *   *

NOTES AND QUESTIONS

1.   The *Rush* case illustrates three ways in which the adjudication in one action may affect a subsequent lawsuit.   The first is one with which you are already familiar: *stare decisis.*   Although neither party in *Rush* had been a party to *Vasu v. Kohler's, Inc.,* both of the lower Ohio courts as well as the dissenting

judge in the Supreme Court of Ohio regarded that case as controlling in *Rush*. Of course, as the *Rush* case itself demonstrates, the binding force of *stare decisis* is not absolute, and the parties to a later action are free to argue that the law announced in an earlier case should be changed. But a court will not lightly depart from precedent even though the parties who are before it were not represented in the case that established the precedent.

When a court has adjudicated a claim between two or more parties and these parties become embroiled in a second action that is related in some way to the first, the decision in the first action binds the parties far more strictly than its force as *stare decisis* would dictate. If the same cause of action is involved in both actions, then, as the holding of the Supreme Court of Ohio illustrates, the second action is precluded and must fail. If plaintiff won in the first action, the cause of action that was asserted is said to have been *merged* in the judgment and cannot be reasserted. If plaintiff lost in the first action the cause of action that was asserted is said to be *barred* by the judgment for defendant. This is the second way in which a former adjudication may affect a case and is called merger and bar, or most often, *res judicata*.[a] It is the subject of Section A of this Chapter.

summary of res judicata

Even if the second suit does not involve the same cause of action as the first, if the parties are the same, then issues decided in the first case are treated as settled between them and cannot be relitigated. Thus both lower courts in *Rush* held that the only issue open in plaintiff's suit for her personal injuries was the amount of her damages, because the issues of negligence, proximate cause, and contributory negligence had all been conclusively determined by her judgment in the earlier action for property damage. Similarly, if A sues B for damages arising out of an accident and wins in spite of B's claim that A was solely at fault, and then B sues A for damages arising out of the same accident, B's suit will be dismissed, because the judgment for A in the first action will have established that B was negligent and A was not. This third way in which a former adjudication may affect a case is called *estoppel by judgment,* or more commonly *collateral estoppel,* and is the subject of Section B of this Chapter.

Among the more valuable sources on res judicata are: 1B Moore, *Federal Practice* (2d ed.); *Restatement, Judgments* (1942); *Restatement (Second), Judgments* (Tent.Draft No. 1, 1973); *Developments in the Law—Res Judicata,* 65 Harv.L.Rev. 818 (1952).

2. Was the critical language in *Vasu* a holding or dictum? Compare UNITED STATES v. TITLE INS. & TRUST CO., 265 U.S. 472, 485–86, 44 S.Ct. 621, 623, 68 L.Ed. 1110, 1114 (1924), in which Mr. Justice Van Devanter said, in connection with an attempt to distinguish an earlier case:

> Enough has been said to make it apparent that that case and this are so much alike that what was said and ruled in that should be equally ap-

---

[a] The Restatement uses the term "res judicata" in "a broad sense as including merger, bar * * * [and] collateral estoppel." *Restatement, Judgments,* Introductory Note to Chapter 3 (1942); *Restatement (Second), Judgments,* Introductory Note to Chapter 3 (Tent.Draft No. 1, 1973). See also *Developments in the Law—Res Judicata,* 65 Harv.L.Rev. 818, 820 n. 1 (1952). Judicial usage on the other hand more commonly identifies the term "res judicata" with what the Restatement terms "merger" and "bar." See Lawlor v. National Screen Serv. Corp., 349 U.S. 322, 326, 75 S.Ct. 865, 867, 99 L.Ed. 1122, 1126 (1955), in which the Supreme Court expressly notes but apparently rejects the Restatement terminology.

plicable in this. But it is urged that what we have described as ruled there was *obiter dictum* and should be disregarded, because the Court there gave a second ground for its decision which was broad enough to sustain it independently of the first ground. The premise of the contention is right but the conclusion is wrong; for where there are two grounds, upon either of which an appellate court may rest its decision, and it adopts both, "the ruling on neither is *obiter,* but each is the judgment of the court and of equal validity with the other."

3. What reasons might plaintiff in *Rush* have had for wishing to sue first on the claim for property damage and then separately for the personal injuries?

———

WEEKES v. ATLANTIC NAT. INS. CO., 370 F.2d 264 (9th Cir. 1966). Rotanzi, driving a rental car insured by Atlantic, collided with a car owned and driven by Weekes. Weekes sued Rotanzi in a federal court for personal injuries, but a dispute arose on the question whether Rotanzi was covered by Atlantic or by California, his own insurer, or both; the parties agreed that the personal-injury action should be stayed while Atlantic brought the instant suit, a declaratory-judgment action against California, Rotanzi, and Weekes to determine the question of coverage. After the personal-injury action was brought, but before the declaratory-judgment action, Weekes sued Rotanzi in a state court for damage to his car. In this action Weekes was not represented by the lawyer who was representing him in the personal injury action, but by a lawyer retained by his own insurer, Allstate. The car-damage action was settled by stipulation and a judgment was entered dismissing Weekes' complaint with prejudice upon payment to him of $1,101.52, the full amount of his claim. Atlantic, California, and Rotanzi each asserted in the declaratory-judgment action—in addition to their contentions respecting coverage—that Weekes' personal-injury claim was now barred by the judgment in the state case. The district court rejected this contention, and the court of appeals affirmed, 2–1. The appellate court held that since there was no proof of the provisions of the Allstate policy or of any payment by Allstate to Weekes for the damage to his car, the case did not come within the exception to the rule against splitting causes of action that permits a separate suit for property damage to be brought on the basis of subrogation by the property's insurer without jeopardizing the owner's claim for personal injuries. But Judge Duniway, writing for the court, said:

> When the car damage case was settled, the personal injury case had been pending in the Federal court for over 2 years. Under F.R.Civ.P. 8(c), *res judicata* must be pleaded; if not so pleaded, it is waived, Rule 12(h). Here, it can only be raised by supplemental answer under Rule 15(d), since the settlement occurred long after the personal injury suit was filed. Such a pleading can be filed only on motion, and the court "may" permit it, "upon such terms as are just." * * * In substance, the court denied a motion for leave to file a supplemental answer in the personal

injury case. We think that it did not abuse its discretion in so doing.

A motion for permission to serve and file a supplemental pleading is addressed to the sound discretion of the court. * * * To uphold the contention that the dismissal is *res judicata* would certainly work an injustice. We hold, as we think that the Arizona courts would hold, that to permit the raising of the defense would work an injustice, and that the court did not abuse its discretion in refusing to permit it.

Id. at 271–72.

NOTES AND QUESTIONS

1. Did Judge Duniway distort the law of pleading in order to reach a just result that he was not willing to achieve by distorting the law of res judicata? How can such an approach be justified? Suppose that after the pleadings in a case have been completed, plaintiff releases the claim against defendant for a modest amount. If the trial judge believes the settlement to have been unfair, but finds that there is no legal or equitable ground for setting it aside, would the court be justified in refusing to permit defendant to amend the answer to allege the release? Would this situation be different from that presented in the *Weekes* case?

2. What should Weekes have done in connection with the state-court action for damage to his car to avoid the problem presented by *Weekes v. Atlantic Nat. Ins. Co.*? (In thinking about this question bear in mind that plaintiff would have had to have had defendant's acquiescence.) See James, *Consent Judgments as Collateral Estoppel*, 108 U.Pa.L.Rev. 173 (1959); Note, *The Consent Judgment as an Instrument of Compromise and Settlement*, 72 Harv.L.Rev. 1314 (1959).

3. "[A] federal court will usually not dismiss or even stay an action *in personam* because of a prior action pending in a state court. The general rule, stated in Kline v. Burke Construction Co., 260 U.S. 226, 230, 43 S.Ct. 79, 81, 67 L.Ed. 226 (1922), is that 'Each court is free to proceed in its own way and in its own time, without reference to the proceedings in the other court.' " GRAZIANO v. PENNELL, 371 F.2d 761, 764 (2d Cir.1967). Would this attitude be any different if two state courts in the same state were involved? What if the two state courts were in different states? See Vestal, *Repetitive Litigation*, 45 Iowa L.Rev. 525, 530 (1960). In light of the thrust of the quotation from *Graziano,* what purpose is served by a doctrine that a defendant waives an objection to the splitting of a cause of action unless the issue is raised at the time the second complaint is filed? See Todd v. Central Petroleum Co., 155 Kan. 249, 124 P.2d 704 (1942); Shaw v. Chell, 176 Ohio St. 375, 199 N.E.2d 869 (1964) (decided after *Rush v. City of Maple Heights*); Annot., 62 A.L.R. 263 (1929). Is the defense of res judicata always subject to waiver? See Ocean Acc. & Guar. Corp. v. United States Fidelity & Guar. Co., 63 Ariz. 352, 162 P.2d 609 (1945).

4. In HYYTI v. SMITH, 67 N.D. 425, 272 N.W. 747 (1937), plaintiff brought a wrongful-death action for the death of her father after having recovered in an earlier action against defendant for her father's hospital and funeral

expenses. The trial court permitted the second suit, and the Supreme Court of North Dakota affirmed:

> Plaintiff's reply * * * alleges that the plaintiff did not know that she had a right of action for damages; that her whole connection with the matter was at the suggestion and advice of an attorney, an associate or member of a firm of attorneys, who represented the defendants herein; that she did not employ said attorney nor any attorney; that she paid no attorney fees; that all the costs, doctor and hospital bills, and judgment were paid by said attorney.
>
> * * *
>
> The plaintiff was a young Finlander who, prior to the accident, lived with her parents, who spoke only the Finnish language. She had very little education, and according to the reply the said attorney, who did know that she had a right of action, fraudulently concealed it and made her believe that everything he was doing for her was being done out of the goodness of his heart.
>
> * * *
>
> The rule against splitting cause of action is for the benefit of defendant, who may waive it or renounce it by agreement with the plaintiff. * * *

Id. at 428–29, 272 N.W. at 749–50.

5. In McCONNELL v. TRAVELERS INDEM. CO., 346 F.2d 219 (5th Cir.1965), plaintiff brought suit in a federal court for $85,000 for personal injuries resulting from an automobile accident. Earlier his wife had brought suit in a state court for $8,500 for injuries she had sustained in the same accident and plaintiff had joined that suit to enforce a claim for her medical expenses. Under Louisiana community-property law, the wife's claim was her separate property, but the claim for plaintiff's personal injuries as well as the claim for the wife's medical expenses belonged to the community; plaintiff, as head of the community, had the sole right to sue on these claims. After the state-court action was submitted, defendant moved in the federal-court action for summary judgment on the ground that plaintiff had split the cause of action by filing the claim for the wife's medical expenses in the state court. The state court then dismissed plaintiff's claim with prejudice, at his request. The federal court then granted summary judgment for defendant on the ground that the dismissal with prejudice was a final judgment of plaintiff's entire claim. The court of appeals affirmed:

> We are aware that the result we reach produces an anomaly. The husband and wife may split their tort claims, but the husband's lawsuit must include any claim for the wife's medical expenses. In effect, therefore, the parties may twice litigate the issue of the wife's injuries. On the other hand, the plaintiff's theory of the case would also produce an anomaly. The purpose of the tort claims is compensation. Under Louisiana law the community of acquets and gains suffers the injury. The plaintiff's theory would divide community damages among several potential lawsuits. It is the Louisiana community property system that causes the anomaly, not the rules of res judicata. This Court must apply the Louisiana law as the Court finds it.

Id. at 223–24. *Cf.* Boland v. Morrill, 275 Minn. 496, 148 N.W.2d 143 (1967).

The source of the former adjudication rules to be applied by the federal courts is discussed in Vestal, *Res Judicata/Preclusion by Judgment: The Law Applied in Federal Courts,* 66 Mich.L.Rev. 1723 (1968).

JONES v. MORRIS PLAN BANK OF PORTSMOUTH

Supreme Court of Appeals of Virginia, 1937.
168 Va. 284, 191 S.E. 608.

GREGORY, Justice.   William B. Jones instituted an action for damages against the Morris Plan Bank of Portsmouth for the conversion of his automobile. * * *

After the plaintiff had introduced all of his evidence and before the defendant had introduced any evidence on its behalf, the latter's counsel moved to strike the evidence of the plaintiff and the court sustained the motion. A verdict for the defendant resulted.

The facts are that the plaintiff purchased from J. A. Parker, a dealer in [Facts] automobiles, a Plymouth sedan, agreeing to pay therefor $595. He paid a part of the purchase price by the delivery of a used car to Parker of the agreed value of $245 and after crediting that amount on the purchase price and adding a finance charge of $78.40, there remained an unpaid balance due the dealer of $428. This latter amount was payable in 12 monthly installments of $35.70 each and evidenced by one note in the principal sum of $428.40. The note contained this provision: "The whole amount of this note (less any payments [Acc. Clause] made hereon) becomes immediately due and payable in the event of nonpayment at maturity of any installment thereof." The note was secured by the usual conditional sales contract * * * in which it was agreed that the title to the car would be retained by the dealer until the entire purchase price was paid in full. * * * [T]he contract was assigned to the defendant * * * and the note was indorsed by Parker and delivered to the defendant at the same time.

Installment payments due on the note for May and June were not made [Non-payment of May-June installment] when payable and for them an action was instituted in the civil and police court of the city of Suffolk. No appearance was made by the defendant (Jones) in that action and judgment was obtained against him for the two payments. Execution issued upon the judgment and it was satisfied * * * by Jones * * *.

Later the defendant instituted another action against Jones in the same court for the July installment which had become due and was unpaid, and to that action Jones filed a plea of res adjudicata, whereupon the * * * [Bank] took a nonsuit.

* * * [T]he defendant * * * took possession of the automobile without the consent of the plaintiff and later sold it and applied the proceeds upon the note.

P's arg:

Afterwards, the plaintiff instituted the present action for conversion to recover damages for the loss of the automobile. His action in the court below was founded upon the theory that when the May and June installments became due and were unpaid, then under the acceleration clause in the note, the entire balance due thereon matured and at once became due and the defendant having elected to sue him for only two installments instead of the entire amount of the note, and having obtained a judgment for the two installments and satisfaction of the execution issued thereon, it waived its right to collect the balance. He also contends that the note was satisfied in the manner narrated and that the conditional sales contract, the sole purpose of which was to secure the payment of the note, served its purpose and ceased to exist, and, therefore, the title to the automobile was no longer retained, but upon the satisfaction of the note, passed to the plaintiff and was his property when the agent of the defendant removed it and converted it to its own use.

P's theory

The position of the defendant is that * * * the title to the automobile, which was the subject of the alleged conversion, was not vested in the plaintiff at the time of the action, nor since, because the condition in the contract was that the title should be retained by the seller (whose rights were assigned to the defendant) until the entire purchase price was paid, and that the purchase price had never been paid * * *.

The defendant also contends that the note and conditional sales contract were divisible; that successive actions could be brought upon the installments as they matured; and that it was not bound, at the risk of waiving its right to claim the balance, to sue for all installments in one action.

The defendant does not deny that the acceleration clause matured all installments upon the default in the payment of the May and June payments.

* * *

Ct's Rationale:

We decide that under the unconditional acceleration provision in the note involved here and in the absence of the usual optional provision reserved to the holder, the entire amount due upon the note became due and payable when default was made in paying an installment. * * *

Was it essential that the defendant here institute an action for all of the installments then due, or could it institute its action for only two of the installments and later institute another action for other installments? The answer to that question depends upon the nature of the transaction. If a transaction is represented by one single and indivisible contract and the breach gives rise to one single cause of action, it cannot be split into distinct parts and separate actions maintained for each.

On the other hand, if the contract is divisible giving rise to more than one cause of action, each may be proceeded upon separately.

1 single note and contract

Was the contract here single and indivisible or was it divisible? Our answer is that the note and conditional sales contract constituted one single contract. The sole purpose of the conditional sales contract was to retain the title in the seller until the note was paid. When that condition was performed, the contract ended.

One of the principal tests in determining whether a demand is single and entire, or whether it is several, so as to give rise to more than one cause of action, is the identity of facts necessary to maintain the action. If the same evidence will support both actions, there is but one cause of action.

In the case at bar, all of the installments were due. The evidence essential to support the action on the two installments for which the action was brought would be the identical evidence necessary to maintain an action upon all of the installments. All installments having matured at the time the action was begun, under well-settled principles, those not embraced in that action are now barred.

* * * At the time the defendant lost its right to institute any action for the remaining installments, the title to the automobile passed to the plaintiff. He was the owner at the time the agent of the defendant took possession of it and exposed it to sale.

It follows that the judgment of the court below will be reversed, and the case will be remanded for the sole purpose of determining the quantum of damages.

Reversed and remanded.

NOTES AND QUESTIONS

1. Why did the court remand only for the purpose of determining damages rather than order a new trial?

2. When a debt is secured by a series of notes or when a bond includes a number of interest coupons, an action on one of the notes or coupons, even though others are due, does not bar a subsequent action on those others. *Restatement, Judgments* § 62, comment *i* (1942); *Restatement (Second), Judgments* § 61, comment *d* (Tent.Draft No. 1, 1973). *Cf.* NESBIT v. RIVERSIDE IND. DISTRICT, 144 U.S. 610, 619, 12 S.Ct. 746, 748, 36 L.Ed. 562, 565 (1892):

> * * * Each matured coupon is a separable promise, and gives rise to a separate cause of action. It may be detached from the bond and sold by itself. Indeed, the title to several matured coupons of the same bond may be in as many different persons, and upon each a distinct and separate action be maintained. So, while the promises of the bond and of the coupons in the first instance are upon the same paper, and the coupons are for interest due upon the bond, yet the promise to pay the coupon is as distinct from that to pay the bond as though the two promises were placed in different instruments, upon different paper.

B.   CAUSE OF ACTION AS A DEFENSE

MITCHELL v. FEDERAL INTERMEDIATE CREDIT BANK

Supreme Court of South Carolina, 1932.
165 S.C. 457, 164 S.E. 136, 83 A.L.R. 629.

[Action for an accounting against defendant bank for proceeds of a crop of potatoes. Plaintiff alleged that in order to obtain loans from defendant he had—at the behest of defendant's agent—sold his potatoes through a growers' association and assigned the proceeds as security for two notes, totalling $9,-000, which had been discounted with defendant; that the potatoes had netted $18,000, but that he had never received any of this, and that the proceeds had been received by defendant or an agent of defendant. In a previous action by defendant on the notes, plaintiff had pleaded in the answer the same facts now the basis of an affirmative claim, but had not counterclaimed or asked relief; judgment had been for him in that action. In the present suit, defendant contended that plaintiff's claim was merged in the earlier judgment. This contention was upheld by the trial court.]

STABLER, J.   *   *   *

We now come to the main question presented by the appeal, namely, Was the circuit judge in error in sustaining the plea in bar to plaintiff's action? Turning to appellant's answer in the federal court case   *   *   * we find that the facts there pleaded by him as a defense to the bank's recovery on its notes are the same as those set out by him in his complaint as the basis of his action in the case at bar, it being alleged that the total amount paid to the bank was in excess of all sums advanced to him on the notes or otherwise, and as a result of the transaction the notes sued upon were fully paid and discharged. In addition, we find in the record of the case before us the following statement by appellant as an admission of fact on his part: "*   *   *   The indebtedness of the bank to Mitchell arising from the embezzlement of the proceeds of the crop was used pro tanto as an offset to the claim of the bank in the Federal Court. The case at bar seeks recovery of the surplusage, over the offset, of the proceeds of the same crop lost by the same embezzlement. The appellant, however, is not seeking to recover in this action the same money that has already been used as an offset."

*   *   *

In support of his position   *   *   *   appellant cites certain decisions of this court, which he claims to be conclusive of the issue, relying especially upon Kirven v. Chemical Co., 77 S.C. 493, 58 S.E. 424, 426.

*   *   *   [T]he record shows that Kirven had bought from the Chemical Company $2,228 worth of fertilizers and had given his note for that amount. The company, upon maturity of the note, brought action against him on his obligation. He at first filed an answer setting up three defenses, the third of which was that the fertilizers furnished were deleterious and destruc-

tive to the crops, and that there was an entire failure of consideration for the note. Later, he was permitted to file a supplemental answer in which he withdrew the third defense. On trial in the federal court, the jury rendered a verdict for the Chemical Company. Thereafter, Kirven brought an action against the company * * * alleging that the defendant caused damage to his crop in the sum of $1,995 by reason of the deleterious effect of the fertilizers furnished. The company set up the defense that the issues in this action were or could have been adjudicated in the [first] suit * * *. A verdict was given Kirven in the amount prayed for, and on appeal * * * it was pointed out that the question raised in the state court was not *actually* litigated and determined in the federal action, and it appears that the court, for that reason, took the view that a bar or estoppel did not exist. Mr. Justice Woods, in his concurring opinion, took the view that, as Kirven elected not to use, as a defense, the fact of *worthlessness,* which might have been available in the action of the company against him, "he was not precluded from using the very different facts of deleteriousness and positive injury caused by appellant's alleged negligence in the manufacture of the fertilizer as the basis of an independent cause of action."

Applnt cites.

Kirven v. Chemical:

Facts not actually litigated in previous Case

We think the facts of the case at bar, however, present a different situation. * * *

O'Connor v. Varney, 10 Gray (Mass.) 231, was an action on contract to recover damages for Varney's failure to build certain additions to a house according to the terms of a written agreement between the parties. The defendant set up as a defense "a judgment recovered by O'Connor in an action brought by Varney against him on that contract to recover the price therein agreed to be paid for the work, in defence of which O'Connor relied on the same nonperformance by Varney, and in which an auditor to whom the case was referred * * * found that Varney was not entitled to recover under the agreement," as the work had been so imperfectly done that it would require a greater sum than the amount sued for to make it correspond with the contract. At the trial of the second action, the trial judge ruled that the judgment in the first suit was a bar, and directed a verdict for the defendant. The plaintiff O'Connor thereupon appealed.

Chief Justice Shaw, who rendered the opinion of the court, said: "The presiding judge rightly ruled that the former judgment was a bar to this action. A party against whom an action is brought on a contract has two modes of defending himself. He may allege specific breaches of the contract declared upon, and rely on them in defence. But if he intends to claim, by way of damages for nonperformance of the contract, more than the amount for which he is sued, he must not rely on the contract in defence, but must bring a cross action, and apply to the court to have the cases continued so that the executions may be set off. He cannot use the same defence, first as a shield, and then as a sword. * * *"

2 Modes of defense in Contract.

It will be noted that Varney was not entitled to recover in the first suit because his dereliction amounted to more than he sued for. This would seem to be exactly the situation in the case at bar.

* * *   When the bank sued * * * [Mitchell] on his two notes, amounting to about $9,000, he had the option to interpose his claim as a defense to that suit or to demand judgment against the bank, by way of counterclaim, for the amount owing him by it. * * *   The transaction out of which the case at bar arises is the same transaction that Mitchell pleaded as a defense in the federal suit. He might, therefore, "have recovered in that action, upon the same allegations and proofs which he there made, the judgment which he now seeks, if he had prayed for it." He did not do this, but attempted to split his cause of action, and to use one portion of it for defense in that suit and to reserve the remainder for offense in a subsequent suit, which, under applicable principles, could not be done. * * *

The judgment of the circuit court is affirmed.

QUESTIONS

1.   Should it make a difference in a case such as *Mitchell* whether under the procedure followed in the court in which the first action was brought, defendant in that court could obtain affirmative relief by asserting a counterclaim? See Derderian v. Union Market Nat. Bank, 326 Mass. 538, 95 N.E.2d 552 (1950) (following the principle of *O'Connor v. Varney* even though no counterclaim could have been filed in the earlier action); *Restatement, Judgments* § 57 (1942).

2.   At common law, would Mitchell's defense in the first action have been in the nature of a recoupment or a set-off? Assuming that the defense would have been one or the other, would this have made a difference as to the right to bring a later suit for the excess? See pp. 505–07, supra.

LINDERMAN MACHINE CO. v. HILLENBRAND CO., 75 Ind.App. 111, 127 N.E. 813 (App.Ct.1920). L sold H a machine, and subsequently sued to recover the purchase price; H answered that the contract had been obtained by fraudulent representations as to the machine's capacity to do H's work, that the machine did not perform as represented, and that H had notified L to remove the machine. Judgment was rendered against L. Subsequently H sued L to recover damages for fraud, alleging that it had incurred great expense in transporting, installing, attempting to operate, and removing the machine. L answered that the action was barred by the judgment in the first suit. The court held for H:

> It is true that a party, when sued, must interpose all defenses which he has, and as to them, whether pleaded or not, the judgment is conclusive; but it is not conclusive as to an affirmative right or cause of action which he may have against the plaintiff, and of which he could have taken advantage by way of cross-complaint. He is not compelled to file his cross-complaint, and, on his failure to do so, his rights with reference thereto will not be adjudged. * * *

[margin handwritten note: Applnts defense in 1st case is bar to c/a in 2nd case.]

There was no issue in the action brought by * * * [L]
to recover the purchase price * * * as to the right of * * *
[H] to recover the expenses which it had been put to in installing
the machinery, and without such issue therein, * * * [L]
is not in position now to invoke against * * * [H] the doctrine of res adjudicata.

Id. at 118, 127 N.E. at 815.

NOTES AND QUESTIONS

1.   Is *Linderman* consistent with *Mitchell*?

2.   Defendant purchased an air conditioner for an onion-drying shed under
a conditional sales agreement with a vendor who assigned the contract to plaintiff. In a suit for the balance of the purchase price, the trial court in FIRST
ACCEPTANCE CORP. v. KENNEDY, 95 F.Supp. 861 (N.D.Iowa 1951),
reversed on other grounds 194 F.2d 819 (8th Cir.1952), permitted defendant
to raise fraud as a total defense to the contract, even though he had not rescinded
the contract. The trial judge's opinion reflects the procedural difficulty in which
a defendant may be placed by the problem involved in *Linderman* and *Mitchell*:

> The defendant claims that the transaction between the United States
> Air Conditioning Corporation and the plaintiff placed him in a legal
> dilemma and that he used the defense of fraud in the only manner left
> open to him. It is the contention of the defendant that rescission was
> legally impossible for the reason that rescission could not be made with
> the United States Air Conditioning Corporation because the title to the
> subject matter of the sale was in the plaintiff; and that rescission could
> not be had with the plaintiff because the sum of $2,800 paid by him under
> the contract had been retained by the United States Air Conditioning
> Corporation and the plaintiff was under no obligation or duty to make
> refund of the $2,800 upon rescission. The defendant points out that
> the United States Air Conditioning Corporation was not subject to service
> of process in Iowa and, therefore, it could not be made a party to this
> action.

> The defendant further claims that the damages sustained by him
> because of the fraud practiced upon him * * * are greatly in excess
> of the amount which the plaintiff seeks to recover herein; and that
> if he asserted part of his damages as an offset or by way of recoupment
> against the plaintiff's claim he would be splitting his cause of action
> and that he then would be unable to recover the balance of his damages
> from the United States Air Conditioning Corporation.

> It is plain that the defendant in his pleadings very carefully refrained
> from attempting to use any part of his damages as an offset or by way
> of recoupment. The position of the defendant is that since rescission
> was impossible and since he could not use part of his claim as an offset
> or by way of recoupment without losing the balance of his claim all that
> he could do was to ask that the contract be not enforced against him
> because of fraud in its procurement.

Id. at 870–71.

2. BAR

A. EFFECT OF DEFENDANT'S JUDGMENT ON PLAINTIFF'S ALTERNATIVE THEORIES AND REMEDIES

SMITH v. KIRKPATRICK

Court of Appeals of New York, 1953.
305 N.Y. 66, 111 N.E.2d 209.

CONWAY, Judge. Plaintiff originally instituted an action against defendant seeking recovery of moneys allegedly due him under a contract of employment. The complaint (hereinafter referred to as the first complaint) alleged that the contract required plaintiff to devote his full time and attention to defendant's business; to solicit export accounts for defendant "with a view to defendant acting as export manager for American manufacturers and purchasing agent for foreign clients"; that plaintiff's remuneration was to be 50% of the income derived from business procured by plaintiff; that over a period of ten months and in compliance with the contract plaintiff solicited for defendant accounts from which an income of $26,000 was or would be derived and that, with the exception of certain payments, defendant failed to compensate plaintiff as agreed.

Defendant denied the existence of the agreement and upon motion made by him for summary judgment, the complaint was dismissed for the reason that the agreement pleaded therein did not comply with the Statute of Frauds. Thereupon plaintiff submitted a proposed order to Special Term granting him leave to serve an amended complaint so that he might sue for the value of his services.

Thereafter, plaintiff served his amended complaint (hereinafter referred to as the *second complaint*) setting forth two causes of action, neither of which sought recovery in "quantum meruit". For a first cause of action, it was alleged that "plaintiff and defendant had an informal oral arrangement [terminable at will] whereby plaintiff conducted some of his business through defendant's office, paying to defendant, as compensation for such use of his office, fifty (50%) percent of the gross profits of any of plaintiff's business handled through defendant's office"; that the business so handled was to be conducted under the name of W. S. Kirkpatrick & Co. but would remain the property of plaintiff; that W. S. Kirkpatrick & Co. earned commissions and profits from accounts obtained by plaintiff but defendant failed to account therefor and appropriated to himself business belonging to plaintiff. As a second cause of action, plaintiff alleged an oral agreement of joint venture the substance of which is essentially the same as that of the agreement alleged in the first cause of action. The relief sought was an accounting, judgment for such sums as were found due, and an order directing defendant to assign to plaintiff such contracts, agreements and arrangements as had been entered into with persons whose accounts had been procured by plaintiff.

A trial was had without a jury and proofs were submitted by both parties. The Justice Presiding directed judgment for defendant and dismissed plaintiff's second complaint upon the merits for the reason that "plaintiff has failed to establish his causes of action by a fair preponderance of the credible evidence." The Justice wrote: "It is clear to the court that the original position taken by the plaintiff correctly represented the relationship between the parties but, unfortunately for the plaintiff, that action was barred by the statute of frauds. * * * It ought to be stated, however, in fairness to the plaintiff, that the defendant was clearly guilty of overreaching the plaintiff, but the bar of the statute of frauds and the failure on the part of the plaintiff to proceed on the theory of quantum meruit have given to the defendant a windfall which in business morals and good conscience he is not entitled to."

[margin note: Π→Δ   P failed to prove and sought recovery under wrong theory.]

Plaintiff took no appeal and subsequently commenced the present action seeking to recover the reasonable value of services rendered by him to defendant at defendant's request. Defendant * * * moved * * * to dismiss the complaint on the ground of res judicata * * *. Upon appeal from the denial of that motion * * * the Appellate Division reversed and dismissed the complaint.

[margin note: "Quantum Meruit" Action.]

There are two questions presented for our consideration (1) whether the present action is barred by the rule of res judicata and, if not so barred, (2) whether by proceeding to judgment on the theories embodied in his second complaint, plaintiff lost what right he had to maintain an action in quantum meruit. We have reached the conclusion that the present action must be permitted to continue. It seems to us that had plaintiff in his first complaint pleaded three causes of action: the first on a contract of employment, the second to establish a partnership and to obtain an accounting, and the third to establish that plaintiff and defendant were joint venturers, and on the trial the first had been dismissed because within the Statute of Frauds, and judgment entered against the plaintiff on the other two because he had failed to establish the existence of the agreements alleged, it would be more readily seen that an action for quantum meruit would still lie. If that be so, the fact that the same position was reached after two actions had been brought by plaintiff should not affect the result.

[margin note: Issue]

[margin note: action for quantum meruit still lies.]

It is familiar law that where a cause of action has been prosecuted to a final adjudication on the merits, the same cause of action may not be again litigated. * * *

[margin note: R/L]

The determination of what constitutes the "same" or "different" causes of action is not a matter free from difficulty. * * * The test for determining whether or not "causes of action" are the "same" for purposes of res judicata has been variously expressed. In De Coss v. Turner & Blanchard, Inc., 267 N.Y. 207, 211, 196 N.E. 28, 30, where an employee twice sought recovery against his employer for the same injury, alleging first that injury was caused by the employer's failure to provide a safe place to work and alleging next that it resulted from the carelessness of a fellow employee, we held that the matter was *res judicata*, Judge Lehman quoting with approval the following definition: " 'A cause of action does not consist of facts, but of the unlawful violation of a right which the facts show. The number and variety of the facts alleged do not establish more than one cause of action so long as their result, whether they be considered severally or in combination, is the violation of but one right by a single legal wrong.' " It has also been said that "there is an identity of causes of action when in both the old and new proceedings the subject-matter and the ultimate issues are the same * * *." Res Judicata, 38 Yale L.J. 299, 313–314. And in the leading case of Schuylkill Fuel Corp. v. B. & C. Nieberg Realty Corp., 250 N.Y. 304, 306–307, 165 N.E. 456, 457, Cardozo, Ch. J., we said that a "judgment in one action is conclusive in a later one, not only as to any matters actually litigated therein, but also as to any that might have been so litigated, when the two causes of action have such a measure of identity that a different judgment in the second would destroy or impair rights or interests established by the first. * * * It is not conclusive, however, to the same extent when the two causes of action are different, not in form only * * * but in the rights and interests affected. The estoppel is limited in such circumstances to the point actually determined. * * *"

By his second complaint, the plaintiff sought to enforce a right which arose out of an express agreement and from defendant's asserted ownership of accounts procured by him. Defendant's alleged wrong was the misappropriation of those accounts and the proceeds thereof. Plaintiff's right to all profits save the 50% intended to compensate defendant for the use of his facilities, sprang from an alleged relationship, established by the express agreement, which, though vaguely expressed in the complaint, appears to have been in the nature of that existing between joint venturers, partners or landlord and tenant. The redress sought was, as we have seen, an accounting, judgment for moneys found due in accordance with the terms fixed by the agreement and the transfer of accounts belonging to plaintiff. In that action it was determined that defendant had no liability by reason of his being a party to the relationships alleged and that plaintiff's title to the accounts was not superior to that of defendant.

In the present action plaintiff's alleged right rests upon an implied contract. The relationship allegedly existing between the parties is somewhat analogous to that found between master and servant. The wrong alleged is defendant's acceptance and retention of benefits, conferred upon him by plaintiff, without payment in return of fair compensation. The relief now sought is merely the reasonable value of the services rendered to defendant at his request or with his consent.

The two actions involve different "rights" and "wrongs". The requisite elements of proof and hence the evidence necessary to sustain recovery vary materially. The causes of action are different and distinct and the rights and interests established by the previous adjudication will not be impaired by a recovery, if that be the outcome, in *quantum meruit*. * * *

Having concluded that the present complaint does not embody the same cause of action * * * the question is whether the matters actually determined are fatal to the instant action. We think not. Plaintiff's failure to recover on the causes stated in his second complaint was due to the fact that he did not establish the existence of the arrangements therein alleged. The decision was not that plaintiff failed to prove compliance with an existing agreement. It was not decided that no services were rendered to defendant with his consent, nor that the services rendered conferred no benefit upon the defendant—those matters are still open and it is those which plaintiff now seeks to prove.

nothing proved in 1st case

* * * Upon the dismissal of the first complaint, plaintiff was given leave to amend. There was no final adjudication on the merits. The conclusiveness of the determination dismissing the first complaint is confined to the precise issue then determined. That being so, the order of dismissal is conclusive only as to the point that the contract alleged in the first complaint did not comply with the Statute of Frauds. That narrow determination is insufficient to preclude the present action * * *.

We turn now to the question of whether or not, having attempted and failed to succeed on the causes involved in the second complaint, plaintiff should be held to have elected his remedy and thus to have lost his right to sue in *quantum meruit*.

In American Woolen Co. v. Samuelsohn, 226 N.Y. 61, 66, 123 N.E. 154, 155, the doctrine of election of remedies was expressed in these words:

"An election of remedies takes place when a choice is exercised between remedies which proceed upon irreconcilable claims of right.

"When an election is made between such claims, with full knowledge of all the facts, an action may not thereafter be maintained upon the inconsistent claim."

Although stating different causes of action, the second complaint is not so inconsistent or irreconcilable with the complaint in the present action in *quantum meruit* that the choice of the former action precludes resort to the present one. Both complaints assumed basically that there existed between the plaintiff and defendant a contractual relationship, and that defendant had reaped benefits at plaintiff's expense. In this State where a litigant fails to establish the right to recover upon an express contract he may, in the same action, recover in *quantum meruit*. * * * If warranted by the pleadings and proof the case may be submitted to a jury on both theories and an election need not be made. * * * It is thus clear that there exists no such irreconcilable inconsistency between the claims asserted by plaintiff in the present and former actions that he may be held to have made an election.

Moreover, where a litigant pursues a remedy which is unavailable because it is inappropriate to the facts alleged and sought to be proved there is no election * * *. And where, as in the case before us, the remedy sought is unavailable because the facts turn out to be different from those supposed by plaintiff, the same rule has been applied, and properly so * * *.

We have said that the doctrine of election of remedies is a harsh one and should not be extended * * *. It has been criticized and the Legislature has indicated its disfavor for at least certain aspects of the doctrine * * *. We are of the opinion that this is not a proper case for the application of the doctrine.

The judgment of the Appellate Division should be reversed and the order of Special Term affirmed, with costs in this court and in the Appellate Division.

NOTES AND QUESTIONS

1. *Election of remedies.* P, while a minor, purchased a car from D, paying $500 down and promising to pay $2,000 more at the end of one year. Midway through the year P reached the age of 21 and had the power to ratify the contract or to repudiate it. At that time P brought an action against D for breach of warranty. May P subsequently amend the complaint to seek rescission on the ground that the contract was made while a minor? Many courts will hold that P may not, but their decision probably will not be based on any idea that having started out to ask for one remedy, plaintiff is precluded from asking for a different one. Rather these courts will say that any action by a person after reaching majority that indicates an intention to continue in force a contract made while a minor will serve to ratify the contract; for example, P's telling D that P considered the contract in force would be such an act; P's suit to enforce a provision of the contract is simply another such act.

Suppose that P moves to amend to ask rescission on the grounds that the breach of warranty was so substantial that plaintiff is entitled to declare the agreement at an end and recover the down payment. Assuming that a suit for rescission would have been appropriate at the outset, most courts ordinarily would allow this type of amendment. But suppose that at the time P brought the suit for breach of warranty, D had offered to take back the car and refund P's down payment because D desired the car for personal use, but P had rejected the offer. If D subsequently has purchased another such car, many courts would deny the amendment, not because P is seeking a different remedy than that first chosen, but because D has changed position in reliance on P's first position.

Some cases still can be found holding that once a plaintiff has sought one remedy, he is precluded from seeking another remedy that is inconsistent. But now that the rules of pleading generally permit alternative and inconsistent allegations, and judgments "grant the relief to which the party * * * is entitled," the following statement of Judge Cardozo is even more accurate than when he uttered it: "[I]t is probable that some element either of ratification or of estoppel is at the root of most cases, if not all, in which an election of remedies, once made, is viewed as a finality." SCHENCK v. STATE LINE TEL. CO., 238 N.Y. 308, 312, 144 N.E. 592, 593 (1924). See Clark, *Code Pleading* § 77 (2d ed. 1947);

5A Corbin, *Contracts* §§ 1214–1227 (1964); *Developments in the Law—Res Judicata,* 65 Harv.L.Rev. 818, 823 (1952). See also Note 2, pp. 408–09, supra.

2. Do the same considerations that persuaded the court to reach the result in *Smith v. Kirkpatrick* apply when the unsuccessful first suit is brought on an implied contract for services rendered, and the second suit is brought on an express contract for compensation? *Cf.* Broz v. Hegwood, 349 Mo. 920, 163 S.W. 2d 1009 (1942).

3. In *Schuylkill Fuel Corp. v. B. & C. Nieberg Realty Corp.,* which is relied upon in *Smith v. Kirkpatrick,* Judge, later Mr. Justice, Cardozo said: "The decisive test is this, whether the substance of the rights or interests established in the first action will be destroyed or impaired by the prosecution of the second." Is this formulation anything more than a statement of the problem? In *Schuylkill Fuel,* Judge Cardozo illustrated the quoted principle as follows:

> * * * Thus, in Reich v. Cochran [151 N.Y. 122, 45 N.E. 367] an order in summary proceedings awarding possession to a landlord for nonpayment of rent was held to bar a suit in equity to declare the lease a mortgage and avoid it on the ground of usury. The relief decreed by the order, the award of possession to one adjudged to be a landlord, would have been nullified altogether, if the same person might thereafter have been declared to be no landlord, but a mortgagee, wrongfully in possession under an agreement void in its inception. * * * Again, in Steinbach v. Relief Fire Insurance Co., 77 N.Y. 498, 33 Am.Rep. 655, the holder of a fire policy sued upon it as it had been written, and then, when found by the court to have broken its conditions, brought suit to reform it and recover the same loss. * * * A different question would have been presented if the loss had been a later one.

250 N.Y. at 308–09, 165 N.E. at 458. Is *Smith v. Kirkpatrick* consistent with the cases Judge Cardozo discusses?

4. Plaintiff in an action against decedent's administrator contended that certain realty belonging to decedent had been purchased with plaintiff's money, and was held by decedent on a resulting trust for plaintiff; judgment was entered for the administrator. Plaintiff then brought a second action against the administrator, alleging that he is entitled to the realty as the common-law husband and heir of the decedent. Should the second action be barred? See Norwood v. McDonald, 142 Ohio St. 299, 52 N.E.2d 67 (1943).

5. See generally Schopflocher, *What is a Single Cause of Action for the Purpose of the Doctrine of Res Judicata?,* 21 Ore.L.Rev. 319 (1942).

MASSARI v. EINSIEDLER

Supreme Court of New Jersey, 1951.
6 N.J. 303, 78 A.2d 572.

BURLING, J. * * *

On September 17, 1948, the Massaris commenced suit in the Superior Court, Law Division, to collect the unpaid balance of the purchase price alleged to be due under a contract between the parties * * * whereby the

Massaris agreed to sell a business owned by them and Einsiedler agreed to purchase the same on a deferred payment plan   * * * the full purchase price being payable within two years. Summary judgment was entered by the trial court in favor of the Massaris * * *. In that suit, Einsiedler's answer admitted the balance due under the contract but pleaded a loan agreement and a security trust agreement, both dated September 25, 1946. The contract dated September 16, 1946, was executed by the Massaris and Einsiedler, whereas the two subsequent agreements were executed solely by Einsiedler. The purport of the latter two agreements was to require the Massaris to accept shares of stock, at their book value, of a corporation to be formed by Einsiedler, in satisfaction of the unpaid balance of the purchase price of the business so sold in the event of a breach by Einsiedler of the contract of sale * * *. The trial court held that the security trust and loan agreements, executed solely by Einsiedler, were inadmissible in evidence to vary the terms of payment as contained in the contract of sale. Einsiedler then filed a petition and supplement thereto seeking to compel the Massaris to accept the aforementioned stock at book value in reduction of the judgment. The petitions were dismissed by the Law Division. On appeal by Einsiedler, the order of dismissal and the summary judgment were affirmed by the Appellate Division. * * *

Einsiedler, in the present proceedings, sought relief by way of reformation, urging that the true agreement between the parties was that expressed by the contract of September 16, 1946, as modified by the loan and security agreements. A petition was filed with the Superior Court, Law Division, and a complaint was filed in the Chancery Division in both of which proceedings reformation and incidental relief was sought. The complaint in the Chancery Division was transferred to the Law Division, where, by subsequent amendment, Einsiedler sought restitution and damages for breach of contract as reformed. These several actions instituted by Einsiedler were consolidated and, on motion of the Massaris, were dismissed by the Law Division. The judgment was affirmed by the Superior Court, Appellate Division. * * *

The primary question to be determined is whether the disposition of the former proceedings is *res judicata* of the right of Einsiedler to seek reformation of the contract of sale and to enforce it as so reformed. The question must be answered in the affirmative.

The litigation in this cause was commenced after the effective date of the Judicial Article of the 1947 Constitution, September 15, 1948, * * * and the disposition of the question involved must be determined by a reference to the 1947 Constitution and the Rules promulgated by the Supreme Court pursuant thereto.

One of the designs of the Judicial Article of the 1947 Constitution was to facilitate and expedite the hearing of causes by disposing of all matters, whether legal or equitable, arising in a controversy in one trial and thus avoid multiple trials of the same case.

     * * *

Under the accepted practice prior to the adoption of the 1947 Constitution a defendant who had unsuccessfully defended a contract action in a law court could then apply to the chancery court for reformation of the contract. * * * Likewise, a plaintiff who had prosecuted an action on a contract to judgment which was rendered for the defendant was not precluded from thereafter seeking reformation of the contract in the chancery court. * * * The reason for the intercession by the equity courts was to prevent the injustice which sometimes resulted from the invulnerability of written instruments in a law court when such instruments did not express the actual intent of the parties but were unassailable in the law court because of the parol evidence rule. * * * Under our present court structure we have a Superior Court which has original general jurisdiction throughout the state in all causes. It is divided into a Law Division and a Chancery Division for the trial of causes. Where adequate relief can be obtained in the Law Division, there is no need for intercession by the Chancery Division since the entire controversy can be determined in the Law Division in one and the same suit. * * *

In the present case, Einsiedler was not only permitted to set up in the original action every equitable defense available to him but, indeed, was required to do so under Rule 3:12–2. It is urged, however, that the reformation of an instrument constitutes affirmative relief and is not an "equitable defense" but rather is properly the subject of a counterclaim. Under the practice in our former Court of Chancery it was generally considered that a defendant should seek affirmative relief by filing a cross-bill and not by way of answer, * * * and that a cross-bill was the proper method of seeking reformation * * *.

* * * [I]t appears that, while preferred procedure for seeking the affirmative relief of reformation by a defendant in our former Court of Chancery was originally by cross-bill and subsequently by a counterclaim * * *, reformation could be sought by a defendant in his answer when the matter could be satisfactorily disposed of in such manner. Be that as it may, the character of the pleading which sought to defeat a claim being prosecuted against a defendant was a *defense* and the character of such pleading was not changed by the manner in which the defense was interposed, whether by answer, cross-bill or counterclaim. Mistake and fraud when pleaded by a defendant were considered to be *defenses*. * * * The fact that affirmative relief could be sought in equity on the basis of such defenses made them equitable defenses. * * *

In Pomeroy's Equity Jurisprudence, Fifth Edition (1941) Vol. 4, § 1369, p. 989, the meaning and nature of an equitable defense is stated as follows: "It is important to determine, in the first place, the nature and meaning of an 'equitable defense'. A defense is a right possessed by the defendant, arising from the facts alleged in his pleadings, which defeats the plaintiff's cause of action or claim for the remedy demanded by his action. An equitable defense is such a right, which exists solely by virtue of equitable doctrines, and which was originally recognized by courts of equity alone. The right constituting an equitable defense may be one which * * * confers upon the defendant some affirmative equitable relief * * * thus defeating the plaintiff's claim; or it may be one * * * which entitles the defendant to no affirmative relief, and which simply operates to bar the plaintiff's action. The general term 'equitable defense' plainly includes both of these classes."

It is clear from the foregoing that mistake and fraud such as would lead to a reformation of a written instrument are "equitable defenses". Rule 3:12–2 provides that "Every defense, legal or equitable," "*shall* be asserted in the answer". (Emphasis supplied.) It follows that Einsiedler should have sought the desired relief in the original action by pleading his equitable defense therein since it was germane to and went to the essence of the Massari cause of action, and if Einsiedler established and proved his defense reformation would have followed as an equitable incident of the right so established.

* * *

Einsiedler's defense in this case was such that under the principles of *res judicata* he could and should have raised it in the original action instituted by Massaris and he was compelled so to do by the provisions of Rule 3:12–2 and since he did not raise such defense, * * * he is deemed to have waived the defense and is concluded by the judgment in the prior action.

* * *

The judgment is affirmed.

NOTES AND QUESTIONS

1. When plaintiff has lost an action on a contract at law because the court interpreted the language of the contract in favor of defendant, should plaintiff be permitted to sue for reformation in equity? What if the court in which the first action was brought did not permit the joinder of legal and equitable causes? See General Discount Corp. v. Sadowski, 183 F.2d 542 (6th Cir.1950). Is permitting the second suit in this context more justifiable than the result in *Smith v. Kirkpatrick?*

2. Is the *Massari* decision properly distinguishable from *Smith v. Kirkpatrick* on the ground that plaintiff in the second suit in *Massari* was defendant in the first? Is there a difference between splitting a cause of action and "splitting a defense"? A result in accord with *Massari,* when the same person was plaintiff in both actions, was reached in Hennepin Paper Co. v. Fort Wayne Corrugated Paper Co., 153 F.2d 822 (7th Cir.1946). See also Sibert v. McAvoy, 15 Ill. 106 (1853).

RESTATEMENT (SECOND), JUDGMENTS (Tent. Draft No. 1, 1973):

§ 61. Dimensions of "Claim" for Purposes of Merger or Bar—General Rule Concerning "Splitting"

(1) When a valid and final judgment rendered in an action extinguishes the plaintiff's claim pursuant to the rules of merger or

bar   *   *   *,   the claim extinguished includes all rights of the plaintiff to remedies against the defendant with respect to all or any part of the transaction, or series of connected transactions, out of which the action arose.

(2) What factual grouping constitutes a "transaction," and what groupings constitute a "series," are to be determined pragmatically, giving weight to such considerations as whether the facts are related in time, space, origin, or motivation, whether they form a convenient trial unit, and whether their treatment as a unit conforms to the parties' expectations or business understanding or usage.

§ 61.1   Exemplifications of General Rule Concerning Splitting

The rule of § 61 applies to extinguish a claim by the plaintiff against the defendant even though the plaintiff is prepared in the second action

(a) To present evidence or grounds or theories of the case not presented in the first action, or

(b) To seek remedies or forms of relief not demanded in the first action.

QUESTIONS

What are the merits and demerits of this "transactional" test? Is it fair to say that it (1) "simplifies the application" of merger and bar, (2) "enhances the benefits" deriving from these rules, and (3) does not cause "undue hardship"? What characteristics would a jurisdiction's procedural system have to possess before you could confidently advocate adoption of the new Restatement's proposed test? Would any of the cases thus far studied in this chapter be decided differently under this standard?

B.   EFFECT OF A DISMISSAL

ROST v. KROKE

Supreme Court of Minnesota, 1935.
195 Minn. 219, 262 N.W. 450, 106 A.L.R. 434.

HILTON, Justice.   *   *   *

In March, 1933, plaintiff instituted an action against these respondents and also against the Standard Oil Company   *   *   *   to recover damages for personal injuries   *   *   *.   The amended complaint alleged substantially that the Standard Oil Company had manufactured and placed upon the market for general sale and use a tar product, designed and intended by it as a substitute for and to take the place of the ordinary tar product, which was intrinsically and inherently dangerous in that it was highly explosive in the ordinary use thereof; that the oil company carelessly, negligently, and unlawfully manufactured and placed its said tar product upon the general commercial retail market without a stamp, label, or warning upon the containers * * *; that * * * the oil company sold to respondents several barrels of said tar compound; that respondents "knew, or but for the want of ordinary and reasonable care and diligence on their part, would have known of the intrinsic and inherent dangerous nature, character and tendency of said tar product to explode"; that * * * respondents carelessly, negligently, and unlawfully sold and delivered five gallons of said tar product to plaintiff and his son to be used by them in their work as contractors and builders and especially for coating the interior of a cistern, without giving them or either of them any notice, information, or warning as to the dangerous character thereof or of its high explosive tendency, etc. There follow allegations with respect to the use by plaintiff of the tar product, its explosion, and injury to him.

The court sustained * * * [a] demurrer [for failure to state facts sufficient to constitute a cause of action] and granted plaintiff twenty days' time within which to amend his complaint, "if so advised." In its memorandum the court cited * * * McCrossin v. Noyes Bros. & Cutler, 143 Minn. 181, 173 N.W. 566, 567, in which this court held that a vendor of another's proprietary product was not "required to analyze or ascertain at his peril whether the same contain any dangerous or poisonous ingredients and give warning accordingly" * * *. No appeal was taken * * * [from the order sustaining the demurrer].

* * * This action was instituted to enforce the same right as was the former, but the complaint alleged that plaintiff ordered tar from respondents and that they "negligently and carelessly sold and delivered to plaintiff five gallons of a tar compound which said defendants knew should be kept away from fire, heat and open flame lights and should not be dropped while contained in a container, and which facts the said defendants negligently and carelessly failed and neglected to inform this plaintiff * * *." Respondents * * * interposed as a defense the judgment and order of the court sustaining the demurrer to the amended complaint in the original action. * * * The court * * * ordered judgment dismissing the action on its merits, holding that the judgment in the former action was a bar to the instant one.

It is well settled that a judgment upon the facts presented in a complaint and confessed by demurrer is as effectual as a bar as if there had been a verdict on the same facts. * * * It is, however, "equally well settled, that, if the plaintiff fails on demurrer in his first action from the omission of an essential allegation in his declaration which is fully supplied in the second suit, the judgment in the first suit is no bar to the second, although the respective actions were instituted to enforce the same right; for the reason that the merits of the cause, as disclosed in the second declaration, were not heard and decided in the first action." Gould v. Evansville & C. R. Co., 91 U.S. 526, 533, 534, 23 L.Ed. 416. * * *

The facts confessed by the demurrer to the amended complaint in the first action were that respondents "knew, or but for the want of ordinary and reasonable care and diligence on their part, would have known of the intrinsic and inherent dangerous nature * * * [etc.]". That confession amounted to nothing more than would an affirmative answer to a question put in the alternative. It did not confess that respondents "knew" that the tar product "should be kept away from fire, heat and open flame lights and should not be dropped while contained in a container," as alleged in the complaint now before us. The order sustaining the demurrer to the amended complaint determined nothing more than that respondents as vendors of another's proprietary product were not required to analyze or ascertain at their peril whether the tar product contained any dangerous substance and give warning accordingly, and that the amended complaint was defective because alleging in the alternative facts upon which a cause of action might be predicated and facts upon which a cause of action could not be based. Actual knowledge on the part of respondents of the dangerous nature of the product and failure to adequately warn thereof would give rise to a good cause of action. * * * That issue has never been litigated, and hence the judgment rendered pursuant to the order sustaining the demurrer to the amended complaint in the former action is not a bar to the instant action. * * * Plaintiff could have again amended the complaint and corrected the defect, as he did in this complaint. We do not understand that he was required to do so in order to present the case on its merits to the court.

* * *

Reversed.

NOTES AND QUESTIONS

1. Plaintiff held defendant's note, which was secured by a deed of trust on land in Virginia. When the note went unpaid, plaintiff foreclosed the deed of trust, but received less than the amount of the note. Plaintiff then brought suit for the deficiency in a North Carolina court, which dismissed the action pursuant to a North Carolina statute that deprived its courts of jurisdiction to enter judgment for a deficiency. In a suit by plaintiff on the same claim in a federal court in North Carolina, should the North Carolina judgment be held to have been "on the merits"? See ANGEL v. BULLINGTON, 330 U.S. 183, 67 S.Ct. 657, 91 L.Ed. 832 (1947). Consider the following comment on the case:

> * * * [J]udgment "on the merits" * * *. We would be better off without this troublesome phrase. The United States Supreme Court held that the judgment of the North Carolina Supreme Court in *Bullington* v. *Angel* was one "on the merits," in the sense that it precluded the second action in a federal court *in North Carolina* and precluded also relitigation of the constitutionality of the statute. * * * This and similar problems would be clarified if, instead of discussing whether a judgment is or is not "on the merits," we simply inquired: What did the judgment determine? The judgment in *Bullington* v.

Angel determined (1) that the statute deprived all North Carolina state courts of jurisdiction to entertain such actions, and (2) that the statute was constitutional as applied to the case before the court. Because of the *Erie* doctrine, the first of these determinations precluded a second action in a North Carolina federal court, if it was constitutional; and the question of constitutionality was res judicata.

B. Currie & Lieberman, *Purchase-Money Mortgages and State Lines: A Study in Conflict-of-Laws Method,* 1960 Duke L.J. 1, 53 n.170.

2. For an extensive autopsy of a prior decision, conducted to determine whether a dismissal in that action was "on the merits," see THOMAS v. CONSOLIDATION COAL CO., 380 F.2d 69 (4th Cir.1967), in which in the earlier action there had been no findings, conclusions, or opinion, and there were fifteen possible grounds for dismissal.

ELFMAN v. GLASER, 313 Mass. 370, 373–74, 378, 47 N.E.2d 925, 927–28, 930 (1943). A demurrer to plaintiff's declaration was sustained "with leave to plaintiff to amend within ten days." Two-and-a-half later plaintiff moved for leave to file a substitute declaration on the grounds that his attorney had continually assured him that the case was proceeding toward trial and that this motion had been filed through another attorney as soon as plaintiff learned that judgment had been entered for defendant on demurrer. Leave was refused and the Supreme Judicial Court affirmed:

> The governing principle, as stated in Whitney v. Whitney, 299 Mass. 547, 550, 551, 13 N.E.2d 401, 403, is as follows: "It is a general rule that a judgment for the defendant founded on a demurrer is not a bar to a second action. The reason for the rule is that such a judgment commonly is based not on the merits but upon the insufficiency of the statement of the cause of action. * * * An exception to that general rule has grown up in cases where the plaintiff has been given leave to amend his pleading and has declined to amend and a judgment has thereafter been entered founded on the sustaining of the defendant's demurrer. * * * In these conditions, where a plaintiff has refused to amend his pleading a judgment rendered on a demurrer causes the matter to become res judicata as between the parties 'as to every issue which was or might have been litigated in that action' and estops the plaintiff 'from contesting the matter further.' * * * The doctrine of res judicata, therefore, applies where the issues have in fact been fully tried and in cases where the plaintiff has had ample opportunity to state his cause of action completely and correctly so as to have the issues tried but has refused to embrace that opportunity." The exception here stated to the rule that ordinarily a judgment founded upon the sustaining of a demurrer does not constitute res judicata is to be distinguished from the exception to this rule "when the demurrer in the earlier action is based on the merits." * * * In the case now before this court the record and pleadings

in the earlier case do not show that the demurrer to the declaration in that case was sustained on the merits. But the exception stated in the Whitney case is applicable * * * when, though the demurrer was sustained by reason of insufficiency of the statement of the cause of action or other defect in form or substance in the declaration, the plaintiff had an opportunity to amend for the purpose of correcting the defect in the declaration and did not avail himself of the opportunity.

* * *

The evidence that the plaintiff was ignorant of the order sustaining the demurrer and giving him leave to amend was immaterial since he was bound to take notice thereof. * * *

ANGUIANO v. TRANSCONTINENTAL BUS SYSTEM, INC.

Supreme Court of Arizona, 1953.
76 Ariz. 246, 263 P.2d 305.

LEVI S. UDALL, Justice. Frank Anguiano, on March 26, 1952, commenced [a] civil action * * * claiming damages for injuries allegedly sustained in a motor vehicle accident. Defendants' motion for security for costs was granted without opposition. Plaintiff wholly ignored the order and failed to comply therewith. Defendants moved under Rule 41(b), Rules of Civil Procedure [b] * * * to dismiss for failure to comply with the order of the court. This motion was unopposed, and the court granted it, thus dismissing the action. This order of dismissal did not state that the same was without prejudice. Plaintiff has never attempted to vacate or set aside this order, nor has he made any attempt to give security for costs.

Instead, on November 1, 1952, he commenced the present action * * * in the same court, his claim for relief being identical with that in the first action. Defendants answered, alleged the prior action had been dismissed, then moved for summary judgment, contending that such prior involuntary dismissal was an adjudication on the merits, under Rule 41(b). The motion was granted * * *.

Plaintiff contends this rule does not apply to all involuntary dismissals, but only to dismissals relating to the trial of the cause or the merits thereof, and that dismissals entered during the preliminary stages of the proceedings, though involuntary, are not on the merits. He argues that the whole pleading reform seen in recent years was meant to do away with harsh and unjust technical rules of pleading and procedure, and requires a decision of all causes upon their merits, and further argues that if Rule 41(b) applies to all involuntary dismissals, cases will be tried upon technicalities rather than the merits.

[b] This rule is in pertinent part identical to Federal Rule 41(b).

Defendants contend that Rule 41(b) is unambiguous and the court should take the words thereof at face value   *   *   *.

*   *   *   In Russo v. Sofia Bros., Inc., D.C., 44 F.Supp. 779,   *   *   * defendant's motion to dismiss the complaint for failure to state a claim was granted   *   *   *. Judgment of dismissal was entered which said nothing of the right to amend. Plaintiff then moved the court for leave to file an amended complaint which corrected the defects in the former pleading and stated a claim. The court discussed the application of Rule 41(b) to this fact situation, emphasized the fact that Rule 41 appears in Chap. 6   *   *   *   [of the Federal Rules] entitled "Trials", said that the rule did not apply because it was primarily one directed to dismissals at or after trial, and granted leave to file the amended complaint.[c]

*   *   *

On the other hand there are many cases supporting defendants' theory. Mas v. Coca Cola Co., 4 Cir., 198 F.2d 380, will serve as illustration. Plaintiff had instituted an earlier suit to have himself adjudged entitled to the design patent for Coca Cola bottles. The cause came on for trial, and after the opening statement of counsel, the court inquired fully into the clean hands of plaintiff, and found that in proceedings before the patent office plaintiff had used a false deposition and uttered forged documents with regard to this same patent. The suit was thereupon dismissed (affirmed on appeal, 4 Cir., 163 F. 2d 505). Thereafter, plaintiff brought this second action to recover damages for the fraudulent appropriation of his bottle design. Defendant pleaded res judicata, and its motion to dismiss the complaint was granted. Upon appeal it was held the prior dismissal operated as an adjudication upon the merits, because the trial court in its order of dismissal did not provide otherwise.

*   *   *

These latter cases have certain features in common: They apply Rule 41(b) to all involuntary dismissals, and recognize that such dismissals, by force of that rule, operate as adjudications upon the merits. If an appeal is perfected, the appellate court will determine if the lower court's discretion was abused in entering such a dismissal. Rule 41(b) is applied to involuntary dismissals without regard to the reasons or causes resulting in such dismissals, and the rule is applied to dismissals at all the preliminary stages of the case. *   *   *

We have concluded that the court in the Russo case (relied upon by plaintiff), reached a just solution on the facts there presented by giving effect to the liberal amendment provisions of the F.R.C.P.   *   *   *   We see no inconsistency in saying that the rule applies to orders of dismissal entered before trial, but that upon proper application such orders may be vacated by exercise of the court's discretion, and leave granted to proceed with the action. We believe the Russo case might better have been decided on these grounds.

    c The motion for leave to amend in the *Russo* case is reported at 2 F.R.D. 80 (S.D. N.Y.1941).

Our analysis of Rule 41 has led us to the same conclusions as the majority of the cases cited. The law provides various avenues by which a complaint may be dismissed. Plaintiff says the Rules have provided for the effect to be given some of these dismissals, but not others: some are saved, and some are damned, while others hang in limbo. He asks us to rule there may be a discretionary and indeterminate number of involuntary dismissals. Such a ruling is incongruous with Rule 41(a) and (d) * * * giving an involuntary dismissal distinct advantages over a voluntary dismissal.

While dismissals may be entered at varying times and for varying reasons, still all dismissals may be dichotomized as voluntary or involuntary. The Rules have adopted this latter classification, and if we were to depart from this and begin classifying dismissals according to the time and reasons for which they were granted, we should conjure up a hydra-headed monster in the field of procedure. * * *

Judgment affirmed.

NOTES AND QUESTIONS

1. Insofar as Rule 41(b) is concerned, should it make any difference whether the dismissal is for lack of jurisdiction, for failure to prosecute or to comply with the rules, or for failure to state a claim for relief? See *Restatement (Second), Judgments* §§ 48, 48.1 (Tent.Draft No. 1, 1973), and comments thereto. Many federal courts have reached the same conclusion as the Arizona Supreme Court reached in *Anguiano* in cases in which the dismissal was based on the last ground. E. g., Rinehart v. Locke, 454 F.2d 313 (7th Cir.1971) (alternative holding); Bartsch v. Chamberlain Co., 266 F.2d 357 (6th Cir.1959); Daley v. Sears, Roebuck & Co., 90 F.Supp. 562 (N.D.Ohio 1950).

2. A Rule 12(b)(6) motion should not be granted "if it is conceivable that, under the allegations of the complaint, a plaintiff can, upon a trial, establish a case which would entitle him to the relief prayed for." SPARKS v. ENGLAND, 113 F.2d 579, 582 (8th Cir.1940). Doesn't it follow that a dismissal in a federal court for failure to state a claim for relief ordinarily would bar a second suit on any closely related claim, even in the absence of Rule 41(b)?

Compare Clark, *Code Pleading* § 73, at 473–74 (2d ed. 1947):

> It has been urged that under the codes, due to a liberal interpretation of the concept *cause of action,* a wide application of the rule against splitting * * * is made. But the rule existed at common law and must exist under any law which at length sets an end to judicial disputes between litigants. The apparently wider application of the rule under the codes is due to two reasons. The first is that various remedies may now be secured in a single action, and hence a litigant no longer need or can bring successive suits to find the remedy which should apply to his wrong. Thus at common law a litigant who brought trespass when he should have brought case is not thereby precluded from starting an action of case * * *. The second reason is that there is probably a tendency constantly to extend the limits of what is considered a "single, entire claim." This is due to a number of causes, including the greater

scope of permissible remedies in the code action, the general extension of rules of joinder in the most modern systems of procedure, and, by no means least, the congested conditions of modern courts. This tendency seems on the whole desirable.

It should be noted, however, that Judge Clark in part predicates his position on the assumption that there are "liberal provisions * * * even for starting a new action where a previous one has failed for reasons not going to the merits * * *." Id. at 474–75.

3. If the court entering the order of dismissal operates under a rule that makes the dismissal a bar to further suit and the court that hears the second action does not follow such a rule, what law governs the question in the second court? See Comment, *Res Judicata in the Federal Courts: Application of Federal or State Law: Possible Differences Between the Two,* 51 Cornell L.Q. 96 (1965).

In GODDARD v. SECURITY TITLE INS. & GUAR. CO., 14 Cal.2d 47, 92 P.2d 804 (1939), plaintiff sued a trustee for a violation of instructions in a California state court. In an earlier action plaintiff had sued the trustee on the same facts in a federal court on a theory of conversion; on demurrer, the district court had dismissed this action, explicitly stating the dismissal to be "with prejudice." (The federal-court action antedated the Federal Rules.) Defendant pleaded the federal-court order as res judicata in the second action. The California court held that the second suit was not barred:

> * * * [I]t is apparent that the prior judgment of dismissal * * * was entered primarily on two grounds, first, that the complaint was framed on a theory of conversion rather than an action on the case; and second, that it was uncertain and insufficient in its pleading * * *. Such a judgment is clearly not on the merits, and * * * is not res judicata.
>
> * * * [I]f the intention of the court, gathered from its order or other source, were the test of the effect of the judgment on subsequent actions, the doctrine of res judicata would disappear as a legal principle and the bar of a judgment would depend wholly upon the whim of the first judge, or more probably, on the form of proposed order drafted by successful counsel. * * * Such a statement, if it has any definite meaning, suggests merely that the court believed that the judgment would finally conclude the controversy. But it is the nature of the action and the character of the judgment that determines whether it is res judicata.

Id. at 53–54, 92 P.2d at 807–08. If a similar case arose today with Rule 41 in force in the federal courts, would *Goddard* be distinguishable?

4. The Full Faith and Credit clause of the United States Constitution, Article IV, Section 1, has been defined by Congress as requiring that judgments "shall have the same full faith and credit in every court within the United States * * * as they have by law or usage in the courts of such State, Territory or Possession from which they are taken." 28 U.S.C. § 1738. The courts of a state are required to give full faith and credit to the judgment of a federal court. Stoll v. Gottlieb, 305 U.S. 165, 59 S.Ct. 134, 83 L.Ed. 104 (1938). *But compare* Phoenix Ins. Co. v. Haney, 235 Miss. 60, 108 So.2d 227, certiorari denied 360 U.S. 917, 79 S.Ct. 1435, 3 L.Ed.2d 1534 (1959) (claim that should have been brought as compulsory counterclaim in earlier federal-court action not barred in state court).

5. Occasionally two actions involving the same dispute will produce inconsistent final judgments. This may occur because the res judicata effect of the first judgment is not raised in the second action or because the court hearing the second action fails to give effect to the first judgment. The generally accepted rule is that the second judgment must be given effect by subsequent courts. See *Restatement (Second), Judgments* § 41.2 (Tent.Draft No. 1, 1973). Is this result sound? Should it make any difference whether the tribunal faced with the problem of two prior judgments is a court that rendered one of the competing judgments or is a third court? For an excellent discussion of this subject, see Ginsburg, *Judgments in Search of Full Faith and Credit: The Last-in-Time Rule for Conflicting Judgments,* 82 Harv.L.Rev. 798 (1969).

---

3. LIMITS ON THE APPLICATION OF RES JUDICATA

ADAMS v. PEARSON

Supreme Court of Illinois, 1952.
411 Ill. 431, 104 N.E.2d 267.

SCHAEFER, Justice. The circuit court of Edgar County entered summary judgment for the plaintiff, Alva F. Adams, in his action of ejectment against the defendant, Milton D. Pearson. The court also denied Pearson's motion for summary judgment on his counterclaim for specific performance against Adams and dismissed the counterclaim for want of equity. * * *

This case is a sequel to Pearson v. Adams, 394 Ill. 391, 68 N.E.2d 777, and the questions now presented relate primarily to the scope and effect of the judgment in that case. * * * In May, 1942, Adams entered into a written contract to sell a farm to Pearson. Pearson made a down payment of $4,000 and agreed to pay the balance of $14,600 when he received payment from the United States for his farm in Indiana * * *. Pearson went into possession of the farm in June, 1942, and has been in possession ever since, and has paid taxes and made improvements. The contract provided for a conveyance to Pearson by warranty deed, executed by Adams and his wife. Adams's wife was not a party to the contract, and she refused to sign the deed. In August, 1942, Adams served notice of his election to rescind, and Pearson tendered the balance of the purchase price, to be turned over to Adams upon delivery of a deed as provided in the contract.

Pearson sued for specific performance, seeking relief of a type which had not theretofore been awarded in Illinois. The prayer was in the alternative, requesting (1) that the value of Mrs. Adams's inchoate dower be ascertained and the purchase price abated by the value of the dower interest, or (2) that the value of the dower interest be paid to Mrs. Adams and a deed free of that interest be executed by the master, or (3) that Adams be required to indemnify

Pearson against the contingency that the dower interest might vest. There was also a prayer for general equitable relief. To this complaint Adams filed an answer, and a counterclaim seeking to rescind the contract and to be restored to possession. The trial court dismissed Pearson's complaint, on the ground that the relief sought was unauthorized, and also dismissed the counterclaim because no showing was made of fraud in the contract for the sale of the land. This court affirmed.

Thereafter the present action in ejectment was instituted by Adams. * * * [The] complaint alleged the contract for the sale of land, and restated all of the pleadings and the judgments of the trial court and of this court in the first case. It alleged further that Pearson had continued in possession of the property but had "failed to pay or tender the unpaid balance of the purchase price for said premises * * * except upon delivery * * * of a warranty deed signed by plaintiff and his wife" and had refused to accept a deed executed by plaintiff alone. The prayer for relief requested judgment for possession and damages by way of mesne profits.

* * * As separate defenses, Pearson's answer alleged that his possession was lawful and that he had paid or tendered the full purchase price; that Mrs. Adams knew of the contract and of expenditures made by Pearson in reliance upon it; that Adams had schemed and colluded with his wife that she should refuse to sign the deed; that Adams had by his counterclaim in the first action sought possession and an accounting * * * and that those claims, having been denied in the first action, are now barred by *res judicata*. Pearson also filed a counterclaim in which he prayed for a decree requiring Adams to perform specifically by delivering a warranty deed executed by Adams alone, without his wife's joinder in the deed. Adams's answer to this counterclaim alleged that Pearson was barred from the relief sought by the operation of *res judicata,* and also by an express election made in the course of the trial of the first case.

* * * A judgment was entered striking Pearson's special defenses, denying his motion for summary judgment, and allowing Adams's motion for summary judgment against Pearson for possession of the property. Leave was granted Pearson to receive from the clerk of the court the money theretofore paid as a tender of the balance of the purchase price and also, to receive from the clerk the $4,000 which had been tendered by Adams * * *. [T]he issue as to an accounting by Pearson * * * [was retained] upon the docket for further consideration. Pearson appeals.

* * * Each of the parties contends that the judgment in the earlier case bars his adversary from the relief now sought.

* * *

In the earlier case, Adams had filed a counterclaim under which he sought to rescind the contract and recover possession of the farm. * * * Adams's claim for possession in the earlier case was based upon four contentions: mistake, fraud, want of consideration and Pearson's failure to tender payment except upon delivery of a deed executed by both Adams and his wife. Both the trial court and this court held that the claims of mistake, fraud and want of consideration were unfounded. The remaining ground upon which Adams sought to recover possession in the earlier case is based upon Pearson's tender of the balance of the purchase price, which was delivered to the clerk of the court to be turned over to Adams "upon the delivery of the deed as in said contract provided." That is the identical basis upon which Adams's claim to possession is predicated in the present ejectment action. In the earlier case, the trial court dismissed Adams's counterclaim for want of equity. Adams assigned cross-error upon this portion of the judgment, but this court affirmed.

The facts upon which Adams now seeks to recover possession of the land existed when the earlier case was heard. And in that case they were presented both to the trial court and to this court as a basis for Adams's claim that he be restored to possession. So far as the record shows, nothing has since occurred which would alter the effect of that adjudication as a bar to the identical claim now presented by Adams. * * *

In behalf of Adams it is argued, however, that the opinion of this court in the former case does not show a specific decision adverse to him upon his claim for possession based upon Pearson's failure to tender the balance of the purchase price except upon the execution of a deed by Adams and his wife. That is true. It is well settled, however, that what has been adjudicated is to be determined not from the opinion rendered but from a consideration of the judgment actually entered in reference to the issues presented for decision. * * * The claim for possession which is now asserted by Adams was presented for decision by his counterclaim in the former case; it was decided adversely to him by the trial court when it dismissed his counterclaim, and that decision was affirmed by this court. Whatever the correctness or error of that decision, it is *res judicata* on the issue. * * *

We turn now to Pearson's claim that he is entitled to a decree directing Adams to perform specifically by conveying title to the extent that he is able to do so by executing his own warranty deed. Adams contends that Pearson is barred from this relief by an election made during the course of the first trial, as well as by the normal operation of the doctrine of *res judicata*. * * *

When Pearson instituted the first action for specific performance, our decisions had held that when a vendor contracted to convey by a deed executed by himself and his wife, and the wife thereafter refused to sign the deed, a court of equity would not attempt to value the wife's inchoate right of dower, nor would it compel the wife to convey or release that right; it would, however, direct the vendor to convey such interest as he could by his own deed, leaving the purchaser to proceed against the vendor for a breach of his covenants. * * * Pearson attempted to induce this court to broaden the relief available to a purchaser so situated by allowing an evaluation of the dower interest, and providing for a corresponding abatement of the purchase price or for an indemnity by the vendor against the possibility that the inchoate right might vest. * * * This court * * * adhered to the rule which denied evaluation of the dower interest in specific performance cases.

It is clear that specific performance by a deed signed by Adams alone was available to Pearson when he instituted his first action. An alternative prayer for that relief could have been included in his complaint, even though that was not the relief which he preferred to obtain. And he could have appealed from a decree which denied the preferred alternative, and thus have obtained the ruling of this court upon his main contentions. * * * Indeed, the relief which he now seeks was then available to him under the prayer for general relief in his complaint. The claim of collusion * * * was likewise available when the former action was instituted.

* * * The relief now sought by Pearson falls within the normal operation of the rules of *res judicata*.

From what has been said it follows that the application of the normal rules of *res judicata* results in a determination that the claim presently made by each of the parties is barred by the adjudication in the former case. The result of such a disposition of the case, however, would be unsatisfactory. Without pursuing the various legal questions which would be generated, it would appear, at best, to leave the parties after nearly ten years of litigation, with actions at law, centering about either the payment of the remainder of the purchase price or the recovery of damages for breach of the contract; and whichever party instituted such an action would have to give up his claim to the farm property. * * *

Application of the doctrine of *res judicata* has, on occasion, produced curious results. * * * These results have been thought to be warranted by the basic public policy against relitigation which supports the rule against splitting a cause of action. But in numerous cases that rule has been relaxed where the omission was due to ignorance, mistake or fraud. * * *

We turn, therefore, to a more detailed consideration of the relative positions of the parties. In the case at bar the equities are clearly with Pearson, the purchaser. The seller's unwarranted effort to rescind the contract precipitated the initial litigation and his continued effort to regain possession of land which he had willingly contracted to sell has resulted in the continuance of the litigation and in the present impasse.

Like considerations do not apply to Pearson. His original action was an effort to secure from a court of equity in this State a type of relief which is regularly afforded by the courts of some other jurisdictions but which had not theretofore been available in Illinois. His belief that the amendment to the Probate Act providing for the evaluation and extinguishment of dower afforded a basis for a broadened type of relief in specific performance actions cannot be said to be unreasonable, even though this court did not accept the arguments he advanced. * * * That his attorney apparently feared that he could not request less satisfactory relief without forfeiting the remedy he actually desired should not subject him to penalty. Here * * * the plaintiff's course of action was influenced by the existence of a grave legal question.

If it were not for the fact that the broadened remedy which Pearson originally sought could have been requested as alternative, instead of exclusive, relief, his situation would fall squarely within the general rule that "Where a judgment is rendered in favor of the defendant because the plaintiff seeks a form of remedy which is not available to him, the plaintiff is not precluded from subsequently maintaining an action in which he seeks an available remedy." Restatement of the Law, Judgments, sec. 65(2). The relief sought by Pearson in his present counterclaim is equitable to both parties; it gives to each what is his due and it is the relief typically awarded in a situation such as this. We hold therefore that under the circumstances of this case the relief sought by Pearson in his counterclaim is not barred by the doctrine of *res judicata*, but is available to him.

     *   *   *   [T]he cause is remanded, with directions   *   *   *   to allow Pearson's motion for summary judgment on his counterclaim against Adams.

     Reversed and remanded, with directions.

NOTES AND QUESTIONS

1. In *Adams v. Pearson* the ordinary principles of res judicata do not solve the problem before the court. Does the court reach its solution by seeking to find the result most consonant with those principles, or does it simply reject those principles and award judgment on the merits of the controversy?

2. Would the decision in *Adams v. Pearson* have been the same if Adams had not cross-assigned error on that portion of the judgment in the first action that dismissed his counterclaim for want of equity?

3. In HAHL v. SUGO, 169 N.Y. 109, 62 N.E. 135, 61 L.R.A. 226 (1901), plaintiff had won an ejectment action against defendant, whose building encroached on plaintiff's property, but the sheriff had returned an execution with the statement that it was impracticable to move defendant's building. Plaintiff subsequently sought an injunction requiring defendant to remove the encroachment but this claim was held to have been merged in the earlier judgment and was dismissed. Is the *Hahl* case distinguishable from *Adams v. Pearson*?

WHITE v. ADLER, 289 N.Y. 34, 43 N.E.2d 798 (1942). Defendant owned 326 shares of stock in a bank. On December 10, 1930, he presented 325 of these for transfer to another person; the transfer had not been registered, however, when on December 11, 1930, the Superintendent of Banks took possession of the bank because it was insolvent. The Superintendent successfully brought suit against defendant as the owner of one share under a statute that rendered bank stockholders liable for the debts of the bank up to an amount equal to the value of their stock. Subsequently the Superintendent brought suit for defendant's liability on the other 325 shares. The Court of Appeals held that the second action was not barred:

     We do not speculate why the Superintendent of Banks in the prior action to enforce the statutory individual liability of the stockholders sought judgment against Henry D. Gasner to the extent of the par value of only one share of stock though *at the time the bank closed* he appeared by the books of the bank to be the holder of 326 shares. Perhaps the reason was that at the time *of the commencement of the action* he appeared to be the holder of only one share, for the transfer of 325 shares had, as we have said, been entered upon the books a few days after the bank was closed but as of December 10th, when the bank was still transacting its regular business and the Superintendent of Banks or his counsel, examining these books in preparation for the enforcement of the liability of the stockholders, may have had no personal knowledge or may have forgotten that the entries in the books of the bank as of December 10th were in fact made thereafter. Perhaps even if that fact was present in their minds they may have failed to recognize its significance, for our decision   *   *   *   [that stockholders remained liable until their stock was transferred on the books] was rendered only in July, 1935. In any event, immediately after that decision the Superintendent of Banks made an additional demand upon these defendants and commenced this action to enforce the additional liability.

     *   *   *   The liability of the stockholder is measured by the number of his shares, but the statute does not create or define a separate liability upon each share of stock or upon each stock certificate in single ownership. Only a single cause of action accrues upon failure to satisfy a single liability.   *   *   *   [T]he recovery upon part of a single cause of action ordinarily bars an action thereafter for the remainder.

     *   *   *   Implicit in   *   *   *   statements of the rule is an assumption that a plaintiff who has split his causes of action has acted inequitably, knowing that he was causing unnecessary vexation to the defendant, or at least careless whether or not he causes such vexation.   *   *   *

     Here the plaintiff is a public officer seeking to enforce a liability created by the State against *all* stockholders of the bank for the benefit of *all* of the creditors. A sound public policy demands that the liability created by the State should be enforced equally against all stockholders—that none should benefit by mistake or even dereliction of duty by the public officer upon whom the duty of enforcing the liability is imposed—nor should those members of the public for whose benefit the liability has been created suffer because of dereliction of duty by the public officer.

     *   *   *   It is not necessary to decide now whether in this State the courts may, in the exercise of a sound discretion, refuse, either in an action at law or in equity, to give full effect to a violation of the rule against splitting causes of action, "as the evident justice of the particular case requires." The stock owned by the defendants was

represented by several stock certificates. Each certificate was assignable by indorsement upon the certificate and delivery. * * * Thus the defendants, by assigning separate stock certificates, did themselves initiate the splitting of liability against them. The assignment * * * created a condition in which there was reasonable doubt about the extent of the recovery which could be had against the defendants. The plaintiff in these circumstances in the prior action sought recovery only for the amount for which the defendants were liable beyond possible doubt. We decide only that in these circumstances the reason for the rule fails * * *.

NOTE

In VARSITY AMUSEMENT CO. v. BUTTERS, 155 Colo. 330, 394 P.2d 603 (1964), an injured employee filed an application for workmen's compensation; while the claim was pending the employee filed a tort action against the employer for injuries, which was settled for $5,000. Subsequently the workmen's compensation commission awarded the employee compensation, with credit for the amount of the civil judgment. Rejecting an argument that the civil judgment was res judicata, the Supreme Court of Colorado said:

> The doctrine of *res judicata* owes its existence to a consideration of public policy; namely, that there should be an end to litigation. We are of the view that a judgment entered by agreement or consent does not have a conclusive effect where to give it that effect would render impotent another important public policy. * * * Certainly the situations in which the doctrine of *res judicata* will yield to considerations of public policy are rare, but the instant case fits into that category. The General Assembly has fixed with indelible clarity the policy of Colorado with respect to the remedy to be pursued when a workman's injuries fall within the coverage of the Workmen's Compensation Act. We decline the * * * invitation to emasculate that policy.

Id. at 339, 394 P.2d at 607.

CLEARY, RES JUDICATA REEXAMINED, 57 Yale L.J. 339, 344–49 (1948):

The grounds commonly advanced to justify the rule of res judicata are: 1. The danger of double recovery; 2. The desirability of stable judicial determinations; 3. Relieving a defendant of the expense and vexation of repeated litigation; 4. Economy of court time. * * *

Danger of Double Recovery

The danger of double recovery obviously exists only in the event the plaintiff has recovered in his first action. If he was successful, then a careful examination of what elements of damages or injury were considered and passed upon should furnish an ample safeguard against further recovery based upon the same elements in the later action. * * *

Whether plaintiff's splitting has been of theory, or arithmetical, or of relief seems to be unimportant in connection with double recovery. The essential inquiry is whether he has already had redress for a particular element of damages or injury. Any doubt should be resolved against plaintiff * * *.

Desirability of Stable Decisions

Effective operation of courts in the social and economic scheme requires that their decisions have the respect of and be observed by the parties, the general public and the courts themselves. According insufficient weight to prior decisions encourages disrespect and disregard of courts and their decisions and invites litigation. However, giving a prior decision effect beyond its actual scope is just as undesirable as according to it an insufficient effect.

The stability of decisions is not affected when plaintiff splits his cause of action arithmetically, or splits his relief. The prior decision remains in full force and is not questioned. * * * A split of theory, on the other hand, presents a very real problem. Policy would seem to indicate that when a plaintiff has once attempted to obtain his entire relief, based upon his entire damages, then the matter should be laid at rest. * * * In deciding such cases, the concept of a cause of action possesses real utility if applied with realization of what actually is at issue and with due regard for the other factors herein discussed.

Freedom from Vexatious Litigation

The elimination of vexatious litigation sounds like a worthy purpose. But what is meant by vexatious litigation? * * * [T]he term seems primarily to be directed against a plaintiff who tries to make two actions do the work of one, by splitting his cause of action arithmetically or by splitting his relief.

* * * A literal reading of the rule that res judicata applies not only to what was litigated but to what might have been litigated, as well, would mean that all procedurally joinable matters between the parties at the time of the former action would now be res judicata, regardless of how unrelated such matters might be in fact. Courts have not gone to that length. * * * If the causes of action are different, it is immaterial * * * that plaintiff might have joined them under rules governing permissive joinder. * * * And so we find a deserving plaintiff denied recovery of very apparent damages for breach of contract because the contract was "entire," and in a former action he had not included damages for anticipatory breach, thus "splitting his cause of action," while in another case plaintiff is permitted to bring as many actions as he holds bonds and coupons of the same identical issue, because each bond and coupon "constitutes a separate cause of action."

* * *

Assuming that sound policy encourages joinder of related matters, a litigant who has split his cause of action arithmetically or as to relief should be penalized to the extent that the splitting has resulted in added expense to the opposing party. The same principle, however, should apply in the case of the plaintiff who brings separate actions * * * which can more economically be tried in one proceeding, e. g., cases where consolidation may be had under present rules if the actions are pending at the same time in the same court. Recoverable expenses should include court costs, counsel fees and other expenses, such as expert witnesses, to the extent that such expenses are increased by the use of more than one action. Thus the desired objective of gathering all related matters into one action may be achieved by the assessment of costs, more effectively than under optional joinder rules and less harshly than under res judicata.

* * *

Economy of Court Time

The final justification of the usual rule of res judicata, the saving in court time, is peculiarly unconvincing. Courts exist for the purpose of trying lawsuits. * * * The fact that a party may waive the defense of res judicata, as seems to be the general rule, indicates that saving the judge's time is more afterthought than reason. * * *

Conclusion

The courts themselves have not been happy over results often apparently required by res judicata. Even Judge Clark is forced to admit [dissenting in Riordan v. Ferguson, 147 F.2d 983, 988 (2d Cir.1945)]:

["The defense of res judicata is universally respected, but actually not very well liked."]

So we find the courts drifting off into somewhat vague dissertations upon the election of remedies * * *. Or we find them making ill-defined exceptions in cases where some items comprising the cause of action have been omitted from the earlier action through ignorance, mistake or fraud. Or * * * the courts may refuse to apply the rule against splitting causes of action in litigation brought by the state, or "involving the public interest." Most of these cases seem to arrive at a desirable result, but the effort has been inartistic, to say the least. * * *

QUESTION

Are "hard cases" of res judicata better handled by an *ad hoc* approach, as exemplified by *Adams, White,* and *Butters,* or by a general rule, such as proposed by Professor Cleary? See also *Restatement (Second), Judgments* § 48.1 (Tent. Draft No. 1, 1973); Blume, *The Scope of a Cause of Action—Elimination of the Splitting Trap,* 38 Mich.St.B.J., Dec. 1959, p. 10; p. 505, Note 4, supra.

SECTION B. COLLATERAL ESTOPPEL

---

1. THE REQUIREMENT OF ACTUAL ADJUDICATION IN THE FIRST ACTION

A. THE BASIC POSTULATE

CROMWELL v. COUNTY OF SAC

Supreme Court of the United States, 1876.
94 U.S. 351, 24 L.Ed. 195.

Error to the Circuit Court of the United States for the District of Iowa.

Mr. Justice FIELD delivered the opinion of the court.

This was an action on four bonds * * * each for $1,000, and four coupons for interest, attached to them, each for $100. The bonds were issued in 1860, and were made payable to bearer, in the city of New York, in the years 1868, 1869, 1870, and 1871, respectively, with annual interest at the rate of ten per cent a year.

To defeat this action, the defendant relied upon the estoppel of a judgment rendered in favor of the county in a prior action brought by one Samuel C. Smith upon certain earlier maturing coupons on the same bonds, accompanied with proof that the plaintiff Cromwell was at the time the owner of the coupons in that action, and that the action was prosecuted for his sole use and benefit.

* * *

In considering the operation of this judgment, it should be borne in mind * * * that there is a difference between the effect of a judgment as a bar or estoppel against the prosecution of a second action upon the same claim or demand, and its effect as an estoppel in another action between the same parties upon a different claim or cause of action. In the former case, the judgment, if rendered upon the merits, constitutes an absolute bar to a subsequent action. It is a finality as to the claim or demand in controversy, concluding parties and those in privity with them, not only as to every matter which was offered and received to sustain or defeat the claim or demand, but as to any other admissible matter which might have been offered for that purpose. Thus, for example, a judgment rendered upon a promissory note is conclusive as to the validity of the instrument and the amount due upon it, although it be subsequently alleged that perfect defences actually existed, of which no proof was offered, such as forgery, want of consideration, or payment. * * * The judgment is as conclusive, so far as future proceedings at law are concerned, as though the defences never existed.   The language, therefore, which is so often used, that a judgment estops not only as to every ground of recovery or defence actually presented in the action, but also as to every ground which might have been presented, is strictly accurate, when applied to the demand or claim in controversy. * * *

But where the second action between the same parties is upon a different claim or demand, the judgment in the prior action operates as an estoppel only as to those matters in issue or points controverted, upon the determination of which the finding or verdict was rendered.   In all cases, therefore, where it is sought to apply the estoppel of a judgment rendered upon one cause of action to matters arising in a suit upon a different cause of action, the inquiry must always be as to the point or question actually litigated and determined in the original action, not what might have been thus litigated and determined. Only upon such matters is the judgment conclusive in another action.

The difference in the operation of a judgment in the two classes of cases mentioned is seen through all the leading adjudications upon the doctrine of estoppel.   Thus, in the case of *Outram v. Morewood*, 3 East, 346, the defendants were held estopped from averring title to a mine, in an action of trespass for digging out coal from it, because, in a previous action for a similar trespass, they had set up the same title, and it had been determined against them.   In commenting upon a decision cited in that case, Lord Ellenborough, in his elaborate opinion, said: "It is not the recovery, but the matter alleged by the party, and upon which the recovery proceeds, which creates the estoppel.   The recovery of itself in an action of trespass is only a bar to the future recovery of damages for the same injury; but the estoppel precludes parties and privies from contending to the contrary of that point or matter of fact, which, having been once distinctly put in issue by them, or by those to whom they are privy in estate or law, has been, on such issue joined, solemnly found against them."

* * *   It was so adjudged by this court in the case of *The Washington, Alexandria, & Georgetown Steam Packet Co. v. Sickles*, reported in the 24th of Howard.   In that case, an action was brought upon a special parol contract for the use of Sickles's cut-off for saving fuel in the working of steamengines, by which the plaintiffs, who had a patent for the cut-off, were to attach one of their machines to the engine of the defendants' boat, and were to receive for its use three-fourths of the saving of fuel thus produced, the payments to be made from time to time when demanded.   To ascertain the saving of fuel an experiment was to be made in a specified manner, and the result taken as the rate of saving during the continuance of the contract.   The plaintiffs in their declaration averred that the experiment had been made, at [sic] the rate of saving ascertained, and that the cut-off had been used on the boat until the commencement of the suit.   In a prior action against the same defendant for an instalment due, where the declaration set forth the same contract in two counts, the first of which was similar to the counts in the second action * * * the plaintiffs had obtained verdict and judgment; and it was insisted that the defendant was estopped by the verdict and judgment produced from proving that there was no such contract as that declared upon, or that no

saving of fuel had been obtained, or that the experiment was not made pursuant to the contract, or that the verdict was rendered upon all the issues, and not upon the first count specially. The Circuit Court assented to these views, and excluded the testimony offered by the defendants to prove those facts. But this court reversed the decision, and held that the defendants were not thus estopped.

"The record produced by the plaintiffs," said the court, "showed that the first suit was brought apparently upon the same contract as the second, and that the existence and validity of that contract might have been litigated. But the verdict might have been rendered upon the entire declaration, and without special reference to the first count. It was competent to the defendants to show the state of facts that existed at the trial, with a view to ascertain what was the matter decided upon by the verdict of the jury. It may have been that there was no contest in reference to the fairness of the experiment, or to its sufficiency to ascertain the premium to be paid for the use of the machine at the first trial * * *. The judgment rendered in that suit * * * is conclusive of all the facts properly pleaded by the plaintiffs; but when it is presented as testimony in another suit, the inquiry is competent whether the same issue has been tried and settled by it."

* * *

Various considerations, other than the actual merits, may govern a party in bringing forward grounds of recovery or defence in one action, which may not exist in another action upon a different demand, such as the smallness of the amount or the value of the property in controversy, the difficulty of obtaining the necessary evidence, the expense of the litigation, and his own situation at the time. A party acting upon considerations like these ought not to be precluded from contesting in a subsequent action other demands arising out of the same transaction. * * *

If, now, we consider the main question presented for our determination * * * its solution will not be difficult. It appears from the findings in the original action of Smith, that the county of Sac, by a vote of its people, authorized the issue of bonds to the amount of $10,000, for the erection of a court-house; that bonds to that amount were issued by the county judge, and delivered to one Meserey, with whom he had made a contract for the erection of the court-house; that immediately upon receipt of the bonds the contractor gave one of them as a gratuity to the county judge; and that the court-house was never constructed by the contractor, or by any other person pursuant to the contract. It also appears that the plaintiff had become, before their maturity, the holder of twenty-five coupons, which had been attached to the bonds, but there was no finding that he had ever given any value for them. * * * The case coming here on writ of error, this court held that the facts disclosed by the findings were sufficient evidence of fraud and illegality in the inception of the bonds to call upon the holder to show that he had given value for the coupons; and, not having done so, the judgment was affirmed. Reading the record of the lower court by the opinion and judgment of this court, it must be considered that the matters adjudged in that case were these: that the bonds were void as against the county in the hands of parties who did not acquire them before maturity and give value for them, and that the plaintiff, not having proved that he gave such value, was not entitled to recover upon the coupons. * * * The finding and judgment upon the invalidity of the bonds, as against the county, must be held to estop the plaintiff here from averring to the contrary. But as the bonds were negotiable instruments * * * they would be held as valid obligations against the county in the hands of a *bona fide* holder taking them for value before maturity * * *. If, therefore, the plaintiff received the bond and coupons in suit before maturity for value, as he offered to prove, he should have been permitted to show that fact. There was nothing adjudged in the former action in the finding that the plaintiff had not made such proof in that case which can preclude the present plaintiff from making such proof here. The fact that a party may not have shown that he gave value for one bond or coupon is not even presumptive, much less conclusive, evidence that he may not have given value for another and different bond or coupon. The exclusion of the evidence offered by the plaintiff was erroneous * * *.

Judgment reversed, and cause remanded for a new trial.

[The dissenting opinion of Mr. Justice CLIFFORD is omitted.]

NOTES AND QUESTIONS

1. In a state that permits separate actions for personal injuries and property damage arising out of the same occurrence, plaintiff brings an action for property damage against defendant who answers with a general denial. Defendant attempts to introduce evidence concerning plaintiff's contributory negligence, but the evidence is excluded on the ground that contributory negligence is an affirmative defense and has not been pleaded. Verdict and judgment for plaintiff. Subsequently plaintiff sues defendant for personal injuries. Is the defense of contributory negligence open to defendant?

2. A physician sues a patient to collect her fee for services rendered. The patient defaults, judgment is entered, and the judgment is satisfied. Later, the patient sues the physician for malpractice. Does the earlier default judgment establish that the physician's services were of value, and not worthless or harmful? *Compare* Gwynn v. Wilhelm, 226 Or. 606, 360 P.2d 312 (1961), *with* Blair v. Bartlett, 75 N.Y. 150, 31 Am.Rep. 455 (1878). See Annot., 77 A.L.R.2d 1410 (1961).

3. See generally *Restatement (Second), Judgments* §§ 68, 68.1 (Tent. Draft No. 1, 1973); Polasky, *Collateral Estoppel—Effects of Prior Litigation,* 39 Iowa L.Rev. 217 (1954); Rosenberg, *Collateral Estoppel in New York,* 44 St. John's L.Rev. 165 (1969); Scott, *Collateral Estoppel by Judgment,* 56 Harv.L. Rev. 1 (1942).

B.   THE THREE COROLLARIES

RUSSELL v. PLACE

Supreme Court of the United States, 1876.
94 U.S. 606, 24 L.Ed. 214.

Appeal from the Circuit Court of the United States for the Northern District of New York.

Mr. Justice FIELD delivered the opinion of the court.

This is a suit for an infringement of a patent to the complainant for an alleged new and useful improvement in the preparation of leather * * *.

The bill of complaint sets forth the invention claimed, the issue of a patent for the same, its surrender for alleged defective and insufficient description of the invention, its reissue with an amended specification, and the recovery of judgment against the defendants for damages in an action at law for a violation of the exclusive privileges secured by the patent.

The bill then alleges the subsequent manufacture, use, and sale by the defendants, without the license of the patentee, of the alleged invention and improvement, and prays that they may be decreed to account for the gains and profits thus acquired by them, and be enjoined from further infringement.

The answer admits the issue of the patent, its surrender and reissue, and, as a defence to this suit, sets up in substance the want of novelty in the invention, its use by the public for more than two years prior to the application for the patent, and that the reissue, so far as it differs from the original patent, is not for the same invention. * * *

The action at law was brought * * * in the ordinary form of such actions for infringement of the privileges secured by a patent. The defendants pleaded the general issue, and set up, by special notice under the act of Congress, the want of novelty in the invention, and its use by the public for more than two years prior to the application for a patent. The plaintiff obtained a verdict for damages, upon which the judgment mentioned was entered; and this judgment, it is now insisted, estops the defendants in this suit from insisting upon the want of novelty in the invention patented, and its prior use by the public, and also from insisting upon any ground going to the validity of the patent which might have been availed of as a defence in that action, and, of course, upon the want of identity in the invention covered by the reissue with that of the original patent.

It is undoubtedly settled law that a judgment of a court of competent jurisdiction, upon a question directly involved in one suit, is conclusive as to that question in another suit between the same parties. But to this operation of the judgment it must appear, either upon the face of the record or be shown by extrinsic evidence, that the precise question was raised and determined in the former suit. If there be any uncertainty on this head in the record—as, for exam-

must be precise
question

ple, if it appear that several distinct matters may have been litigated, upon one or more of which the judgment may have passed, without indicating which of them was thus litigated, and upon which the judgment was rendered—the whole subject-matter of the action will be at large, and open to a new contention, unless this uncertainty be removed by extrinsic evidence showing the precise point involved and determined. * * *

[handwritten margin note: if uncertain as to which issue judgment was rendered ↓ whole subj. matter is open for litig]

Tested by these views, the question presented * * * is of easy solution. The record of that action does not disclose the nature of the infringement for which damages were recovered. The declaration only avers * * * as the infringement complained of, that the defendants have made and used the invention, and have caused others to make and use it. The patent contains two claims: one for the use of fat liquor generally in the treatment of leather, and the other for a process of treating bark tanned lamb or sheep skin by means of a compound composed and applied in a particular manner. Whether the infringement for which the verdict and judgment passed consisted in the simple use of fat liquor in the treatment of leather, or in the use of the process specified, does not appear from the record. A recovery for an infringement of one claim of the patent is not of itself conclusive of an infringement of the other claim, and there was no extrinsic evidence offered to remove the uncertainty upon the record * * *. The verdict may have been for an infringement of the first claim; it may have been for an infringement of the second; it may have been for an infringement of both. The validity of the patent was not necessarily involved, except with respect to the claim which was the basis of the recovery. A patent may be valid as to a single claim *[handwritten margin note: findings]* and not valid as to the others. The record wants, therefore, that certainty which is essential to its operation as an estoppel, and does not conclude the defendants from contesting the infringement or the validity of the patent in this suit.

The record is not unlike a record in an action for money had and received to the plaintiff's use. It would be impossible to affirm from such a record, with certainty, for what moneys thus received the action was brought, without extrinsic evidence showing the fact; and, of course, without such evidence the verdict and judgment would conclude nothing, except as to the amount of indebtedness established.

* * *

Decree affirmed.

Mr. Justice CLIFFORD dissented.

NOTES AND QUESTIONS

1. Plaintiff brings an action against defendant for personal injuries arising out of a collision of their automobiles. Defendant answers, denying negligence and affirmatively pleading contributory negligence. Evidence is presented on both issues, and there is a general verdict for defendant. If defendant subsequently sues plaintiff for his own injuries arising out of the same accident, may defendant rely upon the first judgment as establishing any part of the case? See *Developments in the Law—Res Judicata*, 65 Harv.L.Rev. 818, 845–46 (1952).

2. In KELLEY v. CURTISS, 16 N.J. 265, 273, 108 A.2d 431, 435 (1954), the New Jersey Supreme Court said: "The case against * * * [defendant] having been submitted to the jury with instructions that he was entitled to a verdict of no cause of action if the jury found either that he was not negligent or that * * * [plaintiff] was guilty of contributory negligence, the general verdict is to be considered as determining both grounds in * * * [defendant's] favor." Is this holding consistent with *Russell v. Place?* If not, which case advances the better rule?

3. As a result of the rule in *Russell v. Place,* it frequently is impossible to give any collateral-estoppel effect to an earlier judgment because the judgment could rest on a number of grounds and there is no means of knowing the ground on which it actually was based. Is this a relevant consideration in deciding how rigidly the rules of collateral estoppel should be enforced when it is possible to establish what was determined in the earlier proceeding?

4. In SLATER v. SKIRVING, 51 Neb. 108, 70 N.W. 493 (1897), defendant had brought an action against plaintiffs who suffered a default judgment; a petition by plaintiffs to vacate the judgment on the grounds that it was irregularly obtained, and that jurisdiction had been obtained by fraud on the court and on plaintiffs, was denied. Plaintiffs then sued to enjoin defendant from enforcing the judgment. The Supreme Court of Nebraska said:

> * * * [It] will be observed * * * that in that proceeding there were actually litigated and therein determined the questions now presented, as to whether the original judgment was rendered during term time, or at a time when the court was actually in session, and whether there was presented such a case of casualty or surprise as to justify relief against the judgment. These matters having been in fact litigated, their determination in the former case adversely to the plaintiffs here bars them from again presenting such matters for determination * * *.

> In the former proceeding these plaintiffs also pleaded the facts which they now claim operated as a fraud upon them, and upon the jurisdiction of the court. While, perhaps, such a fraud would render the judgment void, and therefore open to collateral attack, and if so, perhaps, the plaintiffs were not compellable to assert such facts in their former petition, and might have reserved them for use in a collateral attack, still there can be no doubt that they constituted "an irregularity in obtaining the judgment," and "fraud practiced by the successful party in obtaining the judgment." * * * The facts now pleaded with regard to the fraud were therefore properly pleaded in the former proceeding, and, had they been proved, would have compelled a judgment in favor of these plaintiffs.

> * * * Generally speaking, in order that a judgment in one action shall operate as an estoppel in a second action, it must be made to appear, not only that there was a substantial identity of issues, but that the issue as to which the estoppel is pleaded was in the former action actually determined; and, where the record is uncertain, parol evidence is admissible to show what issues were determined in the former suit * * * and we think that, while the authorities are conflicting, their greater weight is in favor of the view that the burden of proof is upon the party pleading the estoppel to establish the fact of the adjudication by

extrinsic evidence, if necessary, and not upon the other party to show that the issue which might have been adjudicated was not. But we conceive that sound principle requires that the record should be conclusive so far as it goes, and that extrinsic evidence must be confined to supplementing the record, and no evidence is admissible to contradict it. To illustrate: If, in the former action, the defendant interposed two different pleas, and recovered a general verdict, extrinsic evidence would be admissible to show that the verdict was based on only one of these pleas, and that the matter involved in the other plea was not adjudicated, because such evidence merely explains the record, the defendant being entitled to judgment if either of his pleas was good. * * * But on the other hand, if the defendant files two pleas, either of which would be good if proved, and the judgment was for plaintiff, then the record shows that both pleas must have been determined adversely to defendant; and to permit extrinsic evidence to show that one plea was abandoned would not supplement the record, but would contradict it. Now, in this case the plaintiffs alleged several facts. If they proved any one of these, the original judgment should have been vacated. Therefore, a general finding against them necessarily involved a determination adversely to the plaintiffs of each one of those facts. The plaintiffs could not avoid the effect of the estoppel merely by failing to introduce evidence in support of the particular averment in question. If they did not desire an adjudication of that issue, they should have amended their petition, and struck out the averments in support thereof. But, the record on these facts requiring an adjudication of this issue in order to justify the judgment rendered, the plaintiffs are bound, whether or not they saw fit to offer evidence in the former action. * * *

Id. at 111–14, 70 N.W. at 494–95.

RIOS v. DAVIS

Court of Civil Appeals of Texas, Eastland, 1963.
373 S.W.2d 386.

COLLINGS, Justice. Juan C. Rios brought this suit against Jessie Hubert Davis in the District Court to recover damages * * * alleged to have been sustained as a result of personal injuries received * * * in an automobile collision. Plaintiff alleged that his injuries were proximately caused by negligence on the part of the defendant. The defendant answered alleging that Rios was guilty of contributory negligence. Also, among other defenses, the defendant urged a plea of res judicata and collateral estoppel based upon the findings and the judgment entered * * * in a suit between the same parties in the County Court at Law of El Paso County. The plea of res judicata was sustained and judgment was entered in favor of the defendant * * *.

It is shown by the record that   *   *   *   Popular Dry Goods Company brought suit against appellee Davis   *   *   *   seeking to recover for damages to its truck in the sum of $443.97, alleged to have been sustained in the same collision here involved.   Davis answered alleging contributory negligence on the part of Popular and joined appellant Juan C. Rios as a third party defendant and sought to recover from Rios $248.50, the alleged amount of damages to his automobile.   The jury   *   *   *   found that Popular Dry Goods Company and Rios were guilty of negligence proximately causing the collision.   However, the jury also found that Davis was guilty of negligence proximately causing the collision, and judgment was entered   *   *   *   denying Popular Dry Goods any recovery against Davis and denying Davis any recovery against Rios.

Appellant Rios in his third point contends that the District Court erred in sustaining appellee's plea of res judicata based upon the judgment of the County Court at Law because the findings on the issues regarding appellant's negligence and liability   *   *   *   were immaterial because the judgment entered in that case was in favor of appellant.   We sustain this point. *   *   *   The sole basis for the judgment   *   *   *   as between Rios and Davis was the findings concerning the negligence of Davis.   The finding that Rios was negligent was not essential or material to the judgment and the judgment was not based thereon.   On the contrary, the finding   *   *   *   that Rios was negligent proximately causing the accident would, if it had been controlling, led [sic] to a different result.   Since the judgment was in favor of Rios he had no right or opportunity to complain of or to appeal from the finding that he was guilty of such negligence even if such finding had been without any support whatever in the evidence.   The right of appeal is from a judgment and not from a finding.   *   *   *   In the case of Word v. Colley, Tex. Civ.App., 173 S.W. 629, at page 634 of its opinion (Error Ref.), the court stated as follows:

> "It is the judgment, and not the verdict or the conclusions of fact, filed by a trial court which constitutes the estoppel, and a finding of fact by a jury or a court which does not become the basis or one of the grounds of the judgment rendered is not conclusive against either party to the suit."

*   *   *

The judgment is, therefore, reversed, and the cause is remanded.

NOTES AND QUESTIONS

1.   The court in *Rios* held that the judgment in the earlier case did not estop Rios from denying his own negligence.   Should the earlier judgment estop Davis from denying his own negligence?

2.   The verdict in the earlier action in *Rios* reflects the consistent practice in Texas courts of submitting a case to the jury on "special issues."   Texas Rules of Civil Procedure 277, 279.   See Dooley, *The Use of Special Issues under the New*

State and Federal Rules, 20 Texas L.Rev. 32 (1941); Green, *Special Issues,* 14 Texas B.J. 521 (1951). Does *Rios* suggest a reason why special verdicts should be used more often?

3. Suppose Davis had not cross-claimed against Rios, merely impleading the latter on a contingent claim for contribution; that Popular had then made a claim against Rios; that at trial Davis and Rios each had argued the other was solely negligent; and that the jury had found for Popular against both of them. In a subsequent suit by Rios against Davis, would the earlier finding that each had been negligent estop Rios from denying negligence? *Compare* Byrum v. Ames & Webb, Inc., 196 Va. 597, 85 S.E.2d 364 (1955) (no), *with* Stangle v. Chicago, R. I. & P. R. R., 295 F.2d 789 (7th Cir.1961) (yes). In both of these cases, the parties in the later action had been named as codefendants by the plaintiff in the earlier action; should it make any difference if one of them had brought the other in by impleader? Should it make any difference if in the earlier case, the jury had found one of them negligent, and the other not negligent?

Generally, a judgment does not act as collateral estoppel between coparties unless they are adversaries, and they are considered adversaries only if there is a claim for relief by one coparty against the other. The fact that their interests clash and that they are on opposite sides of every issue does not make them adversaries for this purpose in the absence of such a claim. See Glaser v. Huette, 232 App.Div. 119, 249 N.Y.S. 374 (1st Dep't 1931), affirmed without opinion 256 N.Y. 686, 177 N.E. 193 (1931); 1B Moore, *Federal Practice* ¶ 0.411[2] (2d ed.); Marks, *Availability of Res Judicata to Litigants Who Were Co-defendants in Prior Suit,* 1963 Ins.L.J. 143.

4. The court in *Rios* supports its view by noting that Rios could not appeal the finding of his negligence in the earlier action. See also *Restatement, Judgments* § 69(2) (1942). Should the prevailing party in the earlier action be permitted in a later action to attack a finding that was necessary to the judgment in the earlier action? Such a situation will not be common, but did arise in an interesting case in Missouri. Plaintiff in the first action sued for partition of an alleged tenancy in common, but defendant answered with a general denial, which in effect disclaimed "all interest or title to the land in dispute." The court found on the basis of the evidence and the pleadings that plaintiff owned the land, and ordered that "plaintiff take nothing by his writ." Subsequently plaintiff sued to eject defendant, who answered that he had title to the land. In BARTLEY v. BARTLEY, 172 Mo. 208, 72 S.W. 521 (1903), the Supreme Court of Missouri held that the finding in the earlier case could not be attacked. *Cf. Partmar Corp. v. Paramount Pictures Theatres Corp.,* p. 1043, supra.

5. *Rios* should be compared with HOME OWNERS FED. SAV. & LOAN ASS'N v. NORTHWESTERN FIRE & MARINE INS. CO., 354 Mass. 448, 238 N.E.2d 55 (1968), in which the majority opinion states, in what may well be dictum, that "certain findings not strictly essential to the final judgment in the prior action * * * may be relied upon if it is clear that the issues underlying them were treated as essential to the prior case by the court and the party to be bound." What advantages does this test have over the *Rios* approach? What disadvantages? Three of the seven justices dissented.

PATTERSON v. SAUNDERS

Supreme Court of Appeals of Virginia, 1953.
194 Va. 607, 74 S.E.2d 204.

HUDGINS, Chief Justice.   Charles C. Patterson filed his motion for judgment against Lillie M. Saunders, J. B. Gray, O. M. King, and Canton Lumber Company, Inc., seeking to recover $50,000 damages for wrongfully cutting and removing timber from a sixty-acre tract of land * * * alleged to be owned by him.   Defendants filed separate pleas of *res judicata*, in which it was alleged that the Circuit Court * * * in a chancery suit brought by the same plaintiff against J. B. Gray and O. M. King, two of the defendants named in his motion for judgment, had held that plaintiff had no title to the same sixty acres of land * * *.   The trial court sustained the pleas and dismissed the case.   * * *

The record of the former proceeding upon which each of the pleas of *res judicata* is based, consists of a bill in chancery, an answer and a decree.   It was alleged in the bill of complaint filed by the same plaintiff * * * that he was the owner in fee of the sixty acres * * * and charged that J. B. Gray and O. M. King "have cut and are cutting 800,000 feet of heavy timber more or less on that portion of my land * * *."   The plaintiff's prayer in the bill was that J. B. Gray and O. M. King be enjoined "from cutting timber and trees on my above said land * * * and * * * from trespassing on my said land in any manner whatsoever."

The defendants in that proceeding filed a short answer denying each and every allegation set forth in the bill.   * * *   [T]he chancellor entered the following decree:

"* * * [T]he Court having heard the evidence, being of the opinion that the complainant has failed to establish his ownership of the property, and having failed to prove that either of the defendants have cut any timber from the complainant's land, and being of the opinion that the complainant is not entitled to any of the relief prayed for, doth adjudge, order and decree that the complainant's petition for a temporary injunction be and the same is hereby denied and this cause is dismissed * * *."

Charles C. Patterson, hereinafter designated "plaintiff," contends that the judgment of the trial court sustaining the pleas of *res judicata* is erroneous * * *: (1) the court of equity in the former proceeding had no jurisdiction to try title to plaintiff's land; (2) even if it had jurisdiction, it did not pass upon the merits of the cause * * *.

The general rule is that in the absence of some peculiar equity arising out of the conduct, situation or relation of the parties, a court of equity is without jurisdiction to settle disputes as to title and boundaries of land.   But where the act done, or threatened to be done, would be destructive of the substance of the estate, or would result in irreparable injury, a court of equity will assume jurisdiction, restrain the perpetration of the wrong and prevent the injury.   Equity having taken jurisdiction, it will then decide the whole controversy, though the issues are legal in their nature and are capable of being tried by a court of law.   *   *   *

Plaintiff's bill   *   *   *   contained the essential averment that plaintiff owned the land, and referred to the deeds by which he claims to have acquired title.   The answer denied this allegation.   Each side was given full opportunity to introduce, and did introduce, evidence on this issue of fact.   The court did more than merely deny the injunction.   It disposed of the controversy on its merits and dismissed the case at the cost of plaintiff.   *   *   *

"A judgment in a case involving two or more issues is treated as conclusive upon all of them, where all are decided in favor of the same litigant and the judgment rests upon them jointly, since the decision of one issue in such case is no less necessary or material than the decision of the other."   30 Am. Jur., Judgments, sec. 185, p. 931.

*   *   *

The plaintiff, in the chancery cause, excepted to the entry of the decree, but took no appeal therefrom.   Whether the decree was or was not supported by the evidence is immaterial.   *   *   *

In the case at bar the equity suit was not dismissed without prejudice. The adjudication was positive.   If the plaintiff had proved that he owned the land, doubtless the court would have performed its duty, issued the injunction and restrained the defendants from cutting and removing the timber   *   *   *.

While the court did not declare that title to the land was in the defendants, or their privies, it did declare that plaintiff was not the owner.   *   *   *

Plaintiff does not allege in his motion for judgment, nor does he contend, that he has acquired any additional right, title or interest in the land since the entry of the final decree against him.

*   *   *

Affirmed.

BUCHANAN, Justice (dissenting).   The opinion of the court in this case, as I believe, extends the doctrine of *res judicata* farther than has been done before and farther than should be done now.   According to the opinion the unsuccessful effort of Patterson at a former time to obtain a temporary injunction to keep Gray and King from cutting timber on land claimed by Patterson   *   *   *   has resulted in his losing all title he then had   *   *   *.

*   *   *   [T]he decree [did not] adjudicate that Patterson had no title. The decree recited that he had "failed to establish his ownership" and "failed to prove that either of the defendants have cut any timber from the complainant's land."   The failure of the complainant that resulted in the denial of his requested relief was a failure to introduce evidence sufficient to support his allegations.   There were only two things alleged—one that he owned the land,

the other that Gray and King were cutting his timber. There is nothing to show what evidence he introduced or why the court held it insufficient. He had not asked the court to adjudicate that he had the true title against all other persons. He merely asked for a temporary injunction to restrain trespassers. Had the relief he asked been granted, it would not have established his title against the defendants in the present motion for judgment. Certainly the denial of the relief he sought did not establish title in any of these defendants, none of whom submitted any claim of title for adjudication in the chancery suit. If the present defendants would not have been barred in the present suit by the granting of an injunction in the chancery suit, then the plaintiff in the present action ought not to be barred by his failure to obtain an injunction in the chancery suit.

* * *

MILLER and WHITTLE, JJ., join in this dissent.

NOTES AND QUESTIONS

1. What policy objectives are served by the rule applied in the principal case? What arguments might be advanced for the contrary rule—that when a prior judgment rests on two or more alternative and independent grounds it is not conclusive as to any of the fact issues that necessarily were found to establish them? See Halpern v. Schwartz, 426 F.2d 102 (2d Cir.1970).

2. Plaintiff brings an action against defendant for personal injuries arising out of a collision of their automobiles. Defendant answers, denying negligence and affirmatively pleading contributory negligence. Evidence is presented on both issues, and the jury returns a special verdict, finding for defendant on both issues. If defendant subsequently sues plaintiff for her injuries arising out of the same accident, may she rely upon the first judgment as establishing any part of her case? How does this question differ from the question in Note 1, p. 1109, supra? Does this difference justify a difference in result? *Compare Restatement, Judgments* § 68, comments *l, n* (1942), *with Restatement (Second), Judgments* § 68, comments *g, i* (Tent.Draft No. 1, 1973); *cf. United States v. Title Ins. & Trust Co.,* p. 1067, supra.

3. Plaintiff-landlord successfully brings suit for the possession of an apartment because of defendant-tenant's nonpayment of $275 in rent. Plaintiff-landlord then institutes an action for the unpaid rent. Should defendant-tenant be collaterally estopped from denying that the rent actually is due? Does it make any difference that the defendant-tenant did not appear in the first action and that it ended in a default judgment? What if the suit for possession had been a summary action in which the court had no jurisdiction to award a judgment for the unpaid rent? See Tutt v. Doby, 459 F.2d 1195 (D.C.Cir.1972).

2. LIMITS ON THE SCOPE OF COLLATERAL ESTOPPEL

A. SUBSTANTIVE POLICIES AS RESTRICTIONS ON THE APPLICATION OF COLLATERAL ESTOPPEL

LYONS v. WESTINGHOUSE ELECTRIC CORP.

United States Court of Appeals, Second Circuit, 1955.
222 F.2d 184.
Certiorari denied 350 U.S. 825, 76 S.Ct. 52, 100 L.Ed. 737.

L. HAND, Circuit Judge. [Westinghouse had sued plaintiffs in a state court for an accounting on a contract the latter had made with Westinghouse to act as its agents for the sale of electric lamps. Plaintiffs pleaded as one defense to this earlier action that Westinghouse and General Electric had conspired to restrain competition in the marketing of such lamps. After trial the state court directed plaintiffs to account, finding *inter alia*, that the "defense of illegality, based upon violation of antitrust laws, has neither been sustained nor established." Plaintiffs appealed from the state court decision.

After the state action was commenced, but before trial, plaintiffs brought this action in a federal court for damages for violation of the antitrust laws. After the decision in the state trial court, Westinghouse moved for a stay of the proceedings in federal court pending the disposition of the state appeal, and the motion was granted. Plaintiffs appealed and in the alternative asked the court to issue a writ of mandamus directing the trial judge to vacate the stay. For that portion of the opinion dealing with mandamus and appeal, see p. 1028, supra.]

    *   *   *

We think that the state court had undoubted jurisdiction, notwithstanding § 15 of Title 15, U.S.C.A., to decide the merits of the first defence, although it involved exactly the same claim as that pleaded in the first count of the action at bar. * * * [I]n Bruce's Juices v. American Can Co., 330 U.S. 743, at page 755, 67 S.Ct. 1015, at page 1020, 91 L.Ed. 1219, in overruling the buyer's defence to the seller's action to recover for goods sold at prices illegally discriminatory under the Robinson-Patman Act, the Court said of the Anti-Trust Act "that where a suit is based upon an agreement * * * which has as its object and effect accomplishment of illegal ends which would be consummated by the judgment sought, the Court will entertain the defense that the contract in suit is illegal under the express provision of that statute. * * * But when the contract sued upon is not intrinsically illegal, the Court has refused to allow property to be obtained under a contract of sale without enforcing the duty to pay for it because of violations of the Sherman Act not inhering in the particular contract in suit."

The upshot of these decisions, if we apprehend them right, is that, if the conspiracy inheres in the contract in suit by a conspirator against a non-conspirator, the conspiracy is a defence, but not otherwise. It is impossible to import any exact boundaries into that word; and we shall not attempt to do so; but, whatever may be its limits, it appears to us that, when a conspirator seeks to enforce a contract between himself and one of his "agents," whom he has employed to carry out the purposes of the illegal enterprise, the conspiracy must "inhere" in the contract. The "agent" is a co-operator with him in his illegal venture, unlike the buyer of the goods monopolized, who has not joined in the undertaking and is therefore not an abettor. * * * Therefore, we think that the state court had jurisdiction to pass upon whether the defence, as alleged, was proved.

It does not, however, follow that final judgment in the state action when entered will be an estoppel in the case at bar. That would be true, we agree, except for § 15 of Title 15, U.S.C.A., because, although the finding that there was no conspiracy involved questions of law as well as questions of fact, it was nevertheless of a kind that courts treat as estoppels. Thus the inquiry comes down to whether, when Congress gave exclusive jurisdiction to the district court over wrongs committed under the Anti-Trust Acts, it only meant that the "person who shall be injured" must sue in the district court to recover damages; or whether it also meant that the district court must have unfettered power to decide the claim, regardless of the findings of any other courts, even when these were essential to the decision of actions over which their jurisdiction was unquestioned. A priori either reading seems permissible, and the decisions give an uncertain answer. The only case that we have discovered in the Supreme Court is Becher v. Contoure Laboratories, Inc., 279 U.S. 388, 49 S.Ct. 356, 73 L.Ed. 752. The action was by the patentee, Becher, for the infringement of his patent; and the defendant was the corporate assignee of the rights of one, Oppenheimer, who had recovered judgment against Becher in a state court, and whose claim had been that the information on which Becher procured the grant of his patent, he had got from Oppenheimer in a confidential relation. Oppenheimer's assignee pleaded the judgment of the state court as a defence, and it was held to be a good estoppel, although the consequence was to invalidate Becher's patent. The meat of the opinion is this, 279 U.S. at page 391, 49 S.Ct. at page 375: "Again, even if the logical conclusion from the establishing of Oppenheimer's claim is that Becher's patent is void, that is not the effect of the judgment. Establishing a fact and giving a specific effect to it by judgment are quite distinct." That looks as though the distinction were between the finding of one of the constituent facts that together make up a claim and the entire congeries of such facts, taken as a unit; an estoppel is good as to the first but not as to the second. It is possible to read § 71 [3] of the Restatement of Judgments with such a limitation: that is to say if "matter" be

---

[3] "Where a court has incidentally determined a matter which it would have had no jurisdiction to determine in an action brought directly to determine it, the judgment is not conclusive in a subsequent action brought to determine the matter directly."

read as all the "operative" facts that together make up a right.   Comment (c)
would also be consonant with this in saying that the finding of a state court, as
a defence to an action on a note, that a patent given as its consideration was invalid, is not an estoppel in an action in a federal court brought upon the patent.
*   *   *   In Loomis v. Loomis, 288 N.Y. 222, 42 N.E.2d 495, 147 A.L.R.
183, the Court of Appeals decided that a finding by the "Family Court"—a division of an inferior court in New York City—that the parties had been divorced did not operate as an estoppel in an action in the Supreme Court for a
declaratory judgment that the divorce was void.   On the other hand in Gera-
cey, Inc., v. Hoover, 77 U.S.App.D.C. 55, 133 F.2d 25, 147 A.L.R. 185, a majority of the Court of Appeals for the District of Columbia held that the judgment of the Municipal Court of the District was an estoppel in an action in the
District Court in the following situation.   The defendant, a landlord, had sued
the plaintiff, his tenant, in the Municipal Court to recover rent, and the plaintiff had pleaded as a set-off that the landlord had damaged his chattels in an
amount greater than the Municipal Court's monetary jurisdiction.   The Municipal Court dismissed the set-off on the merits, and the Court of Appeals held
the finding to be estoppel in an action by the tenant to recover damages in the
full amount.   *   *   *

It is possible that decisions like Loomis v. Loomis   *   *   *   and Gera-
cey, Inc. v. Hoover   *   *   *   depended upon the relative authority of the
court that made the findings compared with that of the court which tried the
cause.   *   *   *   In short, it appears to us that the doctrine, like so many others in the law, must be treated as a compromise between two conflicting interests: the convenience of avoiding a multiplicity of suits and the adequacy of
the remedies afforded for conceded wrongs.

In the case at bar it appears to us that the grant to the district courts of exclusive jurisdiction over the action for treble damages should be taken to imply
an immunity of their decisions from any prejudgment elsewhere; at least on
occasions, like those at bar, where the putative estoppel includes the whole nexus of facts that makes up the wrong.   The remedy provided is not solely civil;
two thirds of the recovery is not remedial and inevitably presupposes a punitive
purpose.   *   *   *   There are sound reasons for assuming that such recovery
should not be subject to the determinations of state courts.   It was part of the
effort to prevent monopoly and restraints of commerce; and it was natural to
wish it to be uniformly administered, being national in scope.   Relief by certiorari would still exist, it is true; but that is a remedy burdensome to litigants
and to the Supreme Court, already charged with enough.   Obviously, an administration of the Acts, at once effective and uniform, would best be accomplished by an untrammeled jurisdiction of the federal courts.

Nor is there anything inconsistent with this in allowing violations of the
Acts to be raised as valid defences to actions brought in state courts upon a
claim against third persons, if it involves a partial enforcement of an undertaking itself forbidden.   It is appropriate to the underlying purpose of the Acts
that such claims shall not succeed   *   *   *.   For these reasons we think that

the situation is one where the delay and expense of a double trial of the same issue, do not balance the importance of an uncommitted enforcement of the remedy provided in § 15.

* * *

[The opinion of MEDINA, Circuit Judge, dissenting in part, is omitted.]

NOTES AND QUESTIONS

1. Plaintiff brought suit in a state court for royalty payments on wheels it alleged defendant had produced under a patent license from plaintiff; the state court found for defendant, holding that the particular wheels were not within the scope of plaintiff's patent. Subsequently, plaintiff brought an action for patent infringement against defendant in a federal court, which held that plaintiff was estopped by the finding in the state court that defendant's wheels were not covered by the patent. On appeal, in VANDERVEER v. ERIE MALLEABLE IRON CO., 238 F.2d 510, 513–15 (3d Cir.1956), the district court's decision was affirmed:

> Although the bringing of actions arising under the patent laws is admittedly restricted to the federal courts it has long been established that actions brought to enforce contracts of which a patent is the subject must in the absence of diversity of citizenship be brought in the state courts. The Supreme Court has held that a state court is empowered to determine questions, as distinguished from cases, arising under the patent laws, * * * and the court has given no indication that the conclusive effect between the parties of the determination of these questions is to be limited to the state courts. Indeed the Supreme Court indicated just the contrary in Becher v. Contoure Laboratories * * *.

> Likewise the contention cannot be accepted that res judicata is not applicable because the question as to which the estoppel is raised is one of law. It may be conceded that the question of construing the claims of a patent is one of law in the sense that, as in the case of other integrated documents, it is a question for the court and not the jury. But the question of infringement involves also questions of fact, such as the nature of the devices alleged to infringe and whether in fact they are within the patent claims as the court has construed them. Thus the finding of infringement is a finding of fact, of the type sometimes called a conclusion of ultimate fact, as to which the doctrine of res judicata is applicable. Indeed * * * even the determination of a pure question of law is ordinarily treated as res judicata in a later suit between the same parties arising out of the same subject matter if no unjust result will follow.

Is *Vanderveer* consistent with *Lyons*? Can the cases be distinguished on the basis of Judge Hand's explanation of *Becher*? Are there reasons why a state court's decision with respect to a patent should be followed, but its decision with respect to an antitrust violation should not? Is it relevant that if a state court holds a patent valid, there may be many others, not bound by the decision, who can challenge the validity of the patent in a federal court, while if the state court holds there is no antitrust violation, the only private party with standing to complain about defendant's conduct may be estopped?

If the state court holds the patent invalid, will this result bind the patentee in a subsequent suit against other persons who are not parties to the original suit? *Cf.* Note 3, p. 1151, infra; *Bernhard v. Bank of America Nat. Trust & Sav. Ass'n,* p. 1138, infra. If the state court holds the patent valid, and in a subsequent action in a federal court involving another party the patent is held invalid, is the losing party in the state action still bound? *Cf. Commissioner of Internal Revenue v. Sunnen,* immediately following these notes.

2. See generally Scott, *Collateral Estoppel by Judgment,* 56 Harv.L.Rev. 1 (1942); Annot., 83 A.L.R.2d 977 (1962). Should a distinction be drawn between those cases in which the prior action was in a court of general jurisdiction, as in *Lyons* and *Vanderveer,* and those cases in which the prior action was in a court of inferior jurisdiction? See Comment, *Article 2226a: Its Effect on Res Judicata and Collateral Estoppel,* 17 Baylor L.Rev. 221 (1965).

COMMISSIONER OF INTERNAL REVENUE v. SUNNEN

Supreme Court of the United States, 1948.
333 U.S. 591, 68 S.Ct. 715, 92 L.Ed. 898.

Certiorari to the United States Circuit Court of Appeals for the Eighth Circuit.

Mr. Justice MURPHY delivered the opinion of the Court.

[Under a series of agreements, a taxpayer had licensed a corporation, which he controlled, to use his patents in exchange for payment of a 10% royalty. At various times, the taxpayer assigned his interest in these agreements to his wife without consideration. Income from these agreements was reported on her income-tax returns, and these taxes were paid. The Commissioner contended that the income was taxable to the taxpayer himself and a deficiency was assessed against him.]

* * * [T]he Tax Court held that, with one exception, all the royalties paid to the wife from 1937 to 1941 were part of the taxable income of the taxpayer. * * * The one exception concerned the royalties of $4,881.35 paid in 1937 under the 1928 agreement. In an earlier proceeding in 1935, the Board of Tax Appeals dealt with the taxpayer's income tax liability for the years 1929–1931; it concluded that he was not taxable on the royalties paid to his wife during those years under the 1928 license agreement. This prior determination by the Board caused the Tax Court to apply the principle of *res judicata* to bar a different result as to the royalties paid pursuant to the same agreement during 1937.

The Tax Court's decision was affirmed in part and reversed in part by the Eighth Circuit Court of Appeals. * * * Approval was given to the Tax

Court's application of the *res judicata* doctrine to exclude from the taxpayer's income the $4,881.35 in royalties paid in 1937 under the 1928 agreement. But to the extent that the taxpayer had been held taxable on royalties paid to his wife during the taxable years of 1937–1941, the decision was reversed on the theory that such payments were not income to him. * * *

If the doctrine of *res judicata* is properly applicable so that all the royalty payments made during 1937–1941 are governed by the prior decision of the Board of Tax Appeals, the case may be disposed of without reaching the merits of the controversy. * * *

* * * [The concepts of res judicata and collateral estoppel] are applicable in the federal income tax field. Income taxes are levied on an annual basis. Each year is the origin of a new liability and of a separate cause of action. Thus if a claim of liability or non-liability relating to a particular tax year is litigated, a judgment on the merits is *res judicata* as to any subsequent proceeding involving the same claim and the same tax year. But if the later proceeding is concerned with a similar or unlike claim relating to a different tax year, the prior judgment acts as a collateral estoppel only as to those matters in the second proceeding which were actually presented and determined in the first suit. Collateral estoppel operates, in other words, to relieve the government and the taxpayer of "redundant litigation of the identical question of the statute's application to the taxpayer's status." Tait v. Western Md. R. Co., 289 U.S. 620, 624, 53 S.Ct. 706, 707, 77 L.Ed. 1405.

But collateral estoppel is a doctrine capable of being applied so as to avoid an undue disparity in the impact of income tax liability. A taxpayer may secure a judicial determination of a particular tax matter, a matter which may recur without substantial variation for some years thereafter. But a subsequent modification of the significant facts or a change or development in the controlling legal principles may make that determination obsolete or erroneous, at least for future purposes. If such a determination is then perpetuated each succeeding year as to the taxpayer involved in the original litigation, he is accorded a tax treatment different from that given to other taxpayers of the same class. As a result, there are inequalities in the administration of the revenue laws, discriminatory distinctions in tax liability, and a fertile basis for litigious confusion. * * * Such consequences, however, are neither necessitated nor justified by the principle of collateral estoppel. That principle is designed to prevent repetitious lawsuits over matters which have once been decided and which have remained substantially static, factually and legally. It is not meant to create vested rights in decisions that have become obsolete or erroneous with time, thereby causing inequities among taxpayers.

And so where two cases involve income taxes in different taxable years, collateral estoppel must be used with its limitations carefully in mind so as to avoid injustice. It must be confined to situations where the matter raised in the second suit is identical in all respects with that decided in the first proceeding and where the controlling facts and applicable legal rules remain unchanged. * * * As demonstrated by Blair v. Commissioner, 300 U.S. 5, 9, 57 S.Ct.

330, 331, 81 L.Ed. 465, a judicial declaration intervening between the two proceedings may so change the legal atmosphere as to render the rule of collateral estoppel inapplicable. But the intervening decision need not necessarily be that of a state court, as it was in the Blair case. While such a state court decision may be considered as having changed the facts for federal tax litigation purposes, a modification or growth in legal principles as enunciated in intervening decisions of this Court may also effect a significant change in the situation. Tax inequality can result as readily from neglecting legal modulations by this Court as from disregarding factual changes wrought by state courts. In either event, the supervening decision cannot justly be ignored by blind reliance upon the rule of collateral estoppel. * * * It naturally follows that an interposed alteration in the pertinent statutory provisions or Treasury regulations can make the use of that rule unwarranted. * * *

Of course, where a question of fact essential to the judgment is actually litigated and determined in the first tax proceeding, the parties are bound by that determination in a subsequent proceeding even though the cause of action is different. * * * And if the very same facts and no others are involved in the second case, a case relating to a different tax year, the prior judgment will be conclusive as to the same legal issues which appear, assuming no intervening doctrinal change. But if the relevant facts in the two cases are separable, even though they be similar or identical, collateral estoppel does not govern the legal issues which recur in the second case. Thus the second proceeding may involve an instrument or transaction identical with, but in a form separable from, the one dealt with in the first proceeding. In that situation, a court is free in the second proceeding to make an independent examination of the legal matters at issue. It may then reach a different result or, if consistency in decision is considered just and desirable, reliance may be placed upon the ordinary rule of *stare decisis*. Before a party can invoke the collateral estoppel doctrine in these circumstances, the legal matter raised in the second proceeding must involve the same set of events or documents and the same bundle of legal principles that contributed to the rendering of the first judgment. * * *

It is readily apparent in this case that the royalty payments growing out of the license contracts which were not involved in the earlier action before the Board of Tax Appeals and which concerned different tax years are free from the effects of the collateral estoppel doctrine. That is true even though those contracts are identical in all important respects with the 1928 contract, the only one that was before the Board, and even though the issue as to those contracts is the same as that raised by the 1928 contract. * * *

A more difficult problem is posed as to the $4,881.35 in royalties paid to the taxpayer's wife in 1937 under the 1928 contract. Here there is complete identity of facts, issues and parties as between the earlier Board proceeding and the instant one. The Commissioner claims, however, that legal principles developed in various intervening decisions of this Court have made plain the error of the Board's conclusion in the earlier proceeding, thus creating a situation like that involved in Blair v. Commissioner, supra. * * *

The principles which have　＊　＊　＊　been recognized and developed by　＊　＊　＊　[Helvering v. Clifford, 309 U.S. 331, 60 S.Ct. 554, 84 L.Ed. 788 (1940), and Helvering v. Horst, 311 U.S. 112, 61 S.Ct. 144, 85 L. Ed. 75, 131 A.L.R. 655 (1940)] are directly applicable to the transfer of patent license contracts between members of the same family. They are guideposts for those who seek to determine in a particular instance whether such an assignor retains sufficient control over the assigned contracts or over the receipt of income by the assignee to make it fair to impose income tax liability on him.

Moreover, the clarification and growth of these principles through the Clifford-Horst line of cases constitute, in our opinion, a sufficient change in the legal climate to render inapplicable in the instant proceeding, the doctrine of collateral estoppel relative to the assignment of the 1928 contract. True, these cases did not originate the concept that an assignor is taxable if he retains control over the assigned property or power to defeat the receipt of income by the assignee. But they gave much added emphasis and substance to that concept, making it more suited to meet the "attenuated subtleties" created by taxpayers. So substantial was the amplification of this concept as to justify a reconsideration of earlier Tax Court decisions reached without the benefit of the expanded notions, decisions which are now sought to be perpetuated regardless of their present correctness. Thus in the earlier litigation in 1935, the Board of Tax Appeals was unable to bring to bear on the assignment of the 1928 contract the full breadth of the ideas enunciated in the Clifford-Horst series of cases. And, as we shall see, a proper application of the principles as there developed might well have produced a different result, such as was reached by the Tax Court in this case in regard to the assignments of the other contracts. Under those circumstances collateral estoppel should not have been used by the Tax Court in the instant proceeding to perpetuate the 1935 viewpoint of the assignment.

＊　＊　＊

The judgment below must therefore be reversed and the case remanded for such further proceedings as may be necessary in light of this opinion.

Reversed.

Mr. Justice FRANKFURTER and Mr. Justice JACKSON believe the judgment of the Tax Court is based on substantial evidence and is consistent with the law, and would affirm that judgment　＊　＊　＊.

NOTES AND QUESTIONS

1. In *Tait v. Western Maryland Ry.*, which is relied upon in the principal case, the Supreme Court had said (289 U.S. at 624, 53 S.Ct. at 707, 77 L.Ed. at 1408):

> ＊　＊　＊　[T]he scheme of the Revenue Acts is an imposition of tax for annual periods, and the exaction for one year is distinct from that for any other. But it does not follow that Congress in adopting this system meant to deprive the government and the taxpayer of relief from redundant litigation of the identical question of the statute's application to the taxpayer's status.

This court has repeatedly applied the doctrine of *res judicata* in actions concerning state taxes, holding the parties concluded in a suit for one year's tax as to the right or question adjudicated by a former judgment respecting the tax of an earlier year. * * * The public policy upon which the rule is founded has been said to apply with equal force to the sovereign's demand and the claims of private citizens. Alteration of the law in this respect is a matter for the law-making body rather than the courts. * * * It cannot be supposed that Congress was oblivious of the scope of the doctrine, and in the absence of a clear declaration of such purpose, we will not infer from the annual nature of the exaction an intent to abolish the rule in this class of cases.

Is this statement consistent with *Sunnen*?

2. In UNITED STATES v. STONE & DOWNER CO., 274 U.S. 225, 47 S.Ct. 616, 71 L.Ed. 1013 (1927), the Supreme Court held that an earlier decision of the Court of Customs Appeals holding certain types of wool to fall into a duty-free classification did not bind the Government in a subsequent effort to collect duties on similar wool imported by the prevailing party in the first proceeding. In *Tait* this decision is explained as follows (289 U.S. at 625, 53 S.Ct. at 707–08, 77 L.Ed. at 1408–09):

The Court of Customs Appeals had from its organization consistently held the rule of *res judicata* inapplicable to its decisions as to the classification of imported commodities for the imposition of tariff duties. * * * After Congress granted a right of review we were urged to overturn the practice and to apply the doctrine of estoppel by judgment in this class of litigation. The court refused to do so, not only because of the settled practice, but also on account of the unique character of the questions presented under the tariff acts. The ruling was justified by considerations which are absent in tax litigation * * *.

What are these considerations?

3. See generally Griswold, *Res Judicata in Federal Tax Cases*, 46 Yale L.J. 1320 (1937).

RACHAL v. HILL, 435 F.2d 59, 63–64 (5th Cir.1970), certiorari denied 403 U.S. 904, 91 S.Ct. 2203, 29 L.Ed.2d 680 (1971). In a proceeding brought by the SEC, the appellants, Rachal and Hunnicutt, had been permanently enjoined from engaging in certain "acts and practices" with regard to the stock of two corporations that were found to violate the federal securities laws. The order issued following a trial without a jury. Hill then brought an action for damages on behalf of himself and his wife, as a representative of all of the stockholders of the corporations, and, derivatively, on behalf of the corporations. Hill successfully moved for summary judgment on the ground that Rachal and Hunnicutt were collaterally estopped from denying that their conduct violated federal law since the issues presented were identical to those in the SEC proceeding. After rejecting appellants' mutuality-of-estoppel argument, see pp. 1134–52, infra, the Fifth Circuit reversed on the following ground:

It is clear that had it not been for the prior adverse determination of the issue of liability by the district court sitting without a jury in the S.E.C. injunction proceeding, the appellants would have been, without question, entitled to a trial by jury as a matter of right under the Seventh Amendment to the United States Constitution and Rule 38, Federal Rules of Civil Procedure. The central question thus presented is whether a litigant can lose his constitutional right to a trial by jury by estoppel when the issue to be decided has been adjudicated adversely to him in a prior proceeding at which there was no right to a trial by jury and his present adversary was not a party.

Although we find no case directly in point, there is a plethora of analogous cases holding under the Seventh Amendment that whenever an equitable claim and a legal claim, the resolution of which depend on the determination of a common factual issue, are joined in the same action, the common issue must be first tried before a jury, even if the equitable claim was brought first or if the legal claim is merely incidental to the equitable. * * * [At this point the court described and quoted from the Supreme Court's opinion in *Beacon Theatres, Inc. v. Westover,* p. 807, supra.]

In light of the great respect afforded in *Beacon Theatres,* supra, and its progeny, for a litigant's right to have legal claims tried first before a jury in an action where legal and equitable claims are joined, it would be anomalous to hold that the appellants have lost their right to a trial by jury on the issue of whether they are liable to respond in damages for violations of the security laws because of a prior adverse determination by the district court of the same issue in an action in which their present adversary was not a party and which arose in a different context from the present action. *Beacon Theatres,* supra, makes it clear that had Hill been a party plaintiff in the S.E.C. injunction action and there presented his claim for damages, the appellants would have received a jury trial on the issue of liability. It hardly makes sense that Hill can now assume a position superior to that to which he would have been entitled if he had been a party to the prior action. Accordingly, we hold that the application of the doctrine of collateral estoppel was not appropriate in view of the particular circumstances presented by this case and that the district court erred in granting summary judgment on the issue of liability.

NOTES AND QUESTIONS

1. For an interesting, and critical, comment on the *Rachal* case, see Shapiro & Coquillette, *The Fetish of Jury Trial in Civil Cases: A Comment on Rachal v. Hill,* 85 Harv.L.Rev. 442 (1971). See also *Restatement (Second), Judgments* § 68, comment *d* (Tent.Draft No. 1, 1973).

2. Should collateral estoppel apply when the first proceeding is before an administrative agency? If so, should any limitations be imposed on its application? See, e. g., Paramount Transp. Systems v. Chauffeurs, Teamsters & Helpers, Local 150, 436 F.2d 1064 (9th Cir.1971).

B. THE ISSUES AFFECTED BY COLLATERAL ESTOPPEL— MEDIATE AND ULTIMATE FACTS

KING, ADMINISTRATOR v. CHASE

Superior Court of Judicature of New Hampshire, 1844.
15 N.H. 9, 41 Am.Dec. 675.

Trespass, for taking and carrying away thirty tons of hay, five tons of corn fodder, and other articles * * *.

On the 27th of June, 1841, the plaintiff took a mortgage from Oliver King, conveying to him all the crops then growing on a certain farm * * * which included the property in question, and also a large quantity of oats growing on said farm, to secure the payment of a note to the testator, executed by said Oliver * * *.

The defendant was [a] sheriff * * * and one James C. Stebbins was his deputy, and, as such deputy, on the 17th day of August took and carried away the property in question and sold it at auction.

The defendant offered evidence tending to show that Oliver King was justly indebted to one George H. Ingersoll in a large sum, who * * * sued out a writ of attachment against him * * * and that Stebbins by virtue thereof attached the property in question, with the oats, as the property of Oliver; and that the conveyance to the plaintiff was fraudulent and void as against creditors.

The defendant contended that the money for which the note described in the mortgage was given, was a gift by the father to Oliver, as an advancement out of his estate, and never to be repaid, and that the note was taken merely as evidence of the sum advanced, and not as evidence of a debt to be repaid, and that the plaintiff knew these facts.

He gave in evidence the record of an action of trover, in which the plaintiff had sued Stebbins for taking the oats described in the same mortgage, and in which there was a verdict and judgment for the defendant * * *.

He then offered parol testimony tending to show that at the trial of the action, the only question submitted to the jury, and by them determined, was, whether the mortgage in question was fraudulent, and that it was so found by the jury. The witness by whom this fact was proved was one of the jurors who tried the case. To this evidence the plaintiff objected * * * but the judge admitted the testimony.

The court instructed the jury that as the deputy, Stebbins, was responsible over to the defendant, they might be considered the same parties in interest; and if the jury were satisfied that the mortgage had been once passed on by another jury, in an action between this plaintiff and Stebbins, and determined to be fraudulent, and that verdict was still in force, they might consider that fact as evidence, though not conclusive, that the mortgage was fraudulent.

The jury returned a verdict for the defendant, and the plaintiff moved for a new trial.

PARKER, C. J. * * *

* * * [T]he judgment is * * * conclusive only upon the matter which was directly in issue upon the former trial; and the question arises, what is to be understood by the "matter in issue." *The Dutchess of Kingston's Case*, 11 State Trials 261, furnishes the rule. It has been repeatedly sanctioned.

"From the variety of cases (said Lord Chief Justice DeGrey, in that case,) relative to judgments being given in evidence in civil suits, these two deductions seem to follow as generally true; first, that the judgment of a court of concurrent jurisdiction, directly upon the point, is as a plea, a bar; or, as evidence, conclusive between the same parties, upon the same matter, directly in question in another court; secondly, that the judgment of a court of exclusive jurisdiction directly upon the point, is, in like manner, conclusive upon the same matter, between the same parties, coming incidentally in question in another court, for a different purpose. But neither the judgment of a concurrent or exclusive jurisdiction is evidence of any matter which came collaterally in question, though within their jurisdiction; nor of any matter incidently cognizable; nor of any matter to be inferred by argument from the judgment."
* * *

All are agreed in the rule, but the difficulty lies, in its application, in determining what is meant by a judgment directly upon the point. * * *

Any fact attempted to be established by evidence, and controverted by the adverse party, may be said to be in issue, in one sense. As, for instance, in an action of trespass, if the defendant alleges and attempts to prove that he was in another place than that where the plaintiff's evidence would show him to have been at a certain time, it may be said that this controverted fact is a matter in issue between the parties. This may be tried, and may be the only matter put in controversy by the evidence of the parties.

But this is not the matter in issue, within the meaning of the rule.

It is that matter upon which the plaintiff proceeds by his action, and which the defendant controverts by his pleadings, which is in issue.

The declaration and pleadings may show specifically what this is, or they may not. If they do not, the party may adduce other evidence to show what was in issue, and thereby make the pleadings as if they were special.

But facts offered in evidence to establish the matters in issue, are not themselves in issue, within the meaning of the rule, although they may be controverted on the trial.   Deeds which are merely offered in evidence are not in issue, even if their authenticity be denied.

When a deed is merely offered as evidence to show a title, whether in a real or personal action, there is no *non est factum* involved in the matters put in issue by the plea of *nul disseizin*, or not guilty, which makes the execution of that deed a matter in issue in the case, notwithstanding the jury may be required to pass upon the fact of its execution.   The verdict and judgment do not establish that fact the one way or the other, so that the finding is evidence. The title is in issue.   The deed comes in controversy directly, in one sense; that is, in the course taken by the evidence it is direct and essential.   But in another sense it is incidental, and collateral.   It is not a matter necessary, of itself, to the finding of the issue.   *   *   *

This may be illustrated by the case before us.   Laying out of consideration the question whether this is a case between the same parties, the former action was for taking certain oats.   The matter in issue was the title to the oats, and the conversion by the defendant in that case.   Upon that the jury passed. They found that the plaintiff had no title, or that the defendant did not convert them, which may be involved in the first.

It may be shown by parol evidence, if necessary, upon which ground the verdict proceeded, and it appears in this case that they found the plaintiff had no title.   The conversion by the defendant in that case was not denied, if the plaintiff had title.

That matter then is settled.   The verdict and judgment may be given in evidence in another action for the oats, between those parties, and is conclusive.   But that is the extent of what was in issue.

It appears that the title set up in that case was by a mortgage.   In finding that the plaintiff had no title, the jury must have been of opinion that the mortgage was fraudulent.   It is contended that this was in issue and the only matter in issue.

But this was only a controversy about a particular matter of evidence, upon which the plaintiff then relied to show title.   If that was the only matter in issue, the plaintiff might bring another suit for those oats, against the same defendant, and, relying upon some other title than that mortgage, try the title to the oats over again.   Can he do so?   Clearly not; and the reason is, that it is his title which has been tried, and he is concluded.

The title, however, which has been tried, was only his title to the oats.

The question whether the mortgage was fraudulent came up only incidentally, by reason of his relying on that as his title.   *   *   *

And while the finding is conclusive on the question of his title to the oats, it is neither conclusive, nor evidence, upon any thing else, because nothing else was in issue.

*   *   *

In this case there might be no great mischief, if the rule was held to apply to the matter in evidence, instead of that in issue. The controversy in the former case seems to have been simple. If the parties were the same, the plaintiff might not complain of injustice if it were held that he is concluded by the finding of the former jury * * *.

But the principle applicable here must be applied in other cases, where the matters in evidence are more complicated, and where it would admit of more doubt how the jury regarded the evidence, and what facts they actually found.

The rule then would have to be confined to what the jury must necessarily have found, which would still shut out as evidence a great many matters actually tried, and as clearly found as any thing found in relation to this mortgage; or it must in many cases be left to the testimony of the jurors what facts they did find, which, when applied to all the controverted matters of evidence arising in a cause, might lead to great uncertainty and confusion.

On the other hand, it would be great injustice to the defendant in the former action to hold that the matter in question was whether the plaintiff's mortgage was fraudulent or not; that this was tried in that case, and not his title generally; and that the plaintiff might commence another suit for the oats and set up another title, because no other title except the mortgage title had been tried.

* * *

Verdict set aside, and new trial.

NOTES AND QUESTIONS

1. Although the rule stated in *King* has not been expressly rejected by many other courts, there certainly are a very great number of cases that would be difficult to reconcile with Chief Justice Parker's opinion. See Annot., 142 A.L.R. 1243 (1943). The relative infrequency of express rejection may result from the close nature of the question of classification in many cases and from the belief that it is not necessary to explain why a fact clearly established in one action should not be relitigated in a second. Some courts, while expressly stating that a fact was not an ultimate fact in the earlier action, nonetheless have held it collateral estoppel in a second suit. E. g., Hanna v. Read, 102 Ill. 596, 40 Am.Rep. 608 (1882) (issue of insanity established in action to set aside deed collateral estoppel in subsequent action involving another deed signed at the same time). See also Dobbins v. Title Guar. & Trust Co., 22 Cal.2d 64, 136 P.2d 572 (1943).

2. Wrongful-death actions for the deaths of A and B were brought in New Hampshire against C who was driving the automobile in which they were killed. The insurer of the car's owner, D, refused to defend on the ground that C was not driving the car with the permission of D. Plaintiffs brought an action in New Hampshire seeking a declaration that it was the insurer's duty to defend; the trial court found that D's son to whom D had lent the car had permitted A and B to use the car only on the condition that C not go with them; on these facts, the New Hampshire Supreme Court found that the car was not being used with D's permission within the meaning of the policy, and that the insurer was not obligated to defend. The actions against C were then voluntarily discontinued.

Subsequently, plaintiffs brought suit against D and his son in New York (where the accident had occurred), relying upon a New York statute that imposes liability upon the owner of a car for the negligence of a person operating the car with his permission. Holding defendant could rely on the judgment entered in favor of their insurer, the Court of Appeals, recognized that the "issue of permission under the insurance policy * * * is not the same as the issue of permission under" the New York statute, but found that the same facts established in the New Hampshire proceeding established a lack of permission under the statute. HINCHEY v. SELLERS, 7 N.Y.2d 287, 197 N.Y.S.2d 129, 165 N.E.2d 156 (1959) (6–1). The opinion states that "the relevant New Hampshire cases seem to be in accord with the general rule that where an issue of fact essential to the judgment is actually litigated and determined by a valid final judgment, the determination is conclusive between the parties and their privies," and cites, among other cases, *King v. Chase.* Do you agree that the New York decision is in accord with *King*?

THE EVERGREENS v. NUNAN

United States Circuit Court of Appeals, Second Circuit, 1944.
141 F.2d 927, 152 A.L.R. 1187.
Certiorari denied 323 U.S. 720, 65 S.Ct. 49, 89 L.Ed. 579.

L. HAND, Circuit Judge. [Taxpayer, a cemetery, owned property of two classes, "fully improved" lots and "partially improved" lots. As to each class, taxpayer's "basis" for the purpose of computing the taxable gain upon the sale of the lots was the value as of March 1, 1913. In an earlier case, the Board of Tax Appeals had held the basis of the "fully improved" lots to be $1.55 per square foot. The Tax Court had accepted this determination as binding with respect to the sale of "fully improved" lots involved in this case; the Commissioner of Internal Revenue did not appeal this ruling. Taxpayer insisted that the basis of the "partially improved" lots—in issue in this case but not in the earlier one—had to be determined by deducting the cost of completing the improvement of the "partially improved" lots from the previously established value of the "fully improved" lots. The Tax Court rejected this contention, however, and determined the basis of the "partially improved" lots from evidence taken in the new proceeding.]

* * *

It is of course well-settled law that a fact, once decided in an earlier suit, is conclusively established between the parties in any later suit, provided it was necessary to the result in the first suit. * * * However, a "fact" may be of two kinds. It may be one of those facts, upon whose combined occurrence the law raises the duty, or the right, in question; or it may be a fact, from whose existence may be rationally inferred the existence of one of the facts upon whose combined occurrence the law raises the duty, or the right. The first kind of fact we shall for convenience call an "ultimate" fact; the second, a "mediate datum." "Ultimate" facts are those which the law makes the occasion for imposing its sanctions.

* * * The next question is whether, after the court in the second suit has learned what the court in the first suit actually did decide, the judgment

conclusively establishes for any purpose any other facts than those which were "ultimate" in the first suit; that is to say, whether any facts decided in the first which were only "mediate data" in that suit, are conclusively established in the second suit. Some courts hold that only facts "ultimate" in the first suit are conclusively established. * * * The same notion was foreshadowed in the often quoted language of Coke: "Every estoppel * * * must be certain to every intent, and not to be taken by argument or inference." Co. Lit. 352b. * * * On the other hand, other courts refuse to distinguish between "ultimate" facts and "mediate data" decided in the first suit, so long as they were necessary to the result. * * * We need not choose between these two doctrines, because * * * the Board decided nothing in the first proceedings which was both a "mediate datum" in that proceeding and necessary to the result.

The important question here is not therefore whether "mediate data" in the first suit are as conclusively established as "ultimate" facts in that suit. On the contrary, we are to decide what are the purposes in the second suit for which anything decided in the first suit—whether "ultimate facts," or "mediate data" therein—are conclusively established. Do the "ultimate" facts, or the "mediate data" decided in the first suit conclusively establish in the second, anything but facts "ultimate" in that suit? Do they also establish "mediate data" in that suit: i.e. premises from which to deduce the existence of any of the facts "ultimate" in that suit?

It is, as we have said, a condition upon the conclusive establishing of any fact that its decision should have been necessary to the result in the first suit. That is a protection, for it means that the issue will be really disputed and that the loser will have put out his best efforts. It can make no difference in this regard whether the original issue was as to an "ultimate" fact or as to a "mediate datum"; the parties can have no interest in what place in the logical hierarchy the issue occupies, if only the final outcome hinges upon it. Altogether different considerations should determine whether any sort of fact, decided in the first suit, should conclusively establish "mediate data" in the second suit. Indeed, it often works very harshly inexorably to make a fact decided in the first suit conclusively establish even a fact "ultimate" in the second. The stake in the first suit may have been too small to justify great trouble and expense in its prosecution or defense; and the chance that a fact decided in it, even though necessary to its result, may later become important between the parties may have been extremely remote. It is altogether right that the judgment shall forever put an end to the first cause of action; but it is not plain that it is always fair that every fact—"ultimate" or "mediate datum"—decided in it, shall be conclusively established between the parties in all future suits, just because the decision was necessary to the result. What jural relevance facts may acquire in the future it is often impossible even remotely to anticipate. Were the law to be recast, it would therefore be a pertinent inquiry whether the conclusiveness, even as to facts "ultimate" in the second suit, of facts decided in the first, might not properly be limited to future controversies which could be thought reasonably in prospect when the first suit was tried. That is of course not the law as it stands; but if it be proposed to make any fact, decided in the first suit, an indisputable datum in the second, from which the winner may make all rational inferences, the loser's risks become enormously enlarged. It is difficult enough to know to what other possible causes of action a fact found in the first suit will later prove to be "ultimate"; but the field is at least somewhat restricted, particularly because the causes of action to which it can apply are apt to be already in existence. But it is utterly impossible to set even the widest boundaries to the situations in which facts found in the first suit may become relevant as data from which to deduce any facts, "ultimate" in all possible future causes of action. Logical relevance is of infinite possibility; there is no conceivable limit which can be put to it. Defeat in one suit might entail results beyond all calculation by either party; a trivial controversy might bring utter disaster in its train. There is no reason for subjecting the loser to such extravagant hazards; unless the decisions compel us to go so far, we will not do so.

We have been able to find very little authority upon the point * * *. Indeed, we have seen that it has not even yet become wholly settled whether facts decided in the first suit, and therein only "mediate data," conclusively establish facts "ultimate" in the second.

* * * Being free to decide, and for the reasons we have given, we do not hesitate to hold that, even assuming arguendo that "mediate data," decided in the first suit, conclusively establish facts, "ultimate" in the second, no fact decided in the first whether "ultimate" or a "mediate datum," conclusively establishes any "mediate datum," in the second, or anything except a fact "ultimate" in that suit.

Order affirmed.

NOTES

1. Collateral estoppel carries a built-in danger that it may be applied loosely to subsequent litigation having such a tenuous connection with the original controversy that application of the doctrine would work an injustice. * * * We would state the limitation * * *: collateral estoppel by judgment is applicable only when it is evident from the pleadings and record that determination of the fact in question was necessary to the final judgment and it was foreseeable that the fact would be of importance in possible future litigation.

HYMAN v. REGENSTEIN, 258 F.2d 502, 510–11 (5th Cir.1958). See also Vestal, *Preclusion/Res Judicata Variables: Nature of the Controversy,* 1965 Wash. U.L.Q. 158, 175.

2. In MOORE v. UNITED STATES, 246 F.Supp. 19, 22 (N.D.Miss. 1965), taxpayers were breeders and sellers of Polled Hereford cattle. Income from the sale of animals that had been held as breeding stock was taxable as capital gains; income from the sale of animals held for sale was taxable as ordinary income. Some of the cattle bred on the ranch were immediately placed in the sale herd; other cattle were placed in a breeding herd, from which they were on occasion culled as unsatisfactory. The critical question from the taxation perspective then was which cattle culled from the breeding herd and sold could be said

to have been held up until then for breeding purposes. A Tax Court proceeding involving earlier years had determined a "cutoff point" in the taxpayers' "method of operations, beyond which animals retained are considered to be held for breeding purposes and prior to which animals sold are considered to have been held for sale in the ordinary course of business." The Government argued that this was a determination of ultimate fact "identical to the ultimate fact which must be found here." The court in the second action said, however:

> The practice of the taxpayers in 1951 through 1953, i. e., the cutoff point * * * was not an ultimate fact in that case nor would it be in this, although it may be mediate datum from which one ultimate fact—the holding purpose—may be inferred. No fact decided in the first case, whether evidentiary or ultimate, is binding on this court unless that precise fact is, in the case here, an ultimate fact necessary to disposition. * * * Other than the length of the holding period, the ultimate facts here are the purposes for which the plaintiffs held the animals in this case before the time of their sale in the years 1957–1960. Regardless of when they were acquired or sold, the plaintiffs' purpose in holding *these* animals was not and could not have been decided by the Tax Court when it dealt with the purpose with which *other* animals were held before the time of their sale in the years 1951–1953. Since no tax consequences arising from the holding of the animals in this case were litigated in the Tax Court, such consequences may be judicially determined here.

3. Is the "ultimate," "mediate," and "evidentiary" fact distinction drawn in *Evergreens* helpful? Are these categories likely to lead to decisions based on the policies that underlie collateral estoppel? In *Restatement (Second), Judgments* § 68, comment *j* (Tent.Draft No. 1, 1973), it is said that the key question "is whether the issue was actually recognized by the parties as important and by the adjudicator as necessary to the first judgment," unless there is a basis for an exception under Section 68.1 of the Restatement—for example, that the significance of the issues for purposes of the subsequent action was not sufficiently foreseeable at the time of the first action. Why?

C. PERSONS BENEFITTED AND PERSONS BOUND BY COLLATERAL ESTOPPEL

RALPH WOLFF & SONS v. NEW ZEALAND INS. CO.

Court of Appeals of Kentucky, 1933.
248 Ky. 304, 58 S.W.2d 623.

STANLEY, Commissioner. The opinion of Wolff v. Niagara Fire Insurance Co., 236 Ky. 1, 32 S.W.2d 548, discloses that H. C. Wolff and R. C. Wolff, partners, suffered the partial loss by fire of their candy factory in December, 1924, and that they had twelve insurance policies on the property for a total sum of $19,500. That case was a consolidation of nine suits on as many policies for the aggregate of $14,500. The verdict was for $2,500 in favor of the plaintiffs "to cover the amount of the loss and damage by fire and water."

That was construed to be a finding that the total property loss was $2,500. Since the insurance involved in the consolidated action was 14500/19500 of the whole coverage, judgment was rendered for that fractional part of the total loss fixed by the jury, that is, for $1,858.90, and that judgment was affirmed.

[Plaintiffs also sued two other insurers, each of whom had insured plaintiffs for $1,000.] * * * Among the several defenses set up in each case was the plea that the policy provided the company should not be liable for a greater proportion of any loss than the amount of the policy bore to the whole insurance covering the property; that in the consolidated cases referred to it had been judicially ascertained and determined that the total loss was $2,500 and by reason thereof the amount of the loss was res judicata and plaintiffs were estopped to assert a greater damage; and that if liable at all it was only for its proportional part, or 1000/19500, to wit $128.20. A demurrer to this plea was overruled * * * and judgment for $128.20 was rendered against each company. * * *

The sole question before us, therefore, is * * * whether the plaintiffs in these suits are bound by the judgment in their cases against the other nine companies.

It is said in Jeter v. Hewitt, 22 How. 352, 364, 16 L.Ed. 345, that "res judicata renders white that which is black, and straight that which is crooked." But all will agree that there are qualifications and that is not true except when there are certain concurring elements, as where one has had a chance, either personally or by representation, to show that black is black and crooked things are crooked. It is conceded, quite naturally, that in order to render a matter res judicata, among other things, there must be identity of parties or their privies; and that is so though the judgment relied upon as a bar involved the same state of facts. * * * The defendants in these actions were not parties to the other one and in no way participated in their defense. There is nothing to show that they even had notice of the pendency of the other suits.

* * * "The fact that persons are interested in the same question or in proving the same facts * * * does not make them privies." Section 438, Freeman on Judgments. * * *

The appellees rest their argument of privity upon what they say is the contractual relation, that is, in effect that as each policy contained the apportionment or contribution clause, they were and are bound together in a common cause. * * * True it is there may be such a contractual relationship that a party becomes bound under certain conditions by the action of another in regard to the matter involved in a suit or by the judgment, such as where he is responsible over, as a warrantor, or as an indemnitor, or as a surety. * * * But we cannot see the application here. The stipulation in the respective contracts of insurance upon the appellants' property was that the company would be liable only for its proportionate share of any loss sustained if other insurance contracts should be made. This, of course, was to avoid duplication of indemnity and to prevent overinsurance. There was no contract nor privity of contract among the insurers. * * * It may be doubted that such would have been claimed had the loss been fixed by the former judgment at what the companies regarded as excessive. To bind the plaintiffs the defendants must also have been bound, for an estoppel is always mutual.

*   *   *

As further refuting the view that the concurrent or pro rata insurance clauses in the several policies so interlocked the contracts as to make them one in effect   *   *   *   it is held that insurers cannot avail themselves of an adjustment by the insured with another insurer either to defeat recovery or reduce the amount of liability under their contract; and that in ascertaining a company's proportionate share of the loss no regard is to be had to the fact that some of the companies have been settled with for a less sum than they were liable for or have paid more than their share.   *   *   *   [T]here can be no difference when the settlement is pursuant to a judicial determination.

*   *   *

It seems to the court, therefore, that the judgment holding the appellants to be bound by the judgment in the former suit is erroneous. It is accordingly reversed, and the case remanded for consistent proceedings.

NOTES AND QUESTIONS

1. Why should it be true, in the words of the court in the principal case, that "to bind the plaintiffs, the defendants must also have been bound"? Is this principle of mutuality based upon any of the purposes we have seen advanced in support of the doctrine of res judicata? Reread the passage from Professor Cleary's article on pp. 1101–03, supra. Might plaintiff in *Ralph Wolff & Sons* have had anything to gain in trying the actions against the insurers in separate groups instead of all at once? Should the answer to the last question affect the decision whether to follow the rule enunciated by the court? Should there be one rule when plaintiff has proceeded so as to obtain separate trials and another rule when plaintiff was unable to avoid separate trials?

2. Would there have been any reasonable basis in the principal case for restricting plaintiff's total recovery to $2,500, while not restricting the possible liability of the two defendants to $128.20 each?

3. A street car and a coal wagon collided. The driver of the wagon sued the street-car company for his injuries and won, the jury finding that he had not been guilty of any want of ordinary care. Subsequently, a pedestrian, against whom the wagon had been thrown, sued the street-car company and the coal company for her injuries. Should the earlier judgment in favor of the wagon driver operate as res judicata on the issue of his lack of negligence? If a verdict is returned against both defendants, should the court order that the judgment contain a provision that execution must be first satisfied out of the property of the street-car company? See Ertel v. Milwaukee Elec. Ry. & Light Co., 164 Wis. 380, 160 N.W. 263 (1916).

4. When an action is brought against one who is entitled to be indemnified by another if he should lose, a judgment against the indemnitee will bind the indemnitor on the issue of the indemnitee's liability in the first action, if the indemnitor has been "vouched in," that is, if notified of the first action and offered an opportunity to defend. See, e. g., First Nat. Bank v. City Nat. Bank, 182 Mass. 130, 65 N.E. 24 (1902) (so holding, even though the indemnitor

was not subject to personal jurisdiction in the state in which the first action was brought). See p. 565, supra.

———

CITY OF ANDERSON v. FLEMING, 160 Ind. 597, 602–03, 67 N.E. 443, 445 (1903). Plaintiff received personal injuries by stepping into an excavation in the street. She sued the contractor who made the excavation, but judgment went against her. Subsequently, she sued the city for the same injuries, and the city pleaded the judgment in favor of the contractor. The Supreme Court of Indiana held for defendant city:

* * * The established rule in this state is that when a street of a municipal corporation is rendered unsafe by the wrongful acts or negligence of a third person, and the corporation is compelled to pay for injuries caused by said unsafe street, it has a right of action over against the person who rendered the same unsafe, for the amount so paid, and, if properly notified of the action, such person is bound and concluded by said judgment recovered against the corporation.

* * * It is clearly established * * * that if appellee was injured, without contributory fault on her part, by reason of said excavations being negligently left open, without proper guards or signals, as alleged, appellant would be entitled to recover from the contractor whatever appellee might recover against it. Such right * * * would rest upon the principles of subrogation. Appellant would be entitled to be subrogated to appellee's right of action against the contractor, but the judgment on the merits in the contractor's favor in appellee's action against him conclusively adjudged that he was not liable to appellee, or any person claiming under her, for the same cause of action. If appellee was not entitled to recover for said injury against the contractor, she is not entitled to recover therefor against appellant.

The contractor had the right, if duly notified by appellant, to appear and set up said former judgment in his favor against appellee in bar of this action against appellant, and appellant has the same right; otherwise the contractor would have to defend the same cause twice on its merits.

NOTES AND QUESTIONS

1. A, an employee acting within the scope of his employment and driving the employer's, B's, car, collides with a car driven by C. C sues A, and judgment is for A. Subsequently B sues C for damages to the car. What effect should the earlier judgment for A have in B's suit against C? See Good Health Dairy Prods. Corp. v. Emery, 275 N.Y. 14, 9 N.E.2d 758, 112 A.L.R. 401 (1937).

2. Suppose on the facts of Question 1 that C had first sued B, and judgment had been for B, and C had then sued A. What effect should the earlier

judgment for B have in C's suit against A? Would your answer be different if the second suit had been by A against C? *Compare* Emery v. Fowler, 39 Me. 326, 63 Am.Dec. 627 (1855), *with* Elder v. New York & Penn. Motor Express, Inc., 284 N.Y. 350, 31 N.E.2d 188 (1940). See generally Note, *Impacts of Defensive and Offensive Assertion of Collateral Estoppel by a Nonparty,* 35 Geo.Wash.L. Rev. 1010 (1967).

3. Suppose that in the first action, A, a real-estate broker, had sued the seller of property, B, for commissions. The trial court dismissed A's action after trial on the ground that A had not produced the person, C, who ultimately had purchased B's property and therefore was not entitled to a brokerage commission. In the second action A sues C for inducing B to breach the brokerage contract causing a loss of the commission. Can C successfully rely on the decision against A in the first action as a bar to A's action against him? Israel v. Wood Dolson Co., 1 N.Y.2d 116, 151 N.Y.S.2d 1, 134 N.E.2d 97 (1956). The New York cases on mutuality of estoppel are discussed at length in 5 Weinstein, Korn & Miller, *New York Civil Practice* ¶¶ 5011.32–.42.

4. When a wrongful-death action for the death of a child has been brought by a personal representative and judgment was for defendant, is the mother estopped by the earlier judgment in an action for her personal injuries arising out of the same accident when she would have been one of the beneficiaries if the first action had been successful? See Smith v. Bishop, 26 Ill.2d 434, 187 N.E.2d 217 (1962). *But cf.* Chicago, R. I. & P. Ry. v. Schendel, 270 U.S. 611, 46 S.Ct. 420, 70 L.Ed. 757 (1926).

BERNHARD v. BANK OF AMERICA NAT. TRUST & SAV. ASS'N

Supreme Court of California, 1942.
19 Cal.2d 807, 122 P.2d 892.

TRAYNOR, Justice. In June, 1933, Mrs. Clara Sather, an elderly woman, made her home with Mr. and Mrs. Charles O. Cook in San Dimas, California. Because of her failing health, she authorized Mr. Cook and Dr. Joseph Zeiler to make drafts jointly against her commercial account in the Security First National Bank of Los Angeles. On August 24, 1933, Mr. Cook opened a commercial account at the First National Bank of San Dimas in the name of "Clara Sather by Charles O. Cook." * * * Thereafter, a number of checks drawn by Cook and Zeiler on Mrs. Sather's commercial account in Los Angeles were deposited in the San Dimas account * * *.

On October 26, 1933, a teller from the Los Angeles Bank called on Mrs. Sather at her request to assist in transferring her money from the Los Angeles Bank to the San Dimas Bank. In the presence of this teller, the cashier of the San Dimas Bank, Mr. Cook, and her physician, Mrs. Sather signed by mark an authorization directing the Security First National Bank of Los Angeles to transfer the balance of her savings account in the amount of $4,155.68 to the First National Bank of San Dimas * * * "for credit to the account of Mrs. Clara Sather." The order was credited by the San Dimas Bank to the account of "Clara Sather by Charles O. Cook." Cook withdrew the entire balance from that account and opened a new account in the same bank in the name of himself and his wife. * * *

Mrs. Sather died in November, 1933. Cook qualified as executor of the estate and proceeded with its administration. After a lapse of several years he filed an account at the instance of the probate court accompanied by his resignation. The account made no mention of the money transferred by Mrs. Sather to the San Dimas Bank; and Helen Bernhard * * * [and other] beneficiaries under Mrs. Sather's will, filed objections to the account for this reason. After a hearing on the objections the court settled the account, and as part of its order declared that the decedent during her lifetime had made a gift to Charles O. Cook of the amount of the deposit in question.

After Cook's discharge, Helen Bernhard was appointed administratrix with the will annexed. She instituted this action against defendant, the Bank of America, successor to the San Dimas Bank, seeking to recover the deposit on the ground that the bank was indebted to the estate for this amount because Mrs. Sather never authorized its withdrawal. In addition to a general denial, defendant pleaded two affirmative defenses: (1) That the money on deposit was paid out to Charles O. Cook with the consent of Mrs. Sather and (2) that this fact is res judicata by virtue of the finding of the probate court * * *. The trial court * * * gave judgment for defendant on the ground that Cook's ownership of the money was conclusively established by the finding of the probate court. * * *

Plaintiff contends that the doctrine of res judicata does not apply because the defendant who is asserting the plea was not a party to the previous action nor in privity with a party to that action and because there is no mutuality of estoppel.

* * *

Many courts have stated the facile formula that the plea of res judicata is available only when there is privity and mutuality of estoppel. * * * Under the requirement of privity, only parties to the former judgment or their privies may take advantage of or be bound by it. * * * A party in this connection is one who is "directly interested in the subject matter, and had a right to make defense, or to control the proceeding, and to appeal from the judgment." * * * A privy is one who, after rendition of the judgment, has acquired an interest in the subject matter affected by the judgment through or under one of the parties, as by inheritance, succession, or purchase. * * * The estoppel is mutual if the one taking advantage of the earlier adjudication would have been bound by it, had it gone against him. * * *

The criteria for determining who may assert a plea of res judicata differ fundamentally from the criteria for determining against whom a plea of res judicata may be asserted. The requirements of due process of law forbid the assertion of a plea of res judicata against a party unless he was bound by the earlier litigation in which the matter was decided. * * * He is bound by that litigation only if he has been a party thereto or in privity with a party thereto. * * * There is no compelling reason, however, for requiring that the party asserting the plea of res judicata must have been a party, or in privity with a party, to the earlier litigation.

No satisfactory rationalization has been advanced for the requirement of mutuality. Just why a party who was not bound by a previous action should be precluded from asserting it as res judicata against a party who was bound by it is difficult to comprehend. See 7 Bentham's Works, Bowring's Ed., 171. Many courts have abandoned the requirement of mutuality and confined the requirement of privity to the party against whom the plea of res judicata is asserted. Coca Cola Co. v. Pepsi-Cola Co., [36 Del. 124, 172 Atl. 260 (1934)] * * *. The commentators are almost unanimously in accord. * * * The courts of most jurisdictions have in effect accomplished the same result by recognizing a broad exception to the requirements of mutuality and privity, namely, that they are not necessary where the liability of the defendant asserting the plea of res judicata is dependent upon or derived from the liability of one who was exonerated in an earlier suit brought by the same plaintiff upon the same facts. * * * Typical examples of such derivative liability are master and servant, principal and agent, and indemnitor and indemnitee. Thus, if a plaintiff sues a servant for injuries caused by the servant's alleged negligence within the scope of his employment, a judgment against the plaintiff of the grounds that the servant was not negligent can be pleaded by the master as res judicata if he is subsequently sued by the same plaintiff for the same injuries. Conversely, if the plaintiff first sues the master, a judgment against the plaintiff on the grounds that the servant was not negligent can be pleaded by the servant as res judicata if he is subsequently sued by the plaintiff. In each of these situations the party asserting the plea of res judicata was not a party to the previous action nor in privity with such a party * * *. Likewise, the estoppel is not mutual since the party asserting the plea, not having been a party or in privity with a party to the former action, would not have been bound by it had it been decided the other way. The cases justify this exception on the ground that it would be unjust to permit one who has had his day in court to reopen identical issues by merely switching adversaries.

In determining the validity of a plea of res judicata three questions are pertinent: Was the issue decided in the prior adjudication identical with the one presented in the action in question? Was there a final judgment on the merits? Was the party against whom the plea is asserted a party or in privity with a party to the prior adjudication?

* * * Since the issue as to the ownership of the money is identical with the issue raised in the probate proceeding, and since the order of the probate court settling the executor's account was a final adjudication of this issue on the merits * * * it remains only to determine whether the plaintiff in the present action was a party or in privity with a party to the earlier proceeding. The plaintiff has brought the present action in the capacity of administratrix of the estate. In this capacity she represents the very same persons and interests that were represented in the earlier hearing on the executor's account. In that proceeding plaintiff and the other legatees who objected to the executor's account represented the estate of the decedent. They were seeking not a personal recovery but, like the plaintiff in the present action, as adminis-

tratrix, a recovery for the benefit of the legatees and creditors of the estate, all of whom were bound by the order settling the account.   *   *   *

The judgment is affirmed.

NOTES AND QUESTIONS

1.   Many of the cases involving mutuality of collateral estoppel that have arisen since *Bernhard* are noted and briefly discussed in the appendix to B. Currie, *Civil Procedure—The Tempest Brews*, 53 Calif.L.Rev. 25, 38–46 (1965).   Other useful discussions of mutuality include B. Currie, *Mutuality of Collateral Estoppel —Limits of the* Bernhard *Doctrine*, 9 Stan.L.Rev. 281 (1957); Moore & Currier, *Mutuality and Conclusiveness of Judgments*, 35 Tul.L.Rev. 301 (1961); Polasky, *Collateral Estoppel—Effects of Prior Litigation*, 39 Iowa L.Rev. 217 (1954); Semmel, *Collateral Estoppel, Mutuality and Joinder of Parties*, 68 Colum.L.Rev. 1457 (1968).

2.   Plaintiff, together with the driver of the car in which she was riding and plaintiff's husband who owned the car, brought suit against defendant for damages arising out of a collision.   The following verdicts were returned: for plaintiff, $371.94 for personal injuries; for the driver, $65.00 for personal injuries; and for the husband, $63.06 for damage to the car.   Judgments were entered for the driver and the husband, but plaintiff moved successfully for a new trial on the ground that the damages awarded her were insufficient.   The judgments in favor of the driver and the husband having become final, plaintiff moved at the new trial to limit the issues to damages since, she argued, those judgments established defendant's liability.   In TAYLOR v. HAWKINSON, 47 Cal.2d 893, 306 P.2d 797 (1957) (6–1), the California Supreme Court, in an opinion by Justice Traynor, held that the *Bernhard* rule should not be applied to these facts:

> There is ample evidence to support the trial court's implied finding that the verdicts following the first trial were compromise verdicts and that the jury did not determine the issue of liability.   The damages awarded plaintiff were less than her special damages * * *.   [H]ad defendant or plaintiff's husband and the driver moved for a new trial, it would have been granted, and their failure to do so was tantamount to accepting the jury's compromise as their own.   * * * Regardless of the effectiveness of such a compromise in extinguishing the causes of action or in settling the rights directly involved therein * * * it does not constitute such a determination of the issues involved as to render them res judicata where distinct rights are sought to be litigated in a separate cause of action.   * * * To hold otherwise would tend to defeat rather than to promote the objective of preventing vexatious litigation with its attendant expense both to the parties and the public.   * * * [Had defendant appealed] more rather than less litigation would have ensued, and plaintiff would have gained nothing.

Id. at 896–97, 306 P.2d at 799.

3.   Would a court following *Bernhard* reach a different result in a case such as *Ralph Wolff & Sons*?   Suppose in the latter case the New Zealand Insurance Company had contributed funds for the defense of the first action?   One who participates in the prosecution or defense of a lawsuit even though not a

party may be bound as though he were. Generally this participation must be such as to give some measure of control over the litigation, and a mere contribution towards the costs of the suit is not enough. See Annot., 139 A.L.R. 9, 29–31 (1942). In light of cases such as *Bernhard*, which has the effect of giving the benefit of favorable judgments to nonparties in many cases, should the general rule be reassessed insofar as unfavorable judgments are concerned?

FIRST NAT. BANK OF CINCINNATI v. BERKSHIRE LIFE INS. CO.

Supreme Court of Ohio, 1964.

176 Ohio St. 395, 199 N.E.2d 863.

This action was commenced by the First National Bank of Cincinnati, as plaintiff * * * against the Berkshire Life Insurance Company, as defendant * * * by the filing of a petition * * * to recover the death benefits on two separate policies of life insurance, each for $5,000, issued respectively on March 16, 1955, and April 11, 1955, to Elroy C. Denton, who, by written assignments dated May 25, 1955, assigned those policies to the bank * * *. Denton died on June 12, 1955.

To this petition * * * the insurer filed an answer denying liability (except for a return of the premiums paid which were tendered into court) on two separate and distinct grounds, first, that Denton was not in "good health" on the respective dates when said policies were delivered and each first premium paid, a condition precedent to the effectiveness of each, and, second, that said policies were procured by false and fraudulent representations made by Denton concerning his health, habits and previous medical attention.

An amended reply of the bank, in addition to general denials, alleges that, on the date of issuance of the second policy (April 11, 1955), the insurer issued a third policy upon the life of Denton for $5,000; that Anna Marie Slate was designated beneficiary of that third policy; that that beneficiary sought recovery of the proceeds of that third policy from defendant-insurer in a Florida court; that defendant filed an answer "interposing the identical defenses as are set forth in its answer filed herein"; that a final judgment was rendered in that Florida case in favor of that beneficiary and against defendant; that "all facts and issues raised by defendant's * * * answer filed herein were raised by defendant's answer in" that Florida case "and decided therein against defendant"; and that "by reason thereof defendant is estopped to assert the same again in this action * * *.

On motion of the defendant, the allegations in the amended reply, except for the general denials thereof, were stricken. * * *

The parties having waived a jury, the case was tried to the court which found (1) that Denton was not "in good health" at the respective times of delivery of the two policies sued on, and (2) that Denton had procured the policies by false and fraudulent representations of which the insurer was without knowledge and except for which the policies would not have been issued. Judgment was rendered for defendant-insurer on both causes of action.

On appeal to the Court of Appeals, that judgment was reversed because of error of the trial court in granting the motion to strike * * *.

TAFT, Chief Justice. * * *

The allegations of the bank's amended reply do describe a judgment against defendant on the third policy issued on April 11, 1955. Recovery by the beneficiary on that policy might determine the good health of Denton on April 11, 1955, but it would not necessarily determine the good health of Denton on March 16, 1955. Denton's good health on March 16, 1955, would not have been an issue in the Florida case based on the policy issued on April 11, 1955.

* * *

It follows that, although proof of the allegations of the bank's amended reply might have established that the Florida judgment could estop defendant from asserting as an affirmative and complete defense to the second policy that Denton was not in good health on April 11, 1955, it could not estop defendant from setting up as an affirmative and complete defense to the first policy that Denton was not in good health on March 16, 1955. * * *

The insurer contends also that the bank cannot assert the Florida judgment as an estoppel against the insurer (even as to the April 11, 1955, policy) because

(1) the bank was neither a party nor in privity with a party to the Florida action, and

(2) no mutuality of estoppel can exist because the insurer could not have relied upon a judgment in the Florida case in its favor as an estoppel against the bank which was not a party to the Florida case. * * *

On the other hand, the bank contends that this court should follow those authorities which have abandoned the requirement of mutuality of estoppel and which permit one not a party or in privity with a party to a judgment to use that judgment as an estoppel against one who was such a party or in privity with such a party to that judgment. * * *

We do not deem it necessary to decide in the instant case whether this court should follow those authorities. The reasons for the conclusions which they reach, as well as the reasons for ever having a judgment operate as an estoppel, militate against use of the Florida judgment as an estoppel in the instant case.

The reasons generally given for estopping a party (even where there is no mutuality of estoppel) to a judgment from relitigating an issue determined against him by that judgment are

(1) that public policy requires an end to litigation, and

(2) that the public is interested in protection of a person from being twice vexed for the same cause. * * *

In the instant case, where the bank has never previously had to oppose or been "vexed" by the insurer's affirmative defense that Denton was not in "good health" on the dates when the bank's policies were delivered, it is obvious that the second reason does not apply.

Also, allowing the bank in the instant case to assert the Florida judgment as an estoppel against the insurer would have no substantial effect in ending litigation between the bank and the insurer. As hereinbefore pointed out, the Florida judgment cannot estop the insurer from litigating the issue as to Denton's "good health" on March 16, 1955, when the first policy was delivered. The same witnesses would necessarily testify at the same time and at the same trial on the similar but not identical issue as to Denton's "good health" on April 11, 1955. Thus, permitting reconsideration of the latter issue, notwithstanding the Florida judgment which determined it against the insurer, would interfere only very slightly, if at all, with the end of litigation between the insurer and the bank.

Furthermore, there are reasons for requiring mutuality of estoppel. Thus, it is stated in Developments in the Law—Res Judicata, 65 Harvard Law Review (1952), 818, 862:

"The justification for this requirement has been said to be that a party may be unwilling to press his case to the utmost in a particular suit, and that it would penalize him to enable strangers to take advantage of his laxity; that an adversary system requires that 'a party to an action should [normally] risk the loss of rights or the creation of liabilities only with reference to his adversaries;' or that a jury may often reach results inconsistent with the truth, and that such a mishap should not affect a losing party outside the particular litigation."

* * *

Such reasons for requiring mutuality of estoppel may generally have little weight. However, that little weight is sufficient to enable them to far outweigh the slight, if any, weight in the instant case of the reasons generally given for estopping a party to a judgment from relitigating an issue determined against him by that judgment.

As hereinbefore pointed out, even the authorities relied upon by the bank will not support the conclusion that the insurer can be estopped by the Florida judgment from litigating the issue as to Denton's "good health" on March 16, 1955. Thus, to permit the bank to assert the Florida judgment as an estoppel against the insurer in the portion of the instant case relating to the second policy issued on April 11, 1955, would result in a holding in the same action for the insurer on the March 16 policy and for the bank on the April 11 policy, even though the evidence in this case clearly discloses that the insured's health was no better on April 11 than it had been on March 16. This would be an anomalous result that would hardly reflect any credit upon our courts.

It may be added here that there may even be a difference between the law of Florida and the law of Ohio, and the insurer had nothing to do with the selection of either jurisdiction as a place in which to litigate. This could explain the result of this judgment which holds for the insurer on one April 11 policy, even though there is a judgment in Florida against the insurer on another policy of the same date involving the same question of insured's good health on that date.

* * *

Judgment reversed.

NOTES AND QUESTIONS

1. Is the *First Nat. Bank* case consistent with *Bernhard*?

2. Would the court have decided differently with respect to the March 16 policy if the bank had been a party to the Florida proceeding? In dealing with the March 16 policy did the court *sub silentio* decide the same question decided by Judge Learned Hand in *Evergreens*?

3. In deciding whether to give collateral-estoppel effect to the findings in an earlier action, should a court consider the following factors: (a) whether or not there are related questions between the parties that must be relitigated in any event; (b) whether or not there already has been a trial in the second action and the findings of fact in that action are different than in the first action; (c) whether or not the first action was tried under different rules of evidence or procedure than would be followed in the second action; (d) whether or not the burden of proof was the same in the first action as it would be in the second; and (e) whether there is any reason to believe that a jury verdict in the first action is the result of bias, compromise, or misconduct?

B. CURRIE, CIVIL PROCEDURE: THE TEMPEST BREWS, 53 Calif.L.Rev. 25, 27–36 (1965):

* * * I was among those who belatedly expressed appreciation for the [*Bernhard*] decision * * * hailing it as "a triumph of judicial statesmanship." [8] I did so, however, with reservations. While there was nothing to be said in defense of the mutuality rule itself * * * the rule had involved, perhaps fortuitously, certain incidental effects that seemed beneficial, and these might be sacrificed to the detriment of law and justice if the broad new criteria substituted by Justice Traynor were applied too literally in factual contexts differing from that of the *Bernhard* case. For immediate purposes it is sufficient to state the reservations as briefly as possible: to jettison the mutuality rule without some saving provision might lead to (1) anomalous results in multiple-claimant cases, such as those resulting from mass disasters, and (2) injustice in those cases in which, by reason of his opponent's astute employment of the initiative, the party against whom the former judgment is invoked did not in the former action have, in a realistic sense, a full and fair opportunity to defend.

* * *

---

[8] * * * [Currie, *Mutuality of Collateral Estoppel: Limits of the* Bernhard *Doctrine*, 9 Stan.L.Rev. 281 (1957)] at 285. * * *

For present purposes, at least, the more important of my reservations is the second of the two that have been stated. It is quite possible that the party against whom the former judgment is pleaded did not in fact enjoy in the former action a full and fair opportunity to present his case, even though the technical requirements of due process for jurisdictional purposes were satisfied. Ideally, the court in each case would examine the circumstances of the former action to determine whether there had or had not been such an opportunity; if there had, the judgment would be treated as conclusive. I was skeptical, however, as to the willingness of the courts to engage in such particularism, and as to the practicability of such a course. Therefore, though recognizing its artificiality, I suggested a rule-of-thumb limitation on the scope of the *Bernhard* doctrine: the plea would not be allowed by one not a party to prior litigation against one who lacked the initiative in that litigation because of the likelihood that, lacking the initiative, he may have lacked a full and fair opportunity to present his case.

It was Justice Traynor himself, I believe, who first shattered the notion that we could be content with a rule of thumb denying the plea against one who lacked the initiative in the former action, irrespective of the circumstances of the individual case. Teitelbaum Furs, Inc. sought to recover on policies insuring against losses by robbery. The insurers invoked a prior judgment convicting Teitelbaum, *alter ego* of the corporation, of staging the robbery himself. Reversing the trial court, the supreme court ordered judgment for the defendants, holding the judgment in the prior criminal case conclusive. The plaintiffs had specifically urged upon the court the argument that one not a party to the prior proceeding should not be allowed to invoke the doctrine of collateral estoppel against one who did not have the initiative in that proceeding.[13] Justice Traynor spurned the rule of thumb:

> Although plaintiffs' president did not have the initiative in his criminal trial, he was afforded a full opportunity to litigate the issue of his guilt with all the safeguards afforded the criminal defendant, and since he was charged with felonies punishable in the state prison * * * he had every motive to make as vigorous and effective a defense as possible.

* * * The decision, as Justice Traynor noted, promoted the policies favoring stability of judgments and expeditious trials, and no injustice was done. In my own defense I can plead only that my rule of thumb was but a second choice; in an "ideal" world the courts would make a detailed inquiry into the circumstances of the former judgment to determine the fairness of allowing the plea of collateral estoppel. But what I failed to recognize was that dedicated judges like Justice Traynor would never accept the easy course of generalization as a substitute for the ideal of justice in the individual case.

Recently another distinguished judge, Henry J. Friendly of the United States Court of Appeals for the Second Circuit, not only followed the *Bernhard* rejection of mutuality, but in so doing rejected also the reservation that the

---

13 58 Cal.2d 601, 606, 375 P.2d 439, 441, 25 Cal.Rptr. 559, 561 (1962).

plea may not be invoked against a party lacking the initiative in the prior action —all this as a matter of federal as distinguished from state law.[17] Two actions, each by a group of employees against a common employer, sought to establish certain seniority rights under the same collective bargaining agreement. The first of these to be filed, known as the *Alexander* case, involved some 160 employees. The second, known as the *Zdanok* case, was filed some two years later and involved only five employees. But it was *Zdanok* that was first litigated while *Alexander* "remained quiescent" * * *. The original *Zdanok* case resulted in a judgment on the merits for the plaintiff employees, giving them the asserted rights of seniority. As soon as this decision had become final *Alexander*, in modified form, came before the same Federal district court in which *Zdanok* had been tried * * *. [S]ince preclusive effect for the *Zdanok* judgment was being urged by persons not parties to the *Zdanok* case the mutuality rule reared its unlovely head. Not only so, but the plea of estoppel was being urged against one who had not enjoyed the initiative in the prior action. The court had little difficulty in rejecting the mutuality requirement itself. * * *

Judge Friendly dealt gently with my suggested limitations of the *Bernhard* doctrine, glossing over the "initiative" reservation as a secondary alternative and concentrating instead on the vital question whether in the former action the defendant had a full and fair opportunity to litigate the issue effectively. He did not hesitate to particularize:

> Here Glidden's opportunity to litigate the Zdanok case was both full and fair. New York was an entirely reasonable forum for litigation of a contract made in New York with respect to residents of New York working in a New York plant; as between state and federal courts in New York, Glidden, in the Zdanok case, had the forum of its choice. * * * And Glidden cannot reasonably argue that it was unfairly surprised * * * or that it would have defended more diligently if the two actions had been combined from the outset. The Zdanok litigation was prosecuted by Glidden with the utmost vigor, up to the Supreme Court of the United States. The Alexander action * * * was known by everyone to be lurking in the wings. * * *

Although Judge Friendly made no great issue of it, the decision in the consolidated *Zdanok* (*Alexander*) litigation necessarily repudiated also my other reservation about abandonment of the mutuality requirement * * *.[d]

> If we are unwilling to treat the judgment against the [defendant] railroad as res judicata when it is the last of a series, all of which

---

[17] Zdanok v. Glidden Co., 327 F.2d 944 (2d Cir.1964) * * * [, certiorari denied 377 U.S. 934, 84 S.Ct. 1338, 12 L.Ed.2d 298 (1964)].

[d] In the following excerpt from his earlier article, *Mutuality of Collateral Estoppel —Limits of the* Bernhard *Doctrine*, 9 Stan.L.Rev. 281 (1957), Professor Currie was discussing a hypothetical situation arising out of a railroad accident. Twenty-five plaintiffs have sued the railroad in successive cases and lost; a twenty-sixth plaintiff has then won. To allow the twenty-seventh plaintiff to rely on the judgment in the twenty-sixth case, he argued, would be anomalous.

except the last were favorable to the railroad, it must follow that we should also be unwilling to treat an adverse judgment as conclusive even though it was rendered in the first action brought, and is the only one of record. Our aversion to the twenty-sixth judgment as a conclusive adjudication stems largely from the feeling that such a judgment in such a series must be an aberration, but we have no warrant for assuming that the aberrational judgment will not come as the first in the series. * * *

* * * We have no readily ascertainable basis for assuming that the plaintiffs in *Zdanok* and *Alexander* exhausted the class of employees similarly situated; therefore the threat of the "multiple-claimant anomaly" was potentially present. But again Judge Friendly turned naturally to the facts of the case instead of to easy and cynical generalization:

> Although the plaintiffs are numerous, and could conceivably, by careful timing of their complaints, have subjected Glidden to such a series of actions as posed in Professor Currie's railroad case, such a course offers little advantage where the matter in issue is not a factual question of negligence subject to the varying appraisals of the facts by different juries, but the construction of a written contract by a judge. * * *

Somewhat earlier, in a district court, Judge Pierson M. Hall had repudiated both of the suggested limitations on the *Bernhard* doctrine * * * in a *jury* case.[33] In 1958 a United Air Lines passenger plane and a jet fighter collided over Nevada, killing all forty-two passengers and the five crew members of the private plane as well as the two Air Force pilots. Suits by survivors were filed in eleven different jurisdictions; we are concerned only with the actions brought by survivors of the passengers against the airline. Of these, twenty-four, brought in the Southern District of California, were consolidated for trial and resulted in a jury verdict for the plaintiffs on the issue of negligence; in time, final judgments were entered on this verdict. Pending before Judge Hall were nine or ten of the remaining cases. * * * [Plaintiffs] moved for summary judgment on the issue of liability on the ground that the California judgment was conclusive.

Note that (1) these plaintiffs had not been parties to the proceeding in California, so that they could not have been bound by a judgment adverse to the plaintiffs in that proceeding; (2) the party against whom the California judgment was pleaded (United Air Lines) lacked the initiative in the former action; (3) there were numerous plaintiffs: the cases tried in California and those pending before Judge Hall did not exhaust the actual, to say nothing of the potential, number of claims arising from the same collision; and (4) the former action had been tried to a jury. Thus the plea of collateral estoppel could not succeed (1) if the requirement of mutuality were followed; (2) if, discarding the mutuality rule, the court were to apply the "initiative" reserva-

---

33 United States v. United Air Lines, Inc., 216 F.Supp. 709 (E.D.Wash., D.Nev.1962), aff'd as to res judicata and mutuality sub nom. United Air Lines v. Wiener, 335 F.2d 379 (9th Cir.1964). * * *

tion as a rule of thumb; (3) if the court were to apply the "multiple-claimant-anomaly" reservation as a rule of thumb; nor (4) if the court were to retain the substance of the mutuality requirement for former judgments based on jury verdicts while departing from it in non-jury cases. Yet Judge Hall confidently and, I think, laudably held the former judgment conclusive. * * *

First, the court rejected the mutuality rule * * *. Second, the court, instead of seizing upon * * * the fact that the airline had not enjoyed the initiative in the former action, stressed that in the circumstances of this particular case it had in fact enjoyed an impeccably full and fair opportunity to make its defense:

> The issue of liability of United Air Lines to the passengers on the plane was litigated to the hilt, by lawyers of the highest competence in their field, in the trial of the 24 cases in Los Angeles. * * * It would be a travesty upon [justice] * * * to now require these plaintiffs who are survivors of passengers for hire on the United Air Lines plane to again re-litigate the issue of liability after it has been so thoroughly and consummately litigated in the trial court in * * * Los Angeles. * * * The defendant has had its day in court on the issue of liability. * * *

Third, for essentially the same reasons, the court did not concern itself with any such limiting concept as the multiple-claimant anomaly. We have merely to permit ourselves to consider the actual circumstances of the case to appreciate the absurdity of any suggestion that the Los Angeles verdict was an "aberration," and certainly there was no collusive maneuvering by the plaintiffs to select an oppressive forum for a test case.

Fourth, the court, so far from regarding the fact that the prior judgment was founded on a jury verdict as an obstacle, seems to have regarded it as an additional circumstance supporting the right of the plaintiffs to invoke the plea against the defendant. Indeed, so long as we retain sufficient faith in the institution of trial by jury to retain it for civil cases at all, what warrant is there for mistrusting the verdict for purposes of collateral estoppel when there is no suggestion that there has been compromise or other impropriety?

In addition to its other virtues, such an application of res judicata principles rather obviously constitutes a powerful instrument for the expeditious and economical handling of massive litigation such as that resulting from major disasters and other events and transactions affecting large numbers of people. * * *

NOTES AND QUESTIONS

1. In BERNER v. BRITISH COMMONWEALTH PACIFIC AIRLINES, LTD., 346 F.2d 532, 540 (2d Cir.1965), certiorari denied 382 U.S. 983, 86 S.Ct. 559, 15 L.Ed.2d 472 (1966), the executors of the estate of concert pianist William Kapell sued for damages arising out of his death in a plane crash. A trial resulted in a jury verdict for defendant, but judgment n. o. v. was granted for plain-

tiffs on the issue of liability, and a new trial on all issues was conditionally ordered. At the second trial, restricted to the issue of damages, the jury returned a verdict for $924,396. On appeal, the court of appeals held that the trial judge had erred in granting judgment n. o. v. and in the conditional order for a new trial, and ordered judgment for defendant. The court rejected plaintiffs' contention that collateral-estoppel effect should be given to an earlier federal-court judgment in California against defendant for a death occurring in the same crash. The court noted that in this action (to which plaintiffs had been parties prior to a dismissal by stipulation) there had been one jury verdict for defendant, and on a new trial a jury had awarded only $35,000 on an ad damnum claim of $500,000.

> * * * [W]hile not necessarily suggesting that BCPA did not have a "full and fair opportunity to litigate" in Halmos, we think it would be unfair in this case to use the result of the second Halmos trial to the disadvantage of BCPA. At the conclusion of the second trial, Zdanok had not been decided. The result of the first trial was a victory for BCPA; of the second, a relatively small judgment. Had it sought still a third trial, it had to weigh victory against a much larger judgment. The failure to appeal for correction of whatever errors may have been made seems altogether reasonable and would very probably not have been the case if BCPA knew then that that judgment would govern the Kapell action in which far more—$7,003,000—was sought as damages. In Zdanok, however, the first action was litigated as strenuously as would seem possible * * * and the issues—interpretation of a collective bargaining contract —were not likely to be decided on the basis of a jury's choice among different factual inferences, as was the case here.

> * * * The rejection of mutuality in United States v. United Airlines, Inc. * * * may be distinguished on the ground that the first judgment involved 24 of 31 pending actions; the gravity of the potential liability is shown by the fact that the ultimate judgments against the airline totalled $2,337,308. * * * Obviously, the airline would have exerted its full efforts with so much at stake. * * * Moreover, the first judgment was being appealed, so that possible errors were not being overlooked. Although the first judgment was affirmed, a reversal would presumably have redounded to the benefit of the defendant in the second action.

2. In 1967, a divided New York Court of Appeals announced that the doctrine of mutuality of estoppel "is a dead letter." B. R. DeWITT, INC. v. HALL, 19 N.Y.2d 141, 278 N.Y.S.2d 596, 225 N.E.2d 195 (1967). The action was brought by the owner of a cement mixing truck against the owner of another vehicle that had collided with the truck. Plaintiff successfully secured summary judgment on the liability question based on the prior recovery of a judgment for personal injuries by the driver of the truck, Farnum, against the same defendant. According to the majority:

> In this case, where the issues, as framed by the pleadings, were no broader and no different than those raised in the first lawsuit; where the defendant here offers no reason for not holding him to the determination in the first action; where it is unquestioned (and probably unquestionable) that the first action was defended with full vigor and opportunity to be heard; and where the plaintiff in the present action, the owner of the vehicle, derives his right to recovery from the plaintiff in the first action, the operator of said vehicle, although they do

not technically stand in the relationship of privity, there is no reason either in policy or precedent to hold that the judgment in the *Farnum* case is not conclusive in the present action * * *.

In dissent, Justice Breitel agreed that mutuality "no longer has standing as an absolute test" but was concerned over some of the "practical effects" of the majority's approach.

> Stated concretely, the issue in this case is whether a defendant * * * owner cast in judgment in a personal injury action brought by the driver of the other automobile involved is bound by that judgment on the issues of liability in the subsequent action by the owner of the other automobile to recover for property damage. There is, of course, no unity of litigation interest between the two plaintiffs and the practical risks of litigation in a personal injury action and a property damage action are different. Perhaps, more important, in this age of widespread liability insurance there is no certainty of identity in the liability carriers for personal injury claims and property damage claims, and, of course, the law may not generally take direct notice of that difference. This is particularly true with respect to commercial or industrial owners of fleets of vehicles. Hence, there is little probability of equal commitment of time, money, and talent in the different litigations. A converse situation could be even more grievous in effect, namely, where the prior judgment may have been for the relatively small amount of property damage incurred, and it is sought to give that judgment binding effect in a personal injury action involving claims for huge sums.

> These are some of the practical disadvantages in a too facile extension of the doctrine of *res judicata* in hitherto unexplored areas. As for the offsetting disadvantage of duplicating the trial of issues in litigation, this does not weigh heavily in measuring the balance of convenience. The present rules in this area have subsisted for a long time and there is no great amount of such duplicated litigation.

Would Justice Breitel be satisfied with the type of judicial inquiry undertaken in *Zdanok* and *Berner* or is he suggesting a full-scale investigation of the relative "time, money, and talent" expended in the two actions? Would that inquiry be a sound expenditure of judicial resources?

Compare MOLINO v. COUNTY OF PUTNAM, 29 N.Y.2d 44, 323 N.Y.S. 2d 817, 272 N.E.2d 323 (1971), in which the Court of Appeals declined to apply collateral estoppel against plaintiff in a wrongful death action, the mother of the deceased driver, even though defendant had successfully sued the deceased's father, the automobile owner. The court reasoned that collateral estoppel should not be applied against someone who had not been a party to the first action and therefore "did not have a full and fair opportunity * * * to contest the issues." The dissenting justices focused on the fact that the prior action against the father had established the fault of the deceased driver and that, despite the absence of any formal privity relationship, both parents should be bound by that determination. Is *Molino* consistent with, or a retreat from, *Hall?*

3. In BLONDER-TONGUE LABORATORIES, INC. v. UNIVERSITY OF ILLINOIS FOUNDATION, 402 U.S. 313, 91 S.Ct. 1434, 28 L.Ed.2d 788 (1971), the Supreme Court abandoned the rule established in Triplett v. Lowell,

297 U.S. 638, 56 S.Ct. 645, 80 L.Ed. 949 (1936) "that an adjudication adverse to any or all the claims of a patent" does not preclude "another suit [by the patentee] upon the same claims against a different defendant." In the course of his opinion for a unanimous Court, Mr. Justice White rationalized this retreat from mutuality as follows:

> The cases and authorities * * * connect erosion of the mutuality requirement to the goal of limiting relitigation of issues where that can be achieved without compromising fairness in particular cases. The courts have often discarded the rule while commenting on crowded dockets and long delays preceding trial. Authorities differ on whether the public interest in efficient judicial administration is a sufficient ground in and of itself for abandoning mutuality, but it is clear that more than crowded dockets is involved. The broader question is whether it is any longer tenable to afford a litigant more than one full and fair opportunity for judicial resolution of the same issue. The question in these terms includes as part of the calculus the effect on judicial administration, but it also encompasses the concern exemplified by Bentham's reference to the gaming table in his attack on the principle of mutuality of estoppel.[e] In any lawsuit where a defendant, because of the mutuality principle, is forced to present a complete defense on the merits to a claim which the plaintiff has fully litigated and lost in a prior action, there is an arguable misallocation of resources. To the extent the defendant in the second suit may not win by asserting, without contradiction, that the plaintiff had fully and fairly, but unsuccessfully, litigated the same claim in the prior suit, the defendant's time and money are diverted from alternative uses—productive or otherwise—to relitigation of a decided issue. And, still assuming that the issue was resolved correctly in the first suit, there is reason to be concerned about the plaintiff's allocation of resources. Permitting repeated litigation of the same issue as long as the supply of unrelated defendants holds out reflects either the aura of the gaming table or "a lack of discipline and of disinterestedness on the part of the lower courts, hardly a worthy or wise basis for fashioning rules of procedure." Kerotest Mfg. Co. v. C-O-Two Co., 342 U.S. 180, 185, 72 S.Ct. 219, 222, 96 L.Ed. 200 (1952). * * *

The opinion went on to demonstrate that mutuality (1) was not "essential to effectuate the purposes of the patent system"; (2) was expensive to those forced to participate in repetitive litigation and led alleged infringers to accept royalty agreements rather than bear the costs and risks of challenging what might be invalid patents; and (3) was productive of some "lengthy patent suits" that might "be fairly disposed of on pleas of estoppel," although any savings in litigation time that might be achieved by overruling *Triplett* was thought to be an "incidental matter" compared to "the economic consequences of continued adherence" to mutuality.

---

e Earlier in his opinion Mr. Justice White had referred to Bentham's attack on mutuality as "a maxim which one would suppose to have found its way from the gaming-table to the bench," which had been quoted by Judge Friendly in the *Zdanok* case.

SECTION C. THE LAW OF THE CASE

Thus far in this Chapter we have been concerned with the way in which adjudication in one case affects the determination of a later case. Issues previously decided recur, however, not only in successive suits but in successive stages of a single suit, and the principles that underlie the rules of res judicata are not without force in the latter situation.

> * * * There is a feeling that the various phases of a lawsuit should be consistent one with another; that the same matter should not be the subject of repetitious, time-consuming hearings; that public confidence must be preserved in the judicial system by adhering to a decision once made. These attitudes have been reflected in numerous cases which have involved the "law of the case" doctrine.

Vestal, *Law of the Case: Single-Suit Preclusion,* 1967 Utah L.Rev. 1.

LINCOLN NAT. LIFE INS. CO. v. ROOSTH

United States Court of Appeals, Fifth Circuit, 1962.
306 F.2d 110.
Certiorari denied 372 U.S. 912, 83 S.Ct. 726, 9 L.Ed.2d 720 (1963).

JOHN R. BROWN, Circuit Judge, joined by TUTTLE, Chief Judge, and RIVES, CAMERON, WISDOM and GEWIN, Circuit Judges. This is the second appearance of this case. On the first trial the District Court after the jury was unable to agree on a verdict, discharged the jury and thereafter entered *j. n. o. v.* for the Insurer * * *. When that judgment for the Insurer came here on appeal, this Court, by a divided vote, reversed and remanded the case for a new trial. * * *

On the retrial pursuant to our mandate, the jury returned a verdict for the beneficiaries of the Assured and against the Insurer. The District Judge made it plain that because of our decision he felt compelled to enter judgment on the verdict against the Insurer. It is equally plain that had it been left to him, he thought the evidence insufficient as a matter of law to sustain any such judgment.

The case then came back again to this Court * * *.

In the routine assignment of cases to the calendar for argument, the second appeal was presented to a panel of this Court different from that deciding the first appeal. After oral argument before that panel, the serious question arose whether * * * the second panel was in agreement with the decision of the former panel that the evidence was legally sufficient to make a jury issue. In view of this, the Court on its own motion and prior to decision of the second panel ordered the case resubmitted to the full Court.

* * * Consideration by the full Court on these briefs verified the initial impression that we are here dealing with a record which is as identical as can ever be achieved considering the unavoidable nuances in the testimony of living witnesses.

The reconsideration of this identical record by the second panel and now by the full Court revealed another thing of equal positiveness. There are no differences among the Judges of this Court on the questions of law as such. The differences, such as they exist, relate to the facts. It is true, of course, that whether the evidence is sufficient to make out a jury case is a question of law. * * * But it is one only in relation to the particular facts of the particular case. There is no disagreement over the controlling standard * * *.

It is that absence of any disagreement on controlling legal principles and the very substantial actual sameness of the two records which leads us to the conclusion that this is a case calling imperatively for the application of the doctrine of the law of the case.

This, we emphasize, is a deliberate choice and is in no sense the product of any erroneous notion that, as a matter of sheer power, application of that doctrine is mandatory. This would, of course, turn our backs on the principle so often recognized by this Court that while this is a rule guiding decision in a given case, the Court is not compelled to follow its former decision. We have too often held that this Court is, and must be, free to determine whether, first, the prior decision was erroneous, and second, and more important, whether the circumstances are such that a different result should be reached. * * *

But we think that when the issue resolves itself, as it does so clearly here, into a question of whether the same body of evidence is enough to permit a jury submission, neither a subsequent, second, or third, panel of this Court, nor the whole Court sitting en banc, should ordinarily undertake to review the correctness of the first decision or, doing so, arrive at a contrary conclusion. * * *

We are aware, of course, that any such approach seemingly gives secondary importance to the intrinsic merits of the particular case, and more serious, to the likelihood of an injustice being done one or more of the litigants. * * * It is the aim and hope, of course, of every tribunal that it can work justice in the cause. But * * * as is true of many procedural as well as substantive requirements, courts of law must recognize that regard should be given to some factors which are not intrinsically a part of the particular case at hand.

Of these other factors, a most important consideration is stability in the law—a sort of permanence and sureness in decision apart from the make-up or composition of the particular tribunal so far as the person of the Judges is concerned. That, of course, is a matter of growing concern to Courts such as this one in which, as a multiple Judge tribunal, we sit by statute in panels of not more than three Judges. * * * In more tranquil days and times, an appeal from a second trial would be heard by the same Court as the first appeal. Now, that is highly unlikely * * *. That puts a premium on multiple appeals. That is so because, without implying any improper purpose to litigants or their counsel, or acknowledging anything more than, as human beings, Judges will unavoidably have differences in emphasis, approach, or views on close questions in given areas, if the practice is followed for each succeeding panel to arrive at its own decisions, the losing party on the first appeal will naturally strive to bring it back a second, or a third, or a fourth time until all are exhausted. * * * One of the vices is that whether a litigant gets a second, or a third time at bat likewise depends so much on chance, or at least on factors making it most unfair that in one situation a second trial and appeal is available while in another one it is lacking. A variety of possibilities will illustrate these unpredictables: the trial Court enters judgment for a plaintiff on a jury verdict, and we reverse for failure to grant an instructed verdict, but send it back for a new trial because no proper motion for *j. n. o. v.* has been made * * *. Another trial Judge, in substantially the same kind of case, takes a bolder course, grants the motion for directed verdict and enters judgment for a defendant which on appeal we affirm. In the former situation, the parties will have a second chance and a second appeal. In the latter, it will be a one-shot affair. Countless other variations may readily be envisioned.

We think that in a multi-Judge Court it is most essential that it acquire an institutional stability by which the immediate litigants of any given case, and equally important, the bar who must advise clients or litigants in situations yet to come, will know that in the absence of most compelling circumstances, the decision on identical questions, once made, will not be re-examined and redecided merely because of a change in the composition of the Court or of the new panel hearing the case.

With that in mind, we are of the clear view that nothing about this case warrants our exercising the undoubted power to overrule the prior decision reached by the Court on the first appeal. * * *

Affirmed.

JOSEPH C. HUTCHESON, Circuit Judge, with whom JONES and GRIFFIN B. BELL, Circuit Judges, join (dissenting). * * *

Although the majority declares that it respects and follows the doctrine, time-honored and well established in this circuit, at least, that the decision on a former appeal is the law of the case on questions of law then and there presented, *unless the former decision is clearly erroneous and works manifest injustice,* and that this doctrine does not constitute a limitation upon the power of the court to reconsider and if necessary overrule the earlier decision, in the light of the action taken, and declined, by the majority, and of the subsequent language in its opinion, it is as plain as anything can be that while the opinion gives lip service to that doctrine it does not adhere to it. Substituted in its stead by the majority is an entirely new rule * * *. It is a rule which apparently attaches to the earlier decision the conclusive effect of res judicata.

* * *

While no disagreement will be found with the proposition that stability and predictability in the law, as well as the expeditious termination of litigation, are desirable goals in the administration of justice, I think it questionable that the rule announced by the majority materially advances those worthy ends. It might if we were a court of last resort. We must not, however, lose sight of the fact that we do not have the infallibility of finality * * *.

> "Our law of the case is not the Supreme Court's law of the case. Our judgment on the second appeal stands or falls on its merits and has no improved standing before the Supreme Court from the fact that it resulted from an application of our law of the case. This being so, it would seem that if on second appeal we thought our earlier opinion was erroneous, we ought sensibly to set ourselves right, rather than to invite reversal above." White v. Higgins, 116 F.2d 312, 317 (1st Cir. 1940).

* * *

NOTES AND QUESTIONS

1. The law-of-the-case doctrine never has been enforced with the rigor that attends the rules of res judicata and collateral estoppel. "In the absence of statute the phrase, 'law of the case' as applied to the effect of previous orders on the later action of the court rendering them in the same case, merely expresses the practice of courts generally to refuse to reopen what has been decided, not a limit to their power." MESSENGER v. ANDERSON, 225 U.S. 436, 444, 32 S.Ct. 739, 740, 56 L.Ed. 1152, 1156 (1912). The doctrine is said to be "contracting in application." Vestal, *Law of the Case: Single-Suit Preclusion*, 1967 Utah L.Rev. 1, 30.

2. Read Alabama Code 1940, tit. 13, § 28 in Part III of the Supplement. Is a provision of this type wise?

3. Should it matter in the application of the doctrine of the law of the case whether the recurring issue previously was decided by the same court, a higher court, or a lower court? Consider the following situations:

(a) A trial judge refuses to order defendant's wife to answer a question asked by plaintiff in the course of a pretrial deposition on the ground that the subject matter is protected by the husband-wife privilege. At trial the same question is addressed to her by plaintiff.

(b) Assume the trial judge refuses to order the wife to answer at trial. Plaintiff appeals from a judgment for defendant, and the appellate court reverses, holding that the wife should have been ordered to answer. At the new trial, the question again is asked by plaintiff.

(c) Assume that in (b) the trial judge at the new trial orders the wife to answer and she does. Defendant then appeals from a judgment for plaintiff, citing as error the trial court's order that the wife answer.

(d) The trial judge refuses to order the wife to answer at the original trial. Plaintiff appeals from a judgment for defendant, but does not raise the evidentiary issue; the appellate court reverses on another ground. At the new trial, the question is again asked by plaintiff.

(e) Assume that in (d) the trial judge at the new trial refuses to order the wife to answer. Plaintiff appeals from a judgment for defendant, citing as error the trial court's refusal to order the wife to answer.

4. Are the reasons for applying the doctrine of the law of the case stronger, as the court in *Roosth* suggests, when the earlier decision was one of fact than when it was one of law? Why?

*

INDEX

FINDINGS OF FACT AND CONCLUSIONS OF LAW
Failure to make findings, 894–898.
Preparation by counsel, 895–897.
Purpose, 897.

FOREIGN LAW
See Judicial Notice.

FORMS OF ACTION
Generally, 329–349.
Assumpsit
General assumpsit, 345–349.
Indebitatus assumpsit, 328, 345–347.
Special assumpsit, 344–345.
Case
Distinguished from trespass, 334–340.
Origins, 332–333.
Covenant, 331, 344.
Debt
Generally, 330, 344–345, 349, 803.
Exclusive jurisdiction in Common Pleas, 323, 345.
Detinue, 330, 340.
Jury trial, significance of, 318.
Quantum meruit, 347.
Quasi-contract, 348–349.
Trespass
Distinguished from case, 334–340.
Necessity of possession, 343, 378.
Origins, 331–333.
Reform of pleading, 378.
Trover, 340–344.
Conversion, 341–342.
Right to possession, 343–344.

FORUM NON CONVENIENS
Generally, 249–255.
Injunction against suit, 254.
Relation to jurisdiction, 94, 152.
Transfer in federal courts, 255–263.
Applicable law, 261.
When venue improper in transferee court, 255–260.
When venue improper in transferor court, 261–263.

FRAUD
See, also, Complaint.
Code pleading, 372.
Equity, 358–359.

FULL FAITH AND CREDIT
Effect of judgments, 69, 1094.

GARNISHMENT
See, also, Jurisdiction, quasi-in-rem jurisdiction, attachment; Enforcement of Judgments, execution.
Due process limitations, 134, 972–974.

JUDGMENT—Continued
Form, generally, 15–16.
Offer of judgment, 770–771.
When entered, see Appellate Review.

JUDGMENT NOTWITHSTANDING VERDICT
See Directed Verdict and Judgment N.O.V.

JUDICIAL NOTICE
Foreign law, 472–473, 695.
In pleading, 471–473.

JUDICIARY ACT OF 1789
All Writs Act, see Extraordinary Writs.
Assignee clause, 209, 529.
Complete diversity requirement, 236.
Mode of proof in equity, 356.
Rules of Decision Act, 266, 936.
Venue, 245–247.
Writ of error, review of fact, 950.

JURISDICTION
See, also, Service of Process.
Attachment, see Quasi-in-rem jurisdiction, this topic.
Challenges to jurisdiction
Answer to merits as waiving error, 179–180.
Res judicata effect of ruling, 182.
Special appearance, 179–183.
Denial of special appearance, 181.
Limited appearance to defend quasi-in-rem, distinguished, 183–186.
Conflicts of law, relation to, 138, 139, 141, 153.
Corporations, 77–88.
Consent, 78.
Doing business, 81, 87–88.
Minimum contacts, 82–87.
Presence, 79.
Single-act statutes, see, Single-act statutes, this topic.
Double liability, danger of, as limiting, 145–146, 535–536.
Due process clause, 69.
Escheat, 145–147.
First amendment, 150–153.
Full faith and credit, 69, 81, 138–139.
Future development, 153–160.
Garnishment, see Quasi-in-rem jurisdiction, attachment, this topic.
In personam and in rem, continued validity of distinction, 117–118, 142–143.
Interstate commerce, 79.
Long-arm statutes, see Single-act statutes, this topic.
Notice, 114–122.
Personal jurisdiction
Generally, 5.
Appearance, 69.
Citizenship, 71–72.
Conflicts of law, relation to, 138, 139, 141, 153.
Consent, 72–73, 168–171.
Fraud and enticement, see Service of Process.
Nonresident motorists, 73, 74–77.